14th Edition
ACCOUNTING PRINCIPLES

PHILIP E. FESS, CPA, PhD
Professor of Accountancy
University of Illinois, Champaign-Urbana

CARL S. WARREN, CPA, PhD
Professor of Accounting
University of Georgia, Athens

Published by
A22 SOUTH-WESTERN PUBLISHING CO.

CINCINNATI   WEST CHICAGO, ILL.   DALLAS   PELHAM MANOR, N.Y.   PALO ALTO, CALIF.

Preface

The fourteenth edition of ACCOUNTING PRINCIPLES is a student-oriented text. It presents the fundamental accounting concepts and procedures in a logical, concise, and clear manner. It provides a foundation that allows instructors to focus on clarifying issues and increasing the student's understanding of accounting and its uses. This student orientation is one of the principal reasons why this text has been used by more students than any other for more than 50 years and why it is still the leader in teaching principles of accounting.

After an "Introduction" which presents a summary of the beginnings of accounting in 1494 to the present, accounting principles and practices are presented in a balanced approach. The fundamental concepts and principles are presented in a business environment that enables students to understand accounting as it is applied in serving not only the business world but all of society. Such an approach is designed to fulfill the needs of college students planning a career in accounting, as well as those studying business administration, liberal arts, law, and other disciplines.

Many innovations are included in this edition of ACCOUNTING PRIN-CIPLES. A section on professional ethics has been added to Chapter 1. In the first five chapters, the focus is on the basic structure of accounting, including accounting for merchandising enterprises. The fundamentals are presented without such complexities as special journals and subsidiary ledgers, and ten-column work sheets are used to facilitate understanding.

Chapter 6 emphasizes the qualities of a properly designed accounting system, including the principles of internal control and the use of special journals and subsidiary ledgers. The remaining chapters build on these first six chapters, which emphasize the foundation of accounting systems.

Chapters 7–11 have been reorganized to present the basic concepts of financial accounting. These chapters begin with cash and, in balance sheet order, proceed through receivables and temporary investments, inventories, plant assets and intangible assets, and current liabilities. Chapter 12 ties together the generally accepted accounting concepts and principles presented in the first 11 chapters and expands the discussion to include additional accounting principles.

Chapter 13, "Reporting Changes in Price Levels", has been added to respond to the increasing emphasis in accounting for changing price levels. Chapters 14–18 present the special accounting issues related to partnerships and corporations. In the concluding chapter, on consolidated financial statements and other reports, the work sheet approach has been added as an aid to preparing consolidated statements. The presentation is such that those instructors who wish to do so may omit the work sheet material. In addition, accounting for foreign operations has been added to Chapter 18.

Chapter 19 continues to emphasize the basic concepts applicable to the use of the statement of changes in financial position. Appendix E has been added for those who wish to use the work sheet in preparing the statement.

Chapters 20–27, which present financial analysis and other managerial concepts, continue to emphasize control accounting and decision-making. For possible use in conjunction with Chapter 22 on accounting for manufacturing enterprises, Appendix F has been added on the manufacturing work sheet. The chapter on income taxes and their effect on business decisions (Chapter 27) has been updated to reflect current changes in the Internal Revenue Code. In Chapter 28, the discussion of personal financial statements has been significantly revised to reflect changes due to the issuance of recent professional pronouncements.

A mini-case has been added at the end of each chapter. The mini-cases are designed to stimulate student interest by presenting situations with which students may easily identify. Each case emphasizes important chapter concepts.

Those familiar with earlier editions will recognize the continuance of many successful features. Learning objectives are presented at the beginning of each chapter to serve as stimuli for the student's study and learning. Five self-examination questions are provided at the end of each chapter. After studying the chapter, the students can answer these questions and compare their answers with those appearing in Appendix C. In this manner, students can assess the degree to which they understand the material presented in each chapter. Appendix C presents an explanation of both the correct and incorrect answers for each question and thus increases understanding and further enhances learning.

A glossary of technical terms and common business and accounting expressions is included as Appendix A. The terms included in the glossary are printed in color the first time they are presented in the text.

As in the preceding edition, the variety and volume of the questions, exercises, and problems presented at the end of each chapter provide a wide choice of subject matter and range of difficulty. They have been carefully written and revised to be both practical and comprehensive. An additional series of problems is provided (Appendix B), and the working papers correlating with the problems are designed to relieve students of the burden of repetitive details so that attention may be more effectively directed to mastery of the underlying concepts. In Appendix G, a complete set of financial statements from the annual reports of two companies and selected statements for other companies are reproduced. Notes to facilitate the use of this appendix are presented in the manual. These notes cross-reference the concept, form, or method illustrated in the appendix to the appropriate chapter in the text, and often include relevant data extracted from *Accounting Trends and Techniques*.

Four manual practice sets and two computerized practice sets are available for use in developing greater student proficiency or for review purposes. Each set requires the recording, analysis, interpretation, and reporting of accounting data. A study guide with solutions, student check sheets, transparencies of solutions to text problems, objective tests (including a set of multiple-choice tests), examination problems, true-false questions, multiple-choice questions, a computerized testing program, teaching outlines, and other teaching aids are also available.

Throughout the text, relevant statements of the Financial Accounting Standards Board and other authoritative publications are discussed, quoted, paraphrased, or footnoted. The authors acknowledge their indebtedness to the American Accounting Association, the American Institute of Certified Public Accountants, and the Financial Accounting Standards Board for permission to use materials from their publications.

The authors acknowledge with gratitude the helpful suggestions received from many instructors who have used earlier editions. Although space limitations prohibit a listing of all of those who have made significant contributions, we acknowledge with sincere thanks the detailed suggestions and recommendations submitted by Professor Gene Willis, University of Illinois, Champaign-Urbana.

Philip E. Fess
Carl S. Warren

Contents

Contents

**Practice Set 2   Skyline Computer
   Systems**
*The narrative accompanies the set, which is available
both with and without business papers. This set provides practice in accounting for a sole proprietorship
using the voucher system.*

TEXT OBJECTIVES | *Describe the evolution and the basic structure of the accounting profession and of the concepts of accounting.*

Describe and illustrate accounting systems for merchandising and manufacturing enterprises.

Describe and illustrate accounting systems for sole proprietorships, partnerships, and corporations.

Describe and illustrate accounting concepts for planning, controlling, and analyzing business operations.

Introduction:

Evolution of Accounting

Accounting has evolved, as have medicine, law, and most other fields of human activity, in response to the social and economic needs of society. As business and society have become more complex over the years, accounting has developed new concepts and techniques to meet the ever increasing needs for financial information. Without such information, many complex economic developments and social programs might never have been undertaken. This introduction is devoted to a brief résumé of the evolution of accounting.

PRIMITIVE ACCOUNTING

People in all civilizations have maintained various types of records of business activities. The oldest known are clay tablet records of the payment of wages in Babylonia around 3600 B.C. There are numerous evidences of record keeping and systems of accounting control in ancient Egypt and in the Greek city-states. The earliest known English records were compiled at the direction of William the Conqueror in the eleventh century to ascertain the financial resources of the kingdom.

For the most part, early accounting dealt only with limited aspects of the financial operations of private or governmental enterprises. There was no systematic accounting for all transactions of a particular unit, only for specific types or portions of transactions. Complete accounting for an enterprise developed somewhat later in response to the needs of the commercial republics of Italy.

DOUBLE-ENTRY SYSTEM

The evolution of the system of record keeping which came to be called "double entry" was strongly influenced by Venetian merchants. The first known description of the system was published in Italy in 1494. The author, a Franciscan monk by the name of Luca Pacioli, was a mathematician who taught in various universities in Perugia, Naples, Pisa, and Florence. Evidence of the position that Pacioli occupied among the intellectuals of his day was his close friendship with Leonardo da Vinci, with whom he collaborated on a mathematics book. Pacioli did the text and da Vinci the illustrations.

Goethe, the German poet, novelist, scientist, and universal genius, wrote about double entry as follows: "It is one of the most beautiful inventions of the human spirit, and every good businessman should use it in his economic under-

1

takings."[1] Double entry provides for recording both aspects of a transaction in such a manner as to establish an equilibrium. For example, if an individual borrows $1,000 from a bank, the amount of the loan is recorded both as cash of $1,000 and as an obligation to repay $1,000. Either of the $1,000 amounts is balanced by the other $1,000 amount. As the basic principles are developed further in the early chapters of this book, it will become evident that "double entry" provides for the recording of all business transactions in a systematic manner. It also provides for a set of integrated financial statements reporting in monetary terms the amount of (1) the profit (net income) for a single venture or for a specified period, and (2) the properties (assets) owned by the enterprise and the ownership rights (equities) to the properties.

When the resources of a number of people were pooled to finance a single venture, such as a voyage of a merchant ship, the double-entry system provided records and reports of the income of the venture and the equity of the various participants. As single ventures were replaced by more permanent business organizations, the double-entry system was easily adapted to meet their needs. In spite of the tremendous development of business operations since 1494, and the ever increasing complexities of business and governmental organizations, the basic elements of the double-entry system have continued virtually unchanged.

INDUSTRIAL REVOLUTION

The Industrial Revolution, which occurred in England from the mid-eighteenth to the mid-nineteenth century, brought many social and economic changes, notably a change from the handicraft method of producing marketable goods to the factory system. The use of machinery in turning out many identical products gave rise to the need to determine the cost of a large volume of machine-made products instead of the cost of a relatively small number of individually handcrafted products. The specialized field of cost accounting emerged to meet this need for the analysis of various costs and for recording techniques.

In the early days of manufacturing operations, when business enterprises were relatively small and often isolated geographically, competition was frequently not very keen. Cost accounting was primitive and focused primarily on providing management with records and reports on past operations. Most business decisions were made on the basis of this historical financial information combined with intuition or hunches about the potential success of proposed courses of action.

As manufacturing enterprises became larger and more complex and as competition among manufacturers increased, the "scientific management concept" evolved. This concept emphasized a systematic approach to the solution of management problems. Paralleling this trend was the development of more sophisticated cost accounting concepts to supply management with analytical techniques for measuring the efficiency of current operations and in planning for future operations. This trend was accelerated in the twentieth century by the advent of the electronic computer with its capacity for manipulating large masses of data and its ability to determine the potential effect of alternative courses of action.

---

[1]Goethe, Johann Wolfgang von, *Samtliche Werke*, edited by Edward von der Hellen (Stuttgart and Berlin: J. G. Cotta, 1902–07), Vol. XVII, p. 37.

CORPORATE
ORGANIZATION

The expanded business operations initiated by the Industrial Revolution required increasingly large amounts of money to build factories and purchase machinery. This need for large amounts of capital resulted in the development of the corporate form of organization, which was first legally established in England in 1845. The Industrial Revolution spread rapidly to the United States, which became one of the world's leading industrial nations shortly after the Civil War. The accumulation of large amounts of capital was essential for establishment of new businesses in industries such as manufacturing, transportation, mining, electric power, and communications. In the United States, as in England, the corporation was the form of organization that facilitated the accumulation of the substantial amounts of capital needed.

Almost all large American business enterprises, and many small ones, are organized as corporations largely because ownership is evidenced by readily transferable shares of stock. The shareholders of a corporation control the management of corporate affairs only indirectly. They elect a board of directors, which establishes general policies and selects officers who actively manage the corporation. The development of a class of owners far removed from active participation in the management of the business created an additional dimension for accounting. Accounting information was needed not only by management in directing the affairs of the corporation but also by the shareholders, who required periodic financial statements in order to appraise management's performance.

As corporations became larger, an increasing number of individuals and institutions looked to accountants to provide economic information about these enterprises. Prospective shareholders and creditors sought information about a corporation's financial status and its prospects for the future. Government agencies required financial information for purposes of taxation and regulation. Employees, union representatives, and customers demanded information upon which to judge the stability and profitability of corporate enterprises. Thus accounting began to expand its function of meeting the needs of a relatively few owners to a public role of meeting the needs of a variety of interested parties.

PUBLIC
ACCOUNTING

The development of the corporation also created a new social need — the need for an independent audit to provide some assurance that management's financial representations were reliable. This audit function, often referred to as the "attest function," was chiefly responsible for the creation and growth of the public accounting profession. Unlike private accountants, public accountants are independent of the enterprises for which they perform services.

Recognizing the need for accounting services of professional caliber, all of the states provide for the licensing of certified public accountants (CPAs). In 1944, fifty years after the enactment of the first CPA law, there were approximately 25,000 CPAs in the United States. During the next three decades the number increased fivefold, and currently the number exceeds 200,000.

Auditing is still a major service offered by CPAs, but presently they also devote much of their time to assisting their clients with problems related to planning, controlling, and decision making. Such services, known as management advisory services, have increased in volume over the years until today they comprise a significant part of the practice of most public accounting firms.

INCOME TAX

Enactment of the federal income tax law in 1913 resulted in a tremendous stimulus to accounting activity. All business enterprises organized as corporations or partnerships, as well as many individuals, were required to maintain sufficient records to enable them to file accurate tax returns. Since that time the income tax laws and regulations have become increasingly complex, many so-called "loopholes" have been closed, and the impact of the tax liability has generally tended to increase. As a consequence businesses have depended upon both private and public accountants for advice on legal methods of tax minimization, for preparing tax returns, and for representing them in tax disputes with governmental agencies.

It should also be noted that accounting has influenced the development of income tax law to a great degree. Had not accounting progressed to a point where periodic net income could be determined, the enactment and enforcement of any tax law undoubtedly would have been extremely difficult, if not impossible.

GOVERNMENT INFLUENCE

Over the years government at various levels has intervened to an increasing extent in economic and social matters affecting ever greater numbers of people. Accounting has played an important role by providing the financial information needed to achieve the desired goals.

As the number and size of corporate enterprises grew and an ever increasing number of shares of stock were traded in the market place, laws regulating the activities of stock exchanges, stockbrokers, and investment companies were enacted for the protection of investors. These regulations involve accounting requirements. To protect the public from excessive charges by railroads and other monopolies, commissions were established to limit their rates to levels yielding net income considered to be a "fair return" on invested capital. This rate-making process required extensive accounting information. Regulated banks and savings and loan associations also had to meet record-keeping and reporting requirements and permit periodic examination of their records by governmental agencies. As labor unions became larger and more powerful, regulatory laws were enacted requiring them to submit periodic financial reports. With the enactment of social security and medicare legislation came record-keeping and reporting requirements for almost all businesses and many individuals.

As the federal government exercised increasing control over economic activities, accounting information became more essential as a basis for formulating legislation. One of the areas in which the government has influenced economic and social behavior has been through the income tax. For example, contributions to charitable organizations have been encouraged by permitting their deduction in determining taxable income. Controls over wages and prices have also been enacted at various times in attempts to control the economy by reducing the rate of inflation. An enormous volume of accounting data must be reported, summarized, and studied before proceeding with the evaluation of various governmental proposals such as the foregoing.

ACCOUNTING'S CAPACITY FOR SERVICE

Accounting is capable of supplying financial information that is essential for the efficient operation and for the evaluation of performance of any economic unit in society. Changes in the environment in which such organizations operate will inevitably be accompanied by alterations in accounting concepts and techniques. Although long-range predictions as to environmental changes are risky and of doubtful value, there are two areas that promise to receive increased attention in the immediate future — international accounting and socioeconomic accounting.

International Accounting

The rapid growth of multinational firms in recent years has had a significant impact on accounting because of the different environments existing in the various countries in which such firms operate. Currently, a major problem is the need to develop more uniform accounting standards among countries. Working toward this end are such international organizations as the International Accounting Standards Committee and the International Federation of Accountants.

Socioeconomic Accounting

The term socioeconomic accounting refers to the measurement and communication of information about the impact of various organizations on society. Three major areas of social measurement can be identified. First, at the societal level the interest is on the total impact of all institutions on matters that affect the quality of life. The second area is concerned with the programs undertaken by the government and socially oriented not-for-profit organizations to accomplish specific social objectives. The third area, sometimes referred to as corporate social responsibility, focuses on the public interest in corporate social performance in such areas as reduction of water and air pollution, conservation of natural resources, improvement in quality of product and customer service, and employment practices regarding minority groups and females. The concept of social measurement is relatively simple as a theory, but much additional study and research will be needed before measurement can be expressed in terms of monetary costs and benefits.

1

CHAPTER

Accounting Principles and Practices

CHAPTER OBJECTIVES

Describe the nature of contemporary accounting and its role in society.

Describe the profession of accounting and its specialized fields.

Identify and illustrate the application of the basic concepts of recording, classifying, summarizing, and reporting business operations.

PART 1

Basic Structure of Accounting

1

CHAPTER

Accounting is often called "the language of business." The acceleration of change in our society has contributed to increasing complexities in this "language," which is used in recording, summarizing, reporting, and interpreting basic economic data for individuals, businesses, governments, and other entities. Sound decisions, based on reliable information, are essential for the efficient distribution and use of the nation's scarce resources. Accounting, therefore, plays an important role in our economic and social system.

Accounting[1] has been defined broadly as:

> . . . the process of identifying, measuring, and communicating economic information to permit informed judgments and decisions by users of the information.[2]

This definition implies that accountants must have a broad knowledge of the socioeconomic environment. Without this knowledge, they would be unable to identify and develop relevant information. Accordingly, the basic structure of accounting is influenced by such factors as the political situation, the various types of institutions that provide society with goods and services, and the legal privileges and restraints within which society lives.

CHARACTER-ISTICS OF ACCOUNTING INFORMATION

Accounting information is composed principally of financial data about business transactions, expressed in terms of money. The recording of transaction data may take various forms, such as pen or pencil markings made by hand, printing by mechanical and electronic devices, or holes or magnetic impressions in cards or tape.

The mere records of transactions are of little use in making "informed judgments and decisions." The recorded data must be sorted and summarized before significant reports and analyses can be prepared. Some of the reports to enterprise managers and to others who need economic information may be made frequently. Other reports are issued only at longer intervals. The usefulness of reports is often improved by various kinds of percentage and trend analyses.

The "basic raw materials" of accounting are composed of business transaction data. Its "primary end products" are composed of various summaries, analyses, and reports.

USERS OF ACCOUNTING INFORMATION

Accounting provides the techniques for gathering and the language for communicating economic data to different individuals and institutions. Investors in a business enterprise need information about its financial status and its future prospects. Bankers and suppliers appraise the financial soundness of a business organization and assess the risks involved before making loans or granting credit. Government agencies are concerned with the financial activities of business organizations for purposes of taxation and regulation. Employees and their union

---

[1]A glossary of terms appears in Appendix A. The terms included in the glossary are printed in color the first time they appear in the text.

[2]A *Statement of Basic Accounting Theory* (Evanston, Illinois: American Accounting Association, 1966), p. 1.

representatives are also vitally interested in the stability and the profitability of the organization that hires them.

The individuals most dependent upon and most involved with the end products of accounting are those charged with the responsibility for directing the operations of enterprises. They are often referred to collectively as "management." Many types of data may be needed by management. For example, in the conduct of day-to-day operations, management relies upon accounting to provide the amount owed to each creditor and by each customer and the date each payment is due. Managers also rely upon accounting information to assist them in evaluating current operations and in planning future operations. For example, comparisons of past performance with planned objectives may reveal the means of accelerating favorable trends and reducing those that are unfavorable.

The process of using accounting to provide information to users is illustrated in the following diagram. First, user groups are identified and their information needs determined. These needs determine which economic data are gathered and

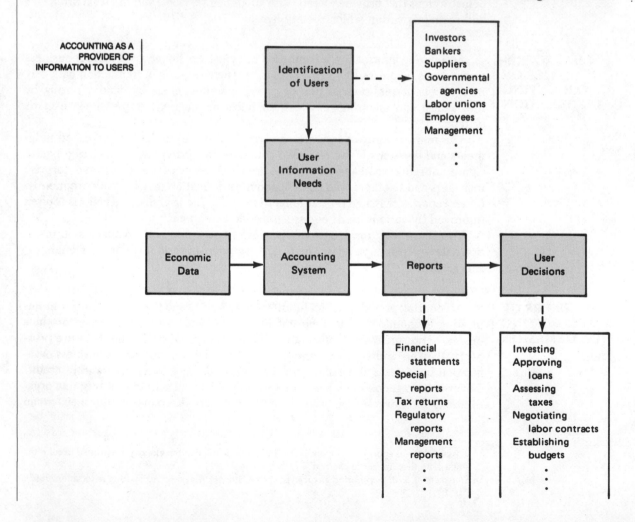

ACCOUNTING AS A
PROVIDER OF
INFORMATION TO USERS

processed by the accounting system. Finally, the accounting system generates reports that communicate essential information to users. For example, investors need information on the financial condition and results of operations of an enterprise to assess the profitability and riskiness of their investments in the enterprise. The accounting system satisfies these needs by recording essential information and periodically summarizing this information in financial reports. Although the information for one category of users may differ markedly from that needed by other users, accounting can provide each user group with economic information to assist them in making decisions regarding future actions.

RELATIONSHIP OF ACCOUNTING TO OTHER FIELDS

Individuals engaged in such areas of business as finance, production, marketing, personnel, and general management need not be expert accountants, but they are more effective if they have a good understanding of accounting principles. Everyone engaged in business activity, from the youngest employee to the manager and owner, comes into contact with accounting. The higher the level of authority and responsibility, the greater is the need for an understanding of accounting concepts and terminology.

A study of U. S. corporations revealed that finance and accounting was the most common background of chief executive officers. Interviews with corporate executives produced the following comments:[3]

"Today, it's vital that the chief executive officer know the corporation and that he have an understanding of accounting."

". . . my training in accounting and auditing practice has been extremely valuable to me throughout."

"A knowledge of accounting carries with it an understanding of the establishment and the maintenance of sound financial controls—an area which is absolutely essential to a chief executive officer."

"I try to have my entire staff understand the financial function and how to use financial data."

The importance of understanding accounting is not limited to the business world. Many employees with specialized training in nonbusiness areas also make use of accounting data and need to understand accounting principles and terminology. For example, an engineer responsible for selecting the most desirable solution to a technical manufacturing problem may consider cost accounting data to be the deciding factor. Lawyers use accounting data in tax cases and in lawsuits involving property ownership and damages from breach of contract. Governmental agencies rely on accounting data in evaluating the efficiency of government operations and for appraising the feasibility of proposed taxation and spending programs. Finally, every adult engages in business transactions and must necessarily be concerned with the financial aspects of life. Accounting plays an important role in

---

[3]John R. Linden, "Rising Corporate Stars: The Accountant as Chief Executive Officer," *The Journal of Accountancy* (September, 1978), pp. 64–71.

modern society and, broadly speaking, all citizens are affected by accounting in some way.

PROFESSION OF ACCOUNTANCY

Accountancy is a profession with stature comparable to that of law or engineering. Accountants employed by a particular business firm or not-for-profit organization, perhaps as chief accountant, controller, or financial vice-president, are said to be engaged in private accounting. Accountants who render accounting services on a fee basis, and staff accountants employed by them, are said to be engaged in public accounting.

Both private and public accounting have long been recognized as excellent training for top managerial responsibilities. Many executive positions in government and in industry are held by men and women with education and experience in accounting.

Private Accounting

The scope of activities and responsibilities of private accountants varies widely. They are frequently referred to as administrative or management accountants, or, if they are employed by a manufacturing concern, as industrial accountants. Various governmental units and other not-for-profit organizations also employ accountants.

The Institute of Management Accounting, which is an affiliate of the National Association of Accountants, grants the certificate in management accounting (CMA) as evidence of professional competence in that field. Requirements for the CMA designation include the baccalaureate degree or equivalent, two years of experience in management accounting, and successful completion of examinations occupying two and one-half days. Participation in a program of continuing professional education is also required for renewal of the certificate. The Institute of Internal Auditors administers a similar program for internal auditors— accountants who review the accounting and operating procedures prescribed by their firms. Accountants qualifying under this program are entitled to use the designation Certified Internal Auditor (CIA).

Public Accounting

In public accounting, an accountant may practice as an individual or as a member of a public accounting firm. Public accountants who have met a state's education, experience, and examination requirements may become certified public accountants, commonly called CPAs.

Qualifications of CPAs

The qualifications required for the CPA certificate differ among the various states. A specified level of education is required, often the completion of a collegiate course of study in accounting. All states require that a candidate pass an examination prepared by the American Institute of Certified Public Accountants (AICPA). The examination is administered twice a year, in May and November. Many states permit candidates to take the examination upon graduation from college or during the term in which they will complete the educational requirements. The examination, which occupies one afternoon and two all-day sessions, is divided into four parts: Accounting Theory, Accounting Practice, Auditing, and Business Law. Some states also require an examination in an additional subject, such as Rules of Professional Conduct. Most states do not permit successful candidates to practice as independent CPAs until they have had from one to three years' experience in public accounting or in employment considered equivalent.

In recent years a majority of the states have enacted laws requiring public practitioners to participate in a program of continuing professional education or forfeit their right to continue in public practice. According to the statutes of one of the states, the continuing education must be a "formal program of learning which contributes directly to the professional competence of an individual after he or she has been licensed to practice public accounting." The states differ as to some of the details of the requirement, such as the number of hours of formal education required for renewal of the permit to practice. The rules adopted by a number of State Boards of Accountancy require 40 hours per year (a fifty-minute class period counts as one hour).

Details regarding the requirements for practice as a CPA in any particular state can be obtained from the respective State Board of Accountancy.

Professional Ethics for CPAs

CPAs have a duty not only to their clients but to their colleagues and the public to perform services competently and with integrity. However, many clients and much of the public do not have the capability of evaluating a CPA's performance. Therefore, standards of conduct have been established to guide CPAs in the conduct of their practices. These standards, called codes of professional ethics, have been established by professional organizations of CPAs, such as the AICPA and state societies of CPAs, and by regulatory agencies, such as State Boards of Accountancy and the Securities and Exchange Commission.

The purpose of codes of professional ethics is to instill confidence in the quality of services rendered by the profession of public accounting. Such codes establish minimum standards of acceptable conduct, which often extend beyond behavior which is otherwise acceptable under the law. For example, under the current AICPA code of professional ethics, CPAs are prohibited from using false, misleading, or deceptive advertising. Such misrepresentations could diminish the profession's usefulness to society.

A CPA who violates the code of ethics is subject to disciplinary proceedings. The AICPA and state societies of CPAs have authority to revoke a CPA's membership in their organizations. If the violation also involves a regulatory agency, such as a State Board of Accountancy or the Securities and Exchange Commission, the CPA's ability to practice within the agency's jurisdiction may be revoked or otherwise limited. The combination of professional organization and regulatory agency sanctions guards against unethical behavior by the public accounting profession.

To meet the public's expectations of the role and responsibilities of the CPA, codes of professional ethics change as society changes. However, ethical conduct is more than simply conforming to written standards of professional behavior. In a true sense, ethical conduct requires a personal commitment to honorable behavior. This thought was best expressed by Marcus Aurelius, who said, "A man should *be* upright; not be *kept* upright."[4]

SPECIALIZED
ACCOUNTING
FIELDS

As in many other areas of human activity during the twentieth century, a number of specialized fields in accounting have evolved as a result of rapid technological advances and accelerated economic growth. The most important accounting fields are described briefly in the following paragraphs.

Financial accounting is concerned with the recording of transactions for a business enterprise or other economic unit and the periodic preparation of various reports from such records. The reports, which may be for general purposes or for a special purpose, provide useful information for managers, owners, creditors, governmental agencies, and the general public. Of particular importance to financial accountants are the rules of accounting, termed **generally accepted accounting principles.** Corporate enterprises must employ such principles in preparing their annual reports on profitability and financial status for their stockholders and the investing public. Comparability of financial reports is essential if the nation's resources are to be divided among business organizations in a socially desirable manner.

Auditing is a field of activity involving an independent review of the accounting records. In conducting an audit, public accountants examine the records supporting the financial reports of an enterprise and give an opinion regarding their fairness and reliability. An important element of "fairness and reliability" is adherence to generally accepted accounting principles. In addition to retaining public accountants for a periodic audit, many corporations have their own permanent staff of internal auditors. Their principal responsibility is to determine if the various operating divisions are following management's policies and procedures.

Cost accounting emphasizes the determination and the control of costs. It is concerned primarily with the costs of manufacturing processes and of manufactured products. In addition, one of the most important duties of the cost accountant is to gather and explain cost data, both actual and prospective. Management uses these data in controlling current operations and in planning for the future.

Management accounting uses both historical and estimated data in assisting management in daily operations and in planning future operations. It deals with specific problems that confront enterprise managers at various organizational levels. The management accountant is frequently concerned with identifying alternative courses of action and then helping to select the best one. For example, the accountant may assist the company treasurer in preparing plans for future financing, or may develop data for use by the sales manager in determining the selling price to be placed on a new product. In recent years, public accountants have realized that their training and experience uniquely qualify them to advise

---

[4]*The Code of Professional Ethics,* American Institute of Certified Public Accountants (New York, 1972), p. 4.

management personnel on policies and administration. This rapidly growing field of specialization by CPAs is frequently called *management advisory services* or *administrative services*.

Tax accounting encompasses the preparation of tax returns and the consideration of the tax consequences of proposed business transactions or alternative courses of action. Accountants specializing in this field, particularly in the area of tax planning, must be familiar with the tax statutes affecting their employer or clients and also must keep up to date on administrative regulations and court decisions on tax cases.

Accounting systems is the special field concerned with the design and implementation of procedures for the accumulation and reporting of financial data. The systems accountant must devise appropriate "checks and balances" to safeguard business assets and provide for information flow that will be efficient and helpful to management. Familiarity with the uses and relative merits of various types of data processing equipment is also essential.

Budgetary accounting presents the plan of financial operations for a period and, through records and summaries, provides comparisons of actual operations with the predetermined plan. A combination of planning and controlling future operations, it is sometimes considered to be a part of management accounting.

International accounting is concerned with the special problems associated with the international trade of multinational business organizations. Accountants specializing in this area must be familiar with the influences that custom, law, and taxation of various countries bring to bear on international operations and accounting principles.

Not-for-profit accounting specializes in recording and reporting the transactions of various governmental units and other not-for-profit organizations such as churches, charities, and educational institutions. An essential element is an accounting system that will insure strict adherence on the part of management to restrictions and other requirements imposed by law, by other institutions, or by individual donors.

Social accounting is the newest field of accounting and is the most difficult to describe in a few words. There have been increasing demands on the profession for measurement of social costs and benefits which have previously been considered to be unmeasurable. One of the engagements in this field involved the measurement of traffic patterns in a densely populated section of the nation. This effort was part of a government study to determine the best use of transportation funds, not only in terms of facilitating trade but also of assuring a good environment for the area's residents. Other innovative engagements have dealt with the best use of welfare funds in a large city, with the public use of state parks, with wildlife in state game preserves, and with statewide water and air pollution.

Accounting instruction, as a field of specialization, requires no explanation. However, in addition to teaching, accounting professors often engage in research, auditing, tax accounting, or other areas of accounting on a part-time or consulting basis.

There is some overlapping among the various fields, and leaders in any particular field are likely to be well versed in related areas. There is also a considerable degree of specialization within a particular field. For example, in auditing one may become an expert in a single type of business enterprise such as department stores or public utilities. In tax accounting one may become a specialist in oil and gas producing companies. In systems one may become an expert in electronic data processing equipment.

OPPORTUNITIES IN ACCOUNTING

The rapid development of accounting theory and technique during the current century has been accompanied by an expansion of the career opportunities in accounting and an increasing number of professionally trained accountants. Among the factors contributing to this growth have been the increase in number, size, and complexity of business corporations; the imposition of new and increasingly complex taxes, particularly the federal income tax; and other governmental restrictions on business operations.

The following table indicates the growth of the profession of accountancy relative to the growth of three other major professions:

Profession	Rate of Increase in Employment 1960–1980
Accountancy	153%
Engineering	66
Law	159
Medicine	78

Source: U. S. Bureau of the Census, Statistical Abstract of the United States: 1981 *(102nd edition) Washington, D. C., 1981.*

During the period 1960–1980, the profession of accountancy grew to approximately one and a half times its size in 1960. As the complexity of the business and social environment continues to increase, employment and advancement opportunities in the profession of accountancy are expected to continue to grow and expand.

BOOKKEEPING AND ACCOUNTING

There is some confusion over the difference between "bookkeeping" and "accounting." This is partly due to the fact that the two are related.

Bookkeeping is the recording of business data in a prescribed manner. A bookkeeper may be responsible for keeping all of the records of a business or of only a small segment, such as a portion of the customer accounts in a department store. Much of the work of the bookkeeper is clerical in nature and is increasingly being handled by mechanical and electronic equipment.

Accounting is primarily concerned with the design of the system of records, the preparation of reports based on the recorded data, and the interpretation of the reports. Accountants often direct and review the work of bookkeepers. The larger the firm, the greater is the number of levels of responsibility and authority. The work of accountants at the beginning levels may possibly include some bookkeeping. In any event, the accountant must have a much higher level of knowledge, conceptual understanding, and analytical skill than is required of the bookkeeper.

PRINCIPLES AND PRACTICE

In accounting, as in the physical and biological sciences, experimentation and change are never-ending. Capable scholars devote their lives and their intellectual energies to the development of accounting principles. Experienced professional accountants contribute their best thinking to the solution of problems continually confronting their clients or employers. The several professional accounting associations periodically issue pronouncements on accounting principles. Authoritative accounting pronouncements are issued by such bodies as the Financial Accounting Standards Board. It is from research, accepted accounting practices, and pronouncements of professional and authoritative bodies that accounting principles evolve to form the underlying basis for accounting practice.

This book is devoted primarily to explanations of accounting principles and, to a lesser extent, to demonstrations of related practices or procedures. It is only through this emphasis on the "why" of accounting as well as on the "how" that the full significance of accounting can be learned.

BUSINESS ENTITY CONCEPT

The business entity concept is based on the applicability of accounting to individual economic units in society. These individual economic units include all business enterprises organized for profit; numerous governmental units, such as states, cities, and school districts; other not-for-profit units such as charities, churches, hospitals, and social clubs; and individual persons and family units. The basic economic data for a unit must first be recorded, followed by analysis and summarization, and finally by periodic reporting. Thus, accounting applies to each separate economic unit.

It is possible, of course, to combine the data for similar economic units to obtain an overall view. For example, accounting data accumulated by each of the airline companies may be assembled and summarized to provide financial information about the entire industry. Similarly, reports on gross national product (GNP) are developed from the accounting records or reports of many separate economic units.

Accounting principles and techniques applicable to family units and not-for-profit organizations are presented in Chapter 28. However, this textbook is concerned primarily with the accounting principles and techniques applicable to profit-making businesses. Such businesses are customarily organized as sole proprietorships, partnerships, or corporations. A sole proprietorship is owned by one individual. A partnership is owned by two or more individuals in accordance with a contractual arrangement. A corporation, organized in accordance with state or federal statutes, is a separate legal entity in which ownership is divided into shares of stock.

BUSINESS TRANSACTIONS

A business transaction is the occurrence of an event or of a condition that must be recorded. For example, the payment of a monthly telephone bill of $68, the purchase of $1,750 of merchandise on credit, and the acquisition of land and a building for $210,000 are illustrative of the variety of business transactions.

The first two transactions are relatively simple: a payment of money in exchange for a service, and a promise to pay within a short time in exchange for goods. The purchase of a building and the land on which it is situated is usually a more complex transaction. The total price agreed upon must be allocated between the land and the building, and the agreement usually provides for spreading the payment of a large part of the price over a period of years and for the payment of interest on the unpaid balance.

A particular business transaction may lead to an event or a condition that results in another transaction. For example, the purchase of merchandise on credit will be followed by payment to the creditor, which is another transaction. Each time a portion of the merchandise is sold, another transaction occurs. Similarly, partial payments for the land and the building are additional transactions, as are periodic payments of interest on the debt. Each of these events must be recorded.

The fact that the life of the building is limited must also be shown in the records. The wearing-out of the building is not an exchange of goods or services between the business and an outsider, but it is nevertheless a significant condition that must be recorded. Transactions of this type, as well as others that are not directly related to outsiders, are sometimes referred to as **internal transactions.**

THE COST PRINCIPLE

Properties and services purchased by a business are recorded in accordance with the **cost principle**, which requires that the monetary record be in terms of *cost*. For example, if a building is purchased at a cost of $150,000, that is the amount used in the purchaser's accounting record. The seller may have been asking $170,000 for the building up to the time of sale; the buyer may have initially offered $130,000 for it; the building may have been assessed at $125,000 for property tax purposes and insured for $135,000; and the buyer may have received an offer of $175,000 for the building the day after it was acquired. These latter amounts have no effect on the accounting records because they do not originate from an exchange transaction. The transaction price, or cost, of $150,000 determines the monetary amount at which the building is recorded.

Continuing the illustration, the $175,000 offer received by the buyer is an indication that it was a bargain purchase at $150,000. To record the building at $175,000, however, would give recognition to an illusory or unrealized profit. If the purchaser should accept the offer and sell the building for $175,000, a profit of $25,000 would be realized, and the new owner would record the building at its $175,000 cost.

The determination of costs incurred and revenues earned is fundamental to accounting. In transactions between buyer and seller, both attempt to get the best price. Only the amount agreed upon is objective enough for accounting purposes. If the monetary amounts at which properties were recorded were constantly revised upward and downward on the basis of mere offers, appraisals, and opinions, accounting reports would soon become so unstable and unreliable as to be meaningless.

ASSETS,
LIABILITIES,
AND CAPITAL

The properties owned by a business enterprise are referred to as **assets** and the rights or claims to the properties are referred to as **equities**. If the assets owned by a business amount to $100,000, the equities in the assets must also amount to $100,000. The relationship between the two may be stated in the form of an equation, as follows:

$$\text{Assets} = \text{Equities}$$

Equities may be subdivided into two principal types: the rights of creditors and the rights of owners. The equities of creditors represent *debts* of the business and are called **liabilities.** The equity of the owners is called **capital**, or **owner's equity**. Expansion of the equation to give recognition to the two basic types of equities yields the following, which is known as the **accounting equation:**

$$\text{Assets} = \text{Liabilities} + \text{Capital}$$

It is customary to place "Liabilities" before "Capital" in the accounting equation because creditors have preferential rights to the assets. The residual claim of the owner or owners is sometimes called owner's equity and is given greater emphasis by transposing liabilities to the other side of the equation, yielding:

$$\text{Assets} - \text{Liabilities} = \text{Owner's Equity} \quad (CAPITOL)$$

The term "capital" is used in this chapter to refer to the equity of the owner. In later chapters, alternative terminology is used.

TRANSACTIONS
AND THE
ACCOUNTING
EQUATION

All business transactions, from the simplest to the most complex, can be stated in terms of the resulting change in the three basic elements of the accounting equation. The effect of these changes on the accounting equation can be demonstrated by studying some typical transactions. As the basis of the illustration, assume that Jerry Miles establishes a sole proprietorship to be known as Miles Taxi. Each transaction or group of similar transactions during the first month of operations is described, followed by an illustration of its effect on the accounting equation.

Transaction (a)

Miles' first transaction is to deposit $10,000 in a bank account in the name of Miles Taxi. The effect of this transaction is to increase the asset cash by $10,000 and to increase capital, on the other side of the equation, by the same amount. After the transaction, the equation for Miles Taxi will appear as follows:

$$
\left. \begin{array}{c} \text{Assets} \\ \hline \text{Cash} \\ \text{(a) } 10{,}000 \end{array} \right\} = \left\{ \begin{array}{c} \text{Capital} \\ \hline \text{Jerry Miles, Capital} \\ 10{,}000 \end{array} \right.
$$

It should be noted that the equation relates only to the business enterprise. Miles' personal assets, such as his home and his personal bank account, and his personal liabilities are excluded from consideration. The business is treated as a separate entity, with cash of $10,000 and owner's equity of $10,000.

Transaction (b)

Miles' next transaction is to purchase land as a future building site, for which $7,500 in cash is paid. This transaction changes the composition of the assets but does not change the total amount. The items in the equation prior to this transaction, the effects of this transaction, and the new balances after the transaction are as follows:

	Assets			Capital
	Cash	+	Land	Jerry Miles, Capital
Bal.	10,000			10,000
(b)	−7,500		+7,500	
Bal.	2,500		7,500	10,000

Miles' current plans are to lease automobiles and other equipment and storage facilities from Ross Bus Company for several months until he can arrange financing for the purchase of automobiles and other equipment and for the construction of storage facilities.

Transaction (c)

During the month Miles purchases $850 of gasoline, oil, and other supplies from various suppliers, agreeing to pay in the near future. This type of transaction is called a purchase _on account_ and the liability created is termed an **account payable**. Consumable goods purchased, such as supplies, are considered to be prepaid expenses, or assets.

In actual practice, each purchase would be recorded as it occurred and a separate record would be kept for each creditor. In this illustration, however, the purchases are recorded as a group. The effect is to increase assets and liabilities by $850, as follows:

	Assets					Liabilities	+	Capital
	Cash	+	Supplies	+	Land	Accounts Payable	+	Jerry Miles, Capital
Bal.	2,500				7,500			10,000
(c)			+850			+850		
Bal.	2,500		850		7,500	850		10,000

Transaction (d)

During the month $400 is paid to creditors on account, thereby reducing both assets and liabilities. The effect on the equation is as follows:

	Assets					Liabilities	+	Capital
	Cash	+	Supplies	+	Land	Accounts Payable	+	Jerry Miles, Capital
Bal.	2,500		850		7,500	850		10,000
(d)	−400					−400		
Bal.	2,100		850		7,500	450		10,000

Transaction (e)

The principal objective of the owner of a business enterprise is to increase capital through earnings. For Jerry Miles this means that the cash and other assets acquired through the sale of taxi services must be greater than the cost of the gasoline and other supplies used, the wages of drivers, the rent, and all of the other expenses of operating the business.

In general, the amount charged to customers for goods or services sold to them is called **revenue**. Other terms may be used for certain kinds of revenue, such as *sales* for the sale of merchandise or business services, *fees earned* for charges by a physician to patients, *rent earned* for the use of real estate or other property, and *fares earned* for Miles Taxi.

In a broad sense, the amount of assets consumed or services used in the process of earning revenue is called **expense**. Expenses would include supplies used, wages of employees, and other assets and services used in operating the business.

The excess of the revenue over the expenses incurred in earning the revenue is called net income or net profit. If the expenses of the enterprise exceed the revenue, the excess is a net loss. It is ordinarily impossible to determine the exact amount of expense incurred in connection with each revenue transaction. Therefore, it is considered satisfactory to determine the net income or the net loss for a stated period of time, such as a month or a year, rather than for each sale or small group of sales.

During the first month of operations Miles Taxi earned fares of $4,500, receiving the amount in cash. The total effect of these transactions is to increase cash by $4,500 and to yield revenue in the same amount. The revenue can be viewed as though it effected a $4,500 increase in capital. At the time expenses of the business are incurred, they are treated as offsets against revenue and hence as reductions in capital. In terms of the accounting equation, the effect of the receipt of cash for services performed is as follows:

	Assets				Liabilities	+	Capital	
	Cash	+ Supplies	+ Land	=	Accounts Payable	+	Jerry Miles, Capital	
Bal.	2,100	850	7,500		450		10,000	
(e)	+4,500						+ 4,500	Fares earned
Bal.	6,600	850	7,500		450		14,500	

Instead of requiring the payment of cash at the time goods or services are sold, a business may make sales *on account*, allowing the customer to pay later. In such cases the firm acquires an **account receivable**, which is a claim against the customer. An account receivable is as much an asset as cash, and the revenue is realized in exactly the same manner as if cash had been immediately received. At a later date, when the money is collected, there is only an exchange of one asset for another, with cash increasing and accounts receivable decreasing.

Transaction (f)

Various business expenses incurred and paid during the month were as follows: wages, $1,125; rent, $850; utilities, $150; miscellaneous, $75. The effect of this group of transactions is to reduce cash and to reduce capital, as indicated in the following manner:

	Assets				Liabilities	+	Capital
	Cash	+ Supplies	+ Land		Accounts Payable	+	Jerry Miles, Capital
Bal.	6,600	850	7,500		450		14,500
(f)	−2,200			=			−1,125 Wages exp.
							− 850 Rent expense
							− 150 Utilities exp.
							− 75 Misc. expense
Bal.	4,400	850	7,500		450		12,300

Transaction (g)

At the end of the month it is determined that the cost of the supplies on hand is $250, the remainder ($850–$250) having been used in the operations of the business. This reduction of $600 in supplies and capital may be shown as follows:

	Assets				Liabilities	+	Capital
	Cash	+ Supplies	+ Land		Accounts Payable	+	Jerry Miles, Capital
Bal.	4,400	850	7,500	=	450		12,300
(g)		−600					−600 Supplies exp.
Bal.	4,400	250	7,500		450		11,700

Transaction (h)

At the end of the month Miles withdraws from the business $1,000 in cash for his personal use. This transaction, which effects a decrease in cash and a decrease in capital, is the exact opposite of an investment in the business by the owner. The withdrawal is not a business expense, and it should be excluded from consideration in determining the net income from operations of the enterprise. The balances in the equation, the effect of the $1,000 withdrawal, and the new balances are as follows:

	Assets				Liabilities	+	Capital
	Cash	+ Supplies	+ Land		Accounts Payable	+	Jerry Miles, Capital
Bal.	4,400	250	7,500	=	450		11,700
(h)	−1,000						−1,000 Drawing
Bal.	3,400	250	7,500		450		10,700

Summary

The business transactions of Miles Taxi are summarized in tabular form, as follows. The transactions are identified by letter, and the balance of each item is shown after each transaction.

	Assets			=	Liabilities +	Capital	
					Accounts	Jerry Miles,	
	Cash +	Supplies +	Land	=	Payable +	Capital	
(a)	+10,000					+10,000	
(b)	− 7,500		+7,500				
	2,500		7,500			10,000	
(c)		+850			+850		
	2,500	850	7,500		850	10,000	
(d)	− 400				−400		
	2,100	850	7,500		450	10,000	
(e)	+ 4,500					+ 4,500	Fares earned
	6,600	850	7,500		450	14,500	
(f)	− 2,200					− 1,125	Wages exp.
						− 850	Rent expense
						− 150	Utilities exp.
						− 75	Misc. expense
	4,400	850	7,500		450	12,300	
(g)		−600				− 600	Supplies exp.
	4,400	250	7,500		450	11,700	
(h)	− 1,000					− 1,000	Drawing
	3,400	250	7,500		450	10,700	

The following observations, which apply to all types of businesses, should be noted:

1. The effect of every transaction can be stated in terms of increases and/or decreases in one or more of the accounting equation elements.
2. The equality of the two sides of the accounting equation is always maintained.

ACCOUNTING STATEMENTS

The principal accounting statements of a sole proprietorship are the balance sheet and the income statement. They are usually accompanied by a less important, but nevertheless useful, statement called the capital statement. The nature of the data presented in each statement, in general terms, is as follows:

Balance sheet
    A list of the assets, liabilities, and capital of a business entity as of a specific date, usually at the close of the last day of a month or a year.
Income statement
    A summary of the revenue and the expenses of a business entity for a specific period of time, such as a month or a year.
Capital statement
    A summary of the changes in capital of a business entity that have occurred during a specific period of time, such as a month or a year.

The basic features of the three statements and their interrelationships are illustrated on page 22. The data for the statements were taken from the summary of transactions of Miles Taxi previously presented.

An additional statement, referred to as the statement of changes in financial position, is also useful in appraising a business enterprise and is an essential part

Miles Taxi
Balance Sheet
August 31, 1984

Assets		
Cash		$ 3 4 0 0 00
Supplies		2 5 0 00
Land		7 5 0 0 00
Total assets		$11 1 5 0 00
Liabilities		
Accounts payable		$ 4 5 0 00
Capital		
Jerry Miles, capital		10 7 0 0 00
Total liabilities and capital		$11 1 5 0 00

Miles Taxi
Income Statement
For Month Ended August 31, 1984

Fares earned		$ 4 5 0 0 00
Operating expenses:		
Wage expense	$ 1 1 2 5 00	
Rent expense	8 5 0 00	
Supplies expense	6 0 0 00	
Utilities expense	1 5 0 00	
Miscellaneous expense	7 5 00	
Total operating expenses		2 8 0 0 00
Net income		$ 1 7 0 0 00

Miles Taxi
Capital Statement
For Month Ended August 31, 1984

Capital, August 1, 1984		$10 0 0 0 00
Net income for the month	$ 1 7 0 0 00	
Less withdrawals	1 0 0 0 00	
Increase in capital		7 0 0 00
Capital, August 31, 1984		$10 7 0 0 00

of financial reports to owners and creditors.[5] The preparation and interpretation of the statement of changes in financial position will be considered in a later chapter after various basic concepts and principles have been explained and illustrated.

All financial statements should be identified by the name of the business, the title of the statement, and the date or period of time. The data presented in the balance sheet are for a specific date. The data presented in the income statement, the capital statement, and the statement of changes in financial position are for a period of time.

The use of indentions, captions, dollar signs, and rulings in the financial statements should be noted. They aid the reader by emphasizing the various distinct sections of the statements.

Balance Sheet

The amounts of Miles Taxi's assets, liabilities, and capital at the end of the first month of operations appear on the last line of the summary on page 21. Minor rearrangements of these data and the addition of a heading yield the balance sheet illustrated on page 22. This form of balance sheet, with the liability and capital sections presented below the asset section, is called the report form. Another arrangement in common use lists the assets on the left and the liabilities and capital on the right. Because of its similarity to the account, a basic accounting device described in the next chapter, it is referred to as the account form of balance sheet.

It is customary to begin the asset section with cash. This item is followed by receivables, supplies, prepaid insurance, and other assets that will be converted into cash or used up in the near future. The assets of a relatively permanent nature, such as land, buildings, and equipment, follow in that order.

In the liabilities and capital section of the balance sheet, it is customary to present the liabilities first, followed by capital. In the illustration on page 22 the liabilities are composed entirely of accounts payable. When there are two or more categories of liabilities, each should be listed and the total amount of liabilities presented in the following manner:

Liabilities		
Notes payable.....................	$1,500	
Accounts payable	1,100	
Salaries payable..................	300	
Total liabilities		$2,900

Income Statement

Revenue earned and expenses incurred during the month were recorded in the equation as increases and decreases in capital, respectively. The details, together with net income in the amount of $1,700, are reported in the income statement on page 22.

The order in which the operating expenses are presented in the income statement varies among businesses. One of the arrangements commonly followed is to

---

[5]*Opinions of the Accounting Principles Board, No. 19,* "Reporting Changes in Financial Position" (New York: American Institute of Certified Public Accountants, 1971), par. 7.

list them in the order of size, beginning with the larger items. Miscellaneous expense is usually shown as the last item regardless of the amount.

Capital Statement

Comparison of the original investment of $10,000 at the beginning of the month with the $10,700 of capital reported in the balance sheet at the end of the month reveals an increase in capital of $700. This net increase is composed of two significant changes in capital that occurred during the period: (1) net income of $1,700 and (2) a withdrawal of $1,000 by the owner. This information is presented in the capital statement on page 22, which serves as a connecting link between the balance sheet and the income statement.

Statements for Corporations

Business enterprises with large aggregations of assets are usually organized as corporations with many stockholders. The corporate form is also used by many small enterprises with a limited number of stockholders. If Miles Taxi had been organized as a corporation with ownership represented by shares of stock, its balance sheet at the end of the first month of operations would appear as follows:

BALANCE SHEET —CORPORATION

Miles Taxi Corporation Balance Sheet August 31, 1984	
Assets	
Cash	$ 3,400
Supplies	250
Land	7,500
Total assets	$11,150
Liabilities	
Accounts payable	$ 450
Capital (STOCKHOLDERS EQUITY)	
Capital stock	$10,000 — Amount PAID IN BY STOCKHOLDERS.
Retained earnings	700
Total capital	10,700
Total liabilities and capital	$11,150

The only differences between the balance sheet shown above and the one illustrated on page 22 occur in the capital section. It is customary on corporation balance sheets to differentiate between the (1) investment of the stockholders ($10,000) and (2) retained earnings, or net income retained in the business ($700). Also, the names of the owners (stockholders) are not shown on corporation balance sheets.

The form of income statement employed by corporate enterprises is similar to the form used by sole proprietorships.

The report of changes in the capital of a corporation follows a somewhat different pattern from that of the capital statement of a sole proprietorship. In corporate enterprises, the emphasis is on the changes in retained earnings that have occurred during the period. Such changes are reported in a **retained earnings statement.** If there have been significant changes in capital stock during a period, such data should be reported in a separate additional statement. The details of minor changes in capital stock need not be reported.

If Miles Taxi had been organized as a corporation, changes in the amount of earnings retained in the business would have resulted from (1) net income and (2) distributions of earnings, called **dividends,** to owners (stockholders). The retained earnings statement for Miles Taxi Corporation for August is as follows:

RETAINED EARNINGS
STATEMENT—
CORPORATION

Miles Taxi Corporation Retained Earnings Statement For Month Ended August 31, 1984	
Net income for the month.....................................	$1,700
Less dividends	1,000
Retained earnings, August 31, 1984	$ 700

Having been in existence only one month, Miles Taxi Corporation had no retained earnings at the beginning of August. For September and most subsequent periods, however, there would be a beginning balance of retained earnings that would be reported on the retained earnings statement. To illustrate, assume that Miles Taxi Corporation reported net income of $2,400 and paid dividends of $1,250 during September. The retained earnings statement for Miles Taxi Corporation for September would appear as follows:

Miles Taxi Corporation Retained Earnings Statement For Month Ended September 30, 1984		
Retained earnings, September 1, 1984		$ 700
Net income for the month........................	$2,400	
Less dividends	1,250	
Increase in retained earnings		1,150
Retained earnings, September 30, 1984		$1,850

1. A profit-making business that is a separate legal entity and in which ownership is divided into shares of stock is known as a:
   A. sole proprietorship   C. partnership
   B. single proprietorship   D. corporation

2. The properties owned by a business enterprise are called:
   A. assets   C. capital
   B. liabilities   D. owner's equity

3. A list of assets, liabilities, and capital of a business entity as of a specific date is:
    A. a balance sheet   C. a capital statement
    B. an income statement   D. a retained earnings statement

4. If total assets increased $20,000 during a period of time and total liabilities increased by $12,000 during the same period, the amount and direction (increase or decrease) of the period's change in capital is:
    A. $32,000 increase   C. $8,000 increase
    B. $32,000 decrease   D. $8,000 decrease

5. If revenue was $45,000, expenses were $37,500, and the owner's withdrawals were $10,000, the amount of net income or net loss was:
    A. $45,000 net income   C. $37,500 net loss
    B. $7,500 net income   D. $2,500 net loss

**Discussion
Questions**

1. Define accounting.

2. Name some of the categories of individuals and institutions who use accounting information.

3. Why is a knowledge of accounting concepts and terminology useful to all individuals engaged in business activities?

4. Distinguish between public accounting and private accounting.

5. Describe in general terms the requirements that an individual must meet to become a CPA.

6. Name some of the specialized fields of accounting activity.

7. Distinguish between the terms *bookkeeping* and *accounting*.

8. What are the three principal forms of profit-making business organizations.

9. What is meant by the cost principle?

10. (a) Land with an assessed value of $71,000 for property tax purposes is acquired by a business enterprise for $132,000. At what amount should the land be recorded by the purchaser?
    (b) Five years later the plot of land in (a) has an assessed value of $105,000 and the business enterprise receives an offer of $196,000 for it. Should the monetary amount assigned to the land in the business records now be increased and, if so, by what amount?
    (c) Assuming that the land was sold for $200,000, (1) how much would capital increase, and (2) at what amount would the purchaser record the land?

11. (a) If the assets owned by a business enterprise total $300,000, what is the amount of the equities of the enterprise? (b) What are the two principal types of equities?

12. (a) An enterprise has assets of $80,000 and liabilities of $25,000. What is the amount of its capital?
    (b) An enterprise has assets of $120,000 and capital of $68,000. What is the total amount of its liabilities?
    (c) A corporation has assets of $270,000, liabilities of $90,000, and capital stock of $100,000. What is the amount of its retained earnings?

(d) An enterprise has liabilities of $40,000 and capital of $110,000. What is the total amount of its assets?

13. Describe how the following business transactions affect the three elements of the accounting equation.
    (a) Invested cash in the business.
    (b) Purchased supplies on account.
    (c) Paid for utilities used in the business.
    (d) Received cash for services performed.

14. (a) A vacant lot acquired for $50,000, on which there is a balance owed of $25,000, is sold for $71,000 in cash. What is the effect of the sale on the total amount of the seller's (1) assets, (2) liabilities, and (3) capital?
    (b) After receiving the $71,000 cash in (a), the seller pays the $25,000 owed. What is the effect of the payment on the total amount of the seller's (1) assets, (2) liabilities, and (3) capital?

15. Operations of a service enterprise for a particular month are summarized as follows:
    Service sales: on account, $42,000; for cash, $12,000
    Expenses incurred: on account, $26,000; for cash, $11,000
    What was the amount of the enterprise's (a) revenue, (b) expenses, and (c) net income?

16. If the expenses of an enterprise exceed the revenue for a particular month, what is this excess of expenses over revenue called?

17. Give the title of a sole proprietorship's three major financial statements illustrated in this chapter, and briefly describe the nature of the information provided by each.

18. What particular item of financial or operating data of a service enterprise, organized as a corporation, appears on (a) both the income statement and the retained earnings statement, and (b) both the balance sheet and the retained earnings statement?

19. If total assets have increased by $19,000 during a specific period of time and capital has decreased by $10,000 during the same period, what was the amount and direction (increase or decrease) of the period's change in total liabilities?

20. The income statement of a sole proprietorship for the month of March indicates a net income of $21,000. During the same period the owner withdrew $28,000 in cash from the business for personal use. Would it be correct to say that the owner incurred a *net loss* of $7,000 during the month? Discuss.

21. Fuber Distributors had a capital balance at the beginning of the period of $120,000. At the end of the period, the company had total assets of $178,000 and total liabilities of $63,000. (a) What was the net income or net loss for the period, assuming no additional investments or withdrawals? (b) What was the net income or net loss for the period, assuming a withdrawal of $25,000 had occurred during the period?

Exercises

Exercise 1-1. The following selected transactions were completed by Castell Delivery Service during November:

(1) Received cash from owner as additional investment, $20,000.
(2) Paid advertising expense, $520.

(3) Purchased supplies of gas and oil for cash, $780.
✓ (4) Received cash from cash customers, $1,500.
(5) Charged customers for delivery services on account, $2,100.
(6) Paid creditors on account, $470.
(7) Paid rent for November, $1,000.
(8) Received cash from customers on account, $1,810.
(9) Paid cash to owner for personal use, $900.
(10) Determined by taking an inventory that $650 of supplies of gas and oil had been used during the month.

Indicate the effect of each transaction on the accounting equation by listing the numbers identifying the transactions, (1) through (10), in a vertical column, and inserting at the right of each number the appropriate letter from the following list:

(a) Increase in one asset, decrease in another asset.
(b) Increase in an asset, increase in a liability.
(c) Increase in an asset, increase in capital.
(d) Decrease in an asset, decrease in a liability.
(e) Decrease in an asset, decrease in capital.

Exercise 1-2. Foreman Corporation, engaged in a service business, completed the following selected transactions during the period:

(1) Issued additional capital stock, receiving cash.
(2) Purchased supplies on account.
(3) Returned defective supplies purchased on account and not yet paid for.
(4) Received cash as a refund from the erroneous overpayment of an expense.
(5) Charged customers for services sold on account.
(6) Paid utilities expense.
(7) Paid a creditor on account.
(8) Received cash on account from charge customers.
(9) Paid cash dividends to stockholders.
(10) Determined the amount of supplies used during the month.

Using a tabular form with four column headings entitled Transaction, Assets, Liabilities, and Capital, respectively, indicate the effect of each transaction. Use + for increase and − for decrease.

Exercise 1-3. C. F. Sirmans is engaged in a service business. Summary financial data for October are presented in equation form as follows. Each line designated by a number indicates the effect of a transaction on the equation. Each increase and decrease in capital, except transaction (5), affects net income.

	Cash	+	Supplies	+	Land	=	Liabilities	+	Capital
Bal.	12,000		540		4,000	=	1,540		15,000
(1)	−6,000				+6,000				
(2)	+3,200								+3,200
(3)	−1,200								−1,200
(4)			+800				+ 800		
(5)	− 750								− 750
(6)	−1,500						−1,500		
(7)			−630						− 630
Bal.	5,750		710		10,000		840		15,620

(a) Describe each transaction.
(b) What is the amount of net decrease in cash during the month?
(c) What is the amount of net increase in capital during the month?
(d) What is the amount of the net income for the month?
(e) How much of the net income of the month was retained in the business?

Exercise 1-4. Four different sole proprietorships, W, X, Y, and Z, show the same balance sheet data at the beginning and end of a year. These data, exclusive of the amount of capital, are summarized as follows:

	Total Assets	Total Liabilities
Beginning of the year	$275,000	$80,000
End of the year.	320,000	85,000

On the basis of the above data and the following additional information for the year, determine the net income (or loss) of each company for the year. (Suggestion: First determine the amount of increase or decrease in capital during the year.)

Company W: The owner had made no additional investments in the business and no withdrawals from the business.

Company X: The owner had made no additional investments in the business but had withdrawn $25,000.

Company Y: The owner had made an additional investment of $50,000 but had made no withdrawals.

Company Z: The owner had made an additional investment of $48,000 and had withdrawn $35,000.

Exercise 1-5. One item is omitted in each of the following summaries of balance sheet and income statement data for four different sole proprietorships, A, B, C, and D.

	A	B	C	D
Beginning of the year:				
Assets.	$100,000	$60,000	$27,000	(d)
Liabilities	40,000	20,000	6,000	$12,600
End of the year:				
Assets.	140,000	75,000	34,000	68,000
Liabilities	50,000	10,000	12,000	37,000
During the year:				
Additional investments in the business	(a)	5,000	12,000	30,000
Withdrawals from the business	12,000	8,000	(c)	21,000
Revenue.	80,000	(b)	42,100	92,000
Expenses.	65,000	30,000	43,600	84,000

Determine the amounts of the missing items, identifying them by letter. (Suggestion: First determine the amount of increase or decrease in capital during the year.)

Exercise 1-6. Financial information related to the sole proprietorship of Tina Pierce Interiors for March and April of the current year is as follows:

	March 31, 19--	April 30, 19--
Accounts Payable..........................	$ 430	$ 690
Accounts Receivable......................	2,560	4,100
Tina Pierce, Capital	?	?
Cash	4,500	5,400
Supplies	840	450

(a) Prepare balance sheets for Tina Pierce Interiors as of March 31 and as of April 30 of the current year.
(b) Determine the amount of net income for April, assuming that the owner had made no additional investments or withdrawals during the month.
(c) Determine the amount of net income for April, assuming that the owner had made no additional investments and had withdrawn $2,500 during the month.

Problems
(Problems in Appendix B: 1-2B, 1-3B, 1-4B.)

Problem 1-1A. On August 1 of the current year C. W. Collins established a sole proprietorship under the name Collins Realty. Collins completed the following transactions during the month:

(a) Opened a business bank account with a deposit of $5,000.
(b) Paid rent on office and equipment for the month, $1,200.
(c) Purchased supplies (stationery, stamps, pencils, ink, etc.) on account, $340.
(d) Paid creditor on account, $250.
(e) Earned sales commissions, receiving cash, $4,850.
(f) Withdrew cash for personal use, $1,000.
(g) Paid automobile expenses (including rental charge) for month, $280, and miscellaneous expenses, $175.
(h) Paid office salaries, $600.
(i) Determined that the cost of supplies used was $65.

Instructions:

(1) Record the transactions and the balances after each transaction, using the following tabular headings:

Assets		Liabilities		Capital
Cash + Supplies	=	Accounts Payable	+	C. W. Collins, Capital

By appropriate notations at the right of each change, indicate the nature of each increase and decrease in capital subsequent to the initial investment.
(2) Prepare an income statement for August, a capital statement for August, and a balance sheet as of August 31.

Problem 1-2A. Following are the amounts of the assets and liabilities of Pioneer Services, a sole proprietorship, at December 31, the *end* of the current year, and its revenue and expenses for the year ended on that date. The capital of E. G. Eberhart, owner, was $10,655 at January 1, the *beginning* of the current year, and the owner withdrew $25,000 during the current year.

Cash......................................	$ 6,150
Accounts receivable	12,260
Supplies....................................	1,200
Prepaid insurance	400
Accounts payable	4,010
Salaries payable...........................	2,100
Sales......................................	91,670
Salary expense............................	25,200
Rent expense	8,000
Utilities expense...........................	7,800
Supplies expense..........................	6,200
Taxes expense	6,000
Insurance expense.........................	4,800
Advertising expense	3,000
Miscellaneous expense.....................	2,425

Instructions:

(1) Prepare an income statement for the current year ending December 31, exercising care to include each item of expense.
(2) Prepare a capital statement for the current year ending December 31.
(3) Prepare a balance sheet as of December 31 of the current year.

Problem 1-3A. Following are the amounts of O'Neal Corporation's assets and liabilities at May 31, the *end* of the current year, and its revenue and expenses for the year ended on that date, listed in alphabetical order. O'Neal Corporation had capital stock of $50,000 and retained earnings of $87,390 on June 1, the *beginning* of the current year. During the current year, the corporation paid cash dividends of $25,000.

Accounts payable	$ 48,320
Accounts receivable	68,840
Advertising expense	14,600
Cash......................................	40,150
Insurance expense.........................	12,000
Land	150,000
Miscellaneous expense.....................	3,140
Notes payable.............................	22,000
Prepaid insurance	2,000
Rent expense	43,100
Salaries payable...........................	18,600
Salary expense............................	186,000
Sales......................................	378,500
Supplies...................................	3,280
Supplies expense..........................	11,700
Taxes expense	16,900
Utilities expense	28,100

Instructions:

(1) Prepare an income statement for the current year ending May 31, exercising care to include each item of expense listed.
(2) Prepare a retained earnings statement for the current year ending May 31.
(3) Prepare a balance sheet as of May 31 of the current year. There was no change in the amount of capital stock during the year.

Problem 1-4A. Dupree Dry Cleaners is a sole proprietorship owned and operated by F. A. Dupree. Currently a building and equipment are being rented pending completion of construction of new facilities. The actual work of dry cleaning is done by another company at wholesale rates. The assets and the liabilities of the business on September 1 of the current year are as follows: Cash, $4,800; Accounts Receivable, $10,400; Supplies, $450; Land, $10,000; Accounts Payable, $6,750. Business transactions during September are summarized as follows:

(a) Received cash from cash customers for dry cleaning sales, $5,150.
(b) Purchased supplies on account, $120.
(c) Paid rent for the month, $600.
(d) Paid creditors on account, $1,260.
(e) Charged customers for dry cleaning sales on account, $3,520.
(f) Received monthly invoice for dry cleaning expense for September (to be paid on October 10), $4,800.
(g) Paid personal expenses by checks drawn on the business, $350, and withdrew $600 in cash for personal use.
(h) Reimbursed a customer $80 for a garment lost by the cleaning company, which agreed to deduct the amount from the invoice received in transaction (f).
(i) Paid the following: wages expense, $1,100; truck expense, $380; utilities expense, $360; miscellaneous expense, $130.
(j) Received cash from customers on account, $4,100.
(k) Determined the cost of supplies used during the month, $170.

Instructions:

(1) State the assets, liabilities, and capital as of September 1 in equation form similar to that shown in this chapter.
(2) Record, in tabular form below the equation, the increases and decreases resulting from each transaction, indicating the new balances after each transaction. Explain the nature of each increase and decrease in capital by an appropriate notation at the right of the amount.
(3) Prepare (a) an income statement for September, (b) a capital statement for September, and (c) a balance sheet as of September 30.

Problem 1-5A. On March 1 of the current year, Express Delivery, Inc. was organized as a corporation. The summarized transactions of the business for its first two months of operations, ending on April 30, are as follows:

(a) Received cash from stockholders for capital stock............ $50,000
(b) Purchased a portion of a delivery service that had been operating as a partnership in accordance with the following details:

Assets acquired by the corporation:		
Accounts receivable..........................	$12,400	
Truck supplies...............................	3,810	
Office supplies..............................	960	$17,170
Liabilities assumed by the corporation:		
Accounts payable............................		8,670
Payment to be made as follows:		
Cash.......................................	$ 2,500	
Three non-interest-bearing notes payable of $2,000 each, due at two-month intervals.........	6,000	$ 8,500

(c) Purchased truck supplies on account	$ 1,615
(d) Paid creditors on account.	5,280
(e) Purchased office supplies for cash.	120
(f) Paid insurance premiums in advance.	600
(g) Received cash from customers on account	8,690
(h) Paid advertising expense	1,100
(i) Paid first of the three notes payable.	2,000
(j) Charged delivery service sales to customers on account	30,550
(k) Paid rent expense on office and trucks	3,025
(l) Paid utilities expense	840
(m) Paid miscellaneous expenses	1,475
(n) Paid wages expense	16,600
(o) Paid taxes expense	220
(p) Truck supplies used.	2,680
(q) Office supplies used.	340
(r) Insurance premiums that expired and became an expense.	200
(s) Purchased land as future building site, paying $8,000 cash and giving a note payable due in 5 years for the balance of $20,000.	28,000
(t) Paid cash dividends to stockholders	750

Instructions:

(1) List the following captions in a single line at the top of a sheet turned sideways.

$$\underline{Cash} + \underline{\begin{matrix}Accounts\\Receivable\end{matrix}} + \underline{\begin{matrix}Truck\\Supplies\end{matrix}} + \underline{\begin{matrix}Office\\Supplies\end{matrix}} + \underline{\begin{matrix}Prepaid\\Insurance\end{matrix}} + \underline{Land} =$$

$$\underline{\begin{matrix}Notes\\Payable\end{matrix}} + \underline{\begin{matrix}Accounts\\Payable\end{matrix}} + \underline{\begin{matrix}Capital\\Stock\end{matrix}} + \underline{\begin{matrix}Retained\\Earnings\end{matrix}} + \underline{\begin{matrix}Retained\ Earnings\\Notations\end{matrix}}$$

(2) Record the original investment in the corporation and the remaining transactions in the appropriate columns, identifying each by letter. Indicate increases by + and decreases by −. *Do not determine the new balances of the items after each transaction.* In the space for retained earnings notations, identify each revenue and expense item and dividends paid to stockholders.

(3) Insert the final balances in each column and determine that the equation is in balance at April 30, the end of the period.

(4) Prepare the following: (a) income statement for the two months, (b) retained earnings statement for the two months, and (c) balance sheet as of April 30.

Mini-Case

Victoria Getz, a sophomore in college, has been seeking ways to earn extra spending money. As an active sports enthusiast, Victoria plays tennis regularly at the Georgetown Golf and Tennis Club, where her father has a family membership. The president of the club recently approached Victoria with the proposal that Victoria manage the club's tennis courts on weekends. Victoria's primary duty would be to supervise the operation of the club's two indoor and six outdoor courts, including court reservations. In return for her services, the club agreed to pay Victoria $50 per weekend, plus Victoria could keep whatever she earned from lessons and the fees from the use of the ball machine. The club and Victoria agreed to a one-month trial, after which both would consider an arrangement for the remaining three years of Victoria's college career. On this basis, Victoria organized Tennis Services Unlimited. During September, Victoria managed the tennis courts and entered into the following transactions:

(a) Opened a business bank account by depositing $350.
(b) Paid $80 for tennis supplies (practice tennis balls, etc.).
(c) Paid $110 for the rental of video tape equipment to be used in offering lessons during September.
(d) Arranged for the rental of a ball machine during September for $40. Paid $20 in advance, with the remaining $20 due October 1.
(e) Received $375 for lessons given during September.
(f) Paid $45 for salaries of part-time employees who answered the telephone and took reservations while Victoria was giving lessons.
(g) Received $60 in fees from the use of the ball machine during September.
(h) Paid $35 for miscellaneous expenses.
(i) Received $200 from the club for managing the tennis courts during September.
(j) Supplies on hand at the end of the month total $55.
(k) Victoria withdrew $300 for personal use on September 30.

As a friend and accounting student, Victoria has asked you to aid her in assessing the venture.

Instructions:

(1) Record the transactions and the balances after each transaction, using the following tabular headings:

	Assets		Liabilities		Capital
Cash	+	Supplies	= Accounts Payable	+	V. Getz, Capital

(2) Prepare an income statement for September.
(3) Prepare a capital statement for September.
(4) Prepare a balance sheet as of September 30.
(5) (a) Assume that Victoria Getz could earn $3.50 per hour working 16 hours per weekend for a fast food restaurant. Evaluate which of the two alternatives, the fast food restaurant or Tennis Services Unlimited, would provide Victoria with the most income per month.
     (b) Discuss any other factors that you believe Victoria should consider before discussing a long-term arrangement with Georgetown Golf and Tennis Club.

2

CHAPTER

The Accounting Cycle

CHAPTER OBJECTIVES

Describe and illustrate the basic accounting concepts for recording, classifying, and summarizing business transactions on a day-to-day basis.

Describe and illustrate the double-entry accounting method of recording transactions.

Describe and illustrate the flow of accounting data through an accounting system.

2

CHAPTER

The transactions completed by an enterprise during a specific period may cause increases and decreases in many different asset, liability, capital, revenue, and expense items. To have the details of these transactions readily available and to prepare periodic financial statements, the effects of the transactions must be recorded in a systematic manner.

The nature of transactions and their effect on business enterprises were described and recorded in Chapter 1 by the use of the accounting equation, Assets = Liabilities + Capital (+ Revenue − Expenses). Although transactions can be analyzed and recorded in terms of their effect on the equation, such a format is not practical as a design for actual accounting systems.

Accountants must have day-to-day information available when they need it and must be able to prepare timely periodic financial statements. Therefore, separate records must be kept for each item that appears on the financial statements. The individual records are then summarized at periodic intervals and the data thus obtained are presented in the financial statements or other reports. For example, it is necessary to have a record used only for recording increases and decreases in cash, another record used only for recording increases and decreases in supplies, another for land, etc. The type of record traditionally used for the purpose of recording individual transactions is called an **account**. A group of related accounts that comprise a complete unit, such as all of the accounts of a specific business enterprise, is called a **ledger**.

NATURE OF AN ACCOUNT

The simplest form of an account has three parts: (1) a title, which is the name of the item recorded in the account; (2) a space for recording increases in the amount of the item, in terms of money; and (3) a space for recording decreases in the amount of the item, also in monetary terms. This form of an account, illustrated below, is known as a **T account** because of its similarity to the letter T.

T ACCOUNT

Title	
Left side	Right side
debit	*credit*

The left side of the account is called the **debit** side and the right side is called the **credit** side.[1] The word **charge** is sometimes used as a synonym for debit. Amounts entered on the left side of an account, regardless of the account title, are called **debits** or **charges** to the account, and the account is said to be **debited** or **charged**. Amounts entered on the right side of an account are called **credits**, and the account is said to be **credited**.

In the following illustration, receipts of cash during a period of time have been listed vertically on the debit side of the cash account. The cash payments for the same period have been listed in similar fashion on the credit side of the account. A memorandum total of the cash receipts for the period to date, $10,950 in the illustration, may be inserted below the last debit at any time the information is

---

[1]Often abbreviated as *Dr.* for "debit" and *Cr.* for "credit," derived from the Latin *debere* and *credere*.

desired. The figures should be small and written in pencil in order to avoid mistaking the amount for an additional debit. (The procedure is sometimes referred to as **pencil footing.**) The total of the cash payments, $6,850 in the illustration, may be inserted on the credit side in a similar manner. Subtraction of the smaller sum from the larger, $10,950 − $6,850, yields the amount of cash on hand, which is called the **balance of the account.** The cash account in the illustration has a balance of $4,100. This amount may be inserted in pencil figures next to the larger pencil footing, which identifies it as a **debit balance.** If a balance sheet were to be prepared at this time, the amount of cash reported thereon would be $4,100.

	Cash	
	3,750	850
	4,300	1,400
	2,900	700
4,100 10,950		2,900
		1,000
		6,850

Balance Sheet Accounts | The manner of recording data in the accounts and the relationship of accounts to the balance sheet are presented in the two illustrations that follow. For the first illustration, assume that R. D. Baker establishes a business venture, to be known as Baker Appliance Repair, by initially depositing $3,500 cash in a bank account for the use of the enterprise. Immediately after the deposit, the balance sheet for the business, in account form, would contain the following information:

Assets	Capital
Cash.................... $3,500	R. D. Baker, capital....... $3,500

The effect of the transaction on accounts in the ledger can be described as a $3,500 debit to Cash and a $3,500 credit to R. D. Baker, Capital. The information can also be stated in a formalized manner by listing the title of the account and the amount to be debited, followed by a similar listing, below and to the right of the debit, of the title of the account and the amount to be credited. This form of presentation is called a **journal entry,** and is illustrated as follows:

Cash...	3,500	
R. D. Baker, Capital.................................		3,500

The data in the journal entry are transferred to the appropriate accounts by a process known as **posting.** The accounts after posting the above journal entry appear as follows:

Cash		R. D. Baker, Capital	
3,500			3,500

Note that the amount of the cash, which is reported on the left side of the account form of balance sheet, is posted to the left (debit) side of Cash. The owner's equity in the business, which is reported on the right side of the balance sheet, is posted to the right (credit) side of R. D. Baker, Capital. When other assets are acquired, the increases will be recorded as debits to the appropriate accounts. As capital is increased or liabilities are incurred, the increases will be recorded as credits.

For the second illustration, assume that after opening the checking account, Baker purchased equipment and tools at a cost of $2,800. Baker paid $1,800 in cash by writing a check on the bank account, and agreed to pay the remaining $1,000 within thirty days. After this transaction, the data reported in the balance sheet would be as follows:

Assets		Liabilities	
Cash....................	$1,700	Accounts payable	$1,000
Equipment...............	2,800	Capital	
		R. D. Baker, capital.........	3,500
Total assets..............	$4,500	Total liabilities and capital....	$4,500

The effect of the transaction can be described as a $2,800 debit (increase) to Equipment, an $1,800 credit (decrease) to Cash, and a $1,000 credit (increase) to Accounts Payable. The same information can be presented in the form of the following journal entry. (An entry composed of two or more debits or of two or more credits is called a **compound journal entry**.)

Equipment...	2,800	
Cash...		1,800
Accounts Payable		1,000

After the journal entry for the second transaction has been posted, the accounts of Baker Appliance Repair appear as follows:

Cash		Accounts Payable	
3,500	1,800		1,000

Equipment		R. D. Baker, Capital	
2,800			3,500

Note that the effect of the transaction was to increase one asset account, decrease another asset account, and increase a liability account. Note also that although the amounts, $2,800, $1,800, and $1,000, are different, the equality of debits and credits was maintained.

In the preceding paragraphs, it was observed that the left side of asset accounts is used for recording increases and the right side is used for recording decreases.

It was also observed that the right side of liability and capital accounts is used to record increases. It naturally follows that the left side of such accounts is used to record decreases. The left side of all accounts, whether asset, liability, or capital, is the debit side and the right side is the credit side. Consequently, a debit may be either an increase or a decrease, depending on the nature of the account affected. A credit may likewise be either an increase or a decrease, depending on the nature of the account. The rules of debit and credit may therefore be stated as follows:

GENERAL RULES OF DEBIT
AND CREDIT

Debit may signify:	*Credit* may signify:
Increase in asset accounts	Decrease in asset accounts
Decrease in liability accounts	Increase in liability accounts
Decrease in capital accounts	Increase in capital accounts

The rules of debit and credit may also be stated in relationship to the accounting equation and the account form of balance sheet, as in the following diagram:

EXPANDED RULES OF DEBIT
AND CREDIT—BALANCE
SHEET ACCOUNTS

Balance Sheet

ASSETS		LIABILITIES	
Asset Accounts		Liability Accounts	
Debit for increases	Credit for decreases	Debit for decreases	Credit for increases

		CAPITAL	
		Capital Accounts	
		Debit for decreases	Credit for increases

Every business transaction affects a minimum of two accounts. Regardless of the complexity of a transaction or the number of accounts affected, the sum of the debits is always equal to the sum of the credits. This equality of debit and credit for each transaction is inherent in the equation $A = L + C$. It is also because of this duality that the system is known as **double-entry accounting**.

Income Statement Accounts

The theory of debit and credit in its application to revenue and expense accounts is based on the relationship of these accounts to capital. The net income or the net loss for a period, as reported on the income statement, is the net increase or the net decrease in capital resulting from operations.

Revenue increases capital. Just as increases in capital are recorded as credits, increases in revenues during an accounting period are recorded as credits.

Expenses have the effect of decreasing capital, and just as decreases in capital are recorded as debits, increases in expense accounts are recorded as debits. Although debits to expense accounts signify *decreases in capital*, they may also be referred to as *increases in expense*. The usual practice is to consider debits to expense accounts in the positive sense (increases in expense) rather than in the negative sense (decreases in capital). The rules of debit and credit as applied to revenue and expense accounts are shown in the following diagram:

EXPANDED RULES OF DEBIT AND CREDIT—INCOME STATEMENT ACCOUNTS

Capital Accounts			
DEBIT *Decreases in capital*		CREDIT *Increases in capital*	
Expense Accounts		Revenue Accounts	
Debit for increases	Credit for decreases	Debit for decreases	Credit for increases

At the end of an accounting period, the revenue and expense account balances are reported in the income statement. Periodically, usually at the end of the accounting year, all revenue and expense account balances are transferred to a summarizing account and the accounts are then said to be *closed*. The balance in the summarizing account, which is the net income or net loss for the period, is then transferred to the capital account (to the retained earnings account for a corporation), and the summarizing account is also closed. Because of this periodic closing of these accounts, they are sometimes called **temporary capital accounts** or **nominal accounts**. The balances of the accounts reported in the balance sheet are carried forward from year to year and because of their permanence are sometimes referred to as **real accounts**.

Drawing Account

The owner of a sole proprietorship may from time to time withdraw cash from the business for personal use. This practice is common if the owner devotes full time to the business or if the business is the owner's principal source of income. Such withdrawals are recorded as debits to an account bearing the owner's name followed by Drawing or Personal. This account is periodically closed to the capital account. Debits to the account may be thought of either as decreases in capital (negative sense) or as increases in drawings (positive sense).

Dividends Account

The dividends account of a corporation is comparable to the drawing account of a sole proprietorship. Distributions of earnings to the stockholders are debited to Dividends, and the account is periodically closed to the retained earnings account. Debits to the account may be regarded either as decreases in capital (negative sense) or as increases in dividends (positive sense).

Normal Balances

The sum of the increases recorded in an account is usually equal to or greater than the sum of the decreases recorded in the account. For this reason, the normal balances of all accounts are positive rather than negative. For example, the total debits (increases) in an asset account will ordinarily be greater than the total credits (decreases). Thus, asset accounts normally have debit balances.

The rules of debit and credit and the normal balances of the various types of accounts are summarized as follows. Note that the drawing, dividends, and expense accounts are considered in the positive sense. Increases in these accounts, which represent decreases in capital, are recorded as debits.

NORMAL ACCOUNT BALANCES	Type of Account	Increase	Decrease	Normal Balance
	Asset	Debit	Credit	Debit
	Liability	Credit	Debit	Credit
	Capital			
	Capital, Capital Stock, Retained Earnings	Credit	Debit	Credit
	Drawing, Dividends	Debit	Credit	Debit
	Revenue	Credit	Debit	Credit
	Expense	Debit	Credit	Debit

When an account that normally has a debit balance actually has a credit balance, or vice versa, it is an indication of an accounting error or of an unusual situation. For example, a credit balance in the office equipment account could result only from an accounting error. On the other hand, a debit balance in an account payable account could result from an overpayment.

CLASSIFICATION OF ACCOUNTS

Accounts in the ledger are customarily classified according to a common characteristic: assets, liabilities, capital, revenue, and expenses. In addition there may be subgroupings within the major categories. The classifications and accounts characteristically used by a small service enterprise are described in the paragraphs that follow. Additional classes and accounts are introduced in later chapters.

Assets

Any physical thing (tangible) or right (intangible) that has a money value is an asset. Assets are customarily divided into groups for presentation on the balance sheet. The two groups used most often are (1) current assets and (2) plant assets.

Current assets. Cash and other assets that may reasonably be expected to be realized in cash or sold or used up usually within a year or less, through the normal operations of the business, are called current assets. In addition to cash, the current assets usually owned by a service business are notes receivable and accounts receivable, and supplies and other prepaid expenses.

Cash is any medium of exchange that a bank will accept at face value. It includes bank deposits, currency, checks, bank drafts, and money orders. **Notes receivable** are claims against debtors evidenced by a written promise to pay a certain sum in money at a definite time to the order of a specified person or to bearer. **Accounts receivable** are also claims against debtors, but are less formal than notes. They arise from sales of services or merchandise on account. **Prepaid**

expenses include supplies on hand and advance payments of expenses such as insurance and property taxes.

Plant assets. Tangible assets used in the business that are of a permanent or relatively fixed nature are called **plant assets** or **fixed assets.** Plant assets include equipment, machinery, buildings, and land. With the exception of land, such assets gradually wear out or otherwise lose their usefulness with the passage of time. They are said to **depreciate.** The concept of depreciation is discussed in more detail in Chapter 3.

Liabilities | Liabilities are debts owed to outsiders (creditors) and are frequently described on the balance sheet by titles that include the word "payable." The two categories occurring most frequently are (1) current liabilities and (2) long-term liabilities.

Current liabilities. Liabilities that will be due within a short time (usually one year or less) and that are to be paid out of current assets are called **current liabilities.** The most common liabilities in this group are **notes payable** and **accounts payable,** which are exactly like their receivable counterparts except that the debtor-creditor relationship is reversed. Other current liability accounts commonly found in the ledger are Salaries Payable, Interest Payable, and Taxes Payable.

Long-term liabilities. Liabilities that will not be due for a comparatively long time (usually more than one year) are called **long-term liabilities** or **fixed liabilities.** As they come within the one-year range and are to be paid, such liabilities become current. If the obligation is to be renewed rather than paid at maturity, however, it would continue to be classed as long-term. When payment of a long-term debt is to be spread over a number of years, the installments due within one year from a balance sheet date are classed as a current liability. When a note is accompanied by security in the form of a mortgage, the obligation may be referred to as *mortgage note payable* or *mortgage payable*.

Capital | *Capital* is the term applied to the owner's equity in the business. It is a residual claim against the assets of the business after the total liabilities are deducted. Other commonly used terms for capital are **owner's equity** and **net worth** (*stockholders' equity, shareholders' equity,* and *shareholders' investment* in referring to a corporation).

Revenue | **Revenue** is the gross increase in capital attributable to business activities. It results from the sale of merchandise, the performance of services for a customer or a client, the rental of property, the lending of money, and other business and professional activities entered into for the purpose of earning income. Revenue from sales of merchandise or sales of services is often identified merely as *sales*. Other terms employed to identify sources of revenue include *professional fees, commissions revenue, fares earned,* and *interest income*. If an enterprise has various types of revenue, a separate account should be maintained for each.

Expense | Costs that have been consumed in the process of producing revenue are **expired costs** or **expenses.** The number of expense categories and individual expense accounts maintained in the ledger varies with the nature and the size of an enterprise. A large business with authority and responsibility spread among many employees may use an elaborate classification and hundreds of accounts as an aid in controlling expenses. For a small service business of the type assumed here, a modest number of expense accounts is satisfactory.

CHART OF ACCOUNTS | The number of accounts maintained by a specific enterprise is affected by the nature of its operations, its volume of business, and the extent to which details are needed for taxing authorities, managerial decisions, credit purposes, etc. For example, one enterprise may have separate accounts for executive salaries, office salaries, and sales salaries, while another may find it satisfactory to record all types of salaries in a single salary expense account.

Insofar as possible, the order of the accounts in the ledger should agree with the order of the items in the balance sheet and the income statement. The accounts are numbered to permit indexing and also for use as posting references.

Although accounts in the ledger may be numbered consecutively as in the pages of a book, a flexible system of indexing is preferable. In the following **chart of accounts,** each account number has two digits. The first digit indicates the major division of the ledger in which the account is placed. Accounts beginning with 1 represent assets; 2, liabilities; 3, capital; 4, revenue; and 5, expenses. The second digit indicates the position of the account within its division. A numbering system of this type has the advantage of permitting the later insertion of new accounts in their proper sequence without disturbing the other account numbers. For a large enterprise with a number of departments or branches, it is not unusual for each account number to have four or more digits.

CHART OF ACCOUNTS FOR COLE PHOTOGRAPHIC STUDIO |

Balance Sheet Accounts	Income Statement Accounts
1. Assets	**4. Revenue**
11 Cash	41 Sales
12 Accounts Receivable	
14 Supplies	**5. Expenses**
15 Prepaid Rent	51 Supplies Expense
18 Photographic Equipment	52 Salary Expense
19 Accumulated Depreciation	53 Rent Expense
	54 Depreciation Expense
2. Liabilities	59 Miscellaneous Expense
21 Accounts Payable	
22 Salaries Payable	
3. Capital	
31 Sara Cole, Capital	
32 Sara Cole, Drawing	
33 Income Summary	

FLOW OF ACCOUNTING DATA | The flow of accounting data from the time a transaction occurs to its recording in the ledger may be diagrammed as follows:

Business
TRANSACTION → Business
DOCUMENT → Entry recorded in
JOURNAL → Entry posted to
LEDGER
occurs   prepared

The initial record of each transaction, or of a group of similar transactions, is evidenced by a business document such as a sales ticket, a check stub, or a cash register tape. On the basis of the evidence provided by the business documents, the transactions are entered in chronological order in a journal. The amounts of the debits and the credits in the journal are then transferred or posted to the accounts in the ledger.

TWO-COLUMN JOURNAL | The basic features of a journal entry were illustrated earlier when the use of debit and credit was introduced. There is great variety in both the design of journals and the number of different journals that can be employed by an enterprise. A business may use a single all-purpose two-column journal, or it may use a number of multicolumn journals, restricting each to a single type of transaction. Examples of more sophisticated journal systems are discussed and illustrated in later chapters. Means by which business documents or various types of automated processing devices may entirely replace journals is also discussed.

The two-column journal, which is still widely used, serves as a valuable device in analyzing transactions. The standard form of the two-column journal is illustrated as follows:

STANDARD FORM OF THE TWO-COLUMN JOURNAL

	DATE		DESCRIPTION	POST. REF.	DEBIT	CREDIT	
1	1984 May	1	Cash	101	1 8 2 2 25		1
2			Sales	401		1 8 2 2 25	2
3			Cash sales for the day.				3
4							4
5		1	Advertising Expense		3 5 0 00		5
6			Cash			3 5 0 00	6
7			Advertisements in Lima News.				7
8							8
9		1	Supplies		1 7 5 00		9
10			Accounts Payable			1 7 5 00	10
11			On account from Crom Co.				11
12							12
13							13

JOURNAL   PAGE 17

The process of recording a transaction in a journal is called **journalizing.** The procedures employed for the two-column journal are as follows:

1. Recording the date:
   a. Year is inserted at top only of Date column of each page, except when the year date changes.
   b. Month is inserted on first line only of Date column of each page, except when the month date changes.
   c. Day is inserted in Date column on first line used for each transaction, regardless of number of transactions during the day.
2. Recording the debit:
   Title of account to be debited is inserted at extreme left of the Description column and amount is entered in the Debit column.
3. Recording the credit:
   Title of account to be credited is inserted below the account debited, moderately indented, and the amount is entered in the credit column.
4. Writing explanation:
   Brief explanations may be written below each entry, moderately indented. Some accountants prefer that the explanation be omitted if the nature of the transaction is obvious. It is also permissible to omit a lengthy explanation of a complex transaction if a reference to the related business document can be substituted.

It should be noted that all transactions are recorded only in terms of debits and credits to specific accounts. The titles used in the entries should be the same as the titles of the accounts in the ledger. For example, supplies purchased should be entered as a debit to Supplies, not to "supplies purchased," and cash received should be entered as a debit to Cash, not to "cash received."

The line following an entry is left blank in order to clearly separate each entry. The column headed Post. Ref. (posting reference) is not used until the debits and credits are posted to the appropriate accounts in the ledger.

TWO-COLUMN ACCOUNT

Accounts in the simple T form are used primarily for illustrative purposes. The addition of special rulings to the T form yields the standard two-column form illustrated as follows:

STANDARD FORM OF THE TWO-COLUMN ACCOUNT

ACCOUNT *Cash* ACCOUNT NO. *11*

DATE		ITEM	POST. REF.	DEBIT	DATE		ITEM	POST. REF.	CREDIT
1984 May	1	Balance	✔	5 2 4 5 00	1984 May	1		17	3 5 0 00
	1		17	1 8 2 2 25		1		17	9 9 5 50
	3		17	9 6 0 40		3		17	1 9 2 00
						3		17	1 8 8 2 25
		4,607.90		8 0 2 7 65					3 4 1 9 75

FOUR-COLUMN ACCOUNT

The standard two-column account form distinguishes to the greatest possible extent between debit entries and credit entries. It is primarily because of this feature that the T form is used at the beginning of introductory accounting courses. In actual practice, there has been a tendency for account forms with balance columns to replace the simpler T form, though the latter is still used. A four-column form is shown as follows:

STANDARD FORM OF THE FOUR-COLUMN ACCOUNT

ACCOUNT *Cash*						ACCOUNT NO. *11*
					BALANCE	
DATE	ITEM	POST. REF.	DEBIT	CREDIT	DEBIT	CREDIT
1984 May 1	Balance	✔			5 2 4 5 00	
1		17	1 8 2 2 25		7 0 6 7 25	
1		17		3 5 0 00	6 7 1 7 25	
1		17		9 9 5 50	5 7 2 1 75	
3		17	9 6 0 40		6 6 8 2 15	
3		17		1 9 2 00	6 4 9 0 15	
3		17		1 8 8 2 25	4 6 0 7 90	

Among the significant advantages of the four-column account form are the following:

1. Only a single date column is required, with each debit and credit appearing in its chronological order.
2. The debit or credit nature of an account balance is more easily determined and more prominently displayed in the account.
3. Having immediately adjacent debit and credit columns makes it easier to examine the data in an account.

When posting machines are used with the four-column form, the new balance of an account is automatically computed and printed in the proper column after each posting. The account balance is thus always readily available. The same procedure may be followed when the posting is done manually. An alternative is to postpone the computation of the balance until all postings for the month have been completed. When this is done, only the final month-end balance is inserted in the appropriate balance column. The exact procedure adopted in a particular situation will depend upon such factors as the availability of adding machines and the desirability of having current account balances visible at all times.

POSTING

In many accounting systems, much or all of the posting to the ledger is done by the use of mechanical or electronic equipment designed for the purpose. When the posting is performed manually, the debits and credits in the journal may be posted in the order that they occur or, if many items are to be posted at one time, all of the debits may be posted first, followed by the credits. The posting of a debit journal entry or a credit journal entry to an account in the ledger is performed in the following manner:

1. Record the date and the amount of the entry in the account.

2. Insert the number of the journal page in the Posting Reference column of the account.

3. Insert the ledger account number in the Posting Reference column of the journal.

These procedures are illustrated as follows by the posting of a debit to the cash account. The posting of a credit uses the same sequence of procedures.

DIAGRAM OF THE POSTING
OF A DEBIT

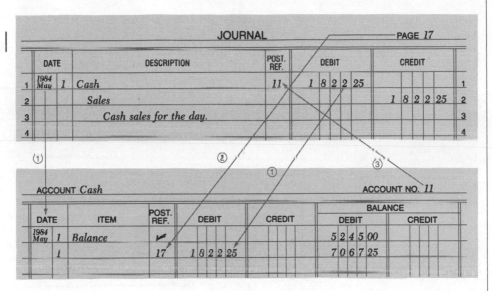

ILLUSTRATIVE   The transactions of a hypothetical business enterprise for a month are used to
PROBLEM   illustrate the recording process. The sequence of steps to be followed in analyzing each part of a transaction is as follows:

1. Determine whether the item affected is asset, liability, capital, revenue, or expense.
2. Determine whether the item affected increases or decreases.
3. Determine whether the effect of the transaction should be recorded as a debit or as a credit.

After a transaction is analyzed in accordance with the preceding outline, the entry is journalized and posted to the accounts in the ledger.

To reduce repetition, some of the following transactions are stated as a summary. For example, sales of services for cash are ordinarily recorded on a daily basis, but in the illustration, summary totals are given only at the middle and end of the month. Similarly, all sales of services on account during the month are summarized as a single transaction. In practice, each sale would be recorded separately.

Mar. 1. Sara Cole operated a photographic business in her home on a part-time basis. She decided to move to rented quarters as of March 1 and to devote full time to the business, which was to be known as Cole Photographic Studio. The following assets were invested in the enterprise: cash, $3,500; accounts receivable, $950; supplies, $1,200; and photographic equipment, $15,000. There were no liabilities transferred to the business.

Analysis: The four asset accounts Cash, Accounts Receivable, Supplies, and Photographic Equipment increase and are debited for $3,500, $950, $1,200, and $15,000, respectively. The owner's equity in these assets is equal to the sum of the assets, or $20,650; hence, Sara Cole, Capital is credited for that amount. (The use of individual accounts receivable from customers is described in a later chapter.)

	DATE		DESCRIPTION	POST. REF.	DEBIT	CREDIT	
			JOURNAL			PAGE 1	
1	1984 Mar.	1	Cash	11	3 5 0 0 00		1
2			Accounts Receivable	12	9 5 0 00		2
3			Supplies	14	1 2 0 0 00		3
4			Photographic Equipment	18	15 0 0 0 00		4
5			Sara Cole, Capital	31		20 6 5 0 00	5

(The ledger to which the illustrative entries are posted is presented on pages 51–53.)

Mar. 1. Paid $2,400 on a lease rental contract, the payment representing three months' rent of quarters for the studio.

Analysis: The asset acquired in exchange for the cash payment is the use of the property for three months. The asset Prepaid Rent increases and is debited for $2,400; the asset Cash decreases and is credited for $2,400. (When rent for a single month is prepaid at the beginning of a month, it is customarily debited to the rent expense account at the time of payment, thus avoiding the necessity of transferring the amount from Prepaid Rent to Rent Expense at the end of the month.)

6							6
7		1	Prepaid Rent	15	2 4 0 0 00		7
8			Cash	11		2 4 0 0 00	8

Mar. 4. Purchased additional photographic equipment on account from Carson Equipment Co. for $2,500.

Analysis: The asset Photographic Equipment increases and is therefore debited for $2,500. The liability Accounts Payable increases and is credited for $2,500. (The use of individual accounts payable to creditors is described in a later chapter.)

9							9
10		4	Photographic Equipment	18	2 5 0 0 00		10
11			Accounts Payable	21		2 5 0 0 00	11

Mar. 5. Received $850 from customers in payment of their accounts.

Analysis: The asset Cash increases and is debited for $850; the asset Accounts Receivable decreases and is credited for $850.

12							12
13	5	Cash	11	8 5 0 00			13
14		Accounts Receivable	12			8 5 0 00	14

Mar. 6. Paid $125 for a newspaper advertisement.

Analysis: Expense accounts are subdivisions of capital. Increases in expense are decreases in capital; hence, an expense account is debited for $125. The asset Cash was decreased by the transaction; therefore that account is credited for $125. (Miscellaneous Expense is debited because total expenditures for advertising during an accounting period are expected to be relatively minor.)

15							15
16	6	Miscellaneous Expense	59	1 2 5 00			16
17		Cash	11			1 2 5 00	17

Mar. 10. Paid $500 to Carson Equipment Co. to apply on the $2,500 debt owed them.

Analysis: This payment decreases the liability Accounts Payable, so that account is debited for $500. It also decreases the asset Cash, which is credited for $500.

18							18
19	10	Accounts Payable	21	5 0 0 00			19
20		Cash	11			5 0 0 00	20

Mar. 13. Paid receptionist $375 for two weeks' salary.

Analysis: Similar to transaction of March 6.

21							21
22	13	Salary Expense	52	3 7 5 00			22
23		Cash	11			3 7 5 00	23

Mar. 16. Received $1,580 from sales for the first half of March.

Analysis: Cash increases and is debited for $1,580. The revenue account Sales, which is a subdivision of capital, increases and is credited for $1,580.

24							24
25	16	Cash	11	1 5 8 0 00			25
26		Sales	41			1 5 8 0 00	26

Mar. 20. Paid $650 for supplies.

Analysis: The asset Supplies increases and is debited for $650; the asset Cash decreases and is credited for $650.

27						27
28	20	Supplies	14	6 5 0 00		28
29		Cash	11		6 5 0 00	29

Mar. 27. Paid receptionist $375 for two weeks' salary.

Analysis: Similar to transaction of March 6.

30						30
31	27	Salary Expense	52	3 7 5 00		31
32		Cash	11		3 7 5 00	32

Mar. 31. Paid $69 for telephone bill for the month.

Analysis: Similar to transaction of March 6.

33						33
34	31	Miscellaneous Expense	59	6 9 00		34
35		Cash	11		6 9 00	35

Mar. 31. Paid $175 for electric bill for the month.

Analysis: Similar to transaction of March 6.

36						36
37	31	Miscellaneous Expense	59	1 7 5 00		37
38		Cash	11		1 7 5 00	38

Mar. 31. Received $1,870 from sales for the second half of March.

Analysis: Similar to transaction of March 16.

	DATE		DESCRIPTION	POST. REF.	DEBIT	CREDIT	
			JOURNAL			PAGE 2	
1	1984 Mar.	31	Cash	11	1 8 7 0 00		1
2			Sales	41		1 8 7 0 00	2

Mar. 31. Sales on account totaled $1,675 for the month.

Analysis: The asset Accounts Receivable increases and is debited for $1,675. The revenue account Sales increases and is credited for $1,675. (Note that the revenue is earned even though no cash is received; the claim against the customers is as much an asset as cash. As customers pay their accounts later, Cash will be debited and Accounts Receivable will be credited.)

3							3
4	31	Accounts Receivable	12	1 6 7 5 00			4
5		Sales	41		1 6 7 5 00		5

Mar. 31. Cole withdrew $1,500 for her personal use.

Analysis: The transaction resulted in a decrease in the amount of capital invested in the business and is recorded by a $1,500 debit to Sara Cole, Drawing; the decrease in business cash is recorded by a $1,500 credit to Cash.

6							6
7	31	Sara Cole, Drawing	32	1 5 0 0 00			7
8		Cash	11		1 5 0 0 00		8

After all the entries for the month have been posted, the ledger will appear as shown below and on pages 52–53. In practice, each account would appear on a separate page in the ledger. Tracing each entry from the journal to the accounts in the ledger will give a clear understanding of the posting process.

The accounts are numbered in accordance with the chart shown on page 43. However, some of the accounts listed in the chart are not shown in the illustrative ledger. The additional accounts will be used later when the work of the accounting cycle is completed.

LEDGER—COLE
PHOTOGRAPHIC STUDIO

ACCOUNT Cash   ACCOUNT NO. 11

DATE	ITEM	POST. REF.	DEBIT	CREDIT	BALANCE DEBIT	BALANCE CREDIT
1984 Mar. 1		1	3 5 0 0 00		3 5 0 0 00	
1		1		2 4 0 0 00	1 1 0 0 00	
5		1	8 5 0 00		1 9 5 0 00	
6		1		1 2 5 00	1 8 2 5 00	
10		1		5 0 0 00	1 3 2 5 00	
13		1		3 7 5 00	9 5 0 00	
16		1	1 5 8 0 00		2 5 3 0 00	
20		1		6 5 0 00	1 8 8 0 00	
27		1		3 7 5 00	1 5 0 5 00	
31		1		6 9 00	1 4 3 6 00	
31		1		1 7 5 00	1 2 6 1 00	
31		2	1 8 7 0 00		3 1 3 1 00	
31		2		1 5 0 0 00	1 6 3 1 00	

LEDGER—COLE
PHOTOGRAPHIC
STUDIO
(CONTINUED)

ACCOUNT Accounts Receivable   ACCOUNT NO. 12

DATE	ITEM	POST. REF.	DEBIT	CREDIT	BALANCE DEBIT	BALANCE CREDIT
1984 Mar. 1		1	9 5 0 00		9 5 0 00	
5		1		8 5 0 00	1 0 0 00	
31		2	1 6 7 5 00		1 7 7 5 00	

ACCOUNT Supplies   ACCOUNT NO. 14

DATE	ITEM	POST. REF.	DEBIT	CREDIT	BALANCE DEBIT	BALANCE CREDIT
1984 Mar. 1		1	1 2 0 0 00		1 2 0 0 00	
20		1	6 5 0 00		1 8 5 0 00	

ACCOUNT Prepaid Rent   ACCOUNT NO. 15

DATE	ITEM	POST. REF.	DEBIT	CREDIT	BALANCE DEBIT	BALANCE CREDIT
1984 Mar. 1		1	2 4 0 0 00		2 4 0 0 00	

ACCOUNT Photographic Equipment   ACCOUNT NO. 18

DATE	ITEM	POST. REF.	DEBIT	CREDIT	BALANCE DEBIT	BALANCE CREDIT
1984 Mar. 1		1	15 0 0 0 00		15 0 0 0 00	
4		1	2 5 0 0 00		17 5 0 0 00	

ACCOUNT Accounts Payable   ACCOUNT NO. 21

DATE	ITEM	POST. REF.	DEBIT	CREDIT	BALANCE DEBIT	BALANCE CREDIT
1984 Mar. 4		1		2 5 0 0 00		2 5 0 0 00
10		1	5 0 0 00			2 0 0 0 00

ACCOUNT Sara Cole, Capital   ACCOUNT NO. 31

DATE	ITEM	POST. REF.	DEBIT	CREDIT	BALANCE DEBIT	BALANCE CREDIT
1984 Mar. 1		1		20 6 5 0 00		20 6 5 0 00

ACCOUNT Sara Cole, Drawing   ACCOUNT NO. 32

DATE	ITEM	POST. REF.	DEBIT	CREDIT	BALANCE DEBIT	BALANCE CREDIT
1984 Mar. 31		2	1 5 0 0 00		1 5 0 0 00	

ACCOUNT Sales   ACCOUNT NO. 41

DATE	ITEM	POST. REF.	DEBIT	CREDIT	BALANCE DEBIT	BALANCE CREDIT
1984 Mar. 16		1		1 5 8 0 00		1 5 8 0 00
31		2		1 8 7 0 00		3 4 5 0 00
31		2		1 6 7 5 00		5 1 2 5 00

LEDGER—COLE
PHOTOGRAPHIC STUDIO
(CONCLUDED)

ACCOUNT Salary Expense						ACCOUNT NO. 52	
						BALANCE	
DATE	ITEM	POST. REF.	DEBIT	CREDIT		DEBIT	CREDIT
1984 Mar. 13		1	3 7 5 00			3 7 5 00	
27		1	3 7 5 00			7 5 0 00	

ACCOUNT Miscellaneous Expense						ACCOUNT NO. 59	
						BALANCE	
DATE	ITEM	POST. REF.	DEBIT	CREDIT		DEBIT	CREDIT
1984 Mar. 6		1	1 2 5 00			1 2 5 00	
31		1	6 9 00			1 9 4 00	
31		1	1 7 5 00			3 6 9 00	

TRIAL
BALANCE

The equality of debits and credits in the ledger should be verified at the end of each accounting period, if not more often. Such a verification, which is called a **trial balance,** may be in the form of an adding machine tape or in the form illustrated as follows. The summary listing of both the balances and the titles of the accounts is also useful in preparing the financial statements.

Cole Photographic Studio								
Trial Balance								
March 31, 1984								
Cash	1	6 3 1	00					
Accounts Receivable	1	7 7 5	00					
Supplies	1	8 5 0	00					
Prepaid Rent	2	4 0 0	00					
Photographic Equipment	17	5 0 0	00					
Accounts Payable					2	0 0 0	00	
Sara Cole, Capital					20	6 5 0	00	
Sara Cole, Drawing	1	5 0 0	00					
Sales					5	1 2 5	00	
Salary Expense		7 5 0	00					
Miscellaneous Expense		3 6 9	00					
	27	7 7 5	00		27	7 7 5	00	

As the first step in preparing the trial balance, the balance of each account in the ledger should be determined. If two-column accounts are used, memorandum pencil footings and balances are inserted in accordance with the procedure illustrated on page 45. If the four-column account form is employed, the balance of each account must be indicated in the appropriate balance column on the same line as the last posting to the account. (In the illustrative ledger the balances were extended after each posting.)

Proof Provided by the Trial Balance   The trial balance does not provide complete proof of the accuracy of the ledger. It indicates only that the *debits* and the *credits* are *equal*. This proof is of value, however, because errors frequently affect the equality of debits and credits. If the two totals of a trial balance are not equal, it is probably due to one or more of the following types of errors:

1. Error in preparing the trial balance, such as:
   a. One of the columns of the trial balance was incorrectly added.
   b. The amount of an account balance was incorrectly recorded on the trial balance.
   c. A debit balance was recorded on the trial balance as a credit, or vice versa, or a balance was omitted entirely.
2. Error in determining the account balances, such as:
   a. A balance was incorrectly computed.
   b. A balance was entered in the wrong balance column.
3. Error in recording a transaction in the ledger, such as:
   a. An erroneous amount was posted to the account.
   b. A debit entry was posted as a credit, or vice versa.
   c. A debit or a credit posting was omitted.

Among the types of errors that will not cause an inequality in the trial balance totals are the following:

1. Failure to record a transaction or to post a transaction.
2. Recording the same erroneous amount for both the debit and the credit parts of a transaction.
3. Recording the same transaction more than once.
4. Posting a part of a transaction correctly as a debit or credit but to the wrong account.

It is readily apparent that care should be exercised both in recording transactions in the journal and in posting to the accounts. The desirability of accuracy in determining account balances and reporting them on the trial balance is equally obvious.

Discovery of Errors   The existence of errors in the accounts may be determined in various ways: (1) by audit procedures, (2) by chance discovery, or (3) through the medium of the trial balance. If the debit and the credit totals of the trial balance are not in agreement, the exact amount of the difference between the totals should be determined before proceeding to search for the error.

The amount of the difference between the two totals of a trial balance sometimes gives a clue as to the nature of the error or where it occurred. For example, a difference of 10, 100, or 1,000 between two totals is frequently the result of an error in addition. A difference between totals can also be due to the omission of a debit or a credit posting or, if it is divisible evenly by 2, to the posting of a debit as a credit, or vice versa. For example, if the debit and the credit totals of a trial balance are $20,640 and $20,236 respectively, the difference of $404 may indicate that a credit posting of that amount was omitted or that a credit of $202 was erroneously posted as a debit.

Two other common types of errors are known as transpositions and slides. A transposition is the erroneous rearrangement of digits, such as writing $542 as $452 or $524. In a slide, the entire number is erroneously moved one or more spaces to the right or the left, such as writing $542.00 as $54.20 or $5,420.00. If an error of either type has occurred and there are no other errors, the discrepancy between the two trial balance totals will be evenly divisible by 9.

A preliminary examination along the lines suggested by the preceding paragraphs will frequently disclose the error. If it does not, the general procedure is to retrace the various steps in the accounting process, beginning with the last step and working back to the original entries in the journal. While there are no rigid rules governing the procedures, the following plan is suggested:

1. Verify the accuracy of the trial balance totals by re-adding the columns.
2. Compare the listings in the trial balance with the balances shown in the ledger, making certain that no accounts have been omitted.
3. Recompute the balance of each account in the ledger.
4. Trace the postings in the ledger back to the journal, placing a small check mark by the item in the ledger and also in the journal. If the error is not found, examine each account to see if there is an entry without a check mark. Do the same with the entries in the journal.
5. Verify the equality of the debits and the credits in the journal.

Ordinarily, errors that have caused the trial balance totals to be unequal will be discovered before all of the procedures outlined above are completed.

Self-Examination Questions
(Answers in Appendix C.)

1. A debit may signify:
   A. an increase in an asset account
   B. a decrease in an asset account
   C. an increase in a liability account
   D. an increase in a capital account

2. The type of account with a normal credit balance is:
   A. an asset
   B. a drawing
   C. a revenue
   D. an expense

3. The current asset category would include:
   A. cash
   B. accounts receivable
   C. supplies on hand
   D. all of the above

4. The receipt of cash from customers in payment of their accounts would be recorded by a:
   A. debit to cash; credit to accounts receivable
   B. debit to accounts receivable; credit to cash
   C. debit to cash; credit to accounts payable
   D. debit to accounts payable; credit to cash

5. The form listing the balances and the titles of the accounts in the ledger on a given date is the:
   A. income statement
   B. capital statement
   C. retained earnings statement
   D. trial balance

A Group of Accounts

A PLACE OR FORM IN WHICH OR ON WHICH YOU RECORD INC. / DEC. IN INDIVIDUAL ASSETS, CAP, LIA, REV, EXP

Discussion Questions

1. Differentiate between an account and a ledger.

2. Do the terms *debit* and *credit* signify increase or decrease, or may they signify either? Explain. *THEY SIGNIFY BOTH DEPENDING on the nature of the A/C*

3. Define posting. *PS A6*

4. Describe the nature of the assets that compose the following categories: (a) current assets, (b) plant assets. *PS 41, 42*

5. As of the time a balance sheet is being prepared, a business enterprise owes a mortgage note payable of $60,000, the terms of which provide for monthly payments of $1,200. How should the liability be classified on the balance sheet?

6. Indicate whether each of the following is recorded by a debit or by a credit: (a) decrease in an asset account, (b) decrease in a liability account, (c) increase in a capital account.

7. What is the effect (increase or decrease) of debits to expense accounts (a) in terms of capital, (b) in terms of expense?

8. Identify each of the following accounts as asset, liability, capital, revenue, or expense, and state in each case whether the normal balance is a debit or a credit: (a) Accounts Payable, (b) Supplies, (c) Interest Expense, (d) M. C. Mullins, Capital, (e) Cash, (f) Accounts Receivable, (g) Salary Expense, (h) M. C. Mullins, Drawing, (i) Equipment, (j) Sales.

9. Bruce Evans Company adheres to a policy of depositing all cash receipts in a bank account and making all payments by check. The cash account as of March 31 has a credit balance of $400 and there is no undeposited cash on hand. (a) Assuming that there were no errors in journalizing or posting, what is the explanation of this unusual balance? (b) Is the $400 credit balance in the cash account an asset, a liability, capital, a revenue, or an expense?

10. Rearrange the following in proper sequence: (a) entry recorded in journal, (b) business document prepared, (c) entry posted to ledger, (d) business transaction occurs.

11. During the month, a business enterprise has a substantial number of transactions affecting each of the following accounts. State for each account whether it is likely to have (a) debit entries only, (b) credit entries only, or (c) both debit and credit entries.

    (1) Interest Income   (5) Cash
    (2) John Gordon, Drawing   (6) Accounts Payable
    (3) Miscellaneous Expense   (7) Notes Receivable
    (4) Accounts Receivable   (8) Sales

12. Describe the three procedures required to post the credit portion of the following journal entry (Sales is account No. 41).

JOURNAL   PAGE 18

19-- May	20	Accounts Receivable	12	1,150	
		Sales			1,150

13. Describe in general terms the sequence of accounts in the ledger.

14. Patterson Brothers performed services in April for a specific customer for which the fee was $2,500. Payment was received in the following May. (a) Was the revenue earned in April or May? (b) What accounts should be debited and credited in (1) April and (2) May?

15. As of June 1, the capital account of a sole proprietorship had a credit balance of $25,000. During the year, the owner's withdrawals totaled $15,000 and the business incurred a net loss of $12,500. There were no additional investments in the business. Assuming that there have been no recording errors, will the balance sheet prepared at May 31 balance? Explain.

16. During the month, a business corporation received $675,000 in cash and paid out $600,000 in cash. Do the data indicate that the corporation earned $75,000 during the month? Explain.

17. (a) Describe the form known as a trial balance. (b) What proof is provided by a trial balance?

18. When a trial balance is prepared, an account balance of $28,500 is listed as $25,800, and an account balance of $6,400 is listed as $640. Identify the transposition and the slide.

19. When a purchase of supplies of $278 for cash was recorded, both the debit and the credit were journalized and posted as $287. (a) Would this error cause the trial balance to be out of balance? (b) Would the answer be the same if the $278 entry had been journalized correctly, the debit to Supplies had been posted correctly, but the credit to Cash had been posted as $287?

20. Indicate which of the following errors, each considered individually, would cause the trial balance totals to be unequal:
    (a) A payment of $12,000 for equipment purchased was posted as a debit of $21,000 to Equipment and a credit of $12,000 to Cash.
    (b) A withdrawal of $1,200 by the owner was journalized and posted as a debit of $120 to Salary Expense and a credit of $120 to Cash.
    (c) A fee of $600 earned and due from a client was not debited to Accounts Receivable or credited to a revenue account because the cash had not been received.
    (d) A receipt of $275 from an account receivable was journalized and posted as a debit of $275 to Cash and a credit of $275 to Sales.
    (e) A payment of $950 to a creditor was posted as a credit of $950 to Accounts Payable and a credit of $950 to Cash.

Exercises

Exercise 2-1. Banister Company has the following accounts in its ledger: Cash; Accounts Receivable; Supplies; Office Equipment; Accounts Payable; Ben Banister, Capital; Ben Banister, Drawing; Fees Earned; Rent Expense; Advertising Expense; Utilities Expense; Miscellaneous Expense.

Record the following transactions, completed during January of the current year, in a two-column journal:

Jan. 2. Paid rent for the month, $700.
       5. Paid cash for supplies, $68.

Jan. 7. Purchased office equipment on account, $2,480.
      8. Paid advertising expense, $100.
     10. Received cash from customers on account, $3,810.
     12. Withdrew cash for personal use, $1,000.
     15. Paid for repairs to office equipment, $45.
     16. Paid creditor on account, $650.
     24. Paid telephone bill for the month, $89.
     30. Fees earned and billed to customers for the month, $4,160.
     31. Paid electricity bill for the month, $220.

Exercise 2-2. Eight transactions are recorded in the following T accounts:

Cash		Equipment		Wayne Meyers, Drawing	
(1) 8,000	(2) 1,500	(2) 10,000		(8) 2,000	
(7) 18,100	(3) 150				
	(4) 1,100				
	(5) 4,800				
	(8) 2,000				

Accounts Receivable		Accounts Payable		Service Revenue	
(6) 22,500	(7) 18,100	(5) 4,800	(2) 8,500		(6) 22,500

Supplies		Wayne Meyers, Capital		Operating Expenses	
(3) 150			(1) 8,000	(4) 1,100	

Indicate for each debit and each credit: (a) the type of account affected (asset, liability, capital, revenue, or expense) and (b) whether the account was increased (+) or decreased (−). Answers should be presented in the following form (transaction (1) is given as an example):

	Account Debited		Account Credited	
Transaction	Type	Effect	Type	Effect
(1)	asset	+	capital	+

Exercise 2-3. Norman Services Co. is a newly organized enterprise. The list of asset, liability, capital, revenue, and expense accounts to be opened in the general ledger is as follows:

Miscellaneous Expense	Accounts Receivable
Retained Earnings	Salary Expense
Sales	Equipment
Accumulated Depreciation	Cash
Rent Expense	Salaries Payable
Supplies	Supplies Expense
Prepaid Rent	Accounts Payable
Capital Stock	Depreciation Expense

List the accounts in the order in which they should appear in the ledger of Norman Services Co. and assign account numbers. Each account number is to have two digits: the first digit is to indicate the major classification ("1" for assets, etc.) and the second digit is to identify the specific account within each major classification ("11" to Cash, etc.).

Exercise 2-4. The accounts (all normal balances) in the ledger of Braves Realty, Inc. as of June 30 of the current year are as follows, in alphabetical order. The balance of the cash account has been intentionally omitted.

Accounts Payable	$ 8,910
Accounts Receivable	12,600
Buildings	225,000
Capital Stock	300,000
Cash	X
Dividends	20,000
Equipment	197,280
Fees Earned	280,000
Land	160,000
Miscellaneous Expense	2,500
Mortgage Note Payable (due 1990)	25,000
Prepaid Insurance	2,400
Retained Earnings	215,000
Salary Expense	180,000
Supplies	4,500
Supplies Expense	3,120
Utilities Expense	11,600

Prepare a trial balance, listing the accounts in their proper order and inserting the missing figure for cash.

Exercise 2-5. The following preliminary trial balance of Hudson Company does not balance. When the ledger and other records are reviewed, you discover the following: (1) the debits and credits in the cash account total $68,600 and $52,140 respectively; (2) a receipt of $600 from a customer on account was not posted to the accounts receivable account; (3) a payment of $1,100 to a creditor on account was not posted to the accounts payable account; (4) the balance of the equipment account is $41,200; (5) each account had a normal balance. Prepare a corrected trial balance.

Hudson Company
Trial Balance
August 31, 19--

Cash	$ 68,600	
Accounts Receivable	14,900	
Prepaid Insurance		$ 300
Equipment	42,100	
Accounts Payable		8,300
Salaries Payable	900	
Elmer Hudson, Capital		51,100
Elmer Hudson, Drawing		4,000
Service Revenue		26,900
Salary Expense	8,400	
Advertising Expense	1,200	
Miscellaneous Expense		240
	$136,100	$90,840

Exercise 2-6. The following errors occurred in posting from a two-column journal:

(1) A credit of $120 to Accounts Payable was posted as a debit.
(2) An entry debiting Advertising Expense and crediting Cash for $250 was not posted.
(3) A debit of $1,500 to Equipment was posted twice.
(4) A debit of $200 to Cash was posted as $2,000.
(5) A debit of $180 to Supplies was posted as $810.
(6) A debit of $350 to Accounts Receivable was not posted.
(7) A credit of $400 to Sales was posted to Cash.

Considering each case individually (i.e., assuming that no other errors had occurred), indicate: (a) by "yes" or "no" whether the trial balance would be out of balance; (b) if answer to (a) is "yes," the amount by which the trial balance totals would differ and (c) the column of the trial balance that would have the larger total. Answers should be presented in the following form (error (1) is given as an example):

Error	(a) Out of Balance	(b) Difference	(c) Larger Total
(1)	yes	$240	debit

Problems
(Problems in Appendix B: 2-1B, 2-3B, 2-4B, 2-6B.)

Problem 2-1A. Amy Metcalf established a sole proprietorship, to be known as Metcalf Decorators, on February 10 of the current year. During the remainder of the month, she completed the following business transactions:

Feb. 10. Metcalf transferred cash from a personal bank account to an account to be used for the business, $10,000.
10. Paid rent for period of February 10 to end of month, $500.
11. Purchased a truck for $12,000, paying $3,000 cash and giving a note payable for the remainder.
12. Purchased equipment on account, $1,460.
14. Purchased supplies for cash, $885.
14. Paid premiums on property and casualty insurance, $170.
15. Received cash for job completed, $360.
16. Purchased supplies on account, $240.
18. Paid wages of employees, $900.
21. Paid creditor for equipment purchased on February 12, $1,460.
24. Recorded sales on account and sent invoices to customers, $2,080.
26. Received an invoice for truck expenses, to be paid in March, $115.
26. Received cash for job completed, $610. This sale had not been recorded previously.
27. Paid utilities expense, $205.
27. Paid miscellaneous expenses, $73.
28. Received cash from customers on account, $1,420.
28. Paid wages of employees, $950.
28. Withdrew cash for personal use, $1,750.

Instructions:

(1) Open a ledger of two-column accounts for Metcalf Decorators, using the following titles and account numbers: Cash, 11; Accounts Receivable, 12; Supplies, 13; Prepaid Insurance, 14; Equipment, 16; Truck, 18; Notes Payable, 21; Accounts

Payable, 22; Amy Metcalf, Capital, 31; Amy Metcalf, Drawing, 32; Sales, 41; Wages Expense, 51; Rent Expense, 53; Utilities Expense, 54; Truck Expense, 55; Miscellaneous Expense, 59.

(2) Record each transaction in a two-column journal, referring to the above list of accounts or to the ledger in selecting appropriate account titles to be debited and credited. (Do not insert the account numbers in the journal at this time.)

(3) Post the journal to the ledger, inserting appropriate posting references as each item is posted.

(4) Determine the balances of the accounts in the ledger, pencil footing all accounts having two or more debits or credits. A memorandum balance should also be inserted in accounts having both debits and credits, in the manner illustrated on page 45. For accounts with entries on one side only (such as Sales), there is no need to insert the memorandum balance in the item column. Accounts containing only a single debit and a single credit (such as Accounts Receivable) need no pencil footings; the memorandum balance should be inserted in the appropriate item column. Accounts containing a single entry only (such as Prepaid Insurance) need neither a pencil footing nor a memorandum balance.

(5) Prepare a trial balance for Metcalf Decorators as of February 28.

Problem 2-2A. Denise Wallace, M.D., completed the following transactions in the practice of her profession during May of the current year:

May   1. Paid office rent for May, $1,400.
        2. Purchased X-ray film and other supplies on account, $680.
        4. Received cash on account from patients, $8,476.
        6. Purchased equipment on account, $5,100.
        6. Paid cash to creditors on account, $4,810.
        8. Sold X-ray film to another doctor at cost, as an accommodation, receiving cash, $120.
      10. Paid invoice for laboratory analyses, $280.
      11. Paid cash for renewal of property insurance policy, $560.
      20. Discovered that the balance of the cash account was understated and the accounts receivable account was overstated as of May 1 by $500. A cash receipt of that amount on account from a patient in April had not been recorded. Journalized the $500 receipt as of May 20.
      24. One of the items of equipment purchased on May 6 was defective. It was returned with the permission of the supplier, who agreed to reduce the account for the amount charged for the item, $800.
      26. Paid cash from business bank account for personal and family expenses, $3,500.
      31. Recorded the cash received in payment of services (on a cash basis) to patients during May, $8,350.
      31. Paid salaries of receptionist and nurses, $3,200.
      31. Paid miscellaneous expenses, $420.
      31. Paid gas and electricity expense, $610.
      31. Paid water expense, $130.
      31. Recorded fees charged to patients on account for services performed in May, $6,180.
      31. Paid telephone expense, $280.

Instructions:

(1) Open a ledger of accounts with balance columns for Dr. Wallace as of May 1 of the current year. The accounts and their balances (all normal balances) as of

May 1 are listed as follows. Enter the balances in the appropriate balance columns and place a check mark (√) in the posting reference column. Cash, 11, $6,170; Accounts Receivable, 12, $14,280; Supplies, 13, $1,240; Prepaid Insurance, 14, $3,600; Equipment, 18, $43,400; Accounts Payable, 22, $7,850; Denise Wallace, Capital, 31, $60,840; Denise Wallace, Drawing, 32; Professional Fees, 41; Salary Expense, 51; Rent Expense, 53; Utilities Expense, 55; Laboratory Expense, 56; Miscellaneous Expense, 59. (It is advisable to verify the equality of the debit and credit balances in the ledger before proceeding with the next instruction.)

(2) Record each transaction in a two-column journal.
(3) Post the journal to the ledger, extending the month-end balances to the appropriate balance columns after all posting is completed.
(4) Prepare a trial balance as of May 31.
(5) Assuming that the expenses which have not been recorded (such as supplies expense and insurance expense) amount to a total of $2,280 for the month, determine the following amounts:
    (a) Net income for the month of May.
    (b) Increase or decrease in capital during May.
    (c) Capital as of May 31.

(If the working papers correlating with the textbook are not used, omit Problem 2-3A.)

Problem 2-3A. The following records of Wiley TV Service are presented in the working papers:

Journal containing entries for the period October 1–31.
Ledger to which the October entries have been posted.
Preliminary trial balance as of October 31, which does not balance.

Locate the errors, supply the information requested, and prepare a corrected trial balance, proceeding in accordance with the following detailed instructions. The balances recorded in the accounts as of October 1 and the entries in the journal are correctly stated. If it is necessary to correct any posted amounts in the ledger, a line should be drawn through the erroneous figure and the correct amount inserted above. Corrections or notations may be inserted on the preliminary trial balance in any manner desired. It is not necessary to complete all of the instructions if equal trial balance totals can be obtained earlier. However, the requirements of instructions (8) and (9) should be completed in any event.

Instructions:

(1) Verify the totals of the preliminary trial balance, inserting the correct amounts in the schedule provided in the working papers.
(2) Compute the difference between the trial balance totals.
(3) Determine whether the difference obtained in (2) is evenly divisible by 9.
(4) If the difference obtained in (2) is an even number, determine half the amount.
(5) Compare the listings in the trial balance with the balances appearing in the ledger.
(6) Verify the accuracy of the balances of each account in the ledger.
(7) Trace the postings in the ledger back to the journal, using small check marks to identify items traced. (Correct any amounts in the ledger that may be necessitated by errors in posting.)
(8) Journalize as of October 31 the purchase of an adjacent piece of land at a cost of $11,000, for which a note payable was given. The transaction had occurred on October 31 but was inadvertently omitted from the journal. Post to the ledger. (Revise any amounts necessitated by posting this entry.)
(9) Prepare a new trial balance.

Problem 2-4A. The following business transactions were completed by Whipple Theatre Corporation during July of the current year:

July   1. Received and deposited in a bank account $60,000 cash for capital stock.

        2. Purchased the Clinton Drive-In Theatre for $100,000, allocated as follows: land, $58,000; buildings, $23,600; equipment, $18,400. Paid $35,000 in cash and gave a mortgage note for the remainder.

        5. Entered into a contract for the operation of the refreshment stand concession at a rental of 20% of the concessionaire's sales, with a guaranteed minimum of $600 a month, payable in advance. Received cash of $600 as the advance payment for the month of July.

        6. Paid premiums for property and casualty insurance policies, $2,750.

        7. Purchased supplies, $420, and equipment, $3,180, on account.

        8. Paid for July billboard and newspaper advertising, $150.

     10. Cash received from admissions for the week, $2,130.

     12. Paid miscellaneous expense, $265.

     15. Paid semimonthly wages, $1,160.

     17. Cash received from admissions for the week, $1,980.

     19. Paid miscellaneous expenses, $310.

     20. Returned portion of supplies purchased on July 7 to the supplier, receiving full credit for the cost, $90.

     23. Paid cash to creditors on account, $1,755.

     24. Cash received from admissions for the week, $2,420.

     26. Purchased supplies for cash, $85.

     26. Paid for advertising leaflets for special promotion during last week in July, $240.

     28. Recorded invoice of $3,500 for rental of film for July. Payment is due on August 15.

     29. Paid electricity and water bills, $920.

     30. Paid semimonthly wages, $950.

     31. Cash received from admissions for remainder of the month, $2,870.

     31. Recorded additional amount owed by the concessionaire for the month of July; sales for the month totaled $4,350. Rental charges in excess of the advance payment of $600 are not due and payable until August 5.

Instructions:

(1) Open a ledger of four-column accounts for Whipple Theatre Corporation, using the following account titles and numbers: Cash, 11; Accounts Receivable, 12; Prepaid Insurance, 13; Supplies, 14; Land, 17; Buildings, 18; Equipment, 19; Accounts Payable, 21; Mortgage Note Payable, 24; Capital Stock, 31; Admissions Income, 41; Concession Income, 42; Wages Expense, 51; Film Rental Expense, 52; Advertising Expense, 53; Electricity and Water Expense, 54; Miscellaneous Expense, 59.

(2) Record the transactions in a two-column journal.

(3) Post the journal to the ledger, extending the month-end balances to the appropriate balance columns after all posting is completed.

(4) Prepare a trial balance as of July 31.

(5) Determine the following:

    (a) Amount of total revenue recorded in the ledger.

    (b) Amount of total expenses recorded in the ledger.

    (c) Amount of net income for July, assuming that additional unrecorded expenses (including supplies used, insurance expired, etc.) totaled $758.

(continued)

(d) The understatement or overstatement of net income for July that would have resulted from failure to record the invoice for film rental until it was paid in August. (See transaction of July 28.)

(e) The understatement or overstatement of liabilities as of July 31 that would have resulted from failure to record the invoice for film rental in July. (See transaction of July 28.)

Problem 2-5A. Seawell Realty, Inc. acts as an agent in buying, selling, renting, and managing real estate. The account balances at the end of July of the current year are as follows:

11	Cash	46,240	
12	Accounts Receivable	23,600	
13	Prepaid Insurance	240	
14	Office Supplies	830	
16	Land	0	
21	Accounts Payable		4,250
22	Notes Payable		0
31	Capital Stock		20,000
32	Retained Earnings		19,606
33	Dividends	2,000	
41	Fees Earned		305,600
51	Salary and Commission Expense	244,480	
52	Rent Expense	12,000	
53	Advertising Expense	10,300	
54	Automobile Expense	8,450	
59	Miscellaneous Expense	1,316	
		349,456	349,456

The following business transactions were completed by Seawell Realty, Inc. during August of the current year.

Aug. 2. Paid rent on office for month, $1,000.
3. Purchased office supplies on account, $250.
5. Received cash from clients on account, $16,280.
7. Paid insurance premiums, $1,400.
12. Paid salaries and commissions, $12,870.
14. Purchased land for a future building site for $20,500, paying $5,500 in cash and giving a note payable for the remainder.
15. Recorded revenue earned and billed to clients during first half of month, $14,160.
18. Paid creditors on account, $2,420.
20. Returned a portion of the supplies purchased on August 3, receiving full credit for their cost, $80.
23. Received cash from clients on account, $10,190.
24. Paid advertising expense, $820.
27. Discovered an error in computing a commission; received cash from the salesperson for the overpayment, $350.
28. Paid automobile expenses (including rental charges), $630.
30. Paid miscellaneous expenses, $216.
31. Recorded revenue earned and billed to clients during second half of month, $16,300.

31. Paid salaries and commissions, $19,840.
31. Paid dividend, $2,000.

Instructions:

(1) Open a ledger of four-column accounts for the accounts listed. Record the balances in the appropriate balance columns as of August 1, write "Balance" in the item section, and place a check mark (√) in the posting reference column.
(2) Record the transactions for August in a two-column journal.
(3) Post to the ledger, extending the month-end balances to the appropriate balance columns after all posting is completed.
(4) Prepare a trial balance of the ledger as of August 31.

Problem 2-6A. The following trial balance for Church Carpet Installation, a sole proprietorship, as of September 30 of the current year, does not balance because of a number of errors:

Cash	3,752	
Accounts Receivable	5,683	
Supplies	1,457	
Prepaid Insurance	100	
Equipment	14,600	
Notes Payable		13,000
Accounts Payable		2,960
Gerri Church, Capital		10,042
Gerri Church, Drawing	3,500	
Sales		38,200
Wages Expense	21,400	
Rent Expense	4,500	
Advertising Expense	200	
Gas, Electricity, and Water Expense	900	
	56,092	64,202

(a) The balance of cash was overstated by $1,000.
(b) A cash receipt of $210 was posted as a debit to Cash of $120.
(c) A debit of $2,000 for a withdrawal by the owner was posted as a credit to the capital account.
(d) The balance of $1,200 in Advertising Expense was entered as $200 in the trial balance.
(e) A debit of $450 to Accounts Receivable was not posted.
(f) A return of $310 of defective supplies was erroneously posted as a $130 credit to Supplies.
(g) The balance of Notes Payable was overstated by $3,000.
(h) An insurance policy acquired at a cost of $200 was posted as a credit to Prepaid Insurance.
(i) Miscellaneous Expense, with a balance of $1,060, was omitted from the trial balance.
(j) A credit of $710 in Accounts Payable was overlooked when determining the balance of the account.

Instructions:

Prepare a corrected trial balance as of September 30 of the current year.

Mini-Case

During May through August, Doug Hally is planning to manage and operate Hally Caddy Service at Milledge Golf and Country Club. Doug will rent a small maintenance building from the country club for $50 per month and will offer caddy services, including cart rentals, to golfers. Doug has had no formal training in record keeping. During May, he kept notes of all receipts and expenses in a shoe box.

An examination of Doug's shoe box records for May revealed the following:

May　1.　Withdrew $500 from a personal bank account to be used to operate the caddy service.

　　　1.　Paid rent to Milledge Golf and Country Club, $50.

　　　3.　Paid for golf supplies (practice balls, etc.), $160.

　　　3.　Paid miscellaneous expenses, $35.

　　　4.　Arranged for the rental of forty regular (pulling) golf carts and ten gasoline-driven carts for $800 per month. Paid $500 in advance, with the remaining $300 due May 20.

　　　7.　Purchased supplies, including gasoline, for the golf carts on account, $305. Milledge Golf and Country Club has agreed to allow Doug to store the gasoline in one of their fuel tanks at no cost.

　　12.　Cash receipts for May 1–12, $870.

　　12.　For May 1–12, accepted IOUs from customers on account, $183.

　　15.　Paid salary of part-time employees, $70.

　　17.　Paid cash to creditors on account, $180.

　　20.　Paid remaining rental on golf carts, $300.

　　22.　Purchased supplies, including gasoline, on account, $280.

　　25.　Received cash in payment of IOUs on account, $141.

　　28.　Paid miscellaneous expenses, $61.

　　31.　Cash receipts for May 13–31, $960.

　　31.　For May 13–31, accepted IOUs from customers on account, $151.

　　31.　Paid electricity (utilities) expense, $55.

　　31.　Paid telephone (utilities) expense, $30.

　　31.　Paid salary of part-time employees, $60.

　　31.　Supplies on hand at the end of May, $200.

Doug has asked you several questions concerning the financial affairs to date, and he has asked you to assist him with his record keeping and reporting of financial data.

Instructions:

(1) To assist Doug with his record keeping, prepare a chart of accounts that would be appropriate for Hally Caddy Service.

(2) Prepare an income statement for May to help Doug assess the profitability of Hally Caddy Service. For this purpose, the use of T accounts may be useful in analyzing the effects of each of the May transactions.

(3) At various times throughout May, Doug took cash from the cash receipts of the caddy service for personal use. If $665 of cash were on hand on May 31, how much did Doug withdraw from the enterprise for personal use?

3

CHAPTER

Completion of the Accounting Cycle

CHAPTER OBJECTIVES

Describe and illustrate the basic procedures for adjusting and summarizing the accounting records prior to the preparation of the financial statements.

Describe and illustrate the preparation of financial statements.

Describe and illustrate the basic procedures for preparing the accounting records for use in accumulating data of the following accounting period.

Describe and illustrate the procedures for correcting errors in accounting records.

3

CHAPTER

The summary of the ledger at the end of an accounting period, as set forth in the trial balance, is a convenient starting point in the preparation of financial statements. Many of the amounts listed on the trial balance can be transferred, without change, to the financial statements. For example, the balance of the cash account is normally the amount of that asset owned by the enterprise on the last day of the accounting period. Similarly, the balance in Notes Payable is likely to be the total amount of that type of liability owed by the enterprise on the last day of the accounting period.

All trial balance amounts are not necessarily correct. The amounts listed for prepaid expenses are normally overstated. The reason for the overstatement is that the day-to-day consumption or expiration of these assets has not been recorded. For example, the balance in the supplies account represents the cost of the inventory of supplies at the beginning of the period plus the cost of those acquired during the period. Some of the supplies would have been used during the period; hence, the balance listed on the trial balance is overstated. In the same manner, the balance in Prepaid Insurance represents the beginning balance plus the cost of insurance policies acquired during the period, and no entries were made for the premiums as they expired. To make entries on a day-to-day basis would be costly and unnecessary. There are two effects on the ledger when the daily reduction in prepaid expenses is not recorded: (1) asset accounts are overstated and (2) expense accounts are understated.

Other data needed for the financial statements may be entirely omitted from the trial balance because revenue or expense related to the period has not been recorded. For example, salary expense incurred between the last pay period and the end of the accounting period would not ordinarily be recorded in the accounts because salaries are customarily recorded only when they are paid. However, such accrued salaries are an expense of the period because the services were rendered during the period. They also represent a liability as of the last day of the period because they are owed to the employees.

MIXED ACCOUNTS AND BUSINESS OPERATIONS

An account with a balance that is partly a balance sheet amount and partly an income statement amount is sometimes called a **mixed account**. Again using the supplies account to illustrate, the balance reported on the trial balance is made up of two elements: the inventory of supplies at the end of the period, which is an **unexpired cost** (asset), and the supplies used during the period, which is an **expired cost** (expense). Before financial statements can be prepared at the end of the period, it is necessary to determine the part of the balance that is an asset and the part that is an expense.

The amount of the asset can be determined by counting the quantity of each of the various commodities, multiplying each quantity by the unit cost of that particular commodity, and totaling the dollar amounts thus obtained. The resulting figure represents the amount of the supplies inventory (asset). The excess of the balance in the supplies account over the supplies inventory is the cost of the supplies used (expense).

The cost of supplies and other prepayments of expenses of future periods may be recorded as expenses at the time of payment, rather than as assets. This alternative treatment will be considered in a later chapter. Meanwhile, all such expenditures will be assumed to be recorded first as assets.

Prepayments of expenses of one accounting period are sometimes made at the beginning of the period to which they apply. When this is the case, the expenditure is ordinarily recorded as an expense rather than as an asset. The expense account debited will be a mixed account during the accounting period, but it will be wholly expense at the end of the period. For example, if rent for March is paid on March 1, it is an asset at the time of payment. The asset expires gradually from day to day, and at the end of the month the entire amount has become an expense. Therefore, if the expenditure is initially recorded as a debit to Rent Expense, no additional entries are needed at the close of the period.

ADJUSTING PROCESS

The entries required at the end of an accounting period to record internal transactions are called adjusting entries. In a broad sense they may be called corrections to the ledger. But bringing the ledger up to date is a planned part of the accounting procedure; it is not caused by errors. The term "adjusting entries" is therefore more appropriate than "correcting entries."

The illustrations of adjusting entries that follow are based on the ledger of Cole Photographic Studio. T accounts are used for illustrative purposes and the adjusting entries, which are shown in the accounts, appear in bold face type to separate them from items that were posted during the month.

Prepaid Expenses

According to Cole's trial balance appearing on page 53, the balance in the supplies account on March 31 is $1,850. Some of these supplies (film, developing agents, etc.) have been used during the past month and some are still in stock. If the amount of either is known, the other can be readily determined. It is more practical to determine the cost of the supplies on hand at the end of the month than it is to keep a record of those used from day to day. Assuming that the inventory of supplies on March 31 is determined to be $890, the amount to be moved from the asset account to the expense account is computed as follows:

Supplies available (balance of account)....	$1,850
Supplies on hand (inventory)..............	890
Supplies used (amount of adjustment)......	$ 960

Increases in expense accounts are recorded as debits and decreases in asset accounts are recorded as credits. Hence at the end of March, the supplies expense account should be debited for $960 and the supplies account should be credited for $960. The adjusting entry is illustrated in the following T accounts:

ADJUSTMENT OF PREPAID EXPENSE

	Supplies					Supplies Expense	
Mar. 1	1,200	Mar. 31	960 →	→Mar. 31	960		
20	650						
	1,850						

After the adjustment, the asset account has a debit balance of $890 and the expense account has a debit balance of $960.

The debit balance of $2,400 in Cole's prepaid rent account represents a prepayment on March 1 of rent for three months, March, April, and May. At the end of March, the rent expense account should be increased (debited) and the prepaid rent account should be decreased (credited) by $800, the rental for one month. The adjusting entry is illustrated in the following T accounts:

ADJUSTMENT OF PREPAID EXPENSE

Prepaid Rent					Rent Expense	
Mar. 1	2,400	Mar. 31	800 ————————→	Mar. 31	800	

The prepaid rent account now has a debit balance of $1,600, which is an asset. The rent expense account has a debit balance of $800, which is an expense.

If the preceding adjustments for supplies ($960) and rent ($800) are not recorded, the financial statements prepared as of March 31 will be incorrect to the extent indicated as follows:

Income statement
Expenses will be understated........................... $1,760
Net income will be overstated.......................... 1,760

Balance sheet
Assets will be overstated.............................. $1,760
Capital will be overstated............................. 1,760

Capital statement
Net income will be overstated.......................... $1,760
Ending capital will be overstated...................... 1,760

Plant Assets

Like supplies, the photographic equipment was used in the operations of the business. Unlike supplies, there is no visible reduction in the quantity of the equipment. However, equipment does wear out as it is used and its usefulness decreases as time passes. This decrease in usefulness is a business expense, which is called depreciation. The factors involved in computing depreciation are discussed in a later chapter.

The adjusting entry to record depreciation is similar in effect to those illustrated in the preceding section. An amount is transferred from an asset account to an expense account. However, for reasons to be described in a later chapter, it is not practical to reduce plant asset accounts by the amount estimated as depreciation. In addition, it is common practice to show on the balance sheet both the original cost of plant assets and the amount of depreciation accumulated since their acquisition. Accordingly, the costs of plant assets are recorded as debits to the appropriate asset accounts and the decreases in usefulness are recorded as credits to the related accumulated depreciation accounts. The latter are called contra asset accounts because they are "offset against" the plant asset accounts. The unexpired or remaining cost of plant assets is determined by subtracting the credit balance in an accumulated depreciation account from the debit balance in the related plant asset account.

Typical titles for plant asset accounts and their related contra asset accounts are as follows:

Plant Asset	*Contra Asset*
Land	_____
Buildings	Accumulated Depreciation — Buildings
Equipment	Accumulated Depreciation — Equipment

The ledger could show more detail by having a separate account for each of a number of buildings. Equipment may also be subdivided according to function, such as Delivery Equipment, Store Equipment, and Office Equipment, with a related accumulated depreciation account for each plant asset account.

The adjusting entry to record depreciation for March for Cole Photographic Studio is illustrated in the following T accounts. The estimated amount of depreciation for the month is assumed to be $175.

ADJUSTMENT FOR DEPRECIATION

Photographic Equipment	Accumulated Depreciation
Mar. 1 15,000	Mar. 31 175
4 2,500	
17,500	

Depreciation Expense
Mar. 31 175

The $175 increase in the accumulated depreciation account represents a subtraction from the $17,500 cost recorded in the related plant asset account. The difference between the two balances is called the book value of the asset, which may be presented on the balance sheet in the following manner:

Plant assets:
Photographic equipment $17,500
Less accumulated depreciation 175 $17,325

Accrued Expenses (Liabilities)

It is customary to pay for some types of services, such as insurance and rent, before they are used. Other types of services are paid for after the service has been performed. Services performed by employees is an example of this type of situation. The wage or salary expense accrues or accumulates as a legal claim hour by hour and day by day, but payment is made only weekly, biweekly, or in accordance with some other period of time. If the last day of a pay period is not the last day of the accounting period, the accrued expense and the related liability must be recorded in the accounts by an adjusting entry.

The data in the following T accounts were taken from the ledger of Cole Photographic Studio. The debits of $375 on March 13 and 27 in the salary expense account were biweekly payments on alternate Fridays for the payroll periods ended on those days. The salaries earned on Monday and Tuesday, March 30 and 31, total $75. This amount is an additional expense of March and is debited to the salary expense account. It is also a liability as of March 31 and is therefore credited to Salaries Payable.

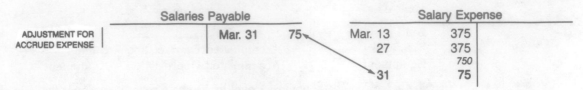

| | ADJUSTMENT FOR ACCRUED EXPENSE |

Salaries Payable   **Salary Expense**

Salaries Payable		Salary Expense	
Mar. 31	75	Mar. 13	375
		27	375
			750
		31	75

After the adjustment, the debit balance of the salary expense account is $825, which is the actual expense for the month. The credit balance of $75 in Salaries Payable is the amount of the liability for salaries owed as of March 31. If the previous adjustment for salaries ($75) is not recorded, the financial statements as of March 31 will be incorrect to the extent indicated as follows:

Income statement
Expenses will be understated $75
Net income will be overstated 75

Balance sheet
Liabilities will be understated. $75
Capital will be overstated 75

Capital statement
Net income will be overstated $75
Ending capital will be overstated 75

WORK SHEET FOR FINANCIAL STATEMENTS

Before journalizing and posting adjustments similar to those just described, it is necessary to determine and assemble the relevant data. For example, it is necessary to determine the cost of supplies on hand and the salaries accrued at the end of the period. Such collections of data, preliminary drafts of financial statements, and other useful analyses prepared by accountants are generally called **working papers.**

A type of working paper frequently used by accountants prior to the preparation of financial statements is called a work sheet. Its use reduces the possibility of overlooking the need for an adjustment, provides a convenient means of verifying arithmetical accuracy, and provides for the arrangement of data in a logical form.

The work sheet for Cole Photographic Studio is presented on pages 74–75. The three lines at the top identify (1) the enterprise, (2) the nature of the form, and (3) the period of time involved. The form has an account title column and ten money columns arranged in five pairs of debit and credit columns. The main headings of the five sets of money columns are:

1. Trial Balance
2. Adjustments
3. Adjusted Trial Balance
4. Income Statement
5. Balance Sheet

Trial Balance Columns

The trial balance data may be assembled directly on the work sheet form or they may be prepared on another sheet first and then copied on the work sheet form.

Adjustments Columns

Both the debit and the credit parts of an adjustment should be inserted on the appropriate lines before going on to another adjustment. Cross-referencing the related debit and credit of each adjustment by letters is useful to anyone who may have occasion to review the work sheet. It is also helpful later when the adjusting entries are recorded in the journal. The sequence of adjustments is not important, except that there is a time and accuracy advantage in following the order in which the adjustment data are assembled. If the titles of some of the accounts to be adjusted do not appear in the trial balance because they had no balance prior to adjustment, they should be inserted below the trial balance totals as they are needed.

The adjusting entries for Cole Photographic Studio were explained and illustrated by T accounts earlier in the chapter. In practice, the adjustments are inserted directly on the work sheet on the basis of the data assembled by the accounting department.

Explanatory notes for the entries in the Adjustments columns of the work sheet follow:

(a) **Supplies.** The supplies account has a debit balance of $1,850; the cost of the supplies on hand at the end of the period is $890; therefore, the supplies expense for March is the difference between the two amounts, or $960. The adjustment is entered by writing (1) *Supplies Expense* in the Account Title column, (2) *$960* in the Adjustments Debit column on the same line, and (3) *$960* in the Adjustments Credit column on the line with Supplies.

(b) **Rent.** The prepaid rent account has a debit balance of $2,400, which represents a payment for three months beginning with March; therefore, the rent expense for March is $800. The adjustment is entered by writing (1) *Rent Expense* in the Account Title column, (2) *$800* in the Adjustments Debit column on the same line, and (3) *$800* in the Adjustments Credit column on the line with Prepaid Rent.

(c) **Depreciation.** Depreciation of the photographic equipment is estimated at $175 for the month. This expired portion of the cost of the equipment is both an expense and a reduction in the asset. The adjustment is entered by writing (1) *Depreciation Expense* in the Account Title column, (2) *$175* in the Adjustments Debit column on the same line, (3) *Accumulated Depreciation* in the Account Title column, and (4) *$175* in the Adjustments Credit column on the same line.

(d) **Salaries.** Salaries accrued but not paid at the end of March amount to $75. This is an increase in expense and an increase in liabilities. The adjustment is entered by writing (1) *$75* in the Adjustments Debit column on the same line with Salary Expense, (2) *Salaries Payable* in the Account Title column, and (3) *$75* in the Adjustments Credit column on the same line.

The final step in completing the Adjustments columns is to prove the equality of debits and credits by totaling and ruling the two columns.

Adjusted Trial Balance Columns

The data in the Trial Balance columns are combined with the adjustments data and extended to the Adjusted Trial Balance columns. For example, the cash and accounts receivable accounts are extended at their original amounts of $1,631 and $1,775, since no adjustments affected either account. Supplies has an initial balance of $1,850 and a credit adjustment (decrease) of $960. The amount to be extended is the debit balance of $890. The same procedure is continued until all account balances have been extended to the Adjusted Trial Balance columns. The Debit and Credit columns are then totaled to prove that no arithmetical errors have been made up to this point.

Income Statement and Balance Sheet Columns

The data in the Adjusted Trial Balance columns are extended to one of the remaining four columns. The amounts of assets, liabilities, capital, and drawing (or dividends) are extended to the Balance Sheet columns, and the revenues and

TEN-COLUMN WORK SHEET

Cole Photographic

Work

For Month Ended

	ACCOUNT TITLE	TRIAL BALANCE		ADJUSTMENTS	
		DEBIT	CREDIT	DEBIT	CREDIT
1	Cash	1 6 3 1 00			
2	Accounts Receivable	1 7 7 5 00			
3	Supplies	1 8 5 0 00			(a) 9 6 0 00
4	Prepaid Rent	2 4 0 0 00			(b) 8 0 0 00
5	Photographic Equipment	1 7 5 0 0 00			
6	Accounts Payable		2 0 0 0 00		
7	Sara Cole, Capital		2 0 6 5 0 00		
8	Sara Cole, Drawing	1 5 0 0 00			
9	Sales		5 1 2 5 00		
10	Salary Expense	7 5 0 00		(d) 7 5 00	
11	Miscellaneous Expense	3 6 9 00			
12		2 7 7 7 5 00	2 7 7 7 5 00		
13	Supplies Expense			(a) 9 6 0 00	
14	Rent Expense			(b) 8 0 0 00	
15	Depreciation Expense			(c) 1 7 5 00	
16	Accumulated Depreciation				(c) 1 7 5 00
17	Salaries Payable				(d) 7 5 00
18				2 0 1 0 00	2 0 1 0 00
19	Net Income				
20					
21					
22					
23					

expenses are extended to the Income Statement columns. An advantage in time and accuracy can be achieved by beginning at the top and proceeding down the page in sequential order.

In the illustrative work sheet, the first account listed is Cash and the balance appearing in the Adjusted Trial Balance Debit column is $1,631. This amount should be extended to the appropriate column. Cash is an asset, it is listed on the balance sheet, and it has a debit balance. Accordingly, the $1,631 amount is extended to the Debit column of the balance sheet section. The balance of Accounts Receivable is extended in similar fashion. The $890 adjusted balance of Supplies is extended to the Balance Sheet Debit column. The same procedure is continued until all account balances have been extended to the appropriate columns. The balances of the capital and drawing accounts are extended to the Balance Sheet columns, because this work sheet does not provide for separate Capital Statement columns.

After all of the balances have been extended, each of the four columns is totaled. The net income or the net loss for the period is the amount of the difference between the totals of the two Income Statement columns. If the Credit

Studio
Sheet
March 31, 1984

| ADJUSTED TRIAL BALANCE | | INCOME STATEMENT | | BALANCE SHEET | | |
DEBIT	CREDIT	DEBIT	CREDIT	DEBIT	CREDIT	
1 6 3 1 00				1 6 3 1 00		1
1 7 7 5 00				1 7 7 5 00		2
8 9 0 00				8 9 0 00		3
1 6 0 0 00				1 6 0 0 00		4
1 7 5 0 0 00				1 7 5 0 0 00		5
	2 0 0 0 00				2 0 0 0 00	6
	2 0 6 5 0 00				2 0 6 5 0 00	7
1 5 0 0 00				1 5 0 0 00		8
	5 1 2 5 00		5 1 2 5 00			9
8 2 5 00		8 2 5 00				10
3 6 9 00		3 6 9 00				11
						12
9 6 0 00		9 6 0 00				13
8 0 0 00		8 0 0 00				14
1 7 5 00		1 7 5 00				15
	1 7 5 00				1 7 5 00	16
	7 5 00				7 5 00	17
2 8 0 2 5 00	2 8 0 2 5 00	3 1 2 9 00	5 1 2 5 00	2 4 8 9 6 00	2 2 9 0 0 00	18
		1 9 9 6 00			1 9 9 6 00	19
		5 1 2 5 00	5 1 2 5 00	2 4 8 9 6 00	2 4 8 9 6 00	20
						21
						22
						23

column total is greater than the Debit column total, the excess is the net income. For the work sheet presented on pages 74–75, the computation of net income is as follows:

Total of Credit column (revenue)...........	$5,125
Total of Debit column (expenses)..........	3,129
Net income (excess of revenue over expenses).................	$1,996

Revenue and expense accounts, which are subdivisions of capital, are temporary in nature. They are used during the accounting period to aid in the accumulation of detailed operating data. After they have served their purpose, the net balance will be transferred to the capital account (or the retained earnings account) in the ledger. This transfer is accomplished on the work sheet by entries in the Income Statement Debit column and the Balance Sheet Credit column, as illustrated on pages 74–75. If there had been a net loss instead of a net income, the amount would have been entered in the Income Statement Credit column and the Balance Sheet Debit column.

After the final entry is made on the work sheet, each of the four statement columns is totaled to verify the arithmetic accuracy of the amount of net income or net loss transferred from the income statement to the balance sheet. The totals of the two Income Statement columns must be equal, as must the totals of the two Balance Sheet columns. The work sheet may be expanded by the addition of a pair of columns solely for capital statement (or retained earnings statement) data. However, because of the very few items involved, this variation is not illustrated.

FINANCIAL STATEMENTS

The income statement, capital statement, and balance sheet prepared from the work sheet of Cole Photographic Studio appear on page 77. Their basic forms correspond to the statements presented in Chapter 1. Some minor variations are illustrated; others will be introduced in later chapters. The remaining portions of this section are devoted to the sources of the data and the manner in which they are reported on the statements.

Income Statement

The work sheet is the source of all of the data reported on the income statement. The sequence of expenses as listed on the work sheet may be changed in order to present them on the income statement in the order of size.

Capital Statement

The amount listed on the work sheet as the capital of a sole proprietorship does not always represent the account balance at the beginning of the accounting period. The proprietor may have invested additional assets in the business during the period. Hence, it is necessary to refer to the account in the ledger to determine the beginning balance and any additional investments. The amount of net income (or net loss) and the amount of the drawings appearing in the Balance Sheet columns of the work sheet are then used to determine the ending capital balance.

INCOME
STATEMENT

Cole Photographic Studio
Income Statement
For Month Ended March 31, 1984

Sales		$ 5,125.00
Operating expenses:		
Supplies expense	$ 960.00	
Salary expense	825.00	
Rent expense	800.00	
Depreciation expense	175.00	
Miscellaneous expense	369.00	
Total operating expenses		3,129.00
Net income		$ 1,996.00

CAPITAL
STATEMENT

Cole Photographic Studio
Capital Statement
For Month Ended March 31, 1984

Capital, March 1, 1984		$20,650.00
Net income for the month	$ 1,996.00	
Less withdrawals	1,500.00	
Increase in capital		496.00
Capital, March 31, 1984		$21,146.00

BALANCE
SHEET

Cole Photographic Studio
Balance Sheet
March 31, 1984

Assets

Current assets:		
Cash	$ 1,631.00	
Accounts receivable	1,775.00	
Supplies	890.00	
Prepaid rent	1,600.00	
Total current assets		$ 5,896.00
Plant assets:		
Photographic equipment	$17,500.00	
Less accumulated depreciation	175.00	17,325.00
Total assets		$23,221.00

Liabilities

Current liabilities:		
Accounts payable	$ 2,000.00	
Salaries payable	75.00	
Total liabilities		$ 2,075.00

Capital

Sara Cole, capital		21,146.00
Total liabilities and capital		$23,221.00

The form of the capital statement can be changed to meet the circumstances of any particular case. In the illustration on page 77, the amount withdrawn by the owner was less than the net income. If the withdrawals had exceeded the net income, the order of the two items could have been reversed. The difference between the two would then be deducted from the beginning capital.

Other factors, such as additional investments or a net loss, also require changes in form, as in the following example:

Capital, January 1, 19--	$45,000.00	
Additional investment during the year	6,000.00	
Total		$51,000.00
Net loss for the year	$ 7,500.00	
Withdrawals	8,600.00	
Decrease in capital		16,100.00
Capital, December 31, 19--		$34,900.00

In an incorporated business, it is necessary to show the difference between changes in capital stock and changes in retained earnings. If the change in the amount of capital stock issued during the period is significant, a capital stock statement should be prepared. Otherwise, such a statement is unnecessary.

Balance Sheet   The balance sheet illustrated on page 77 was expanded by the addition of subcaptions for current assets, plant assets, and current liabilities. If there were any liabilities that were not due until more than a year from the balance sheet date, they would be listed under the caption "Long-term liabilities." An example of a balance sheet illustrating a Long-term liabilities section appears on page 117.

In the illustration on page 77, the plant assets are made up entirely of photographic equipment. When there are two or more categories of plant assets, the cost, accumulated depreciation, and book value of each category should be listed, and the total amount of plant assets should be shown. This presentation is illustrated as follows:

Plant assets:			
Equipment	$40,600		
Less accumulated depreciation	12,100	$28,500	
Automobiles	$22,500		
Less accumulated depreciation	9,600	12,900	
Total plant assets			$41,400

The work sheet is the source of all the data reported on the balance sheet, with the exception of the amount of the sole proprietor's capital, which can be obtained from the capital statement. The capital section of the balance sheet of a corporation is subdivided into capital stock and retained earnings. The amount to be reported for the latter is obtained from the retained earnings statement.

Retained Earnings Statement   The basic form of a retained earnings statement for a corporation is illustrated on page 25. If dividend payments are debited to Dividends, the amount will appear on the work sheet. However, some accountants prefer to debit dividends directly to Retained Earnings. When this is the case, it is necessary to refer to the ledger to determine the beginning balance of Retained Earnings and the amount of the dividends debited during the period.

JOURNALIZING AND POSTING ADJUSTING ENTRIES

At the end of the accounting period, the adjusting entries appearing in the work sheet are recorded in the journal and posted to the ledger. This procedure brings the ledger into agreement with the data reported on the financial statements. The adjusting entries are dated as of the last day of the period, even though they are usually recorded at a later date. Each entry may be supported by an explanation, but a suitable caption above the first adjusting entry is sufficient.

The adjusting entries in the journal of Cole Photographic Studio are presented below. The accounts to which they have been posted appear in the ledger beginning on page 82.

ADJUSTING ENTRIES

	DATE	DESCRIPTION	POST. REF.	DEBIT	CREDIT	
11		Adjusting Entries				11
12	Mar. 31	Supplies Expense	51	9 6 0 00		12
13		Supplies	14		9 6 0 00	13
14						14
15	31	Rent Expense	53	8 0 0 00		15
16		Prepaid Rent	15		8 0 0 00	16
17						17
18	31	Depreciation Expense	54	1 7 5 00		18
19		Accumulated Depreciation	19		1 7 5 00	19
20						20
21	31	Salary Expense	52	7 5 00		21
22		Salaries Payable	22		7 5 00	22
23						23

JOURNAL   PAGE 2

JOURNALIZING AND POSTING CLOSING ENTRIES

The revenue, expense, and drawing (or dividends) accounts are temporary accounts used in classifying and summarizing changes in capital during the accounting period. At the end of the period, the net effect of the balances in these accounts must be recorded in the permanent account. The balances must also be removed from the temporary accounts so that they will be ready for use in accumulating data for the following accounting period. Both of these goals are accomplished by a series of entries called closing entries.

An account titled Income Summary is used for summarizing the data in the revenue and expense accounts. It is used only at the end of the accounting period and is both opened and closed during the closing process. Other account titles used for the summarizing account are Expense and Revenue Summary, Profit and Loss Summary, and Income and Expense Summary.

Four entries are required in order to close the temporary accounts of a sole proprietorship at the end of the period. They are as follows:

1. Each revenue account is debited for the amount of its balance, and Income Summary is credited for the total revenue.
2. Each expense account is credited for the amount of its balance, and Income Summary is debited for the total expense.
3. Income Summary is debited for the amount of its balance (net income), and the capital account is credited for the same amount. (Debit and credit are reversed if there is a net loss.)
4. The drawing account is credited for the amount of its balance, and the capital account is debited for the same amount.

The process of closing is illustrated by the following flowchart:

FLOWCHART OF CLOSING PROCESS

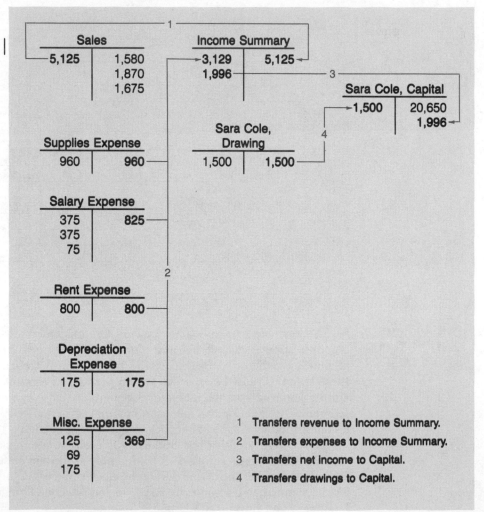

1 Transfers revenue to Income Summary.
2 Transfers expenses to Income Summary.
3 Transfers net income to Capital.
4 Transfers drawings to Capital.

After the closing entries have been journalized, as illustrated below, and posted to the ledger, the balance in the capital account will correspond to the amounts reported on the capital statement and balance sheet. In addition, the revenue, expense, and drawing accounts will have zero balances.

CLOSING ENTRIES

	DATE		DESCRIPTION	POST. REF.	DEBIT	CREDIT	
			JOURNAL			PAGE 2	
24			Closing Entries				24
25	Mar.	31	Sales	41	5 1 2 5 00		25
26			Income Summary	33		5 1 2 5 00	26
27							27
28		31	Income Summary	33	3 1 2 9 00		28
29			Salary Expense	52		8 2 5 00	29
30			Miscellaneous Expense	59		3 6 9 00	30
31			Supplies Expense	51		9 6 0 00	31
32			Rent Expense	53		8 0 0 00	32
33			Depreciation Expense	54		1 7 5 00	33
34							34
35		31	Income Summary	33	1 9 9 6 00		35
36			Sara Cole, Capital	31		1 9 9 6 00	36
37							37
38		31	Sara Cole, Capital	31	1 5 0 0 00		38
39			Sara Cole, Drawing	32		1 5 0 0 00	39
40							40
41							41
42							42
43							43
44							44
45							45

The procedure for closing the temporary accounts of a corporation differs only slightly from the outline described on page 80. Income Summary is closed (entry 3) to Retained Earnings, and Dividends is closed (entry 4) to Retained Earnings.

The account titles and amounts needed in journalizing the closing entries may be obtained from any one of three sources: (1) work sheet, (2) income and capital statements, and (3) ledger. When the work sheet is used, the data for the first two entries are taken from the Income Statement columns. The amount for the third entry is the net income or net loss appearing at the bottom of the work sheet. Reference to the drawing account balance appearing in the Balance Sheet column of the work sheet supplies the information for the fourth, and final, entry.

The ledger of Cole Photographic Studio after the adjusting and closing entries have been posted is presented on pages 82–84. Each posting of an adjusting entry and a closing entry is identified in the item section of the account as an aid to the student. It is not necessary that this be done in actual practice.

LEDGER AFTER THE
ACCOUNTS HAVE BEEN
ADJUSTED AND CLOSED

ACCOUNT Cash   **ACCOUNT NO.** 11

DATE		ITEM	POST. REF.	DEBIT	CREDIT	BALANCE DEBIT	BALANCE CREDIT
1984 Mar.	1		1	3 5 0 0 00		3 5 0 0 00	
	1		1		2 4 0 0 00	1 1 0 0 00	
	5		1	8 5 0 00		1 9 5 0 00	
	6		1		1 2 5 00	1 8 2 5 00	
	10		1		5 0 0 00	1 3 2 5 00	
	13		1		3 7 5 00	9 5 0 00	
	16		1	1 5 8 0 00		2 5 3 0 00	
	20		1		6 5 0 00	1 8 8 0 00	
	27		1		3 7 5 00	1 5 0 5 00	
	31		1		6 9 00	1 4 3 6 00	
	31		1		1 7 5 00	1 2 6 1 00	
	31		2	1 8 7 0 00		3 1 3 1 00	
	31		2		1 5 0 0 00	1 6 3 1 00	

ACCOUNT Accounts Receivable   **ACCOUNT NO.** 12

DATE		ITEM	POST. REF.	DEBIT	CREDIT	BALANCE DEBIT	BALANCE CREDIT
1984 Mar.	1		1	9 5 0 00		9 5 0 00	
	5		1		8 5 0 00	1 0 0 00	
	31		2	1 6 7 5 00		1 7 7 5 00	

ACCOUNT Supplies   **ACCOUNT NO.** 14

DATE		ITEM	POST. REF.	DEBIT	CREDIT	BALANCE DEBIT	BALANCE CREDIT
1984 Mar.	1		1	1 2 0 0 00		1 2 0 0 00	
	20		1	6 5 0 00		1 8 5 0 00	
	31	Adjusting	2		9 6 0 00	8 9 0 00	

ACCOUNT Prepaid Rent   **ACCOUNT NO.** 15

DATE		ITEM	POST. REF.	DEBIT	CREDIT	BALANCE DEBIT	BALANCE CREDIT
1984 Mar.	1		1	2 4 0 0 00		2 4 0 0 00	
	31	Adjusting	2		8 0 0 00	1 6 0 0 00	

ACCOUNT Photographic Equipment   **ACCOUNT NO.** 18

DATE		ITEM	POST. REF.	DEBIT	CREDIT	BALANCE DEBIT	BALANCE CREDIT
1984 Mar.	1		1	15 0 0 0 00		15 0 0 0 00	
	4		1	2 5 0 0 00		17 5 0 0 00	

LEDGER AFTER THE
ACCOUNTS HAVE BEEN
ADJUSTED AND
CLOSED—CONTINUED

ACCOUNT Accumulated Depreciation   **ACCOUNT NO.** 19

DATE		ITEM	POST. REF.	DEBIT	CREDIT	BALANCE DEBIT	BALANCE CREDIT
1984 Mar.	31	Adjusting	2		1 7 5 00		1 7 5 00

ACCOUNT Accounts Payable   **ACCOUNT NO.** 21

DATE		ITEM	POST. REF.	DEBIT	CREDIT	BALANCE DEBIT	BALANCE CREDIT
1984 Mar.	4		1		2 5 0 0 00		2 5 0 0 00
	10		1	5 0 0 00			2 0 0 0 00

ACCOUNT Salaries Payable   **ACCOUNT NO.** 22

DATE		ITEM	POST. REF.	DEBIT	CREDIT	BALANCE DEBIT	BALANCE CREDIT
1984 Mar.	31	Adjusting	2		7 5 00		7 5 00

ACCOUNT Sara Cole, Capital   **ACCOUNT NO.** 31

DATE		ITEM	POST. REF.	DEBIT	CREDIT	BALANCE DEBIT	BALANCE CREDIT
1984 Mar.	1		1		20 6 5 0 00		20 6 5 0 00
	01	Closing	2		1 9 9 6 00		22 6 4 6 00
	31	Closing	2	1 5 0 0 00			21 1 4 6 00

ACCOUNT Sara Cole, Drawing   **ACCOUNT NO.** 32

DATE		ITEM	POST. REF.	DEBIT	CREDIT	BALANCE DEBIT	BALANCE CREDIT
1984 Mar.	01		2	1 5 0 0 00		1 5 0 0 00	
	31	Closing	2		1 5 0 0 00	—	—

ACCOUNT Income Summary   **ACCOUNT NO.** 33

DATE		ITEM	POST. REF.	DEBIT	CREDIT	BALANCE DEBIT	BALANCE CREDIT
1984 Mar.	31	Closing	2		5 1 2 5 00		5 1 2 5 00
	31	Closing	2	3 1 2 9 00			1 9 9 6 00
	31	Closing	2	1 9 9 6 00		—	—

ACCOUNT Sales   **ACCOUNT NO.** 41

DATE		ITEM	POST. REF.	DEBIT	CREDIT	BALANCE DEBIT	BALANCE CREDIT
1984 Mar.	16		1		1 5 8 0 00		1 5 8 0 00
	31		2		1 8 7 0 00		3 4 5 0 00
	31		2		1 6 7 5 00		5 1 2 5 00
	31	Closing	2	5 1 2 5 00		—	

ACCOUNT Supplies Expense   **ACCOUNT NO. 51**

DATE		ITEM	POST. REF.	DEBIT	CREDIT	BALANCE	
						DEBIT	CREDIT
1984 Mar.	31	Adjusting	2	9 6 0 00		9 6 0 00	
	31	Closing	2		9 6 0 00	—	

ACCOUNT Salary Expense   **ACCOUNT NO. 52**

DATE		ITEM	POST. REF.	DEBIT	CREDIT	BALANCE	
						DEBIT	CREDIT
1984 Mar.	13		1	3 7 5 00		3 7 5 00	
	27		1	3 7 5 00		7 5 0 00	
	31	Adjusting	2	7 5 00		8 2 5 00	
	31	Closing	2		8 2 5 00	—	

ACCOUNT Rent Expense   **ACCOUNT NO. 53**

DATE		ITEM	POST. REF.	DEBIT	CREDIT	BALANCE	
						DEBIT	CREDIT
1984 Mar.	31	Adjusting	2	8 0 0 00		8 0 0 00	
	31	Closing	2		8 0 0 00	—	

ACCOUNT Depreciation Expense   **ACCOUNT NO. 54**

DATE		ITEM	POST. REF.	DEBIT	CREDIT	BALANCE	
						DEBIT	CREDIT
1984 Mar.	31	Adjusting	2	1 7 5 00		1 7 5 00	
	31	Closing	2		1 7 5 00	—	

ACCOUNT Miscellaneous Expense   **ACCOUNT NO. 59**

DATE		ITEM	POST. REF.	DEBIT	CREDIT	BALANCE	
						DEBIT	CREDIT
1984 Mar.	6		1	1 2 5 00		1 2 5 00	
	31		1	6 9 00		1 9 4 00	
	31		1	1 7 5 00		3 6 9 00	
	31	Closing	2		3 6 9 00	—	

As the entry to close an account is posted, a line should be inserted in both Balance columns opposite the final entry, as illustrated by Sara Cole, Drawing and the remaining temporary accounts. Transactions affecting the accounts in the following period will be posted in the spaces immediately below the closing entry.

POST-CLOSING TRIAL BALANCE

The last procedure of the accounting cycle is the preparation of a trial balance after all of the temporary accounts have been closed. The purpose of the post-closing (after closing) trial balance is to make sure that the ledger is in balance at the beginning of the new accounting period. The accounts and amounts should agree exactly with the accounts and amounts listed on the balance sheet at the end of the period.

Instead of preparing a formalized post-closing trial balance such as the one illustrated below, it is possible to proceed directly from the ledger to a mechanical or electronic adding device to determine the equality of debit and credit balances in the ledger. Equipment providing a tape record of the amounts introduced into the device should be used — the tape becoming, in effect, the post-closing trial balance. Without such a tape, there are no efficient means of determining whether the cause of an inequality of trial balance totals is due to errors in manipulating the keys or to errors in the ledger.

POST-CLOSING TRIAL BALANCE

Cole Photographic Studio Post-Closing Trial Balance March 31, 1984		
Cash	1 6 3 1 00	
Accounts Receivable	1 7 7 5 00	
Supplies	8 9 0 00	
Prepaid Rent	1 6 0 0 00	
Photographic Equipment	17 5 0 0 00	
Accumulated Depreciation		1 7 5 00
Accounts Payable		2 0 0 0 00
Salaries Payable		7 5 00
Sara Cole, Capital		21 1 4 6 00
	23 3 9 6 00	23 3 9 6 00

FISCAL YEAR

The maximum length of an accounting period is usually one year, which includes a complete cycle of the seasons and of business activities. Income and property taxes are also based on yearly periods and thus require that annual determinations be made.

The annual accounting period adopted by an enterprise is known as its **fiscal year.** Fiscal years ordinarily begin with the first day of the particular month selected and end on the last day of the twelfth month hence. The period most commonly adopted is the calendar year, but other periods are not unusual, particularly for incorporated businesses.

A period ending when a business's activities have reached the lowest point in its annual operating cycle is termed the **natural business year.**

The long-term financial history of a business enterprise may be shown by a succession of balance sheets, prepared every year. The history of operations for the intervening periods is presented in a series of income statements. If the life of a business enterprise is represented by a line moving from left to right, a series of balance sheets and income statements may be diagrammed as follows:

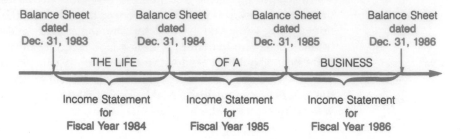

ACCOUNTING
CYCLE

The principal accounting procedures of a fiscal period have been presented in this and the preceding chapter. The sequence of procedures is frequently called the **accounting cycle**. It begins with the analysis and the journalizing of transactions and ends with the post-closing trial balance. The most significant output of the accounting cycle is, of course, the financial statements.

An understanding of all phases of the accounting cycle is essential as a foundation for further study of accounting principles and the uses of accounting data by management. The following outline summarizes the basic phases of the cycle:

1. Transactions are analyzed.
2. Transactions are journalized and posted to the ledger.
3. Trial balance is prepared.
4. Data needed to adjust the accounts are assembled.
5. Work sheet is prepared.
6. Financial statements are prepared.
7. Adjusting entries are journalized and posted to the ledger.
8. Closing entries are journalized and posted to the ledger.
9. Post-closing trial balance is prepared.

INTERIM
STATEMENTS

To reduce the number of transactions and physical space requirements in the illustrative case of Cole Photographic Studio, the entire accounting cycle was completed in a single month. In practice, most business enterprises close the temporary capital accounts only at the end of each fiscal year rather than at the end of each month. They do, however, prepare financial statements at frequent intervals such as monthly, quarterly, or semiannually. Statements issued for periods covering less than a fiscal year are called **interim statements**.

Analyzing and recording transactions (phases 1 and 2 of the accounting cycle) are performed on a continuous basis throughout the fiscal year, regardless of when the accounts are closed. It is also customary to prepare a trial balance (phase 3) at the end of each month or more often. When monthly financial statements (phase 6) are to be prepared, the adjustment data are assembled (phase 4) and a work sheet is completed (phase 5) as of the end of each month.

The amounts of the asset and liability accounts appearing in the balance sheet section of the work sheet are the balances as of the last day of the interim period.

The amounts of the revenue and expenses appearing in the income statement section, however, are the total amounts accumulated since the beginning of the fiscal year. To illustrate, assume that the fiscal year of a hypothetical enterprise is the calendar year. The work sheet prepared at the end of February provides data for an income statement for the two-month period, January–February, and data for a balance sheet as of February 28(29). The work sheet at the end of March provides data for an income statement for the three-month period, January–March, and data for a balance sheet as of March 31. Data for the income statement for a single month only are obtained by subtracting from the amount of each revenue and expense of the current cumulative income statement the corresponding amount from the preceding cumulative income statement. Continuing the illustration, if sales are reported at $190,000 on the cumulative January–March income statement and at $120,000 on the cumulative January–February income statement, the sales reported on the March income statement will be $70,000 ($190,000 − $120,000). The amount of each expense incurred in March and the net income for March is determined in the same manner.

The capital statement or retained earnings statement customarily present cumulative data from the beginning of the fiscal year, but statements for single months can be readily prepared.

CORRECTION OF ERRORS

Occasional errors in journalizing and posting transactions are unavoidable. Procedures used to correct errors in the journal and ledger vary according to the nature of the error and the phase of the accounting cycle in which it is discovered.

When an error in an account title or amount in the journal is discovered before the entry is posted, the correction may be made by drawing a line through the error and inserting the correct title or amount immediately above. If an entry in the journal is prepared correctly but the debit portion is incorrectly posted to the account as a credit (or vice versa), the incorrect posting may be corrected by drawing a line through the error and posting the item correctly. Or if the amount of a single debit or credit posting is in error, such as posting a journal debit of $240 as $420, the correction may be accomplished in a similar manner. If there is any likelihood of questions arising later, the person responsible may initial the correction as in the following illustration:

ACCOUNT WITH CORRECTED POSTING

ACCOUNT Miscellaneous Expense					ACCOUNT NO. 59	
					BALANCE	
DATE	ITEM	POST. REF.	DEBIT	CREDIT	DEBIT	CREDIT
1984 Mar. 6		DC 1	~~1 2 5 00~~ ~~2 1 6 00~~		~~1 2 5 00~~ ~~2 1 6 00~~	

When an erroneous account title appears in a journal entry and the error is not discovered until after posting is completed, the preferable procedure is to journalize and post a correcting entry. To illustrate, assume that a purchase of office equipment, which was paid in cash, was erroneously journalized and posted as a $500 debit to Office Supplies but correctly journalized and posted as a $500 credit to Cash. Before a correcting entry is made, it is advisable to establish clearly both

(1) the debit(s) and credit(s) of the entry in which the error occurred and (2) the debit(s) and credit(s) that should have been recorded. T accounts may be helpful in making this analysis, as in the following example:

Entry in which error occurred:

Office Supplies		Cash	
500			500

Entry that should have been recorded:

Office Equipment		Cash	
500			500

Comparison of the two sets of T accounts shows that the erroneous debit of $500 to Office Supplies may be corrected by a $500 credit to that account and that Office Equipment should be debited for $500. The following correcting entry is then journalized and posted:

CORRECTING
ENTRY

	DATE		DESCRIPTION	POST. REF.	DEBIT	CREDIT	
1	1984 Oct.	31	Office Equipment	18	5 0 0 00		1
2			Office Supplies	15		5 0 0 00	2
3			To correct erroneous debit to				3
4			Office Supplies on Oct. 5.				4
5			See invoice from Allen				5
6			Supply Company. CRN				6
7							7

JOURNAL   PAGE 22

Self-Examination Questions
(Answers in Appendix C.)

1. If the supplies account, before adjustment on May 31, indicated a balance of $2,250, and an inventory of supplies on hand at May 31 totaled $950, the adjusting entry would be:
   A. debit Supplies, $950; credit Supplies Expense, $950
   B. debit Supplies, $1,300; credit Supplies Expense, $1,300
   C. debit Supplies Expense, $950; credit Supplies, $950
   D. debit Supplies Expense, $1,300; credit Supplies, $1,300

2. If the estimated amount of depreciation on equipment for a period is $2,000, the adjusting entry to record depreciation would be:
   A. debit Depreciation Expense, $2,000; credit Equipment, $2,000
   B. debit Equipment, $2,000; credit Depreciation Expense, $2,000
   C. debit Depreciation Expense, $2,000; credit Accumulated Depreciation, $2,000
   D. debit Accumulated Depreciation, $2,000; credit Depreciation Expense, $2,000

3. If the equipment account has a balance of $22,500 and its accumulated depreciation account has a balance of $14,000, the book value of the equipment is:
   A. $36,500   C. $14,000
   B. $22,500   D. $8,500

4. Which of the following accounts would be closed to the income summary account at the end of a period?
   A. Sales   C. Both Sales and Salary Expense
   B. Salary Expense   D. Neither Sales nor Salary Expense

5. The post-closing trial balance would include which of the following accounts?
   A. Cash   C. Salary Expense
   B. Sales   D. All of the above

Discussion Questions

1. What is the term usually used in referring to (a) unexpired costs? (b) expired costs?

2. Why are adjusting entries needed at the end of an accounting period?

3. What is the nature of the balance in the supplies account at the end of the accounting period (a) before adjustment? (b) after adjustment?

4. If the effect of the debit portion of an adjusting entry is to increase the balance of an asset account, which of the following statements describes the effect of the credit portion of the entry: (a) increases the balance of a liability account? (b) increases the balance of a revenue account? (c) decreases the balance of a capital account?

5. Does every adjusting entry have an effect on the determination of the amount of net income for a period? Explain.

6. On October 1 of the current year, an enterprise pays the October rent on the building that it occupies. (a) Do the rights acquired at October 1 represent an asset or an expense? (b) What is the justification for debiting Rent Expense at the time of payment?

7. At the end of March, the first month of the fiscal year, the usual adjusting entry transferring supplies used to an expense account is inadvertently omitted. Which items will be incorrectly stated, because of the error, on (a) the income statement for March and (b) the balance sheet as of March 31? Also indicate whether the items in error will be overstated or understated.

8. (a) Explain the purpose of the two accounts: Depreciation Expense and Accumulated Depreciation. (b) What is the normal balance of each account? (c) Is it customary for the balances of the two accounts to be equal in amount? (d) In what financial statements, if any, will each account appear?

9. What term is applied to the difference between the balance in a plant asset account and its related accumulated depreciation account?

10. Accrued salaries of $3,860 owed to employees for August 29, 30, and 31 are not taken into consideration in preparing the financial statements for the fiscal year ended August 31. Which items will be erroneously stated, because of the error, on (a) the income statement for the year and (b) the balance sheet as of August 31? Also indicate whether the items in error will be overstated or understated.

11. Assume that the error in question 10 was not corrected and that the $3,860 of accrued salaries was included in the first salary payment in September. Which items will be erroneously stated, because of failure to correct the initial error, on (a) the

income statement for the month of September and (b) the balance sheet as of September 30?

12. Is the work sheet a substitute for the financial statements? Discuss.

13. In the Balance Sheet columns of the work sheet for Scott Company for the current year, the Credit column total is $19,450 greater than the Debit column total. Would the income statement report a net income or a net loss? Explain.

14. Why are closing entries required at the end of an accounting period?

15. What type of accounts are closed by transferring their balances to Income Summary (a) as a debit, (b) as a credit?

16. To what account is the income summary account closed for (a) a sole proprietorship? (b) a corporation?

17. To what account in the ledger of a corporation is the account "Dividends" periodically closed?

18. From the following list, identify the accounts that should be closed to Income Summary at the end of the fiscal year: (a) Accounts Payable, (b) Advertising Expense, (c) Capital Stock, (d) Cash, (e) Depreciation Expense, (f) Miscellaneous Expense, (g) Office Equipment, (h) Prepaid Insurance, (i) Retained Earnings, (j) Sales, (k) Supplies, (l) Wages Payable.

19. Are adjusting and closing entries in the journal dated as of the last day of the fiscal period or as of the day the entries are actually made? Explain.

20. Which of the following accounts in the ledger of a corporation will ordinarily appear in the post-closing trial balance? (a) Accounts Receivable, (b) Accumulated Depreciation, (c) Capital Stock, (d) Cash, (e) Depreciation Expense, (f) Dividends, (g) Equipment, (h) Retained Earnings, (i) Sales, (j) Supplies, (k) Wages Expense, (l) Wages Payable.

21. What term is applied to the annual accounting period adopted by a business enterprise?

22. In preparing and posting the journal entry to record the purchase of equipment by issuing a note payable, the accounts payable account was erroneously credited. What is the preferred procedure to correct the error?

Exercises

Exercise 3-1. The balance in the prepaid insurance account before adjustment at the end of the year is $2,780. Journalize the adjusting entry required under each of the following alternatives: (a) the amount of insurance expired during the year is $1,730; (b) the amount of unexpired insurance applicable to future periods is $1,730.

Exercise 3-2. A business enterprise pays weekly salaries of $8,500 on Friday for a five-day week ending on that day. Journalize the necessary adjusting entry at the end of the fiscal period, assuming that the fiscal period ends (a) on Monday, (b) on Wednesday.

Exercise 3-3. On March 1 of the current year, a business enterprise pays $2,400 to the city for taxes (license fees) for the coming year. The same enterprise is also required to pay an annual tax (on property) at the end of the year. The estimated amount of the current year's property tax allocable to March is $550. (a) Journalize the two adjusting entries required to bring the accounts affected by the two taxes up to date as of March 31. (b) What is the amount of tax expense for the month of March?

Exercise 3-4. On December 31, a business enterprise estimates depreciation on equipment used during the first year of operations to be $1,360. (a) Journalize the adjusting entry required as of December 31. (b) If the adjusting entry in (a) were omitted, which items would be erroneously stated on (1) the income statement for the year, and (2) the balance sheet as of December 31?

Exercise 3-5. After all revenue and expense accounts have been closed at the end of the fiscal year, Income Summary has a debit of $312,600 and a credit of $296,500. As of the same date, Jim Higgins, Capital has a credit balance of $60,240 and Jim Higgins, Drawing has a debit balance of $18,300. (a) Journalize the entries required to complete the closing of the accounts. (b) State the amount of Higgins' capital at the end of the period.

Exercise 3-6. Selected accounts from the ledger of Bantam's, Inc. for the current fiscal year ended July 31 are as follows. Prepare a retained earnings statement for the year.

Capital Stock			Dividends			
	Aug. 1	40,000	Oct. 1	2,000	July 31	7,000
			Jan. 1	2,000		
			April 1	2,000		
			July 1	1,000		

Retained Earnings			Income Summary			
July 31	7,000	Aug. 1	112,100	July 31	210,650	July 31	243,500
		July 31	32,850	31	32,850		

Exercise 3-7. Selected accounts from the ledger of J. E. Pittman Company for the current fiscal year ended January 31 are as follows. Prepare a capital statement for the year.

J. E. Pittman, Capital			J. E. Pittman, Drawing			
Jan. 31	20,000	Feb. 1	60,700	April 30	5,000	Jan. 31	20,000
		Jan. 31	18,300	July 31	5,000		
				Oct. 31	5,000		
				Jan. 31	5,000		

Income Summary			
Jan. 31	114,300	Jan. 31	132,600
31	18,300		

Exercise 3-8. A number of errors in journalizing and posting transactions are described below. Present the journal entries to correct the errors.
   (a) Rent of $1,200 paid for the current month was recorded as a debit to Insurance Expense and a credit to Cash.

(b) Cash of $1,610 received from a customer on account was recorded as a $1,160 debit to Cash and credit to Accounts Receivable.

(c) Payment of $1,000 cash to W. C. Townsend, owner of the enterprise, for personal use was recorded as a debit to Miscellaneous Expense and a credit to Cash.

(d) Equipment of $15,000 purchased on account was recorded as a debit to Buildings and a credit to W. C. Townsend, Capital.

(e) A $315 cash payment for supplies was recorded as a debit to Supplies and a credit to Accounts Payable.

Problems
(Problems in Appendix B: 3-1B, 3-2B, 3-3B.)

Problem 3-1A. The trial balance of Sunshine Laundromat at July 31, 1985, the end of the current fiscal year, and the data needed to determine year-end adjustments are as follows:

Sunshine Laundromat
Trial Balance
July 31, 1985

Cash	5,180	
Laundry Supplies	3,850	
Prepaid Insurance	1,200	
Laundry Equipment	87,600	
Accumulated Depreciation		58,700
Accounts Payable		1,620
T. J. Michaels, Capital		34,930
T. J. Michaels, Drawing	10,600	
Laundry Revenue		52,750
Wages Expense	17,900	
Rent Expense	14,000	
Utilities Expense	7,260	
Miscellaneous Expense	410	
	148,000	148,000

Adjustment data:

(a) Inventory of laundry supplies at July 31 .... $ 940
(b) Insurance premiums expired during the year 800
(c) Depreciation on equipment during the year 5,220
(d) Wages accrued but not paid at July 31 850

Instructions:

(1) Record the trial balance on a ten-column work sheet.
(2) Complete the work sheet.
(3) Prepare an income statement, a capital statement (no additional investments were made during the year), and a balance sheet.

(4) On the basis of the adjustment data in the work sheet, journalize the adjusting entries.

(5) On the basis of the data in the work sheet or in the income and capital statements, journalize the closing entries.

Problem 3-2A. As of December 31, the end of the current fiscal year, the accountant for Saunders Company prepared a trial balance, journalized and posted the adjusting entries, prepared an adjusted trial balance, prepared the statements, and completed the other procedures required at the end of the accounting cycle. The two trial balances as of December 31, one before adjustments and the other after adjustments, are as follows:

Saunders Company
Trial Balance
December 31, 19--

	Unadjusted		Adjusted	
Cash	11,200		11,200	
Supplies	8,450		3,240	
Prepaid Rent	7,200		1,200	
Prepaid Insurance	1,800		650	
Land	40,000		40,000	
Buildings	96,000		96,000	
Accumulated Depreciation—				
Buildings		62,400		67,200
Trucks	82,000		82,000	
Accumulated Depreciation—Trucks		32,800		36,900
Accounts Payable		7,120		7,340
Salaries Payable		—		1,450
Taxes Payable		—		920
F. G. Saunders, Capital		120,430		120,430
F. G. Saunders, Drawing	20,500		20,500	
Service Fees Earned		116,680		116,680
Salary Expense	67,200		68,650	
Rent Expense	—		6,000	
Supplies Expense	—		5,210	
Depreciation Expense—Buildings	—		4,800	
Depreciation Expense—Trucks	—		4,100	
Utilities Expense	3,700		3,920	
Taxes Expense	600		1,520	
Insurance Expense	—		1,150	
Miscellaneous Expense	780		780	
	339,430	339,430	350,920	350,920

Instructions:

(1) Present the eight journal entries that were required to adjust the accounts at December 31. None of the accounts was affected by more than one adjusting entry.

(2) Present the journal entries that were required to close the accounts at December 31.

(3) Prepare a capital statement for the fiscal year ended December 31. There were no additional investments during the year.

If the working papers correlating with this textbook are not used, omit Problem 3-3A.

Problem 3-3A. The ledger and trial balance of Lindsey Welding Services as of May 31, the end of the first month of its current fiscal year, are presented in the working papers. The accounts had been closed on April 30.

Instructions:

(1) Complete the ten-column work sheet. Data needed to determine the necessary adjusting entries are as follows:

Inventory of supplies at May 31	$ 364.15
Insurance premiums expired during May	69.30
Depreciation on the building during May	108.63
Depreciation on equipment during May	75.00
Wages accrued but not paid at May 31	1,108.40

(2) Prepare an income statement, a capital statement, and a balance sheet.
(3) Journalize and post the adjusting entries, inserting balances in the accounts affected.
(4) Journalize and post the closing entries. Indicate closed accounts by inserting a line in both Balance columns opposite the closing entry. Insert the new balance of the capital account.
(5) Prepare a post-closing trial balance.

Problem 3-4A. Autoset Lanes, Inc. prepares interim statements at the end of each month and closes its accounts annually as of December 31. The trial balance at September 30 of the current year, the adjustment data needed at September 30, and the interim income statement for the eight months ended August 31 of the current year are as follows:

Autoset Lanes, Inc.
Trial Balance
September 30, 19--

Cash	8,040	
Prepaid Insurance	1,200	
Supplies	1,060	
Land	30,000	
Building	86,500	
Accumulated Depreciation—Building		21,625
Equipment	61,250	
Accumulated Depreciation—Equipment		25,300
Accounts Payable		3,170
Capital Stock		50,000
Retained Earnings		56,245
Dividends	6,500	
Bowling Revenue		80,600
Salaries and Wages Expense	31,150	
Advertising Expense	4,500	
Utilities Expense	4,380	
Repairs Expense	1,320	
Miscellaneous Expense	1,040	
	236,940	236,940

Adjustment data at September 30:
(a) Insurance expired for the period January 1–September 30 . . . . $ 900
(b) Inventory of supplies on September 30 140
(c) Depreciation of building for the period January 1–September 30 . . . 1,620
(d) Depreciation of equipment for the period January 1–September 30. 5,150
(e) Accrued salaries and wages on September 30 1,950

Autoset Lanes, Inc.
Income Statement
For Eight Months Ended August 31, 19--

Bowling revenue		$68,500
Operating expenses:		
Salaries and wages expense	$28,690	
Depreciation expense — equipment	4,400	
Advertising expense	3,755	
Utilities expense	3,702	
Depreciation expense — building	1,440	
Repairs expense	1,148	
Supplies expense	760	
Insurance expense	750	
Miscellaneous expense	827	
Total operating expenses		45,472
Net income		$23,028

Instructions:
(1) Record the trial balance on a ten-column work sheet.
(2) Complete the work sheet. USING ADJUSTMENT DATA
(3) Prepare an interim income statement for the nine months ended September 30.
(4) Prepare an interim retained earnings statement for the nine months ended September 30. (See page 25 for form of statement.)
(5) Prepare an interim balance sheet as of September 30.
(6) On the basis of the income statement for the nine-month period and the income statement for the eight-month period, prepare an interim income statement for the month of September.
(7) Compute the percent of net income to revenue for:
(a) The eight-month period ended August 31.
(b) The nine-month period ended September 30.
(c) The month of September.
(8) Compute the percent of net income for the nine-month period ended September 30 to total capital as of the beginning of the fiscal year. The capital stock account remained unchanged during the nine-month period.

Problem 3-5A. The following selected transactions and errors relate to the accounts of Compton Co. during the current fiscal year:

June   1. Mary Compton established the business with the investment of $29,500 in cash and $11,200 in equipment, on which there was a balance owed of $5,400. The account payable is to be recorded in the ledger of the enterprise.

July 15. Acquired land to be used as a future building site at a contract price of $40,000. The property was encumbered by a mortgage of $24,000. Paid the seller $16,000 in cash and agreed to assume the responsibility for paying the mortgage note.

Sept. 20. Discovered that cash of $810, received from a customer on account, had been journalized and posted as a debit to Cash and a credit to Service Revenue.

Oct. 1. Discovered that a cash payment of $1,700 in partial payment of the account payable incurred with the equipment acquired on June 1 had been journalized and posted as a debit to Accounts Payable of $1,700 and a credit to Equipment of $1,700.

21. Discovered that a withdrawal of $1,200 by the owner had been debited to Salary Expense.

Nov. 1. Discovered that $410 of supplies returned to the supplier for credit had been journalized and posted as a debit to Cash and a credit to Miscellaneous Expense.

Dec. 1. Sold to an employee for cash $200 of supplies at cost for the employee's personal use.

31. Discovered that depreciation of $560 on the equipment acquired on June 1 had been journalized and posted as a debit to Miscellaneous Expense of $650 and a credit to Equipment of $650.

Instructions:

Journalize the transactions and the corrections in a two-column journal. When there are more than two items in an entry, present the entry in compound form.

Mini-Case

Assume that you recently accepted a position with First National Bank as an assistant loan officer. As one of your first duties, you have been assigned the responsibility of evaluating a loan request for $50,000 from Stillwell Pest Control, a small sole proprietorship. In support of the loan application, Alice Stillwell, owner, submitted the following "Statement of Accounts" (trial balance) for the first year of operations ended October 31, 1984:

Stillwell Pest Control
Statement of Accounts
October 31, 1984

Cash.	3,850	
Billings Due from Others	7,400	
Supplies (chemicals, etc.)	16,550	
Trucks	22,300	
Equipment.	15,730	
Amounts Owed to Others		3,420
Investment in Business		40,000
Service Revenue.		86,750
Wages Expense.	56,200	
Utilities Expense	4,210	
Rent Expense.	1,800	
Insurance Expense	1,400	
Other Expenses.	730	
	130,170	130,170

Instructions:

(1) Explain to Alice Stillwell why a set of financial statements (income statement, capital statement, and balance sheet) would be useful to you in evaluating the loan request.

(2) In discussing the "Statement of Accounts" with Alice Stillwell, you discovered that the accounts had not been adjusted at October 31. Through analysis of the "Statement of Accounts", indicate possible adjusting entries that might be necessary before an accurate set of financial statements could be prepared.

(3) Assuming that an accurate set of financial statements will be submitted by Alice Stillwell in a few days, what other considerations or information would you require before making a decision on the loan request?

4

CHAPTER

Accounting for a Merchandising Enterprise

CHAPTER OBJECTIVES

Describe and illustrate accounting for merchandise transactions.

Describe and illustrate the summarizing and reporting procedures for merchandising enterprises at year end.

Describe and illustrate the preparation of financial statements for merchandising enterprises.

Describe and illustrate procedures for preparing the accounting records of a merchandising enterprise for use in accumulating data for the following accounting period.

4

CHAPTER

Merchandising enterprises acquire merchandise for resale to customers. It is the selling of merchandise, instead of a service, that makes the activities of merchandising enterprises differ from the activities of service enterprises. This chapter focuses on the accounting concepts and procedures that are unique to merchandising enterprises—accounting for the purchase and sale of merchandise. In addition, the summarizing and reporting procedures for merchandising enterprises at year end are presented.

PURCHASING AND SELLING PROCEDURES

The procedures followed in purchasing and selling merchandise may vary from business to business. For example, purchases and sales may be made for cash or on credit (on account), and many different arrangements may be made for making payments on account. In addition, policies for the return of merchandise and for the payment of transportation costs may be different. The common procedures for recording transactions between buyers and sellers of merchandise are discussed in the following paragraphs.

ACCOUNTING FOR PURCHASES

Purchases of merchandise are usually identified in the ledger as *Purchases*. A more exact account title, such as "Purchases of Merchandise," could be used, but the briefer title is customarily used. Thus a merchandising enterprise can accumulate in the purchases account the cost of all merchandise purchased for resale during the accounting period.

When purchases are made for cash, the transaction may be recorded as follows:

Jan. 3	Purchases	510	
	Cash		510
	Purchases from supplier, Bowen Co.		

Most purchases of merchandise are made on account and may be recorded as follows:

Jan. 4	Purchases	925	
	Accounts Payable		925
	Purchases from supplier,		
	Thomas Corporation.		

Purchases Discounts

The arrangements agreed upon by the purchaser and the seller as to when payments for merchandise are to be made are called the **credit terms.** If payment is required immediately upon delivery, the terms are said to be "cash" or "net cash." Otherwise, the purchaser is allowed a certain amount of time, known as the **credit period,** in which to pay.

It is usual for the credit period to begin with the date of the sale as shown by the date of the invoice or bill. If payment is due within a stated number of days after the date of the invoice, for example 30 days, the terms are said to be "net 30 days,"[1] which may be written as "n/30." If payment is due by the end of the month in which the sale was made, it may be expressed as "n/eom."

As a means of encouraging payment before the end of the credit period, a discount may be offered for the early payment of cash. Thus the expression "2/10, n/30" means that, although the credit period is 30 days, the purchaser may deduct 2% of the amount of the invoice if payment is made within 10 days of the invoice date. This deduction is known as a cash discount.

From the purchaser's standpoint, it is important to take advantage of all available discounts, even though it may be necessary to borrow the money to make the payment. To illustrate, assume that the following invoice for $1,500 is received by Midtown Electric Corporation:

INVOICE I

Wallace Electronics Supply
3800 MISSION STREET
SAN FRANCISCO, CA 94110-1732

FOR CUSTOMER'S USE ONLY	
Calculations Checked *W. M. L.*	Price Approved *EL.*
Material Received 10-13 19 84 *A. S.* Rec. Cl.	
Date Signature Title	
Audited *L. R. A.*	Final Approval

Customer's Order No. & Date 412 Oct. 9, 1984

Refer to Invoice No. 106-8

Invoice Date Oct. 11, 1984

Vendor's Nos.

SOLD TO Midtown Electric Corporation
1200 San Vicente Blvd.
Los Angeles, CA 90019-2350

Date Shipped Oct. 11, 1984 From San Francisco   Prepaid or Collect?

How Shipped and Route Western Trucking Co.   F.O.B. Los Angeles   Prepaid

Terms 2/10, n/30   Made in U.S.A.

QUANTITY	DESCRIPTION	UNIT PRICE	AMOUNT
20	392E Transformers	75.00	1,500.00

The invoice, with terms of 2/10, n/30, is to be paid within the discount period with money borrowed for the remaining 20 days of the credit period. If an annual interest rate of 12% is assumed, the net savings to the purchaser is $20.20, determined as follows:

Discount of 2% on $1,500	$30.00
Interest for 20 days, at rate of 12%, on $1,470 ($1,500 − $30)	9.80
Savings effected by borrowing	$20.20

Discounts taken by the purchaser for early payment of an invoice are called **purchases discounts**. They are recorded by crediting the purchases discount

[1]The word "net" in this context does not have the usual meaning of a remainder after all relevant deductions have been subtracted, as in "net income," for example.

account and are usually viewed as a deduction from the amount initially recorded as Purchases. To illustrate, the receipt of the purchase invoice presented above and its payment at the end of the discount period may be recorded as follows:

Oct. 11	Purchases	1,500	
	Accounts Payable		1,500
	Invoice 106-8 from Wallace		
	Electronics Supply.		
Oct. 21	Accounts Payable	1,500	
	Cash.		1,470
	Purchases Discount		30
	Invoice 106-8 from Wallace		
	Electronics Supply.		

Purchases Returns and Allowances

When merchandise is returned or a price adjustment is requested, the purchaser usually communicates with the seller in writing. The details may be stated in a letter or the purchaser (debtor) may use a debit memorandum form. This form, illustrated as follows, is a convenient medium for informing the seller (creditor) of the amount the purchaser proposes to debit to the account payable account. It also states the reasons for the return or request for a price reduction.

DEBIT MEMORANDUM

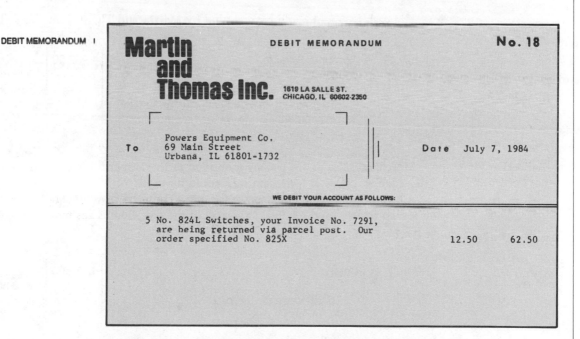

The debtor may use a copy of the debit memorandum as the basis for an entry or may wait for confirmation from the creditor, which is usually in the form of a

credit memorandum. In either event, Accounts Payable must be debited and
Purchases must be credited.[2] To illustrate, the entry by Martin and Thomas, Inc.,
to record the return of the merchandise identified in the debit memo above would
be as follows:

July 7	Accounts Payable	62.50	
	Purchases		62.50
	Debit Memo No. 18.		

When a purchaser returns merchandise or has been granted an allowance prior
to the payment of the invoice, the amount of the debit memorandum is deducted
from the invoice amount before the purchases discount is computed. For example,
assume that the details related to the amount payable to Power Equipment Co.,
for which the debit memo illustrated above was issued, are as follows:

Invoice No. 7291 dated July 1 (terms 2/10, n/30) $2,045.00
Debit Memo No. 18 dated July 7 .... 62.50
Balance of account $1,982.50
Discount (2% of $1,982.50) 39.65
Cash payment, July 11 .... $1,942.85

The cash payment could be recorded by Martin and Thomas, Inc. as follows:

July 11	Accounts Payable	1,982.50	
	Cash....................................		1,942.85
	Purchases Discount		39.65
	Payment of Invoice No. 7291 from Power		
	Equipment Co., less Debit Memo No. 18.		

ACCOUNTING FOR SALES

Merchandise sales are usually identified in the ledger as *Sales*. A more exact
title, such as "Sales of Merchandise," could be used.

A business may sell merchandise for cash. These sales are generally "rung up"
on a cash register and totaled at the end of the day. Such sales may be recorded
as follows:

Jan. 7	Cash....................................	1,872.50	
	Sales		1,872.50
	Cash sales for the day.		

[2]Most businesses credit the purchases account for merchandise returned and allowances granted. This
procedure will be used in the text. However, some businesses prefer to credit a purchases returns
and allowances account. If this alternative is used, the purchases returns and allowances account
can be viewed and reported as a deduction from the amount recorded in the purchases account.

Sales to customers who use bank credit cards (such as MasterCard and VISA) are generally treated as cash sales. The credit card invoices representing these sales are deposited by the seller directly into the bank, along with the currency and checks received from customers. Periodically, the bank charges a service fee for handling these credit card sales. The service fee should be debited to an expense account.

A business may also sell merchandise on account. Such sales result in a debit to Accounts Receivable and a credit to Sales, as illustrated in the following entry:

Jan. 12	Accounts Receivable	510	
	Sales		510
	Invoice No. 7172 to Sims Co.		

Sales made by the use of nonbank credit cards (such as American Express) generally must be reported periodically to the card company before cash is received. Therefore, such sales create a receivable with the card company. Before the card company remits cash, it normally deducts a service fee. To illustrate, assume that nonbank credit card sales of $1,000 are made and reported to the card company on January 20. On January 27, the company deducts a service fee of $50 and remits $950. The transactions may be recorded as follows:

Jan. 20	Accounts Receivable	1,000	
	Sales		1,000
	American Express credit sales.		
Jan. 27	Cash....................................	950	
	Credit Card Collection Expense	50	
	Accounts Receivable		1,000
	Receipt of cash from American Express		
	for sales reported on January 20.		

Sales Discounts The seller refers to the discounts taken by the purchaser for early payment of an invoice as sales discounts. They are recorded by debiting the sales discount account and are considered to be a reduction in the amount initially recorded as sales. To illustrate, if cash is received within the discount period from a previously recorded credit sale of $500, 2/10, n/30, the transaction may be recorded as follows:

June 10	Cash....................................	490	
	Sales Discount	10	
	Accounts Receivable		500
	Collection on Invoice No. 8722 to		
	Carver Co., less discount.		

Sales Returns and Allowances

Merchandise sold may be returned by the customer (sales return) or, because of defects or for other reasons, the customer may be allowed a reduction from the original price at which the goods were sold (sales allowance). If the return or allowance is for a sale on account, the seller usually gives the customer a credit memorandum. This memorandum shows the amount for which the customer is to be credited and the reason therefor. A typical credit memorandum is illustrated as follows:

CREDIT MEMORANDUM

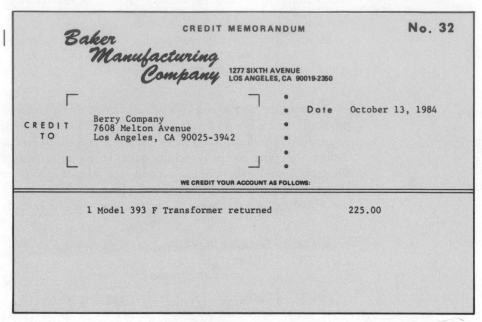

The effect of a sales return or allowance is a reduction in sales revenue and a reduction in cash or accounts receivable. If the sales account is debited, however, the balance of the account at the end of the period will represent net sales, and the volume of returns and allowances will not be disclosed. Because of the loss in revenue resulting from allowances, and the various expenses (transportation, unpacking, repairing, reselling, etc.) related to returns, it is advisable that management know the amount of such transactions. Such a policy will allow management to determine the causes of returns and allowances, should they become excessive, and to take corrective action. It is therefore preferable to debit an account entitled Sales Returns and Allowances. If the original sale is on account, the remainder of the transaction is recorded as a credit to Accounts Receivable. To illustrate, the following entry would be made by Baker Manufacturing Company to record the credit memo presented above:

Oct. 13	Sales Returns and Allowances	225	
	Accounts Receivable		225
	Credit Memo No. 32.		

If a cash refund is made because of merchandise returned or for an allowance, Sales Returns and Allowances is debited and Cash is credited.

TRADE DISCOUNTS

Manufacturers and wholesalers of certain types of merchandise frequently give large reductions from the *list prices* quoted in their catalogs. Such reductions in price are called trade discounts. Trade discounts are an easy method of making changes in prices without reprinting catalogs. As prices go up or down, new schedules of discounts may be issued. Trade discounts may also be used to give various classes of customers different prices.

There is no need to record list prices and their related trade discounts in the accounts. For example, the seller of an article listed at $100 with a trade discount of $40 would record the transaction as a sale of $60. Similarly, the buyer would record the transaction as a purchase of $60. For accounting purposes it is only the agreed price, which in the example is $60, that is important.

TRANSPORTA-TION COSTS

The terms of the agreement between buyer and seller include a provision concerning which party is to bear the cost of delivering the merchandise to the buyer. If the purchaser is to absorb the cost, the terms are stated **FOB shipping point**; if the seller is to assume the cost of transportation, the terms are said to be **FOB destination**.

Costs to Purchaser

When merchandise is purchased on FOB shipping point terms, the transportation costs paid by the purchaser should be debited to Purchases and credited to Cash. Some enterprises maintain an account titled "Freight In" or "Transportation In" for accumulating all separately charged delivery costs on merchandise purchased. The balance of this account is then added to the balance of Purchases to determine the total cost of acquiring the merchandise.

In some cases, the seller may prepay the transportation costs and add them to the invoice, even though the agreement states that the purchaser bear such costs (terms FOB shipping point). If the seller prepays the transportation charges, the purchaser will include the costs in the debit to Purchases and the credit to Accounts Payable. To illustrate, assume that on June 10 the Durban Co. purchases merchandise from Bell Corp. on account, $900, terms FOB shipping point, 2/10, n/30, with prepaid transportation costs of $50 added to the invoice. The entry by Durban Co. would be as follows:

June 10	Purchases	950	
	Accounts Payable		950
	Invoice 73B from Bell Corp.		

When the terms provide for a discount for early payment, the discount is based on the amount of the sale rather than on the invoice total. To illustrate, if Durban Co. pays the amount due on the purchase of June 10 within 10 days, the amount of the discount and the amount of the payment may be determined as follows:

Invoice from Bell Corp., including prepaid transportation
  of $50 . . . . $950
Amount subject to discount $900
Rate of discount 2%
Amount of purchases discount   18
Amount of payment $932

Durban Co. may record the payment as follows:

June 20	Accounts Payable	950	
	Cash		932
	Purchases Discount		18
	Invoice 73B from Bell Corp.		

Costs to Seller

When the agreement states that the seller is to bear the delivery costs (FOB destination), the amounts paid by the seller for delivery are debited to "Delivery Expense," "Transportation Out," or a similarly titled account. The total of such costs incurred during a period is reported on the seller's income statement as a selling expense.

SALES TAXES

Almost all states and many other taxing units levy a tax on sales of merchandise. The liability for the sales tax is ordinarily incurred at the time the sale is made, regardless of the terms of the sale.

Sales Tax for Seller

At the time of a cash sale, the seller collects the sales tax. When a sale is made on account, the customer is charged for the tax. The seller credits the sales account for only the amount of the sale, and credits the tax to Sales Tax Payable. For example, a sale of $100 on account, subject to a tax of 4%, may be recorded by the following entry:

Aug. 12	Accounts Receivable	104	
	Sales		100
	Sales Tax Payable		4
	Invoice No. 339.		

Periodically, the appropriate amount of the sales tax is paid to the taxing unit and Sales Tax Payable is debited.

Sales Tax for Purchaser

The purchaser debits the purchases account for the full amount of the merchandise acquired, including the sales tax. For example, a purchase of $100 on account, subject to a tax of 4%, may be recorded by the following entry:

Aug. 12	Purchases	104	
	Accounts Payable		104
	Invoice No. 339.		

PERIODIC REPORTING FOR MERCHANDISING ENTERPRISES

Although many merchandising enterprises prepare interim statements on a monthly or quarterly basis, a complete cycle of business operations usually occurs every twelve months. At yearly intervals throughout the life of a business enterprise, the operating data for the fiscal year must be summarized and reported for the use of managers, owners, creditors, various governmental agencies, and other interested persons. Summaries of the various assets of the enterprise on the last day of the fiscal year, together with the status of the equities of creditors and owners, must also be reported. The ledger, which contains the basic data for the reports, must then be brought up to date through proper adjusting entries. Finally, the accounts must be prepared to receive entries for transactions that will occur in the following year. The sequence of year-end procedures may be changed slightly, but in general the following outline is typical:

1. Prepare a trial balance of the ledger on a work sheet form.
2. Review the accounts and gather the data required for the adjustments.
3. Insert the adjustments and complete the work sheet.
4. Prepare financial statements from the data in the work sheet.
5. Journalize the adjusting entries and post to the ledger.
6. Journalize the closing entries and post to the ledger.
7. Prepare a post-closing trial balance of the ledger.
8. Journalize the reversing entries required to facilitate the recording of transactions in the following year, and post to the ledger.

Although the summarizing and reporting procedures presented in the remainder of this chapter are similar to those discussed in the preceding chapter, a number of differences should be noted. In a merchandising business, merchandise purchased during the period has been recorded in the purchases account. Some of this merchandise may have been sold during the period, and some may be unsold at the end of the period (ending inventory). This ending inventory becomes the beginning inventory for the next period. This chapter also introduces reversing entries as year-end procedures, and includes illustrations of other forms of the principal financial statements.

MERCHANDISE INVENTORY SYSTEMS

There are two main systems for accounting for merchandise held for sale: periodic and perpetual. Most merchandising enterprises use the periodic system. In this system, the revenues from sales are recorded when sales are made, but no attempt is made on the sales date to record the cost of the merchandise sold. It is only by a detailed listing of the merchandise on hand (called a physical inventory) at the end of the accounting period that a determination is made of (1) the cost of the merchandise sold during the period and (2) the cost of the inventory on hand at the end of the period. The periodic method is used in illustrations in this chapter.

Under the perpetual system, both the sales amount and the cost of merchandise sold amount are recorded when each item of merchandise is sold. In this manner, the accounting records continuously (perpetually) disclose the inventory on hand. The perpetual system is discussed in later chapters.

MERCHANDISE INVENTORY ADJUSTMENTS

For merchandising enterprises using the periodic system, the cost of merchandise sold and the beginning and ending inventories are reported in the income statement in the following manner:

```
Cost of merchandise sold:
  Merchandise inventory, January 1, 1984 ..        $ 59,700
  Purchases ...........................  $530,280
  Less purchases discount ...............     2,525
  Net purchases .........................              527,755
  Merchandise available for sale ..........            $587,455
  Less merchandise inventory,
  December 31, 1984.....................               62,150
      Cost of merchandise sold ............                      $525,305
```

The best method of making the above data readily available is to maintain a separate account entitled Merchandise Inventory. Throughout an accounting period, this account shows the inventory at the beginning of the period. Purchases of merchandise during the period, including costs for transportation and sales taxes, are then debited to the account entitled Purchases. As explained previously, returns and allowances are also recorded directly in the purchases account. Cash discounts are recorded in a purchases discount account.

At the end of the period it is necessary to remove from Merchandise Inventory the amount representing the inventory at the beginning of the period and to replace it with the amount representing the inventory at the end of the period. This is accomplished by two adjusting entries. The first entry transfers the beginning inventory to Income Summary. Since this beginning inventory is part of the cost of merchandise sold, it is debited to Income Summary. It is also a subtraction from the asset account, Merchandise Inventory, and hence is credited to that account. The first adjusting entry is as follows:

```
Dec. 31 | Income Summary ........................ | 59,700 |
        |   Merchandise Inventory .................. |        | 59,700
```

The second adjusting entry debits the cost of the merchandise inventory at the end of the period to the asset account, Merchandise Inventory. The credit portion of the entry effects a deduction of the unsold merchandise from the total cost of the merchandise available for sale during the period. In terms of the illustration of the partial income statement above, the credit portion of the second entry accom-

plishes the subtraction of $62,150 from $587,455 to yield the $525,3
merchandise sold. The second adjusting entry is as follows:

Dec. 31	Merchandise Inventory.....................	62,150	
	Income Summary		62,150

The effect of the two inventory adjustments is indicated by the following T accounts, Merchandise Inventory and Income Summary:

Merchandise Inventory

Dec. 31 Preceding year	59,700	Dec. 31 Current year	59,700
Dec. 31 Current year	62,150		

Income Summary

Dec. 31 Current year	59,700	Dec. 31 Current year	62,150

In the accounts, the inventory of $59,700 at the end of the preceding year (beginning of current year) has been transferred to Income Summary as a part of the cost of merchandise available for sale. It is replaced by a debit of $62,150, the merchandise inventory at the end of the current year. The credit of the same amount to Income Summary is a deduction from the cost of merchandise available for sale.

TRIAL BALANCE AND ADJUSTMENTS ON THE WORK SHEET

After year-end posting of the journal has been completed, a trial balance of the ledger is taken. The trial balance for Midtown Electric Corporation as of December 31, 1984, appears on the work sheet presented on pages 110 and 111. It differs slightly from trial balances illustrated earlier. All of the accounts in the ledger are listed in sequential order, including titles of accounts that have no balances. This variation in format has the advantage of listing accounts in the order in which they will be used when the statements are prepared.

The data needed for adjusting the accounts of Midtown Electric Corporation are summarized as follows:

Merchandise inventory as of December 31, 1984		$62,150
Inventories of supplies as of December 31, 1984:		
Store supplies		960
Office supplies.....................................		480
Insurance expired during 1984 on:		
Merchandise and store equipment	$2,080	
Office equipment and building......................	830	2,910
Depreciation during 1984 on:		
Building		4,500
Office equipment...................................		1,490
Store equipment		3,100
Salaries accrued on December 31, 1984:		
Sales salaries.....................................	$ 780	
Office salaries	372	1,152

WORK
SHEET

ACCOUNT TITLE	TRIAL BALANCE		ADJUSTMENTS	
	DEBIT	CREDIT	DEBIT	CREDIT
Cash	23,590			
Notes Receivable	10,000			
Accounts Receivable	20,880			
Merchandise Inventory ... *BEG. MERCH. INV.*	59,700		(b) 62,150	(a) 59,700
Store Supplies	2,970			(c) 2,010
Office Supplies	1,090			(d) 610
Prepaid Insurance	4,560			(e) 2,910
Land	20,000			
Building	140,000			
Accumulated Depreciation — Building		29,400		(f) 4,500
Office Equipment	15,570			
Accumulated Depreciation — Office Equipment		7,230		(g) 1,490
Store Equipment	27,100			
Accumulated Depreciation — Store Equipment		12,600		(h) 3,100
Accounts Payable		22,420		
Salaries Payable				(i) 1,152
Mortgage Note Payable		25,000		
Capital Stock		100,000		
Retained Earnings		59,888		
Dividends	18,000			
Income Summary *DEBIT INV. EXP.*			(a) 59,700	(b) 62,150
Sales		732,163		
Sales Returns and Allowances	6,140			
Sales Discount	5,822			
Purchases	530,280			
Purchases Discount		2,525		
Sales Salaries Expense	59,264		(i) 780	
Advertising Expense	10,460			
Depreciation Expense — Store Equipment			(h) 3,100	
Insurance Expense — Selling			(e) 2,080	
Store Supplies Expense			(c) 2,010	
Miscellaneous Selling Expense	630			
Office Salaries Expense	20,660		(i) 372	
Heating and Lighting Expense	8,100			
Taxes Expense	6,810			
Depreciation Expense — Building			(f) 4,500	
Depreciation Expense — Office Equipment			(g) 1,490	
Insurance Expense — General			(e) 830	
Office Supplies Expense			(d) 610	
Miscellaneous General Expense	760			
Interest Income		3,600		
Interest Expense	2,440			
	994,826	994,826	137,622	137,622
Net Income				

Explanations of the adjusting entries in the work sheet above are given in the paragraphs that follow.

Merchandise
Inventory

As discussed previously, the $59,700 balance of merchandise inventory appearing in the trial balance represents the amount of the inventory at the end of the preceding year (beginning of the current year). It is a part of the merchandise

Corporation
Sheet
December 31, 1984

ADJUSTED TRIAL BALANCE		INCOME STATEMENT		BALANCE SHEET	
DEBIT	CREDIT	DEBIT	CREDIT	DEBIT	CREDIT
23,590				23,590	
10,000				10,000	
20,880				20,880	
62,150				62,150	
960				960	
480				480	
1,650				1,650	
20,000				20,000	
140,000				140,000	
	33,900				33,900
15,570				15,570	
	8,720				8,720
27,100				27,100	
	15,700				15,700
	22,420				22,420
	1,152				1,152
	25,000				25,000
	100,000				100,000
	59,888				59,888
18,000				18,000	
59,700	62,150	59,700	62,150		
	732,163		732,163		
6,140		6,140			
5,822		5,822			
530,280		530,280			
	2,525		2,525		
60,044		60,044			
10,460		10,460			
3,100		3,100			
2,080		2,080			
2,010		2,010			
630		630			
21,032		21,032			
8,100		8,100			
6,810		6,810			
4,500		4,500			
1,490		1,490			
830		830			
610		610			
760		760			
	3,600		3,600		
2,440		2,440			
1,067,218	1,067,218	726,838	800,438	340,380	266,780
		73,600			73,600
		800,438	800,438	340,380	340,380

available for sale during the year and is hence transferred to Income Summary, where it will be combined with the net cost of merchandise purchased during the year (entry (a) on the work sheet).

The merchandise on hand at the end of the current year, as determined by a physical inventory, is an asset and must be debited to the asset account, Merchandise Inventory. It must also be deducted from the cost of merchandise available for sale (beginning inventory plus purchases less purchases discounts) to yield the cost of the merchandise sold. These objectives are accomplished by debiting Merchandise Inventory and crediting Income Summary for $62,150 (entry (b) on the work sheet).

Supplies | 	The $2,970 balance of the store supplies account in the trial balance is the combined cost of store supplies on hand at the beginning of the year and the cost of store supplies purchased during the year. The physical inventory at the end of the year indicates store supplies on hand totaling $960. The excess of $2,970 over the inventory of $960 is $2,010, which is the cost of the store supplies used during the period. The accounts are adjusted by debiting Store Supplies Expense and crediting Store Supplies for $2,010 (entry (c) on the work sheet). The adjustment for office supplies used is determined in the same manner (entry (d) on the work sheet).

Prepaid Insurance | 	The adjustment for insurance expired is similar to the adjustment for supplies consumed. The balance in Prepaid Insurance is the amount prepaid at the beginning of the year plus the additional premium costs incurred during the year. Analysis of the various insurance policies reveals that a total of $2,910 in premiums has expired, of which $2,080 is related to merchandise and store equipment and $830 is related to office equipment and building. Insurance Expense — Selling is debited for $2,080, Insurance Expense — General is debited for $830, and Prepaid Insurance is credited for $2,910 (entry (e) on the work sheet).

Depreciation of Plant Assets | 	The expired cost of a plant asset is debited to a depreciation expense account and credited to an accumulated depreciation account. A separate account for the current period's expense and for the accumulation of prior periods is maintained for each plant asset account. Thus, the adjustment for $4,500 depreciation of the building is recorded by a debit to Depreciation Expense — Building and a credit to Accumulated Depreciation — Building for $4,500 (entry (f) on the work sheet). The adjustments for depreciation of the office equipment and the store equipment are recorded in a similar manner (entries (g) and (h) on the work sheet).

Salaries Payable | 	The liability for the salaries earned by employees but not yet paid is recorded by a credit of $1,152 to Salaries Payable and debits of $780 and $372 to Sales Salaries Expense and Office Salaries Expense respectively (entry (i) on the work sheet).

COMPLETING THE WORK SHEET | 	After all of the necessary adjustments are entered on the work sheet, the two Adjustments columns are totaled to prove the equality of debits and credits. As illustrated in the preceding chapter, the balances of the accounts in the trial balance columns and the amount of any adjustments are added or deducted as appropriate. The adjusted balances are then extended into the adjusted trial balance columns, which are totaled to prove the equality of debits and credits. Both the debit and credit amounts for Income Summary are extended.

Some accountants prefer to eliminate the adjusted trial balance columns and to extend the adjusted account balances directly to the appropriate statement column. Such an alternative form of work sheet is especially popular if there are only a few items involved.

The process of extending the balances, as adjusted, to the statement columns is accomplished best by beginning with Cash at the top and moving down the work sheet, item by item, in sequential order. An exception to the usual practice of extending only the account balances should be noted. Both the debit and credit amounts for Income Summary are extended to the Income Statement columns. Since both the amount of the debit adjustment (beginning inventory of $59,700) and the amount of the credit adjustment (ending inventory of $62,150) may be reported on the income statement, there is no need to determine the difference between the two amounts.

After all of the items have been extended into the statement sections of the work sheet, the four columns are totaled and the net income or net loss is determined. In the illustration the difference between the credit and the debit columns of the Income Statement section is $73,600, the amount of the net income. The difference between the debit and the credit columns of the Balance Sheet section is also $73,600, which is the increase in capital resulting from net income. Agreement between the two balancing amounts is evidence of debit-credit equality and arithmetical accuracy.

PREPARATION OF FINANCIAL STATEMENTS	The income statement, the retained earnings statement,[3] and the balance sheet are prepared from the account titles and the data in the statement sections of the work sheet.

Many variations are possible in the general format of the principal financial statements, in the terminology used, and in the extent to which details are presented. The forms most frequently used are described and illustrated in the sections that follow.[4]

Income Statement	There are two widely used forms for the income statement, multiple-step and single-step. An income statement in the multiple-step form is presented on page 115. The single-step form is illustrated on page 116.

Multiple-Step Form

The multiple-step income statement is so called because of its many sections, subsections, and intermediate balances. In practice, there is considerable variation in the amount of detail presented in these sections. For example, instead of reporting separately gross sales and the related returns, allowances, and discounts, the statement may begin with net sales. Similarly, the supporting data for the determination of the cost of merchandise sold may be omitted from the statement.

---

[3]For the unincorporated business enterprise, a capital statement replaces the retained earnings statement. Such a statement for a sole proprietorship is illustrated on page 22.

[4]Examples of some of the forms described are also presented in Appendix G.

The various sections of a conventional multiple-step income statement for a mercantile enterprise are discussed briefly in the paragraphs that follow.

Revenue from sales. The total of all charges to customers for merchandise sold, both for cash and on account, is reported in this section. Sales returns and allowances and sales discounts are deducted from the gross amount to yield net sales.

Cost of merchandise sold. The determination of this important figure was explained and illustrated earlier in the chapter. Other descriptive terms frequently employed are **cost of goods sold** and **cost of sales**.

Gross profit. The excess of the net revenue from sales over the cost of merchandise sold is called **gross profit, gross profit on sales,** or **gross margin**. It is called *gross* because operating expenses must be deducted from it.

Operating expenses. The operating expenses of a business may be grouped under any desired number of headings and subheadings. In a retail business of the kind that has been used for illustrative purposes, it is usually satisfactory to subdivide operating expenses into two categories, selling and general.

Expenses that are incurred directly and entirely in connection with the sale of merchandise are classified as **selling expenses**. They include such expenses as salaries of the sales force, store supplies used, depreciation of store equipment, and advertising.

Expenses incurred in the general operations of the business are classified as **general expenses** or **administrative expenses**. Examples of these expenses are office salaries, depreciation of office equipment, and office supplies used. Expenses that are partly connected with selling and partly connected with the general operations of the business may be divided between the two categories. In a small business, however, mixed expenses such as rent, insurance, and taxes are commonly reported as general expenses.

Expenses of relatively small amounts that cannot be identified with the principal accounts are usually accumulated in accounts entitled Miscellaneous Selling Expense and Miscellaneous General Expense.

Income from operations. The excess of gross profit over total operating expenses is called **income from operations**, or **operating income**. The amount of the income from operations and its relationship to capital investment and to net sales are important factors in judging the efficiency of management and the degree of profitability of an enterprise. If operating expenses are greater than the gross profit, the excess is called **loss from operations**.

Other income. Revenue from sources other than the principal activity of a business is classified as **other income**, or **nonoperating income**. In a merchandising business this category often includes income from interest, rent, dividends, and gains resulting from the sale of plant assets.

Other expense. Expenses that cannot be associated definitely with operations are identified as **other expense**, or **nonoperating expense**. Interest expense that results from financing activities and losses incurred in the disposal of plant assets are examples of items that are reported in this section.

MULTIPLE-STEP FORM
OF INCOME STATEMENT

Midtown Electric Corporation
Income Statement
For Year Ended December 31, 1984

Revenue from sales:			
Sales			$732,163
Less: Sales returns and allowances	$ 6,140		
Sales discount	5,822	11,962	
Net sales			$720,201
Cost of merchandise sold:			
Merchandise inventory, January 1, 1984		$ 59,700	
Purchases	$530,280		
Less purchases discount	2,525		
Net purchases		527,755	
Merchandise available for sale		$587,455	
Less merchandise inventory,			
December 31, 1984		62,150	
Cost of merchandise sold			525,305
Gross profit			$194,896
Operating expenses:			
Selling expenses:			
Sales salaries expense	$ 60,044		
Advertising expense	10,460		
Depreciation expense—store equipment	3,100		
Insurance expense—selling	2,080		
Store supplies expense	2,010		
Miscellaneous selling expense	630		
Total selling expenses		$ 78,324	
General expenses:			
Office salaries expense	$ 21,032		
Heating and lighting expense	8,100		
Taxes expense	6,810		
Depreciation expense—building	4,500		
Depreciation expense—office equipment	1,490		
Insurance expense–general	830		
Office supplies expense	610		
Miscellaneous general expense	760		
Total general expenses		44,132	
Total operating expenses			122,456
Income from operations			$ 72,440
Other income:			
Interest income		$ 3,600	
Other expense:			
Interest expense		2,440	1,160
Net income[5]			$ 73,600

[5]This amount is further reduced by corporation income tax. The discussion of income taxes levied on corporate entities is reserved for later chapters.

The two categories of nonoperating items are offset against each other on the income statement. If the total of other income exceeds the total of other expense, the difference is added to income from operations. If the reverse is true, the difference is subtracted from income from operations.

Net income. The final figure on the income statement is labeled net income (or net loss). It is the net increase in capital resulting from profit-making activities. (As noted on the preceding page, the reporting of corporation income tax is discussed later.)

Single-Step Form

The single-step form of income statement derives its name from the fact that the total of all expenses is deducted from the total of all revenues. Such a statement is illustrated as follows for Midtown Electric Corporation. The illustration has been condensed to focus attention on its principal features. Such condensation is not an essential characteristic of the form.

SINGLE-STEP FORM
OF INCOME STATEMENT

Midtown Electric Corporation Income Statement For Year Ended December 31, 1984		
Revenues:		
Net sales		$720,201
Interest income		3,600
Total revenues		$723,801
Expenses:		
Cost of merchandise sold	$525,305	
Selling expenses	78,324	
General expenses	44,132	
Interest expense	2,440	
Total expenses		650,201
Net income		$ 73,600

The single-step form has the advantage of being simple and it emphasizes total revenues and total expenses as the factors that determine net income. An objection to the single-step form is that such relationships as gross profit to sales and income from operations to sales are not as readily determinable as they are when the multiple-step form is used.

Balance Sheet

The traditional arrangement of assets on the left-hand side of the statement, with the liabilities and capital on the right-hand side, is referred to as the account form.[6] If the entire statement is limited to a single page, it is customary to present

---

[6]An account form of balance sheet is illustrated on page 38.

the three sections in a downward sequence, with the total of the assets section equaling the combined totals of the other two sections. The latter form, called the report form, is illustrated in the following balance sheet for Midtown Electric Corporation.

REPORT FORM
OF BALANCE SHEET

Midtown Electric Corporation
Balance Sheet
December 31, 1984

Assets

Current assets:

Cash		$ 23,590
Notes receivable		10,000
Accounts receivable		20,880
Merchandise Inventory		62,150
Store supplies		960
Office supplies		480
Prepaid insurance		1,650
Total current assets		$119,710

Plant assets:

Land			$ 20,000
Building	$140,000		
Less accumulated depreciation	33,900	106,100	
Office equipment	$ 15,570		
Less accumulated depreciation	8,720	6,850	
Store equipment	$ 27,100		
Less accumulated depreciation	15,700	11,400	
Total plant assets			144,350
Total assets			$264,060

Liabilities

Current liabilities:

Accounts payable		$ 22,420
Mortgage note payable (current portion)		5,000
Salaries payable		1,152
Total current liabilities		$ 28,572
Long-term liabilities:		
Mortgage note payable (final payment, 1990)		20,000
Total liabilities		$ 48,572

Capital

Capital stock		$100,000
Retained earnings		115,488
Total capital		215,488
Total liabilities and capital		$264,060

Retained Earnings Statement

The retained earnings statement summarizes the changes which have occurred in the retained earnings account during the fiscal period. It serves as a connecting link between the income statement and the balance sheet. The retained earnings statement for Midtown Electric Corporation is illustrated as follows:

RETAINED EARNINGS STATEMENT

Midtown Electric Corporation Retained Earnings Statement For Year Ended December 31, 1984		
Retained earnings, January 1, 1984		$ 59,888
Net income for the year	$73,600	
Less dividends	18,000	
Increase in retained earnings		55,600
Retained earnings, December 31, 1984		$115,488

It is not unusual to add the analysis of retained earnings at the bottom of the income statement to form a **combined income and retained earnings statement**. The income statement portion of the combined statement may be shown either in multiple-step form or in a single-step form, as in the following illustration:

COMBINED INCOME AND RETAINED EARNINGS STATEMENT

Midtown Electric Corporation Income and Retained Earnings Statement For Year Ended December 31, 1984		
Revenues:		
Net sales		$720,201
Interest income		3,600
		$723,801
Expenses:		
Cost of merchandise sold	$525,305	
Selling expenses	78,324	
General expenses	44,132	
Interest expense	2,440	
Total expenses		650,201
Net income		$ 73,600
Retained earnings, January 1, 1984		59,888
		$133,488
Deduct dividends		18,000
Retained earnings, December 31, 1984		$115,488

The combined statement form emphasizes net income as the connecting link between the income statement and the retained earnings portion of capital and thus helps the reader's understanding. A criticism of the combined statement is that the net income figure is buried in the body of the statement.

ADJUSTING ENTRIES

The analyses required to make the adjustments were completed during the process of preparing the work sheet. It is therefore unnecessary to refer again to the basic data when recording the adjusting entries in the journal. After the entries are posted, the balances of all asset, liability, revenue, and expense accounts correspond exactly to the amounts reported in the financial statements. The adjusting entries for Midtown Electric Corporation are as follows:

ADJUSTING ENTRIES

	DATE		DESCRIPTION	POST. REF.	DEBIT	CREDIT	
1			Adjusting Entries				1
2	1984 Dec.	31	Income Summary	313	59 7 0 0 00		2
3			Merchandise Inventory	114		59 7 0 0 00	3
4							4
5		31	Merchandise Inventory	114	62 1 5 0 00		5
6			Income Summary	313		62 1 5 0 00	6
7							7
8		31	Store Supplies Expense	615	2 0 1 0 00		8
9			Store Supplies	115		2 0 1 0 00	9
10							10
11		31	Office Supplies Expense	717	6 1 0 00		11
12			Office Supplies	116		6 1 0 00	12
13							13
14		31	Insurance Expense — Selling	614	2 0 8 0 00		14
15			Insurance Expense — General	716	8 3 0 00		15
16			Prepaid Insurance	117		2 9 1 0 00	16
17							17
18		31	Depreciation Expense — Building	714	4 5 0 0 00		18
19			Accumulated Depreciation — Building	126		4 5 0 0 00	19
20							20
21		31	Depreciation Expense — Office Equipment	715	1 4 9 0 00		21
22			Accumulated Depr. — Office Equip.	124		1 4 9 0 00	22
23							23
24		31	Depreciation Expense — Store Equipment	613	3 1 0 0 00		24
25			Accumulated Depr. — Store Equip.	122		3 1 0 0 00	25
26							26
27		31	Sales Salaries Expense	611	7 8 0 00		27
28			Office Salaries Expense	711	3 7 2 00		28
29			Salaries Payable	213		1 1 5 2 00	29
30							30
31							31

JOURNAL   PAGE 28

CLOSING ENTRIES

The closing entries are recorded in the journal immediately following the adjusting entries. All of the temporary capital accounts are cleared of their balances, reducing them to zero. The final effect of closing out such balances is a net increase or a net decrease in the retained earnings account. The closing entries for Midtown Electric Corporation are as follows:

CLOSING
ENTRIES

	DATE		DESCRIPTION	POST. REF.	DEBIT	CREDIT	
1			Closing Entries				1
2	1984 Dec.	31	Sales	411	732 1 6 3 00		2
3			Purchases Discount	512	2 5 2 5 00		3
4			Interest Income	812	3 6 0 0 00		4
5			Income Summary	313		738 2 8 8 00	5
6							6
7		31	Income Summary	313	667 1 3 8 00		7
8			Sales Returns and Allowances	412		6 1 4 0 00	8
9			Sales Discount	413		5 8 2 2 00	9
10			Purchases	511		530 2 8 0 00	10
11			Sales Salaries Expense	611		60 0 4 4 00	11
12			Advertising Expense	612		10 4 6 0 00	12
13			Depreciation Expense—Store Equip.	613		3 1 0 0 00	13
14			Insurance Expense—Selling	614		2 0 8 0 00	14
15			Store Supplies Expense	615		2 0 1 0 00	15
16			Miscellaneous Selling Expense	619		6 3 0 00	16
17			Office Salaries Expense	711		21 0 3 2 00	17
18			Heating and Lighting Expense	712		8 1 0 0 00	18
19			Taxes Expense	713		6 8 1 0 00	19
20			Depreciation Expense—Building	714		4 5 0 0 00	20
21			Depreciation Expense—Office Equip.	715		1 4 9 0 00	21
22			Insurance Expense—General	716		8 3 0 00	22
23			Office Supplies Expense	717		6 1 0 00	23
24			Miscellaneous General Expense	719		7 6 0 00	24
25			Interest Expense	911		2 4 4 0 00	25
26							26
27		31	Income Summary	313	73 6 0 0 00		27
28			Retained Earnings	311		73 6 0 0 00	28
29							29
30		31	Retained Earnings	311	18 0 0 0 00		30
31			Dividends	312		18 0 0 0 00	31
32							32

JOURNAL   PAGE 29

The effect of each of these four entries may be described as follows:

1. The first entry closes all income statement accounts with *credit* balances by transferring the total to the *credit* side of Income Summary.
2. The second entry closes all income statement accounts with *debit* balances by transferring the total to the *debit* side of Income Summary.

3. The third entry closes Income Summary by transferring its balance, the net income for the year, to Retained Earnings.
4. The fourth entry closes Dividends by transferring its balance to Retained Earnings.

The income summary account, as it will appear after the merchandise inventory adjustments and the closing entries have been posted, is as follows. Each item in the account is identified as an aid to understanding. Such notations are not an essential part of the posting procedure.

INCOME SUMMARY ACCOUNT

| | | | | | | | | | | | BALANCE | |
DATE		ITEM	POST. REF.	DEBIT		CREDIT		DEBIT		CREDIT	
1984 Dec.	31	Mer. inv., Jan. 1	28	59 7 0 0 00				59 7 0 0 00			
	31	Mer. inv., Dec. 31	28			62 1 5 0 00				2 4 5 0 00	
	31	Revenue, etc.	29			738 2 8 8 00				740 7 3 8 00	
	31	Expense, etc.	29	667 1 3 8 00						73 6 0 0 00	
	31	Net income	29	73 6 0 0 00				—		—	

ACCOUNT Income Summary   ACCOUNT NO. 313

After all temporary capital accounts have been closed, the only accounts with balances are the asset, contra asset, liability, and capital accounts. The balances of these accounts in the ledger will correspond exactly with the amounts appearing on the balance sheet on page 117.

POST-CLOSING TRIAL BALANCE

After the adjusting and closing entries have been recorded, it is advisable to take another trial balance to verify the debit-credit equality of the ledger at the beginning of the following year. This post-closing trial balance may consist of two adding machine listings, one for the debit balances and the other for the credit balances, or its details may be shown in a more formal fashion, as was illustrated in Chapter 3 on page 85.

REVERSING ENTRIES

Some of the adjusting entries recorded at the end of a fiscal year have an important effect on otherwise routine transactions that occur in the following year. A typical example is the adjusting entry for accrued salaries owed to employees at the end of the year. The wage or salary expense of an enterprise and the accompanying liability to employees actually accumulates or accrues day by day, or even hour by hour, during any part of the fiscal year. Nevertheless, the practice of recording the expense only at the time of payment is more efficient. When salaries are paid weekly, an entry debiting Salary Expense and crediting Cash will be recorded 52 or 53 times during the year. If there has been an adjusting entry for accrued salaries at the end of the year, however, the first payment of salaries in the following year will include such year-end accrual. In the absence of some special provision, it will be necessary to debit Salaries Payable for the amount owed for the earlier year and Salary Expense for the portion of the payroll that represents expense for the later year.

To illustrate, assume the following facts for an enterprise that pays salaries weekly and ends its fiscal year on December 31:

1. Salaries are paid on Friday for the five-day week ending on Friday.
2. The balance in Salary Expense as of Friday, December 27, is $62,500.
3. Salaries accrued for Monday and Tuesday, December 30 and 31, total $500.
4. Salaries paid on Friday, January 3, of the following year total $1,250.

The foregoing data may be diagrammed as follows:

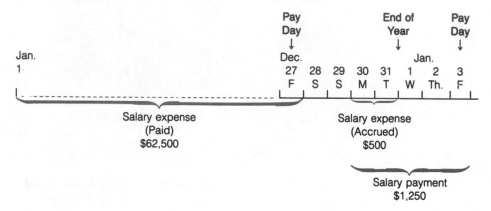

The adjusting entry to record the accrued salary expense and salaries payable for Monday and Tuesday, December 30 and 31, is as follows:

| Dec. 31 | Salary Expense .... | 611 | 500 | |
| | Salaries Payable .... | 213 | | 500 |

After the adjusting entry has been posted, Salary Expense will have a debit balance of $63,000 ($62,500 + $500) and Salaries Payable will have a credit balance of $500. After the closing process is completed, Salary Expense is in balance and ready for entries of the following year, but Salaries Payable continues to have a credit balance of $500. As matters now stand, it would be necessary to record the $1,250 payroll on January 3 as a debit of $500 to Salaries Payable and a debit of $750 to Salary Expense. This means that the employee who records payroll entries must not only record this particular payroll in a different manner from all other weekly payrolls for the year but must also refer to the adjusting entries in the journal or the ledger to determine the amount of the $1,250 payment to be debited to each of the two accounts.

The need to refer to earlier entries and to divide the debit between two accounts can be avoided by an optional procedure of recording a **reversing entry** as of the first day of the following fiscal period. As the term implies, such an entry is the exact reverse of the adjusting entry to which it relates. The amounts and the accounts are the same; the debits and credits are merely reversed.

Continuing with the illustration, the reversing entry for the accrued salaries is as follows:

Jan. 1	Salaries Payable	213	500	
	Salary Expense	611		500

The effect of the reversing entry is to transfer the $500 liability from Salaries Payable to the credit side of Salary Expense. The real nature of the $500 balance is unchanged; it remains a liability. When the payroll is paid on January 3, Salary Expense will be debited and Cash will be credited for $1,250, the entire amount of the weekly salaries. After the entry is posted, Salary Expense will have a debit balance of $750, which is the amount of expense incurred for January 1–3. The sequence of entries, including adjusting, closing, and reversing entries, may be traced in the following accounts:

ACCOUNT **SALARY EXPENSE**
ACCOUNT NO. 611

ADJUSTMENT AND REVERSAL FOR ACCRUED SALARIES

Date		Item	Post. Ref.	Debit	Credit	Balance Debit	Balance Credit
1984 Jan.	5		1	1,240		1,240	
Dec.	6		25	1,300		58,440	
	13		26	1,450		59,890	
	20		27	1,260		61,150	
	27		28	1,350		62,500	
	31	Adjusting	28	500		63,000	
	31	Closing	29		63,000	—	—
1985 Jan.	1	Reversing	29		500		500
	3		29	1,250		750	

ACCOUNT **SALARIES PAYABLE**
ACCOUNT NO. 213

Date		Item	Post. Ref.	Debit	Credit	Balance Debit	Balance Credit
1984 Dec.	31	Adjusting	28		500		500
1985 Jan.	1	Reversing	29	500		—	—

The year-end procedures for Midtown Electric Corporation are completed by journalizing and posting the reversing entry for accrued salaries. The entry is as follows:

REVERSING
ENTRY

			JOURNAL			PAGE 29	
	DATE	DESCRIPTION	POST. REF.	DEBIT		CREDIT	
		Reversing Entry					
32	1985 Jan. 1	Salaries Payable	213	1 1 5 2 00			32
33		Sales Salaries Expense	611			7 8 0 00	33
34		Office Salaries Expense	711			3 7 2 00	34
35							35
36							36
37							37
38							38

After the reversing entry is posted, Salaries Payable is in balance and the liabilities for sales and office salaries appear as credits in the respective expense accounts. The entire amount of the first payroll in January will be debited to the salary expense accounts and the balances of the accounts will then automatically represent the expense of the new period.

Self-Examination Questions *(Answers in Appendix C.)*

1. If merchandise is sold on account to a customer for $1,000, terms FOB shipping point, 1/10, n/30 and the seller prepays $50 in transportation costs, the amount of the discount for early payment would be:
   A. $0   C. $10.00
   B. $5.00   D. $10.50

2. Merchandise is sold on account to a customer for $1,000, terms FOB destination, 1/10, n/30. If the seller pays $50 in transportation costs and the customer returns $100 of the merchandise prior to payment, what is the amount of the discount for early payment?
   A. $0   C. $10.00
   B. $9.00   D. $10.50

3. The amount for merchandise inventory that appears in the trial balance columns of the work sheet represents:
   A. inventory at the beginning of the current period
   B. inventory at the end of the current period
   C. cost of merchandise sold during the current period
   D. none of the above

4. The income statement in which the total of all expenses is deducted from the total of all revenues is termed:
   A. multiple-step form   C. account form
   B. single-step form   D. report form

5. At the end of the fiscal year, the adjusting entry for accrued salaries was inadvertently omitted. The effect of the error (assuming that it is not corrected) would be to:

A. understate expenses for the year
B. overstate net income for the year
C. understate liabilities at the end of the year
D. all of the above

Discussion Questions

1. What is the meaning of (a) 1/10, n/30; (b) n/30; (c) n/eom?

2. What is the term applied to discounts for early payment by (a) the purchaser, (b) the seller?

3. The debits and credits from three related transactions are presented in the following T accounts. (a) Describe each transaction. (b) What is the rate of the discount and on what amount was it computed?

Cash			Accounts Payable			
(3)	8,415		(2)	500	(1)	9,000
			(3)	8,500		

Purchases			Purchases Discount		
(1)	9,000	(2)	500	(3)	85

4. After the amount due on a sale of $1,000, terms 1/10, n/30, is received from a customer within the discount period, the seller consents to the return of the entire shipment. (a) What is the amount of the refund owed to the customer? (b) What accounts should be debited and credited to record the return and the refund?

5. At what amount would a seller record the sale of an item of merchandise with a list price of $1,000 and subject to a trade discount of 30%?

6. Who bears the transportation costs when the terms of sale are (a) FOB shipping point, (b) FOB destination?

7. A retailer is considering the purchase of 5 units of a specific commodity from either of two suppliers. Their offers are as follows:
A: $100 a unit, total of $500, 1/10, n/30, no charge for transportation.
B: $90 a unit, total of $450, 2/10, n/30, plus transportation costs of $65.
Which of the two offers, A or B, yields the lower price?

8. Merchandise is sold on account to a customer for $5,000, terms FOB shipping point, 1/10, n/30, the seller paying the transportation costs of $100. Determine the following: (a) amount of the sale, (b) amount debited to Accounts Receivable, (c) amount of the discount for early payment, (d) amount of the remittance due within the discount period.

9. A sale of merchandise on account for $500 is subject to a 5% sales tax. (a) Should the sales tax be recorded at the time of sale or when payment is received? (b) What is the amount of the sale? (c) What is the amount debited to Accounts Receivable? (d) What is the title of the account to which the $25 is credited?

10. Which type of system for accounting for merchandise held for sale continuously discloses the amount of the inventory on hand?

11. In the following questions, identify the items designated by X:
    (a) Sales − (X + X) = Net sales.
    (b) Purchases − X = Net purchases.
    (c) Merchandise inventory (beginning) + X = Merchandise available for sale.
    (d) Merchandise available for sale − X = Cost of merchandise sold.
    (e) Net sales − cost of merchandise sold = X.

12. The account Merchandise Inventory is listed at $98,500 on the trial balance (before adjustments) as of January 31, the end of the first month in the fiscal year. Which one of the following phrases describes the item correctly?
    (a) Inventory of merchandise at January 1, beginning of the month.
    (b) Purchases of merchandise during January.
    (c) Merchandise available for sale during January.
    (d) Inventory of merchandise at January 31, end of the month.
    (e) Cost of merchandise sold during January.

13. The following data appear in a work sheet as of December 31, the end of the fiscal year:

	Adjustments		Income Statement	
	Dr.	Cr.	Dr.	Cr.
Income Summary	(a) 95,000	(b) 85,000	95,000	85,000

    (a) To what account was the $95,000 credited in adjustment (a)?
    (b) To what account was the $85,000 debited in adjustment (b)?
    (c) What was the amount of the merchandise inventory at January 1, the beginning of the fiscal year?
    (d) What amount will be listed for merchandise inventory on the balance sheet at December 31, the end of the fiscal year?
    (e) If the totals of the Income Statement columns of the work sheet are $910,000 debit and $980,000 credit, what is the amount of the net income for the year?
    (f) Would the amount determined to be net income be affected by extending only the net amount of $10,000 ($95,000 − $85,000) into the Income Statement debit column?

14. For the fiscal year, net sales were $975,000 and net purchases were $650,000. Merchandise inventory at the beginning of the year was $75,000 and at the end of the year it was $80,000. Determine the following amounts:
    (a) Merchandise available for sale.
    (b) Cost of merchandise sold.
    (c) Gross profit.
    (d) Merchandise inventory listed on the balance sheet as of the end of the year.

15. Differentiate between the multiple-step and the single-step forms of the income statement.

16. The following expenses were incurred by a merchandising enterprise during the year. In which expense section of the income statement should each be reported: (a) selling, (b) general, or (c) other?
    (1) Depreciation expense on store equipment.

(2) Interest expense on notes payable.
(3) Salary of salespersons.
(4) Insurance expense on office equipment.
(5) Heating and lighting expense.
(6) Salary of general manager.
(7) Advertising expense.
(8) Office supplies used.

17. What major advantages and disadvantages does the single-step form of income statement have in comparison to the multiple-step statement?

18. Differentiate between the account form and the report form of balance sheet.

19. (a) What two financial statements are frequently combined and presented as a single statement? (b) What is the major criticism directed at the combined statement?

20. Before adjustment at December 31, the end of the fiscal year, the salary expense account has a debit balance of $462,000. The amount of salary accrued (owed but not paid) on the same date is $9,750. Indicate the necessary (a) adjusting entry, (b) closing entry, and (c) reversing entry.

21. (a) What is the effect of closing the revenue, expense, and dividends accounts of a corporation at the end of a fiscal year? (b) After the closing entries have been posted, what type of accounts remain with balances?

22. Immediately after the reversing entries have been recorded, Salary Expense has a credit balance of $9,750. Assuming that there have been no errors, does the balance represent an asset, expense, revenue, liability, contra asset, or contra expense?

23. As of May 1, the first day of the fiscal year, Salary Expense has a credit balance of $5,000. On May 3, the first payday of the year, salaries of $12,500 are paid. (a) What is the salary expense for May 1–3: $5,000, $7,500, $12,500, or $17,500? (b) What entry should be made to record the payment on May 3?

24. Why is it advisable, after closing the accounts at the end of a year, to reverse the adjusting entries that had been made for accrued salaries and other accrued expenses?

Exercises

Exercise 4-1. Determine the amount to be paid in full settlement of each of the following invoices, assuming that credit for returns and allowances was received prior to payment and that all invoices were paid within the discount period.

| | Purchase Invoice | | | |
	Merchandise	Transportation	Terms	Returns and Allowances
(a)	$2,500	—	FOB shipping point, 1/10, n/30	—
(b)	5,000	$80	FOB shipping point, 2/10, n/30	$400
(c)	1,000	—	FOB destination, n/30	100
(d)	1,750	—	FOB destination, 2/10, n/30	50
(e)	2,400	50	FOB shipping point, 1/10, n/30	200

Exercise 4-2. Hume Co. purchases merchandise from a supplier on account, $3,000, terms FOB shipping point, 2/10, n/30. The supplier adds transportation charges of $40 to the invoice. Hume Co. returns some of the merchandise, receiving a credit memorandum for $200, and then pays the amount due within the discount period. Present Hume Co.'s entries to record (a) the purchase, (b) the merchandise return, and (c) the payment. (Hume Co. records merchandise purchases returns and allowances in the purchases account.)

Exercise 4-3. Present entries for the following related transactions:
June 10. Sold merchandise to a customer for $5,000, terms FOB shipping point, 1/10, n/30.
  10. Paid the transportation charges of $70, debiting the amount to Accounts Receivable.
  15. Issued a credit memorandum for $200 to the customer for merchandise returned.
  20. Received a check for the amount due from the sale.

Exercise 4-4. Evans Corp. sells merchandise to Park Co. on account, list price $5,000, trade discount 30%, FOB shipping point, 2/10, n/30. Evans Corp. pays the transportation charges of $100 as an accommodation and adds it to the invoice. Evans Corp. issues a credit memorandum for $150 for merchandise returned and subsequently receives the amount due within the discount period. Present Evans Corp.'s entries to record (a) the sale and the transportation costs, (b) the credit memorandum, and (c) the receipt of the check for the amount due.

Exercise 4-5. Present entries for the following related transactions of F. Barker and Son. Record merchandise purchases returns and allowances in the purchases account.
  (a) Purchased $2,000 of merchandise from Carr Co. on account, terms 2/10, n/30.
  (b) Paid the amount owed on the invoice within the discount period.
  (c) Discovered that some of the merchandise was defective and returned items with an invoice price of $500, receiving credit.
  (d) Purchased an additional $300 of fabrics from Carr Co. on account, terms 2/10, n/30.
  (e) Received a check for the balance owed from the return in (c), after deducting for the purchase in (d).

Exercise 4-6. Two or more items are omitted in each of the following tabulations of income statement data. Determine the amounts of the missing items, identifying them by letter.

Sales	Sales Returns	Net Sales	Beginning Inventory	Net Purchases	Ending Inventory	Cost of Merchandise Sold	Gross Profit
$98,000	$5,000	(a)	$45,000	$80,000	(b)	$70,000	(c)
72,000	(d)	$70,000	19,000	45,000	$20,000	(e)	(f)
89,000	(g)	89,000	(h)	65,000	37,000	(i)	$28,000
65,000	2,000	63,000	22,000	43,000	(j)	(k)	20,000

Exercise 4-7. On the basis of the following data, journalize (a) the adjusting entries at December 31, the end of the current fiscal year, and (b) the reversing entry on January 1, the first day of the following year.

(1) The prepaid insurance account before adjustment on December 31 has a balance of $6,750. An analysis of the policies indicates that $4,850 of premiums has expired during the year.

(2) Store supplies account balance before adjusting, $990; store supplies physical inventory, December 31, $220.

(3) Merchandise inventory: January 1 (beginning) $88,500; December 31 (ending) $87,200.

(4) Sales salaries are uniformly $12,000 for a five-day workweek, ending on Friday. The last payday of the year was Friday, December 27.

Exercise 4-8. Portions of the salary expense account of an enterprise are presented below. (a) Indicate the nature of the entry (payment, adjusting, closing, reversing) from which each numbered posting was made. (b) Present the complete journal entry from which each numbered posting was made.

ACCOUNT Salary Expense   ACCOUNT NO. 52

Date		Item	Post. Ref.	Dr.	Cr.	Balance Dr.	Balance Cr.
19-- Jan.	8		39	3,200		3,200	
Dec.	26	(1)	44	3,350		85,800	
	31	(2)	44	1,350		87,150	
	31	(3)	45		87,150	—	—
19-- Jan.	1	(4)	45		1,350		1,350
	9	(5)	46	3,400		2,050	

Exercise 4-9. Selected account titles and related amounts appearing in the Income Statement and Balance Sheet columns of the work sheet of the Levis Company for December 31 are listed in alphabetical order as follows:

Building	$220,000	Purchases	$735,000
Capital Stock	250,000	Purchases Discount	14,000
Cash	81,500	Retained Earnings	192,500
Dividends	50,000	Salaries Payable	3,100
General Expenses	72,500	Sales	998,000
Interest Expense	5,700	Sales Discount	8,600
Merchandise Inventory (1/1)	170,450	Sales Returns and Allowances	9,200
Merchandise Inventory (12/31)	192,950	Selling Expenses	102,500
Office Supplies	7,100	Store Supplies	6,000

All selling expenses have been recorded in the account entitled "Selling Expenses," and all general expenses have been recorded in the account entitled "General Expenses."

(a) Prepare a multiple-step income statement for the year.

(b) Determine the amount of retained earnings to be reported in the balance sheet at the end of the year.

(c) Journalize the entries to adjust the merchandise inventory.

(d) Journalize the closing entries.

Exercise 4-10. Summary operating data for the Martha Ross Company during the current year ending December 31 are as follows: cost of merchandise sold, $605,000; general expenses, $98,000; interest expense, $22,000; rent income, $40,000; net sales, $950,000; and selling expenses, $142,500. Prepare a single-step income statement.

Exercise 4-11. From the data presented in Exercise 4-10 and assuming that the balance of Retained Earnings was $155,500 on January 1 and that $100,000 of dividends were paid during the year, prepare a combined income and retained earnings statement. (Use the single-step form for the income statement portion of the statement).

Problems
(Problems in Appendix B: 4-1B, 4-3B, 4-4B, 4-6B.)

Problem 4-1A. The following were selected from among the transactions completed by Miller Co. during June of the current year:

June 2. Purchased merchandise on account from Eastwood Co., $5,500, terms FOB destination, 2/10, n/30.
      3. Purchased office supplies for cash, $475.
      6. Purchased merchandise on account from Plymouth Co., $2,200, terms FOB shipping point, 1/10, n/30, with prepaid transportation costs of $70 added to the invoice.
      7. Returned merchandise purchased on June 2 from Eastwood Co., $500.
     10. Sold merchandise for cash, $3,625.
     11. Paid Eastwood Co. on account for purchases of June 2, less returns of June 7 and discount.
     15. Sold merchandise on nonbank credit cards and reported accounts to the card company, $1,950.
     15. Paid Plymouth Co., on account for purchases of June 6, less discount.
     19. Sold merchandise on account to Joan Downs Co., $900, terms 1/10, n/30.
     20. Sold merchandise on account to Bowen and Son, $1,500, terms 1/10, n/30.
     23. Received cash from card company for nonbank credit card sales of June 15, less $117 service fee.
     28. Received cash on account from sale of June 19 to Joan Downs Co., less discount.
     29. Purchased merchandise for cash, $1,000, less trade discount of 40%.
     30. Received merchandise returned by Bowen and Son from sale of June 20, $1,500.

Instructions:
Journalize the transactions in a two-column journal.

Problem 4-2A. The account balances at January 1 of the current year for Spur Company are as follows:

11	Cash	$18,575
12	Accounts Receivable	26,900
13	Merchandise Inventory	40,100
14	Prepaid Insurance	1,250

15	Store Supplies	$ 900
21	Accounts Payable	12,500
31	E. Spur, Capital	75,225
32	E. Spur, Drawing	—
33	Income Summary	—
41	Sales	—
42	Sales Returns and Allowances	—
43	Sales Discount	—
51	Purchases	—
52	Purchases Discount	—
53	Sales Salaries Expense	—
54	Advertising Expense	—
55	Store Supplies Expense	—
56	Miscellaneous Selling Expense	—
57	Office Salaries Expense	—
58	Rent Expense	—
59	Insurance Expense	—
60	Miscellaneous General Expense	—

The following transactions were completed during January of the current year:

Jan. 2. Paid rent for month, $3,000.
   3. Purchased merchandise on account, $9,900.
   4. Received $9,405 cash from customers on account after discounts of $95 were deducted.
   5. Paid creditors $12,250 on account after discounts of $250 had been deducted.
   6. Sold merchandise for cash, $7,500.
   9. Purchased merchandise on account, $11,600.
   10. Sold merchandise on account, $14,200.
   11. Returned merchandise purchased on account on January 9, $600.
   13. Received merchandise returned on account, $500.
   16. Paid sales salaries of $2,100 and office salaries of $1,400.
   18. Paid creditors $10,780 on account after discounts of $220 had been deducted.
   19. Received $14,058 cash from customers on account after discounts of $142 had been deducted.
   20. Sold merchandise for cash, $4,100.
   23. Sold merchandise on account, $11,750.
   27. Refunded $100 cash on sales made for cash.
   29. Paid advertising expense, $1,250.
   30. Sold merchandise for cash, $3,900.
   30. Purchased merchandise on account, $8,800.
   31. Paid sales salaries of $1,970 and office salaries of $1,400.
   31. Paid creditors $9,900 on account, no discount.
   31. Received $16,900 cash from customers on account, no discount.

Instructions:
(1) Open a ledger of four-column accounts for the accounts listed. Record the balances in the appropriate balance column as of January 1, write "Balance" in the item section, and place a check mark (✔) in the posting reference column.
(2) Record the transactions for January in a two-column journal.   *(continued)*

(3) Post to the ledger, extending the month-end balances to the appropriate balance columns after all posting is completed.
(4) Prepare a trial balance of the ledger as of January 31.

Problem 4-3A. The following data for C. Wells and Co. were selected from the ledger after adjustment at December 31, the end of the current fiscal year:

Accounts payable	$ 42,300
Accounts receivable	134,250
Accumulated depreciation—office equipment	34,000
Accumulated depreciation—store equipment	62,700
Capital stock	200,000
Cash	87,550
Cost of merchandise sold	605,500
Dividends	80,000
Dividends payable	20,000
General expenses	89,650
Interest expense	15,200
Merchandise inventory	172,500
Mortgage note payable (due in 1991)	75,000
Office equipment	60,200
Prepaid insurance	8,700
Rent income	12,900
Retained earnings	112,800
Salaries payable	8,100
Sales	942,700
Selling expenses	111,250
Store equipment	145,700

Instructions:
(1) Prepare a combined income and retained earnings statement, using the single-step form for the income statement.
(2) Prepare a balance sheet in report form.

Problem 4-4A. The accounts in the ledger of Whitmore Company, with the unadjusted balances on June 30, the end of the current year, are as follows:

Cash	$ 43,750	Purchases	$610,050
Accounts Receivable	96,150	Sales Salaries Expense	77,400
Merchandise Inventory	145,250	Advertising Expense	24,800
Prepaid Insurance	12,690	Depreciation Expense—	
Store Supplies	8,250	Store Equipment	—
Store Equipment	89,500	Store Supplies Expense	—
Accum. Depreciation—Store		Misc. Selling Expense	4,400
Equipment	25,300	Office Salaries Expense	39,845
Accounts Payable	44,740	Rent Expense	40,000
Salaries Payable	—	Heating and Lighting Exp.	16,100
Capital Stock	180,000	Taxes Expense	8,500
Retained Earnings	81,445	Insurance Expense	—
Dividends	60,000	Misc. General Expense	3,600
Income Summary	—	Gain on Disposal of Equip.	3,800
Sales	945,000		

The data needed for year-end adjustments on June 30 are as follows:

Merchandise inventory on June 30		$150,500
Insurance expired during the year		6,400
Store supplies inventory on June 30		2,150
Depreciation for the current year		19,200
Accrued salaries on June 30:		
Sales salaries	$2,800	
Office salaries	1,300	4,100

Instructions:

(1) Prepare a work sheet for the fiscal year ended June 30, listing all of the accounts in the order given.
(2) Prepare a multiple-step income statement.
(3) Prepare a retained earnings statement.
(4) Prepare a report form balance sheet.
(5) Compute the following:
    (a) Percent of gross profit to sales.
    (b) Percent of income from operations to sales.

Problem 4-5A. The accounts and their balances in the ledger of Abrams Company on December 31 of the current year are as follows:

Cash	$ 30,750
Accounts Receivable	71,500
Merchandise Inventory	92,750
Prepaid Insurance	7,910
Store Supplies	1,525
Office Supplies	1,065
Store Equipment	70,500
Accum. Depreciation—Store Equipment	23,350
Office Equipment	22,750
Accum. Depreciation—Office Equipment	10,000
Accounts Payable	42,115
Salaries Payable	—
Mortgage Note Payable (due 1993)	80,000
C. F. Abrams, Capital	98,500
C. F. Abrams, Drawing	36,000
Income Summary	—
Sales	622,250
Sales Returns and Allowances	3,250
Purchases	410,300
Purchases Discount	2,150
Sales Salaries Expense	56,850
Advertising Expense	17,150
Rent Expense—Selling	16,000
Depreciation Expense—Store Equipment	—
Insurance Expense—Selling	—
Store Supplies Expense	—
Misc. Selling Expense	1,190

Office Salaries Expense	$29,450
Rent Expense–General	8,000
Depreciation Expense–Office Equipment	—
Insurance Expense–General	—
Office Supplies Expense	—
Miscellaneous General Expense	1,225
Gain on Disposal of Plant Assets	9,400
Interest Expense	9,600

The data for year-end adjustments on December 31 are as follows:

Merchandise inventory on December 31		$89,200
Insurance expired during the year:		
Allocable as selling expense	$2,200	
Allocable as general expense	810	3,010
Inventory of supplies on December 31:		
Store supplies		775
Office supplies		415
Depreciation for the year:		
Store equipment		6,750
Office equipment		2,500
Salaries payable on December 31:		
Sales salaries	$2,100	
Office salaries	1,050	3,150

Instructions:
  (1) Prepare a work sheet for the fiscal year ended December 31, listing all accounts in the order given.
  (2) Prepare a multiple-step income statement.
  (3) Prepare a capital statement.
  (4) Prepare a report form balance sheet.
  (5) Journalize the adjusting entries.
  (6) Journalize the closing entries.
  (7) Journalize the reversing entries as of January 1.

Problem 4-6A. A portion of the work sheet of Frank Betts Company for the current year ended June 30 is presented on page 135.

Instructions:
  (1) From the partial work sheet, determine the eight entries that appeared in the adjustments columns and present them in general journal form. The only accounts affected by more than one adjusting entry were Merchandise Inventory and Income Summary. The balance in Prepaid Rent before adjustment was $42,000, representing a prepayment for 14 months' rent at $3,000 a month.
  (2) Determine the following:
    (a) Amount of net income for the year.
    (b) Amount of the owner's capital at the end of the year.

Account Title	Income Statement		Balance Sheet	
	Debit	Credit	Debit	Credit
Cash..			41,750	
Accounts Receivable			140,650	
Merchandise Inventory......................			161,100	
Prepaid Rent			6,000	
Prepaid Insurance.........................			11,950	
Supplies			2,150	
Store Equipment			58,500	
Accumulated Depr.—Store Equipment				22,200
Office Equipment..........................			30,400	
Accumulated Depr.—Office Equipment				10,150
Accounts Payable				62,500
Sales Salaries Payable				3,000
Mortgage Note Payable				100,000
Frank Betts, Capital				212,350
Frank Betts, Drawing			40,000	
Income Summary	172,750	161,100		
Sales		827,050		
Sales Returns and Allowances	8,120			
Purchases	512,410			
Purchases Discount		4,250		
Sales Salaries Expense	72,500			
Delivery Expense..........................	21,200			
Depreciation Expense—Store Equipment....	8,900			
Supplies Expense	1,250			
Miscellaneous Selling Expense	1,200			
Office Salaries Expense....................	40,500			
Rent Expense.............................	36,000			
Heating and Lighting Expense	8,950			
Insurance Expense	7,750			
Depreciation Expense—Office Equipment ...	3,750			
Miscellaneous General Expense	1,320			
Interest Expense	13,500			
	910,100	992,400	492,500	410,200

Your brother operates Tapes Unlimited, Inc., a video tape distributorship that is in its second year of operation. Recently, Ruby Hobbs, the firm's accountant, resigned to enter nursing school. Before leaving, she completed the work sheet for the year ended July 31, 1984, and recorded the necessary adjusting entries. From this work sheet, your brother prepared the following financial statements:

Tapes Unlimited, Inc.
Income Statement
For Year Ended July 31, 1984

Sales		$652,000
Less cost of merchandise sold:		
Purchases	$386,000	
Net decrease in merchandise inventory	8,500	394,500
Gross profit		$257,500
Operating expenses:		
Salaries expense	$126,100	
Heat and lighting expense	12,900	
Insurance expense	6,750	
Depreciation expense—building	4,800	
Depreciation expense—office equipment	2,100	
Depreciation expense—store equipment	3,600	
Supplies expense	7,400	
Miscellaneous expense	2,700	
Delivery expense	23,600	189,950
		$ 67,550
Selling expenses:		
Advertising expense		13,040
Income from operations		$ 54,510
Other income:		
Purchases discount	$ 3,300	
Interest income	1,500	4,800
		$ 59,310
Other expenses:		
Sales returns	$ 3,800	
Dividends	10,000	
Interest expense	12,000	
Taxes expense	6,450	32,250
Net income		$ 27,060

Tapes Unlimited, Inc.
Retained Earnings Statement
For Year Ended July 31, 1984

Retained earnings, August 1, 1983	$13,202
Net income for the year	27,060
Retained earnings, July 31, 1984	$40,262

Tapes Unlimited, Inc.
Balance Sheet
July 31, 1984

Assets

Cash	$ 25,312
Merchandise inventory	103,900
Supplies	4,350
Prepaid insurance	2,800
Accounts receivable	42,600
Store equipment	18,000
Office equipment	10,500
Building	96,000
Land	25,000
Notes receivable	10,000
Total assets	$338,462

Liabilities and Stockholders' Equity

Accumulated depreciation—store equipment	$ 7,200
Accumulated depreciation—office equipment	4,200
Accumulated depreciation—building	9,600
Accounts payable	23,000
Salaries payable	4,200
Mortgage note payable—	
First Federal Savings Bank (due 1995)	80,000
Capital stock	170,000
Retained earnings	40,262
Total liabilities and stockholders' equity	$338,462

As part of the existing loan agreement with First Federal Savings Bank, Tapes Unlimited, Inc. must submit financial statements annually to the bank. In reviewing your brother's statements and supporting records before he submits the statements to the bank, you discover the following information:

Merchandise inventory:		Insurance expense:	
August 1, 1983	$112,400	Selling	$4,200
July 31, 1984	103,900	General	2,550
Supplies inventory at July 31, 1984:		Supplies expense:	
Store supplies	$ 2,610	Store supplies	$4,440
Office supplies	1,740	Office supplies	2,960
Salaries expense:		Miscellaneous expense:	
Sales salaries	$ 90,440	Selling	$1,620
Office salaries	35,660	General	1,080

Instructions:

(1) Revise your brother's statements as necessary to conform to proper form for a multiple-step income statement, a report form of balance sheet, and a retained earnings statement.

(2) Prepare a projected single-step income statement based upon the following data:

Your brother is considering a proposal to increase net income by offering sales discounts of 2/15, n/30, and by shipping all merchandise FOB shipping point. Currently, no sales discount is allowed and merchandise is shipped FOB destination. It is estimated that these credit terms will increase gross sales by 10% and that 75% of all customers will take the discount by paying within the discount period. The remaining 25% will pay within 30 days, which is the current experience for all sales. The ratio of cost of merchandise sold to *gross* sales is 60% and is not expected to change under the proposed plan. Sales returns and allowances are expected to increase proportionately with increased gross sales. All selling and general expenses are expected to remain unchanged, except for store supplies, miscellaneous selling, office supplies, and miscellaneous general expenses, which are expected to increase proportionately with increased gross sales. The other income and other expense items will remain unchanged. The shipment of all merchandise FOB shipping point will eliminate all delivery expenses.

(3) (a) Based upon the projected income statement in (2), would you recommend the implementation of the proposed changes?

(b) Describe any possible concerns you may have related to the proposed changes described in (2).

5

CHAPTER | # Deferrals and Accruals

CHAPTER OBJECTIVES

Identify and describe common classifications of deferrals and accruals.

Describe and illustrate accounting for prepaid expenses, unearned revenues, accrued liabilities, and accrued assets.

5

CHAPTER

Data on revenues earned and expenses incurred by a business enterprise are periodically assembled and reported in an income statement. Such statements always cover a definite period of time, such as a specific month, quarter, half year, or year. The periodic matching of revenues and expenses not only yields the amount of net income or net loss but also yields the amounts for assets, liabilities, and capital to be reported in the balance sheet as of the end of the period.

When cash is received for revenue within the same period that the revenue is earned, there is no question about the period to which the revenue relates. Similarly, when an expense is paid during the period in which the benefits from the service are received, there can be no doubt concerning the period to which the expense should be allocated. Problems of allocation occur when there are differences in the time between the earning of revenues or the incurrence of expenses and the recognition of their respective effects on assets and equities.

The use of adjusting entries helps to allocate expenses to appropriate periods, as was demonstrated in earlier chapters. Deferrals and accruals of some expenses, including insurance, supplies, rent, and wages have been described and illustrated. This chapter further discusses deferrals and accruals of expenses as well as revenues. The underlying purpose of their recognition is to match revenues and expenses in order to determine net income for a specific period of time and the assets and equities as of the last day of that period.

CLASSIFICATION AND TERMINOLOGY

Many kinds of revenues and expenses may require deferral or accrual in certain instances. When such is the case, they are recorded as adjusting entries on the work sheet used in preparing financial statements. If the work sheet is for the fiscal year, the adjustments are also journalized and posted to the ledger. For interim statements, the adjustments may appear only on the work sheet.

Every adjusting entry affects both a balance sheet account and an income statement account. To illustrate, assume that the effect of the credit portion of a particular adjusting entry is to increase a liability account (balance sheet). It follows that the effect of the debit portion of the entry will be either (1) to increase an expense account (income statement) or (2) to decrease a revenue account (income statement). In no case will an adjustment affect only an asset and a liability (both balance sheet) or only an expense and a revenue (both income statement).

Deferral

A deferral is a delay of the recognition of an expense already paid or of a revenue already received.

Deferred expenses expected to benefit a short period of time are listed on the balance sheet among the current assets, where they are called prepaid expenses. Long-term prepayments that can be charged to the operations of several years are presented on the balance sheet in a section called deferred charges.

Deferred revenues may be listed on the balance sheet as a current liability, where they are called unearned revenues or revenues received in advance. If a long period of time is involved, they are presented on the balance sheet in a section called deferred credits.

Accrual | An **accrual** is an expense that has not been paid or a revenue that has not been received. Unrecorded accruals must be recognized before financial statements are prepared.

Accrued expenses may also be described on the balance sheet as **accrued liabilities,** or reference to the accrual may be omitted from the title, as in "Wages payable." The liabilities for accrued expenses are ordinarily due within a year and are listed as current liabilities.

Accrued revenues may also be described on the balance sheet as **accrued assets,** or reference to the accrual may be omitted from the title, as in "Fees receivable." The amounts receivable for accrued revenues are usually due within a short time and are classified as current assets.

PREPAID EXPENSES (DEFERRALS) | Prepaid expenses are the costs of goods and services that have been purchased but not used at the end of the accounting period. The portion of the asset that has been used during the period has become an expense; the remainder will not become an expense until some time in the future. Prepaid expenses include such items as prepaid insurance, prepaid rent, prepaid advertising, prepaid interest, and various kinds of supplies.

At the time an expense is prepaid, it may be debited either to an asset account or to an expense account. The two alternative systems are explained and illustrated in the paragraphs that follow. In any particular situation, either alternative may be elected. The only difference between the systems is in the procedure used. Their effect on the financial statements is the same.

Prepaid Expenses Recorded Initially as Assets | Insurance premiums or other services or supplies that are used may be debited to asset accounts when purchased, even though all or a part of them is expected to be consumed during the accounting period. The amount actually used is then determined at the end of the period and the accounts adjusted accordingly.

To illustrate, assume that the prepaid insurance account has a balance of $2,034 at the end of the year. This amount represents the unexpired insurance at the beginning of the year plus the total of premiums on policies purchased during the year. Assume further that $906 of insurance premiums have expired during the year. The adjusting entry to record the $906 decrease of the asset and the corresponding increase in expense is as follows:

	Adjusting Entry			
Dec. 31	Insurance Expense	716	906	
	Prepaid Insurance	118		906

After this entry has been posted, the two accounts affected appear as follows:

ACCOUNT **INSURANCE EXPENSE**   ACCOUNT NO. **716**

ADJUSTMENT FOR PREPAID EXPENSE RECORDED AS ASSET

Date		Item	Post. Ref.	Debit	Credit	Balance	
						Debit	Credit
1984 Dec.	31	Adjusting	25	906		906	

ACCOUNT PREPAID INSURANCE   ACCOUNT NO. 118

| Date | | Item | Post. Ref. | Debit | Credit | Balance | |
						Debit	Credit
1984							
Jan.	1	Balance	1	1,250		1,250	
Mar.	18		6	225		1,475	
Aug.	26		16	379		1,854	
Nov.	11		20	180		2,034	
Dec.	31	Adjusting	25		906	1,128	

After the $906 of expired insurance is transferred to the expense account, the balance of $1,128 in Prepaid Insurance represents the cost of premiums on various policies that apply to future periods. The $906 expense appears on the income statement for the period and the $1,128 asset appears on the balance sheet as of the end of the period.

Prepaid Expenses Recorded Initially as Expenses

Instead of being debited to an asset account, prepaid expenses may be debited to an expense account at the time of the expenditure, even though all or a part of the prepayment is expected to be unused at the end of the accounting period. The amount actually unused is then determined at the end of the period and the accounts are adjusted accordingly.

To illustrate this alternative system, assume that the insurance expense account has a balance of $2,034 at the end of the year. This amount represents the unexpired insurance at the beginning of the year plus the total premiums on policies purchased during the year. Assume further that $1,128 of the insurance premiums applies to future periods. The adjusting entry to record the $1,128 decrease of the expense and the corresponding increase in the asset is as follows:

		Adjusting Entry			
Dec.	31	Prepaid Insurance.....................	118	1,128	
		Insurance Expense	716		1,128

After this entry has been posted, the two accounts affected appear as follows:

ACCOUNT PREPAID INSURANCE   ACCOUNT NO. 118

ADJUSTMENT FOR PREPAID EXPENSE RECORDED AS EXPENSE

| Date | | Item | Post. Ref. | Debit | Credit | Balance | |
						Debit	Credit
1984							
Dec.	31	Adjusting	25	1,128		1,128	

ACCOUNT INSURANCE EXPENSE   ACCOUNT NO. 716

| Date | | Item | Post. Ref. | Debit | Credit | Balance | |
						Debit	Credit
1984							
Jan.	1	Reversing	1	1,250		1,250	
Mar.	18		6	225		1,475	
Aug.	26		16	379		1,854	
Nov.	11		20	180		2,034	
Dec.	31	Adjusting	25		1,128	906	

After the $1,128 of unexpired insurance is transferred to the asset account, the balance of $906 in Insurance Expense represents the cost of premiums on various policies that has expired during the year. The $1,128 asset appears on the balance sheet at the end of the period and the $906 expense appears on the income statement for the period.

In future periods, the unexpired insurance becomes insurance expense. Therefore, some provision must be made in future periods to transfer the expiration of the insurance from the asset account to the expense account. Although it would be possible to transfer daily the cost of the expiration, a more efficient way of assuring proper allocations in future periods is to add **reversing entries** to the summarizing procedures. Their use eliminates the need to refer to earlier adjustment data to record the expiration of insurance. It also lessens the possibilities of error. The effect of the reversing entry is to transfer the entire balance of the asset account to the expense account immediately after the temporary accounts have been closed for the period. Continuing with the illustration, the reversing entry is as follows:

		Reversing Entry				
Jan.	1	Insurance Expense	716	1,128		
		Prepaid Insurance	118		1,128	

After the reversing entry has been posted to the two accounts, they will appear as follows:

ACCOUNT PREPAID INSURANCE   ACCOUNT NO. 118

Date		Item	Post. Ref.	Debit	Credit	Balance Debit	Balance Credit
1984 Dec.	31	Adjusting	25	1,128		1,128	
1985 Jan.	1	Reversing	26		1,128	—	—

ACCOUNT INSURANCE EXPENSE   ACCOUNT NO. 716

Date		Item	Post. Ref.	Debit	Credit	Balance Debit	Balance Credit
1984 Jan.	1	Reversing	1	1,250		1,250	
Mar.	18		6	225		1,475	
Aug.	26		16	379		1,854	
Nov.	11		20	180		2,034	
Dec.	31	Adjusting	25		1,128	906	
	31	Closing	25		906	—	
1985 Jan.	1	Reversing	26	1,128		1,128	

The reversing entry does not change the basic nature of the $1,128, only its location in the ledger. It is prepaid insurance on January 1, just as it was prepaid insurance on December 31.

After the reversing entry has been posted, the unexpired insurance at January 1 is recorded in the expense account. Furthermore, since past expenditures were debited to the expense account and will probably be treated the same way in the future, all costs for insurance policies in force during the following year will be recorded in the expense account. At the end of the following year, the adjusting and reversing procedures will be repeated in the manner illustrated.

Comparison of the Two Systems

The two systems of recording prepaid expenses and the related entries at the end of an accounting period are summarized as follows:

Prepaid expense *recorded initially as an asset*

Adjusting—Transfers amount used to appropriate expense account.
Closing—Closes balance of expense account.
Reversing—Not required
(Amount prepaid at beginning of new period is in the asset account.)

Prepaid expense *recorded initially as an expense*

Adjusting—Transfers amount unused to appropriate asset account.
Closing—Closes balance of expense account.
Reversing—Transfers amount unused back to expense account.
(Amount prepaid at beginning of new period is in the expense account.)

Either of the two systems may be used for all of the prepaid expenses of an enterprise, or one system may be used for prepayment of some kinds of expenses and the other system for other kinds. Initial debits to the asset account seem to be logical for prepayments of insurance, which are usually for periods of from one to three years. On the other hand, interest charges on notes payable are usually for short periods. Some charges may be recorded when a note is issued; other charges may be recorded when a note is paid; and few, if any, of the debits for interest may require adjustment at the end of the period. It therefore seems logical to record all interest charges initially by debiting the expense account rather than the asset account.[1]

As was noted earlier, the amounts reported as expenses in the income statement and as assets on the balance sheet will not be affected by the system used. To avoid confusion, the system adopted by an enterprise for each kind of prepaid expense should be followed consistently from year to year.

UNEARNED REVENUES (DEFERRALS)

Revenue received during a particular period may be only partly earned by the end of the period. Items of revenue that are received in advance represent a liability that may be termed unearned revenue. The portion of the liability that is discharged during the period through delivery of goods or services has been earned; the remainder will be earned in the future. For example, magazine publishers usually receive advance payment for subscriptions covering periods ranging from a few months to a number of years. At the end of an accounting period, that

---

[1]Notes payable and related interest charges are discussed in more detail in Chapter 11.

portion of the receipts which is related to future periods has not been earned and should, therefore, appear in the balance sheet as a liability.

Other examples of unearned revenue are rent received in advance on property owned, premiums received in advance by an insurance company, tuition received in advance by a school, an annual retainer fee received in advance by an attorney, and amounts received in advance by an advertising firm for advertising services to be rendered in the future.

By accepting advance payment for a good or service, a business commits itself to furnish the good or the service at some future time. At the end of the accounting period, if some portion of the good or the service has been furnished, part of the revenue has been earned. The earned portion appears in the income statement. The unearned portion represents a liability of the business to furnish the good or the service in a future period and is reported in the balance sheet as a liability. As in the case of prepaid expenses, two systems of accounting are explained and illustrated.

Unearned Revenues Recorded Initially as Liabilities

When revenue is received in advance, it may be credited to a liability account. To illustrate, assume that on October 1 a business rents a portion of its building for a period of one year, receiving $7,200 in payment for the entire term of the lease. Assume also that the transaction was originally recorded by a debit to Cash and a credit to the liability account Unearned Rent. On December 31, the end of the fiscal year, one fourth of the amount has been earned and three fourths of the amount remains a liability. The entry to record the revenue and reduce the liability appears as follows:

		Adjusting Entry			
Dec.	31	Unearned Rent.........................	218	1,800	
		Rent Income	812		1,800

After this entry has been posted, the unearned rent account and the rent income account appear as follows:

ACCOUNT **UNEARNED RENT**　　　　　　　　　　　　　　ACCOUNT NO. 218

Date		Item	Post. Ref.	Debit	Credit	Balance	
						Debit	Credit
1984							
Oct.	1		18		7,200		7,200
Dec.	31	Adjusting	25	1,800			5,400

ACCOUNT **RENT INCOME**　　　　　　　　　　　　　　ACCOUNT NO. 812

Date		Item	Post. Ref.	Debit	Credit	Balance	
						Debit	Credit
1984							
Dec.	31	Adjusting	25		1,800		1,800

After the amount earned, $1,800, is transferred to Rent Income, the balance of $5,400 remaining in Unearned Rent is a liability to render a service in the future. It appears as a current liability in the balance sheet because the service is to be rendered within the next accounting period. Rent Income is reported in the Other Income section of the income statement.

Unearned Revenues Recorded Initially as Revenues

Instead of being credited to a liability account, unearned revenue may be credited to a revenue account as the cash is received. To illustrate this alternative, assume the same facts as in the preceding illustration, except that the transaction was originally recorded on October 1 by a debit to Cash and a credit to Rent Income. On December 31, the end of the fiscal year, three fourths of the balance in Rent Income is still unearned and the remaining one fourth has been earned. The entry to record the transfer to the liability account appears as follows:

		Adjusting Entry			
Dec.	31	Rent Income..........................	812	5,400	
		Unearned Rent....................	218		5,400

After this entry has been posted, the unearned rent account and the rent income account appear as follows:

ADJUSTMENT FOR UNEARNED REVENUE RECORDED AS REVENUE

ACCOUNT UNEARNED RENT   ACCOUNT NO. 218

Date		Item	Post. Ref.	Debit	Credit	Balance	
						Debit	Credit
1984 Dec.	31	Adjusting	25		5,400		5,400

ACCOUNT RENT INCOME   ACCOUNT NO. 812

Date		Item	Post. Ref.	Debit	Credit	Balance	
						Debit	Credit
1984 Oct.	1		18		7,200		7,200
Dec.	31	Adjusting	25	5,400			1,800

The unearned rent of $5,400 is listed in the current liability section of the balance sheet, and the rent income of $1,800 is reported in the income statement.

The $5,400 of unearned rent at the end of the year will be earned during the following year. If it is transferred to the income account by a reversing entry immediately after the accounts are closed, no further action will be needed either month by month or at the end of the nine-month period. Furthermore, since the $7,200 rent was credited initially to the income account, all such payments received in the following year will probably be treated the same way. If a reversing entry is not made, there may be balances in both the liability account and the income account at the end of the following year. This would require analysis of both accounts and possibly cause confusion. The reversing entry for the unearned rent, which is the exact reverse of the adjusting entry, is as follows:

		Reversing Entry			
Jan.	1	Unearned Rent......................	218	5,400	
		Rent Income......................	812		5,400

After the foregoing entry is posted to the two accounts, they will appear as follows:

ADJUSTMENT AND
REVERSAL FOR UNEARNED
REVENUE RECORDED AS
REVENUE

ACCOUNT **UNEARNED RENT**   ACCOUNT NO. **218**

Date		Item	Post. Ref.	Debit	Credit	Balance	
						Debit	Credit
1984							
Dec.	31	Adjusting	25		5,400		5,400
1985							
Jan.	1	Reversing	26	5,400		—	—

ACCOUNT **RENT INCOME**   ACCOUNT NO. **812**

Date		Item	Post. Ref.	Debit	Credit	Balance	
						Debit	Credit
1984							
Oct.	1		18		7,200		7,200
Dec.	31	Adjusting	25	5,400			1,800
	31	Closing	25	1,800		—	—
1985							
Jan.	1	Reversing	26		5,400		5,400

At the beginning of the new fiscal year, there is a credit balance of $5,400 in Rent Income. Although the balance is in reality a liability at this time, it will become revenue before the end of the year. Whenever a revenue account needs adjustment for an unearned amount at the end of a period, the adjusting entry should be reversed after the accounts have been closed.

Comparison of the Two Systems

The two systems of recording unearned revenue and the related entries at the end of the accounting period are summarized as follows:

Unearned revenue *recorded initially as a liability*

Adjusting—Transfers amount earned to appropriate revenue account.
Closing—Closes balance of revenue account.
Reversing—Not required.
(Amount unearned at beginning of new period is in the liability account.)

Unearned revenue *recorded initially as revenue*

Adjusting—Transfers amount unearned to appropriate liability account.
Closing—Closes balance of revenue account.
Reversing—Transfers amount unearned back to revenue account.
(Amount unearned at beginning of new period is in the revenue account.)

Either of the systems may be used for all revenues received in advance, or the first system may be used for advance receipts of some kinds of revenue and the second system for other kinds. The results obtained are the same under both systems, but to avoid confusion the system used should be followed consistently from year to year.

ACCRUED LIABILITIES

Some expenses accrue from day to day but are usually recorded only when they are paid. Examples are salaries paid to employees and interest paid on notes payable. The amounts of such accrued but unpaid items at the end of the fiscal period are both an expense and a liability. It is for this reason that such accruals are called **accrued liabilities** or **accrued expenses.**

To illustrate the adjusting entry for an accrued liability, assume that on December 31, the end of the fiscal year, the salary expense account has a debit balance of $72,800. During the year salaries have been paid each Friday for the five-day week then ended. For this particular fiscal year, December 31 falls on Wednesday. The records of the business show that the salary accrued for these last three days of the year amounts to $940. The entry to record the additional expense and the liability is as follows:

	Adjusting Entry			
Dec. 31	Salary Expense	611	940	
	Salaries Payable	214		940

After the adjusting entry has been posted to the two accounts, they appear as follows:

ACCOUNT SALARIES PAYABLE   ACCOUNT NO. 214

ADJUSTMENT FOR ACCRUED LIABILITY

Date		Item	Post. Ref.	Debit	Credit	Balance	
						Debit	Credit
1984 Dec.	31	Adjusting	25		940		940

ACCOUNT SALARY EXPENSE   ACCOUNT NO. 611

Date		Item	Post. Ref.	Debit	Credit	Balance	
						Debit	Credit
1984							
Dec.	26		23	1,425		72,800	
	31	Adjusting	25	940		73,740	

The accrued salaries of $940 recorded in Salaries Payable will appear in the balance sheet of December 31 as a current liability. The balance of $73,740 now recorded in Salary Expense will appear in the income statement for the year ended December 31.

When the weekly salaries are paid on January 2 of the following year, part of the payment will discharge the liability of $940 and the remainder will represent salary expense incurred in January. To avoid the need of analyzing the payment, a reversing entry is made at the beginning of the new year. The effect of the entry, which is illustrated as follows, is to transfer the credit balance in the salaries payable account to the credit side of the salary expense account.

		Reversing Entry			
Jan.	1	Salaries Payable	214	940	
		Salary Expense	611		940

After the reversing entry has been posted, the salaries payable account and the salary expense account appear as follows:

ADJUSTMENT AND REVERSAL FOR ACCRUED LIABILITY

ACCOUNT **SALARIES PAYABLE**   ACCOUNT NO. **214**

Date		Item	Post. Ref.	Debit	Credit	Balance Debit	Balance Credit
1984 Dec.	31	Adjusting	25				940
1985 Jan.	1	Reversing	26	940		—	—

ACCOUNT **SALARY EXPENSE**   ACCOUNT NO. **611**

Date		Item	Post. Ref.	Debit	Credit	Balance Debit	Balance Credit
1984							
Dec.	26		23	1,425		72,800	
	31	Adjusting	25	940		73,740	
	31	Closing	25		73,740	—	—
1985 Jan.	1	Reversing	26		940		940

The liability for salaries on December 31 now appears as a credit in Salary Expense. Assuming that the salaries paid on Friday, January 2, amount to $1,470, the debit to Salary Expense will automatically record the discharge of the liability of $940 and an expense of $530 ($1,470 − $940) for the new period.

The discussion of the treatment of accrued salary expense is illustrative of the method of handling accrued liabilities in general. If, in addition to accrued salaries, there are other accrued liabilities at the end of a fiscal period, separate liability accounts may be set up for each type. When there are many accrued liability items, however, a single account entitled Accrued Payables or Accrued Liabilities may be used. All accrued liabilities may then be recorded as credits to this account instead of to separate accounts.

ACCRUED ASSETS   All assets belonging to the business at the end of an accounting period and all revenues earned during the period should be recorded in the ledger. But during a fiscal period it is common to record some types of revenue only as the cash is received; consequently, at the end of the period there may be items of revenue that have not been recorded. In such cases, the amount of the accrued revenue must be recorded by debiting an asset account and crediting a revenue account. Because of the dual nature of such accruals, they are called **accrued assets** or **accrued revenues**.

To illustrate the adjusting entry for an accrued asset, assume that on December 31, the end of the fiscal year, the fees earned account has a credit balance of $50,500. Assume further that on the same date unbilled services have been performed for a client for $8,050. The entry to record this increase in the amount due from clients and the additional revenue earned is as follows:

	Adjusting Entry			
Dec. 31	Fees Receivable	114	8,050	
	Fees Earned	401		8,050

After this entry has been posted, the fees receivable account and the fees earned account appear as follows:

ACCOUNT **FEES RECEIVABLE**   ACCOUNT NO. **114**

ADJUSTMENT FOR
ACCRUED ASSET

Date		Item	Post. Ref.	Debit	Credit	Balance	
						Debit	Credit
1984 Dec.	31	Adjusting	25	8,050		8,050	

ACCOUNT **FEES EARNED**   ACCOUNT NO. **401**

Date		Item	Post. Ref.	Debit	Credit	Balance	
						Debit	Credit
1984							
Dec.	12		22		4,750		50,500
	31	Adjusting	25		8,050		58,550

The accrued fees of $8,050 recorded in Fees Receivable will appear in the balance sheet of December 31 as a current asset. The credit balance of $58,550 in Fees Earned will appear in the income statement for the year ended December 31.

In the following year, the services for the client, for which the accrued fees of $8,050 were recorded at the end of the year, will be completed and the client billed. Part of the fee collected will cause a reduction in fees receivable and the remainder will represent revenue for the new year. To avoid the inconvenience of analyzing each receipt of fees in the new year, a reversing entry is made immediately after the accounts are closed. The effect of the entry, which is illustrated as follows, is to transfer the debit balance in the fees receivable account to the debit side of the fees earned account.

		Reversing Entry			
Jan.	1	Fees Earned.........................	401	8,050	
		Fees Receivable	114		8,050

After this entry has been posted, the fees receivable account and the fees earned account appear as follows:

ACCOUNT FEES RECEIVABLE   ACCOUNT NO. 114

Date		Item	Post. Ref.	Debit	Credit	Balance	
						Debit	Credit
1984 Dec.	31	Adjusting	25	8,050		8,050	
1985 Jan.	1	Reversing	26		8,050	—	—

ACCOUNT FEES EARNED   ACCOUNT NO. 401

Date		Item	Post. Ref.	Debit	Credit	Balance	
						Debit	Credit
1984							
Dec.	12		22		4,750		50,500
	31	Adjusting	25		8,050		58,550
	31	Closing	25	58,550		—	—
1985 Jan.	1	Reversing	26	8,050		8,050	

The accrual of fees on December 31, $8,050, now appears as a debit in Fees Earned. At the time the client is billed in the following year, the entire amount of the billing will be credited to Fees Earned. This credit will in part represent a reduction in the receivable and in part a revenue of the following period. To illustrate, assume that the client with the unbilled fees of $8,050 on December 31 is billed for $10,000 in the following year. The total amount of fees billed, $10,000, will be credited to Fees Earned, regardless of the amount representing the collection of the receivable and the amount representing revenue of the new period. The effect of the $10,000 credit to Fees Earned is to automatically adjust Fees Earned, so that the balance of the account, $1,950 ($10,000 credit less $8,050 debit), represents revenue for the new year.

The treatment of accrued fees illustrates the method of handling accrued assets in general. If there are other accrued assets at the end of a fiscal period, separate accounts may be set up. Each of these accounts will be similar to the account with fees receivable. When such items are numerous, a single account entitled Accrued

Receivables or Accrued Assets may be used. All accrued assets may then be recorded as debits to this account.

1. If the effect of the debit portion of a specific adjusting entry is to increase an asset account, the effect of the credit portion of the entry would be to:
   A. decrease an asset account   C. decrease a liability account
   B. increase a liability account   D. decrease an expense account

2. Deferred expenses expected to benefit a relatively short period of time are listed on the balance sheet under:
   A. current assets   C. current liabilities
   B. plant assets   D. long-term liabilities

3. The balance in Unearned Rent at the end of a period represents:
   A. an asset   C. a revenue
   B. a liability   D. an expense

4. The office supplies inventory at the beginning of the year was $660, purchases of office supplies during the year were $2,250, and inventory at the end of the year was $595. If office supplies are initially recorded as an expense, the adjusting entry at the end of the year would be:
   A. Dr. Office Supplies, $595; Cr. Office Supplies Expense, $595
   B. Dr. Office Supplies, $2,315; Cr. Office Supplies Expense, $2,315
   C. Dr. Office Supplies Expense, $595; Cr. Office Supplies, $595
   D. Dr. Office Supplies Expense, $2,315; Cr. Office Supplies, $2,315

5. The salary expense account has a credit balance of $500 on January 1, the beginning of the fiscal year, after reversing entries have been posted but before any transactions have occurred. The balance represents:
   A. an asset   C. a revenue
   B. a liability   D. an expense

**Discussion
Questions**

1) INC. LiABility

1. Describe the effect of the credit portion of a specific adjusting entry when the effect of the debit portion is to decrease a revenue account.

2. Where would (a) accrued expenses and (b) accrued revenues, both due within a year, appear on the balance sheet?

3. A purchase of office supplies can be debited to one of two types of accounts. Name the two types of accounts that can be debited.

4. Classify the following items as (a) prepaid expense, (b) unearned revenue, (c) accrued expense, or (d) accrued revenue.
   (1) Receipts from sales of meal tickets by a restaurant.
   (2) Property taxes paid in advance.
   (3) A two-year premium paid on a fire insurance policy.
   (4) Life insurance premiums received by an insurance company.
   (5) Utilities owed but not yet paid.
   (6) Fees earned but not yet received.

(7) Supplies on hand.

(8) Tuition collected in advance by a university.

(9) Storage fees earned but not yet received.

(10) Taxes owed but payable in the following period.

(11) Salary owed but not yet due.

(12) Fees received but not yet earned.

5. From time to time during the fiscal year, an enterprise makes an advance payment of premiums on three-year and one-year property insurance policies. (a) At the end of such fiscal year, will there be a deferral or an accrual for the enterprise? (b) Which of the following types of accounts will be affected by the related adjusting entry at the end of the fiscal year: (1) asset, (2) liability, (3) revenue, (4) expense?

6. (a) Will a business enterprise that occasionally places advertisements in the local newspaper, for which it makes advance payments, always have prepaid advertising at the end of each fiscal year? Explain.

   (b) Will a business enterprise almost always have prepaid property and casualty insurance at the end of each fiscal year? Explain.

   (c) Would it be logical to record prepayments of the type referred to in (a) as expenses and prepayments of the type referred to in (b) as assets? Discuss.

7. On January 3, an enterprise receives $24,000 from a tenant as rent for the current calendar year. The fiscal year of the enterprise is from September 1 to August 31. (a) Will the enterprise's adjusting entry for the rent as of August 31 of the current year be a deferral or an accrual? (b) Which of the following types of accounts will be affected by the adjusting entry as of August 31: (1) asset, (2) liability, (3) revenue, (4) expense? (c) How much of the $24,000 rent should be allocated to the current fiscal year ending August 31?

8. On June 30, the end of its fiscal year, an enterprise owed salaries of $3,100 for an incomplete payroll period. On the first payday in July, salaries of $11,500 are paid. (a) Is the $3,100 a deferral or an accrual as of June 30? (b) Which of the following types of accounts will be affected by the related adjusting entry: (1) asset, (2) liability, (3) revenue, (4) expense? (c) How much of the $11,500 salary payment should be allocated to July?

9. The debit portion of a particular adjustment is to an asset account. (a) If the adjustment is for a deferral, which of the following types of accounts will be credited: (1) asset, (2) liability, (3) revenue, (4) expense? (b) If the adjustment is for an accrual, which of the following types of accounts will be credited: (1) asset, (2) liability, (3) revenue, (4) expense?

10. Each of the following debits and credits represents one half of an adjusting entry. Name the title of the account that would be used for the remaining half of the entry.

    (a) Fees Earned is debited.

    (b) Office Supplies Expense is debited.

    (c) Unearned Subscriptions is credited.

    (d) Salary Expense is debited.

    (e) Property Tax Payable is credited.

    (f) Prepaid Insurance is credited.

    (g) Unearned Rent is debited.

11. There are balances in each of the following accounts after adjustments have been made at the end of the fiscal year. Identify each as (a) asset, (b) liability, (c) revenue, or (d) expense.

(1) Fees Receivable
(2) Supplies Expense
(3) Prepaid Insurance
(4) Insurance Expense
(5) Unearned Subscriptions
(6) Fees Earned

(7) Salary Expense
(8) Rent Income
(9) Prepaid Advertising
(10) Rent Receivable
(11) Taxes Payable
(12) Supplies

12. The accountant for a real estate brokerage and management company uses the following uniform procedures in recording certain transactions:
    (1) Management fees, which are collected for one year in advance, are credited to Unearned Management Fees when received.
    (2) Advertising, which is paid in advance, is debited to Advertising Expense.
    (3) Premiums on fire insurance are debited to Prepaid Insurance.
    Assuming that an adjusting entry is required for each of the foregoing at the end of the fiscal year, (a) give the accounts to be debited and credited for each adjustment and (b) state whether or not each of the adjusting entries should be reversed as of the beginning of the following year.

13. Explain how the reversing of adjustments for accrued assets and accrued liabilities facilitates the recording of transactions.

14. If a particular type of revenue usually collected in advance is always credited to an income account at the time received, why should the year-end adjusting entry be reversed?

15. The status of the accounts listed below is as of the beginning of the fiscal year, after reversing entries have been posted but before any transactions have occurred. Identify each balance as (a) an asset or (b) a liability.
    (1) Utilities Expense, credit balance of $750.
    (2) Rent Income, debit balance of $750.
    (3) Unearned Subscriptions, credit balance of $625.
    (4) Office Supplies, debit balance of $350.
    (5) Insurance Expense, debit balance of $1,225.

Exercises

Exercise 5-1. The store supplies inventory at the beginning of the fiscal year is $610, purchases of store supplies during the year total $2,450, and the inventory at the end of the year is $530.
    (a) Set up T accounts for Store Supplies and Store Supplies Expense, and record the following directly in the accounts, employing the system of initially recording office supplies as an asset (identify each entry by number): (1) beginning balance; (2) purchases for the period; (3) adjusting entry at the end of the period; (4) closing entry.
    (b) Set up T accounts for Store Supplies and Store Supplies Expense, and record the following directly in the accounts, employing the system of initially recording office supplies as an expense (identify each entry by number): (1) beginning balance; (2) purchases for the period; (3) adjusting entry at end of the period; (4) closing entry.

Exercise 5-2. Because of a lack of consistency by the bookkeeper in recording the payment of premiums on property and casualty insurance, there are balances in both the asset and expense accounts at the end of the year before adjustments. Prepaid

Insurance has a debit balance of $1,725 and Insurance Expense has a debit balance of $2,650. You determine that the total amount of insurance premiums allocable to future periods is $2,100.

(a) Assuming that you will instruct the bookkeeper to record all future insurance premiums as an expense, present journal entries: (1) to adjust the accounts, (2) to close the appropriate account, and (3) to reverse the adjusting entry if appropriate.

(b) Assuming that you will instruct the bookkeeper to record all future insurance premiums as an asset, present journal entries: (1) to adjust the accounts, (2) to close the appropriate account, and (3) to reverse the adjusting entry if appropriate.

(c) (1) What is the amount of insurance expense for the year?

(2) What is the amount of prepaid insurance at the end of the year?

Exercise 5-3. The unearned advertising revenue of Chase Advertising Agency at the beginning of the fiscal year is $27,750, revenues received during the year total $280,500, and the unearned advertising revenue at the end of the year is $30,800.

(a) Set up T accounts for Unearned Advertising Revenue and Advertising Revenue and record the following directly in the accounts, employing the system of initially recording advertising fees as a liability (identify each entry by number): (1) beginning balance; (2) revenues received during the period; (3) adjusting entry at the end of the period; (4) closing entry.

(b) Set up T accounts for Unearned Advertising Revenue and Advertising Revenue and record the following directly in the accounts, employing the system of initially recording advertising fees as a revenue (identify each entry by number): (1) beginning balance; (2) revenues received during the period; (3) adjusting entry at the end of the period; (4) closing entry.

Exercise 5-4. In their first year of operations, the Southern Publishing Co. received $290,000 from advertising contracts and $625,000 from magazine subscriptions, crediting the two amounts to Advertising Revenue and Circulation Revenue respectively. At the end of the year, the deferral of advertising revenue amounts to $32,000 and the deferral of circulation revenue amounts to $197,000. (a) If no adjustments are made at the end of the year, will revenue for the year be overstated or understated, and by what amount? (b) Present the adjusting entries that should be made at the end of the year. (c) Present the entries to close the two revenue accounts. (d) Present the reversing entries if appropriate.

Exercise 5-5. Salary Expense has a balance of $722,150 as of June 26.

(a) Present entries for the following:

June 30. Recorded accrued salaries, $6,050.

30. Closed the salaries expense account.

July 1. Recorded a reversing entry for accrued salaries.

3. Recorded salaries paid, $15,700.

(b) Answer the following questions:

(1) What is the balance of the salary expense account on July 1?

(2) Is the balance of the salary expense account on July 1 an asset, a liability, a revenue, or an expense?

(3) What is the balance of the salary expense account on July 3?

(4) Of the $15,700 salary payment on July 3, how much is expense in July?

(5) If there had been no reversing entry on July 1, how should the debit for the salary payment of July 3 have been recorded?

Exercise 5-6. The entries in the following account identified by numbers are related to the summarizing process at the end of the year. (a) Identify each entry as adjusting, closing, or reversing and (b) present for each entry the title of the account to which the related debit or credit was posted.

RENT EXPENSE

Date		Item	Debit	Credit	Balance	
					Debit	Credit
Jan.	1	(1)	600		600	
Jan.	1	Transactions				
to		during the	7,900		8,500	
Dec.	31	year				
	31	(2)		675	7,825	
	31	(3)		7,825	—	—
Jan.	1	(4)	675		675	

Problems
(Problems in Appendix B: 5-1B, 5-2B, 5-5B.)

Problem 5-1A. The accounts listed below appear in the ledger of Knight Company at December 31, the end of the current fiscal year. None of the year-end adjustments have been recorded.

113	Fees Receivable.........	—	
114	Supplies................	$ 675	
115	Prepaid Insurance	3,725	
116	Prepaid Advertising	—	
213	Salaries Payable.........	—	
215	Unearned Rent..........	—	

313	Income Summary	—
411	Fees Earned..........	$62,250
511	Salary Expense	41,700
513	Advertising Expense...	10,340
514	Insurance Expense....	—
515	Supplies Expense	—
611	Rent Income..........	9,100

The following information relating to adjustments at December 31 is obtained from physical inventories, supplementary records, and other sources:

(a) Unbilled fees at December 31, $7,750.

(b) Inventory of supplies at December 31, $190.

(c) The insurance record indicates that $2,100 of insurance has expired during the year.

(d) Of a prepayment of $1,000 for advertising space in a local newspaper, 75% has been used and the remainder will be used in the following year.

(e) Salaries accrued at December 31, $1,140.

(f) Rent collected in advance that will not be earned until the following year, $700.

Instructions:

(1) Open the accounts listed and record the balances in the appropriate balance columns, as of December 31.

(2) Journalize the adjusting entries and post to the appropriate accounts after each entry, extending the balances. Identify the postings by writing "Adjusting" in the item columns.

(3) Prepare a compound journal entry to close the revenue accounts and another compound entry to close the expense accounts.

(4) Post the closing entries, inserting a short line in both balance columns of accounts that are closed. Identify the postings by writing "Closing" in the item columns.

(5) Prepare the reversing journal entries that should be made on January 1 and post to the appropriate accounts after each entry, inserting a short line in both balance columns of accounts that now have zero balances. Write "Reversing" in the item columns.

(If the working papers correlating with the textbook are not used, omit Problem 5-2A.)

Problem 5-2A. John Cox Company prepares interim financial statements at the end of each month and closes its accounts annually on December 31. Its income statement for the two-month period, January and February of the current year, is presented in the working papers. In addition, the trial balance of the ledger as of one month later is presented on a ten-column work sheet in the working papers. Data needed for adjusting entries at March 31, the end of the three-month period, are as follows:

(a) Estimated merchandise inventory at March 31, $247,500.

(b) Insurance expired during the three-month period:
Allocable as selling expense, $360.
Allocable as general expense, $150.

(c) Estimated inventory of store supplies at March 31, $435.

(d) Depreciation for the three-month period:
Store equipment, $1,800.
Office equipment, $600.

(e) Salaries accrued at March 31:
Sales salaries, $1,650.
Office salaries, $250.

(f) Unearned rent income at March 31, $305.

Instructions:

(1) Complete the work sheet for the three-month period ended March 31 of the current year.

(2) Prepare an income statement for the three-month period, using the last three-column group of the nine-column form in the working papers.

(3) Prepare an income statement for the month of March, using the middle three-column group of the nine-column form in the working papers.

(4) Prepare a capital statement for the three-month period. There were no additional investments during the period.

(5) Prepare a balance sheet as of March 31.

Problem 5-3A. The information presented below was obtained from a review of the ledger (before adjustments) and other records of Chin Company at the end of the current fiscal year ended December 31:

(a) As office supplies have been purchased during the year, they have been debited to Office Supplies Expense, which has a balance of $995 at December 31. The inventory of supplies at that date totals $280.

(b) On December 31, Rent Expense has a debit balance of $26,000, which includes rent of $2,000 for January of the following year, paid on December 31 of the preceding year.

(c) Sales commissions are uniformly 1% of net sales and are paid the tenth of the month following the sales. Net sales for the month ended December 31 were $90,500. Only commissions paid have been recorded during the year.

(d) Prepaid Advertising has a debit balance of $7,800 at December 31, which represents the advance payment on March 1 of a yearly contract for a uniform amount of space in 52 consecutive issues of a weekly publication. As of December 31, advertisements had appeared in 44 issues.

(e) Unearned Rent has a credit balance of $14,700, composed of the following: (1) January 1 balance of $2,700, representing rent prepaid for three months, January through March, and (2) a credit of $12,000, representing advance payment of rent for twelve months at $1,000 a month, beginning with April.

(f) Management Fees Earned has a credit balance of $130,750 at December 31. The unbilled fees at December 31 total $7,150.

(g) As advance premiums have been paid on insurance policies during the year, they have been debited to Prepaid Insurance, which has a balance of $1,248 at December 31. Details of premium expirations are as follows:

Policy No.	Premium Cost per Month	Period in Effect During Year
3172	$30	Jan. 1–March 31
D701	25	April 1–Dec. 31
5154	42	Jan. 1–Dec. 31
744B	18	Jan. 1–May 31
649C	22	June 1–Dec. 31

Instructions:

(1) Determine the amount of each adjustment, identifying all principal figures used in the computations.

(2) Journalize the adjusting entries as of December 31 of the current fiscal year, identifying each entry by letter.

(3) Journalize the reversing entries that should be made as of January 1 of the succeeding fiscal year, identifying each entry by the corresponding letter used in (2).

Problem 5-4A. Transactions related to advertising and rent are presented below. Accounts are adjusted and closed only at December 31, the end of the fiscal year.

Advertising

Jan. 1. Debit balance of $1,500 (allocable to January–March).

Apr. 1. Payment of $7,200 (allocable at $600 a month for 12 months beginning April 1).

Rent

Jan. 1. Credit balance of $11,800 ($2,800 allocable to January–April; $9,000 allocable to January–June).

May 1. Receipt of $9,600 (allocable at $800 a month for 12 months beginning May 1).

July 1. Receipt of $19,200 (allocable at $1,600 a month for 12 months beginning July 1).

Instructions:

(1) Open accounts for Prepaid Advertising, Advertising Expense, Unearned Rent, and Rent Income. Using the system of initially recording prepaid expense as an asset and unearned revenue as a liability, record the following directly in the accounts: (a) beginning balances as of January 1; (b) transactions of April 1, May 1, and July 1; (c) adjusting entries at December 31; (d) closing entries at December 31; and (e) reversing entries at January 1, if appropriate. Identify

each entry in the item section of the accounts as balance, transaction, adjusting, closing, or reversing, and extend the balance after each entry.

(2) Open a duplicate set of accounts and follow the remaining instructions in Instruction (1), except to employ the system of initially recording prepaid expense as an expense and unearned revenue as revenue.

(3) Determine the amounts that would appear in the balance sheet at December 31 as asset and liability respectively, and in the income statement for the year as expense and revenue respectively, according to the system employed in Instruction (1) and the system employed in Instruction (2). Present your answers in the following form:

System	Asset	Expense	Liability	Revenue
Instruction (1)	$	$	$	$
Instruction (2)				

Problem 5-5A. Selected accounts from the ledger of Margaret Bynre Co. at the end of the fiscal year are as follows. The account balances are shown before and after adjustment.

	Unadjusted Balance	Adjusted Balance
Fees Receivable	—	$ 3,250
Supplies	$ 2,125	675
Prepaid Insurance	5,600	2,450
Wages Payable	—	2,970
Utilities Payable	—	475
Unearned Rent	—	600
Fees Earned	91,000	94,250
Wages Expense	60,050	63,020
Utilities Expense	4,950	5,425
Insurance Expense	—	3,150
Supplies Expense	—	1,450
Rent Income	7,800	7,200

Instructions:

(1) Journalize the adjusting entries that were posted to the ledger at the end of the fiscal year.

(2) Insert the letter "R" in the date column opposite each adjusting entry that should be reversed as of the first day of the following fiscal year.

Mini-Case

A close friend of your family organized Sullivan Appliance Company on July 1, 1983. Having little training in record keeping, the owner, Thomas Sullivan, kept only cash receipts and disbursements records along with a folder of bills to be paid and a folder listing amounts due from customers. To expand his business, Sullivan has applied for a bank loan of $56,000, with which to purchase a warehouse and land. The bank has requested financial statements, and Sullivan has asked you to aid him in preparing such statements. Following is a summary of Sullivan's records:

Cash receipts (July 1, 1983–September 30, 1984):
(1)	Cash received from Thomas Sullivan to begin the enterprise	$150,000
(2)	Sales (after deducting sales returns and allowances of $4,670 and sales discount of $3,280)	333,150

Cash disbursements (July 1, 1983–September 30, 1984):
(1)	Rent	$ 7,680
(2)	Insurance premiums	2,880
(3)	Purchases (after deducting purchases discounts of $1,960)	265,920
(4)	Utilities	11,200
(5)	Salaries	86,300
(6)	Store equipment	32,000
(7)	Delivery equipment	8,800
(8)	Advertisements in the Carroll Daily News	1,010
(9)	Taxes	3,800
(10)	Supplies	1,850
(11)	Miscellaneous expenses	4,320
(12)	Withdrawals by Thomas Sullivan	10,000
	Total of amounts due on September 30, 1984, from customers	25,400
	Total of unpaid bills on September 30, 1984, from purchases	18,640

Further analysis of the records reveals the following data:
(a)	Merchandise inventory, September 30, 1984	$69,430
(b)	Supplies on hand, September 30, 1984	915
(c)	Prepaid rent, September 30, 1984	480
(d)	Prepaid insurance, September 30, 1984	480
(e)	Depreciation to date on store equipment	3,200
(f)	Depreciation to date on delivery equipment	1,100
(g)	Accrued salaries, September 30, 1984	2,160

Instructions:
(1) Prepare a multiple-step income statement and a capital statement for the 15-month period ended September 30, 1984, and a balance sheet as of September 30, 1984, in report form. For purposes of this case, it is not necessary to distinguish between general and selling expenses.
(2) After receiving the statements in (1), the bank requested a balance sheet as of June 30, 1984, and an income statement and capital statement for the year ended June 30, 1984. Is it possible to prepare such statements? Discuss.

6

Accounting Systems Design

CHAPTER OBJECTIVES

Describe the qualities of a properly designed accounting system.

Describe and illustrate the principles of internal control for directing operations.

Describe and illustrate accounting devices, such as special journals and subsidiary ledgers, and various data processing methods which are useful in accounting systems.

PART 2 | Accounting Systems

6

CHAPTER

The way in which management is given the information for use in conducting the affairs of the business and in reporting to owners, creditors, and other interested parties is called the **accounting system**. In a general sense, an accounting system includes the entire network of communications used by a business organization to provide needed information. Indeed, there are frequent references to accounting systems as the "total informational system" of an enterprise.

PRINCIPLES OF ACCOUNTING SYSTEMS

Because of differences in businesses, in the number of transactions to be processed, and in the uses made of accounting data, accounting systems will vary from business to business. However, there are a number of broad principles discussed in the paragraphs that follow that apply to all systems.

Cost-Effectiveness Balance

An accounting system must be tailored to meet the specific needs of each business. Since costs must be incurred in meeting these needs, one of the major considerations in developing an accounting system is cost effectiveness. For example, although the reports produced by an accounting system are a valuable end product of the system, the value of the reports produced should be at least equal to the cost of producing them. No matter how detailed or informational a report may be, it should not be produced if it costs more than the benefits received by those who use it.

Flexibility to Meet Future Needs

A characteristic of the modern business environment is change. Each business must adapt to the constantly changing environment in which it operates. Whether the changes are the result of new government regulations, changes in accounting principles, organizational changes necessary to meet practices of competing businesses, changes in data processing technology, or other factors, the accounting system must be flexible enough to meet the changing demands made of it. For example, when granting credit to customers became a common practice, it was necessary for many businesses to maintain accounts receivable, accounts payable, and related statistical and other useful information. Regulatory agencies, such as the Securities and Exchange Commission, often require a continually changing variety of reports that require changes in the accounting system.

Adequate Internal Controls

An accounting system must provide the information needed by management in reporting to owners, creditors, and other interested parties and in conducting the affairs of the business. In addition, the system should aid management in controlling operations. The detailed procedures used by management to control operations are called **internal controls**. The broad principles of internal control are discussed later in the chapter.

Effective Reporting

Users of the information provided by the accounting system rely on various reports for relevant information presented in an understandable manner. When these reports are prepared, the requirements and knowledge of the user should be recognized. For example, management may need detailed reports for controlling operations on a weekly or even daily basis, and regulatory agencies often require uniform data and establish certain deadlines for the submission of certain reports.

Adaptation to Organizational Structure

Only by effectively using and adapting to the human resources of a business can the accounting system meet information needs at the lowest cost. Since no two businesses are structured alike, the accounting system must be tailored to the organizational structure of each business. The lines of authority and responsibility will affect the information requirements of each business. In addition, an effective system needs the approval and support of all levels of management.

ACCOUNTING SYSTEM INSTALLATION AND REVISION

Before designing and installing an accounting system for an enterprise, the designer must have a complete knowledge of the business' operations. At the time that a business is organized, however, there are likely to be many unknown factors that will affect such areas of the system as the types and design of the forms needed, the number and titles of the accounts required, and the exact procedures to be used. It is also quite common for a firm to expand its already successful operations into new areas not originally thought about, to increase its volume of transactions, to use additional personnel, and in other ways to "outgrow" its accounting system.

Many large business enterprises maintain an almost continuous review of their accounting system and may constantly be involved in changing some part of it. The job of changing an accounting system, either in its entirety or only in part, is made up of three phases: (1) analysis, (2) design, and (3) implementation.

Systems Analysis

The goal of systems analysis is to determine information needs, the sources of such information, and the deficiencies in procedures and data processing methods presently used. The analysis usually begins with a review of organizational structure and job descriptions of the personnel affected. This is followed by a study of the forms, records, procedures, processing methods, and reports used by the enterprise. A detailed description of the system used by the enterprise, including specific instructions to personnel and minute details of procedures, is of great value to the systems analyst in the fact-finding review. Such a compilation is usually referred to as the firm's *Systems Manual*.

In addition to looking at the shortcomings of the present system, the analyst should determine management's plans for changes in operations (volume, products, territories, etc.) in the foreseeable future.

Systems Design

Accounting systems are changed as a result of the kind of analysis described above. The design of the new system may involve only minor changes from the existing system, such as revision of a particular form and the related procedures and processing methods, or it may be a complete revision of the entire system. Systems designers must have a general knowledge of the qualities of different kinds of data processing equipment, and the ability to evaluate alternatives. Although successful systems design depends to a large extent upon the creativity, imagination, and general capabilities of the designer, observance of the broad principles previously discussed is necessary.

Systems Implementation

The final phase of the creation or revision of an accounting system is to carry out, or implement, the proposals. New or revised forms, records, procedures, and equipment must be installed, and any that are no longer useful must be withdrawn. All personnel responsible for operating the system must be carefully trained and closely supervised until satisfactory efficiency is achieved.

For a large organization, a major revision such as a change from manual processing to electronic processing is usually done gradually over an extended period rather than all at once. With such a procedure, there is less likelihood that the flow of useful data will be seriously slowed down during the critical phase of implementation. Weaknesses and conflicting or unnecessary elements in the design may also become apparent during the implementation phase. They are more easily seen and corrected when changes in a system are adopted gradually, and possible chaos is thereby avoided.

INTERNAL CONTROLS

Internal controls are classified as (1) administrative controls and (2) accounting controls. Internal administrative controls consist of procedures and records that aid management in achieving business goals. For example, with records of defective work by production employees, management can evaluate personnel performance and thus control the quality of the product manufactured. Internal accounting controls consist of procedures and records that are mainly concerned with the reliability of financial records and reports and with the safeguarding of assets. For example, procedures established to make sure that all transactions are recorded according to generally accepted accounting principles help assure reliable financial records. A way of safeguarding assets is to limit access to assets to authorized personnel.

Details of a system of internal control will vary according to the size and type of business enterprise. In a small business where it is possible for the owner-manager to personally supervise the employees and to direct the affairs of the business, few controls are necessary. As the number of employees and the complexities of an enterprise increase, it becomes more difficult for management to maintain control over all phases of operations. As a firm grows, management needs to delegate authority and to place more reliance on the accounting system in controlling operations.

Several broad principles of internal control are discussed in the following paragraphs. Many of these principles should be considered by all businesses, large and small.

Competent Personnel and Rotation of Duties

Successful operation of an accounting system requires people who are able to perform the duties to which they are assigned. Hence it is necessary that all accounting employees be adequately trained and supervised to perform their jobs. It is also advisable to rotate clerical personnel periodically from job to job. In addition to broadening their understanding of the system, the knowledge that others may in the future perform their jobs tends to discourage deviations from prescribed procedures. Occasional rotation is also helpful in disclosing any irregularities that may have occurred. For these same reasons all employees should be required to take annual vacations, with their jobs assigned to others during their absence.

Assignment of Responsibility

If employees are to work efficiently, their responsibilities must be clearly defined. There should be no overlapping or undefined areas of responsibility. For example, if a certain cash register is to be used by two or more salesclerks, each one should be assigned a separate cash drawer and register key. Thus, daily proof of the handling of cash can be obtained for each clerk.

Separation of Responsibility for Related Operations

To decrease the possibility of inefficiency, errors, and fraud, responsibility for a sequence of related operations should be divided among two or more persons. For example, no one individual should be authorized to order merchandise, verify the receipt of the goods, and pay the supplier. To do so would invite such abuses as placing orders with a supplier on the basis of friendship rather than on price, quality, and other objective factors; indifferent and routine verification of the quantity and the quality of goods received; conversion of goods to the personal use of the employee; carelessness in verifying the validity and the accuracy of invoices; and payment of false invoices. When the responsibility for purchasing, receiving, and paying are divided among three persons or departments, the possibilities of such abuses are minimized.

The "checks and balances" provided by distributing responsibility among various departments requires no duplication of effort. The work of each department, as evidenced by the business documents that it prepares, must "fit" with those prepared by the other departments.

Separation of Operations and Accounting

Responsibility for maintaining the accounting records should be separated from the responsibility for engaging in business transactions and for the custody of the firm's assets. By so doing, the accounting records serve as an independent check on the business operations. For example, the employees entrusted with handling cash receipts from credit customers should not have access to the journal or ledger. Separation of the two functions reduces the possibilities of errors and embezzlement.

Proofs and Security Measures

Proofs and security measures should be used to safeguard business assets and assure reliable accounting data. This principle applies to many different techniques and procedures, such as the use of a bank account and other safekeeping measures for cash and other valuable documents. Cash registers are widely used in making the initial record of cash sales. The conditioning of the public to observe the amount recorded as the sale or to accept a printed receipt from the salesclerk increases the machine's effectiveness as a part of internal control.

The use of fidelity insurance is also an aid to internal control. It insures against losses caused by fraud on the part of employees who are entrusted with company assets and serves as a psychological deterrent to the misuse of assets.

Independent Review

To determine whether the other internal control principles are being effectively applied, the system should be periodically reviewed and evaluated by internal auditors. These auditors must be independent of the employees responsible for operations. The auditors should report any weaknesses and recommend changes to correct them. For example, a review of cash disbursements may disclose that invoices were not paid within the discount period, even though enough cash was available.

DATA PROCESSING METHODS

The entire amount of data needed by an enterprise is called its **data base**. Depending upon the variety and the amount of data included in the data base, various processing methods — manual, mechanical, and electronic — may be used. Whether the accounting system for a particular enterprise uses one or a combination of these methods, the basic principles of accounting systems as discussed are applicable.

MANUAL ACCOUNTING SYSTEMS

In preceding chapters, manual accounting systems were used to process accounting data, because they are the easiest systems to understand. If the data base is relatively small, manually kept records may serve a business reasonably well. However, as the data base increases, manual processing becomes too costly and takes too much time. In such a case, the manual system can be changed to reduce costs and more efficiently process accounting data. One way of changing the manual system is to use special journals, in which selected kinds of transactions are recorded, and to use subsidiary ledgers for accounts with a common characteristic.

SPECIAL JOURNALS AND SUBSIDIARY LEDGERS

In the preceding chapters, all transactions were initially recorded in a two-column journal, then posted individually to the appropriate accounts in the ledger. Applying such detailed procedures to a large number of transactions that are often repeated is impractical. For example, if many credit sales are made, each of these transactions would require an entry debiting Accounts Receivable and crediting Sales. In addition, the accounts receivable account in the ledger would include receivables from a large number of customers.

Special Journals

One of the simplest methods of reducing the processing time and expense of recording a large number of transactions is to expand the two-column journal to a **multicolumn journal**. Each money column added to the general purpose journal is restricted to the recording of transactions affecting a certain account. For example, a special column could be used only for recording debits to the cash account and another special column could be used only for recording credits to the cash account. The addition of the two special columns would eliminate the writing of "Cash" in the journal for every receipt and payment of cash. Furthermore, there would be no need to post each individual debit and credit to the cash account. Instead, the "Cash Dr." and "Cash Cr." columns could be totaled periodically and only the totals posted, yielding additional economies. In a similar manner, special columns could be added for recording credits to Sales, debits and credits to Accounts Receivable and Accounts Payable, and for other entries that are repeated. Although there is no exact number of columns that may be effectively used in a single journal, there is a maximum number beyond which the journal would become unmanageable. Also, the possibilities of errors in recording become greater as the number of columns and the width of the page increase.

An all-purpose multicolumn journal is usually satisfactory for a small business enterprise that needs the services of only one bookkeeper. If the number of transactions is enough to require two or more bookkeepers, the use of a single journal is usually not efficient. The next logical development in expanding the system is to replace an all-purpose journal with a number of special journals, each designed to record a single kind of transaction. Special journals would be needed only for the kinds of transactions that occur frequently. Since most enterprises have many transactions in which cash is received and many in which cash is paid out, it is common practice to use a special journal for recording cash receipts and another special journal for recording cash payments. An enterprise that sells services or merchandise to customers on account might use a special journal designed for recording only such transactions. On the other hand, a business that does not give credit would have no need for such a journal.

The transactions that occur most often in a medium-size merchandising firm and the special journals in which they are recorded are as follows:

Transaction:	*Recorded In:*
Purchase of merchandise or other items *on account*	→ Purchases journal
Payment of cash for *any* purpose	→ Cash payments journal
Sale of merchandise *on account*	→ Sales journal
Receipt of cash from *any* source	→ Cash receipts journal

Sometimes the business documents evidencing purchases and sales transactions are used as special journals. When there are a large number of such transactions on a credit basis, the use of this procedure may result in a substantial savings in bookkeeping expenses and a reduction of bookkeeping errors.

The two-column form illustrated in earlier chapters can be used for miscellaneous entries, such as adjusting and closing entries, that do not "fit" in any of the special journals. The two-column form is commonly called the general journal or simply the **journal**.

Subsidiary Ledgers

As the number of purchases and sales on account increase, the need for maintaining a separate account for each creditor and debtor is clear. If such accounts are numerous, their inclusion in the same ledger with all other accounts would cause the ledger to become unmanageable. The chance of posting errors would also be increased and the preparation of the trial balance and the financial statements would be delayed.

When there are a large number of individual accounts with a common characteristic, it is common to place them in a separate ledger called a subsidiary ledger. The principal ledger, which contains all of the balance sheet and income statement accounts, is then called the general ledger. Each subsidiary ledger is represented by a summarizing account in the general ledger called a controlling account. The sum of the balances of the accounts in a subsidiary ledger must agree with the balance of the related controlling account. Thus, a subsidiary ledger may be said to be *controlled* by its controlling account.

The individual accounts with creditors are arranged in alphabetical order in a subsidiary ledger called accounts payable ledger or **creditors ledger**. The related controlling account in the general ledger is Accounts Payable.

A subsidiary ledger for credit customers is needed for most business enterprises. This ledger containing the individual accounts is called the accounts receivable ledger or **customers ledger**. The controlling account in the general ledger that summarizes the debits and credits to the individual customers accounts is Accounts Receivable.

Purchases Journal

Property most frequently purchased on account by a merchandising concern is of the following types: (1) merchandise for resale to customers, (2) supplies for use in conducting the business, and (3) equipment and other plant assets. Because of the variety of items acquired on credit terms, the purchases journal should be designed to allow for the recording of everything purchased on account. The form of purchases journal used by Midtown Electric Corporation is illustrated below.

For each transaction recorded in the purchases journal, the credit is entered in the Accounts Payable Cr. column. The next three columns are used for accumulating debits to the particular accounts most frequently affected. Invoice amounts for merchandise purchased for resale to customers are recorded in the Purchases Dr. column. The purpose of the Store Supplies Dr. and Office Supplies Dr. columns is readily apparent. If supplies of these two categories were purchased only once in a while, the two columns could be omitted from the journal.

PURCHASES JOURNAL

PAGE 19   **PURCHASES**

	DATE		ACCOUNT CREDITED	POST. REF.	ACCOUNTS PAYABLE CR.	
1	1984 Oct.	2	Video-Audio Co.	✔	5 7 2 4 00	
2		3	Marsh Electronics, Inc.	✔	7 4 0 6 00	
3		9	Parker Supply Co.	✔	2 5 7 00	
4		11	Marsh Electronics, Inc.	✔	3 2 0 8 00	
5		16	Dunlap Electric Corporation	✔	3 5 9 3 00	
6		17	Acosta Electronics Supply	✔	1 5 0 0 00	
7		20	Walton Manufacturing Co.	✔	15 1 2 5 00	
8		23	Parker Supply Co.	✔	1 3 2 00	
9		27	Dunlap Electric Corporation	✔	6 3 7 5 00	
10		31			43 3 2 0 00	
11					(2 1 1)	

The final set of columns, under the main heading Sundry Accounts Dr., is used to record acquisitions, on account, of items not provided for in the special debit columns. The title of the account to be debited is entered in the Account column and the amount is entered in the Amount column.

Posting the Purchases Journal

The special journals used in recording most of the transactions affecting creditors accounts are designed to allow the posting of individual transactions to the accounts payable ledger and a single monthly total to Accounts Payable. The basic techniques of posting credits from a purchases journal to an accounts payable ledger and the controlling account are shown in the following flowchart.

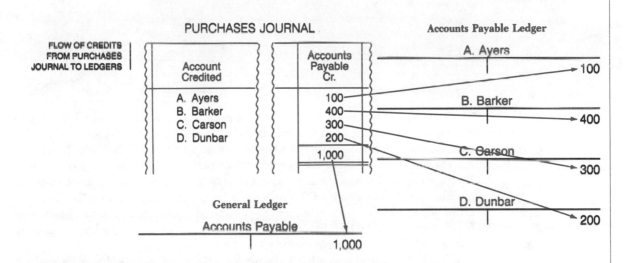

	PURCHASES DR.	STORE SUPPLIES DR.	OFFICE SUPPLIES DR.	SUNDRY ACCOUNTS DR.			
				ACCOUNT	POST. REF.	AMOUNT	
	5 7 2 4 00						1
	7 4 0 6 00						2
		1 3 1 00	1 2 6 00				3
	3 2 0 8 00						4
	3 5 9 3 00						5
	1 5 0 0 00						6
				Store Equipment	121	15 1 2 5 00	7
		7 5 00	5 7 00				8
	6 3 7 5 00						9
	27 8 0 6 00	2 0 6 00	1 8 3 00			15 1 2 5 00	10
	(511)	(115)	(116)			(✓)	11

JOURNAL — PAGE 19

The individual credits of $100, $400, $300, and $200 to Ayers, Barker, Carson, and Dunbar respectively are posted to their accounts in the accounts payable ledger. The sum of the credits to the four individual accounts in the subsidiary ledger is posted as a single $1,000 credit to Accounts Payable, the controlling account in the general ledger.

The source of the entries posted to the subsidiary and general ledgers is indicated in the posting reference column of each account by inserting the letter "P" and the page number of the purchases journal. An account in the accounts payable ledger of Midtown Electric Corporation is presented as an example.

AN ACCOUNT
IN THE ACCOUNTS
PAYABLE LEDGER

NAME	Acosta Electronics Supply					
ADDRESS	3800 Mission Street, San Francisco, California 94110-1732					

DATE	ITEM	POST. REF.	DEBIT	CREDIT	BALANCE
1984 Oct. 17		P19		1 5 0 0 00	1 5 0 0 00

Since the balances in the creditors accounts are usually credit balances, a three-column account form is used instead of the four-column account form illustrated earlier. When a creditor's account is overpaid and a debit balance occurs, such fact should be indicated by an asterisk or parentheses in the Balance column. When an account's balance is zero, a line may be drawn in the Balance column.

The creditors accounts in the subsidiary ledger are not numbered because the order changes each time a new account is inserted alphabetically or an old account is removed. Thus, instead of a number, a check mark (✔) is inserted in the posting reference column of the purchases journal after a credit is posted.

The amounts in the Sundry Accounts Dr. column of the purchases journal are posted to the appropriate accounts in the general ledger and the posting reference ("P" and page number) are inserted in the accounts. As each amount is posted, the related general ledger account number is inserted in the posting reference column of the Sundry Accounts section.

At the end of each month, the purchases journal is totaled and ruled in the manner illustrated on pages 168 and 169. Before posting the totals to the general ledger, the sum of the totals of the four debit columns should be compared with the total of the credit column to prove their equality.

The totals of the four special columns are posted to the appropriate general ledger accounts in the usual manner, with the related account numbers inserted below the columnar totals. Because each amount in the Sundry Accounts Dr. was posted individually, a check mark is placed below the $15,125 total to show that no further action is needed.

Two of the general ledger accounts to which postings were made are presented as examples. The debit posting to Store Equipment was from the Sundry Accounts Dr. column; the credit posting to Accounts Payable was from the total of the Accounts Payable Cr. column.

GENERAL LEDGER
ACCOUNTS AFTER
POSTING FROM
PURCHASES JOURNAL

ACCOUNT Store Equipment						ACCOUNT NO. 121	
DATE	ITEM	POST. REF.	DEBIT	CREDIT	BALANCE DEBIT	BALANCE CREDIT	
1984 Oct. 1	Balance	✔			11 9 7 5 00		
20		P19	15 1 2 5 00		27 1 0 0 00		

ACCOUNT Accounts Payable						ACCOUNT NO. 211	
DATE	ITEM	POST. REF.	DEBIT	CREDIT	BALANCE DEBIT	BALANCE CREDIT	
1984 Oct. 1	Balance	✔				21 9 7 5 00	
31		P19		43 3 2 0 00		65 2 9 5 00	

The flow of data from the purchases journal of Midtown Electric Corporation to its two related ledgers is presented graphically in the diagram below. Two procedures revealed by the flow diagram should be given special attention:

1. Postings are made from the purchases journal to both (a) accounts in the subsidiary ledger and (b) accounts in the general ledger.
2. The sum of the postings to individual accounts payable in the subsidiary ledger equals the columnar total posted to Accounts Payable (controlling account) in the general ledger.

FLOW OF DATA
FROM PURCHASES
JOURNAL TO LEDGERS

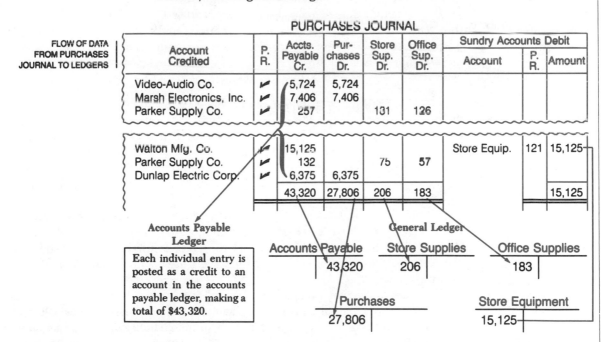

PURCHASES JOURNAL

Purchase Returns and Allowances

When merchandise purchased is returned or a price adjustment is requested, an entry is made in the general journal according to the principles described in Chapter 4. To illustrate, assume that during October, Midtown Electric Corporation issued a debit memorandum for a return of merchandise. The entry may be recorded in a two-column general journal, as follows:

GENERAL JOURNAL ENTRY
FOR RETURNS AND
ALLOWANCES

	DATE		DESCRIPTION	POST. REF.	DEBIT	CREDIT	
JOURNAL						PAGE 18	
17	Oct.	20	Accounts Payable—Dunlap Electric Corp.	211 ✓	9 7 50		17
18			Purchases	511		9 7 50	18
19			Debit Memo No. 20.				19

The debit portion of the entry is posted to the accounts payable account in the general ledger (No. 211) and also to the creditor's account in the subsidiary ledger (✓). The need for posting the debits to two different accounts is indicated, at the time these entries are journalized, by drawing a diagonal line in the posting reference column. The account number and check mark are inserted, in the usual manner, at the time the entry is posted.

After the entry has been recorded, the memorandum is attached to the related unpaid invoice. If the invoice had been paid before the return or allowance was granted, the settlement might be a cash refund.

If goods other than merchandise are returned or a price adjustment is granted, the account to which the goods were first debited should be credited. For example, if a purchase of office equipment is returned, the credit would be to Office Equipment rather than Purchases.

Cash Payments Journal

The standards for determining the special columns to be provided in the cash payments journal are the same as for the purchases journal, namely, the kind of transactions to be recorded and the frequency of their occurrence. It is necessary to have a Cash Cr. column. Payments to creditors on account happen often enough to require columns for Accounts Payable Dr. and Purchases Discount Cr. The cash payments journal illustrated at the top of page 173 has these three columns and an additional column for Sundry Accounts Dr.

All payments by Midtown Electric Corporation are made by check. As each transaction is recorded in the cash payments journal, the related check number is entered in the column at the right of the Date column. The check numbers provide a convenient cross-reference, and their use also is helpful in controlling cash payments.

The Sundry Accounts Dr. column is used to record debits to any account for which there is no special column. For example, on October 2 Midtown Electric Corporation paid $1,275 for a cash purchase of merchandise. The transaction was recorded by writing "Purchases" in the space provided and $1,275 in the Sundry

	DATE	CK. NO.	ACCOUNT DEBITED	POST. REF.	SUNDRY ACCOUNTS DR.	ACCOUNTS PAYABLE DR.	PURCHASES DISCOUNT CR.	CASH CR.	
1	1984 Oct. 2	312	Purchases	511	1 2 7 5 00			1 2 7 5 00	1
2	4	313	Store Equipment	121	3 5 0 00			3 5 0 00	2
3	12	314	Marsh Elec., Inc.	✔		7 4 0 6 00	7 4 06	7 3 3 1 94	3
4	12	315	Sales Salaries Exp.	611	2 5 6 0 00			2 5 6 0 00	4
5	12	316	Office Salaries Exp.	711	8 8 0 00			8 8 0 00	5
6	14	317	Misc. Gen. Exp.	715	5 6 40			5 6 40	6
7	16	318	Prepaid Insurance	117	9 8 4 00			9 8 4 00	7
8	20	319	Marsh Elec., Inc.	✔		3 2 0 8 00	3 2 08	3 1 7 5 92	8
9	20	320	M. B. Heath Co.	✔		4 8 5 0 00		4 8 5 0 00	9
10	21	321	Sales Ret. & Allow.	412	4 6 2 00			4 6 2 00	10
11	23	322	Acosta Elec. Supply	✔		1 5 0 0 00	3 0 00	1 4 7 0 00	11
12	23	323	Video — Audio Co.	✔		7 6 0 0 00		7 6 0 0 00	12
13	23	324	Heat. & Light. Exp.	712	7 8 9 20			7 8 9 20	13
14	24	325	Walton Mfg. Co.	✔		9 5 2 5 00		9 5 2 5 00	14
15	26	326	Sales Salaries Exp.	611	2 5 6 0 00			2 5 6 0 00	15
16	26	327	Office Salaries Exp.	711	8 8 0 00			8 8 0 00	16
17	26	328	Advertising Expense	613	7 8 6 00			7 8 6 00	17
18	27	329	Misc. Selling Exp.	617	4 1 50			4 1 50	18
19	28	330	Office Equipment	122	9 0 0 00			9 0 0 00	19
20	31				12 5 2 4 10	34 0 8 9 00	1 3 6 14	46 4 7 6 96	20
21					(✔)	(211)	(512)	(111)	21

Accounts Dr. and the Cash Cr. columns. The posting reference (511) was inserted later, at the time the debit was posted.

Debits to creditors accounts for invoices paid are recorded in the Accounts Payable Dr. column and credits for the amounts paid are recorded in the Cash Cr. column. If a discount is taken, the debit to the account payable will, of course, differ from the amount of the payment. Cash discounts taken on merchandise purchased for resale are recorded in the purchases Discount Cr. column.

At frequent intervals during the month, the amounts entered in the Accounts Payable Dr. column are posted to the creditors accounts in the accounts payable ledger. After each posting, "CP" and the page number of the journal are inserted in the posting reference column of the account. Check marks are placed in the posting reference column of the cash payments journal to indicate that the amounts have been posted. The items in the Sundry Accounts Dr. column are also posted to the appropriate accounts in the general ledger at frequent intervals. The posting is indicated by writing the account numbers in the posting reference column of the cash payments journal. At the end of the month, each of the money columns in the cash payments journal is footed, the sum of the two debit totals is compared with the sum of the two credit totals to determine their equality, and the journal is ruled.

A check mark is placed below the total of the Sundry Accounts Dr. column to indicate that it is not posted. As each of the totals of the other three columns is posted to a general ledger account, the proper account numbers are inserted below the column totals.

Accounts Payable Control and Subsidiary Ledger

During October, the following postings were made to Accounts Payable in the general ledger of Midtown Electric Corporation:

Credits to Accounts Payable

Oct. 31 Total purchases on account (**purchases journal**) $43,320.00

Debits to Accounts Payable

Oct. 20 A return of merchandise (**general journal**) 97.50
     31 Total cash payments on account (**cash payments journal**) 34,089.00

The accounts payable controlling account and the subsidiary accounts payable ledger of Midtown Electric Corporation as of October 31 are presented below and on the following page.

GENERAL LEDGER

ACCOUNTS PAYABLE ACCOUNT IN THE GENERAL LEDGER AT THE END OF THE MONTH

ACCOUNT Accounts Payable   ACCOUNT NO. 211

DATE	ITEM	POST. REF.	DEBIT	CREDIT	BALANCE DEBIT	BALANCE CREDIT
1984 Oct. 1	Balance	✔				21 975 00
20		J18	97 50			21 877 50
31		P19		43 320 00		65 197 50
31		CP16	34 089 00			31 108 50

ACCOUNTS PAYABLE LEDGER

ACCOUNTS PAYABLE LEDGER AT THE END OF THE MONTH

NAME   Acosta Electronics Supply

ADDRESS   3800 Mission Street, San Francisco, California 94110-1732

DATE	ITEM	POST. REF.	DEBIT	CREDIT	BALANCE
1984 Oct. 17		P19		1 500 00	1 500 00
23		CP16	1 500 00		—

NAME   Dunlap Electric Corporation

ADDRESS   521 Scottsdale Blvd., Phoenix, Arizona 85004-1100

DATE	ITEM	POST. REF.	DEBIT	CREDIT	BALANCE
1984 Oct. 16		P19		3 593 00	3 593 00
20		J18	97 50		3 495 50
27		P19		6 375 00	9 870 50

ACCOUNTS PAYABLE
LEDGER AT THE END OF
THE MONTH—CONCLUDED

NAME   M. B. Heath Co.

ADDRESS   9950 Ridge Ave., Los Angeles, California 90048-3694

DATE		ITEM	POST. REF.	DEBIT	CREDIT	BALANCE
1984 Sept.	21		P18		4 8 5 0 00	4 8 5 0 00
Oct.	20		CP16	4 8 5 0 00	——	

NAME   Marsh Electronics, Inc.

ADDRESS   650 Wilson, Portland, Oregon 97209-1406

DATE		ITEM	POST. REF.	DEBIT	CREDIT	BALANCE
1984 Oct.	3		P19		7 4 0 6 00	7 4 0 6 00
	11		P19		3 2 0 8 00	10 6 1 4 00
	12		CP16	7 4 0 6 00		3 2 0 8 00
	20		CP16	3 2 0 8 00	——	

NAME   Parker Supply Co.

ADDRESS   142 West 8th, Los Angeles, California 90014-1225

DATE		ITEM	POST. REF.	DEBIT	CREDIT	BALANCE
1984 Oct.	9		P19		2 5 7 00	2 5 7 00
	23		P19		1 3 2 00	3 8 9 00

NAME   Video-Audio Co.

ADDRESS   1200 Capitol Ave., Sacramento, California 95814-1048

DATE		ITEM	POST. REF.	DEBIT	CREDIT	BALANCE
1984 Sept.	25		P18		7 6 0 0 00	7 6 0 0 00
Oct.	2		P19		5 7 2 4 00	13 3 2 4 00
	23		CP16	7 6 0 0 00		5 7 2 4 00

NAME   Walton Manufacturing Co.

ADDRESS   9554 W. Colorado Blvd., Pasadena, California 91107-1318

DATE		ITEM	POST. REF.	DEBIT	CREDIT	BALANCE
1984 Sept.	28		P18		9 5 2 5 00	9 5 2 5 00
Oct.	20		P19		15 1 2 5 00	24 6 5 0 00
	24		CP16	9 5 2 5 00		15 1 2 5 00

After all posting has been completed for the month, the sum of the balances in the accounts payable ledger should be compared with the balance of the accounts payable account in the general ledger. If the controlling account and the subsidiary ledger do not agree, the error or errors must be located and corrected. The balances of the individual creditors accounts may be summarized on an adding machine tape, or a schedule such as the following may be prepared. The total of the schedule, $31,108.50, agrees with the balance of the accounts payable account shown on page 174.

SCHEDULE OF
ACCOUNTS PAYABLE

Midtown Electric Corporation Schedule of Accounts Payable October 31, 1984	
Dunlap Electric Corporation.	$ 9,870.50
Parker Supply Co.	389.00
Video-Audio Co.	5,724.00
Walton Manufacturing Co.	15,125.00
Total accounts payable.	$31,108.50

Sales Journal

The **sales journal** is used only for recording *sales of merchandise on account;* sales of merchandise for cash are recorded in the cash receipts journal. Sales of assets not a part of the stock in trade are recorded in the cash receipts journal or the general journal, depending upon whether the sale was made for cash or on account. The sales journal of Midtown Electric Corporation for October is as follows:

SALES JOURNAL
AFTER POSTING

	DATE		INVOICE NO.	ACCOUNT DEBITED	POST. REF.	ACCTS. REC. DR. SALES CR.		
1	1984 Oct.	2	615	R. A. Barnes, Inc.	✔	9 3 5 0 00		1
2		3	616	Standard Supply Co.	✔	1 6 0 4 00		2
3		5	617	David T. Mattox	✔	15 3 0 5 00		3
4		9	618	R. A. Barnes, Inc.	✔	1 3 9 6 00		4
5		10	619	Adler Company	✔	6 7 5 0 00		5
6		17	620	R. E. Hamilton, Inc.	✔	7 8 6 5 00		6
7		23	621	Cooper & Co.	✔	1 5 0 2 00		7
8		26	622	Tracy & Lee, Inc.	✔	3 2 6 0 00		8
9		27	623	Standard Supply Co.	✔	1 9 0 8 00		9
10		31				48 9 4 0 00		10
11						(113)	(411)	11

SALES JOURNAL   PAGE 35

Details of the first sale recorded by Midtown Electric Corporation in October are taken from Invoice No. 615. The customer is R. A. Barnes, Inc., and the invoice total is $9,350. Since the amount of the debit to Accounts Receivable is the same as the credit to Sales, a single amount column in the sales journal is sufficient.

However, if sales are subject to a sales tax, a special column may be added to the sales journal for recording the credit to Sales Tax Payable.

Posting the Sales Journal

The principles used in posting the sales journal compare to those used in posting the purchases journal. The source of the entry being posted is shown in the posting reference column of an account by the letter "S" and the proper page number. A customer's account with a posting from the sales journal is as follows:

AN ACCOUNT
IN THE ACCOUNTS
RECEIVABLE LEDGER

NAME	Adler Company				
ADDRESS	7608 Melton Ave., Los Angeles, California 90025-3942				

DATE	ITEM	POST. REF.	DEBIT	CREDIT	BALANCE
1984 Oct. 10		S35	6 7 5 0 00		6 7 5 0 00

As each debit to a customer's account is posted, a check mark (✔) is inserted in the posting reference column of the sales journal. At the end of each month, the amount column of the sales journal is added, the journal is ruled, and the total is posted as a debit to Accounts Receivable and a credit to Sales. The respective account numbers are then inserted below the total to indicate that the posting is completed.

Sales Returns and Allowances

When merchandise sold is returned or a price adjustment is granted, an entry is made in the general journal according to the principles described in Chapter 4. During October, Midtown Electric Corporation issued a credit memorandum and prepared the following entry in a two-column general journal:

GENERAL JOURNAL ENTRY
FOR SALES RETURNS
AND ALLOWANCES

	DATE	DESCRIPTION	POST. REF.	DEBIT	CREDIT	
			JOURNAL		PAGE 18	
1	1984 Oct. 13	Sales Returns and Allowances	412	2 2 5 00		1
2		Accounts Receivable — Adler Company	113 ✔		2 2 5 00	2
3		Credit Memo No. 32.				3

Note the diagonal line and double posting in the entry to record the credit memorandum. The diagonal line is placed in the posting reference column *at the time the entry is recorded in the general journal.*

If a cash refund is made because of merchandise returned or for an allowance, Sales Returns and Allowances is debited and Cash is credited. The entry would be recorded in the cash payments journal.

Cash Receipts Journal

All transactions that increase the amount of cash are recorded in a **cash receipts journal**. In a typical merchandising business, the most frequent sources of cash receipts are likely to be cash sales and collections from customers on account.

The cash receipts journal has a special column entitled Cash Dr. The frequency of the various kinds of transactions in which cash is received determines the titles of the other columns. The cash receipts journal of Midtown Electric Corporation for October is as follows:

	DATE		ACCOUNT CREDITED	POST. REF.	SUNDRY ACCOUNTS CR.	SALES CR.	ACCOUNTS REC. CR.	SALES DISCOUNT DR.	CASH DR.	
1	1984 Oct.	2	Notes Receivable	112	2 4 0 0 00				2 5 4 4 00	1
2			Interest Income	811	1 4 4 00					2
3		5	R. A. Barnes, Inc.	✔			5 8 0 0 00	1 1 6 00	5 6 8 4 00	3
4		6	Fogarty & Jacobs	✔			2 6 2 5 00	5 2 50	2 5 7 2 50	4
5		7	Sales	✔		3 7 0 0 00			3 7 0 0 00	5
6		10	David T. Mattox	✔			6 0 0 00	1 2 00	5 8 8 00	6
7		13	Standard Supply Co.	✔			1 6 0 4 00	3 2 08	1 5 7 1 92	7
8		14	Sales	✔		1 6 3 2 00			1 6 3 2 00	8
9		17	Adler Company	✔			6 5 2 5 00	1 3 0 50	6 3 9 4 50	9
10		19	R. E. Hamilton, Inc.	✔			4 8 5 0 00		4 8 5 0 00	10
11		21	Sales	✔		1 9 2 0 30			1 9 2 0 30	11
12		23	Purchases	511	8 6 20				8 6 20	12
13		24	B. C. Wallace Corporation	✔			2 2 0 0 00		2 2 0 0 00	13
14		27	R. E. Hamilton, Inc.	✔			7 8 6 5 00	1 5 7 30	7 7 0 7 70	14
15		28	Sales	✔		2 0 8 6 00			2 0 8 6 00	15
16		31	Sales	✔		2 4 2 3 40			2 4 2 3 40	16
17		31			2 6 3 0 20	11 7 6 1 70	32 0 6 9 00	5 0 0 38	45 9 6 0 52	17
18					(✔)	(411)	(113)	(413)	(111)	18
19										19
20										20
21										21
22										22
23										23
24										24

CASH RECEIPTS JOURNAL — CASH RECEIPTS JOURNAL AFTER POSTING — PAGE 14

The Sundry Accounts Cr. column is used for recording credits to any account for which there is no special column. For example, as of October 2, in the illustration, the receipt of $2,544 in payment of an interest-bearing note was recorded by a credit to Notes Receivable of $2,400 and a credit to Interest Income of $144. Both amounts were entered in the Sundry Accounts Cr. column. The posting references for the credits were inserted at the time the amounts were posted.

The Sales Cr. column is used for recording sales of merchandise for cash. Each individual sale is recorded on a cash register, and the totals thus accumulated are recorded in the cash receipts journal daily, weekly, or at other regular intervals. This is illustrated by the entry of October 7 recording weekly sales and cash receipts of $3,700. Since the total of the Sales Cr. column will be posted at the end of the month, a check mark is inserted in the posting reference column to show that the $3,700 item needs no further attention.

Credits to customers accounts for payments of invoices are recorded in the Accounts Receivable Cr. column. The amount of the cash discount granted, if any, is recorded in the Sales Discount Dr. column, and the amount of cash actually received is recorded in the Cash Dr. column. The entry on October 5 illustrates the use of these columns. Cash in the amount of $5,684 was received from R. A. Barnes, Inc. in payment of its account of $5,800, the cash discount being 2% of $5,800, or $116.

Each amount in the Sundry Accounts Cr. column of the cash receipts journal is posted to the proper account in the general ledger at frequent intervals during the month. The posting is indicated by inserting the account number in the posting reference column. At regular intervals the amounts in the Accounts Receivable Cr. column are posted to the customers accounts in the subsidiary ledger and "CR" and the proper page number are inserted in the posting reference columns of the accounts. Check marks are placed in the posting reference column of the journal to show that the amounts have been posted. None of the individual amounts in the remaining three columns of the cash receipts journal are posted.

At the end of the month, all of the amount columns are footed, the equality of the debits and credits is proved, and the journal is ruled. Because each amount in the Sundry Accounts Cr. column has been posted individually to a general ledger account, a check mark is inserted below the column total to indicate that no further action is needed. The totals of the other four columns are posted to the proper accounts in the general ledger and their account numbers are inserted below the totals to show that the posting has been completed.

The flow of data from the cash receipts journal to the ledgers of Midtown Electric Corporation is illustrated in the following diagram:

CASH RECEIPTS JOURNAL

FLOW OF DATA FROM CASH RECEIPTS JOURNAL TO LEDGERS	Account Credited	P. R.	Sundry Accounts Cr.	Sales Cr.	Accounts Receiv- able Cr.	Sales Discount Dr.	Cash Dr.
	Notes Receivable	112	2,400.00				2,544.00
	Interest Income	811	144.00				
	R. A. Barnes, Inc.	✔			5,800.00	116.00	5,684.00
	Fogarty & Jacobs	✔			2,625.00	52.50	2,572.50
	Sales	✔		3,700.00			3,700.00
	David T. Mattox	✔			600.00	12.00	588.00
	Sales	✔		2,423.40			2,423.40
			2,630.20	11,761.70	32,069.00	500.38	45,960.52

Accounts Receivable Ledger

Each individual entry is posted as a credit to an account in the accounts receivable ledger, making a total of $32,069.

General Ledger

Notes Receivable	Accounts Receivable	Sales Discount
2,400.00	32,069.00	500.38

Interest Income	Sales	Cash
144.00	11,761.70	45,960.52

Accounts
Receivable
Control and
Subsidiary Ledger

During October, the following postings were made to Accounts Receivable in the general ledger of Midtown Electric Corporation:

Debits

Oct. 31 Total sales on account (sales journal)............................ $48,940.00

Credits

Oct. 13 A sales return (general journal) 225.00
Oct. 31 Total cash received on account (cash receipts journal)............. 32,069.00

The accounts receivable controlling account of Midtown Electric Corporation as of October 31 is as follows:

GENERAL LEDGER

ACCOUNTS RECEIVABLE
ACCOUNT IN THE GENERAL
LEDGER AT THE END OF
THE MONTH

ACCOUNT Accounts Receivable					ACCOUNT NO. 113	
DATE	ITEM	POST. REF.	DEBIT	CREDIT	BALANCE DEBIT	CREDIT
1984 Oct. 1	Balance	✔			17 2 6 0 00	
13		J18		2 2 5 00	17 0 3 5 00	
31		S35	48 9 4 0 00		65 9 7 5 00	
31		CR14		32 0 6 9 00	33 9 0 6 00	

The posting procedures and determination of the balances of the accounts in the accounts receivable ledger and the preparation of the schedule of accounts receivable are comparable to those for accounts payable and are therefore not illustrated.

MECHANICAL
ACCOUNTING
SYSTEMS

As an enterprise becomes larger and more complex, the manual accounting system may be further changed or perhaps replaced by a system that uses machines. Some of the more common machines that process accounting data are the cash register, adding machine, calculator, and bookkeeping machine. Mechanical cash registers, which are widely used, can record and accumulate totals for credit sales, cash sales, sales taxes, and receipts on account. The new electronic cash registers are faster, quieter, and smaller. They can be used with a computer to help maintain perpetual inventory records, update the accounts receivable ledger, and perform other functions related to merchandising. The use of adding machines and calculators speeds up processing and lessens the annoyance and the expense caused by arithmetical errors.

Conventional bookkeeping machines, which have keyboards, movable carriages, and accumulating devices similar to adding machines, are commonly used in journalizing transactions and posting to ledger accounts. For example, both an account receivable account and the sales journal can be placed in the machine together, so that sales transactions can be recorded in the sales journal and debits can be posted to the accounts receivable ledger at the same time. The sales journal remains in the machine until all sales for the day are recorded and posted to customers accounts in the subsidiary ledger. The total of the debits to Accounts Receivable and credits to Sales for the day are then recorded in the general ledger. Similar techniques are used for recording cash received on account and posting the credits to the customers accounts. Additional forms may also be inserted in the machine with the accounting records, so that monthly statements for customers are prepared at the same time as the recording of the debits for sales on account and the credits for cash receipts on account.

AUTOMATED ACCOUNTING SYSTEMS

Although bookkeeping machines and other mechanical equipment speed up the accounting process and reduce the clerical costs of processing data, large enterprises need equipment that can process data even more efficiently. This demand has stimulated the development of even more elaborate mechanical devices and increasingly sophisticated electronic equipment. There has also been a trend toward bringing the cost of the services of such equipment down to levels that can be afforded by medium- or smaller-size enterprises.

Automated data processing (ADP) is the general term applied to the processing of data by mechanical or electronic equipment that operates with a minimum of manual intervention. When all of the equipment employed by a processing system operates electronically, it may be termed **electronic data processing (EDP)**. Much of the expansion of the role of accounting in systems design and installation has been made possible by the development and ever-widening use of automated data processing equipment.

Self-Examination Questions
(Answers in Appendix C.)

1. The final phase of the revision of an accounting system that involves carrying out the proposals for changes in the system is termed:
   A. systems analysis
   B. systems design
   C. systems implementation
   D. none of the above

2. The detailed procedures adopted by management to control operations are collectively termed:
   A. internal controls
   B. internal accounting controls
   C. internal administrative controls
   D. none of the above

3. A payment of cash for the purchase of merchandise would be recorded in the:
   A. purchases journal
   B. cash payments journal
   C. sales journal
   D. cash receipts journal

4. When there are a large number of individual accounts with a common characteristic, it is common to place them in a separate ledger called a:
   A. subsidiary ledger
   B. creditors ledger
   C. accounts payable ledger
   D. accounts receivable ledger

5. The controlling account in the general ledger that summarizes the debits and credits to the individual customers accounts in the subsidiary ledger is entitled:
   A. Accounts Payable
   B. Accounts Receivable
   C. Sales
   D. Purchases

Discussion Questions

1. The owner of a small successful gift shop uses only two of ten reports provided by its accounting system to analyze monthly sales. What principle of accounting systems is violated by this situation?

2. What is the objective of "systems analysis"?

3. How do internal administrative controls and internal accounting controls differ?

4. How does a policy of rotating clerical employees from job to job aid in strengthening internal control?

5. Why should the responsibility for a sequence of related operations be divided among different persons?

6. The ticket seller at a movie theater doubles as ticket taker for a few minutes each day while the ticket taker is on a "break." Which principle of internal control is violated in this situation?

7. Why should the responsibility for maintaining the accounting records be separated from the responsibility for operations?

8. How does a periodic review by internal auditors strengthen the system of internal control?

9. What is the term applied (a) to the ledger containing the individual customers accounts and (b) to the single account summarizing accounts receivable?

10. The following commodities were purchased on account by a retail hardware store. Indicate the account to which each purchase should be debited.
    (a) Ten garbage cans
    (b) One adding machine for office use
    (c) One cash register
    (d) One gross pads of sales tickets
    (e) One display case
    (f) Two kegs of nails
    (g) Two-year fire insurance policy on building
    (h) Four stepladders

11. During the current month, the following errors occurred in recording transactions in the purchases journal or in posting therefrom. How will each error come to the bookkeeper's attention, other than by chance discovery?
    (a) An invoice for merchandise of $540 was recorded as $450.
    (b) An invoice for merchandise of $810 from Walker Co. was recorded as having been received from Walters Corp., another supplier.
    (c) The accounts payable column of the purchases journal was overadded by $1,000.
    (d) A credit of $850 to Coen & Co. was posted as $85 in the subsidiary ledger.

12. The accounts payable and cash columns in the cash payments journal were unknowingly underadded by $1,000 at the end of the month. (a) Assuming no other errors in recording or posting, will the error cause the trial balance totals to be unequal? (b) Will the creditors ledger agree with the accounts payable controlling account?

13. In recording a cash payment, the bookkeeper enters the correct amount of $1,000 in the Accounts Payable Dr. column and the correct amount of $980 in the Cash Cr.

column, but omits the entry for Purchases Discount. How will the error be found, other than by chance discovery?

14. In recording 500 sales of merchandise on account during a single month, how many times will it be necessary to write "Sales" (a) if each transaction, including sales, is recorded individually in a two-column general journal; (b) if each sale is recorded in a sales journal?

15. How many individual postings to Sales for the month would be needed in Question 14, if the procedure described in (a) had been used; if the procedure described in (b) had been used?

16. In posting the following general journal entry, the bookkeeper posted correctly to Kline's account but failed to post to the controlling account.

    May 5 Sales Returns and Allowances.   402   200
            Accounts Receivable — A. J. Kline . . . .   ✔   200

    (a) How will the error be discovered? (b) Describe the procedure that is designed to prevent oversights of this type.

17. What does a check mark (✔) in the posting reference column of the cash receipts journal, which is illustrated in this chapter, signify (a) when the account being credited is an account receivable; (b) when the account credited is Sales?

18. Assuming the use of the sales journal and the cash receipts journal illustrated in this chapter and a two-column general journal, indicate the journal in which each of the following should be recorded:
    (a) Investment of additional cash in the business by the owner.
    (b) Sale of merchandise for cash.
    (c) Sale of office supplies on account, at cost, to a neighboring business.
    (d) Receipt of cash refund for an overcharge on a purchase of office equipment.
    (e) Receipt of cash on account from customer.
    (f) Receipt of cash in payment of principal and interest on a note.
    (g) Issuance of credit memorandum to customer.
    (h) Sale of merchandise on account.
    (i) Closing of the owner's drawing account at the end of the year.
    (j) Adjustment to record accrued salaries at the end of the year.

19. What do the following initials represent: (a) ADP, (b) EDP?

Exercises

Exercise 6-1. The debits and credits from three related transactions are presented in the following account taken from the creditors ledger. Describe each transaction.

NAME J. W. Sims Co.

ADDRESS 2408 South La Salle St., Chicago, IL 60602-2980

Date		Item	Post. Ref.	Debit	Credit	Balance
19--						
May	2		P28		9,900.00	9,900.00
	7		J8	400.00		9,500.00
	31		CP22	9,500.00		—

Exercise 6-2. The debits and credits from three related transactions are presented in the following account taken from the customers ledger. Describe each transaction.

NAME C. M. Jacobs

ADDRESS 1117 W. Kirby Ave., Champaign, IL 61820-1804

Date		Item	Post. Ref.	Debit	Credit	Balance
19--						
July	10		S36	3,000.00		3,000.00
	14		J11		500.00	2,500.00
	20		CR29		2,500.00	—

Exercise 6-3. Present general journal entries to record the following transactions:

Jan. 3. Issued credit memorandum for return of merchandise sold to T. M. Thomas, Inc., on account on December 30, $750.

7. Received credit memorandum for return of office equipment purchased on account on January 1 from Accord Office Supply, $1,100.

9. Issued debit memorandum for return of merchandise purchased on account on January 4 from B. T. Jones and Co., $3,150.

18. Issued credit memorandum for allowance made to R. T. Roth for defective merchandise sold on account on January 12, $125.

22. Corrected for error of December 31 when a note received from L. M. Carr Co. for $10,000 on account was not recorded.

Exercise 6-4. After Stewart Company had completed all posting for the month of May in the current year, the sum of the balances in the accounts payable ledger did not agree with the balance of the appropriate control account in the general ledger. Assuming that the control account balance of $33,350 has been verified as correct, (a) determine the error(s) in the following accounts and (b) prepare a schedule of accounts payable.

NAME F. W. Edwards Co.

ADDRESS 1959 16th Street

Date		Item	Post. Ref.	Debit	Credit	Balance
19--						
May	1	Balance	✔			3,175
	6		CP19	3,175		—
	22		P31		2,250	2,250
	27		J7	250		2,000

NAME C. Flowers and Son

ADDRESS 707 Main Street

Date		Item	Post. Ref.	Debit	Credit	Balance
May	1	Balance	✔			2,975
	28		CP20	2,975		—
	31		P32		4,500	4,500

NAME W. A. Mann, Inc.

ADDRESS 2250 Broadway

Date		Item	Post. Ref.	Debit	Credit	Balance
May	7		P31		5,750	5,750
	23		P32		6,100	11,650

NAME Reese and Reese Co.

ADDRESS 72 N. Prospect Avenue

Date		Item	Post. Ref.	Debit	Credit	Balance
May	1	Balance	✔			7,850
	8		P31		4,900	12,750
	11		J7	150		12,900
	17		CP20	7,850		5,050

NAME W. W. Wilson Supply

ADDRESS 319 Elm Street

Date		Item	Post. Ref.	Debit	Credit	Balance
May	3		P31		10,250	10,250

Exercise 6-5. Identify each of the posting references in the following purchases journal, indicated by letters, as representing (1) a posting to a general ledger account, (2) a posting to a subsidiary ledger account, or (3) that no posting is required.

(Left page)   PURCHASES JOURNAL

Date	Account Credited	Post. Ref.	Accounts Payable Cr.
19--			
July 2	Ritter Supply Corp	(a)	7,850
5	Thomas Clothes, Inc.............................	(c)	2,200
8	Lane Clothing Co.................................	(d)	4,863
15	Brady & Co	(e)	1,375
18	Ritter Supply Corp	(f)	1,975
22	Thomas Clothes, Inc.............................	(h)	6,615
31			24,878
			(i)

(Right page is on page 186)

(Right Page) PAGE 22

Purchases Dr.	Store Supplies Dr.	Office Supplies Dr.	Sundry Accounts Dr.		
			Account	Post. Ref.	Amount
. . . . .	. . .	. . .	Store Equipment	(b)	7,850
2,200	. . .	. . .	. . . .	. . .	. . . . .
4,863	. . .	. . .	. . . .	. . .	. . . . .
1,375	. . .	. . .	. . . .	. . .	. . . . .
. . . . .	150	275	Office Equipment	(g)	1,550
6,615	. . .	. . .	. . . .	. . .	. . . . .
15,053	150	275			9,400
(j)	(k)	(l)			(m)

Exercise 6-6. Present the general journal entries to correct the following errors, assuming that the incorrect entries had been posted and that the corrections are recorded in the same period in which the errors occurred.

(a) A cash sale of $225 to C. C. Neese was recorded as a sale on account.

(b) A cash receipt of $490 ($500 less 2% discount) from F. G. McGraw Co. was recorded as a $490 debit to Cash and $490 credit to F. G. McGraw Co. (and to Accounts Receivable).

(c) A cash remittance of $65 received from Cox. Co. from payment on account was recorded as a cash sale.

(d) Transportation costs of $80 incurred on office equipment purchased for use in the business had been debited to Purchases.

(e) A $75 cash purchase of merchandise from Moran Co. had been recorded as a purchase on account.

Problems
(Problems in Appendix B: 6-1B, 6-3B, 6-5B, 6-6B, 6-7B.)

Problem 6-1A. Peoria Communications, Inc. is a newly organized enterprise with the following list of asset, liability, and capital accounts, arranged in alphabetical order. The accounts are to be opened in the general ledger, assigned account numbers, and arranged in balance sheet order. Each account number is to be composed of three digits: the first digit is to indicate the major classification ("1" for assets, etc.), the second digit is to indicate the subclassification ("11" for current assets, etc.), and the third digit is to identify the specific account ("111" for Cash, etc.).

Accounts Payable	Notes Receivable (short-term)
Accounts Receivable	Office Equipment
Accumulated Depreciation—Building	Office Supplies
Accumulated Depreciation—Office Equipment	Prepaid Insurance
Accumulated Depreciation—Store Equipment	Retained Earnings
Building	Salaries Payable
Capital Stock	Sales Commissions Payable
Cash	Store Equipment
Dividends	Store Supplies
Land	Taxes Payable
Merchandise Inventory	Unearned Rent
Notes Payable (long-term)	

Instructions:

Construct a chart of accounts for the accounts listed.

Problem 6-2A. Purchases on account and related returns and allowances completed by Robinson Stereo during June of the current year are as follows:

June 1. Purchased merchandise on account from Matzu Co., $7,652.50.
 4. Purchased merchandise on account from Vance Radio Corp., $4,150.75.
 6. Received a credit memorandum from Matzu Co. for merchandise returned, $112.50.
 8. Purchased store supplies on account from Baker Supply Co., $187.50.
 10. Purchased office equipment on account from Mann Equipment Co., $4,200.
 13. Purchased merchandise on account from Matzu Co., $3,250.10.
 17. Purchased merchandise on account from C. Wilson and Son, $875.40.
 19. Received a credit memorandum from Baker Supply Co. for store supplies returned, $37.50.
 20. Purchased merchandise on account from Klos Co., $1,010.
 24. Purchased office supplies on account from Baker Supply Co., $85.25.
 25. Received a credit memorandum from Vance Radio Corp. as an allowance for damaged merchandise, $100.
 27. Purchased merchandise on account from C. Wilson and Son, $475.15.
 30. Purchased store supplies on account from Baker Supply Co., $210.50.

Instructions:

(1) Open the following accounts in the general ledger and enter the balances as of June 1:

114	Store Supplies	$ 442.75	211	Accounts Payable.......	$11,556.75
115	Office Supplies..........	210.10	511	Purchases.............	77,650.50
122	Office Equipment........	22,400.00			

(2) Open the following accounts in the accounts payable ledger and enter the balances in the balance columns as of June 1: Baker Supply Co.; Klos Co.; Mann Equipment Co.; Matzu Co., $4,155.10; Vance Radio Corp., $6,751.50; C. Wilson and Son, $650.15.

(3) Record the transactions for June, posting to the creditors accounts in the accounts payable ledger immediately after each entry. Use a purchases journal similar to the one illustrated on pages 168 and 169 and a two-column general journal.

(4) Post the general journal and the purchases journal to the accounts in the general ledger.

(5) (a) What is the sum of the balances in the subsidiary ledger at June 30?
 (b) What is the balance of the controlling account at June 30?

Problem 6-3A. Britt Clothiers began operations on July 16 of the current year. Transactions related to purchases, returns and allowances, and cash payments during the remainder of the month are as follows:

July 16. Issued Check No. 1 in payment of rent for the remainder of July, $750.
 16. Purchased office equipment on account from Horner Supply Corp., $9,850.
 16. Purchased merchandise on account from Oester Clothing, $11,900.
 17. Issued Check No. 2 in payment of store supplies, $225, and office supplies, $190.

July 17. Purchased merchandise on account from Cedeno Clothing Co., $8,715.

19. Purchased merchandise on account from Boggs Co., $2,150.

20. Received a credit memorandum from Cedeno Clothing Co. for returned merchandise, $715.

Post the journals to the accounts payable ledger.

23. Issued Check No. 3 to Horner Supply Corp. in payment of invoice of $9,850.

23. Received a credit memorandum from Boggs Co. for defective merchandise, $465.

24. Issued Check No. 4 to Oester Clothing, in payment of invoice of $11,900, less 1% discount.

25. Issued Check No. 5 to a cash customer for merchandise returned, $165.

26. Issued Check No. 6 to Cedeno Clothing Co. in payment of the balance owed, less 2% discount.

26. Purchased merchandise on account from Boggs Co., $1,610.

Post the journals to the accounts payable ledger.

30. Purchased the following from Horner Supply Corp. on account: store supplies, $150; office supplies, $75; store equipment, $675.

30. Issued Check No. 7 to Boggs Co. in payment of invoice of $2,150, less the credit of $465.

30. Purchased merchandise on account from Oester Clothing, $3,900.

31. Issued Check No. 8 in payment of incoming transportation charges on merchandise delivered during July, $615.

31. Issued Check No. 9 in payment of sales salaries, $1,775.

31. Received a credit memorandum from Horner Supply Corp. for defect in office equipment, $75.

Post the journals to the accounts payable ledger.

Instructions:

(1) Open the following accounts in the general ledger, using the account numbers indicated.

111	Cash	412	Sales Returns and Allowances
116	Store Supplies	511	Purchases
117	Office Supplies	512	Purchases Discount
121	Store Equipment	611	Sales Salaries Expense
122	Office Equipment	712	Rent Expense
211	Accounts Payable		

(2) Open the following accounts in the accounts payable ledger: Boggs Co.; Cedeno Clothing Co.; Horner Supply Corp.; Oester Clothing.

(3) Record the transactions for July, using a purchases journal similar to the one illustrated on pages 168 and 169, a cash payments journal similar to the one illustrated on page 173, and a two-column general journal. Post to the accounts payable ledger at the points indicated in the narrative of transactions.

(4) Post the appropriate individual entries to the general ledger (Sundry Accounts columns of the purchases journal and the cash payments journal; both columns of the general journal).

(5) Add the columns of the purchases journal and the cash payments journal, and post the appropriate totals to the general ledger. (Because the problem does not include transactions related to cash receipts, the cash account in the ledger will have a credit balance.)

(6) Prepare a schedule of accounts payable.

Problem 6-4A. C. G. Murphy, Inc. was established in June of the current year. Its sales of merchandise on account and related returns and allowances during the remainder of the month are as follows. Terms of all sales were 2/10, n/30, FOB destination.

June 21. Sold merchandise on account to Rusk, Inc., Invoice No. 1, $2,000.

    22. Sold merchandise on account to Allen Co., Invoice No. 2, $850.

    22. Sold merchandise on account to Lane Co., Invoice No. 3, $1,550.

    24. Issued Credit Memorandum No. 1 for $50 to Rusk, Inc. for merchandise returned.

    25. Sold merchandise on account to D. W. Raines, Invoice No. 4, $2,500.

    28. Sold merchandise on account to Unisac, Inc., Invoice No. 5, $2,950.

    29. Issued Credit Memorandum No. 2 for $150 to Allen Co. for merchandise returned.

    30. Sold merchandise on account to Allen Co., Invoice No. 6, $3,100.

    30. Issued Credit Memorandum No. 3 for $90 to D. W. Raines for damages to merchandise caused by faulty packing.

    30. Sold merchandise on account to Lane Co., Invoice No. 7, $725.

Instructions:

(1) Open the following accounts in the general ledger, using the account numbers indicated: Accounts Receivable, 113; Sales, 411; Sales Returns and Allowances, 412.

(2) Open the following accounts in the accounts receivable ledger: Allen Co.; Lane Co.; D. W. Raines; Rusk, Inc.; Unisac, Inc.

(3) Record the transactions for June, posting to the customers' accounts in the accounts receivable ledger and inserting the balance immediately after recording each entry. Use a sales journal similar to the one illustrated on page 176 and a two-column general journal.

(4) Post the general journal and the sales journal to the three accounts opened in the general ledger, inserting the account balances only after the last postings.

(5) (a) What is the sum of the balances of the accounts in the subsidiary ledger at June 30?

    (b) What is the balance of the controlling account at June 30?

If the working papers correlating with the textbook are not used, omit Problem 6-5A.

Problem 6-5A. Three journals, the accounts receivable ledger, and portions of the general ledger of Wilcox Company are presented in the working papers. Sales invoices and credit memorandums were entered in the journals by an assistant. Terms of sales on account are 2/10, n/30, FOB shipping point. Transactions in which cash and notes receivable were received during May are as follows:

May 1. Received $5,586 cash from Nance Co. in payment of April 21 invoice, less discount.

    4. Received $10,300 cash in payment of $10,000 note receivable and interest of $300.

    Post transactions of May 1, 2, and 6 to accounts receivable ledger.

    7. Received $4,312 cash from C. E. Rea and Son in payment of April 27 invoice, less discount.

    8. Received $1,250 cash from Downs & Franks in payment of April 9 invoice, no discount.

    Post transactions of May 7, 8, 10, 12, and 15 to accounts receivable ledger.

    16. Cash sales for first half of May totaled $4,610.

    19. Received $1,000 cash refund for return of defective equipment purchased for cash in April.

May 20. Received $1,470 cash from Nance Co. in payment of balance due on May 10 invoice, less discount.

   21. Received $1,176 cash from Downs & Franks in payment of May 12 invoice, less discount.

   Post transactions of May 18, 20, 21, 22, and 25 to accounts receivable ledger.

   27. Received $40 cash for sale of office supplies at cost.

   31. Received $500 cash and a $2,500 note receivable from Howard Corp. in settlement of the balance due on the invoice of May 1, no discount. (Record receipt of note in the general journal.)

   31. Cash sales for second half of May totaled $4,150.

   Post transactions of May 28, 30, and 31 to accounts receivable ledger.

Instructions:

(1) Record the cash receipts in the cash receipts journal and the note in the general journal. *Before recording a receipt of cash on account, determine the balance of the customer's account.* Post the entries from the three journals, in date sequence, to the accounts receivable ledger in accordance with the instructions in the narrative of transactions. Insert the new balance after each posting to an account.

(2) Post the appropriate individual entries from the cash receipts journal and the general journal to the general ledger.

(3) Add the columns of the sales journal and the cash receipts journal and post the appropriate totals to the general ledger. Insert the balance of each account after the last posting.

(4) Prepare a schedule of the accounts receivable as of May 31 and compare the total with the balance of the controlling account.

Problem 6-6A. Transactions related to sales and cash receipts completed by R & R Company during the period July 16–31 of the current year are as follows. The terms of all sales on account are 2/10, n/30, FOB shipping point.

July 16. Issued Invoice No. 793 to Seaview Co., $4,425.

   18. Received cash from Dumont Co. for the balance due on its account, less discount.

   19. Issued Invoice No. 794 to R. W. Kane Co., $7,500.

   20. Issued Invoice No. 795 to Frank Parker Co., $2,975.

   Post all journals to the accounts receivable ledger.

   23. Received cash from R. W. Kane Co. for the balance owed on July 16; no discount.

   24. Issued Credit Memo No. 35 to Seaview Co., $275.

   25. Issued Invoice No. 796 to R. W. Kane Co., $4,950.

   25. Received $1,560 cash in payment of a $1,500 note receivable and interest of $60.

   Post all journals to the accounts receivable ledger.

   26. Received cash from Seaview Co. for the balance due on invoice of July 16, less discount.

   28. Received cash from R. W. Kane Co. for invoice of July 19, less discount.

   28. Issued Invoice No. 797 to Dumont Co., $2,100.

   30. Issued Credit Memo No. 36 to Dumont Co., $250.

   31. Recorded cash sales for the second half of the month, $8,155.

   Post all journals to the accounts receivable ledger.

Instructions:

(1) Open the following accounts in the general ledger, inserting the balances indicated, as of July 1:

111	Cash	$12,125	412	Sales Returns and	
112	Notes Receivable	5,500		Allowances	—
113	Accounts Receivable	8,725	413	Sales Discount	—
411	Sales	—	811	Interest Income	—

(2) Open the following accounts in the accounts receivable ledger, inserting the balances indicated, as of July 16: Dumont Co., $2,500; R. W. Kane Co., $5,125; Frank Parker Co.; Seaview Co.

(3) The transactions are to be recorded in a sales journal similar to the one illustrated on page 176, a cash receipts journal similar to the one illustrated on page 178, and a 2-column general journal. Insert on the first line of the two special journals "July 16 Total(s) Forwarded ✔" and the following dollar figures in the amount columns:

Sales journal. 20,200
Cash receipts journal: 1,077; 6,950; 21,300; 255; 29,072.

(4) Record the transactions for the remainder of July, posting to the accounts receivable ledger and inserting the balances at the points indicated in the narrative of transactions. *Determine the balance in the customer's account before recording a cash receipt.*

(5) Add the columns of the special journals and post the individual entries and totals to the general ledger. Insert account balances after the last posting.

(6) Determine that the subsidiary ledger agrees with the controlling account in the general ledger.

Problem 6-7A. The transactions completed by Cannon Supply Co. during January, the first month of the current fiscal year, were as follows:

Jan. 2. Issued Check No. 610 for January rent, $1,400.

2. Purchased merchandise on account from Bidwell Co., $2,590.

3. Purchased equipment on account from Weber Equipment Co., $11,100.

5. Issued Invoice No. 940 to W. Cox, Inc., $1,700.

6. Received check for $2,772 from Powell Corp. in payment of $2,800 invoice, less discount.

6. Issued Check No. 611 for miscellaneous selling expense, $310.

9. Received credit memorandum from Bidwell Co. for merchandise returned to them, $290.

9. Issued Invoice No. 941 to Collins Corp., $8,500.

10. Issued Check No. 612 for $9,405 to Howell, Inc. in payment of $9,500 invoice, less 1% discount.

10. Received check for $9,702 from Sax Manufacturing Co. in payment of $9,800 invoice, less discount.

10. Issued Check No. 613 to Bone Enterprises in payment of invoice of $2,120, no discount.

11. Issued Invoice No. 942 to Joy Corp., $3,120.

11. Issued Check No. 614 to Porter Corp. in payment of account, $705, no discount.

12. Received check for $1,683 from W. Cox, Inc. in payment of $1,700 invoice, less discount.

Jan. 13. Issued credit memorandum to Joy Corp. for damaged merchandise, $320.
   13. Issued Check No. 615 for $2,254 to Bidwell Co. in payment of $2,300 balance, less 2% discount.
   16. Issued Check No. 616 for $2,725 for cash purchase of merchandise.
   16. Cash sales for January 2-15, $21,520.
   17. Purchased merchandise on account from Bone Enterprises, $7,920.
   18. Received check for return of merchandise that had been purchased for cash, $790.
   18. Issued Check No. 617 for miscellaneous general expense, $238.
   19. Purchased the following on account from Moore Supply, Inc.: store supplies, $248; office supplies, $197.
   20. Issued Check No. 618 in payment of advertising expense, $1,850.
   23. Issued Invoice No. 943 to Sax Manufacturing Co., $8,172.
   24. Purchased the following on account from Howell, Inc.: merchandise, $5,127; store supplies, $292.
   25. Issued Invoice No. 944 to Collins Corp., $4,650.
   25. Received check for $2,800 from Powell Corp. in payment of $2,800 balance, no discount.
   26. Issued Check No. 619 to Weber Equipment Co. in payment of invoice of January 3, $11,100, no discount.
   27. Issued Check No. 620 to Ann Day as a personal withdrawal, $3,500.
   30. Issued Check No. 621 for monthly salaries as follows: sales salaries, $9,100; office salaries, $3,800.
   31. Cash sales for January 16–31, $18,150.
   31. Issued Check No. 622 for transportation on commodities purchased during the month as follows: merchandise, $720; equipment, $210.

Instructions:

(1) Open the following accounts in the general ledger, entering the balances indicated as of January 1:

111	Cash	$ 9,100	411	Sales	—
113	Accounts Receivable	16,200	412	Sales Returns and Allow.	—
114	Merchandise Inventory	31,500	413	Sales Discount	—
115	Store Supplies	410	511	Purchases	—
116	Office Supplies	225	512	Purchases Discount	—
117	Prepaid Insurance	2,100	611	Sales Salaries Expense	—
121	Equipment	40,650	612	Advertising Expense	—
122	Accumulated Depr.	12,350	619	Miscellaneous Selling Expense	—
211	Accounts Payable	12,325	711	Office Salaries Expense	—
311	Ann Day, Capital	75,510	712	Rent Expense	—
312	Ann Day, Drawing	—	719	Miscellaneous General Expense	—

(2) Record the transactions for January, using a purchases journal (as on pages 168 and 169), a sales journal (as on page 176), a cash payments journal (as on page 173), a cash receipts journal (as on page 178), and a 2-column general journal. The terms of all sales on account are FOB shipping point, 1/10, n/30. Assume that an assistant makes daily postings to the individual accounts in the accounts payable and the accounts receivable ledgers.

(3) Post the appropriate individual entries to the general ledger.

(4) Add the columns of the special journals and post the appropriate totals to the general ledger; insert the account balances.

(5) Prepare a trial balance.

(6) Balances in the accounts in the subsidiary ledgers as of January 31 are listed below. Verify the agreement of the ledgers with their respective controlling accounts.

Accounts Receivable: Balances of $800; $8,500; $2,800; $8,172; $4,650.
Accounts Payable: Balances of $7,920; $5,419; $445.

Mini-Case

For the past few years, your uncle has operated a small jewelry store, Pride Jewelers. Its current annual revenues are approximately $500,000. Because the company's bookkeeper has been taking more and more time each month to record all transactions in a two-column journal and to prepare the financial statements, your uncle is considering improving the company's accounting system by adding special journals and subsidiary ledgers. Your uncle has asked you to help him with this project. He has compiled the following information:

(1)

Type of Transaction	Estimated Frequency per Month
Purchases of merchandise on account	250
Sales on account	160
Daily cash register summaries of cash sales	25
Purchases of merchandise for cash	20
Purchases of office supplies on account	5
Purchases of store supplies on account	5
Cash payments for utilities expenses	4
Cash purchases of office supplies	5
Cash purchases of store supplies	5
Cash receipts from customers on account	160

(2) For merchandise purchases of high dollar-value items, Pride Jewelers issues notes payable at current interest rates to vendors. These notes are issued because many of the high-value items may not sell immediately and the issuance of the notes reduces the need to maintain large balances of cash or assets that can be readily converted to cash. Notes are issued for approximately 10% of the purchases on account.

(3) All purchases discounts are taken when available.

(4) A sales discount of 2/10, n/30 is offered to all credit customers.

(5) A local sales tax of 6% is collected on all intrastate sales of merchandise.

(6) Monthly financial statements are prepared.

Instructions:

(1) Based upon the preceding description of Pride Jewelers, indicate which special journals you would recommend as part of Pride Jewelers' accounting system.

(2) Assume that your uncle has decided to use a sales journal and a purchases journal. Design the format for each journal, giving special consideration to the needs of Pride Jewelers.

(3) Which subsidiary ledgers would you recommend for Pride Jewelers?

7

CHAPTER | Cash

CHAPTER OBJECTIVES

Describe and illustrate the application of internal control principles in controlling cash.

Describe and illustrate accounting for cash.

7
CHAPTER

Earlier chapters have discussed the qualities of a properly designed accounting system and the principles of internal control for directing operations. This chapter presents the application of these internal control principles in the design of an effective system for controlling cash and in accounting for cash transactions.

CONTROL OVER CASH

Because of the high value of money in relation to its mass, and its easy transferability, cash is the asset most likely to be diverted and used improperly by employees. In addition, many transactions either directly or indirectly affect its receipt or payment. It is therefore necessary that cash be effectively safeguarded by special controls.

The Bank Account as a Tool for Controlling Cash

One of the major devices for maintaining control over cash is the bank account. To get the most benefit from a bank account, all cash received must be deposited in the bank and all payments must be made by checks drawn on the bank or from special cash funds. When such a system is strictly followed, there is a double record of cash, one maintained by the business and the other by the bank.

The forms used by the depositor in connection with a bank account are a signature card, deposit ticket, check, and a record of checks drawn.

Signature Card

At the time an account is opened, an identifying number is assigned to the account and the bank requires that a **signature card** be signed by each person authorized to sign checks drawn on the account. The card is used by the bank to determine the authenticity of the signature on checks presented to it for payment.

Deposit Ticket

The details of a deposit are listed by the depositor on a printed form supplied by the bank. **Deposit tickets** may be prepared in duplicate, in which case the copy is stamped or initialed by the bank's teller and given to the depositor as a receipt. The receipt of a deposit may be indicated by means other than a duplicate deposit ticket, but all methods give the depositor written proof of the date and the total amount of the deposit.

Check

A **check** is a written instrument signed by the depositor, ordering the bank to pay a certain sum of money to the order of a designated person. There are three parties to a check: the **drawer,** the one who signs the check; the **drawee,** the bank on which the check is drawn; and the **payee,** the one to whose order the check is drawn. When checks are issued to pay bills, they are recorded as credits to Cash on the day issued, even though they are not presented to the drawer's bank until some later time. When checks are received from customers, they are recorded as debits to Cash, on the assumption that the customer has enough money on deposit.

Check forms may be obtained in many styles. The name and the address of the depositor are often printed on each check, and the checks are usually numbered in sequence to facilitate the depositor's internal control. Most banks use automatic sorting and posting equipment and provide check forms on which the bank's identification number and the depositor's account number are printed along the lower margin in magnetic ink. When the check is presented for payment, the amount for which it is drawn is inserted next to the account number, also in magnetic ink.

Record of Checks Drawn

A memorandum record of the basic details of a check should be prepared at the time the check is written. The record may be a stub from which the check is detached or it may be a small booklet designed to be kept with the check forms. Each type of record also provides spaces for recording deposits and the current bank balance.

Business firms may prepare a copy of each check drawn and then use it as a basis for recording the transaction in the cash payments journal. Checks issued to a creditor on account are usually accompanied by a notification of the specific invoice that is being paid. The purpose of such notification, sometimes called a **remittance advice,** is to make sure that proper credit is recorded in the accounts of the creditor. Mistakes are less likely to happen and the possible need for exchanges of correspondence is reduced. The invoice number or other descriptive data may be inserted in spaces provided on the face or on the back of the check, or on an attachment to the check as in the following illustration:

**CHECK AND REMITTANCE
ADVICE**

MONROE COMPANY			363
813 Greenwood Street	Detroit, MI 48208-4070 ___ April 12 ___ 19 84		8-42 / 720

Pay to the Order of ___ Hammond Office Products Inc. ___ $ 921.20

Nine hundred twenty-one 20/100-- Dollars

AMERICAN NATIONAL BANK
OF DETROIT

K. R. Simms ___ Treasurer

Earl M. Hartman ___ Vice President

DETROIT, MI 48201-2500   (313)232-8547   MEMBER FDIC

⑈072000423⑈ ⑆627042 363

DETACH THIS PORTION BEFORE CASHING

DATE	DESCRIPTION	GROSS AMOUNT	DEDUCTIONS	NET AMOUNT
4/12/84	Invoice No. 529482	940.00	18.80	921.20

MONROE COMPANY

Before depositing the check at the bank, the payee removes the part of the check containing the remittance information. The removed part may then be used by the payee as written proof of the details of the cash receipt.

Bank Statement | Although there are some differences in procedure, banks usually maintain an original and a copy of all checking accounts. When this is done, the original becomes the statement of account that is mailed to the depositor, usually once each month. Like any account with a customer or a creditor, the bank statement shows the beginning balance, debits (deductions by the bank) and credits (additions by the bank), and the balance at the end of the period. The depositor's checks received by the bank during the period may accompany the bank statement, arranged in the order of payment. The paid or canceled checks are perforated or stamped "Paid," together with the date of payment.

Debit or credit memorandums describing other entries in the depositor's account may also be enclosed with the statement. For example, the bank may have debited the depositor's account for service charges or for deposited checks returned because of insufficient funds. It may have credited the account for receipts from notes receivable left for collection or for loans to the depositor. A typical bank statement is illustrated as follows:

BANK STATEMENT |

Bank Reconciliation | When all cash receipts are deposited in the bank and all payments are made by check, the cash account is often called Cash in Bank. This account in the depositor's ledger is the reciprocal of the account with the depositor in the bank's ledger. Cash in Bank in the depositor's ledger is an asset with a debit balance, and the account with the depositor in the bank's ledger is a liability with a credit balance.

It might seem that the two balances should be equal, but they are not likely to be equal on any specific date because of either or both of the following: (1) delay by either party in recording transactions, and (2) errors by either party in recording transactions. Ordinarily, there is a time lag of one day or more between the date a check is written and the date that it is presented to the bank for payment. If the depositor mails deposits to the bank or uses the night depository, a time lag between the date of the deposit and the date that it is recorded by the bank is also probable. Conversely, the bank may debit or credit the depositor's account for transactions about which the depositor will not be informed until later. Examples are service or collection fees charged by the bank and the proceeds of notes receivable sent to the bank for collection.

To determine the reasons for any difference and to correct any errors that may have been made by the bank or the depositor, the depositor's own records should be reconciled with the bank statement. The **bank reconciliation** is divided into two major sections: one section begins with the balance according to the bank statement and ends with the adjusted balance; the other section begins with the balance according to the depositor's records and also ends with the adjusted balance. The two amounts designated as the adjusted balance must be equal. The form and the content of the bank reconciliation are outlined as follows:

FORMAT FOR BANK RECONCILIATION

Bank balance according to bank statement		$xxx
Add: Additions by depositor not on bank statement	$xx	
Bank errors	xx	xx
		$xxx
Deduct: Deductions by depositor not on bank statement	$xx	
Bank errors	xx	xx
Adjusted balance		$xxx
Bank balance according to depositor's records		$xxx
Add: Additions by bank not recorded by depositor	$xx	
Depositor errors	xx	xx
		$xxx
Deduct: Deductions by bank not recorded by depositor	$xx	
Depositor errors	xx	xx
Adjusted balance		$xxx

The following procedures are used in finding the reconciling items and determining the adjusted balance of Cash in Bank:

1. Individual deposits listed on the bank statement are compared with unrecorded deposits appearing in the preceding reconciliation and with deposit receipts or other records of deposits. Deposits not recorded by the bank are added to the balance according to the bank statement.
2. Paid checks are compared with outstanding checks appearing on the preceding reconciliation and with checks listed in the cash payments journal. Checks issued that have not been paid by the bank are outstanding and are deducted from the balance according to the bank statement.
3. Bank credit memorandums are traced to the cash receipts journal. Credit memorandums not recorded in the cash receipts journal are added to the balance according to the depositor's records.

4. Bank debit memorandums are traced to the cash payments journal. Debit memorandums not recorded in the cash payments journal are deducted from the balance according to the depositor's records.
5. Errors discovered during the process of making the foregoing comparisons are listed separately on the reconciliation. For example, if the amount for which a check was drawn had been recorded erroneously by the depositor, the amount of the error should be added to or deducted from the balance according to the depositor's records. Similarly, errors by the bank should be added to or deducted from the balance according to the bank statement.

Illustration of Bank Reconciliation

The bank statement for Monroe Company, reproduced on page 197, indicates a balance of $3,359.78 as of July 31. The balance in Cash in Bank in Monroe Company's ledger as of the same date is $2,234.99. Use of the procedures outlined above reveals the following reconciling items:

1. Deposit of July 31 not recorded on bank statement............ $ 816.20
2. Checks outstanding: No. 812, $1,061.00; No. 878, $435.39; No. 883, $48.60... 1,544.99
3. Note plus interest of $8 collected by bank (credit memorandum), not recorded in cash receipts journal....................... 408.00
4. Bank service charges (debit memorandum) not recorded in cash payments journal.. 3.00
5. Check No. 879 for $732.26 to Taylor Co. on account recorded in cash payments journal as $723.26........................... 9.00

The bank reconciliation based on the bank statement and the reconciling items is as follows:

BANK
RECONCILIATION

Monroe Company
Bank Reconciliation
July 31, 1984

Balance per bank statement.................................		$3,359.78
Add deposit of July 31, not recorded by bank..................		816.20
		$4,175.98
Deduct: Outstanding checks		
No. 812..................................	$1,061.00	
No. 878..................................	435.39	
No. 883..................................	48.60	1,544.99
Adjusted balance.....................................		$2,630.99
Balance per depositor's records.......................		$2,234.99
Add note and interest collected by bank................		408.00
		$2,642.99
Deduct: Bank service charges.......................	$3.00	
Error in recording Check No. 879............	9.00	12.00
Adjusted balance.....................................		$2,630.99

Entries Based on Bank Reconciliation

Bank memorandums not recorded by the depositor and depositor's errors shown by the bank reconciliation require that entries be made in the accounts. The entries may be recorded in the appropriate special journals if they have not already been posted for the month, or they may be recorded in the general journal.

The entries for Monroe Company, based on the bank reconciliation on page 199, are as follows:

July	31	Cash in Bank	408	
		Notes Receivable.....................		400
		Interest Income		8
		Note collected by bank.		
	31	Miscellaneous General Expense	3	
		Accounts Payable — Taylor Co............	9	
		Cash in Bank		12
		Bank service charges and error in recording Check No. 879.		

The data needed for these adjustments are provided by the section of the bank reconciliation that begins with the balance per depositor's records.

After the foregoing entries are posted, the cash in bank account will have a debit balance of $2,630.99, which agrees with the adjusted balance shown on the bank reconciliation. This is the amount of cash available for use as of July 31 and the amount that would be reported on the balance sheet on that date.

Importance of Bank Reconciliation

The bank reconciliation is an important part of the system of internal control because it is a means of comparing recorded cash, per the accounting records, with the amount of cash reported by the bank. It thus provides for finding and correcting errors and irregularities. Greater internal control is achieved when the bank reconciliation is prepared by an employee who does not take part in or record cash transactions with the bank. Without a proper separation of these duties, cash is more likely to be embezzled. For example, an employee who takes part in all of these duties could prepare an unauthorized check, omit it from the accounts, and cash it. Then to account for the canceled check when returned by the bank, the employee could understate the amount of the outstanding checks on future bank reconciliations by the amount of the embezzlement.

INTERNAL CONTROL OF CASH RECEIPTS

Department stores and other retail businesses ordinarily receive cash from two main sources: (1) over the counter from cash customers and (2) by mail from charge customers making payments on account. At the end of the business day, each salesclerk counts the cash in the assigned cash drawer and records the amount on a memorandum form. An employee from the cashier's department removes the cash register tapes on which total receipts were recorded for each cash drawer, counts the cash, and compares the total with the memorandum and the tape, noting any differences. The cash is then taken to the cashier's office and the tapes and memorandum forms are forwarded to the accounting department, where they become the basis for entries in the cash receipts journal.

The employees who open incoming mail compare the amount of cash received with the amount shown on the accompanying remittance advice to be certain that the two amounts agree. If there is no separate remittance advice, an employee prepares one on a form designed for such use. All cash received, usually in the form of checks and money orders, is sent to the cashier's department, where it is combined with the receipts from cash sales and a deposit ticket is prepared. The remittance advices are delivered to the accounting department, where they become the basis for entries in the cash receipts journal and for posting to the customers' accounts in the subsidiary ledger.

The duplicate deposit tickets or other bank receipt forms obtained by the cashier are sent to the controller or other financial officer, who compares the total amount with that reported by the accounting department as the total debit to Cash in Bank for the period.

Cash Short and Over

The amount of cash actually received during a day often does not agree with the record of cash receipts. Whenever there is a difference between the record and the actual cash and no error can be found in the record, it must be assumed that the mistake occurred in making change. The cash shortage or overage is recorded in an account entitled Cash Short and Over. A common method for handling such mistakes is to include in the cash receipts journal a Cash Short and Over Debit column into which all cash shortages are entered, and a Cash Short and Over Credit column into which all cash overages are entered. For example, if the actual cash received from cash sales is less than the amount indicated by the cash register tally, the entry in the cash receipts journal would include a debit to Cash Short and Over. An example for one day's receipts, in general journal form, follows:

```
Cash in Bank . . . . . . . . . . . . . . . . . . . . . . . . . . . . . . . . . . . . .  4,577.60
Cash Short and Over . . . . . . . . . . . . . . . . . . . . . . . . . . . . .      3.16
   Sales. . . . . . . . . . . . . . . . . . . . . . . . . . . . . . . . . . . . . . . . . .           4,580.76
```

If there is a debit balance in the cash short and over account at the end of the fiscal period, it is an expense and may be included in "Miscellaneous general expense" on the income statement. If there is a credit balance, it is revenue and may be listed in the "Other income" section. If the balance becomes larger than may be accounted for by minor errors in making change, the management should take corrective measures.

Cash Change Funds

Retail stores and other businesses that receive cash directly from customers must maintain a fund of currency and coins in order to make change. The fund may be established by drawing a check for the required amount, debiting the account Cash on Hand and crediting Cash in Bank. No additional charges or credits to the cash on hand account are necessary unless the amount of the fund is to be increased or decreased. At the end of each business day, the total amount of cash received during the day is deposited and the original amount of the change fund is retained. The desired composition of the fund is maintained by exchanging bills or coins for those of other denominations at the bank.

INTERNAL CONTROL OF CASH PAYMENTS

It is common practice for business enterprises to require that every payment of cash be evidenced by a check signed by a designated official. As an additional control, some firms require two signatures on all checks or only on checks which are larger than a certain amount. It is also common to use a check protector, which produces amounts on the check that are not easily removed or changed.

When the owner of a business has personal knowledge of all goods and services purchased, the owner may sign checks, with the assurance that the creditors have followed the terms of their contracts and that the exact amount of the obligation is being paid. Disbursing officials are seldom able to have such a complete knowledge of affairs, however. In enterprises of even moderate size, the responsibility for issuing purchase orders, inspecting goods received, and verifying contractual and arithmetical details of invoices is divided among the employees of several departments. It is desirable, therefore, to coordinate these related activities and to link them with the final issuance of checks to creditors. One of the best systems used for this purpose is the voucher system.

Basic Features of the Voucher System

A voucher system is made up of records, methods, and procedures used in proving and recording liabilities and in paying and recording cash payments. A voucher system uses (1) vouchers, (2) a voucher register, (3) a file for unpaid vouchers, (4) a check register, and (5) a file for paid vouchers. As in all areas of accounting systems and internal controls, many differences in detail are possible. The discussion that follows refers to a medium-size merchandising enterprise with separate departments for purchasing, receiving, accounting, and disbursing.

Vouchers

The term voucher is widely used in accounting. In a general sense, it means any document that serves as proof of authority to pay cash, such as an invoice approved for payment, or as evidence that cash has been paid, such as a canceled check. The term has a narrower meaning when applied to the voucher system: a voucher is a special form on which is recorded relevant data about a liability and the details of its payment.

An important characteristic of the voucher system is the requirement that a voucher be prepared for each expenditure. In fact, a check may not be issued except in payment of a properly authorized voucher. Vouchers may be paid immediately after they are prepared or at a later date, depending upon the circumstances and the credit terms.

A voucher form is illustrated on page 203. The face of the voucher provides space for the name and address of the creditor, the date and number of the voucher, and basic details of the invoice or other supporting document, such as the vendor's invoice number and the amount and terms of the invoice. One half

VOUCHER

of the back of the voucher is devoted to the account distribution and the other half to summaries of the voucher and the details of payment. Spaces are also provided for the signature or initials of certain employees.

Vouchers are customarily prepared by the accounting department on the basis of an invoice or a memorandum that serves as proof of an expenditure. This is usually done only after the following comparisons and verifications have been completed and noted on the invoice:

1. Comparison of the invoice with a copy of the purchase order to verify quantities, prices, and terms.
2. Comparison of the invoice with the receiving report to verify receipt of the items billed.
3. Verification of the arithmetical accuracy of the invoice.

After all data except details of payment have been inserted, the invoice or other supporting evidence is attached to the face of the voucher, which is then folded with the account distribution and summaries on the outside. The voucher is then given to the designated official or officials for final approval.

Voucher Register

After approval by the designated official, each voucher is recorded in a journal known as a **voucher register**. It is similar to and replaces the purchases journal described in Chapter 6.

A typical form of a voucher register is illustrated on pages 204 and 205. The vouchers are entered in numerical order, each being recorded as a credit to Accounts Payable (sometimes entitled Vouchers Payable) and as a debit to the account or accounts to be charged for the expenditure.

When a voucher is paid, the date of payment and the number of the check are inserted in the proper columns in the voucher register. These notations provide a ready means of determining at any time the amount of an individual unpaid voucher or of the total amount of unpaid vouchers.

PAGE 11							VOUCHER
DATE	VOU. NO.	PAYEE	DATE PAID	CK. NO.	ACCOUNTS PAYABLE CR.	PURCHASES DR.
19--						
JULY 1	451	ALLIED MFG. CO.	7–8	863	450.00	450.00
1	452	CHAVEZ REALTORS	7–1	856	600.00	
2	453	FOSTER PUBLICATIONS	7–2	857	52.50	
3	454	BENSON EXPRESS CO.	7–3	859	36.80	24.20
3	455	ROBERSON'S SUPPLY CO.			784.20	
3	456	MOORE & CO.	7–11	866	1,236.00	1,236.00
6	457	J. L. BROWN CO.	7–6	860	22.50	
6	458	TURNER CORP.			395.30	395.30
31	477	CENTRAL MOTORS			112.20	
31	478	PETTY CASH	7–31	883	48.60	
31					15,551.60 (212)	11,640.30 (511)

Unpaid Voucher File

After a voucher has been recorded in the voucher register, it is filed in an unpaid voucher file, where it remains until it is paid. The amount due on each voucher represents the credit balance of an account payable, and the voucher itself is like an individual account in a subsidiary accounts payable ledger. Accordingly, a separate subsidiary ledger is not needed.

All voucher systems include some way to assure payment within the discount period or on the last day of the credit period. A simple but effective method is to file each voucher in the unpaid voucher file according to the earliest date that consideration should be given to its payment. The file may be made up of a group of folders, numbered from 1 to 31, the numbers representing days of a month. Such a system brings to the attention of the disbursing official the vouchers that are to be paid on each day. It also provides management with a convenient means of forecasting the amount of cash needed to meet maturing obligations.

When a voucher is to be paid, it is removed from the unpaid voucher file and a check is issued in payment. The date, the number, and the amount of the check are listed on the back of the voucher for use in recording the payment in the check register. Paid vouchers and the supporting documents are often run through a canceling machine to prevent accidental or intentional reuse.

An exception to the general rule that vouchers be prepared for all expenditures may be made for bank charges shown by debit memorandums or notations on the bank statement. For example, such items as bank service charges, safe-deposit box rentals, and returned NSF (Not Sufficient Funds) checks from customers may be charged to the depositor's account without either a formal voucher or a check. For large expenditures, such as the repayment of a bank loan, a supporting voucher may be prepared, if desired, even though a check is not written. The paid note may then be attached to the voucher as evidence of the obligation. All bank debit memorandums are the equivalent of checks as evidence of payment.

REGISTER								PAGE 11
STORE SUPPLIES DR.	ADV. EXP. DR.	DEL. EXP. DR.	MISC. SELLING EXP. DR.	MISC. GENERAL EXP. DR.	SUNDRY ACCOUNTS DR. ACCOUNT	POST. REF.	AMOUNT	
					RENT EXPENSE	712	600.00	
	52.50							
		12.60						
34.20					OFFICE EQUIPMENT	122	750.00	
				22.50				
		112.20						
4.30		16.20	19.50	8.60				
59.80	176.40	286.10	48.30	64.90			3,276.80	
(116)	(612)	(613)	(618)	(710)			(✓)	

Check Register

The payment of a voucher is recorded in a check register, an example of which is illustrated at the bottom of this page. The check register is a modified form of the cash payments journal and is so called because it is a complete record of all checks. It is common to record all checks in the check register in sequential order, including occasional checks that are voided because of an error in their preparation.

Each check issued is in payment of a voucher that has previously been recorded as an account payable in the voucher register. The effect of each entry in the check register is a debit to Accounts Payable and a credit to Cash in Bank (and Purchases Discount, when appropriate).

				CHECK REGISTER					PAGE 14
DATE	CK. NO.	PAYEE	VOU. NO.	ACCOUNTS PAYABLE DR.	PURCHASES DISCOUNT CR.	CASH IN BANK CR.	BANK DEPOSITS	BALANCE	
19--								8,743.10	
JULY 1	856	CHAVEZ REALTORS	452	600.00		600.00	1,240.30	9,383.40	
2	857	FOSTER PUBLICATIONS	453	52.50		52.50		9,330.90	
2	858	HILL AND DAVIS	436	1,420.00	14.20	1,405.80	865.70	8,790.80	
3	859	BENSON EXPRESS CO.	454	36.80		36.80	942.20	9,696.20	
30	879	VOIDED							
30	880	STONE & CO.	460	14.30		14.30		9,521.80	
30	881	EVANS CORP.	448	1,015.00		1,015.00	765.50	9,272.30	
31	882	GRAHAM & CO.	469	830.00	16.60	813.40		8,458.90	
31	883	PETTY CASH	478	48.60		48.60	938.10	9,348.40	
31				17,322.90	198.20	17,124.70			
				(212)	(513)	(111)			

CHECK REGISTER

The memorandum columns for Bank Deposits and Bank Balance appearing in the illustration of the check register are optional. They provide a convenient means of determining the cash available at all times.

When check forms with a remittance advice are prepared in duplicate, the copies retained may make up the check register. At the end of each month, summary totals can be readily obtained for accounts payable debit, purchases discount credit, and cash credit, and the entry recorded in the general journal. If the volume of checks issued is large, a significant amount of clerical expenses may be saved by eliminating the copying of data in a columnar check register.

Paid Voucher File

After payment, vouchers are usually filed in numerical order in a paid voucher file. They are then readily available for examination by employees or independent auditors needing information about a certain expenditure. Eventually the paid vouchers are destroyed according to the firm's policies concerning the retention of records.

Voucher System and Management

The voucher system not only provides effective accounting controls but also aids management in discharging other responsibilities. For example, the voucher system gives greater assurance that all payments are in liquidation of valid liabilities. In addition, current information is always available for use in determining future cash requirements. This in turn enables management to make the best use of cash resources. Invoices on which cash discounts are allowed can be paid within the discount period and other invoices can be paid on the final day of the credit period, thus reducing costs and maintaining a favorable credit standing. Seasonal borrowing for working capital purposes can also be planned more accurately, with a consequent saving in interest costs.

Purchases Discount | In earlier chapters, purchases of merchandise were recorded at the invoice price, and cash discounts taken were credited to the purchases discount account at the time of payment. There are two opposing views on how such discounts should be reported in the income statement.

The most widely accepted view, which has been followed in this textbook, is that purchases discounts should be reported as a deduction from purchases. For example, the cost of merchandise with an invoice price of $1,000, subject to terms of 2/10, n/30, is recorded initially at $1,000. If payment is made within the discount period, the discount of $20 reduces the cost to $980. If the invoice is not paid within the discount period, the cost of the merchandise remains $1,000. This treatment of purchases discounts may be attacked on the grounds that the date of payment should not affect the cost of a commodity. The additional payment required beyond the discount period adds nothing to the value of the commodities purchased.

The second view reports discounts taken as "other income." In terms of the example above, the cost of the merchandise is considered to be $1,000 regardless of the time of payment. If payment is made within the discount period, revenue of $20 is considered to be realized. The objection to this procedure lies in the recognition of revenue from the act of purchasing and paying for a commodity. Theoretically, an enterprise might make no sales of merchandise during an accounting period and yet might report as revenue the amount of cash discounts taken.

A major disadvantage of recording purchases at the invoice price and recognizing purchases discounts at the time of payment is that this method does not measure the cost of failing to take discounts. Well-managed enterprises maintain enough cash to pay within the discount period all invoices subject to a discount, and view the failure to take a discount as an inefficiency. To measure the cost of this inefficiency, purchases invoices may be recorded at the net amount, assuming that all discounts will be taken. Any discounts not taken are then recorded in an expense account called Discounts Lost. This method measures the cost of failure to take cash discounts and gives management an opportunity to take remedial action. Again assuming the same data, the invoice for $1,000 would be recorded as a debit to Purchases of $980 and a credit to Accounts Payable for the same amount. If the invoice is not paid until after the discount period has passed, the entry, in general journal form, would be as follows:

```
Accounts Payable ........................................... 980
Discounts Lost .............................................  20
    Cash in Bank ...........................................       1,000
```

When this method is used with the voucher system, all vouchers are prepared and recorded at the net amount. Any discount lost is noted on the related voucher and recorded in a special column in the check register when the voucher is paid.

Another advantage of this treatment of purchases discounts is that all merchandise purchased is recorded initially at the net price and hence no later adjustments to cost are necessary. An objection, however, is that the amount reported as accounts payable in the balance sheet may be less than the amount needed to discharge the liability.

Petty Cash In most businesses there is a frequent need for the payment of relatively small amounts, such as for postage due, for transportation charges, or for the purchase of urgently needed supplies at a nearby retail store. Payment by check in such cases would result in delay, annoyance, and excessive expense of maintaining the records. Yet because these small payments may occur frequently and therefore amount to a considerable total sum, it is desirable to retain close control over such payments. This may be done by maintaining a special cash fund called **petty cash.**

In establishing a petty cash fund, the first step is to estimate the amount of cash needed for disbursements of relatively small amounts during a certain period such as a week or a month. If the voucher system is used, a voucher is then prepared for this amount and it is recorded in the voucher register as a debit to Petty Cash and a credit to Accounts Payable. The check drawn to pay the voucher is recorded in the check register as a debit to Accounts Payable and a credit to Cash in Bank.

The money obtained from cashing the check is placed in the custody of a specific employee who is authorized to disburse the fund according to restrictions as to maximum amount and purpose. Each time a disbursement is made from the fund, the employee records the essential details on a receipt form, obtains the signature of the payee as proof of the payment, and initials the completed form. A typical petty cash receipt is illustrated as follows:

PETTY CASH
RECEIPT

PETTY CASH RECEIPT

NO. __121__   DATE __August 1, 1984__

PAID TO __Metropolitan Times__   AMOUNT

FOR __Daily newspaper__   3 | 70

CHARGE TO __Miscellaneous General Expense__

PAYMENT RECEIVED:

_____S. O. Hall_____   APPROVED BY _____N. E. R.____

When the amount of money in the petty cash fund is reduced to the predetermined minimum amount, the fund is replenished. If the voucher system is used, the accounts debited on the replenishing voucher are those indicated by a summary of expenditures. The voucher is then recorded in the voucher register as a debit to the various expense and asset accounts and a credit to Accounts Payable. The check in payment of the voucher is recorded in the check register in the usual manner.

After the petty cash fund has been replenished, the fund will be restored to its original amount. It should be noted that the only entry in the petty cash account will be the initial debit, unless at some later time the standard amount of the fund is increased or decreased.

Because disbursements are not recorded in the accounts until the fund is replenished, petty cash funds and other special funds that operate in a like manner should always be replenished at the end of an accounting period. The amount of money actually in the fund will then agree with the balance in the related fund account, and the expenses and the assets for which payment has been made will be recorded in the proper period.

Other Cash Funds   Cash funds may also be established to meet other special needs of a business. For example, money advanced for travel expenses may be accounted for in the same manner as petty cash. An amount is advanced for travel as needed; then periodically after receipt of expense reports, the expenses are recorded and the fund is replenished. A similar procedure may be used to provide a working fund for a sales office located in another city. The amount of the fund may be deposited in a local bank and the sales representative may be authorized to draw checks for payment of rent, salaries, and other operating expenses. Each month, the representative sends the invoices, bank statement, paid checks, bank reconciliation, and other business documents to the home office. The data are audited, the expenditures are recorded, and a reimbursing check is returned for deposit in the local bank.

CASH TRANSACTIONS AND ELECTRONIC FUNDS TRANSFER

Currently most cash payments are made by check or currency and most cash receipts are in the form of currency or check. The broad principles discussed in earlier sections provide the basis for developing an effective system to control such cash transactions. However, the development of electronic funds transfer (EFT) may eventually change the form in which many cash transactions are executed and could affect the processing and controlling of cash transactions.

EFT can be defined as a payment system that uses computerized electronic impulses rather than paper (money, checks, etc.) to effect a cash transaction. For example, a business may pay its employees by means of EFT. Under such a system, employees who want their payroll checks deposited directly in a checking account sign an authorization form. For each pay period, the business' computer produces a magnetic tape with computer-sensitive notations for relevant payroll data. The magnetic tape is delivered to the bank, which automatically debits the business' account for the entire payroll and credits the checking account of each employee. Similar cash payments might be made for other preauthorized payments. The federal government currently processes several million social security checks through EFT.

EFT is also beginning to play a role in retail sales. Through a point-of-sale (POS) system, a customer pays for goods at the time of purchase by presenting a plastic card. The card is used to activate a terminal in the store and thereby effect an immediate transfer from the customer's checking account to the retailer's account at the bank.

Studies have indicated that EFT systems may reduce the cost of processing certain cash transactions and contribute to better control over cash receipts and cash payments. Offsetting these potential advantages are problems of protecting the privacy of information stored in computers, and difficulties in documenting purchase and sale transactions. In any event, developments with EFT systems are likely to be followed very closely by most businesses over the next few years.

Self-Examination Questions
(Answers in Appendix C.)

1. In preparing a bank reconciliation, the amount of checks outstanding would be:
   A. added to the bank balance according to the bank statement
   B. deducted from the bank balance according to the bank statement
   C. added to the cash balance according to the depositor's records
   D. deducted from the cash balance according to the depositor's records

2. Journal entries based on the bank reconciliation are required for:
   A. additions to the cash balance according to the depositor's records
   B. deductions from the cash balance according to the depositor's records
   C. both A and B
   D. neither A nor B

3. The journal used to record liabilities when a voucher system is used is called:
   A. a voucher
   B. an unpaid voucher file
   C. a check register
   D. a voucher register

4. A voucher system is used, all vouchers for purchases are recorded at the net amount, and a purchase is made for $500 under terms 1/10, n/30.
   A. Purchases would be debited for $495 to record the purchase.
   B. Discounts Lost would be debited for $5 if the voucher is not paid within the discount period.
   C. If the voucher is not paid until after the discount period has expired, the discount lost would be reported as an expense on the income statement.
   D. All of the above

5. A petty cash fund is:
   A. used to pay relatively small amounts
   B. established by estimating the amount of cash needed for disbursements of relatively small amounts during a specified period
   C. reimbursed when the amount of money in the fund is reduced to a predetermined minimum amount
   D. all of the above

Discussion Questions

1. Why is cash the asset that often warrants the most attention in the design of an effective internal control system?

2. What name is often given to the notification attached to a check that indicates the specific invoice that is being paid?

3. When checks are received, they are recorded as debits to Cash, the assumption being that the drawer has sufficient funds on deposit. What entry should be made if a check received from a customer and deposited is returned by the bank for lack of sufficient funds (NSF)?

4. What is the purpose of preparing a bank reconciliation?

5. Identify each of the following reconciling items as : (a) an addition to the balance per bank statement, (b) a deduction from the balance per bank statement, (c) an addition to the balance per depositor's records, or (d) a deduction from the balance per depositor's records. (None of the transactions reported by bank debit and credit memorandums have been recorded by the depositor.)
   (1) Deposit in transit, $670.20.
   (2) Note collected by bank, $1,010.
   (3) Outstanding checks, $879.50.
   (4) Check for $20 charged by bank as $200.
   (5) Bank service charge, $17.20.
   (6) Check of a customer returned by bank to depositor because of insufficient funds, $47.
   (7) Check drawn by depositor for $67 but recorded in check register as $76.

6. Which of the reconciling items listed in Question 5 necessitate an entry in the depositor's accounts?

7. The procedures employed by Hardy's for over-the-counter receipts are as follows: At the close of each day's business, the salesclerks count the cash in their respective cash drawers, after which they determine the amount recorded by the register and prepare the memorandum cash form, noting any discrepancies. An employee from the cashier's office counts the cash, compares the total with the memorandum, and takes the cash to the cashier's office. (a) Indicate the weak link in internal control. (b) How can the weakness be corrected?

8. The mailroom employees of Baker Co. send all remittances and remittance advices to the cashier. The cashier deposits the cash in the bank and forwards the remittance advices and duplicate deposit slips to the accounting department. (a) Indicate the weak link in internal control in the handling of cash receipts. (b) How can the weakness be corrected?

9. The combined cash count of all cash registers at the close of business is $2.10 more than the cash sales indicated by the cash register tapes. (a) In what account is the cash overage recorded? (b) Are cash overages debited or credited to this account?

10. The bookkeeper pays all obligations by prenumbered checks. What are the strengths and weaknesses in the internal control over cash disbursements in this situation?

11. What is meant by the term "voucher" as applied to the voucher system?

12. Before a voucher for the purchase of merchandise is approved for payment, three documents should be compared to verify the accuracy of the liability. Name these three documents.

13. (a) When the voucher system is employed, is the accounts payable account in the general ledger a controlling account? (b) Is there a subsidiary creditors ledger?

14. Marvin Maxwell, controller of Carlson Company, approves all vouchers before they are submitted to the treasurer for payment. What procedure can Maxwell add to the system to assure that the documents accompanying the vouchers and supporting the expenditures are not "reused" to improperly support future vouchers?

15. In what order are vouchers ordinarily filed (a) in the unpaid voucher file, and (b) in the paid voucher file? Give reasons for answers.

16. What are the two possibilities for reporting "purchases discounts" on the income statement?

17. Merchandise with an invoice price of $10,000 is purchased subject to terms of 1/10, n/30. Determine the cost of the merchandise according to each of the following systems:

   (a) Discounts taken are treated as deductions from the invoice price.
      (1) The invoice is paid within the discount period.
      (2) The invoice is paid after the discount period has expired.
   (b) Discounts taken are treated as other income.
      (1) The invoice is paid within the discount period.
      (2) The invoice is paid after the discount period has expired.
   (c) Discounts allowable are treated as deductions from the invoice price regardless of when payment is made.
      (1) The invoice is paid within the discount period.
      (2) The invoice is paid after the discount period has expired.

18. What account or accounts are debited when recording the voucher (a) establishing a petty cash fund and (b) replenishing a petty cash fund?

19. The petty cash account has a debit balance of $500. At the end of the accounting period, there is $93 in the petty cash fund along with petty cash receipts totaling $407. Should the fund be replenished as of the last day of the period? Discuss.

20. What is meant by electronic funds transfer?

Exercises

Exercise 7-1. The following data are accumulated for use in reconciling the bank account of C. D. Roberts Co. for May:
(a) Balance per bank statement at May 31, $6,912.15.
(b) Balance per depositor's records at May 31, $6,371.70.
(c) Deposit in transit not recorded by bank, $525.50.
(d) Checks outstanding, $1,059.20.
(e) Bank debit memorandum for service charges, $11.25.
(f) A check for $135 in payment of a voucher was erroneously recorded in the check register as $153.

Prepare a bank reconciliation.

Exercise 7-2. Using the data presented in Exercise 7-1, prepare in general journal form the entry or entries that should be made by the depositor.

Exercise 7-3. Accompanying a bank statement for Wilson Inc. is a credit memorandum for $1,230, representing the principal ($1,200) and interest ($30) on a note that had been collected by the bank. The depositor had been notified by the bank at the time of the collection but had made no entries. In general journal form, present the entry that should be made by the depositor.

Exercise 7-4. Record in general journal form the following selected transactions, indicating above each entry the name of the register in which it should be recorded. Assume the use of a voucher register and a check register similar to those illustrated in this chapter. All invoices are recorded at invoice price.

Oct. 1. Recorded Voucher No. 471 for $5,000, payable to LaMarr Co., for merchandise purchased on terms 1/10, n/30.
2. Recorded Voucher No. 474 for $380, payable to Blum Office Supply, for office equipment repairs, terms 1/10, n/30.
9. Recorded Voucher No. 485 for $2,400, payable to Blair Inc., for office equipment purchased on terms 2/10, n/30.
19. Issued Check No. 464 in payment of Voucher No. 485.
24. Recorded Voucher No. 490 for $184.37 to replenish the petty cash fund for the following disbursements: store supplies, $60.12; office supplies, $49.95; miscellaneous general expense, $39.60; miscellaneous selling expense, $34.70.
25. Issued Check No. 474 in payment of Voucher No. 490.
30. Issued Check No. 479 in payment of Voucher No. 471.
31. Issued Check No. 480 in payment of Voucher No. 474.

Exercise 7-5. Record in general journal form the following related transactions, assuming that invoices for commodities purchased are recorded at their net price after deducting the allowable discount:

> May 5. Voucher No. 610 is prepared for merchandise purchased for Lee Co., $2,000, terms 1/10, n/30.
>
> 15. Voucher No. 621 is prepared for merchandise purchased from Miller Co., $4,500, terms 2/10, n/30.
>
> 25. Check No. 590 is issued, payable to Miller Co., in payment of Voucher No. 621.
>
> June 3. Check No. 599 is issued, payable to Lee Co., in payment of Voucher No. 610.

Exercise 7-6. Prepare in general journal form the entries to record the following:

> (a) Voucher No. 91 is prepared to establish a petty cash fund of $250.
> (b) Check No. 80 is issued in payment of Voucher No. 91.
> (c) The amount of cash in the petty cash fund is now $24.45. Voucher No. 120 is prepared to replenish the fund, based on the following summary of petty cash receipts: office supplies, $77.75; miscellaneous selling expense, $66.50; miscellaneous general expense, $80.85.
> (d) Check No. 110 is issued by the disbursing officer in payment of Voucher No. 120. The check is cashed and the money is placed in the fund.

Exercise 7-7. Record in general journal form the following transactions:

> (a) Voucher No. 112 is prepared to establish a change fund of $200.
> (b) Check No. 101 is issued in payment of Voucher No. 112.
> (c) Cash sales for the day, according to the cash register tapes, were $942.40, and cash on hand is $1,145.10. A bank deposit ticket was prepared for $945.10.

Problems
(Problems in Appendix B: 7-1B, 7-3B, 7-4B, 7-5B.)

Problem 7-1A. The cash in bank account for Martin Co. at July 31 of the current year indicated a balance of $12,192.50 after both the cash receipts journal and the check register for July had been posted. The bank statement indicated a balance of $19,955.65 on July 31. Comparison of the bank statement and the accompanying canceled checks and memorandums with the records revealed the following reconciling items:

> (a) A deposit of $4,015.20, representing receipts of July 31, had been made too late to appear on the bank statement.
> (b) Checks outstanding totaled $9,090.75.
> (c) The bank had collected for Martin Co. $3,045 on a note left for collection. The face of the note was $3,000.
> (d) A check drawn for $470 had been erroneously charged by the bank as $740.
> (e) A check for $72.50 returned with the statement had been recorded in the check register as $7.25. The check was for the payment of an obligation to Shaw Equipment Company for the purchase of office equipment on account.
> (f) Bank service charges for July amounted to $22.15.

Instructions:

(1) Prepare a bank reconciliation.

(2) Journalize the necessary entries. The accounts have not been closed. The voucher system is used.

Problem 7-2A. Anderson Company has just adopted the policy of depositing all cash receipts in the bank and of making all payments by check in conjunction with the voucher system. The following transactions were selected from those completed in May of the current year:

May   1. Recorded Voucher No. 1 to establish a petty cash fund of $150 and a change fund of $750.

1. Issued Check No. 729 in payment of Voucher No. 1.

2. Recorded Voucher No. 3 to establish an advance to salespersons fund of $1,000.

2. Issued Check No. 731 in payment of Voucher No. 3.

15. The cash sales for the day, according to the cash register tapes, totaled $2,917.20. The combined count of all cash on hand (including the change fund) totaled $3,668.70.

20. Recorded Voucher No. 29 to reimburse the petty cash fund for the following disbursements, each evidenced by a petty cash receipt:

May   3. Store supplies, $8.50.

6. Express charges on merchandise purchased, $12.50.

7. Office supplies, $15.75.

9. Office supplies, $9.20.

11. Postage stamps, $20 (Office Supplies).

12. Repair to adding machine, $22.50 (Misc. General Expense).

14. Postage due on special delivery letter, $1.05 (Misc. General Expense).

15. Repair to typewriter, $26.85 (Misc. General Expense).

16. Express charges on merchandise purchased, $5.75.

19. Telegram charges, $3.75 (Misc. Selling Expense).

20. Issued Check No. 760 in payment of Voucher No. 29.

26. The cash sales for the day, according to the cash register tapes, totaled $2,605.50. The count of all cash on hand totaled $3,351.10.

31. Recorded Voucher No. 60 to replenish the advances to salespersons fund for the following expenditures for travel: Frank Bowen, $212.40; Linda James, $301.50; Martha Potter, $297.10.

31. Issued Check No. 773 in payment of Voucher No. 60.

Instructions: Record the transactions in general journal form.

Problem 7-3A. Body 'N Sole had the following vouchers in its unpaid voucher file at July 31 of the current year:

Due Date	Voucher No.	Creditor	Date of Invoice	Amount	Terms
Aug. 5	780	Sports Fashions	July 26	$2,500	2/10, n/30
Aug. 12	768	Ace Tennis	July 13	1,100	n/30
Aug. 13	770	Carr Shoe Co.	July 14	975	n/30

The vouchers prepared and the checks issued during the month of August were as follows:

VOUCHERS

Date	Voucher No.	Payee	Amount	Terms	Distribution
Aug. 1	788	Dale Office Supply Co.	$ 89	cash	Store supplies
4	789	Gibbs Co.	900	2/10, n/30	Purchases
5	790	Powell Co.	1,250	2/10, n/30	Purchases
8	791	The Trophy Shop	500	1/10, n/30	Purchases
13	792	American National Bank	12,700		Note payable, $12,000 Interest, $700
15	793	Smith Office Supply	4,100	n/30	Office equipment
20	794	Sax Printers	215	cash	Office supplies
22	795	Bach Sportswear	1,250	2/10, n/30	Purchases
25	796	The Ski Outlet.	900	1/10, n/30	Purchases
28	797	East Indiana Sports Shop	550	n/30	Purchases
30	798	E. J. Wallace	11,000	cash	Delivery equipment
31	799	Petty Cash	92		Office supplies, $22 Store supplies, $19 Miscellaneous selling expense, $29 Miscellaneous general expense, $22

CHECKS

Date	Check No.	Payee	Voucher Paid	Amount
Aug. 1	760	Dale Office Supply Co.	788	$ 89
5	761	Sports Fashions	780	2,450
12	762	Ace Tennis	768	1,100
13	763	Carr Shoe Co.	770	975
13	764	American National Bank	792	12,700
14	765	Gibbs Co.	789	882
15	766	Powell Co.	790	1,225
18	767	The Trophy Shop	791	495
20	768	Sax Printers	794	215
30	769	E. J. Wallace	798	11,000
31	770	Petty Cash	799	92

Instructions:

(1) Set up a four-column account for Accounts Payable, Account No. 205, and record the balance of $4,575 as of August 1.

(2) Record the August vouchers in a voucher register similar to the one illustrated in this chapter, with the following amount columns: Accounts Payable Cr., Purchases Dr., Store Supplies Dr., Office Supplies Dr., and Sundry Accounts Dr. Purchases invoices are recorded at the gross amount.

(3) Record the August checks in a check register similar to the one illustrated in this chapter, but omit the Bank Deposits and Balance columns. As each check is recorded in the check register, the date and check number should be inserted

in the appropriate columns of the voucher register. (Assume that notations for payment of the July vouchers are made in the voucher register for that month.)

(4) Total and rule the registers and post to Accounts Payable.

(5) Prepare a schedule of unpaid vouchers.

If the working papers correlating with the textbook are not used, omit Problem 7-4A.

Problem 7-4A. Portions of the voucher register, check register, and accounts payable account of R. T. Ritter Inc. are presented in the working papers. Expenditures, cash disbursements, and other selected transactions completed during the period March 25–31 of the current year are described as follows:

Mar. 25. Recorded Voucher No. 491 payable to Lance Co. for merchandise, $4,000, terms 2/10, n/30. (Purchases invoices are recorded at the gross amount.)

25. Issued Check No. 472 to Bowen Co. in payment of Voucher No. 479 for $1,500, less cash discount of 1%.

26. Recorded Voucher No. 492 payable to Southern Automobile Insurance Co. for an insurance policy, $1,584.

26. Issued Check No. 473 in payment of Voucher No. 492.

26. Recorded Voucher No. 493 payable to Hinton Co. for merchandise, $2,400, terms 2/10, n/30.

27. Recorded Voucher No. 494 for $5,100 payable to Palmer National Bank for note payable, $5,000, and interest, $100.

27. Issued Check No. 474 in payment of Voucher No. 494.

28. Issued Check No. 475 to Henry Stevens Co. in payment of Voucher No. 487 for $1,550, less cash discount of 2%.

29. Recorded Voucher No. 495 payable to Danville Times for advertising, $400.

29. Issued Check No. 476 in payment of Voucher No. 495.

31. Recorded Voucher No. 496 payable to Petty Cash for $179.90, distributed as follows: office supplies, $42.50; advertising expense, $31.45; delivery expense, $22.50; miscellaneous selling expense, $47.22; miscellaneous general expense, $36.23.

31. Issued Check No. 477 in payment of Voucher No. 496.

After the journals are posted at the end of the month, the cash in bank account has a debit balance of $16,497.60.

The bank statement indicates a March 31 balance of $19,823.85. A comparison of paid checks with the check register reveals that No. 473, 475, and 476 are outstanding. Check No. 449 for $50.75, which appeared on the February reconciliation as outstanding, is still outstanding. A debit memorandum accompanying the bank statement indicates a charge of $227.50 for a check drawn by Frank Reese, a customer, which was returned because of insufficient funds.

Instructions:

(1) Record the transactions for March 25–31 in the appropriate journals.

(2) Total and rule the voucher register and the check register, and post totals to the accounts payable account.

(3) Complete the schedule of unpaid vouchers. (Compare the total with the balance of the accounts payable account as of March 31.)

(4) Prepare a bank reconciliation and journalize any necessary entries.

Problem 7-5A. Ferris Company employs the voucher system in controlling expenditures and disbursements. All cash receipts are deposited in a night depository after banking hours each Wednesday and Friday. The data required to reconcile the bank statement as of July 31 have been abstracted from various documents and records and are reproduced as follows. To facilitate identification, the sources of the data are printed in capital letters.

CASH IN BANK ACCOUNT:
  Balance as of July 1 . . . . $11,917.15

CASH RECEIPTS JOURNAL:
  Total of Cash in Bank Debit column for month of July 6,772.60

DUPLICATE DEPOSIT TICKETS:
  Date and amount of each deposit in July:

Date	Amount	Date	Amount	Date	Amount
July 2	$760.10	July 12	$589.10	July 23	$792.10
5	819.75	16	797.60	26	601.50
9	784.14	19	701.26	30	927.05

CHECK REGISTER:
  Number and amount of each check issued in July:

Check No.	Amount	Check No.	Amount	Check No.	Amount
414	$ 68.70	421	$202.75	428	$ 291.34
415	620.55	422	VOID	429	179.22
416	319.10	423	VOID	430	882.20
417	627.13	424	918.01	431	982.16
418	103.80	425	558.63	432	62.40
419	220.10	426	530.03	433	675.48
420	238.87	427	338.73	434	97.90

  Total amount of checks issued in July $7,917.10

JULY BANK STATEMENT:
  Balance as of July 1 . . . . $11,899.29
  Deposits and other credits 9,145.65
  Checks and other debits . . . . (8,172.45)
  Balance as of July 31 . . . . $12,872.49

  Date and amount of each deposit in July:

Date	Amount	Date	Amount	Date	Amount
July 1	$725.10	July 11	$784.14	July 21	$701.26
3	760.10	13	589.10	24	792.10
6	819.75	17	797.60	28	601.50

CHECKS ACCOMPANYING JULY BANK STATEMENT:
  Number and amount of each check, rearranged in numerical sequence:

Check No.	Amount	Check No.	Amount	Check No.	Amount
379	$217.60	418	$103.80	426	$530.03
412	97.97	419	220.10	427	338.73
413	219.17	420	238.87	429	179.22
414	68.70	421	212.75	430	882.20
415	620.55	424	918.01	431	982.16
416	319.10	425	558.63	432	62.40
417	627.13			433	675.48

BANK MEMORANDUMS ACCOMPANYING JULY BANK STATEMENT:
Date, description, and amount of each memorandum:

Date	Description	Amount
July 7	Bank credit memo for note collected:	
	Principal	$2,500.00
	Interest	75.00
20	Bank debit memo for check returned because of insufficient	
	funds..	90.10
31	Bank debit memo for service charges.....................	9.75

BANK RECONCILIATION FOR PRECEDING MONTH:

Ferris Company
Bank Reconciliation
June 30, 19--

Balance per bank statement		$11,899.29
Add deposit of June 30, not recorded by bank.........		725.10
		$12,624.39
Deduct outstanding checks:		
No. 379..	$217.60	
407..	172.50	
412..	97.97	
413..	219.17	707.24
Adjusted balance		$11,917.15
Balance per depositor's records.....................		$11,927.65
Deduct service charges		10.50
Adjusted balance		$11,917.15

Instructions:

(1) Prepare a bank reconciliation as of July 31. If errors in recording deposits or checks are discovered, assume that the errors were made by the company. Assume that all deposits are from cash sales. All checks are in payment of vouchers.

(2) Journalize the necessary entries. The accounts have not been closed.

(3) What is the amount of cash in bank that should appear on the balance sheet as of July 31?

Mini-Case

The records of Valdez Company indicate a November 30 cash in bank balance of $18,901.62, which includes undeposited receipts for November 28, 29, and 30. The cash balance on the bank statement as of November 30 is $16,344.41. This balance includes a note of $1,200 plus $30 of interest collected by the bank but not recorded in the cash receipts journal. Checks outstanding on November 30 were as follows: No. 62, $116.25; No. 183, $150.00; No. 284, $253.25; No. 1621, $190.71; No. 1623, $206.80; and No. 1632, $145.28.

On November 1, the Valdez Company cashier submitted his resignation, effective at the end of the month. Before leaving on November 30, the cashier prepared the following bank reconciliation:

Balance per books, November 30		$18,901.62
Add outstanding checks:		
1621	$190.71	
1623	206.80	
1632	145.28	442.79
		$19,344.41
Less undeposited receipts		3,000.00
Balance per bank, November 30		$16,344.41
Deduct unrecorded note with interest		1,230.00
True cash, November 30		$15,114.41

Adding Machine Tape of Outstanding Checks

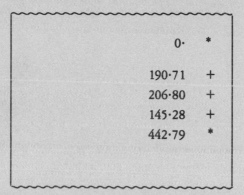

Subsequently, the owner of Valdez Company discovered that the cashier had stolen all undeposited receipts on hand on November 30 in excess of $3,000. The owner, a close family friend, has asked your help in determining the amount that the former cashier has stolen.

Instructions:

(1) Determine the amount the cashier stole from Valdez Company. Show your computations in good form.

(2) How did the cashier attempt to conceal the theft?

(3) (a) Identify two major weaknesses in Valdez Company's internal accounting controls, which allowed the cashier to steal the undeposited cash receipts.

(b) Recommend improvements in Valdez Company's internal accounting controls, so that similar types of thefts of undeposited cash receipts could be prevented.

(AICPA adapted)

8

Receivables and Temporary Investments

CHAPTER OBJECTIVES

Describe and illustrate accounting for receivables.

Describe and illustrate accounting for uncollectible receivables.

Describe and illustrate accounting for temporary investments.

8

CHAPTER

For many businesses, the revenue from sales on a credit basis is the largest factor influencing the amount of net income. As credit is granted, businesses must account for the resulting receivables, which may represent a substantial portion of the total current assets. As the receivables are collected, the cash realized is accounted for in the manner discussed in Chapter 7. If the amount of cash on hand exceeds immediate cash requirements, the excess cash might be invested in securities until needed. These securities are accounted for as temporary investments.

CLASSIFICA-TION OF RECEIVABLES

The term **receivables** includes all money claims against people, organizations, or other debtors. Receivables are acquired by a business enterprise in various kinds of transactions, the most common being the sale of merchandise or services on a credit basis.

Credit may be granted on open account or on the basis of a formal instrument of credit such as a promissory note. Promissory notes are usually used for credit periods of more than sixty days, as in sales of equipment on the installment plan, and for transactions of relatively large dollar amounts. Promissory notes may also be used in settlement of an open account and in borrowing or lending money.

A **promissory note**, frequently referred to simply as a **note**, is a written promise to pay a sum certain in money on demand or at a definite time. As in the case of a check, it must be payable to the order of a certain person or firm, or to bearer. It must also be signed by the person or firm that makes the promise. The one to whose order the note is payable is called the **payee**, and the one making the promise is called the **maker**. The enterprise owning a note refers to it as a **note receivable** and records it as an asset at its face amount.

A note that provides for the payment of interest for the period between the issuance date and the due date is called an **interest-bearing note**. If a note makes no provision for interest, it is said to be **non-interest-bearing**.

The amount that is due at the maturity or due date is called the **maturity value**. The maturity value of a non-interest-bearing note is the face amount. The maturity value of an interest-bearing note is the sum of the face amount and the interest.

From the point of view of the creditor, a claim evidenced by a note has some advantages over a claim in the form of an account receivable. By signing a note, the debtor acknowledges the debt and agrees to pay it according to the terms given. The note is therefore a stronger legal claim if there is court action. It is also more liquid than an open account because the holder can usually transfer it more readily to a bank or other financial agency in exchange for cash.

Accounts and notes receivable originating from sales transactions are sometimes called **trade receivables**. In the absence of other descriptive words or phrases, accounts and notes receivable may be assumed to have originated from sales in the usual course of the business.

Other receivables include interest receivable, loans to officers or employees, and loans to affiliated companies. To facilitate their classification and presentation on the balance sheet, a general ledger account should be maintained for each type of receivable, with proper subsidiary ledgers.

All receivables that are expected to be realized in cash within a year are presented in the current assets section of the balance sheet. Those that are not currently collectible, such as long-term loans, should be listed under the caption "Investments" below the current assets section.

<table>
<tr><td>**DETERMINING**
INTEREST</td><td></td></tr>
</table>

DETERMINING
INTEREST

Interest rates are usually stated in terms of a period of a year, regardless of the actual period of time involved. Thus the interest on $2,000 for a year at 12% would be $240 (12% of $2,000); the interest on $2,000 for one fourth of a year at 12% would be $60 (¼ of $240).

Notes covering a period of time longer than a year ordinarily provide that the interest be paid semiannually, quarterly, or at some other stated interval. The time involved in commercial credit transactions is usually less than a year, and the interest provided for by a note is payable at the time the note is paid. In computing interest for a period of less than a year, agencies of the federal government use the actual number of days in the year. For example, 90 days is considered to be 90/365 of a year. The usual commercial practice is to use 360 as the denominator of the fraction; thus 90 days is considered to be 90/360 of a year.

The basic formula for computing interest is as follows:

$$\text{Principal} \times \text{Rate} \times \text{Time} = \text{Interest}$$

To illustrate the use of the formula, assume that a note for $1,500 is payable in 20 days with interest at 12%. The interest would be $10, computed as follows:

$$\$1,500 \times \frac{12}{100} \times \frac{20}{360} = \$10 \text{ interest}$$

One of the commonly used shortcut methods of computing interest is called the 60-day, 6% method. The 6% annual rate is converted to the effective rate of 1% for a 60-day period (60/360 of 6%). Accordingly, the interest on any amount for 60 days at 6% is determined by moving the decimal point in the principal two places to the left. For example, the interest on $1,500 at 6% for 60 days is $15. The amount obtained by moving the decimal point must be adjusted (1) for interest rates greater or less than 6% and (2) for periods of time greater or less than 60 days. For example, the interest on $1,500 at 6% for 90 days is $22.50 (90/60 of $15). The interest on $1,500 at 12% for 60 days is $30 (12/6 of $15).

Comprehensive interest tables are available and are commonly used by financial institutions and other enterprises that require frequent interest calculations. Nevertheless, students of business should know the mechanics of interest computations well enough to use them with complete accuracy and to recognize major errors in interest amounts that come to their attention.

When the term of a note is stated in months instead of in days, each month may be considered as being 1/12 of a year, or, alternatively, the actual number of days in the term may be counted. For example, the interest on a 3-month note dated June 1 could be computed on the basis of 3/12 of a year or on the basis of 92/360 of a year. It is the usual commercial practice to use the first method, while banks usually charge interest for the exact number of days. For the sake of simplicity, the usual commercial practice will be assumed in all cases.

DETERMINING
DUE DATE

The period of time between the issuance date and the maturity date of a short-term note may be stated in either days or months. When the term of a note is stated in days, the due date is the specified number of days after its issuance. To illustrate, the due date of a 90-day note dated March 16 may be determined as follows:

<table>
<tr><td>DETERMINATION OF DUE
DATE OF NOTE</td><td>Term of the note . . . .</td><td></td><td>90</td></tr>
<tr><td></td><td>March (days) . . . .</td><td>31</td><td></td></tr>
<tr><td></td><td>Date of note . . . .</td><td><u>16</u></td><td><u>15</u></td></tr>
<tr><td></td><td>Number of days remaining . . . .</td><td></td><td>75</td></tr>
<tr><td></td><td>April (days) . . . .</td><td></td><td><u>30</u></td></tr>
<tr><td></td><td></td><td></td><td>45</td></tr>
<tr><td></td><td>May (days) . . . .</td><td></td><td><u>31</u></td></tr>
<tr><td></td><td>Due date, June . . . .</td><td></td><td>14</td></tr>
</table>

When the term of a note is stated as a certain number of months after the issuance date, the due date is determined by counting the number of months from the issuance date. Thus, a 3-month note dated June 5 would be due on September 5. In those cases in which there is no date in the month of maturity that corresponds to the issuance date, the due date becomes the last day of the month. For example, a 2-month note dated July 31 would be due on September 30.

NOTES RECEIVABLE AND INTEREST INCOME

The typical retail enterprise makes most of its sales for cash or on account. If the account of a customer becomes delinquent, the creditor may insist that the account be converted into a note. In this way, the debtor is given more time, and if the creditor needs more funds, the note may be endorsed and transferred to a bank or other financial agency. Notes may also be received by retail firms that sell merchandise on long-term credit. For example, a dealer in household appliances may require a down payment at the time of sale and accept a note or a series of notes for the remainder. Such arrangements usually provide for monthly payments. Wholesale firms and manufacturers are likely to receive notes more often than retailers, although here, too, much depends upon the kind of product and the length of the credit period.

When a note is received from a customer to apply on account, the facts are recorded by debiting the notes receivable account and crediting the accounts receivable controlling account and the account of the customer from whom the note is received. If the note is interest-bearing, interest must also be recorded as appropriate.

To illustrate, assume that the account of W. A. Bunn Co., which has a debit balance of $6,000, is past due. A 30-day, 12% note for that amount, dated December 21, 1984, is accepted in settlement of the account. The entry to record the transaction is as follows:

<table>
<tr><td>Dec. 21</td><td>Notes Receivable . . . .</td><td>6,000</td><td></td></tr>
<tr><td></td><td>Accounts Receivable — W. A. Bunn Co. . . .</td><td></td><td>6,000</td></tr>
<tr><td></td><td>Received a 30-day, 12% note dated
December 21, 1984.</td><td></td><td></td></tr>
</table>

On December 31, 1984, the end of the fiscal year, an adjusting entry would be recorded for the accrual of the interest from December 21 to December 31. The entry to record the accrued revenue of $20 ($6,000 × 12/100 × 10/360) is as follows:

		Adjusting Entry		
Dec.	31	Interest Receivable	20	
		Interest Income		20

Interest receivable is reported on the balance sheet at December 31, 1984, as a current asset. The interest income account is closed at December 31 and the amount is reported in the Other Income section of the income statement for the year ended December 31, 1984.

When the amount due on the note is collected in 1985, part of the interest received will effect a reduction of the interest that was receivable at December 31, 1984, and the remainder will represent revenue for 1985. To avoid the possibility of failing to recognize this division and to avoid the inconvenience of analyzing the receipt of interest in 1985, a reversing entry is made after the accounts are closed. The effect of the entry, which is illustrated as follows, is to transfer the debit balance in the interest receivable account to the debit side of the interest income account.

		Reversing Entry		
Jan.	1	Interest Income	20	
		Interest Receivable		20

At the time the note matures and payment is received, the entire amount of the interest received is credited to Interest Income, as illustrated by the following entry that would be recorded in the cash receipts journal:

Jan. 20	Cash....................................	6,060	
	Notes Receivable		6,000
	Interest Income		60

After the foregoing entries are posted, the interest income account will appear as follows:

ACCOUNT INTEREST INCOME   ACCOUNT NO. 811

Date		Item	Post. Ref.	Debit	Credit	Balance Debit	Balance Credit
1984							
Dec.	12		CR20		120		946
	31	Adjusting	J17		20		966
	31	Closing	J17	966		—	—
1985 Jan.	1	Reversing	J18	20		20	
	20		CR21		60		40

The adjusting and reversing process divided the $60 of interest received on January 20, 1985, into two parts for accounting purposes: (1) $20 representing the interest income for 1984 (recorded by the adjusting entry) and (2) $40 representing the interest income for 1985 (the balance in the interest income account at January 20, 1985).

Discounting Notes Receivable

Instead of being retained by the holder until maturity, notes receivable may be transferred to a bank by endorsement. The **discount** (interest) charged is computed on the maturity value of the note for the period of time the bank must hold the note, namely the time that will pass between the date of the transfer and the due date of the note. The amount of the proceeds paid to the endorser is the excess of the maturity value over the discount.

To illustrate, assume that a 90-day, 12% note receivable for $1,800, dated November 8, is discounted at the payee's bank on December 3 at the rate of 14%. The data used in determining the effect of the transaction are as follows:

Face value of note dated Nov. 8		$1,800.00
Interest on note—90 days at 12%		54.00
Maturity value of note due Feb. 6		$1,854.00
Discount period—Dec. 3 to Feb. 6	65 days	
Discount on maturity value—65 days at 14%		46.87
Proceeds		$1,807.13

The same information is presented graphically in the following flow diagram. In reading the data, follow the direction of the arrows.

DIAGRAM OF DISCOUNTING A NOTE RECEIVABLE

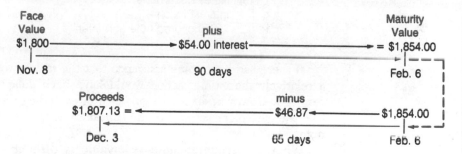

The excess of the proceeds from discounting the note, $1,807.13, over its face value, $1,800, is recorded as interest income. The entry for the transaction, in general journal form, is as follows:

Dec. 3	Cash	1,807.13	
	Notes Receivable		1,800.00
	Interest Income		7.13

It should be observed that the proceeds from discounting a note receivable may be less than the face value. When this happens, the excess of the face value over the proceeds is recorded as interest expense. The amount and direction of the difference between the interest rate and the discount rate will affect the result, as will the relationship between the full term of the note and the length of the discount period.

Without a statement limiting responsibility, the endorser of a note is committed to paying the note if the maker should default. Such potential obligations that will become actual liabilities only if certain events occur in the future are called **contingent liabilities**. Thus, the endorser of a note that has been discounted has a contingent liability that is in effect until the due date. If the maker pays the promised amount at maturity, the contingent liability is removed without any action on the part of the endorser. If, on the other hand, the maker defaults and the endorser is notified according to legal requirements, the liability becomes an actual one.

Significant contingent liabilities should be disclosed on the balance sheet or in an accompanying note. Disclosure requirements for contingent liabilities are discussed and illustrated in Chapter 11.

Dishonored Notes Receivable

If the maker of a note fails to pay the debt on the due date, the note is said to be **dishonored**. A dishonored note receivable is no longer negotiable, and for that reason the holder usually transfers the claim, including any interest due, to the accounts receivable account. For example, if the $6,000, 30-day, 12% note received and recorded on December 21 (page 223) had been dishonored at maturity, the entry to charge the note, including the interest, back to the customer's account would have been as follows:

Jan. 20	Accounts Receivable — W. A. Bunn Co.	6,060	
	Notes Receivable.		6,000
	Interest Income		60
	Dishonored note and interest.		

If there had been some assurance that the maker would pay the note within a relatively short time, action would have been delayed until the matter was resolved. However, for future guidance in extending credit, it may be desirable that the customer's account in the subsidiary ledger disclose the dishonor of the note.

When a discounted note receivable is dishonored, the holder usually notifies the endorser of such fact and asks for payment. If the request for payment and notification of dishonor are timely, the endorser is legally obligated to pay the amount due on the note. The entire amount paid to the holder by the endorser, including the interest, should be debited to the account receivable of the maker. To illustrate, assume that the $1,800, 90-day, 12% note discounted on December 3 (page 225) is dishonored at maturity by the maker, Pryor & Co. The entry to record the payment by the endorser, in general journal form, would be as follows:

Feb. 6	Accounts Receivable — Pryor & Co.	1,854	
	Cash.		1,854

In some cases, the holder of a dishonored note gives the endorser a notarized statement of the facts of the dishonor. The fee for this statement, known as a **protest fee,** is charged to the endorser, who in turn charges it to the maker of the note. If there had been a protest fee of $6 in connection with the dishonor and the payment recorded above, the debit to the maker's account and the credit to Cash would have been $1,860.

UNCOLLECT-IBLE RECEIVABLES

When merchandise or services are sold without the immediate receipt of cash, a part of the claims against customers usually proves to be uncollectible. This is usually the case, regardless of the care used in granting credit and the effectiveness of the collection procedures used. The operating expense incurred because of the failure to collect receivables is called an expense or a loss from **uncollectible accounts, doubtful accounts,** or **bad debts.**[1]

There is no single general rule for determining when an account or a note becomes uncollectible. The fact that a debtor fails to pay an account according to a sales contract or dishonors a note on the due date does not necessarily mean that the account will be uncollectible. Bankruptcy of the debtor is one of the most positive indications of partial or complete worthlessness of a receivable. Other evidence includes closing of the debtor's business, disappearance of the debtor, failure of repeated attempts to collect, and the barring of collection by the statute of limitations.

There are two generally accepted methods of accounting for receivables that are believed to be uncollectible. The **allowance method,** which is sometimes called the **reserve method,** provides in advance for uncollectible receivables. The other procedure, called the **direct write-off method** or **direct charge-off method,** recognizes the expense only when certain accounts are judged to be worthless.

ALLOWANCE METHOD OF ACCOUNTING FOR UNCOLLECT-IBLES

Most large business enterprises provide currently for the amount of their trade receivables estimated to become uncollectible in the future. The advance provision for future uncollectibility is made by an adjusting entry at the end of the fiscal period. As with all periodic adjustments, the entry serves two purposes. In this instance, it provides for (1) the reduction of the value of the receivables to the amount of cash expected to be realized from them in the future and (2) the allocation to the current period of the expected expense resulting from such reduction.

Assumed data for a new business firm will be used to explain and illustrate the allowance method. The enterprise began business in August and chose to use the calendar year as its fiscal year. The accounts receivable account, illustrated as follows, has a balance of $105,000 at the end of the period.

---

[1]If both notes and accounts are involved, both may be included in the title, as in "uncollectible notes and accounts expense," or the general term "uncollectible receivables expense" may be substituted. Because of its wide usage and simplicity, "uncollectible accounts expense" will be used in this book.

ACCOUNT ACCOUNTS RECEIVABLE   ACCOUNT NO. 114

| Date | | Item | Post. Ref. | Debit | Credit | Balance | |
						Debit	Credit
19--							
Aug.	31		S3	20,000		20,000	
Sept.	30		S6	25,000		45,000	
	30		CR4		15,000	30,000	
Oct.	31		S10	40,000		70,000	
	31		CR7		25,000	45,000	
Nov.	30		S13	38,000		83,000	
	30		CR10		23,000	60,000	
Dec.	31		S16	75,000		135,000	
	31		CR13		30,000	105,000	

Among the individual customers accounts making up the $105,000 balance in Accounts Receivable are a number of balances which are a varying number of days past due. No specific accounts are believed to be wholly uncollectible at this time, but it seems likely that some will be collected only in part and that others are likely to become entirely worthless. Based on a careful study, it is estimated that a total of $3,000 will eventually prove to be uncollectible. The amount expected to be realized from the accounts receivable is, therefore, $105,000 − $3,000, or $102,000, and the $3,000 reduction in value is the uncollectible accounts expense for the period.

The $3,000 reduction in accounts receivable cannot yet be identified with specific customers accounts in the subsidiary ledger and should therefore not be credited to the controlling account in the general ledger. The customary practice is to use a contra asset account entitled Allowance for Doubtful Accounts. The adjusting entry to record the expense and the reduction in the asset is as follows:

	Adjusting Entry			
Dec. 31	Uncollectible Accounts Expense	717	3,000	
	Allowance for Doubtful Accounts . . .	115		3,000

The two accounts to which the entry is posted are illustrated as follows:

ACCOUNT UNCOLLECTIBLE ACCOUNTS EXPENSE   ACCOUNT NO. 717

| Date | | Item | Post. Ref. | Debit | Credit | Balance | |
						Debit	Credit
19--							
Dec.	31	Adjusting	J4	3,000		3,000	

ACCOUNT ALLOWANCE FOR DOUBTFUL ACCOUNTS   ACCOUNT NO. 115

| Date | | Item | Post. Ref. | Debit | Credit | Balance | |
						Debit	Credit
19--							
Dec.	31	Adjusting	J4		3,000		3,000

The debit balance of $105,000 in Accounts Receivable is the amount of the total claims against customers on open account, and the credit balance of $3,000 in Allowance for Doubtful Accounts is the amount to be deducted from Accounts Receivable to determine the **expected realizable value.** The $3,000 reduction in the asset was transferred to Uncollectible Accounts Expense, which will in turn be closed to Income Summary.

Uncollectible accounts expense is generally reported on the income statement as a general expense, because the credit-granting and collection duties are the responsibilities of departments within the general administrative framework. The accounts receivable may be listed on the balance sheet at the net amount of $102,000, with a notation in parentheses showing the amount of the allowance, or the details may be presented as shown on the following partial balance sheet. When the allowance account includes provision for doubtful notes as well as accounts, it should be deducted from the total of Notes Receivable and Accounts Receivable.

ACCOUNTS
RECEIVABLE ON
BALANCE SHEET

Richards Company
Balance Sheet
December 31, 19--

Assets

Current assets:

Cash		$ 21,600
Accounts receivable	$105,000	
Less allowance for doubtful accounts	3,000	102,000

Write-Offs to the
Allowance Account

When an account is believed to be uncollectible, it is written off against the allowance account as in the following entry:

Jan. 21	Allowance for Doubtful Accounts	110	
	Accounts Receivable— John Parker		110
	To write off the uncollectible account.		

During the year, as more accounts or portions of accounts are determined to be uncollectible, they are written off against Allowance for Doubtful Accounts in the same manner. Instructions for write-offs should originate with the credit manager or other designated official. The authorizations, which should always be written, serve as objective evidence in support of the accounting entry.

Naturally enough, the total amount written off against the allowance account during the period will rarely be equal to the amount in the account at the beginning of the period. The allowance account will have a credit balance at the end of the period if the write-offs during the period amount to less than the beginning balance. It will have a debit balance if the write-offs exceed the beginning balance. After the year-end adjusting entry is recorded, the allowance account will have a credit balance.

An account receivable that has been written off against the allowance account may later be collected. In such cases the account should be reinstated by an entry that is the exact reverse of the write-off entry. For example, assume that the account of $110 written off in the preceding journal entry is later collected. The entry to reinstate the account would be as follows:

June 10	Accounts Receivable—John Parker.........	110	
	Allowance for Doubtful Accounts..........		110
	To reinstate account written off earlier in the year.		

The cash received in payment would be recorded in the cash receipts journal as a receipt on account. Although it is possible to combine the reinstatement and the receipt of cash into a single debit and credit, the entries in the customer's account, with a proper notation, provide useful credit information.

Estimating Uncollectibles

The estimate of uncollectibles at the end of the fiscal period is based on past experience and forecasts of future business activity. When the trend of general sales volume is upward and there is relatively full employment, the amount of the expense should usually be less than when the trend is in the opposite direction. The estimate is customarily based on either (1) the amount of sales for the entire fiscal period or (2) the amount and the age of the receivable accounts at the end of the fiscal period.

Estimate Based on Sales

Accounts receivable are acquired as a result of sales on account. The amount of such sales during the year may therefore be used to determine the probable amount of the accounts that will be uncollectible. For example, if it is known from past experience that about 1% of charge sales will be uncollectible and the charge sales for a certain year amount to $300,000, the adjusting entry for uncollectible accounts at the end of the year would be as follows:

	Adjusting Entry		
Dec. 31	Uncollectible Accounts Expense	3,000	
	Allowance for Doubtful Accounts.........		3,000

Instead of charge sales, total sales (including those made for cash) may be used in developing the percentage. Total sales is obtainable from the ledger without the analysis that may be needed to determine charge sales. If the ratio of sales on account to cash sales does not change very much from year to year, the results obtained will be equally satisfactory. If in the above example the balance of the sales account at the end of the year is assumed to be $400,000, the application of ¾ of 1% to that amount would also yield an estimate of $3,000.

If it becomes apparent over a period of time that the amount of write-offs is always greater or less than the amount provided by the adjusting entry, the percentage applied to sales data should be changed accordingly. A newly established business enterprise, having no record of credit experience, may obtain data on the probable amount of the expense from trade association journals and other publications containing information on credit and collections.

The estimate-based-on-sales method of determining the uncollectible accounts expense is widely used. It is simple and it provides the best basis for charging uncollectible accounts expense to the period in which the related sales were made.

Estimate Based on Analysis of Receivables

The process of analyzing the receivable accounts is sometimes called **aging the receivables.** The base point for determining age is the due date of the account. The number and breadth of the time intervals used will vary according to the credit terms granted to customers. A portion of a typical analysis is as follows:

ANALYSIS OF ACCOUNTS RECEIVABLE

CUSTOMER	BALANCE	NOT DUE	1–30	31–60	61–90	91–180	181–365	over 365
				DAYS PAST DUE				
Ashby & Co.....	$ 150			$ 150				
B. T. Barr	610					$ 350	$260	
Brock Co.	470	$ 470						
J. Zimmer Co....	160							160
Total	$86,300	$75,000	$4,000	$3,100	$1,900	$1,200	$800	$300

The analysis is completed by adding the columns to determine the total amount of receivables in each age group. A sliding scale of percentages, based on experience, is next applied to obtain the estimated amount of uncollectibles in each group. The manner in which the data may be presented is illustrated as follows:

ESTIMATE OF UNCOLLECTIBLE ACCOUNTS

Age Interval	Balance	Percent	Amount
		Estimated Uncollectible Accounts	
Not due.....................	$75,000	2%	$1,500
1–30 days past due..........	4,000	5	200
31–60 days past due	3,100	10	310
61–90 days past due	1,900	20	380
91–180 days past due	1,200	30	360
181–365 days past due	800	50	400
Over 365 days past due......	300	80	240
Total.....................	$86,300		$3,390

The estimate of uncollectible accounts, $3,390 in the example above, is the amount to be deducted from accounts receivable to yield their expected realizable value. It is thus the amount of the desired balance of the allowance account after adjustment. The excess of this figure over the balance of the allowance account before adjustment is the amount of the current provision to be made for uncollectible accounts expense.

To continue the illustration, assume that the allowance account has a credit balance of $510 before adjustment. The amount to be added to this balance is therefore $3,390 − $510, or $2,880, and the adjusting entry is as follows:

	Adjusting Entry		
Dec. 31	Uncollectible Accounts Expense	2,880	
	Allowance for Doubtful Accounts		2,880

After the adjusting entry is posted, the balance in the allowance account will be $3,390, which is the desired amount. If there had been a debit balance of $300 in the allowance account before the year-end adjustment, the amount of the adjustment would have been $3,390 (the desired balance) + $300 (the negative balance), or $3,690.

Estimation of uncollectible accounts expense based on an analysis of receivables is less common than estimations based on sales volume. It is sometimes preferred because it gives a more accurate estimate of the current realizable value of the receivables.

DIRECT WRITE-OFF METHOD OF ACCOUNTING FOR UNCOLLECTIBLES

If an enterprise sells most of its goods or services on a cash basis, the amount of its expense from uncollectible accounts is usually small in relation to its revenue. The amount of its receivables at any time is also likely to represent a relatively small part of its total current assets. These observations are based on the assumption that the credit period is short, which would be usual if sales are mainly on a cash basis, and that credit policies and collection procedures are adequate. The kind of service or the product sold and the type of customers may also have an important bearing on collection experience. For example, an enterprise that sells most of its output on account to a small number of companies, all of which are financially strong, will have little, if any, expense from failure to collect its accounts.

In such cases, as well as in many small business and professional enterprises, it is satisfactory to delay recognition of uncollectibility until the period in which certain accounts are believed to be worthless and are actually written off as an expense. Accordingly, an allowance account or an adjusting entry is not needed at the end of the period. The entry to write off an account when it is believed to be uncollectible is as follows:

May 10	Uncollectible Accounts Expense	42	
	Accounts Receivable—D. L. Ross.		42
	To write off uncollectible account.		

If an account that has been written off is collected later, the account should be reinstated. If the recovery is in the same fiscal year as the write-off, the earlier entry should be reversed to reinstate the account. To illustrate, assume that the account written off in the May 10 entry above is collected in November of the same fiscal year. The entry to reinstate the account would be as follows:

Nov. 21	Accounts Receivable—D. L. Ross..........	42	
	Uncollectible Accounts Expense..........		42
	To reinstate account written off earlier in		
	the year.		

The receipt of cash in payment of the reinstated amount would be recorded in the cash receipts journal in the usual manner.

When an account that has been written off is collected in a later fiscal year, it may be reinstated by an entry like that just illustrated. An alternative is to credit some other appropriately titled account, such as Recovery of Uncollectible Accounts Written Off. The credit balance in such an account at the end of the year may then be reported on the income statement as a deduction from Uncollectible Accounts Expense, or the net expense only may be reported. Such amounts are likely to be small compared to net income.

TEMPORARY INVESTMENTS

A corporation may have on hand a large amount of cash that is not needed immediately, but this cash may be needed later in operating the business, possibly within the coming year. Rather than allow this excess cash to lie idle until it is actually needed, the corporation may invest all or a part of it in income-yielding securities that can be quickly sold when cash is needed. Such securities are known as **temporary investments** or **marketable securities.** Although they may be retained as an investment for a number of years, they continue to be classified as temporary, provided that: (1) the securities are readily marketable and thus can be sold for cash at any time and (2) management intends to sell them at such time as the enterprise needs more cash for normal operations.

Stocks and bonds held as temporary investments are classified on the balance sheet as current assets. They may be listed after "Cash," or they may be combined with cash and described as "Cash and marketable securities."

A temporary investment in a portfolio of debt securities is usually carried at cost. However, the **carrying amount** (also called **basis**) of a temporary investment in a portfolio of equity securities is the lower of its total cost or market price, determined at the date of the balance sheet.[2] Note that in the following illustration, the carrying amount is based on the comparison between the *total* cost and the *total* market price of the portfolio, rather than the lower of cost or market price of *each item*.

---

[2]*Statement of Financial Accounting Standards, No. 12,* "Accounting for Certain Marketable Securities" (Stamford: Financial Accounting Standards Board, 1975), par. 8.

Temporary Investment Portfolio	Cost	Market	Unrealized Gain (Loss)
Equity security A..........	$150,000	$100,000	$(50,000)
Equity security B..........	200,000	200,000	—
Equity security C..........	180,000	210,000	30,000
Equity security D..........	160,000	150,000	(10,000)
Total....................	$690,000	$660,000	$(30,000)

The marketable equity securities would be reported in the current assets section of the balance sheet at a cost of $690,000 less an allowance for decline to market price of $30,000 to yield a carrying amount of $660,000. The unrealized loss of $30,000 is included in the determination of net income and reported as a separate item on the income statement. If the market value of the portfolio later rises, the unrealized loss is reversed and included in net income, but only to the extent that it does not exceed the original cost. In such cases, the increase is reported separately in the other income section of the income statement and the amount reported on the balance sheet is likewise adjusted.[3]

Self-Examination Questions
(Answers in Appendix C.)

1. What is the maturity value of a 90-day, 12% note for $10,000?
   A. $8,800   C. $10,300
   B. $10,000   D. $11,200

2. An enterprise issues a $5,000, 60-day non-interest-bearing note to the bank which the bank discounts at 9%. The proceeds are:
   A. $4,550   C. $5,000
   B. $4,925   D. $5,075

3. At the end of the fiscal year before the accounts are adjusted, Accounts Receivable has a balance of $200,000 and Allowance for Doubtful Accounts has a credit balance of $2,500. If the estimate of uncollectible accounts determined by aging the receivables is $8,500, the current provision to be made for uncollectible accounts expense would be:
   A. $2,500   C. $8,500
   B. $6,000   D. $200,000

4. At the end of the fiscal year, Accounts Receivable has a balance of $100,000 and Allowance for Doubtful Accounts has a balance of $7,000. The expected realizable value of the accounts receivable is:
   A. $7,000   C. $100,000
   B. $93,000   D. $107,000

5. Under what caption would an investment in stock that is held as a temporary investment be reported in the balance sheet?
   A. Current assets   C. Investments
   B. Plant assets   D. None of the above

[3]*Ibid.*, par. 11.

Discussion Questions

1. What are the advantages, to the creditor, of a note receivable in comparison to an account receivable?

2. In what section should a five-year note receivable from the president of Wilcox Corporation be listed on the corporation's balance sheet?

3. Baker Corporation issued a promissory note to Stevens Company. (a) Name the payee. (b) What is the title of the account employed by Stevens Company in recording the note?

4. If a note provides for payment of principal of $1,000 and interest at the rate of 14%, will the interest amount to $140? Explain.

5. The following questions refer to a 60-day, 12% note for $10,000, dated July 10: (a) What is the face value of the note? (b) What is the amount of interest payable at maturity? (c) What is the maturity value of the note? (d) What is the due date of the note?

6. At the end of the fiscal year, an enterprise holds a 60-day note receivable accepted from a customer fifteen days earlier. (a) Will the interest on the note as of the end of the year represent a deferral or an accrual? (b) Which of the following types of accounts will be affected by the related adjusting entry at the end of the fiscal year: (1) asset, (2) liability, (3) revenue, (4) expense? (c) If the note is held until maturity, what fraction of the total interest should be allocated to the year in which the note is collected?

7. The payee of a 60-day, 12% note for $1,000, dated April 10, endorses it to a bank on April 30. The bank discounts the note at 14%, paying the endorser $1,004.13. Identify or determine the following, as they relate to the note: (a) face value, (b) maturity value, (c) due date, (d) number of days in the discount period, (e) proceeds, (f) interest income or expense recorded by payee, (g) amount payable to the bank if the maker should default.

8. A discounted note receivable is dishonored by the maker and the endorser pays the bank the face of the note, $5,000, the interest, $50, and a protest fee of $8. What entry should be made in the accounts of the endorser to record the payment?

9. During the year, notes receivable of $350,000 were discounted to a bank by an enterprise. By the end of the year, $290,000 of these notes have matured. What is the amount of the endorser's contingent liability for notes receivable discounted at the end of the year?

10. The series of six transactions recorded in the following T accounts were related to a sale to a customer on account and receipt of the amount owed. Briefly describe each transaction.

Cash					Notes Receivable					Accounts Receivable				
(4)	1,882	(5)	1,938		(3)	1,900	(4)	1,900		(1)	2,000	(2)	100
(6)	1,950									(5)	1,938	(3)	1,900
												(6)	1,938

Sales					Interest Income					Interest Expense		
(2)	100	(1)	2,000				(6)	12		(4)	18	

11. Which of the two methods of accounting for uncollectible accounts provides for the recognition of the expense at the earlier date?

12. What kind of an account (asset, liability, etc.) is Allowance for Doubtful Accounts, and is its normal balance a debit or a credit?

13. Give the adjusting entry to increase Allowance for Doubtful Accounts by $11,150.

14. After the accounts are adjusted and closed at the end of the fiscal year, Accounts Receivable has a balance of $197,400 and Allowance for Doubtful Accounts has a balance of $6,100.
    (a) What is the expected realizable value of the accounts receivable?
    (b) If an account receivable of $1,000 is written off against the allowance account, what will be the expected realizable value of the accounts receivable after the write-off, assuming that no other changes in either account have occurred in the meantime?

15. A firm has consistently adjusted its allowance account at the end of the fiscal year by adding a fixed percent of the period's net sales on account. After six years, the balance in Allowance for Doubtful Accounts has become disproportionately large in relationship to the balance in Accounts Receivable. Give two possible explanations.

16. The $750 balance of an account owed by a customer is considered to be uncollectible and is to be written off. Give the entry to record the write-off in the general ledger, (a) assuming that the allowance method is used and (b) assuming that the direct write-off method is used.

17. Which of the two methods of estimating uncollectibles, when advance provision for uncollectible receivables is made, provides for the most accurate estimate of the current realizable value of the receivables?

18. Under what caption should securities held as a temporary investment be reported on the balance sheet?

19. A corporation has two equity securities which it holds as a temporary investment. If they have a total cost of $125,000 and a fair market value of $120,000, at what amount should these securities be reported in the current assets section of the corporation's balance sheet?

Exercises

Exercise 8-1. Determine the interest on the following notes:

Face Amount	Number of Days	Interest Rate
(a) $7,500	60	12%
(b) 3,000	60	14%
(c) 2,000	75	12%
(d) 4,000	75	15%
(e) 7,200	50	10%

Exercise 8-2. Dixon Company issues a 60-day, 12% note for $4,500, dated April 20, to Thomas Corporation on account.
    (a) Determine the due date of the note.

(b) Determine the amount of interest to be paid on the note at maturity.

(c) Present entries, in general journal form, to record the following:

(1) Receipt of the note by the payee.

(2) Receipt by payee of payment of the note at maturity.

Exercise 8-3. (a) Present entries in general journal form for the following:

May 31. Received from Cox Co., on account, a $5,000, 90-day, 12% note dated May 31.

June 30. Recorded an adjusting entry for accrued interest on the note of May 31.

30. Closed the interest income account. The only entry in this account originated from the above adjustment.

July 1. Recorded a reversing entry for accrued interest.

Aug. 29. Received $5,150 from Cox Co. for the note due today.

(b) What is the balance in interest income after the entry of August 29?

(c) How many days' interest·on $5,000 at 12% does the amount reported in (b) represent?

Exercise 8-4. Baxter & Son holds a 90-day, 14% note for $5,000, dated June 20, that was received from a customer on account. On July 20, the note is discounted at the Ogden National Bank at the rate of 16%.

(a) Determine the maturity value of the note.

(b) Determine the number of days in the discount period.

(c) Determine the amount of the discount.

(d) Determine the amount of the proceeds.

(e) Present the entry, in general journal form, to record the discounting of the note on July 20.

Exercise 8-5. Record the following transactions, each in general journal form, in the accounts of C. Reed and Daughter.

May 1. Received a $6,000, 60-day, 14% note dated May 1 from Shaul Corp. on account.

31. Discounted the note at Royal National Bank; discount rate, 15%.

June 30. The note is dishonored; paid the bank the amount due on the note plus a protest fee of $7.

July 30. Received the amount due on the dishonored note plus interest for 30 days at 14% on the total amount debited to Shaul Corp. on June 30.

Exercise 8-6. At the end of the current year, the accounts receivable account has a debit balance of $75,000 and net sales for the year total $800,000. Determine the amount of the adjusting entry to record the provision for doubtful accounts under each of the following assumptions:

(a) The allowance account before adjustment has a credit balance of $700.

(1) Uncollectible accounts expense is estimated at ½ of 1% of net sales.

(2) Analysis of the accounts in the customers ledger indicates doubtful accounts of $5,250.

(b) The allowance account before adjustment has a debit balance of $300.

(1) Uncollectible accounts expense is estimated at ¾ of 1% of net sales.

(2) Analysis of the accounts in the customers ledger indicates doubtful accounts of $5,250.

Exercise 8-7. As of December 31 of the first year of operations, DCA Corporation has the following portfolio of temporary equity securities:

	Cost	Market
Security A	$15,500	$17,750
Security B	8,000	6,200
Security C	22,750	19,500
Security D	85,800	87,000

Describe how the portfolio of temporary equity securities would be reported on the balance sheet and income statement of DCA Corporation.

Problems
(Problems in Appendix B: 8-1B, 8-2B, 8-3B, 8-4B.)

Problem 8-1A. The following were selected from among the transactions completed by D. L. Parton Co. during the current year:

Jan. 9. Sold merchandise on account to Haggart Co., $5,000.
      19. Accepted a 30-day, 12% note for $5,000 from Haggart Co. on account.
Feb. 18. Received from Haggart Co. the amount due on the note of January 19.
May   1. Sold merchandise on account to C. D. Chow Inc., for $2,000, charging an additional $30 for prepaid transportation cost. (Credit Delivery Expense for the $30 charged for prepaid transportation cost.)
      10. Loaned $3,000 cash to John Johnson, receiving a 30-day, 14% note.
      11. Received from C. D. Chow Inc. the amount due on the invoice of May 1, less 2% discount.
June 9. Received the interest due from John Johnson and a new 60-day, 14% note as a renewal of the loan. (Record both the debit and the credit to the notes receivable account.)
Aug. 8. Received from John Johnson the amount due on his note.
Sept. 16. Sold merchandise on account to West and Son, $6,000.
Oct. 11. Received from West and Son a 60-day, 12% note for $6,000.
Nov. 10. Discounted the note from West and Son at the Palmer National Bank at 10%.
Dec. 10. Received notice from Palmer National Bank that West and Son had dishonored its note. Paid the bank the maturity value of the note.
      20. Received from West and Son the amount owed on the dishonored note, plus interest for 10 days at 10% computed on the maturity value of the note.

Instructions:
Record the transactions in general journal form.

Problem 8-2A. During the last three months of the current fiscal year, Denton Co. received the following notes. Notes (1), (2), (3), and (4) were discounted on the dates and at the rates indicated.

	Date	Face Amount	Term	Interest Rate	Date Discounted	Discount Rate
(1)	July 7	$ 9,000	60 days	12%	July 27	10%
(2)	July 20	8,000	60 days	12%	July 30	15%
(3)	Aug. 4	3,000	90 days	10%	Sep. 3	12%
(4)	Aug. 19	7,200	60 days	11%	Sep. 28	12%
(5)	Dec. 11	4,500	30 days	14%	—	—
(6)	Dec. 16	12,000	60 days	13%	—	—

Instructions:
   (1) Determine for each note (a) the due date and (b) the amount of interest due at maturity, identifying each note by number.
   (2) Determine for each of the first four notes (a) the maturity value, (b) the discount period, (c) the discount, (d) the proceeds, and (e) the interest income or interest expense, identifying each note by number.
   (3) Present, in general journal form, the entries to record the discounting of notes (2) and (3) at a bank.
   (4) Assuming that notes (5) and (6) are held until maturity, determine for each the amount of interest earned (a) in the current fiscal year and (b) in the following fiscal year.

Problem 8-3A. Mahan Co. closes its accounts annually as of December 31, the end of the fiscal year. The following data relate to notes receivable and interest from November 1 through February 14 of the following year. (All notes are dated as of the day they are received.)

Nov.   1. Received a $2,000, 12%, 60-day note on account.
      11. Received a $9,000, 14%, 90-day note on account.
Dec. 16. Received a $12,000, 11%, 60-day note on account.
      21. Received a $3,000, 12%, 30-day note on account.
      31. Received $2,040 on note of November 1.
      31. Recorded an adjusting entry for the interest accrued on the notes dated November 11, December 16, and December 21. There are no other notes receivable on this date.
Jan.   1. Recorded a reversing entry for the accrued interest.
      11. Received a $3,500, 12%, 30-day note on account.
      20. Received $3,030 on note of December 21.
Feb.   9. Received $9,315 on note of November 11.
      10. Received $3,535 on note of January 11.
      14. Received $12,220 on note of December 16.

Instructions:
   (1) Open accounts for Interest Receivable (Account No. 116) and Interest Income (Account No. 611), and record a credit balance of $1,150 in the latter account as of November 1 of the current year.
   (2) Present entries in general journal form to record the transactions and other data, posting to the two accounts after each entry affecting them.
   (3) If the reversing entry had not been recorded as of January 1, indicate how each interest receipt in January and February should be allocated. Submit the data in the following form:

Note (Face Amount)	Total Interest Received	Cr. Interest Receivable	Cr. Interest Income
$ 9,000	$	$	$
12,000			
3,000			
3,500			
Total	$	$	$

(continued)

(4) Do the February 14 balances of Interest Receivable and Interest Income obtained by the use of the reversing entry technique correspond to the balances that would have been obtained by analyzing each receipt?

Problem 8-4A. The following transactions, adjusting entries, and closing entries are related to uncollectible accounts. All were completed during the current fiscal year ended December 31.

Feb. 12. Reinstated the account of Charles Ling that had been written off in the preceding year and received $700 cash in full payment.

Apr. 20. Wrote off the $3,125 balance owed by Fuller Co., which has no assets.

July 30. Received 30% of the $6,000 balance owed by L. Born Corp., a bankrupt, and wrote off the remainder as uncollectible.

Nov. 25. Reinstated the account of Lawrence Cox that had been written off two years earlier and received $510 cash in full payment.

Dec. 20. Wrote off the following accounts as uncollectible (compound entry): Colbert and Collins, $375; J. C. Davis Co., $3,700; John Gordon, $390; H. A. Powell Corp., $5,150.

31. Based on an analysis of the $217,550 of accounts receivable, it was estimated that $14,700 will be uncollectible. Recorded the adjusting entry.

31. Recorded the entry to close the appropriate account to Income Summary.

Instructions:

(1) Open the following selected accounts, recording the credit balance indicated as of January 1 of the current fiscal year:

    115 Allowance for Doubtful Accounts.................... $17,300

    313 Income Summary .... ——

    718 Uncollectible Accounts Expense .... ——

(2) Record in general journal form the transactions and the adjusting and closing entries described above. After each entry, post to the three selected accounts affected and extend the new balances.

(3) Determine the expected realizable value of the accounts receivable as of December 31.

(4) Assuming that, instead of basing the provision for uncollectible accounts on an analysis of receivables, the adjusting entry on December 31 had been based on an estimated loss of ½ of 1% of the net sales of $2,700,000 for the year, determine the following:

(a) Uncollectible accounts expense for the year.

(b) Balance in the allowance account after the adjustment of December 31.

(c) Expected realizable value of the accounts receivable as of December 31.

Problem 8-5A. Oakwood Sales Inc. has just completed its fourth year of operations. The direct write-off method of recording uncollectible accounts expense has been employed during the entire period. Because of substantial increases in sales volume and amount of uncollectible accounts, the firm is considering the possibility of changing to the allowance method. Information is requested as to the effect that an annual provision of ½ of 1% of sales would have had on the amount of uncollectible accounts expense reported for each of the past four years. It is also considered desirable to know what the balance of Allowance for Doubtful Accounts would have been at the end of each year. The following data have been obtained from the accounts:

		Uncollectible Accounts Written	Year of Origin of Accounts Receivable Written off as Uncollectible			
Year	Sales	Off	1st	2d	3d	4th
1st	$500,000	$ 500	$ 500			
2d	650,000	2,150	1,500	$ 650		
3d	800,000	3,200	200	2,400	$ 600	
4th	950,000	4,150		600	2,600	$950

Instructions:

(1) Assemble the desired data, using the following columnar captions:

	Uncollectible Accounts Expense			Balance of
Year	Expense Actually Reported	Expense Based on Estimate	Increase in Amount of Expense	Allowance Account, End of Year

(2) Does the estimate of ½ of 1% of sales appear to be reasonably close to the actual experience with uncollectible accounts originating during the first two years?

Mini-Case

For several years, Weberg Furniture's sales have been on a "cash only" basis. On January 1, 1981, however, Weberg began offering credit to selected customers on terms of n/30. The adjusting entry to estimate uncollectible receivables at the end of each year has been based on sales and has been uniformly 1% of credit sales, which is the rate reported as the average for the retail furniture industry. Credit sales and the year-end credit balances in Allowance for Doubtful Accounts for the past four years are as follows:

Year	Credit Sales	Allowance for Doubtful Accounts
1981	$400,000	$2,100
1982	415,000	3,750
1983	395,000	5,100
1984	420,000	6,600

Richard Weberg, president of Weberg Furniture, is concerned that the method of accounting for uncollectible receivables and for the write-off of uncollectible accounts are unsatisfactory. He has asked your advice in the analysis of past operations in this area and recommendations for change.

Instructions:

(1) Determine the amount of (a) the addition to Allowance for Doubtful Accounts and (b) the accounts written off for each of the four years.

(2) Advise Weberg as to whether the estimate of 1% of credit sales appears reasonable.

(3) Assume that after discussing item (2) with Weberg, he asked you what action might be taken to determine what the balance of Allowance for Doubtful Accounts should be at December 31, 1984, and possible changes, if any, you might recommend in accounting for uncollectible receivables. How would you respond?

9

Inventories

CHAPTER OBJECTIVES

Describe and illustrate the importance of inventory in the operations and the accounting for a merchandising firm.

Identify and illustrate the two principal inventory systems.

Identify and illustrate the procedures for the determination of the actual quantity in inventory and the cost of inventory.

Identify and illustrate the proper presentation of inventory in the financial statements.

9

CHAPTER

The term **inventories** is used to designate (1) merchandise held for sale in the normal course of business, and (2) materials in the process of production or held for such use. This chapter discusses the determination of the inventory of merchandise purchased for resale, commonly called **merchandise inventory**. Inventories of raw materials and partially processed materials of a manufacturing enterprise will be considered in a later chapter.

IMPORTANCE OF INVENTORIES

Merchandise, being continually purchased and sold, is one of the most active elements in the operation of wholesale and retail businesses. The sale of merchandise provides the principal source of revenue for such enterprises. When the net income is determined, the cost of merchandise sold is the largest deduction from sales. In fact, it is usually larger than all other deductions combined. In addition, a substantial part of a merchandising firm's resources is invested in inventory. It is frequently the largest of the current assets of such a firm.

Inventory determination plays an important role in matching expired costs with revenues of the period. As was explained and illustrated in Chapter 4, the total cost of merchandise available for sale during a period of time must be divided into two parts at the end of the period. The cost of the merchandise determined to be in the inventory will appear on the balance sheet as a current asset. The other element, which is the cost of the merchandise sold, will be reported on the income statement as a deduction from net sales to yield gross profit. An error in the determination of the inventory figure at the end of the period will cause an equal misstatement of gross profit and net income, and the amount reported for both assets and capital in the balance sheet will be incorrect by the same amount. The effects of understatements and overstatements of merchandise inventory at the end of the period are demonstrated in the following three sets of condensed income statements and balance sheets. The first set of statements is based on a correct inventory of $20,000; the second set, on an incorrect inventory of $12,000; and the third set, on an incorrect inventory of $27,000.

Income Statement for the Year		Balance Sheet at End of Year	
1. Inventory at end of period correctly stated at $20,000.			
Net sales	$200,000	Merchandise inventory	$ 20,000
Cost of merchandise sold	120,000	Other assets	80,000
Gross profit	$ 80,000	Total	$100,000
Expenses	55,000		
Net income	$ 25,000	Liabilities	$ 30,000
		Capital	70,000
		Total	$100,000
2. Inventory at end of period incorrectly stated at $12,000; (understated by $8,000).			
Net sales	$200,000	Merchandise inventory	$ 12,000
Cost of merchandise sold	128,000	Other assets	80,000
Gross profit	$ 72,000	Total	$ 92,000
Expenses	55,000		
Net income	$ 17,000	Liabilities	$ 30,000
		Capital	62,000
		Total	$ 92,000

3. Inventory at end of period incorrectly stated at $27,000; (overstated by $7,000).

Net sales	$200,000	Merchandise inventory	$ 27,000
Cost of merchandise sold ...	113,000	Other assets	80,000
Gross profit	$ 87,000	Total	$107,000
Expenses	55,000	Liabilities	$ 30,000
Net income	$ 32,000	Capital	77,000
		Total	$107,000

Note that in the illustration the total cost of merchandise available for sale was constant at $140,000. It was the way in which the cost was allocated that varied. The variations in allocating the $140,000 of merchandise cost are summarized as follows:

	Merchandise Available		
	Total	Inventory	Sold
1. Inventory correctly stated	$140,000	$20,000	$120,000
2. Inventory understated by $8,000	140,000	12,000	128,000
3. Inventory overstated by $7,000	140,000	27,000	113,000

The effect of the wrong allocations on net income, assets, and capital may also be summarized. Comparison of the amounts reported in financial statements 2 and 3 with the comparable amounts reported in financial statement 1 yields the following:

	Net Income	Assets	Capital
2. Ending inventory understated $8,000	Understated $8,000	Understated $8,000	Understated $8,000
3. Ending inventory overstated $7,000	Overstated $7,000	Overstated $7,000	Overstated $7,000

The inventory at the end of one period becomes the inventory for the beginning of the following period. Thus, if the inventory is incorrectly stated at the end of the period, the net income of that period will be misstated and so will the net income for the following period. The amount of the two misstatements will be equal and in opposite directions. Therefore, the effect on net income of an incorrectly stated inventory, if not corrected, is limited to the period of the error and the following period. At the end of this following period, assuming no additional errors, both assets and capital will be correctly stated.

Elements of the foregoing analyses are closely related to the different inventory systems and methods. A thorough understanding of the effect of inventories on the determination of net income will be helpful when these systems and methods are presented later in this chapter.

INVENTORY SYSTEMS

There are two principal systems of inventory accounting, periodic and perpetual. When the periodic system is used, only the revenue from sales is recorded each time a sale is made. No entry is made at the time of the sale to record the cost of the merchandise that has been sold. Consequently, a physical inventory must be taken in order to determine the cost of the inventory at the end of an accounting period. Ordinarily, it is possible to take a complete physical inventory only at the end of the fiscal year. In the earlier chapters dealing with purchases and sales of merchandise, the use of the periodic system was assumed.

In contrast to the periodic system, the perpetual inventory system uses accounting records that continuously disclose the amount of the inventory. A separate account for each type of merchandise is maintained in a subsidiary ledger. Increases in inventory items are recorded as debits to the proper accounts, and decreases are recorded as credits. The balances of the accounts are called the book inventories of the items on hand. Regardless of the care with which the perpetual inventory records are maintained, their accuracy must be tested by taking a physical inventory of each type of commodity at least once a year. The records are then compared with the actual quantities on hand and any differences are corrected.

The periodic inventory system is often used by retail enterprises that sell many kinds of low unit cost merchandise, such as groceries, hardware, and drugs. The expense of maintaining perpetual inventory records may be prohibitive in such cases. In recent years, however, the application of electronic data processing equipment to such businesses has reduced this expense considerably. Firms selling a relatively small number of high unit cost items, such as office equipment, automobiles, or fur garments, are more likely to use the perpetual system.

Although much of the discussion that follows applies to both systems, the use of the periodic inventory system will be assumed. Later in the chapter, principles and procedures related only to the perpetual inventory system will be presented.

DETERMINING ACTUAL QUANTITIES IN THE INVENTORY

The first stage in the process of "taking" an inventory is to determine the quantity of each kind of merchandise owned by the enterprise. When the periodic system is used, the counting, weighing, and measuring should be done at the end of the accounting period. To accomplish this, the inventory crew may work during the night, or business operations may be stopped until the count is finished.

The details of the specific procedures for determining quantities and assembling the data differ among companies. A common practice is to use teams made up of two persons. One person counts, weighs, or otherwise determines quantity, and the other lists the description and the quantity on inventory sheets. The quantity indicated for high-cost items is verified by a third person at some time during the inventory-taking period. It is also advisable for the third person to verify other items selected at random from the inventory sheets.

All of the merchandise owned by the business on the inventory date, and only such merchandise, should be included in the inventory. It may be necessary to examine purchase and sales invoices of the last few days of the accounting period and the first few days of the following period to determine who has legal title to merchandise in transit on the inventory date. When goods are purchased or sold **FOB shipping point**, title usually passes to the buyer when the goods are shipped. When the terms are **FOB destination**, title usually does not pass to the buyer until the goods are delivered. To illustrate, assume that merchandise purchased FOB shipping point is shipped by the seller on the last day of the buyer's fiscal period. The merchandise does not arrive until the following period and hence is not available for "counting" by the inventory crew. However, such merchandise should be included in the buyer's inventory because title has passed. It is also evident that a debit to Purchases and a credit to Accounts Payable should be recorded by the buyer as of the end of the period, rather than recording it as a transaction of the following period.

Another example, although less common, will further show the importance of closely examining transactions involving shipments of merchandise. Manufacturers sometimes ship merchandise on a consignment basis to retailers who act as the manufacturer's agent when selling the merchandise. The manufacturer retains title until the goods are sold. Obviously, such unsold merchandise is a part of the manufacturer's (consignor's) inventory, even though the manufacturer does not have physical possession. It is just as obvious that the consigned merchandise should not be included in the retailer's (consignee's) inventory.

DETERMINING THE COST OF INVENTORY

The cost of merchandise inventory is made up of the purchase price and all expenditures incurred in acquiring such merchandise, including transportation, customs duties, and insurance against losses in transit. The purchase price can be readily determined, as may some of the other costs. Those that are difficult to associate with specific inventory items may be prorated on some equitable basis. Minor costs that are difficult to allocate may be left out entirely from inventory cost and treated as operating expenses of the period.

If purchases discounts are treated as a deduction from purchases on the income statement, they should also be deducted from the purchase price of items in the inventory. If it is not possible to determine the exact amount of discount applicable to each inventory item, a pro rata amount of the total discount for the period may be deducted instead. For example, if net purchases and purchases discount for the period amount to $200,000 and $3,000 respectively, the discount represents 1½% of net purchases. If the inventory cost, before considering the cash discount, is $30,000, the amount may be reduced by 1½%, or $450, to yield an inventory cost of $29,550.

One of the most significant problems in determining inventory cost comes about when identical units of a certain commodity have been acquired at different unit cost prices during the period. When such is the case, it is necessary to determine the unit prices of the items still on hand. This problem and its relationship to the determination of net income and inventory cost are indicated by the illustration that follows.

Assume that during the fiscal year three identical units of Commodity X, one of which was in the inventory at the beginning of the year, were available for sale to customers. Details as to the dates of purchase and the costs per unit are as follows:

Commodity X	Units	Cost
Jan. 1 Inventory	1	$ 9
Mar. 4 Purchase	1	13
May 9 Purchase	1	14
Total	3	$36
Average cost per unit		$12

During the period, two units of Commodity X were sold, leaving one unit in the inventory at the end of the period. Information is not available as to which two of the three units were sold and which unit remains. Therefore, it becomes necessary to use an arbitrary assumption as to the *flow of costs* of merchandise through the enterprise. The three most common assumptions of determining the cost of the merchandise sold are as follows:

1. Cost flow is in the order in which the expenditures were made.
2. Cost flow is in the reverse order in which the expenditures were made.
3. Cost flow is an average of the expenditures.

Details of the cost of the two units of Commodity X assumed to be sold and the cost of the one unit remaining, determined in accordance with each of these assumptions, are as follows:

	Commodity X Costs		
	Units Available	Units Sold	Unit Remaining
1. In order of expenditures	$36	− ($ 9 + $13) =	$14
2. In reverse order of expenditures	36	− (14 + 13) =	9
3. In accordance with average expenditures	36	− (12 + 12) =	12

In actual practice, it may be possible to identify units with specific expenditures if both the variety of merchandise carried in stock and the volume of sales are relatively small. Ordinarily, however, **specific identification** procedures are too time consuming to justify their use. It is customary, therefore, to use one of the three generally accepted costing methods, each of which is also acceptable in determining income subject to the federal income tax.

First-In, First-Out Method

The first-in, first-out (fifo) method of costing inventory is based on the assumption that costs should be charged against revenue in the order in which they were incurred. Hence the inventory remaining is assumed to be made up of the most recent costs. The illustration of the application of this method is based on the following data for a particular commodity:

Jan. 1 Inventory	200 units at $ 9	$ 1,800
Mar. 10 Purchase	300 units at 10	3,000
Sept. 21 Purchase	400 units at 11	4,400
Nov. 18 Purchase	100 units at 12	1,200
Available for sale during year . .	1,000	$10,400

The physical count on December 31 shows that 300 units of the particular commodity are on hand. In accordance with the assumption that the inventory is composed of the most recent costs, the cost of the 300 units is determined as follows:

Most recent costs, Nov. 18	100 units at $12............	$ 1,200
Next most recent costs, Sept. 21..	200 units at 11............	2,200
Inventory, Dec. 31	300	$ 3,400

Deduction of the inventory of $3,400 from the $10,400 of merchandise available for sale yields $7,000 as the cost of merchandise sold, which represents the earliest costs incurred for this commodity.

In most businesses, there is a tendency to dispose of goods in the order of their acquisition. This would be particularly true of perishable merchandise and goods in which style or model changes are frequent. Thus, the fifo method is generally in harmony with the physical movement of merchandise in an enterprise. To the extent that this is the case, the fifo method approximates the results that would be obtained by specific identification of costs.

Last-In, First-Out Method

The last-in, first-out (lifo) method is based on the assumption that the most recent costs incurred should be charged against revenue. Hence the inventory remaining is assumed to be composed of the earliest costs. Based on the illustrative data presented in the preceding section, the cost of the inventory is determined in the following manner:

Earliest costs, Jan. 1............	200 units at $ 9............	$ 1,800
Next earliest costs, Mar. 10	100 units at 10............	1,000
Inventory, Dec. 31	300	$ 2,800

Deduction of the inventory of $2,800 from the $10,400 of merchandise available for sale yields $7,600 as the cost of merchandise sold, which represents the most recent costs incurred for this particular commodity.

The use of the lifo method was originally confined to the relatively rare situations in which the units sold were taken from the most recently acquired stock. Its use has greatly increased during the past few decades, and it is now often used even when it is not like the physical flow of goods.

Average Cost Method

The average cost method sometimes called the **weighted average method,** is based on the assumption that costs should be charged against revenue according to the weighted average unit costs of the goods sold. The same weighted average unit costs are used in determining the cost of the merchandise remaining in the inventory. The weighted average unit cost is determined by dividing the total cost of the identical units of each commodity available for sale during the period by the related number of units of that commodity. Assuming the same cost data as in the preceding illustrations, the average cost of the 1,000 units and the cost of the inventory are determined as follows:

Average unit cost................ $10,400 ÷ 1,000 = $10.40
Inventory, Dec. 31 ....300 units at $10.40............ $3,120

Deduction of the inventory of **$3,120** from the $10,400 of merchandise available for sale yields **$7,280** as the cost of merchandise sold, which represents the average of the costs incurred for this commodity.

For businesses in which various purchases of identical units of a commodity are mingled, the average method has some relationship to the physical flow of goods.

Comparison of Inventory Costing Methods | Each of the three alternative methods of costing inventories under the periodic system is based on a different assumption as to the flow of costs. If the cost of goods and the prices at which they were sold remained stable, all three methods would yield the same results. Prices do change, however, and as a consequence the three methods will usually yield different amounts for both (1) the inventory at the end of the period and (2) the cost of the merchandise sold and net income reported for the period. The examples presented in the preceding sections illustrated the effect of rising prices. They may be summarized as follows:

	First-In, First-Out	Average Cost	Last-In, First-Out
Merchandise available for sale	$10,400	$10,400	$10,400
Merchandise inventory, December 31	3,400	3,120	2,800
Cost of merchandise sold.....................	$ 7,000	$ 7,280	$ 7,600

The method that yields the lowest figure for the cost of merchandise sold will yield the highest figure for gross profit and net income reported on the income statement. It will also yield the highest figure for inventory reported on the balance sheet. On the other hand, the method that yields the highest figure for the cost of merchandise sold will yield the lowest figure for gross profit and net income and the lowest figure for inventory.

During a period of inflation or rising prices, the use of the first-in, first-out method will result in a greater amount of net income than the other two methods. The reason is that the costs of the units sold is assumed to be in the order in which they were incurred, and the earlier unit costs were lower than the more recent unit costs. Much of the benefit of the larger amounts of gross profit is lost, however, as the inventory is continually replenished at ever higher prices. During the 1970's, when the rate of inflation increased to "double-digit" percentages, the resulting increases in net income were frequently referred to as "inventory profits" or "illusory profits" by the financial press.

In a period of deflation or declining prices the effect described above is reversed, and the fifo method yields the lowest amount of net income. The major criticism of the first-in, first-out method is this tendency to maximize the effect of inflationary and deflationary trends on amounts reported as net income. However, the dollar amount reported as merchandise inventory on the balance sheet will usually be about the same as its current replacement cost.

During a period of rising prices, the use of the last-in, first-out method will result in a lesser amount of net income than the other two methods. The reason is that the cost of the most recently acquired commodities most nearly approximates their cost of replacement. Thus, it can be argued that the use of the lifo method more nearly matches current costs with current revenues. There is also the practical advantage of a saving in income taxes. During the accelerated inflationary trend of the 1970's, many business enterprises changed from fifo to lifo.

In a period of deflation or falling price levels, the effect described above is reversed and the lifo method yields the highest amount of net income. The major justification for lifo is this tendency to minimize the effect of price trends on reported net income and, therefore, to exert a stabilizing influence on the economy. A criticism of the use of lifo is that the dollar amount reported for merchandise inventory on the balance sheet may be quite far removed from current replacement cost. However, in such situations it is customary to indicate the approximate replacement cost (i.e., as though fifo had been used) in a note accompanying published financial statements.

The average cost method of inventory costing is, in a sense, a compromise between fifo and lifo. The effect of price trends is averaged, both in the determination of net income and the determination of inventory cost. For any given series of acquisitions, the average cost will be the same, regardless of the direction of price trends. For example, a complete reversal of the sequence of unit costs presented in the illustration on page 247 would not affect the reported net income or the inventory cost. The time required to assemble the data is likely to be greater for the average cost method than for the other two methods. The additional expense incurred could be large if there are many purchases of a wide variety of merchandise items.

The foregoing comparisons show the importance attached to the selection of the inventory costing method. It is not unusual for manufacturing enterprises to apply one method to a particular class of inventory, such as merchandise ready for sale, and a different method to another class, such as raw materials purchased. The method(s) used may be changed for a valid reason. The effect of any change in method and the reason for the change should be fully disclosed in the financial statements for the fiscal period in which the change occurred.

Throughout the discussion of inventory costing methods, it has been assumed that the goods on hand were salable at normal sales prices. Because of imperfections, shop wear, style changes or other causes, there may be items that are not salable except at prices below cost. Such merchandise should be valued at estimated selling price less any direct cost of disposition, such as sales commission.

VALUATION AT THE LOWER OF COST OR MARKET

A frequently used alternative to valuing inventory at cost is to compare cost with market price and use the lower of the two. It should be noted that regardless of the method used, it is first necessary to determine the cost of the inventory. "Market," as used in the phrase **lower of cost or market** or **cost or market,**

whichever is lower, is interpreted to mean the cost to replace the merchandise on the inventory date. To the extent practicable, the market or replacement price should be based on quantities typically purchased from the usual source of supply. In the discussion that follows, the salability of the merchandise at normal sales prices will be assumed. The valuation of articles that have to be sold at a price below their cost would be determined by the method described in the preceding paragraph.

If the replacement price of an item in the inventory is lower than its cost, the use of the lower of cost or market method provides two advantages: (1) the gross profit (and net income) are reduced for the period in which the decline occurred and (2) an approximately normal gross profit is realized during the period in which the item is sold. To illustrate, assume that merchandise with a unit cost of $70 has sold at $100 during the period, yielding a gross profit of $30 a unit, or 30% of sales. Assume also that at the end of the year, there is a single unit of the commodity in the inventory and that its replacement price has declined to $63. Under such circumstances it would be reasonable to expect that the selling price would also decline, if indeed it had not already done so. Assuming a reduction in selling price to $90, the gross profit based on replacement cost of $63 would be $27, which is also 30% of the selling price. Accordingly, valuation of the unit in the inventory at $63 reduces net income of the past period by $7 and permits a normal gross profit of $27 to be realized on its sale in the following period. If the unit had been valued at its original cost of $70, the net income determined for the past year would have been $7 greater, and the net income attributable to the sale of the item in the following period would have been $7 less.

It would be possible to apply the lower of cost or market basis (1) to each item in the inventory, (2) to major classes or categories, or (3) to the inventory as a whole. The first procedure is the one usually followed in practice. To illustrate the application of the lower of cost or market to individual items, assume that there are 400 identical units of Commodity A in the inventory, each acquired at a unit cost of $10.25. If at the inventory date the commodity would cost $10.50 to replace, the cost price of $10.25 would be multiplied by 400 to determine the inventory value. On the other hand, if the commodity could be replaced at $9.50 a unit, the replacement price of $9.50 would be used for valuation purposes. The following tabulation illustrates one of the forms that may be followed in assembling inventory data.

		Unit Cost Price	Unit Market Price	Total	
DETERMINATION OF INVENTORY AT LOWER OF COST OR MARKET Description	Quantity			Cost	Lower of C or M
Commodity A	400	$10.25	$ 9.50	$ 4,100	$ 3,800
Commodity B	120	22.50	24.10	2,700	2,700
Commodity C	600	8.00	7.75	4,800	4,650
Commodity D	280	14.00	14.00	3,920	3,920
Total				$15,520	$15,070

Although it is not essential to accumulate the data for total cost, as in the illustration, it permits the measurement of the reduction in inventory because of a decline in market prices. When the amount of the market decline is known ($15,520 − $15,070, or $450), it may be reported as a separate item on the income statement. Otherwise, the market decline will be included in the amount reported as the cost of merchandise sold and will reduce gross profit by a corresponding amount. In any event, the amount reported as net income will not be affected. It will be the same, regardless of whether the amount of the market decline is determined and separately stated.

As with the method elected for the determination of inventory cost (first-in, first-out; last-in, first-out; or average cost), the method elected for inventory valuation (cost, or lower of cost or market) must be followed consistently from year to year.

RETAIL METHOD OF INVENTORY COSTING

The **retail inventory method** of inventory costing is widely used by retail businesses, particularly department stores. It is used in connection with the periodic system of inventories and is based on the relationship of the cost of merchandise available for sale to the retail price of the same merchandise. The retail prices of all merchandise acquired are accumulated in supplementary records, and the inventory at retail is determined by deducting sales for the period from the retail price of the goods that were available for sale during the period. The inventory at retail is then converted to cost on the basis of the ratio of cost to selling (retail) price for the merchandise available for sale. Determination of inventory by the retail method is illustrated as follows:

DETERMINATION OF INVENTORY BY RETAIL METHOD

	Cost	Retail
Merchandise inventory, January 1	$19,400	$ 36,000
Purchases in January (net)	42,600	64,000
Merchandise available for sale	$62,000	$100,000
Ratio of cost to retail price: $\frac{\$62,000}{\$100,000} = 62\%$		
Sales for January (net)		70,000
Merchandise inventory, January 31, at retail		$ 30,000
Merchandise inventory, January 31, at approximate cost ($30,000 × 62%)		$ 18,600

There is an inherent assumption in the retail method of inventory costing that the composition or "mix" of the commodities in the ending inventory, in terms of percent of cost to selling price, is comparable to the entire stock of merchandise available for sale. In the illustration, for example, it is unlikely that the retail price of every item was composed of exactly 62% cost and 38% gross profit. It is assumed, however, that the weighted average of the cost percentages of the merchandise in the inventory ($30,000) is the same as in the merchandise available for sale ($100,000). When the inventory is made up of different classes of merchandise with very different gross profit rates, the cost percentages and the inventory should be developed separately for each class.

The use of the retail method does not eliminate the necessity for taking a physical inventory at the end of the year. However, the items are recorded on the inventory sheets at their selling prices instead of their cost prices. The physical inventory at selling price is then converted to cost by applying the ratio of cost to selling (retail) price for the merchandise available for sale. To illustrate, assume that the data presented in the example on page 252 are for an entire fiscal year rather than for the first month of the year only. If the physical inventory taken on December 31 totaled $29,000, priced at retail, it would be this amount rather than the $30,000 that would be converted to cost. Accordingly, the inventory at cost would be $17,980 ($29,000 × 62%) instead of $18,600 ($30,000 × 62%).

One of the major advantages of the retail method is that it provides inventory figures for use in preparing interim statements. Department stores and similar merchandisers usually determine gross profit and operating income each month but take a physical inventory only once a year. In addition to facilitating frequent income determinations, a comparison of the computed inventory total with the physical inventory total, both at retail prices, will show the extent of inventory shortages and the consequent need for corrective measures.

PERPETUAL INVENTORY SYSTEM

The use of a perpetual inventory system for merchandise provides the most effective means of control over this important asset. Although it is possible to maintain a perpetual inventory in memorandum records only or to limit the data to quantities, a complete set of records integrated with the general ledger is preferable. The basic feature of the system is the recording of all merchandise increases and decreases in a manner somewhat similar to the recording of increases and decreases in cash. Just as receipts of cash are debited to Cash, so are purchases of merchandise debited to Merchandise Inventory. Similarly, sales or other reductions of merchandise are recorded in a manner like that used for reductions in Cash, that is, by credits to Merchandise Inventory. Thus, just as the balance of the cash account shows the amount of cash presumed to be on hand, so the balance of the merchandise inventory account represents the amount of merchandise presumed to be on hand.

Inventory Ledger

Unlike cash, merchandise is a mixed mass of goods. Details of the cost of each type of merchandise purchased and sold, together with such related transactions as returns and allowances, must be maintained in a subsidiary ledger, with a separate account for each type. Thus, an enterprise that stocks five hundred kinds of merchandise would need five hundred separate accounts in its **inventory ledger**. In the following illustration of the flow of costs through a subsidiary account, there is a beginning inventory, three purchases, and six sales of the particular commodity during the year. The number of units on hand after each transaction, together with total cost and unit prices, appears in the inventory section of the account.

PERPETUAL
INVENTORY
ACCOUNT

COMMODITY			127B				
		PURCHASED		SOLD		INVENTORY	
DATE	QUANTITY	TOTAL COST	QUANTITY	TOTAL COST	QUANTITY	TOTAL COST	UNIT PRICE
JAN. 1					10	200	20
FEB. 4			7	140	3	60	20
MAR. 10	8	168			3	60	20
					8	168	21
APR. 22			4	81	7	147	21
MAY 18			2	42	5	105	21
AUG. 30	10	220			5	105	21
					10	220	22
OCT. 7			4	84	1	21	21
					10	220	22
NOV. 11			8	175	3	66	22
DEC. 13	10	230			3	66	22
					10	230	23
	18		3	66	10	230	23

With a perpetual system, as in a periodic system of inventory determination, it is necessary to determine the specific cost of each item sold or to use a cost flow assumption. In the foregoing illustration, the first-in, first-out method of cost flow was assumed. Note that after the 7 units of the commodity were sold on February 4, there was a remaining inventory of 3 units at $20 each. The 8 units purchased on March 10 were acquired at a unit cost of $21, instead of $20, and hence could not be combined with the 3 units. The inventory after the March 10 purchase is therefore reported on two lines, 3 units at $20 each and 8 units at $21 each. Next, it should be noted that the $81 cost of the 4 units sold on April 22 is composed of the remaining 3 units at $20 each and 1 unit at $21. At this point, 7 units remain in inventory at a cost of $21 per unit. The remainder of the illustration is explained in a similar manner.

When the last-in, first-out method of cost flow is strictly applied to a perpetual inventory system, the unit cost prices assigned to the ending inventory will not necessarily be those associated with the earliest unit costs of the period. This situation will occur if at any time during a period the number of units of a commodity sold exceeds the number previously purchased during the same period. If this should happen, the excess quantity sold is priced at the cost of the beginning inventory, even though the excess number of units sold is restored later during the period by additional purchases. The effect of such a situation is to depart from the underlying purpose of the lifo costing system, which is to deduct current costs from current sales revenues.

To illustrate the foregoing situation, assume that the beginning inventory includes 100 units of a particular commodity priced at $50 a unit. During the year 70 units are sold, reducing the inventory to 30 units at $50 a unit. Later, near the end of the fiscal year, the inventory is restored to its original number by the purchase of 70 units at $58 a unit. The ending inventory of the commodity would be composed of 30 units at $50 a unit and 70 units at $58 a unit, for a total of $5,560. If the periodic system of inventory determination had been used, the last-in, first-out inventory would have been 100 units at $50 a unit, or $5,000.

One method of avoiding pricing problems of this nature is to maintain the perpetual inventory accounts throughout the period in terms of quantities only, inserting cost data at the end of the period. Another variation in procedure is to record costs in the perpetual inventory accounts in the usual manner in order to provide data needed for interim statements. At the end of the fiscal year, the necessary adjustments to apply the earliest costs to the ending inventory are then made.

The average cost method of cost flow can be applied to the perpetual system, though in a modified form. Instead of determining an average cost price for each type of commodity at the end of a period, an average unit price is computed each time a purchase is made. The unit price is then used to determine the cost of the items sold until another purchase is made. This averaging technique is called a **moving average.**

In earlier chapters, sales of merchandise were recorded by debits to the cash or accounts receivable account and credits to the sales account. The cost of the merchandise sold was not determined for each sale. It was determined only periodically by means of a physical inventory. In contrast to the periodic system, the perpetual system provides the cost data related to each sale. The cost data for sales on account may be accumulated in a special column inserted in the sales journal. Each time merchandise is sold on account, the amount entered in the "cost" column represents a debit to Cost of Merchandise Sold and a credit to Merchandise Inventory. Similar provisions can be made for cash sales. To illustrate sales on account under the perpetual inventory system, assume that the monthly total of the cost column of the sales journal is $140,000 and that the monthly total of the sales column is $210,000. The effect on the general ledger accounts is indicated by the following entries, in general journal form:

Cost of Merchandise Sold 140,000
    Merchandise Inventory 140,000
Accounts Receivable 210,000
    Sales. 210,000

The control feature is the most important advantage of the perpetual system. The inventory of each type of merchandise is always readily available in the subsidiary ledger. A physical count of any type of merchandise can be made at anytime and compared with the balance of the subsidiary account to determine the existence and seriousness of any shortages. When a shortage is discovered, an entry is made debiting Inventory Shortages and crediting Merchandise Inventory for the cost. If the balance of the inventory shortages account at the end of a fiscal period is relatively small, it may be included in miscellaneous general expense on the income statement. Otherwise it may be separately reported in the general expense section.

In addition to the usefulness of the perpetual inventory system in the preparation of interim statements, the subsidiary ledger can be an aid in maintaining inventory quantities at an optimum level. Frequent comparisons of balances with predetermined maximum and minimum levels facilitate both (1) the timely reordering of merchandise to avoid the loss of sales and (2) the avoidance of excess inventory.

Automated Perpetual Inventory Records

A perpetual inventory system may be maintained using manually kept records. However, such a system is often too costly and time consuming for enterprises with a large number of inventory items and/or with many purchase and sales transactions. In such cases, because of the mass of data to be processed, the frequently recurring and routine nature of the processing, and the importance of speed and accuracy, the record keeping is often automated. An automated system may use various combinations of mechanical and electronic equipment that operates with little human intervention.

One means of using electronic equipment in maintaining perpetual inventory records is described in the following outline:

1. The quantity of inventory for each commodity, along with its color, unit size or weight or other descriptive data, storage location, and any other information desired, is recorded on magnetic tape as of the date the system is installed. The tape is the input medium for transferring the data to the storage unit within the computer.

2. Each time the inventory of a commodity increases by purchase or by sales return, or decreases by sale or other cause, the data are recorded and processed by the computer, so that the inventory records in the storage unit are updated.

3. The quantity of inventory and other data for any particular commodity can be displayed on a cathode ray tube, which is similar to a television picture tube, or printed at any time. This assists in filling sales orders and in answering inquiries as to the amount of inventory on hand.

4. At the end of each month, a complete inventory listing is printed and the data representing the beginning inventory and the transactions for the month are removed from storage. Only the new inventory balances are retained within the storage unit of the computer.

5. Data from a physical inventory count are periodically entered into the computer. These data are compared with the current balances and a listing of the overages and shortages is printed. The appropriate commodity balances are adjusted to the quantities determined by the physical count.

By entering additional data, the system described can be extended to aid in maintaining inventory quantities at optimum levels. For example, data on the most economical quantity to be purchased in a single order and the minimum quantity to be maintained for each commodity can be entered into the computer. The equipment is then programmed to compare these data with data on actual inventory and to start the purchasing activity by preparing purchase orders.

PRESENTATION OF MERCHANDISE INVENTORY ON THE BALANCE SHEET

Merchandise inventory is usually presented on the balance sheet immediately following receivables. Both the method of determining the cost of the inventory (lifo, fifo, or average) and the method of valuing the inventory (cost, or lower of cost or market) should be shown. Both are important to the reader. The details may be disclosed by a parenthetical notation or a footnote. The use of a parenthetical notation is illustrated by the following partial balance sheet:

Afro-Arts Company Balance Sheet December 31, 1984		
Assets		
Current assets:		
Cash		$ 19,400
Accounts receivable	$80,000	
Less allowance for doubtful accounts	3,000	77,000
Merchandise inventory — at lower of cost (first-in, first-out method) or market		216,300

It is not unusual for large enterprises with diversified activities to use different costing and pricing methods for different segments of their inventories. The following note from the balance sheet of a merchandising chain is illustrative: "Merchandise inventories in stores are stated at the lower of cost or market, as calculated by the retail method of inventory. Merchandise in warehouses and in transit and food products inventories in restaurants are stated at cost."

GROSS PROFIT METHOD OF ESTIMATING INVENTORIES

When perpetual inventories are maintained or when the retail inventory method is used, the inventory on hand may be closely approximated at any time without the need for a physical count. In the absence of these devices, the inventory may be estimated by the **gross profit method**, which uses an estimate of the gross profit realized during the period.

If the rate of gross profit is known, the dollar amount of sales for a period can be divided into its two components: (1) gross profit and (2) cost of merchandise sold. The latter may then be deducted from the cost of merchandise available for sale to yield the estimated inventory of merchandise on hand.

To illustrate this method, assume that the inventory on January 1 is $57,000, that net purchases during the month amount to $180,000, that net sales during the month amount to $250,000, and finally that gross profit is *estimated* to be 30% of net sales. The inventory on January 31 may be estimated as follows:

Merchandise inventory, January 1		$ 57,000
Purchases in January (net)......................		180,000
Merchandise available for sale		$237,000
Sales in January (net)	$250,000	
Less estimated gross profit ($250,000 × 30%) ...	75,000	
Estimated cost of merchandise sold		175,000
Estimated merchandise inventory, January 31		$ 62,000

The estimate of the rate of gross profit is ordinarily based on the actual rate for the preceding year, adjusted for any changes made in the cost and sales prices during the current period. Inventories estimated in this manner are useful in preparing interim statements. The method may also be used in establishing an estimate of the cost of merchandise destroyed by fire or other disaster.

Self-
Examination
Questions
(Answers in
Appendix C.)

1. If the merchandise inventory at the end of the year is overstated by $7,500, the error will cause an:
   A. overstatement of cost of merchandise sold for the year by $7,500
   B. understatement of gross profit for the year by $7,500
   C. overstatement of net income for the year by $7,500
   D. understatement of net income for the year by $7,500

2. The inventory system employing accounting records that continuously disclose the amount of inventory is called:
   A. periodic   C. physical
   B. perpetual   D. retail

3. The inventory costing method that is based on the assumption that costs should be charged against revenue in the order in which they were incurred is:
   A. fifo   C. average cost
   B. lifo   D. perpetual inventory

4. The following units of a particular commodity were available for sale during the period:

   Beginning inventory.................... 40 units at $20
   First purchase......................... 50 units at $21
   Second purchase....................... 50 units at $22
   Third purchase........................ 50 units at $23

   What is the unit cost of the 35 units on hand at the end of the period as determined under the periodic system by the fifo costing method?
   A. $20   C. $22
   B. $21   D. $23

5. If merchandise inventory is being valued at cost and the price level is steadily rising, the method of costing that will yield the largest net income is:
   A. lifo   C. average
   B. fifo   D. periodic

Discussion Questions

1. The merchandise inventory at the end of the year was inadvertently understated by $10,000. (a) Did the error cause an overstatement or an understatement of the net income for the year? (b) Which items on the balance sheet at the end of the year were overstated or understated as a result of the error?

2. The $10,000 inventory error in Question 1 was not discovered and the inventory at the end of the following year was correctly stated. (a) Will the earlier error cause an overstatement or understatement of the net income for the following year? (b) Which items on the balance sheet at the end of the following year will be overstated or understated as a result of the error in the earlier year?

3. (a) Differentiate between the periodic system and the perpetual system of inventory determination. (b) Which system is more costly to maintain?

4. What is the meaning of the following terms: (a) physical inventory; (b) book inventory?

5. In which of the following types of businesses would a perpetual inventory system be practicable: (a) retail furrier, (b) wholesale office equipment distributor, (c) retail drug store, (d) grocery supermarket, (e) retail hardware store?

6. When does title to merchandise pass from the seller to the buyer if the terms of shipment are (a) FOB shipping point; (b) FOB destination?

7. Which of the three methods of inventory costing, fifo, lifo, or average cost, is based on the assumption that costs should be charged against revenue in the order in which they were incurred?

8. Do the terms *fifo* and *lifo* refer to techniques employed in determining quantities of the various classes of merchandise on hand? Explain.

9. Does the term *last-in* in the lifo method mean that the items in the inventory are assumed to be the most recent (last) acquisitions? Explain.

10. Under which method of cost flow are (a) the earliest costs assigned to inventory; (b) the most recent costs assigned to inventory; (c) average costs assigned to inventory?

11. The following units of a particular commodity were available for sale during the year:

   Beginning inventory................... 8 units at $125
   First purchase....................... 10 units at $130
   Second purchase..................... 10 units at $135

   The firm uses the periodic system and there are 7 units of the commodity on hand at the end of the year. (a) What is their unit cost according to fifo? (b) What is their unit cost according to lifo? (c) Is the average unit cost $130?

12. If merchandise inventory is being valued at cost and the price level is steadily falling, which of the three methods of costing, fifo, lifo, or average cost, will yield (a) the highest inventory cost, (b) the lowest inventory cost, (c) the largest net income, (d) the smallest net income?

13. Which of the three methods of inventory costing, fifo, lifo, or average cost, will in general yield an inventory cost most nearly approximating current replacement cost?

14. An enterprise using "cost" as its method of inventory valuation proposes to value at $900 a group of items having a total cost of $1,400. On what basis could this reduction in value be justified?

15. In the phrase *lower of cost or market*, what is meant by market?

16. The cost of a particular inventory item is $75, the current replacement cost is $70, and the selling price is $110. At what amount should the item be included in the inventory according to the lower of cost or market basis?

17. What are the two principal advantages of using the retail method of inventory costing?

18. An enterprise using a perpetual inventory system sells merchandise to a customer on account for $995; the cost of merchandise was $715. (a) What are the effects of the transaction on general ledger accounts? (b) What is the amount and direction of the net change in the amount of assets and capital resulting from the transaction?

19. What are the three most important advantages of the perpetual inventory system over the periodic system?

20. Under which, if any, of the following systems or methods of inventory determination is a periodic physical inventory unnecessary: (a) periodic inventory system, (b) perpetual inventory system, (c) retail inventory method, (d) gross profit method?

21. What uses can be made of the estimate of the cost of inventory determined by the gross profit method?

Exercises

Exercise 9-1. The beginning inventory and the purchases of Commodity X3C during the year were as follows:

Jan. 1	Inventory	10 units at $135
Mar. 17	Purchase	20 units at $141
July 2	Purchase	20 units at $145
Oct. 30	Purchase	15 units at $144

There are 18 units of the commodity in the physical inventory at December 31 (the periodic system is used). Determine the inventory cost and the cost of merchandise sold by three methods, presenting your answers in the following form:

	Cost	
Inventory Method	Merchandise Inventory	Merchandise Sold
(1) First-in, first-out	$	$
(2) Last-in, first-out		
(3) Average cost		

Exercise 9-2. On the basis of the following data, determine the value of the inventory at the lower of cost or market. Assemble the data in the form illustrated on page 251, in order that the inventory reduction attributable to price declines may be ascertained.

Commodity	Inventory Quantity	Unit Cost	Unit Market
B19	20	$270	$260
H30	32	65	67
N11	10	195	200
S92	45	80	77
V47	8	495	480

Exercise 9-3. On the basis of the following data, estimate the cost of the merchandise inventory at July 31 by the retail method:

		Cost	Retail
July 1	Merchandise inventory	$214,100	$319,500
July 1–31	Purchases (net)	181,870	271,500
July 1–31	Sales (net)		259,000

Exercise 9-4. Beginning inventory, purchases, and sales data for Commodity 92-D are as follows. The enterprise maintains a perpetual inventory system, costing by the first-in, first-out method. Determine the cost of the merchandise sold in each sale and the inventory balance after each sale, presenting the data in the form illustrated on page 254.

July	1.	Inventory..................	24 units at $30
	5.	Sold.....................	10 units
	13.	Purchased	15 units at $31
	19.	Sold.....................	18 units
	22.	Sold.....................	5 units
	30.	Purchased	15 units at $32

Exercise 9-5. Beginning inventory, purchases, and sales data for Commodity 276D for May are as follows:

Inventory, May 1,,....................	20 units at $30
Sales, May 7........................	6 units
15......................	12 units
25......................	5 units
Purchases, May 4	10 units at $31
22	13 units at $33

(a) Assuming that the perpetual inventory system is used, costing by the lifo method, determine the cost of the inventory balance at May 31.

(b) Assuming that the periodic inventory system is used, costing by the lifo method, determine the cost of the 20 units in the physical inventory at May 31.

(c) Determine the amount of the difference between the inventory cost in (a) and (b), and explain the reason for the difference.

Exercise 9-6. The merchandise inventory of Casler Company was destroyed by fire on May 17. The following data were obtained from the accounting records:

Jan. 1	Merchandise inventory	$194,500
Jan. 1–May 17	Purchases (net)	200,000
	Sales (net)........................	310,000
	Estimated gross profit rate...........	35%

Estimate the cost of the merchandise destroyed.

Problems
(Problems in Appendix B: 9-1B, 9-2B, 9-3B, 9-4B.)

Problem 9-1A. Good Vibes employs the periodic inventory system. Details regarding the inventory of television sets at July 1, purchases invoices during year, and the inventory count at June 30 are summarized as follows:

Model	Inventory, July 1	Purchases Invoices			Inventory Count, June 30
		1st	2d	3d	
A29	6 at $150	4 at $150	7 at $155	8 at $155	5
G12	5 at 173	10 at 175	10 at 177	8 at 182	8
J47	4 at 700	2 at 725	2 at 725	2 at 750	2
M59	3 at 520	4 at 531	2 at 549	3 at 542	4
P30	9 at 213	7 at 215	6 at 222	6 at 225	8
T99	6 at 305	3 at 310	3 at 316	4 at 321	5
W71	——	2 at 440	2 at 460	——	1

Instructions:

(1) Determine the cost of the inventory on June 30 by the first-in, first-out method. Present data in columnar form, using the following columnar headings. If the inventory of a particular model is composed of an entire lot plus a portion of another lot acquired at a different unit price, use a separate line for each lot.

Model	Quantity	Unit Cost	Total Cost

(2) Determine the cost of the inventory on June 30 by the last-in, first-out method, following the procedures indicated in instruction (1).
(3) Determine the cost of the inventory on June 30 by the average cost method, using the columnar headings indicated in instruction (1).

Problem 9-2A. The beginning inventory of Commodity P741 and data on purchases and sales for a three-month period are as follows:

April 1.	Inventory	7 units at $180	$1,260
6.	Purchase	10 units at 182	1,820
13.	Sale	10 units at 245	2,450
24.	Sale	3 units at 245	735
May 4.	Purchase	12 units at 183	2,196
6.	Sale	6 units at 250	1,500
19.	Sale	5 units at 250	1,250
25.	Purchase	15 units at 184	2,760
June 5.	Sale	6 units at 250	1,500
12.	Sale	7 units at 250	1,750
19.	Purchase	10 units at 185	1,850
30.	Sale	9 units at 250	2,250

Instructions:

(1) Record the inventory, purchases, and cost of merchandise sold data in a perpetual inventory record similar to the one illustrated on page 254, using the first-in, first-out method.
(2) Determine the total sales and the total cost of Commodity P741 sold for the period and indicate their effect on the general ledger by two entries in general journal form. Assume that all sales were on account.
(3) Determine the gross profit from sales of Commodity P741 for the period.
(4) Determine the cost of the inventory at June 30, assuming that the periodic system of inventory had been employed and that the inventory cost had been determined by the last-in, first-out method.

(If the working papers correlating with the textbook are not used, omit Problem 9-3A.)

Problem 9-3A. Data on the physical inventory of Rodrig Corporation as of June 30, the end of the current fiscal year, are presented in the working papers. The quantity of each commodity on hand has been determined and recorded on the inventory sheet. Unit market prices have also been determined as of June 30 and recorded on the sheet. The inventory is to be determined at cost and also at the lower of cost or market, using the first-in, first-out method. Quantity and cost data from the last purchases invoice of the year and the next-to-the-last purchases invoice are summarized as follows:

Description	Last Purchases Invoice Quantity Purchased	Unit Cost	Next-to-the-Last Purchases Invoice Quantity Purchased	Unit Cost
B16	40	$ 45	35	$ 44
72C	15	120	15	125
GH4	25	90	25	92
6X1	100	25	100	27
23P	6	310	8	320
85J	300	10	200	10
D22	8	400	5	410
EF9	500	6	500	7
Z91	70	17	50	16
39A	5	250	4	260
14P	25	305	25	310
KC2	75	14	100	13
T11	8	48	10	47
L19	150	8	100	9
92Y	50	15	40	16
A72	40	29	50	28
S29	55	28	50	28
G88	8	210	7	215

Instructions:

Record the appropriate unit costs on the inventory sheet and complete the pricing of the inventory. When there are two different unit costs applicable to a commodity, proceed as follows:

(1) Draw a line through the quantity and insert the quantity and unit cost of the last purchase.
(2) On the following line, insert the quantity and unit cost of the next-to-the-last purchase. The first item on the inventory sheet has been completed as an example.

Problem 9-4A. Selected data on merchandise inventory, purchases, and sales for Lane Co. and W. Jones Supply Co. are as follows:

Lane Co.

	Cost	Retail
Merchandise inventory, March 1...........	$277,100	$432,950
Transactions during March:		
Purchases............................	121,600 ⎫	188,300
Purchases discount....................	1,100 ⎭	
Sales		202,100
Sales returns and allowances		2,600

W. Jones Supply Co.

Merchandise inventory, July 1	$417,700
Transactions during July and August:	
Purchases	360,500
Purchases discount	3,600
Sales	510,250
Sales returns and allowances	5,250
Estimated gross profit rate	35%

Instructions:

(1) Determine the estimated cost of the merchandise inventory of Lane Co. on March 31 by the retail method, presenting details of the computations.

(2) Estimate the cost of the merchandise inventory of W. Jones Supply Co. on August 31 by the gross profit method, presenting details of the computations.

Problem 9-5A. The following preliminary income statement of Theis Enterprises Inc. was prepared before the accounts were adjusted or closed at the end of the fiscal year. The company uses the periodic inventory system.

Theis Enterprises Inc.
Income Statement
For Year Ended June 30, 19--

Sales (net)		$817,450
Cost of merchandise sold:		
Merchandise inventory, July 1, 19--	$201,400	
Purchases (net)	511,100	
Merchandise available for sale	$712,500	
Less merchandise inventory, June 30, 19--	220,000	
Cost of merchandise sold		492,500
Gross profit		$324,950
Operating expenses		231,850
Net income		$ 93,100

The following errors in the ledger and on the inventory sheets were discovered by the independent CPA retained to conduct the annual audit:

(a) A number of errors were discovered in pricing inventory items, in extending amounts, and in footing inventory sheets. The net effect of the corrections, exclusive of those described below, was to increase by $2,500 the amount stated as the ending inventory on the income statement.

(b) A sales order for $5,000, dated June 30, had been recorded as a sale on that date, but title did not pass to the purchaser until shipment was made on July 3. The merchandise, which had cost $3,025, was excluded from the June 30 inventory.

(c) A sales invoice for $1,250, dated June 30, had not been recorded. The merchandise was shipped on June 30, FOB shipping point, and its cost, $750, was excluded from the June 30 inventory.

(d) An item of store equipment, received on June 29, was erroneously included in the June 30 merchandise inventory at its cost of $6,425. The invoice had been recorded correctly.

(e) A purchases invoice for merchandise of $750, dated June 29, had been received and correctly recorded, but the merchandise was not received until July 2 and had not been included in the June 30 inventory. Title had passed to Theis Enterprises Inc. on June 29.

(f) A purchases invoice for merchandise of $3,400, dated June 30, was not received until July 2 and had not been recorded by June 30. However, the merchandise, to which title had passed, had arrived and had been included in the June 30 inventory.

Instructions:

(1) Journalize the entries necessary to correct the general ledger accounts as of June 30, inserting the identifying letters in the date column. All purchases and sales were made on account.

(2) Determine the correct inventory for June 30, beginning your analysis with the $220,000 shown on the preliminary income statement. Assemble the corrections in two groupings, "Additions" and "Deductions," allowing six lines for each group. Identify each correction by the appropriate letter.

(3) Prepare a revised income statement.

Problem 9-6A. Parkhill Sales is a distributor of imported mopeds. Its unadjusted trial balance as of the end of the current fiscal year is as follows:

Cash	19,700	
Accounts Receivable	30,600	
Allowance for Doubtful Accounts		675
Merchandise Inventory	41,100	
Equipment	26,000	
Accumulated Depreciation—Equipment		12,250
Accounts Payable		16,750
R. C. Parkhill, Capital		67,500
R. C. Parkhill, Drawing	36,000	
Sales		301,600
Purchases	189,900	
Operating Expenses (control account)	55,575	
Rent Income		1,200
Interest Expense	1,100	
	399,975	399,975

Data needed for adjustments at December 31:

(a) Merchandise inventory at December 31, at lower of cost (first-in, first-out method) or market, $45,800.

(b) Uncollectible accounts expense for current year is estimated at $1,325.

(c) Depreciation on equipment for current year, $2,250.

(d) Accrued wages on December 31, $750.

Instructions:

(1) Journalize the necessary adjusting entries.

(2) Prepare (a) an income statement, (b) a capital statement, and (c) a balance sheet in report form, without the use of a conventional work sheet.

Mini-Case

Eubanks Company began operations in 1984 by selling a single product. Data on purchases and sales for the year were as follows:

Purchases

Date	Units Purchased	Unit Cost	Total Cost
April 10	3,000	$11.00	$ 33,000
May 10	3,000	12.50	37,500
June 8	3,000	14.00	42,000
July 12	3,000	14.20	42,600
September 10	1,000	15.10	15,100
October 12	1,000	15.50	15,500
November 9	600	16.00	·9,600
December 11	600	16.50	9,900
	15,200		$205,200

Sales

April,	1,000 units	September,	1,500 units
May,	1,400 units	October,	1,350 units
June,	1,450 units	November,	1,400 units
July,	1,300 units	December,	1,350 units
August,	1,250 units		

Sales totaled $240,000.

On January 2, 1985, the president of the company, Tony Eubanks, asked for your advice on costing the 3,200-unit physical inventory that was taken on December 31, 1984. Also, since the firm plans to expand its product line, he asked your advice on the use of a perpetual inventory system in the future.

Instructions:

(1) Determine the cost of the December 31, 1984 inventory by the periodic method, using the (a) first-in, first-out method, (b) last-in, first-out method, and (c) average cost method.

(2) Determine the gross profit for the year under each of the three methods in (1).

(3) (a) In your opinion, which of the three inventory costing methods best reflects the results of operations for 1984? Why?

(b) In your opinion, which of the three inventory costing methods best reflects the replacement cost of the inventory on the balance sheet as of December 31, 1984? Why?

(c) Which inventory costing method would you choose to use for income tax purposes?

(4) Discuss the advantages and disadvantages of using a perpetual inventory system. From the data presented in this case, is there any indication of the adequacy of inventory levels during the year?

10
CHAPTER

Plant Assets and Intangible Assets

CHAPTER OBJECTIVES

Describe the characteristics of plant assets and illustrate the accounting for the acquisition of plant assets.

Describe and illustrate the accounting for depreciation, asset disposals, and depletion.

Describe and illustrate the reporting of plant assets and depreciation expense in the financial statements.

Describe and illustrate the accounting for and reporting of intangible assets.

10

CHAPTER

"Long-lived" is a general term that may be applied to assets of a relatively fixed or permanent nature owned by a business enterprise. Such assets that are tangible in nature, used in the operations of the business, and not held for sale in the ordinary course of the business are classified on the balance sheet as plant assets or **fixed assets.** Other descriptive titles frequently used are **property, plant, and equipment,** used either alone or in various combinations. The properties most frequently included in plant assets may be described in more specific terms as equipment, furniture, tools, machinery, buildings, and land. Although there is no standard criterion as to the minimum length of life necessary for classification as plant assets, they must be capable of repeated use and are ordinarily expected to last more than a year. However, the asset need not actually be used continuously or even often. Items of standby equipment held for use in the event of a breakdown of regular equipment or for use only during peak periods of activity are included in plant assets.

Assets acquired for resale in the normal course of business cannot be characterized as plant assets, regardless of their durability or the length of time they are held. For example, undeveloped land or other real estate acquired as a speculation should be listed on the balance sheet in the asset section entitled "Investments."

INITIAL COSTS OF PLANT ASSETS

The initial cost of a plant asset includes all expenditures *necessary* to get it in place and ready for use. Sales tax, transportation charges, insurance on the asset while in transit, special foundations, and installation costs should be added to the purchase price of the related plant asset. Similarly, when a secondhand asset is purchased, the initial costs of getting it ready for use, such as expenditures for new parts, repairs, and painting, are debited to the asset account. On the other hand, costs associated with the acquisition of a plant asset should be excluded from the asset account if they do not increase the asset's usefulness. Expenditures resulting from carelessness or errors in installing the asset, from vandalism, or from other unusual occurrences do not increase the usefulness of the asset and should be allocated to the period as an expense.

The cost of constructing a building includes the fees paid to architects and engineers for plans and supervision, insurance incurred during construction, and all other needed expenditures related to the project. Generally, interest incurred during the construction period on money borrowed to finance construction should also be treated as part of the cost of the building.[1]

The cost of land includes not only the negotiated price but also broker's commissions, title fees, surveying fees, and other expenditures connected with securing title. If delinquent real estate taxes are assumed by the buyer, they also are chargeable to the land account. If unwanted buildings are located on land acquired for a plant site, the cost of their razing or removal, less any salvage recovered, is properly chargeable to the land account. The cost of leveling or otherwise permanently changing the contour is also an additional cost of the land.

---

[1]*Statement of Financial Accounting Standards, No. 34,* "Capitalization of Interest Cost" (Stamford: Financial Accounting Standards Board, 1979), par. 6.

Other expenditures related to the land may be charged to Land, Buildings, or Land Improvements, depending upon the circumstances. If the property owner bears the initial cost of paving the public street bordering the land, either by direct payment or by special tax assessment, the paving may be considered to be as permanent as the land. On the other hand, the cost of constructing walkways to and around the building may be added to the building account if the walkways are expected to last as long as the building. Expenditures for improvements that are neither as permanent as the land nor directly associated with the building may be set apart in a land improvements account and depreciated according to their different life spans. Some of the more usual items of this nature are trees and shrubs, fences, outdoor lighting systems, and paved parking areas.

NATURE OF DEPRECIATION

As time passes, all plant assets with the exception of land lose their capacity to yield services.[2] Accordingly, the cost of such assets should be transferred to the related expense accounts in an orderly manner during their expected useful life. This periodic cost expiration is called depreciation.

Factors contributing to a decline in usefulness may be divided into two categories, *physical* depreciation, which includes wear from use and deterioration from the action of the elements, and *functional* depreciation, which includes inadequacy and obsolescence. A plant asset becomes inadequate if its capacity is not sufficient to meet the demands of increased production. A plant asset is obsolete if the commodity that it produces is no longer in demand or if a newer machine can produce a commodity of better quality or at a great reduction in cost. The continued growth of technological progress during this century has made obsolescence an increasingly important part of depreciation. Although the several factors comprising depreciation can be defined, it is not feasible to identify them when recording depreciation expense.

The meaning of the term "depreciation" as used in accounting is often misunderstood because the same term is also commonly used in business to mean a decline in the market value of an asset. The amount of unexpired cost of plant assets reported in the balance sheet is not likely to agree with the amount that could be realized from their sale. Plant assets are held for use in the enterprise rather than for sale. It is assumed that the enterprise will continue forever as a going concern. Consequently, the decision to dispose of a plant asset is based mainly on its usefulness to the enterprise.

Another common misunderstanding is that depreciation accounting automatically provides the cash needed to replace plant assets as they wear out. The cash account is neither increased nor decreased by the periodic entries that transfer the cost of plant assets to depreciation expense accounts. The misconception probably occurs because depreciation expense, unlike most expenses, does not require an equivalent outlay of cash in the period in which the expense is recorded.

---

[2]Land is here assumed to be used only as a site. Consideration will be given later in the chapter to land acquired for its mineral deposits or other natural resources.

RECORDING
DEPRECIATION

Depreciation may be recorded by an entry at the end of each month, or the adjustment may be delayed until the end of the year. The part of the entry that records the decrease in the plant asset is credited to a contra asset account entitled Accumulated Depreciation or Allowance for Depreciation. The use of a contra asset account permits the original cost to remain unchanged in the plant asset account. This facilitates the computation of periodic depreciation, the listing of both cost and accumulated depreciation on the balance sheet, and the reporting required for property tax and income tax purposes.

An exception to the general procedure of recording depreciation monthly or annually is often made when a plant asset is sold, traded in, or scrapped. As discussed and illustrated later in the chapter, the disposal is recorded by removing from the accounts both the cost of the asset and its related accumulated depreciation as of the date of the disposal. Hence, it is advisable to record the additional depreciation on the item for the current period before recording the transaction disposing of the asset. A further advantage of recording the depreciation at the time of the disposal of the asset is that no additional attention need be given the transaction when the amount of the periodic depreciation adjustment is later determined.

DETERMINING
DEPRECIATION

Factors to be considered in computing the periodic depreciation of a plant asset are its initial cost, its recoverable cost at the time it is retired from service, and the length of life of the asset. It is clear that neither of these latter two factors can be accurately determined until the asset is retired. They must be estimated at the time the asset is placed in service.

The estimated recoverable cost of a depreciable asset as of the time of its removal from service is called **residual, scrap, salvage,** or **trade-in value.** The excess of cost over the estimated residual value is the amount that is to be recorded as depreciation expense during the asset's life. When residual value is expected to be very small in comparison with the cost of the asset, it may be ignored in computing depreciation.

There are no hard-and-fast rules for estimating either the period of usefulness of an asset or its residual value at the end of such period. These two related factors may be greatly affected by management policies. The estimates of a company that provides its sales representatives with a new automobile every year will differ from those of a firm that keeps its cars for three years. Such variables as climate, frequency of use, maintenance, and minimum standards of efficiency will also affect the estimates.

Life estimates for depreciable assets are available in various trade association and other publications. For federal income tax purposes, the Internal Revenue Service has also established guidelines for life estimates. These guidelines may be useful in determining depreciation for financial reporting purposes.

In addition to the many factors that may influence the life estimate of an asset, there is a wide range in the degree of exactness used in the computation. A calendar month is ordinarily the smallest unit of time used. When this period of time is used, all assets placed in service or retired from service during the first half of a month are treated as if the event had occurred on the first day of that month. Similarly, all plant asset additions and reductions during the second half of a month are considered to have occurred on the first day of the next month. In the absence of any statement to the contrary, this practice will be assumed throughout this chapter.

It is not necessary that an enterprise use a single method of computing depreciation for all classes of its depreciable assets. The methods used in the accounts and financial statements may also differ from the methods used in determining income taxes and property taxes. The four methods used most often, straight-line, units-of-production, declining-balance, and sum-of-the-years-digits, are described and illustrated.

Straight-Line Method

The **straight-line method** of determining depreciation provides for equal periodic charges to expense over the estimated life of the asset. To illustrate this method, assume that the cost of a depreciable asset is $16,000, its estimated residual value is $1,000, and its estimated life is 5 years. The annual depreciation is computed as follows:

STRAIGHT-LINE METHOD OF DEPRECIATION

$$\frac{\$16,000 \text{ cost } - \$1,000 \text{ estimated residual value}}{5 \text{ years estimated life}} = \$3,000 \text{ annual depreciation}$$

The annual depreciation of $3,000 would be prorated for the first and the last partial years of use. Assuming a fiscal year ending on December 31 and first use of the asset on October 15, the depreciation for that fiscal year would be $750 (3 months). If usage had begun on October 16, the depreciation for the year would be $500 (2 months).

When the residual value of a plant asset represents a small part of its cost, it is often ignored. In such cases, the annual straight-line depreciation is determined on the basis of cost and the estimated life of the asset is converted to a percentage rate. The conversion to an annual percentage rate is accomplished by dividing 100 by the number of years of life. Thus a life of 50 years is equivalent to a 2% depreciation rate, 20 years is equivalent to a 5% rate, 8 years is equivalent to a 12½% rate, and so on.

The straight-line method is widely used. In addition to its simplicity, it provides a reasonable allocation of costs to periodic revenue when usage is relatively the same from period to period.

Units-of-Production Method

The **units-of-production method** yields a depreciation charge that varies with the amount of asset usage. To apply this method, the length of life of the asset is expressed in terms of productive capacity, such as hours, miles, or number of operations. Depreciation is first computed for the appropriate unit of production, and the depreciation for each accounting period is then determined by multiplying the unit depreciation by the number of units used during the period. To illustrate, assume that a machine with a cost of $16,000 and estimated residual value of $1,000 is expected to have an estimated life of 10,000 hours. The depreciation for a unit of one hour is computed as follows:

$$\frac{\$16,000 \text{ cost} - \$1,000 \text{ estimated residual value}}{10,000 \text{ estimated hours}} = \$1.50 \text{ hourly depreciation}$$

Assuming that the machine was in operation for 2,200 hours during a particular year, the depreciation for that year would be $1.50 × 2,200, or $3,300.

When the amount of usage of a plant asset changes from year to year, the units-of-production method is more logical than the straight-line method. It may yield fairer allocations of cost against periodic revenue.

Declining-Balance Method

The declining-balance method yields a declining periodic depreciation charge over the estimated life of the asset. The most common technique is to double the straight-line depreciation rate, computed without regard to residual value, and apply the resulting rate to the cost of the asset less its accumulated depreciation. For an asset with an estimated life of five years, the rate would be double the straight-line rate of 20%, or 40%. The double rate is then applied to the cost of the asset for the first year of its use and thereafter to the declining book value (cost minus accumulated depreciation). The method is illustrated in the following table:

Year	Cost	Accumulated Depreciation at Beginning of Year	Book Value at Beginning of Year	Rate	Depreciation for Year	Book Value at End of Year
1	$16,000	——	$16,000.00	40%	$6,400.00	$9,600.00
2	16,000	$ 6,400.00	9,600.00	40%	3,840.00	5,760.00
3	16,000	10,240.00	5,760.00	40%	2,304.00	3,456.00
4	16,000	12,544.00	3,456.00	40%	1,382.40	2,073.60
5	16,000	13,926.40	2,073.60	40%	829.44	1,244.16

Note that estimated residual value is not considered in determining the depreciation rate. It is also ignored in computing periodic depreciation, except that the asset should not be depreciated below the estimated residual value. In the above example, it was assumed that the estimated residual value at the end of the fifth year approximates the book value of $1,244.16. If the residual value had been estimated at $1,500, the depreciation for the fifth year would have been $573.60 ($2,073.60 − $1,500) instead of $829.44.

There was an implicit assumption in the above illustration that the first use of the asset coincided with the beginning of the fiscal year. This would usually not occur in actual practice, however, and would require a slight change in the computation for the first partial year of use. If the asset in the example had been placed in service at the end of the third month of the fiscal year, only the pro rata portion of the first full year's depreciation, 9/12 × (40% × $16,000), or $4,800, would be allocated to the first fiscal year. The method of computing the depreciation for the following years would not be affected. Thus, the depreciation for the second fiscal year would be 40% × ($16,000 − $4,800), or $4,480.

Sum-of-the-Years-Digits Method

The **sum-of-the-years-digits method** yields results like those obtained by use of the declining-balance method. The periodic charge for depreciation declines steadily over the estimated life of the asset because a successively smaller fraction is applied each year to the original cost of the asset less the estimated residual value. The denominator of the fraction, which remains the same, is the sum of the digits representing the years of life. The numerator of the fraction, which changes each year, is the number of remaining years of life. For an asset with an estimated life of 5 years, the denominator is $5 + 4 + 3 + 2 + 1$, or 15.[3] For the first year, the numerator is 5, for the second year 4, and so on. The method is illustrated by the following depreciation schedule for an asset with an assumed cost of $16,000, residual value of $1,000, and life of 5 years:

	Year	Cost Less Residual Value	Rate	Depreciation for Year	Accumulated Depreciation at End of Year	Book Value at End of Year
SUM-OF-THE-YEARS-DIGITS METHOD OF DEPRECIATION	1	$15,000	5/15	$5,000	$ 5,000	$11,000
	2	15,000	4/15	4,000	9,000	7,000
	3	15,000	3/15	3,000	12,000	4,000
	4	15,000	2/15	2,000	14,000	2,000
	5	15,000	1/15	1,000	15,000	1,000

When the first use of the asset does not coincide with the beginning of a fiscal year, it is necessary to allocate each full year's depreciation between the two fiscal years benefited. Assuming that the asset in the example was placed in service after three months of the fiscal year had elapsed, the depreciation for that fiscal year would be $9/12 \times (5/15 \times \$15,000)$, or $3,750. The depreciation for the second year would be $4,250, computed as follows:

$3/12 \times (5/15 \times \$15,000)$ $1,250
$9/12 \times (4/15 \times \$15,000)$ 3,000
Total, second fiscal year $4,250

Comparison of Depreciation Methods

The straight-line method provides for uniform periodic charges to depreciation expense over the life of the asset. The units-of-production method provides for periodic charges to depreciation expense that may vary considerably, depending upon the amount of usage of the asset.

Both the declining-balance and the sum-of-the-years-digits methods provide for a higher depreciation charge in the first year of use of the asset and a gradually declining periodic charge thereafter. For this reason they are frequently

---

[3] The denominator can also be determined from the following formula, where S = sum of the digits and N = number of years of estimated life:

$$S = N\left(\frac{N + 1}{2}\right)$$

referred to as **accelerated depreciation methods.** These methods are most appropriate for situations in which the decline in productivity or earning power of the asset is proportionately greater in the early years of its use than in later years. Further justification for their use is based on the tendency of repairs to increase with the age of an asset. The reduced amounts of depreciation in later years are therefore offset to some extent by increased maintenance expenses.

The periodic depreciation charges for the straight-line method and the accelerated methods are compared in the following chart. This chart is based on an asset cost of $16,000, an estimated life of 5 years, and an estimated residual value of $1,000.

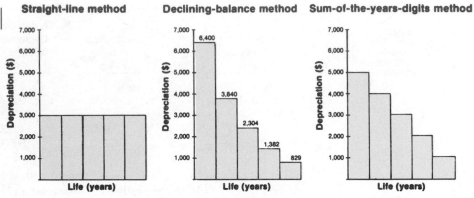

DEPRECIATION FOR FEDERAL INCOME TAX

Each of the four depreciation methods described in the paragraphs above can be used to determine the amount of depreciation for federal income tax purposes for plant assets acquired prior to 1981. The accelerated depreciation methods especially are widely used. Acceleration of the "write-off" of the asset reduces the income tax liability in the earlier years and thus increases the amount of cash available in those years to pay for the asset or for other purposes.

For most plant assets acquired after 1980, the Accelerated Cost Recovery System (ACRS) must be used to determine depreciation deductions for federal income tax purposes. This system provides for deductions that are similar to, or have similar effects as, the accelerated depreciation methods. The subject of federal income tax is covered in more detail in Chapter 27.

REVISION OF PERIODIC DEPRECIATION

Earlier in this chapter, it was noted that two of the factors that must be considered in computing the periodic depreciation of a plant asset — its recoverable cost at the time it is retired from service and its length of life — must be estimated at the time the asset is placed in service. Minor errors resulting from the use of these estimates are normal and tend to be recurring.[4] When such errors occur, the revised estimates are used to determine the amount of the remaining undepreciated asset cost to be charged as an expense in future periods.

---

[4]The correction of material or large errors made in computing depreciation is discussed in Chapter 16.

To illustrate, assume that a plant asset purchased for $130,000 and originally estimated to have a life of 30 years and residual value of $10,000 has been depreciated for 10 years by the straight-line method. At the end of ten years, its book value (undepreciated cost) would be $90,000, determined as follows:

Asset cost......................................	$130,000
Less accumulated depreciation	
($4,000 per year × 10 years)...................	40,000
Book value (undepreciated cost), end of tenth year...	$ 90,000

If during the eleventh year it is estimated that the remaining useful life is 25 years (instead of 20) and that the residual value is $5,000 (instead of $10,000), the depreciation expense for each of the remaining 25 years would be **$3,400**, determined as follows:

Book value (undepreciated cost), end of tenth year...	$90,000
Less revised estimated residual value	5,000
Revised remaining depreciation....................	$85,000
Revised annual depreciation expense	
($85,000 ÷ 25)	$ 3,400

Note that the correction of minor errors in the estimates used in the determination of depreciation does not correct the amounts of depreciation expense recorded in earlier years. The use of estimates, and the resulting likelihood of minor errors in such estimates, is inherent in the accounting process. Therefore when such errors do occur, the amounts recorded for depreciation expense in the past are not corrected; only future depreciation expense amounts are affected.

CAPITAL AND REVENUE EXPENDITURES

In addition to the initial cost of acquiring a plant asset, other costs related to its efficiency or capacity may be incurred during its service life. It is often difficult to recognize the difference between expenditures that add to the utility of the asset for more than one accounting period and those that benefit only the period in which they are incurred. Costs that add to the utility for more than one period are chargeable to an asset account or to a related accumulated depreciation account and are called **capital expenditures**. Expenditures that benefit only the current period are chargeable to expense accounts and are called **revenue expenditures**.

Expenditures for an addition to a plant asset are clearly capital expenditures. For example, the cost of installing an air conditioning unit in an automobile or of adding a wing to a building should be debited to the respective asset accounts. It is equally clear that expenditures for maintenance and repairs of a recurring nature should be classified as revenue expenditures. Thus, the cost of replacing spark plugs in an automobile or of repainting a building should be debited to proper expense accounts. In less obvious situations, several criteria may be considered in classifying the expenditures.

Expenditures that increase operating efficiency or capacity for the remaining useful life of an asset should be capitalized; that is, they should be treated as capital expenditures. For example, if the power unit attached to a machine is replaced by one of greater capacity, the cost and the accumulated depreciation related to the old motor should be removed from the accounts and the cost of the new one added to the asset account.

Expenditures that increase the useful life of an asset beyond the original estimate are also capital expenditures. They should be debited to the appropriate accumulated depreciation account, however, rather than to the asset account. To illustrate, assume that a machine with an estimated life of ten years is substantially rebuilt at the end of its seventh year of use, and that the extraordinary repairs are expected to extend the life of the machine an additional three years beyond the original estimate. In such circumstances the expenditures may be said to restore or "make good" a portion of the depreciation accumulated in prior years, and it is therefore appropriate that they be debited to the accumulated depreciation account.

When the cost of improvements or extraordinary repairs is great or when there is a material change in estimated life, the periodic depreciation allocable to future periods should be redetermined on the basis of the new book value of the asset and the new estimate of the remaining useful life.

Small expenditures are usually treated as repair expense even though they may have the characteristics of capital expenditures. The saving in time and clerical expenses justifies the sacrifice of the small degree of accuracy. Some businesses establish a minimum amount required to classify an item as a capital expenditure.

DISPOSAL OF PLANT ASSETS

Plant assets that are no longer useful may be discarded, sold, or applied toward the purchase of other plant assets. The details of the entry to record a disposal will vary, but in all cases it is necessary to remove the book value of the asset from the accounts. This is done by debiting the proper accumulated depreciation account for the total depreciation to the date of disposal and crediting the asset account for the cost of the asset.

A plant asset should not be removed from the accounts only because it has been depreciated for the full period of its estimated life. If the asset is still useful to the enterprise, the cost and accumulated depreciation should remain in the ledger. Otherwise the accounts would contain no evidence of the continued existence of such plant assets and the control function of the ledger would be impaired. In addition, the cost and the accumulated depreciation data on such assets are often needed in reporting for property tax and income tax purposes.

Discarding Plant Assets

When plant assets are no longer useful to the business and have no market value, they are discarded. If the asset has been fully depreciated, no loss is realized. To illustrate, assume that an item of equipment acquired at a cost of $6,000 became fully depreciated at December 31, the end of the preceding fiscal year, and is now to be discarded as worthless. The entry to record the disposal is as follows:

Mar. 24	Accumulated Depreciation — Equipment	6,000	
	Equipment.		6,000
	To write off equipment discarded.		

If the accumulated depreciation applicable to the $6,000 of discarded equipment had been less than $6,000, there would have been a loss on its disposal. Furthermore, it would have been necessary to record depreciation for the three months of use in the current period before recording the disposal. To illustrate these differences, assume that annual depreciation on the equipment is computed at 10% of cost and that the accumulated depreciation balance is $4,750 after the annual adjusting entry at the end of the preceding year. The entry to record depreciation of $150 for the three months of the current period is as follows:

Mar. 24	Depreciation Expense — Equipment	150	
	Accumulated Depreciation — Equipment . . .		150
	To record current depreciation on equipment discarded.		

The equipment is then removed from the accounts and the loss is recorded by the following entry:

Mar. 24	Accumulated Depreciation — Equipment	4,900	
	Loss on Disposal of Plant Assets.	1,100	
	Equipment.		6,000
	To write off equipment discarded.		

Ordinary losses and gains on the disposal of plant assets are nonoperating items and may be reported in the Other Expense and Other Income sections, respectively, of the income statement.

Sale of Plant Assets   The entry to record the sale of a plant asset is like the entries illustrated in the preceding section, except that the cash or other asset received must also be recorded. If the selling price is more than the book value of the asset, the transaction results in a gain; if the selling price is less than the book value, there is a loss. To illustrate some possibilities, assume that equipment acquired at a cost of $10,000 and depreciated at the annual rate of 10% of cost is sold for cash on October 12 of the eighth year of its use. The accumulated depreciation in the account as of the preceding December 31 is $7,000. The entry to record the depreciation for the nine months of the current year is as follows:

Oct. 12	Depreciation Expense — Equipment	750	
	Accumulated Depreciation — Equipment . . .		750
	To record current depreciation on equipment sold.		

After the current depreciation is recorded, the book value of the asset is $2,250. In general journal form, entries to record the sale under three different assumptions as to selling price are as follows:

Sold at book value, for $2,250. No gain or loss.

Oct. 12	Cash	2,250	
	Accumulated Depreciation — Equipment	7,750	
	Equipment		10,000

Sold below book value, for $1,000. Loss of $1,250.

Oct. 12	Cash	1,000	
	Accumulated Depreciation — Equipment	7,750	
	Loss on Disposal of Plant Assets	1,250	
	Equipment		10,000

Sold above book value, for $3,000. Gain of $750.

Oct. 12	Cash	3,000	
	Accumulated Depreciation — Equipment	7,750	
	Equipment		10,000
	Gain on Disposal of Plant Assets		750

Exchange of Plant Assets

Old equipment is often traded in for new equipment having a similar use. The trade-in allowance is deducted from the price of the new equipment, and the balance owed (**boot**) is paid according to the credit terms. The trade-in allowance given by the seller is often greater or less than the book value of the old equipment traded in. In the past, it was acceptable for financial reporting purposes to recognize the difference between the trade-in allowance and the book value as a gain or a loss. For example, a trade-in allowance of $1,500 on equipment with a book value of $1,000 would have yielded a recognized gain of $500. Such treatment is no longer acceptable for financial reporting purposes on the ground that revenue occurs from the production and sale of items produced by plant assets and not from the exchange of similar plant assets.[5] However, if the trade-in allowance is less than the book value of the old equipment, the loss is recognized immediately.

Nonrecognition of Gain

The acceptable method of accounting for an exchange in which the trade-in allowance exceeds the book value of the old plant asset requires that the cost of the new asset be determined by adding the amount of boot given to the book value of the old asset. To illustrate, assume an exchange based on the following data:

Equipment traded in (old):

Cost of old equipment	$4,000
Accumulated depreciation at date of exchange	3,200
Book value at June 19, date of exchange	$ 800

[5]*Opinions of the Accounting Principles Board, No. 29,* "Accounting for Nonmonetary Transactions" (New York: American Institute of Certified Public Accountants, 1973), **pars.** 16, 21(b), and 22.

Similar equipment acquired (new):

Price of new equipment............................	$5,000
Trade-in allowance on old equipment.................	1,100
Boot given (cash)	$3,900

The cost basis of the new equipment is $4,700, which is determined by adding the boot given ($3,900) to the book value of the old equipment ($800). The compound entry to record the exchange and the payment of cash, in general journal form, is as follows:

June 19 Accumulated Depreciation—Equipment	3,200	
Equipment.....................................	4,700	
Equipment.................................		4,000
Cash......................................		3,900

It should be noted that the nonrecognition of the $300 gain ($1,100 trade-in allowance minus $800 book value) at the time of the exchange is really a postponement. The periodic depreciation expense is based on a cost of $4,700 rather than on the quoted price of $5,000. The unrecognized gain of $300 at the time of the exchange will be matched by a reduction of $300 in the total amount of depreciation taken during the life of the equipment.

Recognition of Loss

To illustrate the accounting for a loss on the exchange of one plant asset for another which is similar in use, assume an exchange based on the following data:

Equipment traded in (old):

Cost of old equipment	$ 7,000
Accumulated depreciation at date of exchange.........	4,600
Book value at September 7, date of exchange	$ 2,400

Similar equipment acquired (new):

Price of new equipment...........................	$10,000
Trade-in allowance on old equipment................	2,000
Boot given (cash)	$ 8,000

The amount of the loss to be recognized on the exchange is the excess of the book value of the equipment traded in ($2,400) over the trade-in allowance ($2,000), or $400. The entry to record the exchange, in general journal form, is as follows:

Sept. 7 Accumulated Depreciation—Equipment	4,600	
Equipment....................................	10,000	
Loss on Disposal of Plant Assets...............	400	
Equipment.................................		7,000
Cash......................................		8,000

Federal Income Tax Requirements

The Internal Revenue Code (IRC) requires that neither gains nor losses be recognized for income tax purposes if (1) the asset acquired by the taxpayer is similar in use to the asset given in exchange and (2) any boot involved is given (rather than received) by the taxpayer. Thus, the treatment of a nonrecognized gain corresponds to the acceptable method prescribed for financial reporting purposes, the boot given being added to the book value of the old equipment. In the first illustration, the cost basis for federal income tax purposes corresponds to the amount recorded as the cost of the new equipment, namely $4,700.

The cost basis of the new equipment in the second illustration, for federal income tax purposes, is determined in a like manner. The boot given ($8,000) is added to the book value of the old equipment ($2,400), yielding a cost basis of $10,400. The unrecognized loss of $400 at the time of the exchange will be matched by an increase of $400 in the total amount of depreciation allowed for income tax purposes during the life of the asset.

SUBSIDIARY LEDGERS FOR PLANT ASSETS   When depreciation is to be computed individually on a large number of assets making up a functional group, it is advisable to maintain a subsidiary ledger. To illustrate, assume that an enterprise owns about 200 items of office equipment with a total cost of about $100,000. Unless the business is newly organized, the equipment would have been acquired over a number of years. The individual cost, estimated residual value, and estimated life would be different in any case, and the makeup of the group will continually change because of acquisitions and disposals.

There are many variations in the form of subsidiary records for depreciable assets. Multicolumn analysis sheets may be used, or a separate ledger account may be maintained for each asset. The form should be designed to provide spaces for recording the acquisition and the disposal of the asset, the depreciation charged each period, the accumulated depreciation to date, and any other pertinent data desired. Following is an example of a subsidiary ledger account for a plant asset:

PLANT ASSET RECORD

ACCOUNT NO.: 123-215   GENERAL LEDGER ACCOUNT: OFFICE EQUIPMENT
ITEM: SF 490 COPIER
SERIAL NO.: AT 47-3926
FROM WHOM PURCHASED: HAMILTON OFFICE MACHINES CO. INC.
ESTIMATED LIFE: 10 YEARS   ESTIMATED RESIDUAL VALUE: $500   DEPRECIATION PER YEAR: $240

| | | ASSET | | ACCUMULATED DEPRECIATION | | | BOOK |
DATE	DEBIT	CREDIT	BALANCE	DEBIT	CREDIT	BALANCE	VALUE
04/08/84	2,900		2,900				2,900
12/31/84					180	180	2,720
12/31/85					240	420	2,480

AN ACCOUNT IN THE OFFICE EQUIPMENT LEDGER

The number assigned to the account illustrated is made up of the number of the office equipment account in the general ledger (123) followed by the number assigned to the specific item of office equipment purchased (215). An identification tag or plaque with the corresponding account number is attached to the asset. Depreciation for the year in which the asset was acquired, computed for nine months on a straight-line basis, is $180; for the following year it is $240. These amounts, together with the corresponding amounts from all other accounts in the subsidiary ledger, provide the figures for the respective year-end adjusting entries debiting the depreciation expense account and crediting the accumulated depreciation account.

The sum of the asset balances and the sum of the accumulated depreciation balances in all of the accounts should be compared periodically with the balances of their respective controlling accounts in the general ledger. When a certain asset is disposed of, the asset section of the subsidiary account is credited and the accumulated depreciation section is debited. This reduces the balances of both sections to zero. The account is then removed from the ledger and filed for possible future reference.

Subsidiary ledgers for plant assets are useful to the accounting department in (1) determining the periodic depreciation expense, (2) recording the disposal of individual items, (3) preparing tax returns, and (4) preparing insurance claims in the event of insured losses. The forms may also be expanded to provide spaces for accumulating data on the operating efficiency of the asset. Such information as number of breakdowns, length of time out of service, and cost of repairs is useful in comparing similar equipment produced by different manufacturers. When new equipment is to be purchased, the data are useful to management in deciding upon size, model, and other specifications and the best source of supply.

Regardless of whether subsidiary equipment ledgers are maintained, plant assets should be inspected periodically in order to determine their state of repair and whether or not they are still in use.

COMPOSITE-RATE DEPRECIATION METHOD

In the preceding illustrations, depreciation has been computed on each individual plant asset and, unless otherwise stated, this procedure will be assumed in the problem materials at the end of the chapter. Another procedure, called the composite-rate depreciation method, is to determine depreciation for entire groups of assets by use of a single rate. The basis for grouping may be similarity in life estimates or other common traits, or it may be broadened to include all assets within a functional class, such as office equipment or factory equipment.

When depreciation is computed on the basis of a composite group of assets of differing life spans, a rate based on averages must be developed. This may be done by (1) computing the annual depreciation for each asset, (2) determining the total annual depreciation, and (3) dividing the sum thus determined by the total cost of the assets. The procedure is illustrated as follows:

COMPOSITE-RATE
METHOD OF
DEPRECIATION

Asset No.	Cost	Estimated Residual Value	Estimated Life	Annual Depreciation
101	$ 20,000	$4,000	10 years	$ 1,600
102	15,600	1,500	15 years	940
147	41,000	1,000	8 years	5,000
Total	$473,400			$49,707

$$\frac{\$49,707 \text{ annual depreciation}}{\$473,400 \text{ cost}} = 10.5\% \text{ composite rate}$$

Although new assets of differing life spans and residual values will be added to the group and old assets will be retired, the "mix" is assumed to remain relatively unchanged. Accordingly, a depreciation rate based on averages (10.5% in the illustration) also remains unchanged for an indefinite time in the future.

When a composite rate is used, it may be applied against total asset cost on a monthly basis, or some reasonable assumption may be made regarding the timing of increases and decreases in the group. A common practice is to assume that all additions and retirements have occurred uniformly throughout the year. The composite rate is then applied to the average of the beginning and the ending balances of the account. Another acceptable averaging technique is to assume that all additions and retirements during the first half of the year occurred as of the first day of that year, and that all additions and retirements during the second half of the year occurred on the first day of the following year.

When assets within the composite group are retired, no gain or loss should be recognized. Instead, the asset account is credited for the cost of the asset and the accumulated depreciation account is debited for the excess of cost over the amount realized from the disposal. Any deficiency in the amount of depreciation recorded on the shorter-lived assets is presumed to be balanced by excessive depreciation on the longer-lived assets.

Regardless of whether depreciation is computed for each individual unit or for composite groups, the periodic depreciation charge is based on estimates. The effect of obsolescence and inadequacy on the life of plant assets is particularly difficult to forecast. Any system that provides for the allocation of depreciation in a systematic and rational manner fulfills the requirements of good accounting.

DEPRECIATION OF PLANT ASSETS OF LOW UNIT COST

Subsidiary ledgers are not usually maintained for classes of plant assets that are made up of individual items of low unit cost. Hand tools and other portable equipment of small size and value are typical examples. Because of hard usage, breakage, and pilferage, such assets may be relatively short-lived and require constant replacement. In such cases, the usual depreciation methods are not practical. One common method of determining cost expiration is to take a periodic inventory of the items on hand, estimate their fair value based on original cost, and transfer the remaining amount from the asset account to an appropriately titled account, such as Tools Expense. Other categories to which the same method is often applied are dies, molds, patterns, and spare parts.

DEPLETION

The periodic allocation of the cost of metal ores and other minerals removed from the earth is called depletion. The amount of the periodic cost allocation is based on the relationship of the cost to the estimated size of the mineral deposit and on the quantity extracted during the particular period. To illustrate, assume that the cost of certain mineral rights is $400,000 and that the deposit is estimated at 1,000,000 tons of ore of uniform grade. The depletion rate would be $400,000 ÷ 1,000,000, or $.40 a ton. If 90,000 tons are mined during the year, the depletion, amounting to $36,000, would be recorded by the following entry:

Adjusting Entry

Dec. 31	Depletion Expense	36,000	
	Accumulated Depletion		36,000

The accumulated depletion account is a contra asset account and is presented in the balance sheet as a deduction from the cost of the mineral deposit.

In determining income subject to the federal income tax, the IRC permits, with certain limitations, a depletion deduction equal to a specified percent of gross income from the extractive operations. Thus, for income tax purposes, it is possible for total depletion deductions to be more than the cost of the property. Detailed examination of the tax law and regulations regarding "percentage depletion" is beyond the scope of this discussion, however.

INTANGIBLE ASSETS

Long-lived assets that are useful in the operations of an enterprise, not held for sale, and without physical qualities are usually classified as **intangible assets.** The basic principles of accounting for intangible assets are like those described earlier for plant assets. The major concerns are the determination of the initial costs and the recognition of periodic cost expiration, called **amortization,** due to the passage of time or a decline in usefulness. Intangible assets often include patents, copyrights, and goodwill.

Patents

Manufacturers may acquire exclusive rights to produce and sell goods with one or more unique features. Such rights are evidenced by **patents,** which are issued to inventors by the federal government. They continue in effect for 17 years. An enterprise may obtain patents on new products developed in its own research laboratories or it may purchase patent rights from others. The initial cost of a purchased patent should be debited to an asset account and then written off, or amortized, over the years of its expected usefulness. This period of time may be less than the remaining legal life of the patent, and the expectations are also subject to change in the future.

To illustrate, assume that at the beginning of its fiscal year an enterprise acquires for $100,000 a patent granted six years earlier. Although the patent will not expire for another eleven years, it is expected to be of value for only five years. A separate contra asset account is normally not credited for the write-off or amortization of patents. In most situations, the credit is recorded directly in the patents account. This practice is common for all intangible assets. The entry to amortize the patent at the end of the fiscal year is as follows:

Adjusting Entry

Dec. 31	Amortization Expense—Patents............	20,000	
	Patents.................................		20,000

Continuing the illustration, assume that after two years of use it appears that the patent will have no value at the end of an additional two years. The cost to be amortized in the third year would be the balance of the asset account, $60,000, divided by the remaining two years, or $30,000. The straight-line method of amortization should be used unless it can be shown that another method is more appropriate.[6]

An enterprise that develops patentable products in its own research laboratories often incurs substantial costs for the experimental work involved. In theory, some accountants believe that such costs, normally referred to as **research and development costs,** should be treated as an asset in the same manner as patent rights purchased from others. However, business enterprises are generally required to treat expenditures for research and development as current operating expenses.[7] The reason for this requirement is that there is a high degree of uncertainty about their future benefits, and therefore expensing these costs as incurred seems most appropriate. In addition, from a practical standpoint, a reasonably fair cost figure for each patent is difficult to establish because a number of research projects may be in process at the same time or work on some projects may extend over a number of years. As a result, a specific relationship between research and development costs and future revenue seldom can be established.

Whether patent rights are purchased from others or result from the efforts of its own research laboratories, an enterprise often incurs substantial legal fees related to the patents. For example, legal fees may be incurred in establishing the legal validity of the patents. Such fees should be debited to an asset account and then amortized over the years of the usefulness of the patents.

Copyrights | The exclusive right to publish and sell a literary, artistic, or musical composition is obtained by a **copyright.** Copyrights are issued by the federal government and extend for 50 years beyond the author's death. The costs assigned to a copyright include all costs of creating the work plus the cost of obtaining the copyright. A copyright that is purchased from another should be recorded at the price paid for it. Because of the uncertainty regarding the useful life of a copyright, it is usually amortized over a relatively short period of time.

Goodwill | In the sense that it is used in business, **goodwill** is an intangible asset that attaches to a business as a result of such favorable factors as location, product superiority, reputation, and managerial skill. Its existence is evidenced by the ability of the business to earn a rate of return on the investment that is in excess of the normal rate for other firms in the same line of business.

Accountants are in general agreement that goodwill should be recognized in the accounts only if it can be objectively determined by an event or transaction, such as the purchase or sale of a business. Accountants also agree that the value

---

[6]*Opinions of the Accounting Principles Board, No. 17,* "Intangible Assets" (New York: American Institute of Certified Public Accountants, 1970), par. 30.

[7]*Statement of Financial Accounting Standards, No. 2,* "Accounting for Research and Development Costs" (Stamford: Financial Accounting Standards Board, 1974), par. 12.

of goodwill eventually disappears and that the recorded costs should be amortized over the years during which the goodwill is expected to be of value. This period should not, however, exceed 40 years.[8]

REPORTING DEPRECIATION EXPENSE, PLANT ASSETS, AND INTANGIBLE ASSETS IN THE FINANCIAL STATEMENTS

The amount of depreciation expense of a period should be set forth separately in the income statement or disclosed in some other manner. A general description of the method or methods used in computing depreciation should also accompany the financial statements.[9]

The balance of each major class of depreciable assets should be disclosed in the financial statements or in notes thereto, together with the related accumulated depreciation, either by major class or in total.[10] When there are too many classes of plant assets to permit such a detailed listing in the balance sheet, a single figure may be presented, supported by a separate schedule.

Intangible assets are usually presented in the balance sheet in a separate section immediately following plant assets. The balance of each major class of intangible assets should be disclosed at an amount net of amortization taken to date.

An illustration of the presentation of plant assets and intangible assets is shown in the following partial balance sheet:

PLANT ASSETS AND INTANGIBLE ASSETS IN THE BALANCE SHEET

Clinton Door Inc.
Balance Sheet
December 31, 19--

Assets

	Cost	Accumulated Depreciation	Book Value	
Total current assets				$462,500
Plant assets:				
Land	$ 30,000	——	$ 30,000	
Buildings.................	110,000	$ 26,000	84,000	
Factory equipment	650,000	192,000	458,000	
Office equipment	120,000	13,000	107,000	
Total plant assets	$910,000	$231,000		679,000
Intangible assets:				
Patents			$ 75,000	
Goodwill			50,000	
Total intangible assets				125,000

---

[8]*Opinions of the Accounting Principles Board, No. 17*, "Intangible Assets," *op. cit.*, par. 29.
[9]*Opinions of the Accounting Principles Board, No. 22*, "Disclosure of Accounting Policies" (New York: American Institute of Certified Public Accountants, 1972), par. 13.
[10]*Opinions of the Accounting Principles Board, No. 12*, "Omnibus Opinion—1967" (New York: American Institute of Certified Public Accountants, 1967), par. 5.

**Self-
Examination
Questions**
*(Answers in
Appendix C.)*

1. Which of the following expenditures incurred in connection with the acquisition of machinery is a proper charge to the asset account?
   A. Transportation charges   C. Both A and B
   B. Installation costs   D. Neither A nor B

2. What is the amount of depreciation, using the sum-of-the-years-digits method, for the first year of use for equipment costing $9,500 with an estimated residual value of $500 and an estimated life of 3 years?
   A. $4,500.00   C. $3,000.00
   B. $3,166.67   D. None of the above

3. An example of an accelerated depreciation method is:
   A. straight-line   C. units of production
   B. sum-of-the-years-digits   D. none of the above

4. A plant asset priced at $100,000 is acquired by trading in a similar asset that has a book value of $25,000. Assuming that the trade-in allowance is $30,000 and that $70,000 cash is paid for the new asset, what is the cost basis for the new asset for financial reporting purposes?
   A. $100,000   C. $30,000
   B. $70,000   D. None of the above

5. Which of the following is an example of an intangible asset?
   A. Patents   C. Copyrights
   B. Goodwill   D. All of the above

**Discussion
Questions**

1. Which of the following qualities of an asset are characteristic of *plant assets?*
   (a) Capable of repeated use in operations of the business.
   (b) Held for sale in normal course of business.
   (c) Tangible.
   (d) Intangible.
   (e) Long-lived.
   (f) Used continuously in operations of the business.

2. Blum Office Supply Co. has a fleet of automobiles and trucks for use by sales-persons and for delivery of office supplies and equipment. Parkhill Auto Sales Inc. has automobiles and trucks for sale. Under what caption would the automobiles and trucks be reported on the balance sheet of (a) Blum Office Supply Co., (b) Parkhill Auto Sales Inc.?

3. John Ryan & Co. acquired an adjacent vacant lot as a speculation. The lot will hopefully be sold in the future at a gain. Where should such real estate be listed in the balance sheet?

4. Indicate which of the following expenditures incurred in connection with the acqui-sition of a printing press should be charged to the asset account: (a) insurance while in transit, (b) freight charges, (c) sales tax on purchase price, (d) fee paid to factory representative for assembling and adjusting, (e) cost of special foundation, (f) new parts to replace those damaged in unloading.

5. Which of the following expenditures incurred in connection with the purchase of a secondhand printing press should be debited to the asset account: (a) new parts to replace those worn out, (b) freight charges, (c) installation costs, (d) repair of vandalism damages occurring during installation?

6. To increase its parking area, Lincolnshire Shopping Center acquired adjoining land for $90,000 and a building located on the land for $50,000. The net cost of razing the building and leveling the land was $10,000, after amounts received from sale of salvaged building materials were deducted. What accounts should be debited for (a) the $90,000, (b) the $50,000, (c) the $10,000?

7. Are the amounts at which plant assets are reported in the balance sheet their approximate market values as of the balance sheet date? Discuss.

8. (a) Does the recognition of depreciation in the accounts provide a special cash fund for the replacement of plant assets? (b) Describe the nature of depreciation as the term is used in accounting.

9. Is it necessary for an enterprise to use the same method of computing depreciation for (a) all classes of its depreciable assets, (b) the financial statements and in determining income taxes?

10. Convert each of the following life estimates to a straight-line depreciation rate, stated as a percent, assuming that residual value of the plant asset is to be ignored: (a) 4 years, (b) 5 years, (c) 10 years, (d) 20 years, (e) 25 years, (f) 40 years, (g) 50 years.

11. A plant asset with a cost of $95,000 has an estimated residual value of $5,000 and an estimated life of 5 years. What is the amount of the annual depreciation, computed by the straight-line method?

12. A plant asset with a cost of $45,000 has an estimated residual value of $5,000 and an estimated productive capacity of 400,000 units. What is the amount of annual depreciation, computed by the units-of-production method, for a year in which production is (a) 40,000 units, (b) 60,000 units?

13. The declining-balance method, at double the straight-line rate, is to be used for an asset with a cost of $25,000, estimated residual value of $1,000, and estimated life of 10 years. What is the depreciation for the first fiscal year, assuming that the asset was placed in service at the beginning of the year?

14. An asset with a cost of $20,750, an estimated residual value of $750, and an estimated life of 4 years is to be depreciated by the sum-of-the-years-digits method. (a) What is the denominator of the depreciation fraction? (b) What is the amount of depreciation for the first full year of use? (c) What is the amount of depreciation for the second full year of use?

15. (a) Name the two accelerated depreciation methods described in this chapter. (b) Why are the accelerated depreciation methods used frequently for income tax purposes?

16. A plant asset with a cost of $125,000 has an estimated residual value of $5,000, an estimated life of 40 years, and is depreciated by the straight-line method. (a) What is the amount of the annual depreciation? (b) What is the book value at the end of the twentieth year of use? (c) If at the start of the twenty-first year it is estimated that the remaining life is 25 years and that the residual value is $5,000, what is the depreciation expense for each of the remaining 25 years?

17. (a) Differentiate between capital expenditures and revenue expenditures. (b) Why are some items that have the characteristics of capital expenditures not capitalized?

18. Immediately after a used truck is acquired, a new motor is installed and the tires are replaced at a total cost of $2,500. Is this a capital expenditure or a revenue expenditure?

19. For a number of subsidiary plant ledger accounts of an enterprise, the balance in accumulated depreciation is exactly equal to the cost of the asset. (a) Is it permissible to record additional depreciation on the assets if they are still in use? (b) When should an entry be made to remove the cost and accumulated depreciation from the accounts?

20. In what sections of the income statement are gains and losses from the disposal of plant assets presented?

21. A plant asset priced at $60,000 is acquired by trading in a similar asset and paying cash for the remainder. (a) Assuming the trade-in allowance to be $25,000, what is the amount of "boot" given? (b) Assuming the book value of the asset traded in to be $20,000, what is the cost basis of the new asset for financial reporting purposes? (c) What is the cost basis of the new asset for the computation of depreciation for federal income tax purposes?

22. Assume the same facts as in question 21, except that the book value of the asset traded in is $30,000. (a) What is the cost basis of the new asset for financial reporting purposes? (b) What is the cost basis of the new asset for the computation of depreciation for federal income tax purposes?

23. The cost of a composite group of equipment is $500,000 and the annual depreciation, computed on the individual items, totals $55,000. (a) What is the composite straight-line depreciation rate? (b) What would the rate be if the total depreciation amounted to $45,000 instead of $55,000?

24. What is the term applied to the periodic charge for (a) ore removed from a mine, and (b) the write-off of the cost of an intangible asset?

25. (a) Over what period of time should the cost of a patent acquired by purchase be amortized? (b) In general, what is the required treatment for research and development costs?

Exercises

Exercise 10-1. A plant asset acquired on January 3 at a cost of $165,000 has an estimated life of 10 years. Assuming that it will have no residual value, determine the depreciation for each of the first two years (a) by the straight-line method, (b) by the declining-balance method, using twice the straight-line rate, and (c) by the sum-of-the-years-digits method.

Exercise 10-2. A diesel-powered generator with a cost of $150,000 and estimated salvage value of $10,000 is expected to have a useful operating life of 70,000 hours. During January, the generator was operated 720 hours. Determine the depreciation for the month.

Exercise 10-3. Balances in Trucks and Accumulated Depreciation — Trucks at the end of the year, prior to adjustment, are $63,800 and $28,970 respectively. Details of the subsidiary ledger are as follows:

Truck No.	Cost	Estimated Residual Value	Estimated Useful Life in Miles	Accumulated Depreciation at Beginning of Year	Miles Operated During Year
1	$24,400	$4,400	200,000	$ 8,500	20,000
2	10,900	2,600	100,000	1,660	25,000
3	19,500	3,000	150,000	11,110	30,000
4	9,000	1,000	100,000	7,700	6,000

(a) Determine the depreciation rates per mile and the amount to be credited to the accumulated depreciation section of each of the subsidiary accounts for the current year. (b) Present the general journal entry to record depreciation for the year.

Exercise 10-4. An item of equipment acquired at the beginning of the fiscal year at a cost of $38,000 has an estimated trade-in value of $2,000 and an estimated useful life of 8 years. Determine the following: (a) the amount of annual depreciation by the straight-line method, (b) the amount of depreciation for the second year computed by the declining-balance method (at twice the straight-line rate), (c) the amount of depreciation for the second year computed by the sum-of-the-years-digits method.

Exercise 10-5. A piece of office equipment acquired at a cost of $15,900 has an estimated residual value of $900 and an estimated life of 5 years. It was placed in service on October 1 of the current fiscal year, which ends on December 31. Determine the depreciation for the current fiscal year and for the following fiscal year (a) by the declining-balance method, at twice the straight-line rate, and (b) by the sum-of-the-years-digits method.

Exercise 10-6. An item of equipment acquired on January 3, 1982, at a cost of $27,500 has an estimated residual value of $2,500 and an estimated life of 10 years. Depreciation has been recorded for each of the first three years ending December 31, 1984, by the straight-line method. Determine the amount of depreciation for the current year ending December 31, 1985, if the revised estimated residual value is $3,800 and the estimated remaining useful life (including the current year) is 9 years.

Exercise 10-7. A number of major structural repairs completed at the beginning of the current fiscal year at a cost of $80,000 are expected to extend the life of a building ten years beyond the original estimate. The original cost of the building was $750,000 and it has been depreciated by the straight-line method for 25 years. Residual value is expected to be negligible and has been ignored. The balance of the related accumulated depreciation account after the depreciation adjustment at the end of the preceding year is $375,000. (a) What has the amount of annual depreciation been in past years? (b) To what account should the $80,000 be debited? (c) What is the book value of the building after the repairs have been recorded? (d) What is the amount of depreciation for the current year, using the straight-line method (assume that the repairs were completed at the very beginning of the year)?

Exercise 10-8. On September 1, Martin Co. acquired a new computer with a list price of $92,500, receiving a trade-in allowance of $12,500 on an old computer of a similar type, paying cash of $20,000, and giving a series of five notes payable for the remainder. The following information about the old computer is obtained from the account in the office equipment ledger: cost $55,000; accumulated depreciation on December 31, the end of the preceding fiscal year, $32,500; annual depreciation, $7,500. Present entries, in general journal form, to record: (a) current depreciation on the old computer to date of trade-in; (b) the transaction on September 1 for financial reporting purposes.

Exercise 10-9. On the first day of the fiscal year, a delivery truck with a list price of $25,000 was acquired in an exchange for an old delivery truck and $21,400 cash. The old truck has a book value of $2,500 at the date of the exchange. The new truck is to be depreciated over 5 years by the straight-line method, assuming a trade-in value of $2,900. Determine the following: (a) annual depreciation for financial reporting purposes, (b) annual depreciation for income tax purposes, (c) annual depreciation for financial reporting purposes, assuming that the book value of the old delivery truck was $5,500, (d) annual depreciation for income tax purposes, assuming the same facts as indicated in (c).

Exercise 10-10. Details of a plant asset account for the fiscal year ended December 31 are as follows. A composite depreciation rate of 12% is applied annually to the account.

Office Equipment			
Jan. 1 Balance	560,400	Apr. 9	8,900
Feb. 10	25,000	Oct. 5	3,800
May 2	6,500	Dec. 17	11,300
Sep. 11	11,900		
Nov. 3	19,800		

Determine the depreciation for the year according to each of the following assumptions: (a) that all additions and retirements have occurred uniformly throughout the year and (b) that additions and retirements during the first half of the year occurred on the first day of that year and those during the second half occurred on the first day of the succeeding year.

Exercise 10-11. On July 1 of the current fiscal year ending December 31, McLevin Co. acquired a patent for $50,000 and mineral rights for $100,000. The patent, which expires in 15 years, is expected to have value for 5 years. The mineral deposit is estimated at 500,000 tons of ore of uniform grade. Present entries to record the following for the current year: (a) amortization of the patent, (b) depletion, assuming that 70,000 tons were mined during the year.

Exercise 10-12. For each of the following unrelated transactions, (a) determine the amount of the amortization or depletion expense for the current year, and (b) present the adjusting entries required to record each expense.
  (1) Governmental and legal costs of $13,300 were incurred at midyear in obtaining a patent with an estimated economic life of 7 years. Amortization is to be for one-half year.
  (2) Goodwill in the amount of $120,000 was purchased on January 5, the first month of the fiscal year. It is decided to amortize over the maximum period allowable.
  (3) Timber rights on a tract of land were purchased for $60,000. The stand of timber is estimated at 600,000 board feet. During the current year, 50,000 feet of timber were cut.

Problems
(Problems in Appendix B: 10-1B, 10-2B, 10-3B, 10-4B.)

Problem 10-1A. The following expenditures and receipts are related to land, land improvements, and buildings acquired for use in a business enterprise. The receipts are identified by an asterisk.

(a) Cost of real estate acquired as a plant site: Land	$150,000
Building	50,000
(b) Finder's fee paid to real estate agency	12,000
(c) Fee paid to attorney for title search	750
(d) Delinquent real estate taxes on property, assumed by purchaser............	18,500
(e) Cost of razing and removing the building	9,000
(f) Proceeds from sale of salvage materials from old building.................	1,500*
(g) Cost of land fill and grading..	7,500
(h) Architect's and engineer's fees for plans and supervision....................	70,000
(i) Premium on 1-year insurance policy during construction	9,000
(j) Cost of paving parking lot to be used by customers	15,250
(k) Cost of trees and shrubbery planted	7,000
(l) Special assessment paid to city for extension of water main to the property ...	2,000
(m) Cost of repairing windstorm damage during construction	3,500
(n) Cost of repairing vandalism damage during construction	800
(o) Proceeds from insurance company for windstorm and vandalism damage.....	3,300*
(p) Interest incurred on building loan during construction	60,000
(q) Money borrowed to pay building contractor...............................	1,000,000*
(r) Paid to building contractor for new building...............................	1,150,000
(s) Refund of premium on insurance policy (i) canceled after 10 months	750*

Instructions:

Assign each expenditure and receipt (indicate receipts by an asterisk) to Land (permanently capitalized), Land Improvements (limited life), Building, or Other Accounts. Identify each item by letter and list the amounts in columnar form, as follows:

Item	Land	Land Improvements	Building	Other Accounts
	$	$	$	$

Problem 10-2A. An item of new equipment, acquired at a cost of $160,000 at the beginning of a fiscal year, has an estimated life of 4 years and an estimated trade-in value of $10,000. The manager requested information (details given in Instruction 1) regarding the effect of alternative methods on the amount of depreciation expense each year. Upon the basis of the data presented to the manager, the declining-balance method was elected.

In the first week of the fourth year, the equipment was traded in for similar equipment priced at $250,000. The trade-in allowance on the old equipment was $25,000, cash of $25,000 was paid, and a note payable was issued for the balance.

Instructions:

(1) Determine the annual depreciation for each of the estimated 4 years of use, the accumulated depreciation at the end of each year, and the book value of the equipment at the end of each year by (a) the straight-line method,

(b) the declining-balance method (at twice the straight-line rate), and (c) the sum-of-the-years-digits method. The following columnar headings are suggested for each schedule:

Year	Depreciation Expense	Accumulated Depreciation, End of Year	Book Value, End of Year

(2) For financial reporting purposes, determine the cost basis of the new equipment acquired in the exchange.

(3) Present the debits and credits required, in general journal form, to record the exchange.

(4) What is the cost basis of the new equipment for purposes of computing the amount of depreciation allowable for income tax purposes?

(5) For financial reporting purposes, determine the cost basis of the new equipment acquired in the exchange, assuming that the trade-in allowance was $10,000 instead of $25,000.

(6) Present the debits and credits required, in general journal form, to record the exchange, assuming the data presented in Instruction (5).

(7) What is the cost basis of the new equipment for purposes of computing the amount of depreciation allowable for income tax purposes, assuming the data presented in Instruction (5)?

(If the working papers correlating with the textbook are not used, omit Problem 10-3A.)

Problem 10-3A. Lakeland Press Co. maintains a subsidiary equipment ledger for the printing equipment and accumulated depreciation accounts in the general ledger. A small portion of the subsidiary ledger, the two controlling accounts, and a general journal are presented in the working papers. The company computes depreciation on each individual item of equipment. Transactions and adjusting entries affecting the printing equipment are described as follows:

1984

June 29. Purchased a power binder (Model 20, Serial No. 70010) from Dunn Manufacturing Co. on account for $72,000. The estimated life of the asset is 12 years, it is expected to have no residual value, and the straight-line method of depreciation is to be used. (This is the only transaction of the year that directly affected the printing equipment account.)

Dec. 31. Recorded depreciation for the year in subsidiary accounts 125–40 to 125–42, and inserted the new balances. (An assistant recorded the depreciation and the new balances in accounts 125–1 to 125–39.)

31. Journalized and posted the annual adjusting entry for depreciation on printing equipment. The depreciation for the year, recorded in subsidiary accounts 125–1 to 125–39, totaled $51,200, to which was added the depreciation entered in accounts 125–40 to 125–42.

1985

Oct. 2. Purchased a Model A7 rotary press from Titus Press Inc., priced at $60,000, giving the Model C8 flatbed press (Account No. 125–41) in exchange plus $20,000 cash and a series of ten $2,500 notes payable, maturing at 6-month intervals. The estimated life of the new press is 10 years and it is expected to have a residual value of $8,500. (Recorded depreciation to date in 1985 on item traded in.)

Instructions:

    (1) Journalize the transaction of June 29. Post to Printing Equipment in the general ledger and to Account No. 125–42 in the subsidiary ledger.

    (2) Journalize the adjusting entry on December 31 and post to Accumulated Depreciation — Printing Equipment in the general ledger.

    (3) Journalize the entries required by the purchase of printing equipment on October 2. Post to Printing Equipment and to Accumulated Depreciation — Printing Equipment in the general ledger and to Account Nos. 125–41 and 125–43 in the subsidiary ledger.

    (4) If the rotary press purchased on October 2 had been depreciated by the declining-balance method at twice the straight-line rate, determine the depreciation on this press for the fiscal years ending (a) December 31, 1985 and (b) December 31, 1986.

Problem 10-4A. The following transactions, adjusting entries, and closing entries were completed by Weberg Furniture Co. during 3 fiscal years ending on June 30. All are related to the use of delivery equipment. The declining-balance method (twice the straight-line rate) of depreciation is used.

1984–1985 Fiscal Year

    July   2. Purchased a used delivery truck for $10,000, paying cash.
            3. Paid $800 to replace the automatic transmission and install new brakes on the truck. (Debit Delivery Equipment.)
    Aug. 21. Paid garage $199 for changing the oil, replacing the oil filter, and tuning the engine on the delivery truck.
    June 30. Recorded depreciation on the truck for the fiscal year. The estimated life of the truck is 8 years, with a trade-in value of $2,000.
          30. Closed the appropriate accounts to the income summary account.

1985–1986 Fiscal Year

    Oct.   8. Paid garage $175 to tune the engine and make other minor repairs on the truck.
         30. Traded in the used truck for a new truck priced at $21,575, receiving a trade-in allowance of $8,000 and paying the balance in cash. (Record depreciation to date in 1985.)
    June 30. Recorded depreciation on the truck. It has an estimated trade-in value of $2,500 and an estimated life of 10 years.
         30. Closed the appropriate accounts to the income summary account.

1986–1987 Fiscal Year

    Apr.   2. Purchased a new truck for $24,000, paying cash.
          3. Sold the truck purchased October 30, 1985, for $16,000. (Record depreciation for the year.)
    June 30. Recorded depreciation on the remaining truck. It has an estimated trade-in value of $3,250 and an estimated life of 8 years.
         30. Closed the appropriate accounts to the income summary account.

Instructions:

    (1) Open the following accounts in the ledger:
        122 Delivery Equipment
        123 Accumulated Depreciation — Delivery Equipment
        616 Depreciation Expense — Delivery Equipment
        617 Truck Repair Expense
        812 Gain on Disposal of Plant Assets   *(continued)*

(2) Record the transactions and the adjusting and closing entries in general journal form. Post to the accounts and extend the balances after each posting.

Problem 10-5A. The following recording errors occurred and were discovered during the current year:

(a) The sale of an electric typewriter for $375 was recorded by a $375 credit to Office Equipment. The original cost of the machine was $1,050 and the related balance in Accumulated Depreciation at the beginning of the current year was $625. Depreciation of $100 accrued during the current year, prior to the sale, had not been recorded.

(b) The $450 cost of repairing factory equipment damaged in the process of installation was charged to Factory Equipment.

(c) Office equipment with a book value of $8,950 was traded in for similar equipment with a list price of $50,000. The trade-in allowance on the old equipment was $15,000, and a note payable was given for the balance. A gain on disposal of plant assets of $6,050 was recorded.

(d) Property taxes of $4,000 were paid on real estate acquired during the year and were debited to Property Tax Expense. Of this amount, $2,800 was for taxes that were delinquent at the time the property was acquired.

(e) The $925 cost of a major motor overhaul expected to prolong the life of a truck one year beyond the original estimate was debited to Delivery Expense. The truck was acquired new three years earlier.

(f) A $190 charge for incoming transportation on an item of factory equipment was debited to Purchases.

(g) The $9,900 cost of repainting the interior of a building was debited to Building. The building had been owned and occupied for ten years.

(h) The cost of a razed building, $40,000, was charged to Loss on Disposal of Plant Assets. The building and the land on which it was located had been acquired at a total cost of $110,000 ($70,000 debited to Land, $40,000 debited to Building) as a parking area for the adjacent plant.

(i) The fee of $5,400 paid to the wrecking contractor to raze the building in (h) was debited to Miscellaneous Expense.

Instructions: Journalize the entries necessary to correct the errors during the current year. Identify each entry by letter.

Problem 10-6A. The trial balance of Nunn Corporation at the end of the current fiscal year, before adjustments, is shown at the top of page 295.

Data needed for year-end adjustments:

(a) Merchandise inventory at December 31, $139,900.

(b) Insurance and other prepaid operating expenses expired during the year, $7,100.

(c) Estimated uncollectible accounts at December 31, $5,250.

(d) Depreciation is computed at composite rates on the average of the beginning and the ending balances of the plant asset accounts. The beginning balances and rates are as follows:

Office equipment, $23,900; 10%   Delivery equipment, $42,650; 20%
Store equipment, $38,500; 8%   Buildings, $190,000; 2%

(e) Amortization of patents computed for the year, $2,000.

(f) Accrued liabilities at the end of the year, $2,800, of which $220 is for interest on the notes and $2,580 is for wages and other operating expenses.

Cash	19,750	
Accounts Receivable.	40,700	
Allowance for Doubtful Accounts		750
Merchandise Inventory	144,500	
Prepaid Expense	14,900	
Land	40,000	
Buildings.	190,000	
Accumulated Depreciation — Buildings.		61,000
Office Equipment	25,100	
Accumulated Depreciation — Office Equipment.		6,900
Store Equipment.	41,500	
Accumulated Depreciation — Store Equipment		20,860
Delivery Equipment	47,350	
Accumulated Depreciation — Delivery Equipment.		21,750
Patents	16,000	
Accounts Payable.		30,250
Notes Payable (short-term).		15,000
Capital Stock.		200,000
Retained Earnings		127,020
Dividends.	45,000	
Sales (net)		989,000
Purchases (net).	711,700	
Operating Expenses (control account)	135,170	
Interest Expense.	860	
	1,472,530	1,472,530

Instructions:

(1) Prepare a multiple-step income statement for the current year.

(2) Prepare a balance sheet in report form, presenting the plant assets in the manner illustrated in this chapter.

Mini-Case

    Joan Palmer, president of J. P. Company, is considering the purchase of machinery for $150,000. The machinery has a useful life of 5 years and no residual value. In the past, all plant assets have been leased. Palmer is considering depreciating the machinery by (1) the straight-line method or (2) the sum-of-the-years-digits method, and has asked your advice as to which method to use.

Instructions:

(1) Compute depreciation for each of the five years of useful life by (a) the straight-line method and (b) the sum-of-the-years-digits method.

(2) Assuming that income before depreciation and income tax is estimated to be uniformly $110,000 per year, that the depreciation method selected will be used for both financial reporting and income tax purposes, and that the income tax rate is 30%, compute the net income for each of the five years of useful life if (a) the straight-line method is used and (b) the sum-of-the-years-digits method is used.

(3) What factors would you present for Palmer's consideration in the selection of a depreciation method?

11

Payroll and Other Current Liabilities; Contingent Liabilities

CHAPTER OBJECTIVES

Describe and illustrate accounting for payrolls, including liabilities arising from employee earnings, deductions from earnings, and employer's payroll taxes.

Describe and illustrate accounting for pensions, notes payable, and leases.

Describe and illustrate accounting for contingent liabilities.

11

CHAPTER

Payables are the opposite of receivables. They are debts owed by an enterprise to its creditors. Money claims against a firm may originate in many ways, such as purchases of merchandise or services on a credit basis, loans from banks, purchases of equipment, and purchases of marketable securities. At any particular moment, a business may also owe its employees for wages or salaries accrued, banks or other creditors for interest accrued on notes, and governmental agencies for taxes.

In addition to known liabilities of a definite or reasonably approximate amount, there may be potential obligations that will materialize only if certain events take place in the future. Such uncertain liabilities are termed **contingent liabilities**.

Some types of current liabilities, such as accounts payable, have been discussed in earlier chapters. Additional types of current liabilities, including liabilities arising from payrolls, pensions, notes payable, and leases, are discussed in this chapter. Contingent liabilities are also discussed. Long-term liabilities are presented in Chapter 17.

PAYROLL |

The term **payroll** is often used to refer to the total amount paid to employees for a certain period. Payroll expenditures are usually significant for several reasons. First, employees are sensitive to payroll errors or irregularities, and maintaining good employee morale requires that the payroll be paid on a timely, accurate basis. Second, payroll expenditures are subject to various federal and state regulations. Finally, the amount of these payroll expenditures and related payroll taxes has a significant effect on the net income of most business enterprises. Although the degree of importance of such expenses varies widely, it is not unusual for a business to expend nearly a third of its sales revenue for payroll and payroll-related expenses. These expenses and their related liabilities are discussed in the following sections.

LIABILITY FOR |
PAYROLL |

The term **salary** is usually applied to payment for managerial, administrative, or similar services. The rate of salary is ordinarily expressed in terms of a month or a year. Remuneration for manual labor, both skilled and unskilled, is commonly called **wages** and is stated on an hourly, weekly, or piecework basis. In practice, the terms salary and wages are often used interchangeably.

The basic salary or wage of an employee may be supplemented by commissions, bonuses, profit sharing, or cost-of-living adjustments. The form in which remuneration is paid generally has no effect on the manner in which it is treated by either the employer or the employee. Although payment is usually in terms of cash, it may take such forms as securities, notes, lodging, or other property or services.

Salary and wage rates are determined, in general, by agreement between the employer and the employees. Enterprises engaged in interstate commerce must also follow the requirements of the Fair Labor Standards Act. Employers covered by this legislation, which is commonly called the Federal Wage and Hour Law, are required to pay a minimum rate of 1½ times the regular rate for all hours worked in excess of 40 hours per week. Exemptions from the requirements are provided for executive, administrative, and certain supervisory positions. Premium rates for overtime or for working at night or other less desirable times are fairly common, even when not required by law, and the premium rates may be as much as twice the base rate.

Determination of Employee Earnings

To illustrate the computation of the earnings of an employee, it is assumed that Thomas C. Johnson is employed at the rate of $19 per hour for the first 40 hours in the weekly pay period and at $28.50 ($19 + $9.50) per hour for any additional hours. His time card shows that he worked 43 hours during the week ended December 27. His earnings for that week are computed as follows:

Earnings at base rate (40 × $19)...............	$760.00
Earnings at overtime rate (3 × $28.50)..........	85.50
Total earnings.............................	$845.50

The foregoing computations can be stated in generalized arithmetic formulas or **algorithms.** If the hours worked during the week are less than or equal to (≤) 40, the formula may be expressed by the following equation, where E represents total earnings, H represents hours worked, and R represents hourly rate:

$$E = H \times R$$

This equation cannot be used to determine the earnings of an employee who has worked more than (>) 40 hours during the week, because the overtime rate differs from the basic rate. The expansion of the equation to include the additional factor of overtime yields the following:

$$E = 40 R + 1.5 R (H - 40)$$

The two equations can be expressed as shown in the following algorithm:

If	Then
$H \leq 40$	$E = H \times R$
$H > 40$	$E = 40R + 1.5R(H - 40)$

After the value of H and R are known for each employee at the end of a payroll period, the earnings of each employee can be computed accurately and speedily. Application of the standardized procedure of the algorithm to mechanized or electronic processing equipment makes it possible to process a payroll routinely, regardless of its size.

Determination of Profit-Sharing Bonuses

Many enterprises pay their employees an annual bonus in addition to their regular salary or wage. The amount of the bonus is often based on the productivity of the employees, as measured by the net income of the enterprise. Such profit-sharing bonuses are treated in the same manner as wages and salaries.

The method used in determining the amount of a profit-sharing bonus is usually stated in the agreement between the employer and the employees. When the amount of the bonus is measured by a certain percentage of income, there are four basic formulas for the computation. The percentage may be applied (1) to income before deducting the bonus and income taxes, (2) to income after deducting the bonus but before deducting income taxes, (3) to income before deducting the bonus but after deducting income taxes, or (4) to net income after deducting both the bonus and income taxes.

Determination of a 10% bonus according to each of the four methods is illustrated as follows, based on the assumption that the employer's income before deducting the bonus and income taxes amounts to $150,000, and that income taxes are levied at the rate of 40% of income. Bonus and income taxes are abbreviated as B and T respectively.

(1) Bonus based on income before deducting bonus and taxes.

$$B = .10 \ (\$150,000)$$
$$\text{Bonus} = \$15,000$$

(2) Bonus based on income after deducting bonus but before deducting taxes.

$$B = .10 \ (\$150,000 - B)$$

Simplifying: $B = \$15,000 - .10B$
Transposing: $1.10B = \$15,000$
$$\text{Bonus} = \$13,636.36$$

(3) Bonus based on income before deducting bonus but after deducting taxes.

B equation: $B = .10 \ (\$150,000 - T)$
T equation: $T = .40 \ (\$150,000 - B)$

Substituting for T in the B equation and solving for B:
$$B = .10 \ [\$150,000 - .40 \ (\$150,000 - B)]$$
Simplifying: $B = .10 \ (\$150,000 - \$60,000 + .40B)$
Simplifying: $B = \$15,000 - \$6,000 + .04B$
Transposing: $.96B = \$9,000$
$$\text{Bonus} = \$9,375$$

(4) Bonus based on net income after deducting bonus and taxes.

B equation: $B = .10 \ (\$150,000 - B - T)$
T equation: $T = .40 \ (\$150,000 - B)$

Substituting for T in the B equation and solving for B:
$$B = .10 \ [\$150,000 - B - .40 \ (\$150,000 - B)]$$
Simplifying: $B = .10 \ (\$150,000 - B - \$60,000 + .40B)$
Simplifying: $B = \$15,000 - .10B - \$6,000 + .04B$
Transposing: $1.06B = \$9,000$
$$\text{Bonus} = \$8,490.57$$

With the amount of the bonus possibilities ranging from the high of $15,000 to the low of $8,490.57, the importance of strictly following the agreement is evident. If the bonus is to be shared by all of the employees, the agreement must also provide for the manner by which the bonus is divided among them. A common method is to express the bonus as a percentage of total earnings for the year. For example, if the bonus were computed to be $15,000 and employee earnings before the bonus had been $100,000, the bonus for each of the employees could be stated as 15% of their earnings.

DEDUCTIONS FROM EMPLOYEE EARNINGS

The total earnings of an employee for a payroll period are often called the **gross pay**. From this amount is subtracted one or more **deductions** to arrive at the **net pay**, which is the amount the employer must pay the employee. The deductions for federal taxes are of the widest applicability and usually the largest in amount. Deductions may also be needed for state or local income taxes and for contributions to state unemployment compensation programs. Other deductions may be made for contributions to pension plans and for items authorized by individual employees.

FICA Tax

Most employers are required by the Federal Insurance Contributions Act (FICA) to withhold a portion of the earnings of each of their employees. The amount of **FICA tax** withheld is the employees' contribution to the combined federal programs for old-age and disability benefits, insurance benefits to survivors, and health insurance for the aged (medicare). With very few exceptions, employers are required to withhold from each employee a tax at a specified rate on earnings up to a specified amount paid in the calendar year. Although both the schedule of future tax rates and the maximum amount subject to tax are revised often by Congress, such changes have no effect on the basic outline of the payroll system.[1] For purposes of illustration, a rate of 7% on maximum annual earnings of $40,000, or a maximum annual tax of $2,800, will be assumed.

Federal Income Tax

Except for certain types of employment, all employers must withhold a portion of the earnings of their employees for payment of the employees' liability for federal income tax. The amount that must be withheld from each employee differs according to the amount of gross pay, marital status, and the estimated deductions and exemptions claimed when filing the annual income tax return.

Other Deductions

Deductions from gross earnings for payment of taxes are compulsory. Neither the employer nor the employee has any choice in the matter. In addition, however, there may be other deductions authorized by individual employees or by the union representing them. For example, an employee may authorize deductions for the purchase of United States savings bonds, for contributions to a United Fund or other charitable organization, for payment of premiums on various types of employee insurance, or for the purchase of a retirement annuity. The union contract may also require the deduction of union dues or other deductions for group benefits.

COMPUTATION OF EMPLOYEE NET PAY

Gross earnings for a payroll period less the payroll deductions yields the amount to be paid to the employee, which is often called the **net pay** or **take-home pay**. The amount to be paid Thomas C. Johnson is $609.30, based on the following summary:

---

[1]Current tax rates may be located in Internal Revenue Service publications and in standard tax reporting services.

Gross earnings for the week		$845.50
Deductions:		
FICA tax	$ 24.50	
Federal income tax	186.70	
U.S. savings bonds	20.00	
United Fund	5.00	
Total deductions		236.20
Net pay		$609.30

As has been indicated, there is a ceiling on the annual earnings subject to the FICA tax, and consequently the amount of the annual tax is also limited. Therefore, when the amount of FICA tax to withhold from an employee is determined for a payroll period, it is necessary to refer to one of the following cumulative amounts:

1. Employee gross earnings for the year prior to the current payroll period, or
2. Employee tax withheld for the year prior to the current payroll period.

To continue with the Johnson illustration, reference to his earnings record shows cumulative earnings of $39,650 prior to the current week's earnings of $845.50. The amount of the current week's earnings subject to FICA tax is therefore the maximum of $40,000 − $39,650, or $350, and the FICA tax to be withheld is 7% of $350, or $24.50. Alternatively, the determination could be based on the amount of FICA tax withheld from Johnson prior to the current payroll period. This amount, according to the employee record, is $2,775.50 and the amount to be withheld is the maximum of $2,800 − $2,775.50, or $24.50.

There is no ceiling on the amount of earnings subject to withholding for income taxes and hence no need to consider the cumulative earnings. The amount of federal income tax withheld would be determined by reference to official withholding tax tables issued by the Internal Revenue Service. For purposes of this illustration, the amount of federal income tax withheld was assumed to be $186.70. The deductions for the purchase of bonds and for the charitable contribution were in accordance with Johnson's authorizations.

As in the determination of gross earnings when overtime rates are a factor, the computation of some deductions can be generalized in the form of algorithms. The algorithm for the determination of the FICA tax deduction, based on the maximum deduction approach, is as follows, where E represents current period's earnings, F represents current period's FICA deduction, and f represents cumulative FICA deductions prior to the current period:

If	Then
$f + (.07E) \leq \$2,800$	$F = .07E$
$f + (.07E) > \$2,800$	$F = \$2,800 - f$

An alternative generalization of the method of determining FICA deductions, based on the maximum taxable earnings approach, is illustrated by the following decision diagram. The additional symbol "e" represents cumulative earnings prior to the current period.

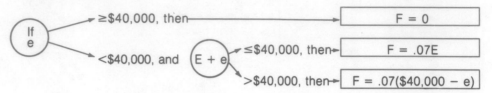

The elements of the decision diagram are examples of standardized instructions that can be applied to computations involving many variables. They are used in many situations as an aid to routine processing of repetitive data, regardless of whether the processing is performed manually, mechanically, or electronically.

LIABILITY FOR EMPLOYER'S PAYROLL TAXES

Thus far the discussion of taxes has been limited to those levied against employees and withheld by employers. Most employers are subject to federal and state taxes based on the amount of remuneration earned by their employees. Such taxes are an operating expense of the business and may amount to a relatively large sum.

FICA Tax

Employers are required to contribute to the Federal Insurance Contributions Act program for each employee. The tax rate and the maximum amount of employee remuneration entering into an employer's tax base are the same as those applicable to employees, which for purposes of illustration are assumed to be 7% and $40,000 respectively.

Federal Unemployment Compensation Tax

Unemployment insurance provides temporary relief to those who become unemployed as a result of economic forces beyond their control. Types of employment subject to the unemployment insurance program are similar to those covered by the FICA tax. The tax of .8% is levied on employers only, rather than on both employers and employees. It is applicable only to the first $7,000 of the remuneration of each covered employee during a calendar year. As with the FICA tax, the rate and the maximum amount subject to federal unemployment compensation tax are revised often by Congress. The funds collected by the federal government are not paid out as benefits to the unemployed, but are allocated among the states for use in administering state programs.

State Unemployment Compensation Tax

The amounts paid as benefits to unemployed persons are obtained, for the most part, by taxes levied upon employers only. A very few states also require employee contributions. The rates of tax and the tax base vary, and in most states, employers who provide steady employment for their employees are awarded reduced rates. The employment experience and the status of each employer's tax account are reviewed annually, and the merit ratings and tax rates are revised accordingly.[2]

[2]As of January 1, 1984, the maximum state rate recognized by the federal unemployment system was 2.7% of the first $7,000 of each employee's earnings during a calendar year. Beginning January 1, 1985, this maximum rate is 5.4%.

ACCOUNTING SYSTEMS FOR PAYROLL AND PAYROLL TAXES

Accounting systems for payroll and payroll taxes are concerned with the records and reports associated with the employer-employee relationship. It is important that the accounting system provide safeguards to insure that payments are in accord with management's general plans and its specific authorizations.

All employees of a firm expect and are entitled to receive their remuneration at regular intervals following the close of each payroll period. Regardless of the number of employees and the difficulties in computing the amounts to be paid, the payroll system must be designed to process the necessary data quickly and assure payment of the correct amount to each employee. The system must also provide adequate safeguards against payments to fictitious persons and other misappropriations of funds.

Various federal, state, and local laws require that employers accumulate certain specified data in their payroll records, not only for each payroll period but also for each employee. Periodic reports of such data must be submitted to the appropriate governmental agencies and remittances made for amounts withheld from employees and for taxes levied on the employer. The records must be retained for specified periods of time and be available for inspection by those responsible for enforcement of the laws. In addition, payroll data may be useful in negotiations with labor unions, in settling employee grievances, and in determining rights to vacations, sick leaves, and retirement pensions.

Although complex organizational structures may necessitate the use of detailed subsystems, the major parts common to most payroll systems are the payroll register, payroll checks, and employee's earnings record. Each of these major payroll components is illustrated and discussed in the following sections. Although the illustrations are relatively simple, many modifications might be introduced in actual practice.

Payroll Register

The multicolumn form used in assembling and summarizing the data needed at the end of each payroll period is called the payroll register. Its design varies according to the number and classes of employees, the extent to which automation is used, and the type of equipment used. A form suitable for a small number of employees is illustrated at the bottom of pages 304 and 305.

The nature of most of the data appearing in the illustrative payroll register is evident from the columnar headings. The number of hours worked and the earnings and deduction data are inserted in the appropriate columns. The sum of the deductions applicable to an employee is then deducted from the total earnings to yield the amount to be paid. Recording the check numbers in the payroll register as the checks are written eliminates the need to maintain other detailed records of the payments.

The two columns under the general heading of Taxable Earnings are used in accumulating data needed to compute the employer's payroll taxes. The last two columns of the payroll register are used to accumulate the total wages or salaries to be charged to the expense accounts. This process is usually termed **payroll distribution**. If there is an extensive account classification of labor expense, the charges may be analyzed on a separate payroll distribution sheet.

The format of the illustrative payroll register aids the determination of arithmetic accuracy before checks are issued to employees and before the summary amounts are formally recorded. Specifically, all columnar totals except those in the Taxable Earnings columns should be cross-verified. The miscellaneous deductions must also be summarized by account classification. The following tabulation illustrates the method of cross-verification. The amounts could be listed on an adding machine, taking the figures directly from the payroll register.

Earnings:		
Regular	$13,328.70	
Overtime	574.00	
Total		$13,902.70
Deductions:		
FICA tax	$ 794.83	
Federal income tax	3,332.18	
U.S. savings bonds	680.00	
United Fund	470.00	
Accounts receivable	50.00	
Total		5,327.01
Paid—net amount		$ 8,575.69
Accounts debited:		
Sales Salaries Expense		$11,122.16
Office Salaries Expense		2,780.54
Total (as above)		$13,902.70

Recording Employees' Earnings

The payroll register may be used as a posting medium in a manner like that in which the voucher register and check register are used. Alternatively, it may be

PAYROLL REGISTER

			PAYROLL FOR WEEK ENDING			
			EARNINGS		TAXABLE EARNINGS	
NAME	TOTAL HOURS	REGULAR	OVERTIME	TOTAL	UNEMPLOY-MENT COMP.	FICA
ARKIN, JOAN E.	40	500.00		500.00	500.00	500.00
DAWSON, LOREN A.	44	392.00	58.80	450.80		450.80
GREEN, MINDY M.		840.00		840.00		
JOHNSON, THOMAS C.	43	760.00	85.50	845.50		350.00
WYATT, WILLIAM R.	40	480.00		480.00		480.00
ZACHS, ANNA H.		525.00		525.00	150.00	525.00
TOTAL		13,328.70	574.00	13,902.70	2,710.00	11,354.70

used as a supporting record for a compound journal entry that records the payroll data. The entry based on the payroll register illustrated is as follows:

Dec. 27	Sales Salaries Expense	11,122.16	
	Office Salaries Expense....................	2,780.54	
	FICA Tax Payable		794.83
	Employees Income Tax Payable...........		3,332.18
	Bond Deductions Payable................		680.00
	United Fund Deductions Payable.........		470.00
	Accounts Receivable—Loren A. Dawson ..		50.00
	Salaries Payable		8,575.69
	Payroll for week ended December 27.		

The total expense incurred for the services of employees is recorded by the debits to the salary expense accounts. Amounts withheld from employees' earnings have no effect on the debits to these accounts. Five of the credits in the entry represent increases in specific liability accounts and one represents a decrease in the accounts receivable account.

Recording and Paying Payroll Taxes

Each time the payroll register is prepared, the amounts of all employees' current earnings entering the tax base are listed in the respective taxable earnings columns. As explained earlier, the cumulative amounts of each employee's earnings just prior to the current period are available in the employee's earnings record.

According to the payroll register illustrated for the week ended December 27, the amount of remuneration subject to FICA tax was $11,354.70 and the amount

DECEMBER 27, 19--

		DEDUCTIONS				PAID		ACCOUNTS DEBITED	
FICA TAX	FEDERAL INCOME TAX	U.S. SAVINGS BONDS	MISCEL- LANEOUS		TOTAL	NET AMOUNT	CHECK NO.	SALES SALARIES EXPENSE	OFFICE SALARIES EXPENSE
35.00	74.10	20.00	UF	10.00	139.10	360.90	6857	500.00	
31.56	62.60		AR	50.00	144.16	306.64	6858		450.80
	186.30	25.00	UF	10.00	221.30	618.70	6859	840.00	
24.50	186.70	20.00	UF	5.00	236.20	609.30	6860	845.50	
33.60	69.20	10.00			112.80	367.20	6880	480.00	
36.75	71.36	5.00	UF	2.00	115.11	409.89	6881		525.00
794.83	3,332.18	680.00	UF	470.00	5,327.01	8,575.69		11,122.16	2,780.54
			AR	50.00					

MISCELLANEOUS DEDUCTIONS: AR—ACCOUNTS RECEIVABLE   UF—UNITED FUND subject to state and federal unemployment compensation taxes was $2,710. Multiplication by the applicable tax rates yields the following amounts:

FICA tax..	$794.83
State unemployment compensation tax (5.4% × $2,710)..........	146.34
Federal unemployment compensation tax (.8% × $2,710).........	21.68
Total payroll taxes expense.................................	$962.85

The general journal entry to record the payroll tax expense for the week and the liability for the taxes accrued is as follows:

Dec. 27	Payroll Taxes Expense......................	962.85	
	FICA Tax Payable		794.83
	State Unemployment Tax Payable		146.34
	Federal Unemployment Tax Payable........		21.68
	Payroll taxes for week ended December 27.		

Payment of the liability for each of the taxes is recorded in the same manner as the payment of other liabilities. Employers are required to compute and report all payroll taxes on the calendar year basis, regardless of the fiscal year they may use for financial reporting and income tax purposes. Details of the federal income tax and FICA tax withheld from employees are combined with the employer's FICA tax on a single return accompanied by the amount of tax due. Payments are required on a weekly, semimonthly, monthly, or quarterly basis, depending on the amount of the combined taxes. Unemployment compensation tax returns and payments are required by the federal government on an annual basis. Earlier payments are required when the tax exceeds a certain minimum. Unemployment compensation tax returns and payments are required by most states on a basis similar to that required by the federal government.

All payroll taxes levied against employers become liabilities at the time the related remuneration is *paid* to employees, rather than at the time the liability to the employees is incurred. Observance of this requirement may cause a problem of expense allocation between fiscal periods. To illustrate, assume that an enterprise using the calendar year as its fiscal year pays its employees on Friday for a weekly payroll period ending the preceding Wednesday, the two-day lag between Wednesday and Friday being needed to process the payroll. Regardless of the day of the week on which the year ends, there will be some accrued wages. If it ends on a Thursday, the accrual will cover a full week plus an extra day. Logically, the unpaid wages and the related payroll taxes should both be charged to the period that benefited from the services performed by the employees. On the other hand, there is legally no liability for the payroll taxes until the wages are paid in January, when a new cycle of earnings subject to tax is begun. The distortion of net income that would result from failure to accrue the payroll taxes might well be insignificant. The practice adopted should be followed consistently.

Payroll
Checks

One of the principal outputs of most payroll systems is a series of **payroll checks** at the end of each pay period. The data needed for this purpose are provided by the payroll register, each line of which applies to an individual employee. It is possible to prepare the checks solely by reference to the Net Amount column of the register. However, the customary practice is to provide each employee with a statement of the details of the computation. The statement may be entirely separate from the check or it may be in the form of a detachable stub attached to the check.

When employees are paid by checks drawn on the regular bank account and the voucher system is used, it is necessary to prepare a voucher for the net amount to be paid the employees. The voucher is then recorded in the voucher register as a debit to Salaries Payable and a credit to Accounts Payable, and payment is recorded in the check register in the usual manner. If the voucher system is not used, the payment would be recorded by a debit to Salaries Payable and a credit to Cash.

It should be understood that the general journal entry derived from the payroll register, such as the compound entry illustrated on page 305, would precede the entries just described. It should also be noted that the entire amount paid may be recorded as a single item, regardless of the number of employees. There is no need to record each check separately in the check register because all of the details are available in the payroll register for future reference.

Most employers with a large number of employees use a special bank account and payroll checks designed specifically for the purpose. After the data for the payroll period have been recorded and summarized in the payroll register, a single check for the total amount to be paid is drawn on the firm's regular bank account and deposited in a special account. The individual payroll checks are then drawn against the special payroll account, and the numbers of the payroll checks are inserted in the payroll register.

The use of special payroll checks relieves the treasurer or other executives of the task of signing a large number of regular checks each payday. The responsibility for signing payroll checks may be given to the paymaster, or mechanical means of signing the checks may be used. Another advantage of this system is that reconciling the regular bank statement is simplified. The paid payroll checks are returned by the bank separately from regular checks and are accompanied by a statement of the special bank account. Any balance shown on the bank's statement will correspond to the sum of the payroll checks outstanding because the amount of each deposit is exactly the same as the total amount of checks drawn. The recording procedures are the same as when checks on the regular bank account are used.

Currency is sometimes used as the medium of payment when the payroll is paid each week or when the business location or the time of payment is such that banking or check-cashing facilities are not readily available to employees. In such cases, a single check, payable to Payroll, is drawn for the entire amount to be paid. The check is then cashed at the bank and the money is inserted in individual pay envelopes. Each employee should be required to sign a receipt which serves as evidence of payment. The procedures for recording the payment correspond to those outlined for payroll checks.

Employee's
Earnings
Record

The necessity of having the cumulative amount of each employee's earnings readily available at the end of each payroll period was discussed earlier. Without such information or the related data on the cumulative amount of FICA tax previously withheld, there would be no means of determining the appropriate amount to withhold from current earnings. It is essential, therefore, that detailed records be maintained for each employee.

A portion of the employee's earnings record is illustrated below and on page 309. The relationship between this record and the payroll register can be seen by tracing the amounts entered on Johnson's earnings record for December 27 back to its source, which is the fourth line of the payroll register illustrated on pages 304 and 305.

In addition to spaces for recording data for each payroll period and the cumulative total of earnings, there are spaces for quarterly totals and the yearly total. These totals are used in various reports for tax, insurance, and other purposes. Copies of one such annual report, known as Form W-2, Wage and Tax Statement, must be given to each employee as well as to the Social Security Administration.

EMPLOYEE'S
EARNINGS
RECORD

THOMAS C. JOHNSON
4990 COLUMBUS AVENUE
STATESVILLE, IOWA 52732–6142   PHONE: 555–3148

MARRIED   NUMBER OF
                           WITHHOLDING   PAY
                           ALLOWANCES: 4   RATE: $760.00 PER WEEK

OCCUPATION: SALESPERSON   EQUIVALENT HOURLY RATE: $19

LINE NO.	PERIOD ENDED	TOTAL HOURS	EARNINGS REGULAR	EARNINGS OVERTIME	TOTAL	CUMULATIVE TOTAL
39	SEPT. 27	41	760.00	28.50	788.50	30,330.50
THIRD QUARTER			9,880.00	256.50	10,136.50	
40	OCT. 4	40	760.00		760.00	31,090.50
46	NOV. 15	41	760.00	28.50	788.50	35,679.00
47	NOV. 22	40	760.00		760.00	36,439.00
48	NOV. 29	42	760.00	57.00	817.00	37,256.00
49	DEC. 6	40	760.00		760.00	38,016.00
50	DEC. 13	40	760.00		760.00	38,776.00
51	DEC. 20	44	760.00	114.00	874.00	39,650.00
52	DEC. 27	43	760.00	85.50	845.50	40,495.50
FOURTH QUARTER			9,880.00	285.00	10,165.00	
YEARLY TOTAL			39,520.00	975.50	40,495.50	

The source of the amounts inserted in the following statement was the employee's earnings record.

WAGE AND TAX STATEMENT

1 Control number	44012	For Paperwork Reduction Act Notice, see back of Copy D. OMB No. 1545-0008	For Official Use Only	

| 2 Employer's name, address, and ZIP code | 3 Employer's identification number 61-843652 | 4 Employer's State number |

Langford Supply Co.
560 Hudson Avenue
Cedar Rapids, Iowa 52731-6148

| 5 Stat. em- ployee | De- ceased | | Legal rep. | 942 emp. | Sub total | | Void |

| 6 Allocated tips | 7 Advance EIC payment |

| 8 Employee's social security number 381-48-9120 | 9 Federal income tax withheld $8,942.06 | 10 Wages, tips, other compensation $40,495.50 | 11 Social security tax withheld $2,800.00 |

| 12 Employee's name (first, middle, last) | 13 Social security wages $40,000.00 | 14 Social security tips |

16 *

Thomas C. Johnson
4990 Columbus Avenue
Statesville, Iowa 52732-6142

| 17 State income tax | 18 State wages, tips, etc. | 19 Name of State |
| 20 Local income tax | 21 Local wages, tips, etc. | 22 Name of locality |

15 Employee's address and ZIP code

Form **W-2 Wage and Tax Statement** 19-- | Copy A For Social Security Administration • See Instructions for Forms W-2 and W-2P | Department of the Treasury Internal Revenue Service

---

SOC. SEC. NO.: 381-48-9120   EMPLOYEE NO.: 814

DATE EMPLOYED: FEBRUARY 15, 1974

DATE OF BIRTH: OCTOBER 4, 1952

DATE EMPLOYMENT TERMINATED:

		DEDUCTIONS			PAID			
FICA TAX	FEDERAL INCOME TAX	U.S. BONDS	OTHER		TOTAL	NET AMOUNT	CHECK NO.	LINE NO.
55.20	174.11	20.00			249.31	539.19	6175	39
700.56	2,238.30	260.00	AR	40.00	3,247.86	6,888.64		
53.20	167.82	20.00	UF	5.00	246.02	513.98	6225	40
55.20	174.11	20.00			249.31	539.19	6530	46
53.20	167.82	20.00			241.02	518.98	6582	47
57.19	180.41	20.00			257.60	559.40	6640	48
53.20	167.82	20.00	UF	5.00	246.02	513.98	6688	49
53.20	167.82	20.00			241.02	518.98	6743	50
61.18	192.99	20.00			274.17	599.83	6801	51
24.50	186.70	20.00	UF	5.00	236.20	609.30	6860	52
711.55	2,244.60	260.00	UF	15.00	3,231.15	6,933.85		
2,800.00	8,942.06	1,040.00	AR	40.00	12,882.06	27,613.44		
			UF	60.00				

PAYROLL | The flow of data within segments of an accounting system may be shown by
SYSTEM | diagrams such as the one illustrated below. It depicts the interrelationships of the
DIAGRAM | principal parts of the payroll system described in this chapter. The requirement of
constant updating of the employee's earnings record is indicated by the dotted line.

FLOW DIAGRAM OF A
PAYROLL SYSTEM

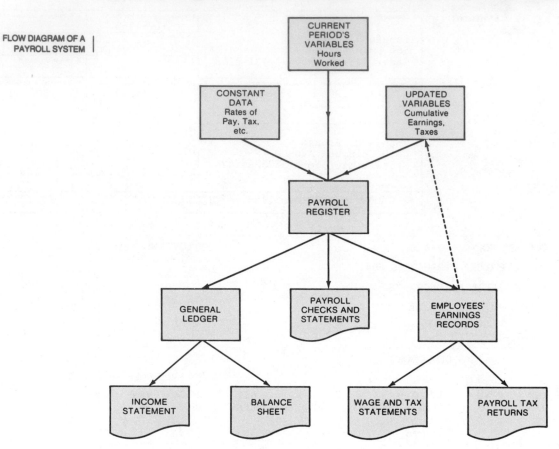

Attention thus far has been directed to the end product or *output* of a payroll
system, namely the payroll register, the checks payable to individual employees,
the earnings records for each employee, and reports for tax and other purposes.
The basic data entering the payroll system are sometimes called the *input* of the
system. Input data that remain relatively unchanged and do not need to be rein-
troduced into the system for each payroll period are characterized as *constants*.
Those that differ from period to period are termed *variables*.

Constants include such data for each employee as name and social security
number, marital status, number of income tax withholding allowances claimed,
rate of pay, functional category (office, sales, etc.), and department where employed. The FICA tax rate, maximum earnings subject to tax, and various tax tables
are also constants which apply to all employees. The variable data for each employee include the number of hours or days worked during each payroll period,

days of sick leave with pay, vacation credits, and cumulative amounts of earnings and taxes withheld. If salespersons are employed on a commission basis, the amount of their sales would also vary from period to period. The forms used in initially recording both the constant and the variable data vary widely according to the complexities of the payroll system and the processing methods used.

INTERNAL
CONTROLS
FOR PAYROLL
SYSTEMS

The large amount of data and the computations necessary to process the payroll are evident. As the number of employees and the mass of data increase, the number of individuals needed to manage and process payroll data likewise increases. Such characteristics, together with the relative magnitude of labor costs, indicate the need for controls that will assure the reliability of the data and minimize the opportunity for misuse of funds.

The expenditure and cash disbursement controls discussed in Chapter 7 are applicable to payrolls. Thus, the use of the voucher system and the requirement that all payments be supported by vouchers are desirable. The addition or deletion of names on the payroll should be supported by written authorizations from the personnel department. It is also essential that employees' attendance records be controlled in such a manner as to prevent errors and abuses. Perhaps the most basic and widely used records are "In and Out" cards, whereby employees indicate, often by "punching" a time clock, their time of arrival and departure. Employee identification cards or badges may also be used in this connection to assure that all salaries and wages paid are paid to the proper individuals.

LIABILITY FOR
PENSIONS

Many companies have established retirement pension plans for their employees. In recent years, such plans have increased rapidly in number, variety, and complexity. Although the details of the plans vary from employer to employer, pension benefits are usually based on factors such as employee age, years of service, and salary level. In 1974, Congress enacted the Employee Retirement Income Security Act (ERISA), which established guidelines for safeguarding employee benefits.

Pension plans may be classified as contributory or noncontributory, funded or unfunded, and qualified or unqualified. A **contributory plan** requires the employer to withhold a portion of each employee's earnings as a contribution to the plan. The employer then makes a contribution according to the provisions of the plan. A **noncontributory plan** requires the employer to bear the entire cost. A **funded plan** requires the employer to set aside funds to meet future pension benefits by making payments to an independent funding agency. The funding agency is responsible for managing the assets of the pension fund and for disbursing the pension benefits to employees. For many pension plans, insurance companies serve as the funding agency. An **unfunded plan** is managed entirely by the employer instead of by an independent agency. A **qualified plan** is designed to comply with federal income tax requirements which allow the employer to deduct pension contributions for tax purposes and which exempt pension fund income from tax. Most pension plans are qualified.

The accounting for pension plans can be complex due to the uncertainties of projecting future pension obligations. Future pension obligations depend upon such factors as employee life expectancies, expected employee compensation levels, and investment income on pension contributions. Pension funding requirements are estimated by individuals known as actuaries, who use sophisticated mathematical and statistical models.

The employer's contribution to a pension plan for **normal pension cost** associated with pension benefits earned by employees in a given year is debited to an operating expense account, Pension Expense. The credit is to Cash if the pension cost is fully funded. If the pension cost is partially funded, any unfunded amount is credited to Pension Contribution Payable. To illustrate, assume that the pension plan of Flossmoor Industries requires an annual pension cost of $25,000, and Flossmoor Industries pays $15,000 to the fund trustee, Equity Insurance Company. The entry to record the transaction in general journal form is as follows:

Pension Expense	25,000	
Cash		15,000
Pension Contribution Payable		10,000

Depending upon when the pension liability is to be paid, the $10,000 will be classified on the balance sheet as either a long-term or a current liability.

An entity's financial statements should fully disclose the nature of its pension plans and pension obligations. The financial statement disclosures should include the pension cost for the year and a description of the pension plan, including the employee groups covered, the entity's accounting and funding policies, and any pension changes affecting comparability among years.[3]

When an employer first adopts or changes a pension plan, special considerations must be given as to whether the employer will grant employees credit for prior years service. If a company does grant credit to employees for past service, a past service cost obligation must be recognized. The funding of **past service cost** is normally provided for over a number of years, thus creating a long-term past service pension cost liability. The complex nature of accounting for past service costs is left for more advanced accounting study.

NOTES PAYABLE AND INTEREST EXPENSE

Notes may be issued to creditors in temporary satisfaction of an account payable created earlier, or they may be issued at the time merchandise or other assets are purchased. To illustrate the former, assume that an enterprise, which owes F. B. Murray Co. $1,000 on an overdue account, issues a 90-day, 12% note for $1,000, dated December 1, 1984, in settlement of the account. The entry to record the transaction is as follows:

Dec. 1	Accounts Payable—F. B. Murray Co.	1,000	
	Notes Payable		1,000
	Issued a 90-day, 12% note on account.		

---

[3]*Statement of Financial Accounting Standards, No. 36,* "Disclosure of Pension Information" (Stamford: Financial Accounting Standards Board, 1980), par. 7.

On December 31, 1984, the end of the fiscal year, an adjusting entry would be recorded for the accrual of the interest from December 1 to December 31. The entry to record the accrued expense of $10 ($1,000 × 12/100 × 30/360) is as follows:

	Adjusting Entry		
Dec. 31	Interest Expense	10	
	Interest Payable		10

Interest payable is reported on the balance sheet at December 31, 1984, as a current liability. The interest expense account is closed at December 31, and the amount is reported in the Other Expense section of the income statement for the year ended December 31, 1984.

When the amount due on the note is paid in 1985, part of the interest paid will effect a reduction of the interest that was payable at December 31, 1984, and the remainder will represent expense for 1985. To avoid the possibility of failing to recognize this division and to avoid the inconvenience of analyzing the payment of interest in 1985, a reversing entry is made after the accounts are closed. The effect of the entry, illustrated as follows, is to transfer the credit balance in the interest payable account to the credit side of the interest expense account.

	Reversing Entry		
Jan. 1	Interest Payable	10	
	Interest Expense		10

At the time the note matures and payment is made, the entire amount of the interest payment is debited to Interest Expense, as illustrated by the following debits and credit that would be recorded in the cash payments journal:

Mar. 1	Notes Payable	1,000	
	Interest Expense	30	
	Cash		1,030

After the foregoing entries are posted, the interest expense account will appear as follows:

ACCOUNT INTEREST EXPENSE   ACCOUNT NO. 911

Date		Item	Post. Ref.	Debit	Credit	Balance	
						Debit	Credit
1984							
~	~	~	~	~	~	~	~
Nov.	10		CP40	250		890	
Dec.	31	Adjusting	J17	10		900	
	31	Closing	J17		900	—	—
1985							
Jan.	1	Reversing	J18		10		10
Mar.	1		CP42	30		20	

The adjusting and reversing process divided the $30 of interest paid on March 1, 1985, into two parts for accounting purposes: (1) $10 representing the interest expense for 1984 (recorded by the adjusting entry) and (2) $20 representing the interest expense for 1985 (the balance in the interest expense account at March 1, 1985).

There are many variations in interest and repayment terms when money is borrowed from banks. The most direct procedure is for the borrower to issue an interest-bearing note for the amount of the loan. For example, assume that on September 19 a firm borrows $4,000 from the First National Bank, with the loan evidenced by the firm's 90-day, 15% note. The effect of this transaction is as follows:

Sept. 19	Cash.	4,000	
	Notes Payable		4,000

On the due date of the note, ninety days later, the borrower owes $4,000, the face amount of the note, and interest of $150. The accounts affected by the payment are as follows:

Dec. 18	Notes Payable	4,000	
	Interest Expense	150	
	Cash.		4,150

A variant of the bank loan transaction just illustrated is to issue a non-interest-bearing note for the amount that is to be paid at maturity. When this plan is followed, the interest is deducted from the maturity value of the note and the borrower receives the remainder. The deduction of interest from a future value is termed **discounting.** The rate used in computing the interest may be termed the **discount rate,** the deduction may be called the **discount,** and the net amount available to the borrower is called the proceeds.

To illustrate the discounting of a note payable, assume that on August 10 an enterprise issued to a bank a $4,000, 90-day, non-interest-bearing note and that the bank discount rate is 15%. The amount of the discount is $150 and the proceeds $3,850. The debits and credit required to record the transaction follow:

Aug. 10	Cash.	3,850	
	Interest Expense	150	
	Notes Payable		4,000

The note payable is recorded at its face value, which is also its maturity value, and the interest expense is recorded at the time the note is issued. When the note is paid, the entry, in general journal form, is as follows:

Nov. 8	Notes Payable	4,000	
	Cash.		4,000

LIABILITY FOR LEASES

A lease is a contractual agreement conveying the right to use an asset for a stated period of time. The two parties to a lease contract are the **lessor** and the **lessee**. The lessor is the party who legally owns the asset and who conveys the rights to use the asset to the lessee. Typical lease transactions include the leasing of automobiles, computers, airplanes, and communication satellites.

In agreeing to a lease, the lessee incurs an obligation to make periodic rent payments for the lease term. In accounting for lease obligations, all leases are classified by the lessee as either capital leases or operating leases. Capital leases are defined as leases which include one or more of the following provisions: (1) the lease transfers ownership of the leased asset to the lessee at the end of the lease term; (2) the lease contains an option for a bargain purchase of the leased asset by the lessee; (3) the lease term extends over most of the economic life of the leased asset; or (4) the lease requires rental payments which approximate the fair market value of the leased asset.[4] Leases which do not meet the preceding criteria for a capital lease are classified as operating leases.

A capital lease is accounted for as if the lessee has, in fact, purchased the asset. Accordingly, when a lease is executed, the lessee would debit an asset account for the fair market value of the leased asset and would credit a long-term lease liability account. The complex accounting procedures applicable to capital leases are discussed in detail in more advanced accounting texts.

In accounting for operating leases, rent expense is recognized as the leased asset is used. Neither future lease obligations nor the future rights to use the leased asset are recognized in the accounts. However, the lessee must disclose future lease commitments in footnotes to the financial statements.[5]

To illustrate, assume that Foster's Jewelers enters into an operating lease requiring a $2,000 refundable deposit and monthly rents of 5% of net sales, payable the fifteenth of each month following the rental month. If the lease is executed on January 1 and January net sales are $10,000, the entries to record the deposit payment and rent obligation for January are as follows, in general journal form:

Jan.	1	Rental Deposit	2,000	
		Cash		2,000
	31	Rent Expense	500	
		Rent Payable		500

The normal entry would be recorded on February 15 for the payment of the rent payable. The rental deposit should be listed on the balance sheet as an "Other asset."

CONTINGENT LIABILITIES

If it is likely that a liability will materialize and if the amount of the liability can be reasonably estimated, it should be recorded in the accounts as a "liability."[6] On

---

[4]*Statement of Financial Accounting Standards, No. 13*, "Accounting for Leases" (Stamford: Financial Accounting Standards Board, 1976), par. 7.

[5]*Ibid.*, par. 16.

[6]*Statement of Financial Accounting Standards, No. 5*, "Accounting for Contingencies" (Stamford: Financial Accounting Standards Board, 1975), pars. 8, 10, 12.

the other hand, if it is not possible to determine whether a liability will materialize or it is not possible to reasonably estimate the amount of a liability, it is deemed to be "contingent." Contingent liabilities arise from discounting notes receivable, litigation, guarantees of products, possible tax assessments, or other causes. Contingent liabilities are normally disclosed in the notes to the financial statements. An example of a note is as follows:

> Due to 1983 weather conditions which caused a peanut crop shortage, the Company was required to allocate available peanuts to customers with whom, in accordance with customary practice, it had entered into firm sales contracts. In accepting or otherwise responding to the allocation arrangements, which generally represented a significant reduction from the contracted quantities, a number of customers indicated that they reserve all their rights to challenge the fairness and reasonableness and other aspects of the allocation program. The Company's management maintains that it is not liable by virtue of the conditions of the 1983 crop and that it allocated its available peanut supply as provided by law. At present, one suit is pending and while no estimate can be made as to the likelihood of other customers challenging the allocations or likelihood of an unfavorable outcome if challenges are made, the Company's management is of the opinion that no material liability will result.

Self-Examination Questions
(Answers in Appendix C.)

1. An employee's rate of pay is $20 per hour, with time and a half for all hours worked in excess of 40 during a week. The following data are available:

Hours worked during current week 45
Cumulative earnings for year prior to current week $39,500
FICA rate, on maximum of $40,000 of annual earnings 7%
Federal income tax withheld . . . . $ 212

Based on these data, the amount of the employee's net pay for the current week is:
A. $500   C. $800
B. $703   D. $950

2. Which of the following taxes are employers required to withhold from employees?
A. Federal income tax
B. Federal unemployment compensation tax
C. State unemployment compensation tax
D. All of the above

3. With limitations on the maximum earnings subject to the tax, employers incur operating costs for which of the following payroll taxes?
A. FICA tax
B. Federal unemployment compensation tax
C. State unemployment compensation tax
D. All of the above

4. The unpaid balance of a mortgage note payable is $50,000 at the end of the current fiscal year. If the terms of the note provide for monthly principal payments of $1,000, how should the liability for the principal be presented on the balance sheet?
   A. $50,000 current liability
   B. $50,000 long-term liability
   C. $12,000 current liability; $38,000 long-term liability
   D. $12,000 long-term liability; $38,000 current liability

5. An enterprise issued a $5,000, 60-day non-interest-bearing note to the bank, and the bank discounts the note at 12%. The proceeds are:
   A. $4,400   C. $5,000
   B. $4,900   D. $5,100

Discussion Questions

1. If an employee is granted a profit-sharing bonus, is the amount of the bonus (a) part of the employee's earnings and (b) deductible as an expense of the enterprise in determining the federal income tax?

2. The general manager of a business enterprise is entitled to an annual profit-sharing bonus of 5%. For the current year, income before bonus and income taxes is $200,000 and income taxes are estimated at 40% of income before income taxes. Determine the amount of the bonus, assuming that the bonus is based on net income after deducting both bonus and income taxes.

3. What is (a) gross pay? (b) net or take-home pay?

4. (a) Identify the federal taxes that most employers are required to withhold from employees. (b) Give the titles of the accounts to which the amounts withheld are credited.

5. For each of the following payroll-related taxes, indicate whether there is a ceiling on the annual earnings subject to the tax: (a) FICA tax, (b) federal income tax, (c) federal unemployment compensation tax?

6. Identify the payroll taxes levied against employers.

7. Prior to the last weekly payroll period of the calendar year, the cumulative earnings of employees E and F are $39,800 and $40,200 respectively. Their earnings for the last completed payroll period of the year are $800 each, which will be paid in January. If the amount of earnings subject to FICA tax is $40,000 and the tax rate is 7%, (a) what will be the employer's FICA tax on the two salary amounts of $800 each; (b) what is the employer's total FICA tax expense for employees E and F for the calendar year just ended?

8. Do payroll taxes levied against employers become liabilities at the time the liabilities for wages are incurred or at the time the wages are paid?

9. Indicate the principal functions served by the employee's earnings record.

10. Explain how a payroll system that is properly designed and operated tends to give assurance (a) that wages paid are based upon hours actually worked, and (b) that payroll checks are not issued to fictitious employees.

11. An employer pays the employees in currency and the pay envelopes are prepared by an employee rather than by the bank. (a) Why would it be advisable to obtain

from the bank the exact amount of money needed for a payroll? (b) How could the exact number of each bill and coin denomination needed be determined efficiently in advance?

12. A company uses a weekly payroll period and a special bank account for payroll. (a) When should deposits be made in the account? (b) How is the amount of the deposit determined? (c) Is it necessary to have in the general ledger an account entitled "Cash—Special Payroll Account"? Explain. (d) The bank statement for the payroll bank account for the month ended August 31 indicates a bank balance of $3,478.30. Assuming that the bank has made no errors, what does this amount represent?

13. Differentiate between a contributory and a noncontributory pension plan.

14. Identify several factors which influence the future pension obligation of an enterprise.

15. How does past service cost arise in a new or revised pension plan?

16. The unpaid balance of a mortgage note payable is $200,000 at the end of the current fiscal year. The terms of the note provide for quarterly principal payments of $10,000. How should the liability for the principal be presented on the balance sheet as of this date?

17. A business enterprise issued a 60-day, 12% note for $10,000 to a creditor on account. Give in general journal form the entries to record (a) the issuance of the note and (b) the payment of the note at maturity, including interest of $200.

18. In borrowing money from a bank, an enterprise issued a $10,000, 60-day, non-interest-bearing note, which the bank discounted at 15%. Are the proceeds $10,000? Explain.

19. Differentiate between an operating lease and a capital lease.

20. How is rental expense recognized under an operating lease?

21. A business firm is contesting a suit for damages of a substantial amount, brought by a customer for an alleged faulty product. Is this a contingent liability for the defendant? If so, should it be disclosed in financial statements issued during the period of litigation? Discuss.

Exercises

Exercise 11-1. Develop an algorithm, in the form illustrated in this chapter, to compute the amount of each employee's weekly earnings subject to state unemployment compensation tax. Assume that the tax is 4.2% on the first $7,000 of each employee's earnings during the year and that the following symbols are to be used:

e — Cumulative earnings subject to state unemployment compensation tax prior to current week
E — Current week's earnings
S — Amount of current week's earnings subject to state unemployment compensation tax

Exercise 11-2. The general manager of a business enterprise is entitled to an annual profit-sharing bonus of 4%. For the current year, income before bonus and income taxes is $320,000 and income taxes are estimated at 40% of income before income taxes.

Determine the amount of the bonus, assuming that (a) the bonus is based on income before deductions for bonus and income taxes and (b) the bonus is based on income after deduction for both bonus and income taxes.

Exercise 11-3. In the following summary of data for a payroll period, some amounts have been intentionally omitted:

Earnings:

(1) At regular rate	——		(7) Union Dues	——
(2) At overtime rate	$2,590.60		(8) Total deductions	$ 9,854.80
(3) Total earnings	——		(9) Net amount paid	36,948.70

Deductions:

Accounts debited:

(4) FICA tax	2,697.50	(10) Factory Wages	33,740.60
(5) Income tax withheld	5,801.70	(11) Sales Salaries	——
(6) Medical insurance . .	469.00	(12) Office Salaries	3,045.00

(a) Determine the totals omitted in lines (1), (3), (7), and (11). (b) Present the general journal entry to record the payroll. (c) Present, in general journal form, the entry to record the voucher for the payroll. (d) Present, in general journal form, the entry to record the payment of the payroll. (e) From the data given in this exercise and your answer to part (a), would you conclude that this payroll was paid sometime during the first few weeks of the calendar year? Explain.

Exercise 11-4. According to a summary of the payroll of Garcia Publishing Co., the amount of earnings for the four weekly payrolls paid in December of the current year was $480,000, of which $40,000 was not subject to FICA tax and $466,000 was not subject to state and federal unemployment taxes. (a) Determine the employer's payroll taxes expense for the month, using the following rates: FICA, 7%; state unemployment, 4.8%; federal unemployment, .8%. (b) Present the general journal entry to record the accrual of payroll taxes for the month of December.

Exercise 11-5. Bryant Corporation maintains a funded pension plan for its employees. The plan requires quarterly installments to be paid to the funding agent, Crawford Insurance Company, by the fifteenth of the month following the end of each quarter. If for the quarter ending December 31 the normal pension cost is $28,000, prepare entries in general journal form to record (a) the accrued pension liability on December 31 and (b) the payment to the funding agent on January 15.

Exercise 11-6. Bingham Co. issues a 120-day, non-interest-bearing note for $80,000 to Republic Bank and Trust Co., and the bank discounts the note at 15%. (a) Present the maker's entries, in general journal form, to record (1) issuance of the note and (2) payment of the note at maturity. (b) Present the payee's entries, in general journal form, to record (1) receipt of the note and (2) receipt of payment of the note at maturity.

Exercise 11-7. In negotiating a 90-day loan, an enterprise has the option of either (1) issuing a $150,000, non-interest-bearing note that will be discounted at the rate of 16%, or (2) issuing a $150,000 note that bears interest at the rate of 16% and that will be accepted at face value.

(a) Determine the amount of the interest expense for each option.
(b) Determine the amount of the proceeds for each option.
(c) Indicate the option that is more favorable to the borrower.

Exercise 11-8. On October 1, Village West purchased land for $250,000 and a building for $600,000, paying $170,000 cash and issuing a 14% note for the balance, secured by a mortgage on the property. The terms of the note provide for seventeen semiannual payments of $40,000 on the principal plus the interest accrued from the date of the preceding payment. Present the entry, in general journal form, to record (a) the transaction on October 1, (b) the adjusting entry on December 31 for accrued interest, (c) the reversing entry on January 1, (d) the payment of the first installment on March 31, and (e) the payment of the second installment the following September 30.

Exercise 11-9. Ryan's, a department store, entered into an operating lease in a new shopping mall on March 1 and paid a refundable deposit of $15,000. The monthly rent is $8.50 per square foot, payable the first of each rental month, plus 1% of gross sales, payable the fifteenth of each month following the rental month. If Ryan's occupies 2,000 square feet and if gross sales for March were $320,000, prepare the general journal entries for March 1, March 31, April 1, and April 15.

Problems
(Problems in Appendix B: 11-1B, 11-2B, 11-4B, 11-5B.)

Problem 11-1A. The president of Schwartz Products is entitled to an annual profit-sharing bonus of 5%. For the current year, income before bonus and income taxes is $206,000 and income taxes are estimated at 40% of income before income taxes.

Instructions:
  (1) Determine the amount of bonus, assuming that:
    (a) The bonus is based on income before deductions for bonus and income taxes.
    (b) The bonus is based on income after deduction for bonus but before deduction for income taxes.
    (c) The bonus is based on income after deduction for income taxes but before deduction for bonus.
    (d) The bonus is based on income after deduction for both bonus and income taxes.
  (2) (a) Which bonus plan would the president prefer? (b) Would this plan always be the president's choice, regardless of Schwartz Products' income level?

Problem 11-2A. The following information relative to the payroll for the week ended December 30 was obtained from the records of C. H. Beal Inc.:

Salaries:		Deductions:	
Sales salaries	$85,800	Income tax withheld	$17,150
Warehouse salaries	18,480	U.S. savings bonds	1,200
Office salaries	9,220	Group insurance	950
	$113,500	FICA tax withheld totals the same amount as the employer's tax.	

Tax rates assumed:
  FICA, 7%
  State unemployment (employer only), 4.2%
  Federal unemployment, .8%

Instructions:
(1) Assuming that the payroll for the last week of the year is to be paid on December 31, present the following entries:
  (a) December 30, to record the payroll. Of the total payroll for the last week of the year, $84,500 is subject to FICA tax and $6,000 is subject to unemployment compensation taxes.
  (b) December 30, to record the employer's payroll taxes on the payroll to be paid on December 31.
(2) Assuming that the payroll for the last week of the year is to be paid on January 3 of the following fiscal year, present the following entries:
  (a) December 31, to record the payroll.
  (b) January 3, to record the employer's payroll taxes on the payroll to be paid on January 3.

Problem 11-3A. The following accounts, with the balances indicated, appear in the ledger of Monico Company on December 1 of the current year:

212	Salaries Payable	—
213	FICA Tax Payable	$ 14,160
214	Employees Federal Income Tax Payable	37,600
215	Employees State Income Tax Payable	11,240
216	State Unemployment Tax Payable	1,460
217	Federal Unemployment Tax Payable	306
218	Bond Deductions Payable	640
219	Medical Insurance Payable	3,280
611	Sales Salaries Expense	531,300
711	Officers Salaries Expense	261,800
712	Office Salaries Expense	68,810
719	Payroll Taxes Expense	82,340

The following transactions relating to payroll, payroll deductions, and payroll taxes occurred during December:

Dec. 3. Prepared Voucher No. 415 for $640, payable to American National Bank, to purchase United States savings bonds for employees.

4. Issued Check No. 621 in payment of Voucher No. 415.

11. Prepared a general journal entry to record the biweekly payroll. A summary of the payroll record follows:
    Deductions: FICA tax, $2,410; federal income tax withheld, $6,640; state income tax withheld, $1,920; bond deductions, $315; medical insurance deductions, $480.
    Salary distribution: sales, $25,400; officers, $12,900; office, $3,200.
    Net amount: $29,735.

11. Prepared Voucher No. 418, payable to Payroll Bank Account, for the net amount of the biweekly payroll.

11. Issued Check No. 627 in payment of Voucher No. 418.

14. Prepared Voucher No. 423 for $51,760, payable to American National Bank, for the amount of employees' federal income tax and FICA tax due on December 15.

14. Issued Check No. 633 in payment of Voucher No. 423.

18. Prepared Voucher No. 429 for $3,280, payable to Wilson Insurance Company, for the semiannual premium on the group medical insurance policy.

21. Issued Check No. 639 in payment of Voucher No. 429.

Dec. 26. Prepared a general journal entry to record the biweekly payroll. A summary of the payroll record follows:

> Deductions: FICA tax, $2,133; federal income tax withheld, $6,342; state income tax withheld, $1,845; bond deductions, $315.
>
> Salary distribution: sales, $23,540; officers, $12,900; office, $3,200. Net amount: $29,005.

26. Prepared Voucher No. 444, payable to Payroll Bank Account, for the net amount of the biweekly payroll.

28. Issued Check No. 671 in payment of Voucher No. 444.

30. Prepared Voucher No. 461 for $630, payable to American National Bank, to purchase United States savings bonds for employees.

30. Issued Check No. 680 in payment of Voucher No. 461.

30. Prepared Voucher No. 462 for $11,240, payable to American National Bank, for employees' state income tax due on December 31.

30. Issued Check No. 681 in payment of Voucher No. 462.

31. Prepared a general journal entry to record the employer's payroll taxes on earnings paid in December. Taxable earnings for the two payrolls, according to the payroll records, are as follows: subject to FICA tax, $64,900; subject to unemployment compensation tax, $8,500. Assume the following tax rates: FICA, 7%; state unemployment, 3.8%; federal unemployment, .8%.

Instructions:

(1) Open the accounts listed and enter the account balances as of December 1.

(2) Record the transactions, using a voucher register, a check register, and a general journal. The only amount columns needed in the voucher register are Accounts Payable Cr. and Sundry Accounts Dr. (subdivided into Account, Post. Ref., and Amount). The only amount columns needed in the check register are Accounts Payable Dr. and Cash in Bank Cr.

(3) Journalize the adjusting entry on December 31 to record salaries for the incomplete payroll period. Salaries accrued are as follows: sales salaries, $8,740; officers salaries, $5,160; office salaries, $1,280. The payroll taxes are immaterial and are not accrued. Post to the accounts.

(4) Journalize the entry to close the salary expense and payroll taxes expense accounts to Income Summary and post to the accounts.

(5) Journalize the entry on January 1 to reverse the adjustment of December 31 and post to the accounts.

Problem 11-4A. Carey Company began business on January 2 of last year. Salaries were paid to employees on the last day of each month, and both FICA tax and federal income tax were withheld in the required amounts. All required payroll tax reports were filed and the correct amount of payroll taxes was remitted by the company for the calendar year. Before the Wage and Tax Statements (Form W-2) could be prepared for distribution to employees and filing with the Social Security Administration, the employees' earnings records were inadvertently destroyed.

None of the employees resigned or were discharged during the year, and there were no changes in salary rates. The FICA tax was withheld at the rate of 7% on the first $40,000 of salary. Data on dates of employment, salary rates, and employees' income taxes withheld, which are summarized as follows, were obtained from personnel records and payroll records.

Employee	Date First Employed	Monthly Salary	Monthly Income Tax Withheld
Altman	Mar. 16	$2,800	$ 471.20
Bayer	Nov. 1	2,500	394.25
Gibbons	Jan. 2	4,200	895.60
Klein	July 16	3,400	636.50
Maxwell	Jan. 2	5,400	1,374.10
Rodgers	May 1	3,600	652.30
Tang	Feb. 16	4,000	864.10

Instructions:

(1) Determine the amounts to be reported on each employee's Wage and Tax Statement (Form W-2) for the year, arranging the data in the following form:

Employee	Gross Earnings	Federal Income Tax Withheld	Earnings Subject to FICA Tax	FICA Tax Withheld

(2) Determine the following employer payroll taxes for the year: (a) FICA; (b) state unemployment compensation at 4.6% on first $7,000; (c) federal unemployment compensation at .8% on first $7,000; (d) total.

(3) In a manner similar to the illustrations in this chapter, develop four algorithms to describe the computations required to determine the four amounts in part (1), using the following symbols:

n = Number of payroll periods
g = Monthly gross earnings
f = Monthly federal income tax withheld
G = Total gross earnings
F = Total federal income tax withheld
T = Total earnings subject to FICA tax
S = Total FICA tax withheld

Problem 11-5A. The following items were selected from among the transactions completed by Califano Co. during the current year:

Feb. 10. Purchased merchandise on account from Tudor Co., $5,200.
Mar. 10. Purchased merchandise on account from Patrick Co., $4,800.
12. Issued a 30 day, 12% note for $5,200 to Tudor Co., on account.
20. Paid Patrick Co. for the invoice of March 10, less 2% discount.
Apr. 11. Paid Tudor Co. the amount owed on the note of March 12.
June 15. Borrowed $8,000 from Merchants National Bank, issuing a 90-day, 13% note for that amount.
25. Issued a 120-day, non-interest-bearing note for $20,000 to Dubuque State Bank. The bank discounted the note at the rate of 15%.
Sept. 13. Paid Merchants National Bank the interest due on the note of June 15 and renewed the loan by issuing a new 30-day, 15% note for $8,000. (Record both the debit and credit to the notes payable account.)
Oct. 13. Paid Merchants National Bank the amount due on the note of September 13.
23. Paid Dubuque State Bank the amount due on the note of June 25.

Dec. 1. Purchased office equipment from Weaver Equipment Co. for $31,250, paying $7,250 and issuing a series of ten 14% notes for $2,400 each, coming due at 30-day intervals.

     31. Paid the amount due Weaver Equipment Co. on the first note in the series issued on December 1.

Instructions:

(1) Record the transactions in general journal form.

(2) Determine the total amount of interest accrued as of December 31 on the nine notes owed to Weaver Equipment Co.

(3) Record the adjusting entry for the accrued interest at December 31 and the reversing entry on January 1.

(4) Assume that a single note for $24,000 had been issued on December 1 instead of the series of ten notes, and that its terms required principal payments of $2,400 each 30 days, with interest at 14% on the principal balance before applying the $2,400 payment. Determine the amount that would have been due and payable on December 31.

Mini-Case

Your father recently retired as president of the family-owned business, Keane Inc. A new president was recruited by an executive search firm under an employment contract calling for an annual base salary of $50,000 plus a bonus of 15% of income after deducting the bonus but before deducting income taxes.

In 1984, the first full year under the new president, Keane Inc. reported income of $805,000 before deducting the bonus and income taxes. On January 2, 1985, the new president was fired, and he demanded immediate payment of a $120,750 bonus for 1984.

Your father was concerned about the accounting practices used during 1984 and has asked you to help him in reviewing the accounting records before the bonus is paid. Upon investigation, you have discovered the following facts:

(a) The payroll for December 26–31, 1984, was not accrued at the end of the year. The salaries for the six-day period and the applicable payroll tax rates are as follows:

Sales salaries $4,800
Warehouse salaries 3,200
Office salaries 2,000

FICA tax.. 7%
State unemployment tax (employer only) 3.2%
Federal unemployment tax......................... .8%

The payroll was paid on January 10, 1985, for the period December 26, 1984, through January 8, 1985.

(b) The semiannual pension cost of $20,000 was not accrued for the last half of 1984. The pension cost was paid to First Equity Insurance Company on January 10, 1985, and was recorded by a debit to Pension Expense and a credit to Cash for $20,000.

(c) On December 1, 1984, Keane Inc. purchased a one-year insurance policy for $2,400, debiting the cost to Prepaid Insurance. No adjusting entry was made for insurance expired at December 31, 1984.

(d) Keane Inc. leases a storeroom in a local shopping mall, which requires a monthly rental of $2,000, payable the first of each month, plus 2% of net sales of the storeroom, payable by the 10th of the following month. The net sales for December were $600,000. The lease payment of 2% of storeroom sales was not accrued on December 31, 1984. On January 10, 1985, the lease payment of $12,000 was made and was recorded as a debit to Rent Expense and a credit to Cash.

Instructions:

(1) Based on reported 1984 income of $805,000 before deducting the bonus and income taxes, was the president's calculation of the $120,750 bonus correct? Explain.

(2) What accounting errors were made in 1984 which would affect the amount of the president's bonus?

(3) Based on the employment contract and your answer to (2), what is the correct amount of the president's bonus for 1984, rounded to the nearest dollar?

(4) How much did the president's demand for a $120,750 bonus exceed the correct amount of the bonus under the employment contract?

(5) Late in 1985, Keane Inc. paid the president the amount of the bonus computed in (3), after which the president sued Keane Inc. for breach of contract. The suit requested compensatory and punitive damages of $500,000. How should the lawsuit be reported on the 1985 financial statements?

(6) Describe the major advantage and disadvantage of using profit-sharing bonuses in employment contracts.

12

Concepts and Principles

CHAPTER OBJECTIVES

Describe the development of accounting concepts and principles.

Identify and illustrate the application of ten basic accounting concepts and principles.

PART 3 | Accounting Principles

12

CHAPTER

The historical development of accounting practice has been closely related to the economic development of the country. In the earlier stages of the American economy, a business enterprise was very often managed by its owner, and the accounting records and reports were used mainly by the owner-manager in conducting the business. Bankers and other lenders often relied on their personal relationship with the owner rather than on financial statements as the basis for making loans for business purposes. If a large amount was owed to a bank or supplier, the creditor often participated in management decisions.

As business organizations grew in size and complexity, "management" and "outsiders" became more clearly differentiated. From the latter group, which includes owners (stockholders), creditors, government, labor unions, customers, and the general public, came the demand for accurate financial information for use in judging the performance of management. In addition, as the size and complexity of the business unit increased, the acounting problems involved in the issuance of financial statements became more and more complex. With these developments came an awareness of the need for a framework of concepts and generally accepted accounting principles to serve as guidelines for the preparation of the basic financial statements.

DEVELOPMENT OF CONCEPTS AND PRINCIPLES

The word "principle" as used in this context does not have the same authoritativeness as universal principles or natural laws relating to the study of astronomy, physics, or other physical sciences. Accounting principles have been developed by individuals to help make accounting data more useful in an ever-changing society. They represent the best possible guides, based on reason, observation, and experimentation, to the achievement of the desired results. The selection of the best method from among many alternatives has come about gradually, and in some subject matter areas a clear consensus is still lacking. These principles are continually reexamined and revised to keep pace with the increasing complexity of business operations. General acceptance among the members of the accounting profession is the criterion for determining an accounting principle.

Responsibility for the development of accounting principles has rested primarily on practicing accountants and accounting educators, working both independently and under the sponsorship of various accounting organizations. These principles are also influenced by business practices and customs, ideas and beliefs of the users of the financial statements, governmental agencies, stock exchanges, and other business groups.

Accounting Organizations

Among the oldest and most influential organizations of accountants are the **American Institute of Certified Public Accountants (AICPA)** and the **American Accounting Association (AAA).** Each organization publishes a monthly or quarterly periodical and, from time to time, issues other publications in the form of research studies, technical opinions, and monographs. There are also other national accounting organizations as well as many state societies and local chapters of the national and state organizations. These groups provide forums for the interchange of ideas and discussion of accounting principles.

From 1959 to 1973, the Accounting Principles Board (APB), provided much of the leadership in the development of generally accepted accounting principles. The APB was composed of eighteen accountants who were members of the AICPA. They served without pay and continued their affiliations with their firms or institutions.

Financial Accounting Standards Board

In 1973, the APB was replaced by the Financial Accounting Standards Board (FASB). The FASB is presently the dominant body in the development of accounting principles. It is composed of seven members, four of whom must be CPAs drawn from public practice. They serve full time, receive a salary, and must resign from the firm or institution with which they have been affiliated. The FASB is assisted by an Advisory Council of approximately twenty members, whose major responsibilities include recommendations as to priorities and agenda, and the review of FASB plans, activities, and statements proposed for issuance. The FASB employs a full-time research staff and administrative staff as well as task forces to study specific matters from time to time.

As problems in financial reporting are identified, the FASB conducts extensive research to identify the principal issues involved and the possible solutions. Generally, after issuing discussion memoranda and preliminary proposals and evaluating comments from interested parties, the Board issues *Statements of Financial Accounting Standards,* which become part of generally accepted accounting principles. To explain, clarify, or elaborate on existing pronouncements, the Board also issues *Interpretations,* which have the same authority as the standards.

Presently, the Board is in the process of developing a broad conceptual framework for financial accounting. This project, which is expected to take many years to complete, is an attempt to develop a "constitution" that can be used to evaluate current standards and can serve as the basis for future standards. The results of this project are being published as *Statements of Financial Accounting Concepts.*

Government Organizations

Of the various governmental agencies with an interest in the development of accounting principles, the Securities and Exchange Commission (SEC) has been the most influential. Established by an act of Congress in 1934, the SEC issues regulations that must be observed in the preparation of financial statements and other reports filed with the Commission.

The Internal Revenue Service (IRS) issues regulations that govern the determination of income for purposes of federal income taxation. Because these regulations sometimes conflict with financial accounting principles, many enterprises maintain two sets of accounts to satisfy both reporting requirements. To avoid this increased record keeping, there have been times when firms have adapted practices that are acceptable for tax purposes as generally accepted accounting principles. A discussion of the nature of the income tax and its effect on accounting and business decisions is presented in more detail in later chapters.

Other regulatory agencies exercise a dominant influence on the accounting principles of the industries under their jurisdiction. In rare situations, Congress may also enact legislation that dictates accounting principles. These situations usually involve controversial issues on which no clear consensus has been reached within the profession.

Other Influential Organizations

The **Financial Executives Institute (FEI)** has influenced the development of accounting principles by encouraging and sponsoring accounting research. The FEI also comments on proposed pronouncements of the FASB, the SEC, and other organizations.

The **National Association of Accountants (NAA)** is one of the largest organizations of accountants. It is primarily concerned with management's use of accounting information in directing business operations. Since management is responsible for the preparation of the basic financial statements, however, the NAA communicates its recommendations on generally accepted accounting principles to appropriate organizations.

Although the organizations mentioned above have traditionally had the most influence upon the establishment of accounting principles, other organizations representing users of accounting reports are increasingly making their views known. Prominent in this group are the **Financial Analysts Federation** (investors and investment advisors) and the **Securities Industry Associates** (investment bankers).

Many accounting principles have been introduced and integrated with discussions in earlier chapters. The remainder of this chapter is devoted to the underlying assumptions, concepts, and principles of the greatest importance and widest applicability. Attention will also be directed to applications of principles to specific situations in order to facilitate better understanding of accounting practices.

BUSINESS ENTITY

The business entity concept assumes that a business enterprise is separate and distinct from the persons who supply its assets. This is true regardless of the legal form of the business organization. The accounting equation, Assets = Equities, or Assets = Liabilities + Capital, is an expression of the entity concept; i.e., the business owns the assets and owes the various claimants. Thus, the accounting process is primarily concerned with the enterprise as a productive economic unit and only secondarily concerned with the investor as a claimant to the assets of the business.

The business entity concept used in accounting for a sole proprietorship is distinct from the legal concept of a sole proprietorship. The nonbusiness assets, liabilities, revenues, and expenses of a sole proprietor are excluded from the business accounts. If a sole proprietor owns two or more dissimilar enterprises, each one is treated as a separate business entity for accounting purposes. Legally, however, a sole proprietor is personally liable for all business debts and may be required to use nonbusiness assets to satisfy the business creditors. Conversely, business assets are not immune from the claims of the sole proprietor's personal creditors.

Differences between the business entity concept and the legal nature of other forms of business organization will be considered in later chapters. For accounting purposes, however, revenues and expenses of any enterprise are viewed as affecting the business assets and liabilities, not the investors' assets and liabilities.

GOING
CONCERN

Only in rare cases is a business organized with the expectation of operating for only a certain period of time. In most cases, it is not possible to determine in advance the length of life of an enterprise, and so an assumption must be made. The nature of the assumption will affect the manner of recording some of the business transactions, which in turn will affect the data reported in the financial statements.

It is customary to assume that a business entity has a reasonable expectation of continuing in business at a profit for an indefinite period of time. This going concern concept provides much of the justification for recording plant assets at acquisition cost and depreciating them in an orderly manner without reference to their current realizable values. It is pointless to report plant assets on the balance sheet at their estimated realizable values if there is no immediate expectation of selling them. This is true regardless of whether the current market value of the plant assets is less than their book value or greater than their book value. If the firm continues to use the assets, the change in market value causes no gain or loss, nor does it increase or decrease the usefulness of the assets. Thus, if the going concern assumption is a valid concept, the investment in plant assets will serve the purpose for which it was made — the investment in the assets will be recovered even though they may be individually marketable only at a loss.

The going concern assumption similarly supports the treatment of prepaid expenses as assets, even though they may not be salable. To illustrate, assume that on the last day of its fiscal year, a wholesale firm receives from a printer a $20,000 order of sales catalogs. If there were no assumption that the firm is to continue in business, the catalogs would be merely scrap paper and the value reported for them on the balance sheet would be small.

When there is conclusive evidence that a business entity has a limited life, the accounting procedures should be appropriate to the expected terminal date of the entity. Changes in the application of normal accounting procedures may be needed for business organizations in receivership or bankruptcy, for example. In such cases, the financial statements should clearly disclose the limited life of the enterprise and should be prepared from the "quitting concern" or liquidation point of view, rather than from a "going concern" point of view.

OBJECTIVE
EVIDENCE

Entries in the accounting records and data reported on financial statements must be based on objectively determined evidence. If this principle is not followed, the confidence of the many users of the financial statements could not be maintained. For example, objective evidence such as invoices and vouchers for purchases, bank statements for the amount of cash in bank, and physical counts for merchandise on hand supports much of accounting. Such evidence is completely objective and can be verified.

Evidence is not always conclusively objective, for there are many cases in accounting in which judgments, estimates, and other subjective factors must be taken into account. In such situations, the most objective evidence available should be used. For example, the provision for doubtful accounts is an estimate of the losses expected from failure to collect sales made on account. Estimation of this amount should be based on such objective factors as past experience in collecting accounts receivable and reliable forecasts of future business activities. To provide accounting reports that can be accepted with confidence, evidence should be developed that will minimize the possibility of error, intentional bias, or fraud.

UNIT OF MEASUREMENT

All business transactions are recorded in terms of money. Other pertinent information of a nonfinancial nature may also be recorded, such as the description of assets acquired, the terms of purchase and sale contracts, and the purpose, amount, and term of insurance policies. But it is only through the record of dollar amounts that the diverse transactions and activities of a business may be measured, reported, and periodically compared. Money is both the common factor of all business transactions and the only feasible unit of measurement that can be used to achieve uniform financial data.

The generally accepted use of the monetary unit for accounting for and reporting the activities of an enterprise has two major limitations: (1) it limits the scope of accounting reports and (2) it assumes a stability of the measurement unit.

Scope of Accounting Reports

Many factors affecting the activities and the future prospects of an enterprise cannot be expressed in monetary terms. In general, accounting does not attempt to report such factors. For example, information regarding the capabilities of the management, the state of repair of the plant assets, the effectiveness of the employee welfare program, the attitude of the labor union, the effectiveness of anti-pollution measures, and the relative strengths and weaknesses of the firm's competitors cannot be expressed in monetary terms. Although such matters are important to those concerned with enterprise operations, at the present time, accountancy does not assume responsibility for reporting information of this kind.

Stability of Monetary Unit

As a unit of measurement, the dollar differs from such quantitative standards as the kilogram, liter, or meter, which have not changed for centuries. The instability of the purchasing power of the dollar is well known, and the disruptive effect of the declining value of the dollar is acknowledged by accountants. In the past, however, this declining value generally was not given recognition in the accounts or in conventional financial statements.

To indicate the nature of the problem, assume that the plant assets acquired by an enterprise for $100,000 twenty years ago are now to be replaced with similar assets which at present price levels will cost $200,000. Assume further that during the twenty-year period the plant assets had been fully depreciated and that the net income of the enterprise had amounted to $300,000. Although the initial outlay of $100,000 for the plant assets was recovered through depreciation charges, the amount represents only one half of the cost of replacing the assets. Instead of considering the current value of the new assets to have increased to double the value of two decades earlier, the dollars recovered can be said to have declined to one half of their earlier value. From either point of view, the firm has suffered a loss in purchasing power, which is the same as a loss of capital. In addition, $100,000 of the net income reported during the period might be said to be illusory, since it must be used to replace the assets.

The use of a monetary unit that is assumed to be stable insures objectivity. In spite of the inflationary trend in the United States, historical-dollar financial statements are considered to be better than statements based on movements of the general price level. Many accountants recommend that businesses use supplemental statements to indicate the effect of changing prices. However, only large companies are required to present selected supplemental information that reflects changing prices.[1] This subject will be discussed again in Chapter 13.

ACCOUNTING PERIOD

A complete and accurate picture of an enterprise's success or failure cannot be obtained until it discontinues operations, converts its assets into cash, and pays off its debts. Then, and only then, is it possible to determine its true net income. But many decisions regarding the business must be made by management and interested outsiders during its existence, and it is therefore necessary to prepare periodic reports on operations, financial position, and changes in financial position.

Reports may be prepared when a certain job or project is completed, but more often they are prepared at specified time intervals. For a number of reasons, including custom and various legal requirements, the longest interval between reports is one year.

This element of periodicity creates many of the problems of accountancy. The basic problem is the determination of periodic net income. For example, the need for adjusting entries discussed in earlier chapters is directly attributable to the division of an enterprise into arbitrary time periods. Problems of inventory costing, of recognizing the uncollectibility of receivables, and of selecting depreciation methods are also directly related to the periodic measurement process. Furthermore, the amounts of the assets and the equities reported on the balance sheet will also be affected by the methods used in determining net income. For example, the cost flow assumption used in determining the cost of merchandise sold during the accounting period will have a direct effect on the amount of cost assigned to the remaining inventory.

MATCHING REVENUE AND EXPIRED COSTS

During the early stages of accounting development, accountants viewed the balance sheet as the principal financial statement. Over the years, the emphasis has shifted to the income statement as the users of financial statements have become more concerned with the results of business operations than with financial position.

The determination of periodic net income is a two-fold problem involving (1) the revenue recognized during the period and (2) the expired costs to be allocated to the period. It is thus a problem of matching revenues and expired costs, the residual amount being the net income or net loss for the period.

Recognition of Revenue

Revenue is measured by the amount charged to customers for merchandise delivered or services rendered to them. The problem created by periodicity is one

---

[1]*Statement of Financial Accounting Standards, No. 33,* "Financial Reporting and Changing Prices" (Stamford: Financial Accounting Standards Board, 1979).

of timing; that is, at what point is the revenue realized? For any particular accounting period, the question is whether revenue items should be recognized and reported as such in the current period or whether their recognition should be delayed to a future period.

Various criteria are acceptable for determining when revenue is realized. In any case, the criteria used should reasonably agree with the terms of the contractual arrangements with the customer and be based insofar as possible on objective evidence. The criteria most often used are described in the remaining paragraphs of this section.

Point of Sale

Revenue from the sale of goods is usually considered to be realized at the time title passes to the buyer. At this point, the sale price has been agreed upon, the buyer acquires the right of ownership in the commodity, and the seller has a legal claim against the buyer. The realization of revenue from the sale of services may be determined in a like manner, although there is often a time lag between the time of the initial agreement and the completion of the service. For example, assume that a contract provides that certain repair services be performed, either for a specified price or on a time and materials basis. The price or terms agreed upon in the initial contract does not become revenue until the work has been performed.

Theoretically, revenue from the production and sale of goods and services emerges continuously as effort is expended. As a practical matter, however, it is usually not possible to make an objective determination until both (1) the contract price has been agreed upon and (2) the seller's portion of the contract has been completed.

Receipt of Payment

The recognition of revenue may be delayed until payment is received. When this criterion is used, revenue is considered to be realized at the time the cash is collected, regardless of when the sale was made. The cash basis is widely used by physicians, attorneys, and other enterprises in which professional services are the source of revenue. It has little theoretical justification but has the practical advantage of simplicity of operation and avoidance of the problem of estimating losses from uncollectible accounts. Its acceptability as a fair method of timing the recognition of revenue from personal services is influenced somewhat by the fact that it may be used in determining income subject to the federal income tax. It is not an appropriate method of measuring revenue from the sale of goods.

Installment Method

In some businesses, especially in the retail field, it is common to make sales on the installment plan. In the typical installment sale, the purchaser makes a down payment and agrees to pay the remainder in specified amounts at stated intervals over a period of time. The seller may retain technical title to the goods or may take other means to make repossession easier in the event that the purchaser defaults on the payments. Despite such provisions, installment sales should ordinarily be treated in the same manner as any other sale on account, in which case the revenue is considered to be realized at the point of sale.[2]

In some exceptional cases, the circumstances are such that the collection of receivables is not reasonably assured. In these cases, another method of determining revenue may be used.[3] The alternative is to consider each receipt of cash to be revenue and to be composed of partial amounts of (1) the cost of merchandise sold and (2) gross profit on the sale. This method may be used for federal income tax purposes by dealers who regularly sell personal property on the installment plan.

As a basis for illustration, assume that in the first year of operations of a dealer in household appliances, installment sales totaled $300,000 and the cost of the merchandise sold amounted to $180,000. Assume also that collections of the installment accounts receivable were spread over three years as follows: 1st year, $140,000; 2d year, $100,000; 3d year, $60,000. According to the point of sale method, all of the revenue would be recognized in the first year and the gross profit realized in that year would be determined as follows:

POINT OF SALE METHOD

Installment sales......................	$300,000
Cost of the merchandise sold	180,000
Gross profit	$120,000

The alternative to the point of sale method, the **installment method,** allocates gross profit according to the amount of receivables collected in each year, based on the percent of gross profit to sales. The rate of gross profit to sales is determined as follows:

$$\frac{\text{Gross Profit}}{\text{Installment Sales}} = \frac{\$120,000}{\$300,000} = 40\%$$

The amounts reported as gross profit for each of the three years, based on collections of installment accounts receivable, are as follows:

INSTALLMENT METHOD

1st year collections: $140,000 × 40%...............	$ 56,000
2d year collections: $100,000 × 40%...............	40,000
3d year collections: $ 60,000 × 40%...............	24,000
Total	$300,000.....................	$120,000

Percentage of Contract Completion

Enterprises engaged in large construction projects may devote several years to the completion of a particular contract. To illustrate, assume that a contractor engages in a project that will require three years to complete, for a contract price

---

[2]*Opinions of the Accounting Principles Board, No. 10,* "Omnibus Opinion — 1966" (New York: American Institute of Certified Public Accountants, 1966), par. 12.
[3]*Ibid.*

of $50,000,000. Further assume that the total cost to be incurred, which will also be spread over the three-year period, is estimated at $44,000,000. According to the point of sale criterion, neither the revenue nor the related costs would be recognized until the project is completed. Therefore, the entire net income from the contract would be reported in the third year.

Whenever the total cost of a long-term contract and the extent of the project's progress can be reasonably estimated, it is preferable to consider the revenue as being realized over the entire life of the contract.[4] The amount of revenue to be recognized in any particular period is then determined on the basis of the estimated percentage of the contract that has been completed during the period. The estimated percentage of completion can be developed by comparing the incurred costs with the most recent estimates of total costs or by estimates by engineers, architects, or other qualified personnel of the progress of the work performed. To continue with the illustration, assume that by the end of the first fiscal year the contract is estimated to be one-fourth completed and the costs incurred during the year were $11,200,000. According to the percentage-of-contract-completion method, the revenue to be recognized and the income for the year would be determined as follows:

Revenue ($50,000,000 × 25%)	$12,500,000
Costs incurred	11,200,000
Income (Year 1).	$ 1,300,000

The costs actually incurred during the year (rather than ¼ of the original cost estimate of $44,000,000, or $11,000,000) are deducted from the revenue recognized.

The use of the percentage-of-contract-completion method, sometimes called the degree-of-contract-completion method, involves some subjectivity, and hence possible error, in the determination of the amount of reported revenue. In spite of estimates, however, the financial statements may be more informative and useful than they would be if none of the revenue were recognized until completion of the contract. The method used should be noted on the financial statements.

A situation somewhat like long-term construction contracts arises in connection with revenue from rentals, loans, and other services that are definitely measurable on a time basis. Neither the point of sale, the receipt of payment, nor the installment method is an appropriate criterion for the recognition of revenue from such sources. Both the amount of total revenue to be realized and the period over which it is to be realized are readily determinable. For example, if a building is leased for a period of 3 years at a rental of $36,000, the revenue is realized at the rate of $1,000 a month. Whether the rent is received in a lump sum at the beginning of the lease, in installments over the life of the lease, or at its termination is irrelevant in determining the amount of revenue realized. According to the concept of the going concern, it is assumed that the owner will supply the use of the building during the term of the lease and that the lessee will complete the contract.

---

[4]*Accounting Research and Terminology Bulletins—Final Edition,* "No. 45, Long-term Construction-type Contracts" (New York: American Institute of Certified Public Accountants, 1961), par. 15.

Allocation of
Costs

Properties and services acquired by an enterprise are generally recorded at cost. "Cost" is the amount of cash or equivalent given to acquire the property or the service. If property other than cash is given to acquire properties or services, the cost is the cash equivalent of the property given. When the properties or the services acquired are sold or used, the costs are deducted from the related revenue to determine the amount of net income or net loss. The costs of properties or services acquired and on hand at any particular time represent assets. Such costs may also be called "unexpired costs." As the assets are sold or used, they become "expired costs" or "expenses."

The techniques of determining and recording cost expirations have been described and illustrated in earlier chapters. In general, there are two approaches to cost allocations: (1) compute the amount of the expired cost or (2) compute the amount of the unexpired cost. For example, it is customary to determine the portion of plant assets that have expired. After the depreciation for the period has been recorded, the balances of the plant asset accounts minus the balances of the related accumulated depreciation accounts represent the unexpired cost of the assets. The alternative approach must be used for merchandise and supplies, unless perpetual inventory records are maintained. If the cost of the merchandise or supplies on hand at the end of the period is determined by taking a physical inventory, the remaining costs in the related accounts are assumed to have expired. It might appear that the first approach emphasizes expired costs and the second emphasizes unexpired costs. This is not the case, however, since the selection of the method is based merely on convenience or practicality.

Many of the costs allocable to a period are treated as an expense at the time of incurrence because they will be wholly expired at the end of the period. For example, when a monthly rent is paid at the beginning of a month, the cost incurred is unexpired and hence it is an asset; but since the cost incurred will be wholly expired at the end of the month, the rental is usually charged directly to the appropriate expense account. This process makes a subsequent adjusting entry unnecessary. The proper allocation of costs among periods is the most important consideration. Any one of many accounting techniques may be used in achieving this objective.

ADEQUATE
DISCLOSURE

Financial statements and their accompanying footnotes or other explanatory materials should contain all of the pertinent data believed essential to the reader's understanding of the enterprise's financial status. Criteria for standards of disclosure often must be based on value judgments rather than on objective facts.

Financial statements are made more useful by the use of headings and subheadings and by merging items in significant categories. For example, detailed information as to the amount of cash in various special and general funds, the amount on deposit in each of several banks, and the amount invested in various marketable government securities is not needed by the reader of financial statements. Such information displayed on the balance sheet would impede rather than aid understanding. On the other hand, if the terms of significant loan agreements provide for a secured claim through a mortgage on an asset, the details should be disclosed.

Some of the matters that accountants agree should be adequately disclosed in the financial statements or the accompanying notes are briefly described and illustrated in the following paragraphs. The illustrations quoted were taken from corporations' annual reports to stockholders, where they appeared in a section variously titled "Statement of Accounting Practices," "Principles Reflected in Financial Statements," and "Notes to Financial Statements."

Accounting Methods Employed

When there are several acceptable alternative methods that could have a significant effect on amounts reported on the statements, the particular method used should be disclosed. Examples include inventory cost flow and pricing methods, depreciation methods, and various criteria of revenue recognition. There is considerable variation in the format used to disclose accounting methods employed. One form is to use a separate "Summary of Significant Accounting Policies" preceding the notes to financial statements or as the initial note.[5]

Note 1   Summary of significant accounting policies:

Inventories. Inventories are carried at cost (about half under the last-in, first-out method and the remainder under the first-in, first-out method), which is substantially less than current market value.

Depreciation. With minor exceptions, depreciation of domestic properties is computed using the sum-of-the-years-digits method. Depreciation of foreign properties is generally computed using the straight-line method.

Revenue recognition. Revenue from long-term construction contracts is recognized by the percentage-of-contract-completion method.

Changes in Accounting Estimates

There are many cases in accounting in which the use of estimates is necessary. These estimates should be revised when additional information or subsequent developments permit better insight or improved judgment upon which to base the estimates. If the effect of such a change on net income is material, it should be disclosed in the financial statements for the year in which the change is adopted.[6]

Note 5—Change in service lives of property:

Effective July 1, 19--, the Company revised its estimates of remaining useful lives of certain machinery and equipment. The revision resulted primarily from a change in conditions and not from a change in accounting principles. As a result of this revision, net income increased $246,000 from what it would have been if the estimated lives had not changed.

Contingent Liabilities

As discussed in Chapter 11, contingent liabilities arise from discounting notes receivable, litigation, guarantees of products, possible tax assessments, or other

---

[5]*Opinions of the Accounting Principles Board, No. 22,* "Disclosure of Accounting Policies" (New York: American Institute of Certified Public Accountants, 1972), par. 15.

[6]*Opinions of the Accounting Principles Board, No. 20,* "Accounting Changes" (New York: American Institute of Certified Public Accountants, 1971), pars. 31–33.

causes. If the amount of the liability can be reasonably estimated, it should be recorded in the accounts. If the amount cannot be reasonably estimated, the details of the contingency should be disclosed.[7] Following is an example of a note disclosing a contingent liability:

Note E—Commitments and contingent liabilities:

...In addition, there are several legal actions pending against the Company. A purported class action is pending in the Supreme Court of the State of New York seeking injunctive relief and $4,001,000,000 for damages suffered as a result of air pollution from the Company's generating plants. Counsel of the Company is of the opinion that the injunctive relief requested will not be granted and that this is not a proper class action under the reported decisions as to New York law. The Attorney General of the State of New York has also commenced an action against the Company alleging that [named a specified installation] is damaging the ecology of the Hudson River. The complaint seeks damages in the amount of $5,000,000 and an injunction against the operation of this plant in such a manner as to damage the river.

Events Subsequent to Date of Statements

Events occurring or becoming known after the close of the period may have a significant effect on the financial statements and should be disclosed.[8] For example, if an enterprise should suffer a crippling loss from a fire or other catastrophe between the end of the year and the issuance of the statements, the facts should be disclosed. Similarly, such occurrences as the issuance of bonds or capital stock, or the purchase of another business enterprise after the close of the period should be made known.

Note 18—Subsequent events:

In April 19--, the Company's Almirante Division (Panama) experienced heavy rains and resultant flooding. As a consequence, banana cultivations and farm installations were damaged. However, property and crop losses cannot be accurately assessed for some time. The Company has insurance coverage, with certain deductibles, on property and installations but not on crop losses. Interruptions in near-term shipping schedules are not expected to be extensive, nor will any serious shortage of fruit result.

CONSISTENCY

A number of accepted alternative principles affecting the determination of income statement and balance sheet amounts have been presented in earlier sections of the text. Recognizing that different methods may be used under varying circumstances, some guide or standard is needed to assure that the periodic financial statements of an enterprise can be compared. It is common practice to compare an enterprise's current income statement and balance sheet with the statements of the preceding year.

---

[7]*Statement of Financial Accounting Standards, No. 5*, "Accounting for Contingencies" (Stamford: Financial Accounting Standards Board, 1975), pars. 8, 10, 12.

[8]*Statement on Auditing Standards, No. 1*, "Codification of Auditing Standards and Procedures" (New York: American Institute of Certified Public Accountants, 1973), par. 560.

The amount and the direction of change in net income and financial position from period to period is very important to readers and may greatly influence their decisions. Therefore, interested persons should be able to assume that successive financial statements of an enterprise are based consistently on the same generally accepted accounting principles. If the principles are not applied consistently, the trends indicated could be the result of changes in the principles used rather than the result of changes in business conditions or managerial effectiveness.

The concept of **consistency** does not completely prohibit changes in the accounting principles used. Changes are permissible when it is believed that the use of a different principle will more fairly state net income and financial position. Examples of changes in accounting principles include a change in the method of inventory pricing, a change in depreciation method for previously recorded assets, and a change in the method of accounting for long-term construction contracts. Consideration of changes in accounting principles must be accompanied by consideration of the general rule for disclosure of such changes, which is as follows:

> The nature of and justification for a change in accounting principle and its effect on income should be disclosed in the financial statements of the period in which the change is made. The justification for the change should explain clearly why the newly adopted accounting principle is preferable.[9]

There are various methods of reporting the effect of a change in accounting principle on net income. The cumulative effect of the change on net income may be reported on the income statement of the period in which the change is adopted. In some cases, the effect of the change could be applied retroactively to past periods by presenting revised income statements for the earlier years affected. Further consideration of the methods of disclosure is reserved for a later chapter.

The application of the consistency concept does not require that a specific accounting method be used uniformly throughout an enterprise. It is not unusual for large enterprises to use different costing and pricing methods for different segments of their inventories. For example, a department store might apply the lower of cost or market, on a first-in, first-out basis, to the merchandise inventory in some departments and employ cost, on a last-in, first-out basis, in determining the inventory of other departments.

MATERIALITY | In following generally accepted accounting principles, the accountant must consider the relative importance of any event, accounting procedure, or change in procedure that affects items on the financial statements. Absolute accuracy in accounting and full disclosure in reporting are not ends in themselves, and there is no need to exceed the limits of practicality. The determination of what is significant and what is not requires the exercise of judgment. Precise criteria cannot be formulated.

To determine **materiality**, the size of an item and its nature must be considered in relationship to the size and the nature of other items. The erroneous classi-

---

[9]*Opinions of the Accounting Principles Board*, No. 20, "Accounting Changes" (New York: American Institute of Certified Public Accountants, 1971), par. 17.

fication of a $10,000 asset on a balance sheet exhibiting total assets of $10,000,000 would probably be immaterial. If the assets totaled only $100,000, however, it would certainly be material. If the $10,000 represented a note receivable from an officer of the enterprise, it might well be material even in the first assumption. If the loan was increased to $100,000 between the close of the period and the issuance of the statements, both the nature of the item at the balance sheet date and the subsequent increase in amount would require disclosure.

The concept of materiality may be applied to procedures used in recording transactions. As was stated in an earlier chapter, small expenditures for plant assets may be treated as an expense of the period rather than as an asset. The saving in clerical costs is justified if the practice does not materially affect the financial statements. In establishing a dollar amount as the dividing line between a revenue expenditure and a capital expenditure, consideration would need to be given to such factors as: (1) amount of total plant assets, (2) amount of plant assets in relationship to other assets, (3) frequency of occurrence of expenditures for plant assets, (4) nature and expected life of plant assets, and (5) probable effect on the amount of periodic net income reported.

Custom and practicality also influence criteria of materiality. Corporate financial statements seldom report the cents amounts or even the hundreds of dollars. A common practice is to round to the nearest thousand. For large corporations, there is an increasing tendency to report financial data in terms of millions, carrying figures to one decimal. For example, an amount stated in millions as $907.4 may be read as nine hundred seven million, four hundred thousand.[10]

A technique known as "whole-dollar" accounting, which is used by some businesses, eliminates the cents amounts from accounting entries at the earliest possible point in the accounting sequence. There are some accounts, such as those with customers and creditors, in which it is not feasible to round to the nearest dollar. Nevertheless, the technique yields savings in office costs and improved productivity. The errors introduced into other accounts by rounding the amounts of individual entries at the time of recording tend to be compensating in nature, and the amount of the final error is not material.

It should not be inferred from the foregoing that whole-dollar accounting encourages or condones errors. The unrecorded cents are not lost; they are merely reported in a manner that reduces bookkeeping costs without materially affecting the accuracy of accounting data.

CONSERVATISM | Periodic statements are affected to a great degree by the selection of accounting procedures and other value judgments. Historically, accountants have tended to be conservative, and in selecting among alternatives they often favored the method or the procedure that yielded the lesser amount of net income or of asset value. This attitude of conservatism was often expressed in the statement to "anticipate no profits and provide for all losses." For example, it is acceptable to price merchandise inventory at lower of cost or market. If market price is higher than cost,

---

[10]Examples are presented in Appendix G.

the higher amount is ignored in the accounts and, if presented in the financial statements, is presented parenthetically. Such an attitude of pessimism has been due in part to the need for an offset to the optimism of business management. It could also be argued that potential future losses to an enterprise from poor management decisions would be lessened if net income and assets were understated.

Current accounting thought has shifted somewhat from this philosophy of conservatism. Conservatism is no longer considered to be a dominant factor in selecting among alternatives. Revenue should be recognized when realized, and expired costs should be matched against revenue according to principles based on reason and logic. The element of conservatism may be considered only when other factors affecting a choice of alternatives are neutral. The concepts of objectivity, consistency, disclosure, and materiality are more important than conservatism, and the latter should be a factor only when the others do not play a significant role.

Self-Examination Questions
(Answers in Appendix C.)

1. Equipment that was acquired for $250,000 has a current book value of $100,000 and an estimated market value of $120,000. If the replacement cost of the equipment is $350,000, at what amount should the equipment be reported in the balance sheet?
   A. $120,000   C. $350,000
   B. $150,000   D. None of the above

2. Merchandise costing $140,000 was sold on the installment plan for $200,000 during the current year. Down payments of $40,000 and installment payments of $35,000 were received during the current year. If the installment method of accounting is employed, what is the amount of gross profit to be realized in the current year?
   A. $22,500   C. $75,000
   B. $60,000   D. None of the above

3. The total contract price for the construction of an ocean liner was $20,000,000 and the estimated construction costs were $17,000,000. During the current year, the project was estimated to be 40% completed and the costs incurred totaled $7,050,000. Under the percentage-of-contract-completion method of accounting, what amount of income would be recognized for the current year?
   A. $950,000   C. $3,000,000
   B. $1,200,000   D. None of the above

4. The concept of consistency requires that the nature of and justification for a change in accounting principle and its effect on income be disclosed in the financial statements of the period in which a change is made. An example of a change in accounting principle is a:
   A. change in method of inventory pricing
   B. change in depreciation method for previously recorded plant assets
   C. change in method of accounting for installment sales
   D. all of the above

5. A corporation's financial statements do not report cents amounts. This is an example of the application of which of the following concepts?
   A. Business entity   C. Consistency
   B. Going concern   D. Materiality

1. Accounting principles are broad guides to accounting practice. (a) How do these principles differ from the principles relating to the physical sciences? (b) Of what significance is acceptability in the development of accounting principles? (c) Why must accounting principles be continually reexamined and revised?

2. Since 1973, what body has been dominant in the development of accounting principles?

3. For accounting purposes, what is the nature of the assumption as to the length of life of an enterprise?

4. Plant assets are reported on the balance sheet at a total cost of $800,000 less accumulated depreciation of $300,000. (a) Is it possible that the assets might realize considerably more or considerably less than $500,000 if the business were discontinued and the assets were sold separately? (b) Why aren't plant assets reported on the balance sheet at their estimated market values?

5. During the current year, a mortgage note payable for $500,000, issued by Wills Company five years ago, becomes due and is paid. Assuming that the general price level has increased by 50% during the five-year period, did the loan result in an increase or decrease in Wills Company's purchasing power? Explain.

6. A machine with a cost of $95,000 and accumulated depreciation of $80,000 will soon need to be replaced by a similar machine that will cost $120,000. (a) At what amount should the machine presently owned be reported on the balance sheet? (b) What amount should management use in planning for the cash required to replace the machine?

7. Conventional financial statements do not give recognition to the instability of the purchasing power of the dollar. How can the effect of the fluctuating dollar on business operations be presented to the users of the financial statements?

8. During May, merchandise costing $92,000 was sold for $150,000 in cash. Because the purchasing power of the dollar has declined, it will cost $100,000 to replace the merchandise. (a) What is the amount of gross profit on sales in May? (b) Assuming that all operating expenses for the month are paid in cash and that the owner withdraws cash for the amount of net income, would there be enough cash remaining from the $150,000 of sales to replace the merchandise sold? Discuss.

9. At which point is revenue from sales of merchandise on account more commonly recognized, time of sale or time of cash receipt?

10. During the current year, merchandise costing $60,000 was sold on the installment plan for $100,000. The down payments and the installment payments received during the current year total $50,000. What is the amount of gross profit considered to be realized in the current year, applying (a) the point-of-sale principle of revenue recognition and (b) the installment method of accounting?

11. During the current year, Davis Construction Company obtained a contract to build an apartment building. The total contract price was $10,000,000 and the estimated construction costs were $8,500,000. During the current year, the project was estimated to be 40% completed and the costs incurred totaled $3,500,000. Under the percentage-of-contract-completion method of recognizing revenue, what amount of (a) revenue, (b) cost, and (c) income should be recognized from the contract for the current year?

12. On Feburary 10 of the current year, Casey Realty Company acquired a twenty-acre tract of land for $200,000. Before the end of the year, $75,000 was spent in subdividing the tract and in paving streets. The market value of the land at the end of the year was estimated at $350,000. Although no lots were sold during the year, the income statement for the year reported revenue of $150,000, expenses of $75,000, and net income of $75,000 from the project. Were generally accepted accounting principles followed? Discuss.

13. Seaver Storage Company constructed a warehouse at a cost of $275,000, after a local contractor had submitted a bid of $325,000. The building was recorded at $325,000 and income of $50,000 was recognized. Were generally accepted accounting principles followed? Discuss.

14. R. D. Bird Company purchased equipment for $290,000 at the beginning of a fiscal year. The equipment could be sold for $300,000 at the end of the fiscal year. It was proposed that since the equipment was worth more at the end of the year than at the beginning of the year, (a) no depreciation should be recorded for the current year and (b) the gain of $10,000 should be recorded. Discuss the propriety of the proposals.

15. When there are several acceptable alternative accounting methods that could be used, the method used by an enterprise should be disclosed in the financial statements. Give examples of accounting methods that fall in this category.

16. If significant changes are made in the accounting principles applied from one period to the next, why should the effect of these changes be disclosed in the financial statements?

17. You have just been employed by a relatively small merchandising business that records its revenues only when cash is received and its expenses only when cash is paid. You are aware of the fact that the enterprise should record its revenues and expenses on the accrual basis. Would changing to the accrual basis violate the principle of consistency? Discuss.

18. Macon Company has used the straight-line method of computing depreciation for many years. For the current year, the sum-of-the-years-digits method was used, depreciation expense for the year amounted to $50,000, and net income amounted to $60,000. Depreciation computed by the straight-line method would have been $35,000. (a) What is the quantitative effect of the change in method on the net income for the current year? (b) Is the effect of the change material? (c) Should the effect of the change in method be disclosed in the financial statements?

19. The accountant for a large wholesale firm charged the acquisition of a pencil sharpener to an expense account, even though the asset had an estimated useful life of 5 years. Which accounting concept supports this treatment of the expenditure?

20. In 1960, Kern Corporation acquired a building with a useful life of 40 years and depreciated it by the declining-balance method. Is this practice conservative (a) for the year 1960 and (b) for the year 1999? Explain.

Exercises

Exercise 12-1. Indicate for each of the following the amount of revenue that should be reported for the current year and the amount that should be postponed to a future period. Give a reason for your answer.

(a) Cash of $15,000 was received in the current year on the sale of gift certificates to be redeemed in merchandise in the following year.

(b) The contract price for building a bridge is $9,000,000. During the current year, the first year of construction, the bridge is estimated to be 20% completed and the costs incurred totaled $1,650,000. Revenue is to be recognized by the percentage-of-contract-completion method.

(c) Leased a tract of land on the first day of the third month of the current year, receiving one year's rent of $30,000.

(d) Merchandise on hand at the end of the current fiscal year, costing $165,000, is expected to be sold in the following year for $231,000.

(e) Thirty days before the end of the current fiscal year, $100,000 was loaned at 12% for 90 days.

(f) Season tickets for a series of six concerts were sold for $90,000. Four concerts were played during the current year.

(g) Sixty days before the end of the current fiscal year, a $75,000, 90-day non-interest-bearing note was accepted at a discount of 12%. Proceeds in the amount of $72,750 were given to the maker of the note.

(h) Salespersons submitted orders in the current year for merchandise to be delivered in the following year. Their merchandise had a cost of $15,500 and a selling price of $21,700.

Exercise 12-2. Carlson Company makes all sales on the installment plan. Data related to merchandise sold during the current fiscal year are as follows:

Sales.	$950,000
Cash received on the $950,000 of installment contracts.	300,000
Merchandise inventory, beginning of year	112,500
Merchandise inventory, end of year.	117,500
Purchases	670,000

Determine the amount of gross profit that would be recognized for the current fiscal year according to (a) the point of sale method and (b) the installment method.

Exercise 12-3. Properties and services acquired by an enterprise are generally recorded at cost. For each of the following, determine the cost:

(a) An adjacent tract of land was acquired for $37,000 to provide additional parking for customers. The structures on the land were removed at a cost of $4,250. The salvage from the structures was sold for $750. The cost of grading the land was $1,500.

(b) Materials and supplies costing $2,750 were purchased and a carpenter was paid $2,000 to build a display case. A similar case would cost $5,500 if purchased from a manufacturer.

(c) Equipment was purchased for $29,500 under terms of n/30, FOB shipping point. The freight amounted to $425 and installation costs totaled $550.

Exercise 12-4. The cost of merchandise inventory at the end of the first fiscal year of operations, according to three different methods, is as follows: fifo, $83,500; average, $79,000; lifo, $71,500. If the average cost method is employed, the net income reported will be $55,000. (a) What will be the amount of net income reported if the lifo method is adopted? (b) What will be the amount of net income reported if the fifo method is adopted? (c) Which of the three methods is the most conservative in terms of net income? (d) Is the particular method adopted of sufficient materiality to require disclosure in the financial statements?

Exercise 12-5. Salespersons for Conley Realty receive a commission of 3% of sales, the amount due on sales of one month being paid in the middle of the following month. At the end of each of the first three years of operations, the accountant failed to record accrued sales commissions expense as follows: first year, $12,000, second year, $9,500, third year, $10,000. In each case, the commissions were paid during the first month of the succeeding year and were charged as an expense of that year. Accrued sales commissions expense was properly recorded at the end of the fourth year. (a) Determine the amount by which net income was overstated or understated for each of the four years. (b) Determine the items on the balance sheet that would have been overstated or understated at the end of each of the four years, and the amount of overstatement or understatement.

Exercise 12-6. Griffin Company sells most of its products on a cash basis but extends short-term credit to a few of its customers. Invoices for sales on account are placed in a file and are not recorded until cash is received, at which time the sale is recorded in the same manner as a cash sale. The net income reported for the first three years of operations was $59,500, $58,000, and $85,000 respectively. The total amount of the uncollected sales invoices in the file at the end of each of the three years was $9,800, $8,750, and $10,500. In each case, the entire amount was collected during the first month of the succeeding year. (a) Determine the amount by which net income was overstated or understated for each of the three years. (b) Determine the items on the balance sheet that were overstated or understated, and the amount, as of the end of each year.

Exercise 12-7. Of the following matters, considered individually, indicate those that are material and that should be disclosed either on the financial statements or in accompanying explanatory notes:
  (a) Between the end of the fiscal year and the date of publication of the annual report, a fire completely destroyed one of three principal plants. The loss is estimated at $1,000,000 and is fully covered by insurance. The net income for the year is $320,000.
  (b) A change in estimates of the remaining usefulness of store equipment increased the amount of net income that would otherwise have been reported from $1,100,000 to $1,107,500.
  (c) A merchandising company employs the last-in, first-out cost flow assumption and prices its inventory at the lower of cost or market.
  (d) A change in accounting for depreciation of plant assets was adopted in the current year. The amount of net income that would otherwise have been reported decreased from $560,000 to $410,000.
  (e) A company is facing litigation involving restraint of trade. Damages might amount to $1,000,000. Annual net income reported in the past few years has ranged from $2,250,000 to $4,000,000.

Exercise 12-8. Each of the following statements represents a decision made by the accountant. State whether or not you agree with the decision. Support your answer with reference to generally accepted accounting principles that are applicable in the circumstances.
  (a) In preparing the balance sheet, detailed information as to the amount due from hundreds of customers on account was omitted. The total amount was presented under the caption "Trade Accounts Receivable."

(b) Merchandise transferred to other parties on a consignment basis and not sold is included in merchandise inventory.

(c) Land, used as a parking lot, was purchased 5 years ago for $75,000. Since its market value is now $105,000, the land account is debited for $30,000 and a gain account is credited for a like amount. The gain is presented as an "Other income" item in the income statement.

(d) Used electronic data processing equipment, with an estimated five-year life and no salvage value, was purchased early in the current fiscal year for $250,000. Since the company planned to purchase new equipment, costing $600,000, to replace this equipment at the end of three years, depreciation expense of $200,000 was recorded for the current year. The depreciation expense thus provided for one third of the cost of the replacement.

(e) All minor expenditures for office equipment are charged to an expense account.

Problems

(Problems in Appendix B: 12-1B, 12-2B, 12-4B, 12-5B, 12-6B.)

Problem 12-1A. You are engaged to review the accounting records of Glenn Allen Company prior to closing of the revenue and expense accounts as of June 30, the end of the current fiscal year. The following information comes to your attention during the review:

(a) Since net income for the current year is expected to be considerably less than it was for the preceding year, depreciation on machinery has not been recorded. Depreciation for the year on machinery, determined in a manner consistent with the preceding year, amounts to $20,195.

(b) Land recorded in the accounts at a cost of $95,000 was appraised at $150,000 by two expert appraisers.

(c) No interest has been accrued on a $30,000, 12%, 90-day note payable, dated May 31 of the current year.

(d) The office supplies account has a balance of $5,000. The cost of the office supplies on hand at June 30, as determined by a physical count, was $1,250.

(e) Merchandise inventory on hand at June 30 of the current year has been recorded in the accounts at cost, $195,000. Current market price of the inventory is $218,750.

(f) Accounts receivable include $2,850 owed by C. L. Linke, a bankrupt. Glenn Allen Company expects to receive twenty cents on each dollar owed. The allowance method of accounting for receivables is employed.

(g) The company is being sued for $500,000 by a customer who claims damages for personal injury allegedly caused by a defective product. Company attorneys and outside legal counsel retained by Glenn Allen Company feel extremely confident that the company will have no liability for damages resulting from this case.

(h) The company received a debit memorandum with the bank statement from Urbana County Bank, indicating that a customer note discounted at the bank has been dishonored. The 12%, 120-day note is from London Co. and has a $25,000 face value. Glenn Allen Company has not recorded the memorandum, which included a protest fee of $7.

Instructions:

Journalize any entries required to adjust or correct the accounts, identifying each entry by letter.

Problem 12-2A. Horowitz Co. makes all sales on the installment basis and recognizes revenue at the point of sale. Condensed income statements and the amounts collected from customers for each of the first three years of operations are as follows:

	First Year	Second Year	Third Year
Sales..................................	$319,000	$340,000	$382,000
Cost of merchandise sold	216,920	227,800	248,300
Gross profit...........................	$102,080	$112,200	$133,700
Operating expenses	40,000	47,500	62,500
Net income	$ 62,080	$ 64,700	$ 71,200
Collected from sales of first year	$ 97,000	$126,000	$ 96,000
Collected from sales of second year......		97,500	140,000
Collected from sales of third year			95,500

Instructions:

Determine the amount of net income that would have been reported in each year if the installment method of recognizing revenue had been employed, ignoring the possible effects of uncollectible accounts on the computation. Present figures in good order.

Problem 12-3A. Video Sales employs the installment method of recognizing gross profit for sales made on the installment plan. Details of a particular installment sale, amounts collected from the purchaser, and the repossession of the item sold are as follows:

First year:
　Sold for $1,200 a color television set having a cost of $960 and received a down payment of $200.
Second year:
　Received twelve monthly payments of $40 each.
Third year:
　The purchaser defaulted on the monthly payments, the set was repossessed, and the remaining 13 installments were canceled. The set was estimated to be worth $450.

Instructions:
　(1) Determine the gross profit to be recognized in the first year.
　(2) Determine the gross profit to be recognized in the second year.
　(3) Determine the gain or loss to be recognized from the repossession of the set.

Problem 12-4A. Day Company began construction on three contracts during 1984. The contract prices and construction activities for 1984, 1985, and 1986 were as follows:

		1984		1985		1986	
Contract	Contract Price	Costs Incurred	Percent Completed	Costs Incurred	Percent Completed	Costs Incurred	Percent Completed
1	$ 5,000,000	$1,780,000	40%	$1,550,000	35%	$1,062,400	25%
2	10,000,000	2,550,000	30	2,625,000	30	2,695,000	30
3	3,600,000	1,495,500	50	1,555,500	50	—	—

Instructions:

Determine the amount of revenue and the income to be recognized for each of the following years: 1984, 1985, and 1986. Revenue is to be recognized by the percentage-of-contract-completion method. Present computations in good order.

Problem 12-5A. Hogan Corporation was organized on January 1, 1984. During its first three years of operations, the company determined uncollectible accounts expense by the direct write-off method, the cost of the merchandise inventory at the end of the period by the first-in, first-out method, and depreciation expense by the straight-line method. The amounts of net income reported and the amounts of the foregoing items for each of the three years were as follows:

	First Year	Second Year	Third Year
Net income reported	$115,000	$142,000	$190,000
Uncollectible accounts expense	1,100	2,800	5,950
Ending merchandise inventory	58,750	80,000	110,000
Depreciation expense	20,000	26,800	35,000

The firm is considering the possibility of changing to the following methods in determining net income for the fourth and subsequent years: provision for doubtful accounts through the use of an allowance account, last-in, first-out inventory, and declining-balance depreciation at twice the straight-line rate. To consider the probable future effect of these changes on the determination of net income, the management requests that net income of the past three years be recomputed on the basis of the proposed methods. The uncollectible accounts expense, inventory, and depreciation expense for the past three years, computed in accordance with the proposed methods, are as follows:

	First Year	Second Year	Third Year
Uncollectible accounts expense	$ 2,500	$ 3,260	$ 4,150
Ending merchandise inventory	57,000	68,100	90,750
Depreciation expense	40,000	38,840	34,100

Instructions:

Recompute the net income for each of the three years, presenting the figures in an orderly manner.

Problem 12-6A. Ann Abby owns and manages The Art Mart on a full-time basis. She also maintains the accounting records. At the end of the first year of operations, she prepared the following balance sheet and income statement:

The Art Mart
Balance Sheet
December 31,19--

Cash	$10,500
Equipment	12,000
Ann Abby	$22,500

The Art Mart
Income Statement
For Year Ended December 31, 19--

Sales		$140,500
Purchases		85,000
Gross profit		$ 55,500
Operating expenses:		
Salary expense	$37,660	
Rent expense	16,800	
Utilities expense	4,225	
Miscellaneous expense.	2,315	
Total operating expenses		61,000
Net loss.		$ 5,500

Because of the large net loss reported by the income statement, Abby is considering discontinuing operations. Before making a decision, she asks you to review the accounting methods employed and, if material errors are found, to prepare revised statements. The following information is elicited during the course of the review:
- (a) The only transactions recorded have been those in which cash was received or disbursed.
- (b) The accounts have not been closed for the year.
- (c) The classification of operating expenses as "selling" and "general" is not considered to be sufficiently important to justify the cost of the analysis.
- (d) The proprietor made no withdrawals during the year.
- (e) The business was established on January 20 by an investment of $20,000 in cash by the owner. An additional investment of $8,000 was made in cash on July 1.
- (f) Accounts receivable from customers at December 31 total $9,150.
- (g) The merchandise inventory at December 31, as nearly as can be determined, has a cost of $23,425.
- (h) Rent Expense includes an advance payment of $1,400 for the month of January in the subsequent year.
- (i) Salaries owed but not paid on December 31 total $850.
- (j) The equipment listed on the balance sheet at $12,000 was purchased for cash on February 1. Equipment purchased March 31 for $4,000 in cash was debited to Purchases. Equipment purchased on December 31 for $7,000, for which a 90-day, 12% note was issued, was not recorded.
- (k) Uncollectible accounts are estimated at $1,200.
- (l) A total of $16,200 is owed to merchandise creditors on account at December 31.
- (m) Depreciation on equipment has not been recorded. The equipment is estimated to have a useful life of 10 years and no salvage value. (Use straight-line method.)
- (n) Insurance premiums of $1,250 were debited to Miscellaneous Expense during the year. The unexpired portion at December 31 is $400.
- (o) Supplies of $2,400 purchased during the year were debited to Purchases. An estimated $800 of supplies were on hand at December 31.

Instructions:
- (1) On the basis of the financial statements presented, prepare an unadjusted trial balance, as of December 31, on an eight-column work sheet.

(2) Record the adjustments and the corrections in the Adjustments columns. Complete the work sheet by extending the adjusted trial balance amounts directly to the appropriate Income Statement or Balance Sheet column.
(3) Prepare a multiple-step income statement, a capital statement, and a report form balance sheet.

Mini-Case

Auto Parts Inc. operates twenty "cash and carry" auto parts stores in the midwest. In an effort to expand sales, the company has decided to offer two additional sales plans:

(1) credit sales to commercial enterprises, such as body and repair shops, with free twenty-four-hour delivery
(2) installment sales of major dollar items, with payments spread over 36 months.

The company president has asked you when the revenue from each of the two new plans would be recognized in the accounting records and statements.

Instructions:

(1) Indicate to the president when the revenue from each type of sale should be recorded in the accounting records.
(2) While discussing the concepts in (1), the president raised the following questions related to various accounting concepts. How would you respond to each?
  (a) "Many businesses cease operating each year; so why do accountants assume a going concern concept when preparing the financial statements?"
  (b) "To assume that the value of the dollar does not change and that we don't have inflation is wrong! An automatic transmission that cost $260 five years ago costs $440 today. Why wouldn't it be better to use current dollars, at least for the inventory?"
  (c) "With so many different accounting methods that can be used, how can I switch methods to improve net income this year?"
  (d) "Our annual bonuses to store managers are based on store profits. It is not fair to 'anticipate no profits and provide for all losses.'"

13

Reporting Changes in Price Levels

CHAPTER OBJECTIVES

Describe and illustrate the effects of price-level changes on conventional financial statements.

Describe and illustrate constant dollar accounting for price-level changes.

Describe and illustrate current cost accounting for price-level changes.

Describe the current financial reporting requirements for price-level changes.

13

CHAPTER

The effects of transactions are recorded in the accounts and reported in the financial statements in terms of money. Although generally accepted accounting principles assume that the monetary unit is stable, the value of money changes over time. Such changes are called **price-level changes.**

The discussion in this chapter focuses on the basic methods of reporting the effects of price-level changes. As noted in Chapter 12, accountants are in general agreement that the effects of price-level changes should be reported in supplemental statements, rather than in the conventional statements to which users are accustomed. The assumption of a stable monetary unit insures objectivity in the conventional statements. In addition, because they report transactions in terms of historical costs arising from arm's-length bargaining, the conventional statements can be independently verified.

TYPES OF PRICE CHANGES

The amount of goods or services that can be purchased with a given amount of money (number of dollars) changes over time. When prices in general are rising, a given number of dollars will buy less and less goods or services and it can be said that the value of the dollar is falling. During the past three decades, the purchasing power of the dollar has generally declined from year to year. Such periods are described as periods of **inflation.** When prices are falling, as was the case in the decades of the 1920's and 1930's, the value of the dollar is rising and the purchasing power of the dollar is increasing. Such periods are described as periods of **deflation.**

Two types of price changes can be identified as affecting business enterprises: (1) general price-level changes and (2) specific price-level changes. A **general price-level change** is the change over time in the amount of money (number of dollars) needed to purchase a general group or market basket of goods and services. To illustrate, assume that such a group of goods and services is composed of X, Y, and Z and that their individual prices and total price at December 31, 1984 and 1983, are as follows:

	December 31		Increase
	1984	1983	(Decrease)
X	$ 6.40	$ 5.00	$ 1.40
Y	20.90	22.00	(1.10)
Z	17.10	10.00	7.10
Total	$44.40	$37.00	$ 7.40

In this illustration, to purchase X, Y, and Z at December 31, 1984, would require an outlay of $7.40 more than would the same purchase at December 31, 1983. The general price level, as measured by the goods X, Y, and Z, has increased by 20% ($7.40 ÷ $37) during 1984. Correspondingly, the purchasing power of the dollar in terms of the amount of X, Y, and Z that can be purchased has decreased by 20%.

A **specific price-level change** is the change over time in the amount of money needed to purchase "individual" goods and services. Prices of individual items may change by a rate that differs from the rate for "general" prices. For example, in the preceding illustration, X increased by 28% ($1.40 ÷ $5) during 1984, Y decreased by 5% ($1.10 ÷ $22), and Z increased by 71% ($7.10 ÷ $10). The general price level for the total of X, Y, and Z increased by 20%.

The effects of general and specific price-level changes on conventional financial statements and two recommendations for reporting these effects are described and illustrated in the remainder of this chapter.

EFFECT OF GENERAL PRICE-LEVEL CHANGES ON FINANCIAL STATEMENTS

The effect of general price-level changes on conventional financial statements depends on (1) the amount and direction of the change in the general purchasing power of the dollar and (2) the composition of the enterprise's assets and liabilities. The following paragraphs describe and illustrate the measurement of general price-level changes and the effect of these changes on different types of assets and liabilities.

Measuring General Price-Level Changes

Using a general price-level index, it is possible to convert conventional financial statement amounts to dollars of common purchasing power as of a given date. A **price-level index** is the ratio of the total cost of a group of goods prevailing at a particular time to the total cost of the same group of goods at an earlier base time. The total cost of the goods at the base time is given a value of 100 and the price-level indexes for all later times are expressed as a ratio to 100. For example, assume that the cost of a selected group of goods amounted to $12,000 at a particular time and $13,200 today. The price index for the earlier, or base, time becomes 100 and the current price index is 110 [($13,200 ÷ $12,000) × 100].

To illustrate the use of general price-level indexes, assume that land is purchased for $10,000 in 1978 when the general price-level index was 100, and that the index is 175 at the current date of December 31, 1984. Using these indexes, the original cost of the land can be restated in current dollars of purchasing power as follows:

$$\frac{\text{Current Price Index}}{\text{Price Index at Date of Purchase}} \times \text{Original Cost} = \text{Restated Amount}$$

$$\frac{175}{100} \times \$10,000 = \$17,500$$

The computation results in a restated amount of $17,500. This $17,500 is the 1984 amount of money that is equivalent in purchasing power to the 1978 amount of $10,000.

Monetary and Nonmonetary Items

The effect of general price-level changes on an enterprise's assets and liabilities depends on the type of asset or liability. For example, cash that is held by a business during a period of inflation always loses some of its purchasing power because the cash will purchase less goods and services at the end of the period than at the beginning. On the other hand, a plant asset, such as land, may increase in value and thus not lose some of its purchasing power during periods of inflation. In periods of inflation, a business gains purchasing power as a result of owing amounts, such as accounts payable, that it must settle in dollars. A gain results because the liability will be paid off in dollars which will purchase less than could have been purchased when the liability was incurred. Thus all assets and liabilities are not affected the same by changes in purchasing power.

For purposes of analyzing the effects of changes in purchasing power, the assets and liabilities of a business are classified as monetary or nonmonetary. A **monetary item** is money or a claim to receive money or an obligation to pay a fixed amount of money. Monetary assets are composed of cash and all claims which are to be settled in cash, such as accounts receivable and notes receivable. Monetary liabilities include virtually all debts, such as accounts payable, notes payable, and bonds payable, because settlement is usually to be made in cash.

All items that are not classified as monetary are classified as **nonmonetary**. The major nonmonetary items are inventories, plant assets, common stock, and retained earnings. Distinguishing monetary and nonmonetary items thus forms the basis for (1) restating nonmonetary items into dollars of current purchasing power and (2) recognizing purchasing power gains and losses related to the monetary items. In this way, the effects of general price-level changes on conventional financial statements are determined.

Monetary Items

Holders of monetary assets and liabilities lose or gain general purchasing power during periods of inflation and deflation as a result of general price-level changes. These gains and losses are called **purchasing power gains and losses**. To illustrate, assume that as of January 1, 1984, a company had a cash balance of $50,000 which it kept throughout the year. If the general price-level index increased during the year from 125 to 150, then a purchasing power loss of **$10,000** has occurred. This purchasing power loss is computed as follows:

Amount needed to maintain the original purchasing power of cash ($50,000 × 150/125)	$60,000
Actual amount of cash at end of year	50,000
Purchasing power loss	$10,000

When the general price-level index increased from 125 to 150 due to inflation, a dollar lost 20% (25/125) of its purchasing power. In this example, the amount of purchasing power loss was $10,000 ($50,000 × 20%). If the price-level index had decreased from 125 to 100, a purchasing power gain of $10,000 would have resulted.

The holding of noncash monetary assets and liabilities also results in purchasing power gains or losses. To illustrate, assume that ten years ago a $100,000 ten-year note receivable was acquired in connection with a sale of property, that the note is now due, and is paid in full.[1] Since the number of dollars received is exactly the same as the number of dollars loaned, it might appear that the lender has been restored to the original position (i.e., ten years earlier). This would be the case only if there had been no change in the general price level between the date of the note and the date of its repayment. If a 50% increase in the price level between the two dates is assumed, the holder of the note has incurred a purchasing power loss of $50,000 during the period. The amount of the loss is measured by the difference between the amount needed to maintain the original purchasing power and the actual amount of money received. The $50,000 purchasing power loss is computed as follows:

Amount needed to maintain original purchasing power of note
    receivable ($100,000 × 150%)............................... $150,000
Actual amount of cash received............................... 100,000
Purchasing power loss .... $ 50,000

The effect of the assumed change in price level on the debtor would be the reverse of the effect on the creditor. During the ten-year period, the purchasing power of the $100,000 original liability increased to $150,000, but only $100,000 is needed to satisfy the obligation. Hence, a purchasing power gain of $50,000 is realized.

Nonmonetary Items

The purchasing power of nonmonetary items tends not to be affected by changes in the price level. For example, the sales price of a nonmonetary item, such as land, will tend to increase as the general price level increases and will therefore retain its purchasing power. Thus, in contrast to monetary items, no purchasing power gains or losses are recognized for nonmonetary items.

CONSTANT DOLLAR STATEMENTS

When historical costs reported in conventional financial statements are converted to dollars of common (or constant) purchasing power, the resulting financial statements are called constant dollar statements or **general price-level statements.** In the conversion process, the purchasing power gain or loss on monetary items is identified.

Constant Dollar Balance Sheet

For purposes of preparing the constant dollar balance sheet, the accounts must be classified into monetary and nonmonetary categories. Because general price-level changes affect monetary and nonmonetary items differently, these items must

---

[1]To simplify the illustration, the periodic interest payments will be excluded from consideration.

be classified correctly. The proper classification of common balance sheet accounts is as follows:

Monetary	Nonmonetary
Cash	Inventory
Accounts Receivable	Land
Notes Receivable	Buildings
Accounts Payable	Accumulated Depreciation — Buildings
Notes Payable	Equipment
Bonds Payable	Accumulated Depreciation — Equipment
	Capital Stock
	Retained Earnings

Monetary assets and liabilities are always stated in current purchasing power dollars and therefore need not be adjusted for price-level changes for the constant dollar balance sheet. However, the net purchasing power gain or loss on monetary items is reported on the constant dollar balance sheet as an adjustment of owners' equity. All other balance sheet accounts — the nonmonetary items — must be restated to constant (current) dollars for the constant dollar balance sheet. By restating the nonmonetary items, recognition is given to the effect of the changes that have occurred in the price level since the items were recorded in the accounts.

To illustrate the preparation of a constant dollar balance sheet, assume that Allen Company was organized on January 1, 1984, when the price-level index was 100. The company's balance sheet was as follows:

Allen Company
Balance Sheet
January 1, 1984

Assets		Stockholders' Equity	
Cash	$10,000	Capital stock..............	$40,000
Land	30,000		
Total assets	$40,000	Total stockholders' equity...	$40,000

For purposes of illustration, assume that Allen Company intends to construct a warehouse on the land and then rent storage space to local businesses. However, because of delays in obtaining necessary construction permits, no transactions were completed during 1984 when the price-level index rose to 125. At December 31, 1984, the conventional balance sheet would appear as above, and the constant dollar balance sheet would appear as follows (the computations are inserted as an aid to understanding):

**Allen Company
Constant Dollar Balance Sheet
December 31, 1984**

Assets		
Cash	$10,000	(Monetary asset stated in constant dollars)
Land	37,500	(Nonmonetary asset restated in constant dollars: $30,000 × 125/100)
Total assets	$47,500	
Stockholders' Equity		
Capital stock	$50,000	(Nonmonetary item restated in constant dollars: $40,000 × 125/100)
Retained earnings (deficit) .	(2,500)	(Purchasing power loss on monetary asset: $10,000 × 125/100 less $10,000)
Total stockholders' equity . .	$47,500	

The determination of the amount reported for each item of the constant dollar balance sheet is explained in the paragraphs that follow.

Cash

The monetary assets are always stated in constant dollars in the accounts. Therefore, cash does not require adjustment for the general price-level change.

Land

Land is a nonmonetary asset and the account amount is restated to end-of-the-year constant dollars by multiplying $30,000 by the ratio of the price-level index of 125 at the end of the year to the price-level index of 100 at the date the asset was purchased (the date the company was organized).

Capital Stock

As a nonmonetary item, capital stock is restated to end-of-the-year constant dollars by multiplying $40,000 by the ratio of the price-level index of 125 at the end of the year to the price-level index of 100 at the date the stock was originally issued (the date the company was organized).

Retained Earnings

Since no transactions were completed during the year, the constant dollar Retained Earnings balance contains only the purchasing power loss on the monetary assets held during the year. The only monetary item was cash, and the purchasing power loss of $2,500 is computed as follows:

Amount needed to maintain the original purchasing power of the monetary item (cash) $10,000 × 125/100	$12,500
Actual amount of monetary item (cash)	10,000
Purchasing power loss	$ 2,500

The basic steps in preparing the constant dollar balance sheet can be summarized as follows:

1. List the monetary assets and liabilities at the account balance amounts because they are always stated in constant (current) dollars.
2. Restate the nonmonetary item account balances to constant dollar equivalents.
3. Reflect the purchasing power gain or loss on monetary items as an adjustment of owners' equity.

Constant Dollar Income Statement

For purposes of preparing the constant dollar income statement, all revenues and expenses are restated to end-of-the-year constant dollars by the use of a price-level index. The net purchasing power gain or loss on monetary items is then determined, and this amount is added or subtracted to arrive at the constant dollar net income or loss for the year.

To illustrate the preparation of a constant dollar income statement, assume that in January, 1985, Allen Company entered into a contract for the construction of a warehouse on the land at a cost of $63,000. The construction was completed and the warehouse was placed in service on June 30, 1985. In settlement of the construction contract, a 16%, two-year note payable, with interest payable monthly, was issued. All revenue during 1985 was for cash and all expenses, except depreciation, were paid in cash. The conventional income statement for the year ended December 31, 1985, and the conventional balance sheet on December 31, 1985, are as follows:

Allen Company
Income Statement
For Year Ended December 31, 1985

Revenues:		
Rental revenue	$43,500	(Rents were collected uniformly during July–December; average price-level index during this period was 145)
Expenses:		
Depreciation expense ...	$ 2,100	(The warehouse was placed in service when the price-level index was 140)
Other rental expenses ...	29,000	(Expenses were paid uniformly during July–December; average price-level index during this period was 145)
Total expenses	31,100	
Net income..................	$12,400	

Allen Company
Balance Sheet
December 31, 1985

Assets

Cash		$ 24,500
Land		30,000
Building	$ 63,000	
Less accumulated depreciation	2,100	60,900
Total assets		$115,400

Liabilities and Stockholders' Equity

Notes payable	$ 63,000
Capital stock	40,000
Retained earnings	12,400
Total liabilities and stockholders' equity	$115,400

If the price-level index at the end of the year was 150, the conventional income statement amounts would be restated to constant dollar equivalents and the constant dollar income statement would appear as follows (the computations are inserted as an aid to understanding):

Allen Company
Constant Dollar Income Statement
For Year Ended December 31, 1985

Revenues:			
Rental revenue		$45,000	(Restated in constant dollars: $43,500 × 150/145)
Expenses:			
Depreciation expense	$ 2,250		(Restated in constant dollars: $2,100 × 150/140)
Other rental expenses	30,000		(Restated in constant dollars: $29,000 × 150/145)
Total expenses		32,250	
Income before purchasing power gain		$12,750	
Purchasing power gain		2,000	(Computed on monetary items held during the year)
Net income		$14,750	

The determination of the amount reported for each item on the constant dollar income statement is explained in the paragraphs that follow.

Rental Revenue

Since the rents were collected uniformly over a period of time, they are restated to end-of-the-year constant dollars by multiplying $43,500 by the ratio of the price-level index of 150 at the end of the year to the average price-level index of 145 for the period July through December.

Depreciation Expense

Since the warehouse was purchased when the price-level index was 140, the depreciation expense is restated to end-of-the-year constant dollars by multiplying $2,100 by the ratio of the price-level index of 150 at the end of the year to the price-level index of 140 at the date of the acquisition of the warehouse.

Other Rental Expenses

As was the case for rental revenues, the other rental expenses, including interest on the note payable, were incurred uniformly throughout the period July through December. Hence, these expenses are restated to end-of-the-year constant dollars by multiplying $29,000 by the ratio of 150 to 145.

Purchasing Power Gain

To determine the net purchasing power gain for the year, it is necessary to compute the purchasing power gains and losses on the monetary items held during the year. For Allen Company, the monetary items were (1) cash and (2) notes payable. The beginning balances and changes in these monetary items during the year, along with the relevant price-level for each, are summarized as follows:

	Amount	Price-Level Index
Monetary assets:		
Cash, January 1, 1985	$10,000	125
Add rental revenue for 1985	43,500	145
Deduct other rental expenses for 1985	(29,000)	145
Cash, December 31, 1985	$24,500	150
Monetary liabilities:		
Notes payable, January 1, 1985	—	—
Issued during 1985	$63,000	140
Notes payable, December 31, 1985	$63,000	150

The net purchasing power gain for the year related to the monetary items is $2,000 and is calculated as shown at the top of page 361.

For each monetary item, the January 1, 1985 balance and changes during 1985 are restated to December 31, 1985 constant dollar amounts. The purchasing power gain or loss on each monetary item is then computed by comparing the December 31, 1985 conventional and constant dollar balance sheet amounts. The sum of the

	Conventional Balance Sheet Amount	Restatement Factor	Constant Dollar Balance Sheet Amount	Purchasing Power Gain (Loss)
Cash:				
January 1 balance......	$10,000	150/125	$12,000	
Add rental revenue for 1985	43,500	150/145	45,000	
Deduct other rental expenses for 1985	(29,000)	150/145	(30,000)	
December 31 balance ..	$24,500		$27,000	$ (2,500)
Notes payable:				
January 1 balance......	—	—		
Issued during 1985	$63,000	150/140	$67,500	
December 31 balance ..	$63,000		$67,500	4,500
Net purchasing power gain...				$ 2,000

purchasing power gains and losses for all monetary items held during 1985 determines the net purchasing power gain or loss for the year.

In the illustration, the January 1, 1985 cash balance is restated to December 31, 1985 constant dollars by multiplying $10,000 by the ratio of the price-level index of 150 at the end of the year to the price-level index of 125 at January 1, 1985. The restatement of cash received from rental revenue and cash paid for other rental expenses to December 31, 1985 constant dollars was described previously and reported on the constant dollar income statement. The $2,500 purchasing power loss from holding cash during 1985 is the difference between the December 31, 1985 constant dollar amount of $27,000 and the actual amount of cash on hand of $24,500 at December 31, 1985.

In a similar manner, the purchasing power gain of $4,500 related to the note payable is computed. The account amount of $63,000 is converted to the constant dollar amount of $67,500 by multiplying $63,000 by the ratio of the price-level index of 150 at the end of the year to the price-level index of 140 at the issuance date. The 1985 net purchasing power gain of $2,000 is the sum of the purchasing power loss of $2,500 from holding cash and the $4,500 purchasing power gain from owing the note payable.

The basic steps in preparing the constant dollar income statement can be summarized as follows:

1. Restate all revenue and expense accounts to constant dollar equivalents by the use of a price-level index.
2. Add or deduct the purchasing power gain or loss on monetary items.

Constant Dollar Retained Earnings Statement

For purposes of preparing a constant dollar retained earnings statement, the beginning balance of Retained Earnings, as reported at the end of the prior period in constant dollars, is restated to end-of-the-year constant dollars. The constant dollar net income or loss for the year is then added or subtracted. Finally, any

dividends for the year are restated to end-of-the-year constant dollars and subtracted to arrive at the constant dollar retained earnings as of the end of the year.

To illustrate, Allen Company's conventional and constant dollar retained earnings statement for the year ended December 31, 1985, are as follows (the computations are inserted as an aid to understanding):

Allen Company
Retained Earnings Statement
For Year Ended December 31, 1985

Retained earnings, January 1, 1985........................	—	
Net income for the year..........	$12,400	(As reported on the 1985 income statement)
Retained earnings, December 31, 1985.........................	$12,400	

Allen Company
Constant Dollar Retained Earnings Statement
For Year Ended December 31, 1985

Retained earnings, January 1, 1985........................	$ (3,000)	(January 1, 1985 constant dollar retained earnings restated to December 31, 1985 constant dollars: $2,500 × 150/125)
Constant dollar net income........	14,750	(As reported on the 1985 constant dollar income statement)
Retained earnings, December 31, 1985.........................	$11,750	

Allen Company reported a constant dollar deficit of $2,500 on its December 31,
1984 constant dollar balance sheet (illustrated on page 357). This beginning-of-the-
year amount must be restated to December 31, 1985 constant dollars by multiplying the $2,500 deficit by the ratio of the price-level index of 150 at the end of
the year to the beginning-of-the-year price-level index of 125. Since no dividends
were declared in 1985, the December 31, 1985 constant dollar retained earnings
of $11,750 is the result of adding the 1985 constant dollar net income of $14,750 to
the restated beginning balance of Retained Earnings.

The basic steps in preparing the constant dollar retained earnings statement
can be summarized as follows:

1. Restate the constant dollar beginning balance of Retained Earnings to end-
of-the-year constant dollars.

2. Add or deduct the constant dollar net income or loss for the year.

3. Deduct constant dollar dividends for the year.

The December 31, 1985 constant dollar retained earnings of $11,750 would appear on the December 31, 1985 constant dollar balance sheet as follows (the computations are inserted as an aid to understanding):

Allen Company
Constant Dollar Balance Sheet
December 31, 1985

Assets

Cash	$ 24,500	(Monetary asset stated in constant dollars)
Land	45,000	(Nonmonetary asset restated to constant dollars: $30,000 × 150/100)
Building	$67,500	(Nonmonetary asset restated to constant dollars: $63,000 × 150/140)
Less accumulated depreciation	2,250 → 65,250	(Nonmonetary contra asset restated to constant dollars: $2,100 × 150/140)
Total assets	$134,750	

Liabilities and Stockholders' Equity

Notes payable	$ 63,000	(Monetary asset stated in constant dollars)
Capital stock	60,000	(Nonmonetary item restated in constant dollars: $40,000 × 150/100)
Retained earnings	11,750	(As reported on the constant dollar retained earnings statement)
Total liabilities and stockholders' equity	$134,750	

EFFECT OF SPECIFIC PRICE-LEVEL CHANGES ON FINANCIAL STATEMENTS

The effect of specific price-level changes on conventional financial statements depends on (1) the amount and direction of the change in specific prices related to the enterprise's assets and liabilities and (2) the composition of the enterprise's assets and liabilities. The following paragraphs describe and illustrate the measurement of specific price-level changes and the effect of these changes on different types of assets and liabilities.

Measuring Specific Price-Level Changes

Accountants disagree concerning the best means to measure the impact of specific price-level changes on an enterprise's assets and liabilities. However, regardless of which of several suggested measures is used, the assets and liabilities are reported at amounts that approximate their current costs (values). The use of current costs permits the identification of gains and losses related to price-level changes for specific assets and liabilities held by an enterprise.

Monetary and Nonmonetary Items

The effect of specific price-level changes depends on the type of asset or liability. For purposes of analyzing the effects of changes in current costs, assets and liabilities of a business are classified as monetary or nonmonetary.

Monetary Items

All monetary assets and liabilities are stated at current costs in the conventional financial statements. For example, since the current cost of a dollar is a dollar, cash is stated at current cost in the conventional balance sheet. Likewise, the current cost of other monetary items to be collected or paid in cash, such as receivables and liabilities, are also stated at current costs in the conventional balance sheet.

Nonmonetary Items

The current cost of the nonmonetary assets, such as the plant assets, is the cost of replacing them with assets of the same age and the same operating capacity. Therefore, because the current cost of such nonmonetary assets tends to increase or decrease over time, the account balances need to be restated for current cost statements. By restating the nonmonetary asset to current cost amounts, it is possible to identify gains and losses that result when the current costs of these assets change. In other words, gains and losses that result from the holding of assets, often called holding gains and losses, are identified and reported in financial statements adjusted for current costs. In conventional financial statements, such holding gains and losses are not reported.

To illustrate the use of and reporting of current costs for nonmonetary assets, assume that land is purchased for $20,000 on January 1, 1985, and that its current cost on December 31, 1985, is $25,000. Restating the land to current costs would result in reporting it at $25,000 on the current-cost-adjusted balance sheet at December 31, 1985. The current-cost-adjusted income statement for the year ended December 31, 1985, would also report an "unrealized" holding gain of $5,000, which represents the increase of the current cost over the original cost of the land. It should be noted that the $5,000 holding gain is identified as "unrealized"; that is, since the land has not been sold, the gain has not been realized. If the land were sold for $25,000—for example, on January 1, 1986—the $5,000 of holding gain would then become realized.

CURRENT COST STATEMENTS

When historical costs reported in the conventional statements are adjusted for specific price-level changes, all elements of the financial statements are reported at their current costs. The resulting financial statements are called current cost statements or specific price-level statements. In the restatement process, the holding gains or losses on nonmonetary assets are identified.

To illustrate the basic concepts of preparing current cost financial statements, assume that Teasley Company was organized on December 31, 1984, by the sale of $150,000 of capital stock for cash. It leased store space and equipment and sold merchandise only for cash. During 1985, merchandise costing $295,000 was purchased, $140,000 of the merchandise was sold for $200,000, and operating expenses were $40,000. A comparative conventional balance sheet for the date of organization and one year later at December 31, 1985, is as follows:

Teasley Company
Comparative Balance Sheet
December 31, 1985 and 1984

Assets	1985	1984
Cash	$ 25,000	$150,000
Merchandise inventory	155,000	—
Total assets	$180,000	$150,000

Liabilities and Stockholders' Equity		
Accounts payable	$ 10,000	
Capital stock	150,000	$150,000
Retained earnings	20,000	
Total liabilities and stockholders' equity	$180,000	$150,000

The conventional income statement for the year ended December 31, 1985, is as follows:

Teasley Company
Income Statement
For Year Ended December 31, 1985

Sales	$200,000
Cost of merchandise sold	140,000
Gross profit	$ 60,000
Operating expenses	40,000
Net income	$ 20,000

The relevant current cost amounts for the preceding financial statement items are as follows:

Cash	$ 25,000
Merchandise inventory	162,000
Accounts payable	10,000
Capital stock	150,000
Sales	200,000
Cost of merchandise sold	154,000
Operating expenses	40,000

| The conventional income statement of Teasley Company is converted to a current cost income statement by restating the revenues and expenses to current costs and by reporting realized and unrealized holding gains or losses. Revenues and expenses are restated to current costs as of the date each revenue and expense transaction takes place. In this way, current cost expenses are matched against current cost revenues. Most revenues are stated in the conventional income statement at amounts that represent the current values at the date the sales transactions occur. Likewise, most expenses which are directly paid for in cash also are stated in the conventional income statement at amounts that represent the current values at the transaction dates.

Based upon the preceding data, the current cost income statement for Teasley Company would appear as follows (the notations are inserted as an aid to understanding):

Teasley Company
Current Cost Income Statement
For Year Ended December 31, 1985

Sales............................	$200,000	(Stated at current cost at the transaction dates)
Cost of merchandise sold	154,000	(Restated to current costs at the transaction dates)
Gross profit.....................	$ 46,000	
Operating expenses	40,000	(Stated at current costs at the transaction dates)
Operating income	$ 6,000	
Realized holding gain...........	14,000	(Holding gain on cost of merchandise sold: $154,000 − $140,000)
Realized income.................	$ 20,000	
Unrealized holding gain.........	7,000	(Holding gain on ending inventory: $162,000 − $155,000)
Net income	$ 27,000	

The determination of the amount reported for each item on the current cost income statement is explained in the paragraphs that follow.

Sales

Since sales are stated in the conventional income statement at amounts that represent the current values at the dates of the sales transactions, the sales amount does not require adjustment for the current cost income statement.

Cost of Merchandise Sold

To determine the current cost of merchandise sold, the current cost of each item of merchandise sold must be identified as of the date of sale. These current cost amounts are then accumulated throughout the year to determine the total current cost of merchandise sold during the year. The total current cost of merchandise sold is then deducted from the current value of sales to arrive at current cost gross profit. For Teasley Company, the accumulated current cost of merchandise sold was determined to be $154,000. Since the original cost of the merchandise sold was $140,000, the amount of the realized holding gain was $14,000.

Operating Expenses

The current cost for operating expenses of $40,000 is the cost of the resources consumed by Teasley Company as measured at the time the expenses were incurred. For this illustration, the conventional amount and the current cost amount is $40,000.[2]

Realized Holding Gain

The $14,000 realized holding gain is the difference between the $154,000 current cost of the merchandise sold and the $140,000 original cost of the merchandise sold. This holding gain is reported as realized, since the merchandise has been sold.

Unrealized Holding Gain

The $7,000 unrealized holding gain is the difference between the $162,000 current cost of the merchandise on hand at the end of the year and its original cost of $155,000. This holding gain is classified as unrealized, since the merchandise has yet to be sold.

It should be noted that the current cost realized income of $20,000 for 1985 equals the conventional income statement net income for 1985. These two financial statement amounts will always be equal, because both the current cost realized income and the conventional financial statement net income include realized holding gains and losses from selling nonmonetary assets.

The basic steps in preparing the current cost income statement can be summarized as follows:

1. List revenues at their current cost amounts.
2. Restate the cost of merchandise sold and other expenses as reported on the conventional income statement to their current cost amounts.
3. Add or deduct the realized and unrealized holding gains and losses.

Current Cost Balance Sheet   For purposes of preparing the current cost balance sheet, the accounts must be classified into monetary and nonmonetary categories. The classification of common balance sheet accounts into monetary and nonmonetary categories was illustrated on page 356.

---

[2]To simplify this illustration, noncash expenses such as depreciation have been excluded from consideration. In current cost financial statements, depreciation would be restated, based upon the average current costs of the depreciable assets held during the year.

Monetary assets and liabilities are always stated in current costs and therefore need not be restated. All nonmonetary assets must be restated to current costs for the current cost balance sheet. By restating the nonmonetary assets, recognition is given to the effect of changes that have occurred in current costs since the assets were initially recorded in the accounts. These changes in current costs are shown in the current cost income statement as holding gains and losses.

Owners' equity accounts are nonmonetary items that must be analyzed separately. The accounts that show investments by stockholders, such as Capital Stock, are stated in the conventional financial statements at the amounts initially received from investors. These amounts represent the current costs of obtaining these funds and do not need to be restated. Other owners' equity accounts, such as Retained Earnings, must be restated to current costs. Retained Earnings is restated to current costs by restating the beginning-of-the-year balance to current costs, then adding current cost net income or subtracting current cost net loss, and subtracting any current cost dividends.

The current cost balance sheet for Teasley Company is as follows (the notations are inserted as an aid to understanding):

Teasley Company
Current Cost Balance Sheet
December 31, 1985

Assets		
Cash	$ 25,000	(Monetary asset stated at current cost)
Merchandise inventory	162,000	(Nonmonetary asset restated to current cost)
Total assets	$187,000	
Liabilities and Stockholders' Equity		
Accounts payable	$ 10,000	(Monetary liability stated at current cost)
Capital stock	150,000	(Nonmonetary capital stated at current cost)
Retained earnings	27,000	(Nonmonetary capital restated to current cost)
Total liabilities and stockholders' equity	$187,000	

The determination of the amount reported for each item on the current cost balance sheet is explained in the paragraphs that follow.

Cash and Accounts Payable

Monetary items are stated at current costs in conventional financial statements and therefore do not require restatement on the current cost balance sheet.

Merchandise Inventory

Merchandise inventory should be stated on the current cost balance sheet at its estimated current cost of $162,000.

Capital Stock

Capital stock is reported in the conventional balance sheet at the amount initially received from investors. This amount represents the current cost of obtaining such funds and does not need to be restated.

Retained Earnings

For Teasley Company, the current cost net income of $27,000 is equal to the December 31, 1985 current cost retained earnings. Preparation of a current cost retained earnings statement is described in the next section.

The basic steps in preparing the current cost balance sheet can be summarized as follows:

1. List the monetary assets and liabilities and capital stock account balances because they are always stated at current costs.
2. Restate the nonmonetary asset account balances to current costs.
3. Compute the current cost retained earnings by restating the beginning balance and changes during the year to current costs.

Current Cost Retained Earnings Statement

For purposes of preparing a current cost retained earnings statement, the beginning balance of Retained Earnings is restated to current costs by referring to the preceding year's current cost financial statements. The current cost net income or loss for the year is then added or subtracted and any current cost dividends are subtracted to arrive at the current cost retained earnings as of the end of the year.

To illustrate, the December 31, 1985 current cost retained earnings statement for Teasley Company is as follows (the notations are inserted as an aid to understanding):

Teasley Company Current Cost Retained Earnings Statement For Year Ended December 31, 1985		
Retained earnings, January 1, 1985	–0–	(The company was organized on December 31, 1984)
Current cost net income	$27,000	(As reported in the 1985 current cost income statement)
Retained earnings, December 31, 1985	$27,000	

Since Teasley Company was organized on December 31, 1984, current cost retained earnings as of January 1, 1985, is zero. No dividends were declared in 1985 and current cost net income is $27,000. The December 31, 1985 current cost retained earnings of $27,000 is reported on the December 31, 1985 current cost balance sheet shown on page 368.

The basic steps in preparing the current cost retained earnings statement are as follows:

1. Restate the beginning balance of retained earnings to current costs.
2. Add or deduct current cost net income or loss for the year.
3. Deduct any current cost dividends for the year.

CURRENT ANNUAL REPORTING REQUIREMENTS FOR PRICE-LEVEL CHANGES

This chapter has described and illustrated two common methods for supplementing conventional financial statements and resolving financial reporting problems created by changing price levels: (1) supplemental financial statements based on constant dollars and (2) supplemental financial statements based on current costs. In 1979, the Financial Accounting Standards Board undertook an experimental program for reporting the effects of changing prices by requiring certain large, publicly held enterprises to annually disclose certain current cost information and constant dollar information as supplemental data.[3] In reaching this decision, the Board determined that both the current cost and constant dollar methods would provide useful information, and that before deciding which method to select, additional experimentation was necessary.

The following paragraphs briefly summarize the most significant annual reporting requirements of the Board. In all cases, the financial statements should contain notes that explain the information disclosed and discuss its significance for the enterprise.[4]

For conventional financial statements, supplementary information for the current year's operations and for the prior five years should be presented. For the current year's operations, schedules or notes should indicate (1) income from continuing operations on both a current cost and constant dollar basis; (2) the current cost amounts of inventory and plant assets and increases or decreases in these amounts for the year, net of the amount of change that would have resulted from the change in the general price index; and (3) the purchasing power gain or loss on net monetary items (assets and liabilities). For each of the five most recent years, schedules or notes should indicate the constant dollar and current cost amounts for (1) net sales and operating revenues, (2) income from continuing operations, in total dollar amounts and on a per share basis, and (3) net assets at

---

[3]*Statement of Financial Accounting Standards, No. 33*, "Financial Reporting and Changing Prices" (Stamford: Financial Accounting Standards Board, 1979). The requirement applies generally only to enterprises having total assets of $1 billion or more, or those having inventory plus cost of plant assets of $125 million or more. It should also be noted that Statement No. 33 uses more technical terms than those used in this chapter. These terminology differences are discussed in more advanced texts.

[4]Appendix G contains illustrations of supplementary price-level reporting.

fiscal year end. Other five-year summary data that should be disclosed include the purchasing power gain or loss on net monetary items and increases or decreases in the current cost amounts of inventory and plant assets held during each fiscal year, net of the amount of change that would have resulted from the change in the general price index.

Self-Examination Questions
(Answers in Appendix C.)

1. A period when prices in general are rising is referred to as a period of:
   A. deflation
   B. inflation
   C. a purchasing power loss
   D. none of the above

2. If a $100,000 investment in stock was made at a time when the general price index was 100, what would be the restated constant dollar amount at a time when the index was 140?
   A. $40,000
   B. $100,000
   C. $140,000
   D. None of the above

3. During a period in which the general price level is rising, which of the following would create a purchasing power gain?
   A. Holding cash
   B. Holding a long-term bond payable
   C. Holding inventory
   D. Holding a note receivable

4. Which of the following is a monetary item?
   A. Cash
   B. Notes receivable
   C. Bonds payable
   D. All of the above

5. Land purchased for $30,000 on April 15, 1984, has a current cost of $40,000 at December 31, 1984. The $10,000 difference between the current cost and the original cost of the land is:
   A. a realized holding gain
   B. a purchasing power gain
   C. an unrealized holding gain
   D. none of the above

Discussion Questions

1. What term is used to refer to periods when the value of the dollar is rising and the purchasing power of the dollar is increasing?

2. Describe the difference between a general price-level change and a specific price-level change.

3. If equipment was purchased for $40,000 when the general price-level index was 220, and the general price-level index has risen to 242 in 1984, what is the original cost restated in current dollars?

4. (a) Describe the difference between monetary and nonmonetary items. (b) Describe a purchasing power gain.

5. Five years ago, Delaney Company accepted an $80,000 long-term note from Mintz Corporation. The note is now due. The general price level has increased by 32% during the five years. (a) What is Delaney Company's purchasing power gain or loss? (b) What is Mintz Corporation's purchasing power gain or loss?

6. During the current year, a mortgage note payable for $310,000, issued by Archer Corporation ten years ago, becomes due and is paid. Assuming that the general price level has increased by 100% during the ten-year period, did the loan result in an increase or decrease in Archer Corporation's purchasing power? Explain.

7. Indicate whether each of the following is a monetary or nonmonetary item:
   (a) Building   (d) Land
   (b) Notes Payable   (e) Accounts Payable
   (c) Cash   (f) Capital Stock

8. During a period of inflation, would an enterprise gain in purchasing power if it held (a) monetary assets or (b) monetary liabilities?

9. Jesse Ward robbed a bank of $50,000 in cash in 1978. Before he was captured and sentenced to prison, he buried the money. In 1984, Ward was released on parole and promptly recovered the buried money. (a) If the general price-level index was 175 in 1978 and 210 in 1984, what was Ward's purchasing power loss while in prison? (b) How many dollars would be necessary in 1984 to equal the purchasing power of the $50,000 stolen in 1978?

10. Sales totaling $210,000 were made uniformly throughout the year. At what amount would sales be reported on the constant dollar income statement if the price-level index at the beginning of the year was 140, the average for the year was 160, and the index at the end of the year was 184?

11. When a constant dollar balance sheet is prepared, which of the following categories of items is restated in terms of constant dollars: (a) monetary items (b) nonmonetary items?

12. Describe the basic steps in preparing a constant dollar (a) balance sheet and (b) income statement.

13. Describe current cost for (a) a monetary asset and (b) a nonmonetary asset.

14. Distinguish between realized holding gains and losses and unrealized holding gains and losses.

15. Land was purchased for $128,000 on May 31, 1983. Subsequently, the current cost of the land was as follows:

    December 31, 1983........$130,000
    December 31, 1984........ 136,000
    December 31, 1985........ 135,000

    (a) What is the unrealized holding gain or loss for each year ending on December 31? (b) If the land were sold on December 31, 1985, for $135,000, what is the realized holding gain or loss?

16. At what amount are sales normally reported on the current cost income statement?

17. When a current cost balance sheet is prepared, which of the following categories of items is restated in current costs: (a) monetary items, (b) nonmonetary assets, (c) paid-in capital accounts, (d) retained earnings?

18. If the current cost concept is used in preparing supplemental statements, what amounts would be reported for (a) land at December 31, 1984, and (b) unrealized gain from holding the land in 1984, based on the following data:

    Land, purchase price, January 2, 1984 .... $60,000
    Land, current cost, December 31, 1984......... 78,000

19. What two amounts in a current cost income statement and a conventional income statement are always equal?

20. Identify two common methods for supplementing conventional financial statements and resolving the financial reporting problems created by increasing price levels?

Exercises

Exercise 13-1. Montgomery Enterprises purchased 3,000 shares of capital stock of Stein Company for $60,000 at a time when the price-level index was 120. On October 11 of the current year when the price-level index was 132, the stock was sold for $71,500.
   (a) Determine the amount of the gain that would be realized according to conventional accounting.
   (b) Indicate the amount of the gain (1) that may be attributed to the change in purchasing power and (2) that may be considered a true gain in terms of current dollars.

Exercise 13-2. Boyd Company was organized on April 1 of the current year. Capital stock was issued for $37,500 cash and land valued at $62,500. Assume that no transactions occurred during the year and that the price-level index was 125 on April 1 and 132 on March 31, the end of the current fiscal year.
   (a) Prepare a conventional balance sheet in report form.
   (b) Prepare a constant dollar balance sheet in report form.

Exercise 13-3. The following selected accounts were extracted from the records of Cordell Company at August 31, the end of the current fiscal year:

Depreciation expense on equipment...........	$ 7,000
Fees earned	112,500
Miscellaneous expense	2,250
Rent and utilities expense	27,000
Supplies expense	1,264
Wages expense............................	72,000

Fees earned, miscellaneous expense, rent and utilities expense, and wages expense occurred evenly throughout the year. Equipment was acquired when the price index was 140, and supplies were acquired when the price index was 158. The price index averaged 150 for the year and was 160 at the end of the year.

Prepare a constant dollar income statement for the current year. The purchasing power loss on monetary items was $6,090.

Exercise 13-4. The beginning balance and changes in cash for the year ended December 31, 1984, along with the relevant price-level indexes for DePew Company, are as follows:

	Amount	Price-Level Index
Cash, January 1, 1984	$ 60,200	172
Add revenue for 1984..............	122,400	180
Deduct expenses for 1984.........	104,400	180
Cash, December 31, 1984.........	$ 78,200	190

Calculate DePew Company's purchasing power loss from holding cash during 1984, using the format shown on page 361.

Exercise 13-5. Fisher Corporation was organized on January 1, 1982, and capital stock was issued for land valued at $60,000. Plans to construct several buildings and to begin operations were never finalized, and the land was sold on January 2, 1985, for $78,500. Assume that no other transactions were completed and that the current cost of the land was as follows:

> December 31, 1982........$61,000
> December 31, 1983........ 72,000
> December 31, 1984........ 78,500

(a) Compute the conventional financial statement net income for the years ended December 31, 1982, 1983, and 1984.
(b) Compute the current cost net income for the years ended December 31, 1982, 1983, and 1984.
(c) Compute the conventional financial statement net income for the year ended December 31, 1985.

Exercise 13-6. Selby Company was organized on January 1, 1984, through the issuance of $50,000 capital stock for cash. The company leases store space and equipment and sells merchandise only for cash. During 1984, merchandise costing $368,600 was purchased, $301,450 of the merchandise was sold for $361,740, and operating expenses were $29,220. At December 31, 1984, the relevant current cost amounts are as follows:

> Cash............................ $ 22,850
> Merchandise inventory............. 81,250
> Accounts payable................. 8,930
> Capital stock 50,000
> Sales 361,740
> Cost of merchandise sold 335,610
> Operating expenses............... 29,220

For the year ended December 31, 1984, prepare (a) a conventional income statement and (b) a current cost income statement.

Exercise 13-7. Based on the data presented in Exercise 13-6, prepare as of December 31, 1984, (a) a conventional balance sheet in report form and (b) a current cost balance sheet in report form.

Problems
(Problems in Appendix B: 13-1B, 13-2B, 13-3B, 13-4B.)

Problem 13-1A. Hodges Company was organized on January 1, 1984, when the price-level index was 200. Capital stock of $140,000 was issued in exchange for cash of $45,000 and land valued at $105,000. The land was subject to property taxes of $10,000 due for the current year. No transactions occurred during 1984, and the price-level index at the end of the year was 210. The income statement for 1985 disclosed the following:

Sales (made uniformly during the year)............................ $347,600
Cost of merchandise sold (purchased when price index was 218).... 272,500
Depreciation expense (asset purchased when price index was 212).. 5,300
Other expenses (incurred uniformly during the year).............. 24,200

The average price-level index for 1985 was 220, and at the end of 1985 it was 240.

Instructions:

(1) Prepare a conventional balance sheet at December 31, 1984, in report form.
(2) Prepare a constant dollar balance sheet at December 31, 1984, in report form.
(3) Prepare a constant dollar income statement for the year ended December 31, 1985. The purchasing power loss for the year was $6,140.

Problem 13-2A. The monetary items held by O'Brien Company throughout the fiscal year ended July 31, 1984, consisted of cash and accounts payable. The beginning balances and changes in these monetary items during the year, along with the relevant price-level index for each, are as follows:

	Amount	Price-Level Index
Monetary asset:		
Cash, August 1, 1983...........................	$ 31,500	210
Add sales	276,750	225
Deduct expenses...............................	196,875	225
Cash, July 31, 1984............................	$111,375	240
Monetary liability:		
Accounts payable, August 1, 1983	$ 16,800	210
Add purchases on account......................	170,550	225
Deduct payments on account...................	154,125	225
Accounts payable, July 31, 1984	$ 33,225	240

Instructions:

Calculate the purchasing power gain or loss for the year ended July 31, 1984, using the format shown on page 361.

Problem 13-3A. MZM Associates, a professional corporation, was organized with the issuance of $62,000 of capital stock on September 1, 1984, and began operations by leasing office space and office equipment. On December 1, 1984, MZM Associates acquired office equipment in exchange for a $12,300, 16%, three-year note payable with interest payable monthly. All services rendered were for cash, and all expenses, except for depreciation, were paid in cash. The conventional income statement for the year ended August 31, 1985, and the conventional balance sheet on August 31, 1985, are shown on page 376.

The average general price-level index for the year ended August 31, 1985, was 170. During the year, the price-level index was as follows:

September 1, 1984......... 155
December 1, 1984 164
August 31, 1985 185

MZM Associates
Income Statement
For Year Ended August 31, 1985

Revenues:			
Professional fees..............		$143,650	(Fees were collected uniformly during year; average price-level index was 170)
Expenses:			
Depreciation expense............	$ 1,640		(The office equipment was purchased when the price-level index was 164)
Other operating expenses...........	128,520		(Expenses were paid uniformly during year; average price-level index was 170)
Total expenses.............		130,160	
Net income....................		$ 13,490	

MZM Associates
Balance Sheet
August 31, 1985

Assets

Cash		$77,130
Office equipment	$12,300	
Less accumulated depreciation	1,640	10,660
Total assets		$87,790

Liabilities and Stockholders' Equity

Notes payable...	$12,300
Capital stock	62,000
Retained earnings	13,490
Total liabilities and stockholders' equity.........................	$87,790

Instructions:

(1) Calculate the purchasing power gain or loss for the year ended August 31, 1985, using the format shown on page 361.
(2) Prepare a constant dollar income statement for the year ended August 31, 1985.
(3) Prepare a constant dollar retained earnings statement for the year ended August 31, 1985.
(4) Prepare a constant dollar balance sheet at August 31, 1985, in report form.

Problem 13-4A. Dunbar Wholesalers Inc. was organized on January 31, 1984, by the sale of $120,000 of capital stock for cash. It leased store space and equipment and sold merchandise only for cash. During 1984, merchandise costing $872,000 was purchased, $615,800 of the merchandise was sold for $862,120, and operating expenses were $182,600. The conventional income statement for the year ended December 31, 1984, and the conventional balance sheet at December 31, 1984, are as follows:

Dunbar Wholesalers Inc.
Income Statement
For Year Ended December 31, 1984

Sales	$862,120
Cost of merchandise sold	615,800
Gross profit	$246,320
Operating expenses	182,600
Net income	$ 63,720

Dunbar Wholesalers Inc.
Balance Sheet
December 31, 1984

Assets

Cash	$ 26,800
Merchandise inventory	256,200
Total assets	$283,000

Liabilities and Stockholders' Equity

Accounts payable	$ 99,280
Capital stock	120,000
Retained earnings	63,720
Total liabilities and stockholders' equity	$283,000

The relevant current cost amounts for the preceding financial statement items are as follows:

Cash	$ 26,800
Merchandise inventory	279,450
Accounts payable	99,280
Capital stock	120,000
Sales	862,120
Cost of merchandise sold	660,500
Operating expenses	182,600

Instructions:

(1) Prepare a current cost income statement for the year ended December 31, 1984.
(2) Prepare a current cost retained earnings statement for the year ended December 31, 1984.
(3) Prepare a current cost balance sheet at December 31, 1984, in report form.

Problem 13-5A. Rowland Company's current cost income statement for the year ended December 31, 1984, and current cost balance sheet as of December 31, 1984, are shown on page 378.

The realized holding gain of $30,850 is identified entirely with the cost of merchandise sold, and $8,000 of the unrealized holding gain of $20,120 pertains to the land. Both the land and all of the ending merchandise inventory were purchased in 1984.

Rowland Company
Current Cost Income Statement
For Year Ended December 31, 1984

Sales	$628,120
Cost of merchandise sold	471,090
Gross profit	$157,030
Operating expenses	146,500
Operating income	$ 10,530
Realized holding gain	30,850
Realized income	$ 41,380
Unrealized holding gain	20,120
Net income	$ 61,500

Rowland Company
Current Cost Balance Sheet
December 31, 1984

Assets

Cash	$ 28,900
Accounts receivable	54,750
Inventory	118,150
Land	50,000
Total assets	$251,800

Liabilities and Stockholders' Equity

Accounts payable	$ 48,230
Capital stock	100,000
Retained earnings	103,570
Total liabilities and stockholders' equity	$251,800

Instructions:

(1) Prepare a conventional income statement for the year ended December 31, 1984.

(2) Prepare a conventional balance sheet as of December 31, 1984.

Mini-Case

On January 2, 1976, Kreps Company, a small privately held company, purchased land for $108,000, paying cash of $16,200 and issuing a $91,800, 12%, 10-year note payable to the seller. The land was located near a proposed interstate highway and was to be used for the construction of a new warehouse and product distribution center. Because of changing business conditions, Kreps Company decided in 1978 to indefinitely defer the warehouse construction but keep the land as an investment. In late 1982, the local zoning commission rezoned the land from commercial use to residential use only. At the beginning of 1982, before the rezoning, the land had an estimated market value of $240,000. At the end of 1982, after the rezoning, the market value of the land dropped to $160,000. On January 4, 1983, Kreps Company sold the land to a real estate developer for $160,000 and paid off the $91,800 note. From January of 1976 to January of 1983, the general price level increased from 176 to 220.

Paul Shuford, a minority shareholder of Kreps Company, has been highly critical of the company's management for the past several years. Shuford has written a letter to Kreps Company's treasurer, questioning management's handling of the land transactions and its reporting of the gain from the sale of the land on the income statement. Excerpts from the letter are as follows:

(a) "Management used poor judgment in not selling the land before the rezoning, and this should be indicated in the 1982 financial statements by reporting an $80,000 ($240,000 − $160,000) loss for the drop in the market value of the land due to the rezoning."

(b) "The land restated in 1983 dollars for general price-level changes is $135,000 ($108,000 × 220/176). Therefore, the maximum gain on the sale of the land that should be reported in 1983 is $25,000 ($160,000 − $135,000) and not the $52,000 as reported on the income statement."

Instructions:

(1) The treasurer has asked you to draft a response to each of Shuford's allegations. How would you respond?

(2) While discussing the points raised in (1), the treasurer asked you the following questions. How would you respond to each?

(a) What is the total amount of purchasing power gain or loss from the issuance and subsequent payment of the note (ignore interest payments)?

(b) If current cost statements were prepared for 1982 and 1983, what would be the amount of realized and unrealized holding gains and losses from the land for each year?

14
CHAPTER

Partnership Formation, Income Division, and Liquidation

CHAPTER OBJECTIVES

Identify basic characteristics of partnership organization and operation which have accounting implications.

Describe and illustrate the accounting for partnerships from formation and admission of new partners to the withdrawal of partners and final liquidation.

Describe and illustrate the preparation of financial statements for partnerships.

PART 4 | Partnerships

14

CHAPTER

The Uniform Partnership Act, which has been adopted by more than ninety percent of the states, defines a partnership as "an association of two or more persons to carry on as co-owners a business for profit." The partnership form of business organization is widely used for comparatively small businesses that wish to take advantage of the combined capital, managerial talent, and experience of two or more persons. In many cases, the alternative to securing the amount of investment needed or the various skills needed to operate a business is to adopt the corporate form of organization. The typical corporate form of organization is sometimes not available, however, to certain professions because of restrictions in state laws or in professional codes of ethics. Hence, a group of physicians, attorneys, or certified public accountants who wish to band together to practice a profession often organize as a partnership. Medical and legal partnerships made up of 20 or more partners are not unusual, and the number of partners in some CPA firms exceeds 1,000.

CHARACTER-ISTICS OF PARTNERSHIPS

Partnerships have several characteristics that have accounting implications. These characteristics are described in the following paragraphs.

A partnership has a **limited life.** Dissolution of a partnership occurs whenever a partner ceases to be a member of the firm for any reason, including withdrawal, bankruptcy, incapacity, or death. Similarly, admission of a new partner dissolves the old partnership. In case of dissolution, a new partnership must be formed if the operations of the business are to be continued without interruption. This is the usual situation with professional partnerships. Their composition may change often as new partners are admitted and others are retired.

Another characteristic of a partnership is **unlimited liability.** Each partner is individually liable to creditors for debts incurred by the partnership. Thus, if a partnership becomes insolvent, the partners must contribute sufficient personal assets to settle the debts of the partnership.

Partners have **co-ownership of partnership property.** The property invested in a partnership by a partner becomes the property of all the partners jointly. Upon dissolution of the partnership and distribution of its assets, the partners' claims against the assets are measured by the amount of the balances in their capital accounts.

A significant right of partners is **participation in income** of the partnership. Net income and net loss are distributed among the partners according to their agreement. In the absence of any agreement, all partners share equally. If the agreement specifies profit distribution but is silent as to losses, the losses are shared in the same manner as profits.

A partnership is created by a voluntary contract containing all the elements essential to any other enforceable contract. It is not necessary that this contract be in writing, nor even that its terms be specifically expressed. However, good business practice dictates that the contract should be in writing and should clearly express the intentions of the partners. The contract, known as the **articles of partnership** or **partnership agreement,** should contain provisions regarding such matters as the amount of investment to be made, limitations on withdrawals of funds, the manner in which net income and net loss are to be divided, and the admission and withdrawal of partners.

ACCOUNTING   Most of the day-to-day accounting for a partnership is the same as the account-
FOR   ing for any other form of business organization. The system described in earlier
PARTNERSHIPS   chapters may, with little change, be used by a partnership. For example, the
journals described may be used without alteration. The chart of accounts, with the
exception of drawing and capital accounts for each partner, does not differ from the
chart of accounts of a similar business conducted by a single owner. It is in the areas
of the formation, income distribution, dissolution, and liquidation of partnerships
that transactions peculiar to partnerships arise. The remainder of the chapter is
devoted to the accounting principles and procedures applicable to these areas.

RECORDING   A separate entry is made for the investment of each partner in a partnership.
INVESTMENTS   The various assets contributed by a partner are debited to the proper asset
accounts. If liabilities are assumed by the partnership, the appropriate liability
accounts are credited. The partner's capital account is credited for the net amount.

To illustrate the entry to record an initial investment, assume that Robert A.
Stevens and Earl S. Foster, who are sole owners of competing hardware stores,
agree to combine their businesses in a partnership. Each is to contribute certain
amounts of cash and other business assets. It is also agreed that the partnership is
to assume the liabilities of the separate businesses. In general journal form, the
entry to record the assets contributed and the liabilities transferred by Robert A.
Stevens is as follows:

Apr.	1	Cash...................................	7,200	
		Accounts Receivable......................	16,300	
		Merchandise Inventory....................	28,700	
		Store Equipment..........................	5,400	
		Office Equipment.........................	1,500	
		Allowance for Doubtful Accounts...........		1,500
		Accounts Payable........................		2,600
		Robert A. Stevens, Capital...............		55,000

The monetary amounts at which the noncash assets are stated are those agreed
upon by the partners. In arriving at an appropriate amount for such assets, consideration should be given to their market values at the time the partnership is
formed. The values agreed upon represent the acquisition cost to the accounting
entity created by the formation of the partnership. These amounts may differ from
the balances appearing in the accounts of the separate businesses before the
partnership was organized. For example, the store equipment stated at $5,400 in
the entry above may have had a book value of $3,500, appearing in Stevens' ledger
at its original cost of $10,000 with accumulated depreciation of $6,500.

Receivables contributed to the partnership are recorded at their face amount,
with a credit to a contra account if provision is to be made for possible future
uncollectibility. Ordinarily, only accounts with reasonable chances of collection are
transferred to the partnership. Again referring to the preceding entry, the accounts
receivable on Stevens' ledger may have totaled $17,600, of which $1,300 was
considered to be worthless. The remaining $16,300 of receivables was recorded in
the partnership accounts by a debit to Accounts Receivable and by debits to the

individual accounts in the subsidiary ledger. Provision for possible future un-collectibility of the accounts receivable contributed to the partnership by Stevens was recorded by a credit of $1,500 to Allowance for Doubtful Accounts.

DIVISION OF NET INCOME OR NET LOSS

As in the case of a sole proprietorship, the net income of a partnership may be said to include a return for the services of the owners, for the capital invested, and for economic or pure profit. Partners are not legally employees of the partnership, nor are their capital contributions a loan. If each of two partners is to contribute equal services and amounts of capital, an equal sharing in partnership net income would be equitable. But if one partner is to contribute a larger portion of capital than the other, provision for unequal capital contributions should be given recognition in the agreement for dividing net income. Or, if the services of one partner are much more valuable to the partnership than those of the other, provision for unequal service contributions should be given recognition in their agreement.

To illustrate the division of net income and the accounting for this division, two possible agreements are to be considered. It should be noted that division of the net income or the net loss among the partners in exact accordance with their partnership agreement is of the utmost importance. If the agreement is silent on the matter, the law provides that all partners share equally, regardless of differences in amounts of capital contributed, of special skills possessed, or of time devoted to the business. The partners may, however, make any agreement they wish in regard to the division of net income and net losses.

Income Division Recognizing Services of Partners

As a means of recognizing differences in ability and in amount of time devoted to the business, articles of partnership often provide for the allocation of a portion of net income to the partners in the form of a salary allowance. The articles may also provide for withdrawals of cash by the partners in lieu of salary payments. A clear distinction must therefore be made between the allocation of net income, which is credited to the capital accounts, and payments to the partners, which are debited to the drawing accounts.

As a basis for illustration, assume that the articles of partnership of Jennifer L. Stone and Crystal R. Mills provide for monthly salary allowances of $2,500 and $2,000 respectively, with the balance of the net income to be divided equally, and that the net income for the year is $75,000. A report of the division of net income may be presented as a separate statement accompanying the balance sheet and the income statement, or it may be added at the bottom of the income statement. If the latter procedure is used, the lower part of the income statement would appear as follows:

Net income			$75,000

Division of net income:	J. L. Stone	C. R. Mills	Total
Salary allowance	$30,000	$24,000	$54,000
Remaining income........................	10,500	10,500	21,000
Net income	$40,500	$34,500	$75,000

The division of net income is recorded as a closing entry, regardless of whether the partners actually withdraw the amounts of their salary allowances. The entry for the division of net income is as follows:

Dec. 31	Income Summary............................	75,000	
	Jennifer L. Stone, Capital................		40,500
	Crystal R. Mills, Capital		34,500

If Stone and Mills had withdrawn their salary allowances monthly, the withdrawals would have accumulated as debits in the drawing accounts during the year. At the end of the year, the debit balances of $30,000 and $24,000 in their drawing accounts would be transferred to their respective capital accounts.

Income Division Recognizing Services of Partners and Investment

Partners may agree that the most equitable plan of income sharing is to allow salaries based on the services rendered and also to allow interest on the capital investments. The remainder is then shared in an arbitrary ratio. To illustrate, assume that Stone and Mills (1) are allowed monthly salaries of $2,500 and $2,000 respectively; (2) are allowed interest at 12% on capital balances at January 1 of the current fiscal year, which amounted to $80,000 and $60,000 respectively; and (3) divide the remainder of net income equally. The division of $75,000 net income for the year could then be reported on the income statement as follows:

	J. L. Stone	C. R. Mills	Total
Net income			$75,000
Division of net income:			
Salary allowance	$30,000	$24,000	$54,000
Interest allowance	9,600	7,200	16,800
Remaining income.........................	2,100	2,100	4,200
Net income	$41,700	$33,300	$75,000

On the basis of the information in the foregoing income statement, the entry to close the income summary account would be recorded in the general journal as follows:

Dec. 31	Income Summary............................	75,000	
	Jennifer L. Stone, Capital................		41,700
	Crystal R. Mills, Capital		33,300

In the illustrations presented thus far, the net income has exceeded the sum of the allowances for salary and interest. If the net income is less than the total of the special allowances, the "remaining balance" will be a negative figure that must be divided among the partners as though it were a net loss. The effect of this situation may be illustrated by assuming the same salary and interest allowances as in the preceding illustration, but changing the amount of net income to $50,000. The salary and interest allowances to Stone total $39,600 and the comparable figure for Mills is $31,200. The sum of these amounts, $70,800, exceeds the net income of $50,000 by $20,800. It is therefore necessary to deduct $10,400 (½ of $20,800) from each partner's share to arrive at the net income, as follows:

	J. L. Stone	C. R. Mills	Total
Net income			$50,000
Division of net income:			
Salary allowance	$30,000	$24,000	$54,000
Interest allowance	9,600	7,200	16,800
Total	$39,600	$31,200	$70,800
Excess of allowances over income	10,400	10,400	20,800
Net income	$29,200	$20,800	$50,000

In closing Income Summary at the end of the year, $29,200 would be credited to Jennifer L. Stone, Capital, and $20,800 would be credited to Crystal R. Mills, Capital.

Partners' Salaries and Interest Treated as Expenses

Although the traditional view among accountants is to treat salary and interest allowances as allocations of net income, as in the foregoing illustrations, some prefer to treat them as expenses of the enterprise. According to this view, the partnership is treated as a distinct legal entity and the partners are considered to be employees and creditors of the firm. When salaries for partners' services and interest on partners' investments are viewed as expenses of the enterprise, withdrawals of the agreed amount are charged to expense accounts rather than to the partners' drawing accounts. The expense accounts are then closed into the income summary account, and the remaining net income is allocated among the partners in the agreed ratio. The amounts considered to be salary expense and interest expense paid to partners should be specifically identified as such on the income statement. Regardless of whether partners' salary and interest are treated as expenses of the partnership or as a division of net income, the total amount allocated to each partner will be the same.

STATEMENTS FOR PARTNERSHIPS

Details of the division of net income should be disclosed in the financial statements prepared at the end of the fiscal period. This may be done by adding a section to the income statement, which has been illustrated in the preceding pages, or by presenting the data in a separate statement.

Details of the changes in partnership capital during the period should also be presented in a capital statement. The purposes of the statement and the data included in it correspond to those of the capital statement of a sole proprietorship. There are a number of variations in form, one of which is illustrated as follows:

	Jennifer L. Stone	Crystal R. Mills	Total
Stone and Mills Capital Statement For Year Ended December 31, 19--			
Capital, January 1, 19--.....................	$ 80,000	$60,000	$140,000
Additional investment during the year		5,000	5,000
	$ 80,000	$65,000	$145,000
Net income for the year	41,700	33,300	75,000
	$121,700	$98,300	$220,000
Withdrawals during the year	24,000	20,000	44,000
Capital, December 31, 19--	$ 97,700	$78,300	$176,000

Under the Internal Revenue Code, enterprises organized as partnerships are not distinct entities and are not required to pay federal income taxes. Instead, the individual partners must report their distributive shares of partnership income on their personal tax returns. However, data on the distributive shares of each partner, as well as a summary of revenue and expense and other financial details of partnership operations, must be reported annually on official "information return" forms. If the agreement requires the payment of salaries or interest to partners, regardless of the amount of net income of the enterprise, such payments must be reported on the partnership information return as an expense. The partners are required, in turn, to combine on their individual returns the amounts received and their distributive shares of net income. Thus, despite the method, the partners report all income in the period that it is earned by the partnership.

PARTNERSHIP DISSOLUTION

One of the basic characteristics of the partnership form of organization is its limited life. Any change in the personnel of the membership results in the dissolution of the partnership. Thus, admission of a new partner dissolves the old firm. Similarly, death, bankruptcy, or withdrawal of a partner causes dissolution.

Dissolution of the partnership is not necessarily followed by the winding up of the affairs of the business. For example, a partnership composed of two partners may admit an additional partner. Or if one of three partners in a business withdraws, the remaining two partners may continue to operate the business. In all such cases, a new partnership is formed and new articles of partnership should be prepared.

Admission of a Partner

An additional person may be admitted to a partnership enterprise only with the consent of all the current partners. It does not follow, however, that a partner's interest, or part of that interest, cannot be disposed of without the consent of the remaining partners. Under common law, if a partner's interest was assigned to an outside party, the partnership was automatically dissolved. Under the Uniform Partnership Act, a partner's interest can be disposed of without the consent of the remaining partners. The person who buys the interest acquires the selling partner's rights to share in net income and assets upon liquidation. The purchaser does not automatically become a partner, however, and has no voice in partnership affairs unless admitted to the firm.

An additional person may be admitted to a partnership through either of two procedures:

1. Purchase of an interest from one or more of the current partners.
2. Contribution of assets to the partnership.

When the first procedure is followed, the capital interest of the incoming partner is obtained from current partners, and neither the total assets nor the total capital of the business is affected. When the second procedure is followed, both the total assets and the total capital of the business are increased.

Admission by Purchase of an Interest

When an additional person is admitted to a firm by purchasing an interest from one or more of the partners, the purchase price is paid directly to the selling partners. Payment is for partnership equity owned by the partners as individuals, and hence the cash or other consideration paid is not recorded in the accounts of the partnership. The only entry needed is the transfer of the proper amounts of capital from the capital accounts of the selling partners to the capital account established for the incoming partner.

As an example, assume that partners Tom Andrews and George Bell have capital balances of $50,000 each. On June 1, each sells one fifth of his respective capital interest to Joe Canter for $10,000 in cash. The only entry required in the partnership accounts is as follows:

June 1	Tom Andrews, Capital	10,000	
	George Bell, Capital	10,000	
	Joe Canter, Capital		20,000

The effect of the transaction on the partnership accounts is presented in the following diagram:

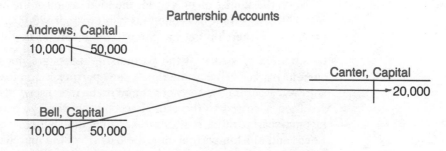

The foregoing entry is made regardless of the amount paid by Canter for the one-fifth interest. If the firm had been earning a high rate of return on the investment and Canter had been very eager to obtain the one-fifth interest, he might have paid considerably more than $20,000. Had other circumstances prevailed, he might have acquired the one-fifth interest for considerably less than $20,000. In either event, the entry to transfer the capital interests would not be affected.

After the admission of Canter, the total capital of the firm is $100,000, in which he has a one-fifth interest, or $20,000. It does not necessarily follow that he will be entitled to a similar share of the partnership net income. Division of net income or net loss will be in accordance with the new partnership agreement.

Admission by Contribution of Assets

Instead of buying an interest from the current partners, the incoming partner may contribute assets to the partnership. In this case, both the assets and the capital of the firm are increased. To illustrate, assume that Donald Lewis and Gerald Morton are partners with capital accounts of $35,000 and $25,000 respectively. On June 1, Sharon Nelson invests $20,000 cash in the business, for which she is to receive an ownership equity of $20,000. The entry to record this transaction, in general journal form, is:

```
June  1  Cash.....................................  20,000
             Sharon Nelson, Capital .................         20,000
```

The major difference between the circumstances of the admission of Nelson above and of Canter in the preceding example may be observed by comparing the following diagram with the one on the preceding page:

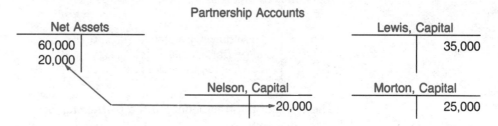

Partnership Accounts

With the admission of Nelson, the total capital of the new partnership becomes $80,000, of which she has a one-fourth interest, or $20,000. The extent of her participation in partnership net income will be governed by the articles of partnership.

Revaluation of assets. If the partnership assets are not fairly stated in terms of current market value at the time a new partner is admitted, the accounts may be adjusted accordingly. The net amount of the increases and decreases in asset values are then allocated to the capital accounts of the old partners according to their income-sharing ratio. To illustrate, assume that in the preceding illustration for the Lewis and Morton partnership, the balance of the merchandise inventory account had been $14,000 and the current replacement price had been $17,000. Prior to Nelson's admission, the revaluation would be recorded as follows, assuming that Lewis and Morton share net income equally:

June	1	Merchandise Inventory	3,000	
		Donald Lewis, Capital		1,500
		Gerald Morton, Capital		1,500

If a number of assets are revalued, the adjustments may be debited or credited to a temporary account entitled Asset Revaluations. After all adjustments are made, the account is closed to the capital accounts.

It is important that the assets be stated in terms of current prices at the time of admission of a new partner. Failure to recognize current prices may result in the new partner participating in gains or losses attributable to the period prior to admission.

Goodwill. When a new partner is admitted to a partnership, goodwill attributable either to the old partnership or to the incoming partner may be recognized. Although there are various methods of estimating goodwill, such factors as the respective shares owned by the partners and the relative bargaining abilities of the partners will influence the final determination. The amount of goodwill agreed upon is recorded as an asset, with a corresponding addition to the appropriate capital accounts.

To illustrate the recognition of goodwill to the old partners, assume that on March 1 the partnership of Marsha Jenkins and Helen Kramer admits William Larson, who is to contribute cash of $15,000. After the tangible assets of the old partnership have been adjusted to current market prices, the capital balances of Jenkins and Kramer are $20,000 and $24,000 respectively. The parties agree, however, that the enterprise is worth $50,000. The excess of $50,000 over the capital balances of $44,000 ($20,000 + $24,000) indicates the existence of $6,000 of goodwill. This $6,000 should be allocated to the capital accounts of the original partners according to their income-sharing agreement.

The entries to record the goodwill and the admission of the new partner, assuming that the original partners share equally in net income, are as follows, in general journal form:

Mar.	1	Goodwill	6,000	
		Marsha Jenkins, Capital		3,000
		Helen Kramer, Capital		3,000
	1	Cash	15,000	
		William Larson, Capital		15,000

If a partnership admits a new partner who is expected to improve the fortunes of the firm, the parties might agree to recognize this high earnings potential. To illustrate, assume that Sandra Ellis is to be admitted to the partnership of Cowen and Dodd for an investment of $30,000. If the parties agree to recognize $5,000 of goodwill attributable to Ellis, the entry to record her admission is as follows, in general journal form:

```
July  1  Cash.....................................    30,000
            Goodwill ...............................     5,000
                Sandra Ellis, Capital ...................            35,000
```

Withdrawal of a Partner

When a partner retires or for some other reason wishes to withdraw from the firm, one or more of the remaining partners may purchase the withdrawing partner's interest and the business may be continued without apparent interruption. In such cases, settlement for the purchase and sale is made between the partners as individuals. The only entry required by the partnership is a debit to the capital account of the partner withdrawing and a credit to the capital account of the partner or partners acquiring the interest.

If the settlement with the withdrawing partner is made by the partnership, the effect is to reduce the assets and the capital of the firm. To determine the ownership equity of the withdrawing partner, the asset accounts should be adjusted to current market prices. The net amount of the adjustments should be allocated among the capital accounts of the partners according to the income-sharing ratio. In the event that the cash or the other available assets are insufficient to make complete payment at the time of withdrawal, a liability account should be credited for the balance owed to the withdrawing partner.

Death of a Partner

The death of a partner dissolves the partnership. In the absence of any contrary agreement, the accounts should be closed as of the date of death, and the net income for the fractional part of the year should be transferred to the capital accounts. It is not unusual, however, for the partnership agreement to stipulate that the accounts remain open to the end of the fiscal year or until the affairs are wound up, if that should occur earlier. The net income of the entire period is then allocated, as provided by the agreement, to the respective periods occurring before and after dissolution.

The balance in the capital account of the deceased partner is then transferred to a liability account with the deceased's estate. The surviving partner or partners may continue the business or the affairs may be wound up. If the former course is followed, the procedures for settling with the estate will conform to those outlined earlier for the withdrawal of a partner from the business.

LIQUIDATION OF A PARTNERSHIP

When a partnership goes out of business, it usually sells most of the assets, pays the creditors, and distributes the remaining cash or other assets to the partners according to their claims. The winding-up process may generally be called **liquidation**. Although liquidation refers specifically to the payment of liabilities, it is often used in a broader sense to include the entire winding-up process.

When the ordinary business activities are discontinued as the partnership goes out of business, the accounts should be adjusted and closed according to the customary procedures of the periodic summary. The only accounts remaining open then will be the various asset, contra asset, liability, and capital accounts.

The sale of the assets is called realization. As cash is realized, it is applied first to the payment of the claims of creditors. After all liabilities have been paid, the remaining cash is distributed to the partners, based on their ownership equities as indicated by their capital accounts.

If the assets are sold piecemeal, the liquidation process may extend over a considerable period of time. This creates no special problem, however, if the distribution of cash to the partners is delayed until all of the assets have been sold.

As a basis for illustration, assume that Farley, Greene, and Hill decide to liquidate their partnership. Their income-sharing ratio is 5:3:2. After discontinuing the ordinary business operations and closing the accounts, the following summary of the general ledger is prepared:

Cash	$11,000	
Noncash Assets	64,000	
Liabilities		$ 9,000
Jane Farley, Capital		22,000
Brad Greene, Capital		22,000
Alice Hill, Capital		22,000
Total	$75,000	$75,000

Accounting for the liquidation will be illustrated by three examples based on the foregoing statement of facts. In all cases, it will be assumed that all noncash assets are disposed of in a single transaction and that all liabilities are paid at one time. This is merely for the sake of brevity. In addition, Noncash Assets and Liabilities will be used as account titles in place of the various asset, contra asset, and liability accounts that in actual practice would be affected by the transactions.

Gain on Realization | Farley, Greene, and Hill sell all noncash assets for $72,000, realizing a gain of $8,000 ($72,000 − $64,000). The gain is divided among the capital accounts in the income-sharing ratio of 5:3:2, the liabilities are paid, and the remaining cash is distributed to the partners according to the balances in their capital accounts. A tabular summary of the transactions follows:

						Capital		
		Noncash				J. Farley	B. Greene	A. Hill
	Cash +	Assets =	Liabilities +			50% +	30% +	20%
Balances before realization	$11,000	$64,000	$ 9,000			$22,000	$22,000	$22,000
Sale of assets and division of gain	+72,000	−64,000				+ 4,000	+ 2,400	+ 1,600
Balances after realization	$83,000		$ 9,000			$26,000	$24,400	$23,600
Payment of liabilities	− 9,000		− 9,000					
Balances	$74,000					$26,000	$24,400	$23,600
Distribution of cash to partners	−74,000					−26,000	−24,400	−23,600

The entries to record the several steps in the liquidation procedure are as follows, in general journal form:

Sale of assets
Cash...	72,000	
Noncash Assets................................		64,000
Loss and Gain on Realization..........................		8,000

Division of gain
Loss and Gain on Realization..........................	8,000	
Jane Farley, Capital............................		4,000
Brad Greene, Capital.....................		2,400
Alice Hill, Capital......................		1,600

Payment of liabilities
| Liabilities.. | 9,000 | |
| Cash... | | 9,000 |

Distribution of cash to partners
Jane Farley, Capital............................	26,000	
Brad Greene, Capital.....................	24,400	
Alice Hill, Capital......................	23,600	
Cash...		74,000

As shown in the foregoing illustration, the distribution of the cash among the partners is determined by reference to the balances of their respective capital accounts after the gain on realization has been allocated. Under no circumstances should the income-sharing ratio be used as a basis for distributing the cash.

Loss on Realization; No Capital Deficiencies | Assume that in the foregoing example, Farley, Greene, and Hill dispose of all noncash assets for $44,000, incurring a loss of $20,000 ($64,000 − $44,000). The various steps in the liquidation of the partnership are summarized as follows:

					Capital		
	Cash	+	Noncash Assets	= Liabilities +	J. Farley 50% +	B. Greene 30% +	A. Hill 20%
Balances before realization...............	$11,000		$64,000	$ 9,000	$22,000	$22,000	$22,000
Sale of assets and division of loss.........	+44,000		−64,000		−10,000	− 6,000	− 4,000
Balances after realization.................	$55,000			$ 9,000	$12,000	$16,000	$18,000
Payment of liabilities....................	− 9,000			− 9,000			
Balances...........................	$46,000				$12,000	$16,000	$18,000
Distribution of cash to partners...........	−46,000				−12,000	−16,000	−18,000

The entries to record the liquidation are as follows, in general journal form:

Sale of assets
Cash...	44,000	
Loss and Gain on Realization..........................	20,000	
Noncash Assets................................		64,000

Division of loss

Jane Farley, Capital..	10,000	
Brad Greene, Capital	6,000	
Alice Hill, Capital	4,000	
Loss and Gain on Realization		20,000

Payment of liabilities

Liabilities	9,000	
Cash		9,000

Distribution of cash to partners

Jane Farley, Capital..	12,000	
Brad Greene, Capital	16,000	
Alice Hill, Capital	18,000	
Cash		46,000

Loss on Realization; Capital Deficiency

In the preceding illustration, the capital account of each partner was more than sufficient to absorb the appropriate share of the loss from realization. The partners shared in the distribution of cash to the extent of the remaining credit balance in their respective capital accounts. However, the share of the loss chargeable to a partner may be such that it exceeds that partner's ownership equity. The resulting debit balance in the capital account, called a **deficiency,** is a claim of the partnership against the partner. Pending collection from the deficient partner, the partnership cash will not be sufficient to pay the other partners in full. In such cases the available cash should be distributed in such a manner that, if the claim against the deficient partner cannot be collected, each of the remaining capital balances will be sufficient to absorb the appropriate share of the deficiency.

To illustrate a situation of this type, assume that Farley, Greene, and Hill sell all of the noncash assets for $10,000, incurring a loss of $54,000 ($64,000 − $10,000). It is readily apparent that the part of the loss allocable to Farley, $27,000 (50% of $54,000), exceeds the $22,000 balance in Farley's capital account. This $5,000 deficiency is a potential loss to Greene and Hill and must be tentatively divided between them in their income-sharing ratio of 3:2 (3/5 and 2/5). The capital balances remaining represent their claims on the partnership cash. The computations may be summarized in the following manner:

		Capital		
	J. Farley 50%	B. Greene 30%	A. Hill 20%	Total
Balances before realization	$ 22,000	$ 22,000	$ 22,000	$ 66,000
Division of loss on realization	−27,000	−16,200	−10,800	−54,000
Balances after realization......................	$− 5,000	$ 5,800	$ 11,200	$ 12,000
Division of potential additional loss	5,000	− 3,000	− 2,000	
Claims to partnership cash		$ 2,800	$ 9,200	$ 12,000

The various transactions that have occurred thus far in the liquidation may then be summarized as follows:

| | | Noncash | | Capital | | |
	Cash	+ Assets	= Liabilities	J. Farley + 50% +	B. Greene 30% +	A. Hill 20%
Balances before realization...............	$11,000	$64,000	$ 9,000	$22,000	$22,000	$22,000
Sale of assets and division of loss.........	+10,000	−64,000		−27,000	−16,200	−10,800
Balances after realization................	$21,000		$ 9,000	$ 5,000 (Dr.)	$ 5,800	$11,200
Payment of liabilities	− 9,000		− 9,000			
Balances	$12,000			$ 5,000 (Dr.)	$ 5,800	$11,200
Distribution of cash to partners...........	−12,000				− 2,800	− 9,200
Balances				$ 5,000 (Dr.)	$ 3,000	$ 2,000

The entries to record the liquidation to this point are as follows, in general journal form:

Sale of assets
Cash..	10,000	
Loss and Gain on Realization............................	54,000	
Noncash Assets......................................		64,000

Division of loss
Jane Farley, Capital.....................................	27,000	
Brad Greene, Capital	16,200	
Alice Hill, Capital	10,800	
Loss and Gain on Realization........................		54,000

Payment of liabilities
Liabilities	9,000	
Cash..		9,000

Distribution of cash to partners
Brad Greene, Capital	2,800	
Alice Hill, Capital	9,200	
Cash..		12,000

The affairs of the partnership are not completely wound up until the claims among the partners are settled. Payments to the firm by the deficient partner are credited to that partner's capital account. Any uncollectible deficiency becomes a loss and is written off against the capital balances of the remaining partners. Finally, the cash received from the deficient partner is distributed to the other partners according to their ownership claims.

To continue with the illustration, the capital balances remaining after the $12,000 cash distribution are as follows: Farley, $5,000 debit; Greene, $3,000 credit; Hill, $2,000 credit. The entries for the partnership, in general journal form, under three different assumptions as to the final settlement, are as follows:

If Farley pays the entire amount of the $5,000 deficiency to the partnership (no loss), the final entries will be:

Receipt of deficiency
Cash.. 5,000
    Jane Farley, Capital....................................   5,000

Distribution of cash to partners
Brad Greene, Capital 3,000
Alice Hill, Capital 2,000
    Cash..   5,000

If Farley pays $3,000 of the deficiency to the partnership and the remainder is considered to be uncollectible ($2,000 loss), the final entries will be:

Receipt of part of deficiency
Cash.. 3,000
    Jane Farley, Capital....................................   3,000

Division of loss
Brad Greene, Capital 1,200
Alice Hill, Capital   800
    Jane Farley, Capital....................................   2,000

Distribution of cash to partners
Brad Greene, Capital 1,800
Alice Hill, Capital 1,200
    Cash..   3,000

If Farley is unable to pay any part of the $5,000 deficiency ($5,000 loss), the loss to the other partners will be recorded by the following entry:

Division of loss
Brad Greene, Capital 3,000
Alice Hill, Capital 2,000
    Jane Farley, Capital....................................   5,000

It should be noted that the type of error most likely to occur in the liquidation of a partnership is improper distribution of cash among the partners. Errors of this type result from confusing the distribution of cash with division of gains and losses on realization.

Gains and losses on realization result from the disposal of assets to outsiders. These gains and losses represent changes in partnership capital and should be divided among the capital accounts in the same manner as net income or net loss from ordinary business operations, namely, in the income-sharing ratio.

On the other hand, the distribution of cash (or other assets) to the partners is an entirely different matter and has no direct relationship to the income-sharing ratio. The distribution of assets to the partners upon liquidation is the exact reverse of the contribution of assets by the partners at the time the partnership was established. The amounts that the partners are entitled to receive from the firm are equal to the credit balances in their respective capital accounts after all gains and losses on realization have been divided and proper allowance has been made for any potential losses.

Self-Examination Questions
(Answers in Appendix C.)

1. As part of the initial investment, a partner contributes office equipment that had originally cost $20,000 and on which accumulated depreciation of $12,500 had been recorded. If the partners agree on a valuation of $9,000 for the equipment, what amount should be debited to the office equipment account?
   A. $7,500   C. $12,500
   B. $9,000   D. $20,000

2. X and Y agree to form a partnership. X is to contribute $50,000 in assets and to devote one-half time to the partnership. Y is to contribute $20,000 and to devote full time to the partnership. How will X and Y share in the division of net income or net loss?
   A. 5:2   C. 1:1
   B. 1:2   D. None of the above

3. X and Y invest $100,000 and $50,000 respectively in a partnership and agree to a division of net income that provides for an allowance of interest at 10% on original investments, salary allowances of $12,000 and $24,000, with the remainder divided equally. What would be X's share of a periodic net income of $45,000?
   A. $22,500   C. $19,000
   B. $22,000   D. $10,000

4. X and Y are partners who share income in the ratio of 2:1 and who have capital balances of $65,000 and $35,000 respectively. If P, with the consent of Y, acquired one half of X's interest for $40,000, for what amount would P's capital account be credited?
   A. $32,500   C. $50,000
   B. $40,000   D. None of the above

5. X and Y share gains and losses in the ratio of 2:1. After selling all assets for cash, dividing the losses on realization, and paying liabilities, the balances in the capital accounts were: X, $10,000 Cr.; Y, $2,000 Dr. How much of the cash would be distributed to X?
   A. $2,000   C. $10,000
   B. $8,000   D. $12,000

Discussion Questions

1. Is it possible for a partner to lose a greater amount than the amount of his or her investment in the partnership enterprise? Explain.

2. In the absence of an agreement, how will net income be distributed among Lisa Roberts and Bob Wilson, partners in the firm of Roberts and Wilson Realty?

3. Frank Baker, Catherine Cox, and John Davis are contemplating the formation of a partnership in which Baker is to invest $70,000 and devote one-fourth time, Cox is to invest $35,000 and devote one-half time, and Davis is to make no investment and devote full time. Would Davis be correct in assuming that since he is not contributing any assets to the firm, he is risking nothing? Explain.

4. As a part of the initial investment, a partner contributes office equipment that had originally cost $50,000 and on which accumulated depreciation of $28,500 had been recorded. The partners agree on a valuation of $25,000. How should the office equipment be recorded in the accounts of the partnership?

5. All partners agree that $50,000 of accounts receivable invested by a partner will be collectible to the extent of 90%. How should the accounts receivable be recorded in the general ledger of the partnership?

6. Ralph Sims and Robert Thomas are contemplating the formation of a partnership in which Sims is to devote one-half time and Thomas is to devote full time. In the absence of any agreement, will the partners share in net income or net loss in the ratio of 1:2?

7. (a) What accounts are debited and credited to record a partner's cash withdrawal in lieu of salary? (b) At the end of the fiscal year, what accounts are debited and credited to record the division of net income among partners? (c) The articles of partnership provide for a salary allowance of $3,000 per month to partner X. If X withdrew only $2,500 per month, would this affect the division of the partnership net income?

8. Must a partnership file a federal income tax return and pay federal income taxes? Explain.

9. Don Klein, a partner in the firm of Klein, Lowell, and Mahan, sells his investment (capital balance of $60,000) to Susan Young. (a) Does the withdrawal of Klein dissolve the partnership? (b) Are Lowell and Mahan required to admit Young as a partner?

10. Explain the difference between the admission of a new partner to a partnership (a) by purchase of an interest from another partner and (b) by contribution of assets to the partnership.

11. Ann Adams and John Bowen are partners who share in net income equally and have capital balances of $85,000 and $95,000 respectively. Adams, with the consent of Bowen, sells one half of her interest to Barbara Potter. What entry is required by the partnership if the sale price is (a) $40,000? (b) $50,000?

12. Why is it important to state all partnership assets in terms of current prices at the time of the admission of a new partner?

13. When a new partner is admitted to a partnership and goodwill is attributable to the old partnership, how should the amount of the goodwill be allocated to the capital accounts of the original partners?

14. Why might a partnership attribute goodwill to a newly admitted partner?

15. (a) Differentiate between "dissolution" and "liquidation" of a partnership. (b) What does "realization" mean when used in connection with liquidation of a partnership?

16. In the liquidation process, (a) how are losses and gains on realization divided among the partners, and (b) how is cash distributed among the partners?

17. Gains and Howell are partners, sharing gains and losses equally. At the time they decide to terminate their partnership, their capital balances are $45,000 and $55,000 respectively. After all noncash assets are sold and all liabilities are paid, there is a cash balance of $80,000. (a) What is the amount of gain or loss on realization? (b) How should the gain or loss be divided between Gains and Howell? (c) How should the cash be divided between Gains and Howell?

18. Roberts, Stevens, and Towns share equally in net income and net loss. After the partnership sells all the assets for cash, divides the losses on realization, and pays the liabilities, the balances in the capital accounts are as follows: Roberts, $10,000

Dr.; Stevens, $14,000 Cr.; Towns, $16,000 Cr. (a) What is the amount of cash on hand? (b) How should the cash be distributed?

19. Black, Clay, and Dunn are partners sharing income 1:2:3. After the firm's loss from liquidation is distributed, Black's capital account has a debit balance of $10,000. If Black is personally bankrupt and unable to pay any of the $10,000, how will the loss be divided between Clay and Dunn?

Exercises

Exercise 14-1. John Allen and Jim Bows decide to form a partnership by combining the assets of their separate businesses. Allen contributes the following assets to the partnership: cash, $9,500; accounts receivable with a face amount of $57,500 and an allowance for doubtful accounts of $8,900; merchandise inventory with a cost of $50,000; and equipment with a cost of $75,000 and accumulated depreciation of $28,000. The partners agree that $3,000 of the accounts receivable are completely worthless and are not to be accepted by the partnership, that $3,500 is a reasonable allowance for the uncollectibility of the remaining accounts, that the merchandise inventory is to be recorded at the current market price of $62,900, and that the equipment is to be priced at $45,000. Present the partnership's entry, in general journal form, to record Allen's investment.

Exercise 14-2. Alice Cahn and Mary Denver form a partnership, investing $50,000 and $75,000 respectively. Determine their participation in the year's net income of $70,000, under each of the following assumptions: (a) no agreement concerning division of income; (b) divided in the ratio of original capital investments; (c) interest at the rate of 12% allowed on original investments and the remainder divided in the ratio of 3:2; (d) salary allowances of $25,000 and $20,000 and the balance divided equally; (e) allowance of interest at the rate of 12% on original investments, salary allowances of $25,000 and $20,000 respectively, and the remainder divided equally.

Exercise 14-3. Determine the participation of Cahn and Denver in the year's net income of $40,000, according to each of the five assumptions as to income division listed in Exercise 14-2.

Exercise 14-4. The capital accounts of Bob Edwards and Jose Ferrara have balances of $82,500 and $65,000 respectively on January 1, the beginning of the current fiscal year. On May 31, Ferrara invested an additional $10,000. During the year, Edwards and Ferrara withdrew $25,000 and $28,000 respectively, and net income for the year was $70,000. The articles of partnership make no reference to the division of net income. (a) Present the journal entries to close (1) the income summary account and (2) the drawing accounts. (b) Prepare a capital statement for the current year.

Exercise 14-5. The capital accounts of Ann Jones and Ed Klein have balances of $120,000 and $80,000 respectively. John Victor and Jane Wicks are to be admitted to the partnership. Victor purchases one third of Jones' interest for $56,000 and one fourth of Klein's interest for $28,000. Wicks contributes $60,000 cash to the partnership, for which she is to receive an ownership equity of $60,000. (a) Present the entries in general journal form to record the admission of (1) Victor and (2) Wicks. (b) What are the capital balances of each partner after the admission of Victor and Wicks?

Exercise 14-6. Jiri Jonas is to retire from the partnership of Jonas and Associates as of March 31, the end of the current fiscal year. After closing the accounts, the capital balances of the partners are as follows: Jiri Jonas, $150,000; Jane Kane, $97,500; and Howard Levy, $67,500. They have shared net income and net losses in the ratio of 3:2:1. The partners agree that the merchandise inventory should be increased by $7,500 and that the allowance for doubtful accounts should be increased by $900. Jonas agrees to accept an interest-bearing note for $100,000 in partial settlement of his ownership equity. The remainder of his claim is to be paid in cash. Kane and Levy are to share in the net income or net loss of the new partnership in the ratio of 2:1. Present entries in general journal form to record (a) the adjustment of the assets to bring them into agreement with current market prices and (b) the withdrawal of Jonas from the partnership.

Exercise 14-7. C. D. Mann and P. E. Nehi, with capital balances of $42,500 and $37,500 respectively, decide to liquidate their partnership. After selling the noncash assets and paying the liabilities, there is $60,000 of cash remaining. If the partners share income and losses equally, how should the cash be distributed?

Exercise 14-8. George Silvers, Bill Tomas, and Mel Unser arrange to import and sell orchid corsages for a university dance. They agree to share the net income or net loss on the venture equally. Silvers and Tomas advance $75 and $125 respectively of their own funds to pay for advertising and other expenses. After collecting for all sales and paying creditors, they have $440 in cash. (a) How should the money be distributed? (b) Assuming that they have only $110 instead of $440, how should the money be distributed? (c) Assuming that the money was distributed as determined in (b), do any of the three have claims against another and, if so, how much?

Exercise 14-9. After the accounts are closed preparatory to liquidating the partnership, the capital accounts of Ivan Bull, Josephine Carter, and Frank Downs are $27,300, $8,050, and $13,650 respectively. Cash and noncash assets total $5,500 and $89,100 respectively. Amounts owed to creditors total $45,600. The partners share income and losses in the ratio of 2:1:1. The noncash assets are sold and sufficient cash is available to pay all of the creditors except one for $5,600. Determine how the claim of the creditors should be settled. Present a summary of the transactions in the form illustrated in the chapter.

Problems
(Problems in Appendix B: 14-1B, 14-2B, 14-5B.)

Problem 14-1A. Noah and Oaks have decided to form a partnership. They have agreed that Noah is to invest $120,000 and that Oaks is to invest $80,000. Noah is to devote one-half time to the business and Oaks is to devote full time. The following plans for the division of income are being considered:

    (a) Equal division.
    (b) In the ratio of original investments.
    (c) In the ratio of time devoted to the business.
    (d) Interest of 10% on original investments and the remainder equally.
    (e) Interest of 12% on original investments, salaries of $15,000 to Noah and $30,000 to Oaks, and the remainder equally.
    (f) Plan (e), except that Oaks is also to be allowed a bonus equal to 20% of the amount by which net income exceeds the salary allowances.

Instructions:

For each plan, determine the division of the net income under each of the following assumptions: net income of $60,000 and net income of $150,000. Present the data in tabular form, using the following columnar headings:

	$60,000		$150,000	
Plan	Noah	Oaks	Noah	Oaks

Problem 14-2A. On July 1 of the current year, Ted Selick and Don Tubbs form a partnership. Selick agrees to invest $9,500 in cash and merchandise inventory valued at $31,500. Tubbs invests certain business assets at valuations agreed upon, transfers business liabilities, and contributes sufficient cash to bring his total capital to $50,000. Details regarding the book values of the business assets and liabilities, and the agreed valuations, follow:

	Tubbs' Ledger Balance	Agreed Valuation
Accounts Receivable	$20,050	$17,500
Allowance for Doubtful Accounts	750	800
Equipment.......................................	68,500	} 45,000
Accumulated Depreciation—Equipment	29,750	
Accounts Payable	11,500	11,500
Notes Payable	10,000	10,000

The articles of partnership include the following provisions regarding the division of net income: interest on original investments at 10%, salary allowances of $17,500 and $20,000 respectively, and the remainder equally.

Instructions:

(1) Prepare the entries, in general journal form, to record the investments of Selick and Tubbs in the partnership accounts.

(2) Prepare a balance sheet as of July 1, the date of formation of the partnership.

(3) After adjustments and the closing of revenue and expense accounts at June 30, the end of the first full year of operations, the income summary account has a credit balance of $66,600 and the drawing accounts have debit balances of $15,000 (Selick) and $18,500 (Tubbs). Present the journal entries to close the income summary account and the drawing accounts at June 30.

Problem 14-3A. The ledger of Bunge and Casale, attorneys-at-law, contains the following accounts and balances after adjustments have been recorded on December 31, the end of the current fiscal year:

Cash.	$ 9,250
Accounts Receivable	24,600
Supplies	650
Land.	35,000
Building......................................	125,000
Accumulated Depreciation—Building	32,500
Office Equipment................................	39,000
Accumulated Depreciation—Office Equipment.......	11,500
Accounts Payable................................	1,750
Salaries Payable	1,250
Claudia Bunge, Capital	65,000
Claudia Bunge, Drawing	20,000
Brian Casale, Capital	80,000
Brian Casale, Drawing	22,500

Professional Fees	$160,500
Salary Expense	60,100
Depreciation Expense — Building	5,150
Property Tax Expense	2,900
Heating and Lighting Expense	2,850
Supplies Expense	1,900
Depreciation Expense — Office Equipment	1,500
Miscellaneous Expense	2,100

Instructions:

(1) Prepare an income statement for the current fiscal year, indicating the division of net income. The articles of partnership provide for salary allowances of $20,000 to Bunge and $25,000 to Casale; that each partner be allowed 12% on their capital balance at the beginning of the fiscal year; and that the remaining net income or net loss be divided equally. An additional investment of $5,000 was made by Casale on May 10 of the current year.

(2) Prepare a capital statement for the current fiscal year.

(3) Prepare a balance sheet as of the end of the current fiscal year.

Problem 14-4A. Bob James and Ed Kane have operated a successful firm for many years, sharing net income and net losses equally. Ann Wilcox is to be admitted to the partnership on May 1 of the current year, in accordance with the following agreement:

(a) Assets and liabilities of the old partnership are to be valued at their book values as of April 30, except for the following:

Accounts receivable amounting to $1,750 are to be written off and the allowance for doubtful accounts is to be increased to 5% of the remaining accounts.

Merchandise inventory is to be valued at $47,900.

Equipment is to be valued at $85,000.

(b) Goodwill of $25,000 is to be recognized as attributable to the firm of James and Kane.

(c) Wilcox is to purchase $40,000 of the ownership interest of James for $55,000 cash and to contribute $20,000 cash to the partnership for total ownership equity of $60,000.

(d) The income-sharing ratio of James, Kane, and Wilcox is to be 2:2:1.

The post-closing trial balance of James and Kane as of April 30 is as follows:

James and Kane
Post-Closing Trial Balance
April 30, 19--

Cash	8,150	
Accounts Receivable	17,750	
Allowance for Doubtful Accounts		550
Merchandise Inventory	42,900	
Prepaid Insurance	625	
Equipment	115,000	
Accumulated Depreciation — Equipment		40,000
Accounts Payable		11,375
Notes Payable		5,000
Bob James, Capital		80,000
Ed Kane, Capital		47,500
	184,425	184,425

Instructions:
(1) Present general journal entries as of April 30 to record the revaluations, using a temporary account entitled Asset Revaluations. The balance in the accumulated depreciation account is to be eliminated.
(2) Present the additional entries, in general journal form, to record the remaining transactions relating to the formation of the new partnership. Assume that all transactions occur on May 1.
(3) Present a balance sheet for the new partnership as of May 1.

(If the working papers correlating with the textbook are not used, omit Problem 14-5A.)

Problem 14-5A. Barbara Coe, Dorothy Due, and Deb Eades decided to discontinue business operations as of December 31 and liquidate their partnership. A summary of the various transactions that have occurred thus far in the liquidation is presented in the working papers.

Instructions:
(1) Assuming that the available cash is to be distributed to the partners, complete the tabular summary of liquidation by indicating the distribution of cash to partners.
(2) Present entries, in general journal form, to record (a) sale of assets, (b) division of loss on sale of assets, (c) payment of liabilities, (d) distribution of cash to partners.
(3) Assuming that Due pays $6,000 of her deficiency to the partnership and the remainder is considered to be uncollectible, present entries, in general journal form, to record (a) receipt of part of deficiency, (b) division of loss, (c) distribution of cash to partners.

Problem 14-6A. On the date the firm of May, Noe, and Owens decides to liquidate the partnership, the partners have capital balances of $50,000, $70,000, and $120,000 respectively. The cash balance is $30,000, the book values of noncash assets total $250,000, and liabilities total $40,000. The partners share income and losses in the ratio of 1:1:3.

Instructions:
Prepare a summary of the liquidation, in the form illustrated in this chapter, for each of the following assumptions:
(1) All of the noncash assets are sold for $300,000 in cash, the creditors are paid, and the remaining cash is distributed to the partners.
(2) All of the noncash assets are sold for $100,000 in cash, the creditors are paid, and the remaining cash is distributed to the partners.
(3) All of the noncash assets are sold for $40,000 in cash, the creditors are paid, and the remaining cash is distributed to the partners. After the available cash is paid to the partners:
   (a) The partner with the debit capital balance pays the amount owed to the firm.
   (b) The additional cash is distributed.
(4) All of the noncash assets are sold for $30,000 in cash, the creditors are paid, and the remaining cash is distributed to the partners. After the available cash is paid to the partners:
   (a) The partner with the debit capital balance pays 50% of his or her deficiency to the firm.
   (b) The additional cash is distributed.
   (c) The remaining partners absorb the remaining deficiency as a loss.

Mini-Case

Doug Burke and Joann Levine formed BLT Company as a partnership fifteen years ago by each contributing $50,000 in capital. The partnership agreement indicated the following division of net income: salary allowances of $12,000 and $18,000 to Burke and Levine, respectively, and all remaining income divided equally.

Levine recently expressed concern with the manner in which profits are being divided. Specifically, the profit-sharing agreement did not consider changes in the amounts invested by each partner as reflected in the balances of their capital accounts. Over the years, Burke has consistently withdrawn more from the partnership than Levine, with the result that the capital balances as of January 1, 1985, indicated an investment of $140,000 by Burke and $260,000 by Levine.

Burke agreed with Levine that a change in the profit-sharing agreement was warranted and accordingly proposed the following two alternatives:

Proposal A

(1) The salary allowances of Burke and Levine would be increased to $24,000 and $36,000, respectively.
(2) Interest at 10% would be allowed on the January 1 balances of the capital accounts.
(3) All remaining income would be divided equally.

Proposal B

(1) The salary allowances of Burke and Levine would not be changed.
(2) No interest would be allowed on the capital balances.
(3) Levine would be allowed a bonus of 20% of the amount by which net income exceeds salary allowances and the remainder would be divided equally.

Levine has asked your advice on which of the two proposals she should accept.

Instructions:

(1) For each proposal, prepare an analysis of the distribution of net income between Burke and Levine for 1985 for income levels of $100,000, $120,000, and $150,000.
(2) Which proposal would you recommend Levine accept?
(3) John Cary has offered to purchase a one-third interest in the partnership capital and net income for $180,000. Assuming that the net tangible assets of the partnership approximate their fair market values at January 1, 1985, how much goodwill is implied by Cary's offer?

15

Corporations: Organization and Operation

CHAPTER OBJECTIVES

Identify basic corporation characteristics which have accounting implications.

Describe and illustrate the accounting for corporate capital.

Describe and illustrate the computation of equity per share of stock.

PART 5 | Corporations

15

CHAPTER

In the Dartmouth College case in 1819, Chief Justice Marshall stated: "A corporation is an artificial being, invisible, intangible, and existing only in contemplation of the law." The concept underlying this definition has become the foundation for the prevailing legal doctrine that a corporation is an artificial person, created by law and having a distinct existence separate and apart from the natural persons who are responsible for its creation and operation. Almost all large business enterprises in the United States are organized as corporations.

Corporations may be classified as **not-for-profit** or **profit.** Not-for-profit corporations include those organized for recreational, educational, charitable, or other philanthropic purposes. For their continuation, they depend upon dues from their members or upon gifts and grants from the public at large. Other not-for-profit corporations include those which render services to the public for a fee, such as cooperative-owned utility companies, but whose objective is rendering services to the public on a cost basis rather than earning a profit. Not-for-profit organizations are discussed in Chapter 28.

Profit corporations are engaged in business activities. They depend upon profitable operations for their continued existence. Large, profit corporations whose shares of stock are widely distributed and traded in a public market are often called **public corporations.** Corporations whose shares are owned by a small group are often called **nonpublic corporations.** Regardless of their nature or purpose, profit corporations are created according to state or federal statutes and are separate legal entities.

CHARACTERISTICS OF A CORPORATION

As a legal entity, the corporation has certain characteristics that make it different from other types of business organizations. The most important characteristics with accounting implications are described briefly in the following paragraphs.

A corporation has a **separate legal existence.** It may acquire, own, and dispose of property in its corporate name. It may also incur liabilities and enter into other types of contracts according to the provisions of its **charter** (also called **articles of incorporation).**

The ownership of a corporation, of which there may be several categories or classes, is divided into **transferable units** known as **shares of stock.** Each share of stock of a certain class has the same rights and privileges as every other share of the same class. The **stockholders** (also called **shareholders**) may buy and sell shares without interfering with the activities of the corporation. The millions of transactions that occur daily on stock exchanges are independent transactions between buyers and sellers. Thus, in contrast to the partnership, the existence of the corporation is not affected by changes in ownership.

The stockholders of a corporation have **limited liability.** A corporation is responsible for its own acts and obligations, and therefore its creditors usually may not look beyond the assets of the corporation for satisfaction of their claims. Thus, the financial loss that a stockholder may suffer is limited to the amount invested. The phenomenal growth of the corporate form of business would not have been possible without this limited liability feature.

The stockholders, who are, in fact, the owners of the corporation, exercise control over the management of corporate affairs indirectly by electing a **board**

of directors. It is the responsibility of the board of directors to meet from time to time to determine the corporate policies and to select the officers who manage the corporation. The following chart shows the **organizational structure** of a corporation:

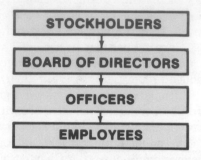

As a separate entity, a corporation is subject to **additional taxes.** It must pay a charter fee to the state at the time of its organization and annual taxes thereafter. If the corporation does business in states other than the one in which it is incorporated, it may also be required to pay annual taxes to such states. The earnings of a corporation may also be subject to a state income tax.

The earnings of a corporation are subject to the federal income tax. When the remaining earnings are distributed to stockholders as dividends, they are again taxed as income to the individuals receiving them. Under certain conditions specified in the Internal Revenue Code, a corporation with a few stockholders may elect to be treated in a manner similar to a partnership for income tax purposes. A corporation electing this optional treatment does not pay federal income taxes. Instead, its stockholders include their distributive shares of corporate income in their own taxable income, regardless of whether the income is distributed to them.

Being a creature of the state and being owned by stockholders who have limited liability, a corporation has less freedom of action than a sole proprietorship and a partnership. There may be **government regulations** in such matters as ownership of real estate, retention of earnings, and purchase of its own stock.

CORPORATE CAPITAL   The owners' equity in a corporation is commonly called **capital, stockholders' equity, shareholders' equity,** or **shareholders' investment.** The two main sources of corporate capital are (1) **paid-in capital,** or investments contributed by the stockholders, and (2) **retained earnings,** or net income retained in the business. As shown in the following illustration, the stockholders' equity section of corporation balance sheets is divided into subsections based on these sources of capital.

Stockholders' Equity

Paid-in capital:	
Common stock	$330,000
Retained earnings	80,000
Total stockholders' equity	$410,000

The capital acquired from the stockholders is recorded in accounts maintained for each class of stock. If there is only one class of stock, the account is entitled Common Stock or Capital Stock.

The retained earnings amount results from transferring the balance in the income summary account to a retained earnings account at the end of a fiscal year. The dividends account, to which distributions of earnings to stockholders have been debited, is also closed to Retained Earnings. If the occurrence of net losses results in a debit balance in Retained Earnings, it is termed a deficit. In the stockholders' equity section of the balance sheet, a deficit is deducted from paid-in capital to determine total stockholders' equity.

There are a number of acceptable variants of the term "retained earnings," among which are *earnings retained for use in the business, earnings reinvested in the business, earnings employed in the business*, and *accumulated earnings*. For many years, the term applied to retained earnings was *earned surplus*. However, the use of this term in published financial statements has generally been discontinued.[1] Because of its connotation as an excess, or something left over, "surplus" was sometimes erroneously interpreted by readers of financial statements to mean "cash available for dividends."

CHARACTER-ISTICS OF STOCK

The general term applied to the shares of ownership of a corporation is capital stock. The number of shares that a corporation is *authorized* to issue is set forth in its charter. The term *issued* is applied to the shares issued to the stockholders. A corporation may, under circumstances discussed later in the chapter, reacquire some of the stock that it has issued. The stock remaining in the hands of the stockholders is then referred to as the stock outstanding.

The shares of capital stock are often assigned an arbitrary monetary figure, known as par. The par amount is printed on the stock certificate, which is the evidence of ownership issued to the stockholder. Stock may also be issued without par, in which case it is called no-par stock. Many states provide that the board of directors must assign a stated value to no-par stock, which makes it similar to par stock.

Because of the limited liability feature, the creditors of a corporation have no claim against the personal assets of stockholders. However, the law requires that some specific minimum contribution by the stockholders be retained by the corporation for the protection of its creditors. This amount, called legal capital, varies among the states but usually includes the par or stated value of the shares of capital stock issued.

Classes of Stock

The major basic rights that accompany ownership of a share of stock are (1) the right to vote, (2) the right to share in distributions of earnings, (3) the right to

---

[1]*Accounting Research and Terminology Bulletins — Final Edition*, "Accounting Terminology Bulletins, No. 1, Review and Résumé" (New York: American Institute of Certified Public Accountants, 1961), par. 65–69.

maintain the same fractional interest in the corporation by purchasing a proportionate number of shares of any additional issuances of stock (preemptive right),[2] and (4) the right to share in assets upon liquidation.

If a corporation issues only common stock, each share has equal rights. In order to appeal to a broader investment market, a corporation may provide for one or more classes of stock with various preferential rights. The preference usually relates to the right to share in distributions of earnings. Such stock is called preferred stock.

The board of directors has the sole authority to distribute earnings to the stockholders. When such action is taken, the directors are said to *declare a dividend*. A corporation cannot guarantee that its operations will be profitable and hence it cannot guarantee dividends to its stockholders. Furthermore, the directors have wide discretionary powers in determining the extent to which earnings should be retained by the corporation to provide for expansion, to offset possible future losses, or to provide for other contingencies.

A corporation with both preferred stock and common stock may declare dividends on the common only after it meets the requirements of the stated dividend on the preferred (which may be stated in monetary terms or as a percent of par). To illustrate, assume that a corporation has 1,000 shares of $10 preferred stock (that is, the preferred has a prior claim to an annual $10 per share dividend) and 4,000 shares of common stock outstanding. Assume also that in the first three years of operations, net income was $30,000, $55,000, and $100,000 respectively. The directors authorize the retention of a portion of each year's earnings and the distribution of the remainder. Details of the dividend distribution are presented in the following tabulation:

	First Year	Second Year	Third Year
Net income	$30,000	$55,000	$100,000
Amount retained	10,000	20,000	40,000
Amount distributed	$20,000	$35,000	$ 60,000
Preferred dividend (1,000 shares)	10,000	10,000	10,000
Common dividend (4,000 shares)	$10,000	$25,000	$ 50,000
Dividends per share:			
Preferred	$10.00	$10.00	$10.00
Common	$ 2.50	$ 6.25	$12.50

Participating and Nonparticipating Preferred Stock

In the foregoing illustration, the holders of preferred stock received an annual dividend of $10 per share, in contrast to the common stockholders, whose annual per share dividends were $2.50, $6.25, and $12.50 respectively. It is apparent from the example that holders of preferred stock have relatively greater assurance than common stockholders of receiving dividends regularly. On the other hand, holders of common stock have the possibility of receiving larger dividends than preferred

---

[2]In recent years the stockholders of a significant number of corporations have, by formal action, given up their preemptive rights.

stockholders. The preferred stockholders' preferential right to dividends is usually limited to a certain amount, which was assumed to be the case in the preceding example. Such stock is said to be **nonparticipating.**

Preferred stock which provides for the possibility of dividends in excess of a certain amount is said to be participating. Preferred shares may participate with common shares to varying degrees, and the contract must be examined to determine the extent of this participation. To illustrate, assume that the contract covering the preferred stock of the corporation in the preceding illustration provides that if the total dividends to be distributed exceed the regular preferred dividend and a comparable dividend on common, the preferred shall share in the excess ratably on a share-for-share basis with the common. According to such terms, the $60,000 dividend distribution in the third year would be allocated as follows:

	Preferred Dividend	Common Dividend	Total Dividends
Regular dividend to preferred (1,000 × $10)	$10,000		$10,000
Comparable dividend to common (4,000 × $10)	—	$40,000	40,000
Remainder to 5,000 shares ratably ($2 per share)	2,000	8,000	10,000
Total	$12,000	$48,000	$60,000
Dividends per share	$12	$12	

Cumulative and Noncumulative Preferred Stock

As was indicated in the preceding section, most preferred stock is nonparticipating. Provision is usually made, however, to assure the continuation of the preferential dividend right if at any time the directors *pass* (do not declare) the usual dividend. This is accomplished by providing that dividends may not be paid on the common stock if any preferred dividends are in arrears. Such preferred stock is said to be cumulative. To illustrate, assume that a corporation has outstanding 5,000 shares of cumulative preferred 9% stock of $100 par and that dividends have been passed for the preceding two years. In the current year, no dividend may be declared on the common stock unless the directors first declare preferred dividends of $90,000 for the past two years and $45,000 for the current year. Preferred stock not having this cumulative right is called **noncumulative.**

Other Preferential Rights

Thus far the discussion of preferential rights of preferred stock has related to dividend distributions. Preferred stock may also be given a preference in its claim to assets upon liquidation of the corporation. If the assets remaining after payment of creditors are not sufficient to return the capital contributions of both classes of stock, payment would first be made to the preferred stockholders and any balance remaining would go to the common stockholders. Another difference between preferred and common stock is that the former may have no voting rights. A corporation may also have more than one class of preferred stock, with differences as to the amount of dividends, priority of claims upon liquidation, and voting rights. In any particular case, the rights of a class of stock may be determined by reference to the charter, the stock certificate, or some other abstract of the agreement.

ISSUING STOCK AT PAR

The entries to record the investment of capital in a corporation are like those of other types of business organizations, in that cash and other assets received are debited and any liabilities assumed are credited. The credit to capital differs, however, in that there are accounts for each class of stock. To illustrate, assume that a corporation, with an authorization of 10,000 shares of preferred stock of $100 par and 100,000 shares of common stock of $20 par, issues one half of each authorization at par for cash. The entry to record the stockholders' investment and the receipt of the cash, in general journal form, is as follows:

```
Cash............................................... 1,500,000
    Preferred Stock................................          500,000
    Common Stock..................................        1,000,000
```

The capital stock accounts (Preferred Stock, Common Stock) are controlling accounts. It is necessary to maintain records of each stockholder's name, address, and number of shares held in order to issue dividend checks, proxy forms, and financial reports. Individual stockholders accounts are kept in a subsidiary ledger known as the **stockholders ledger**.

ISSUING STOCK AT A PREMIUM OR DISCOUNT

Par stock is often issued by a corporation at a price other than par. When it is issued for more than par, the excess of the contract price over par is termed a premium. When it is issued at a price that is below par, the difference is called a discount. Thus, if stock with a par of $50 is issued at $60, the amount of the premium is $10. If the same stock is issued at $45, the amount of the discount is $5.

Theoretically, there is no reason for a newly organized corporation to issue stock at a price other than par. The par designation is merely a part of the plan of dividing capital into a number of units of ownership. Hence, a group of persons investing their funds in a new corporation might all be expected to pay par for the shares. The fortunes of an enterprise do not remain the same, however, even when it is still in the process of organizing. The changing prospects for its future success may affect the price per share at which the incorporators can secure other investors.

A need for additional capital may arise long after a corporation has become established. Losses during the early period may have depleted working capital or the operations may have been successful enough to warrant a substantial expansion of plant and equipment. If the funds are to be obtained by the issuance of additional stock, it is apparent that the current price at which the original stock is selling in the market will affect the price that can be obtained for the new shares.

Generally speaking, the price at which stock can be sold by a corporation is influenced by (1) the financial condition, the earnings record, and the dividend record of the corporation, (2) its potential earning power, (3) the availability of money for investment purposes, and (4) general business and economic conditions and prospects.

Premium on Stock

When capital stock is issued at a premium, cash or other assets are debited for the amount received. The stock account is then credited for the par amount, and a premium account, sometimes called Paid-In Capital in Excess of Par, is credited for the amount of the premium. For example, if Caldwell Company issues 2,000 shares of $50 par preferred stock for cash at $55, the entry to record the transaction would be as follows, in general journal form:

```
Cash..........................................................  110,000
    Preferred Stock......................................          100,000
    Premium on Preferred Stock.....................           10,000
```

The premium of $10,000 is a part of the investment of the stockholders and is therefore a part of paid-in capital. It is distinguished from the capital stock account because usually it is not a part of legal capital and in many states may be used as a basis for dividends to stockholders. However, if the premium is returned to stockholders as a dividend at a later date, it should be emphasized that the dividend is a return of paid-in capital rather than a distribution of earnings.

Discount on Stock

Some states do not permit the issuance of stock at a discount. In others, it may be done only under certain conditions. When stock is issued at less than its par, it is considered to be fully paid as between the corporation and the stockholder. In some states, however, the stockholders are contingently liable to creditors for the amount of the discount. If the corporation is liquidated and there are not enough assets to pay creditors in full, the stockholders may be assessed for an additional contribution up to the amount of the discount on their stock.

When capital stock is issued at a discount, cash or other assets are debited for the amount received, and a discount account is debited for the amount of the discount. The capital stock account is then credited for the par amount. For example, if Caldwell Company issues 20,000 shares of $25 par common stock for cash at $23, the entry to record the transaction would be as follows, in general journal form:

```
Cash..........................................................  460,000
Discount on Common Stock .........................   40,000
    Common Stock.......................................          500,000
```

The discount of $40,000 is a contra paid-in capital account and must be offset against Common Stock to arrive at the amount actually invested by the holders of common stock. The discount is not an asset, nor should it be amortized against revenue as though it were an expense.

Premiums and Discounts on the Balance Sheet

The manner in which premiums and discounts may be presented in the stockholders' equity section of the balance sheet is illustrated as follows, based on the two illustrative entries for Caldwell Company:

Stockholders' Equity

Paid-in capital:

Preferred 10% stock, cumulative, $50 par (2,000 shares authorized and issued)	$100,000	
Premium on preferred stock	10,000	$110,000
Common stock, $25 par (50,000 shares authorized, 20,000 shares issued).	$500,000	
Less discount on common stock	40,000	460,000
Total paid-in capital.		$570,000
Retained earnings		175,000
Total stockholders' equity.		$745,000

The following stockholders' equity section illustrates the reporting of a deficit and some differences in terminology from that in the foregoing example:

Shareholders' Equity

Paid-in capital:

Preferred $3 stock, cumulative, $25 par (10,000 shares authorized and issued)	$ 250,000	
Excess of issuance price over par.	20,000	$ 270,000
Common stock, $10 par (200,000 shares authorized, 100,000 shares issued).	$1,000,000	
Less excess of par over issuance price	100,000	900,000
Total paid in by stockholders.		$1,170,000
Less deficit		75,000
Total shareholders' equity.		$1,095,000

ISSUING STOCK FOR ASSETS OTHER THAN CASH

When capital stock is issued in exchange for assets other than cash, such as land, buildings, and equipment, the assets acquired should be recorded at their fair market price or at the fair market price of the stock issued, whichever is more objectively determinable. The determination of the values to be assigned to the assets is the responsibility of the board of directors.

As a basis for illustration, assume that a corporation acquired land for which the fair market price is not determinable. In exchange, the corporation issued 10,000 shares of its $10 par common stock with a current market price of $12 per share. The transaction could be recorded as follows:

Dec. 5	Land.	120,000	
	Common Stock.		100,000
	Premium on Common Stock		20,000

ISSUING NO-PAR STOCK

In the early days of rapid industrial expansion and increasing use of the corporate form of business organization, it was customary to assign a par of $100 to shares of stock. It is not surprising that unsophisticated investors, mistakenly considering "par value" to be the equivalent of "value," were often induced to invest in mining and other highly speculative enterprises by the simple means of offering $100 par stock at "bargain" prices. Another misleading practice was the use of par in assigning highly inflated values to assets acquired in exchange for stock. For example, stock with a total par of $1,000,000 might be issued in exchange for patents, mineral rights, or other properties with a conservatively estimated value of $50,000. The assets would be recorded at the full par of $1,000,000, whereas in reality the stock had been issued at a discount of $950,000. Balance sheets that were "window-dressed" in this manner were obviously deceptive.

To combat such abuses and also to eliminate the troublesome discount liability of stockholders, stock without par was conceived. The issuance of stock without par was first permitted by New York in 1912. Its use is now authorized in nearly all of the states.

Over the years, questionable practices in the issuance of securities have been virtually eliminated. Today federal and state laws and rules imposed by organized stock exchanges and governmental agencies such as the Securities and Exchange Commission combine to protect the investor from misrepresentations that were common in earlier days.

In most states, both preferred and common stock may be issued without a par designation. However, preferred stock is usually assigned a par. When no-par stock is issued, the entire proceeds may be credited to the capital stock account, even though the issuance price varies from time to time. For example, if at the time of organization a corporation issues no-par common stock at $40 a share and at a later date issues additional shares at $36, the entries, in general journal form, would be:

1. *Original issuance of 10,000 shares of no-par common at $40:*
   Cash 400,000
       Common Stock   400,000

2. *Subsequent issuance of 1,000 shares of no-par common at $36:*
   Cash 36,000
       Common Stock   36,000

The laws of some states require that the entire proceeds from the issuance of no-par stock be regarded as legal capital. The preceding entries conform to this principle, which also conforms to the original concept of no-par stock. In other states, no-par stock may be assigned a stated value per share, and the excess of the proceeds over the stated value may be credited to Paid-In Capital in Excess of Stated Value. Assuming that in the previous example the stated value is $25 and the board of directors wishes to credit the common stock for stated value, the transactions would be recorded as follows, in general journal form:

1. *Original issuance of 10,000 shares of no-par common, stated value $25, at $40:*
   Cash 400,000
       Common Stock   250,000
       Paid-In Capital in Excess of Stated Value   150,000

2. *Subsequent issuance of 1,000 shares of no-par common, stated value $25, at $36:*

Cash	36,000	
Common Stock		25,000
Paid-In Capital in Excess of Stated Value		11,000

It is readily apparent that the accounting for no-par stock with a stated value may follow the same pattern as the accounting for par stock.

SUBSCRIPTIONS AND STOCK ISSUANCE

In some situations involving the initial issue of capital stock or subsequent issuances where the stockholders have waived the preemptive right, a corporation may sell its stock to an **underwriter.** The underwriter then resells the shares to investors at a price high enough to earn a profit from the sale. Under these circumstances, the corporation is relieved of the task of marketing the stock. It receives the entire amount of cash without delay and can proceed immediately with its plans for the use of the funds.

In other situations, a corporation may sell its stock directly to investors or others, such as employees, under stock purchase plans. In such cases, the purchaser may enter into an agreement with the corporation to subscribe to shares at a certain price per share. The terms may provide for payment in full at some future date or for installment payments over a period of time.

When stock is subscribed for at par, the subscription price is debited to the asset account Stock Subscriptions Receivable and credited to the capital stock account Stock Subscribed. When stock is subscribed for at a price above or below par, the stock subscriptions receivable account is debited for the subscription price. The stock subscribed account is credited at par, and the difference between the subscription price and par is debited to a discount account or credited to a premium account, as the case may be.

After a subscriber has completed the agreed payments, the corporation issues the stock certificate. The stock subscribed account is then debited for the total par of the shares issued, and the capital stock account is credited for the same amount.

As the basis for illustrating the entries for subscriptions and stock issuance, assume that the newly organized Ledway Corporation receives subscriptions, collects cash, and issues stock certificates according to the following transactions. The required entries, in general journal form, appear after the statement of the transaction.

1. *Received subscriptions to 10,000 shares of $20 par common stock from various subscribers at $21 per share, with a down payment of 50% of the subscription price.*

Mar. 1 Common Stock Subscriptions Receivable	210,000	
Common Stock Subscribed		200,000
Premium on Common Stock		10,000
1 Cash	105,000	
Common Stock Subscriptions Receivable		105,000

2. *Received 25% of subscription price from all subscribers.*

| May 1 | Cash....................................... | 52,500 | |
| | Common Stock Subscriptions Receivable..... | | 52,500 |

3. *Received final 25% of subscription price from all subscribers and issued the stock certificates.*

July 1	Cash.......................................	52,500	
	Common Stock Subscriptions Receivable.....		52,500
1	Common Stock Subscribed...................	200,000	
	Common Stock............................		200,000

A balance sheet prepared after the transactions of March 1 would list the subscriptions receivable as a current asset and the stock subscribed and the premium as paid-in capital. While it is true that the entire amount has not been "paid in" in cash, the claim against the subscribers is an asset of equivalent value. The presentation of the items in the balance sheet of the Ledway Corporation as of March 1 is as follows:

Ledway Corporation
Balance Sheet
March 1, 19--

Assets		Stockholders' Equity	
Current assets:		Paid-in capital:	
Cash	$105,000	Common stock	
Common stock subscrip-		subscribed	$200,000
tions receivable.......	105,000	Premium on common	
		stock...............	10,000
Total assets	$210,000	Total stockholders' equity..	$210,000

The stock subscriptions receivable account is a controlling account. The individual accounts with each subscriber are maintained in a subsidiary ledger known as a **subscribers ledger.** It is used in much the same manner as the accounts receivable ledger.

After all the subscriptions have been collected, the common stock subscriptions receivable account will have a zero balance. The stock certificates will then be issued and the common stock subscribed account will have a zero balance. The ultimate effect of the series of transactions is a debit to Cash of $210,000, a credit to Common Stock of $200,000, and a credit to Premium on Common Stock of $10,000.

TREASURY STOCK   Although there are some legal restrictions on the practice, a corporation may purchase shares of its own outstanding stock from stockholders. It may also accept shares of its own stock in payment of a debt owed by a stockholder, which in essence is much the same as acquisition by purchase. There are various reasons why a corporation may buy its own stock. For example, it may be to provide shares for resale to employees, for reissuance to employees as a bonus or according to stock purchase agreements, or to support the market price of the stock.

The term treasury stock may be applied only to the issuing corporation's stock that (1) has been issued as fully paid, (2) has later been reacquired by the corporation, and (3) has not been canceled or reissued. In the past, corporations would occasionally list treasury stock on the balance sheet as an asset. The justification for such treatment was that the stock could be reissued and was thus like an investment in the stock of another corporation. The same argument, though indefensible, might well be extended to authorized but unissued stock.

Today, it is generally agreed among accountants that treasury stock should not be reported as an asset. A corporation cannot own a part of itself. Treasury stock has no voting rights, it does not have the preemptive right to participate in additional issuances of stock, nor does it generally participate in cash dividends. When a corporation purchases its own stock, it is returning capital to the stockholders from whom the purchase was made.

There are several methods of accounting for the purchase and the resale of treasury stock. A commonly used method is the **cost basis.** When the stock is purchased by the corporation, the account Treasury Stock is debited for the price paid for it. The par and the price at which the stock was originally issued are ignored. When the stock is resold, Treasury Stock is credited at the price paid for it, and the difference between the price paid and the selling price is debited or credited to an account entitled Paid-In Capital from Sale of Treasury Stock.

As a basis for illustrating the cost method, assume that the paid-in capital of a corporation is composed of common stock issued at a premium, detailed as follows:

Common stock, $25 par (20,000 shares authorized and issued).....	$500,000
Premium on common stock	150,000

The assumed transactions involving treasury stock and the required entries in general journal form are as follows:

1. *Purchased 1,000 shares of treasury stock at $45.*

Treasury Stock	45,000	
Cash		45,000

2. *Sold 200 shares of treasury stock at $55.*

Cash	11,000	
Treasury Stock		9,000
Paid-In Capital from Sale of Treasury Stock.............		2,000

3. *Sold 200 shares of treasury stock at $40.*

Cash	8,000	
Paid-In Capital from Sale of Treasury Stock..............	1,000	
Treasury Stock		9,000

The additional capital obtained through the sale of treasury stock is reported in the paid-in capital section of the balance sheet, and the cost of the treasury stock held by the corporation is deducted from the total of the capital accounts. After the foregoing transactions are completed, the stockholders' equity section of the balance sheet would appear as follows:

Stockholders' Equity

Paid-in capital:		
Common stock, $25 par (20,000 shares authorized and issued)	$500,000	
Premium on common stock	150,000	$650,000
From sale of treasury stock		1,000
Total paid-in capital		$651,000
Retained earnings		130,000
Total......................................		$781,000
Deduct treasury stock (600 shares at cost)		27,000
Total stockholders' equity		$754,000

The stockholders' equity section of the balance sheet indicates that 20,000 shares of stock were issued, of which 600 are held as treasury stock. The number of shares outstanding is therefore 19,400. If cash dividends are declared at this time, the declaration would apply to 19,400 shares of stock. Similarly, 19,400 shares could be voted at a stockholders' meeting.

If sales of treasury stock result in a net decrease in paid-in capital, the decrease may be reported on the balance sheet as a reduction of paid-in capital or it may be debited to the retained earnings account.

EQUITY PER SHARE   The amount appearing on the balance sheet as total stockholders' equity can be stated in terms of the **equity per share.** Another term sometimes used in referring to the equity allocable to a single share of stock is **book value per share.** The latter term is not only less accurate but its use of "value" may also be interpreted by nonaccountants to mean "market value" or "actual worth."

When there is only one class of stock, the equity per share is determined by dividing total stockholders' equity by the number of shares outstanding. For a corporation with both preferred and common stock, it is necessary first to allocate the total equity between the two classes. In making the allocation, consideration must be given to the liquidation rights of the preferred stock, including any participating and cumulative dividend features. After the total is allocated to the two classes, the equity per share of each class may then be determined by dividing the respective amounts by the related number of shares outstanding.

To illustrate, assume that as of the end of the current fiscal year, a corporation has both preferred and common shares outstanding, that there are no preferred dividends in arrears, and that the preferred stock is entitled to receive $105 upon liquidation. The amounts of the stockholders' equity accounts of the corporation and the computation of the equity per share are as follows:

Stockholders' Equity

Preferred $9 stock, cumulative, $100 par	
(1,000 shares outstanding)	$100,000
Premium on preferred stock	2,000
Common stock, $10 par (50,000 shares outstanding)...............	500,000
Premium on common stock.......................................	50,000
Retained earnings	253,000
Total equity	$905,000

Allocation of Total Equity to Preferred and Common Stock

Total equity	$905,000
Allocated to preferred stock:	
Liquidation price	105,000
Allocated to common stock......................................	$800,000

Equity Per Share

Preferred stock: $105,000 ÷   1,000 shares = $105 per share
Common stock: $800,000 ÷ 50,000 shares = $ 16 per share

If it is assumed that the preferred stock is entitled to dividends in arrears in the event of liquidation, and that there is an arrearage of two years, the computations for the foregoing illustration would be as follows:

Allocation of Total Equity to Preferred and Common Stock

Total equity...		$905,000
Allocated to preferred stock:		
Liquidation price....................................	$105,000	
Dividends in arrears................................	18,000	123,000
Allocated to common stock		$782,000

Equity Per Share

Preferred stock: $123,000 ÷   1,000 shares = $123.00 per share
Common stock: $782,000 ÷ 50,000 shares = $ 15.64 per share

Equity per share, particularly of common stock, is often stated in corporation reports to stockholders and quoted in the financial press. It is one of the many factors affecting the **market price,** that is, the price at which a share is bought and sold at a particular moment. However, it should be noted that earning capacity, dividend rates, and prospects for the future usually affect the market price of listed stocks to a much greater extent than does equity per share. So-called "glamour" stocks may at times sell at more than ten times the amount of the equity per share. On the other hand, stock in corporations that have suffered severe declines in earnings or whose future prospects appear to be unfavorable may sell at prices which are much less than the equity per share.

ORGANIZATION COSTS

Expenditures incurred in organizing a corporation, such as legal fees, taxes and fees paid to the state, and promotional costs, are charged to an intangible asset account entitled Organization Costs. Although such costs have no realizable value upon liquidation, they are as essential as plant and equipment, for without the expenditures the corporation could not have been created. If the life of a corporation is limited to a definite period of time, the organization costs should be amortized over the period by annual charges to an expense account. However, at the time of incorporation the length of life of most corporations is indeterminate.

There are two possible extreme viewpoints on the proper accounting for organization costs and other intangibles of indeterminate life. One extreme would consider the cost of intangibles as a permanent asset until there was convincing evidence of loss in value. The other extreme would consider the cost of intangibles as an expense in the period in which the cost is incurred. The practical solution to the problem is expressed in the following quotation:

> . . . . Allocating the cost of goodwill or other intangible assets with an indeterminate life over time is necessary because the value almost inevitably becomes zero at some future date. Since the date at which the value becomes zero is indeterminate, the end of the useful life must necessarily be set arbitrarily at some point or within some range of time for accounting purposes.[3]

The Internal Revenue Code permits the amortization of organization costs ratably over a period of not less than sixty months beginning with the month the corporation commences business. Since the amount of such costs is relatively small in relation to total assets and the effect on net income is ordinarily not significant, amortization of organization costs over sixty months is generally accepted in accounting practice.

Self-Examination Questions
(Answers in Appendix C.)

1. The owners' equity in a corporation is commonly called:
   A. capital
   B. stockholders' equity
   C. shareholders' investment
   D. all of the above

2. If a corporation has outstanding 1,000 shares of $9 cumulative preferred stock of $100 par and dividends have been passed for the preceding three years, what is the amount of preferred dividends that must be declared in the current year before a dividend can be declared on common stock?
   A. $9,000
   B. $27,000
   C. $36,000
   D. None of the above

---

[3]*Opinions of the Accounting Principles Board, No. 17,* "Intangible Assets" (New York: American Institute of Certified Public Accountants, 1970), par. 23.

3. The stockholders' equity section of the balance sheet may include:
   A. Discount on Common Stock   C. Premium on Preferred Stock
   B. Common Stock Subscribed   D. all of the above

4. If a corporation reacquires its own stock, the stock is listed on the balance sheet in the:
   A. current assets section   C. stockholders' equity section
   B. long-term liabilities section   D. none of the above

5. A corporation's balance sheet includes 10,000 outstanding shares of $8 cumulative preferred stock of $100 par; 100,000 outstanding shares of $20 par common stock; premium on common stock of $100,000; and retained earnings of $540,000. If preferred dividends are three years in arrears and the preferred stock is entitled to dividends in arrears plus $110 per share in the event of liquidation, what is the equity per common share?
   A. $20.00   C. $25.40
   B. $23.00   D. None of the above

Discussion Questions

1. Why are most large business enterprises organized as corporations?

2. Contrast the owners' liability to creditors of (a) a partnership (partners) and (b) a corporation (stockholders).

3. Why is it said that the earnings of a corporation are subject to "double taxation"? Discuss.

4. What are the two principal sources of owners' equity for a corporation?

5. The retained earnings account of a corporation at the beginning of the year had a credit balance of $25,000. The only other entry in the account during the year was a debit of $40,000 transferred from the income summary account at the end of the year. (a) What is the term applied to the $40,000 debit? (b) What is the balance in retained earnings at the end of the year? (c) What is the term applied to the balance determined in (b)?

6. The charter of a corporation provides for the issuance of a maximum of 100,000 shares of common stock. The corporation issued 75,000 shares of common stock and two years later it reacquired 5,000 shares. After the reacquisition what is the number of shares of stock (a) authorized, (b) issued, and (c) outstanding?

7. Of two corporations organized at approximately the same time and engaged in competing businesses, one issued $10 par common stock and the other issued $20 par common stock. Do the par designations provide any indication as to which stock is preferable as an investment?

8. (a) Differentiate between common stock and preferred stock. (b) Describe briefly (1) participating preferred stock and (2) cumulative preferred stock.

9. Assume that a corporation has had outstanding 20,000 shares of $10 cumulative preferred stock of $100 par and dividends were passed for the preceding four years. What amount of total dividends must be paid to the preferred stockholders before the common stockholders are entitled to any dividends in the current year?

10. What are some of the factors that influence the market price of a corporation's stock?

11. When a corporation issued stock at a premium, does the premium constitute income? Explain.

12. The stockholders' equity section of a corporation balance sheet is composed of the following items:

Preferred 8% stock	$600,000		
Discount on preferred stock........	50,000	$550,000	
Common stock	$900,000		
Premium on common stock	90,000	990,000	$1,540,000
Retained earnings		280,000	$1,820,000

Determine the following amounts: (a) paid-in capital attributable to preferred stock, (b) paid-in capital attributable to common stock, (c) earnings retained for use in the business, and (d) total stockholders' equity.

13. Land is acquired by a corporation for 2,500 shares of its $50 par, $5 preferred stock which is currently selling for $60 on a national stock exchange. (a) At what value should the land be recorded? (b) What accounts and amounts should be credited to record the transaction?

14. A corporation receives subscriptions to 5,000 shares of $20 par common stock from various subscribers at $30 per share, with a down payment of 25% of the subscription price. Subsequently, another payment of 25% of the subscription price was received. Assuming that financial statements are prepared at this point, determine the following account balances: (a) Subscriptions Receivable, (b) Common Stock Subscribed, (c) Premium on Common Stock, and (d) Common Stock.

15. (a) In what respect does treasury stock differ from unissued stock? (b) For what reasons might a company purchase treasury stock? (c) How should treasury stock be presented on the balance sheet?

16. A corporation reacquires 1,000 shares of its own $10 par common stock for $19,000, recording it at cost. (a) What effect does this transaction have on revenue or expense of the period? (b) What effect does it have on stockholders' equity?

17. The treasury stock in Question 16 is resold for $25,000. (a) What is the effect on the corporation's revenue of the period? (b) What is the effect on stockholders' equity?

18. A corporation that had issued 50,000 shares of $20 par common stock subsequently reacquired 10,000 shares, which it now holds as treasury stock. If the board of directors declares a cash dividend of $2 per share, what will be the total amount of the dividend?

19. Assume that a corporation at the end of the current period has 20,000 shares of preferred stock and 100,000 shares of common stock oustanding, that there are no preferred dividends in arrears, and that the preferred stock is entitled to receive $110 per share upon liquidation. If total stockholders' equity is $4,000,000, determine the following amounts: (a) equity per share of preferred stock, and (b) equity per share of common stock.

20. Common stock has a par of $20 per share, the current equity per share is $49.50, and the market price per share is $83. Suggest reasons for the comparatively high market price in relation to par and to equity per share.

21. (a) What type of expenditure is charged to the organization costs account? (b) Give examples of such expenditures. (c) In what section of the balance sheet is the balance of Organization Costs listed?

22. Identify each of the following accounts as asset, liability, stockholders' equity, revenue, or expense, and indicate the normal balance of each:
    (1) Paid-In Capital from Sale of Treasury Stock
    (2) Preferred Stock
    (3) Common Stock
    (4) Discount on Preferred Stock
    (5) Retained Earnings
    (6) Common Stock Subscribed
    (7) Common Stock Subscriptions Receivable
    (8) Treasury Stock
    (9) Organization Costs
    (10) Premium on Common Stock

Exercises

Exercise 15-1. CMS Inc. has stock outstanding as follows: 5,000 shares of $10 cumulative, nonparticipating preferred stock of $100 par, and 100,000 shares of $20 par common. During its first five years of operations, the following amounts were distributed as dividends: first year, none; second year, $80,000; third year, $130,000; fourth year, $145,000; fifth year, $200,000. Determine the dividends per share on each class of stock for each of the five years.

Exercise 15-2. R and M Company has outstanding stock composed of 2,500 shares of 9%, $100 par, participating preferred stock and 10,000 shares of no-par common stock. The preferred stock is entitled to participate equally with the common, share for share, in any dividend distributions which exceed the regular preferred dividend and a $2 per share common dividend. The directors declare dividends of $60,000 for the current year. Determine the amount of the dividend per share on (a) the preferred stock and (b) the common stock.

Exercise 15-3. On March 10, Benton Company issued for cash 10,000 shares of no-par common stock (with a stated value of $10) at $12, and on July 12 it issued for cash 1,000 shares of $100 par preferred stock at $105. (a) Give the entries, in general journal form, for March 10 and July 12, assuming that the common stock is to be credited with the stated value. (b) What is the total amount invested by all stockholders as of July 12?

Exercise 15-4. On March 30, Wei Company received its charter authorizing 100,000 shares of $10 par common stock. On April 20, the corporation received subscriptions to 50,000 shares of stock at $15. Cash for one half of the subscription price accompanied the subscriptions. On July 31, the remaining half was received from all subscribers and the stock was issued. (a) Present entries, in general journal form, to record the transactions of April 20. (b) Present entries, in general journal form, to record the transactions of July 31. (c) By what amount did the corporation's capital increase on March 30, April 20, and July 31? (d) Name two controlling accounts used in the transactions above and the related subsidiary ledgers.

Exercise 15-5. Montes and Reid Inc., with an authorization of 10,000 shares of preferred stock and 30,000 shares of common stock, completed several transactions involving its capital stock on June 1, the first day of operations. The trial balance at the close of the day follows:

Cash	450,000	
Common Stock Subscriptions Receivable.......	150,000	
Land	110,000	
Buildings.................................	580,000	
Preferred 11% Stock, $100 par		600,000
Premium on Preferred Stock		90,000
Common Stock, $25 par.....................		375,000
Premium on Common Stock..................		100,000
Common Stock Subscribed		125,000
	1,290,000	1,290,000

All shares within each class of stock were sold or subscribed at the same price, the preferred stock was issued in exchange for the land and buildings, and no cash was received on the unissued common stock subscribed. (a) Present the three compound entries, in general journal form, to record the transactions summarized in the trial balance. (b) Prepare the stockholders' equity section of the balance sheet as of June 1.

Exercise 15-6. C. D. Menes Company was organized on January 5 of the current year, with an authorization of 5,000 shares of $4 cumulative preferred stock, $50 par, and 50,000 shares of $10 par common stock.

(a) Record in general journal form the following selected transactions completed during the first year of operations:

Jan.   5.   Sold 10,000 shares of common stock at par for cash.
       5.   Issued 750 shares of common stock to an attorney in payment of legal fees for organizing the corporation.
March 10.   Issued 10,000 shares of common stock in exchange for land, buildings, and equipment with fair market prices of $20,000, $75,000, and $25,000 respectively.
Nov.   30.   Sold 2,500 shares of preferred stock at $46 for cash.

(b) Prepare the stockholders' equity section of the balance sheet as of December 31, the end of the current year. The net income for the year amounted to $30,000.

Exercise 15-7. The capital accounts of Chow Products are as follows: Preferred 9% Stock, $50 par, $500,000; Common Stock, $20 par, $3,000,000; Premium on Common Stock, $300,000; Premium on Preferred Stock, $40,000; Retained Earnings, $1,155,000. (a) Determine the equity per share of each class of stock, assuming that the preferred stock is entitled to receive $60 upon liquidation. (b) Determine the equity per share of each class of stock, assuming that the preferred stock is to receive $60 plus the dividends in arrears in the event of liquidation, and that only the dividends for the current year are in arrears.

Exercise 15-8. The following items were listed in the stockholders' equity section of the balance sheet of May 31: Common stock, $10 par (60,000 shares outstanding), $600,000; Premium on common stock, $100,000; Retained earnings, $140,000. On June 1, the corporation purchased 2,000 shares of its stock for $51,200. (a) Determine the equity per share of stock on May 31. (b) Present the entry, in general journal form, to record the purchase of the stock on June 1. (c) Determine the equity per share on June 1.

Exercise 15-9. The following items were listed in the stockholders' equity section of the balance sheet on April 30: Preferred stock, $50 par, $250,000; Common stock, $10 par,

$500,000; Premium on common stock, $100,000; Deficit, $175,000. On May 1, the board of directors voted to dissolve the corporation immediately. A short time later, after all noncash assets were sold and liabilities were paid, cash of $475,000 remained for distribution to stockholders. (a) Assuming that preferred stock is entitled to preference in liquidation to the extent of 110% of par, determine the equity per share on April 30 of (1) preferred stock and (2) common stock. (b) Determine the amount of the $475,000 that will be distributed for each share of (1) preferred stock and (2) common stock. (c) Explain the reason for the difference between the common stock equity per share on April 30 and the amount of the cash distribution per common share.

Problems
(Problems in Appendix B: 15-2B, 15-3B, 15-5B.)

Problem 15-1A. Landmark Corp. was organized by Gass, Snow, and Thom. The charter authorized 10,000 shares of common stock with a par of $50. The following transactions affecting stockholders' equity were completed during the first year of operations:
  (a) Issued 1,000 shares of stock at par to Gass for cash.
  (b) Issued 100 shares of stock at par to Snow for promotional services rendered in connection with the organization of the corporation, and issued 900 shares of stock at par to Snow for cash.
  (c) Purchased land and a building from Thom. The building is encumbered by a 12%, 18-year mortgage of $65,000, and there is accrued interest of $1,300 on the mortgage note at the time of the purchase. It is agreed that the land is to be priced at $30,000 and the building at $115,000, and that Thom's equity will be exchanged for stock at par. The corporation agreed to assume responsibility for paying the mortgage note and the accrued interest.
  (d) Issued 2,000 shares of stock at $60 to various investors for cash.
  (e) Purchased equipment for $80,000. The seller accepted a 6-month, 14% note for $30,000 and 1,000 shares of stock in exchange for the equipment.

Instructions:
  (1) Prepare entries in general journal form to record the transactions presented above.
  (2) Prepare the stockholders' equity section of the balance sheet as of the end of the first year of operations. Net income for the year amounted to $82,000 and dividends of $5 per share were declared and paid during the year.

Problem 15-2A. The annual dividends declared by C. G. Steinberg Company during a six-year period are presented in the following table:

Year	Total Dividends	Preferred Dividends		Common Dividends	
		Total	Per Share	Total	Per Share
1981	$ 5,000				
1982	30,000				
1983	40,000				
1984	82,000				
1985	112,000				
1986	21,000				

During the entire period, the outstanding stock of the company was composed of 2,000 shares of cumulative, participating, 10% preferred stock, $100 par, and 10,000 shares of common stock, $100 par. The preferred stock contract provides that the preferred stock shall participate in distributions of additional dividends after allowance of a $5 dividend per share on the common stock, the additional dividends to be prorated among common and preferred shares on the basis of the total par of the stock oustanding.

Instructions:

(1) Determine the total dividends and the per share dividends declared on each class of stock for each of the six years, using the headings presented above. There were no dividends in arrears on January 1, 1981.

(2) Determine the average annual dividend per share for each class of stock for the six-year period.

(3) Assuming that the preferred stock was sold at par and the common stock was sold at $55 at the beginning of the six-year period, determine the percentage return on initial shareholders' investment, based on the average annual dividend per share (a) for preferred stock and (b) for common stock.

Problem 15-3A. Selected data from the balance sheets of six corporations, identified by letter, are as follows:

A. Common stock, $20 par .... $ 600,000
   Premium on common stock 120,000
   Deficit 75,000

B. Preferred 10% stock, $25 par............................... $ 500,000
   Common stock, $20 par 1,200,000
   Premium on common stock 130,000
   Retained earnings....................................... 410,000
   Preferred stock has prior claim to assets on liquidation to the extent of par.

C. Preferred 9% stock, $100 par. .... $ 800,000
   Premium on preferred stock.............................. 50,000
   Common stock, no par, 15,000 shares outstanding 1,200,000
   Deficit 237,500
   Preferred stock has prior claim to assets on liquidation to the extent of par.

D. Preferred 11% stock, $50 par............................... $2,500,000
   Premium on preferred stock.............................. 275,000
   Common stock, $25 par 3,750,000
   Deficit 1,240,000
   Preferred stock has prior claim to assets on liquidation to the extent of 110% of par.

E. Preferred $7 stock, $100 par $1,200,000
   Common stock, $50 par 3,100,000
   Premium on common stock 200,000
   Retained earnings....................................... 104,000
   Dividends on preferred stock are in arrears for 2 years, including the dividend passed during the current year. Preferred stock is entitled to par plus unpaid cumulative dividends upon liquidation to the extent of retained earnings.

F. Preferred $2 stock, $25 par $1,000,000
   Discount on preferred stock................................ 80,000
   Common stock, $10 par 3,000,000
   Deficit 130,000
   Dividends on preferred stock are in arrears for 3 years, including the dividend passed during the current year. Preferred stock is entitled to par plus unpaid

cumulative dividends upon liquidation, regardless of the availability of retained earnings.

Instructions:

Determine for each corporation the equity per share of each class of stock, presenting the total stockholders' equity allocated to each class and the number of shares outstanding.

Problem 15-4A. The following accounts and their balances appear in the ledger of C. F. Cammack Co. on June 1 of the current year:

Preferred $5 Stock, par $50 (10,000 shares authorized, 9,000 shares issued)	$450,000
Premium on Preferred Stock	19,000
Common Stock, par $10 (100,000 shares authorized, 75,000 shares issued)	750,000
Premium on Common Stock	120,000
Retained Earnings	190,000

At the annual stockholders' meeting on June 3, the board of directors presented a plan for modernizing and expanding plant operations at a cost of approximately $475,000. The plan provided (a) that the corporation borrow $250,000, (b) that 1,000 shares of the unissued preferred stock be issued through an underwriter, and (c) that a building, valued at $135,000, and the land on which it is located, valued at $35,000, be acquired in accordance with preliminary negotiations by the issuance of 10,000 shares of common stock. The plan was approved by the stockholders and accomplished by the following transactions:

June 12.   Issued 10,000 shares of common stock in exchange for land and building in accordance with the plan.

24.   Issued 1,000 shares of preferred stock, receiving $55 per share in cash from the underwriter.

30.   Borrowed $250,000 from American National Bank, giving a 13% mortgage note.

Instructions:

Assuming for the purpose of the problem that no other transactions occurred during June:

(1) Prepare, in general journal form, the entries to record the foregoing transactions.

(2) Prepare the stockholders' equity section of the balance sheet as of June 30.

Problem 15-5A. The following selected accounts appear in the ledger of Ruiz Corporation on July 1, the beginning of the current fiscal year:

Preferred 9% Stock Subscriptions Receivable	$ 27,500
Preferred 9% Stock, $50 par (10,000 shares authorized, 6,000 shares issued)	300,000
Preferred 9% Stock Subscribed (2,000 shares)	100,000
Premium on Preferred Stock	25,000
Common Stock, $25 par (40,000 shares authorized, 20,000 shares issued)	500,000
Premium on Common Stock	120,000
Retained Earnings	365,500

During the year, the corporation completed a number of transactions affecting the stockholders' equity. They are summarized as follows:
- (a) Purchased 1,000 shares of treasury common for $35,000.
- (b) Received balance due on preferred stock subscribed and issued the certificates.
- (c) Sold 500 shares of treasury common for $20,200.
- (d) Issued 2,500 shares of common stock at $30, receiving cash.
- (e) Received subscriptions to 1,000 shares of preferred 9% stock at $52.50, collecting 20% of the subscription price.
- (f) Sold 250 shares of treasury common for $7,750.

Instructions:
- (1) Prepare entries, in general journal form, to record the transactions listed above. Identify each entry by letter. (The use of T accounts for stockholders' equity accounts will facilitate the determination of the amounts needed in recording some of the transactions and in completing Instruction (2).)
- (2) Prepare the stockholders' equity section of the balance sheet as of June 30. Net income for the year amounted to $192,500. Cash dividends declared and paid during the year totaled $112,000.

Problem 15-6A. Target Company was organized on July 22 of the current year and prepared its first financial statement as of the following December 31, the date that had been adopted as the end of the fiscal year. The following balance sheet was prepared by the bookkeeper as of December 31.

Target Company
Balance Sheet
July 22 to December 31, 19--

Assets		Liabilities	
Cash.......................	$ 45,100	Accounts payable	$ 72,000
Accounts receivable	190,000	Preferred stock..............	150,000
Merchandise inventory	145,000	Common stock	300,000
Prepaid insurance	4,500	Premium on common stock...	50,000
Treasury preferred stock	25,000		
Equipment..................	125,000		
Retained earnings (deficit)....	37,400		
Total assets	$572,000	Total liabilities	$572,000

You are retained by the board of directors to audit the accounts and to prepare a revised balance sheet. The relevant facts developed during the course of your engagement are:
- (a) Stock authorized: 5,000 shares of $50 par, 12% preferred and 100,000 shares of $10 par common.
- (b) Stock issued: 3,000 shares of fully paid preferred at $55 and 25,000 shares of common at $12. The premium on preferred stock was credited to Retained Earnings.
- (c) Stock subscribed but not issued: 5,000 shares of common at par, on which all subscribers have paid one half of the subscription price. Unpaid subscriptions are included in accounts receivable and are collectible in sixty days.
- (d) The company reacquired 500 shares of the issued preferred stock at $60. The difference between par and the price paid was debited to Retained Earnings. (It is decided that the treasury stock is to be recorded at cost.)

(e) Included in merchandise inventory is $1,250 of office supplies.
(f) Land to be used as a future building site cost $25,000 and was charged to Equipment.
(g) No depreciation has been recognized. The equipment is to be depreciated for one-half year by the straight-line method, using an estimated life of 10 years.
(h) Organization costs of $2,500 were charged to Advertising Expense. (None of the organization costs are to be amortized until next year, the first full year of operations.)
(i) No dividends have been declared or paid.
(j) In balancing the common stockholders ledger with the common stock control account, it was discovered that the account with Barbara Jain contained a posting for an issuance of 100 shares, while the copy of the stock certificate indicated that 1,000 shares had been issued. The stock certificate was found to be correct.

Instructions:
(1) Prepare general journal entries where necessary to record the corrections. Corrections of net income should be recorded as adjustments to retained earnings.
(2) Prepare a six-column work sheet, with columns for (a) balances per balance sheet, (b) corrections, and (c) corrected balances. In listing the accounts, leave an extra line blank following the retained earnings account. Complete the work sheet.
(3) Prepare a balance sheet in report form as of the end of the fiscal year.

Mini-Case

Pompano Cooperative Electric Corporation needs $1,500,000 to finance a major plant expansion. To raise the $1,500,000, the chairman of the board of directors suggested that the cooperative first offer common stock for sale at a price equal to the January 1, 1985 equity per share of common stock. The chairman indicated that by setting the price in this way, the value of the current common stockholders' interest in the cooperative would be preserved. Any additional funds that might be needed after this offer expired could be obtained from the issuance of preferred stock.

Since no preferred stock is authorized, the board is considering characteristics of the stock, such as the dividend rate and the cumulative and participating features. So as not to jeopardize common stockholder dividends, the board of directors tentatively approved a dividend rate of 3% for the preferred stock. The board agreed to delay any final action on other aspects of the financing plan until the legal counsel can be contacted to determine the procedures necessary to seek authorization of the preferred stock.

As of January 1, 1985, the stockholders' equity is as follows:

Paid-in capital:		
Common stock, $100 par (50,000 shares authorized, 25,000 shares issued)	$2,500,000	
Premium on common stock	300,000	
Total paid-in capital		$2,800,000
Retained earnings		1,150,000
Total stockholders' equity		$3,950,000

Instructions:
   (1) Determine the equity per share of common stock on January 1, 1985.
   (2) During the board meeting, the chairman asked your opinion of the sugges-
        tion for determining the selling price of the common stock. How would
        you respond?
   (3) What characteristics might you suggest the board consider in designing the
        preferred stock? Comment on the low preferred stock dividend rate tentatively
        approved by the board.

16

CHAPTER

Stockholders' Equity, Earnings, and Dividends

CHAPTER OBJECTIVES

Identify and illustrate alternative terminology used in preparing the stockholders' equity section of the balance sheet.

Describe and illustrate the accounting for corporate income taxes.

Describe and illustrate the accounting for unusual items in the financial statements.

Describe and illustrate the computation of earnings per share.

Describe and illustrate the accounting for appropriations of retained earnings and for dividends and the preparation of a retained earnings statement.

16

As has been indicated, the stockholders' equity section of the balance sheet is divided into two major subdivisions, "paid-in capital" and "retained earnings." Although in practice there is wide variation in the amount of detail presented and the descriptive captions used, sources of significant amounts of capital should be properly disclosed.

The emphasis on disclosure and clarity of expression by the accounting profession has been relatively recent. In earlier days, it was not unusual to present only the amount of the par of the preferred and common stock outstanding and a balancing amount described simply as "Surplus." Readers of the balance sheet could only assume that par represented the amount paid in by stockholders and that surplus represented retained earnings. Although it was possible for a "surplus" of $1,000,000, for example, to be composed solely of retained earnings, it could represent paid-in capital from premiums on stock issued or even an excess of $1,200,000 of such premiums over an accumulated deficit of $200,000 of retained earnings.

PAID-IN CAPITAL

As illustrated in Chapter 15, the main credits to paid-in capital accounts result from the issuance of stock. If par stock is issued at a price above or below par, the difference is recorded in a separate premium or discount account. It is also common to use two accounts in recording the issuance of no-par stock, one for the stated value and the other for the excess over stated value. Another account for paid-in capital discussed in the preceding chapter was Paid-In Capital from Sale of Treasury Stock.

Paid in capital may also originate from donated real estate and redemptions of a corporation's own stock. Civic organizations sometimes give land or land and buildings to a corporate enterprise as an inducement to locate in the community. In such cases, the assets are recorded in the corporate accounts at fair market value, with a credit to Donated Capital. Preferred stock contracts may give to the issuing corporation the right to redeem the stock at varying redemption prices at varying future dates. If the redemption price paid to the stockholder is greater than the original issuance price, the excess is considered to be a distribution of retained earnings. On the other hand, if the amount paid is less than the amount originally received by the corporation, the difference is a retention of capital and should be credited to Paid-In Capital from Preferred Stock Redemption or a similarly titled account.

As with other sections of the balance sheet, there are many variations in terminology and arrangement of the paid-in capital section. Some of these variations are illustrated by the following three examples. The details of each class of stock, including related stock premium or discount, are commonly listed first, followed by the other paid-in capital accounts. Instead of describing the source of each amount in excess of par or stated value, a common practice is to combine all such accounts into a single amount. It is then listed below the capital stock accounts and described as "Additional paid-in capital," "Capital in excess of par (or stated value) of shares," or by a similarly descriptive phrase.

Stockholders' Equity

Paid-in capital:

Common stock, $20 par (50,000 shares authorized, 45,000 shares issued)	$900,000	
Premium on common stock	132,000	$1,032,000
From stock redemption		60,000
From sale of treasury stock		25,000
Total paid-in capital		$1,117,000

Capital

Paid-in capital:

Common stock, $20 par (50,000 shares authorized, 45,000 shares issued)		$ 900,000
Excess of issuance price over par	$132,000	
From redemption of common stock	60,000	
From transactions in own stock	25,000	217,000
Total paid-in capital		$1,117,000

Shareholders' Investment

Contributed capital:

Common stock, $20 par (50,000 shares authorized, 45,000 shares issued)		$ 900,000
Additional paid-in capital		217,000
Total contributed capital		$1,117,000

Significant changes in paid-in capital during the period should also be disclosed. The details of these changes may be presented either in a separate paid-in capital statement or in notes to other financial statements.

CORPORATE EARNINGS AND INCOME TAXES

The determination of the net income or net loss of a corporation is comparable, in most respects, to that of other forms of business organization. Unlike sole proprietorships and partnerships, however, corporations are distinct legal entities. In general, they are subject to the federal income tax and, in many cases, to income taxes levied by states or other political subdivisions. Although the discussion that follows is limited to the income tax levied by the federal government, the basic concepts apply also to state and local income taxes.

For several years, most corporations have been required to estimate the amount of their federal income tax expense for the year and to make advance payments, usually in four installments. To illustrate, assume that a calendar-year corporation estimates its income tax expense for the year to be $84,000. The required entry for each of the four payments of $21,000 (¼ of $84,000), in general journal form, would be as follows:

Income Tax	21,000	
Cash		21,000

At year end, the actual taxable income and the actual tax are determined. If an additional amount is owed, this liability must be recorded. Continuing with the above illustration, assume that the corporation's actual tax, based on actual taxable income, is $86,000 instead of $84,000. The following entry would be required in order to include the income tax expense in the fiscal year in which the related income was earned:

| Dec. 31 | Income Tax............................. | 2,000 | |
| | Income Tax Payable.................... | | 2,000 |

If the amount of the advance payments exceeds the tax liability based on actual income, the amount of the overpayment would be debited to a receivable account and credited to Income Tax.

Income tax returns and related records and documents are subject to review by the taxing authority, usually for a period of three years after the return is filed. Consequently, the determination made by the taxpayer is provisional rather than final. In recognition of the possibility of an assessment for a tax deficiency, the liability for income taxes is sometimes described in the current liability section of the balance sheet as "Estimated income tax payable."

Because of its substantial size in relationship to net income, income tax is often reported on the income statement as a special deduction, as follows:

Palmer Corporation Income Statement For Year Ended December 31, 19--	
Sales..	$980,000
Income before income tax..........................	$200,000
Income tax..	82,500
Net income...	$117,500

INCOME TAX ALLOCATION

The taxable income of a corporation, determined according to the tax laws, is often very different from the amount of income (before income tax) determined from the accounts and reported in the income statement. Differences between the two may be classified as "permanent differences" and "timing differences."[1]

Permanent Differences

The tax laws provide for special treatment of certain revenue and expense items. This results in permanent differences between the amount of income tax

---

[1]*Opinions of the Accounting Principles Board, No. 11,* "Accounting for Income Taxes" (New York: American Institute of Certified Public Accountants, 1967), par. 13.

actually owed and the amount that would be owed if the tax were based on income before income tax. These items may be described as follows:

1. Revenue from a specified source is excludable from taxable income, or an expense for a specified purpose is not deductible in determining taxable income. Example: Interest income on tax-exempt municipal bonds.
2. A deduction is allowed in determining taxable income, but there is no actual expenditure and hence no expense. Example: The excess of the allowable deduction for percentage depletion of natural resources over depletion expense based on cost.

Permanent differences cause no problem for financial reporting. The amount of income tax determined in accordance with the tax laws is the amount reported on the income statement.

Timing Differences

The treatment of certain items results in differences between income before income tax and taxable income, because the items are recognized in one period for income statement purposes and in another period for tax purposes. These timing differences reverse or turn around in later years. The cases in which such differences occur are described as follows:

1. The method used in determining the amount of a specified revenue or expense for income tax purposes differs from the method used in determining net income for reporting purposes. Example: The installment method of determining revenue is used in determining taxable income and the point-of-sale method is used for reporting purposes.
2. The manner prescribed for the treatment of a specified revenue or expense in determining taxable income is contrary to generally accepted accounting principles and hence not acceptable in determining net income for reporting purposes. Example: Revenue received in advance that is to be earned in future years must be included in taxable income in the year received, which is contrary to the basic accounting principle that such revenue be allocated to the years benefited.

Timing differences require special treatment in the accounts. To illustrate the effect of timing differences and their related effect on the amount of income tax reported in corporate financial statements, assume that a corporation that sells its product on the installment basis recognizes the revenue at the time of sale, and maintains its accounts accordingly. At the end of the first year of operations, the income before income tax according to the ledger is $300,000. Realizing the advantage of reducing current income tax, the corporation elects the installment method of determining revenue and cost of merchandise sold, which yields taxable income of only $100,000. Assuming an income tax rate of 45%, the income tax on $300,000 of income would amount to $135,000. The income tax actually due for the year would be only $45,000 (45% of $100,000). The $90,000 difference between the two amounts is due to the timing difference in recognizing revenue. It represents a deferment of $90,000 of income tax to future years. As the installment accounts receivable are collected in later years, the additional $200,000 of income will be included in taxable income and the $90,000 deferment will become a tax liability of those years. The situation may be summarized as follows:

Income before income tax according to ledger	$300,000	
Income tax based on $300,000 at 45%		$135,000
Taxable income according to tax return	$100,000	
Income tax based on $100,000 at 45%		45,000
Income tax deferred to future years		$ 90,000

If the $90,000 of deferred income tax were not recognized in the accounts, the income statement for the first year of operations would report net income as follows:

Income before income tax	$300,000
Income tax	45,000
Net income	$255,000

Failure to allocate the additional income tax of $90,000 to the year in which the revenue is earned may be viewed as an overstatement of net income and an understatement of liabilities of $90,000. To ignore this additional expense of $90,000 and the accompanying deferred liability of $90,000 would be considered by most accountants to be incorrect and unacceptable. It is considered better to allocate the income tax to the period in which the related income is earned. According to this view, the income tax reported on the financial statements will be the total tax expected to result from the net income of the year, regardless of when the tax will become an actual liability.[2] Applying this latter viewpoint to the illustrative data yields the following results, stated in terms of a journal entry:

Income Tax	135,000	
Income Tax Payable		45,000
Deferred Income Tax Payable		90,000

Continuing with the illustration, the $90,000 in Deferred Income Tax Payable will be transferred to Income Tax Payable as the remaining $200,000 of income becomes taxable in later years. If, for example, $120,000 of untaxed income of the first year of the corporation's operations becomes taxable in the second year, the effect would be as follows, stated as a journal entry:

Deferred Income Tax Payable	54,000	
Income Tax Payable		54,000

If installment sales are made in later years, there will be more differences between taxable and reported income, and an accompanying deferment of tax

---

[2]*Ibid*., par. 29.

liability. This will also cause a fluctuation in the balance in the deferred income tax payable account.

In the illustration, the amount in Deferred Income Tax Payable at the end of a year will be reported as a liability. The amount due within one year will be classified as a current liability, and the remainder will be classified as a long-term liability or reported in a Deferred Credits section following the Long-Term Liabilities section.

REPORTING UNUSUAL ITEMS IN THE FINANCIAL STATEMENTS

In recent years, professional accounting organizations have devoted much time to the development of guidelines for reporting unusual items relating to the determination of net income. These items may be divided into four relatively well-defined categories, as follows:

1. Adjustments or corrections of net income of prior fiscal periods.
2. Segregation of the results of discontinued operations from the results of continuing operations.
3. Recognition of extraordinary items of gain or loss.
4. Change from one generally accepted principle to another.

Before examining the guidelines that are presently in effect, a brief summary of earlier viewpoints may be in order. For several years, there were two conflicting theories about the proper function of the income statement: (1) to report the *current operating performance* and (2) to be *all-inclusive*. According to the first theory, only the effects of the ordinary, normal, and recurring operations were to be reported in the income statement. It was considered better to report non-recurring items of significant amount in the retained earnings statement. By so doing, it was argued that readers of the income statement would not draw incorrect conclusions about the "normal operating performance" of an enterprise.

On the other hand, the all-inclusive point of view was exactly the opposite of the current operating performance viewpoint. It required that all revenue and expense items recorded in the current period be reported in the income statement, with significant amounts of a nonrecurring nature properly identified. If nonrecurring items were "buried" in the retained earnings statement, they were likely to be overlooked and the total amount of the periodic net income reported over the entire life of an enterprise could not be determined from its income statements. The all-inclusive viewpoint has prevailed, and most professional accountants agree that it is preferable. The generally accepted guidelines on the subject are discussed briefly in the subsections that follow.

Prior Period Adjustments

Minor accounting errors often result from the use of estimates that are inherent in the accounting process. For example, relatively small errors in amounts provided for income taxes of one or more periods are not unusual. Similarly, annual provisions for the uncollectibility of receivables seldom agree with the amounts of the accounts actually written off. Such errors are normal and tend to be recurring. The effect of these errors should be included with the amounts for the current period.

Errors may also result from mathematical mistakes, mistakes in the application of accounting principles, or oversight or misuse of facts that existed at the time transactions were recorded. The treatment of these errors depends on when they are discovered. Errors that are discovered in the same period in which they occurred were discussed in Chapter 3. The procedure recommended there for correcting erroneous entries that have been posted to the ledger is summarized as follows: (1) set forth the entire entry in which the error occurred by the use of memorandum T accounts or a journal entry; (2) set forth the entry that should have been made, using a second set of T accounts or a journal entry; and (3) formulate the debits and credits needed to bring the erroneous entry into agreement with the correct entry. This procedure is entirely a matter of technique, and no question of principle is involved. After the correction has been made, the account balances are the same as they would have been in the absence of error, and the information given in the income statement and the balance sheet is unaffected.

The effect of material errors that are not discovered within the same fiscal period in which they occurred should not be included in the determination of net income for the current period.[3] Such errors relating to a prior period or periods should be reported as an adjustment of the retained earnings balance at the beginning of the period in which the correction is made. If financial statements are presented only for the current period, the effect of the adjustment on the net income of the preceding period should also be disclosed. If income statements for prior periods are presented in the current annual report, as is preferable, the effect of the adjustment on each statement should be disclosed.

Corrections of this type of error are usually called **prior period adjustments.** For example, the correction of a material error in computing depreciation expense for a prior period would be a prior period adjustment. In addition, a change from an unacceptable accounting principle to an acceptable accounting principle is considered to be a correction of an error and should be treated as a prior period adjustment. An example of such a situation would be the correction resulting from changing from the cash basis to the accrual basis of accounting for a business enterprise that buys and sells merchandise.

Adjustments applicable to prior periods that meet the criteria for a prior period adjustment are rare in modern financial accounting. Annual audits by independent public accountants, combined with the internal control features of accounting systems, lessen the chances of errors justifying such treatment.

Discontinued Operations

A gain or loss resulting from the disposal of a segment of a business should be identified on the income statement as **discontinued operations.** The term *discontinued* refers to "the operations of a segment of a business . . . that has been sold, abandoned, spun off, or otherwise disposed of or . . . is the subject of a formal plan for disposal."[4] The term "segment of a business" refers to a part of an enter-

---

[3]*Statement of Financial Accounting Standards, No. 16,* "Prior Period Adjustments" (Stamford: Financial Accounting Standards Board, 1977), par. 11.

[4]*Opinions of the Accounting Principles Board, No. 30,* "Reporting the Results of Operations" (New York: American Institute of Certified Public Accountants, 1973), par. 8.

prise whose activities represent a major line of business, such as a division or department or a certain class of customer.[5] For example, if an enterprise owning newspapers, television stations, and radio stations were to sell its radio stations, the results of the sale would be reported as a gain or loss on discontinued operations.

When an enterprise discontinues a segment of its operations and identifies the gain or loss therefrom, the results of "continuing operations" should also be identified in the income statement. The net income or loss from continuing operations is presented first, beginning with sales and followed by the enterprise's customary analysis of its costs and expenses. In addition to the data on discontinued operations presented in the body of the statement, such details as the identity of the segment disposed of, the disposal date, a description of the assets and liabilities involved, and the manner of disposal should be disclosed in a note to the financial statements.[6]

Extraordinary Items

Extraordinary gains and losses result from "events and transactions that are distinguished by their unusual nature *and* by the infrequency of their occurrence."[7] Such gains and losses, other than those from the disposal of a segment of a business, should be identified in the income statement as **extraordinary items**. To be so classified, an event or transaction must meet both of the following criteria:

1. *Unusual nature* — the underlying event or transaction should possess a high degree of abnormality and be of a type clearly unrelated to, or only incidentally related to, the ordinary and typical activities of the entity, taking into account the environment in which the entity operates.
2. *Infrequency of occurrence* — the underlying event or transaction should be of a type that would not reasonably be expected to recur in the foreseeable future, taking into account the environment in which the entity operates.[8]

Transactions that meet both of the above criteria are rare. For example, gains and losses on the disposal of plant assets do not qualify as extraordinary items because (1) they are not unusual and (2) they recur from time to time in the ordinary course of business activities. Similarly, gains and losses incurred on the sale of investments are usual and recurring for most enterprises. However, if a company had owned only one investment during its entire existence, a gain or loss on its sale might qualify as an extraordinary item, provided there was no intention of acquiring other investments in the foreseeable future.

The more usual extraordinary items result from major casualties, such as floods, earthquakes, and other rare catastrophes not expected to recur. In addition, gains or losses that result when land or buildings are condemned for public use are considered extraordinary.

---

[5]*Ibid.*, par. 13.
[6]*Ibid.*, par. 18.
[7]*Ibid.*, par. 20.
[8]*Ibid.*

Changes in Accounting Principles

A change in accounting principle "results from adoption of a generally accepted accounting principle different from the one used previously for reporting purposes."[9] The concept of consistency and its relationship to changes in accounting methods were discussed in Chapter 12. A change from one generally accepted accounting principle or method to another generally accepted principle or method should be disclosed in the financial statements of the period in which the change is made. In addition to describing the nature of the change, the justification for the change should be stated and the effect of the change on net income should be disclosed.

The generally accepted procedures for disclosing the effect on net income of a change in principle are as follows: (1) report the cumulative effect of the change on net income of prior periods as a special item on the income statement, and (2) report the effect of the change on net income of the current period. If the financial statements for prior periods are presented in conjunction with the current statements, the effect of the change in accounting principle should also be applied retroactively to the published statements of the prior periods and reported either on their face or in accompanying notes.

The amount of the cumulative effect on net income of prior periods should be reported in a special section of the income statement located immediately prior to the net income. If an extraordinary item or items are reported on the statement, the amount related to the change in principle should follow the extraordinary items.

The procedures should be modified for a change from the lifo assumption for inventory costing to another method or for a change in the method of accounting for long-term construction contracts. For these changes in principle, the cumulative effect on prior years' income is not reported as a special item on the income statement. Instead, the newly adopted principle should be applied retroactively to the income statements of the prior periods and the effect on income disclosed, either on the face of the statements or in accompanying notes. Financial statements of subsequent periods need not repeat the disclosures.[10]

Allocation of Related Income Tax

The amount reported as a prior period adjustment, a discontinued operation, an extraordinary item, or the cumulative effect of a change in accounting principle should be net of the related income tax. The amount of income tax allocable to each item may be disclosed on the face of the appropriate financial statement or by an accompanying note.

Presentation of Unusual Items in the Income Statement

The manner in which discontinued operations, extraordinary items, and the cumulative effect of a change in accounting principle may be presented in the income statement is illustrated as follows. Many variations in terminology and format are possible.

---

[9]*Opinions of the Accounting Principles Board, No. 20,* "Accounting Changes" (New York: American Institute of Certified Public Accountants, 1971), par. 7.

[10]*Ibid.,* pars. 27 and 28.

CAP Corporation
Income Statement
For the Year Ended August 31, 19--

Net sales	$9,600,950

Income from continuing operations before income tax	$1,310,000
Income tax	620,000
Income from continuing operations	$ 690,000
Loss on discontinued operations (Note A)	100,000
Income before extraordinary item and cumulative effect of a change in accounting principle	$ 590,000
Extraordinary item:	
Gain on condemnation of land, net of applicable income tax of $65,000	150,000
Cumulative effect on prior years of changing to a different depreciation method (Note B)	92,000
Net income	$ 832,000

Note A. On July 1 of the current year, the entire electrical products division of the corporation was sold at a loss of $100,000, net of applicable income tax of $50,000. The net sales of the division for the current year were $2,900,000. The assets sold were composed of inventories, equipment, and plant totaling $2,100,000, and the liabilities assumed by the purchaser amounted to $600,000.

Note B. Depreciation of property, plant, and equipment has been computed by the straight-line method at all manufacturing facilities in 19--. Prior to 19--, depreciation of equipment for one of the divisions had been computed on the double-declining balance method. In 19--, the straight-line method was adopted for this division in order to achieve uniformity and to more appropriately match the remaining depreciation charges with the estimated economic utility of such assets. Pursuant to APB Opinion 20, this change in depreciation has been applied retroactively to prior years. The effect of the change was to increase income before extraordinary items for 19-- by approximately $30,000. The adjustment of $92,000 (after reduction for income tax of $88,000) to apply retroactively the new method is also included in income for 19--.

EARNINGS PER COMMON SHARE

Data on earnings per share of common stock are reported on the income statements of public corporations.[11] The data are also often reported in the financial press and by various statistical services. Sometimes called the "bottom line of the income statement," earnings per share is often the item of greatest interest contained in corporate annual reports.

---

[11]Nonpublic corporations are exempt from this requirement, according to *Statement of Financial Accounting Standards, No. 21*, "Suspension of the Reporting of Earnings per Share and Segment Information by Nonpublic Enterprises" (Stamford: Financial Accounting Standards Board, 1978).

The effect of nonrecurring additions to or deductions from income of a period should be considered in computing earnings per share. Otherwise, a single per share amount based on net income would be misleading. To illustrate this point, assume that the corporation whose partial income statement appears above reported net income of $700,000 for the preceding year, with no extraordinary or other special items. Assume also that its capital stock was composed of 200,000 common shares outstanding during the entire two-year period. If the earnings per share of $3.50 ($700,000 ÷ 200,000) for the preceding year were compared with the earnings per share of $4.16 ($832,000 ÷ 200,000) for the current year, it would appear that operations had greatly improved. The per share amount for the current year comparable to $3.50 is in reality $3.45 ($690,000 ÷ 200,000), which indicates a slight downward trend in normal operations.

Data on earnings per share should be presented in conjunction with the income statement. If there are nonrecurring items on the statement, the per share amounts should be presented for (1) income from continuing operations, (2) income before extraordinary items and cumulative effect of a change in accounting principle, (3) cumulative effect of a change in accounting principle, (4) net income.[12] Presentation of per share amounts is optional for gain or loss on discontinued operations and for extraordinary items. The per share data may be shown in parentheses or added at the bottom of the statement, as in the following illustration:

CAP Corporation Income Statement For the Year Ended August 31, 19--	
Income from continuing operations	$690,000
Net income...	$832,000
Earnings per common share:	
Income from continuing operations	$3.45
Loss on discontinued operations	.50
Income before extraordinary item and cumulative effect of a change in accounting principle	$2.95
Extraordinary item...	.75
Cumulative effect on prior years of changing to a different depreciation method	.46
Net income...	$4.16

---

[12]*Opinions of the Accounting Principles Board, No. 15,* "Earnings per Share" (New York: American Institute of Certified Public Accountants, 1969) as amended by *Opinions of the Accounting Principles Board, No. 20* and *Opinions of the Accounting Principles Board, No. 30.*

In computing the earnings per share of common stock, all factors that affect the number of shares outstanding must be considered. If there is an issue of preferred stock or bonds with the privilege of converting to common stock, two different amounts of per share earnings should ordinarily be reported. One amount is computed without regard to the conversion privilege and is referred to as "Earnings per common share — assuming no dilution" or "Primary earnings per share." The other computation is based on the assumption that the convertible preferred stock or bonds are converted to common stock, and the amount is referred to as "Earnings per common share — assuming full dilution" or "Fully diluted earnings per share."[13] These and other complexities of capital structure are discussed in advanced accounting texts.

APPROPRIATION OF RETAINED EARNINGS

The amount of a corporation's retained earnings available for distribution to its shareholders may be limited by action of the board of directors. The amount restricted, which is called an **appropriation** or a **reserve,** remains a part of retained earnings and should be so classified in the financial statements. An appropriation can be effected by transferring the desired amount from Retained Earnings to a special account designating its purpose, such as Appropriation for Plant Expansion.

Appropriations may be initiated by the directors, or they may be required by law or contract. Some states require that a corporation retain earnings equal to the amount paid for treasury stock. For example, if a corporation with accumulated earnings of $200,000 purchases shares of its own issued stock for $50,000, the corporation would not be permitted to pay more than $150,000 in dividends. The restriction is equal to the $50,000 paid for the treasury stock and assures that legal capital will not be impaired by a declaration of dividends. The entry to record the appropriation would be:

| Apr. 24 | Retained Earnings.......................... | 50,000 | |
| | Appropriation for Treasury Stock .... | | 50,000 |

When a part or all of an appropriation is no longer needed, the amount should be transferred back to the retained earnings account. Thus, if the corporation in the above illustration sells the treasury stock, the appropriation would be eliminated by the following entry:

| Nov. 10 | Appropriation for Treasury Stock .... | 50,000 | |
| | Retained Earnings...................... | | 50,000 |

---

[13]*Opinions of the Accounting Principles Board, No. 15,* "Earnings per Share" (New York: American Institute of Certified Public Accountants, 1969), par. 16.

When a corporation borrows a large amount through issuance of bonds or long-term notes, the agreement may provide for restrictions on dividends until the debt is paid. The contract may stipulate that retained earnings equal to the amount borrowed be restricted during the entire period of the loan, or it may require that the restriction be built up by annual appropriations. For example, assume that a corporation borrows $700,000 on ten-year bonds. If equal annual appropriations were to be made over the life of the bonds, there would be a series of ten entries, each in the amount of $70,000, debiting Retained Earnings and crediting an appropriation account entitled Appropriation for Bonded Indebtedness. Even if the bond agreement did not require the restriction on retained earnings, the directors might decide to establish the appropriation. In that case, it would be a *discretionary* rather than a *contractual* appropriation. The entries would be the same in either case.

It must be clearly understood that the appropriation account is not directly related to any certain group of asset accounts. Its existence does not imply that there is an equivalent amount of cash or other assets set aside in a special fund. The appropriation serves the purpose of restricting dividends, but it does not assure that the cash that might otherwise be distributed as dividends will not be invested in additional inventories or other assets, or used to reduce liabilities.

Appropriations of retained earnings may be accompanied by a segregation of cash or marketable securities, in which case the appropriation is said to be funded. Accumulation of such funds is discussed in Chapter 17.

There are other purposes for which the directors may consider appropriations desirable. A company may earmark earnings for specific contingencies, such as inventory price declines or an adverse decision on a pending law suit. Some companies with properties in many locations may assume their own risk of losses from fire, windstorm, and other casualties rather than obtain protection from insurance companies. In such cases, the appropriation account would be entitled Appropriation for Self-Insurance. Such an appropriation is likely to be permanent, although its amount may vary as the total value of properties and the extent of fire protection change. If a loss occurs, it should be debited to a special loss account rather than to the appropriation account. It is definitely a loss of the particular period and should be reported in the income statement.

The details of retained earnings may be presented in the balance sheet in the following manner. The item designated "Unappropriated" is the balance of the retained earnings account.

Retained earnings:		
Appropriated:		
For plant expansion	$ 250,000	
Unappropriated	1,800,000	
Total retained earnings		$2,050,000

Restrictions on retained earnings do not need to be formalized in the ledger. However, following legal requirements and contractual restrictions is necessary, and the nature and the amount of all restrictions should always be disclosed in the balance sheet. For example, the appropriations data appearing in the foregoing illustration could be presented in a note accompanying the balance sheet. Such an alternative might also be used as a means of simplifying or condensing the balance sheet, even though appropriation accounts are maintained in the ledger. The alternative balance sheet presentation, including the note, might appear as follows:

Retained earnings (see note) $2,050,000

Note: Retained earnings in the amount of $250,000 are appropriated for expansion of plant facilities; the remaining $1,800,000 is unrestricted.

NATURE OF DIVIDENDS

A dividend is a distribution by a corporation to its shareholders. It is usually on a pro rata basis for all shares of a certain class. In most cases, dividends represent distributions from retained earnings. In many states, dividends may be declared from the excess of paid-in capital over par or stated value, but such dividends are unusual. The term **liquidating dividend** is applied to a distribution from paid-in capital when a corporation permanently reduces its operations or winds up its affairs completely. The discussion that follows deals with dividends based on accumulated earnings.

Dividends may be paid in cash, in stock of the company, in scrip, or in other property. The two most common types of dividends are **cash dividends** and **stock dividends** (stock of the company issuing the dividend).

Usually there are three prerequisites to paying a cash dividend: (1) sufficient unappropriated retained earnings, (2) sufficient cash, and (3) formal action by the board of directors. A large amount of accumulated earnings does not always mean that a corporation is able to pay dividends. There must also be enough cash in excess of routine requirements. The amount of retained earnings, which represents net income retained in the business, is not directly related to cash. The cash provided by the net income may have been used to purchase assets, to reduce liabilities, or for other purposes. The directors are not required by law to declare dividends, even when both retained earnings and cash appear to be sufficient. When a dividend has been declared, however, it becomes a liability of the corporation.

Corporations with a wide distribution of stock usually try to maintain a stable dividend record. They may retain a large part of earnings in good years in order to be able to continue dividend payments in lean years. Dividends may be paid once a year or on a semiannual or quarterly basis. The tendency is to pay quarterly dividends on both common and preferred stock. In particularly good years, the directors may declare an "extra" dividend on common stock. It may be paid at one of the usual dividend dates or at some other date. The designation "extra" indicates that the board of directors does not anticipate an increase in the amount of the "regular" dividend.

Notice of a dividend declaration is usually reported in financial publications and newspapers. The notice identifies three different dates related to a declaration:

(1) the date of declaration, (2) the date of record, and (3) the date of payment. The first is the date the directors take formal action declaring the dividend, the second is the date as of which ownership of shares is to be determined, and the third is the date payment is to be made. For example, a notice might read: On October 11, the board of directors declared a quarterly cash dividend to stockholders of record as of the close of business on October 21, payable on November 15.

The liability for a dividend is recorded on the declaration date, when the formal action is taken by the directors. No entry is required on the date of record, which merely fixes the date for determining the identity of the stockholders entitled to receive the dividend. The period of time between the record date and the payment date is provided to permit completion of postings to the stockholders ledger and preparation of the dividend checks. The liability of the corporation is paid by the mailing of the checks.

Dividends on cumulative preferred stock do not become a liability of the corporation until formal action is taken by the board of directors. However, dividends in arrears at a balance sheet date should be disclosed by a footnote, a parenthetical notation, or a segregation of retained earnings similar to the following:

Retained earnings:
Required to meet dividends in arrears on preferred
    stock... $30,000
    Remainder, unrestricted........................... 16,000
      Total retained earnings......................... $46,000

Cash Dividends

Dividends payable in cash are by far the most usual form of dividend. Dividends on common stock are usually stated in terms of dollars and cents rather than as a percentage of par. Dividends on preferred stock may be stated either in monetary terms or as a percentage of par. For example, the annual dividend rate on a particular $100 par preferred stock may be stated as either $10 or 10%.

Assuming a sufficient balance in retained earnings, including estimated net income of the current year, the directors usually consider the following factors in determining whether to declare a dividend:

1. The company's working capital position.
2. Resources needed for planned expansion or replacement of facilities.
3. Maturity dates of large liabilities.
4. Future business prospects of the company and forecasts for the industry and the economy generally.

To illustrate the entries required in the declaration and the payment of cash dividends, assume that on December 1 the board of directors declares the regular quarterly dividend of $2.50 on the 5,000 shares of $100 par, 10% preferred stock outstanding (total dividend of $12,500), and a quarterly dividend of 30¢ on the 100,000 shares of $10 par common stock outstanding (total dividend of $30,000). Both dividends are to stockholders of record on December 10, and checks are to be issued to stockholders on January 2. The entry to record the declaration of the dividends is as follows:

| Dec. 1 | Cash Dividends .... | 42,500 | |
| | Cash Dividends Payable .... | | 42,500 |

The balance in Cash Dividends would be transferred to Retained Earnings as a part of the closing process and Cash Dividends Payable would be listed on the balance sheet as a current liability. Payment of the liability on January 2 would be recorded in the usual manner as a debit of $42,500 to Cash Dividends Payable and a credit to Cash.

Stock Dividends

A pro rata distribution of shares of stock to stockholders, accompanied by a transfer of retained earnings to paid-in capital accounts, is called a stock dividend. Such distributions are usually in common stock and are issued to holders of common stock. It is possible to issue common stock to preferred stockholders or vice versa, but such stock dividends are too unusual to warrant their consideration here.

Stock dividends are quite unlike cash dividends, in that there is no distribution of cash or other corporate assets to the stockholders. They are ordinarily issued by corporations that "plow back" (retain) earnings for use in acquiring new facilities or for expanding their operations.

The effect of a stock dividend on the capital structure of the issuing corporation is to transfer accumulated earnings to paid-in capital. The statutes of most states require that an amount equivalent to the par or stated value of a stock dividend be transferred from the retained earnings account to the common stock account. Compliance with this minimum requirement is considered by accountants to be satisfactory for a nonpublic corporation, whose stockholders are presumed to have enough knowledge of the corporation's affairs to recognize the true import of the dividend. However, many investors in the stock of public corporations are often less knowledgeable. An analysis of this latter situation, and the widely accepted viewpoint of professional accountants, has been expressed as follows:

> . . . many recipients of stock dividends look upon them as distributions of corporate earnings and usually in an amount equivalent to the fair value of the additional shares received. Furthermore, it is to be presumed that such views of recipients are materially strengthened in those instances, which are by far the most numerous, where the issuances are so small in comparison with the shares previously outstanding that they do not have any apparent effect upon the share market price and, consequently, the market value of the shares previously held remains substantially unchanged. The committee therefore believes that where these circumstances exist the corporation should in the public interest account for the transaction by transferring from earned surplus to the category of permanent capitalization . . . an amount equal to the fair value of the additional shares issued. Unless this is done, the amount of earnings which the shareholder may

believe to have been distributed to him will be left, except to the extent otherwise dictated by legal requirements, in earned surplus subject to possible further similar stock issuances or cash distributions.[14]

To illustrate the issuance of a stock dividend according to the procedure recommended above, assume the following balances in the stockholders' equity accounts of a corporation as of December 15:

Common Stock, $20 par (2,000,000 shares issued)......	$40,000,000
Premium on Common Stock.........................	9,000,000
Retained Earnings	26,600,000

On December 15, the board of directors declares a 5% stock dividend (100,000 shares, $20 par), to be issued on January 10. Assuming that the average of the high and low market prices on the declaration date is $31 a share, the entry to record the declaration would be as follows:

Dec. 15	Stock Dividends...........................	3,100,000	
	Stock Dividends Distributable.............		2,000,000
	Premium on Common Stock		1,100,000

The $3,100,000 debit to Stock Dividends would be transferred to Retained Earnings as a part of the closing process. The issuance of the stock certificates would be recorded on January 10 as follows:

Jan. 10	Stock Dividends Distributable..............	2,000,000	
	Common Stock.........................		2,000,000

The effect of the stock dividend is to transfer $3,100,000 from the retained earnings account to paid-in capital accounts and to increase by 100,000 the number of shares outstanding. There is no change in the assets, liabilities, or total stockholders' equity of the corporation. If financial statements are prepared between the date of declaration and the date of issuance, the stock dividends distributable account should be listed in the paid-in capital section of the balance sheet.

The issuance of the additional shares does not affect the total amount of a stockholder's equity and proportionate interest in the corporation. The effect of the stock dividend on the accounts of a corporation and on the equity of a stockholder owning 1,000 shares is demonstrated by the following tabulation:

---

[14]*Accounting Research and Terminology Bulletins—Final Edition*, "No. 43, Restatement and Revision of Accounting Research Bulletins" (New York: American Institute of Certified Public Accountants, 1961), Ch. 7, Sec. B, par. 10.

The Corporation	Before Stock Dividend	After Stock Dividend
Common stock	$40,000,000	$42,000,000
Premium on common stock	9,000,000	10,100,000
Retained earnings	26,600,000	23,500,000
Total stockholders' equity	$75,600,000	$75,600,000
Number of shares outstanding	2,000,000	2,100,000
Equity per share	$37.80	$36.00

A Stockholder		
Number of shares owned	1,000	1,050
Total equity	$37,800	$37,800
Portion of corporation owned	.05%	.05%

STOCK SPLITS

Corporations sometimes reduce the par or stated value of their common stock and issue a proportionate number of additional shares. Such a procedure is called a **stock split** or **stock split-up.** For example, a corporation with 10,000 shares of $10 par stock outstanding may reduce the par to $5 and increase the number of shares to 20,000. A stockholder who owned 100 shares before the split would own 200 shares after the split. There are no changes in the balances of any of the corporation's accounts, hence no entry is required. The primary purpose of a stock split is to reduce the market price per share and encourage more investors to enter the market for the company's shares.

DIVIDENDS AND STOCK SPLITS FOR TREASURY STOCK

Cash or property dividends are not paid on treasury stock. To do so would place the corporation in the position of earning income through dealing with itself, an obvious fiction. Accordingly, the total amount of a cash (or property) dividend should be based on the number of shares outstanding at the record date.

When a corporation holding treasury stock declares a stock dividend, the number of shares to be issued may be based on either (1) the number of shares outstanding or (2) the number of shares issued. In practice, the number of shares held as treasury stock represents a small percent of the number of shares issued. Also, the rate of dividend is usually small, so that the difference between the end results of both methods is usually not significant.

There is no legal, theoretical, or practical reason for excluding treasury stock when computing the number of shares to be issued in a stock split. The reduction in par or stated value would apply to all shares of the class, including the unissued, issued, and treasury shares.

RETAINED EARNINGS STATEMENT

The retained earnings statement illustrated in Chapter 1 reported only the changes in the account balance due to earnings and dividends for the period. When there are accounts for appropriations, it is customary to divide the statement into two major sections: (1) appropriated and (2) unappropriated. The first section is composed of an analysis of all appropriation accounts, beginning with the opening balance, listing the additions or the deductions during the period, and ending with the closing balance. The second section is composed of an analysis of the retained earnings account and is similar in form to the first section. The final figure on the statement is the total retained earnings as of the last day of the period. This form of the statement is illustrated as follows:

Shaw Corporation Retained Earnings Statement For Year Ended December 31, 19--			
Appropriated:			
Appropriation for plant expansion, January 1, 19--.........		$ 180,000	
Additional appropriation (see below).....................		100,000	
Retained earnings appropriated, December 31, 19--.......			$ 280,000
Unappropriated:			
Balance, January 1, 19--...............................	$1,414,500		
Net income for the year................................	580,000	$1,994,500	
Cash dividends declared	$ 125,000		
Transfer to appropriation for plant expansion (see above) ..	100,000	225,000	
Retained earnings unappropriated, December 31, 19--.....			1,769,500
Total retained earnings, December 31, 19--			$2,049,500

RETAINED EARNINGS STATEMENT

There are many possible variations in the form of the retained earnings statement. It may also be added to the income statement to form a combined statement of income and retained earnings, which is illustrated in Chapter 4.

Self-
Examination
Questions
(Answers in
Appendix C.)

1. Paid-in capital for a corporation may originate from which of the following sources?
   A. Real estate donated to the corporation
   B. Redemption of the corporation's own stock
   C. Sale of the corporation's treasury stock
   D. All of the above

2. During its first year of operations, a corporation elected to use the straight-line method of depreciation for financial reporting purposes and the sum-of-the-years-digits method in determining taxable income. If the income tax rate is 45% and the amount of depreciation expense is $60,000 under the straight-line method and $100,000 under the sum-of-the-years-digits method, what is the amount of income tax deferred to future years?
   A. $18,000   C. $45,000
   B. $27,000   D. None of the above

3. An item treated as a prior period adjustment should be reported in the financial statements as:
A. an extraordinary item
B. an other expense item
C. an adjustment of the beginning balance of retained earnings
D. none of the above

4. A material gain resulting from the condemnation of land for public use would be reported on the income statement as:
A. an extraordinary item   C. an item of revenue from sales
B. an other income item   D. none of the above

5. An appropriation for plant expansion would be reported on the balance sheet in:
A. the plant assets section   C. the stockholders' equity section
B. the long-term liabilities section   D. none of the above

Discussion Questions

1. Name the titles of the two principal subdivisions of the stockholders' equity section of a corporate balance sheet.

2. If a corporation is given land as an inducement to locate in a particular community, (a) how should the amount of the debit to the land account be determined, and (b) what is the title of the account that should be credited for the same amount?

3. A corporation has paid $250,000 of federal income tax during the year on the basis of its estimated income. What entry should be recorded as of the end of the year if it determines that (a) it owes an additional $25,000? (b) it overpaid its tax by $15,000?

4. The income before income tax reported on the income statement for the year is $400,000. Because of timing differences in accounting and tax methods, the taxable income for the same year is $250,000. Assuming an income tax rate of 50%, state (a) the amount of income tax to be deducted from the $400,000 on the income statement, (b) the amount of the actual income tax that should be paid for the year, and (c) the amount of the deferred income tax liability.

5. Indicate how prior period adjustments would be reported on the financial statements presented only for the current period.

6. Indicate where the following should be reported in the financial statements, assuming that financial statements are presented only for the current year:
   (a) Uninsured loss on building due to flood damage. This was the first time such a loss had been incurred since the firm was organized in 1880.
   (b) Loss on disposal of equipment considered to be obsolete.

7. Classify each of the following revenue and expense items as either (a) normally recurring or (b) extraordinary. Assume that the amount of each item is material.
   (1) Interest expense on notes payable
   (2) Uninsured flood loss (Flood insurance is unavailable because of periodic flooding in the area.)
   (3) Uncollectible accounts expense

(4) Salaries of corporate officers

(5) Loss on sale of plant assets

8. During the current year, five acres of land which cost $50,000 were condemned for construction of an interstate highway. Assuming that an award of $90,000 in cash was received and that the applicable income tax on this transaction is 25%, how would this information be presented in the income statement?

9. A corporation reports earnings per share of $4.25 for the most recent year and $4.75 for the preceding year. The $4.25 includes $.75 per share loss from a rare earthquake. (a) Should the composition of the $4.25 be disclosed in the financial report? (b) What is the amount for the most recent year that is comparable to the $4.75 earnings per share of the preceding year? (c) On the basis of the limited information presented, would you conclude that operations had improved or retrogressed?

10. Appropriations of retained earnings may be (a) required by law, (b) required by contract, or (c) made at the discretion of the board of directors. Give an illustration of each type of appropriation.

11. A credit balance in Retained Earnings does not represent cash. Explain.

12. The board of directors votes to appropriate $50,000 of retained earnings for plant expansion. What is the effect of their action on (a) cash, (b) total retained earnings, and (c) retained earnings available for dividends?

13. What are the three prerequisites to the declaration and the payment of a cash dividend?

14. The dates in connection with the declaration of a cash dividend are May 10, May 24, and June 14. Identify each date.

15. A corporation with both cumulative preferred stock and common stock outstanding has a substantial credit balance in the retained earnings account at the beginning of the current fiscal year. Although net income for the current year is sufficient to pay the preferred dividend of $40,000 each quarter and a common dividend of $70,000 each quarter, the board of directors declares dividends only on the preferred stock. Suggest possible reasons for passing the dividends on the common stock.

16. State the effect of the following actions on a corporation's assets, liabilities, and stockholders' equity: (a) declaration of a stock dividend; (b) issuance of stock certificates for the stock dividend declared in (a); (c) authorization and issuance of stock certificates in a stock split; (d) declaration of cash dividend; (e) payment of the cash dividend declared in (d).

17. An owner of 100 shares of Reed Company common stock receives a stock dividend of 4 shares. (a) What is the effect of the stock dividend on the equity per share of the stock? (b) How does the total equity of 104 shares compare with the total equity of 100 shares before the stock dividend?

18. A corporation with 10,000 shares of no-par common stock issued, of which 500 shares are held as treasury stock, declares a cash dividend of $1 a share. What is the total amount of the dividend?

19. If a corporation with 50,000 shares of common stock outstanding has a 4-for-1 stock split (3 additional shares for each share issued), what will be the number of shares outstanding after the split?

20. If the common stock in Question 19 had a market price of $200 per share before the stock split, what would be an approximate market price per share after the split?

Exercise 16-1. Present entries, in general journal form, to record the following selected transactions of Albin Corporation:

Apr. 15. Paid the first installment of the estimated income tax for the current fiscal year ending December 31, $140,000. No entry had been made to record the liability.

June 15. Paid the second installment of $140,000. (Same note as above.)

Dec. 31. Recorded the additional income tax liability for the year just ended and the deferred income tax liability, based on the two transactions above and the following data:

Income tax rate..	45%
Income before income tax	$1,400,000
Taxable income according to tax return	1,250,000
Third installment paid on September 15	140,000
Fourth installment paid on December 15	140,000

Exercise 16-2. Prior to adjusting and closing the accounts at December 31, the end of the current fiscal year, the accountant discovered the following errors which occurred during the year. Present the entry to correct each error.

(a) The declaration of a cash dividend of $15,000 had been recorded as a debit to Interest Expense and a credit to Interest Payable. Payment of the dividend had been recorded as a debit to Interest Payable and a credit to Cash.

(b) A purchase of $950 of office equipment on account was debited to Office Supplies and credited to Accounts Payable.

(c) Delivery equipment that had cost $17,500 and on which $16,500 of depreciation had accumulated at the time of sale was sold for $2,000. The transaction was recorded by a debit to Cash and a credit to Sales for $2,000.

(d) In recording a purchase of office equipment on December 10, for which a note payable was given, Accounts Payable was credited for $9,500.

Exercise 16-3. On the basis of the following data for the current fiscal year ended June 30, prepare an income statement for Fagan Company, including an analysis of earnings per share in the form illustrated in this chapter. There were 100,000 shares of $10 par common stock outstanding throughout the year.

Cost of merchandise sold	$640,000
Cumulative effect on prior years of changing to a different depreciation method..	74,500
Gain on condemnation of land (extraordinary item).....................	94,500
General expenses	48,600
Income tax applicable to change in depreciation method	22,500
Income tax applicable to gain on condemnation of land	28,500
Income tax reduction applicable to loss from discontinued operations.....	18,750
Income tax applicable to ordinary income.............................	96,300
Loss on discontinued operations	61,750
Sales...	995,000
Selling expenses	82,100

Exercise 16-4. A corporation purchased for cash 2,000 shares of its own $50 par common stock at $75 a share. In the following year, it sold 1,000 of the treasury shares

at $88 a share for cash. (a) Present the entries in general journal form (1) to record the purchase (treasury stock is recorded at cost) and (2) to provide for the appropriation of retained earnings. (b) Present the entries in general journal form (1) to record the sale of the stock and (2) to reduce the appropriation.

Exercise 16-5. The dates in connection with a cash dividend of $50,000 on a corporation's common stock are June 30, July 20, and August 5. Present the entries, in general journal form, required on each date.

Exercise 16-6. The balance sheet of Easso Company indicates common stock (100,000 shares authorized), $10 par, $800,000; premium on common stock, $125,000; and retained earnings, $335,000. The board of directors declares a 5% stock dividend when the market price of the stock is $25 a share. (a) Present entries to record (1) the declaration of the dividend, capitalizing an amount equal to market value, and (2) the issuance of the stock certificates. (b) Determine the equity per share (1) before the stock dividend and (2) after the stock dividend. (c) Frank Rossi owned 100 shares of the common stock before the stock dividend was declared. Determine the total equity of his holdings (1) before the stock dividend and (2) after the stock dividend.

Exercise 16-7. The board of directors of the Corski Corporation authorized the reduction of par of its common shares from $100 to $20, increasing the number of outstanding shares to 500,000. The market price of the stock immediately before the stock split is $220 a share. (a) Determine the number of outstanding shares prior to the stock split. (b) Present the entry required to record the stock split. (c) At approximately what price would a share of stock be expected to sell immediately after the stock split?

Exercise 16-8. Janof Corporation reports the following results of transactions affecting net income and retained earnings for its first fiscal year of operations ending on December 31:

Income before income tax	$135,000
Income tax	42,500
Cash dividends declared	30,000
Appropriation for contingencies	25,000

Prepare a retained earnings statement for the fiscal year ended December 31.

Problems
(Problems in Appendix B: 16-1B, 16-2B, 16-3B, 16-4B, 16-5B.)

Problem 16-1A. Differences in accounting methods between those applied to its accounts and financial reports and those used in determining taxable income yielded the following amounts for the first four years of a corporation's operations:

	First Year	Second Year	Third Year	Fourth Year
Income before income tax	$320,000	$355,000	$451,000	$488,000
Taxable income	295,000	335,000	404,000	438,000

The income tax rate for each of the four years was 45% of taxable income and each year's taxes were promptly paid.

Instructions:

(1) Determine for each year the amounts described in the following columnar captions, presenting the information in the form indicated:

Year	Income Tax Deducted on Income Statement	Income Tax Payments for the Year	Deferred Income Tax Payable	
			Year's Addition (Deduction)	Year-End Balance

(2) Total the first three amount columns.

Problem 16-2A. Selected transactions completed by Tidwell Corporation during the current fiscal year are as follows:

Jan. 22. Purchased 2,000 shares of the corporation's own common stock at $31, recording the stock at cost. (Prior to the purchase, there were 50,000 shares of $20 par common stock outstanding.)

Feb. 10. Discovered that a receipt of $725 cash on account from R. Carter had been posted in error to the account of R. Carson. The transaction was recorded correctly in the cash receipts journal.

Apr. 10. Declared a semiannual dividend of $1.50 on 5,000 shares of preferred stock and a 25¢ dividend on common stock to stockholders of record on April 30, payable on July 10.

July 10. Paid the cash dividends.

Aug. 22. Sold 800 shares of treasury stock at $35, receiving cash.

Oct. 3. Declared semiannual dividends of $1.50 on the preferred stock and 40¢ on the common stock. In addition, a 5% common stock dividend was declared on the common stock outstanding, to be capitalized at the fair market value of the common stock, which is estimated at $30.

Nov. 16. Paid the cash dividends and issued the certificates for the common stock dividend.

Dec. 8. Recorded $96,250 additional federal income tax allocable to net income for the year. Of this amount, $67,500 is a current liability and $28,750 is deferred.

30. The board of directors authorized the appropriation necessitated by the holding of treasury stock.

Instructions:

Record the transactions in general journal form.

Problem 16-3A. The retained earnings accounts of Smid Corporation for the current fiscal year ended December 31 are as follows:

ACCOUNT APPROPRIATION FOR PLANT EXPANSION   ACCOUNT NO. 3201

Date		Item	Debit	Credit	Balance	
					Debit	Credit
19--						
Jan.	1	Balance				200,000
Dec.	31	Retained earnings		50,000		250,000

ACCOUNT APPROPRIATION FOR BONDED INDEBTEDNESS   ACCOUNT NO. 3202

Date		Item	Debit	Credit	Balance	
					Debit	Credit
19--						
Jan.	1	Balance				525,000
Dec.	31	Retained earnings	125,000			400,000

ACCOUNT RETAINED EARNINGS   ACCOUNT NO. 3301

Date		Item	Debit	Credit	Balance	
					Debit	Credit
19--						
Jan.	1	Balance				749,000
Dec.	31	Income summary		165,000		914,000
	31	Appropriation for plant expansion	50,000			864,000
	31	Appropriation for bonded indebtedness		125,000		989,000
	31	Cash dividends	75,000			914,000
	31	Stock dividends	100,000			814,000

ACCOUNT CASH DIVIDENDS   ACCOUNT NO. 3302

Date		Item	Debit	Credit	Balance	
					Debit	Credit
19						
Nov	21		75,000		75,000	
Dec.	31	Retained earnings		75,000	—	—

ACCOUNT STOCK DIVIDENDS   ACCOUNT NO. 3303

Date		Item	Debit	Credit	Balance	
					Debit	Credit
19--						
Dec.	10		100,000		100,000	
Dec.	31	Retained earnings		100,000	—	—

Instructions:
Prepare a retained earnings statement for the fiscal year ended December 31.

Problem 16-4A. The following data were selected from the records of M. C. Yates Inc. for the current fiscal year ended December 31:

Merchandise inventory (January 1)	$115,000
Merchandise inventory (December 31)	138,000
Office salaries expense	40,000
Depreciation expense—store equipment	8,850
Sales	928,500
Sales salaries expense	40,000
Sales commissions expense	52,100
Advertising expense	25,750
Purchases	582,500
Rent expense	21,000

Delivery expense	$17,420
Store supplies expense	7,230
Office supplies expense	1,220
Insurance expense	9,000
Depreciation expense—office equipment	4,120
Miscellaneous selling expense	8,750
Miscellaneous general expense	4,560
Interest expense	24,000
Loss from disposal of a segment of the business	35,750
Gain on condemnation of land	13,000
Income tax:	
Net of amounts allocable to discontinued operations and extraordinary item	26,600
Reduction applicable to loss from disposal of a segment of the business	7,150
Applicable to gain on condemnation of land	2,600

Instructions:

Prepare a multiple-step income statement, concluding with a section for earnings per share in the form illustrated in this chapter. There were 20,000 shares of common stock (no preferred) outstanding throughout the year. Assume that the gain on condemnation of land is an extraordinary item.

Problem 16-5A. The stockholders' equity accounts of Anderson Enterprises Inc., with balances on January 1 of the current fiscal year, are as follows:

Common Stock, stated value $25 (75,000 shares authorized, 40,000 shares issued)	$1,000,000
Paid-In Capital in Excess of Stated Value	125,000
Appropriation for Contingencies	50,000
Appropriation for Treasury Stock	110,000
Retained Earnings	575,500
Treasury Stock (4,000 shares, at cost)	110,000

The following selected transactions occurred during the year:

Jan. 30.   Received land with an estimated fair market value of $50,000 from the city as a donation.

Feb. 1.   Paid cash dividends of $1 per share on the common stock. The dividend had been properly recorded when declared on December 20 of the preceding fiscal year for $36,000.

Mar. 19.   Sold all of the treasury stock for $125,000 cash.

Apr. 29.   Issued 2,000 shares of common stock for $56,000 cash.

June 14.   Declared a 4% stock dividend on common stock, to be capitalized at the market price of the stock, which is $30 a share.

Aug. 18.   Issued the certificates for the dividend declared on June 14.

Nov. 10.   Purchased 1,000 shares of treasury stock for $36,000.

Dec. 21.   The board of directors authorized an increase of the appropriation for contingencies by $10,000.

21.   Declared a $1.20 per share dividend on common stock.

21.   Decreased the appropriation for treasury stock to $36,000.

31.   Closed the credit balance of the income summary account, $219,250.

31.   Closed the two dividends accounts to Retained Earnings.

Instructions:

(1) Open T accounts for the stockholders' equity accounts listed and enter the balances as of January 1. Also open T accounts for the following: Paid-In Capital from Sale of Treasury Stock; Donated Capital; Stock Dividends Distributable; Stock Dividends; Cash Dividends.

(2) Prepare entries in general journal form to record the selected transactions and post to the eleven selected accounts.

(3) Prepare the stockholders' equity section of the balance sheet as of December 31 of the current fiscal year.

Problem 16-6A. The stockholders' equity section of the balance sheet of DTK Co. as of January 1 is as follows:

Stockholders' Equity

Paid-in capital:		
Common stock, $10 par (100,000 shares authorized, 50,000 shares issued)	$500,000	
Premium on common stock	150,000	
Total paid-in capital		$ 650,000
Retained earnings:		
Appropriated for bonded indebtedness	$175,000	
Unappropriated	330,000	
Total retained earnings		505,000
Total		$1,155,000
Deduct treasury stock (5,000 shares at cost)		65,000
Total stockholders' equity		$1,090,000

The following selected transactions occurred during the fiscal year:

Jan. 7. Issued 20,000 shares of stock in exchange for land and buildings with an estimated fair market value of $75,000 and $380,000 respectively. The property was encumbered by a mortgage of $175,000 and the company agreed to assume the responsibility for paying the mortgage note.

Mar. 15. Sold all of the treasury stock for $75,000.

June 25. Declared a cash dividend of $1.50 per share to stockholders of record on July 15, payable on July 30.

July 30. Paid the cash dividend declared on June 25.

Oct. 9. Received additional land valued at $35,000. The land was donated for a plant site by the Urbana Industrial Development Council.

Nov. 1. Issued 2,000 shares of stock to officers as a salary bonus. Market price of the stock is $15 a share. (Debit Officers Salaries Expense.)

Dec. 1. Declared a 4% stock dividend on the stock outstanding to stockholders of record on December 20 to be issued on January 15. The stock dividend is to be capitalized at the market price of $15 a share.

30. Increased the appropriation for bonded indebtedness by $25,000.

31. After closing all revenue and expense accounts, Income Summary has a credit balance of $180,000. Closed the account.

31. Closed the two dividends accounts to Retained Earnings.

Instructions:

   (1) Open T accounts for the accounts appearing in the stockholders' equity section of the balance sheet and enter the balances as of January 1. Also open T accounts for the following: Paid-In Capital from Sale of Treasury Stock; Donated Capital; Cash Dividends; Stock Dividends; Stock Dividends Distributable.

   (2) Prepare entries in general journal form to record the transactions and post to the ten selected accounts.

   (3) Prepare the stockholders' equity section of the balance sheet as of December 31, the end of the fiscal year.

   (4) Prepare a retained earnings statement for the fiscal year ended December 31.

Problem 16-7A. W. C. Hunt Company is in need of additional cash to expand operations. To raise the needed funds, the company is applying to the Miami County Bank for a loan. For this purpose, the bank requests that the financial statements be audited. To assist the auditor, W. C. Hunt Company's accountant prepared the following financial statements related to the current year:

W. C. Hunt Company
Balance Sheet
December 31, 19--

Current assets:		
Cash	$ 52,500	
Accounts receivable	67,660	
Merchandise inventory	81,000	
Supplies	7,050	$208,210
Plant assets:		
Land	$ 85,000	
Buildings	217,500	
Equipment	77,500	
Patents	31,500	411,500
Total assets		$619,710
Current liabilities:		
Accounts payable	$ 35,700	
Salaries payable	2,950	$ 38,650
Deferred charges:		
Accumulated depreciation—buildings	$ 77,000	
Accumulated depreciation—equipment	22,500	
Allowance for doubtful accounts	2,850	102,350
Stockholders' equity:		
Common stock (25,000 shares authorized, $20 par)	$235,000	
Premium on common stock	25,000	
Retained earnings	139,500	
Net income	79,210	478,710
Total liabilities and stockholders' equity		$619,710

W. C. Hunt Company
Income Statement
For Year Ended December 31, 19--

Revenues:
Net sales	$668,150	
Gain on expropriation of land	33,000	
Total revenues		$701,150

Expenses:
Cost of merchandise sold	$400,890	
Salary expense	59,500	
Loss on discontinued operations	31,350	
Depreciation expense—buildings	29,100	
Utilities expense	18,150	
Insurance expense	11,950	
Depreciation expense—equipment	6,200	
Amortization expense—patents	3,500	
Uncollectible accounts expense	2,925	
Miscellaneous general expense	5,875	
Income tax	36,000	
Dividends	16,500	
Total expenses		621,940
Net income		$ 79,210

In the course of the audit, the auditor examined the common stock and retained earnings accounts, which appeared as follows:

ACCOUNT COMMON STOCK ($20 Par) ACCOUNT NO. 6400

Date		Item	Debit	Credit	Balance Debit	Balance Credit
19--						
Jan.	1	Balance—10,000 shares				200,000
	2	Issued 1,000 shares for				
		patents		35,000		235,000

ACCOUNT RETAINED EARNINGS ACCOUNT NO. 6500

Date		Item	Debit	Credit	Balance Debit	Balance Credit
19--						
Jan.	1	Balance				82,000
	30	Error correction	7,500			74,500
June	1	Donation of land		40,000		114,500
Dec.	28	Appropriation for land				
		acquisition		25,000		139,500

A closer examination of the transactions in these and other accounts revealed the following details:

(a) The patent acquired on January 2 by an issuance of 1,000 shares of common stock had a fair market value of $35,000 and an estimated useful life of 10 years.

(b) A computational error was made in the calculation of a prior year's dividend. The corrected amount of the dividend was paid on January 30 and charged to the retained earnings account.

(c) On June 1, W. C. Hunt Company received a donation of a piece of land. The land account was debited for $40,000, the fair market value of the land at that date.

(d) In anticipation of further land acquisition, the board of directors on December 28 authorized a $25,000 appropriation of retained earnings that resulted in a debit to Land and a credit to Retained Earnings.

(e) After three years of using the straight-line method of depreciation for the buildings, the company changed to the sum-of-the-years-digits depreciation method. The following entry recorded this change:

Depreciation Expense — Buildings 17,600
    Accumulated Depreciation — Buildings 17,600

(f) The income tax expense of $36,000 is the estimated tax paid during the year. The expense based on the corrected net income was determined to be $38,210, allocated as follows:

(1) Income from continuing operations $44,590
(2) Loss from discontinued operations 12,540
(3) Gain on expropriation of land 13,200
(4) Cumulative effect of change in depreciation method...... 7,040

The tax owed at December 31 of $2,210 has not been recorded.

(g) A $2 cash dividend declared on December 28 and payable on February 9 of the next fiscal year was not recorded. The $16,500 of dividends expense represents the mid-year cash dividend paid on July 30 of the current year.

Instructions:

(1) Prepare the necessary correcting entries for the items discovered by the independent auditor. Assume that the accounts have not been closed for the current fiscal year.

(2) Prepare a multiple-step income statement for the current fiscal year, including the appropriate earnings per share disclosure.

(3) Prepare the retained earnings statement for the current fiscal year.

(4) Prepare a balance sheet as of the end of the current fiscal year.

Mini-Case

Gambino Co. has paid quarterly cash dividends since 1978. These dividends have steadily increased from $.25 per share to the latest dividend declaration of $.60 per share. The board of directors would like to continue this trend and are hesitant to suspend or decrease the amount of quarterly dividends. Unfortunately, sales of Gambino Co. dropped sharply in the fourth quarter of 1984 due to worsening economic conditions and increased competition. As a result, the board is uncertain as to whether it should declare a dividend for the last quarter of 1984.

On December 1, 1984, Gambino borrowed $500,000 from First City Bank to use in modernizing its retail stores and to expand its product line in reaction to its competition. The terms of the 10-year, 10% loan require Gambino Co. to:

(a) Pay monthly the total interest due,

(b) Pay $50,000 of the principal each December 1, beginning in 1985,

(c) Maintain a current ratio (current assets ÷ current liabilities) of 2:1,

(d) Appropriate $500,000 of retained earnings until the loan is fully paid, and

(e) Maintain a minimum balance of $20,000 (called a compensating balance) in its First City Bank account.

On December 31, 1984, 30% of the $500,000 loan had been disbursed in modernization of the retail stores and in expansion of the product line, and the remainder is temporarily invested in U.S. Treasury notes. Gambino Co.'s balance sheet as of December 31, 1984, is shown on page 462.

The board of directors is scheduled to meet January 8, 1985, to discuss the results of operations for 1984 and to consider the declaration of dividends for the fourth quarter of 1984. The chairman of the board has asked your advice on the declaration of dividends.

Instructions:

(1) What factors should the board consider in deciding whether to declare a cash dividend?

(2) The board is considering the declaration of a stock dividend instead of a cash dividend. Discuss the issuance of a stock dividend from the point of view of (a) a stockholder and (b) the board of directors.

Gambino Co.
Balance Sheet
December 31, 1984

Assets

Current assets:

Cash..............................		$ 30,000
Marketable securities, at cost (market price, $359,500).................		350,000
Accounts receivable	$ 89,500	
Less allowance for doubtful accounts	12,400	77,100
Merchandise inventory...............		135,500
Prepaid expenses		3,400
Total current assets...............		$ 596,000

Plant assets:

Land..............................		$170,000
Buildings	$960,000	
Less accumulated depreciation	213,500	746,500
Equipment.........................	$436,000	
Less accumulated depreciation	114,500	321,500
Total plant assets.................		1,238,000
Total assets.........................		$1,834,000

Liabilities

Current liabilities:

Accounts payable	$ 66,800	
Notes payable (First City Bank)	50,000	
Salaries payable	3,200	
Total current liabilities..............		$120,000

Long-term liabilities:

Notes payable (First City Bank)		450,000
Total liabilities........................		$ 570,000

Stockholders' Equity

Paid-in capital:

Common stock, $30 par (40,000 shares authorized, 15,000 shares issued) ...	$450,000	
Premium on common stock..........	22,500	
Total paid-in capital...............		$472,500

Retained earnings:

Appropriated for provision of First City Bank loan	$500,000	
Unappropriated	291,500	
Total retained earnings.............		$791,500
Total stockholders' equity		1,264,000
Total liabilities and stockholders' equity ..		$1,834,000

17

CHAPTER

Long-Term Liabilities and Investments

CHAPTER OBJECTIVES

Describe and illustrate the impact of borrowing on a long-term basis as a means of financing corporations.

Describe and illustrate the accounting for bonds payable.

Describe and illustrate the accounting for long-term investments in stocks and bonds.

17

CHAPTER

The acquisition of cash and other assets by a corporation through the issuance of its stock has been discussed in earlier chapters. Expansion of corporate enterprises through the retention of earnings, in some instances accompanied by the issuance of stock dividends, has also been explored. In addition to these two methods of obtaining relatively permanent funds, corporations may also borrow money on a long-term basis by issuing notes or bonds. Long-term notes may be issued to relatively few lending agencies or to a single investor such as an insurance company. Bonds are usually sold to underwriters (dealers and brokers in securities), who in turn sell them to investors. Although the discussion that follows will be limited to bonds, the accounting principles involved apply equally to long-term notes.

When funds are borrowed through the issuance of bonds, there is a definite commitment to pay interest and to repay the principal at a stated future date. Bondholders are creditors of the issuing corporation and their claims for interest and for repayment of principal rank ahead of the claims of stockholders.

FINANCING CORPORATIONS

Many factors influence the incorporators or the board of directors in deciding upon the best means of obtaining funds. The subject will be limited here to a brief illustration of the effect of different financing methods on the income of a corporation and the common stockholders. To illustrate, assume that three different plans for financing a $4,000,000 corporation are under consideration by its organizers, and that in each case the securities will be issued at their par or face amount. The incorporators estimate that the enterprise will earn $800,000 annually, before deducting interest on the bonds and income tax estimated at 50% of income. The following tabulation indicates the amount of earnings that would be available to common stockholders under each of the three plans:

	Plan 1	Plan 2	Plan 3
12% bonds	—	—	$2,000,000
9% preferred stock, $50 par	—	$2,000,000	1,000,000
Common stock, $10 par	$4,000,000	2,000,000	1,000,000
Total	$4,000,000	$4,000,000	$4,000,000
Earnings before interest and income tax	$ 800,000	$ 800,000	$ 800,000
Deduct interest on bonds	—	—	240,000
Income before income tax	$ 800,000	$ 800,000	$ 560,000
Deduct income tax	400,000	400,000	280,000
Net income	$ 400,000	$ 400,000	$ 280,000
Dividends on preferred stock	—	180,000	90,000
Available for dividends on common stock	$ 400,000	$ 220,000	$ 190,000
Shares of common stock outstanding	400,000	200,000	100,000
Earnings per share on common stock	$1.00	$1.10	$1.90

If Plan 1 is adopted and the entire financing is from the issuance of common stock, the earnings per share on the common stock would be $1 per share. Under

Plan 2, the effect of using 9% preferred stock for half of the capitalization would result in $1.10 earnings per common share. The issuance of 12% bonds in Plan 3, with the remaining capitalization split between preferred and common stock, would yield a return of $1.90 per share on common stock.

Under the assumed conditions, Plan 3 would obviously be the most attractive for common stockholders. If the anticipated earnings should increase beyond $800,000, the spread between the earnings per share to common stockholders under Plan 1 and Plan 3 would become even greater. But if successively smaller amounts of earnings are assumed, the attractiveness of Plan 2 and Plan 3 decreases. This is illustrated by the following tabulation, in which earnings, before interest and income tax are deducted, are assumed to be $440,000 instead of $800,000:

	Plan 1	Plan 2	Plan 3
12% bonds	—	—	$2,000,000
9% preferred stock, $50 par	—	$2,000,000	1,000,000
Common stock, $10 par	$4,000,000	2,000,000	1,000,000
Total	$4,000,000	$4,000,000	$4,000,000
Earnings before interest and income tax	$ 440,000	$ 440,000	$ 440,000
Deduct interest on bonds..................	—	—	240,000
Income before income tax................	$ 440,000	$ 440,000	$ 200,000
Deduct income tax	220,000	220,000	100,000
Net income	$ 220,000	$ 220,000	$ 100,000
Dividends on preferred stock	—	180,000	90,000
Available for dividends on common stock ...	$ 220,000	$ 40,000	$ 10,000
Shares of common stock outstanding	400,000	200,000	100,000
Earnings per share on common stock	$.55	$.20	$.10

The preceding analysis focused attention on the effect of the different plans on earnings per share of common stock. There are other factors that must be considered when different methods of financing are evaluated. The issuance of bonds represents a fixed annual interest charge that, in contrast to dividends, is not subject to corporate control. Provision must also be made for the eventual repayment of the principal amount of the bonds, in contrast to the absence of any such obligation to stockholders. On the other hand, a decision to finance entirely by an issuance of common stock would require substantial investment by a single stockholder or small group of stockholders who desired to control the corporation.

**CHARACTER-
ISTICS OF
BONDS**

When a corporation issues bonds, it executes a contract with the bondholders known as a **bond indenture** or **trust indenture**. The entire issue is divided into a number of individual bonds, which may be of varying denominations. Usually the principal of each bond, also called the **face value**, is $1,000 or a multiple thereof. The interest on bonds may be payable at annual, semiannual, or quarterly intervals. Most bonds provide for payment on a semiannual basis.

Registered bonds may be transferred from one owner to another only by endorsement on the bond certificate, and the issuing corporation must maintain a record of the name and the address of each bondholder. Interest payments are made by check to the owner of record. Title to **bearer bonds,** which are also called **coupon bonds,** is transferred merely by delivery and the issuing corporation does not know the identity of the bondholders. Interest coupons for the entire term, in the form of checks or drafts payable to bearer, are attached to the bond certificate. At each interest date, the holder detaches the appropriate coupon and presents it to a bank for payment.

When all bonds of an issue mature at the same time, they are called **term bonds.** If the maturities are spread over several dates, they are called **serial bonds.** For example, one tenth of an issue of $1,000,000, or $100,000, may mature eleven years from the issuance date, another $100,000 may mature twelve years from the issuance date, and so on until the final $100,000 matures at the end of the twentieth year.

Bonds that may be exchanged for other securities under certain conditions are called **convertible bonds.** If the issuing corporation reserves the right to redeem the bonds before maturity, they are referred to as **callable bonds.**

A **secured bond** is one that gives the bondholder a claim on specific assets in case the issuing corporation fails to meet its obligations on the bonds. The properties mortgaged or pledged may be specific buildings and equipment, the entire plant, or stocks and bonds of other companies owned by the debtor corporation. Bonds issued on the basis of the general credit of the corporation are called **debenture bonds.**

ACCOUNTING FOR BONDS PAYABLE

When a corporation issues bonds, it usually incurs two distinct obligations: (1) to pay the face amount of the bonds at a specified maturity date, and (2) to pay periodic interest at a specified percentage of the face amount. The interest rate specified in the bond indenture is called the contract or **coupon** rate, which may differ from the rate prevailing in the market at the time the bonds are issued. If the **market** or effective rate is higher than the contract rate, the bonds will sell at a **discount,** or less than their face amount. Conversely, if the market rate is lower than the contract rate, the bonds will sell at a **premium,** or more than their face amount.

Bonds Issued at Face Amount

To illustrate an issuance of bonds, assume that on January 1 a corporation issues for cash $100,000 of 12%, five-year bonds, with interest of $6,000 payable semi-annually. The market rate of interest at the time the bonds are issued is 12%. The bonds will sell at their face amount because this amount is equal to the sum of (1) the present value of $100,000 to be repaid in 5 years plus (2) the present value of 10 semiannual interest payments of $6,000 each.

The sum of the two present value amounts is the price that a buyer is willing to pay now for the future benefits accruing to the owner of the bonds. In determining these present values, the buyer considers the time value or cost of money. That is, the buyer recognizes that a sum of money to be received in the future is not as valuable as the same sum on hand today because money on hand today can be invested to earn income, whereas a sum to be received in the future has no current earnings potential. Therefore, the present value of the two items in the illustration is influenced by the market rate of interest for similar bonds at the time of issuance.

The present value of the 12%, five-year bonds may be analyzed as follows:

Present value of $100,000 due in 5 years, at 12% compounded semiannually...	$ 55,840
Present value of 10 semiannual interest payments of $6,000 at 12% compounded semiannually	44,160
Total present value of the bonds......................................	$100,000

The basic data for the two present values comprising the $100,000 may be obtained from appropriate mathematical tables.[1] However, for a better understanding of the accounting concepts involved, it is helpful to understand the basics of present value determination.

The first of the two amounts, $55,840, is the present value of the $100,000 that is to be repaid in 5 years. If $55,840 were invested at the present time with interest to accumulate at the rate of 12%, compounded semiannually, the sum accumulated at the end of 5 years would be $100,000. The $55,840 is determined by a series of computations. It is first necessary to determine the number of interest compounding periods and the rate of interest for each period. In the illustration, there are 10 periods and the interest rate is 6%. The problem then is to find what amount multiplied 10 successive times by 1.06 (100% + 6%) will total $100,000. It is thus necessary to divide $100,000 by 1.06 and to continue to divide successive quotients by 1.06 until a total of 10 divisions is reached. Details of the computation of the present value of the $100,000, payable in 10 periods, compounded at the rate of 6% per period, are as follows:[2]

PRESENT VALUE
OF BOND
PRINCIPAL

Period	Present Value at Beginning of Period	Divisor		Present Value at End of Period
1	$100,000	÷ 1.06	=	$94,340
2	94,340	÷ 1.06	=	89,000
3	89,000	÷ 1.06	=	83,962
4	83,962	÷ 1.06	=	79,209
5	79,209	÷ 1.06	=	74,725
6	74,725	÷ 1.06	=	70,495
7	70,495	÷ 1.06	=	66,505
8	66,505	÷ 1.06	=	62,741
9	62,741	÷ 1.06	=	59,190
10	59,190	÷ 1.06	=	55,840

[1]Mathematical tables and their use in determining the present value of bond issues appear in Appendix D.

[2]Small differences may exist in the computations in this chapter as a result of rounding.

If the bond indenture provided that no separate interest payments would be made during the entire 5-year period, the bonds would be worth only $55,840 at the time of their issuance. To express the concept of present value from a different viewpoint, the investment of $55,840 with interest at 12% compounded semi-annually would yield $100,000 at the end of 10 semiannual periods.

The second of the two amounts, $44,160, is the total present value of the series of ten $6,000 interest payments. The payments must be successively divided by 1.06 for a differing number of times from 1 to 10 to determine the present value of each. Details are as follows:

PRESENT VALUE
OF BOND INTEREST
PAYMENTS

Payment Number	Interest Payment	Computations	Present Value
1	$6,000	$6,000 ÷ 1.06 =	$ 5,660
2	6,000	5,660 ÷ 1.06 =	5,340
3	6,000	5,340 ÷ 1.06 =	5,038
4	6,000	5,038 ÷ 1.06 =	4,753
5	6,000	4,753 ÷ 1.06 =	4,484
6	6,000	4,484 ÷ 1.06 =	4,230
7	6,000	4,230 ÷ 1.06 =	3,990
8	6,000	3,990 ÷ 1.06 =	3,764
9	6,000	3,764 ÷ 1.06 =	3,551
10	6,000	3,551 ÷ 1.06 =	3,350

Present value of 10 payments of $6,000 each....$44,160

The total present value of $44,160 can also be viewed as the amount of a current deposit earning 12% that would yield ten semiannual withdrawals of $6,000, with the original deposit being reduced to zero by the tenth withdrawal.

The entry to record the issuance of the $100,000 bonds at their face amount is as follows, in general journal form:

```
Jan.  1  Cash......................................  100,000
            Bonds Payable...........................             100,000
```

At six-month intervals following the issuance of the 12% bonds, the interest payment of $6,000 is recorded in the usual manner by a debit to Interest Expense and a credit to Cash. At the maturity date, the payment of the principal sum of $100,000 would be recorded by a debit to Bonds Payable and a credit to Cash.

Bonds Issued at a Discount   If the market rate of interest is 13% and the contract rate is 12%, the bonds will sell at a discount. The present value of the five-year, $100,000 bonds may be analyzed as follows:

Present value of $100,000 due in 5 years, at 13% compounded semiannu-
    ally.. $53,270
Present value of 10 semiannual interest payments of $6,000, at 13% com-
    pounded semiannually   43,133

Total present value of the bonds...................................... $96,403

The two present values that make up the total are both somewhat less than the comparable amounts in the first illustration, where the contract rate and the market rate were exactly the same. The computations from which the present values above could be derived are the same as in the earlier example, except that the divisor is 1.065 (100% + 6.5%) instead of 1.06.

It is customary to record bonds at their face amount, necessitating a separate contra account for the discount. The entry to record the issuance of the 12% bonds, in general journal form, is as follows:

Jan. 1	Cash.....................................	96,403	
	Discount on Bonds Payable	3,597	
	Bonds Payable..........................		100,000

The $3,597 discount may be viewed as the amount that is needed to compensate the investor for accepting a contract rate of interest that is below the prevailing market rate. From another view, the $3,597 represents the additional amount that must be returned by the issuer at maturity; that is, the issuer received $96,403 at the sale date but must return $100,000 at the maturity date. The $3,597 discount must therefore be amortized as additional interest expense over the five-year life of the bonds. There are two widely used methods of allocating bond discount to the various periods: (1) **straight-line** and (2) **interest.** Although the interest method is the recommended method, the straight-line method is acceptable if the results obtained by its use do not materially differ from the results that would be obtained by the use of the interest method.[3]

Amortization of Discount by the Straight-Line Method

The straight-line method is the simpler of the two methods and provides for amortization in equal periodic amounts. Application of this method to the illustration would yield amortization of 1/10 of $3,597, or $359.70, each half year. The amount of the interest expense on the bonds would remain constant for each half year at $6,000 plus $359.70, or $6,359.70. The entry to record the first interest payment and the amortization of the related amount of discount is as follows, in general journal form:

July 1	Interest Expense	6,359.70	
	Discount on Bonds Payable		359.70
	Cash..................................		6,000.00

Amortization of Discount by the Interest Method

In contrast to the straight-line method, which provides for a constant *amount* of interest expense, the interest method provides for a constant *rate* of interest on

---

[3]*Opinions of the Accounting Principles Board, No. 21,* "Interest on Receivables and Payables" (New York: American Institute of Certified Public Accountants, 1971), par. 14.

the **carrying amount** (also called **book value**) of the bonds at the beginning of each period. The interest rate used in the computation is the market rate as of the date the bonds were issued, and the carrying amount of the bonds is their face amount minus the unamortized discount. The difference between the interest expense computed in this manner and the amount of the periodic interest payment is the amount of discount to be amortized for the period. Application of this method to the illustration yields the following data:

AMORTIZATION OF
DISCOUNT ON
BONDS PAYABLE

Interest Payment	A Interest Paid (6% of Face Amount)	B Interest Expense (6½% of Bond Carrying Amount)	C Discount Amortization (B–A)	D Unamortized Discount (D–C)	E Bond Carrying Amount ($100,000–D)
				$3,597	$ 96,403
1	$6,000	$6,266(6½% of $96,403)	$266	3,331	96,669
2	6,000	6,284(6½% of $96,669)	284	3,047	96,953
3	6,000	6,302(6½% of $96,953)	302	2,745	97,255
4	6,000	6,322(6½% of $97,255)	322	2,423	97,577
5	6,000	6,343(6½% of $97,577)	343	2,080	97,920
6	6,000	6,365(6½% of $97,920)	365	1,715	98,285
7	6,000	6,389(6½% of $98,285)	389	1,326	98,674
8	6,000	6,415(6½% of $98,674)	415	911	99,089
9	6,000	6,441(6½% of $99,089)	441	470	99,530
10	6,000	6,470(6½% of $99,530)	470	—	100,000

The following important details should be observed:

1. The interest paid (column A) remains constant at 6% of $100,000, the face amount of the bonds.
2. The interest expense (column B) is computed at 6½% of the bond carrying amount at the beginning of each period, yielding a gradually increasing amount.
3. The excess of the interest expense over the interest payment of $6,000 is the amount of discount to be amortized (column C).
4. The unamortized discount (column D) decreases from the initial balance, $3,597, to a zero balance at the maturity date of the bonds.
5. The carrying amount (column E) increases from $96,403, the amount received for the bonds, to $100,000 at maturity.

The entry to record the first interest payment and the amortization of the related amount of discount is as follows, in general journal form:

July 1	Interest Expense	6,266	
	Discount on Bonds Payable		266
	Cash....................................		6,000

As an alternative to recording the amortization each time the interest is paid, it may be recorded only at the end of the year. When this procedure is used, each interest payment is recorded as a debit to Interest Expense and a credit to Cash. In terms of the illustration, the entry to amortize the discount at the end of the first year would be as follows:

Dec. 31	Interest Expense	550	
	Discount on Bonds Payable		550

The amount of the discount amortized, $550, is made up of the first two semiannual amortization amounts ($266 + $284) from the preceding table.

Bonds Issued at a Premium If the market rate of interest is 11% and the contract rate is 12%, the bonds will sell at a premium. The present value of the five year, $100,000 bonds may be analyzed as follows:

Present value of $100,000 due in 5 years, at 11% compounded semiannually..	$ 58,540
Present value of 10 semiannual interest payments of $6,000 at 11% compounded semiannually	45,226
Total present value of the bonds.....................................	$103,766

In contrast to the first illustration, the two present values making up the total are both greater than the comparable amounts when the contract rate and the market rate were exactly the same. In computing the present values above, the divisor would be 1.055 (100% + 5.5%) instead of 1.06.

The entry to record the issuance of the bonds, in general journal form, is as follows:

Jan. 1 Cash...	103,766	
Bonds Payable..............................		100,000
Premium on Bonds Payable		3,766

Procedures for amortization of the premium and determination of the periodic interest expense are basically the same as those used for bonds issued at a discount.

Amortization of Premium by the Straight-Line Method

Application of the straight-line method to the illustration would yield amortization of 1/10 of $3,766, or $376.60 each half year. Just as bond discount can be viewed as additional interest expense, bond premium can be viewed as a reduction in the amount of interest expense. The entry to record the first interest payment and the amortization of the related amount of premium is as follows, in general journal form:

July 1 Interest Expense	5,623.40	
Premium on Bonds Payable	376.60	
Cash.......................................		6,000.00

Amortization of Premium by the Interest Method

Application of the interest method of amortization yields the following data:

Interest Payment	A Interest Paid (6% of Face Amount)	B Interest Expense (5½% of Bond Carrying Amount)	C Premium Amortization (A–B)	D Unamortized Premium (D–C)	E Bond Carrying Amount ($100,000 + D)
				$3,766	$103,766
1	$6,000	$5,707(5½% of $103,766)	$293	3,473	103,473
2	6,000	$5,691(5½% of $103,473)	309	3,164	103,164
3	6,000	$5,674(5½% of $103,164)	326	2,838	102,838
4	6,000	$5,657(5½% of $102,838)	343	2,495	102,495
5	6,000	$5,638(5½% of $102,495)	362	2,133	102,133
6	6,000	$5,618(5½% of $102,133)	382	1,751	101,751
7	6,000	$5,597(5½% of $101,751)	403	1,348	101,348
8	6,000	$5,575(5½% of $101,348)	425	923	100,923
9	6,000	$5,551(5½% of $100,923)	449	474	100,474
10	6,000	$5,526(5½% of $100,474)	474	—	100,000

The following important details should be observed:

1. The interest paid (column A) remains constant at 6% of $100,000, the face amount of the bonds.
2. The interest expense (column B) is computed at 5½% of the bond carrying amount at the beginning of each period, yielding a gradually decreasing amount.
3. The excess of the periodic interest payment of $6,000 over the interest expense is the amount of premium to be amortized (column C).
4. The unamortized premium (column D) decreases from the initial balance, $3,766, to a zero balance at the maturity date of the bonds.
5. The carrying amount (column E) decreases from $103,766, the amount received for the bonds, to $100,000 at maturity.

The entry to record the first interest payment and the amortization of the related amount of premium is as follows, in general journal form:

```
July 1  Interest Expense ...........................   5,707
           Premium on Bonds Payable ..................     293
           Cash......................................             6,000
```

BOND SINKING FUND | The bond indenture may provide that funds for the payment of bonds at maturity be accumulated over the life of the issue. The amounts set aside are kept separate from other assets in a special fund called a **sinking fund**. Cash deposited in the fund is usually invested in income-producing securities. The periodic deposits plus the earnings on the investments should approximately equal the face amount of the bonds at maturity. Control over the fund may be exercised by the corporation or by a trustee, which is usually a financial corporation.

When cash is transferred to the sinking fund, an account called Sinking Fund Cash is debited and Cash is credited. The purchase of investments is recorded by a debit to Sinking Fund Investments and a credit to Sinking Fund Cash. As interest or dividends are received, the cash is debited to Sinking Fund Cash and Sinking Fund Income is credited.

To illustrate the accounting for a bond sinking fund, assume that a corporation issues $100,000 of 10-year bonds dated January 1, with the provision that equal annual deposits be made in the bond sinking fund at the end of each of the 10 years. The fund is expected to be invested in securities that will yield approximately 14% per year. Reference to the appropriate mathematical table indicates that annual deposits of $5,171 are sufficient to provide a fund of approximately $100,000 at the end of 10 years. A few of the typical transactions and the related entries affecting the sinking fund during the 10-year period are illustrated as follows, in general journal form:

Deposit of cash in the fund

A deposit is made at the end of each of the 10 years.

Entry: Sinking Fund Cash............................. 5,171
       Cash 5,171

Purchase of investments

The time of purchase and the amount invested at any one time vary, depending upon market conditions and the unit price of securities purchased.

Entry: Sinking Fund Investments....................... 5,000
       Sinking Fund Cash........................... 5,000

Receipt of income from investments

Interest and dividends are received at different times during the year. The amount earned per year increases as the fund increases. The entry summarizes the receipt of income for the year on the securities purchased with the first deposit.

Entry: Sinking Fund Cash............................. 700
       Sinking Fund Income......................... 700

Sale of investments

Investments may be sold from time to time and the proceeds reinvested. Prior to maturity, all investments are converted into cash. The entry records the sale of all securities at the end of the tenth year.

Entry: Sinking Fund Cash............................. 85,100
       Sinking Fund Investments..................... 82,480
       Gain on Sale of Investments.................. 2,620

Payments of bonds

The cash available in the fund at the end of the tenth year is composed of the following:

Proceeds from sale of investments (above) . . . . $ 85,100
Income earned during tenth year   11,520
Last annual deposit   5,171
    Total $101,791

The entry records the payment of the bonds and the transfer of the remaining sinking fund cash to the cash account.

Entry: Bonds Payable 100,000
    Cash   1,791
      Sinking Fund Cash.   101,791

In the illustration, the amount of the fund exceeded the amount of the liability by $1,791. This excess was transferred to the regular cash account. If the fund had been less than the amount of the liability, $99,500 for example, the regular cash account would have been drawn upon for the $500 deficiency.

Sinking fund income represents earnings of the corporation and is reported in the income statement as "Other income." The cash and the securities making up the sinking fund are classified in the balance sheet as "Investments," which usually appears immediately below the current assets section.

APPROPRIATION FOR BONDED INDEBTEDNESS

The restriction of dividends during the life of a bond issue is another means of increasing the assurance that the obligation will be paid at maturity. Assuming that the corporation in the preceding example is required by the bond indenture to appropriate $10,000 of retained earnings each year for the 10-year life of the bonds, the following entry would be made annually:

Dec. 31	Retained Earnings.	10,000	
	Appropriation for Bonded Indebtedness . . .		10,000

As was indicated in Chapter 16, an appropriation has no direct relationship to a sinking fund. Each is independent of the other. When there is both a fund and an appropriation for the same purpose, the appropriation may be said to be funded.

BOND REDEMPTION

Callable bonds are redeemable by the issuing corporation within the period of time and at the price stated in the bond indenture. Usually the call price is above the face value. If the market rate of interest declines after the issuance of the bonds, the corporation may sell new bonds at a lower interest rate and use the funds to redeem the original issue. The reduction of future interest expense is always an incentive to bond redemption. A corporation may also redeem all or a portion of its bonds before maturity by purchasing them on the open market.

When a corporation redeems bonds at a price below their carrying amount, the corporation realizes a gain. If the price is in excess of the carrying amount, a loss is incurred. To illustrate redemption, assume that on June 30 a corporation has a bond issue of $100,000 outstanding, on which there is an unamortized premium of $4,000. The corporation has the option of calling the bonds for $105,000, which it exercises on this date. The entry to record the redemption, in general journal form, is:

June 30 Bonds Payable...............................	100,000	
Premium on Bonds Payable	4,000	
Loss on Redemption of Bonds	1,000	
Cash..		105,000

If the bonds were not callable, the corporation might purchase a portion on the open market. Assuming that the corporation purchases one fourth ($25,000) of the bonds for $24,000 on June 30, the entry to record the redemption would be as follows, in general journal form:

June 30 Bonds Payable...............................	25,000	
Premium on Bonds Payable	1,000	
Cash..		24,000
Gain on Redemption of Bonds		2,000

Note that only the portion of the premium relating to the bonds redeemed is written off. The excess of the carrying amount of the bonds purchased, $26,000, over the cash paid, $24,000, is recognized as a gain.

BALANCE SHEET PRESENTATION OF BONDS PAYABLE

Bonds payable are usually reported on the balance sheet as long-term liabilities. If there are two or more bond issues, separate accounts should be maintained and the details of each should be reported on the balance sheet or in a supporting schedule or note. When the balance sheet date is within one year of the bond maturity date, the bonds should be transferred to the current liability classification if they are to be paid out of current assets. If they are to be paid with funds that have been set aside or if they are to be replaced with another bond issue, they should remain in the noncurrent category and their anticipated liquidation disclosed in an explanatory note.

The balance in a discount account should be reported in the balance sheet as a deduction from the related bonds payable. Conversely, the balance in a premium account should be reported as an addition to the related bonds payable. Either in the financial statements or in accompanying notes, the description of the bonds (terms, security, due date, etc.) should also include the effective interest rate and the maturities and sinking fund requirements for each of the next five years.[4]

---

[4]*Statement of Financial Accounting Standards, No. 47,* "Disclosure of Long-Term Obligations" (Stamford: Financial Accounting Standards Board, 1981), par. 10.

INVESTMENTS IN STOCKS AND BONDS

The issuance of bonds and related transactions were discussed in the preceding paragraphs from the standpoint of the issuing corporation. Whenever a corporation records a transaction between itself and the owners of its bonds, there is a reciprocal entry in the accounts of the investor. A similar relationship exists between the issuing corporation and the investor when the corporation issues shares of its stock. In the following discussion, attention will be given to the principles underlying the accounting for investments in **equity securities** (preferred and common shares) and **debt securities** (bonds and notes) that are identified as long-term investments. The principles underlying the accounting for securities known as temporary investments, which are available to meet the needs for additional cash for normal operations and are classified as current assets, were discussed in Chapter 8.

Investments in corporate securities may be purchased directly from the issuing corporation or from other investors. Stocks and bonds may be *listed* on an organized exchange, or they may be *unlisted,* in which case they are said to be bought and sold *over the counter*. The services of a broker are usually employed in buying and selling both listed and unlisted securities. The record of transactions on stock exchanges is reported daily in the financial pages of newspapers. This record usually includes data on the volume of sales and the high, low, and closing prices for each security traded during the day. Prices for stocks are quoted in terms of fractional dollars, ⅛ of a dollar being the usual minimum fraction. Some low-priced stocks are sold in lower fractions of a dollar, such as ¹⁄₁₆ or ¹⁄₃₂. A price of 40⅜ per share means $40.375; a price of 40½ means $40.50. Prices for bonds are quoted as a percentage of the face amount. Thus, the price of a $1,000 bond quoted at 104½ would be $1,045.

Investments that are not intended as a ready source of cash in the normal operations of the business are known as **long-term investments.** A business may make long-term investments simply because it has cash that it cannot use in its normal operations. Cash and securities in bond sinking funds are considered long-term investments, since they are accumulated for the purpose of paying the bond liability. A corporation may also purchase stocks or bonds as a means of establishing or maintaining business relations with the issuing company. Such investments are usually held for an indefinite period and are not sold so long as the relationship remains saisfactory. Corporations may acquire all or a large part of the voting stock of another corporation in order to control its activities. Similarly, a corporation may organize a new corporation for the purpose of marketing a new product or for some other business reason, receiving stock in exchange for the assets transferred to the new corporation.

Securities held as long-term investments are listed in the balance sheet under the caption "Investments," which usually follows the current assets. A long-term investment in debt securities is customarily carried at cost. The carrying amount of a long-term investment in marketable equity securities of a company over which the investor does not exercise significant influence is determined in a manner like that for a temporary investment in such securities. However, market value changes recognized in applying the lower of cost or market rule are not included in the determination of net income. Instead, the effect of such a change in valuation is reported as a separate item in the stockholders' equity section of the balance sheet.[5] If the "decline in market value below cost as of the balance sheet date of an individual security is other than temporary," the cost basis of the individual security is written down and the amount of the write-down is accounted for as a realized loss. After the write-down, the carrying amount of the individual security cannot be changed for subsequent recoveries in market value.[6]

ACCOUNTING FOR INVESTMENTS IN STOCK

There are two methods of accounting for investments in stock: (1) the **cost method** and (2) the **equity method**. The method used depends upon whether the investment is long-term and whether the investor owns enough of the voting stock of the investee (company whose stock is owned by the investor) to have a significant influence over its operating and financing policies. If the investor does not have a significant influence, the cost method (with the lower of cost or market rule) must be used for either a temporary or a long-term investment. If the investor can exercise a significant influence in a long-term investment situation, the equity method must be used. Evidence of such influence includes, but is not limited to, representation on the board of directors, material intercompany transactions, and interchange of managerial personnel. Guidelines to be applied in making the election are as follows:

> In order to achieve a reasonable degree of uniformity in application, the Board concludes that an investment (direct or indirect) of 20% or more of the voting stock of an investee should lead to a presumption that in the absence of evidence to the contrary an investor has the ability to exercise significant influence over an investee. Conversely, an investment of less than 20% of the voting stock of an investee should lead to a presumption that an investor does not have the ability to exercise significant influence unless such ability can be demonstrated.[7]

Cost Method

The cost of stocks purchased includes not only the amount paid to the seller but also other costs related to the purchase, such as broker's commission and postage charges for delivery. When stocks are purchased between dividend dates, there is no separate charge for the pro rata amount of the dividend. Dividends do not accrue from day to day, since they become an obligation of the issuing corporation only when they are declared by the board of directors. The prices of stocks may be affected by the anticipated dividend as the usual declaration date approaches, but this anticipated dividend is only one of many factors that influence stock prices.

The total cost of stocks purchased should be debited to an investment account. To illustrate, assume that 100 shares of Howe Co. common stock are purchased at 55 plus a brokerage fee of $42. The entry to record the transaction, in general journal form, is as follows:

---

[5]*Statement of Financial Accounting Standards, No. 12,* "Accounting for Certain Marketable Securities" (Stamford: Financial Accounting Standards Board, 1975), par. 11.

[6]*Ibid.,* par. 21.

[7]*Opinions of the Accounting Principles Board, No. 18,* "The Equity Method of Accounting for Investments in Common Stock" (New York: American Institute of Certified Public Accountants, 1971), par. 17.

May 7 Investment in Howe Co. Stock 5,542
          Cash.....................................   5,542

When the cost method is used, cash dividends declared on capital stock held as an investment may be recorded as a debit to Dividends Receivable and a credit to Dividend Income. The receivable account is then credited when the cash is received. A common alternative is to delay recognition of the receivable and the income until the dividend income becomes taxable, which occurs when the cash is received.

A dividend in the form of additional shares of stock is usually not income, and therefore no entry is needed beyond a notation as to the additional number of shares acquired. The receipt of a stock dividend does, however, affect the carrying amount of each share of stock. Thus, if a 5-share common stock dividend is received on 100 shares of common stock with a current carrying amount of $4,200 ($42 per share), the unit carrying amount of the 105 shares becomes $4,200 ÷ 105, or $40 per share.

Equity
Method

When the equity method of accounting is used, a stock purchase is recorded at cost as under the cost method. The features that distinguish the equity method from the cost method relate to the net income and cash dividends of the investee and are summarized as follows:

1. The investor records its share of the periodic net income of the investee as an increase in the investment account and as revenue of the period. Conversely, loss for a period is recorded as a decrease in the investment and a loss of the period.
2. The investor records its share of cash or property dividends on the stock as a decrease in the investment account and an increase in the appropriate asset accounts.

To illustrate the foregoing, assume that as of the beginning of the fiscal years of Otto Corporation and Parker Corporation, Otto acquires 60% of the common (voting) stock of Parker for $350,000 in cash, that Parker reports net income of $70,000 for the year, and that Parker declared and paid $30,000 in cash dividends during the year. Entries in the accounts of the investor to record these transactions are as follows, in general journal form:

1. *Record purchase of 60% of Parker Corp. common stock for $350,000 cash.*

    Entry: Investment in Parker Corp. Stock............... 350,000
            Cash.....................................   350,000

2. *Record 60% of Parker Corp. net income of $70,000.*

    Entry: Investment in Parker Corp. Stock.............. 42,000
          Income of Parker Corp.   42,000

3. *Record 60% of cash dividends of $30,000 paid by Parker Corp.*

Entry: Cash.................................... 18,000
              Investment in Parker Corp. Stock.............   18,000

The combined effect of recording 60% of Parker Corporation's income and the dividends received was to increase Cash by $18,000, Investment in Parker Corp. Stock by $24,000, and Income of Parker Corp. by $42,000.

ACCOUNTING FOR INVESTMENTS IN BONDS

The cost of bonds purchased includes the amount paid to the seller plus other costs related to the purchase, such as broker's commission. When bonds are purchased between interest dates, the purchaser pays the seller the interest accrued from the last interest payment date to the date of purchase. The amount of the interest paid should be debited to Interest Income, since it is an offset against the amount that will be received at the next interest date. To illustrate, assume that a $1,000 bond is purchased at 102 plus a brokerage fee of $5.30 and accrued interest of $10.20. The transaction is recorded by the following entry, in general journal form. It should be noted that the cost of the bond is recorded in a single account, i.e., the face amount of the bond and the premium paid are not recorded in separate accounts.

Apr. 2 Investment in Lewis Co. Bonds................ 1,025.30
        Interest Income.............................   10.20
        Cash.....................................   1,035.50

The price investors pay for bonds may be much greater or less than the face amount or the original issuance price. When bonds are purchased with the expectation of holding them indefinitely, the discount or premium should be amortized over the remaining life of the bonds. The amortization of discount increases the amount of the investment account and interest income. The amortization of premium decreases the amount of the investment account and interest income. The procedures for determining the amount of amortization each period correspond to those described and illustrated on pages 469 to 472.

Interest received on bond investments is recorded by a debit to Cash and a credit to Interest Income. At the end of a fiscal year, the interest accrued should be recorded by a debit to Interest Receivable and a credit to Interest Income. The adjusting entry should be reversed after the accounts are closed, so that all receipts of bond interest during the following year may be recorded without referring to the adjustment data.

As a basis for illustrating the transactions associated with long-term investments in bonds, assume that $50,000 of 8% bonds of Nowell Corporation, due in 8¾ years, are purchased on July 1 to yield approximately 11%. The purchase price is $41,706 plus interest of $1,000 accrued from April 1, the date of the last semiannual interest payment. Entries in the accounts of the purchaser at the time of purchase and for the remainder of the fiscal year, ending December 31, are presented as follows in general journal form:

July 1 Payment for bonds and accrued interest

Cost of $50,000 of Nowell Corp. Bonds	$41,706
Interest accrued on $50,000 at 8%, April 1–July 1 (3 months) . . .	1,000
Total	$42,706

Entry: Investment in Nowell Corp. Bonds	41,706	
Interest Income	1,000	
Cash		42,706

October 1 Receipt of semiannual interest

Interest on $50,000 at 8%, April 1–October 1 (6 months), $2,000

Entry: Cash	2,000	
Interest Income		2,000

December 31 Adjusting entries

Interest accrued on $50,000 at 8%, October 1–December 31 (3 months), $1,000

Entry: Interest Receivable	1,000	
Interest Income		1,000

Discount to be amortized by interest method, July 1–December 31 (6 months):

Interest income (5½% of bond carrying amount of $41,706) .	$2,294
Less interest received (4% of face amount of $50,000)	2,000
Amount to be amortized	$ 294

Entry: Investment in Nowell Corp. Bonds	294	
Interest income		294

The entries in the interest income account in the above illustration may be summarized as follows:

July	1 Paid accrued interest—3 months	$(1,000)
Oct.	1 Received interest payment—6 months	2,000
Dec. 31	Recorded accrued interest—3 months	1,000
31	Recorded amortization of discount—6 months	294
	Interest earned—6 months	$ 2,294

SALE OF INVESTMENTS When shares of stock held as an investment are sold, the investment account is credited for the carrying amount of the shares sold and the cash or appropriate receivable account is debited for the proceeds (sales price less commission and other selling costs). The gain or loss on the sale is recorded in an account entitled Gain on Sale of Investments or Loss on Sale of Investments.

A sale of bonds held as an investment is recorded in much the same manner as a sale of stocks. However, in addition to the sale proceeds, the seller receives the interest accrued since the last interest payment date. To illustrate the recording of a sale of bonds held as a long-term investment, assume that the Nowell Corporation bonds of the preceding example are sold for $47,350 plus accrued interest on June 30, seven years after their purchase. The carrying amount of the bonds (cost plus amortized discount) as of January 1 of the year of sale is $47,080. The entries to record the amortization of discount for the current year and the sale of the bonds are as follows, in general journal form.

June 30 Amortization of discount for current year

Discount to be amortized by the interest method, January 1–June 30, $589

Entry:	Investment in Nowell Corp. Bonds	589	
	Interest Income		589

June 30 Receipt of interest and sale of bonds

Interest accrued on $50,000 at 8%, April 1–June 30 (3 months), $1,000

Carrying amount of bonds on January 1 of current year	$47,080
Discount amortized in current year	589
Carrying amount of bonds on June 30	$47,669
Proceeds of sale	47,350
Loss on sale	$ 319

Entry:	Cash	48,350	
	Loss on Sale of Investments	319	
	Interest Income		1,000
	Investment in Nowell Corp. Bonds		47,669

CORPORATION FINANCIAL STATEMENTS

Examples of retained earnings statements, the stockholders' equity section of balance sheets, and sections of income statements affected by the corporate form of organization have been presented in preceding chapters. A complete balance sheet of a corporation, containing items discussed in this and preceding chapters, is illustrated on pages 481a and 481b.

Some of the many variations in the form of corporation financial statements have been described and illustrated. Additional possibilities are presented in later chapters. Attention has also been directed to many of the alternatives in terminology used to describe items in the statements. Selected statements from the annual reports of a number of corporations are presented in Appendix G.

Connor
Balance
December

Assets

Current assets:

Cash			$ 51,379
Marketable securities, at cost (market price, $78,000)			70,000
Accounts and notes receivable............		$156,000	
Less allowance for doubtful receivables ..		6,000	150,000
Inventories, at lower of cost (first-in, first-out) or market			192,880
Prepaid expenses.........................			12,000
Total current assets			$ 476,259

Investments:

Bond sinking fund	$ 53,962
Investment in affiliated company...........	140,000
Total investments	193,962

Plant assets (depreciated by the straight-line method):

	Cost	Accumulated Depreciation	Book Value	
Land	$ 50,000	—	$ 50,000	
Buildings....................	220,000	$ 79,955	140,045	
Machinery and equipment	764,400	166,200	598,200	
Total plant assets	$1,034,400	$246,155		788,245

Intangible assets:

Goodwill	$100,000	
Organization costs	18,000	
Total intangible assets..................		118,000
Total assets		$1,576,466

---

1. If a corporation plans to issue $1,000,000 of 12% bonds at a time when the market rate for similar bonds is 10%, the bonds can be expected to sell:
   A. at their face amount
   B. at a premium
   C. at a discount
   D. at a price below their face amount

2. If the bonds payable account has a balance of $500,000 and the discount on bonds payable account has a balance of $40,000, what is the carrying amount of the bonds?
   A. $460,000
   B. $500,000
   C. $540,000
   D. None of the above

Corporation
Sheet
31, 19--

Liabilities

Current liabilities:

Accounts payable..........................	$108,810	
Income tax payable	30,500	
Dividends payable	24,000	
Accrued liabilities	11,400	
Total current liabilities...................		$ 174,710

Long-term liabilities:

Debenture 8% bonds payable, due		
December 31, 19--....................	$250,000	
Less unamortized discount..............	5,600	244,400

Deferred credits:

Deferred income tax payable,..............		25,500
Total liabilities................................		$ 444,610

Stockholders' Equity

Paid-in capital:

Common stock, $20 par (50,000 shares au-		
thorized, 20,000 shares issued)...........	$400,000	
Premium on common stock.................	320,000	
Total paid-in capital	$720,000	

Retained earnings:

Appropriated:

For bonded indebtedness........ $ 60,000		
For plant expansion 150,000	$210,000	
Unappropriated...........................	201,856	
Total retained earnings	411,856	
Total stockholders' equity		1,131,856
Total liabilities and stockholders' equity........		$1,576,466

3. The balance in the discount on bonds payable account would be reported in the balance sheet in the:

   A. current assets section   C. long-term liabilities section

   B. current liabilities section   D. none of the above

4. If a firm purchases $100,000 of bonds of X Company at 101 plus accrued interest of $2,000 and pays broker's commissions of $50, the amount debited to Investment in X Company Bonds would be:

   A. $100,000   C. $103,000

   B. $101,050   D. none of the above

5. The cash and the securities comprising the sinking fund established for the payment of bonds at maturity are classified on the balance sheet as:
   A. current assets   C. long-term liabilities
   B. investments   D. none of the above

Discussion Questions

1. When underwriters are used by the corporation issuing bonds, what function do the underwriters perform?

2. How are interest payments made to holders of (a) bearer or coupon bonds and (b) registered bonds?

3. Explain the meaning of each of the following terms as they relate to a bond issue: (a) secured, (b) convertible, (c) callable, and (d) debenture.

4. Describe the two distinct obligations incurred by a corporation when issuing bonds.

5. A corporation issues $1,000,000 of 10% coupon bonds to yield interest at the rate of 12½%. (a) Was the amount of cash received from the sale of the bonds greater than $1,000,000 or less than $1,000,000? (b) Identify the following terms related to the bond issue: (1) face amount, (2) market or effective rate of interest, (3) contract or coupon rate of interest, and (4) maturity amount.

6. If bonds issued by a corporation are sold at a premium, is the market rate of interest greater or less than the coupon rate?

7. What is the present value of $5,000 due in 6 months, if the market rate of interest is 11%?

8. If the bonds payable account has a balance of $750,000 and the discount on bonds payable account has a balance of $37,420, what is the carrying amount of the bonds?

9. The following data are related to a $200,000, 12% bond issue for a selected semi-annual interest period:

   Bond carrying amount at beginning of period $212,400
   Interest paid at end of period...................... 12,000
   Interest expense allocable to the period 11,380

   (a) Were the bonds issued at a discount or at a premium? (b) What is the balance of the discount or premium account at the beginning of the period? (c) How much amortization of discount or premium is allocable to the period?

10. A corporation issues 12%, 25-year debenture bonds, with a face amount of $5,000,000, for 102½ at the beginning of the current year. Assuming that the premium is to be amortized on a straight-line basis, what is the total amount of interest expense for the current year?

11. Indicate the title of (a) the account to be debited and (b) the account to be credited in the entry for amortization of (1) discount on bonds payable and (2) premium on bonds payable.

12. When the premium on a bonds payable is amortized by the interest method, does the interest expense increase or decrease over the amortization period?

13. What is the purpose of a bond sinking fund?

14. If the amount accumulated in a sinking fund account exceeds the amount of liability at the redemption date, to what account is the excess transferred?

15. How are cash and securities comprising a sinking fund classified on the balance sheet?

16. Bonds Payable has a balance of $300,000 and Premium on Bonds Payable has a balance of $11,400. If the issuing corporation redeems the bonds at 106, what is the amount of gain or loss on redemption?

17. Indicate how the following accounts should be reported in the balance sheet: (a) Premium on Bonds Payable, and (b) Discount on Bonds Payable.

18. What are two methods of accounting for investments in stock?

19. When stocks are purchased between dividend dates, does the purchaser pay the seller the dividend accrued since the last dividend payment date? Explain.

20. A stockholder owning 500 shares of Sanders Co. common stock, acquired at a total cost of $14,700, receives a common stock dividend of 25 shares. What is the carrying amount per share after the stock dividend?

21. The quoted price of James Corp. bonds on October 1 is 108½. On the same day the interest accrued is 4% of the face amount. (a) Does the quoted price include accrued interest? (b) If $20,000 face amount of James Corp. bonds is purchased on October 1 at the quoted price, what is the cost of the bonds, exclusive of commission?

22. An investor sells $18,000 of bonds of M Corp., carried at $18,450, for $17,900 plus accrued interest of $300. The broker remits the balance due after deducting a commission of $80. Indicate the debits and credits required to record the transaction.

Exercises

Exercise 17-1. Two companies are financed as follows:

	Cohen Co.	Epps Inc.
Bonds payable, 10% (issued at face value).........	$ 500,000	$1,000,000
Preferred 9% stock (nonparticipating).............	500,000	1,000,000
Common stock, $10 par........................	2,000,000	1,000,000

Income tax is estimated at 50% of income. Determine for each company the earnings per share of common stock, assuming the income before bond interest and income tax for each company to be (a) $300,000, (b) $500,000, and (c) $800,000.

Exercise 17-2. E. C. Sheets Company issued $1,000,000 of 15-year, 13½% callable bonds on March 1, 1984, with interest payable on March 1 and September 1. The fiscal year of the company is the calendar year. Present entries, in general journal form, for the following selected transactions:

1984

Mar. 1 Issued the bonds for cash at their face amount.
Sept. 1 Paid the interest.
Dec. 31 Recorded accrued interest for four months.
      31 Closed the interest expense account.

1985

Jan. 1 Reversed the adjusting entry for accrued interest.
Mar. 1 Paid the interest.

1989

Nov. 1 Called the bond issue at 103, the rate provided in the bond indenture. (Omit entry for payment of interest.)

Exercise 17-3. On the first day of its fiscal year, Lea Corporation issued $3,000,000 of 10-year, 10% bonds, interest payable semiannually, at an effective interest rate of 12%, receiving cash of $2,655,885.

(a) Present the entries, in general journal form, to record the following:
   (1) Sale of the bonds.
   (2) First semiannual interest payment. (Amortization of discount is to be recorded annually.)
   (3) Second semiannual interest payment.
   (4) Amortization of discount at the end of the first year, using the straight-line method. Round to the nearest dollar.
(b) Determine the amount of the bond interest expense for the first year.

Exercise 17-4. On the first day of its fiscal year, Morrison Co. issued $5,000,000 of 10-year, 12% bonds at an effective interest rate of 10%, with interest payable semiannually. Compute the following, presenting figures used in your computations and rounding to the nearest dollar:

(a) The amount of cash proceeds from the sale of the bonds. (Use the tables of present values in Appendix D.)
(b) The amount of premium to be amortized for the first semiannual interest payment period, using the interest method.
(c) The amount of premium to be amortized for the second semiannual interest payment period, using the interest method.
(d) The amount of the bond interest expense for the first year.

Exercise 17-5. Davis Corporation issued $900,000 of 30-year bonds on the first day of the fiscal year. The bond indenture provides that a sinking fund be accumulated by 30 annual deposits of $20,000, beginning at the end of the first year.

Present the entries, in general journal form, to record the following selected transactions related to the bond issue:

(a) The required amount is deposited in the sinking fund.
(b) Investments in securities from the first sinking fund deposit total $18,600.
(c) The sinking fund earned $2,790 during the year following the first deposit (summarizing entry).
(d) The bonds are paid at maturity and excess cash of $6,280 in the fund is transferred to the cash account.

Exercise 17-6. On July 22, O'Brien Corporation acquired 1,000 shares of Jones Co. common stock at 26¾ plus commission and postage charges of $250. On September 15, a cash dividend of $1.50 per share and an 8% stock dividend were received. On November 25, 200 shares were sold at 25½ less commission and postage charges of $36. Present entries in general journal form to record (a) purchase of the stock, (b) receipt of the dividends, and (c) sale of the 200 shares.

Exercise 17-7. At a total cost of $2,500,000, Arnold Corporation acquires 125,000 shares of Micro-Systems Co. common stock as a long-term investment. Arnold Corporation uses the equity method of accounting for long-term investments in common stock. Micro-Systems Co. has 312,500 shares of common stock outstanding, including the 125,000 shares acquired by Arnold Corporation. In general journal form, present entries by Arnold Corporation to record the following information:
   (a) Micro-Systems Co. reports net income of $650,000 for the current period.
   (b) A cash dividend of $.40 per common share is paid by Micro-Systems Co. during the current period.

Exercise 17-8. On August 1 of the current fiscal year, Webster Company purchased $200,000 of 10-year, 10% bonds as a long-term investment directly from the issuing company for $177,059. The effective rate of interest is 12% and the interest is payable semiannually. Compute the following for Webster Company, presenting figures used in your computations:
   (a) The amount of discount to be amortized for the first semiannual interest payment period, using the straight-line method.
   (b) The amount of discount to be amortized for the first semiannual interest payment period, using the interest method.

Exercise 17-9. Present entries, in general journal form, to record the following selected transactions of Sampson Corporation:
   (a) Purchased for cash $150,000 of Dohr Co. 10% bonds at 98 plus accrued interest of $3,750.
   (b) Received first semiannual interest.
   (c) Amortized $200 discount on the bond investment at the end of the first year.
   (d) Sold the bonds at 96 plus accrued interest of $1,875. The bonds were carried at $148,000 at the time of the sale.

Problems
(Problems in Appendix B: 17-1B, 17-2B, 17-3B, 17-5B.)

Problem 17-1A. The following transactions were completed by Turner Industries Inc., whose fiscal year is the calendar year:

1984
Mar.   31. Issued $4,000,000 of 10-year, 10% callable bonds dated March 31, 1984, receiving cash of $3,760,880. Interest is payable semiannually on September 30 and March 31.
Sept. 30. Paid the semiannual interest on the bonds.
Dec.   31. Recorded the adjusting entry for interest payable.
       31. Recorded amortization of $10,461 discount on the bonds, using the interest method.
       31. Closed the interest expense account.

1985
Jan.   1. Reversed the adjusting entry for interest payable.
Mar. 31. Paid the semiannual interest on the bonds.
Sept. 30. Paid the semiannual interest on the bonds.
Dec. 31. Recorded the adjusting entry for interest payable.
       31. Recorded amortization of $15,256 discount on the bonds, using the interest method.
       31. Closed the interest expense account.
1992
Mar. 31. Recorded the redemption of the bonds, which were called at 101½. The balance in the bond discount account is $70,369 after the payment of interest and amortization of discount have been recorded. (Record the redemption only.)

Instructions:

(1) Record the foregoing transactions in general journal form.
(2) Indicate the amount of the interest expense in (a) 1984 and (b) 1985.
(3) Determine the effective interest rate (divide the interest expense for 1984 by the bond carrying amount at time of issuance) and express as an annual rate.
(4) Determine the carrying amount of the bonds as of December 31, 1985.

Problem 17-2A. On March 1, 1984, Redding Corporation issued $5,000,000 of 10-year, 12% bonds at an effective interest rate of 11%. Interest on the bonds is payable semiannually on March 1 and September 1. The fiscal year of the company is the calendar year.

Instructions:

(1) Present the entry, in general journal form, to record the amount of the cash proceeds from the sale of the bonds. Use the tables of present values in Appendix D to compute the cash proceeds, rounding to the nearest dollar.
(2) Present the entries in general journal form to record the following:
    (a) The first semiannual interest payment on September 1.
    (b) The amortization of the bond premium on September 1, using the interest method.
    (c) The adjusting entry for accrued interest payable on December 31.
    (d) The amortization of the bond premium on December 31, using the interest method.
    (e) The reversing entry on January 1, 1985, for the interest payable.
(3) Present the entries for Instruction (2), parts (b) and (d), using the straight-line method of amortization.
(4) Determine the total interest expense for 1984 under (a) the interest method of premium amortization and (b) the straight-line method of premium amortization. (c) Will the annual interest expense using the interest method of premium amortization always be greater than the annual interest expense using the straight-line method of premium amortization?

Problem 17-3A. During 1984 and 1985, Plain Company completed the following transactions relating to its $1,000,000 issue of 20-year, 12% bonds dated February 1, 1984. Interest is payable on February 1 and August 1. The corporation's fiscal year is the calendar year.

1984
Feb.   1. Sold the bond issue for $1,080,400 cash.

Aug. 1. Paid the semiannual interest on the bonds.

Dec. 31. Recorded the adjusting entry for interest payable.

      31. Recorded amortization of $3,685 of bond premium, using the straight-line method.

      31. Deposited $30,000 cash in a bond sinking fund.

      31. Appropriated $50,000 of retained earnings for bonded indebtedness.

      31. Closed the interest expense account.

1985

Jan. 1. Reversed the adjustment for interest payable.

     20. Purchased various securities with sinking fund cash, cost $26,700.

Feb. 1. Paid the semiannual interest on the bonds.

Aug. 1. Paid the semiannual interest on the bonds.

Dec. 31. Recorded the receipt of $4,025 of income on sinking fund securities, depositing the cash in the sinking fund.

      31. Recorded the adjusting entry for interest payable.

      31. Recorded amortization of $4,020 of bond premium, using the straight-line method.

      31. Deposited $35,000 cash in the sinking fund.

      31. Appropriated $50,000 of retained earnings for bonded indebtedness.

      31. Closed the interest expense account.

Instructions:

(1) Record the foregoing transactions in general journal form.

(2) Prepare a columnar table, using the following headings, and list the information for each of the two years.

| | | | | | Account Balances at End of Year | | | |
| | | | | | | Sinking Fund | | |
Year	Bond Interest Expense for Year	Sinking Fund Income for Year	Bonds Payable	Premium on Bonds	Cash	Investments	Appropriation for Bonded Indebtedness

Problem 17-4A. The following transactions relate to the issuance of $600,000 of 10-year, 8% bonds dated January 1, 1975, and the accumulations in a fund to redeem the bonds at maturity. Interest on the bonds is payable on June 30 and December 31.

1975

Jan. 3. Sold the bond issue at 100.

June 30. Paid semiannual interest on bonds.

Dec. 31. Paid semiannual interest on bonds and deposited $36,000 in a bond sinking fund.

1976

Mar. 20. Purchased $32,100 of ITS Company common stock with bond sinking fund cash.

June 30. Paid semiannual interest on bonds.

Oct. 20. Received $2,560 of dividends on ITS Company stock.

Dec. 31. Paid semiannual interest on bonds.

(Assume that all intervening transactions have been recorded properly.)

1985

Jan. 4. All investments in the bond sinking fund were sold for $589,800. The sinking fund investments had a book carrying value of $587,200.

Jan. 12. The cash available in the sinking fund at this date was $598,550. The bonds were paid from the sinking fund cash and the regular cash account.

Instructions:

Record the foregoing transactions in general journal form.

Problem 17-5A. The following transactions relate to certain securities acquired as a long-term investment by Brace Company, whose fiscal year ends on December 31:

1984

Apr. 1. Purchased $100,000 of Damen Company 15-year, 12% coupon bonds dated April 1, 1984, directly from the issuing company for $102,400.

May 22. Purchased 500 common shares of Kamp Corporation at 17⅜ plus commission and other costs of $57.50.

June 1. Received the regular cash dividend of 25¢ a share on Kamp Corporation stock.

Oct. 1. Deposited the coupons for semiannual interest on Damen Company bonds.

Dec. 1. Received the regular cash dividend of 25¢ a share plus an extra dividend of 25¢ on Kamp Corporation stock.

　　31. Recorded the adjustment for interest receivable on the Damen Company bonds.

　　31. Recorded the amortization of premium of $120 on the Damen Company bonds, using the straight-line method.

(Assume that all intervening transactions and adjustments have been recorded properly, and that the number of bonds and shares of stocks owned have not changed from December 31, 1984, to December 31, 1989.)

1990

Jan. 1. Reversed the adjustment of December 31, 1989, for interest receivable on the Damen Company bonds.

Apr. 1. Deposited coupons for semiannual interest on the Damen Company bonds.

June 1. Received the regular cash dividend of 25¢ a share and a 6% stock dividend on the Kamp Corporation stock.

July 1. Sold one half of the Damen Company bonds at 103, plus accrued interest. The broker deducted $540 for commission, etc., remitting the balance. Before the sale was recorded, $40 of premium on one half of the bonds was amortized, reducing the carrying amount of those bonds to $50,700.

Aug. 30. Sold 200 shares of Kamp Corporation stock at 17¼. The broker deducted commission and other costs of $34, remitting the balance.

Oct. 1. Deposited coupons for semiannual interest on the Damen Company bonds.

Dec. 1. Received the regular cash dividend at the new rate of 30¢ a share on the Kamp Corporation stock.

　　31. Recorded the adjustment for interest receivable on the Damen Company bonds.

　　31. Recorded the amortization of premium of $80 on the Damen Company bonds, using the straight-line method.

Instructions:

(1) Record the foregoing transactions in general journal form.

(2) Determine the amount of interest earned on the bonds in 1984.

(3) Determine the amount of interest earned on the bonds in 1990.

Problem 17-6A. The accounts in the ledger of Weathersby Industries Inc., with the balances on December 31, 1984, the end of the current fiscal year, are as follows:

Cash	$ 61,800
Accounts Receivable	137,760
Allowance for Doubtful Accounts	1,000
Merchandise Inventory	140,000
Prepaid Insurance	9,120
Store Supplies	4,120
Bond Sinking Fund	71,800
Store Equipment	380,000
Accumulated Depreciation—Store Equipment	84,000
Office Equipment	136,000
Accumulated Depreciation—Office Equipment	51,080
Accounts Payable	58,200
Interest Payable	——
First Mortgage 12% Bonds Payable	160,000
Premium on Bonds Payable	9,800
Common Stock, $10 par	200,000
Retained Earnings	230,372
Income Summary	——
Sales	1,528,000
Purchases	1,129,760
Purchases Discount	14,480
Sales Salaries and Commissions Expense	98,000
Advertising Expense	25,200
Depreciation Expense—Store Equipment	——
Store Supplies Expense	——
Miscellaneous Selling Expense	9,800
Office and Officers Salaries Expense	74,000
Rent Expense	48,000
Depreciation Expense—Office Equipment	——
Uncollectible Accounts Expense	——
Insurance Expense	——
Miscellaneous General Expense	4,080
Interest Expense	16,000
Sinking Fund Income	7,548
Rent Income	960

The data needed for year-end adjustments on December 31, 1984, are as follows:

Merchandise inventory on December 31 (at cost, last-in, first-out)	$148,000
Insurance expired during the year	5,440
Store supplies inventory on December 31	1,520

Depreciation (straight-line method) for the current year on:
   Store equipment . . . . $ 24,800
   Office equipment   18,720
Uncollectible accounts expense is estimated at ¾% of sales.
Bonds payable are due on November 1, 1989. Interest on bonds
  is payable on May 1 and November 1. Premium to be amortized
  on bonds payable, using the straight-line method   1,680

Instructions:
  (1) Prepare a ten-column work sheet for the fiscal year ended December 31.
  (2) Prepare a multiple-step income statement. (Disregard income tax.)
  (3) Prepare a report form balance sheet.

Mini-Case

You hold a 20% common stock interest in the family-owned business, a soft drink bottling distributorship. Your father, who is the manager, has proposed an expansion of plant facilities at an expected cost of $1,000,000. Two alternative plans have been suggested as methods of financing the expansion. Each plan is briefly described as follows:

Plan 1. Issue an additional 10,000 shares of $10 par common stock at $20 per share and $800,000 of 20-year, 15% bonds at face amount.
Plan 2. Issue $1,000,000 of 20-year, 15% bonds at face amount.

The condensed balance sheet of the corporation at the end of the most recent fiscal year is as follows:

Highpoint Bottling of Shelby
Balance Sheet
December 31, 19--

Assets		Liabilities and Capital	
Current assets	$1,600,000	Current liabilities	$1,800,000
Plant assets	6,400,000	Common stock, $10 par	300,000
		Premium on common stock . .	150,000
		Retained earnings	5,750,000
Total assets	$8,000,000	Total liabilities and capital	$8,000,000

Net income has remained relatively constant over the past several years. The expansion program is expected to increase yearly income before bond interest and income tax from $800,000 to $1,080,000. Assume an income tax rate of 50%.

Your father has asked you, as the company treasurer, to prepare an analysis of each financing plan.

Instructions:
  (1) Prepare a tabulation indicating the expected earnings per share on the common stock under each plan.
  (2) List factors other than earnings per share that should be considered in evaluating the two plans.
  (3) Which plan offers the greater benefit to the present stockholders? Give reasons for your opinion.

18
CHAPTER

Consolidated Statements and Other Reports

CHAPTER OBJECTIVES

Describe alternative methods of combining businesses.

Describe and illustrate the accounting for parent-subsidiary affiliations and the preparation of consolidated financial statements.

Describe and illustrate the accounting for foreign operations.

Identify and illustrate the content of annual reports to stockholders.

Describe current regulatory and reporting developments in financial reporting.

18

CHAPTER

The history of business organization in the United States has been characterized by continuous growth in the size of business entities and the combining of separate enterprises to form even larger operating units. The trend toward combining individual businesses engaged either in similar types of activity or in totally different kinds of pursuits has been influenced by such objectives as efficiencies of large-scale production, broadening of markets and sales volume, reduction of competition, diversification of product lines, and savings in income taxes.

METHODS OF COMBINING BUSINESSES

Combinations may be effected (1) through a joining of two or more corporations to form a single unit by either merger or consolidation or (2) through common control of two or more corporations by means of stock ownership that results in a parent-subsidiary affiliation. These methods of combining separate corporations into larger operating units are complex. Therefore, the discussion that follows is intended to be introductory, with major emphasis on the financial statements of business combinations.

Mergers and Consolidations

When one corporation acquires the properties of another corporation and the latter then dissolves, the joining of the two enterprises is called a **merger.** Usually, all of the assets of the acquired company, as well as its liabilities, are taken over by the acquiring company, which continues its operations as a single unit. Payment may be in the form of cash, obligations, or capital stock of the acquiring corporation, or there may be a combination of several kinds of consideration. In any event, the consideration received by the dissolving corporation is distributed to its stockholders in final liquidation.

When two or more corporations transfer their assets and liabilities to a corporation which has been created for purposes of the takeover, the combination is called a **consolidation.** The new corporation usually issues its own securities in exchange for the properties acquired, and the original corporations are dissolved.

There are many legal, financial, managerial, and accounting problems associated with mergers and consolidations. Perhaps the most important matter is the determination of the class and amount of securities to be issued to the owners of the dissolving corporations. In resolving this problem, several factors are considered, including the relative value of the net assets contributed, the relative earning capacities, and the market price of the securities of the respective companies. Bargaining between the parties to the combination may also affect the final outcome.

Parent and Subsidiary Corporations

A common means of achieving a business combination is by one corporation owning a controlling share of the outstanding voting stock of one or more other corporations. When this method is used, none of the participants dissolves. All continue as separate legal entities. The corporation owning all or a majority of the voting stock of another corporation is known as the **parent company.** The corporation that is controlled is known as the **subsidiary company.** Two or more corporations closely related through stock ownership are sometimes called **affiliated** or **associated** companies.

The relationship of a parent and a subsidiary may be accomplished by "purchase" or by a "pooling of interests." When a corporation acquires a controlling share of the voting common stock of another corporation in exchange for cash, other assets, issuance of notes or other debt obligations, or by a combination of these, the transaction is treated as a purchase. It is accounted for by the **purchase method.** When this method of effecting a parent-subsidiary affiliation is used, the stockholders of the acquired company transfer their stock to the parent corporation.

Alternatively, when two corporations become affiliated by means of an exchange of voting common stock of one corporation (the parent) for substantially all of the voting common stock of the other corporation (the subsidiary), the transaction is termed a pooling of interests. It is accounted for by the **pooling of interests method.** When this method of effecting a parent-subsidiary affiliation is used, the former stockholders of the subsidiary become stockholders of the parent company.

The accounting implications of the two affiliation methods are very different. The method first described is a "sale-purchase" transaction in contrast to the second method, in which there is a "joining of ownership interests" in the two companies.

ACCOUNTING FOR PARENT-SUBSIDIARY AFFILIATIONS

Although the corporations that make up a parent-subsidiary affiliation may operate as a single economic unit, they continue to maintain separate accounting records and prepare their own periodic financial reports. The parent corporation uses the equity method of accounting, described on pages 478–479, for its investment in the stock of a subsidiary.

After the parent-subsidiary relationship has been established, the investment account of the parent is periodically increased by its share of the subsidiary's net income and decreased by its share of dividends received from the subsidiary. At the end of each fiscal year, the parent reports the investment account balance on its own balance sheet as a long-term investment, and its current share of the subsidiary's net income on its own income statement as a separate item.

In addition to the interrelationship through stock ownership, there are usually other intercorporate transactions which have an effect on the financial statements of both the parent and the subsidiary. For example, either may own bonds or other evidences of indebtedness issued by the other and either may purchase or sell goods or services to the other.

Because of the central managerial control factor and the intertwining of relationships, it is usually desirable to present the results of operations and the financial position of a parent company and its subsidiaries as if the group were a single company with one or more branches or divisions. Such statements are likely to be more meaningful to stockholders of the parent company than separate statements for each corporation. However, separate statements are preferable for a subsidiary whose operations are totally different from those of the parent (as when the parent is engaged in manufacturing and the subsidiary is a bank, insurance company, or finance company) or because control over the subsidiary's assets and operations is uncertain (as in a subsidiary that is located outside the United States and that is subject to foreign government controls).

The financial statements resulting from the combining of parent and subsidiary statements are generally called consolidated statements. Specifically, such statements may be identified by the addition of "and subsidiary(ies)" to the name of the parent corporation or by modification of the title of the respective statement, as in *consolidated balance sheet* or *consolidated income statement*.[1]

BASIC PRINCIPLES OF CONSOLIDATION OF FINANCIAL STATEMENTS

When the data on the financial statements of the parent corporation and its subsidiaries are combined to form the consolidated statements, special attention should be given to the ties of relationship between the separate corporations. These ties are represented by the intercompany items appearing in their respective ledgers and statements. These intercompany items, called **reciprocals**, must be eliminated from the statements that are to be consolidated. For example, a note representing a loan by a parent corporation to its subsidiary would appear as a note receivable in the parent's balance sheet and a note payable in the subsidiary's balance sheet. When the two balance sheets are combined, the note receivable and the note payable would be eliminated because the consolidated balance sheet is prepared as if the parent and subsidiary were one operating unit. After the proper eliminations are made, the remaining items on the financial statements of the subsidiary are combined with the like items on the financial statements of the parent.

The intercompany accounts of a parent and its subsidiaries may not be entirely reciprocal in amount. Differences may be caused by the manner in which the parent-subsidiary relationship was created, by the extent of the parent's ownership of the subsidiary, or by the nature of their subsequent intercompany transactions. Such factors must be considered when the financial statements of affiliated corporations are consolidated.

To direct attention to the basic concepts of consolidation, most of the data appearing in financial statements will be omitted from many of the illustrations in the following paragraphs. The term "net assets" will be used as a substitute for the specific assets and liabilities that appear in the balance sheet. Explanations will also be simplified by using the term "book equity" in referring to the monetary amount of the stockholders' equity of the subsidiary acquired by the parent. The illustrative companies will be identified as Parent and Subsidiary.

Consolidated Balance Sheet at Date of Acquisition — Purchase Method

When a parent-subsidiary affiliation is effected as a purchase, the parent corporation is deemed to have purchased all or a major part of the subsidiary corporation's net assets. Accordingly, the assets of the subsidiary should be reported on the consolidated balance sheet at their cost to the parent, as measured by the amount of the consideration given in acquiring the stock. In the subsidiary's ledger, the reciprocal of the investment account at the date of acquisition is the composite of all of the subsidiary's stockholders' equity accounts. Any difference between the

---

[1]Examples of consolidated statements are presented in Appendix G.

cost to the parent and the amounts reported on the subsidiary's balance sheet must be given recognition on the consolidated balance sheet.

Income from an investment in assets does not accrue to an investor until after the assets have been purchased. Therefore, subsidiary company earnings accumulated prior to the date of the parent-subsidiary purchase affiliation must be excluded from the consolidated balance sheet and the income statement. Only those earnings of the subsidiary realized subsequent to the affiliation are includable in the consolidated statements.

Wholly Owned Subsidiary Acquired at a Cost Equal to Book Equity

Assume that Parent creates Subsidiary, transferring to it $120,000 of assets and $20,000 of liabilities, and taking in exchange 10,000 shares of $10 par common stock of Subsidiary. The effect of the transaction on Parent's ledger is to replace the various assets and liabilities (net assets of $100,000) with a single account: Investment in Subsidiary, $100,000. The effect on the balance sheet of Parent, together with the balance sheet of Subsidiary prepared immediately after the transaction, is as follows:

	Assets	Capital
Parent:		
Investment in Subsidiary, 10,000 shares.............	$100,000	
Subsidiary:		
Net assets.......................................	$100,000	
Common stock, 10,000 shares, $10 par.............		$100,000

When the balance sheets of the two corporations are consolidated, the reciprocal accounts Investment in Subsidiary and Common Stock are offset against each other, or *eliminated*. The individual assets (Cash, Equipment, etc.) and the individual liabilities (Accounts Payable, etc.) making up the $100,000 of net assets on the balance sheet of Subsidiary are then added to the corresponding items on the balance sheet of Parent. The consolidated balance sheet is completed by listing Parent's paid-in capital accounts and retained earnings.

Wholly Owned Subsidiary Acquired at a Cost Above Book Equity

Instead of creating a new subsidiary, a corporation may acquire an already established corporation by purchasing its stock. In such cases, the subsidiary stock's total cost to the parent usually differs from the book equity of such stock. To illustrate, assume that Parent acquires for $180,000 all of the outstanding stock of Subsidiary, a going concern, from Subsidiary's stockholders. Assume further that the stockholders' equity of Subsidiary is made up of common stock of $100,000 (10,000 shares, $10 par) and $50,000 of retained earnings. Parent records the investment at its cost of $180,000, regardless of the amount of the book equity of Subsidiary. It should also be noted that the $180,000 paid to Subsidiary's stockholders has no effect on the assets, liabilities, or capital of Subsidiary. The situation immediately after the transaction may be presented as follows:

	Assets	Capital
Parent:		
Investment in Subsidiary, 10,000 shares.............	$180,000	
Subsidiary:		
Net assets.......................................	$150,000	
Common stock, 10,000 shares, $10 par.............		$100,000
Retained earnings................................		50,000

It is readily apparent that the reciprocal items on the separate balance sheets differ by $30,000. If the reciprocals were eliminated, as in the preceding illustration, and were replaced solely by Subsidiary's net assets of $150,000, the consolidated balance sheet would be out of balance.

The treatment of the $30,000 difference depends upon the reason that Parent paid more than book equity for Subsidiary's stock. If the amount paid above book equity is due to an excess of fair value over book value of Subsidiary's assets, the values of the appropriate assets should be revised upward by $30,000. For example, if land that Subsidiary had acquired several years previously at a cost of $50,000 (book value) has a current fair value of $80,000, the book amount should be increased from $50,000 to $80,000 when the asset is reported on the consolidated balance sheet. If Parent paid more for Subsidiary's stock because Subsidiary has prospects for high future earnings, the $30,000 should be reported on the consolidated balance sheet under a description such as "Goodwill" or "Excess of cost of business acquired over related net assets." When the additional amount is due to both an excess of fair value over book value of assets and high future earnings prospects, the excess of cost over book equity should be allocated accordingly.[2]

Wholly Owned Subsidiary Acquired at a Cost Below Book Equity

All of the stock of a corporation may be acquired from its stockholders at a cost that is less than book equity. To illustrate, assume that the stock in Subsidiary is acquired for $130,000 and that the composition of the capital of Subsidiary is the same as in the preceding illustration. Parent records the investment at its cost of $130,000. The situation immediately after the transaction is as follows:

	Assets	Capital
Parent:		
Investment in Subsidiary, 10,000 shares.............	$130,000	
Subsidiary:		
Net assets.......................................	$150,000	
Common stock, 10,000 shares, $10 par.............		$100,000
Retained earnings................................		50,000

Elimination of the reciprocal accounts and reporting the $150,000 of net assets of Subsidiary on the consolidated balance sheet creates an imbalance of $20,000.

---

[2]*Opinions of the Accounting Principles Board, No. 16*, "Business Combinations" (New York: American Institute of Certified Public Accountants, 1970), par. 87.

The possible reasons for the apparent "bargain" purchase and the treatment of the "imbalance" are the reverse of those given in explaining acquisition at a price higher than book equity.

Partially Owned Subsidiary Acquired at a Cost Above or Below Book Equity

When one corporation seeks to gain control over another by purchase of its stock, it is not necessary and often not possible to acquire all of the stock. To illustrate this situation, assume that Parent acquires, at a total cost of $190,000, 80% of the stock of Subsidiary, whose book equity is composed of common stock of $100,000 (10,000 shares, $10 par) and $80,000 of retained earnings. The relevant data immediately after the acquisition of the stock are as follows:

	Assets	Capital
Parent:		
Investment in Subsidiary, 8,000 shares.	$190,000	
Subsidiary:		
Net assets	$180,000	
Common stock, 10,000 shares, $10 par		$100,000
Retained earnings		80,000

The explanation of the $10,000 imbalance in the reciprocal items in this illustration is more complex than in the preceding illustrations. Two factors are involved: (1) the amount paid for the stock is greater than 80% of Subsidiary's book equity and (2) only 80% of Subsidiary's stock was purchased. Since Parent acquired 8,000 shares or 80% of the outstanding shares of Subsidiary, only 80% of the stockholders' equity accounts of Subsidiary can be eliminated. The remaining 20% of the stock is owned by outsiders, who are called collectively the minority interest. The eliminations from the partially reciprocal accounts and the amounts to be reported on the consolidated balance sheet, including the minority interest, are determined as follows:

Parent:		
Investment in Subsidiary.	$190,000	
Eliminate 80% of Subsidiary stock	$ 80,000◄	
Eliminate 80% of Subsidiary retained earnings	64,000◄	
Excess of cost over book equity of Subsidiary		
interest		$46,000
Subsidiary:		
Common stock	$100,000	
Eliminate 80% of Subsidiary stock	80,000◄	
Remainder		$20,000
Retained earnings	$ 80,000	
Eliminate 80% of Subsidiary retained earnings	64,000◄	
Remainder		16,000
Minority interest.		$36,000

The excess cost of $46,000 is reported on the consolidated balance sheet as goodwill or the valuation placed on other assets is increased by $46,000, according to the principles explained earlier. The minority interest of $36,000, which is the amount of Subsidiary's book equity allocable to outsiders, is reported on the consolidated balance sheet, usually preceding the stockholders' equity accounts of Parent.[3]

Consolidated Balance Sheet Subsequent to Acquisition— Purchase Method

Subsequent to acquisition of a subsidiary, a parent company's investment account is increased periodically for its share of the subsidiary's earnings and decreased for the related dividends received. Correspondingly, the retained earnings account of the subsidiary will be increased periodically by the amount of its net income and reduced by dividend distributions. Because of these periodic changes in the balances of the reciprocal accounts, the eliminations required in preparing a consolidated balance sheet will change each year.

To illustrate consolidation of balance sheets subsequent to acquisition, assume that Subsidiary in the preceding illustration earned net income of $50,000 and paid dividends of $20,000 during the year subsequent to Parent's acquisition of 80% of its stock. The net effect of the year's transactions on Subsidiary were as follows:

	Net Assets	Common Stock	Retained Earnings
Subsidiary:			
Date of acquisition..................	$180,000	$100,000	$ 80,000
Add net income.....................	50,000		50,000
Deduct dividends	(20,000)		(20,000)
Date subsequent to acquisition	$210,000	$100,000	$110,000

Parent's entries to record its 80% share of subsidiary's net income and dividends are as follows:

Parent:

Investment in Subsidiary	40,000	
Income of Subsidiary		40,000
Cash...	16,000	
Investment in Subsidiary		16,000

The net effect of the foregoing entries on Parent's investment account is to increase the balance by $24,000. Details are as follows:

Parent:
Investment in Subsidiary, 8,000 shares:

Date of acquisition...........................		$190,000
Add 80% of Subsidiary's net income...........	$40,000	
Deduct 80% of Subsidiary's dividends..........	(16,000)	24,000
Date subsequent to acquisition		$214,000

---

[3]*Accounting Trends & Techniques—1982* indicates that minority interest is reported in the long-term liabilities section by most of the companies surveyed.

Continuing the illustration, the eliminations from the partially reciprocal accounts and the amounts to be reported on the consolidated balance sheet are determined as follows:

Parent:
Investment in Subsidiary.......................... $214,000
   Eliminate 80% of Subsidiary stock .... $ 80,000 ←
   Eliminate 80% of Subsidiary retained earnings ....   88,000 ←
   Excess of cost over book equity of Subsidiary
     interest $46,000

Subsidiary:
Common stock $100,000
   Eliminate 80% of Subsidiary stock ....   80,000 ←
   Remainder................................... $20,000
Retained earnings $110,000
   Eliminate 80% of Subsidiary retained earnings ....   88,000 ←
   Remainder...................................   22,000
Minority interest............................... $42,000

A comparison of the data with the analysis as of the date of acquisition shows the following:

1. Minority interest increased $6,000 (from $36,000 to $42,000), which is equivalent to 20% of the $30,000 net increase ($50,000 of net income less $20,000 of dividends) in Subsidiary's retained earnings.
2. Excess of cost over book equity of the subsidiary interest remained unchanged at $46,000.

To avoid additional complexities, it was assumed that the $46,000 excess at the date of acquisition was not due to goodwill or to assets subject to depreciation or amortization.[4]

Work Sheet for Consolidated Balance Sheet—Purchase Method

The preceding discussion focused on the basic concepts associated with the process of preparing consolidated balance sheets. If the consolidation process becomes quite complex or if the amount of data to be processed is substantial, all of the relevant data for the consolidated statements may be assembled on work sheets. Although a work sheet is not essential, it is used in the following illustration to show an alternate method of accumulating all relevant data for the consolidated balance sheet. Whether or not a work sheet is used, the basic concepts and the consolidated balance sheet would not be affected.

To illustrate the use of the work sheet, assume that (as was the case in the illustration in the preceding section) Parent had purchased 80% of Subsidiary

---

[4]Any portion of the excess of cost over book equity assigned to goodwill must be amortized according to *Opinions of the Accounting Principles Board, No. 17,* "Intangible Assets." Similarly, any excess of cost over book equity assigned to plant assets of limited life must be gradually reduced by depreciation. The application of such amortization and depreciation techniques to consolidated statements goes beyond the scope of the discussion here.

stock for $190,000. For the year since the acquisition, Parent had debited the investment account for its share of Subsidiary earnings and had credited the investment account for its share of dividends declared by Subsidiary. Balance sheet data for Parent and Subsidiary as of December 31 of the year subsequent to acquisition appear as follows. Although these data include amounts for land, other assets, and liabilities, the net assets and capital for Subsidiary are the same as in the preceding illustration.

	Parent	Subsidiary
Investment in Subsidiary	$214,000	
Land	100,000	$ 60,000
Other assets	400,000	200,000
	$714,000	$260,000
Liabilities	$164,000	$ 50,000
Common stock:		
Parent	300,000	
Subsidiary		100,000
Retained earnings:		
Parent	250,000	
Subsidiary		110,000
	$714,000	$260,000

The account balances at December 31 and the eliminations from the reciprocal accounts would be entered on the work sheet. The amounts would be determined for the consolidated balance sheet items as follows (the right margin notations are added as an aid to understanding):

Parent and Subsidiary
Work Sheet for Consolidated Balance Sheet
December 31, 19--

	Parent	Subsidiary	Eliminations Debit	Eliminations Credit	Consolidated Balance Sheet	
Investment in Subsidiary ..	214,000			168,000	46,000	Excess of cost over book equity
Land	100,000	60,000			160,000	
Other Assets	400,000	200,000			600,000	
	714,000	260,000			806,000	
Liabilities	164,000	50,000			214,000	
Common Stock:						
Parent	300,000				300,000	
Subsidiary		100,000	80,000		20,000	minority interest
Retained Earnings:						
Parent	250,000				250,000	
Subsidiary		110,000	88,000		22,000	minority interest
	714,000	260,000	168,000	168,000	806,000	

When 80% of Subsidiary common stock and Subsidiary retained earnings is eliminated against the Investment in Subsidiary, as indicated in the eliminations columns of the work sheet, (1) the $46,000 excess of cost over book equity of the subsidiary interest can be identified and (2) the minority interest of $42,000 (consisting of $20,000 related to subsidiary common stock and $22,000 related to subsidiary retained earnings) can be identified. The $46,000 excess of cost over book equity is reported on the consolidated balance sheet according to the principles explained earlier.

In the following balance sheet, it is assumed that the $46,000 is due to an excess of fair value over book value of Subsidiary's land. Thus, the amount for land as reported on the consolidated balance sheet would be $206,000, consisting of the parent's amount of $100,000 plus the subsidiary's amount of $106,000 (the $60,000 book amount plus the $46,000 excess of cost over book equity attributable to the land). The minority interest of $42,000 is also reported on the consolidated balance sheet as explained earlier.

Parent and Subsidiary	
Consolidated Balance Sheet	
December 31, 19--	
Assets	
Land	$206,000
Other assets	600,000
Total assets	$806,000
Liabilities and Stockholders' Equity	
Liabilities..	$214,000
Minority interest in subsidiary..........................	42,000
Common stock	300,000
Retained earnings	250,000
Total liabilities and stockholders' equity..............	$806,000

It should be noted that the work sheet is only an aid for accumulating the data for the consolidated balance sheet. It is not the consolidated balance sheet. Also, if there are other intercompany items that must be eliminated from the statements that are to be consolidated, those eliminations would be entered in the eliminations columns of the work sheet. For example, a loan by a parent to its subsidiary on a note would require an elimination of the amount of the note from both notes receivable and notes payable in the work sheet.

Consolidated Balance Sheet at Date of Affiliation — Pooling of Interests

When a parent-subsidiary affiliation is effected as a pooling of interests, the ownership of the two companies is joined together in the parent corporation. The parent deems its investment in the subsidiary to be equal to the carrying amount of the subsidiary's net assets. Any difference that may exist between such carrying amount and the fair value of the subsidiary's assets does not affect the amount recorded by the parent as the investment. Consequently, no change is needed in the amounts at which the subsidiary's assets should be stated in the consolidated balance sheet. They are reported as they appear in the subsidiary's separate balance sheet.

The credit to the parent company's capital accounts for the stock issued in exchange for the subsidiary company's stock corresponds to the amount debited to the investment account. In addition to the common stock account, the paid-in capital accounts may be affected, as well as the retained earnings account. According to the concept of continuity of ownership interests, earnings accumulated prior to the affiliation should be combined with those of the parent on the consolidated balance sheet. It is as though there had been a single economic unit from the time the enterprises had begun.

To illustrate the procedure for consolidating the balance sheets of two corporations by the pooling of interests method, their respective financial positions immediately prior to the exchange of stock are assumed to be as follows:

	Assets	Capital
Parent:		
Net assets	$230,000	
Common stock, 20,000 shares, $5 par		$100,000
Retained earnings		130,000
Subsidiary:		
Net assets	$150,000	
Common stock, 10,000 shares, $10 par		$100,000
Retained earnings		50,000

Since poolings must involve substantially all (90% or more) of the stock of the subsidiary,[5] the illustration will assume an exchange of 100% of the stock. It is also assumed that the fair value of the net assets of both companies is greater than the amounts reported above and that there appears to be an element of goodwill in both cases. Based on recent price quotations, it is agreed that for the purpose of the exchange, Parent's common stock is to be valued at $9 a share and Subsidiary's at $18 a share.[6] According to the agreement, the exchange of stock is brought about as follows:

Parent issues 20,000 shares valued at $9 per share $180,000

in exchange for

Subsidiary's 10,000 shares valued at $18 per share $180,000

The excess of the $180,000 value of Parent's stock issued over the $150,000 of net assets of Subsidiary may be ignored and the investment recorded as follows:

Parent:

Investment in Subsidiary	150,000	
Common Stock		100,000
Retained Earnings		50,000

---

[5]*Opinions of the Accounting Principles Board, No. 16, op. cit.,* par. 47b.

[6]In practice, it may be necessary to pay cash for fractional shares or for subsidiary shares held by dissenting stockholders.

After the foregoing entry has been recorded, the basic balance sheet data of the two companies are as follows:

	Assets	Capital
Parent:		
Investment in Subsidiary, 10,000 shares............	$150,000	
Other net assets................................	230,000	
Common stock, 40,000 shares, $5 par.............		$200,000
Retained earnings		180,000
Subsidiary:		
Net assets......................................	$150,000	
Common stock, 10,000 shares, $10 par.............		$100,000
Retained earnings		50,000

To consolidate the balance sheets of the two companies, Parent's investment account and Subsidiary's common stock and retained earnings accounts are eliminated. The net assets of the two companies, $230,000 and $150,000, are combined without any changes in valuation, making a total of $380,000. Consolidated capital is composed of common stock of $200,000 and retained earnings of $180,000, for a total of $380,000.

Consolidated Balance Sheet Subsequent to Affiliation — Pooling of Interests

The equity method is used by the parent corporation in recording changes in its investment account subsequent to acquisition. Thus, the account is increased by the parent's share of the subsidiary's earnings and decreased by its share of dividends. Continuing the illustration of the preceding section, assume that Subsidiary's net income and dividends paid during the year subsequent to affiliation with Parent are $20,000 and $5,000 respectively. After Parent has recorded Subsidiary's net income and dividends, the Parent's investment in Subsidiary increases by $15,000 and the Subsidiary's net assets and retained earnings increase by $15,000, yielding the following account balances:

	Assets	Capital
Parent:		
Investment in Subsidiary, 10,000 shares............	$165,000	
Subsidiary:		
Net assets......................................	$165,000	
Common stock, 10,000 shares, $10 par.............		$100,000
Retained earnings		65,000

When the balance sheets of the affiliated corporations are consolidated, the reciprocal accounts are eliminated and the $165,000 of net assets of Subsidiary are combined with those of Parent.

Work Sheet for Consolidated Balance Sheet — Pooling of Interests

To illustrate the use of the work sheet to assemble the relevant data for the consolidated balance sheet for an affiliation effected as a pooling of interests, assume that (as was the case in the illustration in the preceding section) Parent had exchanged 20,000 shares of its common stock for all of the 10,000 shares of Subsidiary common stock. For the year since the acquisition, Parent had debited the

investment account for its share of Subsidiary earnings and had credited the
investment account for its share of dividends declared by Subsidiary. Balance sheet
data for Parent and Subsidiary as of December 31 of the year subsequent to
acquisition appear as follows. As in the purchase illustration, amounts for land,
other assets, and liabilities have been added, but the amounts for net assets and
capital for Subsidiary are the same as in the preceding illustration.

	Parent	Subsidiary
Investment in Subsidiary	$165,000	
Land	80,000	$ 40,000
Other assets	325,000	175,000
	$570,000	$215,000
Liabilities	$140,000	$ 50,000
Common stock:		
Parent	200,000	
Subsidiary		100,000
Retained earnings:		
Parent	230,000	
Subsidiary		65,000
	$570,000	$215,000

The account balances at December 31 and the eliminations from the reciprocal
accounts would be entered on the work sheet and the amounts determined for the
consolidated balance sheet items as follows:

Parent and Subsidiary
Work Sheet for Consolidated Balance Sheet
December 31, 19--

	Parent	Subsidiary	Eliminations Debit	Eliminations Credit	Consolidated Balance Sheet
Investment in Subsidiary ...	165,000			165,000	
Land	80,000	40,000			120,000
Other Assets	325,000	175,000			500,000
	570,000	215,000			620,000
Liabilities	140,000	50,000			190,000
Common Stock:					
Parent	200,000				200,000
Subsidiary		100,000	100,000		
Retained Earnings:					
Parent	230,000				230,000
Subsidiary		65,000	65,000		
	570,000	215,000	165,000	165,000	620,000

After 100% of Subsidiary common stock and Subsidiary retained earnings is eliminated against the Investment in Subsidiary, as indicated in the eliminations columns of the work sheet, the amounts for the two companies are combined, without any changes in valuation, and are then reported on the consolidated balance sheet.

As previously discussed, the work sheet is only an aid for accumulating the data for the consolidated balance sheet. These data are the basis for the consolidated balance sheet, which is prepared in the normal manner.

Consolidated Income Statement and Other Statements

Consolidation of income statements and other statements of affiliated companies usually presents fewer difficulties than those encountered in balance sheet consolidations. The difference is largely because of the inherent nature of the statements. The balance sheet reports cumulative effects of all transactions from the very beginning of an enterprise to a current date, whereas the income statement, the retained earnings statement, and the statement of changes in financial position report selected transactions only and are for a limited period of time, usually a year.

The principles used in the consolidation of the income statements of a parent and its subsidiaries are the same, regardless of whether the affiliation is deemed to be a purchase or a pooling of interests. When the income statements are consolidated, all amounts resulting from intercompany transactions, such as management fees or interest on loans charged by one affiliate to another, must be eliminated. Any intercompany profit included in inventories must also be eliminated. The remaining amounts of sales, cost of goods sold, operating expenses, and other revenues and expenses reported on the income statements of the affiliated corporations are then combined. The eliminations required in consolidating the retained earnings statement and other statements are based largely on data assembled in consolidating the balance sheet and income statement.

ACCOUNTING FOR FOREIGN OPERATIONS

Many U. S. companies conduct business in foreign countries. If the operations of these multinational companies involve currencies other than the dollar, special accounting problems may arise (1) in accounting for transactions with the foreign companies and (2) in the preparation of consolidated statements for domestic and foreign companies that are affiliated. The basic principles used in such situations are presented in the following paragraphs. Details and complexities are reserved for advanced texts.

Accounting for Transactions with Foreign Companies

If transactions with foreign companies are executed in dollars, no special accounting problems arise. Such transactions would be recorded as illustrated in the text. For example, the sale of merchandise to a Japanese company that is billed in and paid in dollars would be recorded by the U. S. company in the normal manner, using dollar amounts. However, if transactions involve receivables or payables that are to be received or paid in a foreign currency, the U. S. company may incur an exchange gain or loss.

Realized Currency Exchange Gains and Losses

When a U. S. company executes a transaction with a company in a foreign country using a currency other than the dollar, one currency needs to be converted into another to settle the transaction. For example, a U. S. company purchasing merchandise from a British company that requires payment in British pounds must exchange dollars ($) for pounds (£) to settle the transaction. This exchange of one currency into another involves the use of an exchange rate. The **exchange rate** is the rate at which one unit of currency (the dollar, for example) can be converted into another currency (the British pound, for example). To continue with the illustration, if the U. S. company had purchased merchandise for £1,000 from a British company on June 1, when the exchange rate was $2.40 per British pound, $2,400 would need to be exchanged for £1,000 to make the purchase.[7] Since the U. S. company maintains its accounts in dollars, the transaction would be recorded as follows, in general journal form:

```
June 1 Purchases .................................   2,400
         Cash.......................................            2,400
         Payment of Invoice No. 1725 from W. A.
         Sterling Co., £1,000; exchange rate, $2.40
         per British pound.
```

Special accounting problems arise when the exchange rate fluctuates between the date of the original transaction (such as a purchase on account) and the settlement of that transaction in cash in the foreign currency (such as the payment of an account payable). In practice, such fluctuations are frequent. To illustrate, assume that on July 10, when the exchange rate was $.004 per yen (Y), a purchase for Y100,000 was made from a Japanese company. Since the U. S. company maintains its accounts in dollars, the entry would be recorded at $400 (Y100,000 × $.004), as follows:

```
July 10 Purchases ................................   400
          Accounts Payable—M. Suzuki and Son.......            400
          Invoice No. 818, Y100,000; exchange rate,
          $.004 per yen.
```

If on the date of payment, August 9, the exchange rate had increased to $.005 per yen, the Y100,000 account payable must be settled by exchanging $500 (Y100,000 × $.005) for Y100,000. In such a case, the U. S. company incurs an exchange loss of $100, because $500 was needed to settle a $400 debt (account payable). The cash payment would be recorded as follows:

---

[7]Foreign exchange rates are quoted in major financial reporting services. Because the exchange rates are quite volatile, those used in this chapter are assumed rates which do not necessarily reflect current rates.

```
Aug.  9 Accounts Payable—M. Suzuki and Son. . . . . . . . . . .      400
        Exchange Loss. . . . . . . . . . . . . . . . . . . . . . . . . . . . . . . .      100
          Cash. . . . . . . . . . . . . . . . . . . . . . . . . . . . . . . . . . . . .              500
            Cash paid on Invoice No. 818, for Y100,000, or
            $400, when exchange rate was $.005 per yen.
```

All transactions with foreign companies can be analyzed in the manner described above. For example, assume that on May 1, when the exchange rate was $.25 per Swiss franc (F), a sale on account for $1,000 to a Swiss company was billed in Swiss francs. The transaction would be recorded as follows:

```
May  1 Accounts Receivable—D. W. Robinson Co. . . . . .    1,000
         Sales. . . . . . . . . . . . . . . . . . . . . . . . . . . . . . . . . . . .            1,000
           Invoice No. 9772, F4,000; exchange rate,
           $.25 per Swiss franc.
```

If the exchange rate had increased to $.30 per Swiss franc on May 31, the date of receipt of cash, the U. S. company would realize an exchange gain of $200. The gain was realized because the F4,000, which had a value of $1,000 on the date of sale, had increased in value to $1,200 (F4,000 × $.30) on May 31 when payment was received. The receipt of the cash would be recorded as follows:

```
May 31 Cash. . . . . . . . . . . . . . . . . . . . . . . . . . . . . . . . . . . .    1,200
          Accounts Receivable—D. W. Robinson Co. . . .            1,000
          Exchange Gain. . . . . . . . . . . . . . . . . . . . . . . . . . .              200
            Cash received on Invoice No. 9772, for
            F4,000, or $1,000, when exchange rate was
            $.30 per Swiss franc.
```

Unrealized Currency Exchange Gains and Losses

In the previous illustrations, the transactions were completed by either the receipt or the payment of cash. Therefore, any exchange gain or loss was realized and, in an accounting sense, was "recognized" at the date of the cash receipt or cash payment. However, if financial statements are prepared between the date of the original transaction (sale or purchase on account, for example) and the date of the cash receipt or cash payment, and the exchange rate has changed since the original transaction, an unrealized gain or loss must be recognized in the statements. To illustrate, assume that a sale on account for $1,000 had been made to a German company on December 20, when the exchange rate was $.50 per deutsche mark (DM), and that the transaction had been recorded as follows:

```
Dec. 20 Accounts Receivable—T. A. Mueller Inc. . . . . . . . .    1,000
           Sales. . . . . . . . . . . . . . . . . . . . . . . . . . . . . . . . . . . .            1,000
             Invoice No. 1793, DM2,000; exchange rate,
             $.50 per deutsche mark.
```

If the exchange rate had decreased to $.45 per deutsche mark on December 31, the date of the balance sheet, the $1,000 account receivable would have a value of only $900 (DM2,000 × $.45). This "unrealized" loss would be recorded as follows:

Dec. 31 Exchange Loss..............................	100	
Accounts Receivable—T. A. Mueller Inc..........		100
Invoice No. 1793, DM2,000 × $.05 decrease in		
exchange rate.		

Assuming that DM2,000 are received on January 19 in the following year, when the exchange rate is $.42, the additional decline in the exchange rate from $.45 to $.42 per deutsche mark must be recognized. The cash receipt would be recorded as follows:

Jan. 19 Cash...	840	
Exchange Loss ($.03 × DM2,000).................	60	
Accounts Receivable—T. A. Mueller Inc..........		900
Cash received on Invoice No. 1793, for		
DM2,000, or $900, when exchange rate was		
$.42 per deutsche mark.		

If the exchange rate had increased between December 31 and January 19, an exchange gain would be recorded on January 19. For example, if the exchange rate had increased from $.45 to $.47 per deutsche mark during this period, Exchange Gain would be credited for $40 ($.02 × DM2,000).

A balance in the exchange loss account at the end of the fiscal period should be reported in the Other Expense section of the income statement. A balance in the exchange gain account should be reported in the Other Income section.

Consolidated Financial Statements with Foreign Subsidiaries

Before the financial statements of domestic and foreign companies are consolidated, the statements for the foreign companies must be converted to U. S. dollars. Asset and liability amounts are normally converted to U. S. dollars by using the exchange rates as of the balance sheet date. Revenues and expenses are normally converted by using the exchange rates that were in effect when those transactions were executed. (For practical purposes, a weighted average rate for the period is generally used.) The adjustments (gains or losses) resulting from the conversion are reported as a separate item in the stockholders' equity section of the balance sheets of the foreign companies.[8]

After the foreign company statements have been converted to U. S. dollars, the financial statements of U. S. and foreign subsidiaries are consolidated in the normal manner as described previously in this chapter.

---

[8]*Statement of Financial Accounting Standards, No. 52,* "Foreign Currency Translation" (Stamford: Financial Accounting Standards Board, 1981).

ANNUAL
REPORTS TO
STOCKHOLDERS

Corporations ordinarily issue to their stockholders and other interested parties annual reports summarizing activities of the past year and any significant plans for the future. Although there are many differences in the form and sequence of the major sections of annual reports, one section is always devoted to the financial statements, including the accompanying notes. In addition, annual reports usually include (a) selected data referred to as financial highlights, (b) a letter from the president of the corporation, which is sometimes also signed by the chairperson of the board of directors, (c) the independent auditors' report, (d) the management report, and (e) a five- or ten-year historical summary of financial data. As a way to strengthen the relationship with stockholders, many corporations also include pictures of their products and officers or other materials. The following subsections describe the portions of annual reports commonly related to financial matters, with the exception of the principal financial statements, examples of which appear in Appendix G.

Financial
Highlights

This section, sometimes called *Results in Brief*, typically summarizes the major financial results for the last year or two. It is usually presented on the first one or two pages of the annual report. Such items as sales, income before income taxes, net income, net income per common share, cash dividends, cash dividends per common share, and the amount of capital expenditures are typically presented. An example of a financial highlights section from a corporation's annual report is as follows:

FINANCIAL
HIGHLIGHTS
SECTION

FINANCIAL HIGHLIGHTS

(Dollars in thousands except per share amounts)

For the Year	Current Year	Preceding Year
Sales...	$1,336,750	$ 876,400
Income before income tax.....................	149,550	90,770
Net income	105,120	66,190
Per common share	4.03	2.62
Dividends declared on common stock	34,990	33,150
Per common share	1.48	1.40
Capital expenditures and investments	265,120	157,050

At Year-End

	Current Year	Preceding Year
Working capital................................	$ 415,410	$ 423,780
Total assets....................................	1,712,170	1,457,240
Long-term debt................................	440,680	457,350
Stockholders' equity	840,350	692,950

There are many variations in format and content of the financial highlights section of the annual report. In addition to the selected income statement data, information about the financial position at year end, such as the amount of working capital (excess of current assets over current liabilities), total assets, long-term debt, and stockholders' equity, is often provided. Other year-end data often reported are the number of common and preferred shares outstanding, number of common and preferred stockholders, and number of employees.

President's
Letter

A letter by the president to the stockholders, discussing such items as reasons for an increase or decrease in net income, changes in existing plant or purchase or construction of new plants, significant new financing commitments, attention given to social responsibility issues, and future prospects, is also found in most annual reports. A condensed version of a president's letter adapted from a corporation's annual report is as follows:

PRESIDENT'S
LETTER SECTION

To the Stockholders:

FISCAL YEAR REVIEWED

The record net income in this fiscal year resulted from very strong product demand experienced for about two thirds of the fiscal year, more complete utilization of plants, and a continued improvement in sales mix. Income was strong both domestically and internationally during this period.

PLANT EXPANSION CONTINUES

Capital expenditures during the year were $14.5 million. Expansions were in progress or completed at all locations. Portions of the Company's major new expansion at one of its West Coast plants came on stream in March of this year and will provide much needed capacity in existing and new product areas. Capital expenditures will be somewhat less during next year.

ENVIRONMENTAL CONCERN

The Company recognizes its responsibility to provide a safe and healthy environment at each of its plants. The Company expects to spend approximately $1 million in the forthcoming year to help continue its position as a constructive corporate citizen.

OUTLOOK

During the past 10 years the Company's net income and sales have more than tripled. Net income increased from $3.1 million to $10.7 million, and sales from $45 million to $181 million.

The Company's employees are proud of this record and are determined to carry the momentum into the future. The current economic slowdown makes results for the new fiscal year difficult to predict. However, we are confident and enthusiastic about the Company's prospects for continued growth over the longer term.

Respectfully submitted,

Frances B. Davis

Frances B. Davis
President

March 24, 19--

During recent years, corporate enterprises have become increasingly active in accepting environmental and other social responsibilities. In addition to the brief discussion that may be contained in the president's letter, a more detailed analysis of the company's social concerns may be included elsewhere in the annual report. Knowledgeable investors recognize that the failure of a business enterprise to meet acceptable social norms can have long-run unfavorable implications. In the near future, an important function of accounting may be to assist management in developing a statement of social responsibilities of corporate enterprises and what management is doing about them.

**Independent
Auditors' Report**

Before issuing annual statements, all publicly held corporations, as well as many other corporations, engage independent public accountants, usually CPAs, to conduct an *examination* of the financial statements. Such an examination is for the purpose of adding credibility to the statements that have been prepared by management. Upon completion of the examination, which for large corporations may engage many accountants for several weeks or longer, an independent auditors' report is prepared. This report accompanies the financial statements. A typical report briefly describes, in two paragraphs, (1) the scope of the auditors' examination and (2) their opinion as to the fairness of the statements. The wording used in the following report conforms with general usage.[9]

**INDEPENDENT
AUDITORS'
REPORT SECTION**

To the Stockholders of X Corporation:

We have examined the balance sheet of X Corporation as of December 31, 19-- and the related statements of income and retained earnings and changes in financial position for the year then ended. Our examination was made in accordance with generally accepted auditing standards, and accordingly included such tests of the accounting records and such other auditing procedures as we considered necessary in the circumstances.

In our opinion, the aforementioned financial statements present fairly the financial position of X Corporation at December 31, 19--, and the results of its operations and the changes in its financial position for the year then ended, in conformity with generally accepted accounting principles applied on a basis consistent with that of the preceding year.

Cincinnati, Ohio
January 28, 19--

Gordon and Staun
Certified Public Accountants

In most instances, the auditors can render a report such as the one illustrated, which may be said to be "unqualified." However, it is possible that accounting methods used by a client do not conform with generally accepted accounting principles or that a client has not been consistent in the application of principles. In such cases, a "qualified" opinion must be rendered and the exception briefly described. If the effect of the departure from accepted principles is sufficiently material, an "adverse" or negative opinion must be issued and the exception described. In rare circumstances, the auditors may be unable to perform sufficient auditing procedures to enable them to reach a conclusion as to the fairness of the financial statements. In such circumstances, the auditors must issue a "disclaimer" and briefly describe the reasons for their failure to be able to reach a decision as to the fairness of the statements.

Professional accountants cannot disregard their responsibility in attesting to the fairness of financial statements without seriously jeopardizing their reputations. This responsibility is described as follows:

[9]*Codification of Statements on Auditing Standards* (New York: American Institute of Certified Public Accountants, 1983), par. 509.07.

The report shall either contain an expression of opinion regarding the financial statements, taken as a whole, or an assertion to the effect that an opinion cannot be expressed. When an overall opinion cannot be expressed, the reasons therefor should be stated. In all cases where an auditor's name is associated with financial statements, the report should contain a clear-cut indication of the character of the auditor's examination, if any, and the degree of responsibility he is taking.[10]

Management Report

Responsibility for the accounting system and the resultant financial statements rests mainly with the principal officers of a corporation. In the **management report,** the chief financial officer or other representative of management (1) states that the financial statements are management's responsibility and that they have been prepared according to generally accepted accounting principles, (2) presents management's assessment of the company's internal accounting control system, and (3) comments on any other pertinent matters related to the accounting system, the financial statements, and the examination by the independent auditor.

Although the concept of a management report is relatively new, an increasing number of corporations are including such a report in the annual report. An example of such a report is as follows:

MANAGEMENT REPORT SECTION

REPORT BY MANAGEMENT

Financial Statements

We prepared the accompanying balance sheet of X Corporation as of December 31, 19‑‑, and the related statements of income, retained earnings, and changes in financial position for the year then ended. The statements have been prepared in conformity with generally accepted accounting principles appropriate in the circumstances, and necessarily include some amounts that are based on our best estimates and judgments.

Internal Accounting Controls

The company maintains an accounting system and related controls to provide reasonable assurance that assets are safeguarded against loss from unauthorized use or disposition and that the financial records are reliable for preparing financial statements and maintaining accountability for assets. The concept of reasonable assurance is based on the recognition that the cost of a system of internal control should not exceed the benefits derived and that the evaluation of those factors requires estimates and judgments by management.

Other Matters

The functioning of the accounting system and related controls is under the general oversight of the board of directors. The accounting system and related controls are reviewed by an extensive program of internal audits and by the company's independent auditors.

James O. Hiller
James O. Hiller
Chief Financial Officer

March 24, 19‑‑

---

[10]*Ibid.*, par. 509.04.

Historical Summary

This section, for which there are many variations in title, reports selected financial and operating data of past periods, usually for five or ten years. It is usually presented in close proximity to the financial statements for the current year, and the types of data reported are varied. An example of a portion of such a report is presented below.

HISTORICAL SUMMARY SECTION

Five-Year Consolidated Financial and Statistical Summary for Years Ended December 31 (Dollar amounts in millions except for per share data)			
For the Year	1984	1983	1980
Net sales	$1,759.7	$1,550.1	$ 997.4
Gross profit	453.5	402.8	270.8
Percent to net sales	25.8%	26.0%	27.2%
Interest expense	33.9	21.3	15.0
Income before income tax	172.7	163.4	87.5
Income tax	82.8	77.8	40.2
Net income	89.9	85.6	47.3
Percent to net sales	5.1%	5.5%	4.7%
Per common share:			
Net income	5.19	4.84	2.54
Dividends	1.80	1.65	1.40
Return on stockholders' equity	15.9%	16.4%	11.2%
Common share market price:			
High	31	41½	40⅝
Low	18	22⅜	22¼
Depreciation and amortization	43.3	41.0	23.6
Capital expenditures	98.5	72.1	55.5
At Year End			
Working capital	$ 443.9	$ 434.8	$ 254.6
Plant assets — gross	704.7	620.3	453.7
Plant assets — net	420.0	362.7	263.4
Stockholders' equity	594.3	536.9	447.6
Stockholders' equity per common share	33.07	29.69	23.02
Number of holders of common shares	39,503	39,275	43,852
Number of employees	50,225	50,134	42,826

GOVERNMENTAL AND EXCHANGE REQUIREMENTS

The Securities and Exchange Commission (SEC) requires corporations whose securities are traded in interstate commerce to file an annual report on *Form 10-K*, which provides a more detailed analysis than annual reports issued to stockholders. The form is available to the public at SEC offices, and corporations will provide a copy to stockholders and financial analysts upon request. Other federal and state agencies also require companies under their jurisdiction to file annual financial statements. In addition, the national stock exchanges require periodic reports of corporations whose securities they list. The exchanges are interested in adequate disclosure policies because they tend to ensure an orderly market.

FINANCIAL
REPORTING
FOR SEGMENTS
OF A BUSINESS

Conglomerates, or companies that diversify their operations, make up a large number of the total business enterprises in the United States. The individual segments of a diversified company ordinarily experience differing rates of profitability, degrees of risk, and opportunities for growth. For example, one prominent diversified company is involved in such diverse markets as telecommunications equipment, industrial products, automotive and consumer products, natural resources, defense and space programs, food processing, financial services, and insurance.

To help financial statement users in assessing the past performance and the future potential of an enterprise, financial reports should disclose such information as the enterprise's operations in different industries, its foreign markets, and its major customers. The required information for each significant reporting segment includes the following: revenue, income from operations, and identifiable assets associated with the segment.[11] This information may be included within the body of the statements or in accompanying notes. An example of a note disclosing segment information is as follows:

REPORTING FOR
SEGMENTS

NOTE 11—SEGMENT REPORTING
The following industry and geographic segment data (dollars in millions) are reported in accordance with *Financial Accounting Standards Board Statement No. 14.*

	Airline Operations	Hotel Operations	Food Services	Total
Revenues:				
United States.........	$ 293.1	$129.7	$ 95.7	$ 518.5
Foreign...............	187.7	46.5	31.3	265.5
Total.............	$ 480.8	$176.2	$127.0	$ 784.0
Income from operations:				
United States.........	$ 4.7	$ 12.1	$ 3.9	$ 20.7
Foreign...............	8.1	5.1	1.0	14.2
Total.............	$ 12.8	$ 17.2	$ 4.9	$ 34.9
Assets:				
United States.........	$1,010.0	$391.5	$112.1	$1,513.6
Foreign...............	617.5	91.2	47.0	755.7
Total.............	$1,627.5	$482.7	$159.1	$2,269.3

[11] *Statement of Financial Accounting Standards, No. 14,* "Financial Reporting for Segments of a Business Enterprise" (Stamford: Financial Accounting Standards Board, 1976). Nonpublic corporations are exempted from this requirement by *Statement of Financial Accounting Standards, No. 21,* "Suspension of the Reporting of Earnings per Share and Segment Information by Nonpublic Enterprises" (Stamford: Financial Accounting Standards Board, 1978).

FINANCIAL
FORECASTS

Many corporations publicize their financial plans and expectations for the year ahead. Such financial forecasts may be issued by various means, such as a press release, a letter to stockholders, and a speech to an assembled group of financial analysts and brokers. In recent years there has been an increasing insistence by stockholders, creditors, and financial analysts that such forecasts be included in corporate annual reports. They contend that management's estimate of the future earning power and financial stability of a corporation can be of great value to investors. In addition, there have been instances in which officers or directors issued informal forecasts to selected persons only, to the harm of investors not so informed.

The accounting profession has not taken a position on whether financial forecasts should be required in annual reports. The AICPA prohibits its members from using their names in a manner which would lead to the belief that a forecast of future transactions is achievable.[12] However, there is no prohibition against CPAs helping their clients in the preparation of the financial forecasts, and many do so.

Several major corporations include financial forecasts in their annual reports. Because there is no standardized approach for presenting such forecasts, varying formats are used. An example of a financial forecast for the current year plus comparisons of the forecast and actual results for the past year is as follows:

FINANCIAL
FORECAST
SECTION

Sales (in millions)	Past Year		Current Year
	Forecast	Actual	Forecast
Recreation			
Lawn & garden equipment...................	$ 42.0	$ 54.9	$ 65.0
Sporting goods.....................	39.0	54.7	84.0
Marine products.............................	48.0	49.8	43.0
Entertainment.............................	45.0	46.5	47.0
Photofinishing	23.0	26.2	29.0
Total recreation...........................	$197.0	$232.1	$268.0
Transportation.............................	147.0	156.6	182.0
Shelter..	85.0	90.5	91.0
Total sales..................................	$429.0	$479.2	$541.0

Among the forecast disclosure issues on which there is presently no general agreement are the following: (a) what financial and operating data (sales, net income, earnings per share, etc.) should be presented, (b) what period of time (six months, one year, two years, etc.) should be covered by the forecast, and (c) whether annual reports should contain a follow-up comparison of the actual results with the forecast. It is apparent that if financial forecasts are increasingly used in the future, the accounting profession will play a major role in directing their development and forms of presentation.

---

[12]*Restatement of the Code of Professional Ethics* (New York: American Institute of Certified Public Accountants, 1972), p. 22.

INTERIM FINANCIAL REPORTS

Corporate enterprises customarily issue interim financial reports to their stockholders. Corporations that are listed on a stock exchange or file reports with the SEC or other regulatory agencies are required to submit interim reports, usually on a quarterly basis. Such reports often have a significant influence on the valuation of a corporation's equity securities on stock exchanges.

Quarterly income statements, which are ordinarily included in interim financial reports, are usually quite brief and report comparative figures for the comparable period of the preceding year. When interim balance sheets or statements of changes in financial position are issued, they are also severely condensed and accompanied by comparative data. Interim reports of an enterprise should disclose such information as gross revenue, costs and expenses, provision for income taxes, extraordinary or infrequently occurring items, net income, earnings per share, contingent items, and significant changes in financial position.[13] The particular accounting principles used on an annual basis, such as depreciation methods and inventory cost flow assumptions, are usually followed in preparing interim statements. However, if changes in accounting principles occur before the end of a fiscal year, there are detailed guidelines for their disclosure.[14]

Much of the value of interim financial reports to the investing public is based on their timeliness. Lengthy delays between the end of a quarter and the issuance of reports would greatly reduce their value. This is one of the reasons that interim reports are usually not audited by independent CPAs. In some cases, the interim reports are subjected to a "limited review" by the CPA and a report on this limited review is issued.

Self-Examination Questions
(Answers in Appendix C.)

1. Which of the following are characteristic of a parent-subsidiary relationship known as a pooling of interests?
   A. Parent acquires a controlling share of the voting stock of subsidiary in exchange for cash
   B. Parent acquires a controlling share of the voting stock of subsidiary in exchange for its bonds payable
   C. Parent acquires a controlling share of the voting stock of subsidiary in exchange for its voting common stock
   D. All of the above

2. P Co. purchased the entire outstanding stock of S Co. for $1,000.000 in cash. If at the date of acquisition, S Co.'s stockholders' equity consisted of $750,000 of com-

---

[13]*Opinions of the Accounting Principles Board*, *No. 28*, "Interim Financial Reporting" (New York: American Institute of Certified Public Accountants, 1973).

[14]*Statement of Financial Accounting Standards*, *No. 3*, "Reporting Accounting Changes in Interim Financial Statements" (Stamford: Financial Accounting Standards Board, 1974).

mon stock and $150,000 of retained earnings, what is the amount of the difference between cost and book equity of the subsidiary interest?

A. Excess of cost over book equity of subsidiary interest, $250,000

B. Excess of cost over book equity of subsidiary interest, $100,000

C. Excess of book equity over cost of subsidiary interest, $250,000

D. None of the above

3. If in Question 2, P Co. had purchased 90% of the outstanding stock of S Co. for $1,000,000, what is the amount of the difference between cost and book equity of subsidiary interest?

A. Excess of cost over book equity of subsidiary interest, $100,000

B. Excess of cost over book equity of subsidiary interest, $190,000

C. Excess of cost over book equity of subsidiary interest, $250,000

D. None of the above

4. Based on the data in Question 3, what is the amount of the minority interest at the date of acquisition?

A. $15,000   C. $100,000

B. $75,000   D. None of the above

5. On July 9, 1984, a sale on account for $10,000 to a Mexican company was billed for 250,000 pesos. The exchange rate was $.04 per peso on July 9 and $.05 per peso on August 8, 1984, when the cash was received on account. Which of the following statements identifies the exchange gain or loss for the fiscal year ended December 31, 1984?

A. Realized exchange loss, $2,500   C. Unrealized exchange loss, $2,500

B. Realized exchange gain, $2,500   D. Unrealized exchange gain, $2,500

Discussion Questions

1. What terms are applied to the following: (a) a corporation that is controlled by another corporation through ownership of a controlling interest in its stock; (b) a corporation that owns a controlling interest in the voting stock of another corporation; (c) a group of corporations related through stock ownership?

2. What are the two methods by which the relationship of parent-subsidiary may be accomplished?

3. P Company purchases for $3,000,000 the entire common stock of S Corporation. What type of accounts on S's balance sheet are reciprocal to the investment account on P's balance sheet?

4. Are the eliminations of the reciprocal accounts in consolidating the balance sheets of P and S in Question 3 recorded in the respective ledgers of the two companies?

5. Palmer Company purchased from stockholders the entire outstanding stock of Sanchez Inc. for a total of $5,000,000 in cash. At the date of acquisition, Sanchez Inc. had $2,000,000 of liabilities and total stockholders' equity of $4,500,000. (a) As of the acquisition date, what was the total amount of the assets of Sanchez Inc.? (b) As of the acquisition date, what was the amount of the net assets of Sanchez

Inc.? (c) What is the amount of difference between the investment account and the book equity of the subsidiary interest acquired by Palmer Company?

6. What is the possible explanation of the difference determined in Question 5(c) and how will it affect the reporting of the difference on the consolidated balance sheet?

7. If, in Question 5, Palmer Company had paid only $4,200,000 for the stock of Sanchez Inc., what would the difference in part (c) have been?

8. Parent Corporation owns 90% of the outstanding common stock of Subsidiary Corporation, which has no preferred stock. (a) What is the term applied to the remaining 10% interest? (b) If the total stockholders' equity of Subsidiary Corporation is $900,000, what is the amount of Subsidiary's book equity allocable to outsiders? (c) Where is the amount determined in (b) reported on the consolidated balance sheet?

9. P Corporation owns 80% of the outstanding common stock of S Co., which has no preferred stock. Net income of S Co. was $150,000 for the year and cash dividends declared and paid during the year amounted to $90,000. What entries should be made by P Corporation to record its share of S Co.'s (a) net income and (b) dividends? (c) What is the amount of the net increase in the equity of the minority interest?

10. (a) What purpose is served by the work sheet for a consolidated balance sheet? (b) Is the work sheet a substitute for the consolidated balance sheet?

11. At the end of the fiscal year, the amount of notes receivable and notes payable reported on the respective balance sheets of a parent and its wholly owned subsidiary are as follows:

	Parent	Subsidiary
Notes Receivable	$275,000	$40,000
Notes Payable	150,000	35,000

If $25,000 of Subsidiary's notes receivable are owed by Parent, determine the amount of notes receivable and notes payable to be reported on the consolidated balance sheet.

12. Sales and purchases of merchandise by a parent corporation and its wholly owned subsidiary during the year were as follows:

	Parent	Subsidiary
Sales	$4,000,000	$850,000
Purchases...........	2,400,000	620,000

If $500,000 of the sales of Parent were made to Subsidiary, determine the amount of sales and purchases to be reported on the consolidated income statement.

13. The relationships of parent and subsidiary were established by the following transactions. Identify each affiliation as a "purchase" or a "pooling of interests."
   (a) Company P receives 100% of the voting common stock of Company S in exchange for cash and long-term bonds payable.
   (b) Company P receives 95% of the voting common stock of Company S in exchange for voting common stock of Company P.

(c) Company P receives 90% of the voting common stock of Company S in exchange for cash.

(d) Company P receives 75% of the voting common stock of Company S in exchange for voting common stock of Company P.

14. Which of the following procedures for consolidating the balance sheet of a parent and wholly owned subsidiary are characteristic of acquisition of control by purchase and which are characteristic of a pooling of interests? (a) Retained earnings of subsidiary at date of acquisition are eliminated. (b) Retained earnings of subsidiary at date of acquisition are combined with retained earnings of parent. (c) Assets are not revalued. (d) Goodwill may not be recognized.

15. On June 30, Polk Corp. issued 9,000 shares of its $10 par common stock, with a total market value of $300,000, to the stockholders of Sapp Inc., in exchange for all of Sapp's common stock. Polk Corp. records its investment at $250,000. The net assets and stockholders' equities of the two companies just prior to the affiliation are summarized as follows:

	Polk Corp.	Sapp, Inc.
Net assets	$810,000	$250,000
Common stock	$600,000	$150,000
Retained earnings	210,000	100,000
	$810,000	$250,000

(a) At what amounts would the following be reported on the consolidated balance sheet as of June 30, applying the pooling of interests method: (1) Net assets, (2) Retained earnings?

(b) Assume that, instead of issuing shares of stock, Polk Corp. had given $300,000 in cash and long-term notes. At what amounts would the following be reported on the consolidated balance sheet as of June 30: (1) Net assets, (2) Retained earnings?

16. Can a U.S. company incur an exchange gain or loss because of fluctuations in the exchange rate if its transactions with foreign countries, involving receivables or payables, are executed in (a) dollars, (b) the foreign currency?

17. A U.S. company purchased merchandise for 5,000 francs on account from a French company. If the exchange rate was $.22 per franc on the date of purchase and $.20 per franc on the date of payment of the account, what was the amount of exchange gain or loss realized by the U.S. company?

18. What two conditions give rise to unrealized currency exchange gains and losses from sales and purchases on account that are to be settled in the foreign currency?

19. (a) What are the major components of an annual report? (b) Indicate the purpose of the financial highlights section and the president's letter.

20. (a) The typical unqualified independent auditors' report consists of two paragraphs. What is reported in each paragraph? (b) Under what conditions does an auditor give a qualified opinion?

21. (a) Why do some investors believe that financial forecasts should be included in the annual report? (b) What position has the American Institute of Certified Public Accountants adopted with respect to reports of financial forecasts?

22. What information is disclosed in interim financial reports?

Exercises

Exercise 18-1. On the last day of the fiscal year, Palmquist Inc. purchased 80% of the common stock of Stowe Company for $550,000, at which time Stowe Company reported the following on its balance sheet: assets, $940,000; liabilities, $290,000; common stock, $10 par, $500,000; retained earnings, $150,000. In negotiating the stock sale, it was determined that the book carrying amounts of Stowe's recorded assets and equities approximated their current market values.

(a) Indicate for each of the following the section, title of the item, and amount to be reported on the consolidated balance sheet as of the date of acquisition:
  (1) Difference between cost and book equity of subsidiary interest.
  (2) Minority interest.
(b) During the following year, Palmquist Inc. realized net income of $725,000, exclusive of the income of the subsidiary, and Stowe Company realized net income of $200,000. In preparing a consolidated income statement, indicate in what amounts the following would be reported:
  (1) Minority interest's share of net income.
  (2) Consolidated net income.

Exercise 18-2. On December 31 of the current year, Pace Corporation purchased 90% of the stock of Sisco Company. The data reported on their separate balance sheets immediately after the acquisition are as follows:

Assets	Pace Corporation	Sisco Company
Cash...	$ 40,500	$ 19,500
Accounts receivable (net)........................	62,500	30,000
Inventories	145,000	54,500
Investment in Sisco Company	350,000	—
Equipment (net)................................	400,000	262,500
	$998,000	$366,500

Liabilities and Stockholders' Equity		
Accounts payable..............................	$ 89,000	$ 27,500
Common stock, $10 par	600,000	250,000
Retained earnings.............................	309,000	89,000
	$998,000	$366,500

The fair value of Sisco Company's assets corresponds to their book carrying amounts, except for equipment, which is valued at $300,000 for consolidation purposes. Prepare a consolidated balance sheet as of that date, in report form, omitting captions for current assets, plant assets, etc. (A work sheet need not be used.)

Exercise 18-3. As of May 31 of the current year, Peak Corporation exchanged 5,000 shares of its $20 par common stock for the 1,000 shares of Saad Company $100 par common stock held by Saad stockholders. The separate balance sheets of the two enterprises, immediately after the exchange of shares, are as follows:

Assets	Peak Corporation	Saad Company
Cash.	$ 41,000	$ 20,500
Accounts receivable (net).	46,500	30,500
Inventories	145,000	57,000
Investment in Saad Company	175,000	—
Equipment (net).	510,000	92,000
	$917,500	$200,000

Liabilities and Stockholders' Equity		
Accounts payable.	$ 77,000	$ 25,000
Common stock.	600,000	100,000
Retained earnings.	240,500	75,000
	$917,500	$200,000

Prepare a consolidated balance sheet as of May 31, in report form, omitting captions for current assets, plant assets, etc. (A work sheet need not be used.)

Exercise 18-4. For the current year ended June 30, the results of operations of Payne Corporation and its wholly owned subsidiary, Saxe Enterprises, are as follows:

	Payne Corporation		Saxe Enterprises	
Sales		$990,000		$310,000
Cost of merchandise sold.	$675,000		$185,000	
Selling expenses	155,000		50,000	
General expenses	75,000		30,000	
Interest income.	(12,000)		—	
Interest expense.	—	893,000	12,000	277,000
Net income		$ 97,000		$ 33,000

During the year, Payne sold merchandise to Saxe for $45,000. The merchandise was sold by Saxe to nonaffiliated companies for $75,000. Payne's interest income was realized from a long-term loan to Saxe.

(a) Prepare a consolidated income statement for the current year for Payne and its subsidiary. Use the single-step form and disregard income taxes. (A work sheet need not be used.)

(b) If none of the merchandise sold by Payne to Saxe had been sold during the year to nonaffiliated companies, and assuming that Payne's cost of the merchandise had been $31,000, determine the amounts that would have been reported for the following items on the consolidated income statement: (1) sales, (2) cost of merchandise sold, (3) net income.

Exercise 18-5. Summarized data from the balance sheets of Pagan Company and Schor Inc., as of April 30 of the current year, are as follows:

	Pagan Company	Schor Inc.
Net assets	$700,000	$80,000
Common stock:		
25,000 shares, $20 par	500,000	
5,000 shares, $10 par		50,000
Retained earnings	200,000	30,000

(a) On May 1 of the current year, the two companies combine. Pagan Company issues 2,500 shares of its $20 par common stock, valued at $95,000, to Schor's stockholders in exchange for the 5,000 shares of Schor's $10 par common stock, also valued at $95,000. Assuming that the affiliation is effected as a pooling of interests, what are the amounts that would be reported for net assets, common stock, and retained earnings as of May 1 of the current year?

(b) Assume that Pagan Company had paid cash of $95,000 for Schor Inc. common stock on May 1 of the current year and that the book value of the net assets of Schor Inc. is deemed to reflect fair value. What are the amounts that would be reported for net assets, common stock, and retained earnings as of May 1 of the current year, using the purchase method? How much goodwill will be reported on the combined balance sheet?

Exercise 18-6. Vance Company makes sales on account to several Mexican companies which it bills in pesos. Record the following selected transactions completed during the current year, in general journal form:

Jan. 12. Sold merchandise on account, 50,000 pesos; exchange rate, $.04 per peso.

Feb. 20. Received cash from sale of January 12, 50,000 pesos; exchange rate, $.05 per peso.

Apr. 30. Sold merchandise on account, 80,000 pesos; exchange rate, $.05 per peso.

July 2. Received cash from sale of April 30, 80,000 pesos; exchange rate, $.04 per peso.

Exercise 18-7. Tudor Company purchases merchandise from a German company that requires payment in deutsche marks. Record the following selected transactions completed during the current year, in general journal form:

July 1. Purchased merchandise on account, net 30, 3,000 marks; exchange rate, $.51 per mark.

31. Paid invoice of July 1; exchange rate, $.52 per mark.

Aug. 10. Purchased merchandise on account, net 30, 6,000 marks; exchange rate, $.52 per mark.

Sep. 9. Paid invoice of August 10; exchange rate, $.50 per mark.

Problems
(Problems in Appendix B: 18-1B, 18-2B, 18-5B, 18-6B.)

Problem 18-1A. On June 30 of the current year, Pondy Company purchased 85% of the stock of Stein Company. On the same date, Pondy Company loaned Stein Company $25,000 on a 90-day note. The data reported on their separate balance sheets immediately after the acquisition and loan are as follows:

Assets	Pondy Company	Stein Company
Cash...	$ 39,000	$ 27,500
Accounts receivable (net)	49,500	35,000
Notes receivable	40,000	——
Inventories......................................	168,000	49,000
Investment in Stein Company	260,000	——
Equipment (net)	375,000	215,000
	$931,500	$326,500

Liabilities and Stockholders' Equity		
Accounts payable	$137,500	$ 22,500
Notes payable	——	25,000
Common stock, $20 par...........................	500,000	——
Common stock, $10 par...........................	——	200,000
Retained earnings	294,000	79,000
	$931,500	$326,500

The fair value of Stein Company's assets correspond to the book carrying amounts, except for equipment, which is valued at $225,000 for consolidation purposes.

Instructions:

(1) Prepare a work sheet for a consolidated balance sheet as of June 30 of the current year.
(2) Prepare in report form a consolidated balance sheet as of June 30, omitting captions for current assets, plant assets, etc.

Problem 18-2A. On January 31, Parr Company purchased 80% of the outstanding stock of Stove Company for $400,000. Balance sheet data for the two corporations immediately after the transaction are as follows:

Assets	Parr Co.	Stove Co.
Cash and marketable securities...................	$ 175,500	$ 23,600
Accounts receivable	246,150	44,150
Allowance for doubtful accounts	(20,100)	(8,050)
Inventories......................................	490,250	122,100
Investment in Stove Company	400,000	——
Land..	140,000	75,000
Building and equipment..........................	729,300	494,600
Accumulated depreciation........................	(232,400)	(261,900)
	$1,928,700	$489,500

Liabilities and Stockholders' Equity		
Accounts payable	$ 205,750	$ 71,150
Income tax payable..............................	42,000	6,050
Bonds payable (due in 1999)	400,000	——
Common stock, $10 par..........................	750,000	——
Common stock, $20 par..........................	——	300,000
Retained earnings	530,950	112,300
	$1,928,700	$489,500

Instructions:

(1) Prepare a work sheet for a consolidated balance sheet as of the date of acquisition.

(2) Prepare in report form a detailed consolidated balance sheet as of the date of acquisition. The fair value of Stove Company's assets are deemed to correspond to the book carrying amounts, except for land, which is to be increased by $50,000.

(3) Assuming that Stove Company earns net income of $90,000 and pays cash dividends of $40,000 during the ensuing fiscal year and that Parr Company records its share of the earnings and dividends, determine the following as of the end of the year:

    (a) The net amount added to Parr Company's investment account as a result of Stove Company's earnings and dividends.

    (b) The amount of the minority interest.

Problem 18-3A. Several years ago, Poll Corporation purchased 18,000 of the 20,000 outstanding shares of stock of Sims Company. Since the date of acquisition, Poll Corporation has debited the investment account for its share of the subsidiary's earnings and has credited the account for its share of dividends declared. Balance sheet data for the two corporations as of March 31 of the current year are as follows:

Assets	Poll Corp.	Sims Co.
Cash	$ 52,500	$ 21,200
Notes receivable	45,000	15,000
Accounts receivable (net)	130,500	49,500
Interest receivable	3,000	600
Dividends receivable	4,500	——
Inventories	190,000	60,000
Prepaid expenses	5,100	1,700
Investment in Sims Co.	180,180	——
Land	75,000	40,000
Buildings and equipment	411,000	240,000
Accumulated depreciation	(200,000)	(95,400)
	$896,780	$332,600

Liabilities and Stockholders' Equity		
Notes payable	$ 40,000	$ 50,000
Accounts payable	89,500	60,500
Income tax payable	30,000	8,900
Dividends payable	15,000	5,000
Interest payable	2,450	3,000
Common stock, $20 par	600,000	——
Common stock, $10 par	——	100,000
Premium on common stock	——	25,000
Retained earnings	119,830	80,200
	$896,780	$332,600

Poll Corporation holds $30,000 of short-term notes of Sims Company, on which there is accrued interest of $3,000. Sims Company owes Poll Corporation $10,000 for a management advisory fee for the year. It has been recorded by both corporations in their respective accounts payable and accounts receivable accounts.

Instructions:

Prepare in report form a detailed consolidated balance sheet as of March 31 of the current year. (A work sheet is not required.) The excess of book equity in Sims Company over the balance of the Poll Corporation's investment account is attributable to overvaluation of Sims Company's land.

Problem 18-4A. On June 1 of the current year, the Park Company, after several months of negotiations, issued 4,500 shares of its own $50 par common stock for all of Shaw Inc.'s outstanding shares of stock. The fair market value of the Park Company shares issued is $75 per share, or a total of $337,500. Shaw Inc. is to be operated as a separate subsidiary. The balance sheets of the two firms on May 31 of the current year are as follows:

Assets	Park Company	Shaw Inc.
Cash...	$ 225,500	$ 18,500
Accounts receivable (net)	240,250	36,900
Inventory	410,000	61,450
Land..	120,000	50,000
Plant and equipment (net)......................	504,250	123,150
	$1,500,000	$290,000

Liabilities and Stockholders' Equity	Park Company	Shaw Inc.
Accounts payable	$ 136,000	$ 12,500
Common stock ($50 par).......................	900,000	150,000
Retained earnings	464,000	97,500
	$1,500,000	$290,000

Instructions:

(1) (a) What entry would be made by Park Company to record the combination as a pooling of interests? (b) Prepare a consolidated balance sheet of Park Company and Shaw Inc. as of June 1 of the current year, assuming that the business combination has been recorded as a pooling of interests. (A work sheet is not required.)

(2) (a) Assume that Park Company paid $150,000 in cash and issued 2,500 shares of Park common stock with a fair market value of $187,500 for all the common stock of Shaw Inc. What entry would Park Company make to record the combination as a purchase? (b) Prepare a consolidated balance sheet as of June 1 of the current year, assuming that the business combination has been recorded as a purchase, and that the book values of the net assets of Shaw Inc. are deemed to represent fair value. (A work sheet is not required.)

(3) Assume the same situation as in (2), except that the fair value of the land of Shaw Inc. was $75,000. Prepare a consolidated balance sheet as of June 1 of the current year. (A work sheet is not required.)

Problem 18-5A. On January 1 of the current year, Pici Corporation exchanged 10,000 shares of its $50 par common stock for 30,000 shares (the entire issue) of Stall Company's $10 par common stock. Stall purchased from Pici Corporation $300,000 of its $500,000 issue of bonds payable, at face amount. All of the items for "interest" appearing on the balance sheets and income statements of both corporations are related to the bonds.

During the year, Pici Corporation sold merchandise with a cost of $151,680 to Stall Company for $189,600, all of which was sold by Stall Company before the end of the year.

Pici Corporation has correctly recorded the income and dividends reported for the year by Stall Company. Data for the income statements of both companies for the current year are as follows:

	Pici Corporation	Stall Company
Revenues:		
Sales	$1,500,000	$400,000
Income of subsidiary	110,000	——
Interest income	——	30,000
	$1,610,000	$430,000
Expenses:		
Cost of merchandise sold	$ 840,000	$205,000
Selling expenses	150,000	42,000
General expenses	125,000	27,000
Interest expense	50,000	——
Income tax	195,000	46,000
	$1,360,000	$320,000
Net income	$ 250,000	$110,000

Data for the balance sheets of both companies as of the end of the current year are as follows:

Assets	Pici Corporation	Stall Company
Cash	$ 75,000	$ 18,300
Accounts receivable (net)	165,000	51,800
Dividends receivable	50,000	——
Interest receivable	——	15,000
Inventories	325,000	126,300
Investment in Stall Co. (30,000 shares)	641,550	——
Investment in Pici Corp. bonds (at face amount)	——	300,000
Plant and equipment	1,350,000	321,950
Accumulated depreciation	(650,000)	(108,350)
	$1,956,550	$725,000

Liabilities and Stockholders' Equity	Pici Corporation	Stall Company
Accounts payable	$ 75,200	$ 27,750
Income tax payable	20,510	5,700
Dividends payable	30,000	50,000
Interest payable	25,000	——
Bonds payable, 10% (due in 1998)	500,000	——
Common stock, $50 par	1,000,000	——
Common stock, $10 par	——	300,000
Premium on common stock	100,000	50,000
Retained earnings	205,840	291,550
	$1,956,550	$725,000

Instructions:

(1) Determine the amounts to be eliminated from the following items in preparing the consolidated balance sheet as of December 31 of the current year: (a) dividends receivable and dividends payable; (b) interest receivable and interest payable; (c) investment in Stall Co. and stockholders' equity; (d) investment in Pici Corp. bonds and bonds payable.

(2) Prepare a detailed consolidated balance sheet in report form.

(3) Determine the amount to be eliminated from the following items in preparing the consolidated income statement for the current year ended December 31: (a) sales and cost of merchandise sold; (b) interest income and interest expense; (c) income of subsidiary and net income.

(4) Prepare a single-step consolidated income statement, inserting the earnings per share in parentheses on the same line with net income.

(5) Determine the amount of the reduction in consolidated inventories, net income, and retained earnings if Stall Company's inventory had included $50,000 of the merchandise purchased from Pici Corporation.

Problem 18-6A. McVoy Company sells merchandise to and purchases merchandise from various Canadian and Mexican companies. These transactions are settled in the foreign currency. The following selected transactions were completed during the current fiscal year:

Jan. 15. Sold merchandise on account to Vega Company, net 30, 200,000 pesos; exchange rate, $.045 per Mexican peso.

Feb. 14. Received cash from Vega Company; exchange rate, $.044 per Mexican peso.

Apr. 1. Purchased merchandise on account from Leafgron Company, net 30, $10,000 Canadian; exchange rate, $.84 per Canadian dollar.

Apr. 30. Issued check for amount owed to Leafgren Company; exchange rate, $.83 per Canadian dollar.

July 31. Sold merchandise on account to Sanchez Company, net 30, 300,000 pesos; exchange rate, $.044 per Mexican peso.

Aug. 30. Received cash from Sanchez Company; exchange rate, $.046 per Mexican peso.

Oct. 10. Purchased merchandise on account from Chevalier Company, net 30, $20,000 Canadian; exchange rate, $.83 per Canadian dollar.

Nov. 9. Issued check for amount owed to Chevalier Company; exchange rate, $.85 per Canadian dollar.

Dec. 10. Sold merchandise on account to Wilson Company, net 30, $30,000 Canadian; exchange rate, $.85 per Canadian dollar.

11. Purchased merchandise on account from Santos Company, net 30, 250,000 pesos; exchange rate, $.047 per Mexican peso.

31. Recorded unrealized currency exchange gain and/or loss on transactions of December 10 and 11. Exchange rates on December 31: $.86 per Canadian dollar; $.048 per Mexican peso.

Instructions:

(1) Present entries in general journal form to record the transactions and adjusting entries for the year.

(2) Present entries in general journal form to record the payment of the purchase of December 11, on January 10, when the exchange rate was $.046 per Mexican peso, and the receipt of cash from the sale of December 10, on January 13, when the exchange rate was $.87 per Canadian dollar.

Mini-Case

Your grandfather recently retired, sold his home in Flint, Michigan, and moved to a retirement community in Naples, Florida. With some of the proceeds from the sale of his home, he is considering investing $75,000 in the stock market.

In the process of selecting among alternative stock investments, your grandfather collected annual reports from twenty different companies. In reviewing these reports, however, he has become confused and has questions concerning several items which appear in the financial reports. He has asked your help and has written down the following questions for you to answer:

(a) "In reviewing the annual reports, I noticed many references to 'consolidated financial statements.' What are consolidated financial statements?"

(b) "'Excess of cost of business acquired over related net assets' appears on the consolidated balance sheets in several annual reports. What does this mean? Is it an asset (it appears with other assets)?"

(c) "What is minority interest?"

(d) "A footnote to one of the consolidated statements indicated interest and the amount of a loan from one company to another had been eliminated. Is this good accounting? A loan is a loan. How can a company just eliminate a loan that hasn't been paid off?"

(e) "How can financial statements for an American company (in dollars) be combined with a Japanese subsidiary (in yen)?"

(f) "Can I rely on the president's letter in an annual report? All of the letters I have read seem to say the same thing. They simply indicate how successful the company has been in the past and how much better things will be in the future."

(g) "I notice that all the companies file with the Securities and Exchange Commission. Does this mean that the companies are a good investment?"

(h) "Should I try to get the latest interim reports before I make any investments?"

Instructions:

(1) Briefly respond to each of your grandfather's questions.

(2) While discussing the items in (1) with your grandfather, he asked your advice on whether he should limit his investments to one stock. What would you advise?

19
CHAPTER

Statement of Changes in Financial Position

CHAPTER OBJECTIVES

Describe the usefulness of reporting changes in financial position.

Describe alternative concepts of funds.

Describe and illustrate the preparation of a statement of changes in financial position based upon the working capital concept of funds.

Describe and illustrate the preparation of a statement of changes in financial position based upon the cash concept of funds.

PART 6

Additional Statements and Analyses

19

CHAPTER

The financial position of an enterprise as of a specified time is reported on its balance sheet. Indications of the changes in financial position that have occurred during the preceding fiscal period can be determined by comparing the individual items on the current balance sheet with the related amounts on the earlier statement. The income statement and retained earnings statement also reveal some of the details of changes in stockholders' equity. However, significant changes in financial position may be overlooked in the process of examining and comparing the statements and still other changes may be completely undisclosed by the statements. For example, if items of equipment or other plant assets were retired and other items acquired during the period, comparison of the balance sheets will disclose only the net amount of change.

The usefulness of a concise statement devoted entirely to changes in financial position has become increasingly apparent during the past several decades. There has been much experimentation and discussion among accountants concerning the scope, format, and terminology to be used, and the inclusion of such statements in financial reports to stockholders has steadily increased. Guidelines for their preparation were issued by the Accounting Principles Board in 1963.[1] Considerable variation in the form and content of the statement was approved and, although not required, its inclusion as a basic statement in annual financial reports was encouraged. Many titles have been used, including *Statement of Source and Application of Funds, Statement of Resources Provided and Applied, and Statement of Changes in Working Capital*. The term often used as a convenience in discussing the statement is **funds statement**. This shorter term will often be used in the discussions that follow.

The 1963 pronouncement of the Accounting Principles Board was followed by a more definitive opinion in 1971. In addition to broadening the scope of the funds statement, the Board directed that it be a basic financial statement for all profit-oriented enterprises and recommended the adoption of the more descriptive title **Statement of Changes in Financial Position.**[2]

CONCEPTS OF FUNDS

In accounting and financial usage, the term **fund** has many meanings. It was first used in this book to mean segregations of cash for a special purpose, as in "change fund" and "petty cash fund." Later it was used to designate the amount of cash and marketable investments segregated in a "sinking fund" for the purpose of liquidating bonds or other long-term obligations at maturity. When used in the plural form, "funds" is often a synonym for cash, as when a drawee bank refuses to honor a check and returns it to the depositor with the notation "not sufficient funds."

The concept used in funds statements has varied somewhat in practice, with resulting variation in the content of the statements. "Funds" can be interpreted

---

[1] *Opinions of the Accounting Principles Board, No. 3*, "The Statement of Source and Application of Funds" (New York: American Institute of Certified Public Accountants, 1963).

[2] *Opinions of the Accounting Principles Board, No. 19*, "Reporting Changes in Financial Position" (New York: American Institute of Certified Public Accountants, 1971).

broadly to mean "working capital" or, more narrowly, to mean "cash" or "cash and marketable securities." Two statements, one based on working capital and the other on cash, may be prepared for the use of management, but only one statement is usually presented in published financial reports.

Regardless of which of the concepts is used for a specific funds statement, financial position may also be affected by transactions that do not involve funds. If such transactions have occurred during the period, their effect, if significant, should be reported in the funds statement.[3]

WORKING CAPITAL CONCEPT OF FUNDS

The excess of an enterprise's total current assets over its total current liabilities at the same point in time may be termed its "net current assets" or working capital. To illustrate, assume that a corporate balance sheet lists current assets totaling $560,000 and current liabilities totaling $230,000. The working capital of the corporation at the balance sheet date is $330,000 ($560,000 − $230,000). The following comparative schedule includes the major categories of current assets and current liabilities:

	December 31 1985	December 31 1984	Increase Decrease*
Current assets:			
Cash..................................	$ 40,000	$ 35,000	$ 5,000
Marketable securities	60,000	40,000	20,000
Receivables (net).......................	100,000	115,000	15,000*
Inventories............................	350,000	295,000	55,000
Prepaid expenses	10,000	15,000	5,000*
Total	$560,000	$500,000	$60,000
Current liabilities:			
Notes payable	$ 70,000	$ 50,000	$20,000
Accounts payable	125,000	145,000	20,000*
Income tax payable....................	10,000	20,000	10,000*
Dividends payable.....................	25,000	25,000	——
Total	$230,000	$240,000	$10,000*
Working capital.........................	$330,000	$260,000	$70,000

The increase or decrease in each item is reported in the third column of the schedule. The increase of $60,000 in total current assets during the year tended to increase working capital. The decrease of $10,000 in total current liabilities also tended to increase working capital. The combined effect was an increase of $70,000 in working capital. Note that working capital is a "net" concept. An increase or decrease in working capital cannot be determined solely by the amount of change in total current assets or solely by the amount of change in total current liabilities.

---

[3]*Ibid.*, par. 8.

The amount of most of the items classified as current assets and current liabilities varies from one balance sheet date to another. Many of the items change daily. Inventories are increased by purchases on account, which also increase accounts payable. Accounts payable are reduced by payment, which also reduces cash. As merchandise is sold on account, inventories decrease and accounts receivable increase. In turn, the collections from customers increase cash and reduce accounts receivable. An understanding of this continuous interaction among the various current assets and current liabilities is essential to an understanding of the concept of working capital and analyses related to it. In the illustration, for example, the absence of increase or decrease in the amount of dividends payable between balance sheet dates should not be thought of as an indication that the account balance remained unchanged throughout the year. If dividends were paid quarterly, four separate liabilities would have been created and four would have been liquidated during the period. Also, the amount of working capital is neither increased nor decreased by a transaction (1) that affects only current assets (such as a purchase of marketable securities for cash), (2) that affects only current liabilities (such as issuance of a short-term note to a creditor on account), or (3) that affects only current assets and current liabilities (such as payment of an account payable).

Working Capital Flow
The working capital schedule on the preceding page shows an increase of $70,000 in working capital, which may be significant in evaluating financial position. However, the schedule gives no indication of the source of the increase. It could have resulted from the issuance of common stock, from the sale of treasury stock, from operating income, or from a combination of these and other sources. It is also possible that working capital would have increased by considerably more during the year had it not been for the purchase of plant assets, the retirement of bonded indebtedness, an adverse judgment as defendant in a damage suit, or other occurrences with a similar effect on working capital.

Both the inflow and the outflow of funds are reported in a funds statement. Those flowing into the enterprise, classified as to source, form the first section of the funds statement. Funds flowing out of the enterprise, classified according to the manner of their use or application, are reported in the second section of the statement. Ordinarily, the totals of the two sections are unequal. If the inflow (sources) has exceeded the outflow (applications), the excess is the amount of the increase in working capital. When the reverse situation occurs, the excess of outflow is a measure of the amount by which working capital has decreased. Accordingly, the difference between the total of the sources and the applications sections of the funds statement is identified as an increase or a decrease in working capital. The details of this balancing amount are presented in a subsidiary section of the statement or in a separate schedule.

Some of the data needed in preparing a funds statement can be obtained from comparing items on the current balance sheet with those on the preceding balance sheet. Information regarding net income may be obtained from the current income statement and dividend data are available in the retained earnings statement.

However, there may be sources and applications of funds that are not disclosed by these statements. Some of the relevant data can be obtained only from an examination of accounts in the ledger or from journal entries.

Although there are many kinds of transactions that affect funds, consideration will be limited here to the most common sources and applications. As a matter of convenience in the discussion that follows, all asset accounts other than current assets will be referred to as "noncurrent assets" and all liability accounts other than current liabilities will be referred to as "noncurrent liabilities."

Sources of Working Capital

The amount of inflow of working capital from various sources can be determined without reviewing and classifying every transaction that occurred during the period. There is also no need to determine the individual effects of a number of similar transactions; summary figures are sufficient. For purposes of discussion, transactions that provide working capital are classified in terms of their effect on noncurrent accounts, as follows:

1. Transactions that **decrease noncurrent assets.**
2. Transactions that **increase noncurrent liabilities.**
3. Transactions that **increase stockholders' equity.**

Decreases in noncurrent assets. The sale of long-term investments, equipment, buildings, land, patents, or other noncurrent assets for cash or on account provides working capital. However, the reduction in the balance of the noncurrent asset account between the beginning and end of the period is not necessarily the amount of working capital provided by the sale. For example, if a patent carried in the ledger at $30,000 is sold during the year for $70,000, the patents account will decrease by $30,000 but the funds provided by the transaction amounted to $70,000. Similarly, if the long-term investments carried at $120,000 at the beginning of the year are sold for $80,000 cash, the transaction provided funds of $80,000 instead of $120,000.

Increases in noncurrent liabilities. The issuance of bonds or long-term notes is a common source of working capital. For example, if bonds with a face value of $600,000 are sold at 100 for cash, the amount of funds provided by the transaction would be indicated by a $600,000 increase in the bonds payable account. If the bonds were issued at a price above or below 100, it would be necessary to refer to the bond premium or discount account, in addition to the bonds payable account, in order to determine the amount of funds provided by the transaction. For example, if the $600,000 of bonds had been issued at 90 instead of 100, the funds provided would have been $540,000 instead of $600,000.

Increases in stockholders' equity. Often the largest and most frequent source of working capital is profitable operations. Revenues realized from the sale of goods or services are accompanied by increases in working capital. Conversely, many of the expenses incurred are accompanied by decreases in working capital. Since the significant details of revenues and expenses appear in the income statement, they need not be repeated in the funds statement. However, the amount of income from operations reported on the income statement is not necessarily equivalent to the working capital actually provided by operations. Such expenses as depreciation of plant assets and amortization of patents are deducted from revenue but have no effect on current assets or current liabilities. Similarly, the amortization of premium on bonds payable, which decreases interest expense and therefore increases operating income, does not affect current assets or current liabilities. The amount reported on the income statement as income from operations must therefore be adjusted upward or downward to determine the amount of working capital so provided. If gains or losses are reported as "extraordinary" items on the income statement, they should be identified as such on the funds statement.[4]

If capital stock is sold during the period, the amount of working capital provided will not necessarily coincide with the amount of the increase in the capital stock account. Consideration must be given to accompanying debits or credits to other paid-in capital accounts. There also may be entries in stockholders' equity accounts that do not affect working capital, such as a transfer of retained earnings to paid-in capital accounts in the issuance of a stock dividend. Similarly, transfers between the retained earnings account and appropriations accounts have no effect on working capital.

Applications of Working Capital

As in the case of working capital sources, it is convenient to classify applications according to their effects on noncurrent accounts. Transactions affecting the outflow or applications of working capital may be described as follows:

1. Transactions that **increase noncurrent assets.**
2. Transactions that **decrease noncurrent liabilities.**
3. Transactions that **decrease stockholders' equity.**

Increases in noncurrent assets. Working capital may be applied to the purchase of equipment, buildings, land, long-term investments, patents, or other noncurrent assets. However, the amount of funds used for such purposes is not necessarily indicated by the net increases in the related accounts. For example, if the debits to the equipment account for acquisitions during the year totaled $160,000 and the credits to the same account for retirements amounted to $30,000, the net change in the account would be $130,000. Such facts can be determined only by reviewing the details in the account.

Decreases in noncurrent liabilities. The liquidation of bonds or long-term notes represents an application of working capital. However, the decrease in the balance of the liability account does not necessarily indicate the amount of working capital applied. For example, if callable bonds issued at their face value of $100,000 are redeemed at 105, the funds applied would be $105,000 instead of $100,000.

---

[4]Extraordinary items are discussed on page 438.

Decreases in stockholders' equity. Probably the most frequent application of working capital in decreases of stockholders' equity results from the declaration of cash dividends by the board of directors. Funds may also be applied to the redemption of preferred stock or to the purchase of treasury stock. As indicated earlier, the issuance of stock dividends does not affect working capital or financial position.

Other Changes in Financial Position

According to the broadened concept of the funds statement, significant transactions affecting financial position should be reported even though they do not affect funds.[5] For example, if an enterprise issues bonds or capital stock in exchange for land and buildings, the transaction has no effect on working capital. Nevertheless, because of the significant effect on financial position, both the increase in the plant assets and the increase in long-term liabilities or stockholders' equity should be reported on the statement. A complete catalog of the kinds of non-fund transactions that usually have a significant effect on financial position is beyond the scope of the discussion here. The following are illustrative of the many possibilities: preferred or common stock may be issued in liquidation of long-term debt, common stock may be issued in exchange for convertible preferred stock, long-term investments may be exchanged for machinery and equipment, and land and buildings may be received from a municipality as a gift.

Transactions of the type indicated in the preceding paragraph may be reported on the funds statement as though there were two transactions: (1) a source of funds and (2) an application of funds. The relationship of the source and the application should be disclosed by proper wording in the descriptive captions or by footnote. To illustrate, assume that common stock of $200,000 par is issued in exchange for $200,000 face amount of bonds payable, on which there is no unamortized discount or premium. The issuance of the common stock should be reported in the sources section of the statement somewhat as follows: "Issuance of common stock at par in retirement of bonds payable, $200,000." The other part of the transaction could be described in the applications section as follows: "Retirement of bonds payable by the issuance of common stock at par, $200,000."

Assembling Data for the Funds Statement Based on Working Capital

Much of the information on funds flow is obtained in the process of preparing the balance sheet, the income statement, and the retained earnings statement. When the volume of data is substantial, experienced accountants may first assemble all relevant facts in working papers designed for the purpose. Specialized working papers are not essential, however. Because of their complexity, they tend to obscure the basic concepts of funds analysis for anyone who is not already familiar with the subject. For this reason, special working papers will not be used in the following discussion. Instead, the emphasis will be on the basic analyses.[6]

---

[5]*Opinions of the Accounting Principles Board, No. 19, op. cit.,* par. 8.

[6]The use of a work sheet as an aid in assembling data for the funds statement is presented in Appendix E.

In the illustration that follows, the necessary information will be obtained from (1) a comparative balance sheet and (2) the ledger accounts for noncurrent assets, noncurrent liabilities, and stockholders' equity. As each change in a noncurrent item is discussed, data from the related account(s) will be presented. Descriptive notations have been inserted in the accounts to facilitate the explanations. Otherwise, it would be necessary to refer to supportive journal entries to determine the complete effect of some of the transactions. The comparative balance sheet in simplified form is as follows:

COMPARATIVE
BALANCE SHEET

T. R. Morgan Corporation Comparative Balance Sheet December 31, 1985 and 1984			
	1985	1984	Increase Decrease*
Assets			
Cash	$ 49,000	$ 26,000	$ 23,000
Trade receivables (net)	74,000	65,000	9,000
Inventories	172,000	180,000	8,000*
Prepaid expenses	4,000	3,000	1,000
Investments (long-term)	——	45,000	45,000*
Land	90,000	40,000	50,000
Building	200,000	200,000	——
Accumulated depreciation—building	(36,000)	(30,000)	(6,000)
Equipment	180,000	142,000	38,000
Accumulated depreciation—equipment	(43,000)	(40,000)	(3,000)
Total assets	$690,000	$631,000	$ 59,000
Liabilities			
Accounts payable (merchandise creditors)	$ 50,000	$ 32,000	$ 18,000
Income tax payable	2,500	4,000	1,500*
Dividends payable	15,000	8,000	7,000
Bonds payable	120,000	245,000	125,000*
Total liabilities	$187,500	$289,000	$101,500*
Stockholders' Equity			
Common stock	$280,000	$230,000	$ 50,000
Retained earnings	222,500	112,000	110,500
Total stockholders' equity	$502,500	$342,000	$160,500
Total liabilities and stockholders' equity	$690,000	$631,000	$ 59,000

Since only the noncurrent accounts reveal sources and applications of funds, it is not necessary to examine the current asset accounts or the current liability accounts. The first of the noncurrent accounts listed on the comparative balance sheet of the T. R. Morgan Corporation is Investments.

Investments

The comparative balance sheet indicates that investments decreased by $45,000. The notation in the following investments account indicates that the investments were sold for $75,000 in cash.

ACCOUNT INVESTMENTS					ACCOUNT NO.	
Date		Item	Debit	Credit	Balance	
					Debit	Credit
1985						
Jan.	1	Balance			45,000	
June	8	Sold for $75,000 cash		45,000	——	——

The $30,000 gain on the sale is included in the net income reported on the income statement. It is necessary, of course, to report also the book value of the investments sold, as an additional source of working capital. To report the entire proceeds of $75,000 as a source of working capital would incorrectly include the gain reported in operating income. Accordingly, to avoid a double reporting of the $30,000 gain, the notation is as follows:

Source of working capital:
Book value of investments sold (excludes $30,000 gain
    reported in net income)............................ $45,000

The proceeds from the sale of investments would appear on the funds statement in two places: (1) book value of investments sold, $45,000, and (2) gain on sale of investments as part of net income, $30,000.

Land

The comparative balance sheet indicates that land increased by $50,000. The notation in the land account, as shown below, indicates that the land was acquired by issuance of common stock at par.

ACCOUNT LAND					ACCOUNT NO.	
Date		Item	Debit	Credit	Balance	
					Debit	Credit
1985						
Jan.	1	Balance			40,000	
Dec.	28	Acquired by issuance of				
		common stock at par	50,000		90,000	

Although working capital was not involved in this transaction, the acquisition represents a significant change in financial position, which may be noted as follows:

Application of working capital:
Purchase of land by issuance of common stock at par... $50,000

Building

According to the comparative balance sheet, there was no change in the $200,000 balance between the beginning and end of the year. Reference to the building account in the ledger confirms the absence of entries during the year and hence the account is not shown here. The credit in the related accumulated depreciation account, shown below, reduced the investment in building, but working capital was not affected.

ACCOUNT ACCUMULATED DEPRECIATION — BUILDING					ACCOUNT NO.	
Date	Item	Debit	Credit	Balance		
				Debit	Credit	
1985						
Jan. 1	Balance					30,000
Dec. 31	Depreciation for year		6,000			36,000

Equipment

The comparative balance sheet indicates that the cost of equipment increased $38,000. The equipment account and the accumulated depreciation account illustrated below reveal that the net change of $38,000 was the result of two separate transactions, the discarding of equipment that had cost $9,000 and the purchase of equipment for $47,000. The equipment discarded had been fully depreciated, as indicated by the debit of $9,000 in the accumulated depreciation account, and no salvage was realized from its disposal. Hence, the transaction had no effect on working capital and is not reported on the funds statement.

ACCOUNT EQUIPMENT					ACCOUNT NO.	
Date	Item	Debit	Credit	Balance		
				Debit	Credit	
1985						
Jan. 1	Balance			142,000		
May 9	Discarded, no salvage		9,000			
July 7	Purchased for cash	47,000		180,000		

ACCOUNT ACCUMULATED DEPRECIATION — EQUIPMENT					ACCOUNT NO.	
Date	Item	Debit	Credit	Balance		
				Debit	Credit	
1985						
Jan. 1	Balance					40,000
May 9	Discarded, no salvage	9,000				
Dec. 31	Depreciation for year		12,000			43,000

The effect on funds of the purchase of equipment for $47,000 was as follows:

Application of working capital:
    Purchase of equipment. $47,000

The credit in the accumulated depreciation account had the effect of reducing the investment in equipment by $12,000 but caused no change in working capital. Further attention will be given to depreciation in a later paragraph.

Bonds Payable

The next noncurrent item listed on the balance sheet, bonds payable, decreased $125,000 during the year. Examination of the bonds payable account, which appears below, indicates that $125,000 of the bonds payable were retired by payment of the face amount.

ACCOUNT BONDS PAYABLE   ACCOUNT NO.

Date		Item	Debit	Credit	Balance Debit	Balance Credit
1985						
Jan.	1	Balance				245,000
June	30	Retired by payment of cash at face amount	125,000			120,000

This transaction's effect on funds is noted as follows:

Application of working capital:
Retirement of bonds payable.......................... $125,000

Common Stock

The increase of $50,000 in the common stock account, as shown below, is identified as stock having been issued in exchange for land valued at $50,000.

ACCOUNT COMMON STOCK   ACCOUNT NO.

Date		Item	Debit	Credit	Balance Debit	Balance Credit
1985						
Jan.	1	Balance				230,000
Dec.	28	Issued at par in exchange for land		50,000		280,000

This change in financial position should be reported on the funds statement and may be noted as follows:

Source of working capital:
Issuance of common stock at par for land.............. $50,000

Retained Earnings

According to the comparative balance sheet, there was an increase of $110,500 in retained earnings during the year. The retained earnings account, as shown below, was credited for $140,500 of net income, which included the gain on sale of investments, and was debited for $30,000 of cash dividends.

ACCOUNT RETAINED EARNINGS						ACCOUNT NO.	
Date		Item	Debit	Credit	Balance		
					Debit	Credit	
1985							
Jan.	1	Balance				112,000	
Dec.	31	Net income		140,500			
	31	Cash dividends	30,000			222,500	

The net income as reported on the income statement must usually be adjusted upward and/or downward to determine the amount of working capital provided by operations. Although most operating expenses either decrease current assets or increase current liabilities, thus affecting working capital, depreciation expense does not do so. The amount of net income understates the amount of working capital provided by operations to the extent that depreciation expense is deducted from revenue. Accordingly, the depreciation expense for the year on the equipment ($12,000) and the building ($6,000), totaling $18,000, must be added back to the $140,500 reported as net income.

The data to be reported as working capital provided by operations is noted as follows:

> *Source of working capital:*
>   Operations during the year:
>   Net income.............................. $140,500
>   Add deduction not decreasing working
>   capital during the year:
>   Depreciation .... __18,000__ $158,500

Working capital is applied to cash dividends at the time the current liability is incurred, regardless of when the dividends are actually paid. The effect of the declaration of cash dividends of $30,000, recorded as a debit in the retained earnings account, is indicated as follows:

> *Application of working capital:*
>   Declaration of cash dividends........................ $30,000

Form of the Funds Statement Based on Working Capital

Although there are many possible variations in the form and the content of the funds statement, the first section is usually devoted to the source of funds, with income from operations presented as the first item.[7] The second section is devoted to the application or use of funds. There may also be a third section in which changes in the amounts of the current assets and the current liabilities are reported.

---

[7]*Opinions of the Accounting Principles Board, No. 19, op. cit.,* par. 10.

The difference between the totals of the sources section and the applications section of the funds statement is identified as the increase or the decrease in working capital. The net change in the amount of working capital reported on the statement should be supported by details of the changes in each of the working capital components.[8] The information may be presented in a third section of the statement, as in the following illustration for T. R. Morgan Corporation, or it may be presented as a separate tabulation accompanying the statement. The data required in either case can be taken from the comparative balance sheet. The two amounts identified as the increase or decrease in working capital ($1,500 increase in the illustration) must agree.

STATEMENT OF
CHANGES IN
FINANCIAL
POSITION—BASED
ON WORKING
CAPITAL

T. R. Morgan Corporation Statement of Changes in Financial Position For Year Ended December 31, 1985			
Sources of working capital:			
Operations during the year:			
Net income............................		$140,500	
Add deduction not decreasing working capital during the year:			
Depreciation		18,000	$158,500
Book value of investments sold (excludes $30,000 gain reported in net income)		45,000	
Issuance of common stock at par for land		50,000	$253,500
Applications of working capital:			
Purchase of land by issuance of common stock at par ..	$ 50,000		
Purchase of equipment..............................	47,000		
Retirement of bonds payable.........................	125,000		
Declaration of cash dividends........................	30,000	252,000	
Increase in working capital.............................		$ 1,500	
Changes in components of working capital:			
Increase (decrease) in current assets:			
Cash	$ 23,000		
Trade receivables (net).............................	9,000		
Inventories	(8,000)		
Prepaid expenses...................................	1,000	$ 25,000	
Increase (decrease) in current liabilities:			
Accounts payable..................................	$ 18,000		
Income tax payable................................	(1,500)		
Dividends payable	7,000	23,500	
Increase in working capital............................		$ 1,500	

---

[8]*Ibid*., par. 12.

ANALYSIS OF
CASH

When the cash concept of funds is used, the analysis is devoted to the movement of cash rather than to the inflow and outflow of working capital.[9] The portion of the statement devoted to operations may report the total revenue that provided cash, followed by deductions for operating costs and expenses requiring the outlay of cash. The usual practice, however, is to begin with net income from operations as was done in the preceding illustration. This basic amount is then adjusted for increases and decreases of all working capital items except cash, using the procedures demonstrated later in the chapter.

There has been much experimentation in the methodology of cash flow analysis and in the form of the related funds statement. The approach that will be used here is patterned after the procedures used in the preceding discussion and illustrations. Although the working capital concept of funds discussed earlier is used more often, particularly in preparing funds statements for reports to stockholders, the cash concept is useful in evaluating financial policies and current cash position. It is especially useful to management in preparing cash budgets.

The format of a funds statement based on the cash concept may be quite similar to the format of a funds statement based on the working capital concept. It is usually divided into two main sections—sources of cash and applications of cash. The difference between the totals of the two sections is the cash increase or decrease for the period. The main parts of the report may be followed by a listing of the cash balance at the beginning of the period, at the end of the period, and the net change. An alternative is to begin the statement with the beginning cash balance, add the total of the sources section, subtract the total of the applications section, and conclude with the cash balance at the end of the period.

Assembling Data for the Funds Statement Based on Cash

The comparative balance sheet of T. R. Morgan Corporation on page 536 and the related accounts presented on the following pages will be used as the basis for illustration.[10] Reference to the earlier analysis discloses that the sale of investments yielded cash and that there were cash outlays for equipment and the retirement of bonds. These transactions may be noted as follows:

> *Source of cash:*
> Book value of investments sold (excludes $30,000 gain
>   reported in net income)............................ $ 45,000
> *Applications of cash:*
> Purchase of equipment............................... $ 47,000
> Retirement of bonds payable......................... 125,000

The earlier analysis also indicated that land was acquired by the issuance of common stock. Although the transaction did not involve cash, it resulted in a significant change in financial position and should be reported on the statement. It is as if the common stock had been issued for cash and the cash received had then

---

[9] The concept may be expanded to include temporary investments that are readily convertible into cash.
[10] The use of a work sheet as an aid in assembling data for the funds statement is presented in Appendix E.

been expended for the parcel of land. The following notation indicates the manner in which the transaction is to be reported in the statement:

Source of cash:
Issuance of common stock at par for land $50,000
Application of cash:
Purchase of land by issuance of common stock at par . . . $50,000

The amount of cash provided by operations usually differs from the amount of net income. The amount of cash used to pay dividends may also differ from the amount of cash dividends declared. The determination of these amounts is discussed in the paragraphs that follow.

Cash Provided by Operations

The starting point in the analysis of the effect of operations on cash is net income for the period. This amount was reported for T. R. Morgan Corporation on page 540 as $140,500. As in the earlier analysis, depreciation expense of $18,000 must be added to the $140,500 because depreciation expense did not decrease the amount of cash. In addition, it is necessary to recognize the relationship of the accrual method of accounting to the movement of cash. Usually, a part of some of the other costs and expenses reported on the income statement, as well as a part of the revenue earned, is not accompanied by cash outflow or inflow.

There is often a period of time between the accrual of a revenue and the receipt of the related cash. Perhaps the most common example is the sale of merchandise or a service on account, for which payment is received at a later point in time. Hence, the amount reported on the income statement as revenue from sales is not likely to correspond with the amount of the related cash inflow for the same period.

Timing differences between the incurrence of an expense and the related cash outflow must also be considered in determining the amount of cash provided by operations. For example, the amount reported on the income statement as insurance expense is the amount of insurance premiums expired rather than the amount of premiums paid during the period. Similarly, supplies paid for in one year may be used and thus converted to an expense in a later year. Conversely, a portion of some of the expenses incurred near the end of one period, such as wages and taxes, may not require a cash outlay until the following period.

The T. R. Morgan Corporation balance sheet (page 536) provides the following data that identify timing differences affecting the amount of cash inflow and outflow from operations:

| | December 31 | | Increase |
Accounts	1985	1984	Decrease*
Trade receivables (net)	$ 74,000	$ 65,000	$ 9,000
Inventories.	172,000	180,000	8,000*
Prepaid expenses	4,000	3,000	1,000
Accounts payable (merchandise creditors)	50,000	32,000	18,000
Income tax payable.	2,500	4,000	1,500*

The effect of timing differences is indicated by the amount and the direction of change in the balances of the asset and liability accounts affected by operations. Decreases in such assets and increases in such liabilities during the period must be added to the amount reported as income from operations. Conversely, increases in such assets and decreases in such liabilities must be deducted from the amount reported as income from operations.

Trade receivables (net) increase. The additions to trade receivables for sales on account during the year were $9,000 more than the deductions for amounts collected from customers on account. The amount reported on the income statement as sales therefore included $9,000 that did not yield cash inflow during the year. Accordingly, $9,000 must be deducted from income to determine the amount of cash provided by operations.

Inventories decrease. The $8,000 decrease in inventories indicates that the merchandise sold exceeded the cost of the merchandise purchased by $8,000. The amount reported on the income statement as a deduction from the revenue therefore included $8,000 that did not require cash outflow during the year. Accordingly, $8,000 must be added to income to determine the amount of cash provided by operations.

Prepaid expenses increase. The outlay of cash for prepaid expenses exceeded by $1,000 the amount deducted as an expense during the year. Hence, $1,000 must be deducted from income to determine the amount of cash provided by operations.

Accounts payable increase. The effect of the increase in the amount owed creditors for goods and services was to include in expired costs and expenses the sum of $18,000 for which there had been no cash outlay during the year. Income was thereby reduced by $18,000, though there was no cash outlay. Hence, $18,000 must be added to income to determine the amount of cash provided by operations.

Income tax payable decrease. The outlay of cash for income taxes exceeded by $1,500 the amount of income tax deducted as an expense during the period. Accordingly, $1,500 must be deducted from income to determine the amount of cash provided by operations.

The foregoing adjustments to income may be summarized as follows in a format suitable for the funds statement:

Source of cash:
  Operations during the year:
    Net income $140,500
    Add deductions not decreasing cash during the year:
      Depreciation $18,000
      Decrease in inventories   8,000
      Increase in accounts payable   18,000   44,000
                                                                                        $184,500
    Deduct additions not increasing cash during the year:
      Increase in trade receivables . . . . $ 9,000
      Increase in prepaid expenses   1,000
      Decrease in income tax payable   1,500   11,500 $173,000

Cash Applied to Payment of Dividends

According to the retained earnings account of T. R. Morgan Corporation (page 540), cash dividends of $30,000 were declared during the year. In the earlier funds flow analysis, this was noted as the amount of working capital applied to the declaration of cash dividends. However, the amounts reported as dividends payable on T. R. Morgan Corporation's comparative balance sheet (page 536) are $15,000 and $8,000 respectively, revealing a timing difference between declaration and payment.

According to the dividends payable account, shown below, dividend payments during the year totaled $23,000.

ACCOUNT	DIVIDENDS PAYABLE				ACCOUNT NO.	
Date		Item	Debit	Credit	Balance	
					Debit	Credit
1985						
Jan	1	Balance				8,000
	10	Cash paid	8,000		—	—
June	20	Dividend declared		15,000		15,000
July	10	Cash paid	15,000		—	—
Dec.	20	Dividend declared		15,000		15,000

The amount of cash applied to dividend payments may be noted as follows:

Application of cash:
Cash dividends declared $30,000
Deduct increase in dividends payable 7,000 $23,000

Form of the Funds Statement Based on Cash

The funds statement based on cash is comparable in form to the funds statement illustrated on page 541. The greatest difference between the two statements is in the section devoted to funds provided by operations. The statement shown at the top of page 546 is supported by a reconciliation of the change in cash, but a funds statement based on cash may conclude with the amount of increase or decrease in cash.

CASH FLOW FROM OPERATIONS

The term **cash flow** is sometimes encountered in reports to stockholders. It may be mentioned in a company president's letter to stockholders, in operating summaries, or elsewhere in the published financial report. Although there are variations in the method of determination, cash flow is approximately equivalent to income from operations plus depreciation, depletion, and any other expenses that had no effect on working capital during the period. Many terms have been used to describe the amount so determined, including "cash flow from operations," "cash income," "cash earnings," and "cash throw-off."

The amount of cash flow from operations for a period may be useful to internal financial management in considering the possibility of retiring long-term debt, in planning replacement of plant facilities, or in formulating dividend policies. How-

T. R. Morgan Corporation
Statement of Changes in Financial Position
For Year Ended December 31, 1985

Sources of cash:
Operations during the year:
Net income............................... $140,500
Add deductions not decreasing cash during
the year:
Depreciation $18,000
Decrease in inventories........ 8,000
Increase in accounts payable.... 18,000   44,000
$184,500
Deduct additions not increasing
cash during the year:
Increase in trade receivables.... $ 9,000
Increase in prepaid expenses... 1,000
Decrease in income tax payable .. 1,500   11,500 $173,000
Book value of investments sold (excludes $30,000 gain re-
ported in net income)   45,000
Issuance of common stock at par for land.............   50,000 $268,000

Applications of cash:
Purchase of land by issuance of common stock at par .. $ 50,000
Purchase of equipment...............................   47,000
Retirement of bonds payable.........................   125,000
Payment of dividends:
Cash dividends declared .... $ 30,000
Deduct increase in dividends payable   7,000   23,000   245,000
Increase in cash.................................... $ 23,000

Change in cash balance:
Cash balance, December 31, 1985 .... $ 49,000
Cash balance, December 31, 1984   26,000
Increase in cash.................................... $ 23,000

ever, when it is presented without reference to the funds statement and its importance stressed in reporting operations to stockholders, it is likely to be misunderstood. The reporting of so-called cash flow per share of stock may be even more misleading, particularly when the amount is larger, which it usually is, than the net income per share. Readers are quite likely to substitute cash flow for net income in appraising the relative success of operations. Guidelines for determining acceptable terminology and practice have been expressed as follows:

The amount of working capital or cash provided from operations is not a substitute for or an improvement upon properly determined net income as a measure of results of operations and the consequent effect on financial position. Terms referring to "cash" should not be used to describe amounts provided from operations unless all non-cash items have been appropriately adjusted.... The Board strongly recommends that isolated statistics of working capital or cash provided from operations, especially per-share amounts, not be presented in annual reports to shareholders. If any per-share data relating to flow of working capital or cash are presented, they should as a minimum include amounts for inflow from operations, inflow from other sources, and total outflow, and each per-share amount should be clearly identified with the corresponding total amount shown in the Statement.[11]

Self-Examination Questions
(Answers in Appendix C.)

1. If an enterprise's total current assets are $225,000 and its total current liabilities are $150,000, its working capital is:
   A. $75,000
   B. $225,000
   C. $375,000
   D. none of the above

2. Which of the following types of transactions would provide working capital?
   A. Transactions that decrease noncurrent assets
   B. Transactions that decrease noncurrent liabilities
   C. Transactions that decrease stockholders' equity
   D. None of the above

3. Which of the following transactions represents an application of working capital?
   A. Sale of common stock for cash
   B. Issuance of bonds payable for cash
   C. Acquisition of equipment for cash
   D. None of the above

4. The net income reported on the income statement for the year was $55,000 and depreciation on plant assets for the year was $22,000. The balances of the current asset and current liability accounts at the beginning and end of the year are as follows:

	End	Beginning
Cash	$ 65,000	$ 70,000
Trade receivables	100,000	90,000
Inventories	145,000	150,000
Prepaid expenses	7,500	8,000
Accounts payable (merchandise creditors)	51,000	58,000

   The total amount reported for working capital provided by operations in the statement of changes in financial position would be:
   A. $33,000
   B. $55,000
   C. $77,000
   D. none of the above

---

[11]*Opinions of the Accounting Principles Board, No. 19, op. cit.*, par. 15.

5. Based on the data presented in Question 4, the total amount reported for the cash provided by operations in the statement of changes in financial position would be:
   A. $33,000   C. $77,000
   B. $55,000   D. none of the above

Discussion Questions

1. What is the shorter term often employed in referring to the statement of changes in financial position?

2. What are the principal concepts of the term *funds,* as employed in referring to the statement of changes in financial position?

3. (a) What is meant by *working capital*? (b) Name another term, other than "funds," that has the same meaning.

4. State the effect of each of the following transactions, considered individually, on working capital:
   (a) Purchased $5,000 of merchandise on account, terms 1/10, n/30.
   (b) Sold, for $900 cash, merchandise that had cost $600.
   (c) Issued 1,000 shares of $100 par preferred stock for $102 a share, receiving cash.
   (d) Received $400 from a customer on account.
   (e) Purchased office equipment for $1,750 on account.
   (f) Issued a $2,000, 30-day non-interest-bearing note to a creditor in temporary settlement of an account payable.
   (g) Borrowed $50,000 cash, issuing a 90-day, 12% note.

5. When the total of the applications section exceeds the total of the sources section on a statement of changes in financial position based on working capital, is this excess identified as an increase or as a decrease in working capital?

6. What is the effect on working capital of writing off $2,500 of uncollectible accounts against Allowance for Doubtful Accounts?

7. A corporation issued $1,000,000 of 20-year bonds for cash at 95. (a) Did the transaction provide funds or apply funds? (b) What was the amount of funds involved? (c) Was working capital affected? (d) Was cash affected?

8. Fully depreciated equipment costing $25,000 was discarded. What was the effect of the transaction on working capital if (a) $500 cash is received, (b) there is no salvage value?

9. A long-term investment in bonds with a cost of $90,000 was sold for $75,000 cash. (a) What was the gain or loss on the sale? (b) What was the effect of the transaction on working capital? (c) How should the transaction be reported in the funds statement?

10. The board of directors declared a cash dividend of $75,000 near the end of the fiscal year, which ends on December 31, payable in January. (a) What was the effect of the declaration on working capital? (b) Did the declaration represent a source or an application of working capital? (c) Did the payment of the dividend in January affect working capital, and if so, how?

11. (a) What is the effect on working capital of the declaration and issuance of a stock dividend? (b) Does the stock dividend represent a source or an application of working capital?

12. On its income statement for the current year, a company reported a net loss of $75,000 from operations. On its statement of changes in financial position, it reported an increase of $50,000 in working capital from operations. Explain the seeming contradiction between the loss and the increase in working capital.

13. What is the effect on working capital of an appropriation of retained earnings for plant expansion?

14. A net loss of $75,000 from operations is reported on the income statement. The only revenue or expense item reported that did not affect working capital was depreciation expense of $45,000. Will the change in financial position attributed to operations appear in the funds statement as a source or as an application of working capital, and at what amount?

15. Assume that a corporation has net income of $200,000 that included a charge of $5,000 for the amortization of bond discount and depreciation expense of $75,000. What amount should this corporation report on its funds statement for working capital provided by operations?

16. A corporation acquired as a long-term investment all of another corporation's capital stock, valued at $10,000,000, by the issuance of $10,000,000 of its own common stock. Where should the transaction be reported on the statement of changes in financial position (a) if the cash concept of funds is employed, and (b) if the working capital concept of funds is employed?

17. A retail enterprise, employing the accrual method of accounting, owed merchandise creditors (accounts payable) $275,000 at the beginning of the year and $240,000 at the end of the year. What adjustment for the $35,000 decrease must be made to income from operations in determining the amount of cash provided by operations? Explain.

18. If revenue from sales amounted to $975,000 for the year and trade receivables totaled $120,000 and $95,000 at the beginning and end of the year respectively, what was the amount of cash received from customers during the year?

19. If salaries payable was $75,000 and $65,000 at the beginning and end of the year respectively, should $10,000 be added to or deducted from income to determine the amount of cash provided by operations? Explain.

20. The board of directors declared cash dividends totaling $100,000 during the current year. The comparative balance sheet indicates dividends payable of $30,000 at the beginning of the year and $25,000 at the end of the year. What was the amount of cash disbursed to stockholders during the year?

Exercises

Exercise 19-1. Using the following schedule of current assets and current liabilities, prepare the section of the statement of changes in financial position entitled "Changes in components of working capital."

	End of Year	Beginning of Year
Cash	$ 49,500	$ 45,400
Trade receivables (net)	55,500	60,000
Inventories	151,250	147,750
Prepaid expenses	4,700	4,550
Accounts payable	55,000	51,500
Dividends payable	15,000	12,500
Salaries payable	9,750	11,000

Exercise 19-2. The net income reported on an income statement for the current year was $79,250. Adjustments required to determine the amount of working capital provided by operations, as well as some other data used for the year-end adjusting entries, are described as follows:

(a) Uncollectible accounts expense, $6,100.
(b) Depreciation expense, $27,500.
(c) Amortization of patents, $4,500.
(d) Interest accrued on notes payable, $1,150.
(e) Income tax payable, $11,500.
(f) Wages accrued but not paid, $3,750.

Prepare the working-capital-provided-by-operations section of the statement of changes in financial position.

Exercise 19-3. On the basis of the details of the following plant asset account, indicate the items to be reported as a source of working capital and as an application of working capital on the statement of changes in financial position.

ACCOUNT LAND   ACCOUNT NO.

Date		Item	Debit	Credit	Balance	
					Debit	Credit
19--						
Jan.	1	Balance			650,000	
Aug.	29	Purchased with long-term mortgage note	200,000			
Dec.	9	Purchased for cash	75,000		925,000	

Exercise 19-4. On the basis of the following stockholders' equity accounts, indicate the items, exclusive of net income, to be reported as a source of working capital and as an application of working capital on the statement of changes in financial position.

ACCOUNT COMMON STOCK, $20 PAR   ACCOUNT NO.

Date		Item	Debit	Credit	Balance	
					Debit	Credit
19--						
Jan.	1	Balance, 40,000 shares				800,000
Feb.	10	5,000 shares issued for cash		100,000		
July	25	1,350 share stock dividend		27,000		927,000

ACCOUNT PREMIUM ON COMMON STOCK   ACCOUNT NO.

Date		Item	Debit	Credit	Balance Debit	Balance Credit
19--						
Jan.	1	Balance				140,000
Feb.	10	5,000 shares issued for cash		50,000		
July	25	Stock dividend		13,500		203,500

ACCOUNT RETAINED EARNINGS   ACCOUNT NO.

Date		Item	Debit	Credit	Balance Debit	Balance Credit
19						
Jan.	1	Balance				425,000
July	25	Stock dividend	40,500			
Dec.	31	Cash dividends	91,350			
	31	Net income		165,000		458,150

Exercise 19-5. An analysis of the general ledger accounts indicated that delivery equipment, which had cost $35,000 and on which accumulated depreciation totaled $29,750 on the date of sale, was sold for $7,000 during the year. Using this information, indicate the items to be reported as a source of working capital and as an application of working capital on the statement of changes in financial position.

Exercise 19-6. The net income reported on an income statement for the current year was $92,125. Depreciation recorded on equipment and building for the year amounted to $34,500. Balances of the current asset and current liability accounts at the beginning and end of the year are as follows:

	End	Beginning
Cash...	$ 69,750	$ 61,250
Trade receivables	80,500	75,000
Inventories.............................	110,000	97,000
Prepaid expenses	6,900	7,400
Accounts payable (merchandise creditors)...........	69,700	72,700
Salaries payable	7,500	6,250

Prepare the cash-provided-by-operations section of a statement of changes in financial position.

Exercise 19-7. The following information was taken from the records of C. D. Collins Co.:
(a) Equipment and land were acquired for cash.
(b) There were no disposals of equipment during the year.
(c) The investments were sold for $80,000 cash.
(d) The common stock was issued for cash.
(e) There was a $76,750 credit to Retained Earnings for net income.
(f) There was a $45,000 debit to Retained Earnings for cash dividends declared.

Based on this information and the following comparative balance sheet, prepare a statement of changes in financial position, employing the working capital concept of funds.

| | June 30 | |
	Current Year	Preceding Year
Cash..	$ 64,200	$ 49,900
Trade receivables (net)	91,500	80,000
Inventories.....................................	105,900	90,500
Investments....................................	——	75,000
Land..	85,000	——
Equipment.....................................	355,000	275,000
Accumulated depreciation........................	(149,000)	(119,000)
	$552,600	$451,400
Accounts payable (merchandise creditors)..........	$ 62,450	$ 55,000
Dividends payable...............................	12,000	10,000
Common stock, $20 par..........................	300,000	250,000
Premium on common stock.......................	22,000	12,000
Retained earnings	156,150	124,400
	$552,600	$451,400

Exercise 19-8. From the data presented in Exercise 19-7, prepare a statement of changes in financial position, employing the cash concept of funds.

Problems
*(Problems in
Appendix B:
19-1B, 19-2B,
19-3B, 19-4B,
19-5B.)*

Problem 19-1A. The comparative balance sheet of Chow Corporation at September 30 of the current year and the preceding year is as follows:

Assets	Current Year	Preceding Year
Cash...	$ 39,600	$ 52,000
Accounts receivable (net)	88,750	70,000
Merchandise inventory	149,550	130,750
Prepaid expenses	4,300	2,700
Plant assets......................................	280,500	260,500
Accumulated depreciation—plant assets	(170,500)	(187,000)
	$392,200	$328,950
Liabilities and Stockholders' Equity		
Accounts payable	$ 68,700	$ 43,200
Mortgage note payable	——	75,000
Common stock, $10 par............................	150,000	100,000
Premium on common stock.........................	40,000	25,000
Retained earnings	133,500	85,750
	$392,200	$328,950

Additional data obtained from the income statement and from an examination of the noncurrent asset, noncurrent liability, and stockholders' equity accounts in the ledger are as follows:

(a) Net income, $87,750.
(b) Depreciation reported on the income statement, $29,500.
(c) An addition to the building was constructed at a cost of $66,000, and fully depreciated equipment costing $46,000 was discarded, no salvage being realized.
(d) The mortgage note payable was not due until 1990, but the terms permitted earlier payment without penalty.
(e) 5,000 shares of common stock were issued at $13 for cash.
(f) Cash dividends declared, $40,000.

Instructions:

Prepare a statement of changes in financial position (working capital concept), including a section on changes in components of working capital.

Problem 19-2A. The comparative balance sheet of Wei Corporation at December 31 of the current year and the preceding year is as follows:

Assets	Current Year	Preceding Year
Cash...	$ 62,750	$ 82,400
Trade receivables (net)........................	148,200	119,200
Inventories....................................	216,350	236,100
Prepaid expenses	4,500	3,900
Land..	100,000	100,000
Buildings	633,300	458,300
Accumulated depreciation — buildings	(202,500)	(185,000)
Machinery and equipment......................	250,000	250,000
Accumulated depreciation — machinery and equipment ..	(130,600)	(108,400)
Patents.......................................	50,000	62,500
	$1,132,000	$1,019,000

Liabilities and Stockholders' Equity		
Accounts payable (merchandise creditors)	$ 36,280	$ 51,780
Dividends payable.............................	25,000	40,000
Salaries payable..............................	18,480	12,480
Mortgage note payable, due 1992....................	100,000	——
Bonds payable................................	——	80,000
Common stock, $10 par........................	450,000	400,000
Premium on common stock.....................	80,000	50,000
Retained earnings	422,240	384,740
	$1,132,000	$1,019,000

An examination of the income statement and the accounting records revealed the following additional information applicable to the current year:

(a) Net income, $62,500.
(b) Depreciation expense reported on the income statement: buildings, $17,500; machinery and equipment, $22,200.

(c) Patent amortization reported on the income statement, $12,500.

(d) A mortgage note for $100,000 was issued in connection with the construction of a building costing $175,000; the remainder was paid in cash.

(e) 5,000 shares of common stock were issued at 16 in exchange for the bonds payable.

(f) Cash dividends declared, $25,000.

Instructions:

Prepare a statement of changes in financial position (working capital concept), including a section for changes in components of working capital.

Problem 19-3A. The comparative balance sheet of Wei Corporation and other data necessary for the analysis of the corporation's funds flow are presented in Problem 19-2A.

Instructions:

Prepare a statement of changes in financial position (cash concept), including a summary of the change in cash balance.

Problem 19-4A. A comparative balance sheet of W. A. Sussman Inc., at December 31 of the current year and the preceding year, and the noncurrent asset accounts, the noncurrent liability accounts, and the stockholders' equity accounts for the current year, are as follows:

Assets	Current Year	Preceding Year
Cash......................................	$ 77,900	$ 62,100
Trade receivables (net).........................	128,800	109,200
Income tax refund receivable	5,000	——
Inventories....................................	184,800	205,000
Prepaid expenses	7,450	8,150
Investments..................................	100,000	200,000
Land...	56,000	100,000
Buildings	550,000	250,000
Accumulated depreciation — buildings.........	(73,100)	(61,500)
Equipment...................................	482,000	392,000
Accumulated depreciation — equipment	(181,620)	(156,420)
	$1,337,230	$1,108,530

Liabilities and Stockholders' Equity		
Accounts payable (merchandise creditors)......	$ 61,400	$ 82,750
Income tax payable...........................	——	9,000
Notes payable	355,000	30,000
Discount on long-term notes payable	(24,750)	(1,500)
Common stock, $20 par.......................	515,000	500,000
Premium on common stock....................	70,000	60,000
Appropriation for contingencies	100,000	75,000
Retained earnings	260,580	353,280
	$1,337,230	$1,108,530

ACCOUNT INVESTMENTS   ACCOUNT NO.

Date		Item	Debit	Credit	Balance Debit	Balance Credit
19-- Jan.	1	Balance			200,000	
Feb.	20	Realized $91,000 cash from sale		100,000	100,000	

ACCOUNT LAND   ACCOUNT NO.

Date		Item	Debit	Credit	Balance Debit	Balance Credit
19-- Jan.	1	Balance			100,000	
May	5	Realized $60,000 from sale		44,000	56,000	

ACCOUNT BUILDINGS   ACCOUNT NO.

Date		Item	Debit	Credit	Balance Debit	Balance Credit
19-- Jan.	1	Balance			250,000	
June	30	Acquired with notes payable	300,000		550,000	

ACCOUNT ACCUMULATED DEPRECIATION—BUILDINGS   ACCOUNT NO.

Date		Item	Debit	Credit	Balance Debit	Balance Credit
19-- Jan.	1	Balance				61,500
Dec.	31	Depreciation for year		11,600		73,100

ACCOUNT EQUIPMENT   ACCOUNT NO.

Date		Item	Debit	Credit	Balance Debit	Balance Credit
19-- Jan.	1	Balance			392,000	
Mar	19	Discarded, no salvage		25,000		
June	2	Purchased for cash	75,000			
Oct.	10	Purchased for cash	40,000		482,000	

ACCOUNT ACCUMULATED DEPRECIATION—EQUIPMENT   ACCOUNT NO.

Date		Item	Debit	Credit	Balance Debit	Balance Credit
19-- Jan.	1	Balance				156,420
Mar.	19	Equipment discarded	25,000			
Dec.	31	Depreciation for year		50,200		181,620

ACCOUNT LONG-TERM NOTES PAYABLE · ACCOUNT NO.

Date		Item	Debit	Credit	Balance Debit	Balance Credit
19--						
Jan.	1	Balance				30,000
June	30	Issued 10-year notes		325,000		355,000

ACCOUNT DISCOUNT ON LONG-TERM NOTES PAYABLE · ACCOUNT NO.

Date		Item	Debit	Credit	Balance Debit	Balance Credit
19--						
Jan.	1	Balance			1,500	
June	30	Notes issued	25,000		26,500	
Dec.	31	Amortization—Jan. 1 Bal.		500		
		June 30 Notes		1,250	24,750	

ACCOUNT COMMON STOCK, $20 PAR · ACCOUNT NO.

Date		Item	Debit	Credit	Balance Debit	Balance Credit
19--						
Jan.	1	Balance				500,000
Dec.	1	Stock dividend		15,000		515,000

ACCOUNT PREMIUM ON COMMON STOCK · ACCOUNT NO.

Date		Item	Debit	Credit	Balance Debit	Balance Credit
19--						
Jan.	1	Balance				60,000
Dec.	1	Stock dividend		10,000		70,000

ACCOUNT APPROPRIATION FOR CONTINGENCIES · ACCOUNT NO.

Date		Item	Debit	Credit	Balance Debit	Balance Credit
19--						
Jan.	1	Balance				75,000
Dec.	31	Appropriation		25,000		100,000

ACCOUNT RETAINED EARNINGS · ACCOUNT NO.

Date		Item	Debit	Credit	Balance Debit	Balance Credit
19--						
Jan.	1	Balance				353,280
Dec.	1	Stock dividend	25,000			
	31	Net loss	17,700			
	31	Cash dividends	25,000			
	31	Appropriated	25,000			260,580

Instructions:

Prepare a statement of changes in financial position (working capital concept), including a section for changes in components of working capital.

Problem 19-5A. The comparative balance sheet of W. A. Sussman Inc. and other data necessary for the analysis of the corporation's funds flow are presented in Problem 19-4A.

Instructions:

Prepare a statement of changes in financial position (cash concept), including a summary of the change in cash balance.

Problem 19-6A. A comparative balance sheet and an income statement of Mills Company are as follows:

Mills Company
Income Statement
For Current Year Ended December 31

Sales...		$990,000
Cost of merchandise sold.............................		615,000
Gross profit		$375,000
Operating expenses (including depreciation of $32,200)..		250,700
Income from operations		$124,300
Other income:		
Gain on sale of land................................	$ 25,000	
Gain on sale of investments........................	3,500	
Interest income	1,100	29,600
		$153,900
Interest expense......................................		18,000
Income before income tax		$135,900
Income tax...		48,100
Net income..		$ 87,800

Mills Company
Comparative Balance Sheet
December 31, Current and Preceding Year

Assets	Current Year	Preceding Year
Cash	$ 36,600	$ 41,500
Marketable securities................................	32,100	——
Trade receivables (net)..............................	110,000	83,000
Inventories...	168,600	147,100
Prepaid expenses	3,750	4,100
Investments	——	80,000
Land	60,000	50,000
Buildings..	305,000	150,000
Accumulated depreciation—buildings	(87,000)	(79,000)
Equipment	402,500	350,000
Accumulated depreciation—equipment................	(145,300)	(121,100)
	$886,250	$705,600

Liabilities and Stockholders' Equity	Current Year	Preceding Year
Accounts payable (merchandise creditors)	$ 67,250	$ 52,900
Income tax payable	5,000	11,500
Dividends payable	25,000	15,000
Mortgage note payable	150,000	——
Bonds payable	100,000	150,000
Common stock, $10 par	340,000	300,000
Premium on common stock	65,000	55,000
Retained earnings	134,000	121,200
	$886,250	$705,600

The following additional information on funds flow during the year was obtained from an examination of the ledger:

(a) Marketable securities were purchased for $32,100.
(b) Investments (long-term) were sold for $83,500.
(c) Equipment was purchased for $52,500. There were no disposals.
(d) A building valued at $155,000 and land valued at $45,000 were acquired by a cash payment of $50,000 and issuance of a five-year mortgage note payable for the balance.
(e) Land which cost $35,000 was sold for $60,000 cash.
(f) Bonds payable of $50,000 were retired by the payment of their face amount.
(g) 4,000 shares of common stock were issued for cash at 12½.
(h) Cash dividends of $75,000 were declared.

Instructions:

(1) Prepare a statement of changes in financial position (working capital concept), including a section for changes in components of working capital.
(2) Prepare a statement of changes in financial position (cash concept), including a summary of the change in cash balance.

Mini-Case

Robert Pickett is the president and majority shareholder of Variety Stores Inc., a small retail store chain. Recently, Pickett submitted a loan application for Variety Stores Inc. to Arcadia State Bank for a $100,000, 14%, 10-year loan to finance the purchase of land and buildings in Clinton, where the company plans to open a new store. The bank's loan officer requested a statement of changes in financial position (based on the working capital concept) in addition to the most recent income statement, balance sheet, and retained earnings statement that Pickett had submitted with the loan application.

As a close family friend, Pickett asked you to prepare a statement of changes in financial position. Using Variety Stores' records, you prepared the following statement:

Variety Stores Inc.
Statement of Changes in Financial Position
For Year Ended December 31, 19--

Sources of working capital:		
Operations during the year:		
Net income..........................	$ 80,000	
Add deduction not decreasing working capital during the year:		
Depreciation......................	20,000	$100,000
Book value of investments sold (excludes $5,000 gain)................		27,000
Issuance of common stock at par for land		50,000 $177,000

Applications of working capital:		
Purchase of land by issuance of common stock at par	$ 50,000	
Purchase of store equipment	25,000	
Declaration of cash dividends..........	20,000	95,000
Increase in working capital		$ 82,000

Changes in components of working capital:		
Increase (decrease) in current assets:		
Cash...............................	$ 16,300	
Trade receivables (net)	24,600	
Inventories	53,600	
Prepaid expenses	(2,500)	$ 92,000

Increase (decrease) in current liabilities:		
Accounts payable	$ 12,400	
Income tax payable.................	2,600	
Dividends payable..................	(5,000)	10,000
Increase in working capital		$ 82,000

After reviewing the statement, Pickett telephoned you and commented, "Are you sure this statement is right?" Pickett then raised the following questions:
  (a) "How can depreciation be a source of working capital?"
  (b) "The issuance of common stock for the land is listed both as a source and an application of working capital. This transaction had nothing to do with working capital! Shouldn't the two items related to this transaction be eliminated from both the sources and applications sections?"
  (c) "Why did you list only the $27,000 book value of the investments sold, excluding the gain of $5,000, as a source of funds? We actually received cash of $32,000 from the sale. Shouldn't the $32,000 be included as a source of working capital?"

(d) "Why not eliminate the 'changes in components of working capital' section of the statement? Since the amount of increase in working capital is already shown in the upper portion of the statement, this section adds nothing."

(e) "Why does the bank need this statement anyway? They can compute the increase in working capital from the balance sheets for the last two years."

After jotting down Pickett's questions, you assured him that this statement was "right". However, to alleviate Pickett's concern, you arranged a meeting for the following day.

Instructions:

(1) How would you respond to each of Pickett's questions?

(2) Do you think that the statement of changes in financial position enhances Variety Stores' chances of receiving the loan? Discuss.

20

CHAPTER | # Financial Statement Analysis

CHAPTER OBJECTIVES

Describe the need for financial statement analysis.

Describe basic financial statement analytical procedures.

Illustrate the application of financial statement analysis in assessing solvency and profitability.

20

CHAPTER

The financial condition and the results of operations of business enterprises are of interest to many groups, including owners, managers, creditors, governmental agencies, employees, and prospective owners and creditors. The principal statements, together with supplementary statements and schedules, present much of the basic information needed to make sound economic decisions regarding business enterprises.

Most of the items in these statements are of limited significance when considered individually. Users of financial statements often gain a clearer picture through studying relationships and comparisons of items (1) within a single year's financial statements, (2) in a succession of financial statements, and (3) with other enterprises. The selection and the preparation of analytical aids are a part of the work of the accountant.

Certain aspects of financial condition or of operations are of greater importance to some interested groups than to others. In general, all groups are interested in the ability of a business to pay its debts as they come due and to earn a reasonable amount of income. These two aspects of the status of an enterprise are called factors of solvency and profitability. An enterprise that cannot meet its obligations to its creditors on a timely basis is likely to experience difficulty in obtaining credit, and this may lead to a decline in its profitability. Similarly, an enterprise whose earnings are less than those of its competitors is likely to be at a disadvantage in obtaining credit or new capital from stockholders. In addition to this interrelationship between solvency and profitability, it is important to recognize that analysis of historical data is useful in assessing both the past performance of an enterprise and in forecasting its future performance.

In this chapter, basic analytical procedures and various types of financial analysis useful in evaluating the solvency and profitability of an enterprise will be discussed.

BASIC ANALYTICAL PROCEDURES

The analytical measures obtained from financial statements are usually expressed as ratios or percentages. For example, the relationship of $150,000 to $100,000 ($150,000/$100,000 or $150,000 : $100,000) may be expressed as 1.5, 1.5 : 1, or 150%. This ease of computation and simplicity of form for expressing financial relationships are major reasons for the widespread use of ratios and percentages in financial analysis.

Analytical procedures may be used to compare the amount of specific items on a current statement with the corresponding amounts on earlier statements. For example, in comparing cash of $150,000 on the current balance sheet with cash of $100,000 on the balance sheet of a year earlier, the current amount may be expressed as 1.5 or 150% of the earlier amount. The relationship may also be expressed in terms of change, that is, the increase of $50,000 may be stated as a 50% increase.

Analytical procedures are also widely used to show the relationships of individual items to each other and of individual items to totals on a single statement. To illustrate, assume that included in the total of $1,000,000 of assets on a balance sheet are cash of $50,000 and inventories of $250,000. In relative terms, the cash balance is 5% of total assets and the inventories represent 25% of total assets. Individual items in the current asset group could also be related to total current assets. Assuming that the total of current assets in the example is $500,000, cash represents 10% of the total and inventories represent 50% of the total.

Increases or decreases in items may be expressed in percentage terms only when the base figure is positive. If the base figure is zero or a negative value, the amount of change cannot be expressed as a percentage. For example, if comparative balance sheets indicate no liability for notes payable on the first, or base, date and a liability of $10,000 on the later date, the increase of $10,000 cannot be stated as a percent of zero. Similarly, if a net loss of $10,000 in a particular year is followed by a net income of $5,000 in the next year, the increase of $15,000 cannot be stated as a percent of the loss of the base year.

In the following discussion and illustrations of analytical procedures, the basic significance of the various measures will be emphasized. The measures developed are not ends in themselves; they are only guides to the evaluation of financial and operating data. Many other factors, such as trends in the industry, changes in price levels, and general economic conditions and prospects may also need consideration in order to arrive at sound conclusions.

Horizontal Analysis

The percentage analysis of increases and decreases in corresponding items in comparative financial statements is called horizontal analysis. The amount of each item on the most recent statement is compared with the corresponding item on one or more earlier statements. The increase or decrease in the amount of the item is then listed, together with the percent of increase or decrease. When the comparison is made between two statements, the earlier statement is used as the base. If the analysis includes three or more statements, there are two alternatives in the selection of the base: the earliest date or period may be used as the basis for comparing all later dates or periods, or each statement may be compared with the immediately preceding statement. The two alternatives are illustrated as follows:

Base: Earliest Year

| | | | | Increase (Decrease*) | | | |
| | | | | 1984–85 | | 1984–86 | |
Item	1984	1985	1986	Amount	Percent	Amount	Percent
A	$100,000	$150,000	$200,000	$ 50,000	50%	$100,000	100%
B	100,000	200,000	150,000	100,000	100%	50,000	50%

Base: Preceding Year

| | | | | Increase (Decrease*) | | | |
| | | | | 1984–85 | | 1985–86 | |
Item	1984	1985	1986	Amount	Percent	Amount	Percent
A	$100,000	$150,000	$200,000	$ 50,000	50%	$ 50,000	33%
B	100,000	200,000	150,000	100,000	100%	50,000*	25%*

Comparison of the amounts in the last two columns of the first analysis with the amounts in the corresponding columns of the second analysis reveals the effect of the base year on the direction of change and the amount and percent of change.

A condensed comparative balance sheet for two years, with horizontal analysis, is illustrated as follows:

COMPARATIVE BALANCE SHEET— HORIZONTAL ANALYSIS

Chung Company Comparative Balance Sheet December 31, 1985 and 1984			Increase (Decrease*)	
	1985	1984	Amount	Percent
Assets				
Current assets............	$ 550,000	$ 533,000	$ 17,000	3.2%
Long-term investments	95,000	177,500	82,500*	46.5%*
Plant assets (net)	444,500	470,000	25,500*	5.4%*
Intangible assets	50,000	50,000	——	
Total assets	$1,139,500	$1,230,500	$ 91,000*	7.4%*
Liabilities				
Current liabilities..........	$ 210,000	$ 243,000	$ 33,000*	13.6%*
Long-term liabilities	100,000	200,000	100,000*	50.0%*
Total liabilities	$ 310,000	$ 443,000	$133,000*	30.0%*
Stockholders' Equity				
Preferred 6% stock, $100 par....................	$ 150,000	$ 150,000	——	——
Common stock, $10 par ...	500,000	500,000	——	——
Retained earnings	179,500	137,500	$ 42,000	30.5%
Total stockholders' equity ..	$ 829,500	$ 787,500	$ 42,000	5.3%
Total liab. & stockholders' equity	$1,139,500	$1,230,500	$ 91,000*	7.4%*

The significance of the various increases and decreases in the items shown cannot be fully determined without additional information. Although total assets at the end of 1985 were $91,000 (7.4%) less than at the beginning of the year, liabilities were reduced by $133,000 (30%) and stockholders' equity increased $42,000 (5.3%). It would appear that the reduction of $100,000 in long-term liabilities was accomplished, for the most part, through the sale of long-term investments. A statement of changes in financial position would provide more definite information about the changes in the composition of the balance sheet items.

The foregoing balance sheet may be expanded to include the details of the various categories of assets and liabilities, or the details may be presented in separate schedules. Opinions differ as to which method presents the clearer picture. A supporting schedule with horizontal analysis is illustrated by the following comparative schedule of current assets:

COMPARATIVE
SCHEDULE OF
CURRENT
ASSETS—
HORIZONTAL
ANALYSIS

Chung Company Comparative Schedule of Current Assets December 31, 1985 and 1984			Increase (Decrease*)	
	1985	1984	Amount	Percent
Cash	$ 90,500	$ 64,700	$25,800	39.9%
Marketable securities......	75,000	60,000	15,000	25.0%
Accounts receivable (net) ..	115,000	120,000	5,000*	4.2%*
Merchandise inventory	264,000	283,000	19,000*	6.7%*
Prepaid expenses........	5,500	5,300	200	3.8%
Total current assets	$550,000	$533,000	$17,000	3.2%

The changes in the current assets would appear to be favorable, particularly in view of the 24.8% increase in net sales, shown in the following comparative income statement with horizontal analysis:

Chung Company Comparative Income Statement For Years Ended December 31, 1985 and 1984			Increase (Decrease*)	
	1985	1984	Amount	Percent
Sales	$1,530,500	$1,234,000	$296,500	24.0%
Sales returns and allow- ances	32,500	34,000	1,500*	4.4%*
Net sales	$1,498,000	$1,200,000	$298,000	24.8%
Cost of merchandise sold ..	1,043,000	820,000	223,000	27.2%
Gross profit	$ 455,000	$ 380,000	$ 75,000	19.7%
Selling expenses	$ 191,000	$ 147,000	$ 44,000	29.9%
General expenses	104,000	97,400	6,600	6.8%
Total operating expenses ..	$ 295,000	$ 244,400	$ 50,600	20.7%
Operating income........	$ 160,000	$ 135,600	$ 24,400	18.0%
Other income............	8,500	11,000	2,500*	22.7%*
	$ 168,500	$ 146,600	$ 21,900	14.9%
Other expense	6,000	12,000	6,000*	50.0%*
Income before income tax ..	$ 162,500	$ 134,600	$ 27,900	20.7%
Income tax..............	71,500	58,100	13,400	23.1%
Net income	$ 91,000	$ 76,500	$ 14,500	19.0%

The reduction in accounts receivable may have come about through changes in credit terms or improved collection policies. Similarly, a reduction in the merchandise inventory during a period of increased sales probably indicates an improvement in the management of inventory.

An increase in net sales, considered alone, is not necessarily favorable. The increase in Chung Company's net sales was accompanied by a somewhat greater percentage increase in the cost of merchandise sold, which indicates a narrowing of the gross profit margin. Selling expenses increased markedly and general expenses increased slightly, making an overall increase in operating expenses of 20.7%, as contrasted with a 19.7% increase in gross profit.

Although the increase in operating income and in the final net income figure is favorable, it would be incorrect for management to conclude that its operations were at maximum efficiency. A study of the expenses and additional analysis and comparisons of individual expense accounts should be made.

The income statement illustrated is in condensed form. Such a condensed statement usually provides enough information for all interested groups except management. If desired, the statement may be expanded or supplemental schedules may be prepared to present details of the cost of merchandise sold, selling expenses, general expenses, other income, and other expense.

A comparative retained earnings statement with horizontal analysis is illustrated as follows:

COMPARATIVE
RETAINED
EARNINGS
STATEMENT—
HORIZONTAL
ANALYSIS

			Increase (Decrease*)	
	1985	1984	Amount	Percent
Chung Company Comparative Retained Earnings Statement For Years Ended December 31, 1985 and 1984				
Retained earnings, January 1	$137,500	$100,000	$37,500	37.5%
Net income for year	91,000	76,500	14,500	19.0%
Total	$228,500	$176,500	$52,000	29.5%
Dividends:				
On preferred stock	$ 9,000	$ 9,000	—	—
On common stock	40,000	30,000	$10,000	33.3%
Total	$ 49,000	$ 39,000	$10,000	25.6%
Retained earnings, December 31	$179,500	$137,500	$42,000	30.5%

Examination of the statement reveals an increase of 30.5% in retained earnings for the year. The increase was attributable to the retention of $42,000 of the net income for the year ($91,000 net income − $49,000 dividends paid).

Vertical
Analysis

Percentage analysis may also be used to show the relationship of the component parts to the total in a single statement. This type of analysis is called vertical analysis. As in horizontal analysis, the statements may be prepared in either detailed or condensed form. In the latter case, additional details of the changes in the various categories may be presented in supporting schedules. If such schedules are prepared, the percentage analysis may be based on either the total of the schedule or the balance sheet total. Although vertical analysis is confined within each individual statement, the significance of both the amounts and the percents is increased by preparing comparative statements.

In vertical analysis of the balance sheet, each asset item is stated as a percent of total assets, and each liability and stockholders' equity item is stated as a percent of total liabilities and stockholders' equity. A condensed comparative balance sheet with vertical analysis is illustrated as follows:

COMPARATIVE BALANCE SHEET— VERTICAL ANALYSIS

Chung Company
Comparative Balance Sheet
December 31, 1985 and 1984

	1985		1984	
	Amount	Percent	Amount	Percent
Assets				
Current assets............	$ 550,000	48.3%	$ 533,000	43.3%
Long-term investments	95,000	8.3	177,500	14.4
Plant assets (net)	444,500	39.0	470,000	38.2
Intangible assets	50,000	4.4	50,000	4.1
Total assets	$1,139,500	100.0%	$1,230,500	100.0%
Liabilities				
Current liabilities..........	$ 210,000	18.4%	$ 243,000	19.7%
Long-term liabilities	100,000	8.8	200,000	16.3
Total liabilities	$ 310,000	27.2%	$ 443,000	36.0%
Stockholders' Equity				
Preferred 6% stock	$ 150,000	13.2%	$ 150,000	12.2%
Common stock	500,000	43.9	500,000	40.6
Retained earnings	179,500	15.7	137,500	11.2
Total stockholders' equity ..	$ 829,500	72.8%	$ 787,500	64.0%
Total liab. & stockholders' equity	$1,139,500	100.0%	$1,230,500	100.0%

The major relative changes in Chung Company's assets were in the current asset and long-term investment groups. In the lower half of the balance sheet, the greatest relative change was in long-term liabilities and retained earnings. Stockholders' equity increased from 64% of total liabilities and stockholders' equity at the end of 1984 to 72.8% at the end of 1985, with a corresponding decrease in the claims of creditors.

In vertical analysis of the income statement, each item is stated as a percent of net sales. A condensed comparative income statement with vertical analysis is illustrated as follows:

COMPARATIVE
INCOME
STATEMENT—
VERTICAL
ANALYSIS

Chung Company Comparative Income Statement For Years Ended December 31, 1985 and 1984				
	1985		1984	
	Amount	Percent	Amount	Percent
Sales	$1,530,500	102.2%	$1,234,000	102.8%
Sales returns and allow-ances	32,500	2.2	34,000	2.8
Net sales	$1,498,000	100.0%	$1,200,000	100.0%
Cost of merchandise sold..	1,043,000	69.6	820,000	68.3
Gross profit	$ 455,000	30.4%	$ 380,000	31.7%
Selling expenses	$ 191,000	12.8%	$ 147,000	12.3%
General expenses	104,000	6.9	97,400	8.1
Total operating expenses ..	$ 295,000	19.7%	$ 244,400	20.4%
Operating income.........	$ 160,000	10.7%	$ 135,600	11.3%
Other income............	8,500	.6	11,000	.9
	$ 168,500	11.3%	$ 146,600	12.2%
Other expense	6,000	.4	12,000	1.0
Income before income tax..	$ 162,500	10.9%	$ 134,600	11.2%
Income tax..............	71,500	4.8	58,100	4.8
Net income	$ 91,000	6.1%	$ 76,500	6.4%

Care must be used in judging the significance of differences between percentages for the two years. For example, the decline of the gross profit rate from 31.7% in 1984 to 30.4% in 1985 is only 1.3 percentage points. In terms of dollars of potential gross profit, however, it represents a decline of approximately $19,500 (1.3% × $1,498,000).

Common-Size Statements

Horizontal and vertical analyses with both dollar and percentage figures are helpful in disclosing relationships and trends in financial condition and operations of individual enterprises. Vertical analysis with both dollar and percentage figures is also useful in comparing one company with another or with industry averages. Such comparisons may be made easier by the use of common-size statements, in which all items are expressed only in relative terms.

Common-size statements may be prepared in order to compare percentages of a current period with past periods, to compare individual businesses, or to compare one business with industry percentages published by trade associations and financial information services. A comparative common-size income statement for two enterprises is illustrated as follows:

Chung Company and Ross Corporation Condensed Common-Size Income Statement For Year Ended December 31, 1985	Chung Company	Ross Corporation
Sales	102.2%	102.3%
Sales returns and allowances	2.2	2.3
Net sales	100.0%	100.0%
Cost of merchandise sold........................	69.6	70.0
Gross profit	30.4%	30.0%
Selling expenses.................................	12.8%	11.5%
General expenses	6.9	4.1
Total operating expenses	19.7%	15.6%
Operating income................................	10.7%	14.4%
Other income....................................	.6	.6
	11.3%	15.0%
Other expense...................................	.4	.5
Income before income tax	10.9%	14.5%
Income tax.......................................	4.8	5.5
Net income......................................	6.1%	9.0%

Examination of the statement reveals that although Chung Company has a slightly higher rate of gross profit than Ross Corporation, the advantage is more than offset by its higher percentage of both selling and general expenses. As a consequence, the operating income of Chung Company is 10.7% of net sales as compared with 14.4% for Ross Corporation, an unfavorable difference of 3.7 percentage points.

Other Analytical Measures

In addition to the percentage analyses discussed above, there are a number of other relationships that may be expressed in ratios and percentages. The items used in the measures are taken from the accounting statements of the current period and hence are a further development of vertical analysis. Comparison of the items with corresponding measures of earlier periods is an extension of horizontal analysis.

Some of the more important ratios useful in the evaluation of solvency and profitability are discussed in the sections that follow. The examples are based on the illustrative statements presented earlier. In a few instances, data from a company's statements of the preceding year and from other sources are also used.

SOLVENCY
ANALYSIS

Solvency is the ability of a business to meet its financial obligations as they come due. Solvency analysis, therefore, focuses mainly on balance sheet relationships that indicate the ability to liquidate current and noncurrent liabilities. Major analyses used in assessing solvency include (1) current position analysis, (2) accounts receivable analysis, (3) merchandise inventory analysis, (4) the ratio of plant assets to long-term liabilities, and (5) the ratio of stockholders' equity to liabilities.

Current Position
Analysis

To be useful, ratios relating to a firm's solvency must show the firm's ability to liquidate its liabilities. The use of ratios showing the ability to liquidate current liabilities is called **current position analysis** and is of particular interest to short-term creditors.

Working Capital

The excess of the current assets of an enterprise over its current liabilities at a certain moment of time is called working capital. The absolute amount of working capital and the flow of working capital during a period of time as reported by a statement of changes in financial position are often used in evaluating a company's ability to meet currently maturing obligations. Although useful for making intra-period comparisons for a company, these absolute amounts are difficult to use in comparing companies of different sizes or in comparing such amounts with industry figures. For example, working capital of $250,000 may be very adequate for a small building contractor specializing in residential construction, but it may be completely inadequate for a large building contractor specializing in industrial and commercial construction.

Current Ratio

Another means of expressing the relationship between current assets and current liabilities is through the current ratio, sometimes referred to as the **working capital ratio** or **bankers' ratio**. The ratio is computed by dividing the total of current assets by the total of current liabilities. The determination of working capital and the current ratio for Chung Company is illustrated as follows:

	1985	1984
Current assets	$550,000	$533,000
Current liabilities	210,000	243,000
Working capital..	$340,000	$290,000
Current ratio	2.6 : 1	2.2 : 1

The current ratio is a more dependable indication of solvency than is working capital. To illustrate, assume that as of December 31, 1985, the working capital of a competing corporation is much greater than $340,000, but its current ratio is only 1.3 : 1. Considering these factors alone, the Chung Company, with its current ratio of 2.6 : 1, is in a more favorable position to obtain short-term credit than the corporation with the greater amount of working capital.

Acid-Test Ratio

The amount of working capital and the current ratio are two solvency measures that indicate a company's ability to meet currently maturing obligations. However, these two measures do not take into account the composition of the current assets. To illustrate the significance of this additional factor, the following current position data for two companies are presented:

	Randall Corporation	Steward Company
Current assets:		
Cash	$ 200,000	$ 550,000
Marketable securities	100,000	100,000
Receivables (net)	200,000	200,000
Inventories	790,000	443,500
Prepaid expenses	10,000	6,500
Total current assets	$1,300,000	$1,300,000
Current liabilities	650,000	650,000
Working capital	$ 650,000	$ 650,000
Current ratio	2 : 1	2 : 1

Both companies have working capital of $650,000 and a current ratio of 2 to 1. But the ability of each company to meet its currently maturing debts is vastly different. Randall Corporation has a large part of its current assets in inventories, which must be sold and the receivables collected before the current liabilities can be paid in full. A considerable amount of time may be required to convert these inventories into cash. Declines in market prices and a reduction in demand could also impair the ability to pay current liabilities. Conversely, Steward Company has almost enough cash on hand to meet its current liabilities.

A ratio that measures the "instant" debt-paying ability of a company is called the acid-test ratio or **quick ratio.** It is the ratio of the sum of cash, receivables, and marketable securities, which are sometimes called quick assets, to current liabilities. The acid-test ratio data for Chung Company are as follows:

	1985	1984
Quick assets:		
Cash	$ 90,500	$ 64,700
Marketable securities	75,000	60,000
Receivables (net)	115,000	120,000
Total	$280,500	$244,700
Current liabilities	$210,000	$243,000
Acid-test ratio	1.3 : 1	1.0 : 1

A thorough analysis of a firm's current position would include the determination of the amount of working capital, the current ratio, and the acid-test ratio. These ratios are most useful when viewed together and when compared with similar ratios for previous periods and with those of other firms in the industry.

Accounts Receivable Analysis

The size and composition of accounts receivable change continually during business operations. The amount is increased by sales on account and reduced by collections. Firms that grant long credit terms tend to have relatively greater amounts tied up in accounts receivable than those granting short credit terms. Increases or decreases in the volume of sales also affect the amount of outstanding accounts receivable.

Accounts receivable yield no revenue, hence it is desirable to keep the amount invested in them at a minimum. The cash made available by prompt collection of receivables improves solvency and may be used to purchase merchandise in larger quantities at a lower price, to pay dividends to stockholders, or for other purposes. Prompt collection also lessens the risk of loss from uncollectible accounts.

Accounts Receivable Turnover

The relationship between credit sales and accounts receivable may be stated as the **accounts receivable turnover.** It is computed by dividing net sales on account by the average net accounts receivable. It is preferable to base the average on monthly balances, which gives effect to seasonal changes. When such data are not available, it is necessary to use the average of the balances at the beginning and the end of the year. If there are trade notes receivable as well as accounts, the two should be combined. The accounts receivable turnover data for Chung Company are as follows. All sales were made on account.

	1985	1984
Net sales on account	$1,498,000	$1,200,000
Accounts receivable (net):		
Beginning of year	$ 120,000	$ 140,000
End of year	115,000	120,000
Total	$ 235,000	$ 260,000
Average	$ 117,500	$ 130,000
Accounts receivable turnover	12.7	9.2

The increase in the accounts receivable turnover for 1985 indicates that there has been an acceleration in the collection of receivables, due perhaps to improvement in either the granting of credit or the collection practices used, or both.

Number of Days' Sales in Receivables

Another means of expressing the relationship between credit sales and accounts receivable is the number of days' sales in receivables. This measure is determined by dividing the net accounts receivable at the end of the year by the average daily sales on account (net sales on account divided by 365), illustrated as follows for Chung Company:

	1985	1984
Accounts receivable (net), end of year............	$ 115,000	$ 120,000
Net sales on account	$1,498,000	$1,200,000
Average daily sales on account.................	$ 4,104	$ 3,288
Number of days' sales in receivables	28.0	36.5

The number of days' sales in receivables gives a rough measure of the length of time the accounts receivable have been outstanding. A comparison of this measure with the credit terms, with figures for comparable firms in the same industry, and with figures of Chung Company for prior years will help reveal the efficiency in collecting receivables and the trends in the management of credit.

Merchandise Inventory Analysis

Although an enterprise must maintain sufficient inventory quantities to meet the demands for its merchandise, it is desirable to keep the amount invested in inventory to a minimum. Inventories in excess of the needs of business reduce solvency by tying up funds. Excess inventories may also cause increases in the amount of insurance, property taxes, storage, and other related expenses, further reducing funds that could be used to better advantage. There is also added risk of loss through price declines and deterioration or obsolescence of the merchandise.

Merchandise Inventory Turnover

The relationship between the volume of merchandise sold and merchandise inventory may be stated as the merchandise inventory turnover. It is computed by dividing the cost of merchandise sold by the average inventory. If monthly data are not available, it is necessary to use the average of the inventories at the beginning and the end of the year. The merchandise inventory turnover data for Chung Company are as follows:

	1985	1984
Cost of merchandise sold	$1,043,000	$820,000
Merchandise inventory:		
Beginning of year	$ 283,000	$311,000
End of year.................................	264,000	283,000
Total	$ 547,000	$594,000
Average....................................	$ 273,500	$297,000
Merchandise inventory turnover	3.8	2.8

The improvement in the turnover resulted from an increase in the cost of merchandise sold, combined with a decrease in average inventory. The variation in types of merchandise is too great to permit any broad generalizations as to what is a satisfactory turnover. For example, a firm selling food should have a much higher turnover than one selling furniture or jewelry, and the perishable foods department of a supermarket should have a higher turnover than the soaps and cleansers department. However, for each business or each department within a business, there is a reasonable turnover rate. A turnover below this rate means that the company or the department is incurring extra expenses such as those for administration and storage, is increasing its risk of loss because of obsolescence and adverse price changes, is incurring interest charges in excess of those considered necessary, and is failing to free funds for other uses.

Number of Days' Sales in Merchandise Inventory

Another means of expressing the relationship between the cost of merchandise sold and merchandise inventory is the **number of days' sales in merchandise inventory**. This measure is determined by dividing the merchandise inventory at the end of the year by the average daily cost of merchandise sold (cost of merchandise sold divided by 365), illustrated as follows for Chung Company:

	1985	1984
Merchandise inventory, end of year	$ 264,000	$283,000
Cost of merchandise sold	$1,043,000	$820,000
Average daily cost of merchandise sold	$ 2,858	$ 2,247
Number of days' sales in inventory	92.4	125.9

The number of days' sales in inventory gives a rough measure of the length of time it takes to acquire, sell, and then replace the average merchandise inventory. Although there was a substantial improvement in the second year, comparison of the measure with those of earlier years and of comparable firms is an essential element in judging the effectiveness of Chung Company's inventory control.

As with many attempts to analyze financial data, it is possible to determine more than one measure to express the relationship between the cost of merchandise sold and merchandise inventory. Both the merchandise inventory turnover and number of days' sales in merchandise inventory are useful for evaluating the efficiency in the management of inventory. Whether both measures are used or whether one measure is preferred over the other is a matter for the individual analyst to decide.

Ratio of Plant Assets to Long-Term Liabilities

Long-term notes and bonds are often secured by mortgages on plant assets. **The ratio of total plant assets to long-term liabilities** provides a solvency measure that shows the margin of safety of the noteholders or bondholders. It also gives an indication of the potential ability of the enterprise to borrow additional funds on a long-term basis. The ratio of plant assets to long-term liabilities of Chung Company is as follows:

	1985	1984
Plant assets (net)...................................	$444,500	$470,000
Long-term liabilities...............................	$100,000	$200,000
Ratio of plant assets to long-term liabilities	4.4 : 1	2.4 : 1

The marked increase in the ratio at the end of 1985 was mainly due to the liquidation of one half of Chung Company's long-term liabilities. If the company should need to borrow additional funds on a long-term basis, it is in a stronger position to do so.

Ratio of Stockholders' Equity to Liabilities

Claims against the total assets of an enterprise are divided into two basic groups, those of the creditors and those of the owners. The relationship between the total claims of the two groups provides a solvency measure that indicates the margin of safety for the creditors and the ability of the enterprise to withstand adverse business conditions. If the claims of the creditors are large in proportion to the equity of the stockholders, there are likely to be substantial charges for interest payments. If earnings decline to the point where the company is unable to meet its interest payments, control of the business may pass to the creditors.

The relationship between stockholder and creditor equity is shown in the vertical analysis of the balance sheet. For example, the balance sheet of Chung Company presented on page 567 indicates that on December 31, 1985, stockholders' equity represented 72.8% and liabilities represented 27.2% of the sum of the liabilities and stockholders' equity (100.0%). Instead of expressing each item as a percent of the total, the relationship may be expressed as a ratio of one to the other, as follows:

	1985	1984
Total stockholders' equity	$829,500	$787,500
Total liabilities....................................	$310,000	$443,000
Ratio of stockholders' equity to liabilities..............	2.7 : 1	1.8 : 1

The balance sheet of Chung Company shows that the major factor affecting the change in the ratio was the $100,000 reduction in long-term liabilities during 1985. The ratio at both dates shows a large margin of safety for the creditors.

PROFITABILITY ANALYSIS

Profitability is the ability of an entity to earn income. It can be assessed by computing various relevant measures, including (1) the ratio of net sales to assets, (2) the rate earned on total assets, (3) the rate earned on stockholders' equity, (4) the rate earned on common stockholders' equity, (5) earnings per share on common stock, (6) the price-earnings ratio, and (7) dividend yield.

Ratio of Net Sales to Assets

The **ratio of net sales to assets** is a profitability measure that shows how effectively a firm utilizes its assets. Assume that two competing enterprises have equal amounts of assets, but the amount of the sales of one is double the amount of the sales of the other. Obviously, the former is making better use of its assets. In computing the ratio, any long-term investments should be excluded from total assets because they are wholly unrelated to sales of goods or services. Assets used in determining the ratio may be the total at the end of the year, the average at the beginning and the end of the year, or the average of the monthly totals. The basic data and the ratio of net sales to assets for Chung Company are as follows:

	1985	1984
Net sales	$1,498,000	$1,200,000
Total assets (excluding long-term investments):		
Beginning of year	$1,053,000	$1,010,000
End of year	1,044,500	1,053,000
Total	$2,097,500	$2,063,000
Average	$1,048,750	$1,031,500
Ratio of net sales to assets	1.4 : 1	1.2 : 1

The ratio improved to a minor degree in 1985, largely due to the increased sales volume. A comparison of the ratio with those of other enterprises in the same industry would be helpful in assessing Chung Company's effectiveness in the utilization of assets.

Rate Earned on Total Assets   The rate earned on total assets is a measure of the profitability of the assets, without regard to the equity of creditors and stockholders in the assets. The rate is therefore not affected by differences in methods of financing an enterprise.

The rate earned on total assets is derived by adding interest expense to net income and dividing this sum by total assets. By adding interest expense to net income, the profitability of the assets is determined without considering the means of financing the acquisition of the assets. The rate earned by Chung Company on total assets is determined as follows:

	1985	1984
Net income	$ 91,000	$ 76,500
Plus interest expense	6,000	12,000
Total	$ 97,000	$ 88,500
Total assets:		
Beginning of year	$1,230,500	$1,187,500
End of year	1,139,500	1,230,500
Total	$2,370,000	$2,418,000
Average	$1,185,000	$1,209,000
Rate earned on total assets	8.2%	7.3%

The rate earned on total assets of Chung Company for 1985 indicates an improvement over that for 1984. A comparison with other companies and with industry averages would also be useful in evaluating the effectiveness of management performance.

It is sometimes preferable to determine the rate of operating income (income before nonoperating income, nonoperating expense, extraordinary items, and income tax) to total assets. If nonoperating income is not considered, the investments yielding such income should be excluded from the assets. The use of income before income tax eliminates the effect of changes in the tax structure on the rate of earnings. When considering published data on rates earned on assets, the reader should note the exact nature of the measure.

Rate Earned on Stockholders' Equity

Another relative measure of profitability is obtained by dividing net income by the total stockholders' equity. In contrast to the rate earned on total assets, the rate earned on stockholders' equity emphasizes the income yield in relationship to the amount invested by the stockholders.

The amount of the total stockholders' equity throughout the year varies for several reasons — the issuance of additional stock, the retirement of a class of stock, the payment of dividends, and the gradual accrual of net income. If monthly figures are not available, the average of the stockholders' equity at the beginning and the end of the year is used, as in the following illustration:

	1985	1984
Net income	$ 91,000	$ 76,500
Stockholders' equity:		
Beginning of year	$ 787,500	$ 750,000
End of year	829,500	787,500
Total	$1,617,000	$1,537,500
Average	$ 808,500	$ 768,750
Rate earned on stockholders' equity	11.3%	10.0%

The rate earned by a thriving enterprise on the equity of its stockholders is usually higher than the rate earned on total assets. The reason for the difference is that the amount earned on assets acquired through the use of funds provided by creditors is more than the interest charges paid to creditors. This tendency of the rate on stockholders' equity to vary disproportionately from the rate on total assets is sometimes called **leverage.** The Chung Company rate on stockholders' equity for 1985, 11.3%, compares favorably with the rate of 8.2% earned on total assets, as reported on the preceding page. The leverage factor of 3.1% (11.3% − 8.2%) for 1985 also compares favorably with the 2.7% (10.0% − 7.3%) differential for the preceding year.

Rate Earned on Common Stockholders' Equity

When a corporation has both preferred and common stock outstanding, the holders of the common stock have the residual claim on earnings. The rate earned on common stockholders' equity is the net income less preferred dividend requirements for the period, stated as a percent of the average equity of the common stockholders.

Chung Company has $150,000 of preferred 6% nonparticipating stock outstanding at both balance sheet dates, hence annual preferred dividends amount to $9,000. The common stockholders' equity is the total stockholders' equity, reduced by the par of the preferred stock ($150,000). The basic data and the rate earned on common stockholders' equity are as follows:

	1985	1984
Net income	$ 91,000	$ 76,500
Preferred dividends	9,000	9,000
Remainder—identified with common stock	$ 82,000	$ 67,500
Common stockholders' equity:		
Beginning of year	$ 637,500	$ 600,000
End of year	679,500	637,500
Total	$1,317,000	$1,237,500
Average	$ 658,500	$ 618,750
Rate earned on common stockholders' equity	12.5%	10.9%

The rate earned on common stockholders' equity differs from the rates earned by Chung Company on total assets and total stockholders' equity. This situation will occur if there are borrowed funds and also preferred stock outstanding, which rank ahead of the common shares in their claim on earnings. Thus the concept of leverage, as discussed in the preceding section, can be applied to the use of funds from the sale of preferred stock as well as from borrowing. Funds from both sources can be used in an attempt to increase the return on common stockholders' equity.

Earnings per Share on Common Stock

One of the profitability measures most commonly quoted in the financial press and included in the income statement in corporate annual reports is earnings per share on common stock. If a company has issued only one class of stock, the earnings per share are determined by dividing net income by the number of shares of stock outstanding. If there are both preferred and common stock outstanding, the net income must be reduced first by the amount necessary to meet the preferred dividend requirements.

Any changes in the number of shares outstanding during the year, such as would result from stock dividends or stock splits, should be disclosed in quoting earnings per share on common stock. Also if there are any nonrecurring (extraordinary, etc.) items in the income statement, as discussed in Chapter 16, the income per share, before such items, should be reported along with net income per share. In addition, if there are convertible bonds or preferred stock outstanding, also discussed in Chapter 16, the amount reported as net income per share should be stated without considering the conversion privilege, followed by net income per share assuming conversion had occurred.

The data on the earnings per share of common stock for Chung Company are as follows:

	1985	1984
Net income	$91,000	$76,500
Preferred dividends	9,000	9,000
Remainder—identified with common stock	$82,000	$67,500
Shares of common stock outstanding	50,000	50,000
Earnings per share on common stock	$1.64	$1.35

Since earnings form the primary basis for dividends, earnings per share and dividends per share on common stock are commonly used by investors in weighing the merits of alternative investment opportunities. Earnings per share data can be presented in conjunction with dividends per share data to indicate the relationship between earnings and dividends and the extent to which the corporation is retaining its earnings for use in the business. The following chart shows this relationship for Chung Company:

CHART OF EARNINGS AND DIVIDENDS ON COMMON STOCK

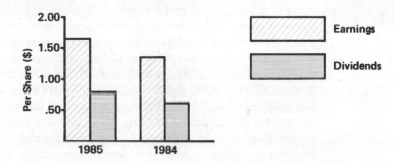

Price-Earnings Ratio

A profitability measure commonly quoted in the financial press is the price-earnings (P/E) ratio on common stock. It is computed by dividing the market price per share of common stock at a specific date by the annual earnings per share. Assuming market prices per common share of 20½ at the end of 1985 and 13½ at the end of 1984, the price-earnings ratio on common stock of Chung Company is as follows:

	1985	1984
Market price per share of common stock	$20.50	$13.50
Earnings per share on common stock	$ 1.64	$ 1.35
Price-earnings ratio on common stock	12.5	10.0

The price-earnings ratio indicates that a share of common stock of Chung Company was selling for 12.5 and 10 times the amount of earnings per share at the end of 1985 and 1984 respectively.

Dividend Yield

The **dividend yield** on common stock is a profitability measure that shows the rate of return to common stockholders in terms of cash dividend distributions. It is of special interest to investors whose main investment objective is to receive a current return on the investment rather than an increase in the market price of the investment. The dividend yield is computed by dividing the annual dividends paid per share of common stock by the market price per share at a specific date. Assuming dividends of $.80 and $.60 per common share and market prices per common share of 20½ and 13½ at the end of 1985 and 1984 respectively, the dividend yield on common stock of Chung Company is as follows:

	1985	1984
Dividends per share on common stock	$ .80	$ .60
Market price per share of common stock...............	$20.50	$13.50
Dividend yield on common stock	3.9%	4.4%

SELECTION OF ANALYTICAL MEASURES

The analytical measures that have been discussed and illustrated are representative of many that can be developed for a medium-size merchandising enterprise. Some of them might well be omitted in analyzing a specific firm, or additional measures could be developed. The type of business activity, the capital structure, and the size of the enterprise usually affect the measures used. For example, in analyzing railroads, public utilities, and other corporations with a high ratio of debt to stockholders' equity, it is customary to express the solvency measure that shows the relative risk of the bondholders in terms of the number of times the interest charges are earned during the year. The higher the ratio, the greater the assurance of continued interest payments in case of decreased earnings. The measure also provides an indication of general financial strength, which is of concern to stockholders and employees, as well as to creditors.

In the following data, the amount available to meet interest charges is not affected by taxes on income because interest is deductible in determining taxable income.

	1985	1984
Income before income tax......................	$ 900,000	$ 800,000
Add interest charges...........................	300,000	250,000
Amount available to meet interest charges	$1,200,000	$1,050,000
Number of times interest charges earned..........	4	4.2

Analyses like the above can be applied to dividends on preferred stock. In such cases, net income would be divided by the amount of preferred dividends to yield the number of times preferred dividends were earned. This measure gives an indication of the relative assurance of continued dividend payments to preferred stockholders.

Percentage analyses, ratios, turnovers, and other measures of financial position and operating results are useful analytical devices. They are helpful in appraising the present performance of an enterprise and in forecasting its future. They are not, however, a substitute for sound judgment nor do they provide definitive guides to action. In selecting and interpreting analytical indexes, proper consideration should be given to any conditions peculiar to the particular enterprise or to the industry of which the enterprise is a part. The possible influence of the general economic and business environment should also be weighed.

To determine trends, the interrelationship of the measures used in appraising a certain enterprise should be carefully studied, as should comparable indexes of earlier fiscal periods. Data from competing enterprises may also be compared in order to determine the relative efficiency of the firm being analyzed. In making such comparisons, however, it is essential to consider the potential effects of any significant differences in the accounting methods used by the enterprises.

Self-Examination Questions
(Answers in Appendix C.)

1. What type of analysis is indicated by the following?

	Amount	Percent
Current assets	$100,000	20%
Plant assets	400,000	80
Total assets	$500,000	100%

   A. Vertical analysis
   B. Horizontal analysis
   C. Differential analysis
   D. None of the above

2. Which of the following measures is useful as an indication of the ability of a firm to liquidate current liabilities?
   A. Working capital
   B. Current ratio
   C. Acid-test ratio
   D. All of the above

3. The ratio determined by dividing total current assets by total current liabilities is:
   A. current ratio
   B. working capital ratio
   C. bankers' ratio
   D. all of the above

4. The ratio of the "quick assets" to current liabilities, which indicates the "instant" debt-paying ability of a firm, is:
   A. current ratio
   B. working capital ratio
   C. acid-test ratio
   D. none of the above

5. A measure useful in evaluating the efficiency in the management of inventory is:
   A. merchandise inventory turnover
   B. number of days' sales in merchandise inventory
   C. both A and B
   D. none of the above

Discussion Questions

1. In the analysis of the financial status of an enterprise, what is meant by *solvency* and *profitability*?

2. Illustrate (a) horizontal analysis and (b) vertical analysis, using the following data taken from a comparative balance sheet:

	Current Year	Preceding Year
Cash.................................	$ 900,000	$ 600,000
Total current assets....................	3,600,000	3,000,000

3. What is the advantage of using comparative statements for financial analysis rather than statements for a single date or period?

4. The current year's amount of net income (after income tax) is 15% larger than that of the preceding year. Does this indicate an improved operating performance? Discuss.

5. What are common-size financial statements?

6. (a) Name the major ratios useful in assessing solvency and profitability.
   (b) Why is it important not to rely on only one ratio or measure in assessing the solvency or profitability of an enterprise?

7. Identify the measure of current position analysis described by each of the following: (a) the excess of the current assets over current liabilities, (b) the ratio of current assets to current liabilities, (c) the ratio of quick assets to current liabilities.

8. The working capital for Robinson Company at the end of the current year is $60,000 greater than the working capital at the end of the preceding year, reported as follows. Does this mean that the current position has improved? Explain.

	Current Year	Preceding Year
Current assets:		
Cash, marketable securities, and receivables	$288,000	$240,000
Merchandise inventory	432,000	260,000
Total current assets	$720,000	$500,000
Current liabilities................................	360,000	200,000
Working capital................................	$360,000	$300,000

9. A company that grants terms of n/30 on all sales has an accounts receivable turnover for the year, based on monthly averages, of 6. Is this a satisfactory turnover? Discuss.

10. What does an increase in the number of days' sales in receivables ordinarily indicate about the credit and collection policy of the firm?

11. (a) Why is it advantageous to have a high merchandise inventory turnover? (b) Is it possible for a merchandise inventory turnover to be too high? (c) Is it possible to have a high merchandise inventory turnover and a high number of days' sales in merchandise inventory? Discuss.

12. What does an increase in the ratio of stockholders' equity to liabilities indicate about the margin of safety for the firm's creditors and the ability of the firm to withstand adverse business conditions?

13. In computing the ratio of net sales to assets, why are long-term investments excluded in determining the amount of the total assets?

14. In determining the rate earned on total assets, why is interest expense added to net income before dividing by total assets?

15. (a) Why is the rate earned on stockholders' equity by a thriving enterprise ordinarily higher than the rate earned on total assets?
    (b) Should the rate earned on common stockholders' equity normally be higher or lower than the rate earned on total stockholders' equity? Explain.

16. The net income (after income tax) of Morgan Company was $10 per common share in the latest year and $15 per common share for the preceding year. At the beginning of the latest year, the number of shares outstanding was doubled by a stock split. There were no other changes in the amount of stock outstanding. What were the earnings per share in the preceding year, adjusted to place them on a comparable basis with the latest year?

17. The price earnings ratio for common stock of Mura Company was 15 at June 30, the end of the current fiscal year. What does the ratio indicate about the selling price of common stock in relation to current earnings?

18. Why would the dividend yield differ significantly from the rate earned on common stockholders' equity?

19. Favorable business conditions may bring about certain seemingly unfavorable ratios, and unfavorable business operations may result in apparently favorable ratios. For example, Almond Company increased its sales and net income substantially for the current year, yet the current ratio at the end of the year is lower than at the beginning of the year. Discuss some possible causes of the apparent weakening of the current position while sales and net income have increased substantially.

Exercises

Exercise 20-1. Revenue and expense data for Eastern Company are as follows:

	1985	1984
Sales	$900,000	$800,000
Cost of merchandise sold	549,000	480,000
Selling expense	117,000	144,000
General expense	81,000	64,000
Income tax	63,000	48,000

(a) Prepare an income statement in comparative form, stating each item for both 1985 and 1984 as a percent of sales.
(b) Comment upon the significant changes disclosed by the comparative income statement.

Exercise 20-2. The following data were abstracted from the balance sheet of Valenzuela Company:

	Current Year	Preceding Year
Cash	$116,000	$101,500
Marketable securities........................	55,000	40,000
Accounts and notes receivable (net)............	159,000	152,500
Merchandise inventory	229,800	160,000
Prepaid expenses	10,200	8,000
Accounts and notes payable (short-term).........	250,000	185,000
Accrued liabilities...........................	50,000	25,000

(a) Determine for each year the (1) working capital, (2) current ratio, and (3) acid-test ratio. (Present figures used in your computations.)
(b) What conclusions can be drawn from these data as to the company's ability to meet its currently maturing debts?

Exercise 20-3. The following data are taken from the financial statements for Lasorta Company:

	Current Year	Preceding Year
Accounts receivable, end of year...............	$ 563,200	$ 462,000
Monthly average accounts receivable (net)	522,500	423,500
Net sales on account.........................	4,180,000	2,964,500

Terms of all sales are 1/10, n/60.
(a) Determine for each year (1) the accounts receivable turnover and (2) the number of days' sales in receivables.
(b) What conclusions can be drawn from these data concerning the composition of accounts receivable?

Exercise 20-4. The following data were abstracted from the income statement of Cowans Corporation:

	Current Year	Preceding Year
Sales.......................................	$4,680,000	$4,575,800
Beginning inventory..........................	588,000	512,000
Purchases	2,424,000	2,496,000
Ending inventory.............................	612,000	588,000

(a) Determine for each year (1) the merchandise inventory turnover and (2) the number of days' sales in merchandise inventory.
(b) What conclusions can be drawn from these data concerning the composition of the merchandise inventory?

Exercise 20-5. The following data were taken from the financial statements of John Concepcion and Co. for the current fiscal year:

Plant assets (net).....................................	$1,104,000

Liabilities:

Current liabilities.......................................		$ 360,000
Mortgage note payable, 10%, issued 1980, due 2000		480,000
Total liabilities		$ 840,000

Stockholders' equity:

Preferred 9% stock, $100 par, cumulative, nonparticipating (no change during year)....................................			$ 180,000
Common stock, $10 par (no change during year)............			900,000
Retained earnings:			
Balance, beginning of year....................	$642,600		
Net income	198,000	$840,600	
Preferred dividends..........................	$ 16,200		
Common dividends	56,400	72,600	
Balance, end of year........................			768,000
Total stockholders' equity................................			$1,848,000

Net sales	$3,295,200
Interest expense.....................................	48,000

Assuming that long-term investments totaled $180,000 throughout the year and that total assets were $2,322,600 at the beginning of the year, determine the following, presenting figures used in your computations: (a) ratio of plant assets to long-term liabilities, (b) ratio of stockholders' equity to liabilities, (c) ratio of net sales to assets, (d) rate earned on total assets, (e) rate earned on stockholders' equity, (f) rate earned on common stockholders' equity.

Exercise 20-6. The net income reported on the income statement of A. B. Virgil Inc. was $2,200,000. There were 200,000 shares of $50 par common stock and 40,000 shares of $50 par 10% preferred stock outstanding throughout the current year. The income statement included two extraordinary items: a $900,000 gain from condemnation of property and a $700,000 loss arising from tornado damage, both after applicable income tax. Determine the per share figures for common stock for (a) income before extraordinary items and (b) net income.

Exercise 20-7. The balance sheet for Henderson Corporation at the end of the current fiscal year indicated the following:

Bonds payable, 11% (issued in 1980, due in 2000)..........	$2,000,000
Preferred 9% stock, $100 par	500,000
Common stock, $20 par	1,500,000

Income before income tax was $660,000 and income taxes were $300,000 for the current year. Cash dividends paid on common stock during the current year totaled

$300,000. The common stock was selling for $42 per share at the end of the year. Determine each of the following: (a) number of times bond interest charges were earned, (b) number of times preferred dividends were earned, (c) earnings per share on common stock, (d) price-earnings ratio, and (e) dividend yield.

Problems
(Problems in Appendix B: 20-1B, 20-3B, 20-5B.)

Problem 20-1A. Data pertaining to the current position of R. Staub, Inc. are as follows:

Cash	$125,000
Marketable securities	60,000
Accounts and notes receivable (net)	295,000
Merchandise inventory	487,000
Prepaid expenses	33,000
Accounts payable	270,000
Notes payable (short-term)	110,000
Accrued liabilities	20,000

Instructions:

(1) Compute (a) working capital (b) current ratio, and (c) acid-test ratio.

(2) List the following captions on a sheet of paper:

Transaction	Working Capital	Current Ratio	Acid-Test Ratio

Compute the working capital, current ratio, and acid-test ratio after each of the following transactions, and record the results in the appropriate columns. Consider each transaction separately and assume that only that transaction affects the data given above.

(a) Paid accounts payable, $150,000.

(b) Received cash on account, $100,000.

(c) Purchased merchandise on account, $70,000.

(d) Paid notes payable, $100,000.

(e) Declared a cash dividend, $50,000.

(f) Declared a common stock dividend on common stock, $100,000.

(g) Borrowed cash from bank on a long-term note, $200,000.

(h) Sold marketable securities, $60,000.

(i) Issued additional shares of stock for cash, $150,000.

(j) Paid cash for store supplies, $40,000.

Problem 20-2A. Revenue and expense data for the current calendar year for Lopez Paper Company and for the paper industry are as follows. The Lopez Paper Company data are expressed in dollars; the paper industry averages are expressed in percentages.

	Lopez Paper Company	Paper Industry Average
Sales	$7,070,000	100.5%
Sales returns and allowances	70,000	.5%
Cost of merchandise sold.	5,040,000	70.0%
Selling expenses	574,000	9.2%
General expenses	434,000	8.0%
Other income.	35,000	.6%
Other expense	84,000	1.4%
Income tax.	406,000	5.5%

Instructions:

(1) Prepare a common-size income statement comparing the results of operations for Lopez Paper Company with the industry average.

(2) As far as the data permit, comment on significant relationships revealed by the comparisons.

Problem 20-3A. For 1985, Rose Company initiated an extensive sales promotion campaign that included the expenditure of an additional $40,000 for advertising. At the end of the year, Frank Rose, the president, is presented with the following condensed comparative income statement:

Rose Company
Comparative Income Statement
For Years Ended December 31, 1985 and 1984

	1985	1984
Sales	$510,000	$303,000
Sales returns and allowances	10,000	3,000
Net sales	$500,000	$300,000
Cost of merchandise sold.	310,000	180,000
Gross profit	$190,000	$120,000
Selling expenses	$ 90,000	$ 48,000
General expenses	20,000	13,500
Total operating expenses	$110,000	$ 61,500
Operating income.	$ 80,000	$ 58,500
Other income.	2,000	900
Income before income tax	$ 82,000	$ 59,400
Income tax.	20,000	15,000
Net income	$ 62,000	$ 44,400

Instructions:

(1) Prepare a comparative income statement for the two-year period, presenting an analysis of each item in relationship to net sales for each of the years.

(2) To the extent the data permit, comment on the significant relationships revealed by the vertical analysis prepared in (1).

Problem 20-4A. Prior to approving an application for a short-term loan, American National Bank required that Trillo Company provide evidence of working capital of at least $400,000, a current ratio of at least 1.5 : 1, and an acid-test ratio of at least 1.0 : 1. The chief accountant compiled the following data pertaining to the current position:

Trillo Company
Schedule of Current Assets and Current Liabilities
December 31, 1984

Current assets:

Cash	$ 52,750
Accounts receivable	262,250
Notes receivable	200,000
Interest receivable	10,000
Marketable securities	150,000
Merchandise inventory	205,000
Supplies	20,000
Total	$900,000

Current liabilities:

Accounts payable	$250,000
Notes payable	200,000
Total	$450,000

Instructions:

(1) Compute (a) working capital, (b) current ratio, and (c) acid-test ratio.

(2) At the request of the bank, a firm of independent auditors was retained to examine data submitted with the loan application. This examination disclosed several errors. Prepare correcting entries for each of the following errors:

(a) Accounts receivable of $42,250 are uncollectible and should be immediately written off. In addition, it was estimated that of the remaining receivables, 5% would eventually become uncollectible and an allowance should be made for these future uncollectible accounts.

(b) Six months' interest had been accrued on the $200,000, 10%, six-month note receivable dated October 1, 1984.

(c) The notes payable is a 12%, 90-day note dated October 17, 1984. No interest had been accrued on the note.

(d) The marketable securities portfolio includes $100,000 of Porter Company stock that is held as a long-term investment.

(e) A canceled check indicates that a bill for $25,000 for repairs on factory equipment had not been recorded in the accounts.

(f) Accrued wages as of December 31, 1984, totaled $30,000.

(g) Received a year's rent of $72,000 for warehouse space leased to Reese Inc., effective October 1, 1984. Upon receipt, rental income was credited for the full amount.

(h) Supplies on hand at December 31, 1984, total $8,000.

(3) Consider each of the preceding errors separately and assume that only that error affects the current position of Trillo Company. Compute (a) working capital, (b) current ratio, and (c) acid-test ratio, giving effect to each of the preceding errors. Use the following column headings for recording your answers.

| Error | Working Capital | Current Ratio | Acid-Test Ratio |

(4) Prepare a revised schedule of working capital as of December 31, 1984, and recompute the current ratio and acid-test ratio, giving effect to the corrections of all of the preceding errors.

(5) Discuss the action you would recommend the bank take regarding the pending loan application.

Problem 20-5A. The comparative financial statements of T. Rice Inc. are as follows. On December 31, 1985 and 1984, the market price of T. Rice Inc. common stock was $107.50 and $154 respectively.

T. Rice Inc.
Comparative Income Statement
For Years Ended December 31, 1985 and 1984

	1985	1984
Sales	$8,585,000	$8,056,000
Sales returns and allowances	85,000	56,000
Net sales	$8,500,000	$8,000,000
Cost of merchandise sold	5,440,000	4,800,000
Gross profit	$3,060,000	$3,200,000
Selling expenses	$1,380,000	$1,250,000
General expenses	595,000	640,000
Total operating expenses	$1,975,000	$1,890,000
Operating income	$1,085,000	$1,310,000
Other income	119,500	120,000
	$1,204,500	$1,430,000
Other expense (interest)	204,500	180,000
Income before income tax	$1,000,000	$1,250,000
Income tax	490,000	610,000
Net income	$ 510,000	$ 640,000

T. Rice Inc.
Comparative Retained Earnings Statement
For Years Ended December 31, 1985 and 1984

	1985	1984
Retained earnings, January 1	$2,200,000	$1,800,000
Add net income for year	510,000	640,000
Total	$2,710,000	$2,440,000
Deduct dividends:		
On preferred stock	$ 80,000	$ 80,000
On common stock	175,000	160,000
Total	$ 255,000	$ 240,000
Retained earnings, December 31	$2,455,000	$2,200,000

T. Rice Inc.
Comparative Balance Sheet
December 31, 1985 and 1984

Assets	1985	1984
Current assets:		
Cash	$ 375,000	$ 330,000
Marketable securities...........................	125,000	120,000
Accounts receivable (net)......................	500,000	450,000
Merchandise inventory	720,000	660,000
Prepaid expenses...............................	80,000	40,000
Total current assets	$1,800,000	$1,600,000
Long-term investments	250,000	200,000
Plant assets	5,150,000	4,800,000
Total assets	$7,200,000	$6,600,000

Liabilities		
Current liabilities.................................	$1,000,000	$ 900,000
Long-term liabilities:		
Mortgage note payable, 10%, due 1990	$ 245,000	——
Bonds payable, 12%, due 1999	1,500,000	$1,500,000
Total long-term liabilities	$1,745,000	$1,500,000
Total liabilities	$2,745,000	$2,400,000

Stockholders' Equity		
Preferred 8% stock, $100 par	$1,000,000	$1,000,000
Common stock, $25 par	1,000,000	1,000,000
Retained earnings	2,455,000	2,200,000
Total stockholders' equity	$4,455,000	$4,200,000
Total liabilities and stockholders' equity	$7,200,000	$6,600,000

Instructions:

Determine for 1985 the following ratios, turnovers, and other measures, presenting the figures used in your computations:
(1) Working capital.
(2) Current ratio.
(3) Acid-test ratio.
(4) Accounts receivable turnover.
(5) Number of days' sales in receivables.
(6) Merchandise inventory turnover.
(7) Number of days' sales in merchandise inventory.
(8) Ratio of plant assets to long-term liabilities.
(9) Ratio of stockholders' equity to liabilities.
(10) Ratio of net sales to assets.
(11) Rate earned on total assets.
(12) Rate earned on stockholders' equity.
(13) Rate earned on common stockholders' equity.
(14) Earnings per share on common stock.
(15) Price-earnings ratio.
(16) Dividend yield.

(continued)

(17) Number of times interest charges earned.
(18) Number of times preferred dividends earned.

Problem 20-6A. Ann Hayden is considering whether to make a substantial investment in T. Rice Inc. The company's comparative financial statements for 1985 and 1984 were given in Problem 20-5A. To assist in the evaluation of the company, Hayden secured the following additional data taken from the balance sheet at December 31, 1983.

Accounts receivable (net)	$ 400,000
Merchandise inventory	600,000
Long-term investments	50,000
Total assets	6,500,000
Total stockholders' equity (preferred and common stock outstanding same as in 1984)	4,000,000

Instructions:

Prepare a report for Hayden, based on an analysis of the financial data presented. In preparing your report, include all ratios and other data that will be useful in arriving at a decision regarding the investment.

Mini-Case

You and your brother are both presidents of companies in the same industry, CMR Inc. and IMR Inc., respectively. Both companies were originally operated as a single-family business; but shortly after your father's death in 1965, the business was divided into two companies. Your brother took over IMR Inc., located in Indianapolis, while you took over CMR Inc., located in Cincinnati.

During a recent family reunion, your brother referred to the much larger rate of return to his stockholders than was the case in your company and suggested that you consider rearranging the method of financing your corporation. Since 1965, the growth in your brother's company has been financed largely through borrowing and yours largely through the issuance of additional common stock. Both companies have about the same volume of sales, gross profit, operating income, and total assets.

The income statements for both companies for the year ended December 31, 1985, and the balance sheets at December 31, 1985, are as follows:

	IMR Inc.	CMR Inc.
Sales	$2,066,800	$1,972,500
Sales returns and allowances	20,800	19,500
Net sales	$2,046,000	$1,953,000
Cost of merchandise sold	1,227,600	1,171,800
Gross profit	$ 818,400	$ 781,200
Selling expenses	$ 375,800	$ 340,400
General expenses	202,400	183,300
Total operating expenses	$ 578,200	$ 523,700
Operating income	$ 240,200	$ 257,500
Interest expense	35,200	7,500
Income before income tax	$ 205,000	$ 250,000
Income tax	82,000	100,400
Net income	$ 123,000	$ 149,600

Assets	IMR Inc.	CMR Inc.
Current assets	$ 42,000	$ 39,000
Plant assets (net)	880,000	906,000
Intangible assets	18,000	5,000
Total assets	$940,000	$950,000

Liabilities		
Current liabilities	$ 18,000	$ 18,500
Long-term liabilities	352,000	75,500
Total liabilities	$370,000	$ 94,000

Stockholders' Equity		
Common stock ($10 par)	$100,000	$500,000
Retained earnings	470,000	356,000
Total stockholders' equity	$570,000	$856,000
Total liabilities and stockholders' equity	$940,000	$950,000

In addition to the 1985 financial statements, the following data were taken from the balance sheets at December 31, 1984:

	IMR Inc.	CMR Inc.
Total assets	$920,000	$910,000
Total stockholders' equity	530,000	834,000

Instructions:

(1) Determine for 1985 the following ratios and other measures for both companies:
   (a) ratio of plant assets to long-term liabilities,
   (b) ratio of stockholders' equity to liabilities,
   (c) ratio of net sales to assets,
   (d) rate earned on total assets, and
   (e) rate earned on stockholders' equity.
(2) For both IMR Inc. and CMR Inc., the rate earned on stockholders' equity is greater than the rate earned on total assets. Explain why.
(3) Why is the rate of return on stockholders' equity for IMR Inc. more than 25% greater than for CMR Inc.?
(4) Comment on your brother's suggestion for rearranging the financing of CMR Inc.

21
CHAPTER

Departments and Branches

CHAPTER OBJECTIVES

Describe and illustrate the accounting for departmental operations.

Describe and illustrate the accounting for branch operations.

PART 7 | Control Accounting

21

CHAPTER

The activities of many business enterprises are performed by separate segments such as departments, divisions, and branches. These units of an operating entity may be organized as separate corporations, with common ownership of the stock and common management at the top. Selection of the organizational structure and the segmentation is often affected by size, volume of business, diversity of activity, and geographic distribution of operations. In any event, the managers of segmented enterprises need accounting reports which are designed to aid them in planning, controlling, and evaluating the performance of the various segments.

Segmentation may occur in service enterprises as well as in businesses engaged mainly in merchandising or manufacturing activities. Segmented accounting reports are useful to management regardless of the type of activity. A merchandising enterprise is used as the basis for discussion and illustration in this chapter. The special accounting concepts and procedures applicable to multiple corporations with common ownership were discussed in a previous chapter.

ACCOUNTING FOR DEPARTMENTAL OPERATIONS

Departmental accounting is more likely to be used by a large business than by a small one, but some degree of departmentalization may be used by a small enterprise. For example, a one-person real estate and property insurance agency could account separately for real estate commissions and for insurance commissions. Analysis of the division of the owner's time between the two activities and of the revenue and expenses by type of activity may show that more time should be devoted to one department and less to the other.

Departmental accounting for a large enterprise is likely to be both feasible and desirable. In a modern department store, for example, there are a number of distinct departments, each under the control of a departmental manager. Departmentalization of accounting and reporting aids in the assignment of responsibility for departmental operations to departmental managers. It assists top management both in evaluating the relative operating efficiencies of individual departments and in planning future operations.

ACCOUNTING REPORTS FOR DEPARTMENTAL OPERATIONS

Accounting reports for departmental operations are generally limited to income statements. Although departmental income statements are usually not issued to stockholders or others outside the management group, the trend is toward providing more information of this type.

The degree to which departmental accounting may be used for a merchandising enterprise varies. Analysis of operations by departments may end with the determination of gross profit or it may extend through the determination of net income. An income statement that includes a departmental breakdown of revenue and expenses categorized by responsibility for the incurrence of costs has been widely used in recent years. The most common departmental income statements are described in the paragraphs that follow.

Gross Profit by Departments

For a merchandising enterprise, the gross profit is one of the most significant figures in the income statement. Since the sales and the cost of merchandise sold are both, to a large extent, controlled by departmental management, the reporting of gross profit by departments is useful in cost analysis and control. In addition, such reports aid management in directing its efforts toward obtaining a mix of sales that will maximize profits. After studying the reports, management may decide to change sales or purchases policies, cut back or expand operations, or shift personnel to achieve a higher gross profit for each department. Caution must be exercised in the use of such reports to insure that proposed changes affecting gross profit do not have an adverse effect on net income. For example, a change that increases gross profit but results in an even greater increase in operating expenses would decrease net income.

To compute gross profit by departments, it is necessary to determine by departments each element entering into gross profit. There are two basic methods of doing this: (1) setting up departmental accounts and identifying each element by department at the time of the transaction, or (2) maintaining only one account for the element and then allocating it among the departments at the time the income statement is prepared. Ordinarily, the first method is used unless the time required in analyzing each transaction is too great. Allocation among departments at the end of a period is likely to yield less accurate results than the first method, but some degree of accuracy may be sacrificed to obtain a saving of time and expense.

The elements that must be departmentalized in order to determine gross profit by departments are merchandise inventory, purchases, sales, and the related cash discounts and returns and allowances. When departmental accounts are maintained for each element, special departmental columns for recording transactions may be provided in the proper journals. For example, in a furniture store that sells furniture and carpeting, the sales journal may have a credit column for Furniture Sales and a credit column for Carpet Sales. To aid in the journalizing of departmental transactions, the supporting documents such as sales invoices, vouchers, and cash register readings must identify the department affected by each transaction. Postings to departmental accounts from the special journals follow the procedures described in earlier chapters.

An income statement showing gross profit by departments for Garrison Company, which has two sales departments, appears on page 596. For illustrative purposes, the operating expenses are shown in condensed form. Usually they would be listed in detail.

| Apportionment of Operating Expenses | Departmental reporting of income may be extended to the various sections of the income statement, such as gross profit less selling expenses (gross selling profit), gross profit less all operating expenses (operating income), income before income tax, or net income. The underlying principle is the same for all degrees of departmentalization, namely, to assign to each department the related revenue and that part of the expenses incurred for its benefit. |

Some expenses may be easily identified with the department benefited. For example, if each salesperson is restricted to a certain sales department, the sales salaries may be assigned to the proper departmental salary accounts each time the payroll is prepared. On the other hand, the salaries of company officers, executives, and office personnel are not identifiable with specific sales departments

Garrison Company
Income Statement
For Year Ended December 31, 19--

	Department A		Department B		Total	
Revenue from sales:						
Sales		$630,000		$270,000		$900,000
Less sales returns and allowances		15,300		7,100		22,400
Net sales		$614,700		$262,900		$877,600
Cost of merchandise sold:						
Merchandise inventory, January 1, 19--		$ 80,150		$ 61,750		$141,900
Purchases	$334,550		$200,350		$534,900	
Less purchases discount	6,200		2,400		8,600	
Merchandise available for sale		$408,500		$259,700		$668,200
Less merchandise inventory, December 31, 19--		85,150		78,950		164,100
Cost of merchandise sold		323,350		180,750		504,100
Gross profit		$291,350		$ 82,150		$373,500
Operating expenses:						
Selling expenses					$113,000	
General expenses					110,200	
Total operating expenses						223,200
Income from operations						$150,300
Other expense:						
Interest expense						2,500
Income before income tax						$147,800
Income tax						64,444
Net income						$ 83,356

INCOME STATEMENT DEPARTMENTALIZED THROUGH GROSS PROFIT

and must therefore be allocated if an equitable and reasonable basis for allocation exists.

Many accountants prefer to apportion all operating expenses to the individual departments only at the end of the accounting period. When this is done, there is no need for departmental expense accounts in the general ledger and fewer postings are needed. The apportionments may be made on a work sheet, which serves as the basis for preparing the departmental income statement.

When operating expenses are allocated, they should be apportioned to the respective departments as nearly as possible in accordance with the cost of services rendered to them. Determining the amount of an expense chargeable to each department is not always a simple matter. In the first place, it requires the exercise of judgment; and accountants of equal ability may well differ in their opinions as to the proper basis for the apportionment of operating expenses. Second, the cost of collecting data for use in making an apportionment must be kept within reasonable bounds. Consequently, information that is readily available and is substantially reliable may be used instead of more accurate information that would be more costly to collect.

To illustrate the apportionment of operating expenses, assume that Garrison Company extends its departmental reporting through income from operations. The company's operating expenses for the calendar year and the methods used in apportioning them are presented in the paragraphs that follow.

Sales Salaries Expense is apportioned to the two departments according to the distributions shown in the payroll records. Of the $84,900 total in the account, $54,000 is chargeable to Department A and $30,900 is chargeable to Department B.

Advertising Expense, covering billboard advertising and newspaper advertising, is apportioned according to the amount of advertising incurred for each department. The billboard advertising totaling $5,000 emphasizes the name and the location of the company. This expense is allocated on the basis of sales, the assumption being that this basis represents a fair allocation of billboard advertising to each department. Analysis of the newspaper space costing $14,000 indicates that 65% of the space was devoted to Department A and 35% to Department B. The apportionment of the total advertising expense is shown in the following tabulation:

	Total	Department A	Department B
Sales—dollars	$900,000	$630,000	$270,000
Sales—percent	100%	70%	30%
Billboard advertising		$ 5,000	$ 3,500	$ 1,500
Newspaper space—percent . .	100%	65%	35%
Newspaper advertising		14,000	9,100	4,900
Advertising expense		$19,000	$12,600	$ 6,400

Depreciation Expense—Store Equipment is apportioned according to the average cost of the equipment in each of the two departments. The computations for the apportionment of the depreciation expense are as follows:

	Total	Department A	Department B
Cost of store equipment:			
January 1	$28,300	$16,400	$11,900
December 31	31,700	19,600	12,100
Total	$60,000	$36,000	$24,000
Average	$30,000	$18,000	$12,000
Percent	100%	60%	40%
Depreciation expense	$ 4,400	$ 2,640	$ 1,760

Officers' Salaries Expense and **Office Salaries Expense** are apportioned on the basis of the relative amount of time devoted to each department by the officers and by the office personnel. Obviously, this can be only an approximation. The number of sales transactions may have some bearing on the matter, as may billing and collection procedures and other factors such as promotional campaigns that might vary from period to period. Of the total officers' salaries of $52,000 and office salaries of $17,600, it is estimated that 60%, or $31,200 and $10,560 respectively, is chargeable to Department A and that 40%, or $20,800 and $7,040 respectively, is chargeable to Department B.

Rent Expense and **Heating and Lighting Expense** are usually apportioned on the basis of the floor space devoted to each department. In apportioning rent expense for a multistory building, differences in the value of the various floors and locations may be taken into account. For example, the space near the main entrance of a department store is more valuable than the same amount of floor space located far from the elevator on the sixth floor. For Garrison Company, rent expense is apportioned on the basis of floor space used because there is no significant difference in the value of the floor areas used by each department. In allocating heating and lighting expense, it is assumed that the number of lights, their wattage, and the extent of use are uniform throughout the sales departments. If there are major variations and the total lighting expense is material, further analysis and separate apportionment may be advisable. The rent expense and the heating and lighting expense are apportioned as follows:

	Total	Department A	Department B
Floor space, square feet	160,000	104,000	56,000
Percent	100%	65%	35%
Rent expense	$15,400	$10,010	$ 5,390
Heating and lighting expense	$ 5,100	$ 3,315	$ 1,785

Property Tax Expense and **Insurance Expense** are related primarily to the value of the merchandise inventory and the store equipment. Although there are differences in the cost of such assets, their assessed value for tax purposes, and their value for insurance purposes, the cost is most readily available and is considered to be satisfactory as a basis for apportioning these expenses. The computation of the apportionment of property tax expense and insurance expense is as follows:

	Total	Department A	Department B
Merchandise inventory:			
January 1....................	$141,900	$ 80,150	$ 61,750
December 31	164,100	85,150	78,950
Total	$306,000	$165,300	$140,700
Average......................................	$153,000	$ 82,650	$ 70,350
Average cost of store equipment (computed previously)...............................	30,000	18,000	12,000
Total	$183,000	$100,650	$ 82,350
Percent....................................	100%	55%	45%
Property tax expense	$ 6,800	$ 3,740	$ 3,060
Insurance expense	$ 3,900	$ 2,145	$ 1,755

Uncollectible Accounts Expense, Miscellaneous Selling Expense, and **Miscellaneous General Expense** are apportioned on the basis of sales. Although the uncollectible accounts expense may be apportioned on the basis of an analysis of accounts receivable written off, it is assumed that the expense is closely related to sales. The miscellaneous selling and general expenses are apportioned on the basis of sales, which are assumed to be a reasonable measure of the benefit to each department. The computation of the apportionment is as follows:

	Total	Department A	Department B
Sales.......................................	$900,000	$630,000	$270,000
Percent....................................	100%	70%	30%
Uncollectible accounts expense	$ 4,600	$ 3,220	$ 1,380
Miscellaneous selling expense	$ 4,700	$ 3,290	$ 1,410
Miscellaneous general expense	$ 4,800	$ 3,360	$ 1,440

An income statement presenting income from operations by departments for Garrison Company appears on the following page. The amounts for sales and cost of merchandise sold are presented in condensed form. Details could be reported, if desired, in the manner illustrated on page 596.

DEPARTMENTAL MARGIN APPROACH TO INCOME REPORTING

Not all accountants agree as to the merits of the type of departmental analysis discussed in the preceding section. Many caution against complete reliance on such departmental income statements on the grounds that the use of arbitrary bases in allocating operating expenses is likely to yield incorrect amounts of departmental operating income. In addition, objection may be made to the reporting of operating income by departments on the grounds that departments are not independent operating units, but segments of a single business enterprise, and that therefore no single department of a business can by itself earn an income. For these reasons, the format of income statements of segmented businesses may follow a somewhat different format than the one illustrated on page 600. The alternative form emphasizes the contribution of each department to the operating expenses incurred on behalf of the business as a unified whole. Income statements

Garrison Company
Income Statement
For Year Ended December 31, 19--

	Department A		Department B		Total	
Net sales		$614,700		$262,900		$877,600
Cost of merchandise sold		323,350		180,750		504,100
Gross profit		$291,350		$ 82,150		$373,500
Operating expenses:						
Selling expenses:						
Sales salaries expense	$ 54,000		$ 30,900		$ 84,900	
Advertising expense	12,600		6,400		19,000	
Depreciation expense—store equipment	2,640		1,760		4,400	
Miscellaneous selling expense	3,290		1,410		4,700	
Total selling expenses		$ 72,530		$ 40,470		$113,000
General expenses:						
Officers' salaries expense	$ 31,200		$ 20,800		$ 52,000	
Office salaries expense	10,560		7,040		17,600	
Rent expense	10,010		5,390		15,400	
Property tax expense	3,740		3,060		6,800	
Heating and lighting expense	3,315		1,785		5,100	
Uncollectible accounts expense	3,220		1,380		4,600	
Insurance expense	2,145		1,755		3,900	
Miscellaneous general expense	3,360		1,440		4,800	
Total general expenses		67,550		42,650		110,200
Total operating expenses		140,080		83,120		223,200
Income (loss) from operations		$151,270		$ (970)		$150,300
Other expense:						
Interest expense						2,500
Income before income tax						$147,800
Income tax						64,444
Net income						$ 83,356

INCOME STATEMENT DEPARTMENTALIZED THROUGH INCOME FROM OPERATIONS

prepared in this alternative form are said to follow the **departmental margin** or **contribution margin** approach to income reporting.

Prior to the preparation of an income statement in the departmental margin format, it is necessary to differentiate between operating expenses that are direct and those that are indirect. The two categories may be described in general terms as follows:

> Direct expense — Operating expenses directly traceable to or incurred for the sole benefit of a specific department and usually subject to the control of the department manager.
>
> Indirect expense — Operating expenses incurred for the entire enterprise as a unit and hence not subject to the control of individual department managers.

The details of departmental sales and cost of merchandise sold are presented on the income statement in the usual manner. The direct expenses of each department are then deducted from the related departmental gross profit, yielding balances which are identified as **departmental margin**. The remaining expenses, including the indirect operating expenses, are not departmentalized. They are reported singly below the total departmental margin.

An income statement in the departmental margin format for the Garrison Company is presented on the following page. The basic revenue, cost, and expense data for the period are identical with those reported in the earlier illustration. The expenses identified as "direct" are sales salaries, property tax, uncollectible accounts, insurance, depreciation, and the newspaper advertising portion of advertising. The billboard portion of advertising, which is for the benefit of the business as a whole, as well as officers' and office salaries, and the remaining operating expenses, are identified as "indirect." Although a $970 net loss from operations is reported for Department B on page 600, a departmental margin of $38,395 is reported for the same department on the statement on page 602.

| DEPARTMENTAL MARGIN ANALYSIS AND CONTROL | The importance of controlling expenses as an essential element of profit maximization has been emphasized throughout this textbook. The value of the departmental margin approach to income reporting derives largely from its emphasis on the assignment of responsibility for control. An accounting system that provides the means for such control is sometimes called **responsibility accounting.** |

With departmental margin analysis, the manager of each department can be held accountable for operating expenses traceable to the department. A reduction in the direct expenses of a department will have a favorable effect on that department's contribution to the net income of the enterprise.

The departmental margin income statement may also be useful to management in making plans for future operations. For example, this type of analysis can be used when the discontinuance of a certain operation or department is being considered. If a specific department yields a departmental margin, it generally should be retained, even though the allocation of the indirect operating expenses would result in a net loss for that department. This observation is based upon the assumption that the department in question represents a relatively small segment of the

INCOME
STATEMENT
DEPARTMEN-
TALIZED THROUGH
DEPARTMENTAL
MARGIN

Garrison Company
Income Statement
For Year Ended December 31, 19--

	Department A		Department B		Total	
Net sales	....	$614,700	....	$262,900	....	$877,600
Cost of merchandise sold................	....	323,350	....	18C,750	....	504,100
Gross profit	....	$291,350	....	$ 82,150	....	$373,500
Direct departmental expenses:						
Sales salaries expense...........	$54,000	....	$30,900	....	$84,900	....
Advertising expense..	9,100	....	4,900	....	14,000	....
Property tax expense.............	3,740	....	3,060	....	6,800	....
Uncollectible accounts expense...........	3,220	....	1,380	....	4,600	....
Depreciation expense—store equipment	2,640	....	1,760	....	4,400	....
Insurance expense ..	2,145	....	1,755	....	3,900	....
Total direct departmental expenses ..	....	74,845	....	43,755	....	118,600
Departmental margin .	....	$216,505	....	$ 38,395	....	$254,900
Indirect expenses:						
Officers' salaries expense	....	....	....	....	$52,000	....
Office salaries expense	....	....	....	....	17,600	....
Rent expense	....	....	....	....	15,400	....
Heating and lighting expense...........	....	....	....	....	5,100	....
Advertising expense..	....	....	....	....	5,000	....
Miscellaneous selling expense...........	....	....	....	....	4,700	....
Miscellaneous general expense...........	....	....	....	....	4,800	....
Total indirect expenses	....	....	....	....	....	104,600
Income from operations	....	....	....	....	....	$150,300
Other expense: Interest expense.....	....	....	....	....	....	2,500
Income before income tax..............	....	....	....	....	....	$147,800
Income tax...........	....	....	....	....	....	64,444
Net income	....	....	....	....	....	$ 83,356

enterprise. Its termination, therefore, would not cause any significant reduction in the amount of indirect expenses.

To illustrate the application of the departmental margin approach to long-range planning, assume that a business occupies a rented three-story building. If the enterprise is divided into twenty departments, each occupying about the same amount of space, termination of the least profitable department would probably not cause any reduction in rent or other occupancy expenses. The space vacated would probably be absorbed by the remaining nineteen departments. On the other hand, if the enterprise were divided into three departments, each occupying approximately equal areas, the discontinuance of one could result in vacating an entire floor and significantly reducing occupancy expenses. When the departmental margin analysis is applied to problems of this type, consideration should be given to proposals for the use of the vacated space.

To further illustrate the departmental margin approach, assume that an enterprise with six departments has earned $70,000 before income tax during the past year, which is fairly typical of recent operations. Assume also that recent income statements, in which all operating expenses are allocated, indicate that Department F has been incurring losses, the net loss having amounted to $5,000 for the past year. Departmental margin analysis shows that, in spite of the losses, Department F should not be discontinued unless there is enough assurance that a proportionate increase in the gross profit of other departments or a decrease in indirect expenses can be effected. The following analysis, which is considerably condensed, shows a possible reduction of $10,000 in net income (the amount of the departmental margin for Department F) if Department F is discontinued.

DEPARTMENTAL ANALYSIS— DISCONTINUANCE OF UNPROFITABLE DEPARTMENT

Proposal to Discontinue Department F
January 25, 19--

	Current Operations			Discontinuance of Department F
	Department F	Departments A–E	Total	
Sales.........................	$100,000	$900,000	$1,000,000	$900,000
Cost of merchandise sold	70,000	540,000	610,000	540,000
Gross profit..................	$ 30,000	$360,000	$ 390,000	$360,000
Direct departmental expenses ...	20,000	210,000	230,000	210,000
Departmental margin	$ 10,000	$150,000	$ 160,000	$150,000
Indirect expenses			90,000	90,000
Income before income tax......			$ 70,000	$ 60,000

In addition to a departmental margin analysis, there are other factors that may need to be considered. For example, there may be problems regarding the displacement of sales personnel. Or customers attracted by the least profitable department may make large purchases in other departments, so that discontinuance of that department may adversely affect the sales of other departments.

The foregoing discussion of departmental income statements has suggested various ways in which income data may be made useful to management in making important policy decisions. Note that the format selected for the presentation of income data to management must be that which will be most useful for evaluating, controlling, and planning departmental operations.

BRANCH OPERATIONS

Just as a business enterprise may add a new department in an effort to increase its sales and income, for similar reasons it also may open new stores (branches) in different locations. Among the types of retail businesses in which branch operations were first successfully developed on a major scale were variety, grocery, and drug stores. There are a number of large corporations with hundreds or thousands of retail branches distributed over a wide area. In addition to the national chain store organizations, there are many of a regional or local nature. The growth of suburban shopping centers has added significantly to the number of firms, especially department stores, that have expanded through the opening of branches.

Although commonly associated with retailing, branch operations are also carried on by banking institutions, service organizations, and many kinds of manufacturing enterprises. Regardless of the nature of the business, each branch ordinarily has a branch manager. Within the framework of general policies set by top management, the branch manager may be given freedom in conducting the business of the branch. Data concerning the amount of business handled and the profitability of operations at each location are essential as a basis for decisions by executive management. It is also necessary to maintain a record of the assets at the branch locations and of liabilities incurred by each branch.

The remainder of this chapter deals with the central office and the single branch of a merchandising business. The fundamental considerations are not greatly affected, however, by the number of branches or by the particular type of business.

SYSTEMS FOR BRANCH ACCOUNTING

There are various systems of accounting for branch operations. The system may be highly centralized, with the accounting for the branch done at the home office. Or the system may be almost completely decentralized, with the branch responsible for the detailed accounting and only summary accounts carried for the branch by the home office. Using some of the elements of both extremes is also common. Many variations are possible, but the two methods of branch accounting described in the following paragraphs are typical.

Centralized System

The branch may prepare only the basic records of its transactions, such as sales invoices, time tickets for employees, and vouchers for liabilities incurred. Copies of all such documents are forwarded to the home office, where they are recorded in proper journals in the usual manner. When this system is used, the branch has no journals or ledgers. If the operating results of the branch are to be determined separately, which is normally the case, separate branch accounts for sales, cost of merchandise sold, and expenses must be maintained in the home office ledger. The principles of departmental accounting will apply in such cases, with the branch being treated as a department.

One important result of centralizing the bookkeeping activities at one location may be substantial savings in office expense. There is also greater assurance of uniformity in accounting methods used. On the other hand, there is some likelihood of delays and inaccuracies in submitting data to the home office, with the result that periodic reports on the operations of a branch may not be available when needed.

Decentralized System

When the accounting for branches is decentralized, each branch maintains its own accounting system with journals and ledgers. The account classification for assets, liabilities, revenues, and expenses in the branch ledger conforms to the classification used by the home office. The accounting processes are like those of an independent business, except that the branch does not have capital accounts. A special account entitled Home Office takes the place of the capital accounts. The process of preparing financial statements and adjusting and closing the accounts is substantially the same as for an independent enterprise. It is this system of branch accounting to which the remainder of the chapter is devoted.

UNDERLYING PRINCIPLES OF DECENTRALIZED BRANCH ACCOUNTING

When the branch has a ledger with a full set of accounts except capital accounts, there must be some tie-in between the branch ledger and the general ledger at the home office. The properties at the branch are a part of the assets of the entire enterprise, and liabilities incurred at the branch are liabilities of the entire enterprise. Although the accounting system at the branch is much like that of an independent company, the branch is not considered a separate entity but only a segment of the business.

The tie-in between the home office and the branch is accomplished by the subsidiary ledger technique, with an added modification that makes the branch ledger a self-contained unit. The basic features of the system are shown in the following chart:

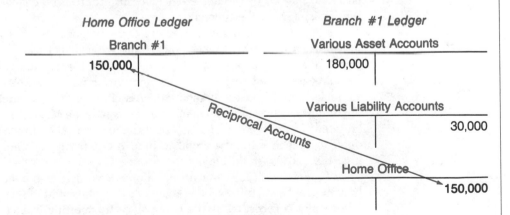

In the home office ledger, the account Branch #1 has a debit balance of $150,000. This balance represents the sum of the assets minus the sum of the liabilities recorded in the ledger at the branch. The various asset and liability accounts in the branch ledger are represented in the chart by one account for all assets ($180,000) and one account for all liabilities ($30,000). To make the branch ledger self-balancing, the account Home Office is added. It has a credit balance of $150,000. The two accounts, Branch #1 in the home office ledger and Home Office in the branch ledger, have equal but opposite balances and are known as reciprocal accounts. The home office account in the branch ledger replaces the capital accounts that would be used if the branch were a separate entity. Actually, the account represents the portion of the capital of the home office that is invested in the branch.

When the home office sends assets to the branch, it debits Branch #1 for the total and credits the proper asset accounts. Upon receiving the assets, the branch debits the proper asset accounts and credits Home Office. To illustrate, assume that the home office begins branch operations by sending $20,000 in cash to the newly appointed branch manager. The entries in the two ledgers are illustrated as follows:

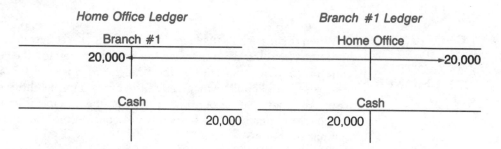

When the branch disburses the cash, it records the transactions as though it were an independent entity. For example, if the branch purchases office equipment for $9,000, paying cash, it debits Office Equipment and credits Cash. No entry is required by the home office because there is no change in the amount of the investment at the branch.

As the branch incurs expenses and earns revenue, it records the transactions in the usual manner. Although such transactions affect the amount of the home office investment at the branch, recognition of the change is delayed until the accounts are closed at the end of the accounting period. At that time, the income summary account in the branch ledger is closed to the account Home Office. If operations have resulted in an operating income, the account Home Office will be credited. In the home office, an operating income at the branch is recorded by a debit to Branch #1 and a credit to Branch Operating Income. For an operating loss, the entries would be just the reverse.

In a merchandising enterprise, all or a large part of the stock in trade of the branch may be supplied by the home office. A shipment of merchandise from the home office is recorded by the home office by debiting Branch #1 and crediting Shipments to Branch #1. The branch records the transaction by debiting Shipments from Home Office and crediting Home Office. It is evident from the following accounts that the two shipments accounts are also reciprocal accounts.

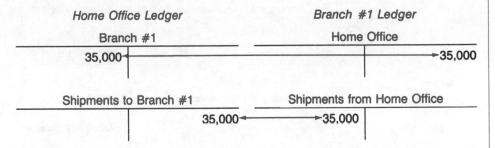

Home Office Ledger	Branch #1 Ledger
Branch #1	Home Office
35,000	35,000
Shipments to Branch #1	Shipments from Home Office
35,000	35,000

The account Shipments to Branch #1 is a contra account representing a reduction in Merchandise Inventory and Purchases in the home office ledger. Shipments from Home Office, in the branch ledger, is like a purchases account. Both accounts are temporary in nature and are periodically closed to the respective income summary accounts.

ILLUSTRATION OF DECENTRALIZED BRANCH ACCOUNTING

A series of entries illustrating the underlying principles applicable to branch accounting on a decentralized basis is presented below and on pages 608 and 609. The illustration begins with the opening of a branch and continues with operations during the remainder of the accounting period. Typical transactions between the home office and the branch are considered, as well as those between the branch and other business enterprises. These transactions are recorded in general journal form. The adjusting and closing entries of the branch and the entry required by the home office to record the operating income of the branch are also presented.

HOME OFFICE ENTRIES[1]	BRANCH ENTRIES

TRANSACTIONS

(1) The home office established Branch #1 near the end of the fiscal year, sending $20,000 in cash and $40,000 in merchandise.

HOME OFFICE ENTRIES	BRANCH ENTRIES

Branch #1 60,000
    Cash 20,000
    Shipments to Br. #1 .. 40,000
	Cash 20,000
	Shipments from H.O. ... 40,000
	    Home Office 60,000

(2) The branch purchased on account $20,000 of merchandise, $30,000 of equipment, and $1,500 of prepaid insurance.

HOME OFFICE ENTRIES	BRANCH ENTRIES
	Purchases .... 20,000 Equipment .... 30,000 Prepaid Insurance ..... 1,500 Accounts Payable ... 51,500

[1]Only the entries and accounts affecting Branch #1 are presented.

HOME OFFICE ENTRIES	BRANCH ENTRIES

(3) The branch sold merchandise for $36,000 in cash and $21,000 on account.

	Cash................. 36,000
	Accounts Receivable... 21,000
	Sales.............. 57,000

(4) The branch paid operating expenses of $11,300.

	Operating Expenses ... 11,300
	Cash.............. 11,300

(5) The branch collected $12,000 on accounts receivable.

	Cash................. 12,000
	Accounts Receivable. 12,000

(6) The branch paid $32,000 on accounts payable.

	Accounts Payable 32,000
	Cash.............. 32,000

(7) The branch sent $10,000 in cash to the home office.

HOME OFFICE	BRANCH
Cash................. 10,000	Home Office 10,000
Branch #1.......... 10,000	Cash............... 10,000

ADJUSTING

(a) To record the branch ending merchandise inventory.

	Mdse. Inventory 22,000
	Income Summary.... 22,000

(b) To record the branch insurance and depreciation expense.

	Operating Expenses ... 700
	Prepaid Insurance ... 200
	Accum. Depreciation . 500

CLOSING

(c) To close the branch sales account.

	Sales................. 57,000
	Income Summary.... 57,000

HOME OFFICE ENTRIES	BRANCH ENTRIES

(d) *To close the branch cost and expense accounts.*

	Income Summary...... 72,000
	Shipments from H.O.. 40,000
	Purchases 20,000
	Operating Expenses . 12,000

(e) *To close the branch income summary account and to record the operating income of the branch in the accounts of the home office.*

HOME OFFICE ENTRIES	BRANCH ENTRIES
Branch #1............ 7,000	Income Summary...... 7,000
Branch #1 Operating	Home Office 7,000
Income 7,000	

After the foregoing entries have been posted, the home office accounts affected and the branch ledger accounts appear as shown below and on pages 610 and 611.

HOME OFFICE LEDGER	BRANCH LEDGER

Cash (Home Office Ledger)

(7)	10,000	(1)	20,000

Cash (Branch Ledger)

(1)	20,000	(4)	11,300
(3)	36,000	(6)	32,000
(5)	12,000	(7)	10,000
		Balance	14,700
	68,000		68,000
Balance	14,700		

Accounts Receivable

(3)	21,000	(5)	12,000
		Balance	9,000
	21,000		21,000
Balance	9,000		

Merchandise Inventory

(a)	22,000		

HOME OFFICE LEDGER	BRANCH LEDGER

Prepaid Insurance

(2)	1,500	(b)		200
		Balance		1,300
	1,500			1,500
Balance	1,300			

Equipment

(2)	30,000

Accumulated Depreciation

	(b)	500

Accounts Payable

(6)	32,000	(2)	51,500
Balance	19,500		
	51,500		51,500
		Balance	19,500

Branch #1

(1)	60,000	(7)	10,000
(e)	7,000	Balance	57,000
	67,000		67,000
Balance	57,000		

Home Office

(7)	10,000	(1)	60,000
Balance	57,000	(e)	7,000
	67,000		67,000
		Balance	57,000

Branch #1 Operating Income

	(e)	7,000

Branch Operating Income will be closed to the income summary account.

Income Summary

(d)	72,000	(a)	22,000
(e)	7,000	(c)	57,000
	79,000		79,000

Sales

(c)	57,000	(3)	57,000

HOME OFFICE LEDGER		BRANCH LEDGER	
Shipments to Branch #1		**Shipments from Home Office**	
	(1) 40,000	(1) 40,000	(d) 40,000
		Purchases	
Shipments to Branch #1 is deducted from the sum of the beginning inventory and purchases. It will be closed to the income summary account.		(2) 20,000	(d) 20,000
		Operating Expenses	
		(4) 11,300	(d) 12,000
		(b) 700	
		12,000	12,000

FINANCIAL
STATEMENTS
FOR HOME
OFFICE AND
BRANCH

Branch financial statements differ from those of a separate business entity in two minor respects. In the branch income statement, shipments from the home office appear in the cost of merchandise sold section following purchases. In the branch balance sheet, the account Home Office takes the place of the capital accounts.

The home office income statement reports details of sales, cost of merchandise sold, expenses, and income or loss from home office operations in the usual manner. The operating income or loss of each branch is then listed, and the operating results for the entire enterprise are reported. The assets section of the balance sheet prepared from the home office ledger will include the controlling accounts for the various branches. The nature and the amounts of the various assets and liabilities at the branch locations will not be disclosed.

The home office statements, together with financial statements for each individual branch, serve a useful purpose for management. They are not usually issued to stockholders and creditors. Accordingly, it is necessary to combine the data on the income statements of the home office and the branches to form one overall income statement. The data on the balance sheets of the home office and of the various branches are also combined to form one balance sheet for the enterprise. The preparation of the combined statements is made easier by the use of work sheets. The work sheets are similar in that each has a column for the home office account balances, a column for the account balances of each branch, a set of columns headed "Eliminations," and a final column to which the combined figures are extended.

The combined income statement and the related work sheet for Keller Corporation are as follows.

Keller Corporation
Work Sheet for Combined Income Statement
For Year Ended March 31, 19--

	Home Office	Branch #1	Eliminations		Combined Income Statement
			Debit	Credit	
Sales	897,000	57,000			954,000
Cost of merchandise sold:					
Mdse. inv., April 1	141,000				141,000
Purchases	652,000	20,000			672,000
	793,000				
Shipments from home office		40,000		40,000	
Less shipments to Branch #1	40,000		40,000		
Mdse. available for sale	753,000	60,000			813,000
Less mdse. inv., March 31	150,000	22,000			172,000
Cost of merchandise sold	603,000	38,000			641,000
Gross profit	294,000	19,000			313,000
Operating expenses	150,500	12,000			162,500
Income before income tax	143,500	7,000	40,000	40,000	150,500
Income tax					66,740
Net income					83,760

Keller Corporation
Income Statement
For Year Ended March 31, 19--

Sales		$954,000
Cost of merchandise sold:		
Merchandise inventory, April 1, 19--	$141,000	
Purchases	672,000	
Merchandise available for sale	$813,000	
Less merchandise inventory, March 31, 19--	172,000	
Cost of merchandise sold		641,000
Gross profit		$313,000
Operating expenses		162,500
Income before income tax		$150,500
Income tax		66,740
Net income (per common share, $4.19)		$ 83,760

The account Shipments from Home Office is canceled by a credit in the Eliminations column, and the account Shipments to Branch #1 is canceled by a debit in the Eliminations column. These eliminations are necessary in the preparation of a combined statement reporting the home office and the branch as a single operating unit. The two accounts merely record a change in location of merchandise within the company.

The combined balance sheet and the related work sheet for Keller Corporation are presented below. The reciprocal account Branch #1 is canceled by a credit elimination; the reciprocal account Home Office is canceled by a debit elimination.

Keller Corporation
Work Sheet for Combined Balance Sheet
March 31, 19--

	Home Office	Branch #1	Eliminations Debit	Eliminations Credit	Combined Balance Sheet
Debit balances:					
Cash	62,000	14,700			76,700
Accounts receivable	81,000	9,000			90,000
Merchandise inventory	150,000	22,000			172,000
Prepaid insurance	8,200	1,300			9,500
Branch #1	57,000			57,000	
Equipment....................	195,000	30,000			225,000
Total	553,200	77,000			573,200
Credit balances:					
Accumulated depreciation	87,000	500			87,500
Accounts payable	110,000	19,500			129,500
Home office		57,000	57,000		
Common stock.................	200,000				200,000
Retained earnings	156,200				156,200
Total	553,200	77,000	57,000	57,000	573,200

Keller Corporation
Balance Sheet
March 31, 19--

Assets

Cash		$ 76,700
Accounts receivable		90,000
Merchandise inventory		172,000
Prepaid insurance		9,500
Equipment	$225,000	
Less accumulated depreciation	87,500	137,500
Total assets		$485,700

Liabilities and Capital

Accounts payable............................		$129,500
Common stock, $10 par	$200,000	
Retained earnings	156,200	356,200
Total liabilities and capital.................		$485,700

SHIPMENTS TO BRANCH BILLED AT SELLING PRICE

In the foregoing discussion and illustrations, the billing for merchandise shipped to the branch has been assumed to be at cost price. When all or most of the merchandise handled by the branch is supplied by the home office, billings are usually made at selling price. An advantage of this procedure is that it provides a convenient control over inventories at the branch. The branch merchandise inventory at the beginning of a period (at selling price), plus shipments during the period (at selling price), less sales for the period yields the ending inventory (at selling price). Comparison of the book amount with the physical inventory taken at selling prices discloses any differences. A significant difference between the physical and the book inventories indicates a need for remedial action by the management.

When shipments to the branch are billed at selling prices, no gross profit will be reported on the branch income statement. The merchandise inventory on the branch balance sheet will also be stated at the billed (selling) price of the merchandise on hand. In combining the branch statements with the home office statements, it is necessary to convert the data back to cost by eliminating the markup from both the shipments accounts and the inventory accounts.

ANALYSES OF OPERATING SEGMENTS

As business units grow ever larger and more diversified, the need for analysis of operations becomes increasingly important. It is necessary to account separately for the various segments that make up the larger unit. Departments and branches are two such segments. Accounting procedures can also be established for other segments of operations such as sales territories and individual products. The accounting procedures for sales territories would follow the principles of departmental accounting, with each territory being treated as a department.

Business operations are often analyzed in terms of individual products. For the merchandising enterprise, accounting procedures like those illustrated for departmental operations could be used. For the manufacturing enterprise, the accounting process would be extended to include the various costs that are necessary in the manufacture of the product. Product cost data are essential in the evaluation of past manufacturing operations, in establishing effective control over costs, and in providing the information useful to management in making decisions. The accounting concepts and procedures applicable to manufacturing operations are discussed in later chapters.

Self-Examination Questions
(Answers in Appendix C.)

1. Which of the following would be the most appropriate basis for allocating rent expense for use in arriving at operating income by departments?
   A. Departmental sales
   B. Physical space occupied
   C. Cost of inventory
   D. Time devoted to departments

2. The term used to describe the excess of departmental gross profit over direct departmental expenses is:
   A. income from operations
   B. net income
   C. departmental margin
   D. none of the above

3. On an income statement departmentalized through departmental margin, sales commissions expense would be reported as:
   A. a direct expense
   B. an indirect expense
   C. an other expense
   D. none of the above

4. In accounting for a firm with a Colony West branch, the *home office* and *Colony West branch* accounts are known as:
   A. home office ledger accounts
   B. branch ledger accounts
   C. reciprocal accounts
   D. none of the above

5. In the work sheet for a combined income statement for the home office and its Northside Branch, what item is eliminated as an offset to Shipments to Northside Branch?
   A. Home Office
   B. Northside Branch
   C. Shipments from Home Office
   D. None of the above.

Discussion Questions

1. Departmental income statements are ordinarily not included in the published annual reports issued to stockholders and other parties outside the business enterprise. For whom are they prepared?

2. The newly appointed general manager of a department store is studying the income statements presenting gross profit by departments in an attempt to adjust operations to achieve the highest possible gross profit for each department. (a) Suggest ways in which an income statement departmentalized through gross profit can be used in achieving this goal. (b) Suggest reasons why caution must be exercised in using such statements.

3. Describe the underlying principle of apportionment of operating expenses to departments for income statements departmentalized through income from operations.

4. For each of the following types of expenses, select the allocation basis listed that is most appropriate for use in arriving at operating income by departments.

   Expense:
   (a) Property tax expense
   (b) Sales salaries
   (c) Rent expense
   (d) Advertising expense

   Basis of allocation:
   (1) Cost of inventory and equipment
   (2) Departmental sales
   (3) Time devoted to departments
   (4) Physical space occupied

5. Describe an appropriate basis for apportioning Officers' Salaries Expense among departments for purposes of the income statement departmentalized through income from operations.

6. Differentiate between a direct and an indirect operating expense.

7. Indicate whether each of the following operating expenses incurred by a department store is a direct or an indirect expense:
   (a) Uncollectible accounts expense
   (b) General manager's salary
   (c) Depreciation of store equipment
   (d) Insurance expense
   (e) Sales commissions
   (f) Heating and lighting expense

8. What term is applied to the dollar amount representing the excess of departmental gross profit over direct departmental expenses?

9. Recent income statements departmentalized through income from operations report operating losses for Department 19, a relatively minor segment of the business.

Management studies indicate that discontinuance of Department 19 would not affect sales of other departments or the volume of indirect expenses. Under what circumstances would the discontinuance of Department 19 result in a decrease of net income of the enterprise?

10. A portion of an income statement in condensed form, departmentalized through income from operations for the year just ended, is as follows:

	Department E
Net sales	$112,300
Cost of merchandise sold............	89,840
Gross profit	$ 22,460
Operating expenses	31,500
Loss from operations................	$ (9,040)

The operating expenses of Dept. E include $20,000 for indirect expenses. It is believed that the discontinuance of Department E would not affect the sales of the other departments nor reduce the indirect expenses of the enterprise. Based on this information, what would have been the effect on the income from operations of the enterprise if Department E had been discontinued prior to the year just ended?

11. Where are the journals and ledgers detailing the operations of a branch maintained in (a) a centralized system for branch accounting and (b) a decentralized system?

12. What is the nature of reciprocal accounts employed in branch accounting?

13. For each of the following accounts appearing in the branch ledger, name the reciprocal account in the home office ledger: (a) Home Office; (b) Shipments from Home Office.

14. In the branch ledger, what is the name of the account that takes the place of the capital accounts common to separate accounting entities?

15. Where, in the branch income statement, is the amount of shipments from home office reported?

16. (a) What home office accounts are debited and credited to record the operating income of the Columbus Branch? (b) What branch accounts are debited and credited to close the Columbus Branch income summary account?

17. In the work sheet for a combined income statement for the home office and its Metro Branch, what item is eliminated as an offset to Shipments from Home Office?

18. In the work sheet for a combined balance sheet for the home office and its Northside Branch, what item is eliminated as an offset to Northside Branch?

19. After the accounts are closed, the asset accounts at Branch #12 total $300,000; the contra asset accounts total $80,000; and liabilities to outsiders total $120,000. (a) What is the title of the remaining account in the branch ledger and what is the amount of its balance? (b) What is the title of the reciprocal account in the home office ledger and what is the amount of its balance? (c) Do these reciprocal items appear in the combined balance sheet?

20. At the end of each accounting period, the home office charges each of its branches with interest on the net investment in the branch. At the end of the current year, the home office debited the branch accounts for various amounts and credited

Interest Income for a total of $61,200. The branches make comparable entries, debiting Interest Expense and crediting Home Office. How should the interest expense and the interest income be treated on the work sheet for the combined income statement?

21. During the first year of operations of the South Plaza Branch, the home office shipped to the branch merchandise that had cost $150,000. The branch was billed for the selling price of $200,000, which would yield a gross profit of 25% of sales. Branch net sales for the year totaled $148,000 (all sales were at the billed price). (a) What should be the amount of the branch ending physical inventory at billed prices? (b) Assuming that there are no inventory shortages at the branch, what is the cost of the ending inventory? (c) Which of the two amounts should be added to the home office inventory for presentation in the combined balance sheet? (d) How much gross profit will be reported in the branch income statement?

Exercises

Exercise 21-1. C. J. Lubin Company occupies a two-story building. The departments and the floor space occupied by each are as follows:

Receiving and Storage........	basement	4,000 sq. ft.
Department 1	basement	6,000 sq. ft.
Department 2	first floor	3,200 sq. ft.
Department 3	first floor	8,000 sq. ft.
Department 4	first floor	4,800 sq. ft.
Department 5	second floor	9,800 sq. ft.
Department 6	second floor	4,200 sq. ft.

The building is leased at an annual rental of $80,000, allocated to the floors as follows: basement, 25%; first floor, 40%; second floor, 35%. Determine the amount of rent to be apportioned to each department.

Exercise 21-2. Mulford Company apportions depreciation expense on equipment on the basis of the average cost of the equipment, and apportions property tax expense on the basis of the combined total of average cost of the equipment and average cost of the merchandise inventories. Depreciation expense on equipment amounted to $110,000 and property tax expense amounted to $26,000 for the year. Determine the apportionment of the depreciation expense and the property tax expense, based on the following data:

	Average Cost	
Departments	Equipment	Inventories
Service:		
R	$ 120,000	
M	60,000	
Sales:		
100	240,000	$160,000
200	420,000	360,000
300	360,000	280,000
Total	$1,200,000	$800,000

Exercise 21-3. M. R. Pierson Company is considering discontinuance of one of its twelve departments. If operations in Department 8 are discontinued, it is estimated that the indirect operating expenses and the level of operations in the other departments will not be affected.

Data from the income statement for the past year ended August 31, which is considered to be a typical year, are as follows:

	Department 8		Other Departments	
Sales		$68,000		$981,000
Cost of merchandise sold		44,200		588,600
Gross profit		$23,800		$392,400
Operating expenses:				
Direct expenses	$18,400		$208,000	
Indirect expenses	9,500	27,900	114,000	322,000
Income (loss) before income tax		$ (4,100)		$ 70,400

(a) Prepare an estimated income statement for the current year ending August 31, assuming the discontinuance of Department 8. (b) On the basis of the data presented, would it be advisable to retain Department 8?

Exercise 21-4. Equifax Company maintains sales offices in several cities. The home office provides the sales manager at each office with a working fund of $12,000 with which to meet payrolls and to pay other office expenses. Prepare the entries, in general journal form, for the home office to record the following:

(a) Sent a check to establish a $12,000 fund for Branch H.
(b) Sent a check to replenish the fund after receiving a report from Branch H indicating the following disbursements: sales salaries, $6,230; office salaries, $2,800; rent, $1,200; utilities expense, $340; miscellaneous general expense, $160.

Exercise 21-5. Prepare the entries, in general journal form, for the Stanfield Branch to record the following selected transactions:

July 1. The home office sent to the branch: cash, $8,000; equipment, $16,750; merchandise at cost, $41,500.
    8. The branch sold merchandise: for cash, $6,460; on account, $2,180.
    9. The branch purchased merchandise on account from outside firms, $5,230.
  16. The branch collected $1,100 on account.
  19. The branch paid accounts payable, $3,800.
  20. The branch received merchandise at cost from the home office, $5,390.
  24. The branch paid operating expenses, $870.
  26. The branch purchased merchandise on account from outside firms, $4,260.
  27. The branch sold merchandise: for cash, $4,910; on account, $1,850.
  31. The branch sent $5,000 to the home office.
  31. The branch reported an operating income of $3,080.

Exercise 21-6. Present the entries, in general journal form, for the home office to record the appropriate transactions in Exercise 21-5.

Exercise 21-7. Peterson Department Store maintains accounts entitled Beaumont Branch and Tyler Branch. Each branch maintains an account entitled Home Office. The Beaumont Branch received instructions from the home office to ship to the Tyler Branch merchandise costing $6,450. The merchandise had been received from the home office. Give the general journal entry to record the transfer of the merchandise in the records of (a) the home office, (b) the Beaumont Branch, and (c) the Tyler Branch.

Exercise 21-8. During the year, the home office shipped to the branch merchandise that had cost $300,000. The branch was billed for $420,000, which was the selling price of the merchandise. No merchandise was purchased from any outside sources. Branch net sales for the year totaled $380,500. All sales were made at the billed price. Merchandise on hand at the beginning of the period totaled $68,300 at the billed price. Merchandise on hand at the end of the period as determined by physical count was $101,470 at the billed price. Determine the amount, at the billed price, of any discrepancy between the book amount and the physical count of inventory.

Problems
(Problems in Appendix B: 21-1B, 21-2B, 21-5B.)

Problem 21-1A. Howington Co. operates two sales departments: Department A for sporting goods and Department B for camping equipment. The trial balance on page 620 was prepared at the end of the current fiscal year, after all adjustments, including the adjustments for merchandise inventory, were recorded and posted.

Merchandise inventories at the beginning of the year were as follows: Department A, $66,000; Department B, $33,300.

The bases to be used in apportioning expenses, together with other essential information, are as follows:

Sales salaries expense—payroll records: Department A, $67,080; Department B, $18,920.

Advertising expense—usage: Department A, $8,250; Department B, $5,500.

Depreciation expense—average cost of equipment. Balances at beginning of year: Department A, $48,600; Department B, $27,300. Balances at end of year: Department A, $59,400; Department B, $44,700.

Store supplies expense—requisitions: Department A, $2,260; Department B, $2,280.

Office salaries expense—Department A, 55%; Department B, 45%.

Rent expense and heating and lighting expense—floor space: Department A, 6,960 sq. ft.; Department B, 5,040 sq. ft.

Property tax expense and insurance expense—average cost of equipment plus average cost of merchandise inventory.

Uncollectible accounts expense, miscellaneous selling expense, and miscellaneous general expense—volume of gross sales.

Howington Co.
Trial Balance
November 30, 19--

Cash	48,150	
Accounts Receivable	83,200	
Merchandise Inventory—Department A	55,400	
Merchandise Inventory—Department B	35,300	
Prepaid Insurance	1,875	
Store Supplies	1,700	
Store Equipment	104,100	
Accumulated Depreciation—Store Equipment		27,760
Accounts Payable		71,680
Income Tax Payable		900
Common Stock		100,000
Retained Earnings		127,045
Cash Dividends	20,000	
Income Summary	99,300	90,700
Sales—Department A		338,000
Sales—Department B		182,000
Sales Returns and Allowances—Department A	3,120	
Sales Returns and Allowances—Department B	2,240	
Purchases—Department A	164,500	
Purchases—Department B	114,800	
Sales Salaries Expense	86,000	
Advertising Expense	13,750	
Depreciation Expense—Store Equipment	6,940	
Store Supplies Expense	4,540	
Miscellaneous Selling Expense	3,640	
Office Salaries Expense	44,200	
Rent Expense	14,400	
Heating and Lighting Expense	11,300	
Property Tax Expense	6,400	
Insurance Expense	3,750	
Uncollectible Accounts Expense	3,200	
Miscellaneous General Expense	1,280	
Interest Expense	1,400	
Income Tax	3,600	
	938,085	938,085

Instructions:

Prepare an income statement departmentalized through income from operations.

Problem 21-2A. Mitchell's Department Store has 18 departments. Those with the least sales volume are Department 16 and Department 17, which were established about a year ago on a trial basis. The board of directors feels that it is now time to consider the retention or the termination of these two departments. The following adjusted trial balance as of May 31, the end of the first month of the current fiscal year, is severely condensed. May is considered to be a typical month. The income tax accrual has no bearing on the decision and is excluded from consideration.

Mitchell's Department Store
Trial Balance
May 31, 19--

Current Assets	333,200	
Plant Assets	642,700	
Accumulated Depreciation — Plant Assets		252,810
Current Liabilities		190,920
Common Stock		100,000
Retained Earnings		291,860
Cash Dividends	15,000	
Sales — Department 16		31,900
Sales — Department 17		24,200
Sales — Other Departments		861,500
Cost of Merchandise Sold — Department 16	22,330	
Cost of Merchandise Sold — Department 17	15,730	
Cost of Merchandise Sold — Other Departments	516,900	
Direct Expenses — Department 16	11,450	
Direct Expenses — Department 17	4,820	
Direct Expenses — Other Departments	126,760	
Indirect Expenses	58,300	
Interest Expense	6,000	
	1,753,190	1,753,190

Instructions:

(1) Prepare an income statement for May, departmentalized through departmental margin.

(2) State your recommendations concerning the retention of Departments 16 and 17, giving reasons.

Problem 21-3A. The bases to be used in apportioning expenses, together with other essential data for the Northwest Corporation, are as follows:

Sales salaries and commissions expense — basic salary plus 6% of sales. Basic salaries for Department A, $54,600; Department B, $26,520.

Advertising expense for brochures distributed within each department advertising specific products — usage: Department A, $12,745; Department B, $6,090.

Depreciation expense — average cost of store equipment: Department A, $78,300; Department B, $56,700.

Insurance expense — average cost of store equipment plus average cost of merchandise inventory. Average cost of merchandise inventory was $58,100 for Department A and $26,900 for Department B.

Uncollectible accounts expense — ⅜% of sales. Departmental managers are responsible for the granting of credit on the sales made by their respective departments.

The following data are obtained from the ledger on April 30, the end of the current fiscal year:

Sales — Department A	740,000
Sales — Department B	296,000

Cost of Merchandise Sold — Department A	495,800	
Cost of Merchandise Sold — Department B	192,400	
Sales Salaries and Commissions Expense	143,280	
Advertising Expense	18,835	
Depreciation Expense — Store Equipment	12,500	
Miscellaneous Selling Expense	2,020	
Administrative Salaries Expense	43,850	
Rent Expense	24,000	
Utilities Expense	14,620	
Insurance Expense	6,500	
Uncollectible Accounts Expense	3,885	
Miscellaneous General Expense	710	
Interest Income		4,400
Income Tax	17,750	

Instructions:

(1) Prepare an income statement departmentalized through departmental margin.
(2) Determine the rate of gross profit for each department.
(3) Determine the rate of departmental margin to sales for each department.

(If the working papers correlating with the textbook are not used, omit Problem 21-4A.)

Problem 21-4A. A work sheet for a combined income statement and a work sheet for a combined balance sheet for O. F. Sanchez Co. and its Clarksville Branch for the current fiscal year ended October 31 are presented in the working papers. Data concerning account titles and amounts have been entered on the work sheets. The amounts on the work sheet for the combined income statement were taken from the adjusted trial balance, and the income of the branch had not been recognized in the revenue accounts of the home office. On the work sheet for the combined balance sheet, the amount in the Clarksville Branch account was adjusted to give effect to the income of the branch for the current year.

Instructions:

(1) Enter the proper amounts in the "Eliminations" columns and complete the work sheets.
(2) Prepare a combined income statement and a combined balance sheet.

Problem 21-5A. Betty R. Bishop and Co. opened a branch office in Shelbyville on June 1 of the current year. Summaries of transactions, adjustments, and year-end closing for branch operations of the current year ended May 31 are as follows:

(a) Received cash advance, $60,000, and merchandise (billed at cost), $114,000, from the home office.
(b) Purchased merchandise on account, $186,000.
(c) Purchased equipment on account, $72,000.
(d) Sales on account, $210,000; cash sales, $90,000.
(e) Received cash from customers on account, $168,000.
(f) Paid creditors on account, $210,000.
(g) Paid operating expenses, $44,520 (all expenses are charged to Operating Expenses, a controlling account).
(h) Sent $30,000 cash to home office.
(i) Recorded accumulated depreciation, $3,600, and allowance for doubtful accounts, $720.

(j) Merchandise inventory at May 31, $82,200.

(k) Closed revenue and expense accounts.

Instructions:

(1) Present, in general journal form, the entries for the branch to record the foregoing. Post to the following T accounts: Cash, Accounts Receivable, Allowance for Doubtful Accounts, Merchandise Inventory, Equipment, Accumulated Depreciation, Accounts Payable, Home Office, Income Summary, Sales, Shipments from Home Office, Purchases, and Operating Expenses.

(2) Prepare an income statement for the year and a balance sheet as of May 31 for the branch.

(3) Present, in general journal form, the entries required on the home office records. Post to a T account entitled Shelbyville Branch.

Mini-Case

Assume that you recently started to work in your family-owned hardware store as an assistant store manager. Your father, the store manager and major stockholder, is considering the elimination of the Garden Supply Department, which has been incurring net losses for several years. Condensed revenue and expense data for the most recent year ended December 31, are presented on the following page. These data are typical of recent years. Bases used in allocating operating expenses among departments are as follows:

Expense	Basis
Sales commissions expense	Actual: 8% of net sales
Advertising expense	Actual: all advertising consists of brochures distributed by the various departments advertising specific products
Depreciation expense	Average cost of store equipment used
Miscellaneous selling expense	Amount of net sales
Administrative salaries expense	Each of the 10 departments apportioned an equal share
Rent expense	Floor space occupied
Utilities expense	Floor space occupied
Insurance and property tax expense	Average cost of equipment used plus average cost of inventory
Miscellaneous general expense	Amount of net sales

Since the Garden Supply Department is under your supervision, your father has asked your opinion as to whether the Garden Supply Department should be eliminated.

Instructions:

Prepare a brief statement of your recommendation to your father, supported by such schedule(s) as you think will be helpful to him in reaching a decision.

Trout Hardware
Income Statement
For Year Ended December 31, 19--

	Garden Supply Department		Other Departments		Total	
Net sales						$216,200
				$199,200		
Cost of merchandise sold				125,000		137,400
		$17,000				
		12,400				
Gross profit		$ 4,600		$ 74,200		$ 78,800
Operating expenses:						
Selling expenses:						
Sales commissions expense	$1,360		$15,936		$17,296	
Advertising expense	510		6,000		6,510	
Depreciation expense—store equipment	400		4,700		5,100	
Miscellaneous selling expense	255		2,988		3,243	
Total selling expenses		$2,525		$29,624		$32,149
General expenses:						
Administrative salaries expense	$1,730		$15,570		$17,300	
Rent expense	568		4,544		5,112	
Utilities expense	511		4,090		4,601	
Insurance and property tax expense	350		3,340		3,690	
Miscellaneous general expense	153		1,793		1,946	
Total general expenses		3,312		29,337		32,649
Total operating expenses		5,837		58,961		64,798
Income (loss) from operations		$ (1,237)		$ 15,239		$ 14,002
Other expense:						
Interest expense						1,200
Income before income tax						$ 12,802
Income tax						1,920
Net income						$ 10,882

22 | Manufacturing and Job Order Cost Systems

CHAPTER

CHAPTER OBJECTIVES

Identify and illustrate concepts and procedures used in accounting for manufacturing operations, including the preparation of a statement of cost of goods manufactured.

Describe and illustrate the flow of data through a cost accounting system of a manufacturing enterprise.

Identify alternative cost accounting systems for manufacturing operations.

Describe and illustrate a job order cost accounting system.

22

CHAPTER

Manufacturers employ labor and use machinery to change materials into finished products. In thus changing the form of goods, their activities differ from those of merchandisers. The furniture manufacturer, for example, changes lumber and other materials into furniture. The furniture dealer in turn purchases the finished goods from the manufacturer and sells them without additional processing.

Some functions of manufacturing companies, such as selling, administration, and financing, are like those of merchandising organizations. The accounting procedures for these functions are the same for both types of enterprises.

Accounting procedures for manufacturing businesses must also provide for the accumulation of the accounting data identified with the production processes. Additional ledger accounts are needed and internal controls must be established over the manufacturing operations. Periodic reports to management and other interested parties must include data that will be useful in measuring the efficiency of manufacturing operations and in guiding future operations.

CONCEPTS OF COST AND EXPENSE

The amount of cash paid or liability incurred for a commodity or service is called the **cost** of the item. As the commodity or service is consumed in the operations of a business enterprise, its cost is said to expire. An expiration of cost is called an **expense**. For example, as office equipment is used, the expiration of its cost is periodically recognized in the accounts as depreciation expense. The unexpired portion of its cost is the excess of the balance of the plant asset account over its related accumulated depreciation account. Expenses (expired costs) are reported periodically in the income statement as deductions from revenue.

The cost of merchandise acquired for resale to customers is treated somewhat differently from the cost of goods and services that will be consumed during operations. The cost of merchandise, which is a composite of invoice prices and various additions and deductions to cover such items as delivery charges, allowances, and cash discounts, does not expire in the usual sense. The merchandise is sold rather than consumed, and the amount sold is called the "cost of merchandise sold."

Determination of the cost of the merchandise available for sale and the cost of the merchandise sold is more difficult for a manufacturing enterprise than for a merchandising business. The cost of manufacturing a commodity includes not only the cost of tangible materials but also the many costs incurred in changing the materials into a finished product ready for sale. This chapter and the next two are concerned mainly with the determination and control of manufacturing costs.

INVENTORIES OF MANUFACTURING ENTERPRISES

Manufacturing businesses maintain three inventory accounts instead of a single merchandise inventory account. Separate accounts are maintained for (1) goods in the state in which they are to be sold, (2) goods in the process of manufacture, and (3) goods in the state in which they were acquired. These inventories are called respectively **finished goods**, **work in process**, and **materials**. The balances in the inventory accounts may be presented in the balance sheet in the following manner:

Inventories:
Finished goods................................... $300,000
Work in process................................. 55,000
Materials 123,000 $478,000

The finished goods inventory and work in process inventory are composed of three separate categories of manufacturing costs: direct materials, direct labor, and factory overhead. **Direct materials** represent the delivered cost of the materials that enter directly into the finished product. **Direct labor** represents the wages of the factory workers who change the materials into a finished product. **Factory overhead** includes all of the remaining costs of operating the factory, such as wages for factory supervision, supplies used in the factory but not entering directly into the finished product, and taxes, insurance, depreciation, and maintenance related to factory plant and equipment.

ACCOUNTING SYSTEMS FOR MANUFACTURING ENTERPRISES

Two basic accounting systems are commonly used by manufacturers: general accounting systems and cost accounting systems. A general accounting system is essentially an extension to manufacturing operations of the system described previously for merchandising enterprises which use periodic inventory procedures. A cost accounting system uses perpetual inventory procedures and provides more detailed information concerning costs of production.

In the remainder of this chapter, a general accounting system is described, followed by a discussion and illustration of one of the two main types of cost accounting systems. The other main type of cost accounting system is discussed in Chapter 23.

GENERAL ACCOUNTING SYSTEM FOR MANUFACTURING OPERATIONS

Although the accounting procedures for manufacturing operations are likely to be more complex than those used in trading operations, the complexity of such procedures varies widely. If only a single product or several similar products are manufactured, and if the manufacturing processes are neither complicated nor numerous, the accounting system may be fairly simple. In such cases, the periodic system of inventory accounting used in merchandising may be extended to the three manufacturing inventories, and the manufacturing accounts may be summarized periodically in an account entitled Manufacturing Summary. It is to such a simple situation that attention will first be directed.

Statement of Cost of Goods Manufactured

Since manufacturing activities differ greatly from selling and general administration activities, it is customary to separate the two groups of accounts in the summarizing process at the end of an accounting period. In addition, the manufacturing group is usually reported in a separate **statement of cost of goods manufactured** in order to avoid a long, complicated income statement. An income statement and its supporting statement of cost of goods manufactured are illustrated as follows:

Ming Manufacturing Company
Income Statement
For Year Ended December 31, 1984

Sales		$915,800
Cost of goods sold:		
Finished goods inventory, January 1, 1984	$ 78,500	
Cost of goods manufactured	550,875	
Cost of finished goods available for sale	$629,375	
Less finished goods inventory, December 31, 1984	91,000	
Cost of goods sold		538,375

STATEMENT OF
COST OF GOODS
MANUFACTURED

Ming Manufacturing Company
Statement of Cost of Goods Manufactured
For Year Ended December 31, 1984

Work in process inventory, January 1, 1984			$ 55,000
Direct materials:			
Inventory, January 1, 1984		$ 62,000	
Purchases		220,800	
Cost of materials available for use		$282,800	
Less inventory, December 31, 1984		58,725	
Cost of materials placed in production		$224,075	
Direct labor		218,750	
Factory overhead:			
Indirect labor	$49,300		
Depreciation of factory equipment	22,300		
Heat, light, and power	21,800		
Property taxes	9,750		
Depreciation of buildings	6,000		
Insurance expired	4,750		
Factory supplies used	2,900		
Miscellaneous factory costs	2,050		
Total factory overhead		118,850	
Total manufacturing costs			561,675
Total work in process during period			$616,675
Less work in process inventory, December 31, 1984			65,800
Cost of goods manufactured			$550,875

In the statement of cost of goods manufactured, the amount listed for the work in process inventory at the beginning of the period is composed of the estimated cost of the direct materials, the direct labor, and the factory overhead applicable to the inventory of partially processed products at the end of the preceding period.

The cost of the direct materials placed in production is determined by adding to the beginning inventory of materials the net cost of the direct materials purchased and deducting the ending inventory. The amount listed for direct labor is determined by referring to the direct labor account. The factory overhead costs, which are determined by referring to the ledger, are listed individually in the statement of cost of goods manufactured or in a separate schedule. The sum of the costs of direct materials placed in production, the direct labor, and the factory overhead represents the total manufacturing costs incurred during the period. Addition of this amount to the beginning inventory of work in process yields the total cost of the work that has been in process during the period. The estimated cost of the ending inventory of work in process is then deducted to yield the cost of goods manufactured. It should be noted that the "cost of goods manufactured" reported in the statement of cost of goods manufactured and income statement is comparable to the "purchases" reported by a merchandising enterprise.

Periodic Inventory Procedures   The process of adjusting the periodic inventory and other accounts of a manufacturing business is like that for a merchandising enterprise. Adjustments to the merchandise inventory account are replaced by adjusting entries for direct materials, work in process, and finished goods. The first two accounts are adjusted through Manufacturing Summary, and the third is adjusted through Income Summary.

At the end of the accounting period, the temporary accounts that appear in the statement of cost of goods manufactured are closed to Manufacturing Summary. This account's final balance, which represents the cost of goods manufactured during the period, is then closed to Income Summary. The remaining temporary accounts (sales, expenses, etc.) are then closed to Income Summary in the usual manner.

The relationship of the manufacturing summary account to the income summary account is illustrated below.

Manufacturing Summary

Dec. 31 Work in process inventory, Jan. 1	55,000	Dec. 31 Work in process inventory, Dec. 31	65,800
31 Direct materials inventory, Jan. 1	62,000	31 Direct materials inventory, Dec. 31	58,725
31 Direct materials purchases	220,800	31 To Income Summary	550,875
31 Direct labor	218,750		
31 Factory overhead	118,850		
	675,400		675,400

Income Summary

Dec. 31 Finished goods inventory, Jan. 1	78,500	Dec. 31 Finished goods inventory, Dec. 31	91,000
31 From Manufacturing Summary	550,875		

COST OF GOODS MANUFACTURED CLOSED TO INCOME SUMMARY

To simplify the illustration, the individual overhead accounts are presented as a total. Note that the balance transferred from the manufacturing summary account to the income summary account, $550,875, is the same as the final figure reported on the statement of cost of goods manufactured.

A work sheet may be used in preparing financial statements for a manufacturing enterprise which uses periodic inventory procedures. A description and illustration of such a work sheet is presented in Appendix F.

COST ACCOUNTING SYSTEM FOR MANUFAC- TURING OPERATIONS

Through the use of perpetual inventory procedures, a cost accounting system achieves greater accuracy in the determination of costs than is possible with a general accounting system such as that described in the preceding sections. Cost accounting procedures also permit far more effective control by supplying data on the costs incurred by each factory department and the unit cost of manufacturing each type of product. Such procedures provide not only data useful to management in minimizing costs but also other valuable information about production methods to use, quantities to produce, product lines to promote, and sales prices to charge.

Perpetual Inventory Procedures

Perpetual inventory controlling accounts and subsidiary ledgers are maintained for materials, work in process, and finished goods in cost accounting systems. Each of these accounts is debited for all additions and is credited for all deductions. The balance of each account thus represents the inventory on hand.

All expenditures incidental to manufacturing move through the work in process account, the finished goods account, and eventually into the cost of goods sold account. The flow of costs through the perpetual inventory accounts and into the cost of goods sold account is illustrated as follows:

FLOW OF COSTS THROUGH PERPETUAL INVENTORY ACCOUNTS

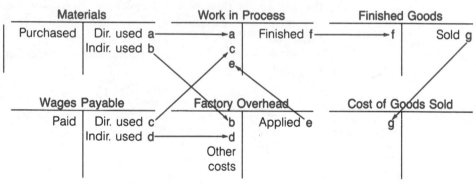

Materials and factory labor used in production are classified as direct and indirect. The materials and the factory labor used directly in the process of manufacturing are debited to Work in Process (**a** and **c** in the diagram). The materials and the factory labor used that do not enter directly into the finished product are debited to Factory Overhead (**b** and **d** in the diagram). Examples of indirect materials are oils and greases, abrasives and polishes, cleaning supplies, gloves, drilling soap, and brushes. Examples of indirect labor are salaries of supervisors, inspectors, material handlers, security guards, and janitors. The proper amount of factory overhead costs are transferred to Work in Process (**e** in the diagram). The costs of the goods finished are transferred from Work in Process to Finished Goods (f in the diagram). When the goods are sold, their costs are transferred from Finished Goods to Cost of Goods Sold (g in the diagram).

The number of accounts presented in the flowchart was limited in order to simplify the illustration. In practice, manufacturing operations may require many processing departments, each requiring separate work in process and factory overhead accounts.

Types of Cost Accounting Systems

There are two main types of cost systems for manufacturing operations — job order cost and process cost. Each of the two systems is widely used, and a manufacturer may use a job order cost system for some of its products and a process cost system for others.

A **job order cost** system provides for a separate record of the cost of each particular quantity of product that passes through the factory. It is best suited to industries that manufacture goods to fill special orders from customers and to industries that produce different lines of products for stock. It is also appropriate when standard products are manufactured in batches rather than on a continuous basis. In a job order cost system, a summary such as the following would show the cost incurred in completing a job.

Job 565
1,000 Units of Product X200

Direct materials used......................	$2,380
Direct labor used	4,400
Factory overhead applied.................	3,080
Total cost	$9,860
Unit cost ($9,860 ÷ 1,000)................	$ 9.86

Under a **process cost** system, the costs are accumulated for each of the departments or processes within the factory. A process system is best used by manufacturers of like units of product that are not distinguishable from each other during a continuous production process.

JOB ORDER COST SYSTEMS

The basic concepts of job order cost systems are illustrated in this chapter, while process cost systems are discussed in Chapter 23. To simplify the illustration, a nondepartmentalized operation is assumed. In factories with departmentalized operations, costs are accumulated in factory overhead and work in process accounts maintained for each department. The discussion focuses attention on the source documents that serve as the basis for the entries in the job order cost system and to the managerial uses of cost accounting in planning and controlling business operations.

Materials

Procedures used in the procurement and issuance of materials differ considerably among manufacturers and even among departments of a particular manufacturer. The discussion that follows is confined to the basic principles, however, and will disregard relatively minor variations and details.

Some time in advance of the date that production of a certain commodity is to begin, the department responsible for scheduling informs the purchasing department, by means of **purchase requisitions,** of the materials that will be needed. The purchasing department then issues the necessary **purchase orders** to suppliers. After the goods have been received and inspected, the receiving department personnel prepare a **receiving report,** showing the quantity received and its condition. Quantities, unit costs, and total costs of the goods billed, as reported on the supplier's invoice, are then compared with the purchase order and the receiving report to make sure that the amounts billed agree with the materials ordered and received. After such verifications, the invoice is recorded in the voucher register or purchases journal as a debit to Materials and a credit to Accounts Payable.

The account Materials in the general ledger is a controlling account. A separate account for each type of material is maintained in a subsidiary ledger called the **materials ledger.** Details as to quantity and cost of materials received are recorded in the materials ledger on the basis of the receiving reports or purchase invoices. A typical form of materials ledger account is illustrated as follows:

MATERIALS LEDGER ACCOUNT

MATERIAL NO. 23								ORDER POINT *1,000*	
RECEIVED			ISSUED			BALANCE			
REC. REPORT NO.	QUAN- TITY	AMOUNT	MAT. REQ. NO.	QUAN- TITY	AMOUNT	DATE	QUAN- TITY	AMOUNT	UNIT PRICE
						Jan. 1	1,200	600.00	.50
			672	500	250.00	4	700	350.00	.50
196	3,000	1,620.00				8	700	350.00	.50
							3,000	1,620.00	.54
			704	800	404.00	18	2,900	1,566.00	.54

The accounts in the materials ledger may also be used as an aid in maintaining proper inventory quantities of stock items. Frequent comparisons of quantity balances with predetermined order points enable management to avoid costly idle time caused by lack of materials. The subsidiary ledger form may also include columns for recording quantities ordered and dates of the purchase orders.

Materials are transferred from the storeroom to the factory in response to **materials requisitions,** which may be issued by the manufacturing department concerned or by a central scheduling department. Storeroom personnel record the issuances on the materials requisition by inserting the physical quantity data. Transfer of responsibility for the materials is evidenced by the signature or initials of the storeroom and factory personnel concerned. The requisition is then routed to the materials ledger clerk, who inserts unit prices and amounts. A typical materials requisition is illustrated as follows:

MATERIALS REQUISITION				
Job No. 62			Requisition No. 704	
Authorized by R. A. Sanders			Date January 18, 19--	
Description	Quantity Authorized	Quantity Issued	Unit Price	Amount
Material No. 23	800	700 100	$.50 .54	$350 54
Total Issued				$404
Issued by M. K.			Received by J. B.	

The completed requisition serves as the basis for posting quantities and dollar data to the materials ledger accounts. In the illustration, the first-in, first-out pricing method was used. A summary of the materials requisitions completed during the month serves as the basis for transferring the cost of materials from the controlling account in the general ledger to the controlling accounts for work in process and factory overhead. The flow of materials into production is illustrated by the following entry:

Work in Process.....................................	13,000	
Factory Overhead	840	
Materials		13,840

The perpetual inventory system for materials has three important advantages: (1) it provides for prompt and accurate charging of materials to jobs and factory overhead, (2) it permits the work of inventory-taking to be spread out rather than concentrated at the end of a fiscal period, and (3) it aids in the disclosure of inventory shortages or other irregularities. As physical quantities of the various materials are determined, the actual inventories are compared with the balances of the respective subsidiary ledger accounts. The causes of significant differences between the two should be determined and the responsibility for the differences assigned to specific individuals. Remedial action can then be taken.

Factory Labor   Unlike materials, factory labor is not tangible, nor is it acquired and stored in advance of its use. Hence, there is no perpetual inventory account for labor. The two main objectives in accounting for labor are (1) determination of the correct amount to be paid each employee for each payroll period, and (2) appropriate allocation of labor costs to factory overhead and individual job orders.

The amount of time spent by an employee in the factory is usually recorded on **clock cards,** which are also called **in-and-out cards.** The amount of time spent by each employee and the labor cost incurred for each individual job, or for factory overhead, are recorded on **time tickets.** A typical time ticket form is illustrated as follows:

TIME
TICKET

Time Ticket				
Employee Name Gail Berry		No. 4521		
Employee No. 240		Date January 18, 19--		
Description of work Finishing		Job No. 62		
Time Started	Time Stopped	Hours Worked	Hourly Rate	Cost
10:00	12:00	2	$6.50	$13.00
1:00	2:00	1	6.50	6.50
Total cost				$19.50
Approved by T. D.				

The times reported on an employee's time tickets are compared with the related clock cards as an internal check on the accuracy of payroll disbursements. A summary of the time tickets at the end of each month serves as the basis for recording the direct and indirect labor costs incurred. The flow of labor costs into production is illustrated by the following entry:

Work in Process......................................	10,000	
Factory Overhead	2,200	
Wages Payable		12,200

Factory Overhead

Factory overhead includes all manufacturing costs, except direct materials and direct labor. Examples of factory overhead costs, in addition to indirect materials and indirect labor, are depreciation, electricity, fuel, insurance, and property taxes. It is customary to have a factory overhead controlling account in the general ledger. Details of the various types of cost are accumulated in a subsidiary ledger.

Debits to Factory Overhead come from various sources. For example, the cost of indirect materials is obtained from the summary of the materials requisitions, the cost of indirect labor is obtained from the summary of the time tickets, costs of electricity and water may be posted from the voucher register, and the cost of depreciation and expired insurance may be recorded as adjustments at the end of the accounting period.

Although factory overhead cannot be specifically identified with particular jobs, it is as much a part of manufacturing costs as direct materials and labor. As the use of machines and automation has increased, factory overhead has represented an ever larger part of total costs. Many items of factory overhead cost are incurred for the entire factory and cannot be directly related to the finished product. The problem is further complicated because some items of factory overhead cost are relatively fixed in amount while others tend to vary according to changes in productivity.

To wait until the end of an accounting period to allocate factory overhead to the various jobs would be quite acceptable from the standpoint of accuracy but highly unsatisfactory in terms of timeliness. If the cost system is to be of maximum usefulness, it is imperative that cost data be available as each job is completed, even though there is a sacrifice in accuracy. It is only through timely reporting that management can make whatever adjustments seem necessary in pricing and manufacturing methods to achieve the best possible combination of revenue and cost on future jobs. Therefore, in order that job costs may be available currently, it is customary to apply factory overhead to production by using a **predetermined factory overhead rate.**

Predetermined Factory Overhead Rate

The factory overhead rate is determined by relating the estimated amount of factory overhead for the forthcoming year to some common activity base, one that will equitably apply the factory overhead costs to the goods manufactured. The common bases include direct labor costs, direct labor hours, and machine hours. For example, if it is estimated that the total factory overhead costs for the year will be $100,000 and that the total direct labor cost will be $125,000, an overhead rate of 80% ($100,000 ÷ $125,000) will be applied to the direct labor cost incurred during the year.

As factory overhead costs are incurred, they are debited to the factory overhead account. The factory overhead costs applied to production are periodically credited to the factory overhead account and debited to the work in process account. The application of factory overhead costs to production (80% of direct labor cost of $10,000) is illustrated by the following entry:

Work in Process....................................	8,000	
Factory Overhead		8,000

Inevitably, factory overhead costs applied and actual factory overhead costs incurred during a particular period will differ. If the amount applied exceeds the actual costs, the factory overhead account will have a credit balance and the overhead is said to be **overapplied** or **overabsorbed.** If the amount applied is less than the actual costs, the account will have a debit balance and the overhead is said to be **underapplied** or **underabsorbed.** Both cases are illustrated in the following account:

ACCOUNT FACTORY OVERHEAD   ACCOUNT NO.

| Date | | Item | Debit | Credit | Balance | |
					Debit	Credit
May	1	Balance				200
	31	Costs incurred	8,320			
	31	Cost applied		8,000	120	

Underapplied Balance

Overapplied Balance

Disposition of Factory Overhead Balance

The balance in the factory overhead account is carried forward from month to month until the end of the year. The amount of the balance is reported on interim balance sheets as a deferred item.

The nature of the balance in the factory overhead account (underapplied or overapplied), as well as the amount, will change during the year. If there is a decided trend in either direction and the amount is substantial, the reason should be determined. If the variation is caused by alterations in manufacturing methods or by substantial changes in production goals, it may be advisable to revise the factory overhead rate. The accumulation of a large underapplied balance is more serious than a trend in the opposite direction and may indicate inefficiencies in production methods, excessive expenditures, or a combination of factors.

Despite any corrective actions that may be taken to avoid an underapplication or overapplication of factory overhead, the account will usually have a balance at the end of the fiscal year. Since the balance represents the underapplied or over-applied factory overhead applicable to the operations of the year just ended, it is not proper to report it in the year-end balance sheet as a deferred item.

There are two main alternatives for disposing of the balance of factory overhead at the end of the year: (1) by allocation of the balance among work in process, finished goods, and cost of goods sold accounts on the basis of the total amounts of applied factory overhead included in those accounts at the end of the year, or (2) by transfer of the balance to the cost of goods sold account. Theoretically, only the first alternative is sound because it represents a correction of the estimated overhead rate and brings the accounts into agreement with the costs actually incurred. On the other hand, much time and expense may be required to make the allocation and to revise the unit costs of the work in process and finished goods inventories. Furthermore, in most manufacturing enterprises, a very large part of the total manufacturing costs for the year passes through the work in process and the finished goods accounts into the cost of goods sold account before the end of the year. Therefore, unless the total amount of the underapplied or overapplied balance is great, it is satisfactory to transfer it to Cost of Goods Sold.

Work in Process   Costs incurred for the various jobs are debited to Work in Process. The job costs described in the preceding sections may be summarized as follows:

Direct materials, $13,000 — Work in Process debited and Materials credited; data obtained from summary of materials requisitions.

Direct labor, $10,000—Work in Process debited and Wages Payable credited; data obtained from summary of time tickets.

Factory overhead, $8,000—Work in process debited and Factory Overhead credited; data obtained by applying overhead rate to direct labor cost (80% of $10,000).

The work in process account to which these costs were charged is illustrated as follows:

Date		Item	Debit	Credit	Balance Debit	Balance Credit
ACCOUNT		WORK IN PROCESS			ACCOUNT NO.	
May	1	Balance			3,000	
	31	Direct materials	13,000		16,000	
	31	Direct labor	10,000		26,000	
	31	Factory overhead	8,000		34,000	
	31	Jobs completed		31,920	2,080	

The work in process account is a controlling account that contains summary information only. The details concerning the costs incurred on each job order are accumulated in a subsidiary ledger known as the cost ledger. Each account in the cost ledger, called a job cost sheet, has spaces for recording all direct materials and direct labor chargeable to the job and for the application of factory overhead at the predetermined rate. Postings to the job cost sheets are made from materials requisitions and time tickets or from summaries of these documents.

The four cost sheets in the subsidiary ledger for the work in process account illustrated are summarized as follows:

COST LEDGER

Job 71 (Summary)	
Balance..................	3,000
Direct materials	2,000
Direct labor...............	2,400
Factory overhead	1,920
	9,320

Job 73 (Summary)	
Direct materials	6,000
Direct labor...............	4,000
Factory overhead	3,200
	13,200

Job 72 (Summary)	
Direct materials	4,000
Direct labor...............	3,000
Factory overhead	2,400
	9,400

Job 74 (Summary)	
Direct materials	1,000
Direct labor...............	600
Factory overhead	480
	2,080

The relationship between the work in process controlling account on page 637 and the subsidiary cost ledger may be observed in the following tabulation:

Work in Process (Controlling)		Cost Ledger (Subsidiary)	
Beginning balance.........	$ 3,000 ⟷	Beginning balance Job 71.................	$ 3,000
Direct materials	$13,000 ⟷	Direct materials	
		Job 71.................	$ 2,000
		Job 72.................	4,000
		Job 73.................	6,000
		Job 74.................	1,000
			$13,000
Direct labor	$10,000 ⟷	Direct labor	
		Job 71.................	$ 2,400
		Job 72.................	3,000
		Job 73.................	4,000
		Job 74.................	600
			$10,000
Factory overhead..........	$ 8,000 ⟷	Factory overhead	
		Job 71.................	$ 1,920
		Job 72.................	2,400
		Job 73.................	3,200
		Job 74.................	480
			$ 8,000
Jobs completed	$31,920 ⟷	Jobs completed	
		Job 71.................	$ 9,320
		Job 72.................	9,400
		Job 73.................	13,200
			$31,920
Ending balance	$ 2,080 ⟷	Ending balance Job 74.................	$ 2,080

The data in the cost ledger were presented in summary form for illustrative purposes. A job cost sheet for Job 72, providing for the current accumulation of cost elements entering into the job order and for a summary when the job is completed, is as follows:

JOB COST SHEET

Job No. 72						Date	May 7, 19--
Item 5,000 Type C Containers						Date wanted	May 23, 19--
For Stock						Date completed	May 21, 19--

Direct Materials		Direct Labor				Summary	
Mat. Req. No.	Amount	Time Summary No.	Amount	Time Summary No.	Amount	Item	Amount
834	800.00	2202	83.60	2248	122.50	Direct	
838	1,000.00	2204	208.40	2250	187.30	materials	4,000.00
841	1,400.00	2205	167.00	2253	155.40	Direct labor	3,000.00
864	800.00	2210	229.00		3,000.00	Factory	
	4,000.00	2211	108.30			overhead	
		2213	107.20			(80% of	
		2216	110.00			direct	
		2222	277.60			labor cost)	2,400.00
		2224	217.40			Total cost	9,400.00
		2225	106.30				
		2231	153.20			No. of units	
		2234	245.20			finished	5,000
		2237	170.00			Cost per unit	1.88
		2242	261.60				

When Job 72 was completed, the direct materials costs and the direct labor costs were totaled and entered in the Summary column. Factory overhead was added at the predetermined rate of 80% of the direct labor cost, and the total cost of the job was determined. The total cost of the job, $9,400, divided by the number of units produced, 5,000, yielded a unit cost of $1.88 for the Type C Containers produced.

Upon the completion of Job 72, the job cost sheet was removed from the cost ledger and filed for future reference. At the end of the accounting period, the sum of the total costs on all cost sheets completed during the period is determined and the following entry is made:

Finished Goods......................................	31,920	
Work in Process		31,920

The remaining balance in the work in process account represents the total cost charged to the uncompleted job cost sheets.

Finished Goods and Cost of Goods Sold

The finished goods account is a controlling account. The related subsidiary ledger, which has an account for each kind of commodity produced, is called the **finished goods ledger** or **stock ledger**. Each account in the subsidiary finished goods ledger provides columns for recording the quantity and the cost of goods manufactured, the quantity and the cost of goods shipped, and the quantity, the total cost, and the unit cost of goods on hand. An account in the finished goods ledger is illustrated as follows:

FINISHED GOODS
LEDGER ACCOUNT

ITEM: TYPE C CONTAINER

MANUFACTURED			SHIPPED			BALANCE			
JOB ORDER NO.	QUAN-TITY	AMOUNT	SHIP. ORDER NO.	QUAN-TITY	AMOUNT	DATE	QUAN-TITY	AMOUNT	UNIT COST
						May 1	2,000	3,920.00	1.96
			643	2,000	3,920.00	8	——	——	——
72	5,000	9,400.00				21	5,000	9,400.00	1.88
			646	2,000	3,760.00	23	3,000	5,640.00	1.88

Just as there are various methods of pricing materials entering into production, there are various methods of determining the cost of the finished goods sold. In the illustration, the first-in, first-out method is used. The quantities shipped are posted to the finished goods ledger from a copy of the shipping order or other memorandum. The finished goods ledger clerk then records on the copy of the shipping order the unit cost and the total amount of the commodity sold. A summary of the cost data on these shipping orders becomes the basis for the following entry:

Cost of Goods Sold	30,168	
Finished Goods		30,168

If goods are returned by a buyer and are put back in stock, it is necessary to debit Finished Goods and credit Cost of Goods Sold for the cost.

Sales

For each sale of finished goods, it is necessary to maintain a record of both the cost price and the selling price of the goods sold. As previously stated, the cost data may be recorded on the shipping orders. The sales journal may be expanded by the addition of a column for recording the total cost of the goods billed. At the end of the month, the total of the column is posted as a debit to Cost of Goods Sold and a credit to Finished Goods. The total of the sales price column is posted as a debit to Accounts Receivable and a credit to Sales.

ILLUSTRATION
OF JOB
ORDER COST
ACCOUNTING

To illustrate further the procedures described in the preceding sections, assume that the Spencer Co. uses a job order cost accounting system. The trial balance of the general ledger on January 1, the first day of the fiscal year, is as follows:

Spencer Co.
Trial Balance
January 1, 19--

Cash	85,000	
Accounts Receivable	73,000	
Finished Goods	40,000	
Work in Process	20,000	
Materials	30,000	
Prepaid Expenses	2,000	
Plant Assets	850,000	
Accumulated Depreciation—Plant Assets		473,000
Accounts Payable		70,000
Wages Payable		15,000
Common Stock		500,000
Retained Earnings		42,000
	1,100,000	1,100,000

A summary of the transactions and the adjustments for January, followed in each case by the related entry in general journal form, is presented below and on pages 642 and 643. In practice, the transactions would be recorded daily in various journals.

(a) Materials purchased and prepaid expenses incurred.

Summary of receiving reports:

Material A	$ 29,000
Material B	17,000
Material C	12,000
Material D	4,000
Total	$ 62,000

Entry: Materials	62,000	
Prepaid Expenses	1,000	
Accounts Payable		63,000

(b) Materials requisitioned for use.

Summary of requisitions:

By Use		
Job 1001	$12,000	
Job 1002	26,000	
Job 1003	22,000	$ 60,000
Factory Overhead		3,000
Total		$ 63,000

By Types

Material A $27,000
Material B 18,000
Material C 15,000
Material D 3,000
Total .... $ 63,000

Entry: Work in Process 60,000
Factory Overhead 3,000
    Materials 63,000

(c) *Factory labor used.*

Summary of time tickets:

Job 1001 .... $ 60,000
Job 1002 30,000
Job 1003 .... 10,000 $100,000
Factory Overhead 20,000
Total $120,000

Entry: Work in Process 100,000
Factory Overhead 20,000
    Wages Payable 120,000

(d) *Other costs incurred.*

Entry: Factory Overhead 56,000
Selling Expenses 25,000
General Expenses 10,000
    Accounts Payable 91,000

(e) *Expiration of prepaid expenses.*

Entry: Factory Overhead 1,000
Selling Expenses 100
General Expenses 100
    Prepaid Expenses 1,200

(f) *Depreciation.*

Entry: Factory Overhead 7,000
Selling Expenses 200
General Expenses 100
    Accumulated Depreciation — Plant Assets 7,300

(g) *Application of factory overhead costs to jobs.* The predetermined rate was 90% of direct labor cost.

Summary of factory overhead applied:

Job 1001 (90% of $60,000).	$ 54,000
Job 1002 (90% of $30,000).	27,000
Job 1003 (90% of $10,000).	9,000
Total	$ 90,000

Entry: Work in Process	90,000	
Factory Overhead		90,000

(h) *Jobs completed.*

Summary of completed job cost sheets:

Job 1001.	$146,000
Job 1002.	83,000
Total	$229,000

Entry: Finished Goods.	229,000	
Work in Process.		229,000

(i) *Sales and cost of goods sold.*

Summary of sales invoices and shipping orders:

	Sales Price	Cost Price
Product X	$ 19,600	$ 15,000
Product Y	165,100	125,000
Product Z	105,300	80,000
Total	$290,000	$220,000

Entry: Accounts Receivable.	290,000	
Sales		290,000
Entry: Cost of Goods Sold	220,000	
Finished Goods		220,000

(j) *Cash received.*

Entry: Cash	300,000	
Accounts Receivable		300,000

(k) *Cash disbursed.*

Entry: Accounts Payable.	190,000	
Wages Payable	125,000	
Cash.		315,000

The flow of costs through the manufacturing accounts, together with summary details of the subsidiary ledgers, is illustrated on page 645. Entries in the accounts are identified by letters to facilitate comparisons with the foregoing summary journal entries.

The trial balance taken from the general ledger of the Spencer Co. on January 31 is as follows:

Spencer Co.
Trial Balance
January 31, 19--

Cash	70,000	
Accounts Receivable	63,000	
Finished Goods	49,000	
Work in Process	41,000	
Materials	29,000	
Prepaid Expenses	1,800	
Plant Assets	850,000	
Accumulated Depreciation—Plant Assets		480,300
Accounts Payable		34,000
Wages Payable		10,000
Common Stock		500,000
Retained Earnings		42,000
Sales		290,000
Cost of Goods Sold	220,000	
Factory Overhead		3,000
Selling Expenses	25,300	
General Expenses	10,200	
	1,359,300	1,359,300

The balances of the three inventory accounts—Materials, Work in Process, and Finished Goods—represent the respective ending inventories on January 31. A comparison of the balances of the general ledger controlling accounts with their respective subsidiary ledgers is as follows:

	Controlling Accounts		*Subsidiary Ledgers*		
	Account	Balance	Account	Balance	
CONTROLLING AND SUBSIDIARY ACCOUNTS COMPARED	Materials	$29,000 ←→	Material A	$17,000	
			Material B	7,000	
			Material C	2,000	
			Material D	3,000	$29,000
	Work in Process	$41,000 ←→	Job 1003		$41,000
	Finished Goods	$49,000 ←→	Product X	$ 5,000	
			Product Y	26,000	
			Product Z	18,000	$49,000

To simplify the illustration, only one work in process account and one factory overhead account have been used. Usually, a manufacturing business has several processing departments, each requiring separate work in process and factory over-

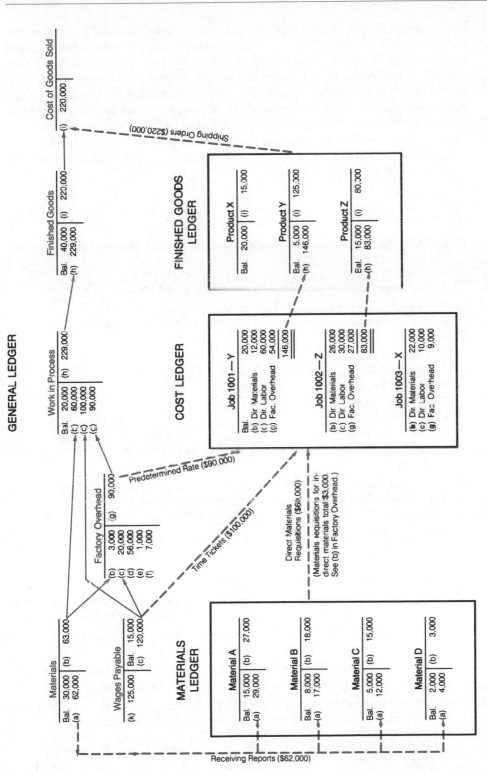

FLOW OF COSTS THROUGH JOB ORDER COST ACCOUNTS

head accounts. In the illustration, one predetermined rate was used in applying the factory overhead to jobs. In a factory with several processing departments, a single factory overhead rate may not provide accurate product costs and effective cost control. A single rate for the entire factory cannot take into consideration such factors as differences among departments in the nature of their operations and in amounts of factory overhead incurred. In such cases, each factory department should have a separate factory overhead rate. For example, in a factory with twenty distinct operating departments, one department might have an overhead rate of 110% of direct labor cost, another a rate of $4 per direct labor hour, and another a rate of $3.50 per machine hour.

Self-Examination Questions
(Answers in Appendix C.)

1. The account maintained by a manufacturing business for inventory of goods in the process of manufacture is:
   A. Finished Goods
   B. Materials
   C. Work in Process
   D. None of the above

2. For a manufacturing business, finished goods inventory includes:
   A. direct materials costs
   B. direct labor costs
   C. factory overhead costs
   D. all of the above

3. An example of a factory overhead cost is:
   A. wages of factory assembly-line workers
   B. salaries for factory plant supervisors
   C. bearings for electric motors being manufactured
   D. all of the above

4. For which of the following would the job order cost system be appropriate?
   A. Antique furniture repair shop
   B. Rubber manufacturer
   C. Coal manufacturer
   D. All of the above

5. If the factory overhead account has a credit balance, factory overhead is said to be:
   A. underapplied
   B. overapplied
   C. underabsorbed
   D. none of the above

Discussion Questions

1. What term refers to an expiration of a cost?

2. Name the three inventory accounts for a manufacturing business and describe what each balance represents at the end of an accounting period.

3. Name and describe the three categories of manufacturing costs included in the cost of finished goods and the cost of work in process.

4. For a manufacturing enterprise, what is the description of the amount that is comparable to a trading concern's net cost of merchandise purchased?

5. Which of the following items are properly classified as part of factory overhead?
   (a) property taxes on factory buildings
   (b) sales commissions
   (c) direct materials
   (d) factory supplies used
   (e) interest expense
   (f) amortization of factory patents

6. Which of the following amounts is not closed to Manufacturing Summary?

    (a) direct materials inventory as of the beginning of the year
    (b) direct materials inventory as of the end of the year
    (c) finished goods inventory as of the beginning of the year
    (d) factory overhead

7. (a) Name the two principal types of cost accounting systems. (b) Which system provides for a separate record of each particular quantity of product that passes through the factory? (c) Which system accumulates the costs for each department or process within the factory?

8. Distinguish between the purchase requisition and the purchase order used in the procurement of materials.

9. Briefly discuss how the purchase order, purchase invoice, and receiving report can be used to assist in controlling cash disbursements for materials acquired.

10. What document is the source for (a) debiting the accounts in the materials ledger, and (b) crediting the accounts in the materials ledger?

11. Briefly discuss how the accounts in the materials ledger can be used as an aid in maintaining appropriate inventory quantities of stock items.

12. How does use of the materials requisition help control the issuance of materials for the storeroom?

13. Discuss the major advantages of a perpetual inventory system over a periodic system for materials.

14. (a) Differentiate between the clock card and the time ticket. (b) Why should the total time reported on an employee's time tickets for a payroll period be compared with the time reported on the employee's clock cards for the same period?

15. Discuss how the predetermined factory overhead rate can be used in job order cost accounting to assist management in pricing jobs.

16. (a) How is a predetermined factory overhead rate determined? (b) Name three common bases used in determining the rate.

17. (a) What is (1) overapplied factory overhead and (2) underapplied factory overhead? (b) If the factory overhead account has a debit balance, was factory overhead underapplied or overapplied? (c) If the factory overhead account has a credit balance at the end of the first month of the fiscal year, where will the amount of this balance be reported on the interim balance sheet?

18. At the end of a fiscal year, there was a relatively minor balance in the factory overhead account. What is the simplest satisfactory procedure for the disposition of the balance in the account?

19. What name is given to the individual accounts in the cost ledger?

20. What document serves as the basis for posting to (a) the direct materials section of the job cost sheet, and (b) the direct labor section of the job cost sheet?

21. Describe the source of the data for debiting Work in Process for (a) direct materials, (b) direct labor, and (c) factory overhead.

22. What account is the controlling account for (a) the materials ledger, (b) the cost ledger, and (c) the finished goods ledger or stock ledger?

Exercises

Exercise 22-1. The following accounts were selected from the pre-closing trial balance of Gregory Co. at March 31, the end of the current fiscal year:

Direct Labor	$256,000
Direct Materials Inventory	68,800
Direct Materials Purchases	306,800
Factory Overhead (control)	102,400
Finished Goods Inventory	102,000
General Expense (control)	73,000
Interest Expense	11,780
Sales	956,800
Selling Expense (control)	102,000
Work in Process Inventory	74,000

Inventories at March 31 were as follows:

Finished Goods	$108,000
Work in Process	79,400
Direct Materials	72,000

Prepare a statement of cost of goods manufactured.

Exercise 22-2. On the basis of the data presented in Exercise 1, prepare journal entries on March 31 to:
(a) Adjust the inventory accounts.
(b) Close the appropriate accounts to Manufacturing Summary.
(c) Close Manufacturing Summary.

Exercise 22-3. The balance of Material F on February 1 and the receipts and issuances during February are as follows:

Balance, February 1, 120 units at $20.00
Received during February:
    Feb. 8, 300 units at $21.00
    Feb. 15, 240 units at $21.30
    Feb. 22, 180 units at $21.60
Issued during February:
    Feb. 10, 180 units for Job 231
    Feb. 18, 150 units for Job 258
    Feb. 27, 210 units for Job 261

Determine the cost of each of the three issuances under a perpetual system, using (a) the first-in, first-out method and (b) the last-in, first-out method.

Exercise 22-4. The issuances of materials for the current month are as follows:

Requisition No.	Material	Job No.	Amount
365	W-8	714	$3,640
366	D-2	706	1,876
367	N-06	General factory use	480
368	I-16	720	2,320
369	Q-4	707	3,564

Present the general journal entry to record the issuances of materials.

Exercise 22-5. A summary of the time tickets for the current month follows:

Job. No.	Amount	Job No.	Amount
901	$1,120	Indirect labor	$1,280
902	3,020	904	3,120
903	1,850	905	2,310

Present the general journal entry to record the factory labor costs.

Exercise 22-6. Wong Company applies factory overhead to jobs on the basis of machine hours in Department 10 and on the basis of direct labor dollars in Department 11. Estimated factory overhead costs, direct labor costs, and machine hours for the year, and actual factory overhead costs, direct labor costs, and machine hours for August are as follows. Departmental accounts are maintained for work in process and factory overhead.

	Department 10	Department 11
Estimated factory overhead cost for year	$57,600	$153,120
Estimated direct labor costs for year		$264,000
Estimated machine hours for year	12,000 hours	
Actual factory overhead costs for August	$ 6,820	$ 12,820
Actual direct labor costs for August		$ 22,500
Actual machine hours for August	1,350 hours	

(a) Determine the factory overhead rate for Department 10. (b) Determine the factory overhead rate for Department 11. (c) Prepare the general journal entry to apply factory overhead to production for August. (d) Determine the balances of the departmental factory overhead accounts as of August 31 and indicate whether the amounts represent overapplied or underapplied factory overhead.

Exercise 22-7. The following account appears in the ledger after only part of the postings have been completed for April:

Work in Process

Balance, April 1	12,250
Direct Materials	30,820
Direct Labor	48,180
Factory Overhead	26,400

Jobs finished during April are summarized as follows:

Job 602	$18,140	Job 611	$29,100
Job 608	32,400	Job 618	18,660

(a) Prepare the general journal entry to record the jobs completed and (b) determine the cost of the unfinished jobs at April 30.

Exercise 22-8. Chien Enterprises Inc. began manufacturing operations on October 1. Jobs 101 and 102 were completed during the month, and all costs applicable to them were recorded on the related cost sheets. Jobs 103 and 104 are still in process at the end of the month, and all applicable costs except factory overhead have been recorded on the related cost sheets. In addition to the materials and labor charged directly to the jobs, $1,050 of indirect materials and $1,890 of indirect labor were used during the month. The cost sheets for the four jobs entering production during the month are as follows, in summary form:

Job 101	
Direct materials..........	8,750
Direct labor	7,000
Factory overhead	3,500
Total.................	19,250

Job 102	
Direct materials	15,680
Direct labor.............	11,200
Factory overhead........	5,600
Total	32,480

Job 103	
Direct materials..........	11,900
Direct labor	9,800
Factory overhead	

Job 104	
Direct materials	3,080
Direct labor..............	4,340
Factory overhead........	

Prepare an entry, in general journal form, to record each of the following operations for the month (one entry for each operation):
(a) Direct and indirect materials used.
(b) Direct and indirect labor used.
(c) Factory overhead applied (a single overhead rate is used, based on direct labor cost).
(d) Completion of Jobs 101 and 102.

Problems
(Problems in Appendix B: 22-1B, 22-2B, 22-3B, 22-6B.)

(If the working papers correlating with the textbook are not used, omit Problem 22-1A.)

Problem 22-1A. The work sheet for Centennial Manufacturing Company, for the current year ended August 31, 1984, is presented in the working papers. Data concerning account titles, trial balance amounts, and selected adjustments have been entered on the work sheet.

Instructions:

(1) Enter the six adjustments required for the inventories on the work sheet. Additional adjustment data are:
Finished goods inventory at August 31 .... $109,200
Work in process inventory at August 31 78,960
Direct materials inventory at August 31 70,470
The adjustments for finished goods inventory should be entered as adjustments to the income summary account, and the work in process and direct materials inventory adjustments should be entered as adjustments to the manufacturing summary account.

(2) Complete the work sheet. The data for the manufacturing summary account and the other manufacturing accounts should be extended to the statement of cost of goods manufactured columns. After all of these data have been extended, the two cost of goods manufactured columns should be totaled and the difference determined. This difference, which is labeled "cost of goods manufactured" in the account title column, is transferred to the income statement

columns by entries in the statement of cost of goods manufactured credit column and the income statement debit column. The remainder of the work sheet is completed in the same manner as is followed for a merchandising business. Appendix F further describes and illustrates the use of a work sheet for manufacturing operations.

(3) Prepare a statement of cost of goods manufactured.

(4) Prepare a multiple-step income statement.

Problem 22-2A. Chatham Printing Company uses a job order cost system. The following data summarize the operations related to production for March, the first month of operations:

(a) Materials purchased on account, $69,850.

(b) Materials requisitioned and factory labor used:

	Materials	Factory Labor
Job 101...............................	$ 9,900	$5,940
Job 102...............................	6,490	4,400
Job 103...............................	8,700	3,190
Job 104...............................	13,090	8,360
Job 105...............................	7,150	4,180
Job 106...............................	4,180	1,870
For general factory use	1,490	1,100

(c) Factory overhead costs incurred on account, $13,250.

(d) Depreciation of machinery and equipment, $4,850.

(e) The factory overhead rate is 80% of direct labor cost.

(f) Jobs completed: 101, 102, 104, and 105.

(g) Jobs 101, 102, and 104 were shipped and customers were billed for $30,800, $19,450, and $38,300 respectively.

Instructions:

(1) Prepare entries in general journal form to record the foregoing summarized operations.

(2) Open T accounts for Work in Process and Finished Goods and post the appropriate entries, using the identifying letters as dates. Insert memorandum account balances as of the end of the month.

(3) Prepare a schedule of unfinished jobs to support the balance in the work in process account.

(4) Prepare a schedule of completed jobs on hand to support the balance in the finished goods account.

(If the working papers correlating with the textbook are not used, omit Problem 22-3A.)

Problem 22-3A. Graco Furniture Company repairs, refinishes, and reupholsters furniture. A job order cost system was installed recently to facilitate (1) the determination of price quotations to prospective customers, (2) the determination of actual costs incurred on each job, and (3) cost reductions.

In response to a prospective customer's request for a price quotation on a job, the estimated cost data are inserted on an unnumbered job cost sheet. If the offer is accepted, a number is assigned to the job and the costs incurred are recorded in the usual manner on the job cost sheet. After the job is completed, reasons for the variances between the estimated and actual costs are noted on the sheet. The data are then available to management in evaluating the efficiency of operations and in preparing quotations on future jobs.

On May 5, an estimate of $510 for reupholstering a couch was given to Jean Ladd. The estimate was based upon the following data:

Estimated direct materials:	
14 meters at $12 per meter.............................	$168
Estimated direct labor:	
10 hours at $15 per hour.................................	150
Estimated factory overhead (60% of direct labor cost).........	90
Total estimated costs	$408
Markup (25% of production costs)	102
Total estimate..	$510

On May 9, the couch was picked up from the residence of Jean Ladd, 1460 Madison Drive, Clearwater, with a commitment to return it on May 20.

The job was completed on May 18. The related materials requisition and time tickets are summarized as follows:

Materials Requisition No.	Description	Amount
1215	10 meters at $12	$120
1219	5 meters at $12	60

Time Ticket No.	Description	Amount
3140	4 hours at $15	$ 60
3146	8 hours at $15	120

Instructions:

(1) Complete that portion of the job order cost sheet that would be completed when the estimate is given to the customer.

(2) Assign number 84-5-6 to the job, record the costs incurred, and complete the job order cost sheet. In commenting upon the variances between actual costs and estimated costs, assume that 1 meter of materials was spoiled, the factory overhead rate has been proved to be satisfactory, and an inexperienced employee performed the work.

Problem 22-4A. The trial balance of the general ledger of Lafayette Corporation as of March 31, the end of the first month of the current fiscal year, is shown at the top of the next page.

As of the same date, balances in the accounts of selected subsidiary ledgers are as follows:

Finished goods ledger:

Commodity A, 2,640 units, $23,760; Commodity B, 6,000 units, $132,000; Commodity C, 3,000 units, $57,000.

Cost ledger:

Job 318, $73,680.

Materials ledger:

Material X, $48,480; Material Y, $37,920; Material Z, $2,160.

Lafayette Corporation
Trial Balance
March 31, 19--

Cash	109,680	
Accounts Receivable	222,360	
Finished Goods	212,760	
Work in Process	73,680	
Materials	88,560	
Plant Assets	949,200	
Accumulated Depreciation — Plant Assets		423,480
Accounts Payable		159,560
Wages Payable		18,000
Capital Stock		720,000
Retained Earnings		300,780
Sales		318,480
Cost of Goods Sold	236,160	
Factory Overhead	1,100	
Selling and General Expenses	46,800	
	1,940,300	1,940,300

The transactions completed during April are summarized as follows:

(a) Materials were purchased on account as follows:

Material X	$66,000
Material Y	46,200
Material Z	1,800

(b) Materials were requisitioned from stores as follows:

Job 318, Material X, $25,440; Material Y, $20,160	$45,600
Job 319, Material X, $32,400; Material Y, $28,560	60,960
Job 320, Material X, $16,560; Material Y, $6,720	23,280
For general factory use, Material Z	1,920

(c) Time tickets for the month were chargeable as follows:

Job 318	$23,520	Job 320	$19,680
Job 319	20,160	Indirect labor	7,200

(d) Factory payroll checks for $77,280 were issued.

(e) Various factory overhead charges of $26,850 were incurred on account.

(f) Depreciation of $10,800 on factory plant and equipment was recorded.

(g) Factory overhead was applied to jobs at 75% of direct labor cost.

(h) Jobs completed during the month were as follows: Job 318 produced 6,720 units of Commodity B; Job 319 produced 4,800 units of Commodity C.

(i) Selling and general expenses of $45,840 were incurred on account.

(j) Payments on account were $171,600.

(k) Total sales on account were $295,080. The goods sold were as follows (use first-in, first-out method): 1,200 units of Commodity A; 6,480 units of Commodity B; 3,600 units of Commodity C.

(l) Cash of $301,200 was received on accounts receivable.

Instructions:

(1) Open T accounts for the general ledger, the finished goods ledger, the cost ledger, and the materials ledger. Record directly in these accounts the balances

as of March 31, identifying them as "Bal." Record the quantities as well as the dollar amounts in the finished goods ledger.

(2) Prepare entries in general journal form to record the April transactions. After recording each transaction, post to the T accounts, using the identifying letters as dates. When posting to the finished goods ledger, record quantities as well as dollar amounts.

(3) Prepare a trial balance.

(4) Prepare schedules of the account balances in the finished goods ledger, the cost ledger, and the materials ledger.

(5) Prepare a multiple-step income statement (to the point of income before income tax) for the two months ended April 30.

Problem 22-5A. The trial balance of Y. M. McInnis Inc., at the end of the eleventh month of the current fiscal year, is as follows:

Y. M. McInnis Inc.
Trial Balance
September 30, 19--

Cash	18,610	
Accounts Receivable	28,550	
Allowance for Doubtful Accounts		780
Finished Goods	35,380	
Work in Process	10,300	
Materials	16,840	
Prepaid Insurance	3,240	
Factory Equipment	166,000	
Accumulated Depreciation—Factory Equipment		70,000
Office Equipment	19,200	
Accumulated Depreciation—Office Equipment		4,640
Accounts Payable		9,800
Income Tax Payable		1,080
Cash Dividends Payable		2,000
Wages Payable		1,640
Interest Payable		—
Mortgage Note Payable (due 1991)		40,000
Common Stock ($10 par)		100,000
Retained Earnings		48,400
Cash Dividends	8,000	
Income Summary		—
Sales		354,000
Cost of Goods Sold	281,000	
Factory Overhead	340	
Selling Expenses	26,760	
General Expenses	11,680	
Interest Expense	2,640	
Income Tax	3,800	
	632,340	632,340

Transactions completed during October and adjustments required on October 31 are summarized as follows:

(a) Materials purchased on account...................... $12,900

(b) Materials requisitioned for factory use:

Direct...	$11,500	
Indirect	170	11,670

(c) Factory labor costs incurred:

Direct...	$ 5,800	
Indirect	520	6,320

(d) Other costs and expenses incurred on account:

Factory overhead	$ 2,610	
Selling expenses.................................	2,480	
General expenses................................	1,000	6,090

(e) Cash disbursed:

Accounts payable...............................	$21,000	
Wages payable	6,080	
Dividends payable	2,000	
Income tax payable	1,080	30,160

(f) Depreciation charged:

Factory equipment	1,600
Office equipment.................................	100

(g) Insurance expired:

Chargeable to factory	$ 140	
Chargeable to selling expenses	20	
Chargeable to general expenses	15	175

(h) Applied factory overhead at a predetermined rate:
80% of direct labor cost.

(i) Total cost of jobs completed 23,000

(j) Sales, all on account:

Selling price......................................	36,000
Cost price..	28,600

(k) Cash received on account 37,000

(l) Uncollectible accounts receivable written off 640

(m) Additional income tax recorded...................... 1,425

(n) Interest accrued on mortgage note payable............ 480

(o) Analysis of accounts in customers ledger indicated doubtful accounts of $800. Adjusted the allowance account.

(p) Balance in Factory Overhead closed to Cost of Goods Sold.

Instructions:

(1) Open T accounts and record the initial balances indicated in the September 30 trial balance, identifying each as "Bal."

(2) Record the transactions and the adjustments directly in the accounts, using the identifying letters in place of dates.

(3) Record the necessary year-end closing entries directly in the accounts, using a capital "C" to designate these entries.

(4) Prepare a multiple-step income statement for the fiscal year ended October 31, 19--

(5) Prepare a report form balance sheet as of October 31, 19--.

Problem 22-6A. Following are selected accounts for Fabco Products. For the purposes of this problem, some of the debits and credits have been omitted.

Accounts Receivable

May	1	Balance	59,500	May 31	Collections	127,300
	31	Sales	(A)			

Materials

May	1	Balance	14,350	May 31	Requisitions	(B)
	31	Purchases	21,070			

Work In Process

May	1	Balance	26,250	May 31	Goods finished	(E)
	31	Direct materials	(C)			
	31	Direct labor	28,000			
	31	Factory overhead	(D)			

Finished Goods

May	1	Balance	48,650	May 31	Cost of goods sold	(G)
	31	Goods finished	(F)			

Factory Overhead

May	1	Balance	140	May 31	Applied (75% of	
	1–31	Costs incurred	22,100		direct labor cost)	(H)

Cost of Goods Sold

May 31		(I)

Sales

	May 31	(J)

Selected balances at May 31:

Accounts receivable	$65,000
Finished goods............................	30,100
Work in process..........................	22,260
Materials	11,760

Materials requisitions for May included $700 of materials issued for general factory use. All sales are made on account, terms n/30.

Instructions:

(1) Determine the amounts represented by the letters (A) through (J), presenting your computations.

(2) Determine the amount of factory overhead overapplied or underapplied as of May 31.

Mini-Case

As an assistant cost accountant for Hanratty Industries, you have been assigned to review the activity base for the predetermined factory overhead rate. The president, G. H. Hanratty, has expressed concern that the over- or underapplied overhead has fluctuated excessively over the years.

An analysis of the company's operations and use of the current overhead base (direct materials usage) have narrowed the possible alternative overhead bases to direct labor cost and machine hours. For the past five years, the following data have been gathered:

	1984	1983	1982	1981	1980
Actual overhead......	$ 580,000	$ 540,000	$ 640,000	$ 490,000	$ 450,000
Applied overhead	575,000	565,000	600,000	500,000	440,000
(Over)underapplied overhead........	$ 5,000	$ (25,000)	$ 40,000	$ (10,000)	$ 10,000
Direct labor cost	$1,800,000	$1,400,000	$2,100,000	$1,150,000	$1,050,000
Machine hours.......	363,500	340,000	402,000	302,000	280,000

Instructions:

(1) Calculate a predetermined factory overhead rate for each alternative base, assuming that the rates would have been determined by relating the amount of factory overhead for the past five years to the base.

(2) For each of the past five years, determine the over- or underapplied overhead, based on the two predetermined overhead rates developed in (1).

(3) Which predetermined overhead rate would you recommend? Discuss the basis for your recommendation.

23

CHAPTER | Process Cost Systems

CHAPTER OBJECTIVES

Distinguish process cost accounting systems from job order cost accounting systems.

Describe and illustrate a process cost accounting system, including the preparation of a cost of production report.

23

CHAPTER

**PROCESS COST
AND JOB
ORDER COST
SYSTEMS
DISTINGUISHED**

In many industries, job orders as described in Chapter 22 are not suitable for scheduling production and accumulating the manufacturing costs. Companies manufacturing cement, flour, or paint, for example, do so on a continuous basis. The principal product is a homogeneous mass rather than a collection of distinct units. No useful purpose would be served by maintaining job orders for particular amounts of a product as the material passes through the several stages of production.

Many of the methods, procedures, and managerial applications presented in the preceding chapter in the discussion of job order cost systems apply equally to process cost systems. For example, perpetual inventory accounts with subsidiary ledgers for materials, work in process, and finished goods are requisites of both systems. In job order cost accounting, however, the costs of direct materials, direct labor, and factory overhead are charged directly to job orders. In process cost accounting, the costs are charged to processing departments, and the cost of a finished unit is determined by dividing the total cost incurred in each process by the number of units produced. Since all goods produced in a department are identical units, it is not necessary to classify production into job orders.

In factories with departmentalized operations, costs are accumulated in factory overhead and work in process accounts maintained for each department. If there is only one processing department in a factory, the cost accounting procedures are simple. The manufacturing cost elements are charged to the single work in process account, and the unit cost of the finished product is determined by dividing the total cost by the number of units produced.

When the manufacturing procedure requires a sequence of different processes, the output of Process 1 becomes the direct materials of Process 2, the output of Process 2 becomes the direct materials of Process 3, and so on until the finished product emerges. Additional direct materials requisitioned from stores may also be introduced during subsequent processes.

A work in process account for a departmentalized factory is illustrated as follows. In this illustration, the total cost of $96,000 is divided by the output, 10,000 units, to obtain a unit cost of $9.60.

Work in Process — Assembly Department

Direct materials	32,000	To Sanding Dept., 10,000 units	96,000
Direct labor	40,000	Cost per unit:	
Factory overhead	24,000	$96,000 ÷ 10,000 = $9.60	
	96,000		96,000

**SERVICE
DEPARTMENTS
AND PROCESS
COSTS**

In a factory with several processes, there may be one or more **service departments** that do not process the materials directly. Examples of service departments are the factory office, the power plant, and the maintenance and repair shop. These departments perform services for the benefit of other production departments.

The costs that they incur, therefore, are part of the total manufacturing costs and must be charged to the processing departments.

The services performed by a service department give rise to internal transactions with the processing departments benefited. These internal transactions are recorded periodically in order to charge the factory overhead accounts of the processing departments with their share of the costs incurred by the service departments. The period usually chosen is a month, although a different period of time may be used. To illustrate, assume that the Power Department produced 500 000 kilowatt-hours during the month at a total cost of $30,000, or 6¢ per kilowatt-hour ($30,000 ÷ 500 000). The factory overhead accounts for the departments that used the power are accordingly charged for power at the 6¢ rate. Assuming that during the month the Assembly Department used 200 000 kwh and the Sanding Department used 300 000 kwh, the accounts affected by the interdepartmental transfer of cost would appear as follows:

SERVICE
DEPARTMENT
COSTS CHARGED
TO PROCESSING
DEPARTMENTS

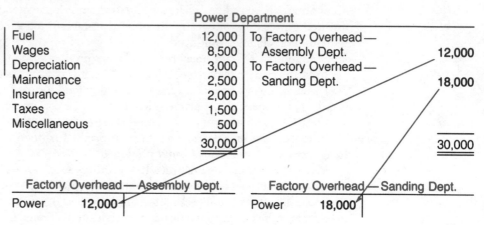

Some service departments render services to other service departments. For example, the power department may supply electric current to light the factory office and to operate data processing equipment. At the same time, the factory office provides general supervision for the power department, maintains its payroll records, buys its fuel, and so on. In such cases, the costs of the department rendering the greatest service to other service departments may be distributed first, despite the fact that it receives benefits from other service departments.

PROCESSING COSTS   The accumulated costs transferred from preceding departments and the costs of direct materials and direct labor incurred in each processing department are debited to the related work in process account. Each work in process account is also debited for the factory overhead applied. The costs incurred are summarized periodically, usually at the end of the month. The costs related to the output of each department during the month are then transferred to the next processing department or to Finished Goods, as the case may be. This flow of costs through a work in process account is illustrated as follows:

Work in Process—Sanding Department

10,000 units at $9.60 from Assembly Dept.		96,000	To Painting Dept., 10,000 units		160,000
Direct labor	36,800		Cost per unit:		
Factory overhead	27,200	64,000	$160,000 ÷ 10,000 = $16		
		160,000			160,000

The three debits in the preceding account may be grouped into two separate categories: (1) direct materials or partially processed materials received from another department, which in this case is composed of 10,000 units received from the Assembly Department, with a total cost of $96,000, and (2) direct labor and factory overhead applied in the Sanding Department, which in this case totaled $64,000. This second group of costs is called the processing cost.

Again referring to the illustration, all of the 10,000 units were completely processed in the Sanding Department and were passed on to the Painting Department. The $16 unit cost of the product transferred to the Painting Department is made up of Assembly Department cost of $9.60 ($96,000 ÷ 10,000 units) and processing cost of $6.40 ($64,000 ÷ 10,000 units) incurred in the Sanding Department.

INVENTORIES OF PARTIALLY PROCESSED MATERIALS	In the preceding illustration, all materials entering a process were completely processed at the end of the accounting period. In such a case, the determination of unit costs is quite simple. The total of costs transferred from other departments, direct materials, direct labor, and factory overhead charged to a department, is divided by the number of units completed and passed on to the next department or to finished goods. Often, however, some partially processed materials remain in various stages of production in a department at the end of a period. In this case, the costs in work in process must be allocated between the units that have been completed and transferred to the next process or to finished goods and those that are only partially completed and remain within the department.

To allocate direct materials and transferred costs between the output completed and transferred to the next process and inventory of goods within the department, it is necessary to determine the manner in which materials are placed in production. For some products, all materials must be on hand before any work begins. For other products, materials may be added to production in about the same proportion as processing costs are incurred. In still other situations, materials may enter the process at relatively few points, which may or may not be evenly spaced throughout the process.

To allocate processing costs between the output completed and transferred to the next process and the inventory of goods within the process, it is necessary to determine (1) the number of *equivalent units* of production during the period and (2) the *processing cost per equivalent unit* for the same period. The **equivalent units** of production are the number of units that could have been manufactured from start to finish during the period. To illustrate, assume that there is no inventory of goods in process in a certain processing department at the beginning of the period, that 1,000 units of materials enter the process during the period, and that at the end of the period all of the units are 75% completed. The equivalent production in the processing department for the period would be 750 units (75% of 1,000). Assuming further that the processing costs incurred during the period totaled $15,000, the processing cost per equivalent unit would be $20 ($15,000 ÷ 750).

Usually there is an inventory of partially processed units in the department at the beginning of the period. These units are normally completed during the period and transferred to the next department along with units started and completed in the current period. Other units started in the period are only partially processed and thus make up the ending inventory. To illustrate the computation of equivalent units under such circumstances, the following data are assumed for the Painting Department:

Inventory within Painting Department on March 1 . . . .   600 units, ⅓ completed
Completed in Painting Department and transferred to
   finished goods during March . . . .   9,800 units, completed
Inventory within Painting Department on March 31 . . . .   800 units, ⅖ completed

The equivalent units of production are determined as follows:

DETERMINATION OF
EQUIVALENT UNITS
OF PRODUCTION

To process units in inventory on March 1	600 units × ⅔	400
To process units started and completed in March . .	9,800 units − 600 units	9,200
To process units in inventory on March 31	800 units × ⅖	320
Equivalent units of production in March.		9,920

The 9,920 equivalent units of production represent the number of units that would have been produced if there had been no inventories within the process either at the beginning or at the end of the period.

Continuing with the illustration, the next step is to allocate the costs incurred in the Painting Department between the units completed during March and those remaining in process at the end of the month. If materials (including transferred costs) were used and processing costs were incurred uniformly throughout the month, the total costs of the process would be divided by 9,920 units to obtain the unit cost. On the other hand, if all materials were introduced at the beginning of the process, the full materials cost per unit must be assigned to the uncompleted units. The processing costs would then be allocated to the finished and the uncompleted units on the basis of equivalent units of production. Entries in the following account are based on the latter assumption:

ACCOUNT WORK IN PROCESS—PAINTING DEPARTMENT   ACCOUNT NO.

Date		Item	Debit	Credit	Balance Debit	Balance Credit
Mar.	1	Bal., 600 units, ⅓ completed			10,200	
	31	Sanding Dept., 10,000 units				
		at $16	160,000		170,200	
	31	Direct labor	26,640		196,840	
	31	Factory overhead	18,000		214,840	
	31	Goods finished, 9,800 units		200,600		
	31	Bal., 800 units, ⅖ completed			14,240	

The processing costs incurred in the Painting Department during March total $44,640 ($26,640 + $18,000). The equivalent units of production for March, determined above, is 9,920. The processing cost per equivalent unit is therefore $4.50 ($44,640 ÷ 9,920). Of the $214,840 debited to the Painting Department, $200,600 was transferred to Finished Goods and $14,240 remained in the account as work in process inventory. The computation of the allocations to finished goods and to inventory is as follows:

<u>Goods Finished During March</u>

ALLOCATION OF
DEPARTMENTAL
CHARGES TO
FINISHED GOODS
AND INVENTORY

600 units:	Inventory on March 1, ⅓ completed...............	$ 10,200
	Processing cost in March:	
	600 × ⅔, or 400 units at $4.50.................	1,800
	Total..	$ 12,000
	(Unit cost: $12,000 ÷ 600 = $20)	
9,200 units:	Materials cost in March, at $16 per unit............	$147,200
	Processing cost in March:	
	9,200 at $4.50 per unit.......................	41,400
	Total..	188,600
	(Unit cost: $188,600 ÷ 9,200 = $20.50)	
9,800 units:	Goods finished during March	$200,600

<u>Painting Department Inventory on March 31</u>

800 units:	Materials cost in March, at $16 per unit............	$ 12,800
	Processing cost in March:	
	800 × ⅖, or 320 at $4.50.....................	1,440
800 units:	Painting Department inventory on March 31	$ 14,240

COST OF PRODUCTION REPORT

A report prepared periodically for each processing department summarizes (1) the units for which the department is accountable and the disposition of these units and (2) the costs charged to the department and the allocation of these costs. This report, termed the **cost of production report**, may be used as the source of the computation of unit production costs and the allocation of the processing costs in the general ledger to the finished and the uncompleted units. More importantly, the report is used to control costs. Each department head is held responsible for the units entering production and the costs incurred in the department. Any differences in unit product costs from one month to another are studied carefully and the causes of significant differences are determined.

The cost of production report based on the data presented in the preceding section for the Painting Department is shown on page 664.

JOINT PRODUCTS

When two or more goods of significant value are produced from a single principal direct material, the products are termed **joint products**. Similarly, the costs incurred in the manufacture of joint products are called **joint costs**. Common examples of joint products are gasoline, naphtha, kerosene, paraffin, benzine, and other related goods, all of which come from the processing of crude oil.

Haworth Manufacturing Company
Cost of Production Report—Painting Department
For the Month Ended March 31, 19--

Quantities:
  Charged to production:
    In process, March 1..............................   600
    Received from Sanding Department   10,000
    Total units to be accounted for   10,600

  Units accounted for:
    Transferred to finished goods   9,800
    In process, March 31.............................   800
    Total units accounted for...........................   10,600

Costs:
  Charged to production:
    In process, March 1.............................. $ 10,200

    March costs:
      Direct materials from Sanding Department ($16 per
        unit)..   160,000

      Processing costs:
        Direct labor .... $ 26,640
        Factory overhead   18,000
        Total processing costs ($4.50 per unit)   44,640
    Total costs to be accounted for..................... $214,840

  Costs allocated as follows:
    Transferred to finished goods:
      600 units at $20 .... $ 12,000
      9,200 units at $20.50........................... 188,600
      Total cost of finished goods..................... $200,600

    In process, March 31:
      Direct materials (800 units at $16) .... $ 12,800
      Processing costs (800 units × 2/5 × $4.50)   1,440
      Total cost of inventory in process, March 31   14,240
    Total costs accounted for $214,840

Computations:
  Equivalent units of production:
    To process units in inventory on March 1:
      600 units × 2/3...................................   400
    To process units started and completed in March:
      9,800 units − 600 units.........................   9,200
    To process units in inventory on March 31:
      800 units × 2/5..................................   320
      Equivalent units of production....................   9,920

  Unit processing cost:
    $44,640 ÷ 9,920..................................... $ 4.50

In management decisions concerning the production and sale of joint products, only the relationship of the total revenue to be derived from the entire group to their total production cost is relevant. Nothing is to be gained from an allocation of joint costs to each product because one product cannot be produced without the others. A decision to produce a joint product is in effect a decision to produce all of the products.

Since joint products come from the processing of a common parent material, the assignment of cost to each separate product cannot be based on actual expenditures. It is impossible to determine the amount of cost incurred in the manufacture of each separate product. However, for purposes of inventory valuation, it is necessary to allocate joint costs among the joint products.

One method of allocation commonly used is the **market (sales) value method.** Its main feature is the assignment of costs to the different products according to their relative sales values. To illustrate, assume that 10,000 units of Product X and 50,000 units of Product Y were produced at a total cost of $63,000. The sales values of the two products and the allocation of the joint costs are as follows:

	Joint Costs	Joint Product	Units Produced	Sales Value per Unit	Total Sales Value
ALLOCATION OF JOINT COSTS	$63,000	{X	10,000	$3.00	$30,000
		{Y	50,000	1.20	60,000
	Total sales value.				$90,000

Allocation of joint costs:

X: $\frac{30,000}{90,000}$ × $63,000 . . . . $21,000

Y: $\frac{60,000}{90,000}$ × $63,000 42,000

Unit cost:

X: $21,000 ← 10,000 units. $2.10

Y: $42,000 ÷ 50,000 units. 84

BY-PRODUCTS

If one of the products resulting from a process has little value in relation to the main product or joint products, it is known as a by-product. The emergence of a by product is only incidental to the manufacture of the main product or joint products. By-products may be leftover materials, such as sawdust and scraps of wood in a lumber mill, or they may be separated from the material at the beginning of production, as in the case of cottonseed from raw cotton.

The amount of manufacturing cost usually assigned to a by-product is the sales value of the by-product reduced by any additional costs necessary to complete and sell it. The amount of cost thus determined is removed from the proper work in process account and transferred to a finished goods inventory account. To illustrate, assume that for a certain period the costs accumulated in Department 4 total $24,400, and that during the same period of time 1,000 units of by-product B, having an estimated value of $200, emerge from the processing in Department 4.

Finished Goods — Product B would be debited for $200 and Work in Process — Department 4 would be credited for the same amount, as illustrated in the following accounts:

Work in Process — Department 4		Finished Goods — Product B	
24,400	200 ──────────→ 200	

The accounting for the manufacturing costs remaining in the work in process account and for sale of the by-product would follow the usual procedures.

ILLUSTRATION OF PROCESS COST ACCOUNTING

To illustrate further the procedures that have been described, assume that Conway Company manufactures one main product designated Product A. The manufacturing activity begins in Department 1, where all materials enter production. The materials remain in Department 1 for a relatively short time and there is usually no inventory of work in process in that department at the end of the accounting period. A by-product, designated Product B, is also produced in Department 1. From Department 1 the materials making up the main product are transferred to Department 2. In Department 2, there are usually inventories at the end of the accounting period. Separate factory overhead accounts are maintained for Departments 1 and 2. Factory overhead is applied at 80% and 50% of direct labor cost for Departments 1 and 2 respectively. There are two service departments, Maintenance and Power.

The trial balance of the general ledger on January 1, the first day of the fiscal year, is as follows:

Conway Company
Trial Balance
January 1, 19--

Cash	38,500	
Accounts Receivable	45,000	
Finished Goods — Product A (1,000 units at $36.50)	36,500	
Finished Goods — Product B (600 pounds at $1.50)	900	
Work in Process — Department 2 (800 units, ½ completed)	24,600	
Materials	32,000	
Prepaid Expenses	6,150	
Plant Assets	510,000	
Accumulated Depreciation — Plant Assets		295,000
Accounts Payable		51,180
Wages Payable		3,400
Common Stock		250,000
Retained Earnings		94,070
	693,650	693,650

To reduce the illustrative entries to a manageable number and to avoid repetition, the transactions and the adjustments for January are stated as summaries. In practice, the transactions would be recorded from day to day in various journals. The descriptions of the transactions, followed in each case by the entry in general journal form, are as follows:

(a) Materials purchased and prepaid expenses incurred.

Entry: Materials	80,500	
Prepaid Expenses	3,300	
Accounts Payable		83,800

(b) Materials requisitioned for use.

Entry: Maintenance Department	1,200	
Power Department	6,000	
Factory Overhead — Department 1	3,720	
Factory Overhead — Department 2	2,700	
Work in Process — Department 1	59,700	
Materials		73,320

(c) Factory labor used.

Entry: Maintenance Department	3,600	
Power Department	4,500	
Factory Overhead — Department 1	2,850	
Factory Overhead — Department 2	2,100	
Work in Process — Department 1	24,900	
Work in Process — Department 2	37,800	
Wages Payable		75,750

(d) Other costs incurred.

Entry: Maintenance Department	600	
Power Department	900	
Factory Overhead — Department 1	1,800	
Factory Overhead — Department 2	1,200	
Selling Expenses	15,000	
General Expenses	13,500	
Accounts Payable		33,000

(e) Expiration of prepaid expenses.

Entry: Maintenance Department	300	
Power Department	750	
Factory Overhead — Department 1	1,350	
Factory Overhead — Department 2	1,050	
Selling Expenses	900	
General Expenses	600	
Prepaid Expenses		4,950

(f) Depreciation.

Entry: Maintenance Department.................... 300
Power Department......................... 1,050
Factory Overhead—Department 1 1,800
Factory Overhead—Department 2 2,700
Selling Expenses 600
General Expenses 300
Accumulated Depreciation—Plant Assets... 6,750

(g) Distribution of Maintenance Department costs.

Entry: Power Department........................ 300
Factory Overhead—Department 1 2,700
Factory Overhead—Department 2 3,000
Maintenance Department.................. 6,000

(h) Distribution of Power Department costs.

Entry: Factory Overhead—Department 1 5,400
Factory Overhead—Department 2 8,100
Power Department....................... 13,500

(i) Application of factory overhead costs to work in process.
The predetermined rates were 80% and 50% of direct labor cost for Departments 1 and 2 respectively. See transaction (c) for the monthly direct labor costs.

Entry: Work in Process—Department 1............. 19,920
Work in Process—Department 2............. 18,900
Factory Overhead—Department 1 19,920
Factory Overhead—Department 2 18,900

(j) Transfer of production costs from Department 1 to Department 2 and to Product B.
4,100 units were fully processed and 800 pounds of Product B, valued at $1.50 per pound, were produced. There is no work in process remaining in Department 1 at the end of the month.

Allocation of total costs of $104,520 charged to Department 1:
Product B, 800 × $1.50......................... $ 1,200
Transferred to Department 2..................... 103,320

Total costs.................................. $104,520

Unit cost of product transferred to Department 2:
$103,320 ÷ 4,100............................. $ 25.20

Entry: Finished Goods—Product B................ 1,200
Work in Process—Department 2............. 103,320
Work in Process—Department 1 104,520

(k) Transfer of production costs from Department 2 to Finished Goods.
4,000 units were completed, and the remaining 900 units were ⅔ completed at the end of the month.

Equivalent units of production:
  To process units in inventory on January 1:
    800 × ½   400
  To process units started and completed in January:
    4,000 − 800 3,200
  To process units in inventory on January 31:
    900 × ⅔   600
  Equivalent units of production in January 4,200

Processing costs:
  Direct labor (c) . . . . $ 37,800
  Factory overhead (i)   18,900
  Total processing costs . . . . $ 56,700
Unit processing costs:
  $56,700 ÷ 4,200 . . . . $ 13.50

Allocation of costs of Department 2:
  Units started in December, completed in January:
    Inventory on January 1, 800 units ½ completed . . $ 24,600
    Processing costs in January, 400 at $13.50   5,400
      Total $30,000 ÷ 800 = $37.50 unit cost) . . . . . $ 30,000

  Units started and completed in January:
    From Department 1, 3,200 units at $25.20 . . . . . $ 80,640
    Processing costs, 3,200 at $13.50   43,200
      Total ($123,840 ÷ 3,200 = $38.70 unit cost) . . .   123,840
      Total transferred to Product A $153,840

  Units started in January, ⅔ completed:
    From Department 1, 900 units at $25.20 . . . . $ 22,680
    Processing costs, 600 at $13.50   8,100
      Total work in process—Department 2   30,780
  Total costs charged to Department 2 . . . . $184,620

  Entry: Finished Goods—Product A   153,840
          Work in Process—Department 2   153,840

(l) *Cost of goods sold.*

Product A, 3,800 units:
  1,000 units at $36.50 . . . . $ 36,500
    800 units at $37.50   30,000
  2,000 units at $38.70   77,400
    Total cost of Product A sold $143,900

Product B, 1,000 pounds:
  1,000 pounds at $1.50   1,500
Total cost of goods sold $145,400

Entry: Cost of Goods Sold...................... 145,400

       Finished Goods — Product A..............   143,900

       Finished Goods — Product B..............   1,500

(m) Sales.

     Entry: Accounts Receivable 210,500

         Sales.....................................   210,500

(n) Cash received.

     Entry: Cash...................................... 200,000

         Accounts Receivable.....................   200,000

(o) Cash disbursed.

     Entry: Accounts Payable 120,000

         Wages Payable............................ 72,500

         Cash....................................   192,500

A chart of the flow of costs from the service and processing department accounts into the finished goods accounts and then to the cost of goods sold account is as follows. Entries in the accounts are identified by letters to aid the comparison with the summary journal entries.

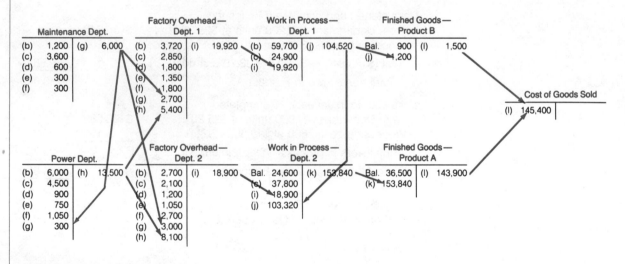

FLOW OF COSTS THROUGH PROCESS COST ACCOUNTS

The trial balance of the general ledger on January 31 is shown at the top of the next page.

On the balance sheet at January 31, the net underapplied factory overhead of $1,650 ($1,950 − $300) would appear as a deferred item. The balance in the cost of goods sold account would appear on the income statement as a deduction from net sales.

Conway Company
Trial Balance
January 31, 19--

Cash	46,000	
Accounts Receivable	55,500	
Finished Goods — Product A (1,200 units at $38.70)	46,440	
Finished Goods — Product B (400 pounds at $1.50)	600	
Work in Process — Department 2 (900 units, ⅔ completed)	30,780	
Materials	39,180	
Prepaid Expenses	4,500	
Plant Assets	510,000	
Accumulated Depreciation — Plant Assets		301,750
Accounts Payable		47,980
Wages Payable		6,650
Common Stock		250,000
Retained Earnings		94,070
Sales		210,500
Cost of Goods Sold	145,400	
Factory Overhead — Department 1		300
Factory Overhead — Department 2	1,950	
Selling Expenses	16,500	
General Expenses	14,400	
	911,250	911,250

1. For which of the following businesses would the process cost system be most appropriate?
   A. Custom furniture manufacturer   C. Crude oil refinery
   B. Commercial building contractor   D. None of the above

2. The group of manufacturing costs referred to as *processing costs* includes:
   A. direct materials and direct labor
   B. direct materials and factory overhead
   C. direct labor and factory overhead
   D. none of the above

3. Information relating to production in Department A for May is as follows:

May 1	Balance, 1,000 units, ¾ completed	$22,150
31	Direct materials, 5,000 units	75,000
31	Direct labor	32,500
31	Factory overhead	16,250

   If 500 units were ¼ completed at May 31 and 5,500 units were completed during May, what was the number of equivalent units of production for May?
   A. 4,500   C. 5,500
   B. 4,875   D. None of the above

4. Based on the data presented in Question 3, what is the unit processing cost?
   A. $10   C. $25
   B. $15   D. None of the above

5. If one of the products resulting from a process has little value in relation to the principal products, it is known as a:

A. joint product

B. by-product

C. direct material

D. none of the above

Discussion Questions

1. Which type of cost system, process or job order, would be best suited for each of the following: (a) washing machine manufacturer, (b) oil refinery, (c) furniture upholsterer, (d) building contractor, (e) paint manufacturer? Give reasons for your answers.

2. In job order cost accounting, the three elements of manufacturing cost are charged directly to job orders. Why is it not necessary to charge manufacturing costs in process cost accounting to job orders?

3. (a) How does a service department differ from a processing department? (b) Give two examples of a service department.

4. Parnell Company maintains a cafeteria for its employees at a cost of $1,400 per month. On what basis would the company most likely allocate the cost of the cafeteria among the production departments?

5. What two groups of manufacturing costs are referred to as processing costs?

6. In the manufacture of 5,000 units of a product, direct materials cost incurred was $15,000, direct labor cost incurred was $8,000, and factory overhead applied was $4,000. (a) What is the total processing cost? (b) What is the processing cost per unit? (c) What is the total manufacturing cost? (d) What is the manufacturing cost per unit?

7. What is meant by the term "equivalent units"?

8. If Department 1 had no work in process at the beginning of the period, 6,000 units were completed during the period, and 2,000 units were 25% completed at the end of the period, what was the number of equivalent units of production for the period?

9. The following information concerns production in Department 14 for January. All direct materials are placed in process at the beginning of production. Determine the number of units in work in process inventory at the end of the month.

WORK IN PROCESS — DEPARTMENT 14

Date		Item	Debit	Credit	Balance Debit	Balance Credit
Jan.	1	Bal., 4,000 units, ¾ completed			6,750	
	31	Direct materials, 15,000 units	7,200			
	31	Direct labor	16,800			
	31	Factory overhead	4,400			
	31	Goods finished, 13,500 units		28,110		
	31	Bal., ___ units, ½ completed			7,040	

10. For No. 9., determine the equivalent units of production for January.

11. What data are summarized in the two principal sections of the cost of production report?

12. What is the most important purpose of the cost of production report?

13. Distinguish between a joint product and a by-product.

14. Department 25 produces two products. How should the costs be allocated (a) if the products are joint products and (b) if one of the products is a by-product?

15. Factory employees in Department 1 of Cargile Co. are paid widely varying wage rates. In such circumstances, would direct labor hours or direct labor cost be the more equitable base for applying factory overhead to the production of the department? Explain.

16. In a factory with several processing departments, a separate factory overhead rate may be determined for each department. Why is a single factory overhead rate often inadequate in such circumstances?

Exercises

Exercise 23-1. Wright & Wright Co. manufactures two products. The entire output of Department 1 is transferred to Department 2. Part of the fully processed goods from Department 2 are sold as Product A and the remainder of the goods are transferred to Department 3 for further processing into Product B. The service department, Factory Office, provides services for each of the processing departments.

Prepare a chart of the flow of costs from the service and processing department accounts into the finished goods accounts and then into the cost of goods sold account. The relevant accounts are as follows:

Cost of Goods Sold   Finished Goods — Product A
Factory Office   Finished Goods — Product B
Factory Overhead — Department 1   Work in Process — Department 1
Factory Overhead — Department 2   Work in Process — Department 2
Factory Overhead — Department 3   Work in Process — Department 3

Exercise 23-2. The Maintenance and Repair Department provides services to processing Departments X, Y, and Z. During June of the current year, the total cost incurred by the Maintenance and Repair Department was $72,000. During June, it was estimated that 36% of the services were provided to Department X, 54% to Department Y, and 10% to Department Z.

Prepare a general journal entry to record the allocation of the Maintenance and Repair Department cost for June to the processing departments.

Exercise 23-3. Upchurch Company manufactures a single product by a continuous process, involving five production departments. The records indicate that $80,500 of direct materials were issued to and $98,000 of direct labor incurred by Department 1 in the manufacture of the product; the factory overhead rate is 40% of direct labor cost; work in process in the department at the beginning of the period totaled $45,150; and work in process at the end of the period totaled $48,650.

Prepare general journal entries to record (a) the flow of costs into Department 1 during the period for (1) direct materials, (2) direct labor, and (3) factory overhead; (b) the transfer of production costs to Department 2.

Exercise 23-4. The chief cost accountant for Pratt Electronics estimates total factory overhead cost for Department 10 for the year at $96,000 and total direct labor costs at $128,000. During August, actual direct labor cost totaled $16,000 and factory overhead cost incurred totaled $11,500. (a) What is the predetermined factory overhead rate based on direct labor cost? (b) Prepare the entry to apply factory overhead to production for August. (c) What is the August 31 balance of the account Factory Overhead —

Department 10? (d) Does the balance in (c) represent overapplied or underapplied factory overhead?

Exercise 23-5. The charges to Work in Process—Department 1 for a period, together with information concerning production, are as follows. All direct materials are placed in process at the beginning of production.

Work in Process—Department 1

1,200 units, 80% completed	25,920	To Dept. 2, 4,200 units	102,258
Direct materials, 3,000 at $12	36,000		
Direct labor	25,200		
Factory overhead	15,138		

Determine the following, presenting your computations: (a) equivalent units of production, (b) processing cost per equivalent unit of production, (c) total and unit cost of product started in prior period and completed in the current period, and (d) total and unit cost of product started and completed in the current period.

Exercise 23-6. Prepare a cost of production report for the Painting Department of McNair Company for July of the current fiscal year, using the following data:

Inventory, July 1, 5,400 units, 60% completed	$131,760
Materials from the Sanding Department, 15,000 units............	324,000
Direct labor for July.......................................	52,200
Factory overhead for July...................................	28,980
Goods finished during July (includes units in process, July 1), 16,400 units...	——
Inventory, July 31, 4,000 units, 40% completed	——

Exericse 23-7. The charges to Work in Process—Department 6, together with units of product completed during the period, are indicated in the following account:

Work in Process—Department 6

From Department 5	172,700	By-product N, 2,000 units
Direct labor	62,800	Joint product R, 12,800 units
Factory overhead	30,900	Joint product S, 6,000 units

There is no inventory of goods in process at either the beginning or the end of the period. The value of N is $2 a unit; R sells at $5 a unit and S sells at $16 a unit.

Allocate the costs to the three products and determine the unit cost of each, presenting your computations.

Problems
(Problems in Appendix B: 23-1B, 23-3B, 23-5B.)

Problem 23-1A. Ferguson Company manufactures Product W. Material C is placed in process in Department 1 where it is ground and partially refined. The output of Department 1 is transferred to Department 2, where Material D is added at the beginning of the process and the refining is completed. On May 1, Ferguson Company had the following inventories:

Finished goods (5,000 units)................................. $121,000
Work in process—Department 1............................. ——
Work in process—Department 2 (1,000 units, ¾ completed)..... 20,100
Materials 27,100

Departmental accounts are maintained for factory overhead and there is one service department, Factory Office. Manufacturing operations for May are summarized
as follows:

(a) Materials purchased on account........................... $48,950
(b) Materials requisitioned for use:
    Material C.. $26,510
    Material D.. 22,000
    Indirect materials—Department 1.......................... 1,760
    Indirect materials—Department 2.......................... 1,265
(c) Labor used:
    Direct labor—Department 1.............................. $55,000
    Direct labor—Department 2.............................. 39,250
    Indirect labor—Department 1 2,090
    Indirect labor—Department 2 1,980
    Factory Office 1,870
(d) Miscellaneous costs incurred on account:
    Department 1... $7,350
    Department 2... 5,170
    Factory Office 2,140
(e) Expiration of prepaid expenses:
    Department 1... $1,045
    Department 2... 715
    Factory Office 300
(f) Depreciation charged on plant assets:
    Department 1... $14,680
    Department 2... 12,520
    Factory Office 950
(g) Distribution of Factory Office costs:
    Department 1.........................75% of total Factory Office costs
    Department 2.........................25% of total Factory Office costs
(h) Application of factory overhead costs:
    Department 1..................................55% of direct labor cost
    Department 2..................................60% of direct labor cost
(i) Production costs transferred from Department 1 to Department 2:
    8,800 units were fully processed and there was no inventory of work in
    process in Department 1 at May 31.
(j) Production costs transferred from Department 2 to finished goods:
    8,000 units, including the inventory at May 1, were fully processed. 1,800
    units were ⅓ completed at May 31.
(k) Cost of goods sold during May:
    9,500 units (use the first-in, first-out method in crediting the finished goods
    account).

Instructions:
(1) Prepare entries in general journal form to record the foregoing operations.
    Identify each entry by letter.
(2) Compute the May 31 work in process inventory for Department 2.

Problem 23-2A. The trial balance of Mathews Inc. at July 31, the end of the first month of the current fiscal year, is as follows:

Mathews Inc.
Trial Balance
July 31, 19--

Cash	78,180	
Marketable Securities	60,000	
Accounts Receivable	210,600	
Allowance for Doubtful Accounts		7,800
Finished Goods—Product P1	85,800	
Finished Goods—Product P2	142,200	
Work in Process—Department 1	18,180	
Work in Process—Department 2	31,620	
Work in Process—Department 3	28,800	
Materials	57,000	
Prepaid Insurance	15,000	
Office Supplies	5,280	
Land	96,000	
Buildings	660,000	
Accumulated Depreciation—Buildings		319,200
Machinery and Equipment	342,000	
Accumulated Depreciation—Machinery and Equipment		216,600
Office Equipment	59,400	
Accumulated Depreciation—Office Equipment		25,560
Patents	60,000	
Accounts Payable		119,400
Wages Payable		17,640
Income Tax Payable		1,950
Mortgage Note Payable (due 1992)		120,000
Common Stock ($10 par)		600,000
Retained Earnings		479,850
Sales		528,600
Cost of Goods Sold	377,700	
Factory Overhead—Department 1	660	
Factory Overhead—Department 2		270
Factory Overhead—Department 3	750	
Selling Expenses	59,520	
General Expenses	39,720	
Interest Expense	960	
Interest Income		300
Income Tax	7,800	
	2,437,170	2,437,170

Instructions:

(1) Prepare a multiple-step income statement.
(2) Prepare a report form balance sheet.

Problem 23-3A. Townsend Company manufactures Product H by a series of three processes, all materials being introduced in Department 1. From Department 1, the materials pass through Departments 2 and 3, emerging as finished Product H. All inventories are priced at cost by the first-in, first-out method.

The balances in the accounts Work in Process — Department 3 and Finished Goods were as follows on October 1:

Work in Process — Department 3 (3,500 units, ½ completed)...... $106,050
Finished Goods (6,000 units at $36.20 a unit)................... 217,200

The following costs were charged to Work in Process — Department 3 during October:

Direct materials transferred from Department 2: 18,500 units at
  $24 a unit.. $444,000
Direct labor... 116,300
Factory overhead.. 70,000

During October, 17,500 units of H were completed and 18,600 units were sold. Inventories on October 31 were as follows:

Work In Process — Department 3: 4,500 units, ⅓ completed
Finished Goods: 4,900 units

Instructions:
(1) Determine the following, presenting computations in good order:
    (a) Equivalent units of production for Department 3 during October.
    (b) Unit processing cost for Department 3 for October.
    (c) Total and unit cost of Product H started in a prior period and finished in October.
    (d) Total and unit cost of Product H started and finished in October.
    (e) Total cost of goods transferred to finished goods.
    (f) Work in process inventory for Department 3, October 31.
    (g) Cost of goods sold (indicate number of units and unit costs).
    (h) Finished goods inventory, October 31.
(2) Prepare a cost of production report for Department 3 for October.

Problem 23-4A. Sikes Products manufactures joint products M and N. Materials are placed in production in Department 1, and after processing, are transferred to Department 2, where more materials are added. The finished products emerge from Department 2. There are two service departments: Factory Office, and Maintenance and Repair.

There were no inventories of work in process at the beginning or at the end of December. Finished goods inventories at December 1 were as follows:

Product M, 4,900 units $56,350
Product N, 940 units 18,330

Transactions related to manufacturing operations for December are summarized as follows:
    (a) Materials purchased on account, $70,000.
    (b) Materials requisitioned for use: Department 1, $32,550 ($28,350 entered directly into the products); Department 2, $22,210 ($18,290 entered directly into the products); Maintenance and Repair, $2,660.
    (c) Labor costs incurred: Department 1, $23,520 ($21,000 entered directly into the products); Department 2, $25,340 ($22,400 entered directly into the products); Factory Office, $3,850; Maintenance and Repair, $9,170.

(d) Miscellaneous costs and expenses incurred on account: Department 1, $3,570; Department 2, $3,150; Factory Office, $1,400; and Maintenance and Repair, $2,170.

(e) Depreciation charged on plant assets: Department 1, $4,900; Department 2, $3,360; Factory Office, $700; and Maintenance and Repair, $980.

(f) Expiration of various prepaid expenses: Department 1, $280; Department 2, $245; Factory Office, $350; and Maintenance and Repair, $490.

(g) Factory office costs allocated on the basis of hours worked: Department 1, 2,240 hours; Department 2, 2,800 hours; Maintenance and Repair, 560 hours.

(h) Maintenance and repair costs allocated on the basis of services rendered: Department 1, 45%; Department 2, 55%.

(i) Factory overhead applied to production at the predetermined rates: 120% and 115% of direct labor cost for Departments 1 and 2 respectively.

(j) Output of Department 1: 5,460 units.

(k) Output of Department 2: 7,050 units of Product M and 2,820 units of Product N. Unit selling price is $16.80 for Product M and $28 for Product N.

(l) Sales on account: 7,750 units of Product M at $16.80 and 2,660 units of Product N at $28. Credits to the finished goods accounts are to be priced in accordance with the first-in, first-out method.

Instructions:

Present entries in general journal form to record the transactions, identifying each by letter. Include as an explanation for entry (k) the computations for the allocation of the production costs for Department 2 to the joint products, and as an explanation for entry (l) the number of units and the unit costs for each product sold.

Problem 23-5A. A process cost system is used to record the costs of manufacturing Product A24C, which requires a series of four processes. The inventory of Work in Process—Department 4 on April 1 and debits to the account during April were as follows:

Balance, 1,600 units, ¼ completed	$ 6,520
From Department 3, 9,200 units	25,760
Direct labor	38,500
Factory overhead	9,625

During April, the 1,600 units in process on April 1 were completed, and of the 9,200 units entering the department, all were completed except 2,200 units, which were ¼ completed.

Charges to Work in Process—Department 4 for May were made as follows:

From Department 3, 8,250 units	$23,925
Direct labor	41,724
Factory overhead	10,431

During May, the units in process at the beginning of the month were completed, and of the 8,250 units entering the department, all were completed except 1,500 units, which were ½ completed.

Instructions:

(1) Set up an account for Work in Process—Department 4. Enter the balance as of April 1 and record the debits and the credits in the account for April. Present

computations for the determination of (a) equivalent units of production, (b) unit processing cost, (c) cost of goods finished, differentiating between units started in the prior period and units started and finished in April and (d) work in process inventory.

(2) Record the transactions for May in the account. Present the computations listed in instruction (1).

(3) Determine the difference in unit cost between the product started and completed in April and the product started and completed in May. Determine also the amount of the difference attributable collectively to operations in Departments 1 through 3 and the amount attributable to operations in Department 4.

Mini-Case

Rivera Inc. manufactures product A68 by a series of four processes. All materials are placed in production in the Die Casting Department and, after processing, are transferred to the Tooling, Assembly, and Painting Departments, emerging as finished product A68.

On April 1, the balance in the account Work in Process — Painting was $336,600, determined as follows:

Direct materials: 12,000 units	$203,400
Direct labor: 12,000 units, ¾ completed	107,550
Factory overhead: 12,000 units, ¾ completed	25,650
Total	$336,600

The following costs were charged to Work in Process — Painting during April:

Direct materials transferred from Assembly Department:	
136,000 units	$2,380,000
Direct labor	1,648,200
Factory overhead	361,800

During April, 138,000 units of A68 were completed and transferred to Finished Goods. On April 30, the inventory in the Painting Department consisted of 10,000 units, one-half completed.

As a new cost accountant for Rivera Inc., you have just received a phone call from George Herschman, the superintendent of the Painting Department. He was extremely upset with the cost of production report, which he says does not balance. In addition, he commented:

"I give up! These reports are a waste of time. My department has always been the best department in the plant, so why should I bother with these reports? Just what purpose do they serve?"

The report to which Herschman referred is as follows:

RIVERA INC.
Cost of Production Report—Painting Department
For Month Ended April 30, 19--

Quantities:
Charged to production:
 In process, April 1 9,000
 Received from Assembly Department................... 136,000
  Total units to be accounted for 145,000

Units accounted for:
 Transferred to finished goods......................... 138,000
 In process, April 30.................................. 5,000
  Total units accounted for 143,000

Costs:
Charged to production:
 In process, April 1.................................. $ 336,600

April costs:
 Direct materials from Assembly Department ($15.70 per
  unit) 2,380,000

 Processing costs:
  Direct labor............................. $1,648,200
  Factory overhead........................ 361,800
   Total processing costs ($13.40 per unit).............. 2,010,000
  Total costs to be accounted for.......................... $4,726,600

Costs allocated as follows:
 Transferred to finished goods:
  138,000 units at $29.10 ($15.70 + $13.40) $4,015,800

 In process, April 30:
  Materials (5,000 units × $15.70) .... $ 78,500
  Processing costs (5,000 units × $13.40) ... 67,000
   Total cost of inventory in process.......... 145,500
  Total costs accounted for................................. $4,161,300

Computations:
 Equivalent units of production:
  To process units in inventory on April 1:
   12,000 units × ¾ 9,000
  To process units started and completed in April 136,000
  To process units in inventory on April 30:
   10,000 units × ½ 5,000
   Equivalent units of production....................... 150,000

 Unit processing cost:
  $2,010,000 ÷ 150,000 .... $ 13.40

Instructions:
(1) Based upon the data for April, prepare a revised cost of production report for the Painting Department.
(2) Assume that for March, the unit direct materials cost was $16.95 and the unit processing cost was $14.80. Determine the change in the direct materials unit cost and unit processing cost for April.
(3) Based upon (2), what are some possible explanations for the changing unit costs?
(4) Describe how you would explain to Herschman that cost of production reports are useful.

24

Budgetary Control and Standard Cost Systems

CHAPTER OBJECTIVES

Describe the nature and objectives of budgeting and the budget process.

Identify the components of the master budget and illustrate the preparation of a master budget for a small manufacturing enterprise.

Describe and illustrate budget performance reports and flexible budgets.

Describe standard costs and illustrate the use of standard costs in planning and controlling operations.

24

CHAPTER

The individuals charged with the responsibility of organizing and directing the operations of a business enterprise are often collectively called the "management." The basic functions of management in which accounting is involved are often classified as (1) planning and (2) control. **Planning** is the process of selecting realistically attainable business objectives and formulating the general policies and the specific directions needed to achieve these objectives. **Control** includes the procedures designed to assure that actual operations conform with management's plans.

Effective planning and control are requisites of successful operations. When the owner of a business can personally supervise every phase of operations, the basic functions of management can be performed with little help from accounting data. Direct supervision of all phases of operations by one person is seldom possible, however, and it is necessary to establish a chain of management command from the chief executive down to department supervisors. Under such circumstances, accounting data are absolutely necessary in providing each management level with the financial and operating data needed to achieve sound planning and effective control.

Various uses of accounting data by management have been described in earlier chapters. The value of financial statements in appraising past operations and planning for the future has been emphasized. Attention has been directed to the principles of internal control designed to safeguard assets, assure accurate accounting data, encourage adherence to management policies, and increase efficiency. The role of cost accounting in planning production and controlling costs has been described. This chapter is devoted to budgeting and standard costs, two additional accounting devices that aid management in planning and controlling the operations of the business.

NATURE AND OBJECTIVES OF BUDGETING

The essentials of budgeting are (1) the establishment of specific goals for future operations and (2) the periodic comparison of actual results with these goals. Although budgeting is commonly associated with profit-making enterprises, it can be used in many other areas. Budgeting plays an important role in operating most instrumentalities of government, ranging from rural school districts and small villages to gigantic agencies of the federal government. It is also an important part of the operations of churches, hospitals, and other not-for-profit institutions. Individuals and family units often use budgeting techniques as an aid to careful management of resources.

A **budget** is a formal written statement of management's plans for the future, expressed in financial terms. A budget charts the course of future action. Thus, it serves management's primary functions in the same manner that the architect's blueprints aid the builder and the navigator's flight plan aids the pilot.

A budget, like a blueprint and a flight plan, should contain sound, attainable objectives. If the budget is to contain such objectives, planning must be based on careful study, investigation, and research. Reliance by management on data thus obtained lessens the role of guesses and intuition in managing a business enterprise.

To be effective, managerial planning must be accompanied by control. The control feature of budgeting lies in periodic comparisons as disclosed by budget performance reports between planned objectives and actual performance. This "feedback" enables management to seek corrective action for areas where significant differences between the budget and actual performance are reported. The role of accounting is to aid management in the investigation phase of budget preparation, to translate management's plans into financial terms, and to prepare budget performance reports and related analyses.

BUDGET PERIOD

Budgets of operating activities usually include the fiscal year of an enterprise. A year is short enough to make possible fairly dependable estimates of future operations, and yet long enough to make it possible to view the future in a reasonably broad context. However, to achieve effective control, the annual budgets must be subdivided into shorter time periods such as quarters of the year, months, or weeks. It is also necessary to review the budgets from time to time and make any changes that become necessary as a result of unforeseen changes in general business conditions, in the particular industry, or in the individual enterprise.

A frequent variant of fiscal-year budgeting, sometimes called **continuous budgeting,** provides for maintenance of a twelve-month projection into the future. At the end of each time interval used, the twelve-month budget is revised by removing the data for the period just ended and adding the newly estimated budget data for the same period next year.

BUDGETING PROCEDURES

The details of budgeting systems are affected by the type and degree of complexity of a particular company, the amount of its revenues, the relative importance of its various divisions, and many other factors. Budget procedures used by a large manufacturer of automobiles would obviously differ in many ways from a system designed for a small manufacturer of paper products. The differences between a system designed for factory operations of any type and a financial enterprise such as a bank would be even more marked.

The development of budgets for a following fiscal year usually begins several months prior to the end of the current year. The responsibility for their development is ordinarily assigned to a committee made up of the budget director and such high-level executives as the controller, treasurer, production manager, and sales manager. The process is started by requesting estimates of sales, production, and other operating data from the various administrative units concerned. It is important that all levels of management and all departments participate in the preparation and submission of budget estimates. The involvement of all supervisory personnel fosters cooperation both within and among departments and also heightens awareness of each department's importance in the overall processes of the company. All levels of management are thus encouraged to set goals and to control operations in a manner that strengthens the possibilities of achieving the goals.

The process of developing budget estimates differs among enterprises. One method is to require all levels of management to start from zero and estimate sales, production, and other operating data as though operations were being started for the first time. Although this concept, called **zero-base budgeting**, has received wide attention in regard to budgeting for governmental units, it is equally useful to commercial enterprises. Another method of developing estimates is for each level of management to modify last year's budgeted amounts in light of last year's operating results and expected changes for the coming year.

The various estimates received by the budget committee are revised, reviewed, coordinated, cross-referenced, and finally put together to form the **master budget**. The estimates submitted should not be substantially revised by the committee without first giving the originators an opportunity to defend their proposals. After agreement has been reached and the master budget has been adopted by the budget committee, copies of the pertinent sections are distributed to the proper personnel in the chain of accountability. Periodic reports comparing actual results with the budget should likewise be distributed to all supervisory personnel.

As a framework for describing and illustrating budgeting, a small manufacturing enterprise will be assumed. The major parts of its master budget are as follows:

Budgeted income statement	**Budgeted balance sheet**
Sales budget	Capital expenditures budget
Cost of goods sold budget	Cash budget
Production budget	
Direct materials purchases budget	
Direct labor cost budget	
Factory overhead cost budget	
Operating expenses budget	

COMPONENTS OF MASTER BUDGET

Sales Budget

The first budget to be prepared is usually the sales budget. An estimate of the dollar volume of sales revenue serves as the foundation upon which the other budgets are based. Sales volume will have a significant effect on all of the factors entering into the determination of operating income.

The sales budget ordinarily shows the amount of each product expected to be sold, classified by area and/or sales representative. The quantity estimates are based on an analysis of past sales and on forecasts of business conditions generally and for the specific industry. The anticipated sales revenue is then determined by multiplying the volume of forecasted sales by the expected unit sales price. A sales budget is illustrated at the top of the next page.

Frequent comparisons of actual sales with the budgeted volume, by product and area, will show differences between the two. Management is then able to investigate the probable cause of the significant differences and attempt corrective action.

Production Budget

The number of units of each commodity expected to be manufactured to meet budgeted sales and inventory requirements is set forth in the production budget. The budgeted volume of production is based on the sum of (1) the expected sales volume and (2) the desired year-end inventory, less (3) the inventory expected to

Bowers Company
Sales Budget
For Year Ending December 31, 19--

Product and Area	Unit Sales Volume	Unit Selling Price	Total Sales
Product X:			
Area A	52,000	$ 9.90	$ 514,800
Area B	40,500	9.90	400,950
Area C	39,500	9.90	391,050
Total			$1,306,800
Product Y:			
Area A	27,900	$16.50	$ 460,350
Area B	19,700	16.50	325,050
Area C	22,400	16.50	369,600
Total			$1,155,000
Total revenue from sales			$2,461,800

be available at the beginning of the year. A production budget is illustrated as follows:

Bowers Company
Production Budget
For Year Ending December 31, 19--

	Units	
	Product X	Product Y
Sales	132,000	70,000
Plus desired ending inventory, December 31, 19--	20,000	15,000
Total...	152,000	85,000
Less estimated beginning inventory, January 1, 19--	22,000	12,000
Total production	130,000	73,000

The production needs must be carefully coordinated with the sales budget to assure that production and sales are kept in balance during the period. Ideally, manufacturing operations should be maintained at normal capacity, with no idle time or overtime, and inventories should be neither excessive nor insufficient to fill sales orders.

Direct Materials Purchases Budget

The production needs shown by the production budget, combined with data on direct materials needed, provide the data for the direct materials purchases budget. The quantities of direct materials purchases necessary to meet production needs is based on the sum of (1) the materials expected to be needed to meet production requirements and (2) the desired year-end inventory, less (3) the inventory expected to be available at the beginning of the year. The quantities of direct materials required are then multiplied by the expected unit purchase price to determine the total cost of direct materials purchases.

In the following direct materials purchases budget, materials A and C are required for Product X and materials A, B, and C are required for Product Y.

DIRECT MATERIALS
PURCHASES
BUDGET

Bowers Company
Direct Materials Purchases Budget
For Year Ending December 31, 19--

| | Direct Materials | | |
	A	B	C
Units required for production:			
Product X....................................	195,000	——	260,000
Product Y....................................	73,000	146,000	147,100
Plus desired ending inventory, Dec. 31, 19--.........	40,000	20,000	60,000
Total	308,000	166,000	467,100
Less estimated beginning inventory, Jan. 1, 19--	51,500	22,000	57,100
Total units to be purchased.....................	256,500	144,000	410,000
Unit price......................................	$ .30	$ .85	$ .50
Total direct materials purchases	$ 76,950	$122,400	$205,000

The timing of the direct materials purchases requires close coordination between the purchasing and production departments so that inventory levels can be maintained within reasonable limits.

Direct Labor Cost Budget

The needs indicated by the production budget provide the starting point for the preparation of the direct labor cost budget. The direct labor hours necessary to meet production needs are multiplied by the estimated hourly rate to yield the total direct labor cost. The manufacturing operations for both Products X and Y are performed in Departments 1 and 2. A direct labor cost budget is illustrated as follows:

DIRECT LABOR
COST BUDGET

Bowers Company
Direct Labor Cost Budget
For Year Ending December 31, 19--

	Department 1	Department 2
Hours required for production:		
Product X.......................................	32,500	26,000
Product Y.......................................	18,250	29,200
Total	50,750	55,200
Hourly rate......................................	$6	$8
Total direct labor cost............................	$304,500	$441,600

Factory Overhead Cost Budget

The factory overhead costs estimated to be necessary to meet production needs are presented in the factory overhead cost budget. For use as a part of the master budget, the factory overhead cost budget usually presents the total estimated cost for each item of factory overhead. Supplemental schedules are often prepared to present the factory overhead cost for each individual department. Such schedules enable department supervisors to direct attention to those costs for which each is solely responsible. They also aid the production manager in evaluating performance in each department. A factory overhead cost budget is illustrated as follows:

FACTORY OVERHEAD COST BUDGET

Bowers Company
Factory Overhead Cost Budget
For Year Ending December 31, 19--

Indirect factory wages	$183,200
Supervisory salaries	90,000
Power and light	76,500
Depreciation of plant and equipment	72,000
Indirect materials	45,700
Maintenance	35,070
Insurance and property taxes	19,800
Total factory overhead cost	$522,270

Cost of Goods Sold Budget   The budget for the cost of goods sold is prepared by combining the relevant estimates of quantities and costs in the budget for (1) direct materials purchases, (2) direct labor costs, and (3) factory overhead costs, with the addition of data on estimated inventories. A cost of goods sold budget is illustrated as follows:

COST OF GOODS SOLD BUDGET

Bowers Company
Cost of Goods Sold Budget
For Year Ending December 31, 19--

Finished goods inventory, January 1, 19--			$ 281,400
Work in process inventory, January 1, 19--		$ 46,100	
Direct materials:			
Direct materials inventory, January 1, 19--	$ 62,700		
Direct materials purchases	404,350		
Cost of direct materials available for use	$467,050		
Less direct materials inventory, December 31, 19--	59,000		
Cost of direct materials placed in production	$408,050		
Direct labor	746,100		
Factory overhead	522,270		
Total manufacturing costs		1,676,420	
Total work in process during period		$1,722,520	
Less work in process inventory, December 31, 19--		55,000	
Cost of goods manufactured			1,667,520
Cost of finished goods available for sale			$1,948,920
Less finished goods inventory, December 31, 19--			298,750
Cost of goods sold			$1,650,170

Operating Expenses Budget | The estimated selling and general expenses are set forth in the operating expenses budget in a format like the factory overhead cost budget illustrated earlier. Detailed schedules based on departmental responsibility should be prepared for major items in the budget. The advertising expense schedule, for example, should include such details as advertising media to be used (newspaper, direct mail, television, etc.), quantities (column inches, number of pieces, minutes, etc.), cost per unit, frequency of use, and sectional totals. It is only through careful attention to details that a realistic budget can be prepared, and through assignment of responsibility to departmental supervisors that effective controls can be achieved.

Budgeted Income Statement | A budgeted income statement can usually be prepared from the estimated data presented in the budgets for sales, cost of goods sold, and operating expenses, with the addition of data on other income, other expense, and income tax. It need not differ in form and arrangement from an income statement based on actual data in the accounts and hence is not illustrated.

The budgeted income statement brings together in condensed form the projection of all profit-making phases of operations and enables management to weigh the effects of the individual budgets on the profit plan for the year. If the budgeted net income in relationship to sales or to stockholders' equity is disappointingly low, additional review of all factors involved should be undertaken in an attempt to improve the plans.

Capital Expenditures Budget | The capital expenditures budget summarizes future plans for acquisition of plant facilities and equipment. Substantial expenditures may be needed to replace machinery and other plant assets as they wear out, become obsolete, or for other reasons fall below minimum standards of efficiency. In addition, an expansion of plant facilities may be planned to keep pace with increasing demand for a company's product or to provide for additions to the product line.

The useful life of many plant assets extends over relatively long periods of time, and the amount of the expenditures for such assets usually changes a great deal from year to year. The customary practice, therefore, is to project the plans for a number of years into the future in preparing the capital expenditures budget. A five-year capital expenditures budget is illustrated as follows:

CAPITAL EXPENDITURES BUDGET

Bowers Company
Capital Expenditures Budget
For Five Years Ending December 31, 1989

Item	1985	1986	1987	1988	1989
Machinery—Department 1...	$100,000			$ 70,000	$ 90,000
Machinery—Department 2...	45,000	$65,000	$140,000	50,000	
Office equipment		22,500			15,000
Total	$145,000	$87,500	$140,000	$120,000	$105,000

The various proposals recognized in the capital expenditures budget must be considered in preparing certain operating budgets. For example, the expected amount of depreciation on new equipment to be acquired in the current year must be taken into consideration when the budgets for factory overhead and operating expenses are prepared. The manner in which the proposed expenditures are to be financed will also affect the cash budget.

Cash Budget

The cash budget presents the expected inflow and outflow of cash for a day, week, month, or longer period. Receipts are classified by source and disbursements by purpose. The expected cash balance at the end of the period is then compared with the amount established as the minimum balance and the difference is the anticipated excess or deficiency for the period.

The minimum cash balance represents a safety buffer for mistakes in cash planning and for emergencies. However, the amount stated as the minimum balance need not remain fixed. It should perhaps be larger during periods of "peak" business activity than during the "slow" season.

The interrelationship of the cash budget with other budgets may be seen from the following illustration. Data from the sales budget, the various budgets for manufacturing costs and operating expenses, and the capital expenditures budget affect the cash budget. Consideration must also be given to dividend policies, plans for equity or long-term debt financing, and other projected plans that will affect cash.

CASH BUDGET

Bowers Company
Cash Budget
For Three Months Ending March 31, 19--

	January	February	March
Estimated cash receipts from:			
Cash sales	$ 42,000	$ 45,000	$ 37,500
Collections of accounts receivable	174,750	179,250	137,250
Other sources (issuance of securities, interest, etc.)	—	—	2,250
Total cash receipts	$216,750	$224,250	$177,000
Estimated cash disbursements for:			
Manufacturing costs	$135,300	$139,050	$134,000
Operating expenses	37,800	37,800	35,200
Capital expenditures	—	36,000	20,000
Other purposes (notes, income tax, etc.)	11,500	5,000	40,000
Total cash disbursements	$184,600	$217,850	$229,200
Cash increase (decrease)	$ 32,150	$ 6,400	$ (52,200)
Cash balance at beginning of month	70,000	102,150	108,550
Cash balance at end of month	$102,150	$108,550	$ 56,350
Minimum cash balance	75,000	75,000	75,000
Excess (deficiency)	$ 27,150	$ 33,550	$ (18,650)

The importance of accurate cash budgeting can scarcely be overemphasized. An unanticipated lack of cash can result in loss of discounts, unfavorable borrowing terms on loans, and damage to the credit rating. On the other hand, an excess amount of idle cash also shows poor management. When the budget shows periods of excess cash, such funds should be used to reduce loans or they should be invested in readily marketable income-producing securities. Reference to the preceding illustration shows excess cash during January and February and a deficiency during March.

Budgeted Balance Sheet

The budgeted balance sheet presents estimated details of financial condition at the end of a budget period, assuming that all budgeted operating and financing plans are fulfilled. It need not differ in form and arrangement from a balance sheet based on actual data in the accounts and hence is not illustrated. If the budgeted balance sheet shows weaknesses in financial position, such as an abnormally large amount of current liabilities in relation to current assets, or excessive long-term debt in relation to stockholders' equity, the relevant factors should be given further study with a view to taking corrective action.

BUDGET PERFORMANCE REPORTS

A budget performance report comparing actual results with the budgeted figures should be prepared periodically for each budget. All significant differences should be investigated immediately to determine their cause and to seek means of preventing their recurrence. If corrective action cannot be taken because of changed conditions that have occurred since the budget was prepared, future budget figures should be revised accordingly. A budget performance report is illustrated as follows:

BUDGET PERFORMANCE REPORT

Bowers Company
Budget Performance Report—Factory Overhead Cost, Department 1
For Month Ended June 30, 19--

	Budget	Actual	Over	Under
Indirect factory wages....................	$15,100	$15,140	$ 40	
Supervisory salaries......................	7,500	7,500		
Power and light..........................	6,400	6,375		$25
Depreciation of plant and equipment.......	6,000	6,000		
Indirect materials	3,800	4,125	325	
Maintenance	2,900	2,870		30
Insurance and property taxes	1,650	1,650		
	$43,350	$43,660	$365	$55

The amounts reported in the "Budget" column were obtained from supplemental schedules accompanying the master budget. The amounts in the "Actual" column are the costs actually incurred. The last two columns show the amounts by which actual costs exceeded or were below budgeted figures. As shown in the illustration, there were differences between the actual and budgeted amounts for some of the items of overhead cost. The cause of the significant difference in indirect materials cost should be investigated, and an attempt made to find means of corrective action.

FLEXIBLE
BUDGETS

In the discussion of budget systems, it has been assumed that the amount of sales and the level of manufacturing activity achieved during a period approximated the goals established in the budgets. When substantial changes in expectations occur during a budget period, the budgets should be revised to give effect to such changes. Otherwise, they will be of questionable value as incentives and instruments for controlling costs and expenses.

The effect of changes in volume of activity can be "built in" to the system by what are termed flexible budgets. Particularly useful in estimating and controlling factory overhead costs and operating expenses, a flexible budget is in reality a series of budgets for varying rates of activity. To illustrate, assume that because of extreme variations in demand and other uncontrollable factors, the output of a particular manufacturing enterprise fluctuates widely from month to month. In such circumstances, the total factory overhead costs incurred during periods of high activity are certain to be greater than during periods of low activity. It is equally certain, however, that fluctuations in total factory overhead costs will not be exactly proportionate to the volume of production. For example, if $100,000 of factory overhead costs are usually incurred during a month in which production totals 10,000 units, the factory overhead for a month in which only 5,000 units are produced would unquestionably be more than $50,000.

Items of factory cost and operating expense that tend to remain constant in amount regardless of changes in volume of activity may be said to be fixed. Real estate taxes, property insurance, and depreciation expense on buildings are examples of fixed costs. The amounts incurred are substantially independent of the level of operations. Costs and expenses which tend to fluctuate in amount according to changes in volume of activity are called variable. Supplies and indirect materials used and sales commissions are examples of variable costs and expenses. The degree of variability is not the same for all variable items; few, if any, vary in exact proportion to sales or production. The terms semivariable or semifixed are sometimes applied to items that have both fixed and variable characteristics to a significant degree. An example is electric power, for which there is often an initial flat fee and a rate for additional usage. For example, the charge for electricity used might be $700 for the first 10 000 kwh consumed during a month and $.05 per kwh used above 10 000.

In the following flexible budget for factory overhead cost, a single manufacturing department and a single product are assumed, with budgeted costs stated at three different levels of production. In practice, the number of production levels and the interval between levels will vary with the range of production volume. For example, instead of budgeting for 8,000, 9,000, and 10,000 units of product, it might be necessary to provide for levels, at intervals of 500, from 6,000 to

12,000 units. Alternative bases may also be used in measuring volume of activity, such as hours of departmental operation or direct labor hours.

Collins Manufacturing Company Monthly Factory Overhead Cost Budget			
Units of product	8,000	9,000	10,000
Variable cost:			
Indirect factory wages	$ 32,000	$ 36,000	$ 40,000
Electric power	24,000	27,000	30,000
Indirect materials	12,000	13,500	15,000
Total variable cost	$ 68,000	$ 76,500	$ 85,000
Fixed cost:			
Supervisory salaries	$ 40,000	$ 40,000	$ 40,000
Depreciation of plant and equipment	25,000	25,000	25,000
Property taxes	15,000	15,000	15,000
Insurance	12,000	12,000	12,000
Electric power	10,000	10,000	10,000
Total fixed cost	$102,000	$102,000	$102,000
Total factory overhead cost	$170,000	$178,500	$187,000

STANDARD COSTS

The determination of the unit cost of products manufactured is basic to cost accounting. The process cost and job order cost systems discussed in the preceding chapters were designed to determine *actual* or *historical* unit costs. The aim of both systems is to provide management with timely data on actual manufacturing costs and to aid in cost control and profit maximization.

The use of budgetary control procedures is often extended to the point of unit cost projections for each commodity produced. Cost systems using detailed estimates of each element of manufacturing cost entering into the finished product are sometimes called **standard cost systems.** Such systems enable management to determine how much a product should cost (standard), how much it does cost (actual), and the causes of any difference (variance) between the two. Standard costs thus serve as a measuring device for determination of efficiency. If the standard cost of a product is $5 per unit and its current actual cost is $5.50 per unit, the factors responsible for the excess cost can be determined and remedial measures taken. Thus, supervisors have a device for controlling the costs for which they are responsible, and employees become more cost conscious.

Standard costs may be used in either the process type of production or the job order type of production. For more effective control, standard costs should be used for each department or cost center in the factory. It is possible, however, to use standard costs in some departments and actual costs in others.

A wide variety of management skills are needed in setting standards, and the joint effort of accounting, engineering, personnel administration, and other managerial areas is also needed. Time and motion studies of each operation are made, and the work force is trained to use the most efficient methods. Direct materials and productive equipment are subjected to detailed study and tests in an effort to achieve maximum productivity for a given level of costs.

VARIANCES FROM STANDARDS

Production management's goal is the attainment of properly determined standards. Differences between the standard costs of a department or product and the actual costs incurred are termed variances. If actual cost incurred is less than standard costs, the variance is favorable. If actual cost exceeds standard cost, the variance is unfavorable. When actual costs are compared with standard costs, only the "exceptions" or variances are reported to the person responsible for cost control. This reporting by the "principle of exceptions" enables the one responsible for cost control to concentrate on the cause and correction of the variances.

The total variance for a certain period is usually made up of several variances, some of which may be favorable and some unfavorable. There may be variances from standards in direct materials costs, in direct labor costs, and in factory overhead costs. The remainder of the chapter is devoted to illustrations and analyses of these variances for a manufacturing enterprise. For illustrative purposes, it is assumed that only one type of direct material is used, that there is a single processing department, and that Product X is the only commodity manufactured by the enterprise.

Direct Materials Cost Variance

Two major factors enter into the determination of standards for direct materials cost: (1) the quantity (usage) standard and (2) the price standard. If the actual quantity of direct materials used in producing a commodity differs from the standard quantity, there is a quantity variance. If the actual unit price of the materials differs from the standard price, there is a price variance. To illustrate, assume that the standard direct materials cost of producing 10,000 units of Product X and the direct materials cost actually incurred during June were as follows:

Standard: 20,000 pounds at $1.00 . . . . $20,000
Actual: 20,600 pounds at $1.04   21,424

The unfavorable variance of $1,424 resulted in part from an excess usage of 600 pounds of direct materials and in part from an excess cost of $.04 per pound. The analysis of the materials cost variance is as follows:

DIRECT MATERIALS COST VARIANCE

Quantity variance:
  Actual quantity . . . . 20,600 pounds
  Standard quantity . . . . 20,000 pounds
    Variance — unfavorable . . . .   600 pounds × standard price, $1 . . . . $ 600

Price variance:
  Actual price . . . . $1.04 per pound
  Standard price . . . .   1.00 per pound
    Variance — unfavorable . . . . $ .04 per pound × actual quantity, 20,600 .   824

Total direct materials cost variance — unfavorable $1,424

The physical quantity and the dollar amount of the quantity variance should be reported to the factory superintendent and other personnel responsible for production. If excessive amounts of direct materials were used because of the malfunction of equipment or some other failure within the production department, those responsible should correct the situation. However, an unfavorable direct materials quantity variance is not necessarily the result of inefficiency within the production department. If the excess usage of 600 pounds of materials in the example above had been caused by inferior materials, the purchasing department should be held responsible.

The unit price and the total amount of the materials price variance should be reported to the purchasing department, which may or may not be able to control this variance. If materials of the same quality could have been purchased from another supplier at the standard price, the variance was controllable. On the other hand, if the variance resulted from a marketwide price increase, the variance was not subject to control.

Direct Labor Cost Variance

As in the case of direct materials, two major factors enter into the determination of standards for direct labor cost: (1) the time (usage or efficiency) standard, and (2) the rate (price or wage) standard. If the actual direct labor hours spent producing a product differ from the standard hours, there is a time variance. If the wage rate paid differs from the standard rate, there is a rate variance. The standard cost and the actual cost of direct labor in the production of 10,000 units of Product X during June are assumed to be as follows:

Standard:	8,000 hours at $8.00	$64,000
Actual:	7,900 hours at 8.20	64,780

The unfavorable direct labor variance of $780 is made up of a favorable time variance and an unfavorable rate variance, determined as follows:

DIRECT LABOR COST VARIANCE

Time variance:
Standard time	8,000 hours	
Actual time	7,900 hours	
Variance—favorable	100 hours × standard rate, $8	$ 800

Rate variance:
Actual rate	$8.20 per hour	
Standard rate	8.00 per hour	
Variance—unfavorable . .	$ .20 per hour × actual time, 7,900 hours . . .	1,580
Total direct labor cost variance—unfavorable		$ 780

The control of direct labor cost is often in the hands of production supervisors. To aid them, daily or weekly reports analyzing the cause of any direct labor variance may be prepared. A comparison of standard direct labor hours and actual direct labor hours will provide the basis for an investigation into the efficiency of direct labor (time variance). A comparison of the rates paid for direct labor with the standard rates highlights the efficiency of the supervisors or the personnel department in selecting the proper grade of direct labor for production (rate variance).

Some of the difficulties encountered in allocating factory overhead costs among products manufactured have been considered in earlier chapters. These difficulties stem from the great variety of costs that are included in factory overhead and their nature as indirect costs. For the same reasons, the procedures used in determining standards and variances for factory overhead cost are more complex than those used for direct materials cost and direct labor cost.

A flexible budget is used to establish the standard factory overhead rate and to aid in determining subsequent variations from standard. The standard rate is determined by dividing what the factory overhead costs should be by the standard amount of productive activity, generally expressed in direct labor hours, direct labor cost, or machine hours. A flexible budget showing the standard factory overhead rate for a month is as follows:

FACTORY
OVERHEAD COST
BUDGET
INDICATING
STANDARD
FACTORY
OVERHEAD RATE

W. Ballard and Company
Factory Overhead Cost Budget
For Month Ending June 30, 19--

	80%	90%	100%	110%
Percent of normal productive capacity	80%	90%	100%	110%
Direct labor hours	8,000	9,000	10,000	11,000
Budgeted factory overhead:				
Variable cost:				
Indirect factory wages	$12,800	$14,400	$16,000	$17,600
Power and light	5,600	6,300	7,000	7,700
Indirect materials	3,200	3,600	4,000	4,400
Maintenance	2,400	2,700	3,000	3,300
Total variable cost	$24,000	$27,000	$30,000	$33,000
Fixed cost:				
Supervisory salaries	$ 5,500	$ 5,500	$ 5,500	$ 5,500
Depreciation of plant and equipment ...	4,500	4,500	4,500	4,500
Insurance and property taxes	2,000	2,000	2,000	2,000
Total fixed cost	$12,000	$12,000	$12,000	$12,000
Total factory overhead cost	$36,000	$39,000	$42,000	$45,000
Factory overhead rate per direct labor hour ($42,000 ÷ 10,000)....			$4.20	

The standard factory overhead cost rate is determined on the basis of the projected factory overhead costs at 100% of normal productive capacity, where this level of capacity represents the general expectation of business activity under normal operating conditions. In the illustration, the standard factory overhead rate is $4.20 per direct labor hour. This rate can be subdivided into $3 per hour for variable factory overhead ($30,000 ÷ 10,000 hours) and $1.20 per hour for fixed factory overhead ($12,000 ÷ 10,000 hours).

Variances from standard for factory overhead cost result (1) from operating at a level above or below 100% of normal capacity and (2) from incurring a total amount of factory overhead cost greater or less than the amount budgeted for the level of operations achieved. The first factor results in the volume variance, which is a measure of the penalty of operating at less than 100% of normal productive capacity or the benefit from operating at a level above 100% of normal productive capacity. The second factor results in the controllable variance, which is the difference between the actual amount of factory overhead incurred and the amount of factory overhead budgeted for the level of production achieved during the period. To illustrate, assume that the standard cost and actual cost of factory overhead for the production of 10,000 units of Product X during June were as follows:

Standard:	8,000 hours at $4.20		$33,600
Actual:	Variable factory overhead.	$24,600	
	Fixed factory overhead	12,000	36,600

The unfavorable factory overhead cost variance of $3,000 is made up of a volume variance and a controllable variance, determined as follows:

<table>
<tr><td rowspan="12">FACTORY
OVERHEAD COST
VARIANCE</td><td colspan="3">Volume variance:</td></tr>
<tr><td>Normal productive capacity of 100%. . . . .</td><td>10,000 hours</td><td></td></tr>
<tr><td>Standard for product produced . . . .</td><td>8,000 hours</td><td></td></tr>
<tr><td>Productive capacity not used . . . .</td><td>2,000 hours</td><td></td></tr>
<tr><td>Standard fixed factory overhead cost rate . . . .</td><td>× $1.20</td><td></td></tr>
<tr><td>Variance — unfavorable. . . . .</td><td></td><td>$2,400</td></tr>
<tr><td>Controllable variance:</td><td></td><td></td></tr>
<tr><td>Actual factory overhead cost incurred . . . .</td><td>$36,600</td><td></td></tr>
<tr><td>Budgeted factory overhead for standard product produced. .</td><td>36,000</td><td></td></tr>
<tr><td>Variance — unfavorable. . . . .</td><td></td><td>600</td></tr>
<tr><td>Total factory overhead cost variance — unfavorable . . . .</td><td></td><td>$3,000</td></tr>
</table>

Volume Variance

When the amount of the volume variance is determined, the productive capacity not used (or the productive capacity used in excess of 100%) is multiplied by the standard fixed factory overhead cost rate. In the illustration, the 2,000 hours of idle productive capacity is multiplied by $1.20, the standard fixed factory overhead cost rate. The $2,400 unfavorable volume variance can be viewed as the cost of the available but unused productive capacity.

The variable portion of the factory overhead cost rate was ignored in determining the volume variance. Variable factory overhead costs vary with the level of production. Thus, a curtailment of production should be accompanied by a comparable reduction of such costs. On the other hand, fixed factory overhead costs are not affected by changes in the volume of production. The fixed factory overhead costs represent the costs of providing the capacity for production, and the volume variance measures the amount of the fixed factory overhead cost due to the variance between capacity used and 100% of capacity.

The idle time that resulted in a volume variance may be due to such factors as failure to maintain an even flow of work, machine breakdowns or repairs causing work stoppages, and failure to obtain enough sales orders to keep the factory operating at full capacity. Management should determine the causes of the idle time and should take corrective action. A volume variance caused by failure of supervisors to maintain an even flow of work, for example, can be remedied. Volume variances caused by lack of sales orders may be corrected through increased advertising or other sales effort, or it may be advisable to develop other means of using the excess plant capacity.

Controllable Variance

The amount and the direction of the controllable variance show the degree of efficiency in keeping the factory overhead costs within the limits established by the budget. Most of the controllable variance is related to the cost of the variable factory overhead items because generally there is little or no variation in the costs incurred for the fixed factory overhead items. Therefore, responsibility for the control of this variance generally rests with department supervisors.

In the illustration, the standard direct labor hours for the product manufactured during June was 8,000, which represents 80% of normal productive capacity. According to the factory overhead cost budget on page 696, the overhead budgeted at this level of production is $36,000. The excess of the $36,600 of overhead costs actually incurred over the $36,000 budgeted yields the unfavorable controllable variance of $600.

Reporting Factory Overhead Cost Variance

The best means of presenting standard factory overhead cost variance data is through a factory overhead cost variance report. Such a report, illustrated on page 699, can present both the controllable variance and the volume variance in a format that pinpoints the causes of the variances and aids in placing the responsibility for control.

The variance in many of the individual cost items in factory overhead can be subdivided into quantity and price variances, as were the variances in direct materials and direct labor. For example, the indirect factory wages variance may include both time and rate variances and the indirect materials variance may be made up of both a quantity variance and a price variance.

The foregoing brief introduction to analysis of factory overhead cost variance suggests the many difficulties that may be encountered in actual practice. The rapid increase of automation in factory operations has been accompanied by in-

FACTORY
OVERHEAD COST
VARIANCE REPORT

W. Ballard and Company
Factory Overhead Cost Variance Report
For Month Ended June 30, 19--

Normal production capacity for the month................ 10,000 hours
Actual production for the month........................ 8,000 hours

	Budget	Actual	Variances Favorable	Variances Unfavorable
Variable cost:				
Indirect factory wages	$12,800	$13,020		$ 220
Power and light	5,600	5,550	$50	
Indirect materials..................	3,200	3,630		430
Maintenance......................	2,400	2,400		
Total variable cost..............	$24,000	$24,600		
Fixed cost:				
Supervisory salaries	$ 5,500	$ 5,500		
Depreciation of plant and equipment...	4,500	4,500		
Insurance and property taxes........	2,000	2,000		
Total fixed cost..................	$12,000	$12,000		
Total factory overhead cost...........	$36,000	$36,600		
Total controllable variances...........			$50	$ 650

Net controllable variance—unfavorable........................... $ 600
Volume variance—unfavorable:
  Idle hours at the standard rate for fixed factory overhead—
  2,000 × $1.20... 2,400
Total factory overhead cost variance—unfavorable $3,000

creased attention to factory overhead costs. The use of predetermined standards and the analysis of variances from such standards provides management with the best possible means of establishing responsibility and controlling factory overhead costs.

STANDARDS IN THE ACCOUNTS

Although standard costs can be used solely as a statistical device apart from the ledger, it is generally considered preferable to incorporate them in the accounts. One approach, when this plan is used, is to debit the work in process account for the actual cost of direct materials, direct labor, and factory overhead entering into production. The same account is credited for the standard cost of the product completed and transferred to the finished goods account. The balance remaining in the work in process account is then made up of the ending inventory of work in process and the variances of actual cost from standard cost. In the following illustrative accounts, there is assumed to be no ending inventory of work in process. The balance in the account is the sum of the variances (unfavorable) between standard and actual costs.

ACCOUNT WORK IN PROCESS   ACCOUNT NO.

Date		Item	Debit	Credit	Balance	
					Debit	Credit
June	30	Direct materials (actual)	21,424		21,424	
	30	Direct labor (actual)	64,780		86,204	
	30	Factory overhead (actual)	36,600		122,804	
	30	Units finished (standard)		117,600		
	30	Balance (variances)			5,204	

ACCOUNT FINISHED GOODS   ACCOUNT NO.

Date		Item	Debit	Credit	Balance	
					Debit	Credit
June	1	Inventory (standard)			88,800	
	30	Units finished (standard)	117,600		206,400	
	30	Units sold (standard)		113,500	92,900	

Variances from standard costs are usually not reported to stockholders and others outside of management. However, it is customary to disclose the variances on income statements prepared for management. An interim monthly income statement prepared for internal use is illustrated as follows:

W. Ballard and Company
Income Statement
For Month Ended June 30, 19--

	Favorable	Unfavorable	
Sales			$185,400
Cost of goods sold—at standard.			113,500
Gross profit—at standard			$ 71,900
Less variances from standard cost:			
Direct materials quantity		$ 600	
Direct materials price.		824	
Direct labor time.	$800		
Direct labor rate		1,580	
Factory overhead volume		2,400	
Factory overhead controllable		600	5,204
Gross profit			$ 66,696
Operating expenses:			
Selling expenses.		$22,500	
General expenses		19,225	41,725
Income before income tax			$ 24,971

At the end of the fiscal year, the variances from standard are usually transferred to the cost of goods sold account. However, if the variances are significant or if many of the products manufactured are still on hand, the variances should be allocated to the work in process, finished goods, and cost of goods sold accounts. The result of such an allocation is to convert these account balances from standard cost to actual cost.

1. The budget that summarizes future plans for acquisition of plant facilities and equipment is the:
   A. cash budget
   B. sales budget
   C. capital expenditures budget
   D. none of the above

2. The system that "builds in" the effect of fluctuations in volume of activity into the various budgets is termed:
   A. budget performance reporting
   B. continuous budgeting
   C. flexible budgeting
   D. none of the above

3. The standard and actual direct materials cost for producing a specified quantity of product is as follows:

   Standard: 50,000 pounds at $5.00 . . . . $250,000
   Actual: 51,000 pounds at $5.05 257,550

   The direct materials price variance is:
   A. $2,500 unfavorable
   B. $2,550 unfavorable
   C. $7,550 unfavorable
   D. none of the above

4. The standard and actual factory overhead cost for producing a specified quantity of product is as follows:

   Standard: 19,000 hours at $6 ($4 variable and $2 fixed). . . . $114,000
   Actual: Variable factory overhead. $72,500
              Fixed factory overhead 40,000   112,500

   If 1,000 hours of productive capacity were unused, the factory overhead volume variance would be:
   A. $1,500 favorable
   B. $2,000 unfavorable
   C. $4,000 unfavorable
   D. none of the above

5. Variances from standard costs are reported on interim income statements as:
   A. selling expenses
   B. general expenses
   C. other expenses
   D. none of the above

Discussion Questions

1. What is a budget?

2. (a) Name the two basic functions of management in which accounting is involved. (b) How does a budget aid management in the discharge of these basic functions?

3. What is a budget performance report?

4. What is meant by *continuous budgeting*?

5. Why should all levels of management and all departments participate in the preparation and submission of budget estimates?

6. Which budgetary concept requires all levels of management to start from zero and estimate sales, production, and other operating data as though the operations were being initiated for the first time?

7. Why should the production requirements as set forth in the production budget be carefully coordinated with the sales budget?

8. Why should the timing of direct materials purchases be closely coordinated with the production budget?

9. What is a capital expenditures budget?

10. (a) Discuss the purpose of the cash budget. (b) If the cash budget for the first quarter of the fiscal year indicates excess cash at the end of each of the first two months, how might the excess cash be used?

11. What is a flexible budget?

12. Which of the following costs incurred by a manufacturing enterprise tend to be fixed and which tend to be variable: (a) rent on factory building, (b) cost of raw materials entering into finished product, (c) depreciation on factory building, (d) real estate taxes on factory building, (e) salary of factory superintendent, (f) direct labor, (g) factory supplies?

13. What is a semivariable (or semifixed) cost?

14. Haas Corporation uses flexible budgets. For each of the following variable operating expenses, indicate whether there has been a saving or an excess of expenses, assuming that actual sales were $400,000.

Expense Item	Actual Amount	Budget Allowance Based on Sales
Factory supplies expense	$ 7,850	2%
Uncollectible accounts expense	17,840	4%

15. What are the basic objectives in the use of standard costs?

16. As the term is used in reference to standard costs, what is a *variance*?

17. What is meant by reporting by the "principle of exceptions" as the term is used in reference to cost control?

18. (a) What are the two types of variances between actual cost and standard cost for direct materials? (b) Discuss some possible causes of these variances.

19. (a) What are the two types of variances between actual cost and standard cost for direct labor? (b) Who generally has control over the direct labor cost?

20. (a) Describe the two variances between actual costs and standard costs for factory overhead. (b) What is a factory overhead cost variance report?

Exercises

Exercise 24-1. Kipling Company manufactures two models of heating pads, HP-1 and HP-2. Based on the following production and sales data for April of the current year, prepare (a) a sales budget and (b) a production budget.

	HP-1	HP-2
Estimated inventory (units), April 1	30,000	13,800
Desired inventory (units), April 30	36,000	12,000
Expected sales volume (units):		
Area 20	21,000	5,400
Area 30	10,800	2,400
Unit sales price	$9.60	$13.20

Exercise 24-2. Humphreys Company uses flexible budgets. Prepare a flexible operating expenses budget for February of the current year for sales volumes of $400,000, $500,000, and $600,000, based on the following data:

Sales commissions	9% of sales
Advertising expense	$20,000 for $400,000 of sales
	$24,000 for $500,000 of sales
	$28,000 for $600,000 of sales
Miscellaneous selling expense	$2,000 plus 1% of sales
Office salaries expense	$18,600
Office supplies expense	1½% of sales
Miscellaneous general expense	$850 plus 1% of sales

Exercise 24-3. The operating expenses incurred during February of the current year by Humphreys Company were as follows:

Sales commissions	$46,500
Advertising expense	22,000
Miscellaneous selling expense	7,200
Office salaries expense	18,600
Office supplies expense	8,100
Miscellaneous general expense	5,600

Assuming that the total sales for February were $500,000, prepare a budget performance report for operating expenses on the basis of the data presented above and in Exercise 24-2.

Exercise 24-4. The following data relating to direct materials cost for June of the current year are taken from the records of D. J. Drury Company:

Quantity of direct materials used	28 000 kilograms
Unit cost of direct materials	$2 per kilogram
Units of finished product manufactured	10,100 units
Standard direct materials per unit of finished product . . .	2.5 kilograms
Direct materials quantity variance—unfavorable	$5,720
Direct materials price variance—favorable	$2,240

Determine the standard direct materials cost per unit of finished product, assuming that there was no inventory of work in process at either the beginning or the end of the month. Present your computations.

Exercise 24-5. Standard costs and actual costs for direct materials, direct labor, and factory overhead incurred for the manufacture of 3,000 units of product were as follows:

	Standard Costs	Actual Costs
Direct materials	3,000 pounds at $20	2,900 pounds at $21.50
Direct labor	4,500 hours at $12	4,800 hours at $12.50
Factory overhead	Rates per direct labor hour, based on normal capacity of 5,000 labor hours:	
	Variable cost, $4.20	$20,500 variable cost
	Fixed cost, $2.80	$14,000 fixed cost

Determine (a) the quantity variance, price variance, and total direct materials cost variance; (b) the time variance, rate variance, and total direct labor cost variance; and (c) the volume variance, controllable variance, and total factory overhead cost variance.

Exercise 24-6. Wade Company prepared the following factory overhead cost budget for Department I for June of the current year. The company expected to operate the department at normal capacity of 20,000 direct labor hours.

Variable cost:		
Indirect factory wages	$18,000	
Power and light	15,300	
Indirect materials	5,400	
Total variable cost		$38,700
Fixed cost:		
Supervisory salaries	$14,850	
Depreciation of plant and equipment	7,300	
Insurance and property taxes	5,850	
Total fixed cost		28,000
Total factory overhead cost		$66,700

During June, the department was operated for 15,000 direct labor hours, and the factory overhead costs incurred were: indirect factory wages, $13,600; power and light, $11,200; indirect materials, $4,250; supervisory salaries, $14,850; depreciation of plant and equipment, $7,300; and insurance and property taxes, $5,850.

Prepare a standard factory overhead variance report for June. To be useful for cost control, the budgeted amounts should be based on 15,000 direct labor hours.

Exercise 24-7. Prepare an income statement for presentation to management, using the following data from the records of Briscoe Company for July of the current year:

Cost of goods sold (at standard)	$277,770
Direct materials quantity variance — favorable	1,860
Direct materials price variance — favorable	2,550
Direct labor time variance — favorable	690
Direct labor rate variance — unfavorable	2,535
Factory overhead volume variance — unfavorable	3,000

(continued)

Factory overhead controllable variance—favorable	$ 1,140
General expenses	16,290
Sales	362,700
Selling expenses	29,970

Problems
(Problems in Appendix B: 24-1B, 24-3B, 24-4B.)

Problem 24-1A. Grant Company prepared the following factory overhead cost budget for the Sanding Department for April of the current year:

Grant Company
Factory Overhead Cost Budget—Sanding Department
For Month Ending April 30, 19--

Direct labor hours:		
Normal productive capacity		18,000
Hours budgeted		15,300
Variable cost:		
Indirect factory wages	$20,060	
Indirect materials	14,280	
Power and light	5,440	
Total variable cost		$39,780
Fixed cost:		
Supervisory salaries	$18,300	
Indirect factory wages	12,100	
Depreciation of plant and equipment	8,100	
Insurance	6,800	
Power and light	5,450	
Property taxes	3,250	
Total fixed cost		54,000
Total factory overhead cost		$93,780

Instructions:

(1) Prepare a flexible budget for April, indicating capacities of 13,500, 15,300, 18,000, and 21,600 direct labor hours and the determination of a standard factory overhead rate per direct labor hour.

(2) Prepare a standard factory overhead cost variance report for April. The Sanding Department was operated for 15,300 direct labor hours and the following factory overhead costs were incurred:

Indirect factory wages	$32,600
Supervisory salaries	18,300
Indirect materials	13,950
Power and light	11,200
Depreciation of plant and equipment	8,100
Insurance	6,800
Property taxes	3,250
Total factory overhead cost incurred	$94,200

Problem 24-2A. The budget director of Feinberg Company requests estimates of sales, production, and other operating data from the various administrative units every month. Selected information concerning sales and production for March of the current year are summarized as follows:

(a) Estimated sales for March by sales territory:
   East:
   Product P1 . . . . 10,000 units at $75 per unit
   Product P2 . . . . 12,000 units at $88 per unit
   Midwest:
   Product P1 . . . . 8,000 units at $75 per unit
   Product P2 . . . . 11,500 units at $88 per unit
   West:
   Product P1 . . . . 14,000 units at $75 per unit
   Product P2 . . . . 18,000 units at $88 per unit

(b) Estimated inventories at March 1:
   Direct materials:
   Material E: 10,600 lbs.
   Material F: 9,200 lbs.
   Material G: 4,800 lbs.
   Material H: 11,500 lbs.
   Finished products:
   Product P1:   4,000 units
   Product P2:   7,100 units

(c) Desired inventories at March 31:
   Direct materials:
   Material E: 12,000 lbs.
   Material F: 8,000 lbs.
   Material G: 5,000 lbs.
   Material H: 10,000 lbs.
   Finished products:
   Product P1:   5,000 units
   Product P2:   6,000 units

(d) Direct materials used in production:
   In manufacture of Product P1:
   Material E: 3.0 lbs. per unit of product
   Material F: 1.6 lbs. per unit of product
   Material G: 2.2 lbs. per unit of product
   In manufacture of Product P2:
   Material E: 1.5 lbs. per unit of product
   Material F: 1.0 lbs. per unit of product
   Material H: 3.0 lbs. per unit of product

(e) Anticipated purchase price for direct materials:
   Material E: $ .45 per lb.
   Material F: $1.80 per lb.
   Material G: $ .80 per lb.
   Material H: $ .75 per lb.

(f) Direct labor requirements:
   Product P1:
      Department 10: 1.0 hour at $12 per hour
      Department 20: 1.5 hours at $15 per hour
   Product P2:
      Department 10: 2.0 hours at $12 per hour
      Department 30: 1.5 hours at $18 per hour

Instructions:

   (1) Prepare a sales budget for March.
   (2) Prepare a production budget for March.
   (3) Prepare a direct materials purchases budget for March.
   (4) Prepare a direct labor cost budget for March.

Problem 24-3A. Delwood Inc. maintains perpetual inventory accounts for materials, work in process, and finished goods and uses a standard cost system based on the following data:

	Standard Cost per Unit
Direct materials: 2 kilograms at $3.50 per kg...........	$ 7
Direct labor: 4 hours at $17.50 per hr.................	70
Factory overhead: $1.50 per direct labor hour...........	6
Total..	$83

There was no inventory of work in process at the beginning or end of October, the first month of the current fiscal year. The transactions relating to production completed during October are summarized as follows:
   (a) Materials purchased on account, $62,480.
   (b) Direct materials used, $55,025. This represented 15 500 kilograms at $3.55 per kilogram.
   (c) Direct labor paid, $560,700. This represented 31,500 hours at $17.80 per hour. There were no accruals at either the beginning or the end of the period.
   (d) Factory overhead incurred during the month was composed of depreciation on plant and equipment, $18,650; indirect labor, $14,300; insurance, $8,000; and miscellaneous factory costs, $9,550. The indirect labor and miscellaneous factory costs were paid during the period, and the insurance represents an expiration of prepaid insurance. Of the total factory overhead of $50,500, fixed costs amounted to $27,200 and variable costs were $23,300.
   (e) Goods finished during the period, 8,000 units.

Instructions:

   (1) Prepare entries in general journal form to record the transactions, assuming that the work in process account is debited for actual production costs and credited with standard costs for goods finished.
   (2) Prepare a T account for Work in Process and post to the account, using the identifying letters as dates.
   (3) Prepare schedules of variances for direct materials cost, direct labor cost, and factory overhead cost. Normal productive capacity for the plant is 34,000 direct labor hours.
   (4) Total the amount of the standard cost variances and compare this total with the balance of the work in process account.

Problem 24-4A. The treasurer of Epstein Company instructs you to prepare a monthly cash budget for the next three months. You are presented with the following budget information:

	August	September	October
Sales	$480,000	$450,000	$510,000
Manufacturing costs	284,000	230,000	288,000
Operating expenses	162,000	150,000	176,000
Capital expenditures	——	200,000	——

The company expects to sell about 30% of its merchandise for cash. Of sales on account, 80% are expected to be collected in full in the month following the sale and the remainder the following month. Depreciation, insurance, and property taxes represent $12,000 of the estimated monthly manufacturing costs and $4,000 of the probable monthly operating expenses. Insurance and property taxes are paid in June and December respectively. Of the remainder of the manufacturing costs and operating expenses, 60% are expected to be paid in the month in which they are incurred and the balance in the following month.

Current assets as of August 1 are composed of cash of $58,500, marketable securities of $50,000, and accounts receivable of $474,500 ($383,500 from July sales and $91,000 from June sales). Current liabilities as of August 1 are composed of an $80,000, 15%, 120-day note payable due September 15, $82,500 of accounts payable incurred in July for manufacturing costs, and accrued liabilities of $48,200 incurred in July for operating expenses.

It is expected that $1,800 in dividends will be received in August. An estimated income tax payment of $26,000 will be made in October. Epstein Company's regular semiannual dividend of $15,000 is expected to be declared in September and paid in October. Management desires to maintain a minimum cash balance of $50,000.

Instructions:
  (1) Prepare a monthly cash budget for August, September, and October.
  (2) On the basis of the cash budget prepared in (1), what recommendation should be made to the treasurer?

Problem 24-5A. As a preliminary to requesting budget estimates of sales, costs, and expenses for the fiscal year beginning January 1, 1984, the following tentative trial balance as of December 31 of the preceding year is prepared by the accounting department of Bromley Company:

Cash	58,000	
Accounts Receivable	56,000	
Finished Goods	102,200	
Work in Process	59,200	
Materials	34,800	
Prepaid Expenses	6,800	
Plant and Equipment	540,000	
Accumulated Depreciation—Plant and Equipment		216,000
Accounts Payable		66,000
Notes Payable		40,000
Common Stock, $10 par		100,000
Retained Earnings		435,000
	857,000	857,000

Factory output and sales for 1984 are expected to total 40,000 units of product, which are to be sold at $18 per unit. The quantities and costs of the inventories (lifo method) at December 31, 1984, are expected to remain unchanged from the balances at the beginning of the year.

Budget estimates of manufacturing costs and operating expenses for the year are summarized as follows:

| | Estimated Costs and Expenses | |
	Fixed (Total for Year)	Variable (Per Unit Sold)
Cost of goods manufactured and sold:		
Direct materials	——	$2.30
Direct labor	——	5.60
Factory overhead:		
Depreciation of plant and equipment	$28,800	——
Other factory overhead.........................	19,200	1.70
Selling expenses:		
Sales salaries and commissions..................	40,000	.90
Advertising	20,500	——
Miscellaneous selling expense....................	1,500	.10
General expenses:		
Office and officers salaries	50,000	.40
Supplies..	3,400	.10
Miscellaneous general expense..................	2,600	.05

Balances of accounts receivable, prepaid expenses, and accounts payable at the end of the year are expected to differ from the beginning balances by only inconsequential amounts.

For purposes of this problem, assume that federal income tax of $24,000 on 1984 taxable income will be paid during 1984. Regular quarterly cash dividends of $.20 a share are expected to be declared and paid in March, June, September, and December. It is anticipated that plant and equipment will be purchased for $125,000 cash in September.

Instructions:

  (1) Prepare a budgeted income statement for 1984 in multiple-step form.

  (2) Prepare a budgeted balance sheet as of December 31, 1984, in report form.

Mini-Case   Daughtrey Company operates a plant in Mountain View, Missouri, where you have been assigned as the new cost analyst. To familiarize yourself with your new responsibilities, you have gathered the cost variance data for October, shown on the following page. During October, 30,600 units of product were manufactured.

Factory Overhead Cost Variance Report

Normal production capacity for the month .... 18,000 hours
Standard for product produced during month .... 15,300 hours

	Budget	Actual	Favorable	Unfavorable
Variable cost:				
Indirect factory wages	$ 22,185	$ 22,600		$ 415
Power and light	42,840	42,590	$250	
Indirect materials.................	7,650	8,000		350
Maintenance......................	5,355	5,500		145
Total variable cost..............	$ 78,030	$ 78,690		
Fixed cost:				
Supervisory salaries	$ 32,500	$ 32,500		
Depreciation of plant and equipment ..	8,500	8,500		
Insurance and property taxes	2,200	2,200		
Total fixed cost	$ 43,200	$ 43,200		
Total factory overhead cost...........	$121,230	$121,890		
Total controllable variances			$250	$ 910

Net controllable variance—unfavorable .... $ 660
Volume variance—unfavorable:
  Idle hours at the standard rate for
    fixed factory overhead—2,700 × $2.40 6,480
Total factory overhead cost variance—unfavorable **$7,140**

Direct Materials Cost Variance

Quantity variance:
  Actual quantity .... 48,300 pounds
  Standard quantity........... 45,900 pounds
    Variance—unfavorable.... 2,400 pounds × standard price, $1.40.... $ 3,360
Price variance:
  Actual price................ $1.60 per pound
  Standard price .... 1.40 per pound
    Variance—unfavorable.... $ .20 per pound × actual quantity, 48,300.. 9,660
Total direct materials cost variance—unfavorable **$13,020**

Direct Labor Cost Variance

Time variance:
  Actual time................. 15,450 hours
  Standard time .... 15,300 hours
    Variance—unfavorable.... 150 hours × standard rate, $16 .... $ 2,400
Rate variance:
  Standard rate .... $16.00 per hour
  Actual rate................. 15.60 per hour
    Variance—favorable...... $ .40 per hour × actual hours, 15,450.... 6,180
Total direct labor cost variance—favorable .... **$ 3,780**

After your review of the October cost variance data, you arranged a meeting with the factory superintendent to discuss manufacturing operations. During this meeting, the factory superintendent made the following comment:

"Why do you have to compute a factory overhead volume variance? I don't have any control over the level of operations. I can only control costs for the level of production at which I am told to operate. Why not just eliminate the volume variance from the factory overhead cost variance report?"

You next discussed the direct materials variance analyses with the purchasing department manager, who made the following comment:

"The materials price variance is computed incorrectly. The computations should be actual price minus standard price times the standard quantity of materials for the product produced. By multiplying the difference in the actual and standard price by the actual quantity of materials used, my department is being penalized for the inefficiencies of the production department."

During November, the standard costs were not changed, normal productive capacity was 18,000 hours, and the following data were taken from the records for the production of 24,000 units of product:

Quantity of direct materials used	37,900 pounds
Cost of direct materials.	$ 1.62 per pound
Quantity of direct labor used	12,260 hours
Cost of direct labor	$15.70 per hour
Factory overhead costs:	
Power and light.	$33,520
Supervisory salaries	32,500
Indirect factory wages	18,100
Depreciation of plant and equipment	8,500
Indirect materials	6,940
Maintenance	4,250
Insurance and property taxes	2,200

Instructions:
(1) Prepare a factory overhead cost variance report for November.
(2) Determine (a) the quantity variance, price variance, and total direct materials cost variance, and (b) the time variance, rate variance, and total direct labor cost variance for November.
(3) Based upon the cost variances for October and November, what areas of operations would you investigate and why?
(4) How would you respond to the comments of the factory superintendent?
(5) How would you respond to the comments of the manager of the purchasing department?

25

CHAPTER

Cost and Revenue Concepts for Management

CHAPTER OBJECTIVES

Describe the importance of accounting in providing data that management can use in studying and resolving current problems and making plans for the future.

Describe some alternative concepts of cost and revenue that are useful to management in making decisions.

Illustrate uses of alternative concepts of cost and revenue in managerial decision making.

PART 8 | Decision Making

25

CHAPTER

One of the main objectives of accounting is the determination of net income. For this purpose, costs are classified either as assets or as expenses. The costs of properties and prepaid services owned at any time represent assets. As the assets are sold or used, they become expenses. This concept of cost has been explored in detail in earlier chapters. Various criteria for determining when revenues should be recognized and reported in the income statement have also been discussed.

Another important objective of accounting is to provide data that management can use in studying and resolving current problems and making plans for the future. For any particular business problem or proposed project, there may be several possible courses of action, only one of which can be selected. Much of the analysis of alternatives concerns costs and revenues. Useful data on past costs and revenues may be available in the ledger, but data relevant to some situations, particularly those related to proposed new projects, cannot always be found there. In any case, the record of past events alone is usually not an adequate basis for a decision affecting the future. This chapter considers the application of revenue and cost concepts to decision making.

HISTORICAL COST AND REPLACEMENT COST

Used broadly, the term "cost" means the amount of money or other property expended, or liability or other obligation incurred, for goods or services purchased. References to the amount of property expended or liability incurred for goods or services acquired may be expressed by the shorter phrase "cash or equivalent." Time is important in discussions of cost, often requiring the use of the adjective "historical" or "replacement."

Historical cost is the cash or equivalent outlay for goods or services actually acquired. Another term, **actual cost,** is often used when comparisons with estimated or standard cost are made. Historical costs are recorded in the ledgers and other basic accounting records. The expired portions are reported as expenses in the income statement and the unexpired portions are reported as assets in the balance sheet. Historical costs are relevant in determining periodic net income and current financial status, but they may be of little, if any, importance in planning for the future.

Replacement cost is the cost of replacing an asset at current market prices. In many planning situations, the cost of replacing an asset is of greater significance than its historical cost. To illustrate, assume that an offer is received for goods to be manufactured at a certain price. Assume also that there are enough unprocessed materials in stock that were acquired at a much higher cost than current market prices. A decision to accept the offer depends upon the replacement cost of the materials. It might be advisable to accept the offer even though, on the basis of historical costs, a loss is likely to result.

Replacement cost analysis is also useful in planning the replacement of worn-out or obsolete plant assets. The cost of the replacement asset is likely to differ from the cost of the original asset, in part because of changes in price levels. In addition, because of technological improvements and other changes in physical characteristics, a new plant asset is usually not the same as the asset it replaces.

It is often useful to compare annual depreciation expense based on historical cost with depreciation based on estimated replacement cost. The difference between the two represents the estimated amount of operating income that should be retained in order to maintain the productive capacity of the physical plant. If, for example, depreciation expense recorded for the year is $120,000 and depreciation based on estimated replacement cost is $200,000, it may be wise for the board of directors to authorize an $80,000 appropriation of retained earnings for "replacement of facilities." In any event, management should realize that if the replacement of facilities is not to be financed in part by earnings, it may be necessary to issue more stock or debt obligations.

The significance of replacement cost, adjusted for depreciation, in the admission or the withdrawal of a partner was discussed in an earlier chapter. Similar analyses play an important role in negotiations for the purchase and sale of a going business and in the merging of two separate enterprises. In such cases, the values finally placed on plant assets are greatly influenced by the bargaining process, but consideration of replacement cost is often the starting point.

ABSORPTION COSTING AND VARIABLE COSTING

The cost of manufactured products consists of direct materials, direct labor, and factory overhead. All such costs become a part of the finished goods inventory and remain there as an asset until the goods are sold. This conventional treatment of manufacturing costs is sometimes called absorption costing because all costs are "absorbed" into finished goods. Although the concept is necessary in determining historical costs and taxable income, another costing concept may be more useful to management in making decisions.

In variable costing, which is also termed **direct costing**, the cost of products manufactured is composed only of those manufacturing costs that increase or decrease as the volume of production rises or falls. According to this point of view, the cost of finished goods includes, in addition to direct materials and direct labor, only those factory overhead costs which vary with the rate of production. The remaining factory overhead costs, which are the nonvariable or fixed items, are related to the productive capacity of the manufacturing plant and are not affected by changes in the quantity of product manufactured. Accordingly, the nonvariable factory overhead does not become a part of the costs of finished goods but is considered to be an expense of the period.

VARIABLE COSTING AND THE INCOME STATEMENT

The arrangement of data in the variable costing income statement differs considerably from the format of the conventional income statement. Variable costs and expenses are presented separately from fixed costs and expenses, with significant summarizing amounts inserted at intermediate points. As a basis for illustrating the differences between the two forms, assume the following information:

	Total Cost or Expense	Number of Units	Unit Cost
Manufacturing costs:			
Variable..........................	$375,000	15,000	$25
Fixed..............................	150,000	15,000	10
Total............................	$525,000		$35
Selling and general expenses:			
Variable..........................	$ 60,000		
Fixed..............................	50,000		
Total............................	$110,000		

The two income statements prepared from this information are as follows. The computations in parentheses are shown as an aid to understanding.

Absorption Costing Income Statement		
Sales...		$600,000
Cost of goods sold:		
Cost of goods manufactured (15,000 × $35)........	$525,000	
Less ending inventory (3,000 × $35)..............	105,000	
Cost of goods sold...........................		420,000
Gross profit.................................		$180,000
Selling and general expenses ($60,000 + $50,000)....		110,000
Income from operations.........................		$ 70,000

Variable Costing Income Statement		
Sales...		$600,000
Variable cost of goods sold:		
Variable cost of goods manufactured (15,000 × $25) .	$375,000	
Less ending inventory (3,000 × $25)..............	75,000	
Variable cost of goods sold....................		300,000
Manufacturing margin..........................		$300,000
Variable selling and general expenses..............		60,000
Contribution margin...........................		$240,000
Fixed costs and expenses:		
Fixed manufacturing costs......................	$150,000	
Fixed selling and general expenses...............	50,000	200,000
Income from operations.........................		$ 40,000

The absorption costing income statement does not distinguish between variable and fixed costs and expenses. All manufacturing costs incurred are included in the cost of finished goods. The deduction of the cost of goods sold from sales yields the intermediate amount, gross profit. Deduction of selling and general expenses then yields income from operations.

In contrast, the variable costing income statement includes only the variable manufacturing costs in the cost of goods manufactured and cost of goods sold. Deduction of the cost of goods sold from sales yields an intermediate amount, termed manufacturing margin. Deduction of the variable selling and general expenses yields the contribution margin or **marginal income**. The fixed costs and expenses are then deducted from the contribution margin to yield income from operations.

The $30,000 difference in the amount of income from operations ($70,000 − $40,000) is due to the different treatment of the fixed manufacturing costs. The entire amount of the $150,000 of fixed manufacturing costs is included as an expense of the period in the variable costing statement. The ending inventory in the absorption costing statement includes $30,000 (3,000 × $10) of fixed manufacturing costs. This $30,000, by being included in inventory on hand, is thus excluded from current cost of goods sold and instead is deferred to another period. For any period in which the quantity of inventory at the end of the period is larger than that at the beginning of the period, such as in the illustration, the operating income reported by absorption costing will be larger than the operating income reported by variable costing. When the quantity of the ending inventory is less than the beginning inventory, the effect is reversed; that is, a smaller operating income will be reported if absorption costing is used.

VARIABLE COSTING AS A MANAGERIAL AID

Various concepts of cost and revenue are useful to management in making decisions. Some of them, however, are not acceptable for published financial statements in which the results of operations and financial condition are reported to stockholders, creditors, and others outside the management group. Variable costing is one such concept.[1] Although it cannot be used for published financial statements or generally for federal income tax purposes, variable costing can be very useful to management in making decisions relating to cost control, product pricing, production planning, and other management functions.

Cost Control

All costs are controllable by someone within a business enterprise, but they are not all controllable at the same level of management. For example, plant supervisors, as members of operating management, are responsible for controlling the use of direct materials in their departments. They have no control, however, of the amount of insurance coverage or premium costs related to the buildings housing their departments. For a specific level of management, **controllable costs** are costs that it controls directly, and **uncontrollable costs** are costs that another level of management controls. This distinction, as applied to specific levels of management, is useful in fixing the responsibility for incurrence of costs and then for reporting the cost data to those responsible for cost control.

---

[1] *Accounting Research and Terminology Bulletins — Final Edition*, "No. 43, Restatement and Revision of Accounting Research Bulletins" (New York: American Institute of Certified Public Accountants, 1961), pp. 28–29.

Variable manufacturing costs are controlled at the operating level because the amount of such costs varies with changes in the volume of production. By including only variable manufacturing costs in the cost of the product, variable costing provides a product cost figure that can be controlled by operating management. The fixed factory overhead costs are ordinarily the responsibility of a higher level of management. When the fixed factory overhead costs are reported as a separate item in the variable costing income statement, they are easier to identify and control than when they are spread among units of product as they are under absorption costing.

As is the case with the fixed and variable manufacturing costs, the control of the variable and fixed operating expenses is usually the responsibility of different levels of management. Under variable costing, the variable selling and general expenses are reported in a separate category from the fixed selling and general expenses. Because they are reported in this manner, both types of operating expenses are easier to identify and control than is the case under absorption costing, where they are not reported separately.

Product Pricing

Many factors enter into the determination of the selling price of a product. The cost of making the product is clearly significant. Microeconomic theory deduces, from a set of restrictive assumptions, that income is maximized by expanding output to the volume where the revenue realized by the sale of the final unit (marginal revenue) equals the cost of that unit (marginal cost). Although the degree of exactness assumed in economic theory is rarely attainable, the concepts of marginal revenue and marginal cost are useful in setting selling prices.

In the short run, an enterprise is committed to the existing capacity of its manufacturing facilities. The pricing decision should be based upon making the best use of such capacity. The fixed costs and expenses cannot be avoided, but the variable costs and expenses can be eliminated if the company does not manufacture the product. The selling price of a product, therefore, should at least be equal to the variable costs and expenses of making and selling it. Any price above this minimum selling price contributes an amount toward covering fixed costs and expenses and providing operating income. Variable costing procedures yield data that emphasize these relationships.

In the long run, plant capacity can be increased or decreased. If an enterprise is to continue in business, the selling prices of its products must cover all costs and expenses and provide a reasonable operating income. Hence, in establishing pricing policies for the long run, information provided by absorption costing procedures is needed.

There are no simple solutions to most pricing problems. Consideration must be given to many factors of varying importance. Accounting can contribute by preparing analyses of various pricing plans for both the short run and the long run.

Production Planning

Production planning also has both short-run and long-run implications. In the short run, production is limited to existing capacity, and operating decisions must be made quickly before opportunities are lost. For example, a company manufacturing products with a seasonal demand may have an opportunity to obtain an off-season order that will not interfere with its production schedule nor reduce the sales of its other products. The relevant factors for such a short-run decision are the revenues and the variable costs and expenses. If the revenues from the special order will provide a contribution margin, the order should be accepted because it will increase the company's operating income. For long-run planning, management must also consider the fixed costs and expenses.

Additional Managerial Uses of Variable Costing

To control and plan operations, management needs information on the profitability of the various segments of its business, such as types of products and sales territories. Variable costing makes a significant contribution to management decision making in providing data for effective profit planning in such areas. Two aspects of profit planning are (1) determination of the most profitable sales mix of a company's products and (2) determination of the contribution being made by each sales territory.

Sales Mix Studies

Sales mix is generally defined as the relative distribution of sales among the various products manufactured. Some products are more profitable than others, and management should concentrate its sales efforts on those that will provide the maximum total operating income. Two very important factors that should be determined for each product are (1) the production facilities needed for its manufacture and (2) the amount of contribution margin to be gained from its manufacture.

The following statement is an example of the type of data needed for an evaluation of sales mix. The enterprise, which manufactures two products and is operating at full capacity, is considering whether to change the emphasis of its advertising and other promotional efforts.

CONTRIBUTION MARGIN STATEMENT—UNIT OF PRODUCT

Contribution Margin by Unit of Product
April 15, 19--

	Product A	Product B
Sales price	$6.00	$8.50
Variable cost of goods sold	3.50	5.50
Manufacturing margin	$2.50	$3.00
Variable selling and general expenses	1.00	1.00
Contribution margin	$1.50	$2.00

The statement indicates that Product B yields a greater amount of contribution margin per unit than Product A. Therefore, Product B provides the larger contribution to the recovery of fixed costs and expenses and realization of operating income. If the amount of production facilities used for each product is assumed to be equal, it would be desirable to increase the sales of Product B. However, if it is assumed that Product B requires twice the amount of production facilities that are needed for Product A, the conclusion would be different. Under the latter assumption, the production of one additional unit of Product B would require a decrease of two units of Product A. The effect on the contribution margin would be an increase of $2 (Product B) and a decrease of $3 (Product A), or a net decrease of $1. Under such circumstances, a change in sales mix designed to increase sales of Product A would be desirable.

Sales mix studies are based on assumptions, such as the ability to sell one product in place of another and the ability to convert production facilities to accommodate manufacture of one product instead of another. Proposed changes in the sales mix often affect only small segments of a company's total operations. In such cases, changes in sales mix may be possible within the limits of existing capacity, and the presentation of cost and revenue data in the variable costing form is useful in achieving the most profitable sales mix.

Contribution of Sales Territories

An income statement presenting the contribution margin by sales territories is often useful to management in appraising past performance and in directing future efforts. The following income statement is prepared in such a format, in abbreviated form:

CONTRIBUTION MARGIN STATEMENT— SALES TERRITORIES

<table>
<tr><td colspan="4">Contribution Margin Statement by Sales Territory
For Month Ended July 31, 19--</td></tr>
<tr><td></td><td>Territory A</td><td>Territory B</td><td>Total</td></tr>
<tr><td>Sales ....</td><td>$315,000</td><td>$502,500</td><td>$817,500</td></tr>
<tr><td>Less variable costs and expenses.........</td><td>189,000</td><td>251,250</td><td>440,250</td></tr>
<tr><td>Contribution margin ....</td><td>$126,000</td><td>$251,250</td><td>$377,250</td></tr>
<tr><td>Less fixed costs and expenses...........</td><td></td><td></td><td>242,750</td></tr>
<tr><td>Income from operations ....</td><td></td><td></td><td>$134,500</td></tr>
</table>

In addition to sales volume and contribution margin, the contribution margin ratio (contribution margin ÷ sales) for each territory is useful in comparing sales territories, evaluating performance, and directing operations toward more profitable activities. For Territory A, the ratio is 40% ($126,000 ÷ $315,000); for Territory B, it is 50% ($251,250 ÷ $502,500).

DIFFERENTIAL ANALYSIS

Planning for future operations is chiefly decision making. For some decisions, revenue and cost information drawn from the general ledger and other basic accounting records is very useful. For example, historical cost data in the absorption costing format are helpful in setting pricing policies for the long run. Historical cost data in the variable costing format are useful for pricing decisions affecting the short run. However, the revenue and cost data needed to evaluate courses of future operations or to choose among competing alternatives are often not available in the basic accounting records.

The relevant revenue and cost data in the analysis of future possibilities are the differences between the alternatives under consideration. The amounts of such differences are called **differentials** and the area of accounting concerned with the effect of alternative courses of action on revenues and costs is called differential analysis.

Differential revenue is the amount of increase or decrease in revenue expected from a particular course of action as compared with an alternative. To illustrate, assume that certain equipment is being used to manufacture a product that provides revenue of $150,000. If the equipment could be used to make another product that would provide revenue of $175,000, the differential revenue from the alternative would be $25,000.

Differential cost is the amount of increase or decrease in cost that is expected from a particular course of action as compared with an alternative. For example, if an increase in advertising expenditures from $100,000 to $150,000 is being considered, the differential cost of the action would be $50,000.

Differential analyses can be used advantageously by management in arriving at decisions on a variety of alternatives, such as (1) whether equipment should be leased or sold, (2) whether to accept additional business at a special price, (3) whether to discontinue an unprofitable segment, (4) whether to manufacture or purchase a needed part, (5) whether to replace usable plant assets, (6) whether to expand or contract production capacity, and (7) whether to introduce new products or abandon old products. The following sections relate to the use of differential analysis in analyzing some of these alternatives.

Lease or Sell

The main advantage of differential analysis is its selection of relevant revenues and costs related to alternative courses of action. Differential analysis reports emphasize the significant factors bearing on the decision, help to clarify the issues, and save the time of the reader.

To illustrate, assume that an enterprise is considering the disposal of an item of equipment that is no longer needed in the business. Its original cost is $200,000 and accumulated depreciation to date totals $120,000. A tentative offer has been received to lease the machine for a number of years for a total of $160,000, after which the machine would be sold as scrap for a small amount. The repair, insurance, and property tax expenses during the period of the lease are estimated at $35,000. Alternatively, the equipment can be sold through a broker for $100,000 less a 6% commission. The decision to be made is whether the equipment should be leased or sold. The report of the analysis is as follows:

DIFFERENTIAL ANALYSIS REPORT—LEASE OR SELL

Proposal to Lease or Sell Equipment
June 22, 19--

Differential revenue from alternatives:		
Revenue from lease..................................	$160,000	
Revenue from sale..................................	100,000	
Differential revenue from lease........................		$60,000
Differential cost of alternatives:		
Repair, insurance, and property tax expenses............	$ 35,000	
Commission expense on sale..........................	6,000	
Differential cost of lease..............................		29,000
Net advantage of lease alternative........................		$31,000

It should be noted that it was not necessary to consider the $80,000 book value ($200,000 − $120,000) of the equipment. The $80,000 is a **sunk cost**; that is, it is a cost that will not be affected by later decisions. In the illustration, the expenditure to acquire the equipment had already been made, and the choice is now between leasing or selling the equipment. The relevant factors to be considered are the differential revenues and differential costs associated with the lease or sell decision. The undepreciated cost of the equipment is irrelevant. The validity of the foregoing report can be shown by the following conventional analysis:

Lease alternative:
Revenue from lease..............................		$160,000
Depreciation expense..........................	$80,000	
Repair, insurance, and property tax expenses	35,000	115,000
Net gain.......................................		$45,000
Sell alternative:		
Sale price		$100,000
Book value of equipment........................	$80,000	
Commission expense	6,000	86,000
Net gain.......................................		14,000
Net advantage of lease alternative...................		$31,000

The alternatives presented in the illustration were relatively uncomplicated. Regardless of the number and complexity of the additional factors that may be involved, the approach to differential analysis remains basically the same. Two factors that often need to be considered are (1) the differential revenue from investing the funds generated by the alternatives and (2) the income tax differential. In the example on the preceding page, there would undoubtedly be a differential advantage to the immediate investment of the $94,000 net proceeds from the sale over the investment of the net proceeds from the lease arrangement, which would become available over a period of years. The income tax differential would be that related to the differences in timing of the income from the alternatives and the differences in the amount of investment income.

Acceptance of Business at a Special Price	In determining whether to accept additional business at a special price, management must consider the differential revenue that would be provided and the differential cost that would be incurred. If the company is operating at full capacity, the additional production will increase both fixed and variable production costs. But if the normal production of the company is below full capacity, additional business may be undertaken without increasing fixed production costs. In the latter case, the variable costs will be the differential cost of the additional production. Variable costs are the only costs to be considered in making a decision to accept or reject the order. If the operating expenses are likely to increase, these differentials must also be considered.

To illustrate, assume that the usual monthly production of an enterprise is 10,000 units of a certain commodity. At this level of operation, which is well below capacity, the manufacturing cost is $20 per unit, composed of variable costs of $12.50 and fixed costs of $7.50. The selling price of the product in the domestic market is $30. The manufacturer receives an offer from an exporter for 5,000 units of the product at $18 each. Production can be spread over a three-month period without interfering with normal production or incurring overtime costs. Pricing policies in the domestic market will not be affected. Comparison of a sales price of $18 with the present unit cost of $20 would indicate that this offer should be rejected. However, if attention is limited to the differential cost, which in this case is composed of the variable costs and expenses, the conclusion is quite different. The essentials of the analysis are presented in the following brief report:

DIFFERENTIAL
ANALYSIS
REPORT—SALE AT
REDUCED PRICE

Proposal to Sell to Exporter
March 10, 19--

Differential revenue from acceptance of offer:	
Revenue from sale of 5,000 additional units at $18	$90,000
Differential cost of acceptance of offer:	
Variable costs and expenses of 5,000 additional units at $12.50	62,500
Gain from acceptance of offer	$27,500

Proposals to sell an increased output in the domestic market at a reduced price may require additional considerations of a difficult nature. It would clearly be unwise to increase sales volume in one territory by means of a price reduction if sales volume would thereby be jeopardized in other areas. Manufacturers must also exercise care to avoid violations of the Robinson-Patman Act, which prohibits price discrimination within the United States unless the difference in price can be justified by a difference in the cost of serving different customers.

Discontinuance of an Unprofitable Segment

When a department, branch, territory, or other segment of an enterprise has been operating at a loss, management should consider eliminating the unprofitable segment. It might be natural to assume (mistakenly) that the total operating income of the enterprise would be increased if the operating loss could be eliminated. Discontinuance of the unprofitable segment will usually eliminate all of the related variable costs and expenses. However, if the segment represents a relatively small part of the enterprise, the fixed costs and expenses (depreciation, insurance, property taxes, etc.) will not be reduced by its discontinuance. It is entirely possible in this situation for the total operating income of a company to be reduced rather than increased by eliminating an unprofitable segment. As a basis for illustrating this type of situation, the following income statement is presented for the year just ended, which was a normal year. For purposes of the illustration, it is assumed that discontinuance of Product A, on which losses are incurred annually, will have no effect on total fixed costs and expenses.

Condensed Income Statement
For Year Ended August 31, 19--

	Product			
	A	B	C	Total
Sales............................	$100,000	$400,000	$500,000	$1,000,000
Cost of goods sold:				
Variable costs...................	$ 60,000	$200,000	$220,000	$ 480,000
Fixed costs	20,000	80,000	120,000	220,000
Total cost of goods sold.........	$ 80,000	$280,000	$340,000	$ 700,000
Gross profit.......................	$ 20,000	$120,000	$160,000	$ 300,000
Operating expenses:				
Variable expenses...............	$ 25,000	$ 60,000	$ 95,000	$ 180,000
Fixed expenses	6,000	20,000	25,000	51,000
Total operating expenses........	$ 31,000	$ 80,000	$120,000	$ 231,000
Income (loss) from operations	$ (11,000)	$ 40,000	$ 40,000	$ 69,000

Data on the estimated differential revenue and differential cost related to discontinuing Product A, on which an operating loss of $11,000 was incurred during the past year, may be assembled in a report such as the following. This report emphasizes the significant factors bearing on the decision, helps clarify the issues, and saves the time of the reader.

DIFFERENTIAL
ANALYSIS
REPORT—
DISCONTINUANCE
OF UNPROFITABLE
SEGMENT

Proposal to Discontinue Product A
September 29, 19--

Differential revenue from annual sales of product:		
Revenue from sales		$100,000
Differential cost of annual sales of product:		
Variable cost of goods sold	$60,000	
Variable operating expenses	25,000	85,000
Annual differential income from sales of Product A........		$ 15,000

Instead of an increase in annual operating income to $80,000 (Product B, $40,000; Product C, $40,000) that might seem to be indicated by the income statement, the discontinuance of Product A would reduce operating income to an estimated $54,000 ($69,000 − $15,000). The validity of this conclusion can be shown by the conventional analysis on the next page.

For purposes of the illustration, it was assumed that the discontinuance of Product A would not cause any significant reduction in the volume of fixed costs and expenses. If plant capacity made available by discontinuance of a losing operation can be used in some other manner or if plant capacity can be reduced with a resulting reduction in fixed costs and expenses, additional analysis would be needed.

Proposal to Discontinue Product A
September 29, 19--

| | Current Operations | | | Discontinuance of Product A |
	Product A	Products B and C	Total	
Sales.........................	$100,000	$900,000	$1,000,000	$900,000
Cost of goods sold:				
Variable costs................	$ 60,000	$420,000	$ 480,000	$420,000
Fixed costs	20,000	200,000	220,000	220,000
Total cost of goods sold......	$ 80,000	$620,000	$ 700,000	$640,000
Gross profit....................	$ 20,000	$280,000	$ 300,000	$260,000
Operating expenses:				
Variable expenses.............	$ 25,000	$155,000	$ 180,000	$155,000
Fixed expenses	6,000	45,000	51,000	51,000
Total operating expenses.....	$ 31,000	$200,000	$ 231,000	$206,000
Income (loss) from operations.....	$ (11,000)	$ 80,000	$ 69,000	$ 54,000

In decisions involving the elimination of an unprofitable segment, management must also consider such other factors as its effect on employees and customers. If a segment of the business is discontinued, some employees may have to be laid off and others may have to be relocated and retrained. Also important is the possible decline in sales of the more profitable products to customers who were attracted to the firm by the discontinued product.

Make or Buy

The assembly of many parts is often a substantial element in manufacturing operations. Many of the large factory complexes of automobile manufacturers are specifically called assembly plants. Some of the parts of the finished automobile, such as the motor, are produced by the automobile manufacturer, while other parts, such as tires, are often purchased from other manufacturers. Even in manufacturing the motors, such items as spark plugs and nuts and bolts may be acquired from suppliers in their finished state. When parts or components are purchased, management has usually evaluated the question of "make or buy" and has concluded that a savings in cost results from buying the part rather than manufacturing it. However, "make or buy" options are likely to arise anew when a manufacturer has excess productive capacity in the form of unused equipment, space, and labor.

As a basis for illustrating such alternatives, assume that a manufacturer has been purchasing a component, Part X, for $5 a unit. The factory is currently operating at 80% of capacity, and no significant increase in production is anticipated in the near future. The cost of manufacturing Part X, determined by absorption costing methods, is estimated at $1 for direct materials, $2 for direct labor, and $3 for factory overhead (at the predetermined rate of 150% of direct labor cost), or a total of $6. The decision based on a simple comparison of a "make" price of $6 with a "buy" price of $5 is obvious. However, to the extent that unused capacity could be used in manufacturing the part, there would be no increase in the total amount of fixed factory overhead costs. Hence, only the variable factory overhead costs need to be considered. Variable factory overhead costs such as power and maintenance are determined to amount to approximately 65% of the direct labor cost of $2, or $1.30. The cost factors to be considered are summarized in the following report:

Proposal to Manufacture Part X
February 15, 19--

DIFFERENTIAL
ANALYSIS
REPORT—MAKE
OR BUY

Purchase price of part....................................		$5.00
Differential cost to manufacture part:		
Direct materials...	$1.00	
Direct labor	2.00	
Variable factory overhead...............................	1.30	4.30
Cost reduction from manufacturing Part X..................		$ .70

Other possible effects of a change in policy should also be considered, such as the possibility that a future increase in volume of production would require the use of the currently idle capacity of 20%. The possible effect of the alternatives on employees and on future business relations with the supplier of the part, who may be providing other essential components, are additional factors that might need study.

Equipment Replacement

The usefulness of plant assets may be impaired long before they are considered to be "worn out." Equipment may no longer be ideally adequate for the purpose for which it is used, but on the other hand it may not have reached the point of complete inadequacy. Similarly, the point in time when equipment becomes obsolete may be difficult to determine. Decisions to replace usable plant assets should be based on studies of relevant costs rather than on whims or subjective opinions. The costs to be considered are the alternative future costs of retention as opposed to replacement. The book values of the plant assets being replaced are sunk costs and are irrelevant.

To illustrate some of the factors involved in replacement decisions, assume that an enterprise is considering the disposal of several identical machines having a total book value of $100,000 and an estimated remaining life of five years. The old machines can be sold for $25,000. They can be replaced by a single high-speed machine at a cost of $250,000, with an estimated useful life of five years and no residual value. Analysis of the specifications of the new machine and of accompanying changes in manufacturing methods indicate an estimated annual reduction in variable manufacturing costs from $225,000 to $150,000. No other changes in the manufacturing costs or the operating expenses are expected. The basic data to be considered are summarized in the following report:

DIFFERENTIAL
ANALYSIS
REPORT—
EQUIPMENT
REPLACEMENT

Proposal to Replace Equipment
November 28, 19--

Annual variable costs—present equipment.............	$225,000	
Annual variable costs—new equipment.................	150,000	
Annual differential decrease in cost.....................	$ 75,000	
Number of years applicable............................	× 5	
Total differential decrease in cost......................	$375,000	
Proceeds from sale of present equipment	25,000	$400,000
Cost of new equipment................................		250,000
Net differential decrease in cost, 5-year total............		$150,000
Annual differential decrease in cost—new equipment		$ 30,000

Complicating features could be added to the foregoing illustration, such as a disparity between the remaining useful life of the old equipment and the estimated life of the new equipment, or possible improvement in the product due to the new machine, with a resulting increase in selling price or volume of sales. Another factor that should be considered is the importance of alternative uses for cash outlay needed to obtain the new equipment. The amount of income that would result from the best available alternative to the proposed use of cash or its equivalent is sometimes called opportunity cost. If, for example, it is assumed that the cash outlay of $250,000 for the new equipment, less the $25,000 proceeds from the sale of the present equipment, could be used to yield a 10% return, the opportunity cost of the proposal would amount to 10% of $225,000, or $22,500.

The term "opportunity cost" introduces a new concept of "cost." In reality, it is not a cost in any usual sense of the word. Instead, it represents the forgoing of possible income associated with a lost opportunity. Although opportunity cost computations do not appear as a part of historical accounting data, they are unquestionably useful in analyses involving choices between alternative courses of action.

Self-
Examination
Questions
(Answers in
Appendix C.)

1. The concept that considers the cost of products manufactured to be composed only of those manufacturing costs that vary with the rate of production is known as:
   A. absorption costing
   B. variable costing
   C. replacement cost
   D. none of the above

2. In an income statement prepared under the variable costing concept, the deduction of the variable cost of goods sold from sales yields an intermediate amount referred to as:
   A. gross profit
   B. contribution margin
   C. manufacturing margin
   D. none of the above

3. Sales were $750,000, variable cost of goods sold was $400,000, variable selling and general expenses were $90,000, and fixed costs and expenses were $200,000. The contribution margin was:
   A. $60,000
   B. $260,000
   C. $350,000
   D. none of the above

4. The amount of increase or decrease in cost that is expected from a particular course of action as compared with an alternative is referred to as:
   A. differential cost
   B. replacement cost
   C. sunk cost
   D. none of the above

5. The amount of income that would result from the best available alternative to a proposed use of cash or its equivalent is referred to as:
   A. actual cost
   B. historical cost
   C. opportunity cost
   D. none of the above

Discussion Questions

1. What term is commonly used to refer to the amount of money or other property expended, or liability or other obligation incurred, for goods or services purchased?

2. (a) Differentiate between historical cost and replacement cost. (b) Why would replacement costs be more useful than historical costs in preparing a capital expenditures budget?

3. What types of costs are customarily included in the cost of manufactured products under (a) the *absorption costing* concept and (b) the *variable costing* concept?

4. Which of the following costs would be included in the cost of a manufactured product according to the variable costing concept? (a) property taxes on factory building, (b) salary of factory supervisor, (c) direct labor, (d) rent on factory building, (e) depreciation on factory equipment, (f) direct materials, and (g) electricity purchased to operate factory equipment.

5. In the variable costing income statement, how are the fixed manufacturing costs reported and how are the fixed selling and general expenses reported?

6. In the following equations, based on the variable costing income statement, identify the items designated by **X**:
   (a) Net sales − **X** = manufacturing margin
   (b) Manufacturing margin − **X** = contribution margin
   (c) Contribution margin − **X** = income from operations

7. If the quantity of ending inventory is smaller than that of beginning inventory, will the amount of income from operations determined by absorption costing be greater than or less than the amount determined by variable costing? Explain.

8. Is variable costing generally acceptable for use in (a) published financial statements and (b) federal income tax returns?

9. Since all costs of operating a business are controllable, what is the significance of the term *uncontrollable cost*?

10. As the terms are used in microeconomic theory, what is meant by (a) marginal revenue and (b) marginal cost?

11. Discuss how financial data prepared on the basis of variable costing can assist management in the development of short-run pricing policies.

12. What term is used to refer to the relative distribution of sales among the various products manufactured?

13. A company, operating at full capacity, manufactures two products, with Product A requiring twice the production facilities as Product B. The contribution margin is $30

per unit for Product A and $12 per unit for Product B. How much would the total contribution margin be increased or decreased for the coming year if the sales of Product A could be increased by 500 units by changing the emphasis of promotional efforts?

14. What term is applied to the type of analysis that emphasizes the difference between the revenues and costs for proposed alternative courses of action?

15. Explain the meaning of (a) *differential revenue* and (b) *differential cost*.

16. Norton Lumber Company incurs a cost of $60 per thousand board feet in processing a certain "rough-cut" lumber which it sells for $115 per thousand board feet. An alternative is to produce a "finished-cut" at a total processing cost of $82 per thousand board feet, which can be sold for $150 per thousand board feet. What is the amount of (a) the differential revenue and (b) the differential cost associated with the alternative?

17. (a) What is meant by *sunk costs*? (b) A company is contemplating replacing an old piece of machinery which cost $210,000 and has $180,000 accumulated depreciation to date. A new machine costs $300,000. What is the sunk cost in this situation?

18. The condensed income statement for Yancey Company for the current year is as follows:

| | Product | | | |
	M	N	O	Total
Sales..................................	$60,000	$380,000	$340,000	$780,000
Less variable costs and expenses.........	44,400	260,000	233,400	537,800
Contribution margin......................	$15,600	$120,000	$106,600	$242,200
Less fixed costs and expenses	20,000	80,000	76,000	176,000
Income (loss) from operations	$(4,400)	$ 40,000	$ 30,600	$ 66,200

Management decided to discontinue the manufacture and sale of Product M. Assuming that the discontinuance will have no effect on the total fixed costs and expenses or on the sales of Products N and O, has management made the correct decision? Explain.

19. (a) What is meant by *opportunity cost*? (b) Draper Company is currently earning 12% on $100,000 invested in marketable securities. It proposes to use the $100,000 to acquire plant facilities to manufacture a new product that is expected to add $20,000 annually to net income. What is the opportunity cost involved in the decision to manufacture the new product?

Exercises

Exercise 25-1. Kittle Company is contemplating the expansion of its operations through the purchase of the net assets of Weldon Lumber Company. Included among the assets is lumber which was purchased for $129,000 and which has a replacement cost of $141,000. (a) At what amount should the inventory of lumber be included on the balance sheet of Weldon Lumber Company? Briefly explain the reason for your answer. (b) How much might Kittle Company be expected to pay for the inventory if it purchases the net assets of Weldon Lumber Company? Briefly explain the reason for your answer.

Exercise 25-2. Borg Company began operations on October 1 and operated at 100% of capacity during the first month. The following data summarize the results for October:

Sales (6,000 units).....................................		$90,000
Production costs (8,000 units):		
Direct materials	$20,000	
Direct labor.......................................	36,000	
Variable factory overhead	6,000	
Fixed factory overhead.............................	10,000	72,000
Selling and general expenses:		
Variable selling and general expenses...............	$ 8,400	
Fixed selling and general expenses	4,800	13,200

(a) Prepare an income statement in accordance with the absorption costing concept. (b) Prepare an income statement in accordance with the variable costing concept. (c) What is the reason for the difference in the amount of operating income reported in (a) and (b)?

Exercise 25-3. DeLorenzo Company expects to operate at 80% of productive capacity during July. The total manufacturing costs for July for the production of 12,500 grinders are budgeted as follows:

Direct materials.......................................	$ 56,250
Direct labor	156,250
Variable factory overhead.............................	75,000
Fixed factory overhead	31,250
Total manufacturing costs...........................	$318,750

The company has an opportunity to submit a bid for 3,000 grinders to be delivered by July 31 to a governmental agency. If the contract is obtained, it is anticipated that the additional activity will not interfere with normal production during July or increase the selling or general expenses. (a) What is the present unit product cost on an absorption costing basis? (b) What is the present unit product cost on a variable costing basis? (c) What is the unit cost below which the DeLorenzo Company should not go in bidding on the government contract? (d) Is a unit cost figure based on absorption costing or one based on variable costing more useful in arriving at a bid on this contract? Explain.

Exercise 25-4. Farley Company has a plant capacity of 50,000 units and current production is 35,000 units. Monthly fixed costs and expenses are $140,000 and variable costs and expenses are $12.50 per unit. The present selling price is $18 per unit. On February 3, the company received an offer from Wong Yu Company for 5,000 units of the product at $15 each. The Wong Yu Company will market the units in a foreign country under its own brand name. The additional business is not expected to affect the regular selling price or quantity of sales of Farley Company. (a) Prepare a differential analysis report for the proposed sale to Wong Yu Company. (b) Briefly explain the reason why the acceptance of this additional business will increase operating income. (c) What is the minimum price per unit that would produce a contribution margin?

Exercise 25-5. A condensed income statement by product line for McCaffrey Co. indicated the following for Product X for the past year:

Sales	$160,000
Cost of goods sold	108,000
Gross profit	$ 52,000
Operating expenses	72,000
Loss from operations	$(20,000)

It is estimated that 15% of the cost of goods sold represents fixed factory overhead costs and that 20% of operating expenses is fixed. Since Product X is only one of many products, the fixed costs and expenses will not be materially affected if the product is discontinued. (a) Prepare a differential analysis report, dated January 2 of the current year, for the proposed discontinuance of Product X. (b) Should Product X be retained? Explain.

Exercise 25-6. Quigley Company has been purchasing carrying cases for its portable typewriters at a delivered cost of $18.75 per unit. The company, which is currently operating below full capacity, charges factory overhead to production at the rate of 60% of direct labor cost. The direct materials and direct labor costs per unit to produce comparable carrying cases are expected to be $5 and $12 respectively. If Quigley Company manufactures the carrying cases, fixed factory overhead costs will not increase and variable factory overhead costs associated with the cases are expected to be 20% of direct labor costs. (a) Prepare a differential analysis report, dated March 6 of the current year, for the make or buy decision. (b) On the basis of the data presented, would it be advisable to make or to continue buying the carrying cases? Explain.

Exercise 25-7. Rowe Company produces a commodity by applying a machine and direct labor to the direct material. The original cost of the machine is $180,000, the accumulated depreciation is $108,000, its remaining useful life is 8 years, and its salvage value is negligible. On January 18, a proposal was made to replace the present manufacturing procedure with a fully automatic machine that will cost $340,000. The automatic machine has an estimated useful life of 8 years and no significant salvage value. For use in evaluating the proposal, the accountant accumulated the following annual data on present and proposed operations:

	Present Operations	Proposed Operations
Sales	$440,000	$440,000
Direct materials	184,800	184,800
Direct labor	79,200	——
Power and maintenance	13,600	31,500
Taxes, insurance, etc.	8,800	12,800
Selling and general expenses	35,200	35,200

(a) Prepare a differential analysis report for the proposal to replace the machine. Include in the analysis both the net differential decrease in costs and expenses anticipated over the 8 years and the annual differential decrease in costs and expenses anticipated. (b) Based only on the data presented, should the proposal be accepted? (c) What are some of the other factors that should be considered before a final decision is made?

Exercise 25-8. On April 1, Muller Company is considering leasing a building and purchasing the necessary equipment to operate a public warehouse. The project would be financed by selling $500,000 of 10% U.S. Treasury bonds that mature in 15 years. The bonds were purchased at face value and are currently selling at face value. The following data have been assembled:

Cost of equipment..	$500,000
Life of equipment	15 years
Estimated residual value of equipment	$ 80,000
Yearly costs to operate the warehouse, in addition to depreciation of equipment...	$ 48,500
Yearly expected revenues—first 5 years	$120,000
Yearly expected revenues—next 10 years......................	$150,000

(a) Prepare a differential analysis report presenting the differential revenue and the differential cost associated with the proposed operation of the warehouse for the 15 years as compared with present conditions. (b) Based upon the results disclosed by the differential analysis, should the proposal be accepted? (c) If the proposal is accepted, what is the total estimated income from operation of the warehouse for the 15 years?

Problems
(Problems in Appendix B: 25-1B, 25-2B, 25-4B.)

Problem 25-1A. Ingersoll Refining Inc. refines Product C in batches of 80,000 gallons, which it sells for $.28 per gallon. The associated unit costs and expenses are currently as follows:

	Per Gallon
Direct materials	$.144
Direct labor	.040
Variable factory overhead	.020
Fixed factory overhead.......................	.012
Sales commissions	.028
Fixed selling and general expenses	.008

The company is presently considering a proposal to put Product C through several additional processes to yield Products C and D. Although the company had determined such further processing to be unwise, new processing methods have now been developed. Existing facilities can be used for the additional processing, but since the factory is operating at full 8-hour-day capacity, the processing would have to be performed at night. Additional costs of processing would be $3,200 per batch and there would be an evaporation loss of 15%, with 60% of the processed material evolving as Product C and 25% as Product D. The selling price of Product D is $.80 per gallon. Sales commissions are a uniform percentage based on the sales price.

Instructions:

(1) Prepare a differential analysis report as of March 14, presenting the differential revenue and the differential cost per batch associated with the processing to produce Products C and D, compared with processing to produce Product C only.

(2) Briefly report your recommendations.

Problem 25-2A. Packard Company is considering the replacement of a machine that has been used in its factory for three years. Relevant data associated with the operations of the old machine and the new machine, neither of which has any residual value, are as follows:

<u>Old Machine</u>

Cost of machine, 8-year life	$270,000
Annual depreciation	33,750
Annual manufacturing costs, exclusive of depreciation	425,000
Related annual operating expenses	280,000
Associated annual revenue	940,000
Estimated selling price of old machine	190,000

<u>New Machine</u>

Cost of machine, 5-year life	$525,000
Annual depreciation	105,000
Estimated annual manufacturing costs, exclusive of depreciation	325,000

Annual operating expenses and revenue are not expected to be affected by purchase of the new machine.

Instructions:

(1) Prepare a differential analysis report as of January 4 of the current year, comparing operations utilizing the new machine with operations using the present equipment. The analysis should indicate the total differential decrease or increase in costs that would result over the 5-year period if the new machine is acquired.

(2) List other factors that should be considered before a final decision is reached.

Problem 25-3A. Edens Company is planning a one-month campaign for August to promote sales of one of its two products. A total of $120,000 has been budgeted for advertising, contests, redeemable coupons, and other promotional activities. The following data have been assembled for their possible usefulness in deciding which of the products to select for the campaign:

	Product A	Product B
Unit selling price	$100	$120
Unit production costs:		
Direct materials	$28	$36
Direct labor	20	28
Variable factory overhead	16	16
Fixed factory overhead	12	12
Total unit production costs	$ 76	$ 92
Unit variable operating expenses	10	10
Unit fixed operating expenses	6	6
Total unit costs and expenses	$ 92	$108
Operating income per unit	$ 8	$ 12

No increase in facilities would be necessary to produce and sell the increased output. It is anticipated that 18,000 additional units of Product A or 12,500 additional units of Product B could be sold without changing the unit selling price of either product.

Instructions:

(1) Prepare a differential analysis report as of July 6 of the current year, presenting the additional revenue and additional costs and expenses anticipated from the promotion of Product A and Product B.

(2) The sales manager had tentatively decided to promote Product B, estimating that operating income would be increased by $30,000 ($12 operating income per unit for 12,500 units, less promotion expenses of $120,000). It was also believed that the selection of Product A would increase operating income by only $24,000 ($8 operating income per unit for 18,000 units, less promotion expenses of $120,000). State briefly your reasons for supporting or opposing the tentative decision.

Problem 25-4A. The demand for Product D, one of numerous products manufactured by UGA Inc., has dropped sharply because of recent competition from a similar product. The company's chemists are currently completing tests of various new formulas, and it is anticipated that the manufacture of a superior product can be started on October 1, one month hence. No changes will be needed in the present production facilities to manufacture the new product because only the mixture of the various materials will be changed.

The controller has been asked by the president of the company for advice on whether to continue production during September or to suspend the manufacture of Product D until October 1. The controller has assembled the following pertinent data:

UGA Inc.
Estimated Income Statement—Product D
For Month Ending August 31, 19--

Sales (50,000 units)	$375,000
Cost of goods sold	294,000
Gross profit	$ 81,000
Selling and general expenses	95,000
Loss from operations	$ 14,000

The estimated production costs and selling and general expenses, based on a production of 50,000 units, are as follows:

Direct materials	$2.30 per unit
Direct labor	1.60 per unit
Variable factory overhead	.70 per unit
Variable selling and general expenses	1.15 per unit
Fixed factory overhead	$64,000 for August
Fixed selling and general expenses	$37,500 for August

Sales for September are expected to drop about 40% below those of the preceding month. No significant changes are anticipated in the production costs or operating expenses. No extra costs will be incurred in discontinuing operations in the portion of the plant associated with Product D. The inventory of Product D at the beginning and end of September is expected to be inconsequential.

Instructions:

(1) Prepare an estimated income statement in absorption costing form for September for Product D, assuming that production continues during the month.

(2) Prepare an estimated income statement in variable costing form for September for Product D, assuming that production continues during the month.

(3) State the estimated operating loss arising from the activities associated with Product D for September if production is temporarily suspended.

(4) Prepare a brief statement of the advice the controller should give.

Problem 25-5A. R. A. Frazier Company manufactures three styles of folding chairs, X, Y, and Z. The income statement has consistently indicated a net loss for Style Z and management is considering three proposals: (1) continue Style Z, (2) discontinue Style Z and reduce total output accordingly, or (3) discontinue Style Z and conduct an advertising campaign to expand the sales of Style Y so that the entire plant capacity can continue to be used.

If Proposal 2 is selected and Style Z is discontinued and production curtailed, the annual fixed production costs and fixed operating expenses could be reduced by $14,500 and $8,000 respectively. If Proposal 3 is selected, it is anticipated that an additional annual expenditure of $20,000 for advertising Style Y would yield an increase of 35% in its sales volume, and that the increased production of Style Y would utilize the plant facilities released by the discontinuance of Style Z.

The sales, costs, and expenses have been relatively stable over the past few years and they are expected to remain so for the foreseeable future. The income statement for the past year ended December 31 is:

| | Style | | | |
	X	Y	Z	Total
Sales	$400,000	$432,000	$126,000	$958,000
Cost of goods sold:				
Variable costs	$220,000	$246,000	$ 88,200	$554,200
Fixed costs	80,000	84,000	28,000	192,000
Total cost of goods sold	$300,000	$330,000	$116,200	$746,200
Gross profit	$100,000	$102,000	$ 9,800	$211,800
Less operating expenses:				
Variable expenses	$ 40,000	$ 43,200	$ 12,600	$ 95,800
Fixed expenses	24,000	24,000	10,500	58,500
Total operating expenses	$ 64,000	$ 67,200	$ 23,100	$154,300
Income from operations	$ 36,000	$ 34,800	$(13,300)	$ 57,500

Instructions:

(1) Prepare an income statement for the past year in the variable costing format. Use the following headings:

| | Style | | | |
	X	Y	Z	Total

Data for each style should be reported through contribution margin. The fixed costs and expenses should be deducted from the total contribution margin as reported in the "total" column to determine income from operations.

(2) Based on the income statement prepared in (1) and the other data presented above, determine the amount by which total annual operating income would be reduced below its present level if Proposal 2 is accepted.

(3) Prepare an income statement in the variable costing format, indicating the projected annual operating income if Proposal 3 is accepted. Use the following headings:

Style		
X	Y	Total

Data for each style should be reported through contribution margin. The fixed costs and expenses should be deducted from the total contribution margin as reported in the "total" column. For purposes of this problem, the additional expenditure of $20,000 for advertising can be added to the fixed operating expenses.

(4) By how much would total annual income increase above its present level if Proposal 3 is accepted? Explain.

Mini-Case

Your father operates a family-owned automotive dealership. Recently, the city government has requested bids on the purchase of 20 sedans for use by the city police department. Although the city prefers to purchase from local dealerships, state law requires the acceptance of the lowest bid. The past several contracts for automotive purchases have been granted to dealerships from surrounding communities.

The following data were taken from the dealership records for the normal sale of the automobile for which current bids have been requested:

Retail list price of sedan......................................	$12,100
Cost allocated to normal sale:	
Dealer cost from manufacturer............................	8,470
Fixed overhead	1,200
Shipping charges from manufacturer.......................	500
Preparation charges	100
Sales commission based on selling price....................	5%

Your father has asked you to help him in arriving at a "winning" bid price for this contract. In the past, your father has always bid $250 above the total cost (including fixed overhead). No sales commissions will be paid if the bid is accepted, and your father has indicated that the bid price must contribute at least $250 per car to the profits of the dealership.

Instructions:

(1) Do you think that your father has used good bidding procedures for prior contracts? Explain.

(2) What should be the bid price, based upon your father's profit objectives?

(3) Explain why the bid price determined in (2) would not be an acceptable price for normal customers.

26

CHAPTER

Management Reports and Special Analyses

CHAPTER OBJECTIVES

Describe the purpose of management reports and special analyses.

Describe and illustrate typical special analyses and reports used by management.

26

CHAPTER

A basic function of accounting is to provide the data needed to report the results of the economic activities of an enterprise to all interested parties. One group making extensive use of accounting data is operating management. Managers of even very small businesses need financial data to help them in making decisions. As the size and the complexity of businesses increase, the importance of accounting as a tool in directing operations becomes more apparent.

In assisting management, the accountant relies upon a variety of methods of analysis. The use of cost accounting and of cost relationships as they affect planning and controlling operations was discussed in earlier chapters. In this chapter, additional reports and analyses for the use of management are explained and illustrated.

The term **management reports** refers to various statements, schedules, and summaries prepared solely for the use of management. There are no standardized patterns for such reports. They may be devoted to a very small segment of the activities of the enterprise or to special problems facing management. They often contain forecasts rather than historical data, and timeliness is more important than complete accuracy. In all cases, they should be easy to understand and should give sufficient but not excessive detail.

RESPONSIBILITY REPORTING

One of the basic functions of management is to direct operations in such a way as to achieve as nearly as possible the predetermined objectives of the enterprise. Establishing effective control over operations requires the assignment of definite responsibilities to personnel at the various managerial levels. The accountant can then aid management by providing revenue and expense data for use in measuring actual performance on the basis of the responsibilities assigned.

A term often used to describe this process of reporting operating data by areas of responsibility is **responsibility reporting**. The reports are designed according to the plan of responsibility for each operating segment. Reports prepared for the top level of management should usually be broad in scope, presenting summaries of data rather than small details. They should be departmentalized to the extent needed to assign responsibility. On the other hand, reports for personnel at the lower end of the managerial range should usually be narrow in scope and contain detailed data. To illustrate, assume that the responsibility for the manufacturing operations of an enterprise is as represented in the following organization chart:

ORGANIZATION CHART DEPICTING MANAGEMENT RESPONSIBILITY FOR PRODUCTION

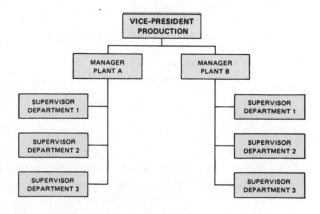

In the illustration, there are three levels of management responsibility. At the operating level are the department supervisors who are responsible for operations within their departments and who are accountable to the plant managers. The plant managers, in turn, are responsible for overall plant operations and are accountable to the vice-president in charge of production — the executive level of management.

Management reports aid each level of management in carrying out assigned responsibilities. To illustrate, the following budget performance reports are part of a responsibility reporting system for an enterprise:

RESPONSIBILITY
REPORTING

Budget Performance Report — Vice-President, Production
For Month Ended October 31, 19--

	Budget	Actual	Over	Under
Administration	$ 19,500	$ 19,700	$ 200	
Plant A	467,475	470,330	2,855	
Plant B	395,225	394,300		$925
	$882,200	$884,330	$3,055	$925

Budget Performance Report — Manager, Plant A
For Month Ended October 31, 19--

	Budget	Actual	Over	Under
Administration	$ 17,500	$ 17,350		$150
Department 1	109,725	111,280	$1,555	
Department 2	190,500	192,600	2,100	
Department 3	149,750	149,100		650
	$467,475	$470,330	$3,655	$800

Budget Performance Report — Supervisor, Department 1-Plant A
For Month Ended October 31, 19--

	Budget	Actual	Over	Under
Direct materials	$ 30,000	$ 31,700	$1,700	
Direct labor	48,000	47,750		$250
Factory overhead:				
Indirect factory wages	10,100	10,250	150	
Supervisory salaries	6,400	6,400		
Power and light	5,750	5,690		60
Depreciation of plant and equipment	4,000	4,000		
Indirect materials	2,500	2,525	25	
Maintenance	2,000	1,990		10
Insurance and property taxes	975	975		
	$109,725	$111,280	$1,875	$320

The amount of detail presented in the budget performance report depends upon the level of management to which the report is directed. The reports prepared for the department supervisors present details of the budgeted and actual manufacturing costs for their departments. Each supervisor can then concentrate on the individual items that resulted in significant variations. In the illustration, the budget performance report for Department 1-Plant A indicates a significant variation between the budget and actual amounts for direct materials. It is clear that supplemental reports providing detailed data on the causes of the variation would aid the supervisor in taking corrective action. One such report, a scrap report, is illustrated as follows. This report indicates the cause of a significant part of the variation.

SCRAP
REPORT

Direct Materials Scrap Report—Department 1-Plant A
For Month Ended October 31, 19--

Material No.	Units Spoiled	Unit Cost	Dollar Loss	Remarks
A392	50	$3.10	$ 155.00	Machine malfunction
C417	76	.80	60.80	Inexperienced employee
G118	5	1.10	5.50	
J510	120	8.25	990.00	Substandard materials
K277	2	1.50	3.00	
P719	7	2.10	14.70	
V112	22	4.25	93.50	Machine malfunction
			$1,322.50	

The scrap report is one example of the type of supplemental report that can be provided to department supervisors. Other examples would include reports on direct labor rate variance, direct labor usage variance, and cost of idle time.

The budget performance reports for the plant managers contain summarized data on the budgeted and actual costs for the departments under their jurisdiction. These reports enable them to identify the department supervisors responsible for significant variances. The report for the vice-president in charge of production summarizes the data by plant so that the persons responsible for plant operations can be held accountable for significant variations from predetermined objectives.

GROSS PROFIT ANALYSIS

Gross profit is often considered the most significant intermediate figure in the income statement. It is common to determine its percentage relationship to sales and to make comparisons with prior periods. However, the mere knowledge of the percentages and the degree and direction of change from prior periods is insufficient. Management needs information about the causes. The procedure used in developing such information is termed **gross profit analysis**.

Since gross profit is the excess of sales over the cost of goods sold, a change in the amount of gross profit can be caused by (1) an increase or decrease in the amount of sales and (2) an increase or decrease in the amount of cost of goods sold. An increase or decrease in either element may in turn be due to (1) a change in the number of units sold and (2) a change in the unit price. The effect of these two factors on either sales or cost of goods sold may be stated as follows:

1. **Quantity factor.** The effect of a change in the number of units sold, assuming no change in unit price.
2. **Price factor.** The effect of a change in unit price on the number of units sold.

The following data are to be used as the basis for illustrating gross profit analysis. For the sake of simplicity, a single commodity is assumed. The amount of detail entering into the analysis would be greater if a number of different commodities were sold, but the basic principles would not be affected.

	1985	1984	Increase Decrease*
Sales....................................	$900,000	$800,000	$100,000
Cost of goods sold	650,000	570,000	80,000
Gross profit.............................	$250,000	$230,000	$ 20,000
Number of units sold.....................	125,000	100,000	25,000
Unit sales price	$7.20	$8.00	$.80*
Unit cost price	$5.20	$5.70	$.50*

The following analysis of these data shows that the favorable increase in the number of units sold was partially offset by a decrease in unit selling price. Also, the increase in the cost of goods sold due to increased quantity was partially offset by a decrease in unit cost.

GROSS PROFIT ANALYSIS REPORT

Analysis of Increase in Gross Profit
For Year Ended December 31, 1985

Increase in amount of sales attributed to:
Quantity factor:
    Increase in number of units sold in 1985 ...   25,000
    Unit sales price in 1984................... × $8 $200,000
Price factor:
    Decrease in unit sales price in 1985 .... $.80
    Number of units sold in 1985.............. ×125,000 100,000
Net increase in amount of sales $100,000
Increase in amount of cost of goods sold attributed to:
Quantity factor:
    Increase in number of units sold in 1985 ...   25,000
    Unit cost price in 1984 .... × $5.70 $142,500
Price factor:
    Decrease in unit cost price in 1985 .... $.50
    Number of units sold in 1985.............. ×125,000 62,500
Net increase in amount of cost of goods sold .   80,000
Increase in gross profit .... $ 20,000

The data presented in the report may be useful both in evaluating past performance and in planning for the future. The importance of the cost reduction of $.50 a unit is quite clear. If the unit cost had not changed from the preceding year, the net increase in the amount of sales ($100,000) would have been more than offset by the increase in the cost of goods sold ($142,500), causing a decrease of $42,500 in gross profit. The $20,000 increase in gross profit actually attained was made possible, therefore, by the ability of management to reduce the unit cost of the commodity.

The means by which the reduction in the unit cost of the commodity was accomplished is also significant. If it was due to the spreading of fixed factory overhead costs over the larger number of units produced, the decision to reduce the sales price in order to achieve a larger volume was probably wise. On the other hand, if the $.50 reduction in unit cost was due to operating efficiencies entirely unrelated to the increased production, the $.80 reduction in the unit sales price was unwise. The accuracy of the conclusion is demonstrated by the following analysis, which shows the possible loss of an opportunity to have realized an additional gross profit of $30,000 ($280,000 − $250,000).

	Actual		Hypothetical	
Number of units sold...............	125,000		100,000	
Unit sales price	$7.20		$8.00	
Sales..............................		$900,000		$800,000
Unit cost price	$5.20		$5.20	
Cost of goods sold		650,000		520,000
Gross profit.......................		$250,000		$280,000

If the reduction in unit cost had been achieved by a combination of the two means, the approximate effects of each could be determined by additional analyses. The methods used in gross profit analysis may also be extended, with some changes, to the analysis of changes in selling and general expenses.

COST-VOLUME-PROFIT RELATIONSHIPS
The determination of the selling price of a product is a complex matter that is often affected by forces partially or entirely beyond the control of management. Nevertheless, management must establish pricing policies within the bounds permitted by the market place. Accounting can play an important role in the development of policy by supplying management with special reports on the relative profitability of its various products, the probable effects of changes in selling price, and other cost-volume-profit relationships.

The unit cost of producing a commodity is affected by such factors as the inherent nature of the product, the efficiency of operations, and the volume of production. An increase in the quantity produced is usually accompanied by a decrease in unit cost, provided the volume attained remains within the reasonable limits of plant capacity.

Quantitative data relating to the effect on income of changes in unit selling price, sales volume, production volume, production costs, and operating expenses help management to improve the relationship among these variables. If a change in selling price appears to be desirable or, because of competitive pressure, unavoidable, the possible effect of the change on sales volume and product cost needs to be studied. Inquiry into a promotional sales campaign's likely effect on income is another example of special studies that may be undertaken.

For purposes of cost-volume-profit analysis, all operating costs and expenses must be subdivided into two categories: (1) fixed and (2) variable. Analyses of this type are made easier by the use of variable costing procedures, which require that costs and expenses be so classified. When conventional absorption costing systems are used, it is necessary first to divide the relevant cost data between the fixed and variable categories. Types of analyses used in appraising the interactions of selling price, sales and production volume, variable cost and expense, fixed cost and expense, and income are described and illustrated in the next three sections.

Break-Even Analysis

The point in the operations of an enterprise at which revenues and expired costs are exactly equal is called the **break-even point**. At this level of operations, an enterprise will neither realize an operating income nor incur an operating loss. Break-even analysis can be applied to past periods, but it is most useful when applied to future periods as a guide to business planning, particularly if either an expansion or a curtailment of operations is expected. In such cases, it is concerned with future prospects and future operations and hence relies upon estimates. The reliability of the analysis is greatly influenced by the accuracy of the estimates.

The break-even point can be computed by means of a mathematical formula or it can be determined from a graphic presentation of the relationship between revenue, costs, and volume of productive capacity. In either case the data required are (1) total estimated fixed costs and expenses for a future period, such as a year, and (2) the total estimated variable costs and expenses for the same period, stated as a percent of net sales. To illustrate, assume that fixed costs and expenses are estimated at $90,000 and that variable costs and expenses are expected to be 60% of sales. The break-even point is $225,000 of sales, computed as follows:

Break-Even Sales (in $) = Fixed Costs (in $) + Variable Costs (as % of Break-Even Sales)
$$S = \$90,000 + 60\%S$$
$$40\%S = \$90,000$$
$$S = \$225,000$$

Break-even analysis may also be used in estimating the sales volume needed to yield a specified amount of operating income. The formula stated above can be changed for use in this computation by adding at the end of the equation the desired amount of operating income. For example, the sales volume needed to yield operating income of $40,000 for the enterprise above would be $325,000, computed as follows:

Sales = Fixed Costs + Variable Costs + Operating Income
$$S = \$90,000 + 60\%S + \$40,000$$
$$40\%S = \$130,000$$
$$S = \$325,000$$

Presentation of break-even analysis in chart form is often preferred over the equation form. From such a chart, the approximate operating income or operating loss associated with any given sales volume or percentage of capacity can be readily determined. The following break-even chart is based on the foregoing data:

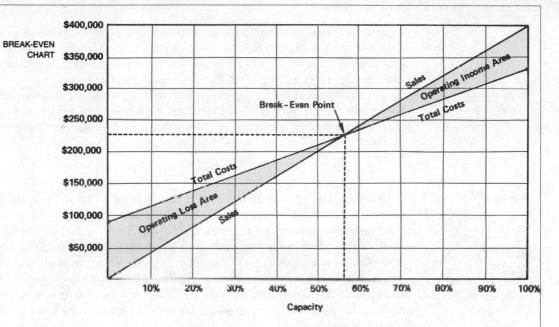

A break-even chart is constructed in the following manner:

1. Percentages of productive capacity of the enterprise are spread along the horizontal axis, and dollar amounts representing operating data are spread along the vertical axis. The outside limits of the chart represent 100% of productive capacity and the maximum sales potential at that level of production.
2. A diagonal line representing sales is drawn from the lower left corner to the upper right corner.
3. A point representing fixed costs is plotted on the vertical axis at the left and a point representing total costs at maximum capacity is plotted at the right edge of the chart. A diagonal line representing total costs at various percentages of capacity is then drawn connecting these two points. In the illustration, the fixed costs are $90,000 and the total costs at maximum capacity amount to $330,000 ($90,000 plus variable costs of 60% of $400,000).
4. Horizontal and vertical lines are drawn at the point of intersection of the sales and cost lines, which is the break-even point, and the areas representing operating income and operating loss are identified.

Relying as it does on rigid assumptions concerning the behavior of sales and costs, break-even analysis should be used with caution. If the selling price of a product is increased or decreased or if the amount of cost changes, the analysis prepared prior to such action will no longer be valid. In addition, the assumptions underlying the classification of costs as fixed or variable must be recognized. Among these is the assumption of relatively stable use of plant facilities. In the foregoing illustration, for example, it is quite possible that at 80% and 100% of capacity the fixed costs would be $90,000, while if production were only 10% of capacity the fixed costs would be less than $90,000. Under conditions of substantial change in the use of plant facilities, very few costs would be fixed. Since substantial changes in the use of plant facilities are uncommon in practice, break-even analysis can often be used quite effectively in decision making.

A break-even chart for an enterprise selling two or more products must be based on a certain "product mix." Changes in the mix would require more analysis and construction of a new chart. Recognition of the inherent assumptions and the limitations of break-even analysis is essential to its effective use in management planning.

Margin of Safety

Business enterprises do not use the break-even point as their goal for future operations. Rather, they seek to achieve the largest possible volume of sales above the break-even point. The difference between the current sales revenue and the sales at the break-even point is called the **margin of safety**. It represents the possible decrease in sales revenue that may occur before an operating loss results, and it may be stated either in terms of dollars or as a percentage of sales. For example, if the volume of sales is $250,000 and sales at the break-even point amount to $200,000, the margin of safety is $50,000 or 20%, as shown by the following computation:

$$\text{Margin of Safety} = \frac{\text{Sales} - \text{Sales at Break-Even Point}}{\text{Sales}}$$

$$\text{Margin of Safety} = \frac{\$250,000 - \$200,000}{\$250,000} = 20\%$$

The margin of safety is useful in evaluating past operations and as a guide to business planning. For example, if the margin of safety is low, management should carefully study forecasts of future sales because even a small decline in sales revenue will result in an operating loss.

Contribution Margin Ratio

Another relationship between cost, volume, and profits that is especially useful in business planning because it gives an insight into the profit potential of a firm is the **contribution margin ratio**, sometimes called the **profit-volume ratio**. This ratio indicates the percentage of each sales dollar available to cover the fixed expenses and to provide operating income. For example, if the volume of sales is $250,000 and variable expenses amount to $175,000, the contribution margin ratio is 30%, as shown by the following computation:

$$\text{Contribution Margin Ratio} = \frac{\text{Sales} - \text{Variable Expenses}}{\text{Sales}}$$

$$\text{Contribution Margin Ratio} = \frac{\$250,000 - \$175,000}{\$250,000} = 30\%$$

The contribution margin ratio permits the quick determination of the effect on operating income of an increase or a decrease in sales volume. To illustrate, assume that the management of a firm with a contribution margin ratio of 30% is studying the effect on operating income of adding $25,000 in sales orders. Multiplying the ratio (30%) by the change in sales volume ($25,000) indicates an increase in operating income of $7,500 if the additional orders are obtained. In using the analysis in such a case, factors other than sales volume, such as the amount of fixed expenses, the percentage of variable expenses to sales, and the unit sales price, are assumed to remain constant. If these factors are not constant, the effect of any change in these factors must be considered in applying the analysis.

The contribution margin ratio is also useful in setting business policy. For example, if the contribution margin ratio of a firm is large and production is at a level below 100% capacity, a comparatively large increase in operating income can be expected from an increase in sales volume. On the other hand, a comparatively large decrease in operating income can be expected from a decline in sales volume. A firm in such a position might decide to devote more effort to additional sales promotion because of the large change in operating income that will result from changes in sales volume. On the other hand, a firm with a small contribution margin ratio will probably want to give more attention to reducing costs and expenses before concentrating large efforts on additional sales promotion.

RATE OF RETURN ON ASSETS

The **rate of return on assets,** sometimes called the rate of return on investment (**ROI**), is a useful measure of managerial efficiency. The determination of the rate can be quite complicated or it can be relatively simple, depending upon the exactness with which a certain amount of income can be allocated to a certain group of assets.

An example of a fairly simple problem is the determination of the rate of return on the securities owned by an enterprise. If a portfolio of stocks and bonds acquired at a cost of $200,000 and owned throughout the year yields income of $11,700, the rate of return is 5.85% ($11,700 ÷ $200,000). If, however, there were any significant changes in the amount invested during the year, a weighted average should be computed and the rate based thereon. A part of the administrative expenses and income taxes could be deducted from income in determining the rate of return. The computation could also be based on market value instead of cost.

The rate of return on assets can be determined for an enterprise as a whole and also for each department. Comparisons of departmental rates are valuable aids in measuring efficiency and the resulting managerial decisions. It is common, in evaluating the various segments of an enterprise, to exclude interest on borrowed funds. It is the income generated by the assets, regardless of the source of the funds used in their acquisition, that is important. The incurrence of interest and other nonoperating costs is also beyond the control of division managers.

To illustrate a somewhat more complex situation than the rate of return on securities, assume that the past year's sales volume of the two operating divisions of a business did not differ greatly and yielded approximately the same amount of income from operations. Assume also that the book value of the assets used was substantially greater for one division than for the other. Details in the following report clearly show a difference in the rates of return for the two divisions.

Rate of Return on Assets
For Year Ended December 31, 19--

	Division A	Division B
Sales	$400,000	$435,000
Operating expenses	350,000	380,000
Income from operations	$ 50,000	$ 55,000
Average assets employed	$500,000	$300,000
Rate of return on assets	10%	18.3%

The data presented in the above report disclose a great difference in the effectiveness of the two divisions, and, therefore, a need for a careful study of their operating policies. It is only through an awareness of the situation, followed by a careful analysis, that the causes of the substantial difference in the rates of return can be determined and corrective action taken.

There are other ways in which the rate of return on assets may be used, both as a control device and in planning. If a minimum rate is established, it can be used in measuring the relative efficiency of the various segments of a business. The measure can be used in estimating a new product's price required to yield a needed rate of return on the assets to be used. It may also be used in evaluating proposed purchases of additional plant assets.

ANALYSIS OF PROPOSED CAPITAL EXPENDITURES

With the fast growth of American industry, increasing attention has been given to accounting analyses designed to evaluate plans requiring large outlays for plant replacement, improvement, and expansion. Three types of analysis commonly used in evaluating proposals for major capital expenditures are described.

Average Rate of Return

The expected average rate of return is a measure of the expected profitability of an investment in plant assets. The amount of income expected to be earned from the investment is stated as an annual average over the number of years the asset is to be used. The amount of the investment may be considered to be the original cost of the plant assets, or recognition may be given to the effect of depreciation on the amount of the investment. According to the latter view, the investment gradually declines from the original cost to the estimated residual value at the end of its useful life. Assuming straight-line depreciation and no residual value, the average investment would be equal to one half of the original expenditure.

To illustrate, assume that management is considering the purchase of a certain machine at a cost of $50,000. The machine is expected to have a useful life of 4 years, with little residual value, and its use during the 4 years is expected to yield total income of $20,000. The expected average annual income is therefore $5,000 ($20,000 ÷ 4) and the average investment is $25,000 [($50,000 cost + $0 residual value) ÷ 2]. Accordingly, the expected average rate of return on the average investment is 20%, computed as follows:

$$\frac{\$20,000 \div 4}{\$50,000 \div 2} = 20\% \text{ average rate of return}$$

Comparison of this expected rate of return with the rate established by management as the minimum reward for the risks involved in the investment in additional equipment will show the comparative attractiveness of the proposed purchase. A significant objection to the use of this measure is its lack of consideration of (1) the timing of the expected recovery of the amount invested in plant assets and (2) the timing of the income that such investment is expected to produce. This "timing" is important because funds coming from an investment can be reinvested in other income-producing activities. Therefore, the sooner the funds become available, the more income that can be generated from their reinvestment. A project that recovers a high proportion of its investment and yields high income early in its life is more desirable than a project with the same average rate of return but with lower cost recovery and income in the earlier years.

Cash Payback Period

The expected period of time that will pass between the date of a capital expenditure and the complete recovery in cash (or equivalent) of the amount invested is called the cash payback period. To simplify the analysis, the revenues and the out-of-pocket operating expenses expected to be associated with the operation of the plant assets are assumed to be entirely in the form of cash. The excess of the cash flowing in from revenue over the cash flowing out for expenses is termed **net cash flow.** The time required for the net cash flow to equal the initial outlay for the plant asset is the payback period.

For purposes of illustration, assume that the proposed expenditure for a plant asset with an 8-year life is $200,000 and that the annual net cash flow is expected to be $40,000. The estimated cash payback period for the expenditure is 5 years, computed as follows:

$$\frac{\$200,000}{\$40,000} = \text{5-year cash payback period}$$

The cash payback concept is widely used in evaluating proposals for expansion and for investment in new projects. A relatively short payback period is desirable, because the sooner the cash is recovered the sooner it becomes available for reinvestment in other projects. In addition, there is likely to be less possibility of loss from changes in economic conditions and other unavoidable risks when the commitment is short-term. The cash payback concept is also of interest to bankers and other creditors who may be dependent upon net cash flow for the repayment of claims associated with the initial capital expenditure.

The major limitation of the cash payback period as a basis for decisions is its failure to take into consideration the expected profitability of a proposal. A project with a very short payback period coupled with relatively poor profitability would be less desirable than one with a longer payback period but with satisfactory profitability.

Discounted Cash Flow

An expenditure for plant and equipment may be looked upon as the acquisition of a series of future net cash flows composed of two elements: (1) recovery of the initial expenditure and (2) income. Both the absolute and the relative amounts of these two elements are important. The period of time over which the net cash flows will be received is also important. Any specified amount of cash that is to be received at some date in the future is not the equivalent of the same amount of cash held at an earlier date. Cash on hand can be immediately used. The income that can be earned by earlier investment may be an important factor. This element of timing is given recognition in **discounted cash flow analysis.** The expected future net cash flows coming from proposed present capital expenditures are reduced to their present values.

The concept of present value of future payments was noted in earlier chapters in connection with the determination of the issuance price of bonds and amortization of bond discount and premium. Application of the concept of discounted cash flow analysis may be illustrated by computing the amount to be deposited at a given rate of interest that will yield a specified sum at a later date. If the rate of interest is 6% and the sum to be accumulated in one year is $1,000, the amount to be invested is $943.40 ($1,000 ÷ 1.06). If the funds were to be invested one year earlier (two years in all), with the interest compounded at the end of the first year, the amount of the deposit would be $890.00 ($943.40 ÷ 1.06).

Instead of determining the present value of future sums by a series of divisions in the manner just illustrated, it is common to find the present value of 1 from a table of present values and to multiply it by the amount of the future sum. Reference to the following partial table shows that the present value of $1 to be received two years hence, with interest at the rate of 6% a year, is .890. Multiplication of .890 by $1,000 yields the same amount that was determined in the preceding paragraph by two successive divisions.

	Years	6%	10%	12%	15%	20%
PRESENT VALUE OF 1 AT COMPOUND INTEREST	1	.943	.909	.893	.870	.833
	2	.890	.826	.797	.756	.694
	3	.840	.751	.712	.658	.579
	4	.792	.683	.636	.572	.482
	5	.747	.621	.567	.497	.402
	6	.705	.564	.507	.432	.335
	7	.665	.513	.452	.376	.279
	8	.627	.467	.404	.327	.233
	9	.592	.424	.361	.284	.194
	10	.558	.386	.322	.247	.162

The particular rate of return selected in discounted cash flow analysis is affected by the nature of the business enterprise and its relative profitability, the purpose of the capital expenditure, and other related factors. If the present value of the net cash flow expected from a proposed expenditure, at the selected rate, equals or exceeds the amount of the expenditure, the proposal is desirable. For purposes of illustration, assume a proposal for the acquisition of $200,000 of equipment with an expected useful life of 5 years and a minimum desired rate of return of 10%. The anticipated net cash flow for each of the 5 years and the analysis of the proposal are as follows. The report shows that the proposal is expected to recover the investment and provide more than the minimum rate of return.

DISCOUNTED
CASH FLOW
ANALYSIS
REPORT—
EQUIPMENT
ACQUISITION

Analysis of Proposal to Acquire Equipment
June 30, 19--

Year	Present Value of 1 at 10%	Net Cash Flow	Present Value of Net Cash Flow
1	.909	$ 70,000	$ 63,630
2	.826	60,000	49,560
3	.751	50,000	37,550
4	.683	40,000	27,320
5	.621	40,000	24,840
Total		$260,000	$202,900

Amount to be invested in equipment...................... 200,000

Excess of present value over amount to be invested......... $ 2,900

Each of the three methods of analyzing proposals for capital expenditures has both advantages and limitations. It is often wise to use a combination of methods in evaluating the various economic aspects of major projects. Obviously, estimates play a substantial role in all analyses of future expectations. Such factors as product pricing, improvements in products, availability and training of personnel, marketing procedures, and pressure of competition must also be given consideration in arriving at decisions.

MANAGERIAL USES OF QUANTITATIVE TECHNIQUES

Each of the previously discussed uses of accounting data in planning and controlling business operations has been concerned with a limited number of objectives or variables. In recent years, more sophisticated quantitative techniques have been developed to assist management in solving problems. This framework of quantitative techniques, sometimes called operations research, uses mathematical and statistical models with a large number of interdependent variables. The accounting system is the source of much of the quantitative data needed by many operations research techniques.

One of the areas for which operations research is often used is inventory control. For business enterprises that need large quantities of inventories to meet sales orders or production requirements, it is important to know the ideal quantity to be purchased in a single order and the minimum and maximum quantities to be on hand at any time. Such factors as economies of large-scale buying, storage costs, work interruption due to shortages, and seasonal and cyclical changes in production schedules need to be considered. Two quantitative techniques that may be used to assist in inventory control are (1) the economic order quantity formula and (2) linear programming.

Economic Order Quantity Formula

The economic order quantity (EOQ) is the optimum quantity of specified inventoriable materials to be ordered at one time. Important factors to be considered in determining the optimum quantity are the costs involved in processing an order for the materials and the costs involved in storing the materials.

The annual cost of processing orders for a specified material (cost of placing orders, verifying invoices, processing payments, etc.) increases as the number of orders placed increases. On the other hand, the annual cost of storing the materials (taxes, insurance, occupancy of storage space, etc.) decreases as the number of orders placed increases. The economic order quantity is therefore that quantity that will minimize the combined annual costs of ordering and storing materials.

The combined annual cost incurred in ordering and storing materials can be computed under various assumptions as to the number of orders to be placed during a year. To illustrate, assume the following data for an inventoriable material which is used at the same rate during the year:

<u>Material A732</u>

Units required during the year	1,200
Ordering cost, per order placed	$10.00
Storage cost, per unit	.60

If a single order were placed for the entire year's needs, the cost of ordering the 1,200 units would be $10. The average number of units held in inventory during the year would therefore be 600 (1,200 units ÷ 2) and would result in an annual storage cost of $360 (600 units × $.60). The combined order and storage costs for placing only one order during the year would thus be $370 ($10 + $360). If, instead of a single order, two orders were placed during the year, the order cost would be $20 (2 × $10), 600 units would need to be purchased on each order, the average inventory would be 300 units, and the annual storage costs would be $180 (300 units × $.60). Accordingly, the combined order and storage costs for placing two orders during the year would be $200 ($20 + $180). Successive computations will disclose the EOQ when the combined cost reaches its lowest point and starts upward. The following table shows an optimum of 200 units of material per order, with 6 orders per year, at a combined cost of $120.

			Order and Storage Costs		
Number of Orders	Number of Units Per Order	Average Units in Inventory	Order Cost	Storage Cost	Combined Cost
1	1,200	600	$10	$360	$370
2	600	300	20	180	200
3	400	200	30	120	150
4	300	150	40	90	130
5	240	120	50	72	122
6	200	100	60	60	120
7	171	86	70	52	122

TABULATION OF ECONOMIC ORDER QUANTITY

The economic order quantity may also be determined by a formula based on differential calculus. The formula and its application to the illustration is as follows:

ECONOMIC ORDER QUANTITY FORMULA

$$EOQ = \sqrt{\frac{2 \times \text{Annual Units Required} \times \text{Cost per Order Placed}}{\text{Storage Cost per Unit}}}$$

$$EOQ = \sqrt{\frac{2 \times 1,200 \times \$10}{\$.60}}$$

$$EOQ = \sqrt{40,000}$$

$$EOQ = 200 \text{ units}$$

The foregoing brief introduction to the determination of the economic order quantity suggests the many aspects of inventory control that may be encountered in actual practice. Formulas can be developed to incorporate such factors as economies of large-scale buying and seasonal and cyclical changes in volume of production.

Linear Programming | One of the techniques used in selecting the most favorable action from among a number of alternatives is called **linear programming**. It is sometimes used in solving business problems in which there are many variables and alternatives. The technique, which ordinarily uses many algebraic expressions, can be effectively used with a computer. Although a discussion of the technique is appropriate for more advanced courses, the following simplified illustration demonstrates the type of problem to which linear programming can be applied.

A manufacturing company purchases Part P for use at both its West Branch and East Branch. Part P is available in limited quantities from two suppliers. The total unit cost price varies considerably for parts acquired from the two suppliers mainly because of differences in transportation charges. The relevant data bearing upon the decision as to the most economical purchase arrangement are summarized in the following diagram:

Supplier A

Units available	75
Unit cost delivered to:	
West Branch	$ 70
East Branch	$ 90

West Branch

40 units required

Supplier B

Units available	75
Unit cost delivered to:	
West Branch	$ 80
East Branch	$120

East Branch

75 units required

It might appear that the most economical course of action would be to purchase (1) the 40 units required by West Branch from Supplier A at $70 a unit, (2) 35 units for East Branch from Supplier A at $90 a unit, and (3) the remaining 40 units required by East Branch from Supplier B at $120 a unit. If this course of action were followed, the total cost of the parts needed by the two branches would amount to $10,750, as indicated by the following computation:

| | Cost of Purchase | | |
	For West Branch	For East Branch	Total
From Supplier A:			
40 units at $70	$2,800		$ 2,800
35 units at $90		$3,150	3,150
From Supplier B:			
40 units at $120		4,800	4,800
Total.................................	$2,800	$7,950	$10,750

Although many different purchasing programs are possible, the most economical course of action would be to purchase (1) the 75 units required by East Branch from Supplier A at $90 a unit and (2) the 40 units required by West Branch from Supplier B at $80 a unit. If this plan were used, no units would be purchased at the lowest available unit cost, and the total cost of the parts would be $9,950, calculated as follows:

| | Cost of Purchase | | |
	For West Branch	For East Branch	Total
From Supplier A:			
75 units at $90		$6,750	$6,750
From Supplier B:			
40 units at $80	$3,200		3,200
Total.................................	$3,200	$6,750	$9,950

Self-Examination Questions
(Answers in Appendix C.)

1. If sales totaled $800,000 for the current year (80,000 units at $10 each) and $765,000 for the preceding year (85,000 units at $9 each), the effect of the quantity factor on the change in sales is:
   A. a $50,000 increase
   B. a $35,000 decrease
   C. a $45,000 decrease
   D. none of the above

2. If sales are $500,000, variable costs and expenses are $200,000, and fixed costs and expenses are $240,000, what is the break-even point?
   A. $200,000
   B. $240,000
   C. $400,000
   D. None of the above

3. Based on the data presented in Question 2, what is the margin of safety?
   A. 20%
   B. 40%
   C. 60%
   D. None of the above

4. Based on the data presented in Question 2, what is the contribution margin ratio?
   A. 40%
   B. 48%
   C. 88%
   D. None of the above

5. As used in analysis of proposed capital expenditures, the expected period of time that will elapse between the date of a capital expenditure and the complete recovery of the amount of cash invested is called:
   A. the average rate of return period
   B. the cash payback period
   C. the discounted cash flow period
   D. none of the above

Discussion Questions

1. What are management reports?

2. What is meant by responsibility reporting?

3. What determines the amount of detail presented in a budget performance report?

4. Discuss the two factors affecting both sales and cost of goods sold to which a change in gross profit can be attributed.

5. The analysis of increase in gross profit for a company includes the effect that an increase in the quantity of goods sold has had on the cost of goods sold. How is this figure determined?

6. (a) What is the break-even point? (b) How can the break-even point be determined?

7. (a) If fixed costs and expenses are $420,000 and variable costs and expenses are 70% of sales, what is the break-even point? (b) What sales are required to realize operating income of $150,000 under the conditions described in (a)?

8. What is the advantage of presenting break-even analysis in the chart form over the equation form?

9. Both McBride Company and Sherwood Company had the same sales, total costs and expenses, and operating income for the current fiscal year, yet McBride Company had a lower break-even point than Sherwood Company. Explain the reason for this difference in break-even points.

10. (a) What is meant by the term "margin of safety"? (b) If sales are $750,000, net income $60,000, and sales at the break-even point $480,000, what is the margin of safety?

11. What ratio indicates the percentage of each sales dollar that is available to cover fixed costs and expenses and to provide a profit?

12. (a) If sales are $350,000 and variable costs and expenses $210,000, what is the contribution margin ratio? (b) What is the contribution margin ratio if variable costs and expenses are 55% of sales?

13. An examination of the accounting records of Valentine Company disclosed a high contribution margin ratio and production at a level below maximum capacity. Based on this information, suggest a likely means of improving operating income. Explain.

14. What does the rate of return on assets measure?

15. Why is interest on borrowed funds ordinarily not considered in computing the rate of return on assets for the various operating divisions of a business enterprise?

16. What is a significant objection to the use of the average rate of return method in evaluating capital expenditure proposals?

17. (a) As used in analyses of proposed capital expenditures, what is the cash payback period? (b) Discuss the principal limitation of this method for evaluating capital expenditure proposals.

18. Which method of evaluating capital expenditure proposals reduces their expected future net cash flows to present values?

19. What is operations research?

20. What is the purpose of using the economic order quantity formula?

21. What is the operations research technique that is employed in selecting the most favorable action from among a number of alternatives in which there are many variables?

Exercises

Exercise 26-1. The chief accountant of Emerson Company prepares weekly reports of idleness of direct labor employees. These reports for the plant manager classify the idle time by departments. Idle time data for the week ended March 20 of the current year are as follows:

Department	Standard Hours	Productive Hours
1	4,200	3,990
2	2,800	2,800
3	6,100	5,978
4	1,900	1,786

The hourly direct labor rates are $18.60, $14.00, $16.50, and $15.50 respectively for Departments 1 through 4. The idleness was caused by a machine breakdown in Department 1, a materials shortage in Department 3, and a lack of sales orders in Department 4.

Instructions:

Prepare an idle time report, classified by departments, for the week ended March 20. Use the following columnar headings for the report:

	Production			Idle Time		
Dept.	Standard Hours	Actual Hours	Percentage of Standard	Hours	Cost of Idle Time	Remarks

Exercise 26-2. From the following data for Gossage Company, prepare an analysis of the decrease in gross profit for the year ended December 31, 1985:

	1985		1984	
Sales.................	40,000 units @ $18	$720,000	48,000 units @ $16.80	$806,400
Cost of goods sold.......	40,000 units @ $12	480,000	48,000 units @ $11.20	537,600
Gross profit		$240,000		$268,800

Exercise 26-3. For the coming year, Margo Company anticipates fixed costs and expenses of $240,000 and variable costs and expenses equal to 60% of sales.
(a) Compute the anticipated break-even point.
(b) Compute the sales required to realize operating income of $80,000.
(c) Construct a break-even chart, assuming sales of $1,000,000 at full capacity.
(d) Determine the probable operating income if sales total $750,000.

Exercise 26-4. (a) If Pridemore Company, with a break-even point at $600,000 of sales, has actual sales of $750,000, what is the margin of safety expressed (1) in dollars and (2) as a percentage of sales? (b) If the margin of safety for Strauss Company was 36%, fixed costs and expenses were $180,000, and variable costs and expenses were 55% of sales, what was the amount of actual sales?

Exercise 26-5. (a) If Torino Company budgets sales of $800,000, fixed costs and expenses of $224,000, and variable costs and expenses of $512,000, what is the anticipated contribution margin ratio? (b) If the contribution margin ratio for Underwood Company is 40%, sales were $2,400,000, and fixed costs and expenses were $670,000, what was the operating income?

Exercise 26-6. For the past year, Zeller Company had sales of $650,000, a margin of safety of 20%, and a contribution margin ratio of 45%. Compute:
    (a) The break-even point.
    (b) The variable costs and expenses.
    (c) The fixed costs and expenses.
    (d) The operating income.

Exercise 26-7. For 1984, a company had sales of $2,400,000, fixed costs and expenses of $600,000, and a contribution margin ratio of 30%. During 1985, the variable costs and expenses were 70% of sales, the fixed costs and expenses did not change from the previous year, and the margin of safety was 20%.
    (a) What was the operating income for 1984?
    (b) What was the break-even point for 1985?
    (c) What was the amount of sales for 1985?
    (d) What was the operating income for 1985?

Exercise 26-8. The sales, income from operations, and asset investments of two divisions in the same company are as follows:

	Division X	Division Y
Sales	$ 800,000	$550,000
Income from operations	120,000	82,500
Assets	1,000,000	412,500

    (a) What is the percentage of operating income to sales for each division of the company?
    (b) What is the rate of return on assets for each division?
    (c) As far as the data permit, comment on the relative performance of these two divisions.

Exercise 26-9. Walsh Company is considering the acquisition of machinery at a cost of $200,000. The machinery has an estimated life of 4 years and no salvage value. It is expected to provide yearly income of $30,000 and yearly net cash flows of $80,000. The company's minimum desired rate of return for discounted cash flow analysis is 15%. Compute the following:
    (a) The average rate of return, giving effect to depreciation on investment.
    (b) The cash payback period.
    (c) The excess or deficiency of present value over the amount to be invested as determined by the discounted cash flow method. Use the table of present values appearing in this chapter.

Exercise 26-10. Fernandez Company estimates that 1,680 units of material F will be required during the coming year. Past experience indicates that the storage costs are $.80 per unit and the cost to place an order is $42. Determine the economic order quantity to be purchased.

Problems
(Problems in Appendix B: 26-1B, 26-2B, 26-3B, 26-5B, 26-6B.)

(If the working papers correlating with the textbook are not used, omit Problem 26-1A.)

Problem 26-1A. The organization chart for manufacturing operations for Carlos Inc. is presented in the working papers. Also presented are the budget performance reports for the three departments in Plant 3 and a partially completed budget performance report prepared for the vice-president in charge of production.

In response to an inquiry into the cause of the direct labor variance in the Plating Shop-Plant 3, the following data were accumulated:

Job No.	Budgeted Hours	Actual Hours	Hourly Rate
940	110	116	$14.00
942	120	124	14.50
944	80	78	14.00
945	100	112	15.00
950	128	120	15.50
951	90	95	14.80
952	130	130	15.00
958	105	115	14.60

The significant variations from budgeted hours were attributed to machine breakdown on Jobs 940 and 942, to an inexperienced operator on Job 951, and to the fact that Jobs 945 and 958 were of types that were being done for the first time. Experienced operators were assigned to Jobs 944 and 950.

Instructions:

(1) Prepare a direct labor time variance report for the Plating Shop-Plant 3.
(2) Prepare a budget performance report for the use of the manager of Plant 3, detailing the relevant data from the three departments in the plant. Assume that the budgeted and actual administration expenses for the plant were $11,340 and $11,520, respectively.
(3) Complete the budget performance report for the vice-president in charge of production.

Problem 26-2A. Gibbons Company manufactures only one product. In 1984, the plant operated at full capacity. At a meeting of the board of directors on December 18, 1984, it was decided to raise the price of this product from $32, which had prevailed last year, to $35, effective January 1, 1985. Although the cost price was expected to rise about $1.50 per unit in 1985 because of a direct materials and direct labor wage increase, the increase in selling price was expected to cover this increase and also add to operating income. The comparative income statement for 1984 and 1985 is as follows:

	1985		1984	
Sales.		$420,000		$480,000
Cost of goods sold: variable	$150,000		$165,000	
fixed.	120,000	270,000	120,000	285,000
Gross profit		$150,000		$195,000
Operating expenses: variable	$ 43,200		$52,500	
fixed.	75,000	118,200	75,000	127,500
Operating income		$ 31,800		$ 67,500

Instructions:

(1) Prepare a gross profit analysis report for the year 1985.
(2) At a meeting of the board of directors on March 2, 1986, the president, after reading the gross profit analysis report, made the following comment:

"It looks as if the increase in unit cost price was $3.50 and not the anticipated $1.50. The failure of operating management to keep these costs within the bounds of those in 1984, except for the anticipated $1.50 increase in direct materials and direct labor cost, was a major factor in the decrease in gross profit."

Do you agree with this analysis of the increase in unit cost price? Explain.

Problem 26-3A. Blier Company expects to maintain the same inventories at the end of 1985 as at the beginning of the year. The total of all production costs for the year is therefore assumed to be equal to the cost of goods sold. With this in mind, the various department heads were asked to submit estimates of the expenses for their departments during 1985. A summary report of these estimates is as follows:

	Estimated Fixed Expense	Estimated Variable Expense (per unit sold)
Production costs:		
Direct materials	$ —	$7.50
Direct labor	—	5.70
Factory overhead	284,000	1.80
Selling expenses:		
Sales salaries and commissions	104,000	.90
Advertising	63,000	—
Travel	30,900	—
Miscellaneous selling expense	16,300	.30
General expenses:		
Office and officers' salaries	135,100	—
Supplies	16,900	.15
Miscellaneous general expense	9,800	.15
	$660,000	$16.50

It is expected that 80,000 units will be sold at a selling price of $27.50 a unit. Capacity output is 100,000 units.

Instructions:

(1) Determine the break-even point (a) in dollars of sales, (b) in units, and (c) in terms of capacity.
(2) Prepare an estimated income statement for 1985.
(3) Construct a break-even chart, indicating the break-even point in dollars of sales.
(4) What is the expected margin of safety?
(5) What is the expected contribution margin ratio?

Problem 26-4A. Portnoy Company operated at full capacity during 1984. Its income statement for 1984 is as follows:

Sales..	$3,300,000
Cost of goods sold	1,872,000
Gross profit.....................................	$1,428,000
Operating expenses:	
Selling expenses $648,000	
General expenses 180,000	
Total operating expenses.....................	828,000
Operating income	$ 600,000

An analysis of costs and expenses reveals the following division of costs and expenses between fixed and variable:

	Fixed	Variable
Cost of goods sold.......	25%	75%
Selling expenses........	20%	80%
General expenses	68%	32%

Management is considering a plant expansion program that will permit an increase of $700,000 in yearly sales. The expansion will increase fixed costs and expenses by $120,000, but will not affect the relationship between sales and variable costs and expenses.

Instructions:
(1) Determine for present capacity (a) the total fixed costs and expenses and (b) the total variable costs and expenses.
(2) Determine the percentage of total variable costs and expenses to sales.
(3) Compute the break-even point under present conditions.
(4) Compute the break-even point under the proposed program.
(5) Determine the amount of sales that would be necessary under the proposed program to realize the $600,000 of operating income that was earned in 1984.
(6) Determine the maximum operating income possible with the expanded plant.
(7) If the proposal is accepted and sales remain at the 1984 level, what will the operating income be for 1985?
(8) Based upon the data given, would you recommend accepting the proposal? Explain.

Problem 26-5A. Kaufman Company is considering the addition of a new product to its line. For 1984, production was at 70% of capacity, the assets employed were $2,500,000 (original cost), and the income statement showed an operating income of $300,000, computed as follows:

Sales		$2,250,000
Less: Cost of goods sold.....................	$1,350,000	
Selling expenses	440,000	
General expenses	160,000	1,950,000
Operating income		$ 300,000

If the new product is added, market research indicates that 6,000 units can be sold in 1985 at an estimated selling price of $75 per unit. The idle capacity will be utilized to produce the product, but an additional $480,000 in plant assets will be required. The cost data per unit for the new product are as follows:

Direct materials	$19.50
Direct labor	18.00
Factory overhead (includes depreciation on additional investment)	12.50
Selling expenses	9.00
General expenses	4.00
	$63.00

Instructions:

(1) Prepare an estimated income statement for 1985 for the new product.
(2) Prepare a schedule indicating the rate of return on assets under present conditions and for the new product. Use the original cost of the assets in your computations.
(3) Would you recommend addition of the new product? Would you require other data before you make your decision? If so, what additional data would you require?

Problem 26-6A. The capital expenditures budget committee is considering two projects. The estimated operating income and net cash flows from each project are as follows:

	Project A		Project B	
Year	Operating Income	Net Cash Flow	Operating Income	Net Cash Flow
1	$12,000	$ 40,000	$10,800	$ 24,000
2	9,000	30,000	10,800	24,000
3	6,000	20,000	7,200	36,000
4	6,000	20,000	3,600	24,000
5	3,000	6,000	3,600	8,000
	$36,000	$116,000	$36,000	$116,000

Each project requires an investment of $80,000, with no residual value expected. The committee has selected a rate of 12% for purposes of the discounted cash flow analysis.

Instructions:

(1) Compute the following:
  (a) The average rate of return for each project, giving effect to depreciation on the investment.
  (b) The excess or deficiency of present value over amount to be invested, as determined by the discounted cash flow method for each project. Use the present value table appearing in this chapter.
(2) Prepare a brief report for the budget committee, advising it on the relative merits of the two projects.

Mini-Case

Hardman Company manufactures product P, which sold for $20 per unit in 1984. For the past several years, sales and net income have been declining. On sales of $540,000 in 1984, the company operated near the break-even point and used only 60% of its productive capacity. John Hardman, your father-in-law, is considering several proposals to reverse the trend of declining sales and net income, to more fully use production facilities, and to increase profits. One proposal under consideration is to reduce the unit selling price to $19.20.

Your father-in-law has asked you to aid him in assessing the proposal to reduce the sales price by $.80. For this purpose, he provided the following summary of the estimated fixed and variable costs and expenses for 1985, which are unchanged from 1984:

Variable costs and expenses:
Production costs .... $8.60 per unit
Selling expenses .... 2.00 per unit
General expenses .... 1.40 per unit

Fixed costs and expenses:
Production costs...................... $100,000
Selling expenses 40,000
General expenses 60,000

Instructions:

(1) Determine the break-even point for 1985 in dollars, assuming (a) no change in sales price and (b) the proposed sales price.
(2) How much additional sales are necessary for Hardman Company to break even in 1985 under the proposal?
(3) Determine the net income for 1985, assuming (a) no change in sales price and volume from 1984 and (b) the new sales price and no change in volume from 1984.
(4) Determine the maximum net income for 1985, assuming the proposed sales price.
(5) Briefly list factors that you would discuss with your father-in-law in evaluating the proposal.

27

CHAPTER

Income Taxes and Their Effect on Business Decisions

CHAPTER OBJECTIVES

Describe the federal income tax system and the basic accounting methods that can be used for federal tax purposes.

Describe and illustrate the basic components and computations for determining federal income taxes of individuals and corporations.

Describe and illustrate various legal means of minimizing income taxes.

27

CHAPTER

The federal government and more than three fourths of the states levy an income tax. In addition, some of the states permit municipalities or other political subdivisions to levy income taxes. Because of the complex nature of income determination, accounting and income taxes are interrelated. An understanding of any but the simplest aspects of income taxes is almost impossible without some knowledge of accounting concepts.

Because the tax can be a significant expenditure, taxpayers try to plan their affairs so that the amount of the tax can be kept to a minimum. For this reason, managers of business enterprises make few decisions about proposals for new ventures or about significant changes in business practices without first giving careful consideration to the tax consequences.

There are many cases in which an enterprise or an individual taxpayer may choose from among two or more optional accounting methods. The particular method chosen may have a great effect on the amount of income tax, not only in the year in which the choice is made but also in later years. Examples of such cases described in earlier chapters are cost-flow assumptions for inventories (first-in, first-out; last-in, first-out; etc.) and revenue recognition practices (point of sale, installment method, etc.).

Before the impact of income taxes on business decisions can be discussed in a meaningful way, a knowledge of the basic structure of the federal income tax is necessary. The explanations and illustrations of the federal system presented in this chapter are brief and relatively free of the many complexities encountered in actual practice. In addition, it should be noted that the federal tax laws are often changed and the current law should be examined before making decisions. Nevertheless, the following discussion should be useful in demonstrating the essential characteristics of the tax system and their effect on business decisions.

FEDERAL INCOME TAX SYSTEM

The present system of federal income tax began with the Revenue Act of 1913, which was enacted soon after the ratification of the Sixteenth Amendment to the Constitution. All current income tax statutes, as well as other federal tax laws, are now codified in the **Internal Revenue Code (IRC)**.

The executive branch of the government charged with responsibility in tax matters is the Treasury Department. The branch of the Department concerned specifically with enforcement and collection of the income tax is the **Internal Revenue Service (IRS)**, headed by the Commissioner of Internal Revenue. Interpretations of the law and directives formulated according to express provisions of the IRC are issued in various forms. The most important and comprehensive are the "Regulations," which extend to more than two thousand pages.

Taxpayers alleged by the IRS to be deficient in reporting or paying their tax may, if they disagree with the determination, present their case in informal conferences at district and regional levels. Unresolved disputes may be taken to the federal courts for settlement. The taxpayer may seek relief in the Tax Court or may pay the disputed amount and sue to recover it.

The data required for the determination of income tax liability are supplied by the taxpayer on official forms and supporting schedules that are referred to collectively as a **tax return**. Failure to receive the forms from the appropriate governmental agency or failure to maintain adequate records does not relieve taxpayers of their legal obligation to file annual tax returns. Willful failure to comply with the income tax laws may result in the imposition of severe penalties, both civil and criminal.

The income tax is not imposed upon business units as such, but upon taxable entities. The principal taxable entities are individuals, corporations, estates, and trusts. Business enterprises organized as sole proprietorships are not taxable entities. The revenues and expenses of such business enterprises are reported in the individual tax returns of the owners. Partnerships are not taxable entities but are required to report in an informational return the details of their revenues, expenses, and allocations to partners. The partners then report on their individual tax returns the amount of net income and other special items allocated to them on the partnership return.

Corporations engaged in business for profit are generally treated as distinct taxable entities. However, it is possible for two or more corporations with common ownership to join in filing a consolidated return. Subchapter S of the IRC also permits a nonpublic corporation that conforms to specified requirements to elect to be treated in a manner similar to a partnership. The effect of the election is to tax the shareholders on their distributive shares of the net income instead of taxing the corporation.

ACCOUNTING METHODS

Although neither the IRC nor the Regulations provide uniform systems of accounting for use by all taxpayers, detailed procedures are prescribed in certain cases. In addition, the IRS has the authority to prescribe accounting methods where those used by a taxpayer fail to yield a fair determination of taxable income. In general, taxpayers have the option of using either the cash basis or the accrual basis.

Cash Basis

Because of its greater simplicity, the cash method of determining taxable income is usually used by individuals whose sources of income are limited to salary, dividends, and interest. Employers are required to use the cash basis in determining the salary amounts which they report to their employees and also to the IRS in connection with the withholding of income tax. Payments of interest and dividends by business enterprises are also required to be reported according to the cash method.

Professional and other service enterprises (e.g., physicians, attorneys, insurance agencies) also ordinarily use the cash basis in determining net income. One of the advantages is that the fees charged to clients or customers are not considered to be earned until payment is received. Accordingly, no provisions need be made for uncollectible accounts expense. Similarly, it is not necessary to accrue expenses incurred but not paid within the tax year. Rent, electricity, wages, and other items of expense are recorded only at the time of cash payment. It is not permissible, however, to treat the entire cost of long-lived assets as an expense of the period in which the cash payment is made. Deductions for depreciation on equipment and buildings used for business purposes may be claimed in the same manner as under the accrual basis, regardless of when payment is made. Similarly, when advance payments for insurance premiums or rentals on business property exceed a period of one year, the total cost must be prorated over the life of the contract.

Recognition of revenue according to the cash method is not always contingent upon the actual receipt of cash. In some cases, revenue is said to be *constructively received* at the time it becomes available to the taxpayer, regardless of when it is actually converted to cash. For example, a check for services rendered which is received before the end of a taxable year is income of that year, even though the check is not deposited or cashed until the following year. Other examples of constructive receipt are bond interest coupons due within the taxable year and interest credited to a savings account as of the last day of the taxable year.

Accrual Basis

For businesses in which production or trading in merchandise is an important factor, purchases and sales must be accounted for on the accrual basis. Thus, revenues from sales must be reported in the year in which the goods are sold, regardless of when the cash is received. Similarly, the cost of goods purchased must be reported in the year in which the liabilities are incurred, regardless of when payment is made. The usual adjustments must also be made for the beginning and ending inventories in order to determine the cost of goods sold and the gross profit. However, manufacturing and mercantile enterprises are not required to extend the accrual basis to every other phase of their operations. A mixture of the cash and accrual methods of accounting is permissible, if it yields reasonable results and is used consistently from year to year.

INCOME TAX ON INDIVIDUALS

Methods of accounting in general, as well as many of the regulations affecting the determination of net business or professional income, are not affected by the legal nature or the organizational structure of the taxpayer. On the other hand, the tax base and the tax rate structure for individuals differ markedly from those which apply to corporations.

The individual's tax base, upon which the amount of income tax is determined, is called **taxable income**. Taxable income is determined as follows:

DETERMINATION OF TAXABLE INCOME

GROSS INCOME
minus
DEDUCTIONS FROM GROSS INCOME
equals
ADJUSTED GROSS INCOME
minus
EXCESS ITEMIZED DEDUCTIONS AND EXEMPTIONS
equals
TAXABLE INCOME

After taxable income is determined, most individual taxpayers use one of two basic methods for determining the tax: (1) the tax table, the simpler procedure, or (2) the tax rate schedules. Generally, the tax table must be used if taxable income is less than $50,000. Taxpayers with income above $50,000 must use the tax rate schedules.

The basic concepts underlying the determination of taxable income and the use of the tax table and tax rate schedules are discussed in the paragraphs that follow.

Gross Income

Items of gross income subject to tax are sometimes called **taxable gross income** or **includable gross income**. Items of gross income not subject to tax are often termed **nontaxable gross income** or **excludable gross income**. A list of some of the ordinary items of gross income inclusions and exclusions of individuals is presented below.

TAXABLE ITEMS	NONTAXABLE ITEMS
Wages and other remuneration from employer.	Federal old-age pension benefits.
Tips and gratuities for services rendered.	Value of property received as a gift.
Amount in excess of $100 for dividends from domestic sources.[1]	Value of property received by bequest, devise, or inheritance.
Portion of pensions, annuities, and endowments representing income.	Dividends of $100 or less from domestic sources.[1]
Rents and royalties.	Life insurance proceeds received because of death of insured.
Income from a business or profession.	Interest on obligations of a state or political subdivision.
Taxable gains from the sale of real estate, securities, and other property.	Scholarships for which no services are required.
Distributive share of partnership income.	Portion of pensions, annuities, and endowments representing return of capital invested.
Income from an estate or trust.	Compensation for injuries or for damages related to personal or family rights.
Prizes won in contests.	
Gambling winnings.	Worker's compensation insurance for sickness or injury.
Jury fees.	Limited disability pay benefits.
Gains from illegal transactions.	Child support received.
Alimony received.	

PARTIAL LIST OF TAXABLE AND NONTAXABLE ITEMS

Wholly excludable items of gross income, such as interest on state bonds, are not reported on the tax return. Partly excludable items, such as dividends, are reported in their entirety and the excludable portion is then deducted.

The amount of gross income, in conjunction with age, marital status, and joint return election, determines whether an individual is required to file a return. Unmarried individuals under 65 years of age as of the last day of the year must file a return if their gross income for the year is $3,300 or more. Those who are 65 or over need file only if their gross income is $4,300 or more. Married individuals may combine the gross income and deductions of both spouses in one tax return called a **joint return.** If both spouses are under 65 years of age and they elect a joint return, they must file if their gross income is $5,400 or more. The limit is increased by $1,000 for each spouse who is 65 or over. Married individuals who elect separate returns must file if their gross income is $1,000 or more.

---

[1]In a joint return of husband and wife, the amount is $200.

A dependent of another taxpayer must file a return if the dependent has dividends, interest, or other unearned income of $1,000 or more.

When an individual meets the applicable gross income test, a return must be filed, even though the allowable deductions and exemptions exceed the gross income. A return must also be filed, regardless of the applicable gross income test, for taxpayers to receive a tax refund.

Deductions from Gross Income | Business expenses and other expenses related to earning certain types of revenue are deductible from gross income to yield **adjusted gross income**. The categories of such expenses that are of general applicability are described in the following paragraphs.

Business Expenses Other Than as an Employee

Ordinary and necessary expenses incurred in the operation of a sole proprietorship are deductible from gross income. The tax forms provide spaces for reporting sales, cost of goods sold, gross profit, salaries, depreciation, and other business expenses, and finally net income, which is the adjusted gross income derived from the business.

Expenses that are directly connected with earning rent or royalty income are allowable as deductions from gross income in determining adjusted gross income. Expenses commonly incurred in connection with rental properties include depreciation, taxes, repairs, wages of custodian, and interest on indebtedness incurred to purchase the income-producing property.

Losses from a sale or exchange of property are deductible from gross income, provided the property was acquired or held for the production of income. Thus, losses from the sale of rental property or of investments in stocks and bonds are deductible within carefully stated limitations.

Business Expenses of an Employee

For an employee, the types and amounts of employment-related expenses that may be deducted from salary and similar remuneration are limited by the statutes and regulations. Generally four types of unreimbursed expenses are deductible from gross income by an employee. If the employer reimburses the employee for a part of the expenses, only the amount by which the expenses exceed the amount of the reimbursement is deductible. If the amount of the reimbursement is more than the expenses incurred, the excess is included in gross income. The four types of qualifying expenses are described briefly in the following paragraphs.

Transportation expenses. Employment-related costs of public transportation and the cost of operating an employee-owned automobile are deductible from gross income. Instead of deducting actual automobile expenses, the taxpayer may elect a standard mileage rate of 20.5¢ a mile for the first 15,000 business miles driven during the year and 11¢ a mile for the excess over 15,000 miles. The cost of commuting between the employee's home and place of employment is not deductible.

Travel expenses. Deductible travel expenses include transportation expense and the cost of meals and lodging if incurred by an employee when away from home overnight.

Outside salesperson's expenses. In addition to transportation and travel, outside salespersons can deduct expenses incurred in soliciting business away from the employer's establishment. Such expenses include telephone, secretarial help, meals for customers, and entertainment.

Moving expenses. The expenses incurred by an employee in changing place of residence in connection with beginning work in a new location, either because of a transfer in an existing job or for new employment, are deductible from gross income. The distance moved and the length of time employed in the new location must meet specified minimum requirements.

Deduction for Retirement Plan Contribution

A self-employed individual may establish a qualified retirement fund and deduct the annual contributions from gross income in determining adjusted gross income. The IRC and related regulations state many limitations on the amount of the contributions, the nature and control of the fund, and the time (based on age) when pension benefits must be paid. When the retirement benefits are received in the form of a pension, they must be included in the gross income of the taxpayer.

In 1982, Congress enacted a provision allowing employees to establish retirement funds referred to as **Individual Retirement Accounts.** Contributions to these accounts may be deducted from gross income in determining adjusted gross income. Prior to this legislation, employees who were covered by an employer-sponsored plan were not permitted to establish Individual Retirement Accounts.

Alimony

Alimony is deductible by the payer (and is taxable to the payee). Child support payments are not deductible by the payer nor taxable to the payee.

Two-Earner Married Couples

For married taxpayers, filing a joint return normally results in lower taxes than does filing separate returns. When both spouses have nearly equal incomes, however, the joint tax liability could exceed the total both would owe if they were single and filing separately. To compensate for this "marriage penalty", 10% of the earnings of the spouse with the smaller income can be deducted, up to a maximum deduction of $3,000.

Adjusted Gross Income

Each category of expenses described in the preceding section is deducted from an amount of related gross income. The sum of the resulting figures is the adjusted gross income. If the adjusted gross income from a certain source is a negative amount, such as a net loss from business operations or from property rentals, it is deducted from the positive amounts in the other categories. The system of assembling data for each type of gross income and its related deductions is illustrated by the following summary for a single taxpayer:

DETERMINATION OF
ADJUSTED GROSS
INCOME

Salary from employment..............................	$36,200	
Deductions for employee business expenses........	900	$35,300
Rental income.......................................	$ 9,500	
Deductions for expenses attributable to rental property	10,100	(600)
Interest on bank deposits............................		400
Dividends from corporation stocks...................	$ 1,225	
Exclusion	100	1,125
Adjusted gross income..............................		$36,225

Deductions from Adjusted Gross Income

After the amount of adjusted gross income of an individual is determined, the excess itemized deductions and exemptions are subtracted to yield taxable income. These two deductions from adjusted gross income are described in the following paragraphs.

Excess Itemized Deductions

Certain specified expenditures and losses may be *itemized* and deducted from adjusted gross income. Although some taxpayers are required to itemize their deductions, most taxpayers itemize them only if doing so will reduce the amount of the tax.

As an alternative to itemizing deductions, taxpayers may compute their tax using the zero bracket amount. The **zero bracket amount** is based upon the taxpayer's filing status (single, married filing a joint return, etc.) without regard to the amount of income. The effect of the zero bracket amount is to allow the taxpayer an automatic specified deduction without requiring a detailed listing of itemized deductions. This zero bracket amount is built in to both the tax table and the tax rate schedules. Therefore, only if the deductions are itemized and they exceed the zero bracket amount (thus the term **excess itemized deductions**) will the computation of the tax be affected. Single taxpayers would itemize deductions only if the total exceeded $2,300 (the zero bracket amount for single taxpayers), while married taxpayers filing joint returns would do so only if their itemized deductions exceeded $3,400 (the zero bracket amount for such taxpayers).

The deductions that are generally available to individuals who itemize deductions are described in the paragraphs that follow.

Nonbusiness expenses. Expenses in this category are those related to the production or conservation of income but which do not qualify as "business" expenses or other categories of expenses that are deductible from gross income in determining adjusted gross income. Specifically, nonbusiness expenses are the expenses attributable to (1) the production or collection of income, (2) the maintenance or management of income-producing property, or (3) the determination, collection, or refund of any tax that does not qualify as a deduction from gross income. For example, job-related travel expenses and labor union dues are both attributable to the "production of income," but only the former is deductible from *gross income*. The latter is deductible from *adjusted gross income* as a nonbusiness expense. Other examples of nonbusiness expenses are fees paid for the preparation of a personal income tax return, the cost of investment advisory services and subscriptions to financial periodicals, and the cost of job uniforms that are unsuitable for street wear.

Charitable contributions. Contributions made by an individual to domestic organizations created exclusively for religious, charitable, scientific, literary, or educational purposes, or for the prevention of cruelty to children or animals are deductible, provided the organization is nonprofit and does not devote a substantial part of its activities to influencing legislation. Contributions to domestic governmental units and to organizations of war veterans are also deductible.

The limitation on the amount of qualified contributions that may be deducted ranges from 20% of adjusted gross income for contributions to private foundations to 50% of adjusted gross income for contributions to public charities, with 50% being the overall maximum. There are other intermediate limitations related to contributions of various types of property other than cash.[2]

Interest expense. Interest expense of an entirely personal nature, such as on indebtedness incurred to buy a home or an automobile, is deductible.

Taxes. Most of the taxes levied by the federal government are not deductible from adjusted gross income. Some of the taxes of a nonbusiness or personal nature levied by states or their political subdivisions are deductible from adjusted gross income. The deductible status of the more common state and local taxes is as follows:

Deductible: Real estate, personal property, income, and general sales taxes.
Nondeductible: Gift, inheritance, estate, gasoline, cigarette, and alcoholic beverages taxes.

Medical expenses. Amounts paid for prescription drugs and insulin and other medical expenses are deductible to the extent that they exceed 5% of adjusted gross income. Other medical expenses include medical care insurance, doctors' fees, hospital expenses, etc.

Casualty and theft losses. Property losses not compensated for by insurance, resulting from a casualty such as fire, storm, or automobile accident or from theft, are deductible to the extent that the total loss for the year exceeds 10% of adjusted gross income. In computing the total loss, the loss from any one casualty or theft is included only to the extent it exceeds $100. Payments to another person for property damage or personal injury caused by the taxpayer are not casualty losses.

---

[2]For taxpayers who do not itemize deductions, a portion of their contributions may be deducted from adjusted gross income. This provision is scheduled to expire in 1986.

Exemptions

Each taxpayer is entitled to a personal exemption of $1,000. An additional exemption is allowed for each dependent.

In general, a dependent is a person who satisfies all of the following requirements: (1) is closely related to the taxpayer, (2) received over one half of his or her support from the taxpayer during the year, (3) had less than $1,000 of gross income during the year, and (4) if married, does not file a joint return. However, the $1,000 limitation on gross income does not apply to a child of the taxpayer who is either under 19 years of age at the end of the taxable year or who has been a full-time student at an educational institution for at least five months of the year.

An additional exemption is allowed to a taxpayer and/or spouse who is 65 years of age or older on the last day of the taxable year. An additional exemption is also allowed to a taxpayer and/or spouse who is blind at the end of the taxable year. Neither of these additional exemptions is available for dependents of the taxpayer.

Determination of Income Tax

There are four filing methods, classified as follows:

1. Single taxpayers.
2. Married taxpayers filing joint returns and qualifying widows and widowers.
3. Married taxpayers filing separate returns.
4. Unmarried (or legally separated) taxpayers who qualify as heads of household.

It is usually advantageous for married taxpayers (not legally separated) to file joint returns. If all of the income subject to tax is earned exclusively by one spouse, a joint return will invariably yield a smaller tax liability than a separate return. In some cases, separate returns may result in a smaller amount of income tax. When there is any question concerning the filing method to be used, the total tax liability should be determined by both methods.

To qualify as a head of household, an individual must be unmarried at the end of the taxable year and must, in general, maintain as his or her home a household in which at least one of the following persons lives: (1) an unmarried son, daughter, or descendent, (2) a married son, daughter, or descendent who qualifies as a dependent of the taxpayer, or (3) any other close relative who qualifies as a dependent of the taxpayer. The head of household status may also be claimed by an unmarried taxpayer who maintains his or her dependent parent in a separate household.

As discussed in preceding paragraphs, taxpayers determine their tax by use of either the tax table or the tax rate schedules. A portion of the tax table and two tax rate schedules are presented on page 771.[3]

To illustrate the use of the tax table, assume that a single taxpayer has taxable income of $19,710. Reference to the tax table indicates that the income tax in this situation is $3,134.

_____

[3]The income tax table and rate schedules are often changed by Congress. For example, current plans are to adjust them from year to year for inflation.

TAX TABLE	If taxable income is—		And you are—			
	Over	But not over	Single	Married Filing Jointly	Married Filing Separately	Head of Household
			Your tax is—			
	2,300	2,350	3	0	69	3
	2,350	2,400	8	0	74	8
	2,400	2,450	14	0	80	14
	2,450	2,500	19	0	85	19
	5,500	5,550	399	234	483	366
	5,550	5,600	405	240	490	372
	5,600	5,650	413	246	497	378
	5,650	5,700	420	252	504	384
	19,700	19,750	3,134	2,412	3,838	2,900
	19,750	19,800	3,147	2,421	3,855	2,912
	19,800	19,850	3,160	2,430	3,871	2,924
	19,850	19,900	3,173	2,439	3,888	2,936

NOTE: The zero bracket amount has been built into the tax table.

TAX RATE SCHEDULES

Single Taxpayers				Married Taxpayers Filing Joint Returns and Qualifying Widows and Widowers			
If taxable income is:			The tax is:	If taxable income is:			The tax is:
Not over $2,300....			–0–	Not over $3,400....			–0–
Over—	But not over—		of the amount over—	Over—	But not over—		of the amount over—
$2,300	$3,400	11%	$2,300	$3,400	$5,500	11%	$3,400
$3,400	$4,400	$121 + 12%	$3,400	$5,500	$7,600	$231 + 12%	$5,500
$4,400	$6,500	$241 + 14%	$4,400	$7,600	$11,900	$483 + 14%	$7,600
$6,500	$8,500	$535 + 16%	$6,500	$11,900	$16,000	$1,085 + 16%	$11,900
$8,500	$10,800	$835 + 16%	$8,500	$16,000	$20,200	$1,741 + 18%	$16,000
$10,800	$12,900	$1,203 + 18%	$10,800	$20,200	$24,600	$2,497 + 22%	$20,200
$12,900	$15,000	$1,581 + 20%	$12,900	$24,600	$29,900	$3,465 + 25%	$24,600
$15,000	$18,200	$2,001 + 23%	$15,000	$29,900	$35,200	$4,790 + 28%	$29,900
$18,200	$23,500	$2,737 + 26%	$18,200	$35,200	$45,800	$6,274 + 33%	$35,200
$23,500	$28,800	$4,115 + 30%	$23,500	$45,800	$60,000	$9,772 + 38%	$45,800
$28,800	$34,100	$5,705 + 34%	$28,800	$60,000	$85,600	$15,168 + 42%	$60,000
$34,100	$41,500	$7,507 + 38%	$34,100	$85,600	$109,400	$25,920 + 45%	$85,600
$41,500	$55,300	$10,319 + 42%	$41,500	$109,400	$162,400	$36,630 + 49%	$109,400
$55,300	$81,800	$16,115 + 48%	$55,300	$162,400	$215,400	$62,600 + 50%	$162,400
$81,800	$108,300	$28,835 + 50%	$81,800	$215,400	....	$89,100 + 50%	$215,400
$108,300	....	$42,085 + 50%	$108,300				

Note: The zero bracket amount has been built into these Tax Rate Schedules.

To illustrate the use of the tax rate schedules, assume that married taxpayers filing a joint return have taxable income of $52,000. Their tax is determined as follows:

Tax on	$45,800	$ 9,772
Tax on	6,200 at 38%	2,356
Total on	$52,000	$12,128

The tax schedules and the tax table provide for a graduated series of tax rates; that is, successively higher rates are applied to successively higher segments of income. Because of this progression of rates, the income tax is sometimes termed a **progressive tax.** The highest rate applied to the income of any particular taxpayer is sometimes called the taxpayer's **marginal tax rate.** In the illustration above, the marginal tax rate is 38%.

Capital Gains and Losses | Gains and losses resulting from individuals selling or exchanging certain types of assets, called **capital assets,** are given special treatment for income tax purposes. Capital assets most commonly owned by taxpayers are stocks and bonds. Under certain conditions, land, buildings, and equipment used in business may also be treated as capital assets.

The gains and losses from the sale or exchange of capital assets are classified as **short-term** or **long-term,** based on the length of time the assets are held (owned). The holding period for short-term gains and losses is one year or less. For long-term gains and losses, the holding period is more than one year.

The aggregate of all short-term gains and losses during a taxable year is called a **net short-term capital gain** (or **loss**) and the aggregate of all long-term gains and losses is similarly identified as a **net long-term capital gain** (or **loss**). The net short-term and net long-term results are then combined to form the **net capital gain** (or **loss**).

Net Capital Gain

If there is a net capital gain, it is reported as gross income. To the extent that a net capital gain is composed of an excess of a net long-term gain over a net short-term loss (if any), 60% of such excess is deducted from gross income to yield adjusted gross income from capital gains. The application of the foregoing provisions is demonstrated by the following illustration:

	A	B	C
Net short-term capital gain (loss)...............	($ 2,000)	$12,000	$ 5,000
Net long-term capital gain (loss)	12,000	(2,000)	5,000
Net capital gain — gross income	$10,000	$10,000	$10,000
Long-term capital gain deduction	6,000	—	3,000
Adjusted gross income from capital gain	$ 4,000	$10,000	$ 7,000

Although the net capital gain is $10,000 in each of the three examples, the adjusted gross income from capital gain is $4,000, $10,000, and $7,000 respectively. There is thus a distinct advantage in having capital gains qualify as long-term.

A gain from the sale of a taxpayer's principal residence is treated as a capital gain (a loss is not deductible). The tax on the gain may be postponed if a new home is purchased within 24 months at a cost equal to or more than the adjusted sales price of the old home. If a new home is not purchased, or if the purchase price of a new home is less than the adjusted sales price of the old home, some or all of the gain is subject to tax. Taxpayers who are 55 or older may choose a one-time exclusion of $125,000 of the gain if they lived in the home for three of the five years prior to the sale. Any remaining gain may be postponed by replacing the residence (if certain conditions with respect to replacement cost are met).

Net Capital Loss

When the taxpayer's transactions in capital assets during the year result in a net capital loss instead of a net capital gain, the deductibility of the loss is severely limited. The loss can be deducted from gross income only to the extent of $3,000.

As in the case of a net capital gain, the composition of the "net loss" must be considered. If it is composed of short-term loss, each dollar of loss provides an equivalent dollar deduction from gross income. If it is composed of long-term loss, two dollars of loss are needed to yield one dollar of deduction. If there is both a net short-term loss and a net long-term loss, the former is deducted from gross income first. The excess of net capital loss is carried over and may be used in future years. The application of these provisions is illustrated as follows:

	A	B	C
Net short-term capital gain (loss)	($9,000)	$2,000	($4,000)
Net long-term capital gain (loss)	2,000	(9,000)	(3,000)
Net capital loss	($7,000)	($7,000)	($7,000)
Capital loss used to reduce adjusted gross income by $3,000	(3,000)	(6,000)	(3,000)
Capital loss carryover to future years:			
Short-term carryover	($4,000)	—	($1,000)
Long-term carryover	—	($1,000)	(3,000)

If there is a net capital loss, it is advantageous to have it qualify as short-term rather than long-term, which is the reverse of net capital gain.

Credits Against the Tax | After the amount of the income tax has been determined, the tax may be reduced on a dollar-for-dollar basis by the amount of various credits. These credits are therefore quite different from deductions and exemptions, which are reductions of the income subject to tax. The most common credits are described in the paragraphs that follow.

Political Contributions

Concern over the high cost of financing political campaigns and the potential political influence of a few large donors prompted Congress to encourage small cash contributions to political funds. A credit against the tax liability may therefore be claimed for one half of the contributions, with a maximum credit of $50 ($100 for joint returns).

Residential Energy Credit

Owners and renters of homes are eligible for a credit of 15% of the first $2,000 they spend on new qualifying home energy conservation items with an expected life of three or more years. An additional credit of up to 40% of the first $10,000 is granted on expenditures for solar, wind-powered, or geothermal property for the home. These expenditures must be for new property installed in the taxpayer's principal home and must have a useful life of at least five years.

Investment Credit

The investment tax credit was enacted in 1962 to encourage businesses to purchase equipment and thereby stimulate the economy. Since its original enactment, the IRC has been changed often in attempts to fine tune the economy. In general, the credit is granted for purchases of certain new or used tangible personal property with a useful life of at least 3 years that is used in the taxpayer's trade or business. The maximum credit is 10% of the cost of property with a life of 5 years or more and 6% for property with a life of less than five years. In determining depreciation, the cost of the asset is generally reduced by one half of the amount of the credit. The basic reduction can be avoided if the taxpayer elects to take a smaller investment credit (8% for property with a life of five years or more, 4% for property with a life of less than 5 years). Also, the maximum amount of the credit in any year is limited if the potential credit is more than $25,000.

Credit for the Elderly

Some elderly taxpayers receive nontaxable retirement income, such as social security, while others receive taxable retirement income. The credit for the elderly is an attempt to overcome this perceived inequity. Generally, a taxpayer who is 65 or older, with less than $2,500 from nontaxable pensions and annuities and an adjusted gross income of less than $12,500 ($15,000 for a joint return), is eligible for the credit. The formula for determining the credit is complex and the IRC should be consulted for the details.

Child and Disabled Dependent Care Expenses Credit

Taxpayers who maintain a household are allowed a tax credit for expenses, including household expenses, involved in the care of a dependent child under age 15 or a physically or mentally incapacitated dependent or spouse, provided the expenses were incurred to enable the taxpayer to be gainfully employed. The amount of the credit is on a sliding scale, depending on the amount of adjusted gross income and the number of dependents. The following table shows the allowable amount of the credit:

	Maximum Amount of Child Care Credit	
Adjusted Gross Income	One Dependent	Two or More Dependents
$10,000	$720	$1,440
20,000	600	1,200
30,000 and above	480	960

Earned Income Credit

This credit against the tax is available to low-income workers who maintain a household for at least one of their dependent children and who have *earned income* (wages and self-employment income) and an adjusted gross income of less than $10,000. The credit is determined by reference to a special earned income credit table and is limited to a maximum of $500.

Unlike the other credits, which cannot exceed the amount of the tax before applying the credit, if the earned income credit reduces the tax liability below zero, the negative amount is paid to the taxpayer. For example, if a worker's tax liability before applying the credit is $150 and the earned income credit is $375, the taxpayer will receive a direct payment of $225. Direct payments of tax revenues to individuals who have no liability for federal income tax is a new concept with significant socio-economic implications. The concept is often called a "negative income tax."

Filing Returns; Payment of Tax

The income tax withheld from an employee's earnings by the employer represents current payments on account. An individual whose income is not subject to withholding, or only partially so, or an individual whose income is fairly large must estimate the income tax in advance. The estimated tax for the year, after deducting the estimated amount to be withheld and any credit for overpayment from prior years, must be paid currently, usually in four installments.

Annual income tax returns must be filed at the appropriate Internal Revenue Service office within 3½ months following the end of the taxpayer's taxable year. Any balance owed must accompany the return. If there has been an overpayment of the tax liability, the taxpayer may request that the overpayment be refunded or credited against the estimated tax for the following year.

To illustrate the assembly of income tax information and the determination of tax liability, the following data are given for a married couple who file a joint return. The husband owns and operates a retail enterprise. The wife owns a building, which she leases. She also works part-time. Each is entitled to one personal exemption and there are two additional exemptions for their dependent children. Sources and amounts of includable gross income, itemized deductions and exemptions, and other data are presented in condensed form. In practice, the data would be reported in much greater detail on official tax forms.

Ann G. and John P. May
Summary of Federal Income Tax Data
For Calendar Year 19--

Gross Income and Deductions from Gross Income:

Salary			$13,090
Dividends on stock:			
Husband	$ 690		
Wife	180	$ 870	
Exclusion		200	670
Rents:			
Gross income		$ 18,600	
Expenses		7,400	11,200
Business:			
Sales		$280,000	
Cost of merchandise sold		197,000	
Gross profit		$ 83,000	
Expenses		44,400	
Net income		$ 38,600	
Deduction for retirement plan contribution		5,790	32,810
Capital gains and losses:			
Net long-term capital gain		$ 5,000	
Net short-term capital loss		1,000	
Net capital gain		$ 4,000	
Long-term capital gain deduction		2,400	1,600
Adjusted gross income			$59,370

Excess itemized deductions and exemptions:

Interest on residence mortgage note	$ 1,810		
Charitable contributions	1,730		
Real estate tax on residence	1,525		
State income tax	1,409		
State sales tax	472		
Safe-deposit box rental	24		
Total	$ 6,970		
Zero bracket amount	3,400		
Excess itemized deductions		$ 3,570	
Exemptions (4 × $1,000)		4,000	7,570
Taxable income			$51,800

Income Tax Liability:

On $45,800		$ 9,772	
On $6,000 at 38%		2,280	$12,052

Advance Payments and Tax Credit:

Tax withheld from salary	$ 495		
Payments of estimated tax	11,000	$ 11,495	
Political contributions credit		100	11,595
Balance due			$ 457

Special
Situations

There are two special situations that may significantly affect the amount of the tax liability. One situation is referred to as *income averaging,* and the other is the *alternative minimum tax*. Special forms are used for assembling the data and computing the tax liability in both cases. The two situations are briefly described in the following sections.

Income Averaging

Individual taxpayers whose taxable income for a taxable year is unusually large in comparison with the average taxable income of the four preceding years may qualify for computing their income tax by the averaging method. The method permits a portion of the unusually large income of the current year to be taxed in lower tax brackets through an averaging technique. The tax savings achieved by the averaging technique can be substantial.

Alternative Minimum Tax

In the past, some taxpayers who had very large incomes were paying very little tax because of allowable deductions from income, such as the deduction for long-term capital gains. To ensure that such taxpayers pay some tax, certain so-called tax preferences (such as the deduction for long-term capital gains) are added to adjusted gross income to determine a "minimum tax base". The alternative minimum tax is then computed and is payable if it exceeds the taxpayer's regular tax. The alternative minimum tax is computed at 20% of the amount by which the minimum tax base exceeds $30,000 ($40,000 for joint returns).

INCOME TAX
ON
CORPORATIONS

Certain classes of corporations are given special treatment because the sources and nature of their income differ from that of general business corporations. Included in the special categories are insurance companies, mutual savings banks, regulated investment companies, farm cooperatives, and corporations specifically exempt by statute.

Excluding the special classes from consideration, the taxable income of a corporation is determined, in general, by deducting its ordinary business expenses from the total amount of its includable gross income. Of the many variations from this general procedure, there are three of broad applicability that deserve brief consideration.

Dividends
Received
Deduction

All dividends received on shares of stock in other corporations are includable in gross income. However, 85% of such dividends is usually allowed as a special deduction from gross income. Certain corporations which are members of an affiliated group may deduct the entire amount of dividends received.

Charitable
Contributions

The deduction for charitable contributions is limited to 10% of taxable income, computed without regard to the contributions and the special deduction for dividends received. Contributions in excess of the 10% limitation may be carried over to the five succeeding years, with deductions in the succeeding years also being subject to the 10% maximum.

Capital Gains and Losses

As in the case of individuals, capital gains and losses of corporations are classified as short-term and long-term according to the schedule presented earlier. The excess of a net long-term capital gain over a net short-term capital loss is included in its entirety in taxable income. However, the tax thereon is limited to a maximum of 28%. No part of a net capital loss may be deducted from ordinary income. However, it may be carried back to the third year preceding the year of the loss and applied against net capital gain of such year. Regardless of its nature (long-term or short-term) in the year incurred, the loss is treated as short-term in the carryback years. Any unused amount of the carryback is then carried to the succeeding years to the extent of a five-year carryover from the loss year.

DETERMINATION OF CORPORATION INCOME TAX

The corporate income tax is progressive, but the steps for the graduated series of rates are fewer than is the case for the rates for individuals. The corporate tax rates are as follows:

CORPORATE INCOME TAX RATES

Taxable Income		Tax Rate
$0 — $25,000	....	15%
Over $25,000 — $50,000	....	18%
Over $50,000 — $75,000	....	30%
Over $75,000 — $100,000	....	40%
Over $100,000	....	46%

For taxable income of $70,000, the corporate tax rates would be applied as follows:

Tax on first $25,000 at 15%		$ 3,750
Tax on next 25,000 at 18%		4,500
Tax on next _20,000_ at 30%		_6,000_
Total on _$70,000_ of taxable income		$14,250

There are two additional taxes which are designed to limit the use of the corporate form as a means of avoiding income tax on individuals. Although the statutes which provide for these "loophole closing" taxes are too voluminous for detailed explanations, their basic nature deserves brief consideration.

Accumulated Earnings Tax

An additional income tax may be assessed against corporations that accumulate earnings in order to avoid the income tax that would be levied on shareholders if such earnings were distributed as dividends. Ordinarily, accumulated earnings of up to $250,000 are exempt from this tax. Additional accumulations are subject to the additional tax unless it can be proved that they are not in excess of the reasonable needs of the business. The tax rate is 27.5% of the first $100,000 of accumulated taxable income and 38.5% of the excess over $100,000.

Personal Holding Company Tax

The statutory definition of a personal holding company is quite technical. In general, the special tax is designed to discourage individuals from transferring their investment properties to a corporation in exchange for its stock, or to "incorporate" their personal talents or services. The additional income tax, which is levied at the rate of 50% of the undistributed personal holding company income, is an effective deterrent to the use of the corporation as a device for the accumulation of "tax-sheltered" income.

TAX PLANNING TO MINIMIZE INCOME TAXES

There are various legal means of minimizing or reducing federal income taxes, some of which are of broader applicability than others. Much depends upon the volume and the sources of a taxpayer's gross income, the nature of the expenses and other deductions, and the accounting methods used.

The amount of income tax that may be saved by any particular proposal can be determined by estimating the total tax, assuming that the proposal is to be adopted, and comparing that amount with the estimated tax according to the alternative proposals under consideration. In many cases it is possible to determine the tax effect of a proposal by computing the tax at the *marginal* rate on the amount of taxable income differential. To illustrate the latter procedure, assume that a married couple filing a joint return has taxable income of $52,800 and that they use the zero bracket amount instead of itemizing deductions. According to the applicable rate schedule on page 771, their marginal tax rate is 38%, which is the rate for the segment of taxable income in the $45,800 to $60,000 bracket. If an analysis of the couple's check stubs and other records should disclose excess itemized deductions of $1,000, they would save $380 (38% × $1,000) by itemizing their deductions.

Additional examples of means to minimize income taxes are presented in the following paragraphs.

Form of Business Organization

One of the most important considerations in selecting the form of organization to use in operating a business enterprise is the impact of the federal income tax. If a business is a sole proprietorship, income must be reported on the owner's personal income tax return. In a partnership, each individual partner is taxed on the distributive share of the business income in much the same manner as a sole proprietor. If the business is incorporated, the corporation must pay an income tax on its earnings. When the remaining earnings are distributed in the form of dividends, they are taxed to the owners (shareholders).

The double taxation feature of the corporation form might seem to outweigh any possible advantages of using it for a family enterprise or other nonpublic business. This is not necessarily the case, however. For most business enterprises, there are likely to be both advantages and disadvantages in the corporate form. Among the many factors that need to be considered are the following: (1) amount of net income, (2) changes in net income from year to year, (3) disposition of aftertax income (withdrawn from the enterprise or used for expansion), (4) method of financing, (5) number of owners and shares of ownership, and (6) the owners' income from other sources. The type of analysis needed to appraise the relative merits of alternative forms of organization is described in the paragraphs that follow.

For purposes of illustration, assume that a married couple engaged in a business partnership are considering incorporation. The business, in which personal services and capital investment are material income-producing factors, has been yielding adjusted gross income of $85,000 and other investments yield income of $16,000 (after the dividend exclusion). Itemized deductions in excess of the zero bracket amount plus the allowance for personal exemptions total $8,000. A joint return is filed. Partners' business withdrawals totaling $50,000 a year would be treated as salary expense if the enterprise were to be incorporated. The federal income tax consequences under the two forms of organization are as follows, using the tax rates presented in this chapter.

Organized as a Partnership

Tax on individuals:

Business income	$ 85,000	
Other income	16,000	
Adjusted gross income	$101,000	
Deductions from adjusted gross income	8,000	
Taxable income	$ 93,000	
Income tax liability:		
On $85,600	$ 25,920	
On $7,400 at 45%	3,330	
Total income tax—partnership form		$29,250

Organized as a Corporation

Tax on corporation:

Taxable income, $85,000 − $50,000 (salary expense)	$ 35,000	
Income tax liability:		
On $25,000 at 15%	$ 3,750	
On $10,000 at 18%	1,800	$ 5,550

Tax on individuals:

Salary	$ 50,000	
Other income	16,000	
Adjusted gross income	$ 66,000	
Deductions from adjusted gross income	8,000	
Taxable income	$ 58,000	
Income tax liability:		
On $45,800	$ 9,772	
On $12,200 at 38%	4,636	14,408
Total income tax—corporation form		$19,958

Comparison of the two tax liabilities indicates that an annual tax savings of $9,292 ($29,250 − $19,958) could be effected by using the corporate form. However, the possible distribution of the corporation's net income as dividends was not taken into consideration. If the corporation's aftertax income of $29,450 were to be paid as dividends to the owners, their taxable income would total $87,450 instead of $58,000. The resulting increase in their personal income tax, amounting to approximately $12,345, would convert the expected $9,292 advantage of the corporate form to a $3,053 disadvantage.

Earnings accumulated by the corporation in the foregoing example might at some future time become available to the stockholders through sale of their stock. They would thus be converted into long-term capital gains, of which only 40% would be included in taxable income. However, retention of earnings beyond the $250,000 exemption could result in imposition of the accumulated earnings tax. If additional accumulations were beyond the reasonable needs of the business, the shareholders might then elect partnership treatment under Subchapter S and thus avoid the double tax on corporate earnings. Additional information about the intentions of the owners and prospects for the future would be needed to explore additional ramifications of the problem.

The best form of organization, from the standpoint of the federal income tax, can be determined only by a detailed analysis of the particular situation. Generalizations are likely to be of little benefit and may even be misleading. The impact of state and local taxes also varies according to the form of business organization, and the importance of such nontax factors as limited liability and transferability of ownership should be weighed.

Timing of Transactions and Reporting	"Timing" is an important element in the effect of management's decisions on liability for income tax. The selection of the fiscal year, the choice of accounting methods, and the acceleration or deferment of gross income or expense are some of the time factors that need to be considered. Applications of timing considerations to relatively common situations are described in the following paragraphs.

Cash Basis v. Accrual Basis

Corporations that regularly have taxable income in excess of $100,000, and thus have a marginal tax rate of 46%, are unlikely to be greatly affected by their choice of the cash or accrual basis of accounting. A small corporation whose taxable income tends to fluctuate above and below $100,000 from year to year may be better able to control the fluctuation if the cash basis is used. For example, near the end of a taxable year in which taxable income is likely to exceed $100,000, some of the excess which will be subject to the tax rate of 46% may be shifted to the following year when the marginal rate may be less than 46%. It may be possible to postpone the receipt of gross income by delayed billings for services, or expenses may be increased by payment of outstanding bills before the end of the year. The timing of expenditures and payments for such expenses as redecorating, repairs, and advertising may also be readily subject to control.

Unincorporated businesses may also be able to reduce fluctuations in net income and thus lower the marginal tax rate of the owners. Even individual taxpayers whose income is mainly from salary may have opportunities to save a modest amount by careful planning of payment of deductible items. For example, if a large amount of medical expense is incurred near the end of the year, it would be preferable to pay all such bills before the end of the year if by so doing the medical expense deduction and other itemized deductions will exceed the zero bracket amount. On the other hand, if early payment would not yield a reduction in taxes for the current year, postponement of payment to the following year might be beneficial.

A closely related technique is to alternate from year to year between electing the zero bracket amount and claiming excess itemized deductions. To illustrate, assume that a married couple has average annual itemized deductions of $2,900. Use of the zero bracket amount of $3,400 in lieu of itemizing deductions would reduce taxable income by $500. However, if they could schedule cash payments so as to move $900 of deductible expenses from one year to another, they could then alternate between itemizing deductions of $3,800 ($2,900 + $900) and using the zero bracket amount of $3,400. By so doing, they would realize tax savings by gaining an additional $400 in deductions over the two-year period.

Installment Method

The installment method of determining gross income from sales of merchandise on the installment plan, which was described in Chapter 12, is widely used for income tax purposes. The method may also be used in reporting the net gain from a sale of real estate or from a casual sale of personal property. Tax savings may be effected by reporting gain on the sale of a capital asset by the installment method, particularly if the amount of the gain is large in relation to other income.

Capital Gains and Losses

The timing of capital gains and losses is usually subject to a high degree of control because the taxpayer can select the time to sell the capital assets. Delaying a sale by only one day can result in a substantial tax saving. To illustrate, assume that the only sale of a capital asset by an individual during the taxable year is the sale of listed stocks that had been held for exactly one year, realizing a gain of $4,000. The gain would be classified as a short-term capital gain and taxed as ordinary income. Assuming that the taxpayer's marginal tax rate is 45%, the tax on the $4,000 gain would be $1,800. Alternatively, if the individual had held the securities at least one additional day before selling them, the $4,000 gain (assuming no change in selling price) would have qualified as a long-term capital gain, of which only 40% would be taxed. Thus, if the sale had occurred at least one day later, there would have been a tax of only 45% of $1,600, or $720, for a tax saving of $1,080.

When a taxpayer owns various lots of an identical security that were acquired at different dates and at different prices, it may be possible to choose between realizing a gain and realizing a loss, and perhaps to a limited extent to govern the amount realized. For example, a taxpayer who has realized gains from the sale of securities may wish to offset them, in whole or in part, by losses from the sales of other securities. To illustrate, assume that a taxpayer who owns three 100-share lots of common stock in the same corporation, purchased at $40, $48, and $60 a share respectively, plans to sell 100 shares at the current market price of $52. Depending upon which of the three 100-share lots is sold, the taxpayer will realize a gain of $1,200, a gain of $400, or a loss of $800. If the identity of the particular lot sold cannot be determined, the first-in, first-out cost flow assumption must be used. The use of average cost is not permitted.

Depreciation

The IRC specifies the use of the Accelerated Cost Recovery System (ACRS) for determining depreciation, or the "cost recovery deduction," for plant asset acquisitions. ACRS generally provides for three classes for most business property (3-year, 5-year, and 15-year classes) and provides for depreciation that approximates the use of the 150 percent declining-balance method. The 3-year class includes automobiles, while most machinery and equipment is included in the 5-year class and buildings fall into the 15-year class.

ACRS simplifies depreciation accounting by eliminating the need to estimate useful life and salvage value and to decide upon a depreciation method. Although a short-run saving can usually be realized by using the regular ACRS cost recovery allowance, a taxpayer may elect to use a straight-line deduction based on the property classes prescribed under ACRS. The accelerated write-off of depreciable assets provided by ACRS does not, however, effect a long-run net saving in income tax. The tax reduction of the early years of use is offset by higher taxes as the annual cost recovery allowance diminishes. The possibility of changes in tax rates in future years adds to the uncertainty of the real merits of accelerated write-off. Nevertheless, the additional funds made available by current tax savings are usually considered to be advantageous enough to justify the use of ACRS.

Taxpayers may also choose to deduct, as a current expense, a limited amount of the cost of plant asset acquisitions that qualify for the investment tax credit. Amounts expended under this provision are not available for computing the investment tax credit or the cost recovery allowance.

Equalization Among Taxable Entities

In some situations, a saving in income taxes may be effected by transfers of income-producing properties among members of a family group. For example, if taxpayers with high marginal tax rates give securities or other income-producing properties to their children, grandchildren, or other close relatives of modest means, the income will be taxed to the new owner at a lower rate. It is also possible to accomplish a reduction in income taxes by establishing trust funds.

Nontaxable Investment Income

Interest on bonds issued by a state or political subdivision is exempt from the federal income tax. Such investments are especially attractive to taxpayers with a high marginal tax rate. To illustrate, the following table compares the income after tax on a $100,000 investment in a 10% industrial bond and a $100,000 investment in a 6% municipal bond for an individual with a marginal tax rate of 50% and a corporation with a marginal tax rate of 46%.

	Taxable 10% Industrial Bond	Nontaxable 6% Municipal Bond
Individual taxpayer:		
Income	$10,000	$6,000
Tax (50% of $10,000)	5,000	—
Income after tax	$ 5,000	$6,000
Corporate taxpayer:		
Income	$10,000	$6,000
Tax (46% of $10,000)	4,600	—
Income after tax	$ 5,400	$6,000

Although the interest rate on the municipal bond (6%) is less than the rate on the industrial bond (10%), the aftertax income to both taxpayers is larger from the investment in the municipal bond.

Use of Debt for Corporate Financing

If a corporation is in need of relatively permanent funds, it generally considers borrowing money on a long-term basis or issuing stock. Since interest on debt is a deductible expense in determining taxable income and dividends paid on stock are not, this impact on income tax is one of the important factors to consider in evaluating the two methods of financing. To illustrate, assume that a corporation with a marginal tax rate of 46% is considering issuing (1) $1,000,000 of 10% bonds or (2) $1,000,000 of 10% cumulative preferred stock. If the bonds are issued, the deduction of the yearly $100,000 of interest in determining taxable income results in an annual net borrowing cost of $54,000 ($100,000 less tax savings of 46% of $100,000). If the preferred stock is issued, the dividends are not deductible in determining taxable income and the net annual outlay for this method of financing is $100,000. Thus, issuing bonds instead of preferred stock reduced the annual financing expenditures by $46,000 ($100,000 − $54,000). Although there are other factors to consider in making such decisions, the impact of income taxes favors the issuance of the bonds.

When a corporation owns shares of another domestic corporation and receives dividends on the stock, 85% of the dividends received are generally allowed as a special deduction. Thus, only 15% of such dividends are taxable. When a corporation borrows money, the interest expense is deductible in determining taxable income. The aftertax cost of borrowing is therefore less than the interest expense. These two tax provisions can be used to convert an apparently uneconomical transaction into a profit. For example, a corporation with a marginal tax rate of 46% has an opportunity to invest $100,000 in preferred stock yielding 10%. However, it will need to borrow the $100,000 at 15% to make the investment. On the surface, this investment looks unattractive. As the following table shows, however, the investment provides an annual net profit of $1,210 after taxes.

Dividend income ($100,000 × 10%)		$10,000
Tax on dividend income:		
Dividend.	$10,000	
Dividend exclusion	8,500	
Taxable amount	$ 1,500	
Tax rate	× 46%	
Tax		690
Net dividend income after tax		$ 9,310
Interest expense ($100,000 × 15%)		$15,000
Tax savings on interest:		
Interest deduction	$15,000	
Tax rate	× 46%	6,900
Net interest expense after tax		$ 8,100
Net dividend income after tax		$ 9,310
Net interest expense after tax		8,100
Net profit		$ 1,210

IMPACT OF INCOME TAXES GENERALLY

The foregoing description of the federal income tax system and discussion of tax minimization, together with explanations in other chapters, demonstrates the importance of income taxes to business enterprises. The most important factor influencing a business decision is often the federal income tax. Many accountants, in both private and public practice, devote their entire attention to tax planning for their employers or their clients. The statutes and the administrative regulations, which are often changed, must be studied continuously by anyone who engages in this phase of accounting.

Self-Examination Questions
(Answers in Appendix C.)

1. Which of the following is included in the gross income of a single taxpayer?
   A. Dividends received, $100   C. Tips for services rendered, $1,450
   B. Gift from father, $1,000   D. None of the above

2. Which of the following is deductible from gross income by a self-employed taxpayer in determining adjusted gross income?
   A. Interest on home mortgage note
   B. Real estate taxes on a personal residence
   C. Contributions to a qualified retirement fund
   D. None of the above

3. What is the adjusted gross income from capital gain if net short-term capital losses total $8,000 and net long-term capital gains total $20,000?
   A. $4,800   C. $20,000
   B. $12,000   D. None of the above

4. Which of the following results in a credit against the federal income tax for a single taxpayer?
   A. Depreciation on rental property, $9,000
   B. Interest on mortgage note on personal residence, $3,100
   C. Contribution to political party, $100
   D. None of the above

5. Which of the following is granted special treatment in determining the taxable income for a corporation?
   A. Dividends received on stock in other corporations
   B. Charitable contributions
   C. Excess of net long-term capital gain over net short-term capital loss
   D. All of the above

Discussion Questions

1. Does the failure (a) to receive the tax forms from the appropriate governmental agency or (b) to maintain adequate records qualify as a legitimate means of tax avoidance?

2. A particular individual owns three unincorporated business enterprises, maintaining a separate accounting system for each. (a) Is a separate income tax return required for each enterprise? (b) May the owner elect to file a separate return and determine the tax on each enterprise separately?

3. Describe briefly the system employed in subjecting the income of partnerships to the federal income tax.

4. The adjusted gross income of a sole proprietorship for the year was $60,000, of which the owner withdrew $45,000. What amount of income from the business enterprise must be reported on the owner's income tax return?

5. Do corporations electing partnership treatment (Subchapter S) pay federal income tax? Discuss.

6. Which of the two methods of accounting, cash or accrual, is more commonly used by individual taxpayers?

7. During the year, a CPA who uses the cash basis of determining taxable income spends $1,300 for a two-year insurance policy and determines that a $750 fee billed to a client during the year is uncollectible. Discuss the status of these two items as allowable deductions from gross income.

8. Describe *constructive receipt* of gross income as it applies to (a) a salary check received from an employer, (b) interest credited to a savings account, and (c) bond interest coupons.

9. Arrange the following items in their proper sequence for the determination of taxable income of an individual.
   (a) Adjusted gross income
   (b) Gross income
   (c) Excess itemized deductions and exemptions
   (d) Taxable income
   (e) Expenses related to business or specified revenue

10. Which of the following items are includable in gross income by a single taxpayer in determining taxable income?

(a) Rent proceeds.
(b) Interest on municipal bonds.
(c) Shares of corporation stock received as a gift.
(d) Dividends in excess of $100 on stock acquired in (c).
(e) Insurance proceeds received by beneficiary because of death of insured.
(f) Alimony payments received from former spouse.
(g) Compensation received for personal injury.
(h) Scholarship received from State University by a sophomore.
(i) Tips received for services rendered.

11. Which of the following are required to file an income tax return?
    (a) Corporation with net loss of $90,000.
    (b) Unmarried college student, supported by father, with unearned income of $1,350.
    (c) Unmarried person, 20 years old, with gross income of $8,950.
    (d) Husband and wife, filing jointly, both 68 years of age, with gross income of $6,500.

12. Discuss the circumstances under which a single taxpayer would generally elect to itemize deductions from adjusted gross income.

13. Classify the following items paid by an individual operating a business as a sole proprietorship as (a) deductible from gross income in determining adjusted gross income, (b) deductible from adjusted gross income as excess itemized deductions in determining taxable income, or (c) not deductible. (Ignore any possible limitations on the amount of the deduction.)
    (1) Contribution to State University by the business enterprise.
    (2) Loss from sale of property held for the production of income.
    (3) Federal excise tax on commodities purchased for family use.
    (4) Transportation expenses incurred for the business enterprise.
    (5) Contribution to a pension retirement program as a self-employed individual.
    (6) State income tax.
    (7) Loss incurred on sale of corporation securities.
    (8) State alcoholic beverage tax.
    (9) State tax on gasoline used in family automobile.
    (10) Interest paid on mortgage on taxpayer's residence.
    (11) State sales taxes on commodities purchased for family use.
    (12) Property tax on residence.
    (13) Property taxes on apartment building held as an investment.

14. According to this chapter's tax rate schedule for single taxpayers, the tax on taxable income of $55,000 is $15,989. (a) What is the approximate percentage of the tax to the $55,000 of taxable income? (b) What is the marginal tax rate at this level of taxable income?

15. Jane Mautz is considering whether to reject an opportunity to earn an additional $1,500 of taxable income, on the grounds that doing so would put her in a higher tax bracket. How would you advise her?

16. A single taxpayer had a net long-term capital gain of $25,000 and a net short-term capital loss of $8,000 during the year. (a) What is the amount of the adjusted gross income from net capital gain? (b) Assuming that the taxpayer's taxable income, exclusive of capital gains and losses, is $122,500 (marginal tax rate of 50%), what is the income tax on the net capital gain?

17. An individual taxpayer had a net short-term capital gain of $6,000 and a net long-term capital loss of $15,000. What is the amount of (a) the net capital loss, (b) the allowable deduction from adjusted gross income, and (c) the carryover?

18. If a single taxpayer's income tax before consideration of the following items or tax credits is $225, what is the amount of the tax after allowable credits for: (a) political contributions, $100, (b) earned income credit, $310?

19. Are the following federal income taxes termed progressive: (a) tax on individual taxpayer (b) tax on corporate taxpayer?

20. Dan Lowe, the president and major stockholder of D. Lowe Corporation, received in salary and income from other investments an amount which places him in the 50% income tax bracket. (a) Which corporate policy would be more advantageous to him—retention of earnings or distribution in dividends? (b) Describe the deterrent to retention of earnings provided by the IRC.

21. A taxpayer with a marginal tax rate of 50% has an investment in a 7% tax-exempt municipal bond. What rate would need to be earned on a taxable bond to yield the same aftertax return as is being earned on the present investment?

Exercises

Exercise 27-1. Ellen Aims is an employee who does not qualify as an outside salesperson. She received a salary of $36,250 during the year and incurred the following unreimbursed expenses related to her employment: (a) automobile, $850 for 5,000 miles of travel; and lunches, $695, incurred while calling on customers within the city in which she lives; (b) travel away from home overnight, $1,050; and (c) customer entertainment, $490. Determine her adjusted gross income from salary.

Exercise 27-2. Using the following data, determine the adjusted gross income from salary for employees A, B, and C.

	A	B	C
Salary	$34,000	$26,900	$48,250
Reimbursement allowance received from employer for travel expenses	975	750	1,750
Travel expenses incurred and paid by the employee when away overnight	720	915	1,750

Exercise 27-3. A taxpayer has adjusted gross income of $25,000 for the year. Amounts paid for medical expenses during the year were as follows: medical care insurance premiums, $350; prescription drugs, $480; other medical expenses, $1,250. Determine the amount of the allowable deduction for medical expenses. Assume that the taxpayer itemizes deductions.

Exercise 27-4. Married taxpayers who file a joint return have adjusted gross income of $32,250 and expended the following amounts during the year:

Fee paid to CPA for preparation of tax return	$ 125
Charitable contributions	975
Interest expense on home mortgage	2,250
Interest expense on family automobile	910
Real estate taxes on home	1,400

State sales taxes	$ 295
State gasoline taxes	75
Medical care insurance premiums	395
Doctor's fees	290
Repair of family automobile damaged in accident (reimbursed by insurance company after deduction of $100 under policy deductible clause)	1,500
Contributions to political fund	100
Insurance on family automobile	475

(a) Determine the amount of itemized deductions. (b) Should the taxpayers itemize deductions or elect the zero bracket amount? Explain.

Exercise 27-5. A single taxpayer is entitled to two exemptions, including one for a younger sister. The taxpayer's adjusted gross income for the year is $22,325 and total itemized deductions are $2,900. Using the tax table presented in this chapter, determine the tax. Present details of the computation.

Exercise 27-6. Taxpayer husband and wife, entitled to one exemption each and two additional exemptions for dependents, file a joint return. Other summary data related to their tax return are as follows:

Includable gross income	$55,500
Allowable deductions from gross income	1,250
Total allowable itemized deductions from adjusted gross income	3,175
Political contributions	150
Tax withheld from salary	9,072
Payments of estimated tax	2,500

Determine the following: (a) adjusted gross income; (b) taxable income; (c) total income tax, using the tax rate schedule appearing in this chapter; and (d) overpayment or balance due.

Exercise 27-7. The capital gains and losses of an individual taxpayer during the year are listed as follows, with losses identified by parentheses:

Short-term: $(9,000), $7,500, $(1,500)
Long-term: $12,000, $5,000, $(4,000)

Determine the following: (a) net short-term capital gain or loss; (b) net long-term capital gain or loss; (c) net capital gain or loss; (d) long-term capital gain deduction, if any; and (e) adjusted gross income from capital gain.

Exercise 27-8. Taxpayer husband and wife file a joint return. Summary data related to their possible tax credits are as follows:

Political fund contributions	$ 150
Payment on qualifying home energy conservation items	2,500
Purchase of qualifying new tangible personal property used in taxpayer's business, 5-year life	5,000

Determine their total income tax credits.

Exercise 27-9. The data required for the determination of a particular corporation's income tax for the current year are summarized as follows:

Dividends received from other corporations	$ 35,000
Net short-term capital loss	11,500
Net long-term capital gain	30,500
Includable gross income from ordinary operations (i.e., in addition to the three items listed above)	210,000
Allowable deductions, exclusive of special deduction for dividends received	80,000

Using the rates appearing in this chapter and assuming an 85% dividends received deduction, determine (a) taxable income, exclusive of capital gains and losses, (b) excess of net long-term capital gain over net short-term capital loss, and (c) total income tax.

Problems
(Problems in Appendix B: 27-1B, 27-2B, 27-3B.)

Problem 27-1A. Donald Dodds owns a small apartment building from which he receives rental income. He uses the cash method of determining income, depositing in a special bank account all rents received from tenants. All disbursements related to the building, as well as occasional unrelated disbursements, are paid by checks drawn on the same account. During the current taxable year ending December 31, Dodds deposited $95,000 of rent receipts in the special bank account.

Disbursements from the special bank account during the current year are summarized as follows:

Interest on mortgage note payable on land and building		$19,750
Installment payments of principal on mortgage note payable		16,250
Wages of custodian and maintenance employee:		
Withheld for FICA tax and paid to IRS	$ 1,260	
Withheld for income tax and paid to IRS	1,750	
Paid to custodian	14,990	18,000
Utilities expense		9,300
Repainting interior of several apartments		2,950
Premium on a two-year insurance policy on the building, effective January 3		800
Repairs to heating and plumbing equipment		975
Payroll tax expense		1,260
Contributions:		
United Fund		500
American Cancer Society		75
Political committee		100
Miscellaneous expense incurred in earning rentals		995
Purchases of various stocks		17,000
Real estate tax on land and building		3,700

In addition to the foregoing data, you determine from other records and the tax return for the preceding year that the total allowable deduction for depreciation expense for the current year is $12,500 and that current expirations of insurance premiums paid in earlier years total $525.

Instructions:

Prepare a statement of adjusted gross income from rents, identifying each of the allowable deductions from gross income.

Problem 27-2A. Alice Bowen, unmarried and entitled to one exemption for herself, is a CPA. She uses the cash method of determining taxable income and reports on the calendar-year basis. Her cash receipts and disbursements for the current year are summarized as follows:

Cash Receipts

Professional fees	$122,200
Borrowed from bank (professional purposes)	20,000
From sale of A Corporation stock (long-term capital gain was $5,000)	16,000
Dividends	610

Cash Disbursements

Wages of employees	$ 34,750
Payroll taxes	2,780
Office rent	12,000
Telephone expense (office)	1,250
Electricity (office)	2,750
Office supplies expense	695
Insurance on office equipment (3-year policy, dated January 1)	300
Professional liability insurance (1-year policy, dated January 1)	1,200
Partial repayment of bank loan (professional purposes)	4,000
Interest on bank loan (professional purposes)	2,200
Charitable contributions	950
Payment on principal of residence mortgage note	3,200
Interest on residence mortgage note	2,050
Personal property tax on office equipment	50
Real estate tax on home	750
State sales tax on purchases for personal use	275
Political contributions	120
Automobile operating expense (exclusive of depreciation)	1,500
Office equipment (purchased at various times during year)	5,000
Purchase of 100 shares of C Corporation stock	8,400
Payments of estimated income tax for current year	16,250

The automobile was used 70% of the time for professional purposes. The total depreciation expense for the year was $1,800. Allocate 70% of the depreciation and other automobile expenses to professional purposes.

The cost of the office equipment purchased during the year is indicated in the summary of cash payments and is to be expensed during the year. Depreciation expense for equipment purchased in prior years is $750.

Instructions:

Prepare a summary of federal income tax data for Bowen, applying the appropriate schedule of tax rates presented in this chapter.

Problem 27-3A. The following preliminary income statement of Naples Video was prepared as of the end of the calendar year in which the business was established. You are engaged to examine the statement, review the business records, revise the accounting system to the extent necessary, and determine the adjusted gross income.

Sales..........................		$122,000
Purchases		90,150
Gross profit.....................		$ 31,850
Operating expenses:		
Salaries	$32,000	
Rent	9,650	
Store equipment.................	12,000	
Insurance......................	960	
Fuel..........................	850	
Utilities	1,105	
Advertising	650	
Payroll taxes	1,360	
Donations......................	160	
Miscellaneous..................	950	59,685
Net loss		$ 27,835

You obtain the following information during your examination:

(a) The preliminary income statement is a summary of cash receipts and disbursements. Sales on account are not recorded until cash is received. They are evidenced only by duplicate sales tickets. Similarly, invoices for merchandise and other purchases are not recorded until payment is made. In the meantime, they are filed in an unpaid file.

(b) Uncollected sales to customers on account at December 31 amount to $5,375.

(c) Unpaid invoices at December 31 for expenditures of the past year are summarized as follows:

Merchandise	$7,450
Fuel...................	96
Utilities	105

(d) Merchandise inventory at December 31 amounted to $21,900.

(e) Withdrawals of $15,000 by the owner of the enterprise were included in the amount reported as Salaries.

(f) The agreement with the three part-time salesclerks provides for a bonus equal to 1% of cash collected on sales during the year, payable in January of the following year.

(g) The rent for January of the following year ($650) was paid and recorded in December.

(h) The store equipment reported in the preliminary income statement was installed on March 3, and $7,500 is to be expensed during the year. Depreciation expense allowable during the year is $1,375.

(i) A total of $405 of insurance premiums was unexpired at December 31.

(j) Accrued salaries as of the end of the year amount to $350.

(k) Payments classified as Donations were contributions to charitable, religious, and educational organizations.

(l) Payments classified as Miscellaneous included $300 of personal expenses of the owner.

Instructions:

Prepare a statement of adjusted gross income from the business for submission with the income tax return of Don Powell, the owner, using the accrual method of accounting.

Problem 27-4A. Three married individuals, A, B, and C, are engaged in related types of businesses as sole proprietors, but plan to combine their enterprises to form Allen Co. They have discussed the relative merits of the partnership and the corporation forms of organization, exclusive of the effect of the federal income tax. You are engaged to assemble and analyze the relevant data and to determine the immediate income tax consequences to each of them of the two forms of organization. The consolidation is planned to take effect as of January 1, the beginning of the company's fiscal year.

The combined annual net income of the three separate enterprises has typically totaled $150,000. It is anticipated that economies of operation and other advantages of the consolidation will have the immediate effect of increasing annual net income by $30,000, making a total of $180,000 before deducting owners' salaries totaling $90,000.

Each of the owners is to be assigned managerial duties as a partner or, alternatively, be designated an officer of the corporation. In either event, each is to be paid an annual salary, which is to be treated as an operating expense of the enterprise. In addition, they plan to distribute $27,000 of earnings annually, which are to be allocated among them in accordance with their original investments (the income-sharing ratio). It is anticipated that the remaining earnings will be retained for use in expanding operations. The agreed capital investments, salaries, and distributions of earnings are to be as follows:

	A	B	C	Total
Capital investment...........	$150,000	$200,000	$150,000	$500,000
Salary.......................	27,000	36,000	27,000	90,000
Distribution of earnings........	8,100	10,800	8,100	27,000

For each individual and his or her spouse, the estimated adjusted gross income from sources other than Allen Co. and other pertinent data are as follows. The amount of income reported for each includes dividends in excess of the allowable exclusion, and each files a joint return for the calendar year, prepared in accordance with the cash method.

	A	B	C
Ordinary adjusted gross income, exclusive of salary and net income of Allen Co.	$27,000	$16,000	$30,000
Total itemized deductions	5,400	6,400	4,400
Exemptions	2,000	4,000	5,000

Instructions:

(1) Present the following reports of estimated results of the first year of operations, assuming that Allen Co. is to be organized as a partnership: (a) estimated capital statement of the partners of Allen Co. and (b) statement of estimated federal income tax of A, B, and C, applying the appropriate schedule of tax rates presented in this chapter.

(2) Present the following reports of estimated results of the first year of operations, based on the assumption that Allen Co. is to be organized as a corporation: (a) statement of estimated federal income tax of Allen Co., applying the corporation tax rates presented in this chapter; (b) estimated statement of stockholders' equity of each of the stockholders in Allen Co., allocating each increase and decrease in the manner employed in (1a) above; and (c) estimated federal income tax of A, B, and C, applying the appropriate schedule of tax rates presented in this chapter.

(3) Present a report comparing the estimated federal income tax effects of the two methods of organization on each of the three individuals. For purposes of this report, the income tax on the corporation should be allocated among the individuals as in (2b).

Problem 27-5A. Joan and Frank Adams, each of whom is entitled to one exemption, have 2 dependent children. Frank also contributed more than half of the cost of supporting his mother, who received gross income of $950 during the year. During the current year ended December 31, Joan realized a net short-term capital gain of $1,925 and incurred a net long-term capital loss of $1,525. The Adams' residence also suffered windstorm damages of $1,750. Other details of receipts and disbursements during the year are as follows:

Cash Receipts

Joan Adams:	
Withdrawals of net income from Adams & Associates, a partnership in which she is a partner (distributive share of the net income for the year, $19,500)	$15,000
Rent from property owned	9,800
Insurance proceeds (death of mother)	25,000
Dividends on corporation stock	200
Frank Adams:	
Salary as sales manager of Martin Co.	37,700
(Earnings, $60,000. Withholding: income tax, $14,100; FICA tax, $2,800; purchases of Martin Co. stock, $5,400)	
Interest on bonds of City of Rantoul	600
Dividends on corporation stocks	750
Interest on U.S. Treasury bills	450

Cash Disbursements

Joan Adams:	
Rental property:	
Real estate tax	700
Insurance (one-year policies purchased January 3)	390
Painting and repairs	275
Mortgage note payments:	
Principal	4,250
Interest	1,800
(Building was acquired for $50,000 several years ago, and allowable depreciation is $2,000)	
Charitable contributions	350
Political contributions	100

Frank Adams:

Real estate tax on residence...............................	$ 1,720
State sales tax on items purchased for personal use	380
State gasoline tax (family cars)............................	195
State income tax	1,850
Damages for accidental injury suffered by visitor, not compensated by insurance	2,000
Charitable contributions	2,500
Political contributions	100
Interest on mortgage on residence	2,150
Automobile license fees (family cars)	80
Payments of estimated income tax for current year............	6,000

Instructions:

Prepare a summary of federal income tax data for the Adams', applying the schedule of tax rates for joint returns presented in this chapter.

Mini-Case

Your father recently signed a contract for the purchase of a vacation cottage on a nearby mountain lake. A $15,000 down payment is required by December 11, 1984. To raise the $15,000, your father is considering selling 150 of the 200 shares of CBC common stock that he acquired on January 20, 1984, at a total cost of $18,000.

Your father has asked your advice as to whether he should sell the stock or borrow the $15,000 for a maximum of 60 days at the current short-term interest rate of 12%. The stock is currently selling at $101 per share, and brokerage fees are expected to be $150 if the 150 shares are sold.

Instructions:

(1) Assuming that your father is in the 50% marginal tax bracket and itemizes deductions, how much tax would be due if the stock is sold on December 11, 1984?

(2) What would you suggest that your father consider concerning the selling of the stock? Discuss.

28

Accounting for Individuals and Nonprofit Organizations

CHAPTER OBJECTIVES

Describe and illustrate accounting systems and the preparation of financial statements for individuals.

Describe the characteristics of not-for-profit organizations.

Describe and illustrate accounting concepts and the preparation of financial statements for not-for-profit organizations.

PART 9

Individuals and Nonprofit Organizations

28

CHAPTER

Preceding chapters have discussed accounting concepts and procedures used by business enterprises organized to make a profit. Although many of these concepts and procedures apply to individuals and not-for-profit organizations, there are also many differences.

The term **individuals,** as used in the chapter title, may refer to a person or to a family unit, such as a husband, wife, and children. **Not-for-profit,** or **nonprofit,** entities are usually organized as informal associations or as corporations in accordance with applicable laws and regulations. Such organizations may be classified as either (1) governmental units or (2) charitable, religious, or philanthropic units (hereafter referred to simply as "charitable"). The first category includes the federal government and state, city, and county governments. The second category includes churches, hospitals, private schools and universities, medical research facilities, and many other types of organizations that are financed wholly or in part by donations.

ACCOUNTING SYSTEMS FOR INDIVIDUALS

Accounting systems for individuals differ widely. Some individuals may use a system based on the accrual method and double-entry accounting, with a complete set of journals, ledgers, and reports. Such an elaborate system is needed by individuals who have complex reporting obligations and many financial transactions of large amounts. For other individuals, a rather simple system based on the cash method is sufficient. The basics of such a system are described briefly in the sections that follow. Even with the use of such a simple system, however, it still may be wise to seek the services of a professional accountant to assist in the preparation of financial statements, tax returns, and other reports.

Budgets for Individuals

The use of budgets by an individual or a family unit is an important part of successful financial planning. A budget provides a systematic and orderly method of managing money. It enables individuals to spend their money wisely and to live within their income. The cash basis is ordinarily used in preparing budgets for individuals because most of their transactions are cash transactions evidenced by bank deposits and checks. In addition, the cash basis is required for an individual's reports to state taxing authorities and to the Internal Revenue Service for income taxes and FICA taxes.

The first step in preparing a budget is to determine as accurately as possible the cash income expected during a certain period of time, ordinarily a calendar year. Money to be received from salary or wages (net take-home pay), interest on bonds or savings accounts, dividends on shares of stock, and any other cash income should be included in the estimate. The second step is to develop a realistic plan for allocating the estimated income among the various goods and services most wanted by the individual or family and to provide for savings. There is no magic formula for determining the amount to be saved or the allocation of expenditures among various "essentials" and "luxuries." Much depends on such factors as the size of the family unit, its needs, tastes, wants, and the priorities assigned to each.

The process of estimating income and expenditures is often complicated by the fact that not all income is received on a regularly recurring basis and not all expenditures are incurred on a regularly recurring basis. Some income may be received on a weekly, biweekly, monthly, quarterly, or semiannual basis. For example, if salary is received biweekly, twenty-six amounts are used in determining the yearly amount. On the other hand, dividends on shares of stock are ordinarily received quarterly and four amounts would be used in estimating the yearly amount. Heating and lighting expenses ordinarily vary as the seasons change, thus requiring the consideration of twelve different monthly estimates to determine the yearly amount.

After the estimate of total income and expenditures for the year has been completed, the next step is to divide total income and each category of expenditure by 12, which provides the data for the monthly budget. Such a budget for a family composed of husband and wife and two children is illustrated as follows:

MONTHLY BUDGET |

**Susan and Henry Rice
Monthly Budget**

Income	**$1,950**
Allocations for expenditures:	
Housing and house operation	$675
Food and sundries	560
Transportation	200
Clothing	130
Medical care	90
Recreation and education	80
Contributions and gifts	70
Savings	70
Miscellaneous	75
Total allocations for expenditures	**$1,950**

Basic to the budgeting process is the requirement that the budget balance, that is, that the allocations among planned expenditures and savings do not exceed cash income. The need to maintain a balanced budget requires that priorities on spending be established if the individual or family unit is to be able to do those things that give it the most satisfaction. Thus, if the preliminary budget shows an excess of cash outflow over cash income, as is often the case, consideration should be given to possibilities of increasing earnings, reducing expenditures, omitting savings, borrowing money, or drawing upon accumulated savings from earlier periods. If the reverse situation occurs, the excess cash income may be added to savings or used to reduce outstanding liabilities.

Budget Performance Record for Individuals

An essential part of budgeting is the necessity of keeping a record of actual expenditures and making frequent comparisons with budgeted amounts. This record, termed the **budget performance record,** is then used to help control expenditures and to help the individuals to live within their budget.

The budget performance record is a multicolumn form that shows (1) the monthly budget allocations for each category of expenditures, (2) the actual individual expenditures made during the month and the end-of-month total of each category, and (3) the amount by which each total is over or under the budgeted amounts. Budget performance records for January, the first month of the budget period, and for a portion of February are illustrated below. The budget allocations are based on the budget appearing on the preceding page.

Susan and Henry Rice
Budget Performance Record—January, 19--

	Housing & house operation	Food & sundries	Trans-portation	Clothing	Medical care	Recrea-tion & education	Contri-butions & gifts	Savings	Miscella-neous
January allocation	675	560	200	130	90	80	70	70	75
January payments:									
January 1			15			18			8
2........................		57							7
4........................					12				
5........................		41							
7........................		25							11
8........................	15		16		10	12			
9........................	83	80		65					
10........................	55						50		
12........................		47							5
14........................		32				9			
15........................	156	38	14						
17........................		35							15
19........................		45	49			5			
21........................						11			18
23........................	30	27	15	22					
26........................	75								
27........................		52					30		
29........................		38	12						
30........................	360				35			70	
31........................		58	51	10		24			8
Total	774	575	172	105	57	79	80	70	72
Over* or under budget, Feb. 1	99*	15*	28	25	33	1	10*	—	3

Susan and Henry Rice
Budget Performance Record—February, 19--

	Housing & house operation	Food & sundries	Trans-portation	Clothing	Medical care	Recrea-tion & education	Contri-butions & gifts	Savings	Miscella-neous
Over* or under budget, Feb. 1....	99*	15*	28	25	33	1	10*	—	3
February allocation	675	560	200	130	90	80	70	70	75
Total budget, February	576	545	228	155	123	81	60	70	78
February payments:									
February 1		15				17			
2........................			14	18					16
3........................		19							8
5........................		62							
7........................	14						10		
8........................		25	12			24			
9........................	82				5				7
10........................		41		40					5

The January payments were recorded during the month and totaled at the end of the month for each category. These totals were then subtracted from the budget allocations to determine the over or under budget amounts as of February 1. For example, the allocation for housing and house operation for January was $675 and the total payments made during January amounted to $774. The payments exceeded the budgeted amount by $99. An investigation determined that this budget variance was the result of seasonal fluctuations in expenditures, namely, higher than average expenditures necessary for heat and light during the month and payment of a semiannual premium on property insurance. The over budget amount of $99, therefore, was carried forward to the budget performance record for February.

The actual expenditures will often vary from the monthly allocations and the causes of the "over budget" amounts should be carefully examined. If they are fairly small in amount and are the result of seasonal fluctuations in expenditures, as in the illustration, the balances should be carried forward to the next month and no revisions of the monthly budget are necessary. On the other hand, if the balances are significant and cannot be attributed to seasonal fluctuations, the monthly budget for the succeeding months should be revised accordingly. For example, a large expenditure for medical care that had not been anticipated may require a revision of the budgeted allocations for expenditures and savings for the next several months.

Records for Individuals

In addition to the budget performance record described in the preceding section, the record keeping system ordinarily consists of (1) a checkbook, (2) a file for bills and statements of account representing unpaid liabilities, (3) a file for documents supporting cash payments, and (4) a property inventory record.

As cash is received, it is deposited in the checking account and the amount is recorded in the checkbook, either on a "stub" or "check register" provided by the bank for the purpose of keeping a record of deposits, checks, and cash balance. As each check is written, the amount of the disbursement and its purpose should be entered on the stub or check register and the remaining balance recorded. The disbursement should also be entered in the budget performance record. The checkbook "cash balance" should be reconciled with the monthly bank statement as described in Chapter 7.

Individuals, like business enterprises, often need to make small expenditures. Payment by check in such cases would result in delay, annoyance, and excessive writing of checks. Instead, a check for a moderate sum can be "cashed" and the money used for small disbursements in a manner similar to a business enterprise's use of a petty cash fund. A pocket note pad may be carried for purposes of recording such expenditures. As a check is written to replenish the "pocket" cash, the memoranda recorded in the note pad may be summarized for recording on the stub or check register and in the budget performance record.

A simple but effective method of handling unpaid liabilities is to maintain a file box or folder in which bills and statements of account are placed. When the liabilities are paid, the documents are marked with the number of the check written to make the payment and are filed in a paid file. This file should be retained as long as is legally required for such purposes as verification of income tax deductions claimed, or as long as it may be needed for informational purposes.

The property inventory record contains detailed information, such as description and cost data, about valuable pieces of property such as personal residence (including improvements), investments, jewelry, silverware, and china. Such a record is especially useful for insurance purposes and for establishing gain or loss on sale of property.

FINANCIAL STATEMENTS FOR INDIVIDUALS

Financial statements are often prepared for an individual or for related individuals such as a husband and wife as a family unit. Such statements may be used in arranging a loan of a large amount, as an aid in planning for retirement, for estate and income tax planning, or for disclosure by public officials or candidates for public office.

Financial statements for individuals should be prepared according to generally accepted accounting principles for personal financial statements.[1] These principles primarily focus on an individual's assets and liabilities, which are reported at estimated current values rather than historical costs.

Statement of Financial Condition

The main financial statement for individuals is the **statement of financial condition**, sometimes called the statement of assets and liabilities. This statement, illustrated on pages 802–803, presents the (1) estimated current values of assets, (2) estimated current amounts of liabilities, (3) estimated income tax on unrealized appreciation of assets, and (4) net worth.

The assets and liabilities are reported on the accrual basis. Current and noncurrent classifications are not used, because working capital is generally not relevant to users of personal financial statements. The notes accompanying the statement describe the methods used in determining the current values and other relevant details.

Assets

Assets, such as real estate and securities, are reported in the order of liquidity at their estimated current values. The current values of most assets other than listed securities may be estimated by examining recent transactions involving similar assets or by using appraisals by independent experts in particular fields, such as art or jewelry. Any estimated costs of disposal of an asset, such as commissions, are deducted in arriving at estimated current values.

Investments. The estimated current values of corporate securities, real estate, interests in sole proprietorships or partnerships, and life insurance must be deter-

---

[1]*Statement of Position, No. 82-1*, "Accounting and Financial Reporting for Personal Financial Statements" (New York: American Institute of Certified Public Accountants, 1982).

mined as accurately as possible. Quoted market prices of marketable securities are usually available in the financial press. The estimated current market value of real estate can be obtained from a competent real estate appraiser. Data on recent sales of similar real estate may also be available. An offer to purchase the net assets of a sole proprietorship or other business unit or an estimate of liquidation values may

Bruce A. and Jennifer S. McCord
Statement of Financial Condition
December 31, 19--

Assets	
Cash (Note 2)	$ 18,250
Marketable securities (Note 3)	115,600
Cash value of life insurance ($300,000 face value)	36,500
Investment in real estate (Note 4)	130,000
Equity interest in McCord and Associates (Note 5)	183,000
Automobiles	17,000
Residence, pledged against mortgage (Note 4)	225,000
Household furnishings	28,500
Jewelry and paintings (Note 4)	50,000
Vested interest in AB Corp. pension trust	49,700
Total assets	$853,550
Liabilities	
Accounts payable and accrued liabilities	$ 7,700
Income tax payable	8,775
Note payable, 12%, due May 31, 19--	40,000
Mortgage note payable, 11%, final payment due July 1, 19-- (Note 6)	148,500
Total liabilities	$204,975
Estimated income tax on unrealized appreciation of assets (Note 7)	28,000
Net worth	620,575
Total liabilities, estimated income tax on unrealized appreciation of assets, and net worth	$853,550

Note 1–Current values and amounts

The accompanying statement of financial condition includes the assets and liabilities of Bruce A. and Jennifer S. McCord. Assets are stated at their estimated current values and liabilities at their estimated current amounts.

Note 2–Cash

The cash amount of $18,250 includes $17,500 deposited in money market accounts. These accounts allow unrestricted withdrawal without penalty.

Note 3–Marketable securities

Marketable securities consist of the following (estimated current value is the quoted market price on December 31, 19--, less estimated broker commissions):

	Shares or Face Amount	Current Value
Stocks:		
American Manufacturing...............................	500	$ 48,700
Jackson Tool Company...............................	200	9,800
Pontiac Power Company.............................	100	5,500
United Products, Inc..................................	50	20,900
Bonds:		
Pontiac Power Company, 10⅛%, due 20--..............	$ 5,000	10,300
U.S. Government, 9½%, due 19--....................	10,000	20,400
Total..		$115,600

Note 4–Investment in real estate and residence and personal effects

The estimated market price of investment in real estate and residence, jewelry, and paintings is based on independent appraisals made by Hunt and Associates.

Note 5–Equity interest in McCord and Associates

The estimated market price of the equity interest of Bruce A. McCord in McCord and Associates partnership is based on an offer made on October 10, 19-- to purchase the net assets of the partnership. The offer was rejected.

Note 6–Mortgage note payable

The terms of the mortgage note provide for monthly payments of $760, which includes the interest accrued on the loan.

Note 7–Estimated income tax on unrealized appreciation of assets

Estimated income taxes have been provided on the unrealized appreciation of the estimated current values of assets over their tax bases as if the estimated current values of the assets had been realized on the statement date, using applicable tax laws and regulations. This estimate will probably differ from the amounts of income taxes that eventually might be paid because of possible changes in the current values of the assets and in the tax laws which might be in effect at the time of disposal of the assets.

be used as the estimated market price of such investments. Life insurance is reported at its cash surrender value, which is obtainable from the policy contract or from the insurer, less the amount of any loans against it. The face amount of life insurance should also be disclosed.

Residences and personal effects. Ordinarily, a residence and household furnishings, automobiles, objects of art, and jewelry are reported in the statement of financial condition if their value is material in relation to total assets. The estimated current values of especially significant assets may be determined by independent appraisers or estimated on the basis of advertised prices of similar items.

Future interests. Individuals may have future interests in pensions, profit-sharing plans, trusts, or similar future rights. If the individual has a definite (rather than contingent) legal right to future benefits, such a right is said to be "vested" in the individual. The present value of such interests should be reported on the statement.

Liabilities

Commitments to pay future sums that are fixed in amount are listed on the statement of financial condition at their present values in the order of dates of maturity. Examples of such commitments include fixed amounts of alimony and charitable pledges. Commitments that depend upon a future contingency or the rendering of services by others should be disclosed in a note.

Estimated Income Tax on Unrealized Appreciation of Assets

An estimate of the income tax that would be owed if the assets were sold at their current values should be reported as a separate item below the total liabilities. This provision is necessary because the current values of the assets cannot be realized without the incurrence of a tax liability.

Net Worth

The equity of the individual(s) is called **net worth.** At the financial statement date, net worth can be determined as the difference between (1) the total assets and (2) the total of the liabilities plus the estimated income tax on the unrealized appreciation of the assets. On the statement of financial condition, net worth is reported below the estimated income tax on unrealized appreciation of assets.

Other Financial Statements for Individuals

For most uses, a single statement of financial condition is sufficient. In some situations, comparative statements for at least two years may be useful. When comparative statements are presented, an additional statement is often included. This statement, referred to as the statement of changes in net worth, presents the major sources of increases and decreases in net worth.

Although personal financial statements are presented on the basis of estimated current values, users may sometimes request certain historical cost data. Such data may be included as supplementary information in the statements.

CHARACTER-ISTICS OF NONPROFIT ORGANIZATIONS

Entities engaged in business transactions may be classified as profit-making or nonprofit. Profit-making organizations respond to a demand for a product or a service with the expectation of earning net income. The accounting concepts and procedures applicable to such organizations were discussed in preceding chapters. The distinguishing characteristics of nonprofit organizations are: (1) there is neither a conscious profit motive nor an expectation of earning net income; (2) no part of any excess of revenues over expenditures is distributed to those who contributed support through taxes or voluntary donations; and (3) any excess of revenues over expenditures that results from operations in the short run is ordinarily used in later years to further the purposes of the organization.

Nonprofit organizations provide goods or services that fulfill a social need, often for those who do not have the purchasing power to acquire these goods or services for themselves.

Some nonprofit organizations, such as a government-owned electric utility or a public transportation company, are created to provide services to the citizens of the area for a fee that is close to the cost of providing the service. After the initial investment, they tend to be self-sustaining; that is, the revenues earned support their operations. Because the activities of such organizations are financed mainly by charges to the customers using the services, the accounting concepts and procedures used are those appropriate to a commercial enterprise. Most nonprofit organizations, however, are established to provide a service to society without levying against the user a direct charge equal to the full cost of the service. The concepts and procedures applicable to nonprofit organizations of the latter type are discussed in the remainder of the chapter. The explanations and illustrations presented are necessarily brief and relatively free of the complexities encountered in actual practice.

ACCOUNTING FOR NONPROFIT ORGANIZATIONS

With the increase in the sense of social responsibility in society has come a corresponding increase in the number of nonprofit organizations and in the volume of their activities. Approximately one third of the volume of business in the United States is conducted by governmental units and charitable organizations. As such organizations play an increasingly significant role, accounting for these organizations is receiving more and more attention. For example, a Governmental Accounting Standards Board (GASB), similar to the Financial Accounting Standards Board (FASB), has been proposed. This body would be responsible for establishing accounting standards for state and local governmental units. Accounting for other nonprofit organizations, such as churches and hospitals, is also receiving attention by the American Institute of Certified Public Accountants and other professional accounting groups.

The accounting systems for all nonprofit organizations must provide financial data to internal management for use in planning and controlling operations and to external parties, such as taxpayers and donors, for use in determining the effectiveness of operations. The basic double-entry system, an effective system of internal control, and the periodic determination of and reporting of financial position and results of operations are essential for nonprofit organizations. In addition, accounting systems for nonprofit organizations should include mechanisms (1) to ensure that management observes the restrictions imposed upon it by law, charter, by-laws, etc., and (2) to provide for reports to taxpayers and donors that such restrictions have been respected. For these reasons, a nonprofit organization often applies the concept of "fund accounting" in conjunction with a budget and appropriations technique to account for the assets received by the organization and to ensure that expenditures are made only for authorized purposes.

Fund Accounting

In this book, the term "fund" has been used with a variety of meanings. Fund has been used to denote segregations of cash for a special purpose, for example, in "petty cash fund," or to designate the amount of cash and marketable securities segregated in a "sinking fund" to pay long-term obligations at maturity. The term was also used in the context of the funds statement, where funds can be interpreted broadly to mean "working capital" or more narrowly to mean "cash" or "cash and marketable securities." The term "fund" as used in accounting for nonprofit organizations has still another meaning.

In accounting for nonprofit organizations, fund is defined as an accounting entity with accounts maintained for recording assets, liabilities, capital (usually called "fund balance"), revenues, and expenditures for a particular purpose according to specified restrictions or limitations. Funds may be established by law, provisions of a charter, administrative action, or by a special contribution to a charitable organization. For example, cities usually maintain a "General Fund" for recording transactions related to many community services, such as fire and police protection, street lighting and repairs, and maintenance of water and sewer mains. Additional funds may be maintained for special tax assessments, bond redemption, and for other specified purposes. It is possible to have transactions between funds, as when one fund borrows money from another fund, in which case the transaction is recorded in the accounts of both funds.

Both public and private universities usually maintain a number of separate funds in addition to a General Fund. For example, there may be a number of scholarship funds, named for alumni or other donors, with many restrictions concerning the recipients, such as high scholastic attainment, residing in a specified area, and enrolled in a particular course of study.

Charitable organizations often have a number of funds, sometimes called "endowment funds," from which only the income may be spent. The amounts contributed to such funds are often invested in various income-yielding bonds and stocks. For fund balances of modest amount, however, it is not feasible to identify each bond or share with a particular fund. In such situations, the investments are commingled, each fund having a claim on the investment pool equal to its fund balance. The income is periodically divided among the various participating funds in proportion to the respective fund balances at the beginning of the period. The same technique is used by governmental units, such as state universities, for the temporary investment of large amounts of cash that would otherwise yield no income.

Estimated Revenues and Appropriations

Budgeting is an important part of an accounting system for nonprofit organizations. The budget is prepared by management and subsequently reviewed, revised, and approved by the governing body (council, directors, trustees, etc.) of the organization. The official budget sets the specific goals for the fiscal period and, through appropriations, designates the manner in which the revenues of each fund are to be used to accomplish these goals. The estimated revenues may be viewed as potential assets and the **appropriations** as potential liabilities.

Many governmental units apply the concept of **zero-base budgeting** in developing budget estimates. This concept requires all levels of management to start from zero and estimate revenues and appropriations as if there had been no previous activities in their unit.

After the budget for the general fund has been approved by the governing body, the estimated revenues and appropriations are recorded in controlling accounts by an entry such as the following:

Estimated Revenues	1,900,000	
Appropriations		1,850,000
Fund Balance		50,000

The effect of the recording of the budgeted amounts in the general fund accounts is presented in the following diagram:

General Fund Accounts

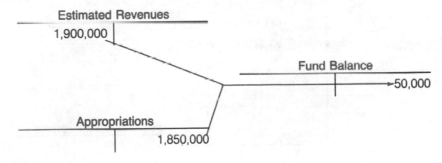

When the budget shows an excess of estimated revenues over appropriations, as in the illustration, the account Fund Balance is credited. The amount in Fund Balance represents the estimated accumulated capital of the general fund. If the budget had shown an excess of appropriations over estimated revenues, the excess would be debited to the account Fund Balance. The subsidiary ledgers for Estimated Revenues and Appropriations contain accounts for the various sources of expected revenue (property taxes, sales taxes, etc.) and the various purposes of appropriations (general government, streets and roads, libraries, etc.). By recording this budgetary information in the accounts, periodic reports comparing actual with budget can be prepared readily.

Revenues

The realization of revenues requires an entry debiting accounts for the assets acquired and crediting the revenues account. For example, a portion of the estimated revenues from property taxes, sales taxes, etc., may be realized in the form of cash during the first month of the fiscal year. To summarize these receipts, an entry would be made as follows, in general journal form:

```
Cash.............................................  152,500
     Revenues......................................          152,500
```

Revenues is a controlling account. In practice, it is customary to use a single subsidiary ledger, called the revenue ledger, for both Estimated Revenues and Revenues. Each subsidiary account is used for recording the estimated revenues and the actual revenues. The relationship between the general ledger accounts and the subsidiary revenue ledger is illustrated in the following diagram:

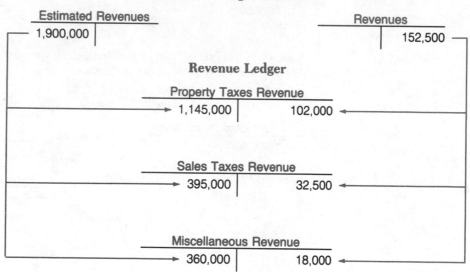

At any point in time, the difference between the two general ledger controlling accounts, Estimated Revenues and Revenues, would be equal to the sum of the balances of the accounts in the subsidiary revenue ledger. A debit balance in a subsidiary ledger account indicates the amount of the excess of estimated revenues over actual revenues. If actual revenues exceed the amount estimated, the account balance would be a credit.

Expenditures

As regularly recurring expenditures, such as payrolls, are incurred, the account Expenditures is debited and the appropriate liability accounts or cash are credited. For example, the entry for the biweekly payroll would be as follows:

| Expenditures...................................... | 31,200 | |
| Wages Payable .... | | 31,200 |

Encumbrances

There is usually a lapse of time between the placing of an order and delivery of the goods or services ordered. When contracts such as those for road or building construction are executed, the time lag may extend over relatively long periods. All legally binding commitments to pay money eventually become expenditures. These commitments, called **encumbrances,** should be recorded in the accounts when a contract is entered into in order to ensure that expenditures do not exceed amounts appropriated. The means of preventing overexpenditures is illustrated by the following entry:

| Encumbrances...................................... | 10,000 | |
| Reserve for Encumbrances....................... | | 10,000 |

When orders are filled or contracts completed for amounts encumbered, the entry that recorded the encumbrance is reversed and the expenditure is recorded, as illustrated by the following entries:

Reserve for Encumbrances.........................	10,000	
Encumbrances....................................		10,000
Expenditures......................................	10,000	
Accounts Payable		10,000

The effect of these two entries is to (1) cancel the original entry in which the encumbrance was recorded and (2) record the expenditure and the related liability.

When encumbrances are recorded, the sum of the balances of the accounts Encumbrances and Expenditures can be viewed as offsets to the account Appropriations. The difference obtained by subtracting the balance of Encumbrances and Expenditures from the amount of Appropriations is the amount of commitments that can still be made. For example, if appropriations of $1,850,000 were approved when the budget was adopted and $1,500,000 and $240,000 have been recorded in Expenditures and Encumbrances, respectively, only $110,000 is available for commitment during the remainder of the fiscal year.

Expenditure Ledger

Appropriations, Encumbrances, and Expenditures are controlling accounts. In practice, it is customary to use a single subsidiary ledger, called the expenditure ledger, in which each account indicates appropriations, encumbrances, and expenditures.

When a budget is approved, appropriations are recorded in the proper accounts in the expenditure ledger to indicate the uncommitted balance. As order commitments are made, the amounts of the encumbrances are recorded in the proper expenditure ledger account (by a debit) and the uncommitted balance is adjusted accordingly. When orders are filled, the expenditure and the credit to encumbrances are recorded in the proper columns. At any point in time, the accounts in the expenditure ledger indicate the balance of the encumbrances outstanding and the uncommitted balance.

In the following illustration of an account in the expenditure ledger, the budget appropriation for police department supplies is $250,000 as of July 1. On July 5, a purchase order that encumbered $10,000 was recorded and the encumbrances balance of $10,000 and the uncommitted balance of $240,000 were recorded. When the invoice of $10,000 was received on July 17, the encumbrances balance was reduced to zero and the $10,000 expenditure was recorded.

ACCOUNT POLICE DEPARTMENT—SUPPLIES								ACCOUNT NO. 200-21
Date		Item	Encumbrances			Expenditures		Uncommitted Balance
			Debit	Credit	Balance	Item	Total	
July	1	Budget appropriation						250,000
	5	Purchase order	10,000		10,000			240,000
	17	Invoice		10,000	———	10,000	10,000	240,000
	30	Purchase order	7,500		7,500			232,500

Long-Lived Assets

When long-lived assets are purchased, they are usually recorded as debits to the account Expenditures in the same manner as supplies and other ordinary expenses. A separate record of the individual assets can be maintained for the purpose of assigning responsibility for the custody and use of these assets.

The practice of recording the purchase of long-lived assets as an expenditure and the related failure to record depreciation expense has been severely criticized for many years. Most governmental units and charitable organizations still fail to differentiate between long-lived assets and ordinary recurring expenses. This practice is supported by the fact that the acquisition of plant assets is often authorized by a special appropriation, perhaps financed by a bond issue for a local government unit or by donations or special fund-raising drives for a charitable organization.

Periodic Reporting A nonprofit organization should prepare interim statements comparing actual revenues and expenditures with the related budgeted amounts. Variations between the two should be investigated immediately to determine their cause and to consider possible corrective actions.

At the end of the fiscal year, closing entries are recorded and the operating data are summarized and reported. The entry to close the revenues and estimated revenues accounts is illustrated as follows:

Revenues..	1,920,000	
Estimated Revenues		1,900,000
Fund Balance		20,000

In the illustration, actual revenues exceeded the amount estimated. If the actual revenues had been less than the amount estimated, the capital account, Fund Balance, would have been decreased by a debit. The effect of this entry is to adjust Fund Balance to the actual amount of the revenues for the period.

The entry to close the appropriations and expenditures accounts is illustrated as follows:

Appropriations	1,850,000	
Expenditures		1,825,000
Fund Balance		25,000

In the illustration, appropriations exceeded the actual expenditures. If the appropriations had been less than the actual expenditures, the capital account, Fund Balance, would have been decreased by a debit. The effect of this entry is to adjust Fund Balance to the actual amount of the expenditures for the period.

The entry to close the encumbrances account, which represents the commitments outstanding at the end of the year, is illustrated as follows:

Fund Balance	20,000	
Encumbrances		20,000

Inevitably, some orders placed during the year will remain unfilled at the end of the year. To indicate the commitment to pay for these orders, Reserve for Encumbrances is not closed and is included in the year-end balance sheet. When the orders are filled in the next year, Reserve for Encumbrances will be debited and Accounts Payable credited.

Financial statements for each fund and combined financial statements for all funds should be prepared periodically. These statements should also be accompanied by adequate disclosures, including a summary of significant accounting policies.

The principal financial statements prepared at the end of each fiscal year are: (1) statement of revenues and expenditures—budget and actual, (2) balance sheet, and (3) statement of changes in fund balance. Because of the absence of the profit motive and the presence of controls imposed upon nonprofit organizations by law or dictate of donors, the operating statement shows budgeted and actual results instead of a net income figure. The balance sheet is similar to a balance sheet for commercial enterprises. A statement of changes in fund balance, although similar to the Retained Earnings Statement for a commercial enterprise, has a unique format. These statements are illustrated in the following section.

ILLUSTRATION OF NONPROFIT ACCOUNTING

To illustrate further the concepts and procedures that have been described, assume that the trial balance of the General Fund of the City of Lewiston, as of July 1, the beginning of the fiscal year, is as follows:

City of Lewiston—General Fund
Trial Balance
July 1, 19--

Cash	242,500	
Savings Accounts.................................	250,000	
Property Taxes Receivable.........................	185,000	
Investment in U.S. Treasury Notes	350,000	
Accounts Payable.................................		162,600
Wages Payable...................................		30,000
Fund Balance		834,900
	1,027,500	1,027,500

The transactions completed during the year for the General Fund are summarized and recorded as follows, in general journal form. In practice, the transactions would be recorded from day to day in various journals.

(a) *Estimated revenues and appropriations.*

Entry: Estimated Revenues..................... 9,100,000
           Appropriations......................... 9,070,000
           Fund Balance.......................... 30,000

(b) *Revenues from property tax levy.*

Entry: Property Taxes Receivable 6,500,000
           Revenues 6,500,000

(c) *Collection of property taxes and other taxes on a cash basis, such as sales
taxes, motor vehicle license fees, municipal court fines, etc.*

Entry: Cash 9,105,000
           Property Taxes Receivable.............. 6,470,000
           Revenues 2,635,000

(d) *Expenditures for payrolls.*

Entry: Expenditures........................... 3,280,000
           Wages Payable........................ 3,280,000

(e) *Expenditures encumbered.*

Entry: Encumbrances.......................... 5,800,000
           Reserve for Encumbrances 5,800,000

(f) *Liquidation of encumbrances and receipt of invoices.*

Entry: Reserve for Encumbrances 5,785,000
           Encumbrances........................ 5,785,000

          Expenditures 5,785,000
           Accounts Payable..................... 5,785,000

(g) Cash disbursed.

    Entry: Accounts Payable 5,800,000
               Wages Payable......................... 3,270,000
                  Cash   9,070,000

(h) Revenues and estimated revenues accounts closed.

    Entry: Revenues 9,135,000
               Estimated Revenues...................   9,100,000
               Fund Balance........................   35,000

(i) Appropriations and expenditures accounts closed.

    Entry: Appropriations......................... 9,070,000
               Expenditures   9,065,000
               Fund Balance........................   5,000

(j) Encumbrances account closed.

    Entry: Fund Balance 15,000
               Encumbrances.......................   15,000

After the foregoing entries have been posted, the general ledger accounts, the trial balance, and the balance sheet for the General Fund appear as follows. Entries in the accounts are identified by letters to facilitate comparison with the summary journal entries.

Cash				Accounts Payable		
Balance	242,500	(g)	9,070,000	(g)	5,800,000	Balance	162,600
(c)	9,105,000	Balance	277,500	Balance	147,600	(f)	5,785,000
	9,347,500		9,347,500		5,947,600		5,947,600
Balance	277,500					Balance	147,600

Savings Accounts		Wages Payable		
Balance	250,000	(g)	3,270,000	Balance	30,000
		Balance	40,000	(d)	3,280,000
			3,310,000		3,310,000
				Balance	40,000

Property Taxes Receivable			
Balance	185,000	(c)	6,470,000
(b)	6,500,000	Balance	215,000
	6,685,000		6,685,000
Balance	215,000		

Reserve for Encumbrances			
(f)	5,785,000	(e)	5,800,000
Balance	15,000		
	5,800,000		5,800,000
		Balance	15,000

Investment in U.S. Treasury Notes	
Balance	350,000

Fund Balance

(j)	15,000	Balance	834,900
Balance	889,900	(a)	30,000
		(h)	35,000
	904,900	(i)	5,000
			904,900
		Balance	889,900

Appropriations

(i)	9,070,000	(a)	9,070,000

Expenditures

(d)	3,280,000	(i)	9,065,000
(f)	5,785,000		
	9,065,000		9,065,000

Estimated Revenues

(a)	9,100,000	(h)	9,100,000

Revenues

(h)	9,135,000	(b)	6,500,000
		(c)	2,635,000
	9,135,000		9,135,000

Encumbrances

(e)	5,800,000	(f)	5,785,000
		(j)	15,000
	5,800,000		5,800,000

City of Lewiston—General Fund
Trial Balance
June 30, 19--

Cash	277,500	
Savings Accounts	250,000	
Property Taxes Receivable	215,000	
Investment in U.S. Treasury Notes	350,000	
Accounts Payable		147,600
Wages Payable		40,000
Reserve for Encumbrances		15,000
Fund Balance		889,900
	1,092,500	1,092,500

BALANCE SHEET

City of Lewiston—General Fund
Balance Sheet
June 30, 19--

Assets

Cash	$ 277,500
Savings accounts	250,000
Property taxes receivable	215,000
Investment in U.S. Treasury notes	350,000
Total assets	$1,092,500

Liabilities and Fund Balance

Accounts payable	$ 147,600
Wages payable	40,000
Reserve for encumbrances	15,000
Fund balance	889,900
Total liabilities and fund balance	$1,092,500

To simplify the illustration, the subsidiary ledgers were not presented. Such ledgers provide data for the following statement of revenues and expenditures— budget and actual.

City of Lewiston — General Fund
Statement of Revenues and Expenditures—Budget and Actual
For Year Ended June 30, 19--

	Budget	Actual	Over	Under
Revenues:				
General property taxes	$6,480,000	$6,500,000	$20,000	
Sales taxes	1,835,500	1,850,500	15,000	
Motor vehicle licenses	312,250	310,250		$ 2,000
Municipal court fines	257,000	255,750		1,250
Interest	35,000	35,000		
Building permits	27,100	27,500	400	
Miscellaneous	153,150	156,000	2,850	
Total revenues	$9,100,000	$9,135,000	$38,250	$ 3,250
Expenditures:				
General government	$2,450,000	$2,465,250	$15,250	
Police department—personnel services	1,250,000	1,256,000	6,000	
Police department—supplies	299,000	290,500		$ 8,500
Police department—equipment	190,000	182,750		7,250
Police department—other charges	30,000	27,500		2,500
Fire department—personnel services	1,035,000	1,039,000	4,000	
Fire department—supplies	320,600	315,600		5,000
Fire department—equipment	200,500	197,750		2,750
Fire department—other charges	16,400	18,200	1,800	
Streets and roads	1,530,000	1,521,850		8,150
Sanitation	741,000	739,500		1,500
Public welfare	630,000	632,600	2,600	
Libraries	377,500	378,500	1,000	
Total expenditures	$9,070,000	$9,065,000	$30,650	$35,650
Excess of revenues over expenditures	$ 30,000	$ 70,000		

Although there are many variations in form, the following statement of changes in fund balance has the advantages of indicating (1) the excess of estimated revenues over appropriations, (2) the excess of revenues over estimated revenues, (3) the excess of appropriations over expenditures, and (4) the encumbrances outstanding at the end of the year. These four items represent the effect of the four entries made in the fund account during the year.

City of Lewiston—General Fund
Statement of Changes in Fund Balance
For Year Ended June 30, 19--

Balance, July 1, 19--				$834,900
Add:				
Excess of estimated revenues over appro-priations:				
Estimated revenues	$9,100,000			
Appropriations	9,070,000	$30,000		
Excess of revenues over estimated reve-nues:				
Revenues	$9,135,000			
Estimated revenues	9,100,000	35,000		
Excess of appropriations over expendi-tures:				
Appropriations	$9,070,000			
Expenditures	9,065,000	5,000	70,000	
				$904,900
Deduct:				
Encumbrances, June 30, 19--				15,000
Balance, June 30, 19--				$889,900

1. Assets in the statement of financial condition for individuals are reported at:
   A. cost
   B. estimated current values
   C. lower of cost or market
   D. none of the above

2. The caption for the equity of the individual in the statement of financial condition is:
   A. proprietorship
   B. capital
   C. net worth
   D. none of the above

3. In accounting for nonprofit organizations, the term employed to represent an accounting entity with accounts for assets, liabilities, capital, revenues, and expenditures for a particular purpose is:
   A. fund
   B. appropriation
   C. encumbrance
   D. none of the above

4. In accounting for nonprofit organizations, the account that represents the capital of an accounting entity is:
   A. Retained Earnings
   B. Accumulated Earnings
   C. Fund Balance
   D. none of the above

5. The financial statement for a nonprofit organization that is similar to the retained earnings statement for a commercial enterprise is:
   A. statement of changes in fund balance
   B. trial balance
   C. balance sheet
   D. none of the above

1. How does the use of budgets assist an individual or family unit in financial planning?

2. If the preliminary monthly budget for an individual indicates an excess of cash outflow over cash income, what courses of action might the individual consider to achieve a balanced budget?

3. What name is given to the record that indicates the relationship between actual expenditures made by an individual and the allocations for expenditures provided in the budget?

4. In addition to a budget performance record, what four other records are ordinarily included in an individual's record keeping system?

5. In what respects does the statement of financial condition prepared for individuals differ from the conventional balance sheet prepared for commercial enterprises?

6. In what order are (a) assets and (b) liabilities listed in the statement of financial condition?

7. Why should the statement of financial condition include an amount for estimated income tax on unrealized appreciation of assets?

8. In the statement of financial condition, what caption is used to identify the equity of an individual?

9. What characteristics distinguish commercial enterprises from nonprofit organizations?

10. As the term is used in reference to accounting for nonprofit organizations, what is meant by "fund accounting"?

11. What concept requires all levels of management of a governmental unit to start from zero and estimate revenues and appropriations as if there had been no previous activities in their unit?

12. In recording estimated revenues and appropriations as expressed in the budget, would Fund Balance be debited or credited if estimated revenues exceed appropriations?

13. If an account in the revenue ledger indicated that revenues exceeded estimated revenues, will the account have a debit or a credit balance?

14. What is the purpose of recording encumbrances in the accounts?

15. If the appropriations, expenditures, and encumbrances accounts have balances of $900,000, $600,000, and $250,000 respectively, what amount is available for commitments during the remainder of the fiscal year?

16. In the subsidiary expenditure ledger, the libraries account shows an uncommitted balance. Does this balance indicate that appropriations for the year exceed the sum of encumbrances outstanding and expenditures incurred to date?

17. (a) What account in the general ledger of a nonprofit organization is debited for purchases of long-lived assets? (b) Is depreciation generally recorded on such assets?

18. When the closing entry for the appropriations and expenditures accounts is prepared, in what account is the difference between the balances in the two accounts recorded?

19. In which financial statement will the year-end balance of the following accounts appear: (a) Reserve for Encumbrances and (b) Encumbrances?

20. What statement for a commercial corporate enterprise is similar to the statement of changes in fund balance that is prepared for each fund of a nonprofit organization?

Exercises

Exercise 28-1. Julie and John Milton applied to the Eastern Pacific Bank for a loan. The bank requested a statement of financial condition. Summary financial data accumulated as of May 1 are as follows:

(a) Present value of accounts payable and accrued liabilities, $19,050.
(b) Automobiles: cost, $38,500; estimated market price, $27,000.
(c) Cash, including money market funds, $27,000.
(d) Cash value of $200,000 face value life insurance policy, $34,400.
(e) Household furnishings: cost, $127,750; estimated market price, $102,200.
(f) Marketable securities: cost, $288,500; estimated current value, $380,000.
(g) Present value of 10% mortgage note payable, final payment due September 1, 19--, $167,700.
(h) Residence (pledged against mortgage note): cost $240,000; estimated market price, $308,000.

Prepare a statement of financial condition (exclusive of notes to the statement) as of May 1. Assume that the estimated income tax on unrealized appreciation of assets is $18,400.

Exercise 28-2. The budget approved for the fiscal year by the city council of Spirit Lake for the general fund indicated appropriations of $2,715,000 and estimated revenues of $2,760,000. Present the general journal entry to record the financial data indicated by the budget.

Exercise 28-3. An order was placed by a nonprofit organization for $19,250 of supplies. Subsequently, $16,850 of the supplies were received and $2,400 were back ordered. Present entries to record (a) the placement of the order and (b) the receipt of the supplies and the invoice for $16,850, terms n/30.

Exercise 28-4. Selected account balances from the general fund ledger of Truesdell Foundation at the end of the current fiscal year are as follows:

Appropriations	$676,000
Encumbrances	10,000
Estimated Revenues	672,000
Expenditures	664,000
Fund Balance	92,400
Reserve for Encumbrances	10,000
Revenues	680,000

Prepare the appropriate closing entries.

Exercise 28-5. Selected account balances from the ledger of the University of Amarillo Alumni Association—General Fund are as follows:

Accounts Payable	$ 2,730
Cash in Bank	8,330
Fund Balance	80,780
Marketable Securities	35,000
Petty Cash	280
Reserve for Encumbrances	2,100
Savings Accounts	42,000

Prepare a balance sheet as of August 31.

Exercise 28-6. Data from two subsidiary ledgers of Dexter College—Intercollegiate Athletics Fund, at June 30, are as follows:

Revenue Ledger

	Debits	Credits
Basketball	87,500	86,250
Football	275,000	279,000
Other	7,500	8,550

Expenditure Ledger

	Expen- ditures	Budget Appropriations
Administration	43,000	42,000
Basketball	58,200	60,800
Football	185,900	187,600
Maintenance of facilities	31,800	33,600
Publicity	11,400	11,000
Other	27,700	25,000

Prepare a statement of revenues and expenditures—budget and actual for the fiscal year ended June 30.

Exercise 28-7. Selected account balances before closing on June 30, the end of the current fiscal year for C. R. Corbin Foundation—General Fund, are as follows. The fund balance account had a balance of $792,800 on July 1, the beginning of the current year.

Appropriations	$4,160,000
Encumbrances	20,000
Estimated Revenues	4,240,000
Expenditures	4,016,000
Revenues	4,120,000

Prepare a statement of changes in fund balance.

Problems
(Problems in
Appendix B:
28-1B, 28-3B,
28-4B.)

Problem 28-1A. Mark Kaye is a partner in the firm of Kaye and Associates, and Jean Kaye owns and manages The Studio. They applied to the Atlantic National Bank for a loan to be used to build an apartment complex. The bank requested a statement of financial condition and they assembled the following data for this purpose at October 31:

(a) Cash in bank, savings, and money market accounts, $17,800. (Unrestricted withdrawals are allowed without penalty.)

(b) Marketable securities (current value is quoted market price on October 31, 19--, less estimated broker commissions):

	Cost	Current Value
Stocks:		
MGM Industries, 500 shares	$13,000	$17,750
Harris Manufacturing Inc., 300 shares	10,000	12,500
Bell Food Stores Inc., 1,000 shares	40,000	58,000
Bonds:		
U.S. Treasury, 8%, $50,000 face amount, due 19--	45,600	47,250
Nall Motors Inc., 10%, $15,000 face amount, due 20--	13,500	14,200

(c) Mark Kaye's equity interest in Kaye and Associates: cost, $80,000; estimated market, $120,000. Jean Kaye's equity interest in The Studio: cost, $30,000; estimated market, $50,000. Estimated market prices were determined by an independent appraisal made by Warner Realty.

(d) Cash value of $400,000 face value life insurance policy, $70,000.

(e) Residence: cost $150,000; estimated market, $280,000. The estimated market price was determined by an independent appraisal made by Lawler and Associates. The residence is pledged against a 9½% mortgage note payable, final installment due July 1, 19--. The present value of the monthly mortgage payments of $910, including interest, is $74,600.

(f) Household furnishings: cost, $70,000; estimated market, $56,000.

(g) Automobiles: cost, $41,500; estimated market, $28,000.

(h) Jewelry and paintings: cost, $40,000; estimated market, $62,000. The estimated market price was determined by an independent appraisal made by Lawler and Associates.

(i) Present value of vested interest in Harris Corporation Pension Trust, $18,200.

(j) Present value of accounts payable and accrued liabilities, $13,500.

(k) Income tax payable, $6,500.

(l) Present value of 12% note payable, due March 1, 19--, $26,000.

(m) Estimated income tax on unrealized appreciation of salable assets, $17,400.

Instructions:

Prepare a statement of financial condition as of October 31 of the current year. Notes to the statement should be presented as appropriate.

Problem 28-2A. Scott and Elaine Heinze maintain a budget performance record. The over-under budget amounts as of April 1 and the monthly allocations for expenditures as indicated by the monthly budget were as follows:

	Over*-Under Budget	Allocations
Housing and house operation	$120	$1,200
Food and sundries	40*	600
Transportation	50	160
Clothing.	80	90
Medical care	210*	80
Recreation and education.	60*	100
Contributions and gifts.	20	40
Savings	50	50
Miscellaneous	42	70

The expenditures for April are summarized as follows:

April   1. Food and sundries, $60; recreation and education, $48.
4. Transportation, $25; miscellaneous, $12.
6. Food and sundries, $74.
8. Medical care, $30; miscellaneous, $16.
10. Food and sundries, $125; clothing, $40.
11. Housing and house operation, $720; food and sundries, $80; transportation, $30.
13. Food and sundries, $40; transportation, $22.
15. Clothing, $39; miscellaneous, $20.
16. Housing and house operation, $265; recreation and education, $28.
18. Food and sundries, $32; transportation, $36; contributions, $30.
19. Transportation, $12; recreation and education, $40.
21. Housing and house operation, $130; food and sundries, $74; miscellaneous, $12.
22. Transportation, $41; clothing, $43.
26. Housing and house operation, $40; food and sundries, $28.
27. Food and sundries, $86; medical care, $60; miscellaneous, $35.
30. Housing and house operation, $110; transportation, $34; savings, $60.

Instructions:

Prepare a budget performance record for April.

(If the working papers correlating with the textbook are not used, omit Problem 28-3A.)

Problem 28-3A. After the closing entries were posted, the account balances in the ledger of the general fund for Woodbury on June 30, the end of the current year, are as follows:

Accounts Payable.	$114,300
Cash in Bank	162,900
Cash on Hand	23,500
Fund Balance.	654,700
Investments in Marketable Securities	240,000
Property Taxes Receivable	213,000
Reserve for Encumbrances.	21,300
Savings Accounts	180,000
Wages Payable	29,100

Estimated revenues, revenues, appropriations, encumbrances, and expenditures from the respective subsidiary ledgers have been entered in the statement of revenues and expenditures—budget and actual in the working papers. The fund balance account had a balance of $631,400 on July 1, the beginning of the current year.

Instructions:

(1) Complete the statement of revenues and expenditures—budget and actual.
(2) Prepare a statement of changes in fund balance.
(3) Prepare a balance sheet.

Problem 28-4A. The trial balance for the City of Covington—General Fund at the beginning of the current year is as follows:

City of Covington—General Fund
Trial Balance
July 1, 19--

Cash	455,000	
Savings Accounts	140,000	
Property Taxes Receivable	245,000	
Investment in U.S. Treasury Notes	280,000	
Accounts Payable		245,000
Wages Payable		38,500
Fund Balance		836,500
	1,120,000	1,120,000

The following data summarize the operations for the current year.

(a) Estimated revenues, $6,370,000; appropriations, $6,300,000.
(b) Revenues from property tax levy, $4,900,000.
(c) Cash received from property taxes, $5,000,000; other revenues, $1,540,000.
(d) Expenditures for payrolls, $2,870,000.
(e) Expenditures encumbered and evidenced by purchase orders, $3,535,000.
(f) Liquidation of encumbrances and vouchers prepared, $3,510,000.
(g) Cash disbursed for vouchers, $3,515,000; for payment of wages, $2,880,000; for savings accounts, $100,000.

Instructions:

(1) Prepare entries in general journal form to record the foregoing summarized operations.
(2) Open T accounts for the accounts appearing in the trial balance and enter the balances as of July 1, identifying them as "Bal."
(3) Open T accounts for Reserve for Encumbrances, Estimated Revenues, Revenues, Appropriations, Expenditures, and Encumbrances. Post the entries recorded in (1) to the accounts, using the identifying letters in place of dates.
(4) Prepare the appropriate entries to close the accounts as of June 30 and post to the accounts, using the letter "C" to identify the postings.
(5) Prepare a trial balance as of June 30.

Problem 28-5A. The account balances in the general fund ledger of the City of Tallulah Falls on June 30, the end of the current fiscal year, are as follows:

Cash on Hand	$	3,000
Cash in Bank		204,600
Savings Accounts		250,000
Property Taxes Receivable		100,000

Accounts Payable	$	40,200
Wages Payable		25,800
Reserve for Encumbrances		11,200
Estimated Revenues		3,375,000
Revenues		3,390,000
Appropriations		3,350,000
Expenditures		3,353,500
Encumbrances		11,200

The total of the debits and credits in the revenue ledger are as follows:

	Debits	Credits
General property taxes	2,580,000	2,600,000
Sales taxes	612,000	601,000
Motor vehicle licenses	116,000	118,000
Interest on savings accounts	25,000	26,500
Miscellaneous	42,000	44,500

Data from the expenditure ledger are as follows:

	Expenditures	Budget Appropriations
General government	1,123,500	1,110,000
Police department	660,000	666,000
Fire department	514,900	528,000
Streets and roads	490,000	402,000
Sanitation	353,100	354,000
Public welfare	204,000	210,000

The encumbrances balances in the expenditure ledger are as follows:

General government	4,300
Fire department	2,500
Sanitation	4,400

Instructions:

(1) Prepare a statement of revenues and expenditures—budget and actual.
(2) Prepare a statement of changes in fund balance. The fund balance account had a balance of $455,100 on July 1, the beginning of the current fiscal year.
(3) Prepare a balance sheet.

Mini-Case

Joseph Leone, your former college roommate, is running for the office of state representative of the fifth legislative district. A major campaign issue has been the incumbent's challenge that Leone disclose his personal financial statement, even though state law does not require such disclosures. Leone has decided to meet this challenge and has asked you to prepare such a statement. Leone has assembled the following data at October 15:

(a) Cash in bank, savings, and money market accounts, $37,400. (Unrestricted withdrawals are allowed without penalty.)

(b) Marketable securities (current value is quoted market price on October 15, 19--, less estimated broker commissions):

	Cost	Current Value
Stocks:		
FMA Industries, 1,000 shares	$ 65,000	$ 78,000
Morgan Manufacturing Inc., 30,000 shares.......	750,000	1,260,000
Edelman Food Stores Inc., 5,000 shares	100,000	120,000
Bonds:		
U.S. Treasury, 10%, $100,000 face amount, due 19--	88,600	90,800
Hurst Motors Inc., 12%, $50,000 face amount, due 20--	50,000	51,200

(c) Joseph Leone's equity interest in Leone & Associates: cost, $500,000; estimated market value, $1,400,000. Estimated market prices were determined by independent appraisal made by Temple Realty.

(d) Cash value of $400,000 face value life insurance policy, $65,000.

(e) Residence: cost $260,000; estimated market, $450,000. The estimated market price was determined by an independent appraisal made by Hastings and Associates. The residence is pledged against a 9½% mortgage note payable, final installment due October 1, 19--. Present value of monthly mortgage payments of $2,500, including interest, is $120,000.

(f) Household furnishings: cost, $150,000; estimated market, $100,000.

(g) Automobiles: cost, $60,000; estimated market, $45,000.

(h) Jewelry and paintings; cost, $80,000; estimated market, $110,000. The estimated market price was determined by an independent appraisal made by Hastings and Associates.

(i) Vested interest in Morgan Corporation pension trust: estimated market, $21,000.

(j) Present value of accounts payable and accrued liabilities, $18,600.

(k) Income tax payable, $15,000.

(l) Present value of 9% note payable, due January 31, 19--, $90,000.

(m) Estimated income tax on unrealized appreciation of salable assets, $320,000.

Instructions:

(1) Prepare a statement of financial condition as of October 15. Notes to the statement should be presented as appropriate.

(2) After reviewing the statement of financial condition prepared in (1), Leone objects to the caption "Estimated income tax on unrealized appreciation of assets." He argues that this disclosure will give voters the impression that he is delinquent on payment of his taxes. How would you respond?

(3) If Leone publishes the statement of financial condition prepared in (1), how could it embarrass him in the eyes of the voters and possibly reduce his chances of election?

Glossary

A

Absorption costing. The concept that considers the cost of manufactured products to be composed of direct materials, direct labor, and factory overhead.

Accelerated Cost Recovery System (ACRS). The system described in the Internal Revenue Code for determining depreciation (cost recovery) of plant asset acquisitions.

Accelerated depreciation method. A depreciation method that provides for a high depreciation charge in the first year of use of an asset and gradually declining periodic charges thereafter.

Account. The form used to record additions and deductions for each individual asset, liability, capital, revenue, and expense.

Account form of balance sheet. A balance sheet with assets on the left-hand side and liabilities and capital on the right-hand side.

Accounting. The process of identifying, measuring, and communicating economic information to permit informed judgments and decisions by users of the information.

Accounting cycle. The principal accounting procedures employed to process transactions during a fiscal period.

Accounting equation. The expression of the relationship between assets, liabilities, and capital; most commonly stated as Assets = Liabilities + Capital.

Accounting Principles Board. The AICPA board that provided most of the leadership in the development of accounting principles from 1959 to 1973.

Account payable. A liability created by a purchase made on credit.

Account receivable. A claim against a customer for sales made on credit.

Accounts payable ledger. The subsidiary ledger containing the individual accounts with suppliers (creditors).

Accounts receivable ledger. The subsidiary ledger containing the individual accounts with customers (debtors).

Accounts receivable turnover. The relationship between credit sales and accounts receivable, computed by dividing net sales on account by the average net accounts receivable.

Accrual. An expense or a revenue that gradually increases with the passage of time.

Accrual basis accounting. The reporting of all revenues in the period earned, all expenses in the period consumed, all assets in the period purchased, and all liabilities in the period incurred; contrasted with the cash basis of accounting.

Accumulated depreciation account. The contra asset account used to accumulate the depreciation recognized to date on plant assets.

Acid-test ratio. The ratio of the sum of cash, receivables, and marketable securities to current liabilities.

Adjusted gross income. An amount determined for federal income tax purposes, computed as gross income less business expenses and other expenses connected with earning certain types of income.

Adjusting entry. An entry required at the end of an accounting period to record an internal transaction and to bring the ledger up to date.

Affiliated companies. Two or more corporations closely related through stock ownership.

Aging the receivables. The process of analyzing the accounts receivable and classifying them according to various age groupings, with the due date being the base point for determining age.

Algorithm. Generalized arithmetic formula.

Allowance method. The method of accounting for uncollectible receivables, by which advance provision for the uncollectibles is made.

American Institute of CPAs (AICPA). The national professional organization of CPAs.

Amortization. **The periodic expense attributed to the decline in usefulness of an intangible asset or the allocation of bond premium or discount over the life of a bond issue.**

Appropriation. A designated use of revenues for which a potential liability is recognized by nonprofit organizations.

Appropriation of retained earnings. The amount of a corporation's retained earnings that has been restricted and therefore is not available for distribution to shareholders as dividends.

Articles of partnership. The formal written contract creating a partnership.

Asset. Property owned by a business enterprise.

Automated data processing (ADP). The general term applied to the processing of data by mechanical or electronic equipment that operates with a minimum of manual intervention.

Average cost method. The method of inventory costing that is based on the assumption that costs should be charged against revenue in accordance with the weighted average unit costs of the commodities sold.

Average rate of return. A method of analysis of proposed capital expenditures that focuses on the anticipated profitability of the investment.

B

Balance of an account. The amount of difference between the debits and the credits that have been entered into an account.

Balance sheet. A financial statement listing the assets, liabilities, and capital of a business entity as of a specific date.

Bank reconciliation. The method of analysis that details the items that are responsible for the difference between the cash balance reported in the bank statement and the balance of the cash account in the ledger.

Bond. A form of interest-bearing note employed by corporations to borrow on a long-term basis.

Bond discount. Excess of the face amount of bonds over the issue price.

Bond indenture. The contract between a corporation issuing bonds and the bondholders.

Bond premium. Excess of the issue price of bonds over the face amount.

Bookkeeping. The recording of business data in a prescribed manner.

Book value of an asset. The cost of an asset less the balance of any related contra asset account.

Boot. The balance owed the supplier when old equipment is traded for new equipment.

Break-even point. The point in the operations of an enterprise at which revenues and expired costs are equal.

Budgeting. The process of establishing specific goals for future operations and making periodic comparisons of actual results with these goals.

Budget performance record. A record used by individuals to compare actual expenditures with budgeted amounts.

Budget performance report. A report comparing actual results with budget figures.

Business entity concept. The concept that assumes that accounting applies to individual economic units and that each unit is separate and distinct from the persons who supply its assets.

Business transaction. The occurrence of an event or of a condition that must be recorded in the accounting records.

By-product. A product resulting from a manufacturing process and having little value in relation to the principal product or joint products.

C

Capital. The rights (equity) of the owners in a business enterprise.

Capital expenditure. A cost that adds to the utility of an asset for more than one accounting period.

Capital expenditures budget. The budget summarizing future plans for acquisition of plant facilities and equipment.

Capital gain or loss. A gain or loss resulting from the sale or exchange of a capital asset, as defined by the Internal Revenue Code and given special treatment for federal income tax purposes.

Capital lease. A lease which includes one or more of four provisions that result in treating the leased asset as a purchased asset in the accounts.

Capital statement. A summary of the changes in the capital of a business entity during a specific period of time.

Capital stock. Shares of ownership of a corporation.

Cash. Any medium of exchange that a bank will accept at face value.

Cash basis accounting. The reporting of all revenues and expenses in the period during which cash is received or paid.

Cash discount. The deduction allowable if an invoice is paid by a specified date.

Cash dividend. A distribution of cash by a corporation to its shareholders.

Cash payback period. The expected period of time that will elapse between the date of a capital ex-

penditure and the complete recovery in cash (or equivalent) of the amount invested.

Cash payments journal. The journal in which all cash payments are recorded.

Cash receipts journal. The journal in which all cash receipts are recorded.

Certified Public Accountant (CPA). An accountant who meets state licensing requirements for engaging in the practice of public accounting as a CPA.

Chart of accounts. A listing of all the accounts used by a business enterprise.

Check register. A modified form of the cash payments journal used to record all transactions paid by check.

Closing entry. An entry necessary to eliminate the balance of a temporary account in preparation for the following accounting period.

Codes of professional ethics. Standards of conduct established by professional organizations of CPAs to guide CPAs in the conduct of their practices.

Common-size statement. A financial statement in which all items are expressed only in relative terms.

Common stock. The basic ownership class of corporate capital stock.

Composite-rate depreciation method. A method of depreciation based on the use of a single rate that applies to entire groups of assets.

Conservatism. The concept that dictates that in selecting among alternatives, the method or procedure that yields the lesser amount of net income or asset value should be selected.

Consistency. The concept that assumes that the same generally accepted accounting principles have been applied in the preparation of successive financial statements.

Consolidated statement. A financial statement resulting from combining parent and subsidiary company statements.

Consolidation. The creation of a new corporation by the transfer of assets and liabilities from two or more existing corporations.

Constant dollar statements. The financial statements that result when historical costs reported in conventional statements are converted to dollars of common (or constant) purchasing power.

Contingent liability. A potential obligation that will materialize only if certain events occur in the future.

Contra asset account. An account that is offset against an asset account.

Contract rate of interest. The interest rate specified on a bond.

Contribution margin. Sales less variable cost of goods sold and variable selling and general expenses.

Contribution margin ratio. The percentage of each sales dollar that is available to cover the fixed expenses and provide an operating income.

Controlling account. The account in the general ledger that summarizes the balances of a subsidiary ledger.

Corporation. A separate legal entity that is organized in accordance with state or federal statutes and in which ownership is divided into shares of stock.

Cost ledger. A subsidiary ledger employed in a job order cost system and which contains an account for each job order.

Cost method. A method of accounting for an investment in stock, by which the investor recognizes as income the share of property dividends of the investee.

Cost of production report. A report prepared periodically by a processing department, summarizing (1) the units for which the department is accountable and the disposition of these units and (2) the costs charged to the department and the allocation of these costs.

Cost principle. The principle that assumes that the monetary record for properties and services purchased by a business should be maintained in terms of cost.

Credit. (1) The right side of an account; (2) the amount entered on the right side of an account; (3) to enter an amount on the right side of an account.

Credit memorandum. The form issued by a seller to inform a debtor that a credit has been posted to the debtor's account receivable.

Cumulative preferred stock. Preferred stock that is entitled to current and past dividends before dividends may be paid on common stock.

Current asset. Cash or another asset that may reasonably be expected to be realized in cash or sold or consumed, usually within a year or less, through the normal operations of a business.

Current cost statements. The financial statements that result when historical costs reported in conventional statements are adjusted for specific price-level changes, so that all elements of the statements are reported at their current costs.

Current liability. A liability that will be due within a short time (usually one year or less) and that is to be paid out of current assets.

Current ratio. The ratio of current assets to current liabilities.

D

Debit. (1) The left side of an account; (2) the amount entered on the left side of an account; (3) to enter an amount on the left side of an account.

Debit memorandum. The form issued by a purchaser to inform a creditor that a debit has been posted to the creditor's account payable.

Debt security. A bond or a note payable.

Declining-balance depreciation method. A method of depreciation that provides declining periodic depreciation charges to expense over the estimated life of an asset.

Deferral. A postponement of the recognition of an expense already paid or a revenue already received.

Deficiency. The debit balance in the capital account of a sole proprietor or a partner.

Deficit. A debit balance in the retained earnings account.

Deflation. A period when prices in general are falling and the purchasing power of money is increasing.

Departmental margin. Departmental gross profit less direct departmental expenses.

Depletion. The cost of metal ores and other minerals removed from the earth.

Depreciation. The periodic cost expiration of all plant assets except land.

Differential analysis. The area of accounting concerned with the effect of alternative courses of action on revenues and costs.

Differential cost. The amount of increase or decrease in cost that is expected from a particular course of action compared with an alternative.

Differential revenue. The amount of increase or decrease in revenue expected from a particular course of action as compared with an alternative.

Direct expense. An expense directly traceable to or incurred for the sole benefit of a specific department and ordinarily subject to the control of the department manager.

Direct labor. Wages of factory workers who convert materials into a finished product.

Direct labor rate variance. The cost associated with the difference between the actual rate paid for direct labor used in producing a commodity and the standard rate for the commodity.

Direct labor time variance. The cost associated with the difference between the actual direct labor hours spent producing a commodity and the standard hours for the commodity.

Direct materials. The cost of materials that enter directly into the finished product.

Direct materials price variance. The cost associated with the difference between the actual price of direct materials used in producing a commodity and the standard price for the commodity.

Direct materials quantity variance. The cost associated with the difference between the actual quantity of direct materials used in producing a commodity and the standard quantity for the commodity.

Direct write-off method. A method of accounting for uncollectible receivables, whereby an expense is recognized only when specific accounts are judged to be uncollectible.

Discounted cash flow analysis. The method of analysis of proposed capital expenditures that gives consideration to the timing of the net cash flows.

Discount on stock. The excess of the par amount of stock over its sales price.

Discount rate. The rate used in computing the interest to be deducted from the maturity value of a note.

Dishonored note receivable. A note which the maker fails to pay on the due date.

Dividend. A distribution of earnings of a corporation to its owners (stockholders).

Double-entry accounting. A system for recording transactions based on recording increases and decreases in accounts so that debits always equal credits.

E

Earnings per share (EPS) on common stock. The profitability ratio of net income available to common shareholders to the number of common shares outstanding.

Economic order quantity (EOQ). The optimum quantity of specified inventoriable materials to be ordered at one time.

Effective rate of interest. The market rate of interest at the time bonds are issued.

Electronic data processing. The term applied to the processing of data by electronic equipment.

Employee's earnings record. A detailed record of each employee's earnings.

Encumbrance. A commitment by a nonprofit organization to incur expenditures in the future.

Equity. The right or claim to the properties of a business enterprise.

Equity method. A method of accounting for investments in common stock, by which the investment account is adjusted for the investor's share of periodic net income and property dividends of the investee.

Equity per share. The ratio of stockholders' equity to the related number of shares of stock outstanding.

Equity security. Preferred or common stock.

Equivalent units of production. The number of units that could have been manufactured from start to finish during a period.

Excess itemized deductions. The amount that is deducted from adjusted gross income in computing the federal income tax and that represents the amount by which the total itemized deductions exceed the zero bracket amount.

Exchange rate. The rate at which one unit of a currency can be converted into another currency.

Exemption. An allowable deduction from adjusted gross income, available to the taxpayer in accordance with the Internal Revenue Code.

Expense. The amount of assets consumed or services used in the process of earning revenue.

Extraordinary item. An event or transaction that is unusual and infrequent.

F

Factory overhead. All of the costs of operating the factory except for direct materials and direct labor.

Factory overhead controllable variance. The difference between the actual amount of factory overhead cost incurred and the amount of factory overhead budgeted for the level of operations achieved.

Factory overhead volume variance. The cost or benefit associated with operating at a level above or below 100% of normal productive capacity.

Federal unemployment compensation tax. A federal tax paid by employers and used to provide temporary relief to those who become unemployed.

FICA tax. Federal Insurance Contributions Act tax used to finance federal programs for old-age and disability benefits and health insurance for the aged.

Fifo (first-in, first-out). A method of inventory costing based on the assumption that the costs of merchandise sold should be charged against revenue in the order in which the costs were incurred.

Financial Accounting Standards Board (FASB). The current authoritative body for the development of accounting principles.

Financial forecast. A statement indicating an enterprise's financial plans and expectations for the future.

Finished goods. Goods in the state in which they are to be sold.

Fiscal year. The annual accounting period adopted by an enterprise.

Fixed expense. An expense that tends to remain constant in amount regardless of variations in volume of activity.

Flexible budget. A series of budgets for varying rates of activity.

FOB destination. Terms of agreement between buyer and seller, requiring the seller to absorb the transportation costs.

FOB shipping point. Terms of agreement between buyer and seller, requiring the buyer to absorb the transportation costs.

Fund. A term with multiple meanings, including (1) segregations of cash for a special purpose, (2) working capital or cash as reported in the funds statement, (3) in accounting for nonprofit organizations, an accounting entity with accounts maintained for recording assets, liabilities, capital (called fund balance), revenues, and expenditures for a particular purpose.

Funded. An appropriation of retained earnings accompanied by a segregation of cash or marketable securities.

Funds statement. The statement of changes in financial position.

G

General expense. Expense incurred in the general operation of a business.

General journal. The two-column form used to record journal entries that do not "fit" in any special journals.

General ledger. The principal ledger, when used in conjunction with subsidiary ledgers, that contains all of the balance sheet and income statement accounts.

Generally accepted accounting principles. Generally accepted guidelines for the preparation of financial statements.

General price-level change. The change over time in the amount of money needed to purchase a general group of goods and services.

Going concern concept. The concept that assumes that a business entity has a reasonable expectation of continuing in business at a profit for an indefinite period of time.

Goodwill. An intangible asset that attaches to a business as a result of such favorable factors as location, product superiority, reputation, and managerial skill.

Gross pay. The total earnings of an employee for a payroll period.

Gross profit. The excess of net revenue from sales over the cost of merchandise sold.

Gross profit analysis. The procedure used to develop information concerning the effect of changes in quantities and unit prices on sales and cost of goods sold.

Gross profit method. A means of estimating inventory on hand without the need for a physical count.

H

Historical cost. The cash or equivalent outlay for goods or services acquired.

Holding gains and losses. Gains and losses that result from the holding of nonmonetary assets.

Horizontal analysis. The percentage analysis of increases and decreases in corresponding items in comparative financial statements.

I

Income from operations. The excess of gross profit over total operating expenses.

Income statement. A summary of the revenues and expenses of a business entity for a specific period of time.

Income summary account. The account used in the closing process for summarizing the revenue and expense accounts.

Independent auditors' report. A report accompanying financial statements, in which CPAs express an opinion as to the fairness of the statements.

Indirect expense. An expense that is incurred for an entire business enterprise as a unit and that is not subject to the control of individual department managers.

Inflation. A period when prices in general are rising and the purchasing power of money is declining.

Installment method. The method of recognizing revenue, whereby each receipt of cash from installment sales is considered to be composed of partial payment of cost of merchandise sold and gross profit.

Intangible asset. A long-lived asset that is useful in the operations of an enterprise, is not held for sale, and is without physical qualities.

Interim statement. A financial statement issued for a period covering less than a fiscal year.

Internal accounting controls. Procedures and records that are mainly concerned with the reliability of financial records and reports and with the safeguarding of assets.

Internal administrative controls. Procedures and records that aid management in achieving business goals.

Internal controls. The detailed procedures adopted by an enterprise to control its operations.

Internal Revenue Code (IRC). The codification of current federal tax statutes.

Internal Revenue Service (IRS). The branch of the U.S. Treasury Department concerned with enforcement and collection of the income tax.

Invoice. The bill provided by the seller (referred to as a sales invoice) to a purchaser (referred to as a purchase invoice) for items purchased.

J

Job cost sheet. An account in the cost ledger in which the costs charged to a particular job order are recorded.

Job order cost system. A type of cost system that provides for a separate record of the cost of each particular quantity of product that passes through the factory.

Joint cost. The cost common to the manufacture of two or more products (joint products).

Joint products. Two or more commodities of significant value produced from a single principal direct material.

L

Lease. A contractual agreement conveying the right to use an asset for a stated period of time.

Ledger. The group of accounts used by an enterprise.

Leverage. The tendency of the rate earned on stockholders' equity to vary from the rate earned on total assets because the amount earned on assets acquired through the use of funds provided by creditors varies from the interest paid to these creditors.

Liability. A debt of a business enterprise.

Lifo (last-in, first-out). A method of inventory costing based on the assumption that the most recent costs incurred should be charged against revenue.

Linear programming. A quantitative technique employed in selecting the most favorable course of action from among a number of alternatives.

Liquidating dividend. A distribution out of paid-in capital when a corporation permanently reduces its operations or winds up its affairs completely.

Liquidation. The winding-up process when a partnership goes out of business.

Long-term investment. An investment that is not intended to be a ready source of cash in the normal operations of a business and that is listed in the "investments" section of the balance sheet.

Long-term liability. A liability that is not due for a comparatively long time (usually more than one year).

Lower of cost or market. A method of costing inventory or valuing temporary investments that carries those assets at the lower of their cost or current market prices.

M

Manufacturing margin. Sales less variable cost of goods sold.

Marginal tax rate. The highest rate applied to the income of any particular taxpayer.

Margin of safety. The difference between current sales revenue and the sales at the break-even point.

Marketable security. An investment in a security that can be readily sold when cash is needed.

Master budget. The comprehensive budget plan encompassing all the individual budgets related to sales, cost of goods sold, operating expenses, capital expenditures, and cash.

Matching. The principle of accounting that all revenues should be matched with the expenses incurred in earning those revenues during a period of time.

Materiality. The concept that recognizes the practicality of ignoring small or insignificant deviations from generally accepted accounting principles.

Materials. Goods in the state in which they were acquired for use in manufacturing operations.

Materials requisition. The form used by the appropriate manufacturing department to authorize the issuance of materials from the storeroom.

Maturity value. The amount due at the maturity or due date of a note.

Merchandise inventory. Merchandise on hand and available for sale.

Merchandise inventory turnover. The relationship between the volume of merchandise sold and merchandise inventory, computed by dividing the cost of merchandise sold by the average inventory.

Merger. The fusion of two corporations by the acquisition of the properties of one corporation by another, with the dissolution of one of the corporations.

Minority interest. The portion of a subsidiary corporation's capital stock that is not owned by the parent corporation.

Monetary items. Money or a claim to receive money or an obligation to pay a fixed amount of money.

Mortgage. A form of security for a debt which gives the creditor a lien or claim to property owned by the debtor in the event the debtor defaults on an obligation.

Moving average. An averaging technique used when the average cost method of inventory costing is applied in a perpetual inventory system.

Multiple-step income statement. An income statement with numerous sections and subsections with several intermediate balances before net income.

N

Natural business year. A year that ends when a business's activities have reached the lowest point in its annual operating cycle.

Net income. The final figure in the income statement when revenues exceed expenses.

Net loss. The final figure in the income statement when expenses exceed revenues.

Net pay. Gross pay less payroll deductions; the amount the employer is obligated to pay the employee.

Net worth. The owner's equity in a business.

Nominal account. A revenue or expense account periodically closed to the income summary account; a temporary capital account.

Nonmonetary items. All items, such as inventories, plant assets, common stock, and retained earnings, that are not classified as monetary items.

Normal pension cost. The cost of pension benefits earned by employees during the current year of service.

Note payable. A written promise to pay, representing an amount owed by a business.

Note receivable. A written promise to pay, representing an amount to be received by a business.

Number of days' sales in merchandise inventory. The relationship between the volume of merchandise sold and merchandise inventory, computed by dividing the merchandise inventory at the end of the year by the average daily cost of merchandise sold.

Number of days' sales in receivables. The relationship between credit sales and accounts receivable, computed by dividing the net accounts receivable at the end of the year by the average daily sales on account.

O

Operating lease. A lease which does not meet the criteria for a capital lease, and thus which is accounted for as an operating expense, so that neither future lease obligations nor future rights to use the leased asset are recognized in the accounts.

Operations research. Quantitative techniques which often utilize mathematical and statistical models encompassing a large number of interdependent variables and which assist management in planning and controlling business operations.

Opportunity cost. The amount of income that would result from the best available alternative to a proposed use of cash or its equivalent.

Other expense. An expense that cannot be associated definitely with operations.

Other income. Revenue from sources other than the principal activity of a business.

Overapplied factory overhead. The amount of factory overhead applied in excess of the actual factory overhead costs incurred for production during a period.

Owner's equity. The rights of the owners in a business enterprise.

P-Q

Paid-in capital. The capital acquired from stockholders.

Par. The arbitrary monetary figure printed on a stock certificate.

Parent company. The company owning all or a majority of the voting stock of another corporation.

Participating preferred stock. Preferred stock that could receive dividends in excess of the specified amount granted by its preferential rights.

Partnership. A business owned by two or more individuals.

Past service cost. The cost of pension benefits granted to employees for prior years of service.

Payroll. The total amount paid to employees for a certain period.

Payroll register. A multi-column form used to assemble and summarize payroll data at the end of each payroll period.

Percentage-of-contract-completion method. The method of recognizing revenue from long-term contracts over the entire life of the contract.

Periodic inventory system. A system of inventory accounting in which only the revenue from sales is recorded each time a sale is made; the cost of merchandise on hand at the end of a period is determined by a detailed listing (physical inventory) of the merchandise on hand.

Perpetual inventory system. A system of inventory accounting that employs records that continually disclose the amount of the inventory.

Petty cash fund. A special cash fund used to pay relatively small amounts.

Physical inventory. The detailed listing of merchandise on hand.

Plant asset. A tangible asset of a relatively fixed or permanent nature owned by a business enterprise.

Pooling of interests method. A method of accounting for an affiliation of two corporations resulting from an exchange of voting stock of one corporation for substantially all of the voting stock of the other corporation.

Post-closing trial balance. A trial balance prepared after all of the temporary accounts have been closed.

Posting. The process of transferring debits and credits from a journal to the accounts.

Predetermined factory overhead rate. The rate used to apply factory overhead costs to the goods manufactured.

Preemptive right. The right of each shareholder to maintain the same fractional interest in the corporation by purchasing a proportionate number of shares of any additional issuances of stock.

Preferred stock. A class of stock with preferential rights over common stock.

Premium on stock. The excess of the sales price of stock over its par amount.

Prepaid expense. A purchased commodity or service that has not been consumed at the end of an accounting period.

Present value. The estimated present worth of an amount of cash to be received (or paid) in the future.

Price-earnings (P/E) ratio. The ratio of the market price per share of common stock, at a specific date, to the annual earnings per share.

Prior period adjustment. Correction of a material error related to a prior period or periods, excluded from the determination of net income.

Private accounting. The profession whose members are accountants employed by a business firm or nonprofit organization.

Proceeds. The net amount available from discounting a note.

Process cost system. A type of cost system that accumulates costs for each of the various departments or processes within a factory.

Processing cost. The direct labor and factory overhead costs associated with the manufacture of a product.

Profitability. The ability of a firm to earn income.

Promissory note. A written promise to pay a sum in money on demand or at a definite time.

Public accounting. The profession whose members render accounting services on a fee basis.

Purchase method. The accounting method employed when a parent company acquires a controlling share of the voting stock of a subsidiary other than by the exchange of voting common stock.

Purchase order. The form issued by the purchasing department to suppliers, requesting the delivery of materials.

Purchase requisition. The form used to inform the purchasing department that items are needed by a business.

Purchases discount. An available discount taken by the purchaser for early payment of an invoice.

Purchases journal. The journal in which all items purchased on account are recorded.

Purchasing power gains and losses. Gains and losses that result from holding monetary items during periods of price-level change.

Quick assets. The sum of cash, receivables, and marketable securities.

R

Rate earned on common stockholders' equity. A measure of profitability computed by dividing net income, reduced by preferred dividend requirements, by common stockholders' equity.

Rate earned on stockholders' equity. A measure of profitability computed by dividing net income by total stockholders' equity.

Rate earned on total assets. A measure of the profitability of assets, without regard to the equity of creditors and stockholders in the assets.

Rate of return on investment (ROI). A measure of managerial efficiency in the use of investments in assets.

Real account. A balance sheet account.

Realization. The sale of assets when a partnership is being liquidated.

Receiving report. The form used by the receiving department to indicate that materials have been received and inspected.

Reciprocal accounts. Accounts that have equal but opposite balances in two different ledgers.

Replacement cost. The cost of replacing an asset at current market prices.

Report form of balance sheet. The form of balance sheet with the liability and capital sections presented below the asset section.

Residual value. The estimated recoverable cost of a depreciable asset as of the time of its removal from service.

Responsibility reporting. The process of reporting operating data by areas of responsibility.

Retail inventory method. A method of inventory costing based on the relationship of the cost and retail price of merchandise.

Retained earnings. Net income retained in a corporation.

Retained earnings statement. A statement for a corporate enterprise, summarizing the changes in retained earnings during a specific period of time.

Revenue. The amount charged to customers for goods sold or services rendered.

Revenue expenditure. An expenditure that benefits only the current period.

Reversing entry. An entry that reverses a specific adjusting entry to facilitate the recording of routine transactions in the subsequent period.

S

Sales discount. An available discount granted by the seller for early payment of an invoice.

Sales journal. The journal in which all sales of merchandise on account are recorded.

Sales mix. The relative distribution of sales among the various products available for sale.

Sales returns and allowances. Reductions in sales, resulting from merchandise returned by customers or from the seller's reduction in the original sales price.

Securities and Exchange Commission (SEC). The federal agency that exercises a dominant influence over the development of accounting principles for most companies whose securities are traded in interstate commerce.

Selling expense. An expense incurred directly and entirely in connection with the sale of merchandise.

Semivariable cost. A cost with both fixed and variable characteristics.

Serial bonds. Bonds of an issue with maturities spread over several dates.

Service department. A factory department that does not process materials directly but renders services for the benefit of production departments.

Single-step income statement. An income statement with the total of all expenses deducted from the total of all revenues.

Sinking fund. Assets set aside in a special fund to be used for a specific purpose.

Slide. The erroneous movement of all digits in a number, one or more spaces to the right or the left, such as writing $542 as $5,420.

Sole proprietorship. A business owned by one individual.

Solvency. The ability of a firm to pay its debts as they come due.

Special journal. A journal designed to record a single type of transaction.

Specific price-level change. The change over time in the amount of money needed to purchase individual goods and services.

Standard costs. Detailed estimates of what a product should cost.

Stated value. An amount assigned by the board of directors to each share of no-par stock.

Statement of changes in financial position. A basic financial statement devoted exclusively to reporting changes in financial position for a specified period of time.

Statement of changes in fund balance. The statement for a nonprofit enterprise that is similar to the retained earnings statement for a commercial enterprise.

Statement of cost of goods manufactured. A separate statement for a manufacturer that reports the cost of goods manufactured during a period.

Statement of financial condition. The principal financial statement for individuals, presenting the estimated current values of assets, current amounts of liabilities, estimated income tax on unrealized appreciation of assets, and net worth.

Statements of Financial Accounting Standards. Pronouncements issued by the Financial Accounting Standards Board which become part of generally accepted accounting principles.

State unemployment compensation tax. A state tax generally paid by employers and used to provide temporary relief to those who become unemployed.

Stock dividend. Distribution of a company's own stock to its shareholders.

Stockholders' equity. The equity of the shareholders in a corporation.

Stock outstanding. The stock in the hands of the stockholders.

Stock split. A reduction in the par or stated value of a share of common stock and the issuance of a proportionate number of additional shares.

Straight-line depreciation method. A method of depreciation that provides for equal periodic charges to expense over the estimated life of an asset.

Subscribers ledger. The subsidiary ledger containing the individual accounts of each subscriber to a stock issue.

Subsidiary company. The corporation that is controlled by a parent company.

Subsidiary ledger. A ledger containing individual accounts with a common characteristic.

Sum-of-the-years-digits depreciation method. A method of depreciation that provides for declining periodic depreciation charges to expense over the estimated life of an asset.

Sunk cost. A cost that is not affected by subsequent decisions.

Systems analysis. The determination of the informational needs, the sources of such information, and the deficiencies in the current system.

T

T account. A form of account resembling the letter T.

Taxable income. The base on which the amount of income tax is determined.

Temporary capital account. A revenue or expense account periodically closed to the income summary account; a nominal account.

Temporary investment. An investment in securities that can be readily sold when cash is needed.

Term bonds. Bonds of an issue, all of which mature at the same time.

Trade discount. The reduction allowable from the list price of goods offered for sale.

Transposition. The erroneous arrangement of digits in a number, such as writing $542 as $524.

Treasury stock. A corporation's own outstanding stock that has been reacquired.

Trial balance. A summary listing of the balances and the titles of the accounts.

U-V

Underapplied factory overhead. The amount of actual factory overhead in excess of the factory overhead applied to production during a period.

Unearned revenue. Revenue received in advance of its being earned.

Units-of-production depreciation method. A method of depreciation that provides for depreciation expense based on the expected productive capacity of an asset.

Variable costing. The concept that considers the cost of products manufactured to be composed only of those manufacturing costs that increase or decrease as the volume of production rises or falls (direct materials, direct labor, and variable factory overhead).

Variable expense. An expense that tends to fluctuate in amount in accordance with variations in volume of activity.

Variances from standard. Difference between standard cost and actual cost.

Vertical analysis. The percentage analysis of component parts in relation to the total of the parts in a single financial statement.

Voucher. A document that serves as evidence of authority to pay cash.

Voucher register. The journal in which all vouchers are recorded.

Voucher system. Records, methods, and procedures employed in verifying and recording liabilities and paying and recording cash payments.

W-Z

Working capital. The excess of total current assets over total current liabilities at some point in time.

Work in process. Goods in the process of manufacture.

Work sheet. A working paper used to assist in the preparation of financial statements.

Zero-base budgeting. A concept of budgeting that requires all levels of management to start from zero and estimate budget data as if there had been no previous activities in their unit.

Zero bracket amount. An amount built in to the tax table and tax rate schedules, representing an automatic specified deduction from adjusted gross income and used in lieu of itemizing deductions.

Series B Problems

CHAPTER 1 | **Problem 1-2B.** Following are the amounts of the assets and liabilities of Kelley's Personnel Service, a sole proprietorship, at June 30, the *end* of the current year, and its revenue and expenses for the year ended on that date. The capital of T. P. Kelley, owner, was $12,900 at July 1, the *beginning* of the current year, and the owner withdrew $12,000 during the current year.

Cash.	$ 5,420
Accounts receivable	9,850
Supplies.	620
Prepaid insurance	150
Accounts payable	1,440
Salaries payable.	600
Fees earned	58,025
Salary expense.	24,500
Rent expense	6,000
Advertising expense	5,200
Utilities expense.	3,800
Supplies expense	2,600
Taxes expense	1,400
Insurance expense	600
Miscellaneous expense	825

Instructions:
(1) Prepare an income statement for the current year ending June 30, exercising care to include each item of expense.
(2) Prepare a capital statement for the current year ending June 30.
(3) Prepare a balance sheet as of June 30 of the current year.

Problem 1-3B. Following are the amounts of Tucker Corporation's assets and liabilities at October 31, the *end* of the current year, and its revenue and expenses for the year ended on that date, listed in alphabetical order. Tucker Corporation had capital stock of $20,000 and retained earnings of $15,755 on November 1, the *beginning* of the current year. During the current year, the corporation paid cash dividends of $5,000.

Accounts payable	$ 6,175
Accounts receivable	12,840
Advertising expense	1,750

Cash	$ 8,175
Insurance expense	720
Land	36,000
Miscellaneous expense	580
Notes payable	3,000
Prepaid insurance	120
Rent expense	14,400
Salaries payable	2,430
Salary expense	38,960
Sales	84,160
Supplies	865
Supplies expense	2,910
Taxes expense	2,800
Utilities expense	6,400

Instructions:

(1) Prepare an income statement for the current year ending October 31, exercising care to include each item of expense listed.

(2) Prepare a retained earnings statement for the current year ending October 31

(3) Prepare a balance sheet as of October 31 of the current year. There was no change in the amount of capital stock during the year.

Problem 1-4B. Dupree Dry Cleaners is a sole proprietorship owned and operated by F. A. Dupree. Currently a building and equipment are being rented pending expansion of operations to new facilities. The actual work of dry cleaning is done by another company at wholesale rates. The assets and the liabilities of the business on May 1 of the current year are as follows: Cash, $5,400; Accounts Receivable, $3,700; Supplies, $410; Land, $9,500; Accounts Payable, $2,380. Business transactions during May are summarized as follows:

(a) Paid rent for the month, $850.

(b) Charged customers for dry cleaning sales on account, $5,646.

(c) Paid creditors on account, $1,680.

(d) Purchased supplies on account, $254.

(e) Received cash from cash customers for dry cleaning sales, $2,894.

(f) Received cash from customers on account, $2,750.

(g) Paid personal expenses by checks drawn on the business, $260, and withdrew $500 in cash for personal use.

(h) Received monthly invoice for dry cleaning expense for May (to be paid on June 10), $3,416.

(i) Paid the following: wages expense, $675; truck expense, $310; utilities expense, $260; miscellaneous expense, $89.

(j) Reimbursed a customer $50 for a garment lost by the cleaning company, which agreed to deduct the amount from the invoice received in transaction (h).

(k) Determined the cost of supplies used during the month, $328.

Instructions:

(1) State the assets, liabilities, and capital as of May 1 in equation form similar to that shown in this chapter.

(2) Record, in tabular form below the equation, the increases and decreases resulting from each transaction, indicating the new balances after each

transaction. Explain the nature of each increase and decrease in capital by an appropriate notation at the right of the amount.

(3) Prepare (a) an income statement for May, (b) a capital statement for May, and (c) a balance sheet as of May 31.

CHAPTER 2 | Problem 2-1B. Ling Chin established a sole proprietorship, to be known as Chin Decorators, on October 12 of the current year. During the remainder of the month, she completed the following business transactions:

Oct. 12. Chin transferred cash from a personal bank account to an account to be used for the business, $8,000.

12. Paid rent for period of October 12 to end of month, $360.

14. Purchased office equipment on account, $980.

15. Purchased a used truck for $8,500, paying $2,500 cash and giving a note payable for the remainder.

16. Purchased supplies for cash, $420.

17. Received cash for job completed, $240.

18. Paid wages of employees, $300.

20. Paid premiums on property and casualty insurance, $210.

22. Recorded sales on account and sent invoices to customers, $1,460.

24. Received an invoice for truck expenses, to be paid in November, $154.

26. Received cash for job completed, $650. This sale had not been recorded previously.

28. Paid creditor for equipment purchased on October 14, $980.

28. Purchased supplies on account, $178.

29. Paid utilities expense, $390.

29. Paid miscellaneous expenses, $86.

30. Received cash from customers on account, $815.

30. Paid wages of employees, $320.

31. Withdrew cash for personal use, $800.

Instructions:

(1) Open a ledger of two-column accounts for Chin Decorators, using the following titles and account numbers: Cash, 11; Accounts Receivable, 12; Supplies, 13; Prepaid Insurance, 14; Equipment, 16; Truck, 18; Notes Payable, 21; Accounts Payable, 22; Ling Chin, Capital, 31; Ling Chin, Drawing, 32; Sales, 41; Wages Expense, 51; Rent Expense, 53; Utilities Expense, 54; Truck Expense, 55; Miscellaneous Expense, 59.

(2) Record each transaction in a two-column journal, referring to the above list of accounts or to the ledger in selecting appropriate account titles to be debited and credited. (Do not insert the account numbers in the journal at this time.)

(3) Post the journal to the ledger, inserting appropriate posting references as each item is posted.

(4) Determine the balances of the accounts in the ledger, pencil footing all accounts having two or more debits or credits. A memorandum balance should also be inserted in accounts having both debits and credits, in the manner illustrated on page 45. For accounts with entries on one side only (such as Sales), there is no need to insert the memorandum balance in the item column. Accounts containing only a single debit and a single credit (such as Accounts Receivable) need no pencil footings; the memorandum balance should be inserted in the appropriate item column. Accounts containing a single entry only

(such as Prepaid Insurance) need neither a pencil footing nor a memorandum balance.

(5) Prepare a trial balance for Chin Decorators as of October 31.

(If the working papers correlating with the textbook are not used, omit Problem 2-3B.)

Problem 2-3B. The following records of Wiley TV Service are presented in the working papers:

Journal containing entries for the period October 1–31.
Ledger to which the October entries have been posted.
Preliminary trial balance as of October 31, which does not balance.

Locate the errors, supply the information requested, and prepare a corrected trial balance, proceeding in accordance with the following detailed instructions. The balances recorded in the accounts as of October 1 and the entries in the journal are correctly stated. If it is necessary to correct any posted amounts in the ledger, a line should be drawn through the erroneous figure and the correct amount inserted above. Corrections or notations may be inserted on the preliminary trial balance in any manner desired. It is not necessary to complete all of the instructions if equal trial balance totals can be obtained earlier. However, the requirements of instructions (8) and (9) should be completed in any event.

Instructions:

(1) Verify the totals of the preliminary trial balance, inserting the correct amounts in the schedule provided in the working papers.

(2) Compute the difference between the trial balance totals.

(3) Determine whether the difference obtained in (2) is evenly divisible by 9.

(4) If the difference obtained in (2) is an even number, determine half the amount.

(5) Compare the listings in the trial balance with the balances appearing in the ledger.

(6) Verify the accuracy of the balances of each account in the ledger.

(7) Trace the postings in the ledger back to the journal, using small check marks to identify items traced. (Correct any amounts in the ledger that may be necessitated by errors in posting.)

(8) Journalize as of October 31 the payment of $112 for gas and electricity. The bill had been paid on October 31 but was inadvertently omitted from the journal. Post to the ledger. (Revise any amounts necessitated by posting this entry.)

(9) Prepare a new trial balance.

Problem 2-4B. The following business transactions were completed by Southern Theatre Corporation during April of the current year:

Apr. 1. Deposited in a bank account $80,000 cash received for capital stock.

2. Purchased the King Drive-In Theatre for $125,000, allocated as follows: land, $75,000; buildings, $36,000; equipment, $14,000. Paid $70,000 in cash and gave a mortgage note for the remainder.

5. Entered into a contract for the operation of the refreshment stand concession at a rental of 25% of the concessionaire's sales, with a guaranteed minimum of $500 a month, payable in advance. Received cash of $500 as the advance payment for the month of April.

5. Paid for advertising leaflets for April, $120.

6. Paid premiums for property and casualty insurance policies, $3,200.

7. Purchased supplies, $864, and equipment, $2,960, on account.

8. Paid for April billboard and newspaper advertising, $1,280.

10. Cash received from admissions for the week, $4,120.

12. Paid miscellaneous expense, $179.

Apr. 15. Paid semimonthly wages, $1,540.
   17. Cash received from admissions for the week, $3,810.
   19. Paid miscellaneous expenses, $258.
   19. Returned portion of supplies purchased on April 7 to the supplier, receiving full credit for the cost, $160.
   21. Paid cash to creditors on account, $2,350.
   24. Cash received from admissions for the week, $3,980.
   26. Purchased supplies for cash, $282.
   26. Recorded invoice of $4,800 for rental of film for April. Payment is due on May 5.
   28. Paid electricity and water bills, $574.
   30. Paid semimonthly wages, $1,410.
   30. Cash received from admissions for remainder of the month, $4,450.
   30. Recorded additional amount owed by the concessionaire for the month of April; sales for the month totaled $5,280. Rental charges in excess of the advance payment of $500 are not due and payable until May 12.

Instructions:

(1) Open a ledger of four-column accounts for Southern Theatre Corporation, using the following account titles and numbers: Cash, 11; Accounts Receivable, 12; Prepaid Insurance, 13; Supplies, 14; Land, 17; Buildings, 18; Equipment, 19; Accounts Payable, 21; Mortgage Note Payable, 24; Capital Stock, 31; Admissions Income, 41; Concession Income, 42; Wages Expense, 51; Film Rental Expense, 52; Advertising Expense, 53; Electricity and Water Expense, 54; Miscellaneous Expense, 59.

(2) Record the transactions in a two-column journal.

(3) Post the journal to the ledger, extending the month-end balances to the appropriate balance columns after all posting is completed.

(4) Prepare a trial balance as of April 30.

(5) Determine the following:

(a) Amount of total revenue recorded in the ledger.

(b) Amount of total expenses recorded in the ledger.

(c) Amount of net income for April, assuming that additional unrecorded expenses (including supplies used, insurance expired, etc.) totaled $2,280.

(d) The understatement or overstatement of net income for April that would have resulted from failure to record the additional amount owed by the concessionaire for the month of April until it was paid in May. (See transaction of April 30.)

(e) The understatement or overstatement of assets as of April 30 that would have resulted from failure to record the additional amount owed by the concessionaire in April. (See transaction of April 30.)

Problem 2-6B. The trial balance at the top of the next page, for Winder Photography, a sole proprietorship, as of March 31 of the current year, does not balance because of a number of errors.

(a) The balance of cash was understated by $650.

(b) A cash receipt of $810 was posted as a debit to Cash of $180.

(c) A debit of $250 to Accounts Receivable was not posted.

(d) A return of $123 of defective supplies was erroneously posted as a $231 credit to Supplies.

(e) An insurance policy acquired at a cost of $400 was posted as a credit to Prepaid Insurance.

Cash............................	1,260	
Accounts Receivable	3,920	
Supplies.........................	1,012	
Prepaid Insurance.................	50	
Equipment.......................	9,950	
Notes Payable....................		3,600
Accounts Payable		2,252
Steve Holmes, Capital.............		8,760
Steve Holmes, Drawing	2,250	
Sales...........................		24,650
Wages Expense...................	13,800	
Rent Expense....................	1,500	
Advertising Expense...............	138	
Gas, Electricity, and Water Expense ..	980	
	34,860	39,262

(f) The balance of Notes Payable was understated by $1,200.

(g) A credit of $68 in Accounts Payable was overlooked when the balance of the account was determined.

(h) A debit of $750 for a withdrawal by the owner was posted as a credit to the capital account.

(i) The balance of $1,380 in Advertising Expense was entered as $138 in the trial balance.

(j) Miscellaneous Expense, with a balance of $480, was omitted from the trial balance.

Instructions:

Prepare a corrected trial balance as of March 31 of the current year.

CHAPTER 3 | Problem 3-1B. The trial balance of Sno-White Laundromats at October 31, 1985, the end of the current fiscal year, and the data needed to determine year-end adjustments are as follows:

Sno-White Laundromats
Trial Balance
October 31, 1985

Cash	12,650	
Laundry Supplies	6,410	
Prepaid Insurance	2,800	
Laundry Equipment	92,100	
Accumulated Depreciation............................		55,200
Accounts Payable.....................................		4,900
S. M. White, Capital		36,960
S. M. White, Drawing	10,000	
Laundry Revenue.......................................		111,600
Wages Expense	42,300	
Rent Expense	28,500	
Utilities Expense.......................................	11,200	
Miscellaneous Expense............................	2,700	
	208,660	208,660

Adjustment data:

   (a) Inventory of laundry supplies at October 31 .... $3,100
   (b) Insurance premiums expired during the year. 2,000
   (c) Depreciation on equipment during the year 4,600
   (d) Wages accrued but not paid at October 31 1,750

Instructions:

   (1) Record the trial balance on a ten-column work sheet.
   (2) Complete the work sheet.
   (3) Prepare an income statement, a capital statement (no additional investments were made during the year), and a balance sheet.
   (4) On the basis of the adjustment data in the work sheet, journalize the adjusting entries.
   (5) On the basis of the data in the work sheet or in the income and capital statements, journalize the closing entries.

Problem 3-2B. As of April 30, 1985, the end of the current fiscal year, the accountant for Aaron Company prepared a trial balance, journalized and posted the adjusting entries, prepared an adjusted trial balance, prepared the statements, and completed the other procedures required at the end of the accounting cycle. The two trial balances as of April 30, one before adjustments and the other after adjustments, are as follows:

Aaron Company
Trial Balance
April 30, 1985

	Unadjusted		Adjusted	
Cash	6,138		6,138	
Supplies	7,526		1,430	
Prepaid Rent	14,400		1,200	
Prepaid Insurance	1,180		262	
Equipment	69,750		69,750	
Accumulated Depreciation—Equipment ...		33,480		36,270
Automobiles	36,500		36,500	
Accumulated Depreciation—Automobiles..		18,250		21,900
Accounts Payable		4,310		4,500
Salaries Payable.		—		3,480
Taxes Payable.		—		1,200
H. T. Aaron, Capital		31,730		31,730
H. T. Aaron, Drawing	18,000		18,000	
Service Fees Earned		182,722		182,722
Salary Expense.	112,300		115,780	
Rent Expense	—		13,200	
Supplies Expense	—		6,096	
Depreciation Expense—Equipment	—		2,790	
Depreciation Expense—Automobiles	—		3,650	
Utilities Expense.	2,130		2,320	
Taxes Expense	858		2,058	
Insurance Expense	—		918	
Miscellaneous Expense	1,710		1,710	
	270,492	270,492	281,802	281,802

Instructions:

(1) Present the eight journal entries that were required to adjust the accounts at April 30. None of the accounts was affected by more than one adjusting entry.

(2) Present the journal entries that were required to close the accounts at April 30.

(3) Prepare a capital statement for the fiscal year ended April 30. There were no additional investments during the year.

(If the working papers correlating with this textbook are not used, omit Problem 3-3B.)

Problem 3-3B. The ledger and trial balance of Lindsey Welding Services as of May 31, the end of the first month of its current fiscal year, are presented in the working papers. The accounts had been closed on April 30.

Instructions:

(1) Complete the ten-column work sheet. Data needed to determine the necessary adjusting entries are as follows:

Inventory of supplies at May 31	$ 465.10
Insurance premiums expired during May	82.32
Depreciation on the building during May	120.60
Depreciation on equipment during May	94.50
Wages accrued but not paid at May 31	1,006.50

(2) Prepare an income statement, a capital statement, and a balance sheet.

(3) Journalize and post the adjusting entries, inserting balances in the accounts affected.

(4) Journalize and post the closing entries. Indicate closed accounts by inserting a line in both Balance columns opposite the closing entry. Insert the new balance of the capital account.

(5) Prepare a post-closing trial balance.

CHAPTER 4 | Problem 4-1B. The following were selected from among the transactions completed by Perez Company during July of the current year.

July 1. Purchased merchandise for cash, $5,000, less trade discount of 30%.

3. Purchased merchandise on account from Wei Co., $7,500, terms FOB destination, 1/10, n/30.

5. Returned merchandise purchased on July 3 from Wei Co., $1,500.

6. Sold merchandise on account to J. W. Valdez Co., $4,000, terms 2/10, n/30.

9. Purchased office supplies for cash, $170.

12. Purchased merchandise on account from A. C. Simon, Inc., $3,500, terms FOB shipping point, 1/10, n/30, with prepaid transportation costs of $65 added to the invoice.

July 12. Paid Wei Co. on account for purchases of July 3, less returns of July 5 and discount.
   15. Received cash on account from sale of July 6 to J. W. Valdez Co., less discount.
   17. Sold merchandise on nonbank credit cards and reported accounts to the card company, $1,625.
   20. Sold merchandise on account to Alice Block and Co., $1,400, terms 2/10, n/30.
   21. Paid A. C. Simon, Inc. on account for purchases of July 12, less discount.
   24. Received cash from card company for nonbank credit card sales of July 17, less $96 service fee.
   26. Sold merchandise for cash, $2,150.
   28. Received merchandise returned by Alice Block and Co. from sale of July 20, $175.

Instructions:

Journalize the transactions in a two-column journal.

Problem 4-3B. The following data for C. C. Romano Co. were selected from the ledger after adjustment at June 30, the end of the current fiscal year:

Accounts payable	$ 45,800
Accounts receivable	88,750
Accumulated depreciation—office equipment	20,500
Accumulated depreciation—store equipment	60,700
Capital stock	200,000
Cash	30,150
Cost of merchandise sold	572,360
Dividends	40,000
Dividends payable	10,000
General expenses	72,500
Interest expense	18,750
Merchandise inventory	310,200
Mortgage note payable (due in 1991)	100,000
Office equipment	72,750
Prepaid insurance	3,500
Rent income	12,650
Retained earnings	197,630
Salaries payable	3,750
Sales	827,150
Selling expenses	113,720
Store equipment	155,500

Instructions:

(1) Prepare a combined income and retained earnings statement, using the single-step form for the income statement.
(2) Prepare a balance sheet in report form.

Problem 4-4B. The accounts in the ledger of Snyder Company, with the unadjusted balances on December 31, the end of the current fiscal year, are as follows:

Cash....................	$ 22,200	Purchases..............	$642,450
Accounts Receivable.....	66,700	Sales Salaries Expense ...	103,550
Merchandise Inventory....	151,850	Advertising Expense......	29,150
Prepaid Insurance........	3,100	Depreciation Expense—	
Store Supplies...........	2,650	Store Equipment.......	—
Store Equipment.........	207,750	Store Supplies Expense...	—
Accum. Depreciation—		Misc. Selling Expense	2,010
Store Equipment.......	105,800	Office Salaries Expense...	65,350
Accounts Payable........	39,950	Rent Expense...........	30,000
Salaries Payable.........	—	Heating and Lighting Exp..	21,100
Capital Stock............	100,000	Taxes Expense...........	9,800
Retained Earnings........	150,600	Insurance Expense.......	—
Dividends..............	20,000	Misc. General Expense ...	3,050
Income Summary........	—	Loss on Disposal of	
Sales..................	985,600	Equip................	1,240

The data needed for year-end adjustments on December 31 are as follows:

Merchandise inventory on December 31.........	$125,800
Insurance expired during the year..............	1,950
Store supplies inventory on December 31.......	700
Depreciation for the current year..............	11,700
Accrued salaries on December 31:	
Sales salaries............................ $2,200	
Office salaries............................ 1,550	3,750

Instructions:

(1) Prepare a work sheet for the fiscal year ended December 31, listing all of the accounts in the order given.
(2) Prepare a multiple-step income statement.
(3) Prepare a retained earnings statement.
(4) Prepare a report form balance sheet.
(5) Compute the following:
    (a) Percent of gross profit to sales.
    (b) Percent of income from operations to sales.

Problem 4-6B. A portion of the work sheet of Benton Supply Co. for the current year ended May 31 is presented on page 848.

Instructions:

(1) From the partial work sheet, determine the eight entries that appeared in the adjustments columns and present them in general journal form. The only accounts affected by more than one adjusting entry were Merchandise Inventory and Income Summary. The balance in Prepaid Rent before adjustment was $26,000, representing 13 month's rent at $2,000 per month.
(2) Determine the following:
    (a) Amount of net income for the year.
    (b) Amount of the owner's capital at the end of the year.

Account Title	Income Statement		Balance Sheet	
	Debit	Credit	Debit	Credit
Cash.			48,250	
Accounts Receivable			102,100	
Merchandise Inventory			277,600	
Prepaid Rent.			2,000	
Prepaid Insurance			1,950	
Supplies.			1,150	
Store Equipment.			126,900	
Accumulated Depr. — Store Equipment				42,500
Office Equipment			37,600	
Accumulated Depr. — Office Equipment				29,150
Accounts Payable				97,200
Sales Salaries Payable				3,750
Mortgage Note Payable				200,000
Alice Benton, Capital.				212,500
Alice Benton, Drawing			36,000	
Income Summary.	295,100	277,600		
Sales.		850,000		
Sales Returns and Allowances	17,010			
Purchases	514,755			
Purchases Discount.		4,910		
Sales Salaries Expense	102,500			
Delivery Expense	13,650			
Depreciation Expense — Store Equipment	7,500			
Supplies Expense	795			
Miscellaneous Selling Expense.	3,100			
Office Salaries Expense	55,000			
Rent Expense	24,000			
Heating and Lighting Expense	19,950			
Insurance Expense	4,950			
Depreciation Expense — Office Equipment	3,800			
Miscellaneous General Expense.	1,950			
Interest Expense	20,000			
	1,084,060	1,132,510	633,550	585,100

CHAPTER 5 | **Problem 5-1B.** The accounts listed below appear in the ledger of Hunter Company at June 30, the end of the current fiscal year. None of the year-end adjustments have been recorded:

113	Fees Receivable	—	411	Fees Earned	$188,800
114	Supplies	$ 1,950	511	Salary Expense.	115,750
115	Prepaid Insurance	4,800	513	Advertising Expense	25,500
116	Prepaid Advertising	—	514	Insurance Expense	—
213	Salaries Payable	—	515	Supplies Expense.	—
215	Unearned Rent	—	611	Rent Income	19,500
313	Income Summary	—			

The following information relating to adjustments at June 30 is obtained from physical inventories, supplementary records, and other sources.

(a) Of a prepayment of $7,500 for newspaper advertising, 70% has been used and the remainder will be used in the following year.

(b) Rent collected in advance that will not be earned until the following year, $1,500.

(c) Salaries accrued at June 30, $2,975.

(d) Unbilled fees at June 30, $8,500.

(e) The insurance record indicates that $1,600 of insurance relates to future years.

(f) Inventory of supplies at June 30, $675.

Instructions:

(1) Open the accounts listed and record the balances in the appropriate balance columns, as of June 30.

(2) Journalize the adjusting entries and post to the appropriate accounts after each entry, extending the balances. Identify the postings by writing "Adjusting" in the item columns.

(3) Prepare a compound journal entry to close the revenue accounts and another compound entry to close the expense accounts.

(4) Post the closing entries, inserting a short line in both balance columns of accounts that are closed. Identify the postings by writing "Closing" in the item columns.

(5) Prepare the reversing journal entries that should be made on July 1 and post to the appropriate accounts after each entry, inserting a short line in both balance columns of accounts that now have zero balances. Write "Reversing" in the item columns.

(If the working papers correlating with the textbook are not used, omit Problem 5-2B.)

Problem 5-2B. John Cox Company prepares interim financial statements at the end of each month and closes its accounts annually on December 31. Its income statement for the two-month period, January and February of the current year, is presented in the working papers. In addition, the trial balance of the ledger as of one month later is presented on a ten-column work sheet in the working papers. Data needed for adjusting entries at March 31, the end of the three-month period, are as follows:

(a) Estimated inventory of store supplies at March 31, $435.

(b) Salaries accrued at March 31:
    Sales salaries, $1,750.
    Office salaries, $350.

(c) Depreciation for the three-month period:
    Store equipment, $1,800.
    Office equipment, $600.

(d) Insurance expired during the three-month period:
    Allocable as selling expense, $360.
    Allocable as general expense, $150

(e) Estimated merchandise inventory at March 31, $246,100.

(f) Unearned rent income at March 31, $305.

Instructions:

(1) Complete the work sheet for the three-month period ended March 31 of the current year.

(2) Prepare an income statement for the three-month period, using the last three-column group of the nine-column form in the working papers.

(3) Prepare an income statement for the month of March, using the middle three-column group of the nine-column form in the working papers.

(4) Prepare a capital statement for the three-month period. There were no additional investments during the period.

(5) Prepare a balance sheet as of March 31.

Problem 5-5B. Selected accounts from the ledger of Linens and Things at the end of the fiscal year are as follows. The account balances are shown before and after adjustment.

	Unadjusted Balance	Adjusted Balance
Fees Receivable..	—	$ 11,250
Supplies...	$ 2,325	975
Prepaid Insurance..	5,900	2,650
Wages Payable...	—	3,090
Advertising Payable..	—	3,750
Unearned Rent...	—	500
Fees Earned...	187,000	198,250
Wages Expense..	79,100	82,190
Insurance Expense...	—	3,250
Advertising Expense.......................................	20,250	24,000
Supplies Expense..	—	1,350
Rent Income...	6,500	6,000

Instructions:

(1) Journalize the adjusting entries that were posted to the ledger at the end of the fiscal year.

(2) Insert the letter "R" in the date column opposite each adjusting entry that should be reversed as of the first day of the following fiscal year.

CHAPTER 6 | Problem 6-1B. Earhardt Supply Co. is a newly organized enterprise with the following list of asset, liability, and capital accounts, arranged in alphabetical order. The accounts are to be opened in the general ledger, assigned account numbers, and arranged in balance sheet order. Each account number is to be composed of three digits: the first digit is to indicate the major classification ("1" for assets, etc.), the second digit is to indicate the subclassification ("11" for current assets, etc.), and the third digit is to identify the specific account ("111" for Cash, etc.).

Accounts Payable
Accounts Receivable
Accumulated Depreciation—Building
Accumulated Depreciation—Delivery Equipment
Accumulated Depreciation—Office Equipment
Accumulated Depreciation—Store Equipment
Building
Capital Stock
Cash
Delivery Equipment
Dividends
Interest Payable

Land
Merchandise Inventory
Mortgage Note Payable (long-term)
Notes Payable (short-term)
Office Equipment
Office Supplies
Prepaid Insurance
Retained Earnings
Salaries Payable
Store Equipment
Store Supplies
Taxes Payable

Instructions:

Construct a chart of accounts for the accounts listed.

Problem 6-3B. Bergner Co. was established in March of the current year. Transactions related to purchases, returns and allowances, and cash payments during the remainder of the month are as follows:

Mar. 17. Issued Check No. 1 in payment of rent for March, $950.
   17. Purchased store equipment on account from Horner Supply Corp., $10,100.
   17. Purchased merchandise on account from Oester Clothing, $3,150.
   18. Issued Check No. 2 in payment of store supplies, $95, and office supplies, $35.
   19. Purchased merchandise on account from Cedeno Clothing Co., $4,920.
   20. Purchased merchandise on account from Boggs Co., $2,250.
   22. Received a credit memorandum from Cedeno Clothing Co. for returned merchandise, $70.
       Post the journals to the accounts payable ledger.
   25. Issued Check No. 3 to Horner Supply Corp. in payment of invoice of $10,100.
   25. Received a credit memorandum from Boggs Co. for defective merchandise, $250.
   26. Issued Check No. 4 to Oester Clothing, in payment of invoice of $3,150, less 2% discount.
   28. Issued Check No. 5 to a cash customer for merchandise returned, $25.
   28. Issued Check No. 6 to Cedeno Clothing Co. in payment of the balance owed, less 2% discount.
   28. Purchased merchandise on account from Boggs Co., $3,100.
       Post the journals to the accounts payable ledger.
   30. Purchased the following from Horner Supply Corp. on account: store supplies, $48; office supplies, $42; office equipment, $3,420.
   30. Issued Check No. 7 to Boggs Co. in payment of invoice of $2,250, less the credit of $250 and 1% discount.
   30. Purchased merchandise on account from Oester Clothing, $1,200.
   31. Issued Check No. 8 in payment of incoming transportation charges on merchandise delivered during March, $195.
   31. Issued Check No. 9 on payment of sales salaries, $2,125.
   31. Received a credit memorandum from Horner Supply Corp. for defect in office equipment, $25.
       Post the journals to the accounts payable ledger.

Instructions:

(1) Open the following accounts in the general ledger, using the account numbers indicated.

111	Cash	412	Sales Returns and Allowances
116	Store Supplies	511	Purchases
117	Office Supplies	512	Purchases Discount
121	Store Equipment	611	Sales Salaries Expense
122	Office Equipment	712	Rent Expense
211	Accounts Payable		

(2) Open the following accounts in the accounts payable ledger: Boggs Co.; Cedeno Clothing Co.; Horner Supply Corp.; Oester Clothing.

(3) Record the transactions for March, using a purchases journal similar to the one illustrated on pages 168 and 169, a cash payments journal similar to the one

illustrated on page 173, and a two-column general journal. Post to the accounts payable ledger at the points indicated in the narrative of transactions.

(4) Post the appropriate individual entries to the general ledger (Sundry Accounts columns of the purchases journal and the cash payments journal; both columns of the general journal).

(5) Add the columns of the purchases journal and the cash payments journal, and post the appropriate totals to the general ledger. (Because the problem does not include transactions related to cash receipts, the cash account in the ledger will have a credit balance.)

(6) Prepare a schedule of accounts payable.

(If the working papers correlating with the textbook are not used, omit Problem 6-5B.)

Problem 6-5B. Three journals, the accounts receivable ledger, and portions of the general ledger of Henson Company are presented in the working papers. Sales invoices and credit memorandums were entered in the journals by an assistant. Terms of sales on account are 1/10, n/30, FOB shipping point. Transactions in which cash and notes receivable were received during May of the current year are as follows:

May   1. Received $5,643 cash from Nance Co. in payment of April 21 invoice, less discount.

3. Received $10,200 cash in payment of $10,000 note receivable and interest of $200.
Post transactions of May 1, 2, and 6 to accounts receivable ledger.

8. Received $4,356 cash from C. E. Rea and Son in payment of April 27 invoice, less discount.

9. Received $1,250 cash from Downs & Franks in payment of April 9 invoice, no discount.

15. Cash sales for first half of May totaled $15,015.
Post transactions of May 8, 9, 10, 12, and 15 to accounts receivable ledger.

17. Received $440 cash refund for return of defective equipment purchased for cash in April.

19. Received $1,485 cash from Nance Co. in payment of balance due on May 10 invoice, less discount.

22. Received $1,188 cash from Downs & Franks in payment of May 12 invoice, less discount.
Post transactions of May 18, 19, 22, and 25 to accounts receivable ledger.

28. Received $50 cash for sale of office supplies at cost.

31. Received $500 cash and a $2,500 note receivable from Howard Corp. in settlement of the balance due on the invoice of May 2, no discount. (Record receipt of note in general journal.)

31. Cash sales for the second half of May totaled $13,100.
Post transactions of May 28, 30, and 31 to accounts receivable ledger.

Instructions:

(1) Record the cash receipts in the cash receipts journal and the note in the general journal. *Before recording a receipt of cash on account, determine the balance of the customer's account.* Post the entries from the three journals, in date sequence, to the accounts receivable ledger in accordance with the instructions in the narrative of transactions. Insert the new balance after each posting to an account.

(2) Post the appropriate individual entries from the cash receipts journal and the general journal to the general ledger.

(3) Add the columns of the sales journal and the cash receipts journal and post the appropriate totals to the general ledger. Insert the balance of each account after the last posting.

(4) Prepare a schedule of the accounts receivable as of May 31 and compare the total with the balance of the controlling account.

Problem 6-6B. Transactions related to sales and cash receipts completed by Veal Company during the period January 16–31 of the current year are as follows. The terms of all sales on account are 1/10, n/30, FOB shipping point.

July 16. Issued Invoice No. 512 to Seaview Co., $4,550.
    17. Received cash from Dumont Co. for the balance owed on its account, less discount.
    18. Issued Invoice No. 513 to R. W. Kane Co., $5,200.
    19. Issued Invoice No. 514 to Frank Parker Co., $1,650.
    Post all journals to the accounts receivable ledger.
    22. Received cash from R. W. Kane Co. for the balance owed on July 16; no discount.
    24. Issued Credit Memo No. 40 to Seaview Co., $150.
    24. Issued Invoice No. 515 to R. W. Kane Co., $6,000.
    25. Received $609 cash in payment of a $600 note receivable and interest of $9.
    Post all journals to the accounts receivable ledger.
    27. Received cash from Seaview Co. for the balance due on invoice of July 16, less discount.
    28. Received cash from R. W. Kane Co. for invoice of July 18, less discount.
    29. Issued Invoice No. 516 to Dumont Co., $3,500.
    31. Recorded cash sales for the second half of the month, $9,222.
    31. Issued Credit Memo No. 30 to Dumont Co., $50.
    Post all journals to the accounts receivable ledger.

Instructions:
(1) Open the following accounts in the general ledger, inserting the balances indicated, as of July 1:

111	Cash	$12,125	412	Sales Returns and	
112	Notes Receivable	5,500		Allowances	—
113	Accounts Receivable	8,725	413	Sales Discount	—
411	Sales	—	811	Interest Income	—

(2) Open the following accounts in the accounts receivable ledger, inserting the balances indicated, as of July 16: Dumont Co., $2,500; R. W. Kane Co., $5,125; Frank Parker Co.; Seaview Co.

(3) The transactions are to be recorded in a sales journal similar to the one illustrated on page 176, a cash receipts journal similar to the one illustrated on page 178, and a 2-column general journal. Insert on the first line of the two special journals "July 16 Total(s) Forwarded ✔" and the following dollar figures in the respective amount columns:
    Sales journal: 20,200
    Cash receipts journal: 1,077; 6,950; 21,300; 255; 29,072.

(4) Record the transactions for the remainder of July, posting to the accounts receivable ledger and inserting the balances at the points indicated in the

narrative of transactions. *Determine the balance in the customer's account before recording a cash receipt.*

(5) Add the columns of the special journals and post the individual entries and totals to the general ledger. Insert account balances after the last posting.

(6) Determine that the subsidiary ledger agrees with the controlling account in the general ledger.

Problem 6-7B. The transactions completed by Cannon Supply Co. during January, the first month of the current fiscal year, were as follows:

Jan. 2. Issued Check No. 810 for January rent, $1,500.
2. Purchased merchandise on account from Dane Corp., $2,250.
2. Purchased equipment on account from Lee Equipment Co., $3,700.
3. Issued Invoice No. 942 to C. Block, Inc., $1,320.
7. Received check for $2,744 from Nichols Corp. in payment of $2,800 invoice, less discount.
7. Issued Check No. 811 for miscellaneous selling expense, $205.
8. Received credit memorandum from Dane Corp. for merchandise returned to them, $150.
8. Issued Invoice No. 943 to Jackson Co., $5,000.
9. Issued Check No. 812 for $9,310 to Easterly, Inc. in payment of $9,500 invoice, less 2% discount.
9. Received check for $9,604 from Baker Manufacturing Co. in payment of $9,800 invoice, less discount.
10. Issued Check No. 813 to Collins Enterprises in payment of invoice of $2,120, no discount.
10. Issued Invoice No. 944 to Nichols Corp., $3,225.
11. Issued Check No. 814 to Peak Corp. in payment of account, $705, no discount.
12. Received check from C. Block, Inc. on account, $775, no discount.
14. Issued credit memorandum to Nichols Corp. for damaged merchandise, $225.
15. Issued Check No. 815 for $2,058 to Dane Corp. in payment of $2,100 balance, less 2% discount.
15. Issued Check No. 816 for $1,250 for cash purchase of merchandise.
15. Cash sales for January 2–15, $18,942.
17. Purchased merchandise on account from Collins Enterprises, $6,420.
18. Received check for return of merchandise that had been purchased for cash, $75.
18. Issued Check No. 817 for miscellaneous general expense, $130.
21. Purchased the following on account from Bunn Supply, Inc.: store supplies, $215; office supplies, $170.
22. Issued Check No. 818 in payment of advertising expense, $610.
23. Issued Invoice No. 945 to Baker Manufacturing Co., $1,950.
24. Purchased the following on account from Easterly, Inc.: merchandise, $3,125; store supplies, $110.
25. Issued Invoice No. 946 to Jackson Co., $3,290.
25. Received check for $2,940 from Nichols Corp. in payment of $3,000 balance, less discount.
26. Issued Check No. 819 to Lee Equipment Co. in payment of invoice of January 2, $3,700, no discount.

Jan. 29. Issued Check No. 820 to Ann Day as a personal withdrawal, $2,500.

30. Issued Check No. 821 for monthly salaries as follows: sales salaries, $9,600; office salaries, $3,800.

31. Cash sales for January 16–31, $19,250.

31. Issued Check No. 822 for transportation on commodities purchased during the month as follows: merchandise, $275; equipment, $115.

Instructions:

(1) Open the following accounts in the general ledger, entering the balances indicated as of January 1:

111	Cash................	$ 9,100	412	Sales Returns and Allow.....	—
113	Accounts Receivable ..	16,200	413	Sales Discount.............	—
114	Merchandise Inventory	31,500	511	Purchases.................	—
115	Store Supplies	410	512	Purchases Discount	—
116	Office Supplies	225	611	Sales Salaries Expense	—
117	Prepaid Insurance....	2,100	612	Advertising Expense........	—
121	Equipment...........	40,650	619	Miscellaneous Selling	
122	Accumulated Depr....	12,350		Expense	—
211	Accounts Payable	12,325	711	Office Salaries Expense.....	—
311	Ann Day, Capital	75,510	712	Rent Expense..............	—
312	Ann Day, Drawing	—	719	Miscellaneous General	
411	Sales	—		Expense	—

(2) Record the transactions for January, using a purchases journal (as on pages 168 and 169), a sales journal (as on page 176), a cash payments journal (as on page 173), a cash receipts journal (as on page 178), and a 2-column general journal. The terms of all sales on account are FOB shipping point, 2/15, n/60. Assume that an assistant makes daily postings to the individual accounts in the accounts payable ledger and the accounts receivable ledger.

(3) Post the appropriate individual entries to the general ledger.

(4) Add the columns of the special journals and post the appropriate totals to the general ledger; insert the account balances.

(5) Prepare a trial balance.

(6) Balances in the accounts in the subsidiary ledgers as of January 31 are listed below. Verify the agreement of the ledgers with their respective controlling accounts.

Accounts Receivable: Balances of $2,825; $1,320; $5,000; $1,950; $3,290.

Accounts Payable: Balances of $6,420; $385; $3,235.

CHAPTER 7 | Problem 7-1B. The cash in bank account for R. C. Graziano Co. at April 30 of the current year indicated a balance of $7,424.95 after both the cash receipts journal and the check register for April had been posted. The bank statement indicated a balance of $11,740.50 on April 30. Comparison of the bank statement and the accompanying canceled checks and memorandums with the records revealed the following reconciling items:

(a) Checks outstanding totaled $4,840.75.

(b) A deposit of $2,672.10, representing receipts of April 30, had been made too late to appear on the bank statement.

(c) The bank had collected for R. C. Graziano Co. $2,050 on a note left for collection. The face of the note was $2,000.

(d) A check for $24.50 returned with the statement had been recorded in the check register as $42.50. The check was for the payment of an obligation to Rey Office Supply Co. for the purchase of office supplies on account.

(e) A check drawn for $100 had been erroneously charged by the bank as $10.

(f) Bank service charges for April amounted to $11.10.

Instructions:

(1) Prepare a bank reconciliation.

(2) Journalize the necessary entries. The accounts have not been closed. The voucher system is used.

Problem 7-3B. Wei Co. had the following vouchers in its unpaid voucher file at March 31 of the current year:

Due Date	Voucher No.	Creditor	Date of Invoice	Amount	Terms
April 6	476	Avery Co.	March 27	$ 900	1/10, n/30
April 15	460	Hall Inc.	March 16	1,700	n/30
April 27	489	Wells Co.	March 28	750	n/30

The vouchers prepared and the checks issued during the month of April were as follows:

VOUCHERS

Date	Voucher No.	Payee	Amount	Terms	Distribution
April 2	493	Fox Co.	$ 800	1/10, n/30	Purchases
3	494	Love & Son	77	cash	Office supplies
7	495	Coe Co.	750	2/10, n/30	Purchases
8	496	Moe Express	46	cash	Delivery expense
10	497	Moore Co.	1,250	2/10, n/30	Purchases
13	498	Hunt Supply	120	cash	Store supplies
16	499	Commercial Savings	5,300		Note payable, $5,000 Interest, $300
19	500	Jones Office Co.	1,450	n/30	Office equipment
20	501	Case & Co.	950	2/10, n/30	Purchases
24	502	R. Day & Co.	2,200	cash	Store equipment
26	503	Gove Co.	3,100	2/10, n/30	Purchases
30	504	Petty Cash	80		Store supplies, $17 Office supplies, $16 Miscellaneous selling expense, $27 Miscellaneous general expense, $20

CHECKS

Date	Check No.	Payee	Voucher Paid	Amount
April 3	460	Love & Son	494	$ 77
6	461	Avery Co.	476	891
8	462	Moe Express	496	46
12	463	Fox Co.	493	792
13	464	Hunt Supply	498	120
15	465	Hall Inc.	460	1,700
16	466	Commercial Savings	499	5,300
17	467	Coe Co.	495	735
20	468	Moore Co.	497	1,225
24	469	R. Day & Co.	502	2,200
27	470	Wells Co.	489	750
30	471	Case & Co.	501	931
30	472	Petty Cash	504	80

Instructions:

(1) Set up a four-column account for Accounts Payable, Account No. 205, and record the balance of $3,350 as of April 1.

(2) Record the April vouchers in a voucher register similar to the one illustrated in this chapter, with the following amount columns: Accounts Payable Cr., Purchases Dr., Store Supplies Dr., Office Supplies Dr., and Sundry Accounts Dr. Purchases invoices are recorded at the gross amount.

(3) Record the April checks in a check register similar to the one illustrated in this chapter, but omit the Bank Deposits and Balance columns. As each check is recorded in the check register, the date and check number should be inserted in the appropriate columns of the voucher register. (Assume that notations for payment of the March vouchers are made in the voucher register for March.)

(4) Total and rule the registers and post to Accounts Payable.

(5) Prepare a schedule of unpaid vouchers.

(If the working papers correlating with the textbook are not used, omit Problem 7-4B.)

Problem 7-4B. Portions of the voucher register, check register, and accounts payable account of R. T. Ritter Inc. are presented in the working papers. Expenditures, cash disbursements, and other selected transactions completed during the period March 25–31 of the current year are described as follows:

Mar. 25. Issued Check No. 632 to Nelson Co. in payment of Voucher No. 487 for $2,000, less cash discount of 2%.

25. Recorded Voucher No. 495 payable to Wilson Co. for merchandise, $5,000, terms 1/10, n/30. (Purchases invoices are recorded at the gross amount.)

26. Recorded Voucher No. 496 payable to Western Auto Insurance Co. for an insurance policy, $1,860.

26. Issued Check No. 633 in payment of Voucher No. 496.

27. Recorded Voucher No. 497 payable to James Co. for merchandise, $3,300, terms, 1/10, n/30.

27. Recorded Voucher No. 498 for $9,360 payable to First National Bank for note payable, $9,000, and interest, $360.

Mar. 27. Issued Check No. 634 in payment of Voucher No. 498.
   28. Recorded Voucher No. 499 payable to Oakwood Press for advertising, $410.
   28. Issued Check No. 635 in payment of Voucher No. 499.
   29. Recorded Voucher No. 500 payable to Petty Cash for $193.05, distributed as follows: office supplies, $54.40; advertising expense, $18.35; delivery expense, $40.10; miscellaneous selling expense, $38.15; miscellaneous general expense, $42.05.
   29. Issued Check No. 636 in payment of Voucher No. 500.
   31. Issued Check No. 637 to Quartz Co. in payment of Voucher No. 481 for $1,050, no discount.

After the journals are posted at the end of the month, the cash in bank account has a debit balance of $20,387.90.

The bank statement indicates a March 31 balance of $22,890.45. A comparison of paid checks with the check register reveals that Nos. 633 and 637 are outstanding. Check No. 601 for $79.95, which appeared on the February reconciliation as outstanding, is still outstanding. Debit memorandums accompanying the bank statement indicate a charge of $475.50 for a check drawn by C. A. Moyer, a customer, which was returned because of insufficient funds, and $11.90 for service charges.

Instructions:

   (1) Record the transactions for March 25–31 in the appropriate journals.
   (2) Total and rule the voucher register and the check register, and post totals to the accounts payable account.
   (3) Complete the schedule of unpaid vouchers. (Compare the total with the balance of the accounts payable account as of March 31.)
   (4) Prepare a bank reconciliation and journalize any necessary entries.

Problem 7-5B. M. C. Levin Co. employs the voucher system in controlling expenditures and disbursements. All cash receipts are deposited in a night depository after banking hours each Wednesday and Friday. The data required to reconcile the bank statement as of June 30 have been abstracted from various documents and records and are reproduced as follows. To facilitate identification, the sources of the data are printed in capital letters.

CASH IN BANK ACCOUNT:
   Balance as of June 1 .... $7,016.50

CASH RECEIPTS JOURNAL:
   Total of Cash in Bank Debit column for month of June 7,812.50

DUPLICATE DEPOSIT TICKETS:
   Date and amount of each deposit in June:

Date	Amount	Date	Amount	Date	Amount
June 1	$978.36	June 10	$791.71	June 22	$999.90
3	849.40	15	957.85	24	876.71
8	901.50	17	946.47	29	510.60

CHECK REGISTER:
Number and amount of each check issued in June:

Check No.	Amount	Check No.	Amount	Check No.	Amount
615	$401.70	622	$490.90	629	$ 97.75
616	232.45	623	Void	630	249.75
617	401.90	624	640.13	631	113.95
618	604.84	625	376.77	632	907.95
619	506.88	626	299.37	633	359.60
620	117.25	627	537.01	634	601.50
621	298.66	628	380.95	635	486.39

Total amount of checks issued in June........................ $8,105.70

JUNE BANK STATEMENT:

Balance as of June 1	$7,019.57
Deposits and other credits......................................	8,516.15
Checks and other debits	(7,638.55)
Balance as of June 30	$7,897.17

Date and amount of each deposit in June:

Date	Amount	Date	Amount	Date	Amount
June 1	$690.25	June 9	$910.50	June 18	$946.47
2	978.36	11	791.71	23	999.90
4	849.40	16	957.85	30	876.71

CHECKS ACCOMPANYING JUNE BANK STATEMENT:
Number and amount of each check, rearranged in numerical sequence:

Check No.	Amount	Check No.	Amount	Check No.	Amount
606	$112.15	619	$506.88	626	$299.37
613	301.40	620	117.25	627	537.01
614	60.55	621	298.66	628	380.95
615	401.70	622	490.90	630	249.75
616	232.45	624	640.13	631	113.95
617	401.90	625	376.77	632	907.95
618	604.84			635	486.39

BANK MEMORANDUMS ACCOMPANYING JUNE BANK STATEMENT:
Date, description, and amount of each memorandum:

Date	Description	Amount
June 15	Bank credit memo for note collected:	
	Principal	$500.00
	Interest	15.00
20	Bank debit memo for check returned because of insufficient funds...	103.50
30	Bank debit memo for service charges........................	14.10

BANK RECONCILIATION FOR PRECEDING MONTH:

M. C. Levin Co.
Bank Reconciliation
May 31, 19--

Balance per bank statement			$7,019.57
Add deposit of May 31, not recorded by bank			690.25
			$7,709.82
Deduct outstanding checks:			
No. 606		$112.15	
611		219.22	
613		301.40	
614		60.55	693.32
Adjusted balance			$7,016.50
Balance per depositor's records			$7,026.00
Deduct service charges			9.50
Adjusted balance			$7,016.50

Instructions:

(1) Prepare a bank reconciliation as of June 30. If errors in recording deposits or checks are discovered, assume that the errors were made by the company. Assume that all deposits are from cash sales. All checks are in payment of vouchers.

(2) Journalize the necessary entries. The accounts have not been closed.

(3) What is the amount of cash in bank that should appear on the balance sheet as of June 30?

CHAPTER 8 | Problem 8-1B. The following were selected from among the transactions completed by Michael Levin and Co. during the current year:

Jan. 15. Loaned $6,000 cash to Frank Reilly, receiving a 90-day, 12% note.

Mar. 1. Sold merchandise on account to A-1 Supply, $3,000, charging an additional $75 for prepaid transportation cost. (Credit Delivery Expense for the $75 charged for prepaid transportation cost.)

11. Received from A-1 Supply the amount due on the invoice of March 1, less 1% discount.

12. Sold merchandise on account to Caldwell Co., $4,000.

Apr. 11. Accepted a 30-day, 15% note for $4,000 from Caldwell Co. on account.

15. Received the interest due from Frank Reilly and a new 90-day, 14% note as a renewal of the loan. (Record both the debit and the credit to the notes receivable account.)

May 11. Received from Caldwell Co. the amount due on the note of April 11.

July 12. Sold merchandise on account to Swartz and Sons, $10,000.

14. Received from Frank Reilly the amount due on his note of April 15.

Aug. 11. Received from Swartz and Sons a 60-day, 12% note for $10,000.

Sept. 10. Discounted the note from Swartz and Sons at the Commercial National Bank at 14%.

Oct. 13. Received notice from the Commercial National Bank that Swartz and Sons had dishonored its note. Paid the bank the maturity value of the note.

Nov. 9. Received from Swartz and Sons the amount owed on the dishonored note, plus interest for 30 days at 12% computed on the maturity value of the note.

Instructions:

Record the transactions in general journal form.

Problem 8-2B. During the last three months of the current fiscal year, Bailey Co. received the following notes. Notes (1), (2), (3), and (4) were discounted on the dates and at the rates indicated.

Date	Face Amount	Term	Interest Rate	Date Discounted	Discount Rate
(1) Oct. 2	$4,800	60 days	14%	Oct. 22	12%
(2) Oct. 6	7,500	30 days	12%	Oct. 21	14%
(3) Oct. 28	3,100	90 days	14%	Dec. 27	15%
(4) Nov. 3	4,000	60 days	12%	Nov. 13	16%
(5) Dec. 16	6,000	60 days	11%	—	—
(6) Dec. 21	8,700	30 days	12%	—	—

Instructions:

(1) Determine for each note (a) the due date and (b) the amount of interest due at maturity, identifying each note by number.

(2) Determine for each of the first four notes (a) the maturity value, (b) the discount period, (c) the discount, (d) the proceeds, and (e) the interest income or interest expense, identifying each note by number.

(3) Present, in general journal form, the entries to record the discounting of notes (2) and (4) at a bank.

(4) Assuming that notes (5) and (6) are held until maturity, determine for each the amount of interest earned (a) in the current fiscal year and (b) in the following fiscal year.

Problem 8-3B. B. Olin Co. closes its accounts annually as of December 31, the end of the fiscal year. The following data relate to notes receivable and interest from November 1 through February 29 of the following year. (All notes are dated as of the day they are received.)

Nov. 1. Received a $4,500, 12%, 60-day note on account.

Dec. 1. Received a $10,000, 15%, 90-day note on account.

16. Received a $12,000, 13%, 60-day note on account.

21. Received a $6,000, 12%, 30-day note on account.

31. Received $4,590 on note of November 1.

31. Recorded an adjusting entry for the interest accrued on the notes dated December 1, December 16, and December 21. There are no other notes receivable on this date.

Jan. 1. Recorded a reversing entry for the accrued interest.

20. Received $6,060 on note of December 21.

21. Received a $3,500, 12%, 30-day note on account.

Feb. 14. Received $12,260 on note of December 16.

20. Received $3,535 on note of January 21.

29. Received $10,375 on note of December 1.

Instructions:

(1) Open accounts for Interest Receivable (Account No. 116) and Interest Income (Account No. 611), and record a credit balance of $1,410 in the latter account as of November 1 of the current year.
(2) Present entries in general journal form to record the transactions and other data, posting to the two accounts after each entry affecting them.
(3) If the reversing entry had not been recorded as of January 1, indicate how each interest receipt in January and February should be allocated. Submit the data in the following form:

Note (Face Amount)	Total Interest Received	Cr. Interest Receivable	Cr. Interest Income
$ 6,000	$	$	$
12,000			
3,500			
10,000			
Total	$	$	$

(4) Do the February 29 balances of Interest Receivable and Interest Income obtained by use of the reversing entry technique correspond to the balances that would have been obtained by analyzing each receipt?

Problem 8-4B. The following transactions, adjusting entries, and closing entries are related to uncollectible accounts. All were completed during the current fiscal year ended December 31.

Mar. 10. Received 40% of the $10,000 balance owed by Porter Co., a bankrupt, and wrote off the remainder as uncollectible.

Apr. 18. Reinstated the account of Virginia Babb that had been written off three years earlier and received $725 cash in full payment.

June 15. Wrote off the $2,900 balance owed by Vance Corp., which has no assets.

Sept. 5. Reinstated the account of Suburban Cleaners that had been written off in the preceding year and received $925 cash in full payment.

Dec. 30. Wrote off the following accounts as uncollectible (compound entry): Baker and Dodds, $1,120; Flowers, Inc., $2,975; McMann Distributors, $7,100; J. J. Stevens, $420.

31. Based on an analysis of the $420,000 of accounts receivable, it was estimated that $22,700 will be uncollectible. Recorded the adjusting entry.

31. Recorded the entry to close the appropriate account to Income Summary.

Instructions:

(1) Open the following selected accounts, recording the credit balance indicated as of January 1 of the current fiscal year:

115 Allowance for Doubtful Accounts $19,500
313 Income Summary.................................... —
718 Uncollectible Accounts Expense .... —

(2) Record in general journal form the transactions and the adjusting and closing entries described above. After each entry, post to the three selected accounts affected and extend the new balances.
(3) Determine the expected realizable value of the accounts receivable as of December 31.

(4) Assuming that, instead of basing the provision for uncollectible accounts on an analysis of receivables, the adjusting entry on December 31 had been based on an estimated loss of ½ of 1% of the net sales of $4,700,000 for the year, determine the following:
  (a) Uncollectible accounts expense for the year.
  (b) Balance in the allowance account after the adjustment of December 31.
  (c) Expected realizable value of the accounts receivable as of December 31.

CHAPTER 9 | Problem 9-1B. A & W Associates employs the periodic inventory system. Details regarding the inventory of television sets at January 1, purchases invoices during the year, and the inventory count at December 31 are summarized as follows:

Model	Inventory, Jan. 1	Purchases Invoices 1st	2d	3d	Inventory Count, Dec. 31
72B	3 at $119	2 at $125	4 at $130	5 at $133	6
11D	6 at 77	5 at 82	8 at 89	8 at 99	10
19X	4 at 108	4 at 110	5 at 118	6 at 130	4
32C	8 at 88	4 at 79	3 at 85	6 at 92	8
97A	1 at 250	1 at 260	2 at 271	2 at 275	2
42L	6 at 175	2 at 200	2 at 210	5 at 220	7
66P	—	4 at 150	4 at 200	2 at 205	7

Instructions:
  (1) Determine the cost of the inventory on December 31 by the first-in, first-out method. Present data in columnar form, using the following columnar headings. If the inventory of a particular model is composed of an entire lot plus a portion of another lot acquired at a different unit price, use a separate line for each lot.

Model	Quantity	Unit Cost	Total Cost

  (2) Determine the cost of the inventory on December 31 by the last-in, first-out method, following the procedures indicated in instruction (1).
  (3) Determine the cost of the inventory on December 31 by the average cost method, using the columnar headings indicated in instruction (1).

Problem 9-2B. The beginning inventory of soybeans at the Champaign Farmer's Co-Op and data on purchases and sales for a three month harvest period are as follows:

June	1. Inventory.......	30,000 bushels at	$6.90	$207,000
	15. Purchase.......	70,000 bushels at	7.10	497,000
	20. Sale...........	35,000 bushels at	7.50	262,500
	30. Sale...........	20,000 bushels at	7.45	149,000
July	8. Sale...........	10,000 bushels at	7.40	74,000
	16. Purchase.......	40,000 bushels at	6.75	270,000
	17. Sale...........	35,000 bushels at	7.35	257,250
	28. Sale...........	15,000 bushels at	7.30	109,500
Aug.	10. Purchase.......	60,000 bushels at	6.60	396,000
	15. Sale...........	50,000 bushels at	7.20	360,000
	18. Purchase.......	50,000 bushels at	6.50	325,000
	30. Sale...........	40,000 bushels at	7.00	280,000

Instructions:

(1) Record the inventory, purchases, and cost of merchandise sold data in a perpetual inventory record similar to the one illustrated on page 254, using the first-in, first-out method.

(2) Determine the total sales and the total cost of soybeans sold for the period and indicate their effect on the general ledger by two entries in general journal form. Assume that all sales were on account.

(3) Determine the gross profit from sales of soybeans for the period.

(4) Determine the cost of the inventory at August 31, assuming that the periodic system of inventory had been employed and that the inventory cost had been determined by the last-in, first-out method.

(If the working papers correlating with the textbook are not used, omit Problem 9-3B.)

Problem 9-3B. Data on the physical inventory of Bargh Corporation as of June 30, the end of the current fiscal year, are presented in the working papers. The quantity of each commodity on hand has been determined and recorded on the inventory sheet. Unit market prices have also been determined as of June 30 and recorded on the sheet. The inventory is to be determined at cost and also at the lower of cost or market, using the first-in, first-out method. Quantity and cost data from the last purchases invoice of the year and the next-to-the-last purchases invoice are summarized as follows:

	Last Purchases Invoice		Next-to-the-Last Purchases Invoice	
Description	Quantity Purchased	Unit Cost	Quantity Purchased	Unit Cost
B16	40	$ 45	50	$ 44
72C	15	130	10	128
GH4	20	90	25	92
6X1	100	22	50	23
23P	4	305	6	310
85J	300	10	100	10
D22	10	380	5	385
EF9	500	6	500	6
Z91	80	17	50	18
39A	5	250	4	260
14P	30	315	2	320
KC2	70	15	50	15
T11	7	48	5	49
L19	150	8	50	9
92Y	60	16	40	17
A72	50	29	25	28
S29	75	26	60	25
G88	8	210	7	215

Instructions:

Record the appropriate unit costs on the inventory sheet and complete the pricing of the inventory. When there are two different unit costs applicable to a commodity, proceed as follows:

(1) Draw a line through the quantity and insert the quantity and unit cost of the last purchase.

(2) On the following line, insert the quantity and unit cost of the next-to-the-last purchase. The first item on the inventory sheet has been completed as an example.

Problem 9-4B. Selected data on merchandise inventory, purchases, and sales for Hendricks Co. and Fiore Co. are as follows:

Hendricks Co.

	Cost	Retail
Merchandise inventory, June 1	$216,500	$310,000
Transactions during June:		
Purchases	305,700⎫	
Purchases discount	2,450⎭	432,500
Sales...		450,000
Sales returns and allowances		5,000

Fiore Co.

Merchandise inventory, November 1	$606,150
Transactions during November and December:	
Purchases	384,900
Purchases discount	4,900
Sales..	635,500
Sales returns and allowances	4,500
Estimated gross profit rate.......................	40%

Instructions:

(1) Determine the estimated cost of the merchandise inventory of Hendricks Co. on June 30 by the retail method, presenting details of the computations.

(2) Estimate the cost of the merchandise inventory of Fiore Co. on December 31 by the gross profit method, presenting details of the computations.

CHAPTER 10 | Problem 10-1B. The following expenditures and receipts are related to land, land improvements, and buildings acquired for use in a business enterprise. The receipts are identified by an asterisk.

(a)	Cost of real estate acquired as a plant site: Land..........................	$100,000
	Building	40,000
(b)	Delinquent real estate taxes on property assumed by purchaser..............	7,500
(c)	Cost of razing and removing the building	4,650
(d)	Fee paid to attorney for title search....................................	950
(e)	Cost of land fill and grading	5,500
(f)	Architect's and engineer's fees for plans and supervision..................	50,000
(g)	Premium on 1-year insurance policy during construction....................	4,800
(h)	Paid to building contractor for new building	675,000
(i)	Cost of repairing windstorm damage during construction	1,500
(j)	Cost of paving parking lot to be used by customers.......................	9,750
(k)	Cost of trees and shrubbery planted...............................	12,000
(l)	Special assessment paid to city for extension of water main to the property....	1,200
(m)	Cost of repairing vandalism damage during construction	500
(n)	Interest incurred on building loan during construction	22,000
(o)	Cost of floodlights installed on parking lot................................	6,000
(p)	Proceeds from sale of salvage materials from old building	1,100*
(q)	Money borrowed to pay building contractor	600,000*
(r)	Proceeds from insurance company for windstorm damage.................	1,000*
(s)	Refund of premium on insurance policy (g) canceled after 11 months	300*

Instructions:

Assign each expenditure and receipt (indicate receipts by an asterisk) to Land (permanently capitalized), Land Improvements (limited life), Building, or Other Accounts. Identify each item by letter and list the amounts in columnar form, as follows:

Item	Land	Land Improvements	Building	Other Accounts
	$	$	$	$

Problem 10-2B. An item of new equipment, acquired at a cost of $80,000 at the beginning of a fiscal year, has an estimated life of 5 years and an estimated trade-in value of $5,000. The manager requested information (details given in Instruction 1) regarding the effect of alternative methods on the amount of depreciation expense each year. Upon the basis of the data presented to the manager, the declining-balance method was elected.

In the first week of the fifth year, the equipment was traded in for similar equipment priced at $140,000. The trade-in allowance on the old equipment was $15,000, cash of $25,000 was paid, and a note payable was issued for the balance.

Instructions:

(1) Determine the annual depreciation (round to nearest dollar) for each of the estimated 5 years of use, the accumulated depreciation at the end of each year, and the book value of the equipment at the end of each year by (a) the straight-line method, (b) the sum-of-the-years-digits method, and (c) the declining balance method (at twice the straight-line rate). The following columnar headings are suggested for each schedule:

Year	Depreciation Expense	Accumulated Depreciation, End of Year	Book Value, End of Year

(2) For financial reporting purposes, determine the cost basis of the new equipment acquired in the exchange.

(3) Present the debits and credits required, in general journal form, to record the exchange.

(4) What is the cost basis of the new equipment for purposes of computing the amount of depreciation allowable for income tax purposes?

(5) For financial reporting purposes, determine the cost basis of the new equipment acquired in the exchange, assuming that the trade-in allowance was $10,000 instead of $15,000.

(6) Present the debits and credits required, in general journal form, to record the exchange, assuming the data presented in Instruction (5).

(7) What is the cost basis of the new equipment for purposes of computing the amount of depreciation allowable for income tax purposes, assuming the data presented in Instruction (5)?

(If the working papers correlating with the textbook are not used, omit Problem 10-3B.)

Problem 10-3B. Nessinger Press Inc. maintains a subsidiary equipment ledger for the printing equipment and accumulated depreciation accounts in the general ledger. A small portion of the subsidiary ledger, the two controlling accounts, and a general journal are presented in the working papers. The company computes depreciation on each individual item of equipment. Transaction and adjusting entries affecting the printing equipment are described as follows:

1984

Sept. 3. Purchased a power binder (Model 17, Serial No. P73) from Wise Manufacturing Co. on account for $30,000. The estimated life of the asset is 10 years, it is expected to have no residual value, and the straight-line method of depreciation is to be used. (This is the only transaction of the year that directly affected the printing equipment account.)

Dec. 31. Recorded depreciation for the year in subsidiary accounts 125-40 to 125-42, and inserted the new balances. (An assistant recorded the depreciation and the new balances in accounts 125-1 to 125-39.)

31. Journalized and posted the annual adjusting entry for depreciation on printing equipment. The depreciation for the year, recorded in subsidiary accounts 125-1 to 125-39, totaled $48,200, to which was added the depreciation entered in accounts 125-40 to 125-42.

1985

Mar. 30. Purchased a Model B3 rotary press from Carson Press, Inc., priced at $50,000, giving the Model C8 flatbed press (Account No. 125-41) in exchange plus $6,000 cash and a series of eight $3,000 notes payable, maturing at 6-month intervals. The estimated life of the new press is 10 years and it is expected to have a residual value of $5,000. (Recorded depreciation to date in 1985 on item traded in.)

Instructions:

(1) Journalize the transaction of September 3. Post to Printing Equipment in the general ledger and to Account No. 125-42 in the subsidiary ledger.

(2) Journalize the adjusting entry required on December 31 and post to Accumulated Depreciation—Printing Equipment in the general ledger.

(3) Journalize the entries required by the purchase of printing equipment on March 30. Post to Printing Equipment and to Accumulated Depreciation—Printing Equipment in the general ledger and to Account Nos. 125-41 and 125-43 in the subsidiary ledger.

(4) If the rotary press purchased on March 30 had been depreciated by the declining-balance method at twice the straight-line rate, determine the depreciation on this press for the fiscal years ending (a) December 31, 1985 and (b) December 31, 1986.

Problem 10-4B. The following transactions, adjusting entries, and closing entries were completed by Jane Barr Furniture Co. during a 3-year period. All are related to the use of delivery equipment. The declining-balance method (twice the straight-line rate) of depreciation is used.

1984

Jan. 2. Purchased a used delivery truck for $7,200, paying cash.

5. Paid $800 for major repairs to the truck.

July 20. Paid garage $210 for miscellaneous repairs to the truck.

Dec. 31. Recorded depreciation on the truck for the fiscal year. The estimated life of the truck is 4 years, with a trade-in value of $1,200.

31. Closed the appropriate accounts to the income summary account.

1985

July 3. Traded in the used truck for a new truck priced at $15,000, receiving a trade-in allowance of $3,500 and paying the balance in cash. (Record depreciation to date in 1985.)

Dec. 21. Paid garage $250 for miscellaneous repairs to the truck.

Dec. 31. Recorded depreciation on the truck. It has an estimated trade-in value of $2,000 and an estimated life of 5 years.

   31. Closed the appropriate accounts to the income summary account.

1986

Oct. 1. Purchased a new truck for $16,200, paying cash.

   2. Sold the truck purchased in 1985 for $9,000. (Record depreciation to date in 1986.)

Dec. 31. Recorded depreciation on the remaining truck. It has an estimated trade-in value of $2,200 and an estimated life of 6 years.

   31. Closed the appropriate accounts to the income summary account.

Instructions:

(1) Open the following accounts in the ledger:

    122 Delivery Equipment
    123 Accumulated Depreciation—Delivery Equipment
    616 Depreciation Expense—Delivery Equipment
    617 Truck Repair Expense
    812 Gain on Disposal of Plant Assets

(2) Record the transactions and the adjusting and closing entries in general journal form. Post to the accounts and extend the balances after each posting.

CHAPTER 11 | Problem 11-1B. The president of Minish Products is entitled to an annual profit-sharing bonus of 4%. For the current year, income before bonus and income taxes is $480,000 and income taxes are estimated at 40% of income before income taxes.

Instructions:

(1) Determine the amount of bonus, assuming that:

(a) The bonus is based on income before deductions for bonus and income taxes.

(b) The bonus is based on income after deduction for bonus but before deduction for income taxes.

(c) The bonus is based on income after deduction for income taxes but before deduction for bonus.

(d) The bonus is based on income after deduction for both bonus and income taxes.

(2) (a) Which bonus plan would the president prefer? (b) Would this plan always be the president's choice, regardless of Minish Products' income level?

Problem 11-2B. The following information relative to the payroll for the week ended December 30 was obtained from the records of E. Thurmond Inc.:

Salaries:		Deductions:	
Sales salaries	$109,200	Income tax withheld	$23,850
Warehouse salaries	16,280	U.S. savings bonds	2,400
Office salaries	7,020	Group insurance	1,800
	$132,500	FICA tax withheld totals the same amount as the employer's tax.	

Tax rates assumed:
  FICA, 7%
State unemployment (employer only), 3.8%
Federal unemployment, .8%

Instructions:

(1) Assuming that the payroll for the last week of the year is to be paid on December 31, present the following entries:

    (a) December 30, to record the payroll. Of the total payroll for the last week of the year, $92,800 is subject to FICA tax and $10,000 is subject to unemployment compensation taxes.

    (b) December 30, to record the employer's payroll taxes on the payroll to be paid on December 31.

(2) Assuming that the payroll for the last week of the year is to be paid on January 4 of the following year, present the following entries:

    (a) December 30, to record the payroll.

    (b) January 4, to record the employer's payroll taxes on the payroll to be paid on January 4.

Problem 11-4B. Jaffe Company began business on March 1 of last year. Salaries were paid to employees on the last day of each month, and both FICA tax and federal income tax were withheld in the required amounts. All required payroll tax reports were filed and the correct amount of payroll taxes was remitted by the company for the calendar year. Before the Wage and Tax Statements (Form W-2) could be prepared for distribution to employees and filing with the Social Security Administration, the employees' earnings records were inadvertently destroyed.

None of the employees resigned or were discharged during the year, and there were no changes in salary rates. The FICA tax was withheld at the rate of 7% on the first $40,000 of salary. Data on dates of employment, salary rates, and employees' income taxes withheld, which are summarized as follows, were obtained from personnel records and payroll records.

Employee	Date First Employed	Monthly Salary	Monthly Income Tax Withheld
Choi	June 2	$3,500	$ 637.25
Gramm	Mar. 15	4,200	854.50
Kaufman	Dec. 1	3,800	748.15
Marlin	Mar. 1	5,800	1,492.75
Rodriguez	Oct. 16	3,600	652.30
Sherman	Apr. 15	2,800	461.10
Wylie	Mar. 1	5,200	1,261.40

Instructions:

(1) Determine the amounts to be reported on each employee's Wage and Tax Statement (Form W-2) for the year, arranging the data in the following form:

Employee	Gross Earnings	Federal Income Tax Withheld	Earnings Subject to FICA Tax	FICA Tax Withheld

(2) Determine the following employer payroll taxes for the year: (a) FICA; (b) state unemployment compensation at 3.8% on first $7,000; (c) federal unemployment compensation at .8% on first $7,000; (d) total.

(continued)

(3) In a manner similar to the illustrations in this chapter, develop four algorithms to describe the computations required to determine the four amounts in part (1), using the following symbols:

n = Number of payroll periods
g = Monthly gross earnings
f = Monthly federal income tax withheld
G = Total gross earnings
F = Total federal income tax withheld
T = Total earnings subject to FICA tax
S = Total FICA tax withheld

Problem 11-5B. The following items were selected from among the transactions completed by Valentine Co. during the current year:

Mar.   2. Purchased merchandise on account from J. W. Stokes Co., $3,600.
       8. Purchased merchandise on account from York Co., $7,000.
      12. Paid J. W. Stokes Co. for the invoice of March 2, less 3% discount.
Apr.   1. Issued a 60-day, 12% note for $7,000 to York Co. on account.
May   22. Issued a 120-day, non-interest-bearing note for $30,000 to Garden City Bank. The bank discounted the note at the rate of 14%.
      31. Paid York Co. the amount owed on the note of April 1.
Aug.   5. Borrowed $7,500 from First Financial Corporation, issuing a 60-day, 14% note for that amount.
Sept. 19. Paid Garden City Bank the amount due on the note of May 22.
Oct.   4. Paid First Financial Corporation the interest due on the note of August 5 and renewed the loan by issuing a new 30-day, 16% note for $7,500. (Record both the debit and the credit to the notes payable account.)
Nov.   3. Paid First Financial Corporation the amount due on the note of October 4.
      15. Purchased office equipment from Powell Equipment Brokers Inc. for $24,000, paying $3,000 and issuing a series of seven 12% notes for $3,000 each, coming due at 30-day intervals.
Dec. 15. Paid the amount due Powell Equipment Brokers Inc. on the first note in the series issued on November 15.

Instructions:
(1) Record the transactions in general journal form.
(2) Determine the total amount of interest accrued as of December 31 on the six notes owed to Powell Equipment Brokers Inc.
(3) Record the adjusting journal entry for the accrued interest at December 31 and the reversing entry on January 1.
(4) Assume that a single note for $21,000 had been issued on November 15 instead of the series of seven notes, and that its terms required principal payments of $3,000 each 30 days, with interest at 12% on the principal balance before applying the $3,000 payment. Determine the amount that would have been due and payable on December 15.

CHAPTER 12 | **Problem 12-1B.** You are engaged to review the accounting records of Parker Company prior to closing of the revenue and expense accounts as of December 31, the end of the current fiscal year. The following information comes to your attention during the review:
(a) Accounts receivable include $4,625 owed by H. L. Moore Co., a bankrupt. There is no prospect of collecting any of the receivable. The allowance method of accounting for receivables is employed.

(b) No interest has been accrued on a $50,000, 12%, 120-day note receivable, dated November 1 of the current year.

(c) Merchandise inventory on hand at December 31 of the current year has been recorded in the accounts at cost, $227,150. Current market price of the inventory is $236,500.

(d) The prepaid insurance account has a balance of $5,175. At December 31, the unexpired premiums were $2,200.

(e) Since net income for the current year is expected to be considerably less than it was for the preceding year, depreciation on equipment has not been recorded. Depreciation for the year on equipment, determined in a manner consistent with the preceding year, amounts to $43,500.

(f) Land recorded in the accounts at a cost of $50,000 was appraised at $97,500 by two expert appraisers.

(g) The company is being sued for $750,000 by a customer who claims damages for personal injury allegedly caused by a defective product. Company attorneys and outside legal counsel retained by Parker Company feel extremely confident that the company will have no liability for damages resulting from this case.

Instructions:

Journalize any entries required to adjust or correct the accounts, identifying each by letter.

Problem 12-2B. J. A. Horn Inc. makes all sales on the installment basis and recognizes revenue at the point of sale. Condensed income statements and the amounts collected from customers for each of the first three years of operations are as follows:

	First Year	Second Year	Third Year
Sales	$300,000	$340,000	$400,000
Cost of merchandise sold	195,000	224,400	256,000
Gross profit	$105,000	$115,600	$144,000
Operating expenses	57,500	68,500	87,500
Net income	$ 47,500	$ 47,100	$ 56,500
Collected from sales of first year	$ 75,000	$125,000	$100,000
Collected from sales of second year		110,000	180,000
Collected from sales of third year			105,000

Instructions:

Determine the amount of net income that would have been reported in each year if the installment method of recognizing revenue had been employed, ignoring the possible effects of uncollectible accounts on the computation. Present figures in good order.

Problem 12-4B. Cosell Company began construction on three contracts during 1984. The contract prices and construction activities for 1984, 1985, and 1986 were as follows:

Contract	Contract Price	1984 Costs Incurred	1984 Percent Completed	1985 Costs Incurred	1985 Percent Completed	1986 Costs Incurred	1986 Percent Completed
1	$6,000,000	$2,150,000	40%	$3,250,000	60%	—	—
2	3,000,000	525,000	20	1,075,000	40	$1,100,000	40%
3	3,500,000	305,000	10	985,000	30	1,675,000	50

Instructions:

Determine the amount of revenue and income to be recognized from the contracts for each of the following years: 1984, 1985, and 1986. Revenue is to be recognized by the percentage-of-contract-completion method. Present computations in good order.

Problem 12-5B. Carlton Company was organized on January 1, 1983. During its first three years of operations, the company determined uncollectible accounts expense by the direct write-off method, the cost of the merchandise inventory at the end of the period by the first-in, first-out method, and depreciation expense by the straight-line method. The amounts of net income reported and the amounts of the foregoing items for each of the three years were as follows:

	First Year	Second Year	Third Year
Net income reported	$46,200	$60,750	$70,900
Uncollectible accounts expense	950	2,350	4,250
Ending merchandise inventory	50,500	54,750	58,900
Depreciation expense	19,000	19,900	20,900

The firm is considering the possibility of changing to the following methods in determining net income for the fourth and subsequent years: provision for doubtful accounts through the use of an allowance account, last-in, first-out inventory, and declining-balance depreciation at twice the straight-line rate. To consider the probable future effect of these changes on the determination of net income, the management requests that net income of the past three years be recomputed on the basis of the proposed methods. The uncollectible accounts expense, inventory, and depreciation expense for the past three years, computed in accordance with the proposed methods, are as follows:

	First Year	Second Year	Third Year
Uncollectible accounts expense	$ 1,550	$ 2,900	$ 4,100
Ending merchandise inventory	53,750	53,650	60,400
Depreciation expense	38,000	32,000	27,520

Instructions:

Recompute the net income for each of the three years, presenting the figures in an orderly manner.

Problem 12-6B. Frank White owns and manages The Gallery on a full-time basis. He also maintains the accounting records. At the end of the first year of operations, he prepared the following balance sheet and income statement:

The Gallery
Balance Sheet
December 31, 19--

Cash	$ 6,500
Equipment	13,500
Frank White	$20,000

The Gallery
Income Statement
For Year Ended December 31, 19--

Sales		$96,200
Purchases		71,500
Gross profit		$24,700
Operating expenses:		
Salary expense	$16,850	
Rent expense	13,000	
Utilities expense	3,100	
Miscellaneous expense	1,750	
Total operating expenses		34,700
Net loss		$10,000

Because of the large net loss reported by the income statement, White is considering discontinuing operations. Before making a decision, he asks you to review the accounting methods employed and, if material errors are found, to prepare revised statements. The following information is elicited during the course of the review:

(a) The only transactions recorded have been those in which cash was received or disbursed.

(b) The accounts have not been closed for the year.

(c) The business was established on January 2 by an investment of $25,000 in cash by the owner. An additional investment of $5,000 was made in cash on August 10.

(d) The equipment listed on the balance sheet at $10,500 was purchased for cash on January 3. Equipment purchased July 1 for $5,000 in cash was debited to Purchases. Equipment purchased on December 31 for $6,000, for which a 60-day, 12% note was issued, was not recorded.

(e) Depreciation on equipment has not been recorded. The equipment is estimated to have a useful life of 10 years and no salvage value. (Use straight-line method.)

(f) Accounts receivable from customers at December 31 total $7,700.

(g) Uncollectible accounts are estimated at $525.

(h) The merchandise inventory at December 31, as nearly as can be determined, has a cost of $12,750.

(i) Insurance premiums of $950 were debited to Miscellaneous Expense during the year. The unexpired portion at December 31 is $420.

(j) Supplies of $1,000 purchased during the year were debited to Purchases. An estimated $250 of supplies were on hand at December 31.

(k) A total of $4,000 is owed to merchandise creditors on account at December 31.

(l) Rent Expense includes an advance payment of $1,000 for the month of January in the subsequent year.

(m) Salaries owed but not paid on December 31 total $350.

(n) The classification of operating expenses as "selling" and "general" is not considered to be sufficiently important to justify the cost of the analysis.

(o) The proprietor made no withdrawals during the year.

Instructions:

(1) On the basis of the financial statements presented, prepare an unadjusted trial balance, as of December 31, on an eight-column work sheet.

(continued)

(2) Record the adjustments and the corrections in the Adjustments columns. Complete the work sheet by extending the adjusted trial balance amounts directly to the appropriate Income Statement or Balance Sheet column.

(3) Prepare a multiple-step income statement, a capital statement, and a report form balance sheet.

CHAPTER 13 | Problem 13-1B. Lin Chin Company was organized on March 1, 1984, when the price-level index was 140. Capital stock of $98,000 was issued in exchange for cash of $25,000 and land valued at $81,200. The land was subject to property taxes of $8,200 due for the current year. No transactions occurred in the year ended April 30, 1985, and the price-level index at the end of the year was 154. The income statement for the year ended April 30, 1986, disclosed the following:

Sales (made uniformly during the year)................................ $196,800
Cost of merchandise sold (purchased when price index was 162)...... 129,600
Depreciation expense (asset purchased when price index was 156).... 9,672
Other expenses (incurred uniformly during the year) 36,080

The average price index for the year ended April 30, 1986, was 164, and at the end of the year it was 172.

Instructions:

(1) Prepare a conventional balance sheet at April 30, 1985, in report form.

(2) Prepare a constant dollar balance sheet at April 30, 1985, in report form.

(3) Prepare a constant dollar income statement for the year ended April 30, 1986. The purchasing power gain for the year was $2,680.

Problem 13-2B. The monetary items held by Melton Company throughout 1984 consisted of cash and accounts payable. The beginning balances and changes in these monetary items during the year, along with the relevant price-level index for each, are as follows:

	Amount	Price-Level Index
Monetary asset:		
Cash, January 1, 1984	$ 47,500	190
Add sales	175,480	205
Deduct expenses..............................	154,775	205
Cash, December 31, 1984	$ 68,205	220
Monetary liability:		
Accounts payable, January 1, 1984..............	$ 29,640	190
Add purchases on account.....................	135,300	205
Deduct payments on account...................	136,325	205
Accounts payable, December 31, 1984	$ 28,615	220

Instructions:

Calculate the purchasing power gain or loss for the year ended December 31, 1984, using the format shown on page 361.

Problem 13-3B. P. R. Murray & Associates, a professional corporation, was organized with the issuance of $30,000 of capital stock on January 1, 1984, and began operations by leasing office space and office equipment. On April 30, 1984, P. R. Murray & Associates acquired office equipment in exchange for a $25,000, 18%, three-year note payable with interest payable monthly. All services rendered were for cash, and all expenses, except for depreciation, were paid in cash. The conventional income statement for the year ended December 31, 1984, and the conventional balance sheet on December 31, 1984, are as follows:

P. R. Murray & Associates
Income Statement
For Year Ended December 31, 1984

Revenues:		
Professional fees............	$132,300	(Fees were collected uniformly during year; average price-level index was 252)
Expenses:		
Depreciation expense........	$ 3,000	(The office equipment was purchased when the price-level index was 250)
Other operating expenses.......	114,030	(Expenses were paid uniformly during year; average price-level index was 252)
Total expenses	117,030	
Net income..................	$ 15,270	

P. R. Murray & Associates
Balance Sheet
December 31, 1984

Assets		
Cash		$48,270
Office equipment	$25,000	
Less accumulated depreciation	3,000	22,000
Total assets		$70,270

Liabilities and Stockholders' Equity	
Notes payable...	$25,000
Capital stock	30,000
Retained earnings	15,270
Total liabilities and stockholders' equity.........................	$70,270

The average general price-level index for 1984 was 252. During the year, the price-level index was as follows:

January 1, 1984............	240
April 30, 1984	250
December 31, 1984	264

Instructions:

(1) Calculate the purchasing power gain or loss for the year ended December 31, 1984, using the format shown on page 361.

(2) Prepare a constant dollar income statement for the year ended December 31, 1984.

(3) Prepare a constant dollar retained earnings statement for the year ended December 31, 1984.

(4) Prepare a constant dollar balance sheet at December 31, 1984, in report form.

Problem 13-4B. Waller Company was organized on July 1, 1984, by the sale of $80,000 of capital stock for cash. It leased store space and equipment and sold merchandise only for cash. During the year ended June 30, 1985, merchandise costing $248,500 was purchased, $201,650 of the merchandise was sold for $262,145, and operating expenses were $31,261. The conventional income statement for the year ended June 30, 1985, and the conventional balance sheet at June 30, 1985, are as follows:

Waller Company
Income Statement
For Year Ended June 30, 1985

Sales	$262,145
Cost of merchandise sold	201,650
Gross profit	$ 60,495
Operating expenses	31,261
Net income	$ 29,234

Waller Company
Balance Sheet
June 30, 1985

Assets

Cash	$104,895
Merchandise inventory	46,850
Total assets	$151,745

Liabilities and Stockholders' Equity

Accounts payable	$ 42,511
Capital stock	80,000
Retained earnings	29,234
Total liabilities and stockholders' equity	$151,745

The relevant current cost amounts for the preceding financial statement items are as follows:

Cash	$104,895
Merchandise inventory	68,650
Accounts payable	42,511
Capital stock	80,000
Sales	262,145
Cost of merchandise sold	234,150
Operating expenses	31,261

Instructions:

(1) Prepare a current cost income statement for the year ended June 30, 1985.
(2) Prepare a current cost retained earnings statement for the year ended June 30, 1985.
(3) Prepare a current cost balance sheet at June 30, 1985, in report form.

CHAPTER 14 | **Problem 14-1B.** Virginia Fox and June Gove have decided to form a partnership. They have agreed that Fox is to invest $60,000 and that Gove is to invest $90,000. Fox is to devote full time to the business and Gove is to devote one-half time. The following plans for the division of income are being considered:

(a) Equal division.
(b) In the ratio of original investments.
(c) In the ratio of time devoted to the business.
(d) Interest of 12% on original investments and the remainder in the ratio of 3 : 2.
(e) Interest of 12% on original investments, salaries of $30,000 to Fox and $15,000 to Gove, and the remainder equally.
(f) Plan (e), except that Fox is also to be allowed a bonus equal to 20% of the amount by which net income exceeds the salary allowances.

Instructions:

For each plan, determine the division of the net income under each of the following assumptions: net income of $75,000 and net income of $51,000. Present the data in tabular form, using the following columnar headings:

	$75,000		$51,000	
Plan	Fox	Gove	Fox	Gove

Problem 14-2B. On June 1 of the current year, Manny Santos and John Tull form a partnership. Santos agrees to invest $5,000 in cash and merchandise inventory valued at $42,000. Tull invests certain business assets at valuations agreed upon, transfers business liabilities, and contributes sufficient cash to bring his total capital to $50,000. Details regarding the book values of the business assets and liabilities, and the agreed valuations, follow:

	Tull's Ledger Balance	Agreed Valuation
Accounts Receivable	$18,600	$17,500
Allowance for Doubtful Accounts	200	500
Merchandise Inventory	22,700	23,250
Equipment	41,000	22,500
Accumulated Depreciation — Equipment	22,750	
Accounts Payable	6,700	6,700
Notes Payable.....................................	10,000	10,000

The articles of partnership include the following provisions regarding the division of net income: interest of 10% on original investments, salary allowances of $24,000 and $18,000 respectively, and the remainder equally.

Instructions:

(1) Prepare the entries, in general journal form, to record the investments of Santos and Tull in the partnership accounts. *(continued)*

(2) Prepare a balance sheet as of June 1, the date of formation of the partnership.

(3) After adjustments and the closing of revenue and expense accounts at May 31, the end of the first full year of operations, the income summary account has a credit balance of $55,000 and the drawing accounts have debit balances of $21,000 (Santos) and $18,500 (Tull). Present the journal entries to close the income summary account and the drawing accounts at May 31.

(If the working papers correlating with the textbook are not used, omit Problem 14-5B.)

Problem 14-5B. Barbara Coe, Dorothy Due, and Del Eades decided to discontinue business operations as of December 31 and liquidate their partnership. A summary of the various transactions that have occurred thus far in the liquidation is presented in the working papers.

Instructions:

(1) Assuming that the available cash is to be distributed to the partners, complete the tabular summary of liquidation by indicating the distribution of cash to partners.

(2) Present entries, in general journal form, to record (a) sale of assets, (b) division of loss on sale of assets, (c) payment of liabilities, (d) distribution of cash to partners.

(3) Assuming that Due pays $4,500 of her deficiency to the partnership and the remainder is considered to be uncollectible, present entries, in general journal form, to record (a) receipt of part of deficiency, (b) division of loss, (c) distribution of cash to partners.

CHAPTER 15 | Problem 15-2B. The annual dividends declared by Valentine Company during a six-year period are presented in the following table:

Year	Total Dividends	Preferred Dividends Total	Per Share	Common Dividends Total	Per Share
1981	$ 79,000				
1982	127,000				
1983	10,000				
1984	5,000				
1985	6,000				
1986	43,000				

During the entire period, the outstanding stock of the company was composed of 1,000 shares of cumulative, participating, $9 preferred stock, $100 par, and 20,000 shares of common stock, $10 par. The preferred stock contract provides that the preferred stock shall participate in distributions of additional dividends after allowance of a $2 dividend per share on the common stock, the additional dividends to be prorated among common and preferred shares on the basis of the total par of the stock outstanding.

Instructions:

(1) Determine the total dividends and the per share dividends declared on each class of stock for each of the six years, using the headings presented above. There were no dividends in arrears on January 1, 1981.

(2) Determine the average annual dividend per share for each class of stock for the six-year period.

(3) Assuming that the preferred stock was sold at par and common stock was sold at $15 at the beginning of the six-year period, determine the percentage return on initial shareholders' investment, based on the average annual dividend per share (a) for preferred stock and (b) for common stock.

Problem 15-3B. Selected data from the balance sheets of six corporations, identified by letter, are as follows:

A. Common stock, no par, 100,000 shares outstanding $1,050,000
   Deficit   130,000

B. Preferred 12% stock, $50 par . . . . $ 500,000
   Premium on preferred stock   25,000
   Common stock, $5 par 2,000,000
   Discount on common stock   190,000
   Deficit   235,000
   Preferred stock has prior claim to assets on liquidation to the extent of par.

C. Preferred 9% stock, $25 par $1,250,000
   Common stock, $10 par 1,000,000
   Premium on common stock   50,000
   Retained earnings   450,000
   Preferred stock has prior claim to assets on liquidation to the extent of par.

D. Preferred 10% stock, $100 par . . . . $ 750,000
   Premium on preferred stock   90,000
   Common stock, $25 par 2,500,000
   Deficit   65,000
   Preferred stock has prior claim to assets on liquidation to the extent of 110% of par.

E. Preferred $11 stock, $100 par . . . . $ 800,000
   Common stock, $5 par 1,250,000
   Premium on common stock   200,000
   Retained earnings   104,000
   Dividends on preferred stock are in arrears for 2 years, including the dividend passed during the current year. Preferred stock is entitled to par plus unpaid cumulative dividends upon liquidation to the extent of retained earnings.

F. Preferred $2 stock, $25 par . . . . $ 500,000
   Discount on preferred stock   40,000
   Common stock, $10 par 1,500,000
   Deficit   65,000
   Dividends on preferred stock are in arrears for 3 years, including the dividend passed during the current year. Preferred stock is entitled to par plus unpaid cumulative dividends upon liquidation, regardless of the availability of retained earnings.

Instructions:
Determine for each corporation the equity per share of each class of stock, presenting the total stockholders' equity allocated to each class and the number of shares outstanding.

Problem 15-5B. The following selected accounts appear in the ledger of Heston Corporation on July 1, the beginning of the current fiscal year:

Preferred $10 Stock Subscriptions Receivable . . . . $ 68,750
Preferred $10 Stock, $100 par (20,000 shares authorized,
   10,000 shares issued) 1,000,000

Preferred $10 Stock Subscribed (2,500 shares)	$ 250,000
Premium on Preferred Stock	125,000
Common Stock, $10 par (500,000 shares authorized, 300,000 shares issued)	3,000,000
Premium on Common Stock	900,000
Retained Earnings	1,105,000

During the year, the corporation completed a number of transactions affecting the stockholders' equity. They are summarized as follows:

(a) Received balance due on preferred stock subscribed and issued the certificates.

(b) Purchased 10,000 shares of treasury common for $150,000.

(c) Sold 3,000 shares of treasury common for $55,000.

(d) Received subscriptions to 2,000 shares of preferred $10 stock at $105, collecting 25% of the subscription price.

(e) Issued 50,000 shares of common stock at $14, receiving cash.

(f) Sold 2,000 shares of treasury common for $28,000.

Instructions:

(1) Prepare entries in general journal form to record the transactions listed above. Identify each entry by letter. (The use of T accounts for the stockholders' equity accounts will facilitate the determination of the amounts needed in recording some of the transactions and in completing Instruction (2).)

(2) Prepare the stockholders' equity section of the balance sheet as of June 30. Net income for the year amounted to $620,000. Cash dividends declared and paid during the year totaled $300,000.

CHAPTER 16 | Problem 16-1B. Differences in accounting methods between those applied to its accounts and financial reports and those used in determining taxable income yielded the following amounts for the first four years of a corporation's operations:

	First Year	Second Year	Third Year	Fourth Year
Income before income tax	$390,000	$350,000	$460,000	$440,000
Taxable income	340,000	320,000	470,000	460,000

The income tax rate for each of the four years was 45% of taxable income and each year's taxes were promptly paid.

Instructions:

(1) Determine for each year the amounts described in the following columnar captions, presenting the information in the form indicated:

Year	Income Tax Deducted on Income Statement	Income Tax Payments for the Year	Deferred Income Tax Payable	
			Year's Addition (Deduction)	Year-End Balance

(2) Total the first three amount columns.

Problem 16-2B. Selected transactions completed by the Golan Corporation during the current fiscal year are as follows:

Jan. 30. Declared a semiannual dividend of $4 on the 10,000 shares of preferred stock and a 50¢ dividend on the 40,000 shares of $10 par common stock to stockholders of record on February 14, payable on March 1.

Mar. 1. Paid the cash dividends.

Apr. 9. Purchased 5,000 shares of the corporation's own common stock at $21, recording the stock at cost.

May 15. Discovered that a receipt of $950 cash on account from J. M. Jones Co. had been posted in error to the account of J. Jones. The transaction was recorded correctly in the cash receipts journal.

June 23. Sold 1,000 shares of treasury stock at $24, receiving cash.

July 30. Declared semiannual dividends of $4 on the preferred stock and 50¢ on the common stock. In addition, a 4% common stock dividend was declared on the common stock outstanding, to be capitalized at the fair market value of the common stock, which is estimated at $25.

Sep. 10. Paid the cash dividends and issued the certificates for the common stock dividend.

Nov. 8. Discovered that an invoice of $825 for utilities expense for the month of October was debited to Office Supplies.

Dec. 31. Recorded $97,500 additional federal income tax allocable to net income for the year. Of this amount, $73,000 is a current liability and $24,500 is deferred.

31. The board of directors authorized the appropriation necessitated by the holding of treasury stock.

Instructions:

Record the transactions in general journal form.

Problem 16-3B. The retained earnings accounts of SMID Corporation for the current fiscal year ended December 31 are as follows:

ACCOUNT APPROPRIATION FOR PLANT EXPANSION   ACCOUNT NO. 3201

Date		Item	Debit	Credit	Balance	
					Debit	Credit
19--						
Jan.	1	Balance				300,000
Dec.	31	Retained earnings	50,000			250,000

ACCOUNT APPROPRIATION FOR BONDED INDEBTEDNESS   ACCOUNT NO. 3202

Date		Item	Debit	Credit	Balance	
					Debit	Credit
19--						
Jan.	1	Balance				450,000
Dec.	31	Retained earnings		75,000		525,000

ACCOUNT RETAINED EARNINGS   ACCOUNT NO. 3301

| Date | | Item | Debit | Credit | Balance | |
					Debit	Credit
19--						
Jan.	1	Balance				675,000
Dec.	31	Income summary		270,000		945,000
	31	Appropriation for plant expansion		50,000		995,000
	31	Appropriation for bonded indebtedness	75,000			920,000
	31	Cash dividends	100,000			820,000
	31	Stock dividends	150,000			670,000

ACCOUNT CASH DIVIDENDS   ACCOUNT NO. 3302

| Date | | Item | Debit | Credit | Balance | |
					Debit	Credit
19--						
Feb.	10		50,000		50,000	
Aug.	12		50,000		100,000	
Dec.	31	Retained earnings		100,000	—	—

ACCOUNT STOCK DIVIDENDS   ACCOUNT NO. 3303

| Date | | Item | Debit | Credit | Balance | |
					Debit	Credit
19--						
Aug.	12		150,000		150,000	
Dec.	31	Retained earnings		150,000	—	—

Instructions:

Prepare a retained earnings statement for the fiscal year ended December 31.

Problem 16-4B. The following data were selected from the records of M. C. Yates, Inc. for the current fiscal year ended December 31:

Advertising expense	$ 22,100
Delivery expense	9,750
Depreciation expense — office equipment	3,750
Depreciation expense — store equipment	9,900
Gain on condemnation of land	50,000
Income tax:	
Net of amounts allocable to discontinued operations and extraordinary item	49,500
Reduction applicable to loss from disposal of a segment of a business	5,200
Applicable to gain on condemnation of land	15,000
Insurance expense	7,800
Interest expense	18,000
Loss from disposal of a segment of the business	17,200
Merchandise inventory (January 1)	112,500
Merchandise inventory (December 31)	108,800

Miscellaneous general expense		$ 3,050
Miscellaneous selling expense		3,600
Office salaries expense		44,000
Office supplies expense		1,950
Purchases		582,600
Rent expense		30,400
Sales		995,000
Sales commissions expense		45,700
Sales salaries expense		55,500
Store supplies expense		2,700

Instructions:

Prepare a multiple-step income statement, concluding with a section for earnings per share in the form illustrated in this chapter. There were 20,000 shares of common stock (no preferred) outstanding throughout the year. Assume that the condemnation of land is an extraordinary item.

Problem 16-5B. The stockholders' equity accounts of Santos Enterprises, Inc., with balances on January 1 of the current fiscal year, are as follows:

Common Stock, stated value $20 (50,000 shares authorized,		
35,000 shares issued)		$700,000
Paid-In Capital in Excess of Stated Value		105,000
Appropriation for Contingencies		100,000
Appropriation for Treasury Stock		37,500
Retained Earnings		505,500
Treasury Stock (1,500 shares, at cost)		37,500

The following selected transactions occurred during the year:

Jan. 21. Paid cash dividends of $1 per share on the common stock. The dividend had been properly recorded when declared on December 19 of the preceding fiscal year.

Mar. 15. Sold all of the treasury stock for $45,000 cash.

Apr. 9. Issued 5,000 shares of common stock for $130,000 cash.

May 11. Received land with an estimated fair market value of $50,000 from the Gibson City Council as a donation.

June 20. Declared a 5% stock dividend on common stock, to be capitalized at the market price of the stock, which is $30 a share.

July 27. Issued the certificates for the dividend declared on June 20.

Aug. 8. Purchased 2,500 shares of treasury stock for $65,000.

Dec. 20. Declared a $1 per share dividend on common stock.

20. The board of directors authorized the increase of the appropriation for contingencies by $25,000.

20. Increased the appropriation for treasury stock to $65,000.

31. Closed the credit balance of the income summary account, $163,000.

31. Closed the two dividends accounts to Retained Earnings.

Instructions:

(1) Open T accounts for the stockholders' equity accounts listed and enter the balances as of January 1. Also open T accounts for the following: Paid-In Capital from Sale of Treasury Stock; Donated Capital; Stock Dividends Distributable; Stock Dividends; Cash Dividends. *(continued)*

(2) Prepare entries in general journal form to record the selected transactions and post to the eleven selected accounts.

(3) Prepare the stockholders' equity section of the balance sheet as of December 31 of the current fiscal year.

CHAPTER 17 | **Problem 17-1B.** The following transactions were completed by Evans Co., whose fiscal year is the calendar year:

1984

Oct.   1. Issued $5,000,000 of 10-year, 12% callable bonds dated October 1, 1984, for cash of $5,623,160. Interest is payable semiannually on October 1 and April 1.

Dec. 31. Recorded the adjusting entry for interest payable.

      31. Recorded amortization of $9,421 premium on the bonds, using the interest method.

      31. Closed the interest expense account.

1985

Jan.   1. Reversed the adjusting entry for interest payable.

Apr.   1. Paid the semiannual interest on the bonds.

Oct.   1. Paid the semiannual interest on the bonds.

Dec. 31. Recorded the adjusting entry for interest payable.

      31. Recorded amortization of $39,592 premium on the bonds, using the interest method.

      31. Closed the interest expense account.

1991

Oct.   1. Recorded the redemption of the bonds, which were called at 104. The balance in the bond premium account is $253,882 after the payment of interest and amortization of premium have been recorded. (Record the redemption only.)

Instructions:

(1) Record the foregoing transactions in general journal form.

(2) Indicate the amount of the interest expense in (a) 1984 and (b) 1985.

(3) Determine the effective interest rate (divide the interest expense for 1984 by the bond carrying amount at time of issuance) and express as an annual rate.

(4) Determine the carrying amount of the bonds as of December 31, 1985.

Problem 17-2B. On October 1, 1984, Meltzer Corporation issued $4,000,000 of 10-year, 10% bonds at an effective interest rate of 11%. Interest on the bonds is payable semiannually on April 1 and October 1. The fiscal year of the company is the calendar year.

Instructions:

(1) Present the entry, in general journal form, to record the amount of the cash proceeds from the sale of the bonds. Use the tables of present values in Appendix D to compute the cash proceeds, rounding to the nearest dollar.

(2) Present the entries in general journal form to record the following:

   (a) The adjusting entry for the accrued interest payable on December 31, 1984.

   (b) The amortization of the bond discount on December 31, 1984, using the interest method.

(c) The reversing entry on January 1, 1985, for the interest payable.
(d) The first semiannual interest payment on April 1, 1985.
(e) The amortization of the bond discount on April 1, 1985, using the interest method.
(f) The amortization of the bond discount on October 1, 1985, using the interest method.

(3) Present the entries for Instruction (2), parts (b) and (f), using the straight-line method of discount amortization.

(4) Determine the total interest expense for 1984 for (a) the interest method of discount amortization and (b) the straight-line method of discount amortization. (c) Will the annual interest expense using the interest method of discount amortization always be less than the annual interest expense using the straight-line method of discount amortization?

Problem 17-3B. During 1984 and 1985, Mitchum Company completed the following transactions relating to its $3,000,000 issue of 30-year, 11% bonds dated September 1, 1984. Interest is payable on March 1 and September 1. The corporation's fiscal year is the calendar year.

1984

Sept. 1. Sold the bond issue for $2,798,400 cash.
Dec. 31. Recorded the adjusting entry for interest payable.
      31. Recorded amortization of $2,240 of bond discount, using the straight-line method.
      31. Deposited $60,000 cash in a bond sinking fund.
      31. Appropriated $100,000 of retained earnings for bonded indebtedness.
      31. Closed the interest expense account.

1985

Jan. 1. Reversed the adjustment for interest payable.
Feb. 20. Purchased various securities with sinking fund cash, cost $55,600.
Mar. 1. Paid the semiannual interest on the bonds.
Sept. 1. Paid the semiannual interest on the bonds.
Nov. 30. Recorded the receipt of $6,670 of income on sinking fund securities, depositing the cash in the sinking fund.
Dec. 31. Recorded the adjusting entry for interest payable.
      31. Recorded amortization of $6,720 of bond discount, using the straight-line method.
      31. Deposited $65,000 cash in the sinking fund.
      31. Appropriated $100,000 of retained earnings for bonded indebtedness.
      31. Closed the interest expense account.

Instructions:

(1) Record the foregoing transactions in general journal form.
(2) Prepare a columnar table, using the following headings, and list the information for each of the two years.

					Account Balances at End of Year		
					Sinking Fund		
	Bond Interest Expense	Sinking Fund Income	Bonds	Discount			Appropriation For Bonded
Year	for Year	for Year	Payable	on Bonds	Cash	Investments	Indebtedness

Problem 17-5B. The following transactions relate to certain securities acquired by Hardigree Company, whose fiscal year ends on December 31:

1984

Feb. 10. Purchased 2,000 common shares of Doyle Corporation at 35 plus commission and other costs of $350.

May 15. Received the regular cash dividend of 80¢ a share on Doyle Corporation stock.

Aug. 1. Purchased $400,000 of Moody Company 20-year, 9% coupon bonds dated August 1, 1984, directly from the issuing company for $388,000.

Nov. 15. Received the regular cash dividend of 80¢ a share plus an extra dividend of 10¢ a share on Doyle Corporation stock.

Dec. 31. Recorded the adjustment for interest receivable on the Moody Company bonds.

31. Recorded the amortization of discount of $250 on the Moody Company bonds, using the straight-line method.

(Assume that all intervening transactions and adjustments have been recorded properly, and that the number of bonds and shares of stocks owned have not changed from December 31, 1984, to December 31, 1988.)

1989

Jan. 1. Reversed the adjustment of December 31, 1988, for interest receivable on the Moody Company bonds.

Feb. 1. Deposited the coupons for semiannual interest on the Moody Company bonds.

May 1. Sold one half of the Moody Company bonds at 98 plus accrued interest. The broker deducted $1,240 for commission, etc., remitting the balance. Before the sale was recorded, $100 of discount on one half of the bonds was amortized, increasing the carrying amount of those bonds to $195,425.

15. Received the regular cash dividend of 80¢ a share and a 5% stock dividend on the Doyle Corporation stock.

Aug. 1. Deposited coupons for semiannual interest on the Moody Company bonds.

Oct. 8. Sold 750 shares of Doyle Corporation stock at 36. The broker deducted commission and other costs of $640, remitting the balance.

Nov. 15. Received a cash dividend at the new rate of 84¢ a share on the Doyle Corporation stock.

Dec. 31. Recorded the adjustment for interest receivable on the Moody Company bonds.

31. Recorded the amortization of discount of $300 on the Moody Company bonds.

Instructions:

(1) Record the foregoing transactions in general journal form.

(2) Determine the amount of interest earned on the bonds in 1984.

(3) Determine the amount of interest earned on the bonds in 1989.

CHAPTER 18 | **Problem 18-1B.** On May 1 of the current year, Pena Company purchased 90% of the stock of Shea Company. On the same date, Pena Company loaned Shea Company $50,000 on a 120-day note. The data reported on their separate balance sheets immediately after the acquisition and loan are as follows:

Assets	Pena Company	Shea Company
Cash	$ 41,500	$ 22,750
Accounts receivable (net)............................	48,250	35,000
Notes receivable.....................................	50,000	—
Inventories	164,250	52,250
Investment in Shea Company	290,000	—
Equipment (net)	360,000	215,000
	$954,000	$325,000

Liabilities and Stockholders' Equity		
Accounts payable.....................................	$175,000	$ 19,500
Notes payable..	—	50,000
Common stock, $10 par	500,000	—
Common stock, $20 par	—	200,000
Retained earnings	279,000	55,500
	$954,000	$325,000

The fair value of Shea Company's assets corresponds to the book carrying amounts, except for equipment, which is valued at $250,000 for consolidation purposes.

Instructions:

(1) Prepare a work sheet for a consolidated balance sheet as of May 1 of the current year.

(2) Prepare in report form a consolidated balance sheet as of May 1, omitting captions for current assets, plant assets, etc.

Problem 18-2B. On June 30, Pile Company purchased 80% of the outstanding stock of Salem Company for $600,000. Balance sheet data for the two corporations immediately after the transaction are as follows:

Assets	Pile Company	Salem Company
Cash and marketable securities	$ 96,700	$ 51,750
Accounts receivable	110,500	98,600
Allowance for doubtful accounts	(9,500)	(2,200)
Inventories	475,000	192,400
Investment in Salem Company	600,000	—
Land	100,000	35,000
Building and equipment	760,000	495,000
Accumulated depreciation	(210,000)	(110,000)
	$1,922,700	$760,550

Liabilities and Stockholders' Equity		
Accounts payable...................................	$ 152,500	$ 71,650
Income tax payable.................................	41,500	9,900
Bonds payable (due in 2000)	500,000	—
Common stock, $20 par	900,000	—
Common stock, $25 par	—	500,000
Retained earnings	328,700	179,000
	$1,922,700	$760,550

Instructions:

(1) Prepare a work sheet for a consolidated balance sheet as of the date of acquisition.

(2) Prepare in report form a detailed consolidated balance sheet as of the date of acquisition. The fair value of Salem Company's assets are deemed to correspond to the book carrying amounts, except for land, which is to be increased by $50,000 for consolidation purposes.

(3) Assuming that Salem Company earns net income of $95,000 and pays cash dividends of $50,000 during the ensuing fiscal year and that Pile Company records its share of the earnings and dividends, determine the following as of the end of the year:

(a) The net amount added to Pile Company's investment account as a result of Salem Company's earnings and dividends.

(b) The amount of the minority interest.

Problem 18-5B. On January 1 of the current year, Penn Corporation exchanged 10,000 shares of its $20 par common stock for 25,000 shares (the entire issue) of Shay Company's $10 par common stock. Later in the year, Shay purchased from Penn Corporation $125,000 of its $250,000 issue of bonds payable, at face amount. All of the items for "interest" appearing on the balance sheets and income statements of both corporations are related to the bonds.

During the year, Penn Corporation sold merchandise with a cost of $140,000 to Shay Company for $200,000, all of which was sold by Shay Company before the end of the year.

Penn Corporation has correctly recorded the income and dividends reported for the year by Shay Company. Data for the income statements of both companies for the current year are as follows:

	Penn Corporation	Shay Company
Revenues:		
Sales	$1,870,000	$615,000
Income of subsidiary	115,000	—
Interest income	—	3,125
	$1,985,000	$618,125
Expenses:		
Cost of merchandise sold	$1,199,600	$320,500
Selling expenses	180,000	57,525
General expenses	135,000	37,000
Interest expense	12,500	—
Income tax	155,100	88,100
	$1,682,200	$503,125
Net income	$ 302,800	$115,000

Data for the balance sheets of both companies as of the end of the current year are as follows:

Assets	Penn Corporation	Shay Company
Cash	$ 96,400	$ 37,150
Accounts receivable (net).	128,500	62,800
Dividends receivable.	12,500	—
Interest receivable	—	3,125
Inventories	549,250	199,000
Investment in Shay Co. (25,000 shares)	505,800	—
Investment in Penn Corp. bonds (at face amount)	—	125,000
Plant and equipment	917,650	312,000
Accumulated depreciation	(210,100)	(164,075)
	$2,000,000	$575,000

Liabilities and Stockholders' Equity		
Accounts payable.	$ 106,900	$ 48,600
Income tax payable	17,500	8,100
Dividends payable	20,000	12,500
Interest payable	6,250	—
Bonds payable, 10% (due in 1997)	250,000	—
Common stock, $20 par	1,000,000	—
Common stock, $10 par	—	250,000
Premium on common stock	40,000	80,000
Retained earnings	559,350	175,800
	$2,000,000	$575,000

Instructions:
(1) Determine the amounts to be eliminated from the following items in preparing the consolidated balance sheet as of December 31 of the current year: (a) dividends receivable and dividends payable; (b) interest receivable and interest payable; (c) investment in Shay Co. and stockholders' equity; (d) investment in Penn Corp. bonds and bonds payable.
(2) Prepare a detailed consolidated balance sheet in report form.
(3) Determine the amount to be eliminated from the following items in preparing the consolidated income statement for the current year ended December 31: (a) sales and cost of merchandise sold; (b) interest income and interest expense; (c) income of subsidiary and net income.
(4) Prepare a single-step consolidated income statement, inserting the earnings per share in parentheses on the same line with net income.
(5) Determine the amount of the reduction in consolidated inventories, net income, and retained earnings if Shay Company's inventory had included $50,000 of the merchandise purchased from Penn Corporation.

Problem 18-6B. Allen Company sells merchandise to and purchases merchandise from various Canadian and Mexican companies. These transactions are settled in the foreign currency. The following selected transactions were completed during the current fiscal year:

Feb. 1 Purchased merchandise on account from Bianchi Company, net 30, $20,000 Canadian; exchange rate, $.85 per Canadian dollar.

Mar. 2 Issued check for amount owed to Bianchi Company; exchange rate, $.86 per Canadian dollar.

Apr. 15 Sold merchandise on account to Ruiz Company, net 30, 300,000 pesos; exchange rate, $.045 per Mexican peso.

May 15 Received cash from Ruiz Company; exchange rate, $.046 per Mexican peso.

June 10 Purchased merchandise on account from Blume Company, net 30, $30,000 Canadian; exchange rate, $.86 per Canadian dollar.

July 9 Issued check for amount owed to Blume Company; exchange rate, $.85 per Canadian dollar.

Sept. 30 Sold merchandise on account to Mendoza Company, net 30, 200,000 pesos; exchange rate, $.044 per Mexican peso.

Oct. 30 Received cash from Mendoza Company; exchange rate, $.043 per Mexican peso.

Dec. 20 Sold merchandise on account to Adams Company, net 30, $30,000 Canadian; exchange rate, $.85 per Canadian dollar.

21 Purchased merchandise on account from Orta Company, net 30, 250,000 pesos; exchange rate, $.047 per Mexican peso.

31 Recorded unrealized currency exchange gain and/or loss on transactions of December 20 and 21. Exchange rates on December 31: $.84 per Canadian dollar; $.046 per Mexican peso.

Instructions:

(1) Present entries in general journal form to record the transactions and adjusting entries for the year.

(2) Present entries in general journal form to record the payment of the purchase of December 21, on January 20, when the exchange rate was $.048 per Mexican peso, and the receipt of cash from the sale of December 20, on January 23, when the exchange rate was $.83 per Canadian dollar.

CHAPTER 19 | **Problem 19-1B.** The comparative balance sheet of Meyers Corporation at June 30 of the current year and the preceding year is as follows:

Assets	Current Year	Preceding Year
Cash	$ 47,300	$ 45,300
Accounts receivable (net)	59,400	58,500
Merchandise inventory	77,250	91,850
Prepaid expenses	5,600	4,950
Plant assets	375,000	310,000
Accumulated depreciation—plant assets	(117,500)	(125,000)
	$447,050	$385,600

Liabilities and Stockholders' Equity		
Accounts payable	$ 55,250	$ 38,800
Mortgage note payable	—	50,000
Common stock, $25 par	250,000	200,000
Premium on common stock	35,000	25,000
Retained earnings	106,800	71,800
	$447,050	$385,600

Additional data obtained from the income statement and from an examination of the noncurrent asset, noncurrent liability, and stockholders' equity accounts in the ledger are as follows:

(a) Net income, $75,000.
(b) Depreciation reported on the income statement, $27,500.
(c) An addition to the building was constructed at a cost of $100,000, and fully depreciated equipment costing $35,000 was discarded, no salvage being realized.
(d) The mortgage note payable was not due until 1989, but the terms permitted earlier payment without penalty.
(e) 2,000 shares of common stock were issued at 30 for cash.
(f) Cash dividends declared, $40,000.

Instructions:

Prepare a statement of changes in financial position (working capital concept), including a section on changes in components of working capital.

Problem 19-2B. The comparative balance sheet of Brown Corporation at December 31 of the current year and the preceding year is as follows:

Assets	Current Year	Preceding Year
Cash	$ 55,100	$ 42,500
Trade receivables (net)	91,350	61,150
Inventories	104,500	109,500
Prepaid expenses	3,600	2,700
Land	50,000	50,000
Buildings	325,000	245,000
Accumulated depreciation—buildings	(120,600)	(110,400)
Machinery and equipment	255,000	255,000
Accumulated depreciation—machinery and equipment	(92,000)	(65,000)
Patents	35,000	40,000
	$706,950	$630,450

Liabilities and Stockholders' Equity		
Accounts payable (merchandise creditors)	$ 61,150	$ 75,000
Dividends payable	15,000	10,000
Salaries payable	6,650	7,550
Mortgage note payable, due 1990	50,000	—
Bonds payable	—	75,000
Common stock, $20 par	300,000	250,000
Premium on common stock	100,000	75,000
Retained earnings	174,150	137,900
	$706,950	$630,450

An examination of the income statement and the accounting records revealed the following additional information applicable to the current year:

(a) Net income, $96,250.
(b) Depreciation expense reported on the income statement: buildings, $10,200; machinery and equipment, $27,000.

(c) Patent amortization reported on the income statement, $5,000.
(d) A mortgage note for $50,000 was issued in connection with the construction of a building costing $80,000; the remainder was paid in cash.
(e) 2,500 shares of common stock were issued at 30 in exchange for the bonds payable.
(f) Cash dividends declared, $60,000.

Instructions:

Prepare a statement of changes in financial position (working capital concept), including a section for changes in components of working capital.

Problem 19-3B. The comparative balance sheet of Brown Corporation and other data necessary for the analysis of the corporation's funds flow are presented in Problem 19-2B.

Instructions:

Prepare a statement of changes in financial position (cash concept), including a summary of the change in cash balance.

Problem 19-4B. The comparative balance sheet of D. A. Ruiz Inc., at December 31 of the current year and the preceding year, and the noncurrent asset accounts, the noncurrent liability accounts, and the stockholders' equity accounts for the current year, are as follows:

Assets	Current Year	Preceding Year
Cash	$ 58,000	$ 64,500
Trade receivables (net)	103,325	91,725
Inventories	208,100	188,000
Prepaid expenses	6,850	7,100
Investments	—	50,000
Land	65,000	65,000
Buildings	285,000	185,000
Accumulated depreciation—buildings	(76,400)	(69,000)
Equipment	480,500	410,500
Accumulated depreciation—equipment	(143,500)	(129,000)
	$986,875	$863,825

Liabilities and Stockholders' Equity		
Accounts payable (merchandise creditors)	$ 60,075	$ 77,600
Income tax payable	5,500	2,800
Notes payable	105,000	—
Discount on long-term notes payable	(4,625)	—
Common stock, $20 par	624,000	600,000
Premium on common stock	67,000	55,000
Appropriation for contingencies	35,000	25,000
Retained earnings	94,925	103,425
	$986,875	$863,825

ACCOUNT INVESTMENTS   ACCOUNT NO.

Date		Item	Debit	Credit	Balance Debit	Balance Credit
19-- Jan.	1	Balance			50,000	
June	29	Realized $57,500 cash from sale		50,000	—	—

ACCOUNT LAND   ACCOUNT NO.

Date		Item	Debit	Credit	Balance Debit	Balance Credit
19-- Jan.	1	Balance			65,000	

ACCOUNT BUILDINGS   ACCOUNT NO.

Date		Item	Debit	Credit	Balance Debit	Balance Credit
19-- Jan.	1	Balance			185,000	
Apr.	1	Acquired with notes payable	100,000		285,000	

ACCOUNT ACCUMULATED DEPRECIATION—BUILDINGS   ACCOUNT NO.

Date		Item	Debit	Credit	Balance Debit	Balance Credit
19-- Jan.	1	Balance				69,000
Dec.	31	Depreciation for year		7,400		76,400

ACCOUNT EQUIPMENT   ACCOUNT NO.

Date		Item	Debit	Credit	Balance Debit	Balance Credit
19-- Jan.	1	Balance			410,500	
Feb.	8	Discarded, no salvage		35,000		
July	2	Purchased for cash	60,000			
Nov.	1	Purchased for cash	45,000		480,500	

ACCOUNT ACCUMULATED DEPRECIATION—EQUIPMENT   ACCOUNT NO.

Date		Item	Debit	Credit	Balance Debit	Balance Credit
19-- Jan.	1	Balance				129,000
Feb.	8	Equipment discarded	35,000			
Dec.	31	Depreciation for year		49,500		143,500

ACCOUNT LONG-TERM NOTES PAYABLE   ACCOUNT NO.

| Date | | Item | Debit | Credit | Balance | |
					Debit	Credit
19--						
Apr.	1	Issued 10-year notes		105,000		105,000

ACCOUNT DISCOUNT ON LONG-TERM NOTES PAYABLE   ACCOUNT NO.

| Date | | Item | Debit | Credit | Balance | |
					Debit	Credit
19--						
Apr.	1	Notes issued	5,000		5,000	
Dec.	31	Amortization		375	4,625	

ACCOUNT COMMON STOCK, $20 PAR   ACCOUNT NO.

| Date | | Item | Debit | Credit | Balance | |
					Debit	Credit
19--						
Jan.	1	Balance				600,000
July	10	Stock dividend		24,000		624,000

ACCOUNT PREMIUM ON COMMON STOCK   ACCOUNT NO.

| Date | | Item | Debit | Credit | Balance | |
					Debit	Credit
19--						
Jan.	1	Balance				55,000
July	10	Stock dividend		12,000		67,000

ACCOUNT APPROPRIATION FOR CONTINGENCIES   ACCOUNT NO.

| Date | | Item | Debit | Credit | Balance | |
					Debit	Credit
19--						
Jan.	1	Balance				25,000
Dec.	31	Appropriation		10,000		35,000

ACCOUNT RETAINED EARNINGS   ●   ACCOUNT NO.

| Date | | Item | Debit | Credit | Balance | |
					Debit	Credit
19--						
Jan.	1	Balance				103,425
July	10	Stock dividend	36,000			
Dec.	31	Net income		127,500		
	31	Cash dividends	90,000			
	31	Appropriated	10,000			94,925

Instructions:

Prepare a statement of changes in financial position (working capital concept), including a section for changes in components of working capital.

Problem 19-5B. The comparative balance sheet of D. A. Ruiz Inc. and other data necessary for the analysis of the corporation's funds flow are presented in Problem 19-4B.

Instructions:

Prepare a statement of changes in financial position (cash concept), including a summary of the change in cash balance.

CHAPTER 20 | **Problem 20-1B.** Data pertaining to the current position of Carol Cavitt and Company are as follows:

Cash	$120,000
Marketable securities	50,000
Accounts and notes receivable (net)	130,000
Merchandise inventory	275,000
Prepaid expenses	25,000
Accounts payable	165,000
Notes payable (short-term)	100,000
Accrued liabilities	35,000

Instructions:

(1) Compute (a) working capital, (b) current ratio, and (c) acid-test ratio.
(2) List the following captions on a sheet of paper:

Transaction	Working Capital	Current Ratio	Acid-Test Ratio

Compute the working capital, current ratio, and acid-test ratio after each of the following transactions, and record the results in the appropriate columns. Consider each transaction separately and assume that only that transaction affects the data given above.

(a) Declared a cash dividend, $50,000.
(b) Issued additional shares of stock for cash, $100,000.
(c) Purchased merchandise on account, $40,000.
(d) Paid accounts payable, $60,000.
(e) Borrowed cash from bank on a long-term note, $50,000.
(f) Paid cash for office supplies, $25,000.
(g) Received cash on account, $75,000.
(h) Paid notes payable, $100,000.
(i) Declared a common stock dividend on common stock, $150,000.
(j) Sold marketable securities, $50,000.

Problem 20-3B. For 1985, Chapman Company initiated an extensive sales promotion campaign that included the expenditure of an additional $75,000 for advertising. At the end of the year, Susan Chapman, the president, is presented with the condensed comparative income statement shown at the top of page 896.

Instructions:

(1) Prepare a comparative income statement for the two-year period, presenting an analysis of each item in relationship to net sales for each of the years.
(2) To the extent the data permit, comment on the significant relationships revealed by the vertical analysis prepared in (1).

Chapman Company
Comparative Income Statement
For Years Ended December 31, 1985 and 1984

	1985	1984
Sales	$845,625	$689,520
Sales returns and allowances	20,625	9,520
Net sales	$825,000	$680,000
Cost of merchandise sold	528,000	442,000
Gross profit	$297,000	$238,000
Selling expenses	$198,000	$102,000
General expenses	36,300	40,800
Total operating expenses	$234,300	$142,800
Operating income	$ 62,700	$ 95,200
Other expense	3,300	3,400
Income before income tax	$ 59,400	$ 91,800
Income tax	14,025	23,800
Net income	$ 45,375	$ 68,000

Problem 20-5B. The comparative financial statements of R. C. Jain Company are as follows. On December 31, 1985 and 1984, the market price of R. C. Jain Company common stock was $60 and $47 respectively.

R. C. Jain Company
Comparative Income Statement
For Years Ended December 31, 1985 and 1984

	1985	1984
Sales	$4,590,000	$3,272,500
Sales returns and allowances	90,000	72,500
Net sales	$4,500,000	$3,200,000
Cost of merchandise sold	3,060,000	2,080,000
Gross profit	$1,440,000	$1,120,000
Selling expenses	$ 585,000	$ 464,000
General expenses	292,500	224,000
Total operating expenses	$ 877,500	$ 688,000
Operating income	$ 562,500	$ 432,000
Other income	22,500	19,200
	$ 585,000	$ 451,200
Other expense (interest)	129,200	110,000
Income before income tax	$ 455,800	$ 341,200
Income tax	210,800	150,200
Net income	$ 245,000	$ 191,000

R. C. Jain Company
Comparative Retained Earnings Statement
For Years Ended December 31, 1985 and 1984

	1985	1984
Retained earnings, January 1	$723,000	$602,000
Add net income for year	245,000	191,000
Total	$968,000	$793,000
Deduct dividends:		
On preferred stock	$ 40,000	$ 40,000
On common stock	45,000	30,000
Total	$ 85,000	$ 70,000
Retained earnings, December 31	$883,000	$723,000

R. C. Jain Company
Comparative Balance Sheet
December 31, 1985 and 1984

Assets	1985	1984
Current assets:		
Cash	$ 225,000	$ 175,000
Marketable securities	100,000	—
Accounts receivable (net)	425,000	325,000
Merchandise inventory	720,000	480,000
Prepaid expenses	30,000	20,000
Total current assets	$1,500,000	$1,000,000
Long term investments	250,000	225,000
Plant assets	2,093,000	1,948,000
Total assets	$3,843,000	$3,173,000
Liabilities		
Current liabilities	$ 750,000	$ 650,000
Long-term liabilities:		
Mortgage note payable, 12%, due 1989	$ 410,000	—
Bonds payable, 10%, due 1995	800,000	$ 800,000
Total long-term liabilities	$1,210,000	$ 800,000
Total liabilities	$1,960,000	$1,450,000
Stockholders' Equity		
Preferred $4 stock, $50 par	$ 500,000	$ 500,000
Common stock, $20 par	500,000	500,000
Retained earnings	883,000	723,000
Total stockholders' equity	$1,883,000	$1,723,000
Total liabilities and stockholders' equity	$3,843,000	$3,173,000

Instructions:

Determine for 1985 the following ratios, turnovers, and other measures, presenting the figures used in your computations:

(1) Working capital.
(2) Current ratio.
(3) Acid-test ratio.
(4) Accounts receivable turnover.
(5) Number of days' sales in receivables.
(6) Merchandise inventory turnover.
(7) Number of days' sales in merchandise inventory.
(8) Ratio of plant assets to long-term liabilities.
(9) Ratio of stockholders' equity to liabilities.
(10) Ratio of net sales to assets.
(11) Rate earned on total assets.
(12) Rate earned on stockholders' equity.
(13) Rate earned on common stockholders' equity.
(14) Earnings per share on common stock.
(15) Price-earnings ratio.
(16) Dividend yield.
(17) Number of times interest charges earned.
(18) Number of times preferred dividends earned.

CHAPTER 21 | Problem 21-1B. Lawson Appliances operates two sales departments: Department A for small appliances, such as radios and televisions, and Department B for large appliances, such as refrigerators and washing machines. The trial balance on page 899 was prepared at the end of the current fiscal year, after all adjustments, including the adjustments for merchandise inventory, were recorded and posted:

Merchandise inventories at the beginning of the year were as follows: Department A, $26,400; Department B, $62,800.

The bases to be used in apportioning expenses, together with other essential information, are as follows:

Sales salaries expense—payroll records: Department A, $12,900; Department B, $43,600.

Advertising expense—usage: Department A, $5,600; Department B, $8,750.

Depreciation expense—average cost of equipment. Balances at beginning of year: Department A, $18,600; Department B, $59,200. Balances at end of year: Department A, $22,200; Department B, $70,000.

Store supplies expense—requisitions: Department A, $1,200; Department B, $1,500.

Office salaries expense—Department A, 30%; Department B, 70%.

Rent expense and heating and lighting expense—floor space: Department A, 4,800 sq. ft.; Department B, 7,200 sq. ft.

Property tax expense and insurance expense—average cost of equipment plus average cost of merchandise inventory.

Uncollectible accounts expense, miscellaneous selling expense, and miscellaneous general expense—volume of gross sales.

Instructions:

Prepare an income statement departmentalized through income from operations.

Lawson Appliances
Trial Balance
July 31, 19--

Cash	29,300	
Accounts Receivable	84,500	
Merchandise Inventory — Department A	20,300	
Merchandise Inventory — Department B	70,500	
Prepaid Insurance	600	
Store Supplies	550	
Store Equipment	92,200	
Accumulated Depreciation — Store Equipment		21,280
Accounts Payable		17,700
Income Tax Payable		5,525
Common Stock		100,000
Retained Earnings		98,491
Cash Dividends	10,000	
Income Summary	89,200	90,800
Sales — Department A		197,080
Sales — Department B		560,920
Sales Returns and Allowances — Department A	2,780	
Sales Returns and Allowances — Department B	6,800	
Purchases — Department A	109,884	
Purchases — Department B	369,232	
Sales Salaries Expense	56,500	
Advertising Expense	14,350	
Depreciation Expense — Store Equipment	6,100	
Store Supplies Expense	2,700	
Miscellaneous Selling Expense	4,450	
Office Salaries Expense	48,000	
Rent Expense	18,000	
Heating and Lighting Expense	16,800	
Property Tax Expense	6,200	
Insurance Expense	2,400	
Uncollectible Accounts Expense	2,200	
Miscellaneous General Expense	3,150	
Interest Expense	3,000	
Income Tax	22,100	
	1,091,796	1,091,796

Problem 21-2B. Kearney Fashions has 16 departments. Those with the least sales volume are Department 13 and Department 15, which were established about eighteen months ago on a trial basis. The board of directors believes that it is now time to consider the retention or the termination of these two departments. The following adjusted trial balance as of August 31, the end of the first month of the current fiscal year, is severely condensed. August is considered to be a typical month. The income tax accrual has no bearing on the decision and is excluded from consideration.

Kearney Fashions
Trial Balance
August 31, 19--

Current Assets.	236,200	
Plant Assets.	672,400	
Accumulated Depreciation—Plant Assets		168,100
Current Liabilities		118,100
Common Stock		200,000
Retained Earnings		403,304
Cash Dividends.	30,000	
Sales—Department 13		32,500
Sales—Department 15		21,400
Sales—Other Departments		948,600
Cost of Merchandise Sold—Department 13	21,125	
Cost of Merchandise Sold—Department 15	14,980	
Cost of Merchandise Sold—Other Departments.	569,160	
Direct Expenses—Department 13	8,125	
Direct Expenses—Department 15	7,490	
Direct Expenses—Other Departments	227,664	
Indirect Expenses.	94,860	
Interest Expense.	10,000	
	1,892,004	1,892,004

Instructions:

(1) Prepare an income statement for August, departmentalized through departmental margin.
(2) State your recommendations concerning the retention of Departments 13 and 15, giving reasons.

Problem 21-5B. Stockman Products opened a branch office in Trenton on March 1 of the current year. Summaries of transactions, adjustments, and year-end closing for branch operations of the ten months ended December 31 are as follows:

(a) Received cash advance, $65,000, and merchandise (billed at cost), $86,750, from the home office.
(b) Purchased equipment on account, $48,800.
(c) Purchased merchandise on account, $61,340.
(d) Sales on account, $76,260; cash sales, $32,140.
(e) Received cash from customers on account, $61,100.
(f) Paid creditors on account, $98,800.
(g) Sent $25,000 cash to home office.
(h) Paid operating expenses, $16,350 (all expenses are charged to Operating Expenses, a controlling account).
(i) Recorded accumulated depreciation, $2,440, and allowance for doubtful accounts, $180.
(j) Merchandise inventory at December 31, $83,050.
(k) Closed revenue and expense accounts.

Instructions:

(1) Present, in general journal form, the entries for the branch to record the foregoing. Post to the following T accounts: Cash, Accounts Receivable, Allowance for Doubtful Accounts, Merchandise Inventory, Equipment, Accumulated

Depreciation, Accounts Payable, Home Office, Income Summary, Sales, Shipments from Home Office, Purchases, and Operating Expenses.

(2) Prepare an income statement for the ten-month period and a balance sheet as of December 31 for the branch.

(3) Present, in general journal form, the entries required on the home office records. Post to a T account entitled Trenton Branch.

CHAPTER 22

(If the working papers correlating with the textbook are not used, omit Problem 22-1B).

Problem 22-1B. The work sheet for Centennial Manufacturing Company, for the current year ended August 31, 1984, is presented in the working papers. Data concerning account titles, trial balance amounts, and selected adjustments have been entered on the work sheet.

Instructions:

(1) Enter the six adjustments required for the inventories on the work sheet. Additional adjustment data are:

Finished goods inventory at August 31	$112,030
Work in process inventory at August 31	81,200
Direct materials inventory at August 31	61,800

The adjustments for finished goods inventory should be entered as adjustments to the income summary account, and the work in process and direct materials inventory adjustments should be entered as adjustments to the manufacturing summary account.

(2) Complete the work sheet. The data for the manufacturing summary account and the other manufacturing accounts should be extended to the statement of cost of goods manufactured columns. After all of these data have been extended, the two cost of goods manufactured columns should be totaled and the difference determined. This difference, which is labeled "cost of goods manufactured" in the account title column, is transferred to the income statement columns by entries in the statement of cost of goods manufactured credit column and the income statement debit column. The remainder of the work sheet is completed in the same manner as is followed for a merchandising business. Appendix F further describes and illustrates the use of a work sheet for manufacturing operations.

(3) Prepare a statement of cost of goods manufactured.

(4) Prepare a multiple-step income statement.

Problem 22-2B. Pendaflex Printing Company uses a job order cost system. The following data summarize the operations related to production for September, the first month of operations:

(a) Materials purchased on account, $47,850.

(b) Materials requisitioned and factory labor used:

	Materials	Factory Labor
Job 1001	$9,720	$7,630
Job 1002	2,780	1,640
Job 1003	7,100	3,910
Job 1004	3,570	1,580
Job 1005	5,680	2,410
Job 1006	5,150	3,850
For general factory use	1,540	2,380

(c) Factory overhead costs incurred on account, $9,390.
(d) Depreciation of machinery and equipment, $4,510.
(e) The factory overhead rate is 60% of direct labor cost.
(f) Jobs completed: 1001, 1002, 1003, and 1004.
(g) Jobs 1001, 1002, and 1004 were shipped and customers were billed for $30,100, $7,300, and $8,500 respectively.

Instructions:

(1) Prepare entries in general journal form to record the foregoing summarized operations.
(2) Open T accounts for Work in Process and Finished Goods and post the appropriate entries, using the identifying letters as dates. Insert memorandum account balances as of the end of the month.
(3) Prepare a schedule of unfinished jobs to support the balance in the work in process account.
(4) Prepare a schedule of completed jobs on hand to support the balance in the finished goods account.

(If the working papers correlating with the textbook are not used, omit Problem 22-3B.)

Problem 22-3B. Rubinstein Furniture Company repairs, refinishes, and reupholsters furniture. A job order cost system was installed recently to facilitate (1) the determination of price quotations to prospective customers, (2) the determination of actual costs incurred on each job, and (3) cost reductions.

In response to a prospective customer's request for a price quotation on a job, the estimated cost data are inserted on an unnumbered job cost sheet. If the offer is accepted, a number is assigned to the job and the costs incurred are recorded in the usual manner on the job cost sheet. After the job is completed, reasons for the variances between the estimated and actual costs are noted on the sheet. The data are then available to management in evaluating the efficiency of operations and in preparing quotations on future jobs.

On November 18, an estimate of $742 for reupholstering a chair and couch was given to Chris Joel. The estimate was based upon the following data:

Estimated direct materials:	
20 meters at $16 per meter	$320
Estimated direct labor:	
14 hours at $10 per hour	140
Estimated factory overhead (50% of direct labor cost)	70
Total estimated costs	$530
Markup (40% of production costs)	212
Total estimate	$742

On November 21, the chair and couch were picked up from the residence of Chris Joel, 4810 Beekman Place, Racine, with a commitment to return it on November 30. The job was completed on November 28.

The related materials requisitions and time tickets are summarized as follows:

Materials Requisition No.	Description	Amount
715	6 meters at $16	$ 96
718	10 meters at $16	160
723	6 meters at $16	96

Time Ticket No.	Description	Amount
471	4 hours at $10	$ 40
478	8 hours at $10	80
481	3 hours at $10	30

Instructions:

(1) Complete that portion of the job order cost sheet that would be completed when the estimate is given to the customer.

(2) Assign number 85-11-8 to the job, record the costs incurred, and complete the job order cost sheet. In commenting upon the variances between actual costs and estimated costs, assume that 2 meters of materials were spoiled, the factory overhead rate has been proved to be satisfactory, and an inexperienced employee performed the work.

Problem 22-6B. Following are selected accounts for Gould Industrial Products. For the purposes of this problem, some of the debits and credits have been omitted

Accounts Receivable

Aug.	1 Balance	40,800	Aug. 31 Collections	60,175
	31 Sales	(A)		

Materials

Aug.	1 Balance	10,050	Aug. 31 Requisitions	(B)
	31 Purchases	15,190		

Work in Process

Aug.	1 Balance	11,775	Aug. 31 Goods finished	(E)
	31 Direct materials	(C)		
	31 Direct labor	24,000		
	31 Factory overhead	(D)		

Finished Goods

Aug.	1 Balance	5,585	Aug. 31 Cost of goods sold	(G)
	31 Goods finished	(F)		

Factory Overhead

Aug.	1 Balance	200	Aug. 31 Applied (80% of	
	1–31 Costs incurred	18,790	direct labor cost)	(H)

Cost of Goods Sold

Aug.	31	(I)		

Sales

			Aug. 31	(J)

Selected balances at August 31:

Accounts receivable $44,375
Finished goods.   11,195
Work in process   14,070
Materials   7,620

Materials requisitions for August included $750 of materials issued for general factory use. All sales are made on account, terms n/30.

Instructions:

(1) Determine the amounts represented by the letters (A) through (J), presenting your computations.
(2) Determine the amount of factory overhead overapplied or underapplied as of August 31.

CHAPTER 23 | Problem 23-1B. Rutherford Company manufactures Product G. Material A is placed in process in Department 1, where it is ground and partially refined. The output of Department 1 is transferred to Department 2, where Material B is added at the beginning of the process and the refining is completed. On March 1, Rutherford Company had the following inventories:

Finished goods (4,100 units) $71,750
Work in process — Department 1 . . . .   —
Work in process — Department 2 (2,100 units, ⅔ completed)   34,230
Materials   40,980

Departmental accounts are maintained for factory overhead and there is one service department, Factory Office. Manufacturing operations for March are summarized as follows:

(a) Materials purchased on account $21,800
(b) Materials requisitioned for use:
Material A $34,470
Material B   6,560
Indirect materials — Department 1   1,440
Indirect materials — Department 2   360
(c) Labor used:
Direct labor — Department 1 . . . . $48,700
Direct labor — Department 2   20,500
Indirect labor — Department 1   2,800
Indirect labor — Department 2   1,280
Factory Office   2,300
(d) Depreciation charged on plant assets:
Department 1 . . . . $19,900
Department 2   9,600
Factory Office   1,100
(e) Miscellaneous costs incurred on account:
Department 1 . . . . $ 3,690
Department 2   2,310
Factory Office   1,200

(f) Expiration of prepaid expenses:

Department 1... $ 2,280
Department 2...   490
Factory Office   750

(g) Distribution of Factory Office costs:

Department 1........................ 60% of total Factory Office costs
Department 2........................ 40% of total Factory Office costs

(h) Application of factory overhead costs:

Department 1.............................. 70% of direct labor cost
Department 2.............................. 80% of direct labor cost

(i) Production costs transferred from Department 1 to Department 2:

8,200 units were fully processed and there was no inventory of work in process in Department 1 at March 31.

(j) Production costs transferred from Department 2 to finished goods:

7,500 units, including the inventory at March 1, were fully processed. There were 2,800 units ¾ completed at March 31.

(k) Cost of goods sold during March:

8,000 units (use the first-in, first-out method in crediting the finished goods account).

Instructions:

(1) Prepare entries in general journal form to record the foregoing operations. Identify each entry by letter.

(2) Compute the March 31 work in process inventory for Department 2.

Problem 23-3B. Pugh Company manufactures Product J by a series of four processes, all materials being introduced in Department 1. From Department 1, the materials pass through Departments 2, 3, and 4, emerging as finished Product J. All inventories are priced at cost by the first-in, first-out method.

The balances in the accounts Work in Process—Department 4 and Finished Goods were as follows on March 1:

Work in Process—Department 4 (4,000 units, ¾ completed)......... $40,100
Finished Goods (7,200 units at $12.50 a unit)...................... 90,000

The following costs were charged to Work in Process—Department 4 during March:

Direct materials transferred from Department 3: 24,000 units
at $4.80 a unit.. $115,200
Direct labor... 127,260
Factory overhead.. 42,420

During March, 21,600 units of J were completed and 20,800 units were sold. Inventories on March 31 were as follows:

Work in Process—Department 4: 6,400 units, ¼ completed
Finished Goods: 8,000 units

Instructions:

(1) Determine the following, presenting computations in good order:

(a) Equivalent units of production for Department 4 during March.

(b) Unit processing cost for Department 4 for March.

(c) Total and unit cost of Product J started in a prior period and finished in March.

(d) Total and unit cost of Product J started and finished in March.

(continued)

(e) Total cost of goods transferred to finished goods.
(f) Work in process inventory for Department 4, March 31.
(g) Cost of goods sold (indicate number of units and unit costs).
(h) Finished goods inventory, March 31.
(2) Prepare a cost of production report for Department 4 for March.

Problem 23-5B. A process cost system is used to record the costs of manufacturing Product CE5, which requires a series of three processes. The inventory of Work in Process—Department 3 on August 1 and debits to the account during August were as follows:

Balance, 2,400 units, ⅔ completed	$ 23,280
From Department 2, 10,500 units	18,900
Direct labor	101,352
Factory overhead	25,338

During August, the 2,400 units in process on August 1 were completed, and of the 10,500 units entering the department, all were completed except 4,000 units, which were ¾ completed.

Charges to Work in Process—Department 3 for September were as follows:

From Department 2, 12,200 units	$ 21,350
Direct labor	127,000
Factory overhead	31,750

During September, the units in process at the beginning of the month were completed, and of the 12,200 units entering the department, all were completed except 1,500 units, which were ⅔ completed.

Instructions:

(1) Set up an account for Work in Process—Department 3. Enter the balance as of August 1 and record the debits and the credits in the account for August. Present computations for the determination of (a) equivalent units of production, (b) unit processing cost, (c) cost of goods finished, differentiating between units started in the prior period and units started and finished in August, and (d) work in process inventory.

(2) Record the transactions for September in the account. Present the computations listed in instruction (1).

(3) Determine the difference in unit cost between the product started and completed in August and the product started and completed in September. Determine also the amount of the difference attributable collectively to operations in Departments 1 and 2 and the amount attributable to operations in Department 3.

CHAPTER 24 | Problem 24-1B. Barnes Inc. prepared the following factory overhead cost budget for the Painting Department for January of the current year:

Barnes Inc.
Factory Overhead Cost Budget — Painting Department
For Month Ending January 31, 19--

Direct labor hours:

Normal productive capacity........................	24,000
Hours budgeted	21,600

Variable cost:

Indirect factory wages............................	$13,905
Indirect materials	10,935
Power and light.....................................	9,720
Total variable cost	$34,560

Fixed cost:

Supervisory salaries...............................	$12,950
Indirect factory wages............................	4,820
Depreciation of plant and equipment..................	4,460
Insurance......	2,600
Power and light.,..................................	2,350
Property taxes.....................................	1,620
Total fixed cost	28,800
Total factory overhead cost	$63,360

Instructions:

(1) Prepare a flexible budget for January, indicating capacities of 19,200, 21,600, 24,000, and 26,400 direct labor hours and the determination of a standard factory overhead rate per direct labor hour.

(2) Prepare a standard factory overhead cost variance report for January. The Painting Department was operated for 21,600 direct labor hours and the following factory overhead costs were incurred:

Indirect factory wages	$19,120
Supervisory salaries	12,950
Power and light	13,050
Indirect materials......................................	10,600
Depreciation of plant and equipment....................	4,460
Insurance	2,600
Property taxes	1,620
Total factory overhead cost incurred	$64,400

Problem 24-3B. McCloskey Inc. maintains perpetual inventory accounts for materials, work in process, and finished goods and uses a standard cost system based on the following data:

	Standard Cost per Unit
Direct materials: 5 kilograms at $2.80 per kg	$14
Direct labor: 2 hours at $18 per hour	36
Factory overhead: $2.50 per direct labor hour	5
Total	$55

There was no inventory of work in process at the beginning or end of August, the first month of the current fiscal year. The transactions relating to production completed during August are summarized as follows:

(a) Materials purchased on account, $89,600.

(b) Direct materials used, $92,220. This represented 31 800 kilograms at $2.90 per kilogram.

(c) Direct labor paid, $227,500. This represented 13,000 hours at $17.50 per hour. There were no accruals at either the beginning or the end of the period.

(d) Factory overhead incurred during the month was composed of depreciation on plant and equipment, $14,600; indirect labor, $11,750; insurance, $3,000; and miscellaneous factory costs, $5,500. The indirect labor and miscellaneous factory costs were paid during the period, and the insurance represents an expiration of prepaid insurance. Of the total factory overhead of $34,850, fixed costs amounted to $19,600 and variable costs were $15,250.

(e) Goods finished during the period, 6,400 units.

Instructions:

(1) Prepare entries in general journal form to record the transactions, assuming that the work in process account is debited for actual production costs and credited with standard costs for goods finished.

(2) Prepare a T account for Work in Process and post to the account, using the identifying letters as dates.

(3) Prepare schedules of variances for direct materials cost, direct labor cost, and factory overhead cost. Normal productive capacity for the plant is 14,000 direct labor hours.

(4) Total the amount of the standard cost variances and compare this total with the balance of the work in process account.

Problem 24-4B. The treasurer of Donovan Company instructs you to prepare a monthly cash budget for the next three months. You are presented with the following budget information:

	May	June	July
Sales	$300,000	$245,000	$350,000
Manufacturing costs	195,000	160,000	227,000
Operating expenses	45,000	37,000	56,000
Capital expenditures	—	100,000	—

The company expects to sell about 20% of its merchandise for cash. Of sales on account, 75% are expected to be collected in full in the month following the sale and the remainder the following month. Depreciation, insurance, and property taxes represent $15,000 of the estimated monthly manufacturing costs and $3,000 of the probable monthly operating expenses. Insurance and property taxes are paid in March and August respectively. Of the remainder of the manufacturing costs and operating expenses, 70% are expected to be paid in the month in which they are incurred and the balance in the following month.

Current assets as of May 1 are composed of cash of $31,000, marketable securities of $20,000, and accounts receivable of $265,000 ($220,000 from April sales and $45,000 from March sales). Current liabilities as of May 1 are composed of a $30,000, 14%, 120-day note payable due June 10, $60,400 of accounts payable incurred in April for manufacturing costs, and accrued liabilities of $14,100 incurred in April for operating expenses.

It is expected that $2,200 in dividends will be received in June. An estimated income tax payment of $12,500 will be made in June. Donovan Company's regular quarterly dividend of $5,000 is expected to be declared in June and paid in July. Management desires to maintain a minimum cash balance of $35,000.

Instructions:

(1) Prepare a monthly cash budget for May, June, and July.

(2) On the basis of the cash budget prepared in (1), what recommendation should be made to the treasurer?

CHAPTER 25 | Problem 25-1B. Ladner Refining Inc. refines Product X in batches of 200,000 gallons, which it sells for $3.20 per gallon. The associated unit costs and expenses are currently as follows:

	Per Gallon
Direct materials	$1.84
Direct labor	.48
Variable factory overhead	.18
Fixed factory overhead	.12
Sales commissions	.16
Fixed selling and general expenses	.08

The company is presently considering a proposal to put Product X through several additional processes to yield Products X and Z. Although the company had determined such further processing to be unwise, new processing methods have now been developed. Existing facilities can be used for the additional processing, but since the factory is operating at full 8-hour-day capacity, the processing would have to be performed at night. Additional costs of processing would be $11,650 per batch and there would be an evaporation loss of 8%, with 70% of the processed material evolving as Product X and 22% as Product Z. The selling price of Product Z is $4.80 per gallon. Sales commissions are a uniform percentage based on the sales price.

Instructions:

(1) Prepare a differential analysis report as of November 12, presenting the differential revenue and the differential cost per batch associated with the processing to produce Products X and Z, compared with processing to produce Product X only.

(2) Briefly report your recommendations.

Problem 25-2B. Fedder Company is considering the replacement of a machine that has been used in its factory for two years. Relevant data associated with the operations of the old machine and the new machine, neither of which has any residual value, are as follows:

Old Machine

Cost of machine, 8-year life	$224,000
Annual depreciation	28,000
Annual manufacturing costs, exclusive of depreciation	372,000
Related annual operating expenses	193,600
Associated annual revenue	600,000
Estimated selling price of old machine	116,000

New Machine

Cost of machine, 6-year life....................................... $384,000
Annual depreciation   64,000
Estimated annual manufacturing costs, exclusive of depreciation   300,000

Annual operating expenses and revenue are not expected to be affected by purchase of the new machine.

Instructions:

(1) Prepare a differential analysis report as of January 3 of the current year, comparing operations utilizing the new machine with operations using the present equipment. The analysis should indicate the total differential decrease or increase in costs that would result over the 6-year period if the new machine is acquired.

(2) List other factors that should be considered before a final decision is reached.

Problem 25-4B. The demand for Product G, one of numerous products manufactured by Bolton Inc., has dropped sharply because of recent competition from a similar product. The company's chemists are currently completing tests of various new formulas, and it is anticipated that the manufacture of a superior product can be started on May 1, one month hence. No changes will be needed in the present production facilities to manufacture the new product because only the mixture of the various materials will be changed.

The controller has been asked by the president of the company for advice on whether to continue production during April or to suspend the manufacture of Product G until May 1. The controller has assembled the following pertinent data:

Bolton Inc.
Estimated Income Statement — Product G
For Month Ending March 31, 19--

Sales (20,000 units).........................	$320,000
Cost of goods sold	280,000
Gross profit................................	$ 40,000
Selling and general expenses.................	75,000
Loss from operations........................	$ 35,000

The estimated production costs and selling and general expenses, based on a production of 20,000 units, are as follows:

Direct materials....................................	$3.40 per unit
Direct labor	6.50 per unit
Variable factory overhead..........................	.80 per unit
Variable selling and general expenses	2.20 per unit
Fixed factory overhead	$66,000 for March
Fixed selling and general expenses.................	$31,000 for March

Sales for April are expected to drop about 30% below those of the preceding month. No significant changes are anticipated in the production costs or operating expenses. No extra costs will be incurred in discontinuing operations in the portion of the plant associated with Product G. The inventory of Product G at the beginning and end of April is expected to be inconsequential.

Instructions:

(1) Prepare an estimated income statement in absorption costing form for April for Product G, assuming that production continues during the month.
(2) Prepare an estimated income statement in variable costing form for April for Product G, assuming that production continues during the month.
(3) State the estimated operating loss arising from the activities associated with Product G for April if production is temporarily suspended.
(4) Prepare a brief statement of the advice the controller should give.

CHAPTER 26 | **Problem 26-1B.** The organization chart for manufacturing operations for Carlos Inc. is presented in the working papers. Also presented are the budget performance reports for the three departments in Plant 3 and a partially completed budget performance report prepared for the vice-president in charge of production.

(If the working papers correlating with the textbook are not used, omit Problem 26-1B.)

In response to an inquiry into the cause of the direct labor variance in the Plating Shop-Plant 3, the following data were accumulated:

Job No.	Budgeted Hours	Actual Hours	Hourly Rate
940	70	75	$16.00
942	120	113	17.00
944	115	119	16.50
945	90	105	18.00
950	80	80	17.20
951	119	128	17.00
952	100	94	15.50
958	65	67	16.50

The significant variations from budgeted hours were attributed to the fact that Job 945 was of a type that was being done for the first time, to machine breakdown on Jobs 940, 944, and 958, and to an inexperienced operator on Job 951. Experienced operators were assigned to Jobs 942 and 952.

Instructions:

(1) Prepare a direct labor time variance report for the Plating Shop-Plant 3.
(2) Prepare a budget performance report for the use of the manager of Plant 3, detailing the relevant data from the three departments in the plant. Assume that the budgeted and actual administration expenses for the plant were $12,400 and $12,210, respectively.
(3) Complete the budget performance report for the vice-president in charge of production.

Problem 26-2B. Maloney Company manufactures only one product. In 1984, the plant operated at full capacity. At a meeting of the board of directors on December 12, 1984, it was decided to raise the price of this product from $16, which had prevailed for the past few years, to $18, effective January 1, 1985. Although the cost price was expected to rise about $1.20 per unit in 1985 because of a direct materials and direct labor wage increase, the increase in selling price was expected to cover this increase and also add to operating income. The comparative income statement for 1984 and 1985 is as follows:

	1985		1984	
Sales.....................................		$612,000		$640,000
Cost of goods sold: variable.............	$289,000		$292,000	
fixed	136,000	425,000	136,000	428,000
Gross profit.............................		$187,000		$212,000
Operating expenses: variable.............	$ 71,400		$ 72,000	
fixed	36,000	107,400	36,000	108,000
Operating income		$ 79,600		$104,000

Instructions:

(1) Prepare a gross profit analysis report for 1985.
(2) At a meeting of the board of directors on February 3, 1986, the president, after reading the gross profit analysis report, made the following comment:

> "It looks as if the increase in unit cost price was $1.80 and not the anticipated $1.20. The failure of operating management to keep these costs within the bounds of those in 1984, except for the anticipated $1.20 increase in direct materials and direct labor cost, was a major factor in the decrease in gross profit."

Do you agree with this analysis of the increase in unit cost price? Explain.

Problem 26-3B. W. F. Epstein Company expects to maintain the same inventories at the end of 1985 as at the beginning of the year. The total of all production costs for the year is therefore assumed to be equal to the cost of goods sold. With this in mind, the various department heads were asked to submit estimates of the expenses for their departments during 1985. A summary report of these estimates is as follows:

	Estimated Fixed Expense	Estimated Variable Expense (per unit sold)
Production costs:		
Direct materials	—	$ 9.20
Direct labor..............................	—	4.80
Factory overhead.........................	$174,000	2.00
Selling expenses:		
Sales salaries and commissions.............	80,400	1.20
Advertising	21,600	—
Travel	3,600	—
Miscellaneous selling expense	2,400	.48
General expenses:		
Office and officers' salaries................	70,500	—
Supplies.................................	4,500	.24
Miscellaneous general expense............	3,000	.08
	$360,000	$18.00

It is expected that 70,000 units will be sold at a selling price of $24 a unit. Capacity output is 75,000 units.

Instructions:

(1) Determine the break-even point (a) in dollars of sales, (b) in units, and (c) in terms of capacity.
(2) Prepare an estimated income statement for 1985.   *(continued)*

(3) Construct a break-even chart, indicating the break-even point in dollars of sales.
(4) What is the expected margin of safety?
(5) What is the expected contribution margin ratio?

Problem 26-5B. Glick Company is considering the addition of a new product to its line. For 1984, production was at 80% of capacity, the assets employed were $1,000,000 (original cost), and the income statement showed an operating income of $140,000, computed as follows:

Sales		$740,000
Less: Cost of goods sold	$468,000	
Selling expenses	107,000	
General expenses	25,000	600,000
Operating income		$140,000

If the new product is added, market research indicates that 5,000 units can be sold in 1985 at an estimated selling price of $20 per unit. The idle capacity will be utilized to produce the product, but an additional $112,500 in plant assets will be required. The cost data per unit for the new product are as follows:

Direct materials	$ 6.50
Direct labor...	4.80
Factory overhead (includes depreciation on additional investment)	2.60
Selling expenses	1.55
General expenses	.95
	$16.40

Instructions:
(1) Prepare an estimated income statement for 1985 for the new product.
(2) Prepare a schedule indicating the rate of return on assets under present conditions and for the new product. Use the original cost of the assets in your computations.
(3) Would you recommend addition of the new product? Would you require other data before you make your decision? If so, what additional data would you require?

Problem 26-6B. The capital expenditures budget committee is considering two projects. The estimated operating income and net cash flows from each project are as follows:

	Project A		Project B	
Year	Operating Income	Net Cash Flow	Operating Income	Net Cash Flow
1	$19,950	$ 60,000	$28,000	$ 75,000
2	13,300	60,000	14,000	75,000
3	13,300	50,000	14,000	50,000
4	13,300	30,000	7,000	20,000
5	10,150	30,000	7,000	10,000
	$70,000	$230,000	$70,000	$230,000

Each project requires an investment of $160,000, with no residual value expected. The committee has selected a rate of 15% for purposes of the discounted cash flow analysis.

Instructions:

(1) Compute the following:

    (a) The average rate of return for each project, giving effect to depreciation on the investment.

    (b) The excess or deficiency of present value over amount to be invested, as determined by the discounted cash flow method for each project. Use the present value table appearing in this chapter.

(2) Prepare a brief report for the budget committee, advising it on the relative merits of the two projects.

CHAPTER 27 | **Problem 27-1B.** Ana Jonas owns a small apartment building from which she receives rental income. She uses the cash method of determining income, depositing in a special bank account all rents received from tenants. All disbursements related to the building, as well as occasional unrelated disbursements, are paid by checks drawn on the same account. During the current taxable year ending December 31, she deposited $86,000 of rent receipts in the special bank account.

Disbursements from the special bank account during the current year are summarized as follows:

Wages of custodian and maintenance employee:		
Withheld for FICA tax and paid to IRS	$ 1,365	
Withheld for income tax and paid to IRS	1,495	
Paid to custodian	16,640	$19,500
Interest on mortgage note payable on land and building		15,200
Installment payments of principal on mortgage note payable		12,750
Purchases of various securities		11,500
Utilities expense		10,800
Real estate tax on land and building		4,700
Repainting interior of apartments		4,500
Premium on a three-year insurance policy on the building, effective January 3		1,590
Repairs to heating and plumbing equipment		1,575
Payroll tax expense		1,365
Contributions:		
United Fund		250
Salvation Army		100
Political committee		50
Miscellaneous expense incurred in earning rentals		1,120

In addition to the foregoing data, you determine from other records and the tax return for the preceding year that the total allowable deduction for depreciation expense for the current year is $9,800 and that current expirations of insurance premiums paid in earlier years total $245.

Instructions:

Prepare a statement of adjusted gross income from rents, identifying each of the allowable deductions from gross income.

Problem 27-2B. James Rea, unmarried and entitled to one exemption for himself, is an attorney. He uses the cash method of determining taxable income and reports on the calendar-year basis. His cash receipts and disbursements for the current year are summarized as follows:

Cash Receipts

Professional fees	$129,400
Borrowed from bank (professional purposes)	25,000
From sale of X Corporation stock (long-term capital gain was $5,000)	19,900
Dividends	1,250

Cash Disbursements

Wages of employees	$ 41,000
Payroll taxes	3,280
Office rent	12,000
Electricity (office)	6,250
Telephone expense (office)	1,750
Office supplies expense	950
Insurance on office equipment (2-year policy, dated January 1)	300
Professional liability insurance (1-year policy, dated January 1)	1,750
Automobile operating expense (exclusive of depreciation)	1,600
Partial repayment of bank loan (professional purposes)	6,750
Interest on bank loan (professional purposes)	3,250
Charitable contributions	1,300
Payment on principal of residence mortgage note	4,750
Interest on residence mortgage note	2,250
Personal property tax on office equipment	60
Real estate tax on home	1,150
State sales tax on purchases for personal use	315
Political contributions	150
Office equipment (purchases at various times during year)	4,000
Purchase of Z Corporation stock	15,000
Payments of estimated income tax for current year	14,600

The automobile was used 80% of the time for professional purposes. The total depreciation expense for the year was $1,750. Allocate 80% of the depreciation and other automobile expenses to professional purposes.

The cost of the office equipment purchased during the year is indicated in the summary of cash payments and is to be expensed during the year. Depreciation expense for equipment purchased in prior years is $850.

Instructions:

Prepare a summary of federal income tax data for Rea, applying the appropriate schedule of tax rates presented in this chapter.

Problem 27-3B. The following preliminary income statement of Bigley's Stereo was prepared as of the end of the calendar year in which the business was established. You are engaged to examine the statement, review the business records, revise the accounting system to the extent necessary, and determine the adjusted gross income.

Sales...............................		$137,500
Purchases		92,400
Gross profit.......................		$ 45,100
Operating expenses:		
Salaries	$38,500	
Rent	9,600	
Store equipment.................	12,000	
Insurance.......................	500	
Fuel............................	1,025	
Utilities	950	
Advertising	800	
Payroll taxes	1,640	
Donations.......................	250	
Miscellaneous...................	775	66,040
Net loss		$ 20,940

You obtain the following information during your examination:

(a) The preliminary income statement is a summary of cash receipts and disbursements. Sales on account are not recorded until cash is received. They are evidenced only by duplicate sales tickets. Similarly, invoices for merchandise and other purchases are not recorded until payment is made. In the meantime, they are filed in an unpaid file.

(b) Uncollected sales to customers on account at December 31 amount to $6,600.

(c) Unpaid invoices at December 31 for expenditures of the past year are summarized as follows:

Merchandise	$5,400
Fuel	105
Utilities	75

(d) Merchandise inventory at December 31 amounted to $20,200.

(e) Withdrawals of $18,000 by the owner of the enterprise were included in the amount reported as Salaries. Accrued salaries at the end of the year amount to $750.

(f) The agreement with the salesclerks provides for a bonus equal to 1% of sales during the year, payable in January of the following year.

(g) The rent for January of the following year ($700) was paid and recorded in December.

(h) The store equipment reported in the preliminary income statement was installed on February 1, and $7,500 is to be expensed during the year. Depreciation expense allowable during the year is $1,400.

(i) A total of $210 of insurance premiums was unexpired at December 31.

(j) Payments classified as Donations were contributions to charitable, religious, and educational organizations.

(k) Payments classified as Miscellaneous included $250 of personal expenses of the owner.

Instructions:

Prepare a statement of adjusted gross income from the business for submission with the income tax return of Joan Bigley, the owner, using the accrual method of accounting.

CHAPTER 28 | Problem 28-1B. Stacy Triplett is a partner in the firm of Evert, Spaulding, and Associates, and Dwight Triplett owns and manages Southern Motor Inn. They applied to the First National Bank for a loan to be used to build an apartment complex. The bank requested a statement of financial condition, and they assembled the following data for this purpose at August 31:

(a) Cash in bank, savings, and money market accounts, $24,300. (Unrestricted withdrawals are allowed without penalty.)

(b) Marketable securities (current value is quoted market price on August 31, 10 , less estimated broker commissions):

	Cost	Current Value
Stocks:		
TVR Industries, 200 shares	$ 9,000	$12,300
Majik Manufacturing Inc., 300 shares	15,000	18,000
Sunshine Food Stores Inc., 1,500 shares	22,500	25,500
Bonds:		
U. S. Treasury, 9¾%, $30,000 face amount, due 19-- . .	27,600	28,500
Dudley Motors Inc., 10%, $20,000 face amount,		
due 19--	20,000	19,500

(c) Stacy Triplett's equity interest in Evort, Spaulding, and Associates: cost, $40,000; estimated market, $160,000. Dwight Triplett's equity interest in the Southern Motor Inn: cost, $50,000; estimated market, $70,000. The estimated market prices were determined by an independent appraisal made by Rhodes Realty.

(d) Cash value of $100,000 face value life insurance policy, $36,500.

(e) Residence: cost, $160,000; estimated market, $210,000. The estimated market price was determined by an independent appraisal made by Jamison and Associates. The residence is pledged against a 10½% mortgage note payable, final installment due November 1, 19--. The present value of the monthly mortgage payments of $1,240, including interest, is $76,800.

(f) Household furnishings: cost, $53,500; estimated market, $40,000.

(g) Automobiles: cost, $36,500; estimated market, $23,000.

(h) Jewelry and paintings: cost, $9,800; estimated market, $14,000. The estimated market price was determined by an independent appraisal made by Jamison and Associates.

(i) Present value of vested interest in Puritan Mills Corporation Pension Trust, $18,400.

(j) Present value of accounts payable and accrued liabilities, $7,500.
(k) Income tax payable, $8,500.
(l) Present value of 13% note payable, due October 1, 19--, $15,000.
(m) Estimated income tax on unrealized appreciation of salable assets, $18,500.

Instructions:

Prepare a statement of financial condition as of August 31 of the current year. Notes to the statement should be presented as appropriate.

(If the working papers correlating with the textbook are not used, omit Problem 28-3B.)

Problem 28-3B. After the closing entries were posted, the accounts in the ledger of the general fund for Woodbury on June 30, the end of the current year, are as follows:

Accounts Payable	$ 52,500
Cash in Bank	18,400
Savings Accounts	50,000
Cash on Hand	5,600
Fund Balance	170,750
Investments in Marketable Securities	150,000
Property Taxes Receivable	72,650
Reserve for Encumbrances	41,000
Wages Payable	32,400

Estimated revenues, revenues, appropriations, encumbrances, and expenditures from the respective subsidiary ledgers have been entered in the statement of revenues and expenditures—budget and actual in the working papers. The fund balance account had a balance of $167,150 on July 1, the beginning of the current year.

Instructions:

(1) Complete the statement of revenues and expenditures—budget and actual.
(2) Prepare a statement of changes in fund balance.
(3) Prepare a balance sheet.

Problem 28-4B. The trial balance for the City of Waycross—General Fund at the beginning of the current year is as follows:

City of Waycross—General Fund
Trial Balance
July 1, 19--

Cash	72,600	
Savings Accounts	220,000	
Property Taxes Receivable	190,600	
Investment in U. S. Treasury Notes	80,000	
Accounts Payable		81,700
Wages Payable		26,120
Fund Balance		455,380
	563,200	563,200

The following data summarize the operations for the current year.
(a) Estimated revenues, $4,600,000; appropriations, $4,560,000.
(b) Revenues from property tax levy, $3,320,000.

(c) Cash received from property taxes, $3,040,000; other revenues, $1,320,000.

(d) Expenditures encumbered and evidenced by purchase orders, $2,660,000.

(e) Expenditures for payrolls, $1,850,000.

(f) Liquidation of encumbrances and vouchers prepared, $2,600,000.

(g) Cash disbursed for vouchers, $2,530,000; for payment of wages, $1,840,000; for savings accounts, $50,000.

Instructions:

(1) Prepare entries in general journal form to record the foregoing summarized operations.

(2) Open T accounts for the accounts appearing in the trial balance and enter the balances as of July 1, identifying them as "Bal."

(3) Open T accounts for Reserve for Encumbrances, Estimated Revenues, Revenues, Appropriations, Expenditures, and Encumbrances. Post the entries recorded in (1) to the accounts, using the identifying letters In place of dates.

(4) Prepare the appropriate entries to close the accounts as of June 30 and post to the accounts, using the letter "C" to identify the postings.

(5) Prepare a trial balance as of June 30.

Answers to Self-Examination Questions

CHAPTER 1

1. **D** A corporation, organized in accordance with state or federal statutes, is a separate legal entity in which ownership is divided into shares of stock (answer D). A sole proprietorship, sometimes referred to as a single proprietorship (answers A and B), is a business enterprise owned by one individual. A partnership (answer C) is a business enterprise owned by two or more individuals.

2. **A** The properties owned by a business enterprise are referred to as assets (answer A). The debts of the business are called liabilities (answer B), and the equity of the owners is called capital or owner's equity (answers C and D).

3. **A** The balance sheet is a listing of the assets, liabilities, and capital of a business entity at a specific date (answer A). The income statement (answer B) is a summary of the revenue and expenses of a business entity for a specific period of time. The capital statement (answer C) summarizes the changes in capital for a sole proprietorship or partnership during a specific period of time. The retained earnings statement (answer D) summarizes the changes in retained earnings for a corporation during a specific period of time.

4. **C** The accounting equation is:

Assets = Liabilities + Capital

Therefore, if assets increased by $20,000 and liabilities increased by $12,000, capital must have increased by $8,000 (answer C) as indicated in the following computation.

Assets = Liabilities + Capital
$20,000 = $12,000 + Capital
$20,000 − $12,000 = Capital
$ 8,000 = Capital

5. **B** Net income is the excess of revenue over expenses, or $7,500 (answer B). If expenses exceed revenue, the difference is a net loss. Withdrawals by the owner are the opposite of the owner's investing in the business and do not affect the amount of net income or net loss.

CHAPTER 2

1. **A** A debit may signify an increase in asset accounts (answer A) or a decrease in liability and capital accounts. A credit may signify a decrease in asset accounts (answer B) or an increase in liability and capital accounts (answers C and D).

2. **C** Liability, capital, capital stock, retained earnings and revenue (answer C) accounts have normal credit balances. Asset (answer A), drawing (answer B), dividend, and expense (answer D) accounts have normal debit balances.

3. **D** The current asset category includes cash and other assets that may reasonably be expected to be realized in cash or sold or consumed usually within a year or less and therefore would include cash (answer A), accounts receivable (answer B), and supplies on hand (answer C).

4. **A** The receipt of cash from customers on account increases the asset cash and decreases the asset accounts receivable as

920

indicated by answer A. Answer B has the debit and credit reversed and answers C and D involve transactions with creditors (accounts payable) and not customers (accounts receivable).

5. D The trial balance (answer D) is a listing of the balances and the titles of the accounts in the ledger on a given date, so that the equality of the debits and credits in the ledger can be verified. The income statement (answer A) is a summary of revenue and expenses for a period of time, the capital statement (answer B) is a summary of changes in capital of a sole proprietorship or partnership over a period of time, and the retained earnings statement (answer C) is a summary of the changes in retained earnings for a corporation over a period of time.

CHAPTER 3

1. D The balance in the supplies account, before adjustment, represents the amount of supplies available. From this amount ($2,250) is subtracted the amount of supplies on hand ($950) to determine the supplies used ($1,300). Since increases in expense accounts are recorded by debits and decreases in asset accounts are recorded by credits, answer D is the correct entry.

2. C Since increases in expense accounts (such as depreciation expense) are recorded by debits and it is customary to record the decreases in usefulness of plant assets as credits to accumulated depreciation accounts, answer C is the correct entry.

3. D The book value of a plant asset is the difference between the balance in the asset account and the balance in the related accumulated depreciation account, or $22,500 − $14,000, as indicated by answer D ($8,500).

4. C Since all revenue and expense accounts are closed at the end of the period, both Sales (revenue) and Salary Expense (expense) would be closed to Income Summary (answer C).

5. A Since the post-closing trial balance includes only balance sheet accounts (all of the revenue, expense, and drawing accounts have been previously closed), Cash (answer A) would appear on the trial balance. Both Sales (answer B) and Salary Expense (answer C) are temporary accounts that are closed prior to the preparation of the post-closing trial balance.

CHAPTER 4

1. C The amount of discount for early payment is $10 (answer C), or 1% of $1,000. Although the $50 of transportation costs paid by the seller are debited to the customer's account, the customer is not entitled to a discount on that amount.

2. B The customer is entitled to a discount of $9 (answer B) for early payment. This amount is 1% of $900, which is the sales price of $1,000 less the return of $100. The $50 of transportation costs is an expense of the seller.

3. A The amount of merchandise inventory appearing in the trial balance columns of the work sheet represents the inventory at the beginning of the period (answer A). This amount and the amount of the merchandise inventory at the end of the period (answer B) are included on the work sheet as inventory adjustments. These two adjustments and the net cost of merchandise purchased provide the data to determine the cost of merchandise sold (answer C).

4. B The single-step form of income statement (answer B) is so named because the total of all expenses is deducted from the total of all revenues. The multiple-step form (answer A) includes numerous sections and subsections with several intermediate balances before arriving at net income. The account form (answer C) and the report form (answer D) are two common forms of the balance sheet.

5. D The omission of the adjustment for accrued salaries at the end of the year understates expenses (answer A) and consequently overstates net income (answer B) for the year. The liability for salaries payable is also omitted and results in understating liabilities at the end of the year (answer C).

CHAPTER 5

1. D Every adjusting entry affects both a balance sheet account and an income statement account. Therefore if the debit portion of an

adjusting entry increases an asset (balance sheet) account, the credit portion of the entry must affect an income statement account, as would be the case for a decrease in an expense account (answer D).

2. A Deferred expenses are assets, and those expected to benefit a relatively short period of time are listed on the balance sheet among the current assets (answer A).

3. B Unearned revenues are revenues received in advance that will be earned in the future. They represent a liability (answer B) of the business to furnish the service in a future period.

4. A Under the system of initially recording office supplies as an expense, the office supplies expense account would have a balance of $2,910 ($660 plus $2,250) before adjustment, representing the combined cost of office supplies on hand at the beginning of the year and the cost of office supplies purchased during the year. The accounts are therefore adjusted by debiting Office Supplies and crediting Office Supplies Expense for $595 (answer A). The adjustment transfers $595, representing the unconsumed supplies on hand at the end of the year, to the asset account.

5. B The $500 credit balance in salary expense on January 1, the beginning of the fiscal year, before any transactions have occurred, resulted from a reversing entry that transferred the credit balance in the salaries payable account at the end of the preceding year to the salary expense account. This credit balance is a liability (answer B) that will be paid as a portion of the first salary payment of the fiscal year. Therefore, the first salary payment of the fiscal year will discharge the liability of $500 and the remainder of the payment will represent salary expense incurred.

CHAPTER 6

1. C The task of revising an accounting system is composed of three phases. Systems analysis (answer A) is the initial phase involving the determination of the informational needs, sources of such information, and deficiencies in the processing methods currently employed. Systems design (answer B) is the phase in which proposals for changes are developed.

Systems implementation (answer C) is the final phase involving carrying out or implementing the proposals for changes.

2. A The detailed procedures adopted by management to control operations are collectively termed internal controls (answer A). Internal controls are classified as administrative controls (answer C) and accounting controls (answer B). Internal administrative controls consist of procedures and records that assist management in achieving business objectives. Internal accounting controls consist of procedures and records that are primarily concerned with the reliability of financial records and reports and with the safeguarding of assets.

3. B All payments of cash for any purpose are recorded in the cash payments journal (answer B). Only purchases of merchandise or other items *on account* are recorded in the purchases journal (answer A). All sales of merchandise on account are recorded in the sales journal (answer C) and all receipts of cash are recorded in the cash receipts journal (answer D).

4. A The general term used to describe the type of separate ledger that contains a substantial number of individual accounts with a common characteristic is subsidiary ledger (answer A). The creditors ledger (answer B), sometimes called the accounts payable ledger (answer C), is a specific subsidiary ledger containing only individual accounts with creditors. Likewise, the accounts receivable ledger (answer D), also referred to as the customers ledger, is a specific subsidiary ledger containing only individual accounts with customers.

5. B The controlling account for the customers ledger (the ledger that contains the individual accounts with customers) is Accounts Receivable (answer B). The accounts payable account (answer A) is the controlling account for the creditors ledger. There are no subsidiary ledgers for the sales (answer C) and purchases (answer D) accounts.

CHAPTER 7

1. B On any specific date, the cash in bank account in a depositor's ledger may not agree

with the reciprocal account in the bank's ledger because of delays by either party in recording transactions, and/or errors made by either party in recording transactions. The purpose of a bank reconciliation, therefore, is to determine the reasons for any discrepancies between the two account balances. All errors should then be corrected by the depositor or the bank as appropriate. In arriving at the adjusted (correct) balance according to the bank statement, outstanding checks must be deducted (answer B) to adjust for checks that have been written by the depositor but that have not yet been presented to the bank for payment.

2. C All reconciling items that are added to and deducted from the "balance per depositor's records" on the bank reconciliation (answer C) require that journal entries be made by the depositor to correct errors made in recording transactions or to bring the cash account up to date for delays in recording transactions.

3. D A voucher (answer A) is the form on which is recorded pertinent data about a liability. After a voucher is approved by the designated official, it is recorded in the voucher register (answer D). The voucher is filed in an unpaid vouchers file (answer B) until it is due for payment. It is then removed from the file and a check is issued in payment and an entry is made in the check register (answer C).

4. D A major advantage of recording purchases at the net amount (answer A) is that the cost of failing to take discounts is recorded in the accounts (answer B) and then reported as an expense on the income statement (answer C).

5. D To avoid the delay, annoyance, and expense that is associated with paying all obligations by check, relatively small amounts (answer A) are paid from a petty cash fund. The fund is established by estimating the amount of cash needed to pay these small amounts during a specified period (answer B) and it is then reimbursed when the amount of money in the fund is reduced to a predetermined minimum amount (answer C).

CHAPTER 8

1. C Maturity value is the amount that is due at the maturity or due date. The maturity value of

$10,300 (answer C) is determined as follows:

Face amount of note...............	$10,000
Plus interest ($10,000 × 12/100	
× 90/360)......................	300
Maturity value of note.............	$10,300

2. B The net amount available to a borrower from discounting a note payable is termed the proceeds. The proceeds of $4,925 (answer B) is determined as follows:

Face amount of note...............	$5,000
Less discount ($5,000 × 9/100	
× 60/360).....................	75
Proceeds.......................	$4,925

3. B The estimate of uncollectible accounts, $8,500, is the amount of the desired balance of Allowance for Doubtful Accounts *after adjustment*. The amount of the current provision to be made for uncollectible accounts expense is thus $6,000 (answer B), which is the amount that must be added to the Allowance for Doubtful Accounts credit balance of $2,500 so that the account will have the desired balance of $8,500.

4. B The amount expected to be realized from accounts receivable is the balance of Accounts Receivable, $100,000, less the balance of Allowance for Doubtful Accounts, $7,000, or $93,000 (answer B).

5. A Securities held as temporary investments are classified on the balance sheet as current assets (answer A).

CHAPTER 9

1. C The overstatement of inventory by $7,500 at the end of a period will cause the cost of merchandise sold for the period to be understated by $7,500, the gross profit for the period to be overstated by $7,500, and the net income for the period to be overstated by $7,500 (answer C).

2. B The perpetual system (answer B) continuously discloses the amount of inventory. The periodic inventory system (answer A) relies upon a detailed listing of the merchandise on hand, called a physical inventory (answer C), to determine the cost of inventory at the end of a

period. The retail inventory method (answer D) is employed in connection with the periodic system and is based on the relationship of the cost of merchandise available for sale to the retail price of the same merchandise.

3. A The fifo method (answer A) is based on the assumption that costs are charged against revenue in the order in which they were incurred. The lifo method (answer B) charges the most recent costs incurred against revenue, and the average cost method (answer C) charges a weighted average of unit costs of commodities sold against revenue. The perpetual inventory system (answer D) is a system that continuously discloses the amount of inventory.

4. D The fifo method of costing is based on the assumption that costs should be charged against revenue in the order in which they were incurred (first-in, first-out). Thus the most recent costs are assigned to inventory. The 35 units would be assigned a unit cost of $23 (answer D).

5. B When the price level is steadily rising, the earlier unit costs are lower than recent unit costs. Under the fifo method (answer B), these earlier costs are matched against revenue to yield the largest possible net income. The periodic inventory system (answer D) is a system and not a method of costing.

CHAPTER 10

1. C All expenditures necessary to get a plant asset (such as machinery) in place and ready for use are proper charges to the asset account. In the case of machinery acquired, the transportation costs (answer A) and the installation costs (answer B) are both (answer C) proper charges to the machinery account.

2. A The periodic charge for depreciation under the sum-of-the years-digits method is determined by multiplying a fraction by the original cost of the asset after the estimated residual value has been subtracted. The denominator of the fraction, which remains constant, is the sum of the digits representing the years of life, or 6 (3 + 2 + 1), in the question. The numerator of the fraction, which changes each year, is the number of years of remaining life, or 3 for the first year, 2 for the second year, and 1 for

the third year in the question. The $4,500 (answer A) of depreciation for the first year is determined as follows:

$$\frac{\text{Years of Life Remaining}}{\text{Sum of Digits for Years of Life}} \times \text{Cost} - \text{Estimated Residual Value}$$

$$\frac{3}{3 + 2 + 1} \times (\$9,500 - \$500)$$

$$= \frac{1}{2} \times \$9,000 = \$4,500$$

3. B Depreciation methods that provide for a higher depreciation charge in the first year of the use of an asset and a gradually declining periodic charge thereafter are referred to as accelerated depreciation methods. Examples of such methods are the sum-of-the-years-digits (answer B) and the declining balance methods.

4. D The acceptable method of accounting for an exchange of similar assets in which the trade-in allowance ($30,000) exceeds the book value of the old asset ($25,000) requires that the cost of the new asset be determined by adding the amount of boot given ($70,000) to the book value of the old asset ($25,000), which totals $95,000.

5. D Long-lived assets that are useful in operations, not held for sale, and without physical qualities are referred to as intangible assets. Patents, goodwill, and copyrights are examples of intangible assets (answer D).

CHAPTER 11

1. B The amount of net pay of $703 (answer B) is determined as follows:

Gross pay:
| 40 hours at $20 | $800 | |
| 5 hours at $30 | 150 | $950 |

Deductions:
Federal income tax withheld	$212	
FICA ($500 × .07)	35	247
Net pay		$703

2. A Employers are required to withhold a portion of the earnings of their employees for payment of federal income taxes (answer A). Generally, federal (answer B) and state (answer C) unemployment compensation taxes are levied

against the employer only and thus are not deducted from employee earnings.

3. D The employer incurs operating costs for FICA tax (answer A), federal unemployment compensation tax (answer B), and state unemployment compensation tax (answer C). These costs add significantly to the total labor costs for most businesses.

4. C Liabilities due within a year should be presented as current liabilities and those with a more distant future date should be presented as long-term liabilities on the balance sheet. Therefore the 12 monthly payments of $1,000 each, for a total of $12,000, represent a current liability and the remaining $38,000 is a long-term liability (answer C).

5. B The net amount available to a borrower from discounting a note payable is termed the proceeds. The proceeds of $4,900 (answer B) is determined as follows:

Face amount of note $5,000
Less discount ($5,000 × 12/100
    × 60/360) 100
Proceeds $4,900

CHAPTER 12

1. D In the balance sheet, the equipment should be reported at its cost less accumulated depreciation, $100,000. The effect of the declining value of the dollar on plant assets, the market value of plant assets, and the replacement cost of plant assets are not recognized in the basic historical cost statements.

2. A Under the installment basis of accounting, gross profit is realized in accordance with the amount of cash collected in each year, based on the percent of gross profit to sales. For the question, the amount of gross profit to be realized for the current year is $22,500 (answer A), determined as follows:

Percent of gross profit to sales:
    $60,000 ÷ $200,000 = 30%
Gross profit realized:
    $75,000 × 30% = $22,500

3. A Under the percentage-of-contract-completion method of accounting, the amount of revenue

to be recognized during a period is determined on the basis of the estimated percentage of the contract that has been completed during the period. The costs incurred during the period are deducted from this revenue to yield the income from the contract. The $950,000 of income for the question is determined as follows:

Revenue to be recognized
    (40% × $20,000,000)........ $8,000,000
Costs incurred 7,050,000
Income..................... $ 950,000

4. D In some situations, there are a number of accepted alternative principles that could be used. To assure a high degree of comparability of the financial statements between periods, appropriate disclosure should be made when a change is made from one accepted principle to another. A change in method of inventory pricing (answer A), a change in depreciation method for previously recorded plant assets (answer B), and a change in method of accounting for installment sales (answer C) are examples of changes in accepted alternative principles that should be appropriately disclosed.

5. D The concept of materiality (answer D) relates to the acceptance of a procedure that deviates from absolute accuracy for insignificant or immaterial items, such as reporting cents on financial statements.

CHAPTER 13

1. B A decline in the general purchasing power caused by rising prices is termed inflation (answer B), while an increase in general purchasing power caused by declining prices is deflation (answer A). A purchasing power loss (answer C) is created by holding monetary items during periods of inflation or deflation.

2. C The restated constant dollar amount would be $140,000 (answer C), determined as follows:

$$\frac{140}{100} \times \$100,000 = \$140,000$$

3. B Purchasing power gains are created by holding monetary liabilities such as bonds payable

(answer B) during periods in which the general price level is rising. Cash (answer A) and notes receivable (answer D) are monetary assets which, if held during periods of increasing general price levels, create purchasing power losses. Inventory (answer C) is a nonmonetary asset. Nonmonetary assets do not create purchasing power gains or losses.

4. D Cash (answer A), notes receivable (answer B), and bonds payable (answer C) are all monetary items representing cash or claims to a fixed amount of cash.

5. C An increase in the current cost of the land over the original cost is termed an unrealized holding gain (answer C). When the land is sold, the gain becomes a realized holding gain (answer A). A purchasing power gain (answer B) is created by holding monetary items during periods of general price-level changes.

CHAPTER 14

1. B Noncash assets contributed to a partnership should be recorded at the amounts agreed upon by the partners. The preferable practice is to record the office equipment at $9,000 (answer B).

2. C Net income and net loss are divided among the partners in accordance with their agreement. In the absence of any agreement, all partners share equally (answer C).

3. C X's share of the $45,000 of net income is $19,000 (answer C), determined as follows:

	X	Y	Total
Interest allowance	$10,000	$ 5,000	$15,000
Salary allowance	12,000	24,000	36,000
Total	$22,000	$29,000	$51,000
Excess of allowances over income	3,000	3,000	6,000
Net income distribution	$19,000	$26,000	$45,000

4. A When an additional person is admitted to a partnership by purchasing an interest from one or more of the partners, the purchase price is paid directly to the selling partner(s). The amount of capital transferred from the capital account(s) of the selling partner(s) to the capital account of the incoming partner is the capital interest acquired from the selling partner. In the question, the amount is $32,500

(answer A), which is one half of X's capital balance of $65,000.

5. B Partnership cash would be equal to the net balance in the partners' capital accounts, or $8,000. This cash would be distributed in accordance with the credit balances in the partners' capital accounts, after considering the potential loss that might result from the inability to collect from a deficient partner. Therefore the $8,000 (answer B) would be distributed to X (X's $10,000 capital balance less the potential loss from Y's $2,000 deficiency).

CHAPTER 15

1. D The owners' equity in a corporation is commonly called capital (answer A), stockholders' equity (answer B), shareholders' investment (answer C), or shareholders' equity.

2. C If a corporation has cumulative preferred stock outstanding, dividends that have been passed for prior years plus the dividend for the current year must be paid before dividends may be declared on common stock. In this case, dividends of $27,000 ($9,000 × 3) have been passed for the preceding three years and the current year's dividends are $9,000, making a total of $36,000 (answer C) that must be paid to preferred stockholders before dividends can be declared on common stock.

3. D The stockholders' equity section of corporate balance sheets is divided into two principal subsections: (1) investments contributed by the stockholders and (2) net income retained in the business. Included as part of the investments by stockholders is the excess of par over issued price of stock, such as discount on common stock (answer A); the par of stock subscribed, such as common stock subscribed (answer B); and the excess of issued price of stock over par, such as premium on preferred stock (answer C).

4. C Reacquired stock, known as treasury stock, should be listed in the stockholders' equity section (answer C) of the balance sheet. The price paid for the treasury stock is deducted from the total of all of the capital accounts.

5. B The total stockholders' equity is determined as follows:

Preferred stock......................	$1,000,000
Common stock........................	2,000,000
Premium on common stock.............	100,000
Retained earnings	540,000
Total equity	$3,640,000

The amount allocated to common stock is determined as follows:

Total equity		$3,640,000
Allocated to preferred stock:		
Liquidation price	$1,100,000	
Dividends in arrears	240,000	1,340,000
Allocated to common stock		$2,300,000

The equity per common share is determined as follows:

$2,300,000 ÷ 100,000 shares = $23 per share

CHAPTER 16

1. **D** Paid-in capital is one of the two major subdivisions of the stockholders' equity of a corporation. It may result from many sources, including the receipt of donated real estate (answer A), the redemption of a corporation's own stock (answer B), and the sale of a corporation's treasury stock (answer C).

2. **A** The amount of income tax deferred to future years is $18,000 (answer A), determined as follows:

Depreciation expense, sum-of-the-years-digits method..............	$100,000
Depreciation expense, straight-line method........................	60,000
Excess expense in determination of taxable income.................	$ 40,000
Income tax rate....................	× 45%
Income tax deferred to future years..	$ 18,000

3. **C** The correction of a material error related to a prior period should be excluded from the determination of net income of the current period and reported as an adjustment of the balance of retained earnings at the beginning of the period (answer C).

4. **A** Events and transactions that are distinguished by their unusual nature and by the infrequency of their occurrence, such as a gain on condemnation of land for public use, are reported in the income statement as extraordinary items (answer A).

5. **C** An appropriation for plant expansion is a portion of total retained earnings and would be reported in the stockholders' equity section of the balance sheet (answer C).

CHAPTER 17

1. **B** Since the contract rate on the bonds is higher than the prevailing market rate, a rational investor would be willing to pay more than the face amount, or a premium (answer B), for the bonds. If the contract rate and the market rate were equal, the bonds could be expected to sell at their face amount (answer A). Likewise, if the market rate is higher than the contract rate, the bonds would sell at a price below their face amount (answer D) or at a discount (answer C).

2. **A** The bond carrying amount, sometimes called the book value, is the face amount plus unamortized premium or less unamortized discount. For this question, the carrying amount is $500,000 less $40,000, or $460,000 (answer A).

3. **C** The balance of Discount on Bonds Payable is reported as a deduction from Bonds Payable in the long-term liabilities section (answer C) of the balance sheet. Likewise, a balance in a premium on bonds payable account would be reported as an addition to Bonds Payable in the long-term liabilities section of the balance sheet.

4. **B** The amount debited to the investment account is the cost of the bonds, which includes the amount paid to the seller for the bonds (101% × $100,000) plus broker's commissions ($50), or $101,050 (answer B). The $2,000 of accrued interest that is paid to the seller should be debited to Interest Income, since it is an offset against the amount that will be received as interest at the next interest date.

5. **B** Although the sinking fund may consist of cash as well as securities, the fund is listed on the

balance sheet as an investment (answer B) because it is to be used to pay the long-term liability at maturity.

CHAPTER 18

1. **C** When parent acquires a controlling share of the voting stock of subsidiary in exchange for its voting common stock (answer C), the affiliation is termed a "pooling of interests." When parent acquires a controlling share of the voting stock of subsidiary in exchange for cash (answer A), other assets, issuances of debt obligations (answer B), or a combination of the foregoing, it is termed a "purchase."

2. **B** The excess of cost over book equity of interest in S Co. is $100,000 (answer B), determined as follows:

Investment in S Co. (cost)	$1,000,000
Eliminate 100% of S Co. stock	(750,000)
Eliminate 100% of S Co. retained earnings	(150,000)
Excess of cost over book equity of subsidiary interest	$ 100,000

3. **B** The excess of cost over book equity of interest in S Co. is $190,000 (answer B), determined as follows:

Investment in S Co. (cost)	$1,000,000
Eliminate 90% of S Co. stock	(675,000)
Eliminate 90% of S Co. retained earnings	(135,000)
Excess of cost over book equity of subsidiary interest	$ 190,000

4. **D** The 10% of the stock owned by outsiders is referred to as the minority interest. It amounts to $90,000, determined as follows:

10% of common stock	$75,000
10% of retained earnings	15,000
Total minority interest	$90,000

5. **B** The 250,000 pesos ($10,000 ÷ $.04) representing the billed price, which had a value of $10,000 on July 9, 1984, had increased in

value to $12,500 (250,000 pesos × $.05) on August 8, 1984, when payment was received. The gain, which was realized because the transactions were completed by the receipts of cash, was $2,500 (answer B).

CHAPTER 19

1. **A** Working capital is the excess of total current assets over total current liabilities; that is, $225,000 less $150,000, or $75,000 (answer A) in the question.

2. **A** Working capital is provided by transactions that decrease noncurrent assets (answer A), such as the sale of a plant asset for cash. Transactions that decrease noncurrent liabilities (answer B), such as the redemption of long-term liabilities for cash, and transactions that decrease stockholders' equity (answer C), such as the declaration of cash dividends, are applications of working capital.

3. **C** The acquisition of equipment for cash (answer C) decreases cash and working capital and is therefore an application of working capital. The sale of common stock for cash (answer A) and the issuance of bonds payable for cash (answer B) both increase cash and working capital and therefore are sources of working capital.

4. **C** The operations section of the statement of changes in financial position would report a total of $77,000 (answer C) for the working capital provided by operations, determined as follows:

Operations during the year:

Net income	$55,000	
Add deduction not decreasing working capital during the year:		
Depreciation	22,000	$77,000

5. **D** The operations section of the statement of changes in financial position would report a total of $65,500 for the cash provided by operations, determined as follows:

Operations during the year:

Net income		$55,000
Add deductions not de-creasing cash during the year:		
Depreciation	$22,000	
Decrease in inventories . . .	5,000	
Decrease in prepaid expenses	500	27,500
		$82,500
Deduct additions not increasing cash during the year:		
Increase in trade re-ceivables	$10,000	
Decrease in accounts payable	7,000	17,000
		$65,500

CHAPTER 20

1. **A** Percentage analysis indicating the relationship of the component parts to the total in a financial statement, such as the relationship of current assets to total assets (20% to 100%) in the question, is called vertical analysis (answer A). Percentage analysis of increases and decreases in corresponding items in comparative financial statements is called horizontal analysis (answer B). An example of horizontal analysis would be the presentation of the amount of current assets in the preceding balance sheet along with the amount of current assets for the current year, with the increase or decrease in current assets between the periods expressed as a percentage. Differential analysis (answer C), as discussed in Chapter 25, is the area of accounting concerned with the effect of alternative courses of action on revenue and expenses.

2. **D** Various solvency measures, categorized as current position analysis, indicate a firm's ability to meet currently maturing obligations. Each measure contributes in the analysis of a firm's current position and is most useful when viewed with other measures and when compared with similar measures for other periods and for other firms. Working capital (answer A) is the excess of current assets over current liabilities; the current ratio (answer B) is the

ratio of current assets to current liabilities; and the acid-test ratio (answer C) is the ratio of the sum of cash, receivables, and marketable securities to current liabilities.

3. **D** The ratio of current assets to current liabilities is usually referred to as the current ratio (answer A) and is sometimes referred to as the working capital ratio (answer B) or bankers' ratio (answer C).

4. **C** The ratio of the sum of cash, receivables, and marketable securities (sometimes called "quick assets") to current liabilities is called the acid-test ratio (answer C) or quick ratio. The current ratio (answer A) and working capital ratio (answer B) are two terms that describe the ratio of current assets to current liabilities.

5. **C** As with many attempts at analyzing financial data, it is possible to determine more than one measure that is useful for evaluating the efficiency in the management of inventory. Both the merchandise inventory turnover (answer A), which is determined by dividing the cost of merchandise sold by the average inventory, and the number of days' sales in merchandise inventory (answer B), which is determined by dividing the merchandise at the end of the year by the average daily cost of merchandise sold, express the relationship between the cost of merchandise sold and merchandise inventory.

CHAPTER 21

1. **B** Operating expenses should be apportioned to the various departments as nearly as possible in accordance with the cost of services rendered to them. For rent expense, generally the most appropriate basis is the floor space devoted to each department (answer B).

2. **C** When the departmental margin approach to income reporting is employed, the direct departmental expenses for each department are deducted from the gross profit for each department to yield departmental margin for each department (answer C). The indirect expenses are deducted from the total departmental margin to yield income from operations (answer A). The final total income is identified as net income (answer B).

3. **A** Operating expenses traceable to or incurred for the sole benefit of a specific department, such as sales commissions expense, are termed direct expenses (answer A) and should be so reported on the income statement departmentalized through departmental margin.

4. **C** The home office account in the branch ledger and the Colony West branch account in the home office ledger have equal but opposite balances and are known as reciprocal accounts (answer C).

5. **C** In the work sheet for the combined income statement, the account Shipments to Northside Branch is eliminated against the account Shipments from Home Office (answer C) because these two accounts record a change in location of merchandise within the company.

CHAPTER 22

1. **C** Three inventory accounts are maintained by manufacturing businesses for (1) goods in the process of manufacture (Work in Process — answer C), (2) goods in the state in which they are to be sold (Finished Goods — answer A), and (3) goods in the state in which they were acquired (Materials — answer B).

2. **D** The finished goods inventory is composed of three categories of manufacturing costs: direct materials (answer A), direct labor (answer B), and factory overhead (answer C).

3. **B** Factory overhead includes all manufacturing costs, except direct materials and direct labor. Salaries of plant supervisors (answer B) is an example of a factory overhead item. Wages of factory assembly-line workers (answer A) is a direct labor item, and bearings for electric motors (answer C) are direct materials.

4. **A** Job order cost systems are best suited to businesses manufacturing for special orders from customers, such as would be the case for a repair shop for antique furniture (answer A). A process cost system is best suited for manufacturers of homogeneous units of product, such as rubber (answer B) and coal (answer C).

5. **B** If the amount of factory overhead applied during a particular period exceeds the actual overhead costs, the factory overhead account

will have a credit balance and is said to be overapplied (answer B) or overabsorbed. If the amount applied is less than the actual costs, the account will have a debit balance and is said to be underapplied (answer A) or underabsorbed (answer C).

CHAPTER 23

1. **C** The process cost system is most appropriate for a business where manufacturing is conducted by continuous operations and involves a series of uniform production processes, such as the processing of crude oil (answer C). The job order cost system is most appropriate for a business where the product is made to customers' specifications, such as custom furniture manufacturing (answer A) and commercial building construction (answer B).

2. **C** The manufacturing costs that are necessary to convert direct materials into finished products are referred to as processing costs. The processing costs include direct labor and factory overhead (answer C).

3. **B** The number of units that could have been produced from start to finish during a period is termed equivalent units. The 4,875 equivalent units (answer B) is determined as follows:

To process units in inventory on May 1:	
1,000 units × ¼	250
To process units started and completed in May: 5,500 units − 1,000 units	4,500
To process units in inventory on May 31:	
500 units × ¼	125
Equivalent units of production in May	4,875

4. **A** The processing costs (direct labor and factory overhead) totaling $48,750 are divided by the number of equivalent units (4,875) to determine the unit processing cost of $10 (answer A).

5. **B** The product resulting from a process that has little value in relation to the principal product or joint products is known as a by-product (answer B). When two or more commodities of significant value are produced from a single direct material, the products are termed joint products (answer A). The raw material that

enters directly into the finished product is termed direct material (answer C).

CHAPTER 24

1. **C** The capital expenditures budget (answer C) summarizes the plans for a number of years into the future for the acquisition of plant facilities and equipment. The cash budget (answer A) presents the expected inflow and outflow of cash for a budget period, and the sales budget (answer B) presents the expected sales for the budget period.

2. **C** Flexible budgeting (answer C) provides a series of budgets for varying rates of activity and thereby builds into the budgeting system the effect of fluctuations in volume of activity. Budget performance reporting (answer A) is a system of reports that compares actual results with budgeted figures. Continuous budgeting (answer B) is a variant of fiscal-year budgeting that provides for the maintenance of a twelve-month projection into the future at all times. This is achieved by periodically deleting from the current budget the data for the elapsed period and adding newly estimated budget data for the same period next year.

3. **B** The unfavorable direct materials price variance of $2,550 (answer B) is determined as follows:

Actual price . . . . $5.05 per pound
Standard price. . . . . 5.00 per pound
  Price variance — unfavorable $ .05 per pound

.05 × 51,000 actual quantity = $2,550

4. **B** The unfavorable factory overhead volume variance of $2,000 (answer B) is determined as follows:

Productive capacity not used . . . . 1,000 hours
Standard fixed factory overhead cost
  rate . . . . × $2
  Factory overhead volume variance
   — unfavorable. $2,000

5. **D** Since variances from standard costs represent the differences between the standard

cost of manufacturing a product and the actual costs incurred, the variances relate to the product. Therefore, they should be reported on interim income statements as an adjustment to gross profit — at standard.

CHAPTER 25

1. **B** Under the variable costing concept (answer B), the cost of products manufactured are composed of only those manufacturing costs that increase or decrease as the volume of production rises or falls. Those costs include direct materials, direct labor, and variable factory overhead. Under the absorption costing concept (answer A), all manufacturing costs become a part of the cost of the products manufactured. The absorption costing concept is required in the determination of historical cost and taxable income. The variable costing concept is often useful to management in making decisions.

2. **C** In the variable costing income statement, the deduction of the variable cost of goods sold from sales yields the manufacturing margin (answer C). Deduction of the variable selling and general expenses from manufacturing margin yields the contribution margin (answer B).

3. **B** The contribution margin of $260,000 (answer B) is determined by deducting all of the variable costs and expenses ($400,000 + $90,000) from sales ($750,000).

4. **A** Differential cost (answer A) is the amount of increase or decrease in cost that is expected from a particular course of action compared with an alternative. Replacement cost (answer B) is the cost of replacing an asset at current market prices, and sunk cost (answer C) is a past cost that will not be affected by subsequent decisions.

5. **C** The amount of income that could have been earned from the best available alternative to a proposed use of cash is called opportunity cost (answer C). Actual cost (answer A) or historical cost (answer B) is the cash or equivalent outlay for goods or services actually acquired.

CHAPTER 26

1. **C** A change in sales from one period to another can be attributed to (1) a change in the number of units sold—quantity factor and (2) a change in the unit price—price factor. The $45,000 decrease (answer C) attributed to the quantity factor is determined as follows:

   Decrease in number of units sold in
      current year...................... 5,000
   Unit sales price in preceding year...... × $9
   Quantity factor—decrease $45,000

   The price factor can be determined as follows:

   Increase in unit sales price in current
      year.............................. $1
   Number of units sold in current year.... ×80,000
   Price factor—increase $80,000

   The increase of $80,000 attributed to the price factor less the decrease of $45,000 attributed to the quantity factor accounts for the $35,000 increase in total sales for the current year.

2. **C** The break-even point of $400,000 (answer C) is that point in operations at which revenue and expired costs are exactly equal and is determined as follows:

   $$\text{Break-Even Sales (in \$)} = \text{Fixed Costs (in \$)} + \text{Variable Costs (as \% of Sales)}$$
   $$S = \$240,000 + 40\%S$$
   $$60\%S = \$240,000$$
   $$S = \$400,000$$

3. **A** The margin of safety of 20% (answer A) represents the possible decrease in sales revenue that may occur before an operating loss results and is determined as follows:

   $$\text{Margin of Safety} = \frac{\text{Sales} - \text{Sales at Break-Even Point}}{\text{Sales}}$$
   $$\text{Margin of Safety} = \frac{\$500,000 - \$400,000}{\$500,000}$$
   $$= 20\%$$

   The margin of safety can also be expressed in terms of dollars and would amount to

$100,000, determined as follows:

   Sales $500,000
   Less sales at break-even point...... 400,000
   Margin of safety.................$100,000

4. **D** The contribution margin ratio indicates the percentage of each sales dollar available to cover the fixed expenses and provide operating income and is determined as follows:

   $$\text{Contribution Margin Ratio} = \frac{\text{Sales} - \text{Variable Expenses}}{\text{Sales}}$$
   $$\text{Contribution Margin Ratio} = \frac{\$500,000 - \$200,000}{\$500,000}$$
   $$= 60\%$$

5. **B** Of the three methods of analyzing proposals for capital expenditures, the cash payback period method (answer B) refers to the expected period of time required to recover the amount of cash to be invested. The average rate of return method (answer A) is a measure of the anticipated profitability of a proposal. The discounted cash flow method (answer C) reduces the expected future net cash flows originating from a proposal to their present values.

CHAPTER 27

1. **C** Dividends of $100 or less (answer A) for a single taxpayer and the value of property received as a gift (answer B) are nontaxable items. Tips for services rendered, although sometimes not included in the wages from employers (answer C), are taxable.

2. **C** Interest (answer A) and real estate taxes (answer B) on personal residence are deductible from adjusted gross income only if the taxpayer itemizes deductions and claims excess itemized deductions. Contributions (within prescribed limits) to a qualified retirement fund (answer C) are deductible from gross income by self-employed taxpayers to determine adjusted gross income.

3. **A** Since 60% of the excess of a net long-term capital gain over a short-term capital loss is deducted from gross income, the adjusted gross income from capital gains is $4,800 (answer A), determined as follows:

Net long-term capital gain. $20,000
Net short-term capital loss 8,000
Net capital gain — gross income. $12,000
Long-term capital gain deduction 7,200
Adjusted gross income from capital
   gain. . . . . $ 4,800

4. C Depreciation on rental property (answer A) is a deduction from gross income in determining adjusted gross income, and interest on mortgage note on personal residence (answer B) is deductible from adjusted gross income if deductions are itemized. Both of these items therefore reduce taxable income. One half of the contribution to a political party (answer C), with a maximum credit of $50 for a single taxpayer, is a direct credit against the tax.

5. D Generally, the taxable income of a corporation is determined by deducting its ordinary business expenses from its total includable gross income. However, the following three items are granted special consideration: 85% of dividends from other corporations (answer A) is excluded from gross income; charitable contributions for the current year (answer B) are limited to 5% of taxable income; and the tax on the excess of a net long-term capital gain over a short-term capital loss (answer C) is limited to a maximum of 28%.

CHAPTER 28

1. B Personal financial statements are used for many purposes, such as income tax planning and arranging for a loan. For such multiple purposes, reporting of assets at estimated current values (answer B) is most useful.

2. C The caption "net worth" (answer C) is used in the statement of financial condition for the individual's equity. Titles such as proprietorship (answer A) and capital (answer B) are usually associated with commercial enterprises.

3. A In accounting for nonprofit organizations, the term used to represent an accounting entity with appropriate accounts for a particular purpose is "fund" (answer A). Potential liabilities of a fund are referred to as appropriations (answer B), and a fund's binding commitments to pay money eventually are referred to as encumbrances (answer C).

4. C The account that represents the capital for a nonprofit organization is termed Fund Balance (answer C). For a commercial enterprise, the capital resulting from earnings retained in the enterprise is referred to by various terms, including Retained Earnings (answer A) and Accumulated Earnings (answer B).

5. A A statement of changes in fund balance (answer A), although similar to the retained earnings statement of a commercial enterprise, has a unique format. It indicates the balance at the beginning of the year in fund balance, plus or minus, as appropriate, the difference for the fiscal year of (1) estimated revenues and appropriations, (2) revenues and estimated revenues, and (3) appropriations and expenditures. Finally, the encumbrances outstanding at the end of the year are deducted to arrive at the end-of-the-year balance of the fund balance account. The trial balance (answer B) and balance sheet (answer C) for nonprofit organizations are similar to such statements for commercial enterprises.

D

APPENDIX

Present Value

Mathematical tables reporting various interest rates for various time periods are always based on $1. The reason is that a value for $1, selected from the appropriate table, can be used in determining the effect of any number of dollars. Tables were not used in the illustrations in Chapter 17 because a better understanding of the concepts is achieved through the more laborious detailed computations.

The following sections present mathematical tables and the formulas used in deriving the tables. The tables are limited to 20 periods for a small number of interest rates and the amounts are carried to only four decimal places. Books of tables are available with as many as 360 periods, 45 interest rates (including many fractional rates), and amounts carried to eight decimal places.

The examples used are based on the illustrations in Chapter 17. Slight discrepancies between the amounts obtained in Chapter 17 and those obtained from the tables are due to rounding the decimals to four places.

PRESENT VALUE OF $1 AT COMPOUND INTEREST

The formula for determining the *present value* of $1 at compound interest is $Pv = \dfrac{1}{(1 + i)^n}$ where "Pv" is the present value of $1, "i" the periodic interest rate, and "n" the number of periods.

The table on the next page may be used to determine the present value of the face amount of the $100,000, 12%, 5-year bond issue (pages 466–472) based on assumed market rates of 11%, 12%, and 13%. The contract rate is, of course, 12% in all three examples. It should also be noted that the 10 semiannual interest payments are excluded from consideration in the following computations.

Bonds issued at face amount, market rate of 12%:
"Pv" of $1 for 10 periods at 6% is $0.5584
The present value of the face of the bonds is:
$100,000 × $0.5584 = $55,840

934

Bonds issued at a discount, market rate of 13%:
"Pv" of $1 for 10 periods at 6½% is $0.5327
The present value of the face of the bonds is:
$100,000 × $0.5327 = $53,270

Bonds issued at a premium, market rate of 11%:
"Pv" of $1 for 10 periods at 5½% is $0.5854
The present value of the face of the bonds is:
$100,000 × $0.5854 = $58,540

PRESENT VALUE OF
$1 AT COMPOUND
INTEREST

Periods	5%	5½%	6%	6½%	7%	7½%	8%	8½%
1	0.9524	0.9479	0.9434	0.9390	0.9346	0.9302	0.9259	0.9217
2	0.9070	0.8985	0.8900	0.8817	0.8734	0.8653	0.8573	0.8495
3	0.8638	0.8516	0.8396	0.8278	0.8163	0.8050	0.7938	0.7829
4	0.8227	0.8072	0.7921	0.7773	0.7629	0.7488	0.7350	0.7216
5	0.7835	0.7651	0.7473	0.7299	0.7130	0.6966	0.6806	0.6650
6	0.7462	0.7252	0.7050	0.6853	0.6663	0.6480	0.6302	0.6129
7	0.7107	0.6874	0.6651	0.6435	0.6228	0.6028	0.5835	0.5649
8	0.6768	0.6516	0.6274	0.6042	0.5820	0.5607	0.5403	0.5207
9	0.6446	0.6176	0.5919	0.5674	0.5439	0.5216	0.5002	0.4799
10	0.6139	0.5854	0.5584	0.5327	0.5083	0.4852	0.4632	0.4423
11	0.5847	0.5549	0.5268	0.5002	0.4751	0.4513	0.4289	0.4076
12	0.5568	0.5260	0.4970	0.4697	0.4440	0.4199	0.3971	0.3757
13	0.5303	0.4986	0.4688	0.4410	0.4150	0.3906	0.3677	0.3463
14	0.5051	0.4726	0.4423	0.4141	0.3878	0.3633	0.3405	0.3191
15	0.4810	0.4479	0.4173	0.3888	0.3624	0.3380	0.3152	0.2941
16	0.4581	0.4246	0.3936	0.3651	0.3387	0.3144	0.2919	0.2711
17	0.4363	0.4024	0.3714	0.3428	0.3166	0.2925	0.2703	0.2499
18	0.4155	0.3815	0.3503	0.3219	0.2959	0.2720	0.2502	0.2303
19	0.3957	0.3616	0.3305	0.3022	0.2765	0.2531	0.2317	0.2122
20	0.3769	0.3427	0.3118	0.2838	0.2584	0.2354	0.2145	0.1956

Periods	9%	10%	11%	12%	13%	14%	15%	16%
1	0.9174	0.9091	0.9009	0.8929	0.8850	0.8772	0.8696	0.8621
2	0.8417	0.8264	0.8116	0.7972	0.7831	0.7695	0.7561	0.7432
3	0.7722	0.7513	0.7312	0.7118	0.6931	0.6750	0.6575	0.6407
4	0.7084	0.6830	0.6587	0.6355	0.6133	0.5921	0.5718	0.5523
5	0.6499	0.6209	0.5935	0.5674	0.5428	0.5194	0.4972	0.4761
6	0.5963	0.5645	0.5346	0.5066	0.4803	0.4556	0.4323	0.4104
7	0.5470	0.5132	0.4817	0.4523	0.4251	0.3996	0.3759	0.3538
8	0.5019	0.4665	0.4339	0.4039	0.3762	0.3506	0.3269	0.3050
9	0.4604	0.4241	0.3909	0.3606	0.3329	0.3075	0.2843	0.2630
10	0.4224	0.3855	0.3522	0.3220	0.2946	0.2697	0.2472	0.2267
11	0.3875	0.3505	0.3173	0.2875	0.2607	0.2366	0.2149	0.1954
12	0.3555	0.3186	0.2858	0.2567	0.2307	0.2076	0.1869	0.1685
13	0.3262	0.2897	0.2575	0.2292	0.2042	0.1821	0.1625	0.1452
14	0.2992	0.2633	0.2320	0.2046	0.1807	0.1597	0.1413	0.1252
15	0.2745	0.2394	0.2090	0.1827	0.1599	0.1401	0.1229	0.1079
16	0.2519	0.2176	0.1883	0.1631	0.1415	0.1229	0.1069	0.0930
17	0.2311	0.1978	0.1696	0.1456	0.1252	0.1078	0.0929	0.0802
18	0.2120	0.1799	0.1528	0.1300	0.1108	0.0946	0.0808	0.0691
19	0.1945	0.1635	0.1377	0.1161	0.0981	0.0829	0.0703	0.0596
20	0.1784	0.1486	0.1240	0.1037	0.0868	0.0728	0.0611	0.0514

PRESENT
VALUE OF AN
ANNUITY OF $1
PER PERIOD AT
COMPOUND
INTEREST

An **annuity** is a series of equal payments at fixed intervals. The **present value** of an annuity is the sum of the present value of each payment, at compound interest. Thus, the first payment is discounted for one period, the second payment for two periods, etc., as is illustrated in Chapter 17.

The formula for determining the present value of an annuity of $1 is

$$PvA = \frac{1 - \frac{1}{(1 + i)^n}}{i}$$

where "PvA" is the present value of an annuity of $1, "i" the periodic interest rate, and "n" the number of equal payments.

The table below may be used to determine the present value of the 10 equal payments of $6,000 associated with the $100,000, 12%, 5-year bond issue (pages 466–472), based on the three assumed rates of interest.

PRESENT VALUE OF
ANNUITY OF $1
AT COMPOUND
INTEREST

Periods	5%	5½%	6%	6½%	7%	7½%	8%	8½%
1	0.9524	0.9479	0.9434	0.9390	0.9346	0.9302	0.9259	0.9217
2	1.8594	1.8463	1.8334	1.8206	1.8080	1.7956	1.7833	1.7711
3	2.7232	2.6979	2.6730	2.6485	2.6243	2.6005	2.5771	2.5540
4	3.5460	3.5052	3.4651	3.4258	3.3872	3.3493	3.3121	3.2756
5	4.3295	4.2703	4.2124	4.1557	4.1002	4.0459	3.9927	3.9406
6	5.0757	4.9955	4.9173	4.8410	4.7665	4.6938	4.6229	4.5536
7	5.7864	5.6830	5.5824	5.4845	5.3893	5.2966	5.2064	5.1185
8	6.4632	6.3346	6.2098	6.0888	5.9713	5.8573	5.7466	5.6392
9	7.1078	6.9522	6.8017	6.6561	6.5152	6.3789	6.2469	6.1191
10	7.7217	7.5376	7.3601	7.1888	7.0236	6.8641	6.7101	6.5613
11	8.3064	8.0925	7.8869	7.6890	7.4987	7.3154	7.1390	6.9690
12	8.8633	8.6185	8.3838	8.1587	7.9427	7.7353	7.5361	7.3447
13	9.3936	9.1171	8.8527	8.5997	8.3577	8.1258	7.9038	7.6910
14	9.8986	9.5896	9.2950	9.0138	8.7455	8.4892	8.2442	8.0101
15	10.3797	10.0376	9.7123	9.4027	9.1079	8.8271	8.5595	8.3042
16	10.8378	10.4622	10.1059	9.7678	9.4467	9.1415	8.8514	8.5753
17	11.2741	10.8646	10.4773	10.1106	9.7632	9.4340	9.1216	8.8252
18	11.6896	11.2461	10.8276	10.4325	10.0591	9.7060	9.3719	9.0555
19	12.0853	11.6077	11.1581	10.7347	10.3356	9.9591	9.6036	9.2677
20	12.4622	11.9504	11.4699	11.0185	10.5940	10.1945	9.8181	9.4633

Periods	9%	10%	11%	12%	13%	14%	15%	16%
1	0.9174	0.9091	0.9009	0.8929	0.8850	0.8772	0.8696	0.8621
2	1.7591	1.7355	1.7125	1.6901	1.6681	1.6467	1.6257	1.6052
3	2.5313	2.4869	2.4437	2.4018	2.3612	2.3216	2.2832	2.2459
4	3.2397	3.1699	3.1024	3.0373	2.9745	2.9137	2.8550	2.7982
5	3.8897	3.7908	3.6959	3.6048	3.5172	3.4331	3.3522	3.2743
6	4.4859	4.3553	4.2305	4.1114	3.9976	3.8887	3.7845	3.6847
7	5.0330	4.8684	4.7122	4.5638	4.4226	4.2883	4.1604	4.0386
8	5.5348	5.3349	5.1461	4.9676	4.7988	4.6389	4.4873	4.3436
9	5.9952	5.7590	5.5370	5.3283	5.1317	4.9464	4.7716	4.6065
10	6.4177	6.1446	5.8892	5.6502	5.4262	5.2161	5.0188	4.8332
11	6.8052	6.4951	6.2065	5.9377	5.6869	5.4527	5.2337	5.0286
12	7.1607	6.8137	6.4924	6.1944	5.9176	5.6603	5.4206	5.1971
13	7.4869	7.1034	6.7499	6.4235	6.1218	5.8424	5.5831	5.3423
14	7.7862	7.3667	6.9819	6.6282	6.3025	6.0021	5.7245	5.4675
15	8.0607	7.6061	7.1909	6.8109	6.4624	6.1422	5.8474	5.5755
16	8.3126	7.8237	7.3792	6.9740	6.6039	6.2651	5.9542	5.6685
17	8.5436	8.0216	7.5488	7.1196	6.7291	6.3729	6.0472	5.7487
18	8.7556	8.2014	7.7016	7.2497	6.8399	6.4674	6.1280	5.8178
19	8.9501	8.3649	7.8393	7.3658	6.9380	6.5504	6.1982	5.8775
20	9.1285	8.5136	7.9633	7.4694	7.0248	6.6231	6.2593	5.9288

Bonds issued at face amount, market rate of 12%:
"PvA" of $1 for 10 periods at 6% is $7.3601
The present value of the 10 payments of $6,000 is:
$6,000 × $7.3601 = $44,161

Bonds issued at a discount, market rate of 13%:
"PvA" of $1 for 10 periods at 6½% is $7.1888
The present value of the 10 payments of $6,000 is:
$6,000 × $7.1888 = $43,133

Bonds issued at a premium, market rate of 11%:
"PvA" of $1 for 10 periods at 5½% is $7.5376
The present value of the 10 payments of $6,000 is:
$6,000 × $7.5376 = $45,226

The present value of the face of the bonds plus the present value of the interest payments, determined by use of the tables, corresponds to the results obtained in the three illustrations on pages 466–472, except for minor differences due to rounding the tables to four decimal places.

Work Sheet for Statement of Changes in Financial Position

Some accountants prefer to use a work sheet to assist them in assembling data for the statement of changes in financial position (funds statement). Although a work sheet is not essential, it is especially useful when a large number of transactions must be analyzed. Also, whether or not a work sheet is used, the concepts of funds and the funds statement are not affected.

The following sections describe and illustrate the use of the work sheet. Attention is directed to its use in preparing the funds statement (1) based on working capital and (2) based on cash. The data that appear in Chapter 19 for T. R. Morgan Corporation are used for the illustrations.

WORK SHEET PROCEDURES FOR FUNDS STATEMENT BASED ON WORKING CAPITAL

The comparative balance sheet and additional data obtained from the accounts of T. R. Morgan Corporation are presented on page 939. The work sheet prepared from these data is presented on page 940.

The procedures to prepare the work sheet for the funds statement based on working capital are outlined as follows:

1. List the title of each noncurrent account in the Description column. For each account, enter that debit or credit representing the change (increase or decrease) in the account balance for the year in the Change During Year column.

2. Add the debits and credits in the Change During Year column and determine the subtotals. Enter the change (increase or decrease) in working capital during the year in the appropriate column to balance the totals of the debits and credits.

3. Provide space in the bottom portion of the work sheet for later use in identifying the various (1) sources of working capital and (2) applications of working capital.

4. Analyze the change during the year in each noncurrent account in order to determine the sources and/or applications of working capital related to the transactions recorded in each account. Record these sources and applications

in the bottom portion of the work sheet by means of entries in the Work Sheet Entries columns.

5. Complete the work sheet.

These procedures are explained in detail in the following paragraphs.

T. H. Morgan Corporation
Comparative Balance Sheet
December 31, 1985 and 1984

	1985	1984	Increase Decrease*
Assets			
Cash	$ 49,000	$ 26,000	$ 23,000
Trade receivables (net)	74,000	65,000	9,000
Inventories	172,000	180,000	8,000*
Prepaid expenses	4,000	3,000	1,000
Investments (long-term)	—	45,000	45,000*
Land	90,000	40,000	50,000
Building	200,000	200,000	—
Accumulated depreciation building	(36,000)	(30,000)	(6,000)
Equipment	180,000	142,000	38,000
Accumulated depreciation—equipment	(43,000)	(40,000)	(3,000)
Total assets	$690,000	$631,000	$ 59,000
Liabilities			
Accounts payable (merchandise creditors)	$ 50,000	$ 32,000	$ 18,000
Income tax payable	2,500	4,000	1,500*
Dividends payable	15,000	8,000	7,000
Bonds payable	120,000	245,000	125,000*
Total liabilities	$187,500	$289,000	$101,500*
Stockholders' Equity			
Common stock	$280,000	$230,000	$ 50,000
Retained earnings	222,500	112,000	110,500
Total stockholders' equity	$502,500	$342,000	$160,500
Total liabilities and stockholders' equity	$690,000	$631,000	$ 59,000

Additional data:

(1) Net income, $140,500.

(2) Cash dividends declared, $30,000.

(3) Common stock issued at par for land, $50,000.

(4) Bonds payable retired for cash, $125,000.

(5) Depreciation for year: equipment, $12,000; building, $6,000.

(6) Fully depreciated equipment discarded, $9,000.

(7) Equipment purchased for cash, $47,000.

(8) Book value of investments sold for $75,000 cash, $45,000.

T. R. Morgan Corporation
Work Sheet for Statement of Changes in Financial Position
For Year Ended December 31, 1985

Description	Change During Year Debit	Change During Year Credit	Work Sheet Entries Debit	Work Sheet Entries Credit
Investments		45,000	(j) 45,000	
Land	50,000			(i) 50,000
Building......................	—	—		
Accumulated depreciation— building......................		6,000	(h) 6,000	
Equipment	38,000		(f) 9,000	(g) 47,000
Accumulated depreciation— equipment		3,000	(e) 12,000	(f) 9,000
Bonds payable	125,000			(d) 125,000
Common stock		50,000	(c) 50,000	
Retained earnings		110,500	(a) 140,500	(b) 30,000
	213,000	214,500		
Increase in working capital	1,500			
Totals........................	214,500	214,500		
Sources of working capital: Operations:				
Net income				(a) 140,500
Depreciation of equipment...................				(e) 12,000
Depreciation of building				(h) 6,000
Issuance of common stock for land.............				(c) 50,000
Book value of investments sold.................				(j) 45,000
Applications of working capital:				
Declaration of cash dividends..................			(b) 30,000	
Retirement of bonds..........................			(d) 125,000	
Purchase of equipment........................			(g) 47,000	
Purchase of land by issuance of common stock...			(i) 50,000	
Totals...			514,500	514,500

Noncurrent Accounts

Since the analysis of transactions recorded in the noncurrent accounts reveals the sources and applications of working capital, the work sheet focuses on the noncurrent accounts. For this purpose, the titles of the noncurrent accounts are entered in the Description column. Next, the debit or credit change for the year in each account balance is entered in the Change During Year column. For example, the beginning and ending balances of Investments were $45,000 and zero, respectively. Thus, the change for the year was a decrease, or credit, of $45,000. The beginning and ending balances of Land were $40,000 and $90,000, respectively. Thus, the change for the year was an increase, or debit, of $50,000. The changes in the other accounts are determined in a like manner.

Change in Working Capital	Since transactions that result in changes in working capital (the current accounts) also result in changes in the noncurrent accounts, the change in working capital for the period will equal the change in the noncurrent accounts for the period. Thus, if a subtotal of the debits and credits for the noncurrent accounts (as indicated in the Change During Year column) is determined, the increase or decrease in working capital for the period can be inserted in the appropriate column and the two columns will balance. In the illustration, the subtotal of the credit column ($214,500) exceeds the subtotal of the debit column ($213,000) by $1,500, which is identified as the increase in working capital. By entering the $1,500 as a debit in the Change During Year column, the debit and credit columns are balanced. This $1,500 increase in working capital will be reported on the funds statement as the difference between the total of the sources section and the total of the applications section. This change is supported by details of the change in each of the working capital components, as follows:

CHANGES IN COMPONENTS OF WORKING CAPITAL	Changes in components of working capital:

Increase (decrease) in current assets:		
Cash	$23,000	
Trade receivables (net)	9,000	
Inventories	(8,000)	
Prepaid expenses	1,000	$25,000
Increase (decrease) in current liabilities:		
Accounts payable	$18,000	
Income tax payable	(1,500)	
Dividends payable	7,000	23,500
Increase in working capital		$ 1,500

If the subtotals in the Change During Year columns indicate that the debits exceed the credits, the balancing figure would be identified as a decrease in working capital.

Sources and Applications Sections	After the Change During Year columns are totaled and ruled, "Sources of working capital" is written in the Description column. Several lines are skipped, so that at a later time the various sources of working capital can be entered, and "Applications of working capital" is written in the Description column. When the work sheet is completed, this bottom portion will contain the data necessary to prepare the sources section and the applications section of the funds statement.
Analysis of Noncurrent Accounts	As was discussed on pages 532–535, transactions that result in sources and applications of working capital can be classified in terms of their effect on the noncurrent accounts. Therefore, to determine the various sources and applications for the year, the changes in the noncurrent accounts are analyzed. As each account is analyzed, entries made in the work sheet relate specific sources or

applications of working capital to the noncurrent account. It should be noted that the work sheet entries are not entered into the accounts. They are, as is the entire work sheet, strictly an aid in assembling the data for later use in preparing the funds statement.

The sequence in which the noncurrent accounts are analyzed is unimportant. However, because it is more convenient and efficient, and the chance for errors is reduced, the analysis illustrated will begin with the retained earnings account and proceed upward in the listing in sequential order.

Retained Earnings

The work sheet indicates that there was an increase of $110,500 in retained earnings for the year. The additional data, taken from an examination of the account, indicate that the increase was the result of two factors: (1) net income of $140,500 and (2) declaration of cash dividends of $30,000. To identify the sources and applications of working capital, two entries are made on the work sheet. These entries also serve to account for, or explain, the increase of $110,500.

Net income. In closing the accounts at the end of the year, the retained earnings account was credited for $140,500, representing the net income. The $140,500 is also reported on the funds statement as a source of working capital. An entry on the work sheet to debit retained earnings and to credit "Sources of working capital — operations: net income" accomplishes the following: (1) the credit portion of the closing entry (to retained earnings) is accounted for, or in effect canceled, and (2) the source of working capital is identified in the bottom portion of the work sheet. The entry on the work sheet is as follows:

(a) Retained Earnings............................. 140,500
    Sources of Working Capital — Operations:
      Net Income................................... 140,500

Dividends. In closing the accounts at the end of the year, the retained earnings account was debited for $30,000, representing the cash dividends declared. The $30,000 is also reported on the funds statement as an application of working capital. An entry on the work sheet to debit "Applications of working capital — declaration of cash dividends" and to credit retained earnings accomplishes the following: (1) the debit portion of the closing entry (to retained earnings) is accounted for, or in effect canceled, and (2) the application of working capital is identified in the bottom portion of the work sheet. The entry on the work sheet is as follows:

(b) Applications of Working Capital — Declaration
    of Cash Dividends 30,000
      Retained Earnings............................. 30,000

Common Stock

The next noncurrent item on the work sheet, common stock, increased by $50,000 during the year. The additional data, taken from an examination of the account, indicate that the stock was exchanged for land. The work sheet entry to account for this increase and to identify the source of working capital is as follows:

(c) Common Stock   50,000
      Sources of Working Capital—Issuance of
      Common Stock for Land   50,000

It should be noted that the effect of the exchange will also be analyzed when the land account is examined.

Bonds Payable

The decrease of $125,000 in the bonds payable account during the year resulted from the retirement of the bonds for cash. The work sheet entry to record the effect of this transaction on working capital is as follows:

(d) Applications of Working Capital—Retirement of
      Bonds Payable.   125,000
      Bonds Payable.   125,000

Accumulated Depreciation—Equipment

The work sheet indicates that the accumulated depreciation—equipment account increased by $3,000 during the year. The additional data indicate that the increase resulted from (1) depreciation expense of $12,000 (credit) for the year and (2) discarding $9,000 (debit) of fully depreciated equipment. Since depreciation expense does not affect working capital but does decrease the amount of net income, it should be added to net income to determine the amount of working capital from operations. This effect is indicated on the work sheet by the following entry:

(e) Accumulated Depreciation—Equipment.   12,000
      Sources of Working Capital—Operations:
      Depreciation of Equipment   12,000

It should be noted that the notation in the Description column is placed so that the $12,000 can be added to "Sources of working capital—operations: net income."

Since the discarding of the fully depreciated equipment did not affect working capital, the following entry is made on the work sheet in order to fully account for the change of $3,000 in the accumulated depreciation—equipment account:

(f) Equipment   9,000
      Accumulated Depreciation—Equipment.   9,000

It should be noted that this entry, like the transaction that was recorded in the accounts, does not affect working capital. It serves only to complete the accounting for all transactions that resulted in the change in the account during the year and thus helps assure that no transactions affecting working capital are overlooked in the analysis.

Equipment

The work sheet indicated that the equipment account increased by $38,000 during the year. The additional data, determined from an examination of the ledger account, indicated that the increase resulted from (1) discarding $9,000 of fully depreciated equipment and (2) purchasing $47,000 of equipment. The discarding of the equipment was included in, or accounted for, in (f) and needs no additional attention. The application of working capital to the purchase of equipment is recognized by the following entry on the work sheet:

```
(g) Applications of Working Capital — Purchase
       of Equipment ...................................   47,000
           Equipment ...................................            47,000
```

Accumulated Depreciation — Building

The $6,000 increase in the accumulated depreciation — building account during the year resulted from the entry to record depreciation expense. Since depreciation expense does not affect working capital but does decrease the amount of net income, it should be added to net income to determine the amount of working capital from operations. This effect is accomplished by the following entry on the work sheet:

```
(h) Accumulated Depreciation — Building ...............   6,000
       Sources of Working Capital — Operations:
          Depreciation of Building ........................            6,000
```

Building

There was no change in the beginning and ending balances of the building account and reference to the account confirms that no entries were made in it during the year. Hence, no entry is necessary on the work sheet.

Land

As indicated in the analysis of the common stock account, the $50,000 increase in land resulted from a purchase by issuance of common stock. The work sheet entry to indicate this application of working capital is as follows:

```
(i) Applications of Working Capital — Purchase of
       Land by Issuance of Common Stock ..............   50,000
           Land.........................................            50,000
```

Investments

The work sheet indicates that investments decreased by $45,000. The examination of the ledger account indicates that investments were sold for $75,000. As was explained on page 537, the $30,000 gain on the sale is already included in net income and consequently has already been accounted for as a source of working capital. Only the $45,000 book value of the investments sold would be reported as a source of working capital. To indicate this source on the work sheet, the following entry is made:

```
(j) Investments .....................................   45,000
        Sources of Working Capital—Book Value of
        Investments Sold.............................           45,000
```

Completing the Work Sheet

After all of the noncurrent accounts have been analyzed, all of the sources and applications are identified in the bottom portion of the work sheet. To assure the equality of the work sheet entries, the last step is to total the Work Sheet Entries columns.

Preparation of the Funds Statement

The data for the sources section and the applications section of the funds statement are obtained from the bottom portion of the work sheet. Some modifications are made to the work sheet data for presentation on the statement. For example, in presenting the working capital provided by operations, the additions to net income are labeled "Add deductions not decreasing working capital during the year." Another example is the reporting of the total depreciation expense ($18,000) instead of the two separate amounts ($12,000 and $6,000).

The increase (or decrease) in working capital that is reported on the statement is also identified on the work sheet. The funds statement prepared from the work sheet, including the details of the changes in each working capital component, is presented on page 946.

WORK SHEET PROCEDURES FOR FUNDS STATEMENT BASED ON CASH

The work sheet used to assemble the data for the funds statement based on working capital is also used to assemble data for the funds statement based on cash. The procedures differ in that the focus for the statement based on cash is on the analysis of the *noncash* accounts instead of the *noncurrent* accounts, as was the case when the statement was based on working capital. In other words, *in addition* to analyzing the changes in the noncurrent accounts, all of the current accounts *except cash* are analyzed in preparing the work sheet for the funds statement based on cash. To illustrate such a work sheet, the data for T. R. Morgan Corporation presented on page 939 are used. The work sheet prepared from these data is presented on page 947.

The procedures to prepare the work sheet for the funds statement based on cash are outlined as follows:

1. List the title of each *noncash* account in the Description column. For each account, enter the debit or credit representing the change (increase or decrease) in the account balance for the year in the Change During Year column.
2. Add the debits and credits in the Change During Year column and determine the subtotals. Enter the change (increase or decrease) in cash during the year in the appropriate column to balance the totals of the debits and credits.

T. R. Morgan Corporation
Statement of Changes in Financial Position
For Year Ended December 31, 1985

Sources of working capital:
  Operations during the year:
    Net income........................... $140,500
    Add deduction not decreasing working
    capital during the year:
      Depreciation 18,000 $158,500
  Issuance of common stock at par for land   50,000
  Book value of investments sold (excludes $30,000
    gain reported in net income) 45,000 $253,500
Applications of working capital:
  Declaration of cash dividends..................... $ 30,000
  Retirement of bonds payable......................   125,000
  Purchase of equipment...........................   47,000
  Purchase of land by issuance of common stock
    at par..   50,000   252,000
Increase in working capital.......................... $ 1,500

Changes in components of working capital:
  Increase (decrease) in current assets:
    Cash .... $ 23,000
    Trade receivables (net)........................   9,000
    Inventories ....   (8,000)
    Prepaid expenses...............................   1,000 $ 25,000
  Increase (decrease) in current liabilities:
    Accounts payable............................... $ 18,000
    Income tax payable.............................   (1,500)
    Dividends payable..............................   7,000   23,500
Increase in working capital.......................... $ 1,500

3. Provide space in the bottom portion of the work sheet for later use in identifying the various (1) sources of cash and (2) applications of cash.

4. Analyze the change during the year in each noncash account to determine the sources and/or applications of cash related to the transactions recorded in each account. Record these sources and applications in the bottom portion of the work sheet by means of entries in the Work Sheet Entries columns.

5. Complete the work sheet.

These procedures are explained in detail in the following paragraphs.

Noncash Accounts

Since the analysis of transactions recorded in the noncash accounts reveals the sources and applications of cash, the work sheet focuses on noncash accounts. For this purpose, the titles of the noncash accounts are entered in the Description

WORK SHEET FOR STATEMENT OF CHANGES IN FINANCIAL POSITION BASED ON CASH

T. R. Morgan Corporation
Work Sheet for Statement of Changes in Financial Position
For Year Ended December 31, 1985

Description	Change During Year Debit	Change During Year Credit	Work Sheet Entries Debit	Work Sheet Entries Credit
Trade receivables	9,000			(p) 9,000
Inventories..........................		8,000	(o) 8,000	
Prepaid expenses	1,000			(n) 1,000
Accounts payable		18,000	(m) 18,000	
Income tax payable.................	1,500			(l) 1,500
Dividends payable...................		7,000	(k) 7,000	
Investments........................		45,000	(j) 45,000	
Land............................	50,000			(i) 50,000
Building	—	—		
Accumulated depreciation—building..		6,000	(h) 6,000	
Equipment	38,000		(f) 9,000	(g) 47,000
Accumulated depreciation— equipment......................		3,000	(e) 12,000	(f) 9,000
Bonds payable.....................	125,000			(d) 125,000
Common stock.....................		50,000	(c) 50,000	
Retained earnings		110,500	(a) 140,500	(b) 30,000
	224,500	247,500		
Increase in cash....................	23,000			
Totals	247,500	247,500		

Sources of cash:		
Operations:		
Net income		(a) 140,500
Depreciation of equipment		(e) 12,000
Depreciation of building........................		(h) 6,000
Decrease in income tax payable	(l) 1,500	
Increase in accounts payable....................		(m) 18,000
Increase in prepaid expenses	(n) 1,000	
Decrease in inventories		(o) 8,000
Increase in trade receivables	(p) 9,000	
Issuance of common stock for land..............		(c) 50,000
Book value of investments sold		(j) 45,000
Applications of cash:		
Declaration of cash dividends......................	(b) 30,000	
Increase in dividends payable		(k) 7,000
Retirement of bonds	(d) 125,000	
Purchase of equipment............................	(g) 47,000	
Purchase of land by issuance of common stock	(i) 50,000	
Totals	559,000	559,000

column. To facilitate reference in the illustration, noncash current accounts are listed first, followed by the noncurrent accounts. The order of the listing is not important.

The debit or credit change for the year in each account balance is entered in the Change During Year column. For example, the beginning and ending balances of Trade Receivables were $65,000 and $74,000, respectively. Thus, the change for the year was an increase, or debit, of $9,000. The changes in the other accounts are determined in a like manner.

Change in Cash

Since transactions that result in changes in cash also result in changes in the noncash accounts, the change in cash for the period will equal the change in the noncash accounts for the period. Thus, if a subtotal of the debits and credits for the noncash accounts (as indicated in the Change During Year column) is determined, the increase or decrease in cash for the period can be inserted in the appropriate column and the two columns will balance. In the illustration, the subtotal of the credit column ($247,500) exceeds the subtotal of the debit column ($224,500) by $23,000, which is identified as the increase in cash. By entering the $23,000 as a debit in the Change During Year column, the debit and credit columns are balanced. This $23,000 increase in cash will be reported on the funds statement as the difference between the total of the sources section and the total of the applications section.

If the subtotals in the Change During Year columns indicate that the debits exceed the credits, the balancing figure would be identified as a decrease in cash.

Sources and Applications of Cash

After the Change During Year columns are totaled and ruled, "Sources of cash" is written in the Description column. Several lines are skipped, so that at a later time the various sources of cash can be entered, and "Applications of cash" is written in the Description column. When the work sheet is completed, this bottom portion will contain the data necessary to prepare the sources section and the applications section of the funds statement.

To determine the various sources and applications of cash for the year, the changes in the noncash accounts are analyzed. As each account is analyzed, entries made in the work sheet relate specific sources or applications of cash to the noncash accounts. For purposes of discussion, the noncash accounts can be classified as (1) noncurrent accounts and (2) current accounts (except cash).

The analysis of the noncurrent accounts for T. R. Morgan Corporation, discussed on pages 533–535, revealed (as does the additional data presented on page 939) that the sale of investments yielded cash, that there were cash outlays for equipment and the retirement of bonds, and that land was acquired by the issuance of common stock. The effect of these transactions on both cash and working capital is therefore the same. For the statement based on cash, it is necessary to add the analysis of the current accounts (except cash).

Analysis of Noncurrent Accounts

The entries resulting from the analysis of the noncurrent accounts are summarized as follows (the letters refer to those used on the work sheet to identify the entries). These entries are identical to the entries shown on pages 942–945, except that they have been adjusted to reflect the cash concept.

(a) Retained Earnings...........................	140,500	
Sources of Cash—Operations: Net Income......		140,500
(b) Applications of Cash—Declaration of Cash		
Dividends.....................................	30,000	
Retained Earnings...........................		30,000
(c) Common Stock	50,000	
Sources of Cash—Issuance of Common Stock		
for Land....................................		50,000
(d) Applications of Cash—Retirement of Bonds		
Payable......................................	125,000	
Bonds Payable..............................		125,000
(e) Accumulated Depreciation—Equipment...........	12,000	
Sources of Cash—Operations: Depreciation		
of Equipment		12,000
(f) Equipment	9,000	
Accumulated Depreciation—Equipment........		9,000
(g) Applications of Cash—Purchase of Equipment.....	47,000	
Equipment		47,000
(h) Accumulated Depreciation—Building	6,000	
Sources of Cash—Operations: Depreciation		
of Building		6,000
(i) Applications of Cash—Purchase of Land by		
Issuance of Common Stock	50,000	
Land..		50,000
(j) Investments	45,000	
Sources of Cash—Book Value of Investments		
Sold		45,000

Analysis of Current Accounts (Except Cash)

The amount of cash used to pay dividends may differ from the amount of cash dividends declared. Timing differences between the incurrence of an expense and the related cash outflow and the recognition of revenue and the receipt of cash must be considered in determining the amount of cash provided by operations. Therefore, the current accounts (other than cash) are analyzed to determine (1) cash applied to payment of dividends and (2) cash provided by operations.

Cash Applied to Payment of Dividends

The additional data indicate that $30,000 of dividends had been declared, which was identified as an application in entry (b). The $7,000 credit in the Change During Year column of the work sheet for Dividends Payable reveals a timing difference between the declaration and the payment. In other words, the $7,000 increase in Dividends Payable for the year indicates that dividends paid were $7,000 less than dividends declared. The work sheet entry to adjust the dividends declared of $30,000 to reflect the dividends paid of $23,000 is as follows:

(k) Dividends Payable 7,000
    Applications of Cash—Declaration of Cash
    Dividends: Increase in Dividends Payable.......... 7,000

When the $7,000, which represents the increase in dividends payable, is deducted from the $30,000 of "application of cash—declaration of cash dividends," $23,000 is subsequently reported on the funds statement as an application of cash.

Cash Provided by Operations

The starting point in the analysis of the effect of operations on cash is net income for the period. The effect of this amount, $140,500, is indicated by entry (a). As in the earlier analysis, depreciation expense of $18,000 must be added [(e) and (h)] to the $140,500 because depreciation expense did not decrease the amount of cash. In addition, it is necessary to recognize the relationship of the accrual method of accounting to the movement of cash. Ordinarily, a portion of some of the other costs and expenses reported on the income statement, as well as a portion of the revenue earned, is not accompanied by cash outflow or inflow.

The effect of timing differences is indicated by the amount and the direction of change in the balances of the asset and liability accounts affected by operations. Decreases in such assets and increases in such liabilities during the period must be added to the amount reported as net income to determine the amount of cash provided by operations. Conversely, increases in such assets and decreases in such liabilities must be deducted from the amount reported as net income.

The noncash current accounts (except Dividends Payable) provide the following data that indicate the effect of timing differences on the amount of cash inflow and outflow from operations:

Accounts	Increase Decrease*
Trade receivables (net).....................................	$ 9,000
Inventories...	8,000*
Prepaid expenses	1,000
Accounts payable (merchandise creditors)....................	18,000
Income tax payable..	1,500*

The sequence in which the noncash current accounts are analyzed is unimportant. However, to continue the sequence used in analyzing preceding accounts, the analysis illustrated will begin with the income tax payable account and proceed upward in the listing in sequential order.

Income tax payable decrease. The outlay of cash for income taxes exceeded by $1,500 the amount of income tax deducted as an expense during the period. Accordingly, $1,500 must be deducted from income to determine the amount of cash provided by operations. This procedure is indicated on the work sheet by the following entry:

(l) Sources of Cash—Operations: Decrease in Income
    Tax Payable...................................... 1,500
    Income Tax Payable 1,500

Accounts payable increase. The effect of the increase in the amount owed creditors for goods and services was to include in expired costs and expenses the sum of $18,000. Income was thereby reduced by $18,000 for which there had been no cash outlay during the year. Hence, $18,000 must be added to income to determine the amount of cash provided by operations. The work sheet entry is as follows:

(m) Accounts Payable	18,000	
Sources of Cash—Operations: Increase in		
Accounts Payable		18,000

Prepaid expenses increase. The outlay of cash for prepaid expenses exceeded by $1,000 the amount deducted as an expense during the year. Hence, $1,000 must be deducted from income to determine the amount of cash provided by operations. The work sheet entry is as follows:

(n) Sources of Cash—Operations: Increase in Prepaid		
Expenses..	1,000	
Prepaid Expenses		1,000

Inventories decrease. The $8,000 decrease in inventories indicates that the merchandise sold exceeded the cost of the merchandise purchased by $8,000. The amount reported on the income statement as a deduction from the revenue therefore included $8,000 that did not require cash outflow during the year. Accordingly, $8,000 must be added to income to determine the amount of cash provided by operations. The work sheet entry is as follows:

(o) Inventories..	8,000	
Sources of Cash—Operations: Decrease in		
Inventories......................................		8,000

Trade receivables (net) increase. The additions to trade receivables for sales on account during the year exceeded by $9,000 the deductions for amounts collected from customers on account. The amount reported on the income statement as sales therefore included $9,000 that did not yield cash inflow during the year. Accordingly, $9,000 must be deducted from income to determine the amount of cash provided by operations. The work sheet entry is as follows:

(p) Sources of Cash—Operations: Increase in Trade		
Receivables.....................................	9,000	
Trade Receivables...............................		9,000

Completing the Work Sheet   After all of the noncash accounts have been analyzed, all of the sources and applications are identified in the bottom portion of the work sheet. To assure the equality of the work sheet entries, the last step is to total the Work Sheet Entries columns.

The data for the sources section and the applications section of the funds statement are obtained from the bottom portion of the work sheet. The increase (or decrease) in cash that is reported on the statement is also identified on the work sheet. The funds statement prepared from the work sheet, including the details of the changes in the cash account, is as follows:

T. R. Morgan Corporation
Statement of Changes in Financial Position
For Year Ended December 31, 1985

Sources of cash:
  Operations during the year:
    Net income. $140,500
    Add deductions not decreasing cash
    during the year:
      Depreciation $18,000
      Increase in accounts payable . . .   18,000
      Decrease in inventories.   8,000   44,000
                                                                $184,500
    Deduct additions not increasing
    cash during the year:
      Decrease in income tax payable . $ 1,500
      Increase in prepaid expenses . . .   1,000
      Increase in trade receivables. . . .   9,000   11,500 $173,000
  Issuance of common stock at par for land   50,000
  Book value of investments sold (excludes $30,000 gain
    reported in net income). 45,000 $268,000
Applications of cash:
  Payment of dividends:
    Cash dividends declared . . . . $ 30,000
    Deduct increase in dividends payable . . . . .   7,000 $ 23,000
  Retirement of bonds payable.   125,000
  Purchase of equipment   47,000
  Purchase of land by issuance of common stock at par . .   50,000   245,000
Increase in cash. . . . . $ 23,000

Change in cash balance:
  Cash balance, December 31, 1985 . . . . $ 49,000
  Cash balance, December 31, 1984   26,000
Increase in cash. . . . . $ 23,000

APPENDIX F

Manufacturing Work Sheet

Many accountants use a work sheet to assist them in the preparation of financial statements. The use of a work sheet for a merchandising enterprise was illustrated in Chapters 3 and 4. In a like manner, a work sheet may be used for a manufacturing enterprise. Such a work sheet was not illustrated in Chapter 22 so that the discussion could focus on the basic concepts applicable to accounting for manufacturing operations.

The following sections describe and illustrate the use of a work sheet for manufacturing operations. The illustration is based on the presentation of a general accounting system, which is described on pages 627–630.

WORK SHEET PROCEDURES

The work sheet used in preparing financial statements for a merchandising business, which was illustrated in Chapter 4, is expanded for manufacturing enterprises using periodic inventory procedures by adding a pair of columns for the statement of cost of goods manufactured as shown on page 955. All items that enter into the determination of the cost of goods manufactured are extended to these two columns. After all these data have been extended, the two cost of goods manufactured columns should be totaled and the difference determined. This difference, which is labeled "Cost of Goods Manufactured" in the account title column, is transferred to the income statement columns by entries in the statement of cost of goods manufactured credit column and the income statement debit column. The remainder of the work sheet is completed in the same manner as is followed for a merchandising business.

To illustrate the use of a work sheet for a manufacturing enterprise, data are taken from the accounts and records of Ming Manufacturing Company, which uses periodic inventory procedures. The unadjusted trial balance at the end of 1984 is reported in the first two columns of the work sheet presented on pages 954 and 955. The data needed for year-end adjustments on December 31, 1984, are summarized as follows:

Inventories on December 31, 1984:
Finished goods	$91,000
Work in process	65,800
Direct materials	58,725
Factory supplies	1,800

Depreciation for the year:
Factory buildings .... $ 6,000
Factory equipment 22,300
Accruals on December 31, 1984:
Wages and salaries:
Direct labor 4,500
Indirect labor 950

Adjusting Entries The adjusting entries are recorded on the work sheet in the usual manner illustrated in the merchandising enterprise chapters, except for inventories of work in process and direct materials. Each of the adjusting entries pertaining to the

MING MANUFACTURING
Work
For Year Ended

ACCOUNT TITLE	TRIAL BALANCE		ADJUSTMENTS	
	DEBIT	CREDIT	DEBIT	CREDIT
Cash..	18,200			
Accounts Receivable.........................	66,100			
Allowance for Doubtful Accounts		1,500		
Finished Goods	78,500		(b) 91,000	(a) 78,500
Work in Process..............................	55,000		(d) 65,800	(c) 55,000
Direct Materials..............................	62,000		(f) 58,725	(e) 62,000
Factory Supplies...............................	4,700			(g) 2,900
Prepaid Insurance	1,250			
Land...	50,000			
Factory Buildings	240,000			
Accumulated Depreciation—Factory Buildings........		30,000		(h) 6,000
Factory Equipment..................................	446,000			
Accumulated Depreciation—Factory Equipment........		111,500		(i) 22,300
Accounts Payable		45,600		
Wages and Salaries Payable.........................				(j) 5,450
Income Tax Payable		13,200		
Common Stock ($10 par)......................		200,000		
Retained Earnings		497,325		
Income Summary.............................			(a) 78,500	(b) 91,000
Manufacturing Summary......................			(c) 55,000	(d) 65,800
			(e) 62,000	(f) 58,725
Sales..		915,800		
Direct Materials Purchases	220,800			
Direct Labor..................................	214,250		(j) 4,500	
Indirect Factory Labor........................	48,350		(j) 950	
Depreciation—Factory Equipment....................			(i) 22,300	
Factory Heat, Light, and Power.....................	21,800			
Factory Property Taxes.........................	9,750			
Depreciation—Factory Buildings			(h) 6,000	
Insurance Expense—Factory.....................	4,750			
Factory Supplies Expense			(g) 2,900	
Miscellaneous Factory Expense	2,050			
Selling Expenses	130,500			
General Expenses	88,700			
Income Tax...................................	52,225			
	1,814,925	1,814,925	447,675	447,675
Cost of Goods Manufactured......................				
Net Income				

inventories of finished goods, work in process, and direct materials is briefly described below.

The finished goods inventory account is adjusted through the income summary account in the same manner as the merchandise inventory of a merchandising enterprise. The beginning finished goods inventory is transferred to the income summary account by crediting Finished Goods and debiting Income Summary for $78,500 (entry (a) on the work sheet). The ending finished goods inventory is recorded by debiting Finished Goods and crediting Income Summary for $91,000 (entry (b) on the work sheet).

As explained in Chapter 22, the work in process inventory account is adjusted through Manufacturing Summary. The inventory of work in process at the beginning of the period is transferred to the manufacturing summary account by

COMPANY
Sheet
December 31, 1984

STATEMENT OF COST OF GOODS MANUFACTURED		INCOME STATEMENT		BALANCE SHEET	
DEBIT	CREDIT	DEBIT	CREDIT	DEBIT	CREDIT
				18,200	
				66,100	
					1,500
				91,000	
				65,800	
				58,725	
				1,800	
				1,250	
				50,000	
				240,000	
					36,000
				446,000	
					133,800
					45,600
					5,450
					13,200
					200,000
					107,325
		78,500	91,000		
55,000	65,800				
62,000	58,725				
			915,800		
220,800					
218,750					
49,300					
22,300					
21,800					
9,750					
6,000					
4,750					
2,900					
2,050					
		130,500			
		88,700			
		52,225			
675,400	124,525				
	550,875	550,875			
675,400	675,400	900,800	1,006,800	1,038,875	932,875
		106,000			106,000
		1,006,800	1,006,800	1,038,875	1,038,875

crediting Work in Process and by debiting Manufacturing Summary for $55,000 (entry (c) on the work sheet). The ending work in process inventory is recorded by debiting Work in Process and by crediting Manufacturing Summary for $65,800 (entry (d) on the work sheet).

Like the work in process inventory, the direct materials inventory at the beginning of the fiscal period is transferred to the manufacturing summary account by crediting Direct Materials and by debiting Manufacturing Summary for $62,000 (entry (e) on the work sheet). The direct materials inventory at the end of the period is recorded by debiting Direct Materials and crediting Manufacturing Summary for $58,725 (entry (f) on the work sheet).

Completing the Work Sheet

After all the adjustments have been entered on the work sheet, each account balance, as adjusted, is then extended to the appropriate column. In this illustration, the adjusted trial balance columns which appear in the work sheets illustrated in Chapters 3 and 4 have been eliminated. Experienced accountants often omit these columns in order to save time in preparing the work sheet. Under this approach, the adjusted account balances are entered directly into the proper financial statement columns. The temporary accounts that appear in the statement of cost of goods manufactured are extended to the statement of cost of goods manufactured columns. The other accounts are extended to the income statement and balance sheet columns in the usual manner. Note that the beginning and ending inventory amounts appearing opposite Income Summary and Manufacturing Summary in the adjustments column are extended individually rather than as the net figure, since both amounts will be used in preparing the statements.

After all of the amounts have been extended to the appropriate columns, the work sheet is completed in the following manner:

(1) The statement of cost of goods manufactured columns are totaled. In the illustration, the total of the Dr. column is $675,400 and the total of the Cr. column is $124,525.

(2) The amount of the difference between the two statement of cost of goods manufactured columns is determined and entered in the statement of cost of goods manufactured Cr. column and the income statement Dr. column. This amount ($550,875 in the illustration) is the cost of goods manufactured for the period.

(3) The totals of the columns are then entered. The statement of cost of goods manufactured columns should now be in balance.

(4) The amount of net income is determined and is recorded in the income statement Dr. column and in the balance sheet Cr. column.

(5) The totals of the last four columns, which should now be in balance, are entered.

FINANCIAL STATEMENTS

The completed work sheet provides the information necessary for preparing the financial statements. For Ming Manufacturing Company, the income statement, statement of cost of goods manufactured, and balance sheet are shown on pages 957–958.

Ming Manufacturing Company
Income Statement
For Year Ended December 31, 1984

Sales		$915,800
Cost of goods sold:		
Finished goods inventory, January 1, 1984.	$ 78,500	
Cost of goods manufactured	550,875	
Cost of finished goods available for sale	$629,375	
Less finished goods inventory, December 31, 1984	91,000	
Cost of goods sold		538,375
Gross profit		$377,425
Operating expenses:		
Selling expenses.	$130,500	
General expenses	88,700	
Total operating expenses		219,200
Income before income tax		$158,225
Income tax.		52,225
Net income (per share, $5.30).		$100,000

Ming Manufacturing Company
Statement of Cost of Goods Manufactured
For Year Ended December 31, 1984

Work in process inventory, January 1, 1984			$ 55,000
Direct materials:			
Inventory, January 1, 1984	$ 62,000		
Purchases	220,800		
Cost of materials available for use	$282,800		
Less inventory, December 31, 1984	58,725		
Cost of materials placed in production	$224,075		
Direct labor	218,750		
Factory overhead:			
Indirect labor	$49,300		
Depreciation of factory equipment	22,300		
Heat, light, and power.	21,800		
Property taxes.	9,750		
Depreciation on buildings.	6,000		
Insurance expired.	4,750		
Factory supplies used	2,900		
Miscellaneous factory costs	2,050		
Total factory overhead.		118,850	
Total manufacturing costs.			561,675
Total work in process during period.			$616,675
Less work in process inventory, December 31,			
1984.			65,800
Cost of goods manufactured			$550,875

Ming Manufacturing Company
Balance Sheet
December 31, 1984

Assets

Current assets:

Cash		$ 18,200	
Accounts receivable	$ 66,100		
Less allowance for doubtful accounts	1,500	64,600	
Inventories:			
Finished goods	$ 91,000		
Work in process	65,800		
Direct materials	58,725	215,525	
Factory supplies		1,800	
Prepaid insurance		1,250	
Total current assets			$301,375

Plant assets:

Land		$ 50,000	
Buildings	$240,000		
Less accumulated depreciation	36,000	204,000	
Factory equipment	$446,000		
Less accumulated depreciation	133,800	312,200	
Total plant assets			566,200
Total assets			$867,575

Liabilities

Current liabilities:

Accounts payable	$ 45,600	
Wages and salaries payable	5,450	
Income tax payable	13,200	
Total current liabilities		$ 64,250

Stockholders' Equity

Common stock, $10 par	$200,000	
Retained earnings	603,325	
Total stockholders' equity		803,325
Total liabilities and stockholders' equity		$867,575

APPENDIX

Specimen Financial Statements

This appendix contains financial statements based on the actual statements of a small, privately held manufacturing company, the complete financial section of the annual report of The Coca Cola Company, and selected statements and notes for other companies. Because privately held companies are not required to release their financial statements to the public, the Carter Manufacturing Company statements were modified to protect the confidentiality of the company. We are grateful for the assistance of the public accounting firm of Deloitte Haskins & Sells and Mr. Mark Young in developing these statements.

AUDITORS' OPINION

Carter Manufacturing Company:

We have examined the balance sheets of Carter Manufacturing Company as of December 31, 1982 and 1981, and the related statements of income and retained earnings and of changes in financial position for the years then ended. Our examinations were made in accordance with generally accepted auditing standards and, accordingly, included such tests of the accounting records and such other auditing procedures as we considered necessary in the circumstances.

In our opinion, the accompanying financial statements present fairly the financial position of Carter Manufacturing Company as of December 31, 1982 and 1981, and the results of its operations and the changes in its financial position for the years then ended, in conformity with generally accepted accounting principles consistently applied.

Masters & Young

February 22, 1983
Atlanta, Georgia

CARTER MANUFACTURING COMPANY

BALANCE SHEETS, DECEMBER 31, 1982 and 1981

ASSETS	NOTES	1982	1981
CURRENT ASSETS:			
Cash:			
Cash in bank............................		$ 38,526	$ 88,443
Petty cash............................		7,650	12,300
Savings certificates		375,000	235,344
Marketable securities	2,5	332,238	361,842
Receivables:			
Customers—less allowance for doubtful accounts of $486,000 in 1982 and $45,000 in 1981	3	2,979,197	2,809,352
Dividends...............................		2,157	2,091
Interest.................................		16,680	6,288
Other..................................		20,736	8,034
Inventories..............................	4	5,927,631	6,033,126
Prepaid insurance		38,604	45,234
Other prepayments		22,566	32,586
Total current assets.......................		9,760,985	9,634,640
PLANT AND EQUIPMENT:			
Machinery and equipment		2,901,148	2,788,225
Delivery equipment		745,893	771,873
Furniture and fixtures		214,119	214,437
Leasehold improvements		97,758	94,011
Total		3,958,918	3,868,546
Less accumulated depreciation and amortization............................		2,172,171	2,085,417
Plant and equipment—net..................		1,786,747	1,783,129
TOTAL ASSETS...........................		$11,547,732	$11,417,769

See notes to financial statements.

LIABILITIES AND SHAREHOLDERS' EQUITY	NOTES	<u>1982</u>	<u>1981</u>
CURRENT LIABILITIES:			
Trade accounts payable....................		$ 1,804,807	$ 1,700,652
Due under line of credit	5	120,000	180,000
Current portion of long-term debt	6	266,676	236,709
Accrued salaries, wages and commissions		369,009	194,910
Accrued and withheld payroll taxes		69,267	144,111
Income taxes payable........................		48,081	37,287
Contributions to employee benefit plans	8	277,521	100,647
Accrued rent		67,500	270,000
Total current liabilities.....................		3,022,861	2,864,316
LONG-TERM DEBT	6,7,9	1,028,682	1,295,358
DEFERRED INCOME TAXES................		56,091	44,877
SHAREHOLDERS' EQUITY:			
Capital stock—authorized and outstanding,			
172,000 shares of $3 par value.............		516,000	516,000
Additional paid-in capital....................		36,927	36,927
Retained earnings		6,887,171	6,660,291
Shareholders' equity		7,440,098	7,213,218
TOTAL LIABILITIES AND SHAREHOLDERS' EQUITY		$11,547,732	$11,417,769

CARTER MANUFACTURING COMPANY

STATEMENTS OF INCOME AND RETAINED EARNINGS FOR THE YEARS ENDED DECEMBER 31, 1982 AND 1981

	NOTE	1982	1981
SALES (Less returns of $237,782 in 1982 and $345,762 in 1981)		$23,555,271	$23,401,635
COST OF GOODS SOLD		17,130,648	17,767,857
GROSS PROFIT		6,424,623	5,633,778
SELLING AND GENERAL EXPENSES		6,136,161	5,406,762
INCOME FROM OPERATIONS		288,462	227,016
OTHER INCOME (EXPENSES):			
Interest		167,978	84,732
Dividends		50,268	50,124
Sale of waste materials, etc.		183,526	91,365
Gain from sale of property and equipment		4,581	3,600
Unrealized loss on marketable securities	2	(28,824)	(80,388)
Interest expense		(233,385)	(112,641)
Cash discount lost		(63,924)	(108,987)
Total		80,220	(72,195)
INCOME BEFORE INCOME TAXES		368,682	154,821
INCOME TAX EXPENSE:			
Federal:			
Current		112,336	31,410
Deferred		9,303	18,036
Total federal		121,639	49,446
State:			
Current		18,252	11,955
Deferred		1,911	3,021
Total state		20,163	14,976
Total		141,802	64,422
NET INCOME		226,880	90,399
RETAINED EARNINGS, BEGINNING OF YEAR		6,660,291	6,569,892
RETAINED EARNINGS, END OF YEAR		$ 6,887,171	$ 6,660,291

See notes to financial statements.

CARTER MANUFACTURING COMPANY

STATEMENTS OF CHANGES IN FINANCIAL POSITION FOR THE YEARS ENDED DECEMBER 31, 1982 AND 1981

	1982	1981
SOURCES OF WORKING CAPITAL:		
Net income	$ 226,880	$ 90,399
Add charges not requiring an outlay of working capital:		
Depreciation and amortization........................	173,145	181,638
Deferred income taxes	11,214	21,057
Total from operations	411,239	293,094
Proceeds from sale of plant and equipment—net of gains		
included in operations..............................	11,019	1,800
Increase in long-term debt..........................		1,295,358
Total	422,258	1,590,252
USES OF WORKING CAPITAL:		
Purchase of plant and equipment......................	187,782	1,322,398
Reduction of long-term debt..........................	266,676	
Total	454,458	1,322,398
INCREASE (DECREASE) IN WORKING CAPITAL	$ (32,200)	$ 267,854
COMPONENTS OF CHANGE IN WORKING CAPITAL:		
Cash and savings certificates and account.............	$ 85,089	$ 325,572
Marketable securities...............................	(29,604)	(80,388)
Receivables.......................................	193,005	290,889
Inventories.......................................	(105,495)	(3,918)
Prepaid expenses	(16,650)	77,820
Trade accounts payable	(104,155)	(1,177)
Due under line of credit	60,000	(60,000)
Current portion of long-term debt	(29,967)	(236,709)
Accrued salaries, wages and commissions	(174,099)	(28,560)
Accrued and withheld payroll taxes	74,844	(102,966)
Income taxes payable—net	(10,794)	(35,937)
Contributions to employee benefit plans................	(176,874)	123,228
Accrued rent	202,500	
INCREASE (DECREASE) IN WORKING CAPITAL	$ (32,200)	$ 267,854

See notes to financial statements.

CARTER MANUFACTURING COMPANY

NOTES TO FINANCIAL STATEMENTS FOR THE YEARS ENDED DECEMBER 31, 1982 AND 1981

1. SIGNIFICANT ACCOUNTING POLICIES

Nature of Business — The Company is principally engaged in the manufacture and sale of metal products.

Inventories

For the year ended December 31, 1980, the Company changed its method of accounting for inventories to a last-in, first-out (lifo) method. During a time of rapid price increases, the lifo method provides a better matching of revenue and expense than does the fifo method. The total effect of the change was included in the 1980 financial statements, and no restatement was made of amounts reported in prior years. The effect of this change was to reduce net income for 1980 by $298,944.

Plant and Equipment

Plant and equipment are stated at cost less accumulated depreciation and amortization. Depreciation on plant and equipment acquired after 1978 is computed using the straight-line method for financial reporting and accelerated methods for income tax purposes. Depreciation on previously acquired plant and equipment is computed using accelerated methods for financial reporting and income tax purposes, except that the straight-line method is used for tax purposes at such time as it results in a greater deduction than would result from continued use of an accelerated method. Rates are based upon the following estimated useful lives:

Classification	Useful Life
Machinery and equipment	7-10 Years
Delivery equipment	6-7 Years
Furniture and fixtures	8-10 Years
Leasehold improvements	5-6 Years

Revenue Recognition — Revenue from merchandise sales is recognized when the merchandise is shipped to the customer.

Deferred Income Taxes

Deferred income taxes are provided for timing differences between reported financial income before income taxes and taxable income. The timing differences arise from depreciation deductions for income tax purposes in excess of depreciation expense for financial reporting purposes.

2. MARKETABLE SECURITIES

The Company's marketable securities are stated at the lower of cost or market. At December 31, 1982 and 1981, the Company's investments had a cost of $582,876 and

$583,656 respectively. To reduce the carrying amount of this investment to market, which was lower than cost at December 31, 1982 and 1981, valuation allowances of $250,638 and $221,814, respectively, were established. This resulted in a charge to earnings of $28,824 in 1982 and a charge to earnings of $80,388 in 1981.

3. RECEIVABLE DUE FROM A SINGLE CUSTOMER

At December 31, 1982, approximately $700,000 was due from a single distributor. Approximately $435,000 of the allowance for doubtful accounts at December 31, 1982, relates specifically to this receivable.

At December 31, 1981, approximately $350,000 was due from the distributor.

4. INVENTORIES

At December 31, 1982 and 1981, inventories (see Note 1) consisted of the following:

	1982	1981
Raw materials.	$1,654,563	$1,491,876
Work in process	2,427,513	2,255,574
Finished goods	2,684,409	2,839,278
Total cost.	6,766,485	6,586,728
Less lifo reserve	838,854	553,602
Total lifo.	$5,927,631	$6,033,126

5. LINE OF CREDIT

The Company has an agreement with a bank for a line of credit, of which $180,000 was unused at December 31, 1982. Borrowings under the line are at an interest rate (14% at December 31, 1982) of 2% above the bank's prime lending rate. The Company's marketable securities are pledged as collateral for borrowings under the line.

6. LONG-TERM DEBT

At December 31, 1982 and 1981, the Company had three installment notes, payable to a bank as follows:

	1982	1981
Note dated February 2, 1981, due in $60,000 semi-annual installments, with interest payable monthly at 12.625%	$ 120,000	$ 240,000
Note dated March 2, 1981, due in $10,000 semiannual installments, with interest payable monthly at 14.125%	20,000	40,000
Note dated December 12, 1981, due in 120 monthly payments of increasing amounts with interest at 14.00%.	1,155,358	1,252,067
Total	1,295,358	1,532,067
Less amount due within one year.	266,676	236,709
Total	$1,028,682	$1,295,358

CARTER MANUFACTURING COMPANY

NOTES TO FINANCIAL STATEMENTS

7. LONG-TERM LIABILITIES

The long-term liabilities have the following aggregate minimum maturities during the next five years:

1983	$ 266,676
1984	131,122
1985	135,103
1986	140,503
1987	146,299
After 1987	475,655
Total	$1,295,358

8. EMPLOYEE BENEFIT PLANS

The Company has a profit-sharing plan for its salaried employees and a defined benefit retirement plan for its hourly paid employees. Both plans are noncontributory, are funded annually, and have been amended to comply with the Employee Retirement Income Security Act of 1974.

The contributions to the profit-sharing plan are made at the discretion of the Board of Directors and were $138,261 for 1982 and $57,750 for 1981.

Annual contributions to the retirement plan were $139,260 for 1982 and $42,897 for 1981. The plan is being funded based upon actuarial computations of costs which include consideration of normal cost, interest on the unfunded prior service cost, and amortization of the prior service cost over a forty-year period.

At January 1, 1982 and 1981, net assets available for retirement plan benefits were $824,214 and $622,518 respectively; the actuarial present values of vested plan benefits were $984,666 and $885,435, respectively; and nonvested accumulated plan benefits were $87,522 and $90,788, respectively. The assumed rate of return used in determining the actuarial present values of accumulated plan benefits was 5%.

9. OPERATING LEASE

The Company leases land and buildings under a 5-year noncancelable operating lease which expires on December 31, 1985. Future minimum lease payments are as follows:

1983	$ 300,000
1984	330,000
1985	360,000
Total	$ 990,000

Consolidated Statements Of Income
(In thousands except per share data)

The Coca-Cola Company and Subsidiaries

Year Ended December 31,	1982	1981	1980
Net operating revenues	$6,249,718	$5,889,035	$5,620,749
Cost of goods and services	3,453,493	3,307,574	3,197,733
Gross Profit	2,796,225	2,581,461	2,423,016
Selling, administrative and general expenses	1,901,962	1,782,875	1,681,861
Operating Income	894,263	798,586	741,155
Interest income	106,177	70,632	40,099
Interest expense	74,561	38,349	35,102
Other income (deductions)—net	6,112	(23,615)	(9,425)
Income From Continuing Operations			
Before Income Taxes	931,991	807,254	736,727
Income taxes	419,759	360,184	330,409
Income From Continuing Operations	512,232	447,070	406,318
Discontinued operations:			
Income from discontinued operations			
(net of applicable income taxes of $7,271 in 1981,			
and $11,782 in 1980)	—	5,641	15,790
Gain on disposal of discontinued operations			
(net of applicable income taxes of $13,274)	—	29,071	—
Net Income	$ 512,232	$ 481,782	$ 422,108
Per Share:			
Continuing operations	$ 3.95	$ 3.62	$ 3.29
Discontinued operations	—	.28	.13
Net income	$ 3.95	$ 3.90	$ 3.42
Average Shares Outstanding	129,793	123,610	123,578

See Notes to Consolidated Financial Statements

Consolidated Balance Sheets
(In thousands except share data)

The Coca-Cola Company and Subsidiaries
December 31,

Assets	1982	1981
Current		
Cash	$ 177,530	$ 120,908
Marketable securities, at cost (approximates market)	83,381	218,634
Trade accounts receivable, less allowances of $21,336 in 1982 and $8,579 in 1981	751,775	483,491
Inventories and unamortized film costs	808,799	750,719
Prepaid expenses and other assets	255,080	62,494
Total Current Assets	2,076,565	1,636,246
Investments, Film Costs and Other Assets		
Investments, at cost	221,909	176,332
Unamortized film costs	211,460	—
Other assets	241,395	211,086
	674,764	387,418
Property, Plant and Equipment		
Land and improvements	126,201	96,468
Buildings	602,475	570,356
Machinery and equipment	1,383,668	1,271,065
Containers	333,472	306,243
	2,445,816	2,244,132
Less allowances for depreciation	907,250	834,676
	1,538,566	1,409,456
Goodwill and Other Intangible Assets	633,415	131,661
	$4,923,310	$3,564,781

Liabilities and Shareholders' Equity	1982	1981
Current		
Loans and notes payable	$ 70,561	$ 89,647
Current maturities of long-term debt	50,623	5,515
Accounts payable and accrued expenses	792,250	672,049
Participations and other entertainment obligations	154,803	—
Accrued taxes—including income taxes	258,574	239,114
Total Current Liabilities	1,326,811	1,006,325
Participations and Other Entertainment Obligations	190,408	—
Long-Term Debt	462,344	137,278
Deferred Income Taxes	165,093	150,406
Shareholders' Equity		
Common stock, no par value— Authorized—140,000,000 shares; Issued: 136,099,741 shares in 1982 and 124,024,735 shares in 1981	68,427	62,389
Capital surplus	478,308	114,194
Retained earnings	2,300,217	2,109,542
Foreign currency translation adjustment	(54,486)	—
	2,792,466	2,286,125
Less treasury stock, at cost (359,338 shares in 1982; 401,338 shares in 1981)	13,812	15,353
	2,778,654	2,270,772
	$4,923,310	$3,564,781

See Notes to Consolidated Financial Statements

Consolidated Statements of Shareholders' Equity   *The Coca-Cola Company and Subsidiaries*

(In thousands except per share data)

Three Years Ended December 31, 1982

	Number of Shares		Amount				
	Common Stock	Treasury Stock	Common Stock	Capital Surplus	Retained Earnings	Foreign Currency Translation	Treasury Stock
Balance January 1, 1980	123,960	401	$62,357	$112,333	$1,759,367	$ —	$(15,353)
Sales to employees exercising stock options and appreciation rights	30	—	15	711	—	—	—
Tax benefit from sale of option shares by employees	—	—	—	128	—	—	—
Net income	—	—	—	—	422,108	—	—
Dividends (per share—$2.16)	—	—	—	—	(266,928)	—	—
Balance December 31, 1980	123,990	401	62,372	113,172	1,914,547	—	(15,353)
Sales to employees exercising stock options and appreciation rights	35	—	17	841	—	—	—
Tax benefit from sale of option shares by employees	—	—	—	181	—	—	—
Net income	—	—	—	—	481,782	—	—
Dividends (per share—$2.32)	—	—	—	—	(286,787)	—	—
Balance December 31, 1981	124,025	401	62,389	114,194	2,109,542	—	(15,353)
Effect of restating asset and liability balances as of January 1, 1982 for adoption of SFAS No. 52 (net of income taxes of $2,316)	—	—	—	—	—	(11,657)	—
Sales to employees exercising stock options and appreciation rights	121	—	61	3,685	—	—	—
Tax benefit from sale of option shares by employees	—	—	—	814	—	—	—
Purchase of Columbia Pictures Industries, Inc.	11,954	—	5,977	359,579	—	—	—
Translation adjustments (net of income taxes of $11,188)	—	—	—	—	—	(42,829)	—
Treasury stock issued to officers	—	(42)	—	36	—	—	1,541
Net income	—	—	—	—	512,232	—	—
Dividends (per share—$2.48)	—	—	—	—	(321,557)	—	—
Balance December 31, 1982	136,100	359	$68,427	$478,308	$2,300,217	$(54,486)	$(13,812)

See Notes to Consolidated Financial Statements

**Consolidated Statements of
Changes in Financial Position** (In thousands)

The Coca-Cola Company and Subsidiaries

Year Ended December 31,	1982	1981	1980
Source Of Working Capital			
From operations:			
Income from continuing operations	$ 512,232	$447,070	$ 406,318
Add charges not requiring outlay of working capital during the year:			
Depreciation	148,856	136,868	131,042
Amortization of noncurrent film costs	43,495	—	—
Deferred income taxes	50,807	23,692	31,500
Other (principally amortization of goodwill and container adjustments)	34,304	61,009	37,932
Total From Continuing Operations	789,694	668,639	606,792
Discontinued operations (excludes provisions for depreciation, amortization and deferred income taxes of $2,429 in 1981, and $4,521 in 1980)	—	37,141	20,311
Total From Operations	789,694	705,780	627,103
Common stock issued	370,152	1,090	854
Increase in long-term debt	249,392	4,057	99,415
Transfer of noncurrent film costs to current	93,909	—	—
Disposals of property, plant and equipment	44,467	71,788	77,053
Decrease in investments and other assets	21,836	—	—
Other	5,153	—	—
	1,574,603	782,715	804,425
Application Of Working Capital			
Cash dividends	321,557	286,787	266,928
Acquisitions of purchased companies excluding net current assets:			
Property, plant and equipment—net	56,739	9,814	5,885
Other assets net of other liabilities	89,693	103	(2,862)
Goodwill	516,115	10	10,455
Additions to property, plant and equipment	325,016	319,792	287,186
Additions to noncurrent film costs	95,804	—	—
Increase in investments and other assets	—	85,131	95,254
Foreign currency translation	21,693	—	—
Other	28,153	11,830	2,348
	1,454,770	713,467	665,194
Increase In Working Capital	$ 119,833	$ 69,248	$ 139,231
Increase (Decrease) In Working Capital By Component			
Cash	$ 56,622	$ (8,777)	$ 22,799
Marketable securities	(135,253)	117,233	59,716
Trade accounts receivable	268,284	(39,632)	88,044
Inventories and unamortized film costs	58,080	(59,516)	140,621
Prepaid expenses and other current assets	192,586	4,685	5,470
Loans and notes payable	19,086	(2,060)	16,229
Current maturities of long-term debt	(45,108)	2,013	(3,144)
Accounts payable and accrued expenses	(120,201)	60,974	(156,161)
Participations and other entertainment obligations	(154,803)	—	—
Accrued taxes—including income taxes	(19,460)	(5,672)	(34,343)
Increase In Working Capital	$ 119,833	$ 69,248	$ 139,231

See Notes to Consolidated Financial Statements

Notes to Consolidated Financial Statements

The Coca-Cola Company and Subsidiaries

1. Accounting Policies. The major accounting policies and practices followed by the Company and its subsidiaries are as follows:

Consolidation

The consolidated financial statements include the accounts of the Company and its majority-owned subsidiaries. All significant inter-company accounts and transactions are eliminated in consolidation.

Inventories and Unamortized Film Costs

Inventories are valued at the lower of cost or market. The last-in, first-out (LIFO) method of inventory valuation is used for sugar and other sweeteners used in beverages in the United States, for certain major citrus concentrate and wine products, for substantially all inventories of United States bottling subsidiaries and for certain other operations. All other inventories are valued on the basis of average cost or first in, first-out (FIFO) methods. The excess of current costs over LIFO stated values amounted to approximately $72 million and $76 million at December 31, 1982 and 1981, respectively.

Unamortized film costs include film production, print, pre-release and national advertising costs, and capitalized interest. The individual film forecast method is used to amortize these costs based on the revenues recognized in proportion to management's estimate of ultimate revenues to be received.

The costs of feature and television films are classified as current assets to the extent such costs are expected to be recovered through the respective primary markets. Other costs relating to film production are classified as noncurrent.

Revenues from theatrical exhibition of feature films are recognized on the dates of exhibition. Revenues from television licensing agreements are recognized when films are available for telecasting.

Property, Plant and Equipment

Property, plant and equipment is stated at cost, less allowance for depreciation, except that foreign subsidiaries carry bottles and shells in service at amounts (less than cost) which generally correspond with deposit prices obtained from customers. Approximately 89% of depreciation expense was determined by the straight-line method for 1982 and approximately 87% for both 1981 and 1980. Investment tax credits are accounted for by the flow-through method.

Goodwill and Other Intangible Assets

Goodwill and other intangible assets are stated on the basis of cost and, if purchased subsequent to October 31, 1970, are being amortized, principally on a straight-line basis, over the estimated future periods to be benefited (not exceeding 40 years). Accumulated amortization amounted to $26 million and $16 million at December 31, 1982 and 1981, respectively.

Capitalized Interest

Interest capitalized as part of the cost of acquisition, construction or production of major assets (including film costs)

was $14 million, $8 million and $6 million in 1982, 1981, and 1980, respectively.

Foreign Currency Translation

In the second quarter of 1982, the Company adopted Statement of Financial Accounting Standards No. 52, "Foreign Currency Translation" (SFAS 52), effective as of January 1, 1982, and restated the results for the first quarter. Exchange gains (gains and losses on foreign currency transactions and translation of balance sheet accounts of operations in hyperinflationary economies) included in income were $27 million for 1982. Under the translation rules used in prior years, such gains would have been approximately $10 million. The impact on 1981 and 1980 operating results is not material and such financial statements have not been restated.

An equity adjustment ($11.7 million) was recorded as of January 1, 1982, for the cumulative effect of SFAS 52 on prior years.

2. Inventories and Unamortized Film Costs. Inventories and unamortized film costs are comprised of the following (in thousands):

	December 31,	
	1982	1981
Finished goods	$219,000	$259,391
Work in process	96,305	92,464
Raw materials and supplies	368,730	398,864
Unamortized film costs (includes in process costs of $23,260)	124,764	—
	$808,799	$750,719
Noncurrent—Unamortized film costs		
Completed	$113,527	$
In process	97,933	—
	$211,460	$ —

3. Short-Term Borrowings and Credit Arrangements. Loans and notes payable include amounts payable to banks of $71 million and $61 million at December 31, 1982 and 1981, respectively.

Under line of credit arrangements for short-term debt with various financial institutions, the Company and its subsidiaries may borrow up to $768 million. These lines of credit are subject to normal banking terms and conditions. At December 31, 1982, the unused portion of the credit lines was $674 million. Some of the financial arrangements require compensating balances which are not material.

Notes to Consolidated Financial Statements (continued)

4. Accounts Payable and Accrued Expenses are composed of the following amounts (in thousands):

	December 31,	
	1982	1981
Trade accounts payable	$647,061	$565,697
Deposits on bottles and shells	67,725	67,489
Other	77,464	38,863
	$792,250	$672,049

5. Accrued Taxes are composed of the following amounts (in thousands):

	December 31,	
	1982	1981
Income taxes	$190,790	$175,753
Sales, payroll and miscellaneous taxes	67,784	63,361
	$258,574	$239,114

6. Long-Term Debt consists of the following amounts (in thousands):

	December 31,	
	1982	1981
$9^7/8\%$ notes due June 1, 1985	$ 99,928	$ 99,898
$11^3/4\%$ notes due October 1, 1989	97,548	—
$10^3/8\%$ notes due June 1, 1988	23,200	—
Short-term borrowings to be refinanced with long-term debt	173,000	—
Other	119,291	42,895
	512,967	142,793
Less current portion	50,623	5,515
	$462,344	$137,278

The $9^7/8\%$ notes may not be redeemed before June 1, 1983. After that date, the notes may be redeemed at the option of the Company in whole or in part at 100% of their principal amount, plus accrued interest.

The $11^3/4\%$ notes were issued in international markets and may not be redeemed prior to October 1, 1986, except under certain limited conditions. After that date, the notes may also be redeemed at the option of the Company in whole or in part at 101% of the principal amount during the succeeding twelve month period, and thereafter at 100% of the principal amount, together in each case with accrued interest.

The principal amount of the $10^3/8\%$ notes is $100 million. The notes were issued in the international markets on a partly paid basis, whereby 25% of the issue price was received on December 1, 1982, and the remaining 75% will be received on June 1, 1983. These notes may not be redeemed prior to maturity, except under certain limited conditions.

At December 31, 1982, $173 million of short-term borrowings have been classified as long-term debt as management intends to repay such borrowings with proceeds from the remaining installment of the $10^3/8\%$ notes, and from the proceeds of an additional $100 million of partly paid notes issued on February 2, 1983 (these notes have an annual coupon rate of $9^7/8\%$, require payment in installments of 30% on February 2, 1983, and 70% on August 1, 1983, and mature on August 1, 1992).

Other long-term debt consists of various mortgages and notes with maturity dates ranging from 1983 to 2010. Interest on a portion of this debt varies with the changes in the prime rate, and the weighted average interest rate applicable to the remainder is approximately 11.3%.

The above notes and other long-term debt instruments include various restrictions, none of which are presently significant to the Company.

Maturities of long-term debt for the five years succeeding December 31, 1982, are as follows (in thousands):

1983	$ 50,623
1984	12,822
1985	110,357
1986	8,856
1987	10,990

The Company is contingently liable for guarantees of indebtedness by its independent bottling companies and others in the approximate amount of $70 million at December 31, 1982.

7. Foreign Operations. The Company's identifiable assets and liabilities outside the United States and Puerto Rico are shown below (in thousands):

	December 31,	
	1982	1981
Current assets	$ 776,095	$ 751,835
Property, plant and equipment—net	585,320	567,179
Other assets	77,003	121,903
	1,438,418	1,440,917
Liabilities	626,888	637,015
Net assets	$ 811,530	$ 803,902

Appropriate United States and foreign income taxes have been provided for on earnings of subsidiary companies which are expected to be remitted to the parent company in the near future. Accumulated unremitted earnings of foreign subsidiaries which are expected to be required for use in the foreign operations amounted to approximately $63 million at December 31, 1982, exclusive of amounts which if remitted would result in little or no tax.

Notes to Consolidated Financial Statements (continued)

8. Stock Options. The Company's 1979 stock option plan provides for the granting of stock appreciation rights and stock options to certain officers and employees. Stock appreciation rights permit the holder, upon surrendering all or part of the related stock option, to receive cash, common stock, or a combination thereof, in an amount up to 100% of the difference between the market price and the option price. Included in options outstanding at December 31, 1982, are various options granted under a previous plan and other options granted not as a part of an option plan.

Further information relating to options is as follows:

	1982	1981	1980
Options outstanding at January 1	1,406,360	1,392,457	1,259,886
Options granted in the year	288,300	244,975	362,350
Options exercised in the year	(120,791)	(35,651)	(29,559)
Options cancelled in the year	(66,707)	(195,421)	(200,220)
Options outstanding at December 31	1,507,162	1,406,360	1,392,457
Options exercisable at December 31	781,906	755,598	728,067
Shares available at December 31 for options which may be granted	25,261	278,121	400,408
Option prices per share			
Exercised in the year	$22-$44	$22-$34	$19-$25
Unexercised at year-end	$25-$68	$22-$68	$19-$68

Not included above are options assumed in connection with the purchase of Columbia Pictures Industries, Inc. covering 504,997 shares of the Company's common stock. The value of these options in excess of the option price has been included in the acquisition cost. At December 31, 1982, options for 263,281 such shares were outstanding at an average option price of $31.

9. Pension Plans. The Company and its subsidiaries sponsor and/or contribute to various pension plans covering substantially all domestic employees and certain employees in foreign countries. Pension expense for continuing operations determined under various actuarial cost methods, principally the aggregate level cost method, amounted to approximately $37 million in 1982, $35 million in 1981, and $32 million in 1980. Amendments which resulted in improved benefits for retired employees increased 1982 pension expense by $1.2 million and increased the value of vested benefits by $12 million at January 1, 1982.

The actuarial present value of accumulated benefits, as estimated by consulting actuaries, and net assets available for benefits of Company and subsidiary-sponsored domestic plans are presented below (in thousands):

	January 1,	
	1982	1981
Actuarial present value of accumulated plan benefits:		
Vested	$178,343	$146,884
Nonvested	14,284	12,669
	$192,627	$159,553
Net assets available for benefits	$234,836	$193,268

The weighted average assumed rates of return used in determining the actuarial present value of accumulated plan benefits were approximately 10% for 1982 and 9% for 1981. Changes in the assumed rates of return reduced the actuarial present value of accumulated plan benefits by approximately $18 million and $19 million at January 1, 1982 and 1981, respectively.

The Company has various foreign pension plans which are not required to report to certain governmental agencies pursuant to the Employee Retirement Income Security Act (ERISA) and do not otherwise determine the actuarial present value of accumulated plan benefits or net assets available for benefits as calculated and disclosed above. For such plans, the value of the pension funds and balance sheet accruals exceeded the actuarially computed value of vested benefits as of January 1, 1982 and 1981, as estimated by consulting actuaries.

Notes to Consolidated Financial Statements (continued)

10. Income Taxes. The components of income before income taxes for both continuing and discontinued operations consisted of the following (in thousands):

	Year Ended December 31,		
	1982	1981	1980
United States	$357,063	$309,654	$251,807
Foreign	574,928	552,857	512,492
	$931,991	$862,511	$764,299

Income taxes for continuing and discontinued operations consisted of the following amounts (in thousands):

	Year Ended December 31,		
	United States	State & Local	Foreign	Total
---	---	---	---	---
1982				
Current	$79,605	$22,638	$266,709	$368,952
Deferred	33,281	1,363	16,163	50,807
1981				
Current	$86,589	$22,461	$248,292	$357,342
Deferred	15,574	1,646	6,167	23,387
1980				
Current	$63,636	$17,438	$228,013	$309,087
Deferred	25,518	2,390	5,196	33,104

Total tax expense differed from the amount computed by applying the statutory federal income tax rate to income before income taxes principally because of investment tax credits which had the effect of reducing the tax provision by approximately $24 million in 1982, $14 million in 1981 and $11 million in 1980.

Deferred taxes are provided principally for depreciation and film costs which are recognized in different years for financial statement and income tax purposes.

11. Acquisitions. On June 21, 1982, the Company acquired all of the outstanding capital stock of Columbia Pictures Industries, Inc. ("Columbia") in a purchase transaction. The purchase price, consisting of cash and common stock of the Company, is valued at approximately $692 million. The values assigned to assets acquired and liabilities assumed are based on studies conducted to determine their fair values. The excess cost over net fair value is being amortized over forty years using the straight-line method; amortization amounted to $6 million in 1982.

The pro forma consolidated results of operations of the Company, as if Columbia had been acquired as of January 1, 1981, are as follows (in thousands, except per share data):

	Year Ended December 31,	
	1982	1981
Net operating revenues	$6,602,571	$6,623,775
Income from continuing operations	498,692	456,452
Income from continuing operations per share	3.67	3.36

The pro forma results include adjustments to reflect interest expense on $333 million of the purchase price assumed to be financed with debt bearing interest at an annual rate of 11%, the amortization of the unallocated excess cost over net assets of Columbia, the income tax effects of pro forma adjustments and the issuance of 12.2 million shares of the Company's common stock.

The pro forma results for the twelve months ended December 31, 1981, have been further adjusted to reflect Columbia's repurchase in February, 1981, of 2.4 million shares of Columbia common stock from certain shareholders as if such repurchase had been consummated as of January 1, 1981. Accordingly, interest expense has been increased for amounts necessary to fund the cash portion of the purchase price, legal expenses incurred in litigation with such shareholders have been eliminated and income taxes have been adjusted.

In June 1982, the Company purchased Associated Coca-Cola Bottling Co., Inc. ("Associated") at a cost of approximately $419 million. Associated was acquired with the intent of selling its properties to other purchasers as part of the Company's strategy to assist in restructuring the bottler system. Accordingly, the acquisition has been accounted for as a temporary investment under the cost method of accounting. At December 31, 1982, approximately 70% of Associated's operating assets had been sold for cash equal to the allocated costs of such assets. A substantial portion of such assets were sold for $245 million to a corporation principally owned by a former director of the Company.

The remaining investment in Associated of $120 million at December 31, 1982 is included in other current assets.

In September 1982, the Company purchased Ronco Foods Company, a manufacturer and distributor of pasta products, for cash. This transaction had no significant effect on the Company's operating results.

12. Discontinued Operations. In 1981, the Company sold Aqua-Chem, Inc., a wholly-owned subsidiary which produced steam generators, industrial boilers and water treatment equipment. In February 1982, the Company sold its Tenco Division for approximately book value. Tenco was an operating unit which manufactured and distributed private label instant coffees and teas.

Net sales of discontinued operations were $240 million and $292 million in 1981 and 1980, respectively.

Notes to Consolidated Financial Statements (continued)

13. Industry Segments. The Company operates principally in the soft drink industry. Carbonated and noncarbonated beverages and Hi-C fruit drinks are classified as soft drinks. In June 1982, the Company acquired Columbia Pictures Industries, Inc., which operates in the entertainment industry. Citrus, coffee, wine and plastic products are included in other industries. Inter-segment transfers are not material. Information concerning operations in different industries is as follows (in thousands):

Year Ended December 31,	1982	1981	1980
Net operating revenues:*			
Soft drinks	$4,515,813	$4,683,467	$4,522,048
Entertainment	457,305	—	—
Other industries	1,276,600	1,205,568	1,098,701
Total	$6,249,718	$5,889,035	$5,620,749
Income from industry segments:*			
Soft drinks	$ 893,221	$ 803,748	$ 731,783
Entertainment	35,535	—	—
Other industries	127,196	113,759	101,138
Total	1,055,952	917,507	832,921
Other income, net of other deductions	(50,089)	(37,671)	(37,893)
General expenses	(73,872)	(72,582)	(58,301)
Income from continuing operations before income taxes	$ 931,991	$ 807,254	$ 736,727
Identifiable assets at year-end:*			
Soft drinks	$2,521,410	$2,472,533	$2,436,192
Entertainment	1,309,837	—	—
Other industries	615,872	578,588	529,184
Total	4,447,119	3,051,121	2,965,376
Corporate assets (principally marketable securities, investments and fixed assets)	476,191	452,693	289,202
Discontinued operations	—	60,967	151,380
Total	$4,923,310	$3,564,781	$3,405,958
Capital expenditures by industry segment including fixed assets of purchased companies:			
Soft drinks	$ 249,529	$ 251,539	$ 224,152
Entertainment	53,913	—	—
Other industries	53,686	58,422	40,924
Depreciation of fixed assets and amortization of intangible assets by industry segment:*			
Soft drinks	$ 118,404	$ 112,476	$ 108,126
Entertainment	8,296	—	—
Other industries	26,455	22,817	20,731

*Amounts for 1980 have been restated to reflect the sale of the Company's Aqua-Chem, Inc., subsidiary and Tenco Division.

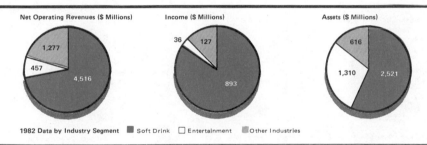

Net Operating Revenues ($ Millions) — 1,277 / 457 / 4,516

Income ($ Millions) — 36 / 127 / 893

Assets ($ Millions) — 616 / 1,310 / 2,521

1982 Data by Industry Segment ■ Soft Drink □ Entertainment ▨ Other Industries

Notes to Consolidated Financial Statements (continued)

14. Operations in Geographic Areas. Information about the Company's operations in different geographic areas is presented below (in thousands). Africa, which is not a significant geographic area as defined by SFAS 14, has been grouped with Europe in accordance with the Company's management organizational structure. Other insignificant geographic areas are combined as Canada and Pacific. Inter-company transfers between geographic areas are not material.

Year Ended December 31,	1982	1981	1980
Net operating revenues:*			
United States and Puerto Rico	$3,580,140	$3,238,673	$3,059,953
Latin America	516,336	608,110	560,164
Europe and Africa	1,155,564	1,096,257	1,170,294
Canada and Pacific	997,678	945,995	830,338
Total	$6,249,718	$5,889,035	$5,620,749
Income from geographic areas:*			
United States and Puerto Rico	$ 417,542	$ 337,522	$ 279,315
Latin America	174,742	179,739	148,055
Europe and Africa	276,279	248,802	278,707
Canada and Pacific	187,389	151,444	126,844
Total	1,055,952	917,507	832,921
Other income, net of other deductions	(50,089)	(37,671)	(37,893)
General expenses	(73,872)	(72,582)	(58,301)
Income from continuing operations before income taxes	$ 931,991	$ 807,254	$ 736,727
Identifiable assets at year-end:*			
United States and Puerto Rico	$3,008,701	$1,631,123	$1,604,490
Latin America	435,879	436,215	420,197
Europe and Africa	582,037	583,017	579,851
Canada and Pacific	420,502	400,766	360,838
Total	4,447,119	3,051,121	2,965,376
Corporate assets (principally marketable securities, investments and fixed assets)	476,191	452,693	289,202
Discontinued operations	—	60,967	151,380
Total	$4,923,310	$3,564,781	$3,405,958

*Amounts for 1980 have been restated to reflect the sale of the Company's Aqua-Chem, Inc., subsidiary and Tenco Division.

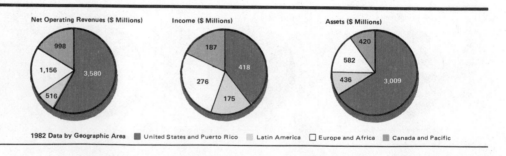

Net Operating Revenues ($ Millions)   Income ($ Millions)   Assets ($ Millions)

1982 Data by Geographic Area   ■ United States and Puerto Rico   Latin America   □ Europe and Africa   ■ Canada and Pacific

Report of Independent Accountants

The Coca-Cola Company and Subsidiaries

Board of Directors and Shareholders
The Coca-Cola Company
Atlanta, Georgia

We have examined the consolidated balance sheets of The Coca-Cola Company and subsidiaries as of December 31, 1982 and 1981, and the related consolidated statements of income, shareholders' equity and changes in financial position for each of the three years in the period ended December 31, 1982. Our examinations were made in accordance with generally accepted auditing standards and, accordingly, included such tests of the accounting records and such other auditing procedures as we considered necessary in the circumstances.

In our opinion, the financial statements referred to above present fairly the consolidated financial position of The Coca-Cola Company and subsidiaries at December 31, 1982 and 1981, and the consolidated results of their operations and the changes in their financial position for each of the three years in the period ended December 31, 1982, in conformity with generally accepted accounting principles consistently applied during the period except for the change in 1982, with which we concur, in the method of accounting for foreign currency translation as described in Note 1 to the consolidated financial statements.

Atlanta, Georgia
February 14, 1983

Ernst & Whinney

Report of Management

Management is responsible for the preparation and integrity of the consolidated financial statements appearing in this Annual Report. The financial statements were prepared in conformity with generally accepted accounting principles appropriate in the circumstances and, accordingly, include some amounts based on management's best judgments and estimates. Other financial information in this Annual Report is consistent with that in the financial statements.

Management is responsible for maintaining a system of internal accounting controls and procedures to provide reasonable assurance, at an appropriate cost/benefit relationship, that assets are safeguarded and that transactions are authorized, recorded and reported properly. The internal accounting control system is augmented by a program of internal audits and appropriate reviews by management, written policies and guidelines, careful selection and training of qualified personnel and a written Code of Business Conduct adopted by the Board of Directors, applicable to all employees of the Company and its subsidiaries. Management believes that the Company's internal accounting controls provide reasonable assurance that assets are safeguarded against material loss from unauthorized use or disposition and that the financial records are reliable for preparing financial statements and other data and maintaining accountability for assets.

The Audit Committee of the Board of Directors, composed solely of Directors who are not officers of the Company, meets with the independent accountants, management and internal auditors periodically to discuss internal accounting controls, auditing and financial reporting matters. The Committee reviews with the independent accountants the scope and results of the audit effort. The Committee also meets with the independent accountants without management present to ensure that the independent accountants have free access to the Committee.

The independent accountants, Ernst & Whinney, are recommended by the Audit Committee of the Board of Directors, selected by the Board of Directors and ratified by the shareholders. Ernst & Whinney are engaged to examine the financial statements of The Coca-Cola Company and subsidiaries and conduct such tests and related procedures as they deem necessary in conformity with generally accepted auditing standards. The opinion of the independent accountants, based upon their examination of the consolidated financial statements, is contained in this Annual Report.

Roberto C. Goizueta
Chairman, Board of Directors,
and Chief Executive Officer

Sam Ayoub
Senior Executive Vice President
and Chief Financial Officer

February 14, 1983

Unaudited Quarterly Data
(For the years ended December 31, 1982 and 1981)

The Coca-Cola Company and Subsidiaries

Quarterly Results of Operations
(In thousands except per share data)

	Net Operating Revenues		Gross Profit	
	1982	1981	1982	1981
First quarter	$1,271,289	$1,346,462	$ 589,071	$ 584,925
Second quarter	1,567,851	1,600,247	727,885	701,879
Third quarter	1,745,157	1,529,810	747,365	661,166
Fourth quarter	1,665,421	1,412,516	731,904	633,491
	$6,249,718	$5,889,035	$2,796,225	$2,581,461

	Income From Continuing Operations		Net Income	
	1982	1981	1982	1981
First quarter	$ 107,616	$ 97,633	$ 107,616	$ 100,097
Second quarter	139,821	126,992	139,821	128,876
Third quarter	143,463	116,219	143,463	146,581
Fourth quarter	121,332	106,226	121,332	106,228
	$ 512,232	$ 447,070	$ 512,232	$ 481,782

	Income Per Share From Continuing Operations		Net Income Per Share	
	1982	1981	1982	1981
First quarter	$ .87	$ .79	$ .87	$ .81
Second quarter	1.13	1.03	1.13	1.04
Third quarter	1.06	.94	1.06	1.19
Fourth quarter	.89	.86	.89	.86
	$ 3.95	$ 3.62	$ 3.95	$ 3.90

Net operating revenues and gross profit for the first three quarters of 1981 have been restated to reflect the sale of the Company's Aqua-Chem, Inc., subsidiary and Tenco Division.

Supplemental Information on the Effects of Changing Prices (Unaudited)

The Coca-Cola Company and Subsidiaries

General. The following unaudited disclosures were prepared in accordance with Statement Nos. 33 and 70 issued by the Financial Accounting Standards Board and are intended to quantify the impact of inflation on earnings and production facilities. The inflation-adjusted data is presented under the specific price changes method (current cost). Only those items most affected by inflation have been adjusted; i.e., inventories, property, plant and equipment, the related costs of goods and services sold and depreciation and amortization expense. Although the resulting measurements cannot be used as precise indicators of the effects of inflation, they do provide an indication of the effect of increases in specific prices of the Company's inventories and properties.

The adjustments for specific price changes involve a substantial number of judgments as well as the use of various estimating techniques employed to control the cost of accumulating the data. The data reported should not be thought of as precise measurements of the assets and expenses involved, or of the amount at which the assets could be sold. Rather, they represent reasonable approximations of the price changes that have occurred in the business environment in which the Company operates.

Inflation-adjusted data based on the constant dollar method is not presented because a significant part of the Company's operations is in foreign locations whose functional currency is not the U.S. dollar.

A brief explanation of the current cost method is presented below.

Current Cost. The current cost method attempts to measure the effect of increases in the specific prices of the Company's inventories and properties. It is intended to estimate what it would cost in 1982 dollars to replace the Company's inventories and existing properties.

Under this method, cost of goods sold valued on the average method is adjusted to reflect the current cost of inventories at the date of sale. That portion of cost of goods sold valued on the LIFO method approximates the current cost of inventory at the date of sale and generally remains unchanged from the amounts presented in the primary financial statements.

Current cost depreciation expense is based on the average current cost of properties in the year. The depreciation methods, salvage values and useful lives are the

Statement of Income Adjusted for Changing Prices

(In millions except per share data)

Year Ended December 31, 1982	As Reported in the Primary Statements	Adjusted for Changes in Specific Prices (Current Costs)
Net operating revenues	$6,249.7	$6,249.7
Cost of goods and services (excluding depreciation)	3,386.8	3,412.0
Depreciation and amortization	156.9	235.4
Other operating expenses	1,817.6	1,817.6
Net of other (income) and deductions	(43.6)	(41.3)
Income from continuing operations before income taxes	932.0	826.0
Income taxes	419.8	419.8
Income from continuing operations	$ 512.2	$ 406.2
Income per share from continuing operations	$ 3.95	$ 3.13
Effective income tax rate	45.0%	50.8%
Purchasing power gain from holding net monetary liabilities in the year		$ 17.7
Increase in specific prices of inventories and property, plant and equipment held in the year		$ 261.8
Less effect of increase in general price level		147.2
Increase in specific prices over increase in the general price level		$ 114.6
Estimated translation adjustment		$ (300.0)
Inventory and film costs	$1,020.3	$1,109.7
Property, plant and equipment—net	$1,538.5	$2,342.8

A significant part of the Company's operations are measured in functional currencies other than the U.S. dollar. Adjustments to reflect the effects of general inflation were determined on the translate-restate method using the U.S. CPI(U).

Supplemental Information on the Effects of Changing Prices (Unaudited) (continued)

same as those used in the primary statements.

The current cost of finished products inventory was approximated by adjusting historical amounts to reflect current costs for material, labor and overhead expenses as well as current cost depreciation, where applicable. The current cost for inventories other than finished products was determined on the basis of price lists or appropriate supplier quotations and by other managerial estimates consistent with established purchasing and production procedures.

Since motion picture films are the result of a unique blending of the artistic talents of many individuals and are produced under widely varying circumstances, it is not feasible to develop the current cost of film inventories, particularly since the Company would rarely, if ever, attempt to duplicate an existing film property. As a result, film inventories have been valued based on studies conducted to determine their fair value in connection with the purchase price allocation process.

Direct supplier quotations, published price lists, engineering estimates, construction quotations, appraisals, published and internally developed indexes were the methods used to determine the current cost of property, plant and equipment.

Under current cost accounting, increases in specific prices (current cost) of inventories and properties held during the year are not included in income from continuing operations.

Income Taxes. Taxes on income included in the supplementary statement of income are the same as reported in the primary financial statements. In most countries, present tax laws do not allow deductions for the effects of inflation. Thus, taxes are levied on the Company at rates which, in real terms, exceed established statutory rates.

Purchasing Power Gain. During periods of inflation, monetary assets, such as cash, marketable securities and accounts receivable, lose purchasing power since they will buy fewer goods when the general price level increases. The holding of monetary liabilities, such as accounts payable, accruals and debt, results in a gain of purchasing power because cheaper dollars will be used to repay the obligations. The Company has benefited from a net monetary liability position in recent years, resulting in a net gain in purchasing power. This gain does not represent an increase in funds available for distribution to shareholders and does not necessarily imply that incurring more debt would be beneficial to the Company.

Increase in Specific Prices. Shown separately are the total changes in current costs for inventories and properties, that component of the total change due to general inflation and that component of the change attributable to fluctuations in exchange rates.

Five-Year Comparison of Selected Supplemental Financial Data Adjusted for Effects of Changing Prices (In Average 1982 Dollars)
(In millions except per share data)

Year Ended December 31,	1982	1981	1980	1979	1978
Net operating revenues	$6,249.7	$6,258.6	$6,595.5	$6,245.9	$6,069.6
Current cost information:					
Income from continuing operations	406.2	372.7	310.7	369.0	
Income per share from continuing operations	3.13	3.02	2.51	2.99	
Increase in specific prices over (under) increase in the general price level, including translation adjustments	(185.4)	(220.0)	25.9	213.8	
Net assets at year-end	3,622.8	3,334.2	3,733.3	3,768.4	
Purchasing power gain on net monetary items	17.7	26.0	50.6	27.6	
Cash dividends declared per share:					
As reported	2.48	2.32	2.16	1.96	1.74
Adjusted for general inflation	2.48	2.47	2.53	2.61	2.58
Market price per common share at year-end:					
Historical amount	52.00	34.75	33.375	34.50	43.875
Adjusted for general inflation	52.00	36.93	39.16	45.96	65.03
Average Consumer Price Index—Urban	289.6	272.5	246.8	217.4	195.4

Statement of earnings

General Electric Company and consolidated affiliates

For the years ended December 31 (In millions) (note 1)	1982	1981	1980
Sales Sales of products and services to customers	$26,500	$27,240	$24,959
Operating costs Cost of goods sold	18,605	19,476	18,171
Selling, general and administrative expense	4,506	4,435	3,838
Depreciation, depletion and amortization	984	882	707
Operating costs (notes 2 and 3)	24,095	24,793	22,716
Operating margin	2,405	2,447	2,243
Other income (note 4)	692	614	564
Interest and other financial charges (note 5)	(344)	(401)	(314)
Earnings Earnings before income taxes and minority interest	2,753	2,660	2,493
Provision for income taxes (note 6)	(900)	(962)	(938)
Minority interest in earnings of consolidated affiliates	(36)	(46)	(21)
Net earnings applicable to common stock	$ 1,817	$ 1,652	$ 1,514
Earnings per common share (in dollars) (note 7)	$8.00	$7.26	$6.65
Dividends declared per common share (in dollars)	$3.35	$3.15	$2.95
Operating margin as a percentage of sales	9.1%	9.0%	9.0%
Net earnings as a percentage of sales	6.9%	6.1%	6.1%

Statement of retained earnings

General Electric Company and consolidated affiliates

For the years ended December 31 (In millions) (note 1)	1982	1981	1980
Retained earnings Balance January 1	$8,088	$7,151	$6,307
Net earnings	1,817	1,652	1,514
Dividends declared on common stock	(760)	(715)	(670)
Balance December 31	$9,145	$8,088	$7,151

The information on pages 32 and 36-44 is an integral part of these statements.

CONSOLIDATED BALANCE SHEETS

Hershey Foods Corporation

(in thousands of dollars)

December 31	1982	1981
ASSETS		
Current Assets:		
Cash and short-term investments	$ 17,820	$ 53,879
Accounts receivable—trade (less allowances for doubtful accounts of $3,040 and $2,792)	65,129	56,241
Inventories (Note 1)	178,585	151,890
Other current assets	13,411	25,020
Total current assets	274,945	287,030
Property, Plant and Equipment, at cost: (Notes 1 and 4)		
Land	51,050	46,592
Buildings	183,387	174,705
Machinery and equipment	474,918	358,446
Capitalized leases	19,920	18,238
	729,275	597,981
Less—accumulated depreciation and amortization	189,361	157,797
	539,914	440,184
Excess of Cost Over Net Assets of Businesses Acquired (Note 1)	52,609	53,911
Investments and Other Assets	20,603	25,675
	$888,071	$806,800

December 31	1982	1981

LIABILITIES AND STOCKHOLDERS' EQUITY

Current Liabilities:

Accounts payable	$ 45,288	$ 48,085
Accrued liabilities		
Payroll and other compensation costs	29,208	23,916
Advertising and promotional expenses	12,805	14,415
Other	23,281	18,702
	65,294	57,033
Accrued income taxes	11,399	10,006
Current portion of long-term debt (Note 4)	19,579	2,131
Total current liabilities	141,560	117,255
Long-Term Debt (Notes 4 and 5)	140,250	158,182
Deferred Income Taxes (Note 2)	73,766	61,699

Stockholders' Equity: (Note 1)

Common stock without par value (stated value $1 per share)— authorized 20,000,000 shares; outstanding 15,668,556 shares	15,669	15,669
Additional paid-in capital	54,006	54,006
Retained earnings	462,820	399,989
Total stockholders' equity	532,495	469,664
	$888,071	$806,800

The accompanying notes are an integral part of these balance sheets.

CONSOLIDATED STATEMENTS OF INCOME AND RETAINED EARNINGS

(in thousands of dollars except per share amounts)

For the years ended December 31	1982	1981	1980
Net Sales	$1,565,736	$1,451,151	$1,335,289
Costs and Expenses:			
Cost of sales	1,084,748	1,015,767	971,714
Selling, general and administrative	301,586	267,930	224,615
Total costs and expenses	1,386,334	1,283,697	1,196,329
Income from Operations	179,402	167,454	138,960
Interest expense, net (Note 1)	7,859	12,512	14,100
Income before Taxes	171,543	154,942	124,860
Provision for income taxes (Note 2)	77,375	74,580	62,805
Net Income	94,168	80,362	62,055
Retained Earnings at January 1	399,989	345,131	304,316
Less—Cash Dividends	31,337	25,504	21,240
Retained Earnings at December 31	$ 462,820	$ 399,989	$ 345,131
Net Income per Common Share (Note 1)	$ 6.01	$ 5.61	$ 4.38
Cash Dividends per Common Share	$ 2.00	$ 1.75	$ 1.50

The accompanying notes are an integral part of these statements.

SUPPLEMENTARY INFORMATION REGARDING THE EFFECTS OF INFLATION (Unaudited)

The Company's consolidated financial statements are prepared based upon the historical prices in effect when the transactions occurred. The following supplementary information reflects certain effects of inflation upon the Company's operations in accordance with the requirements of Statement of Financial Accounting Standards No. 33, "Financial Reporting and Changing Prices", issued by the Financial Accounting Standards Board.

The effects of inflation on income have been measured in two ways as described below and presented in the following statements. The first method, "constant dollar", measures the effect of general inflation determined by using the 1982 average Consumer Price Index for all Urban Consumers (CPI-U) to recompute results of operations. The second method, "current cost", is more specific to the Company in that it measures inflation by recomputing results of operations using the current cost of inventory and property, plant and equipment rather than the historical cost of such assets. Current costs of property, plant and equipment were developed from external price indices, quotations or similar measurements.

The inflation-adjusted information presented may not necessarily be comparable with other companies within the same industry because of differences in assumptions and judgments. However, of the two methods required, the Company believes the current cost method is more meaningful because it better measures the effects of inflation on Company operations.

Depreciation expense increased under both methods because of inflation. Current cost depreciation exceeds constant dollar depreciation because the cumulative increases in the Company's specific cost of property, plant and equipment have exceeded the general inflation rate. Both methods represent costs of property, plant and equipment currently used in operations. However, the Company generally takes advantage of the latest technological improvements when actual replacement occurs.

The adjustment to current cost of sales is not significant because substantial portions of inventories in the historical financial statements are stated at LIFO cost. Under LIFO cost, current costs are included in cost of sales in the historical financial statements. During 1982, the costs of non-LIFO components of cost of sales increased only slightly, resulting in a minor increase in current cost over historical cost of sales.

The statement shows that the historical effective income tax rate for 1982 of 45.1% increases under both methods since Federal Income Tax Regulations do not provide for a tax deduction for these inflation adjustments.

The gain from decline of purchasing power of net amounts owed set forth in the following schedule presents the Company's gain from holding more monetary liabilities (requiring fixed future cash settlements) than monetary assets (right to receive fixed amounts of future cash) during periods of inflation, thereby requiring less purchasing power to satisfy such future obligations. However, since this gain will not be realized until the obligations are repaid, it is excluded from inflation-adjusted net income.

Five-Year Comparison

The five-year comparison on page 35 shows the effect of adjusting historical net sales, net income, dividends per common share, market price per common share, net assets and other information, to dollar amounts expressed in terms of average 1982 dollars, as measured by the average Consumer Price Index. After adjustment for inflation, net sales have increased 38% from 1978 through 1982.

Management recognizes the impact of inflation and has taken various steps to minimize its impact on the Company's businesses. The use of LIFO inventory accounting for the major portion of its inventories reduces reported earnings, thereby reducing taxes and improving cash flow, in periods of inflation by matching current costs with current revenues. The capital expenditure program, through investment in modern plant and equipment, not only improves productivity and manufacturing efficiencies, but also provides for future sales growth. Programs designed to identify cost reductions and productivity improvements which would result in improved margins are a continuing part of the Company's approach to inflation management. In 1982, the Company achieved approximately an 11% increase in current cost net income compared with a 17% increase in historical dollar net income.

The Company also recognizes that the purchasing power of the dollar significantly affects its stockholders and has attempted to maintain or improve the inflation-adjusted dividend. In 1982, the Company provided real growth of 7.5% in dividends paid per common share. Dividends paid in 1982 are approximately 41% of earnings per share when stated in both constant dollar and current cost amounts compared with a 33% historical dollar basis.

The increase in specific prices compared with general inflation increases has changed annually since costs for agricultural commodities often do not follow the trend of general inflation. Comparisons of other amounts for years prior to 1979 were neither readily available nor required by Statement No. 33. Historical cost data presented for 1979 includes results of Friendly Ice Cream Corporation subsequent to its acquisition in January 1979.

FIVE-YEAR COMPARISON OF SELECTED SUPPLEMENTARY FINANCIAL DATA ADJUSTED FOR EFFECTS OF INFLATION (Unaudited)

(in thousands of average 1982 dollars except per share amounts)

For the years ended December 31	1982	1981	1980	1979	1978
Net sales					
As reported	$1,565,736	1,451,151	1,335,289	1,161,295	767,880
In constant dollars	$1,565,736	1,540,117	1,564,149	1,544,298	1,136,101
Net Income					
As reported . . . . $	94,168	80,362	62,055	53,504	41,456
In constant dollars . . . . $	77,171	64,982	53,302	52,357	
At current cost . . . . $	76,536	69,148	50,564	56,837	
Net Income per share					
As reported . . . . $	6.01	5.61	4.38	3.78	3.02
In constant dollars . . . . $	4.93	4.54	3.76	3.70	
At current cost . . . . $	4.88	4.83	3.57	4.02	
Dividends per common share					
As reported . . . . $	2.00	1.75	1.50	1.35	1.225
In constant dollars . . . . $	2.00	1.86	1.76	1.80	1.81
Market price per common share at year-end					
As reported . . . . $	56.38	36.00	23.50	24.63	20.63
In constant dollars . . . . $	55.74	36.97	26.29	30.97	29.39
Net assets at year-end					
As reported . . . . $	532,495	469,664	361,550	320,730	284,389
In constant dollars . . . . $	797,098	752,957	631,159	590,342	
At current cost . . . . $	836,224	854,152	845,134	804,996	
Gain from decline in purchasing power of net amounts owed . . . $	10,595	22,872	31,974	35,360	
Excess of increase in general price level over decrease in specific prices . . . . $	62,011	90,376	(210)	(28,712)	
Average Consumer Price Index (1967 = 100)	289.1	272.4	246.8	217.4	195.4

CONSOLIDATED STATEMENT OF INCOME ADJUSTED FOR EFFECTS OF INFLATION (Unaudited)

(in thousands of dollars)

For the year ended December 31, 1982	As Reported in the Primary Statement	Adjusted for General Inflation	Adjusted for Changes in Specific Prices
	(historical dollars)	(constant dollar)	(current cost)
Net sales	$1,565,736	$1,565,736	$1,565,736
Cost of sales . . . . (excluding depreciation)	1,057,761	1,061,054	1,059,505
Selling, general and administrative expenses . . . . (excluding depreciation)	297,892	297,892	297,892
Depreciation expense	30,681	44,385	46,569
Interest expense—net	7,859	7,859	7,859
Income before taxes	171,543	154,546	153,911
Income taxes	77,375	77,375	77,375
Net income	$ 94,168	$ 77,171	$ 76,536
Effective tax rate	45.1%	50.1%	50.3%
Gain from decline of purchasing power of net amounts owed		$ 10,595	$ 10,595
Decrease in specific prices (current cost) of inventories and property, plant and equipment held during the year (see Note).			$ (24,924)
Effect of increase in general price level of inventories and property, plant and equipment			37,087
Excess of increase in general price level over decrease in specific prices			$ 62,011

Note: At December 31, 1982, current cost of inventory was $240.7 million and current cost of property, plant and equipment, net of accumulated depreciation was $778.6 million.

Hilton Hotels Corporation
and Subsidiaries

Consolidated Statements of Income
(In thousands of dollars
except share data)

Year Ended December 31,		1982	1981	1980
Revenue	Rooms	$223,627	218,952	216,153
	Food and beverage	163,920	161,411	155,010
	Casino	163,302	145,054	141,095
	Casino promotional allowances	(25,168)	(20,746)	(19,392)
	Management and franchise fees	37,234	34,586	30,229
	Interest and dividends	20,965	27,481	21,266
	Other	36,604	45,966	31,232
		620,484	612,704	575,593
Expenses	Rooms	67,541	63,557	59.523
	Food and beverage	126,041	118,330	112,581
	Casino	64,892	50,690	45,509
	Other operating expenses	123,888	112,777	102,606
	Property operations	59,008	51,003	44,971
	Lease rentals	6,491	6,591	5,923
	Property taxes	12,776	10,837	12,892
	Interest (net of $3,813, $1,926 and $2,625 capitalized)	8,962	10,955	8,572
	Depreciation	37,826	29,603	26,493
		507,425	454,343	419,070
Income from Operations		113,059	158,361	156,523
	Earnings from unconsolidated affiliates	25,645	38,222	38,785
Income Before Property Transactions		138,704	196,583	195,308
	Property transactions	2,764	—	—
Income Before Income Taxes		141,468	196,583	195,308
	Federal and state income taxes	58,095	83,960	89,176
Net Income		$ 83,373	112,623	106,132
Net Income per Share		$3.12	4.22	4.00

See notes to financial statements

International Business Machines Corporation
and Subsidiary Companies

Consolidated Statement of Financial Position
at December 31:

(Dollars in millions)	1982		1981*	
Assets				
Current Assets:				
Cash	$ 405		$ 454	
Marketable securities, at lower of cost or market	2,895		1,575	
Notes and accounts receivable–trade, less allowance:				
1982, $216; 1981, $187	4,976		4,382	
Other accounts receivable	457		410	
Inventories	3,492		2,803	
Prepaid expenses	789		685	
		$ 13,014		$ 10,309
Rental Machines and Parts	16,527		16,599	
Less: Accumulated depreciation	7,410		7,347	
		9,117		9,252
Plant and Other Property	14,240		12,702	
Less: Accumulated depreciation	5,794		5,157	
		8,446		7,545
Deferred Charges and Other Assets		1,964		2,001
		$ 32,541		$ 29,107
Liabilities and Stockholders' Equity				
Current Liabilities:				
Taxes	$ 2,854		$ 2,412	
Loans payable	529		773	
Accounts payable	983		872	
Compensation and benefits	1,959		1,556	
Deferred income	402		390	
Other accrued expenses and liabilities	1,482		1,323	
		$ 8,209		$ 7,326
Deferred Investment Tax Credits		323		252
Reserves for Employees' Indemnities and Retirement Plans		1,198		1,184
Long Term Debt		2,851		2,669
Stockholders' Equity:				
Capital stock, par value $1.25 per share	5,008		4,389	
Shares authorized: 750,000,000				
Issued: 1982–602,406,128; 1981–592,293,624				
Retained earnings	16,259		13,909	
Translation adjustments	(1,307)		(622)	
		19,960		17,676
		$ 32,541		$ 29,107

*Restated. See Accounting Change–
Foreign Currency Translation note on page 36.

The notes on pages 35 through 42 are an integral part of this statement.

Kidde, Inc. and Subsidiaries

Consolidated Statements of Income for the years ended December 31:

	1982	1981	1980
	(dollars in thousands except per share amounts)		
Net Sales	$2,655,335	$2,849,170	$2,539,275
Costs, Expenses and Other:			
Cost of sales	1,949,846	2,118,365	1,885,193
Selling, general and administrative expenses	488,716	495,712	449,443
Interest and debt expense, net	70,996	64,174	55,037
Other, net	587	(2,379)	(3,666)
Taxes on income	60,980	74,085	65,881
	2,571,125	2,749,957	2,451,888
Net Income	$ 84,210	$ 99,213	$ 87,387
Per share—primary	$4.02	$4.87	$4.30
Per share—fully diluted	$3.60	$4.22	$3.71

The accompanying notes are an integral part of these statements.

SFN Companies, Inc. and Subsidiaries

Consolidated Statements of Earnings

For the years ended April 30, 1982, 1981 and 1980 (in thousands except per share amounts)

	1982	1981 Restated	1980 Restated
Revenues:			
Net sales	$251,102	$270,813	$254,151
Royalties and miscellaneous	999	4,905	5,054
Total revenues	$252,101	$275,718	$259,205
Operating Costs:			
Cost of goods sold (Note 3)	$ 63,147	$ 74,107	$ 70,126
Selling and shipping expenses	59,199	57,353	51,380
Publishing and editorial expenses	40,050	41,627	39,562
Administrative and general expenses	35,931	33,771	30,705
Depreciation and amortization	16,109	12,825	10,998
Operating Income	$ 37,665	$ 56,035	$ 56,434
Interest expense	(540)	(617)	(661)
Investment income	9,832	4,491	4,929
Gain on sale of subsidiary (Note 10)	—	8,763	—
Earnings Before Taxes Based on Income	$ 46,957	$ 68,672	$ 60,702
Taxes Based on Income (Note 6)	21,029	32,681	28,887
Earnings Before Cumulative Effect of a Change In Accounting Principle	$ 25,928	$ 35,991	$ 31,815
Cumulative effect as of May 1, 1981 of change in method of accounting for investment tax credit (Note 2)	1,736	—	—
Net Earnings for the Year	$ 27,664	$ 35,991	$ 31,815
Per Common Share:			
Earnings before cumulative effect of a change In accounting principle	$2.27	$3.08	$2.73
Cumulative effect as of May 1, 1981 of change in method of accounting for investment tax credit	.16	—	—
Net earnings	$2.43	$3.08	$2.73
Pro Forma Data:			
Pro forma amounts, assuming retroactive application of the 1982 change to the flow-through method of accounting for investment tax credit, are as follows:			
Net earnings	$ 25,928	$ 36,391	$ 31,942
Net earnings per common share	$2.27	$3.11	$2.75

The accompanying notes are an integral part of these statements.

SFN Companies, Inc. and Subsidiaries

Consolidated Statements of Changes in Financial Position

For the years ended April 30, 1982, 1981 and 1980. (in thousands)

	1982	1981 Restated	1980 Restated
Source of Funds:			
Net earnings for the year	$ 27,664	$ 35,991	$ 31,815
Depreciation and amortization	16,109	12,825	10,998
Provision for deferred income taxes	(1,922)	2,963	498
Writedown of long-term investment	—	1,861	—
Funds derived from operations	$ 41,851	$ 53,640	$ 43,311
Long-term portion of note receivable becoming current	3,429	—	—
Property, non-current assets and liabilities, disposed of through sale of subsidiary	—	6,886	—
Common stock issued to retire preferred stock	707	583	420
	$ 45,987	$ 61,109	$ 43,731
Application of Funds:			
Acquisition of treasury shares	$ 26,558	$ —	$ —
Net increase to property, plant, equipment, and book plates	17,545	16,916	12,955
Business acquisition, net of working capital acquired	2,778	—	—
Note receivable acquired through sale of subsidiary	—	16,508	—
Dividends	12,035	10,792	9,361
Prepayment of long-term debt	—	—	250
Long-term debt becoming current	1,540	1,410	1,279
Redemption and conversion of preferred stock	801	679	927
Other items—net	655	(2,152)	1,045
	$ 61,912	$ 44,153	$ 25,817
Increase (Decrease) in Working Capital	$ (15,925)	$ 16,956	$ 17,914
Increase (Decrease) in Working Capital:			
Cash and temporary investments	$ (10,468)	$ 9,895	$ 11,192
Accounts receivable	(5,712)	6,626	1,009
Note receivable	(3,540)	7,041	—
Inventories	3,131	1,117	13,064
Other current assets	551	336	913
Accounts payable	(1,733)	3,747	(5,403)
Accrued royalties	—	129	(296)
Income taxes	3,483	(2,221)	(1,579)
Other current liabilities	(1,637)	(1,814)	(986)
Working capital disposed of through sale of subsidiary	—	(7,900)	—
Increase (Decrease) in Working Capital	$ (15.925)	$ 16,956	$ 17,914

The accompanying notes are an integral part of these statements.

TELEDYNE, INC. AND SUBSIDIARIES

Consolidated Balance Sheets
December 31, 1982 and 1981
(In millions)

	1982	1981
ASSETS		
Current Assets:		
Cash and marketable securities	$ 723.3	$ 448.4
Receivables	329.4	385.0
Inventories	128.0	164.4
Prepaid expenses	7.1	7.2
Total current assets	1,187.8	1,005.0
Investments in Unconsolidated Subsidiaries	1,624.2	1,463.8
Property and Equipment	395.7	364.9
Other Assets	34.4	34.5
	$3,242.1	$2,868.2
LIABILITIES AND SHAREHOLDERS' EQUITY		
Current Liabilities:		
Accounts payable	$ 105.8	$ 122.1
Accrued liabilities	246.2	216.4
Accrued income taxes	12.0	15.2
Current portion of long-term debt	29.0	33.5
Total current liabilities	393.0	387.2
Long-Term Debt	570.6	595.9
Deferred Income Taxes	157.8	156.6
Other Long-Term Liabilities	34.3	22.0
Shareholders' Equity	2,086.4	1,706.5
	$3,242.1	$2,868.2

The accompanying notes are an integral part of these balance sheets.

Index

1-D

LERMA, ROBERT